[illegible]
9th November 1984
(8/9)

[illegible]

VOLUME NINETEEN

A

B

C

D

E

F

G

H

I

J

K

L

M

N

O

P

R

S

T

U

V

W

Y

ILLUSTRATIONS

Photographs — half-tone and (c) colour

Line illustrations and (c/a) cutaway drawings

Tone illustrations and colour (c) drawings

PRINTED BY CARFAX CARDS LIMITED, BARNES, LONDON.

Volume 19 Number 1 July 1980

Managing Editor *William Green*
Editor *Gordon Swanborough*
Modelling Editor *Fred J Henderson*
Contributing Artist *Dennis Punnett*
Contributing Photographer *Stephen Peltz*
Editorial Representative, Washington *Norman Polmar*
Managing Director *Donald Syner*
Publisher *Keith Attenborough*
Financial Director *Claire Sillette*
Advertising Director *Elizabeth Baker*
Advertising Manager *Roger Jewers*
Subscription Manager *Sheilagh Campbell*
Distribution Manager *William Streek*

Editorial Offices:
The AIR INTERNATIONAL, PO Box 16, Bromley, BR2 7RB Kent.

Subscription, Advertising and Circulation Offices:
The AIR INTERNATIONAL, De Worde House, 283 Lonsdale Road, London SW13 9QW. Telephone 01-878 2454. US and Canadian readers may address subscriptions and general enquiries to AIR INTERNATIONAL PO Box 353, Whitestone, NY 11357 for onward transmission to the UK, from where all correspondence is answered and orders despatched.

MEMBER OF THE AUDIT BUREAU OF CIRCULATIONS ABC

Subscription rates, inclusive of postage, direct from the publishers, per year:

United Kingdom	£7·50
Overseas	£8·00
USA/Canada	$20·00

Rates for other countries and for air mail subscriptions available on request from the Subscription Department at the above address.

The AIR INTERNATIONAL is published monthly by Fine Scroll Limited, distributed by Ducimus Books Ltd and printed by William Caple & Company Ltd, Chevron Press, Leicester, England.

Second Class postage approved at New York, NY. USA Mailing Agents: Air-Sea Freight Inc, 527 Madison Avenue, New York, NY 10022.

ISSN 0306-5634

CONTENTS

FRONT COVER An SH 37 Viggen all-weather maritime reconnaissance and attack aircraft of F 17 based at Kallinge.

WRENDEZVOUS WITH WREN

"Advanced Technology Intruder For Sneaking Under Enemy Radar."

AIRSCENE

MILITARY AFFAIRS

AUSTRALIA

The government has decided to fund **design and development of a new basic trainer** to replace the CT-4A Airtrainer in the RAAF training syllabus from about 1986 onwards, by which time the CT-4A will have seen only a decade of service. Tenders have been invited from CAC, Hawker DH and the GAF for up to 100 aircraft representing a programme cost of up to Aus$50m (£24·75m) in 1980 terms. Some factions within both the service and industry would prefer to see greater priority assigned to a successor for the ageing MB 326 then to the newer CT-4A.

In order to augment **plans for increased Indian Ocean surveillance** agreed in Washington earlier this year by the governments of the USA, Australia and New Zealand, it is anticipated that one of the RAAF's two P-3 Orion squadrons will be transferred from Edinburgh to one of the two existing West Australian bases as a temporary measure pending construction of the new base at Derby, in the north-west, for which Aus$47m (£23·27m) is included in the current defence budget. At the present time, Orions assigned to Indian Ocean surveillance must overfly two-thirds of the continent before reaching their designated patrol area. The air base at Derby, which will be capable of accepting any of the RAAF's firstline aircraft, is not likely to be available until the mid-'eighties.

The flight **test programme of** the first of three **F-111Cs** being converted for the reconnaissance rôle at Amberley commenced in April. The first conversion was conducted by General Dynamics at Fort Worth last year, this involving installation of Fairchild KA-56E low-altitude panoramic cameras, Fairchild KS-87C split vertical cameras, Honeywell AN/AAD-5 IR line scanners and a Cardion Electronics TV system, and the four modified aircraft will complement the 16 surviving F-111Cs in No 82 Strike Wing.

BRAZIL

The *Força Aérea Brasileira* now anticipates receiving a total of 144 examples of the **lightweight strike fighter** based on the Aeritalia-Aermacchi AMX, with six annual production authorisations each of 24 aircraft being envisaged commencing 1984, the estimated total value of the aircraft being some £380m excluding R&D. The minimally modified version of the AMX to be produced by EMBRAER for the FAB is now being referred to as the ABX, and Italy has agreed to fund a proportion of Brazilian production, and sufficient technical assistance is to be provided to enable EMBRAER to build almost the entire airframe indigenously in return for Brazil's one-third contribution to the estimated £186m R&D cost of the AMX/ABX programme.

CANADA

The **first** of eighteen Lockheed **CP-140 Aurora** maritime surveillance aircraft — actually the fourth to roll off the Burbank assembly line — was **delivered** to the Canadian Armed Forces in May and all 18 Auroras are scheduled to have been taken into the CAF inventory by April of next year. The first and second Auroras have been engaged in some 900 hours of flight test and systems proving, which was scheduled to be completed last month (June) — the Aurora combines the avionics of the S-3 Viking with a P-3 Orion airframe — and the third aircraft has been engaged on crew training under Lockheed supervision. When the Aurora enters CAF service later this year, the main support base will be Greenwood, Nova Scotia, on Canada's East Coast, which will eventually house 14 of the aircraft, the home base for the remaining four aircraft being Comox, British Columbia, on the West Coast.

DENMARK

The first of eight Westland **Lynx** helicopters for the Royal Danish Navy's air component, *Søvaernets Flyvetjaeneste*, was **handed over** on 15 May after landing aboard the Danish Navy's platform-equipped fishery protection frigate *Hvidbjørnen* moored on the Thames, in the Pool of London. The five vessels of the *Hvidbjørnen* and *Beskytteren* classes from which the Danish Lynx helicopters will operate during deployments from their home base at Vaerløse are the smallest ships for which the Westland helicopter has so far been ordered, and the Lynx will serve primarily in the Atlantic, in the vicinity of the Faeroes and Southern Greenland.

FEDERAL GERMANY

The *Bundesmarine* is currently planning reconfiguration of its Westland **Sea King** Mk 41 SAR helicopters **for** the interim **maritime strike** rôle in the mid 'eighties to enable the *Marineflieger* to gain experience of strike helicopter operations prior to definition of a specification for a five-*tonne* helicopter for this mission which it is anticipated will enter service in the early 'nineties. The *Bundesmarine* is currently examining the potentialities of the principal European anti-ship missiles as Sea King armament, the SISTEL Sea Killer, already fitted to Italian Sea Kings, being the frontrunner, with the BAeD Sea Skua and Aérospatiale AS-15TT as strong contenders.

FINLAND

Follow-on orders are to be placed on behalf of *Ilmavoimat* for five **additional Mil Mi-8 helicopters** increasing the Finnish fleet of this type to 11 machines. The first Mi-8s, which serve primarily for SAR tasks with the transport squadron, or *Kuljetuslentoläivue*, at Utti, were received by *Ilmavoimat* mid-1973.

FRANCE

Formation of the **third** *Aéronavale* **squadron to receive** the Dassault-Breguet **Super Etendard** began on 21 March at Landivisiau with delivery of the 35th production aircraft, and this unit, *Flottille* 17F, is scheduled to achieve operational status at Hyères later this year with a complement of 12 aircraft. By the time formation of *Flottille* 17F commenced, the two existing Super Etendard squadrons, *Flottille* 11F and *Flottille* 14F, had respectively accumulated some 4,000 and 1,650 flying hours, the former unit having made 600 deck landings since it received its first aircraft in August 1978.

The **last of** the planned total of nine *Armée de l'Air* **Jaguar squadrons**, *Escadre de Chasse* 4/7 *Limousin*, was **commissioned** on 1 April at St Dizier. This unit is scheduled to be detached to Istres next month (August) after an initial period of working up and will achieve operational status by the year's end. The Jaguars of EC 4/7 are equipped to carry the AN 52 nuclear weapon. *Armée de l'Air* Jaguar flying hours have now surpassed 120,000.

By late 1984, when the last of the additional batch of 25 Transall C.160 transports have been delivered to the *Armée de l'Air*, only 40 of the aged **Nord Noratlas** transports are expected to remain in the service's inventory and this figure will have been reduced to 15 by late 1986. Approximately 100 Noratlases are currently **in French service**, the majority being with the 64e *Escadre* at Evreux, and one of the three component squadrons of this unit is to disband on 1 July next year, each of the two remaining squadrons progressively converting by flights of three or four aircraft to the C.160 throughout 1983 and 1984, until they each reach a statutory strength of 12 Transalls.

In April, the Aérospatiale **SA 342M HOT Gazelle** achieved **operational** service with the army air component (ALAT), and by the end of the year the 2e *Régiment d'Hélicoptères de Combat* will comprise three anti-armour flights each with 12 SA 342Ms based at Freiburg and Brisgau in Federal Germany.

INDONESIA

On 20 May, Indonesia's Minister of Defence, General Mohammud Jusuf, announced that the Indonesian Armed Forces — Air Force *(Tentara Nasional Indonesia — Angkatan Udara)*, or TNI-AU, will shortly receive three **new squadrons of fighters, bombers and trainers**. Gen Jusuf was referring to 16 Northrop F-5 Tiger IIs (12 single-seat F-5Es and four two-seat F-5Fs), the first eight of which were delivered to Indonesia in May with the remaining eight to be delivered this month (July); 16 McDonnell Douglas A-4 Skyhawks (14 A-4Es and two TA-4Fs) scheduled to be delivered later this year, and eight BAe Hawks also scheduled for delivery within the coming months — four Hawks are to participate in the National Day flypast over Jakarta on 5 October. Replacement of the TNI-AU's ageing Fuji-built Beech T-34A Mentor trainers — 30 of which were delivered in 1963 — is to begin next year with the commencement of deliveries of FFA AS.202 Bravos from Switzerland, 20 of which have been ordered under a SwFr 6m (£1·57m) contract recently awarded.

IRAQ

Agusta has received a **contract** from the Iraqi government **for** a batch — reported to be eight — of **AB 212ASW** anti-submarine and anti-surface vessel helicopters which are intended for operations over the Persian Gulf. Previously, Agusta had received an Iraqi order for six VIP-equipped AS 61TS transport helicopters, which, like the AB 212ASW helicopters, are to be operated by the Iraqi Air Force.

JAPAN

On 17 April, the Maritime Self-Defence Force formed its **fifth ASR squadron** at the Ozuki Air Base with two Sikorsky S-62 helicopters. The MSDF anticipates forming its 6th ASR squadron next year at the Iwojima Air Base and is planning replacement in the near term of its current fleet of six S-62s with S-61As.

Following completion of deliveries of Mitsubishi F-1 close air support fighters to the 3rd and 8th squadrons of the 3rd Air Wing at Misawa AB, the ASDF began **conversion of** the **third** planned **F-1 unit**, the 6th Squadron of the 8th Air Wing at Tsuiki AB, in April, marking commencement of the final stage of the phase out of the F-86F Sabre from the ASDF inventory. The 6th Squadron will be fully equipped with the F-1 by March of next year.

The Defence Agency is devoting maximum effort to an attempt to complete the current **defence build-up programme** (1980-84) one year **in advance of schedule** as a result of pressure from the US government. On 30 April, the

Defence Minister, Mr Kichizo Hosoda, ordered that priority attention be given by the self-defence forces in their Fiscal 1981 budget presentations to the following: procurement of four additional E-2C Hawkeye AEW aircraft; acceleration of the C-130 Hercules procurement feasibility study; acceleration of indigenous development of ECM and ECCM systems; an increase in mobile 3-D radar and communications units; acceleration of replacement of the Base Air Defence Ground Environment by a more modern system; an increase in air base defence capabilities; modernisation of an airfield on Iwojima for use as a training facility and acceleration of the replacement of current Hawk SAMs with an improved version.

KENYA
Initial BAe **Hawk** export deliveries were made in April when the first three of 12 aircraft ordered for the Kenya Air Force were **delivered** by KAF pilots trained by BAe at Dunsfold. The first Kenyan Hawk flew in December and participated in weapons firing trials in January.

PAKISTAN
With deliveries continuing of the 32 Mirage IIIs ordered for the Pakistan Air Force in 1978, **discussions** are continuing with France **concerning possible procurement of** another **follow-on** batch comprising 18 **aircraft**, which, bringing total procurement of Mirage IIIs and 5s by the PAF since 1969 to 114 aircraft, would permit phase-out of the Chaen-6bin (MiG-19S) acquired from China. Discussions between Pakistan and France concerning additional fighter procurement are reported to relate also to acquisition of between 30 and 40 Mirage F1Cs at a fly-away unit cost of some £3·9m as compared with about £2·4m being quoted the PAF for the Mirage III. The PAF is also taking delivery of MATRA 550 Magic dogfight AAMs and is discussing procurement of the MATRA Super 530 AAM. Some French personnel are now based in Pakistan at Kamrah to assist in Mirage overhaul, repair and modification.

SINGAPORE
The US Congress has been notified of the proposed sale of a **follow-on batch of** six Northrop F-5E **Tiger IIs**, together with spares and support equipment, with a total contract value of approximately $33·8m (£14·7m) to the Singapore Air Force, supplementing 15 F-5Es and three F-5Fs recently delivered. Subject to Congressional approval, the additional aircraft are said to be needed to maintain readiness and to train replacement pilots for operational units.

USA
The USAF Military **Airlift Command** is **reserving** 127,000 hours of heavyweight **lift time on** Lockheed C-5A **Galaxies** while the fleet undergoes its wing modification programme during 1982-87 in order to cater for any contingencies. This will demand a complex balancing act to keep the requisite lift time available as Galaxies enter and leave the modification cycle.

AIRCRAFT AND INDUSTRY

BRAZIL
EMBRAER has announced that it is developing a **pressurised version of** the **Bandeirante** as the EMB-110P3, for delivery from the spring of 1983. Powered by 1,173 shp PT6A-65 turboprops, it will have a cabin differential of 2·5 psi (0,18 kg/cm²), to give a 10,000 ft (3 050 m) equivalent when cruising at 17,000 ft (5 182 m); the cruising speed will be 265 kt (490 km/h) and the range will be better than 600 naut mls (1 062 km). As well as pressurisation, the 19-seat EMB-110P3 will differ from existing Bandeirantes in having a T-tail and a new undercarriage developed by the French company ERAM.

EMBRAER has concluded its **negotiations with Neiva** (see *Airscene*/May 1980) by acquiring the entire stock of the latter company, which will be retained as a fully-owned subsidiary. The Neiva factory, with a workforce of about 400, will be used primarily to handle light aircraft production (Piper types and the Ipenema), making more space available in the EMBRAER plant for Bandeirante, Brasilia and T-27 production.

CANADA
De Havilland Canada announced on 20 May that 17 companies have signed **letters of intent** in respect of 55 of the new 32/36-passenger **Dash 8 commuterliners** (see pp 34-35). First deliveries, to norOntair, are to be made in mid-1984 and the aircraft covered by the commitments now announced will all have been delivered by early 1986. The list of 15 airlines (eight USA, four Canadian, one UK, one Columbian and one Pacific) and two oil companies planning to acquire Dash 8s is as follows: Golden Gate Airlines, 12; Pennsylvania Commuter Airlines, 6; Southern Jersey Airways, 4; Golden West Airlines, 3; Henson Airlines, 3; Ransome Airlines, 3; Rio Airlines, 3; Air Oregon, 2; Time Air, 4; norOntair, 2; Trans North Turbo Air, 2; Aerolineas Centrales de Colombia, 2; Brymon Airways, 2; South Pacific Island Airways, 2; Dome Petroleum, 1; unnamed western Canadian carrier, 3 and unnamed Canadian oil company, 1.

CHINA
Three **prototypes of the Y-10** four-engined 140-seat airliner are reported to be in various stages of completion at the Shanghai Aircraft Factory, and first flight is expected to be made this year. One of the three airframes is believed to be assigned to structural testing and the other two will be used for flight testing. Powered by four Pratt & Whitney JT3D-3 turbofans, the Y-10 is of the same configuration as the Boeing 707 but is slightly smaller than the 707-320. The engines are drawn from a substantial stock of spares purchased in 1972 when 10 Boeing 707s were ordered by CAAC, but Boeing engineers who have visited China discount the view that the Y-10 is a "Chinese copy" of the American aircraft, and have been told by Chinese officials that project design of the Y-10 began in 1970 with a view to developing China's technical capabilities. A **new version of the Y-11** twin-engined utility transport is also reported to be under development at the Harbin Aircraft Factory, to be powered by Pratt & Whitney PT6A-110 turboprops in place of locally-powered piston radial engines. Production of the PT6A may take place in China under licence.

FEDERAL GERMANY
Dornier has introduced **new designations for** its current and future models of the **Skyservant**, taking the place of the previous Do 28D nomenclature. The basic Do 28D-2 with 380 hp Lycoming IO-540-A1E piston engines is now known as the Dornier 128-2, while the newly-launched Do 28D-6 with Pratt & Whitney PT6A-110 turboprops is now the Dornier 128-6. The new Do 28E variants, which feature the TNT wing and retractable undercarriage, will be Dornier 228s — the 228-100 with 15-passenger accommodation and the 228-200 with lengthened fuselage for 19 passengers. The first flight of the Dornier 228-100 is expected to be made during 1981, and the first batch of aircraft will have 715 shp Garrett AiResearch TPE331-5 turboprops. In due course, Dornier expects to offer Pratt & Whitney and Lycoming engine options.

Dornier began flight testing during March a **Skyservant** fitted **with** Lycoming TIGO-540 **turbosupercharged engines** and designated the Do 28D-2T. The conversion has been sponsored by the Federal Ministry of Defence and is intended to be applied to the 120 Do 28D-2 Skyservants that are in service with the *Luftwaffe* and *Marineflieger*.

FRANCE
Aérospatiale has confirmed that it is **ending** its effort to market the **Fouga 90** derivative of the Magister basic trainer. The single prototype totalled some 250 hrs of testing and has provided useful data for the definition of a new transition trainer for the *Armée de l'Air*, but the evaluation also showed that the characteristics of the Fouga 90 were too different from those of modern jet fighters to be acceptable to the *Armée de l'Air*. Without an order from the latter, Aérospatiale concluded that it would be impossible to export the Fouga 90, and attention is now being switched to the development of a completely new transition trainer which will have a lower total weight and a higher wing loading. The *Armée de l'Air* is expected to need a replacement for about 200 Magisters in the 1985-1990 period.

The **fourth** and last single-seat prototype of the Dassault-Breguet **Mirage 2000** made its **first flight** at Istres on 12 May. Piloted by Guy Mitaux-Maurouard, the Mirage 2000-04 reached $M = 1{\cdot}5$ and 42,000 ft (12 800 m) on its first flight, which was the 495th Mirage 2000 flight.

Sales of the SOCATA TB10 **Tobago and Tampico** continue to mount and by 31 March 1980, just under 11 months since marketing began, a total of 149 aircraft had been ordered. This total included 44 Tobago and 13 Tampico for French customers and 75 and 17 respectively for export. The production rate of the two types at Tarbes is now 19 aircraft a month. In the 15 months to 31 March 1980, SOCATA also took orders for 102 Rallyes, including 68 for export.

Dassault-Breguet announced that **sales of the Falcon 50** had reached 119 by the end of April, including 99 sold in North America by Falcon Jet Corporation. Aircraft No 3 — which in October 1978 flew non-stop from Chicago to Paris — recently carried 11 passengers from Honolulu to St Louis, a distance of 3,660 naut mls (6 771 km). Another long flight was made in April when the No 1 Falcon 50 flew from Teterboro to Hanover, a distance of 3,382 naut mls (6 264 km) in 8 hrs 21 min. Current sales totals for the Falcon 10 and Falcon 20 are 194 and 459 respectively.

Following the successful operation of a modified **Douglas DC-6 water-bomber** in the fire-fighting rôle in France during 1979, alongside the *Protection Civile* fleet of Canadair CL-215s, the French government has ordered the conversion of three more DC-6s for use later this year. The modification will be made by UTA, which was responsible for the first conversion.

INTERNATIONAL
VFW has completed the first **conversion of** an Airbus **A300B4-100 to -200** standard, permitting an increase in gross weight from 347,200 lb (157 500 kg) to 363,800 lb (165 000 kg). The conversion involves structural strengthening of the fuselage and modification of the undercarriage and results in an increase of 300 naut mls (556 km) in the range with max payload. The first aircraft converted was one of the Air France fleet; a second for Air France and one for Hapag Lloyd are to be converted shortly. Airbus Industrie is now offering **higher** landing and zero fuel **weights as customer options** for both the B4-100 and the B4-200;

compared with the standard landing weight of 295,300 lb (134 000 kg) and zero fuel weight of 273,300 lb (124 000 kg), the new figures are 300,000 lb (136 000 kg) and 277,700 lb (126 000 kg) respectively. These same higher weights will also apply to the A300-600 which (see *Airscene*/March 1980) will have a redesigned interior to allow one more seat row, and the tail cone and some other new features of the A310. Probably using later versions of the CF6-50 or JT9D engine, the A300-600 will also have more underfloor cargo space and larger cargo loading doors; it is likely to be available in 1984.

ISRAEL

FAA **certification of** the IAI **Westwind 2** was obtained on 17 April and the prototype of this new version (with SIGMA wing and winglets) was delivered to Helcol (Avianca) in Colombia on 16 May. Deliveries of production Westwind 2s to customers in the USA will begin in September. In the last four months, IAI has sold 41 Westwinds, and the production rate is now four a month; a fully descriptive feature article on the Westwind will appear in our next issue.

The four IAI **Westwinds** recently **ordered by Rhein Flugzeugbau** and to be operated by that company on behalf of the *Marineflieger* will be used to tow radar-reflective targets at speeds up to 300 kt (530 km), primarily for anti-aircraft training. The target-towing system is being designed and developed partly by IAI and will provide for targets to be changed in flight. The first of the Westwinds will be delivered early in 1981 and the others in the course of the same year.

ITALY

The prototype **Tyne-engined** Aeritalia **G.222L** general-purpose military transport made an **initial flight** of 2 hrs 03 mins on 15 May with the Aeritalia chief test pilot, Cmdt Bellio, at the controls. Production deliveries of the G.222L are scheduled to commence early next year at a rate of one per month. Production of the 44 T64-powered G.222s for the Italian *Aeronautica Militare* is now essentially complete, the most recent order for this version having been placed by Somalia for three.

The **Agusta A 109A** has now been **certificated for** single-pilot **IFR** operations by both the British and West German authorities, at a gross weight of 5,730 lb (2 600 kg). Following this approval, the first A 109A on the British register was delivered to Barratt Developments Ltd, through the UK agents, Alan Mann Helicopters Ltd.

JAPAN

Kawasaki has completed the preliminary design of an **improved version of** the **KV-107-2** tandem rotor helicopter which it builds under licence from Boeing Vertol. Expected to be purchased by the JASDF in the search-and-rescue rôle, the new version features 1,700 shp General Electric CT7 engines (in place of 1,400 shp CT58s), retractable landing gear, composite main rotors and fuel stowed in streamlined external tanks. Principal characteristics include a max speed of 138 kt (256 km/h), range of 740 naut mls (1 370 km), payload of 9,900 lb (4 500 kg) and loiter time of 2·9 hr at a distance of 200 naut mls (370 km) from base. Gross weight is increased from 21,390 lb (9 700 kg) to 22,930 lb (10 400 kg).

SOVIET UNION

A Tupolev **Tu-144**, bearing the registration CCCP-77106 and therefore apparently the aircraft used to fly the first regular (freight and mail) service between Moscow and Alma Ata on 26 December 1975, has been **added to** the exhibits of the **aviation museum** at Monino. According to Soviet reports, the aircraft landed on the unpaved runway at Monino, using three braking parachutes to help it to stop in the available distance.

UNITED KINGDOM

British Aerospace has started a nine-month **fatigue test** schedule **on a Lightning F Mk 6**, in order to confirm an increase in the planned service life of the fighter. The RAF has already announced its plans to prolong the in-service life of the aircraft and to extend the training and operational rôle of the two present squadrons flying Lightnings in Strike Command. A third squadron is to be formed from reserve stocks next year. The increased emphasis on low-altitude operation has changed the fatigue spectrum since the Lightning first entered service in 1960 as a high-altitude interceptor, and the new test will simulate several thousands of hours of sub- and supersonic flying, using an airframe that has already completed a substantial service life.

USA

Boeing has ended its flight test programme with the Model **707 powered by four CFM56** turbofans and has indicated that it **will not proceed** further with its tentative plans to offer a retrofit programme for the 707-320s to be modified to 707-700s with the new engines. A total of 164 hrs was flown in 86 flights by the prototype, which is now to be modified back to 707-320C standard and is likely to become the last commercial 707 sold. The decision not to proceed with the 707-700 reflects Boeing's failure to secure the required minimum number of orders for conversions from airlines that required either the lower noise levels or the greater range offered by use of the CFM56. The decision does not affect the programme to convert the USAF's fleet of KC-135A tankers to KC-135RE type with CFM56 engines and the company is also continuing to study a possible derivative of the E-3A Sentry (itself based on the 707-320 airframe) powered by CFM56 engines to meet the current USN requirements for a new TACAMO aircraft as a follow-on for the EC-130Q Hercules used as a communications link with submerged submarines.

Uprated engines and a lengthened upper deck to seat about 65-70 passengers are among the **improvements planned** by Boeing **for Model 747s** to be delivered from 1982 onwards. All of the "big three" engine manufacturers are expected to have uprated versions of their turbofans available in the 1982-84 timescale, starting with the 53,000 lb st (24 040 kgp) Rolls-Royce RB.211-524D4 in March 1982 and already ordered by Qantas and Air New Zealand. Pratt & Whitney expects to certificate before the end of 1982 the 54,750 lb st (24 835 kgp) JT9D-7R4G-2, a variant in the -7R4 series of engines already adopted to power the Boeing 767. Finally, in 1984, General Electric will have available the 56,000 lb st (25 400 kgp) CF6-80C/C1, also derived from that company's engine for the Boeing 767. Extending aft the upper fuselage deck will increase its capacity from 32 to about 67, and a straight stairway access is also now being offered for the upper deck in place of the spiral stairway, making it possible to load tourist class passengers onto the upper deck by way of the second entrance door rather than through the forward door and first class cabin area.

Boeing is continuing with its studies of a **stretched derivative of the 737** as the Model 737-300, although it has not yet made specific offers to airlines or reached a final definition. Interest centres upon a version with the fuselage lengthened by 6 ft 8 in (2,03 m) to give 12 more seats in mixed-class arrangements, and making use of the improved flight deck developed for the 737-200s now in production for British Airways and Lufthansa, with advanced digital avionics and improved control systems. Engines on the 737-300, if it goes ahead, are almost certain to be either the CFM56-3 or the more recently launched Rolls-Royce/Japan RJ-500, both of which are in the 19,000-20,000 lb st (8 618-9 072 kgp) thrust bracket and are small enough to be accommodated under the 737 wing without modifying the landing gear.

Some preliminary studies have been made by General Dynamics' Convair Division of a **retrofit programme for the CV-880**, substituting a pair of CFM56 turbofans for the four General Electric CJ805s. Of 43 Convair 880s reported to be current at the end of 1979, 24 are owned by Gulfstream American, which has developed its own all-cargo conversion scheme for the aircraft and is the prime prospect for the engine retrofit programme. The other CV-880s are owned in ones and twos.

Hiller Aviation Inc, which has been producing the three-seat UH-12E helicopter at Porteville, California, since 1973, has now **purchased** all **rights in** the **FH-1100** from Fairchild Industries, including tooling, engineering documentation and type certification. Production of the FH-1100 — which was originally designed by Hiller for the Army LOH competition in the mid 'sixties — will be resumed in California next year. Fairchild had acquired the FH-1100 from the earlier Hiller Aircraft company in 1966 and built some 246 examples up to 1973, when production ceased. Hiller plans to use a 420 shp Allison 250-C20B engine in place of the less powerful C18 used previously.

En route to Germany to make its first public appearance at the Hanover Air Show at the end of April, the prototype Gulfstream American **Gulfstream III set** two world class **records** with a non-stop flight from Savannah to Hanover. The distance of 4,600 mls (7 400 km/h) was covered at an average speed of 511 mph (822 km/h). With certification expected by mid-summer, the Gulfstream III is now backed by nearly 60 orders.

Bellanca Aircraft Corp has **suspended production** of the Citabria, Decathlon and Scout high-wing monoplanes at its Osceola, Wisconsin, plant and has laid off all its production personnel at that site. At Alexandria, Minnesota, more than half the production workforce has been laid off and production of the Viking low-wing monoplane has been halted. Work is continuing on the Aries T-250, the first production example of which was delivered to a dealer on 17 April, and on the Eagle agricultural biplane, produced under licence for Eagle Aircraft Co.

Bristow Helicopters has decided **not to convert** into a firm order its **options on** five Boeing Vertol 234LR **Chinooks** and a similar decision has been taken in respect of three options held by Helikopter Service A/S of Norway. The eight Chinooks were intended to be operated by the two companies as a joint venture in the British and Norwegian sectors of the North Sea, starting in 1982, and represented a total order value of $143m. In an unusually frank statement regarding its decision, Bristow indicated that intensive analysis and negotiations over many months had failed to convince the company that the Commercial Chinook could be guaranteed to meet the stringent demands of operation in the 'eighties. Specifically, Bristow said that "Boeing Vertol ... forecasted that four years from the Chinook entering commercial service only about 60 per cent of the dynamic components would reach their targetted TBO's" and that in the opinion of the two operators "Boeing Vertol's warranty terms were totally inadequate". Similarly, it was claimed of the

AL5512 engines that Avco Lycoming "did not envisage the attainment of an overhaul cycle of 4,000 hrs until about four years after first entry into commercial service" and "was not prepared to guarantee the obtaining of a 2½-minute single-engined contingency rating". Notwithstanding the Bristow/Helikopter Service decision, Boeing Vertol is continuing to develop the Commercial Chinook, for which it now holds orders for seven (including six for British Airways) and five options. First flight is expected to be made this month (July).

Delivery of the **10,000th** Pratt & Whitney **JT8D turbofan**, to the Boeing company for use in a 727, sets a new record in commercial jet engine production. Since introduction in 1964, the JT8Ds have flown more than 164 million hours, powering over 3,000 aircraft in service with 175 operators, including Boeing 727s and 737s, Douglas DC-9s, Super Caravelles and Dassault Mercures. More than 1,000 additional JT8Ds are at present on order.

The **second prototype** of the **Citation III** joined the **flight test** programme on 2 May at Wichita. At that time, the first prototype had completed 180 hrs of testing, with speeds up to Mach 0·85 achieved. First customer deliveries are scheduled for the beginning of 1982, and production is sold out to the end of 1984.

Boeing has developed a "jet-mixer" **sound suppressor for** use on the JT8D engines of the **Boeing 737**. Mixing the high-velocity hot gases with slower-moving cold air from the front fan serves to reduce the noise levels below the take-off path by about three decibels. The mixer has been flight-tested and its first application will be on the 32 Advanced 737-200s ordered by Lufthansa for delivery from the end of this year.

Martin Marietta Aerospace has been selected as the **supplier of** the **TADS/PNVS** fire control and sensor system **for the Hughes AH-64A** attack helicopter, following a fly-off competition with a system developed by Northrop. Martin has been awarded a 26-month contract for the final development phase, leading to full production starting in December 1981. The equipment comprises two independently functioning subsystems — the target acquisition and designation sight (TADS) and the pilot night-vision sensor (PNVS).

To meet the USAF requirement for a new generation trainer (NGT) replacing the Cessna T-37B, **Vought Corp** has proposed a **design based on** the Rhein Flugzeugbau **Fantrainer**. The submission is made jointly by Vought and VFW (the parent company of RFB) and is competing with proposals made by Cessna, Fairchild, Rockwell, General Dynamics and Gulfstream American (see *Airscene*/May 1980). The Vought/VFW project is in effect a scaled up version of the Fantrainer as recently evaluated by the *Luftwaffe*, differing in having side-by-side rather than tandem seating and a pair of 625 shp Allison 250-C30 or Avco-Lycoming LTS-101 engines in place of the single 425 shp turboprop in the German prototype. Gross weight of the projected trainer is about 5,000 lb (2 270 kg).

Deliveries of **Enstrom helicopters** were **resumed** on 20 March, after a five-month interruption (see *Airscene*/April 1980), with Turbo Shark F-280s going to Californian and French dealers. Certification work on the Hawk has also now been resumed.

Lockheed has begun flight testing of a C-130H **Hercules** fitted **with** two small **ventral fins** on the rear fuselage beneath the tailplane. By smoothing out air flow round the tail and rear fuselage, the fins reduce aerodynamic drag and are claimed to cut fuel consumption by about three per cent in the long-range cruise. They were developed as part of USAF efforts to reduce its fuel bills.

Flight **testing of** the **prototype Beech Commuter C99** was expected to start last month (June). The aircraft is c/n U50, a Model 99 Airliner purchased from Allegheny Commuter last year with 15,000 hrs flown. The aircraft has been completely stripped and refurbished and has had new PT6A-34 engines installed. It was being painted during April and after instrumentation during May will be used for development flying and FAA certification, to be completed by October. It will then embark on a nationwide demonstration tour. Delivery of new-production C99s will begin in mid-1981.

As part of its participation in the **Boeing 767** programme, Kawasaki is designing an **optional larger door** for the forward underfloor cargo compartment, with a width of 134 in (3,40 m) compared with the standard 70-in (1,78-m) door. The larger door will be first fitted in the No 14 Boeing 767 and Kawasaki expects that a substantial proportion of customers will specify this feature. Meanwhile, production of 767 components is proceeding on schedule in Japan, with Kawasaki to deliver the first wing rib set and front/centre fuselage units in June/July, the first aft fuselage section leaving Mitsubishi's Nagoya plant in August and Fuji delivering the first wing/fuselage fairing sets in October.

Bell is investigating, in company-funded programmes, **possible improvements in** the **AH-1 Cobra** series. Two separate prototypes are in flight test: one is an AH-1S fitted with a four-bladed main rotor similar to that of the Bell Model 412 but of 2-ft (0,61-m) less diameter; the other, more extensive, modification replaces the Pratt & Whitney T400-WV-402 Twin Pac of the standard AH-1T with two General Electric CT7-2 engines plus the transmission and plastics-construction blades of the Model 214ST. With gross power increased by more than 50 per cent, this AH-1T Plus has a greatly-improved high-altitude and single-engined performance, and the potential to fly at gross weights up to 40 per cent greater than the standard AH-1T.

Riley Aircraft of Carlsbad, Calif, has flown the **prototype** of its Cessna 421C Golden Eagle conversion with turboprops. Known as the **Riley Turbine Eagle,** it is powered by Pratt & Whitney PT6A-135 engines flat-rated at 780 shp. The aircraft is thus comparable with Cessna's own Corsair which differs from the Turbine Eagle in having a longer span (Cessna 414-type) wing and dihedral on the tailplane. In another programme, Schafer Aircraft Modifications of Clifton, Texas, offers a PT6A-135 conversion of the Cessna 404, with gross weight of 8,400 lb (3 810 kg) and cruising speed of 285 mph (459 km/h).

The Piper **Navajo** is the subject of two **conversion schemes** currently on offer in the USA. The Panther Navajo is the latest programme of the Colemill company, featuring 350 hp Lycoming TIO-540-J2BD engines and four-bladed propellers in place of the standard 310 hp engines, the new installation being similar to that of the Navajo Chieftain. The Panther follows earlier Colemill conversions of the Cessna 310 and Beech Baron 55 to, respectively, the Executive 600 and President 600, both with increased engine power. At Clifton, Tex, Schafer Aircraft Modifications is converting pressurised Navajos to have PT6A-135 turboprops; with a gross weight of 8,350 lb (3 788 kg), the cruising speed is 285 mph (459 km/h). Flight testing of a prototype began recently and conversions are to be made at the rate of 10 a year.

CIVIL AFFAIRS

AUSTRALIA

The Australian regional carrier East-West Airlines has taken over responsibility for the operation of **air services in the** country's **Northern Territory**, replacing Connair. A new airline is being set up, named Northern, in which EWA holds a 51 per cent share and the balance is being offered for sale to local residents. The new airline is expected to operate Swearingen Metros in place of Connair's piston-engined types.

FEDERAL GERMANY

LTU put its first Lockheed **L-1011-500 TriStar into** regular **service** on 15 May, one week after delivery, and has scheduled an average daily utilisation of more than 17 hrs, six days a week. Its schedule includes a weekly Düsseldorf-Los Angeles flight which is the longest regular operation by TriStar with a distance of 5,980 mls (9 622 km). LTU has five L-1011-1s in its fleet and has a second Dash 500 on order for delivery later this year.

FRANCE

The *Service de la Formation Aéronautique et du Controle Technique* **(SFACT)**, a department of the French *Direction Generale de l'Aviation Civile*, has **ordered 18** Robin **Aiglon** light four-seaters. They will have modified cockpits with an inclined instrument panel, increasing pilot comfort and making space for a Badin-Crouzet radio to be installed. A new control console is also fitted.

JAPAN

Japanese **carriers** expect to carry 42-43 million passengers in 1980, up from about 38 million in 1979, and **will introduce** a number of **new aircraft** in the course of the year. JAL expects to take delivery of five DC-10 Srs 40s, two Boeing 747Bs, two 747SRs and a 747F (leaving three DC-10s and three 747s on order for 1981 delivery) and will retire six DC-8s during the year. All Nippon Airways will receive six more Boeing 747SRs during the year, joining a 97-aircraft fleet. TDA expects to receive three A300s and five DC-9 Super 80s (leaving six and three, respectively, on order) to join a 62-aircraft fleet that includes 40 YS-11s. Two of the DC-9 Srs 41s will be retired and three more will be modified to have advanced automatic braking systems to permit operations at 5,000-ft (1 500-m) airfields, like five already in service. Japan Asia Airways will lease two DC-10s from JAL, in place of DC-8s, for its charter operations between Tokyo and Taipei.

UNITED KINGDOM

Loganair has **resumed** its **Translink operations**, with effect from 28 April, to link Prestwick International Airport with Aberdeen, Edinburgh and Belfast on a daily basis and (from 3 May) with the Isle of Man on Saturdays and Sundays. The Translink service was launched in 1979, using a Shorts 330, but was suspended at the end of the summer season when traffic declined. The resumed service is operated by Twin Otters and the company's newly-delivered Bandeirante.

British Caledonian was granted a **licence** by the CAA to operate scheduled services between **London** (Gatwick) **and Hong Kong;** applications by Laker and Hong Kong-based Cathay Pacific were rejected. The licence provides competition for British Airways, which has been the sole operator on the route and has been criticised for not providing an adequate service. B.Cal subsequently said it would inaugurate service in August, using DC-10 Srs 30s and building up to daily service by November. The fare structure will include a £100 one-way fare for "Eleventh Hour" stand-by seats.

USA

Regular operations by a new **helicopter operator** were scheduled to begin **in the San Francisco area** at the end of June. Backed by Hanson Aviation, SFO Helicopter Airlines Inc is operating two 18-passenger Sikorsky S-58T helicopters (acquired from Bristow Helicopters and Okanagan Helicopters in the UK and Canada respectively), initially to fly 20 return trips a day between San Francisco and Oakland International Airports.

The CAB has given tentative approval to the planned **acquisition of Hughes Airwest by Republic Airlines** and has given final and unanimous approval of the **acquisition of Seaboard** World Airlines **by Tiger International**, to effect a merger with Flying Tiger Line. The latter decision has, however, drawn opposition from the US Justice Department, which at press-time was considering taking the case to the US Court of Appeals. Such action, even if not resulting in a reversal of the decision, would make it impossible for the merger to be concluded within the projected three-month period and with Seaboard continuing to lose money, this would jeopardise the deal. In another deal, **Midwest Charter Express**, which operates a fleet of 54 aircraft for overnight package deliveries, has been **acquired by Airborne Freight Corp**. The latter is a forwarding company which has been using Midwest services almost exclusively. The fleet includes six Caravelles and 13 NAMC YS-11s as well as a mixture of smaller types. Most of the latter are expected to be sold by the new owners and plans have been announced to acquire a mix of 10-12 second-hand Boeing 727s and 737s in the near future.

Following delivery of the first of 12 Lockheed **L-1011-500 TriStars** to Pan American on 11 April at Palmdale, Calif, the airline put the new type **into revenue service** on 1 May between New York and Caracas, one month ahead of schedule. The Pan Am TriStars are the first in service to feature an active control system (see AIR INTERNATIONAL/April 1980) which, together with the use of a computerised performance management system and the latest RB.211-524B engines, contribute to an eight per cent reduction in fuel consumption, compared with earlier TriStar versions. With six L-1011s to be delivered this year and six more next year, Pan Am plans to use its TriStars primarily to replace its Boeing 707-320s, of which it has 20 in service and seven retired; all will be out of service by November.

Air Florida and **Northwest Orient Airlines** are the newest airlines to inaugurate **transatlantic service,** respectively flying a weekly schedule between Miami and Amsterdam with effect from 1 June and a daily service between London Gatwick and Minneapolis/St Paul, starting on 2 June.

CIVIL CONTRACTS AND SALES

Aérospatiale/BAe Concorde: Air France received a fifth Concorde, No 213, to allow additional services to be flown on the North Atlantic and for "better management of the present Concorde fleet". Delivery was made on 9 May and the aircraft entered service 14 May.

Aérospatiale Corvette: Sales of two more SN 601s from existing stocks were announced, one each to Air Foyal in Martinique and Taxi Leadair at Le Bourget, Paris.

Airbus A310: Austrian Airlines' previously-announced interest has been confirmed with a firm order for two, to be delivered late 1985/early 1986, with two more on option. The Austrian company has specified Pratt & Whitney JT9D-7R4 engines for its A310s.

Boeing 727: JAT Yugoslav Airlines ordered two more 727s to bring its total to 11; delivery will be made in May and June 1981. □ American Airlines confirmed that it had ordered 12 more 727s for 1981 delivery but has cancelled options on 10 for 1982.

Boeing 737: Noga SA Import and Export Company of Geneva has ordered one high-gross-weight 737-200 for executive use, with an additional 3,000 US gal (11 356 l) of fuel. Delivery will be made in December 1981. □ Ladeco in Chile ordered four Advanced 737-200s for delivery from July 1980 to November 1982. □ International Lease Finance Corp ordered another 737-200 for March 1981 delivery.

Boeing 747: All Nippon Airways order for six more 747SRs has been confirmed by Boeing, making 13 in all. Powered by CF6 engines, the new aircraft will be delivered from May this year to March 1981. □ Libyan Arab Airlines has abandoned its efforts to obtain an export licence for three 747 Combis, two of which have been completed; delivery has been blocked by the US State Department and Boeing is now expected to make the aircraft available to other customers. □ Lufthansa ordered four more 747s with CF6-50 engines. They comprise one 747F for September 1981 delivery, two 747C Combis for December 1981 and February 1982 and a -200B for March 1982. Options were taken on two more 747s.

British Aerospace 748: The Frankfurt-based commuter airline DLT ordered three 52-seat 748 Srs 2Bs for 1981 delivery with three more on option.

CASA C-212 Aviocar: Indonesia's Ministry of Communication has ordered 14 more NC-212s from Nurtanio, of which 12 are to be made available to Merpati Nusantara Airlines and two will be used by the LPPU Aviation Training Centre. Nurtanio's sales of NC-212s now total 99 of which 19 have been delivered, including two supplied from the CASA production line.

EMBRAER EMB-110 Bandeirante: Lucas Aigle Azur, a French charter company based in Pontoise, has acquired one EMB-110P1. It has initially been leased to Air Littoral, which will soon take delivery of its own (third) Bandeirante.

EMBRAER EMB-120 Brasilia: Brazilian regional airline TAM has taken options on 10 Brasilias and VOTEC is expected to take options on five.

Fokker F28: Aerolineas Argentinas has taken delivery of one F28 Mk 4000, supplementing three Mk 1000s in service for several years.

GAF Nomad: The Airline of the Marshall Islands, newly founded to operate domestic routes and services linking the 36 islands in the territory, has acquired one 12-passenger N22B and one 16-passenger N24A. The aircraft are fitted with nose-mounted search radar and OMEGA navaids to allow for their use also on maritime surveillance to detect fishing poachers around the islands.

Hughes 500D: Les Helicopteres La Verendrye Inc of Montreal ordered 15 more Hughes 500Ds, adding to six in course of delivery.

MBB BO 105: The Indonesian Ministry of Agriculture followed up its letter of intent for Nurtanio-built BO 105s (this column last month) by placing a firm order for 12 of the helicopters, half to be delivered this year and six in 1981. □ The Indonesian Ministry of Communications ordered one BO 105, for use by the Aviation Training Centre in West Java. The order brings total sales of the helicopter by Nurtanio to 107, of which 33 had been delivered by April (including six supplied from MBB production).

McDonnell Douglas DC-9: Republic Airlines has confirmed an order for 10 Super 80s and has taken options on four more. Southern Airways, which merged with North Central to form Republic, was one of the launch customers for the Super 80 but subsequently cancelled the order while the fleet needs were re-assessed following the merger. □ Toa Domestic has sold six Srs 41s to Finnair, to be delivered between December 1980 and February 1983.

Mitsubishi MU-2: Recent sales of the MU-2 series include a Solitaire to Bristow Helicopters for operation jointly with Shell Oil in Africa from Lagos, and a Marquise to TAW Leasing Corp in Abidjan, Ivory Coast, for use as a demonstrator. Sales now exceed 640.

Shorts 330: Olympic Airways has ordered two 330s for operation by Olympic Aviation on feeder services on the Greek mainland and throughout the Aegean islands. Delivery was being made in May and June, and options have been taken on four more.

Swearingen Metro II: Big Sky Airlines has taken delivery of two Metro IIs and has two on order for 1981, operating scheduled services in Montana and Wyoming.

MILITARY CONTRACTS

Agusta-Bell AB 212ASW: Agusta has received a contract for a number — unofficially reported as eight — of AB 212ASW helicopters for use by the Iraqi Air Force.

Beech T-34C Turbine Mentor: At the beginning of May, the air component of the Ecuadorian Navy took delivery of three T-34C-1 trainers under a $3·5m (£1·52m) contract which also includes a single Super King Air (for early 1981 delivery), operational equipment and spares. This purchase follows earlier procurement of 20 T-34C-1s by the Ecuadorian Air Force.

De Havilland Canada DHC-5D Buffalo: The Air Wing of the Tanzanian Defence Force has placed a follow-on order for two DHC-5D Buffalo STOL transports to increase the Wing's fleet of this type to six aircraft.

EMBRAER EMB-110P1 Bandeirante: The *Force Aérienne Gabonaise* has placed an order with EMBRAER for three EMB-110P1 light utility transports and one EMB-111 maritime surveillance aircraft with deliveries scheduled for completion by the end of 1981.

FFA AS.202 Bravo: The Indonesian government has placed a SwFr6m (£1·57m) contract with FFA for the supply of 20 AS.202 Bravo primary trainers.

IAI Arava: The *Fuerza Aérea Colombiana* took delivery of three Arava STOL utility transports in March.

Westland Lynx: On 29 May, Westland announced orders for 32 Lynx helicopters, valued, with spares, etc, at £65m. These orders comprised 10 for the Royal Navy (to supplement 60 previously ordered), 14 for France's *Aéronavale* (26 previously ordered) and eight for an unspecified export customer.

Westland/Aérospatiale Puma: On 23 May, Westland handed over to the RAF the first of a new batch of eight Pumas. Previously, the RAF had received 40 Pumas with deliveries completed in 1972.

JAKTVIGGEN

MAJOR BOOST FOR SWEDISH AIR DEFENCE

Ten years ago, the Swedish Air Defence Committee completed what was asserted at the time to be the most fundamental investigation into Sweden's air defences ever carried out. One vital conclusion was that, as stated unequivocally in its final report to the Supreme Commander, a version of the Saab 37 Viggen optimised for the intercept rôle offered the most efficacious answer to the demands of the Swedish airspace defence scenario postulated for the 'eighties. Today, a decade on, the highly effective warplane which this conclusion launched on its development cycle has completed intensive service trials and is on the threshold of fully operational status.

DURING THIS SUMMER, when one of the *divisioner*, or squadrons, of the *Bråvalla Flygflottilj* (F 13) at Norrköping, some 110 miles (175 km) south-east of Stockholm, is declared combat ready on the *JaktViggen*, Sweden's Air Force will be able to claim with justification that it has brought to operational status what is undoubtedly the most advanced all-weather all-altitude air defence system of European design yet to have achieved production.

That Sweden, a nation of fewer than eight-and-a-half millions and possessor of an aerospace industry with barely 12,000 personnel, can field modern combat aeroplanes of indigenous design and manufacture no longer gives rise to astonishment. This Scandinavian country has now maintained its extraordinary unilateral posture in the front echelon of advanced warplane manufacturing nations for some three decades. What *is* surprising is the fact that the Swedish aircraft industry has established a lead over other and much larger West European industries of some four years in bringing to full-scale production and service a fighter which, in capability, can be matched only by the very latest — and vastly more expensive — US fighters, such as the F-15 Eagle. The situation is not without its element of irony when it is considered that more than one of the immensely more populous and industrially more powerful West European nations sadly lack a defensive warplane of the calibre of the *JaktViggen*.

The Viggen *per se* is no newcomer to the European aeronautical scene. What visitor to any major international air show with a European venue in recent years does not retain a vivid impression of this Swedish warplane literally hurling itself into the air within something less than 550 yards, attended by an ear-searing cacophony; of its awe-evoking turns, as often as not within the airfield perimeter, and its constant-attitude arrival preceding a startlingly truncated landing run — no aerial frivolities these for the amusement of spectators but demonstrations for their edification of capabilities intrinsic to the concept of this uniquely configured warplane.

But if the aircraft responsible for these memorable displays of aeronautical verve is no newly-presented débutante — indeed, Viggen, in its AJ 37 version, began to enter the ranks of *Flygvapnet* nine years ago — and the *JaktViggen*, now occupying the Saab-Scania assembly line at Linköping and about to attain combat status at Norrköping, displays only modest external dissimilarities to the Viggen first delivered to F 7 at Såtenäs in the summer of 1971, it should not be supposed that differences between the two models are nominal. On the contrary, beneath the skin the *JaktViggen* is a *very* different aeroplane to Viggens of the first generation, the last of which, an SF 37 reconnaissance model, was completed at Linköping on 1 February and delivered to F 21 at Luleå.

Whereas the initial Viggen model, the AJ 37, was essentially an attack aircraft with secondary fighter capability, the *JaktViggen*, or JA 37, is optimised for the fighter mission while retaining some attack capability, as is indicated by the transposition of the functional letters (J = Jakt, or Fighter, and A = Attack) prefixing the numerical designation. Entirely new radar and avionics have been applied to an airframe refined and reinforced to permit increase of the load spectrum, mated with an improved and more powerful engine, and coupled with new weapons for the air-air rôle, to result in what is indisputably one of the world's most advanced air defence systems. Yet, withal, external similarity between first-generation attack aircraft and second-generation fighter remains surprisingly close — much more so, for example, than between IDS and ADV versions of Tornado — and the greatly enhanced mission capabilities have apparently been attained without any sacrifice of fundamental qualities — such as ease of piloting and maintenance, and amenability to operational deployment on secondary fields and roads — for which the AJ 37 Viggen has justifiably gained acclaim.

A decade of development

From the outset of Viggen development, the new warplane was based on the "standardised platform" concept; a basic design more or less readily adaptable to fulfil the four primary rôles of attack, interception, reconnaissance and training, with each mission-optimised version having a secondary rôle (eg, the attack model having a secondary fighter capability, the reconnaissance variants possessing secondary attack faculty). The specification was as comprehensive as any conceived to that time — few have attempted to meet so demanding a specification since — and could only be met by a highly sophisticated aeroplane, and by the time that design definition was completed in 1962 and a development contract signed in October of that year, the project that was to be assigned the appellation of Viggen (Thunderbolt) was certainly sophisticated from every viewpoint.

Development priority was assigned to the AJ 37 attack variant and to the tandem two-seat SK 37 conversion training model — the early stage at which the latter was fed into the Linköping assembly line was to prove a vital factor in the successful service phase-in of Viggen — while evolution of the fighter variant was viewed as a somewhat longer term programme paced by development of adequately advanced intercept radar and air-air weapons necessary to provide the quantum advance in air defence capability sought by *Flygvapnet*. In fact, whereas changes to be introduced to suit Viggen for the training (SK 37) and reconnaissance (SH 37 and SF 37) tasks were minimal and confined almost solely to those dictated by mission requirements, those foreseen for the fighter (JA 37) were to be more fundamental and, indeed, such that this variant was soon being viewed as a second-generation aircraft.

Preliminary design work on the JA 37 and its systems commenced in 1968, and, because of priorities and workload imposed by other Viggen versions, proceeded in relatively low key until the early 'seventies, but in October 1972, the Swedish Defence Material Administration let major development contracts for the future *JaktViggen* and the programme accelerated. These contracts, which were intended to cover development up to 1 February 1975, were placed with Saab-Scania for continued development and production preparations (SKr 230m); Volvo Flygmotor for continued development of the RM 8B engine optimised for use by the future fighter (SKr 160m); the Kearfott Division of the Singer Company for inertial navigation system development (SKr 9m); Garrett AiResearch for digital air data equipment development (SKr 2m); L M Ericsson for the development of a target acquisition system (SKr 70m), and Svenska Radio for the continued development of the (EP-12) electronic display equipment (SKr 28m).

The flight testing of selected systems, including a prototype radar, commenced in the following year, utilising an adapted Saab 32 Lansen as a test vehicle, and four AJ 37 prototype airframes were assigned to JA 37 R&D, each of these being devoted to a specific aspect of the *JaktViggen* programme, while a fifth test aeroplane, to be built from the outset to what was then seen as the definitive JA 37 standard and was to be viewed in consequence as a pre-series aircraft rather than a prototype, was laid down. The first modified AJ 37 joined the JA 37 R&D programme on 4 June 1974, this aircraft being used primarily for stability and control system testing (and later being fitted with a pre-production RM 8B engine), the second, for RM 8B development, flew on 27 September 1974 (but was lost at an early stage in the programme), while the third AJ 37 to join the programme flew with JA 37 electronics

The JA 37 Viggen, seen here at Norrköping where F 13 is currently working up on this new interceptor, possesses what is probably the best short-field performance of any aircraft in its category. Externally, the JA 37 differs little from the earlier AJ 37, apart from the extension of the vertical tail surfaces which it shares with the two-seat SK 37 version.

Seen above with a full complement of AAMs — two Sky Flashes on the inboard wing pylons and four Sidewinders on the outboard wing and fuselage pylons — which, with the ventral KCA cannon, endow this Viggen with considerable potency in the air-air rôle, the JA 37 will more than double the effectiveness of Swedish air defence. The cannon installation is so designed that a ventral fuel tank may still be carried on the centreline pylon, as seen both above and below right.

on 22 November 1974 (this later being fitted with a pre-production radar). The fourth AJ 37, which flew on 30 May 1975, was also assigned to electronics testing initially, but was later to be assigned to weapon system development. The next *JaktViggen* R&D aircraft to fly was the newly-built pre-series aircraft, which, flown on 15 December 1975, was equipped with an RM 8B engine and pre-production avionics, and was primarily used for verifying performance tests with the electronic systems under various mission types and conditions. The stable of R&D aircraft was restored to full strength at the end of September 1976, when a fifth modified AJ 37 flew as an engine trials aircraft with a production standard RM 8B to replace the engine platform aircraft which had been lost earlier.

Meanwhile, on 6 September 1974, Saab-Scania received a contract for an initial batch of 30 JA 37s — at which time it was envisaged that service introduction would commence in 1978 — against a planned total of 149 aircraft to equip eight squadrons. The remaining 119 JA 37s were to be subsequently ordered in increments of 60 and 59 (the funding for the final batch being completed in March of this year). The first production JA 37 was to fly on 4 November 1977, with the first deliveries being effected to F 13 at Norrköping in 1979 to initiate an intensive service trials period during which the *JaktViggen* flew more than 300 operational missions against "live" targets in regular air defence exercises. The outcome of these trials was the pronouncement that the JA 37 fully meets the very stringent requirements of *Flygvapnet*, and the Swedish service endorsed Saab-Scania's claim that the *JaktViggen* is the most efficacious all-weather all-altitude fighter of European design yet to achieve production.

Advanced systems approach

The efficacy of the JA 37 of course owes much to its advanced systems approach, and of all its sub-systems its radar is the most vital element, this, after six years of flight testing, being cited by its manufacturer, L M Ericsson, as the first multi-mode pulse-doppler airborne radar system to attain series production. This intercept radar, designated PS-46/A, offers all-hemisphere coverage and all-altitude and look-down capability, as well as air-to-ground ranging, and during more than 1,000 hours of flight testing has consistently yielded detection ranges against typical "live" targets in excess of 30 miles (50 km) in look-down modes.

Representing a noteworthy pioneering achievement on the part of L M Ericsson, and a key factor in the JA 37's performance, the multi-mode PS-46/A can be configured to provide target search, target acquisition (either automatic via the head-up display or semi-automatic via the head-down display), target track (track-while-scan or continuous tracking), target illumination and air-to-ground ranging. Unaffected by variations of weather or altitude, the PS-46/A is virtually impervious to ground clutter and its design stresses resistance to electronic countermeasures. An extremely high level of reliability is claimed, this being achieved by a failure

A total of 329 Viggens has been ordered for Flygvapnet of which 149 will be JA 37s, these following 180 first-generation Viggens including 110 AJ 37s and the remainder comprising a mix of SK 37s, SF 37s and SH 37s. The photographs on these pages illustrate (above) an SF 37 of F 13's reconnaissance squadron with a camera nose and (port fuselage pylon) night camera and illumination pod; (below and top right) AJ 37s of F 7, and (below right) a JA 37 of F 13 (also illustrated at head of page 7).

13
FARA

rate corresponding to an MTBF of 100 hours and redundant modes of operation, and ease of maintenance is ensured by extensive built-in test facilities and functional partitioning into rapidly replaceable units which are readily interchangeable on the flight line. Unit replacement calls for the use of only two sizes of socket wrench, and specified elapsed time for replacement of, say, the data processor, is eight minutes, while the transmitter may be replaced within 12 minutes. The autonomous operation capability of the system is noteworthy as it provides *Flygvapnet* with the ability to fill any gaps in the ground radar coverage of Sweden's extensive borders that may arise during hostilities.

A less dramatic but nevertheless important contribution to the efficacy of the *JaktViggen* is its entirely new cockpit presentation system which, offering significant improvements over that of the AJ 37, itself widely praised, has been evolved by Saab-Scania in concert with Svenska Radio. The system is built up around three main electronic displays providing flight data and weapon aiming and delivery information: the head-up display (HUD) developed by Smiths Industries in collaboration with Svenska Radio for low-level flight and close-in air combat; the head-down display (HDD) for all-weather interception, and the tactical display for *en route* navigation or combat situation assessment and embodying a synthetic video map. All three displays can be read even in bright ambient light.

The HUD restricts symbology to essential information in order to offer good look-through capability and includes an optical aiming mode for close-in air combat, a "quick access switch" on the throttle lever clearing the HUD for optical aiming and bringing all other systems (ie, radar search and lock-on, autopilot, and weapon selection and aiming) into line. The HDD affords the pilot all the information that he needs during radar search (ie, heading, speed, altitude, attitude and terrain warning) without necessitating consultation of any other instrument, the data presentation being a mix of analogue and digital information, both aircraft-generated after target lock-on and ground control-derived. The tactical display provides basic geographic information, and the pilot may insert manually, via the central computer, reference points and other information, tactical information for intercept, navigation and landing being superimposed on the map.

Other features of the JA 37's avionics include Singer-Kearfott's SKC-2037 digital central computer, licence-manufactured by Saab-Scania as the CD 107, and offering a capacity five times that of the computer installed in the AJ 37. The computer's display system reduces the pilot's workload by limiting the information presented to that specifically required for a particular phase of the mission. Singer-Kearfott is also responsible for the JA 37's inertial navigation system, which, well integrated and demanding no pilot participation for normal operation, uses rapid-alignment dry gyros and offers

Saab JA 37 Viggen specification

Power Plant: One Volvo Flygmotor RM 8B turbofan with maximum ratings of 16,200 lb (7 350 kg) unreheated and 28,110 lb (12 750 kg) with full reheat. Fuel distributed between saddle tank over engine, one tank in each side of the fuselage, one tank aft of the cockpit and one tank in each wing.
Performance: Max speed (with two Rb 24 Sidewinder and two Rb 71 Sky Flash AAMs), 1,255-1,365 mph (2 020-2 195 km/h), or Mach=1·9-2·1, above 36,000 ft (11 000 m), 838 mph (1 350 km/h), or Mach=1·1, at 1,000 ft (305 m); patrol endurance, 1·5-2·0 hrs; tactical radius (HI-LO-HI), 620 mls (1 000 km) plus; time to 32,810 ft (10 000 m) from brakes off, 1·5 min; approach speed (approx), 137 mph (220 km/h); take-off run, 437 yds (400 m); landing roll, 547 yds (500 m).
Weights: Normal loaded (two Rb 24s and two Rb 71s), (approx) 37,480 lb (17 000 kg).
Dimensions: Span, 34 ft 9¼ in (10,60 m); length (excluding probe), 50 ft 8¼ in (15,45 m), (including probe), 53 ft 9½ in (16,40 m); height, 19 ft 4¼ in (5,90 m), (fin folded), 13 ft 1½ in (4,00 m); wing area (including foreplanes), 561·88 sq ft (52,20 m²).
Armament: One 30-mm Oerlikon KCA revolver-type cannon with 150 rounds, two Rb 71 Sky Flash radar-homing AAMs and two or four Rb 24 Sidewinder infrared-homing AAMs.

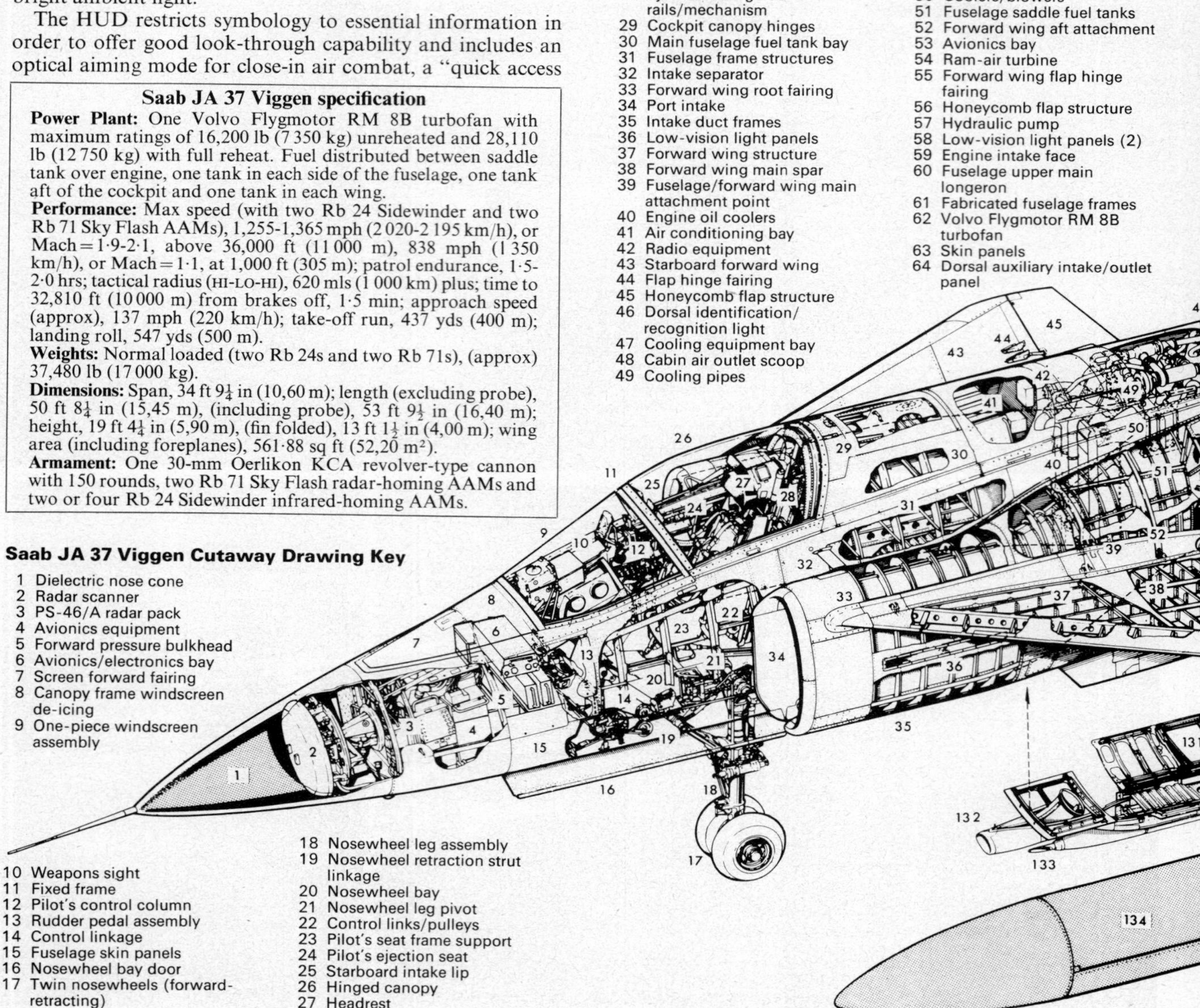

Saab JA 37 Viggen Cutaway Drawing Key

1 Dielectric nose cone
2 Radar scanner
3 PS-46/A radar pack
4 Avionics equipment
5 Forward pressure bulkhead
6 Avionics/electronics bay
7 Screen forward fairing
8 Canopy frame windscreen de-icing
9 One-piece windscreen assembly
10 Weapons sight
11 Fixed frame
12 Pilot's control column
13 Rudder pedal assembly
14 Control linkage
15 Fuselage skin panels
16 Nosewheel bay door
17 Twin nosewheels (forward-retracting)
18 Nosewheel leg assembly
19 Nosewheel retraction strut linkage
20 Nosewheel bay
21 Nosewheel leg pivot
22 Control links/pulleys
23 Pilot's seat frame support
24 Pilot's ejection seat
25 Starboard intake lip
26 Hinged canopy
27 Headrest
28 Ejection seat guide-rails/mechanism
29 Cockpit canopy hinges
30 Main fuselage fuel tank bay
31 Fuselage frame structures
32 Intake separator
33 Forward wing root fairing
34 Port intake
35 Intake duct frames
36 Low-vision light panels
37 Forward wing structure
38 Forward wing main spar
39 Fuselage/forward wing main attachment point
40 Engine oil coolers
41 Air conditioning bay
42 Radio equipment
43 Starboard forward wing
44 Flap hinge fairing
45 Honeycomb flap structure
46 Dorsal identification/recognition light
47 Cooling equipment bay
48 Cabin air outlet scoop
49 Cooling pipes
50 Coolers/blowers
51 Fuselage saddle fuel tanks
52 Forward wing aft attachment
53 Avionics bay
54 Ram-air turbine
55 Forward wing flap hinge fairing
56 Honeycomb flap structure
57 Hydraulic pump
58 Low-vision light panels (2)
59 Engine intake face
60 Fuselage upper main longeron
61 Fabricated fuselage frames
62 Volvo Flygmotor RM 8B turbofan
63 Skin panels
64 Dorsal auxiliary intake/outlet panel

navigational accuracy of 1 NM (1,85 km) per hour. The Garrett-AiResearch LD-5 digital air data computer is derived from the system employed by the F-14 Tomcat and is built up around solid-state quartz pressure transducers, and a particularly important contribution to piloting ease — on which emphasis has been placed throughout the development of the *JaktViggen* cockpit — is made by the Honeywell/Saab-Scania SA 07 digital automatic flight control system which has the advantage of being controlled with the stick and having its indicators and operating controls high on the panel, close to the pilot's line of sight for head-up flying. Claimed to be the world's first production digital flight control system, the SA 07 offers high combined load factor and roll rate command capability throughout the flight envelope, and besides the normal functional modes, it offers a special aiming mode for interception.

The air defence mission and its more stringent requirements than those demanded by the attack mission — especially in terms of raising the surge margin throughout the flight envelope — dictated the development by Volvo Flygmotor of a version of the RM 8 turbofan for the JA 37 offering increased functional flexibility. This, the RM 8B, differs from the RM 8A of the AJ 37 primarily in combining a three-stage fan with a three-stage low-pressure compressor rather than a two-stage fan and a four-stage low-pressure unit. Another significant feature of the RM 8B engine is the increased thrust, which, of the order of 10 per cent, is achieved at a somewhat higher

continued on page 51

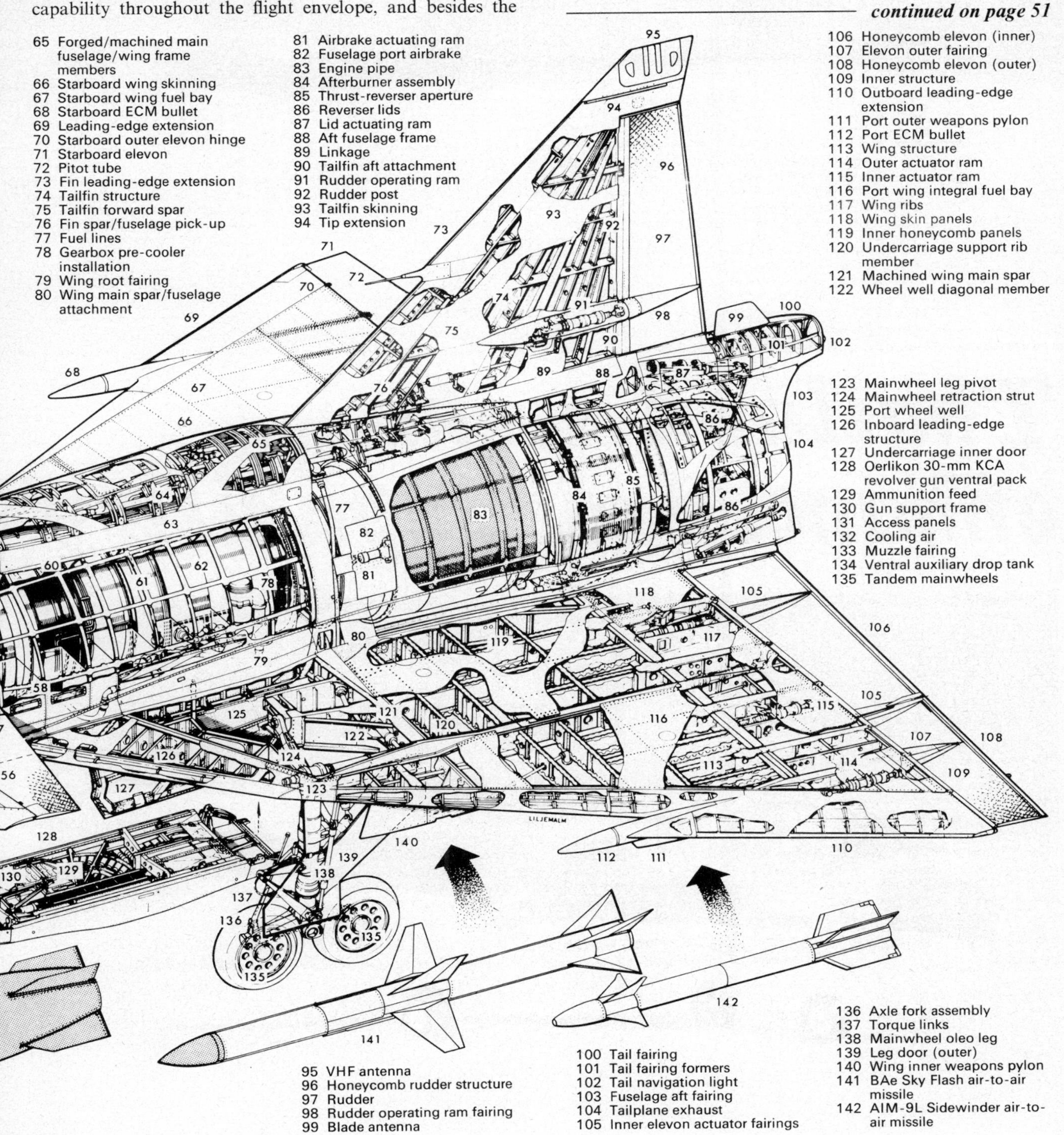

Thailand seeks enhanced air capability

THE CURRENT FORCE STRUCTURE of the Royal Thai Air Force is *not* adequate to meet the threat now posed Thailand, according to the service's Commander-in-Chief, Air Chief Marshal Panieng Kantarat. "We have to get more aircraft to perform our most vital missions — more fighters for interception and more transport aircraft so that we may provide greater support for the Army," he said when interviewed. He stressed that *some* rectification of these most pressing shortages is imminent, however. A second interceptor squadron is forming on a second batch of Tiger IIs (15 single-seat F-5Es and three two-seat F-5Fs), completion of deliveries of which is imminent, and is scheduled to achieve operational status shortly, and in a major boost of the RTAF logistic support capability, the first of three C-130H Hercules transports is expected to enter the inventory "sometime this year".

When, five years ago, the fighting in Vietnam came to an end, the South-East Asian strategic centre of gravity moved inexorably westward to Thailand, which, for long politically orientated towards the west, has faced the most overt threat to its continued independence since the Vietnamese invasion and occupation of neighbouring Kampuchea, with all its implications and possible consequences.

Marginally larger than Spain, with an area of 198,455 square miles (513 996 km²) and a population of some 47 millions, Thailand occupies a geostrategic position between the Indian Ocean and the South China Sea. By South-East Asian standards, it offers a unique combination of relative political stability and traditions of independence — the Thais have successfully defended their national independence for eight centuries — thus providing an enclave of sanity in a region of almost ceaseless turmoil.

Today, with a Vietnamese-influenced and hostile Laos to the east, a Vietnamese-occupied Kampuchea to the south-east, and China, long covetous of the rich Thai rice basin and valuable mineral deposits, a mere three score miles away in the north, Thailand, by consensus, has never been at greater risk. Spurred by the ominous events of recent years, the Thai armed forces are making strenuous efforts to upgrade their defensive capabilities, but budgetary strictures and diminishing US grant aid equipment supply are imposing lower modernisation and growth rate levels than service commanders believe vital to ensure Thailand's continued independence.

The Royal Thai Air Force, in particular, is suffering from funding constraints, but this year will see some capability upgrading as was revealed by the C-in-C of the service, Air Chief Marshal Panieng Kantarat, in an interview conducted recently at his Headquarters at Don Muang Air Base, Bangkok.

Military Assistance Program aid from the USA ended in 1978, but most of the equipment in the RTAF's future procurement programmes is still likely to come from the United States under the cash buy provisions of the Foreign Military Sales system, but the value of acquisitions under FMS is at present and is likely to continue to be constrained by the limited funding available for equipment procurement. With a Fiscal 1980 budget allocation of some 4,145m *Bahts*, equivalent to about £92m, only a proportion of which can be applied to equipment purchase, the RTAF can hardly be numbered among the world's wealthier air forces.

Nevertheless, relatively substantial procurement — by Thai standards — is sought over the next few years and the next major programme is expected to encompass acquisition of attack aircraft, initially to replace the service's remaining squadron of aged piston-engined T-28D counter-insurgency machines and, eventually, the squadron of Cessna A-37Bs. "My staff is now studying which aircraft we should have and I am awaiting its report," ACM Panieng said. "We are certainly looking at the [refurbished] A-4 Skyhawk as three other ASEAN* countries, Singapore, Malaysia and Indonesia, either have this type now or will soon do so, and it may prove suitable for us too. Of course, if we were threatened by a column of tanks, the Fairchild A-10 might be the solution, or," he added, presumably with budgetary realities in mind, "we might acquire another squadron of [second-hand] F-5As to add to the existing one."

The bulk of the RTAF's present combat strength is, in fact, made up by what would generically be regarded elsewhere as counter-insurgency aircraft, but which, as ACM Panieng pointed out, are "attack" aircraft under Thai nomenclature. In this category, in addition to one squadron each of T-28Ds, A-37Bs and F-5As, the RTAF fields two squadrons of OV-10C Broncos, one of Fairchild AU-23A Peacemakers and

**Association of South-East Asian Nations.*

THE HISTORY OF THE ROYAL THAI AIR FORCE

ALTHOUGH the Royal Thai Air Force traces its existence as a separate and autonomous arm back only two score and four years, to October 1936, when the Royal Siamese Aeronautical Service was raised in status from a component of the Army to that of an independent member of the Siamese armed forces, its history stretches back to the dawn of military aviation and 18 January 1911. On that date, the Siamese Ministry of Defence decided to send three officers of the Royal Siamese Engineers to France to study flying and aircraft maintenance. All three obtained pilot's certificates, and in 1913, the senior member of the trio, Maj Phya Chalerm Arkas — who, in 1937, was to become the first C-in-C of the Royal Siamese Air Force (as the RTAF was then known) — also received a military aviation certificate from the French War Ministry.

In November 1913, the three officers returned to Siam, as Thailand was then known, accompanying four Breguet and four Nieuport aircraft, and in the following January, work began on an airfield at Don Muang, just north of Bangkok, and training of both pilots and mechanics initiated. On 23 March 1914, the Royal Siamese Flying Corps was established under the aegis of the Royal Siamese Engineers. The workshops at Don Muang were progressively enlarged and, in May 1915, a Breguet biplane built entirely from indigenous materials was flown. In July 1917, the Kingdom of Siam, at that time an autocracy, declared war on the Central Powers, sending an expeditionary force to Europe to fight alongside the Allies, this including a contingent of the Flying Corps. Ninety-five Siamese officers and non-commissioned officers subsequently qualified as military pilots at the French Army's flying schools at Avord and Istres, 28 completing fighter conversion courses at Poix, 37 passing through the bomber school at Le Crotoy and five going to the reconnaissance school at Chapelle-la-Reine, Siamese pilots flying their first operational missions over the Western Front during the closing weeks of WW I.

With the end of hostilities, the Siamese contingent formed part of the Allied Army of Occupation in the Rhineland, returning to Siam in August 1919 with a number of SPAD S VII and S XIII, and Nieuport-Delage NiD 29 single-seat fighters, Breguet XIV A2 and B2 reconnaissance and bomber aircraft, and various Nieuport trainers to equip a much-expanded air arm, which, meanwhile, had been restyled the Royal Siamese Aeronautical Service, although still a component of the Army. While Don

One of the Vought V.100 Corsairs built in the mid-'thirties.

The RTAF has 18 twin-turbine Sikorsky S-58Ts in its inventory (such as that illustrated left) converted from CH-34s by Thai-Am, an aircraft servicing and maintenance organisation originally formed by Thai International Airways and Pan American World Airways, from kits supplied between September 1977 and March 1978. The RTAF currently has four Swearingen Merlin IVs (below) in its inventory, three having been procured for the photographic rôle and two as 15-passenger VIP transports for use by the Royal Family and its entourage. One of the latter was lost in an accident following a training flight in November 1979, and no replacement has yet been obtained.

one of Douglas AC-47s. The service is seeking more Broncos, which it describes as "very good" for the counter-insurgency rôle, to make up attrition losses among the 38 OV-10Cs supplied in two batches of 16 from 1971 onwards and a further six in 1977. "The problem," said the C-in-C, "is that this aircraft is out of production. If we were to place an order independently, it would cost too much, and so we have to await the placing of an order by another country. We could then add our order and reduce the unit cost. If someone were to order, say, 30 aircraft, then the unit cost might come down sufficiently to enable us to have 10, but if such an order be for only 20 aircraft we would probably have to settle for eight."

The T-28Ds, which have now seen almost a score of years in Thai service, are regarded as well-suited for the counter-insurgency task — "slow, carries a good ordnance load and permits accurate gunnery" — but along with the OV-10C obviously lacks the versatility for use against other than guerilla targets. Apart from its lack of flexibility, the fairly early replacement of the T-28D is dictated by the likelihood of spares shortages developing in the not-too-distant future. Some realignment of combat squadrons took place recently in preparation for the arrival of the previously-mentioned additional batch of Tiger IIs, and the two remaining squadrons of T-28Ds, totalling some 40 aircraft, were combined into one squadron so that, as ACM Panieng

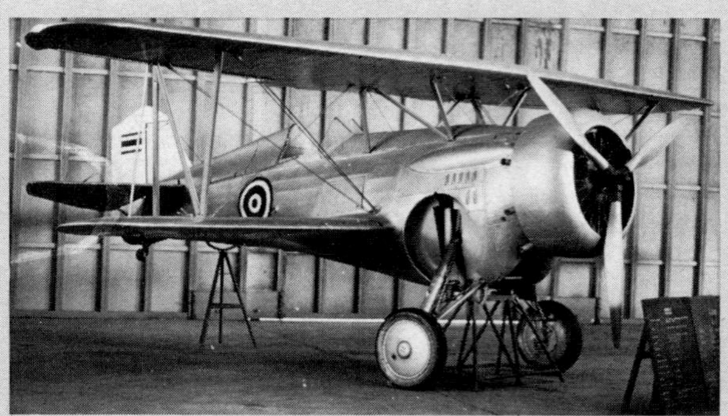

The Curtiss Hawk III served with the RTAF from 1935 to late '40s.

Muang remained the principal base, additional airfields and airstrips were constructed, and from 1920, the Service operated an internal airline. At this time, the RSAS comprised the 1st (Pursuit) Group with SPAD S XIIIs and NiD 29s, and the 2nd (General-Purpose) Group divided into a reconnaissance and topographical survey wing, and a transport and liaison wing equipped primarily with the Breguet XIV. During the late 'twenties, personnel were sent for training to Europe and the USA, and competitive trials were conducted between the Avro 504N and the Fleet PT-1 for adoption by the RSAS as a standard trainer, the former being selected, 20 being procured from the UK in March 1930, and licence production being initiated thereafter in the RSAS workshops where more than 50 were to be built during 1930-33. The Avro 504N was to remain standard *ab initio* equipment until 1945.

The purchase of more modern combat aircraft was at that time considered less urgent and a somewhat protracted evaluation of potential replacements for existing flying equipment followed. During the fighter selection process, a single Heinkel Hd 43 was acquired from Germany; two Bristol Bulldog IIAs were delivered from the UK in January 1930, and two examples of the Boeing 100E followed in November 1931, but, in the event, the Curtiss Hawk II was selected, with a batch of 12 being procured in 1934. To succeed the ageing Breguet XIV, the Vought V.100 was chosen in 1933, licence manufacture of this type being undertaken by the RSAS Workshops at Bangsue and a total of 72 machines eventually being built. Subsequently, the Curtiss Hawk III fighter was also to be built at Bangsue, 25 being completed in 1937 following procurement of 24 from the parent company between August 1935 and February 1936.

Siam had meanwhile (in 1932) become, technically, a constitutional monarchy, and, as previously related, in October 1936, the RSAS was granted autonomous status as a separate service, being redesignated Royal Siamese Air Force in the following April. At this time, the service comprised the Flying Training School and No 1 Wing (Fighters) at Don Muang, Nos 2 and 4 Wings (Observation and Fighters respectively) at Lopburi, No 3 Wing (Bombers) at Nagorn Rajasima and No 5 Wing (Fighters) at Prachuab Kirikhan. Continuing what had now become an established policy of procuring its principal

Backbone of the logistic support element, the C-123K Provider, equipping two squadrons, must either be re-engined or replaced during the first half of the present decade. The feasibility of a re-engining programme is currently under study and contingency studies of such types as the Aeritalia G.222, the DHC Buffalo and even the Transall C.160 have been made in case favoured re-engining proves impracticable.

explained, the pilots of one of the squadrons previously flying T-28Ds could take over the squadron of A-37Bs, whose pilots, in turn, converted to the F-5E with the existing squadron of this type and have since taken over the new Northrop fighters as they have arrived, the second Tiger II squadron thus being likely to achieve operational status almost immediately after the final aircraft arrive. The first F-5E squadron, a component unit of the 1st Wing at Don Muang, achieved operational status in 1978, and some attrition suffered by the unit was made up in August last year with the delivery of four replacement aircraft.

Future airlift capability

No priority is currently attached to replacing the RTAF's fast reconnaissance aircraft, which currently consist of a few RF-5As and RT-33As assigned to the F-5A squadron — "We have many T-33As which we cannibalise to keep the RT-33As flying." The need for increased airlift capacity, on the other hand, is a matter of some urgency. This will in part be met by delivery of the C-130H Hercules, the numbers of which are expected to remain at three for the foreseeable future as, in the words of ACM Panieng, "we don't have enough money for more". It is anticipated that a new squadron will be formed to operate the Hercules, but a question mark hangs over the survival in RTAF service of the sizeable fleet of Fairchild C-123B and K Providers, the two squadrons of which, with an inventory of some 40 aircraft, currently provide most of the service's transport capability.

"These aircraft consume a lot of 100 and 130 octane fuel, so we have to restrict our flying time," the C-in-C said. The feasibility of re-engining the entire fleet of aircraft with turboprops is currently under study and if such a solution proves practical the work will be carried out in Thailand using imported modification kits. A negative report on the feasibility of re-engining the Providers will certainly not be welcomed by the RTAF, which will then have to find the substantial funding needed to procure a replacement type. A contingency study is in hand. "We are looking at the de Havilland Canada Buffalo, the Aeritalia G.222 and the Transall C.160," ACM Panieng commented. A similar fuel problem is, of course, presented by

equipment from the USA, the Siamese government ordered six Martin 139 twin-engined bombers in 1937 for the re-equipment of part of No 3 Wing.

On 24 June 1939, it was announced that Siam would thenceforth be known as Thailand and the national air arm thus became the Royal Thai Air Force. In the previous year, 12 Curtiss Hawk 75N fighters had been ordered as a further stage in a continuing modernisation programme, deliveries having commenced in November 1938, this purchase being followed by an order for 10 North American NA-69 attack bombers and, in 1940, one for six North American NA-68 single-seat fighters. At this time, some factions in the Thai government were favourably impressed by the Japanese Greater Asia Co-Prosperity Sphere, one result being the widening of Thai weapons procurement to embrace Japan and the RTAF acquiring nine Mitsubishi Ki.21-I twin-engined bombers and nine Tachikawa Ki.55 advanced trainers. In the event, neither NA-69 attack bombers nor NA-68 fighters were to be added to the RTAF inventory, the former being seized in the Philippines while *en route* to Thailand (and placed in US Army service as A-27s) and the latter being seized aboard ship in Hawaii.

In January 1941, Thai forces invaded French Indo-China following a dispute with the Vichy government concerning areas along the border between Thailand and French territory. French bombers attacked Bangkok and other targets within Thailand on 10 January, and the RTAF reciprocated by sending Ki.21-I and V.100 Corsair bombers, escorted by Hawk 75Ns, to attack the French airfield at Nakorn Wat, destroying one Farman 221 on the ground for the loss of two aircraft to intercepting M.S.406s and anti-aircraft fire. The pilot of one of the RTAF Corsair biplanes became disorientated and landed in French territory. Fighting between Thai and French forces, with sporadic aerial activity, continued until a truce was arranged between the combatants by the Japanese, and on 9 May 1941, the Vichy government ceded some Indo-Chinese territory to Thailand under a convention signed in Tokyo. The French also agreed to Japanese use of three Indo-Chinese airfields, this being followed by peaceable occupation of the whole of Indo-China by Japanese forces which were thus placed on the Thai border.

The Japanese played on the memory of the humiliation suffered by King Chulalongkorn (of "Anna" fame) at the hands of the French in 1893, promising the return to Thailand of lost territories if the Thai government would permit the "peaceful

A dozen Hawk 75N fighters were procured by the RTAF during 1938-39.

The Northrop F-5E Tiger II now possesses primary responsibility for Thai air defence, with one RTAF squadron of this type fully operational and a second currently working up. The F-5E Tiger II (above) is considered ideally suited to Thai requirements and no further procurement of aircraft optimised for the air defence rôle is foreseen before the mid-'eighties. The ageing RT-33A (left) shares the tactical reconnaissance task with a few RF-5As and is expected to remain in the RTAF inventory for some years.

the Douglas C-47, which equips one squadron of the transport force as well as one combat squadron in its gunship form, while a further half-dozen C-47s serve in the photo reconnaissance rôle alongside three of the RTAF's remaining four Swearingen Merlin IVAs. Similar possibilities of re-engining to those being investigated for the Provider are under consideration for the C-47. "We might change to a triple turboprop arrangement [*à la* Tri Turbo-3]," said the C-in-C, "which would be a lot cheaper than buying new aircraft. In any case, there is no *real* replacement for the C-47, only aircraft that are lighter or heavier!"

concluded on page 20

Early post-WW II RTAF procurement included a number of Tiger Moths.

transit" of the Japanese Army on its way to Malaya and Singapore, and subsequently declare war on the Allies. The Thai government agreed, but neglected to inform some Army and RTAF units of the agreement. In consequence, some elements of the Japanese forces, anticipating no opposition, were surprised by spirited opposition. At Watana Nakorn, on Thailand's eastern border, a squadron of Hawk IIIs of the 1st Wing fought vastly superior Japanese formations, claiming a number of "kills", while, to the south, Hawk 75Ns of the 5th Wing from Prachuab Kirikhan also fought the Japanese, losing one-third of the Wing's entire personnel strength before a frantic message from Bangkok ordering a ceasefire finally reached the commander of the Wing!

On 25 January 1942, Thailand declared war on the Allies — an act that was virtually ignored by the US and British governments — and became ostensibly a co-belligerent of Japan. Insofar as the RTAF was concerned, a strange twilight existence now began in which, while ostensibly fighting alongside the Japanese, it was, for a large part, actively assisting Japan's enemies, the RTAF Headquarters at Don Muang actually becoming the centre of a well-organised underground movement. Radio contact was established with the Allies who were soon flying agents into Thailand and, with RTAF connivance, landing them directly on central airfields from where they were ferried south to Bangkok by the RTAF. In fact, a regular shuttle service was soon operating under the noses of the Japanese, and Allied pilots forced down over Thailand were rescued and flown by the RTAF to bases from which they could safely be collected by Allied aircraft. Some RTAF personnel were sent to India to operate with the British Force 136 and the American OSS, and information concerning Japanese dispositions was constantly

Late 'forties purchase of Spitfire XIVs upgraded RTAF capability.

relayed to the Allies. Frequently, RTAF units moved from permanent bases in deference to the Japanese "allies", the bases promptly being attacked by RAF or USAAF bombers.

Only the most reliable portions of the RTAF could be assigned to these clandestine activities, some staunchly pro-Japanese elements existing in the north, and as the Japanese looked upon the RTAF as a co-belligerent force, some Thai personnel received training in Japan, and a number of Japanese combat aircraft were delivered to the service, these including 12 Nakajima Ki.27 fighters and, later, 12 Nakajima Ki.43-II Hayabusa fighters, nine Mitsubishi Ki.30 light bombers and several Mansyu Ki.79 advanced trainers. Pro-Japanese RTAF personnel were carefully segregated from those favouring the Allies and were mostly sent to units in the north, near the borders of Burma and China, where, from time to time, they were encountered by the US 13th Air Force.

With the end of WW II and the signing of Peace Treaties between Thailand and the Allies, the RTAF found itself possessor of a motley inventory of aircraft ranging from the totally obsolete to, at best, the patently obsolescent. Apart from wartime Japanese aircraft acquisitions, to which had been added some Mitsubishi A6M2 and A6M5 Zero-Sen fighters abandoned by the Japanese Navy and for which few spares existed, the old Hawk III biplane was still in first-line service, together with the V.100 Corsair. Plans were immediately formulated for the reorganisation and modernisation of the RTAF, which, in 1947, it was proposed should have a strength of six operational wings.

The RTAF began an intensive phase of reconstruction, initially with the assistance of RAF personnel, and in the summer of 1948, batches of 20 ex-RAF Miles Magister primary trainers and 42 Harvards were acquired from surplus stocks, together with 10 Douglas C-47s. Thai purchasing commissions visited the UK, Canada and the USA, procurement including a number of surplus Tiger Moths, a batch of Canadian-built Chipmunk trainers, and 30 reconditioned Spitfire FR Mk XIVs, availability of the last-mentioned permitting withdrawal of the remaining Hawk IIIs and A6M5s. With the rising tide of Communist successes in South-East Asia, however, culminating in 1950 in the complete overrunning of the Chinese mainland, it became increasingly obvious that further modernisation and expansion of the RTAF was becoming a matter of the utmost urgency. In 1951, after the arrival of an American Military Advisory Group in the previous year, an initial batch of 50 F8F-1D and -1DB Bearcats was delivered, together with 63 T-6s, RTAF pilots receiving 130 hours on the latter before 60 hours operational conversion on the former, the Bearcats equipping No 13 Sqdn in the 1st Wing and Nos 22 and 23 Sqdns in the 2nd Wing, other squadrons simultaneously re-equipping with armed Texans for the counter-insurgency rôle. The RTAF was eventually to receive 129 Bearcats (100 F8F-1Ds and 29 F8F-1DBs) and, some years later, in 1957, a further 75 T-6 Texans for COIN missions.

Other equipment procured by the RTAF in the mid-'fifties included Stinson L-5 Sentinels and Piper L-18 Super Cubs, later supplemented by Cessna O-1 Bird Dogs for the AOP and FAC tasks, Fairchild 24Ws, Cessna 170s and Beech C-45s for liaison and light transport missions, and a number of helicopters, including Sikorsky S.55s and Hiller 360s from the USA, and four Westland-built S.51s from the UK. A major infusion of modern equipment began in February 1957, when the RTAF received the first of 30 F-84G Thunderjets as its initial jet combat aircraft, these going to No 12 Sqdn at Don Muang, its companion unit, No 11 Sqdn, receiving a mix of T-33As for advanced training and RT-33As for reconnaissance.

By 1962, the last of the piston-engined Bearcats had been phased out of the first-line inventory and, in March of that year, deliveries were completed of 40 F-86F Sabres which replaced the Thunderjets in No 12 Sqdn and also equipped an additional unit, No 13 Sqdn, formed within the 1st Wing at Don Muang. Two years later, in 1964, some limited all-weather capability was introduced in the form of F-86L Sabres which re-equipped No 12 Sqdn, and in April 1966, No 13 Sqdn began re-equipping with MAP-supplied Northrop F-5s (18 single-seat F-5As and two two-seat F-5Bs), the surviving F-86F Sabres going to No 43 Sqdn in the 4th Wing at Takhli.

Meanwhile, the Thai forces had been fighting a constant battle with guerrilla forces — opportunistic raids across the Mekong from Laos and from Cambodia's Battambang district, ranging from the northern to the southern extremities of eastern Thailand, had necessitated a state of constant mobilisation for years — and the RTAF began to place increased emphasis on counter-insurgency capability, the armed T-6G Texans being supplemented (and eventually replaced) by more than 60 T-28Ds which equipped Nos 21, 22 and 23 squadrons within the 2nd Wing at Chieng Mai, Ubol and Udon respectively, the Texans going to No 53 Sqdn of the 5th Wing at Prachuab, No 62 Sqdn of the 6th Wing at Don Muang and No 73 Sqdn of the 7th Wing at Satahip. Airlift capability was gradually increased by the provision of additional C-47s and the progressive delivery of C-123B Providers.

The RTAF began to receive the F8F-1D Bearcat from 1951.

In 1954, Thailand had signed the South-East Asia Collective Defence Treaty, and as the conflict in Vietnam escalated, Thai airfields increasingly served as bases for USAF strikes against North Vietnam. Seven major USAF bases had been established in Thailand by the late 'sixties, some of these bases being shared by the RTAF which enjoyed a major infusion of MAP aid, including the supply of T-37B basic trainers, CH-34C transport and a few HH-43B rescue helicopters, and various other second-line aircraft types, including further C-123 Provider transports. These were supplemented in the early 'seventies with substantial quantities of UH-1H Iroquois helicopters and 16 A-37B light strike aircraft.

Under the Foreign Military Sales (FMS) programme, the RTAF procured 16 OV-10C Bronco counter-insurgency aircraft from the beginning of 1971 as the first stage in the upgrading of the service's anti-guerrilla capability, a further batch of 16 Broncos following from mid-1973, and from mid-1975, 20 Fairchild AU-23 Peacemaker STOL counter-insurgency aircraft were obtained under FMS to supplement 13 transferred from the USAF after completion of the *Credible Chase* evaluation. Together with the T-28Ds, the Broncos and Peacemakers were to provide the backbone of the RTAF anti-guerrilla force formed primarily by the 2nd Wing which progressively phased out its T-6G Texans. At the same time, the RTAF was engaged in modernising its flying training equipment and, in this respect, evinced a tendency to diversify its sources of procurement for the first time in two decades, placing an order in 1972 with New Zealand for 24 CT-4 Airtrainers to supplant the ageing Chipmunk for grading and the primary phase of the training syllabus, following this with an order with Italy for 12 Siai Marchetti SF 260MT basic trainers to supplement and partly replace the T-6G Texan, the CT-4 and SF 260 entering Thai service from 1973 and 1974 respectively.

With the impending withdrawal of remaining USAF combat squadrons from Thai bases in 1975, and the decision to phase out the South-East Asia Collective Defence Treaty (SEATO), to which Thailand was a signatory, the Thai government began to pay increased attention to air defence and, in 1976, accepted a US letter of offer covering 13 F-5E Tiger II fighters and three two-seat F-5Fs, their delivery permitting final phase-out of the aged F-86F Sabres. Whereas the 1976 budget showed an 11 per cent increase over the previous year for defence expenditure, the 1977 figure showed a phenomenal 26 per cent increase. Six additional Broncos were obtained in 1977 to make up attrition, and in 1978, the conversion of 18 CH-34 helicopters to twin-turbine S-58T configuration was initiated for the service. Late in the year, three Swearingen Merlin IVAs configured for the photographic rôle were ordered, as were a further 15 F-5Es and three F-5Fs for 1980 delivery, three C-130H Hercules transports, with the first

The OV-10C Bronco equips two RTAF counter-insurgency squadrons and more aircraft of this type are currently sought to make up attrition, but cost is an inhibiting factor and it is impracticable to reinstate the Bronco in production for the small quantity required by the RTAF.

The RTAF is not, in fact, any stranger to re-engining programmes, having phased into service in 1978 a batch of 18 Sikorsky H-34 helicopters converted to turbine-powered S-58T standard by the Thai-Am concern in Bangkok. The pronounced success of this programme is doubtless one of the reasons that the service is willing to consider such a solution as the first option in prolonging the service lives of its main transport aircraft types. The S-58Ts equip one of the RTAF's two helicopter squadrons, the other operating the UH-1H Iroquois. According to its commander, the service has no plans to acquire more helicopters. "We have enough for our missions and no longer assist the Army as we did before as Army Aviation now possesses a substantial helicopter force of its own."

Training, centred at Korat, utilises a syllabus based on three types, grading and primary instruction being provided on the NZAI CT-4A Airtrainer, from which the pupil progresses to the Siai Marchetti SF 260MT for basic instruction, future jet pilots then converting to the Cessna T-37B for advanced instruction, and the RTAF professes itself happy with all three aircraft. However, there is some possibility that the next trainer to enter the RTAF inventory may be of indigenous design and construction. A prototype of a tandem two-seat twin-boom pusher design, the RTAF-5, has been under development for some considerable time in the air force workshops at Don Muang and, according to ACM Panieng, should fly "sometime this year". Powered by a 380 hp Avco Lycoming IGSO-540-A engine, the RTAF-5 is expected to have a maximum speed of 180 mph (290 km/h) at sea level and an initial climb rate of 1,600 ft/min (8,13 m/sec), and maximum take-off weight is calculated at 3,500 lb (1 588 kg). Depending on the results of flight testing, ACM Panieng believes that the RTAF-5 could be placed in production around 1983, with an in-service date of 1984. The number of aircraft likely to be ordered is as yet a matter for speculation. "It might replace both the CT-4A and the SF 260MT, and as it could also perform the forward air control mission it might also replace the O-1 Bird Dog which currently serves in that rôle."

One possible area of future procurement by the RTAF could be in equipment for the ground defence of its bases. The service's nine operational airfields are each assigned a battalion of RTAF troops, but not all are at full strength. These troops, essentially infantry formations, operate within a radius of 2-3 miles (3-5 km) of each base, anti-aircraft defence being provided by an attached AA company currently equipped with rather old 20-mm and 40-mm guns, and 0·5-in (12,7-mm) machine guns. Surface-to-air missiles for base defence must assuredly have a relatively high priority in RTAF procurement planning.

The Thai government firmly rejected a Soviet offer last year of military equipment and economic aid in return for port facilities for the Soviet Pacific Fleet, emphasising that neither does it want US troops, aircraft or ships based in Thailand, despite the fact that for political, economic and logistical reasons, it anticipates that the bulk of future procurement for its armed forces will continue to be from the United States. Insofar as the RTAF is concerned, ACM Panieng believes that the current expansion of the interceptor fighter component, and the planned upgrading of the ground attack element and the transport fleet, should be sufficient to enable the service to retain its effectiveness over the first half of this new decade. "But if the threat increases, then we will have to think of something else!" □

This feature incorporates, with permission, material published in a recent issue of Defence Attaché magazine.

scheduled for delivery in the third quarter of 1980, and a number of mobile radar units. The year 1978 also saw some revision of

The F-86F Sabre served the RTAF from the early '60s to late '70s.

the structure of the RTAF, the Tactical Air Command, within which all flying units other than training formations had been embodied, was disbanded, all air wings being directly subordinated to RTAF Headquarters.

Today, the RTAF, with some 38,000 personnel, possesses one F-5E Tiger II-equipped interceptor squadron, with a second now in process of working up, three attack squadrons equipped respectively with the F-5A, the A-37B and the T-28D, and four counter-insurgency squadrons, two equipped with the OV-10C Bronco, one with the AU-23A Peacemaker and one with the AC-47 "gunship". There is a small tactical reconnaissance element with RF-5As and RT-33As, and three tactical transport squadrons, two operating the C-123B and K Provider and one flying the C-47. There is also a photographic squadron with a mix

The F-84G Thunderjet was the first RTAF jet combat aircraft in 1957.

of C-47s and Merlin IVAs, and several helicopter squadrons with UH-1Hs and S-58Ts. Although still positively pro-western, the Thai government pursues a more neutralistic policy than it has in the past, despite increased threat from neighbouring Communist states, but reliance primarily on the USA for the bulk of the equipment of the RTAF is likely to continue unchanged in the foreseeable future. □

The T-6 Texan served in the COIN rôle from late '40s to late '70s.

BY B R A BURNS

EFFICACIOUS AIR INTAKES

Since the first jet aircraft appeared about 40 years ago, intake design has become a progressively more complex and specialised subject. On early jet fighters the intakes were sized for high speed flight and shaped for minimum drag, with few concessions to "off-design" performance. Nowadays intake location and detail design has become a major item in configuration design, requiring continued testing and refinement throughout the development programme to achieve optimum performance in all phases of flight. The quality of intake design can make or mar a combat aeroplane. In this final article in the "Fundamentals of Design" series, the considerations affecting intake design and location are reviewed and the reasons for adopting alternative design features explained.

THE primary considerations in the design of intakes include: (1) pressure recovery, (2) minimum distortion and turbulence, (3) low external drag, (4) avoidance of "buzz" and (5) avoidance of spray and debris ingestion. The first of these objectives is to minimise pressure losses at the intake face and down the duct; that is, to deliver the air to the engine face at the maximum pressure, as near as possible to free stream total pressure. Every percent loss in pressure represents an equal percentage loss in thrust at static conditions and a proportionately higher loss at forward speed; typically, the losses are magnified two to one at transonic speed. The second objective is to achieve as even as possible a distribution of pressure/velocity, free from swirl, at the engine face, to provide smooth operating conditions for the compressor, to reduce the risk of compressor stall and engine surge.

Achieving low external drag is an obvious necessity. Intake "buzz", mentioned at (4) above, is an instability of the shock system on a supersonic intake, resulting from shock/boundary layer interaction, which causes pressure disturbances down the duct at a frequency and amplitude akin to that of gun firing. Also, it is necessary to avoid ingestion of spray and debris on take-off, gun and missile gases in flight and the ingestion of hot gas "fountain" on V/STOL designs (see "Fundamentals of Design-II"/April 1979).

Sizing the intake

The amount of air ingested by a jet engine does not depend directly on intake size or on forward speed. The engine takes in what it demands; air is not forced into it. The rotational speed (RPM) of the compressor determines the inlet flow rate at the engine face: moving upstream to the intake, the narrower the duct, the higher the local velocity. At the intake face, therefore, the local velocity (determined by engine RPM and duct area distribution) is, in general, different from flight velocity.

At low forward speed/high RPM, the "capture stream tube" is larger than the intake and the air streams must converge and accelerate into the intake, giving a "sucking" condition. At high forward speeds, with the engine throttled, the capture stream tube is smaller than the intake, which then has to "spill" some of it away, around the intake lips. On a supersonic combat aeroplane, the intake is usually sized for operation at high subsonic speed, that is, the intake area is matched to the maximum engine demand and the duct internal area must increase downstream to match the engine inlet velocity (typically, a Mach number of 0·4).

Cowl shape

Efficient low speed operation, with the flow converging into the intake, requires a large lip radius to prevent separation of the flow inside the lip and consequent pressure losses, distortion and turbulence. This is most important for V/STOL operations; every percent reduction in installed thrust represents one per cent off the maximum VTO weight and a much larger percentage reduction in weapon load or range. For CTOL aeroplanes with high thrust/weight ratios, a few percent loss in intake efficiency at the slow end of the take-off has little effect on take-off distance and so sharp lips may be tolerable, as on the Lightning, for instance.

However, the dominant consideration may be uniform, smooth flow at the engine face rather than just intake efficiency, particularly with modern multi-spool, high compression by-pass engines which tend to be more "fussy" in this respect than their pure jet predecessors. Thick, rounded lips would result in unacceptable supersonic drag penalties, so a compromise small radius is usually the solution, augmented by auxiliary doors which open at low forward speeds under the influence of duct suction. These give a larger effective intake area, reducing the suction inside the lips to eliminate separation, yielding improved efficiency and smoother, more uniform flow in the duct.

At high forward speeds, or at moderate speeds with the engine throttled for cruise or endurance, the intake is usually spilling. This does not necessarily incur a drag penalty subsonically; suitable shaping of the forward-facing area of the cowl can induce suction forces on the cowl to cancel spillage drag. However, additional forward area on the cowl inevitably causes drag at supersonic speed, so a compromise is necessary.

At supersonic speed, therefore, intake spillage incurs an increasingly important drag penalty as speed increases, an effect which can be alleviated only by reducing intake area to match the reduced demand. This can be done by various

(Below) The enlarged "deep breather" intakes applied to the Meteor F Mk 8 in the mid-'fifties (the original, smaller-diameter intakes being seen above). The enlarged intakes benefited climb performance at the expense of max speed and cruise efficiency.

means — fore and aft-moving half-cones (in French, *souris*=mice) on Mirage variants, pivoted half-cones on the TSR-2, variable internal ramps on the Tornado, to name only a few examples. However, the weight and complexity of these devices has to be justified by the performance improvement which they offer; broadly speaking variable intake throat area is unlikely to pay off unless the design Mach number exceeds about 1·7.

Compression surfaces

The only means of decelerating an air stream supersonically is to make use of a shock wave. A shock incurs pressure loss and the higher the Mach number ahead of the shock, the lower the Mach number behind it and the greater the pressure loss. The pressure loss is minimised by generating a number of weak shocks rather than a single strong one. (Theoretically, a pointed body, suitably shaped with continuously increasing curvature against the flow, can decelerate a supersonic air stream without pressure loss — a series of infinitely weak shocks in effect.) The air stream entering the intake must be decelerated to subsonic speed before the intake throat, so that it continues to decelerate subsonically inside the duct. The supersonic deceleration, or compression (because it involves an increase in density), upstream of the throat is achieved most efficiently by surfaces inclined against the flow, to generate an initial shock, so that the second "normal" shock (that is, at right angles to the flow, with subsonic flow downstream of it) is comparatively weak. Without any pre-compression surface a single normal shock occurs and the pressure loss is very high at high supersonic speed (seven per cent at M=1·5, and 27 per cent at M=2·0).

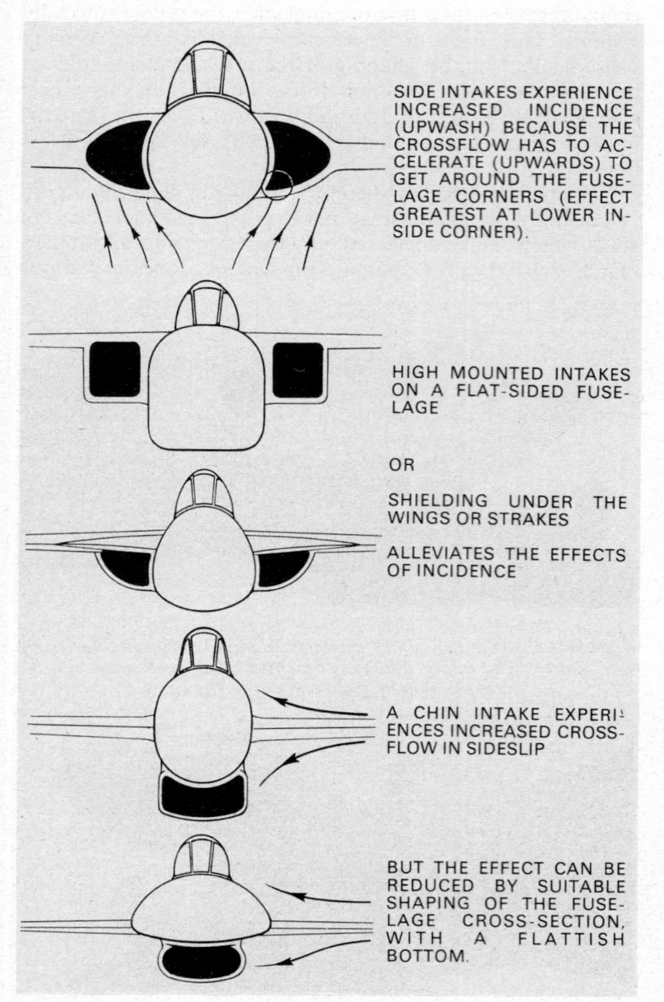

SIDE INTAKES EXPERIENCE INCREASED INCIDENCE (UPWASH) BECAUSE THE CROSSFLOW HAS TO ACCELERATE (UPWARDS) TO GET AROUND THE FUSELAGE CORNERS (EFFECT GREATEST AT LOWER INSIDE CORNER).
HIGH MOUNTED INTAKES ON A FLAT-SIDED FUSELAGE
OR
SHIELDING UNDER THE WINGS OR STRAKES
ALLEVIATES THE EFFECTS OF INCIDENCE
A CHIN INTAKE EXPERIENCES INCREASED CROSSFLOW IN SIDESLIP
BUT THE EFFECT CAN BE REDUCED BY SUITABLE SHAPING OF THE FUSELAGE CROSS-SECTION, WITH A FLATTISH BOTTOM.

Examples of subsonic nose pitot intakes are provided by the MiG-15bis (left) and the F-84F Thunderstreak (right).

There are two basic classes of compression surfaces, external and internal. Examples of external compression surfaces on intakes are the centre body cones on the Lightning and MiG-21, vertical ramps on the Phantom, Su-15 *Flagon* and F-18, half-cones on the Mirages and F-104, horizontal wedges on the F-14, F-15, Tornado, MiG-25 *Foxbat*, and many others. With suitably designed surfaces, the pressure loss through the intake shock system can be reduced from the crippling 27 per cent due to a normal shock to a value of seven or eight per cent at M=2·0. However the compression surfaces do themselves produce some drag which penalises subsonic and transonic performance and, of course, weight, both of which impair transonic acceleration. Whether they are worthwhile depends on the emphasis on supersonic performance in the design specification. If the design Mach number is less than about 1·5, a simple pitot intake is probably the best choice. Even above M=1·5, if it is acceleration rather than top speed that is wanted, the addition of compression surfaces may not be justified.

Internal compression can be achieved, theoretically, by means of a convergent duct just inside the intake face, followed by subsonic deceleration in a divergent section of the duct downstream. Such an intake would have no external drag and good internal performance at the design point, where internal geometry is matched to the flight Mach number and engine airflow, with the intersecting internal shocks sitting in exactly the right place, close to the intake throat. The main drawback of this type of intake is that any variation in flight Mach number or engine airflow results in a rapid deterioration in performance, usually to that of a pitot intake with an expelled normal shock. This renders the internal compression intake unsuitable, at least for combat aeroplanes which have to operate efficiently over a wide range of speed. External compression is much less sensitive because the intake shock system is not reflected internally.

Diverter design

The purpose of a diverter is to prevent the sluggish air in the boundary layer on the surfaces ahead of the intake from entering the intake, to the detriment of performance and quality of internal flow. Early examples were the "shouldered" diverters on the Vampire and the slotted diverter on the Lockheed F-80/T-33. Later transonic and supersonic designs tended to move the intakes more firmly away from the fuselage sides and the diverter surfaces behind the intake lips, to reduce the chance of turgid boundary layer air spilling into the intakes at extreme flow conditions (eg, low speed, high incidence). Examples are the Buccaneer, Phantom, Jaguar and Tornado. Side intakes situated under the wings or strakes as on the F-111 and F-18 complicate diverter design, because both fuselage and underwing boundary layers and particularly the corner region where they overlap have to be diverted. On the F-111 the intake-to-fuselage spacing had to be increased at an early stage of its development to increase the diverter area. The F-18 diverters are carefully shaped, there being three diverter paths — upwards through the strake slots, downwards, and sideways between the upper lip and the strake undersurface. The F-18 also employs bleed holes on the intake splitter plate to remove the boundary layer of that surface ahead of the intake throat.

Intake location

The natural place for the intake, with fuselage-mounted engines, is at the nose and indeed many early jet fighters (F-84, F-86, Ouragan, Mystère, MiG-15, MiG-17, Saab J 29, etc) were configured thus. A nose intake requires no diverter and is therefore simple on that account. It results in a long duct — good from the point of view of settling any pressure disturbances that might originate at the intake lips at high incidence and sideslip — but an overlong duct incurs a significant pressure loss due to the "scrubbing" drag of the internal flow.

A nose intake is not suitable with rear-mounted engines, generally favoured nowadays, but is satisfactory with centrally mounted engines as on earlier generations of fighters, named above. A nose intake widens the fuselage dimensions, adding surface area and therefore drag. A central pre-compression body in a nose intake, as on the Lightning or MiG-21, is a convenient location for a small radar, but the size is not compatible with today's larger radar dishes. (The days of the "eyeball" fighter are gone.)

Side intakes have been adopted for most of the combat aeroplanes of the 'sixties and 'seventies, freeing the nose for the installation of radar and other operational equipment, but requiring a diverter to ensure a high level of efficiency. Side intakes are also subject, in general, to magnified incidence effects due to upwash around the fuselage contours and an uneven distribution of incidence across the intake face for the same reason. The upwash is strongest closest to the fuselage side, at the bottom corner, reducing upwards and outwards from that point. This may require careful shaping of the lower lip to avoid separation of the captured flow at high incidence and low speed, an important consideration for both airfield performance and for combat.

Incidence effects on side intakes are alleviated by a high intake location on a flat-sided fuselage, as on the Jaguar for example. Other means of improving intake performance at high incidence are:

*Extending the upper lip forward of the lower, as on the A-5 Vigilante, F-14, F-15, Tornado and MiG-25 *Foxbat*. The upper lip can also act as a horizontal compression wedge for supersonic operation.

*Situating the intake under the wing (F-111) or strake (F-18), although this complicates diverter design, as noted earlier.

*Tilting the intakes downward at high incidence, as on the F-15.

Other forms of variable geometry, such as variable lower lips or lower surface auxiliary doors, may be considered.

Sideslip effects can also be troublesome on side intakes, particularly the flow on the leeward side of the fuselage. With a single engine, a splitter plate dividing the duct right to the engine face has been required on some designs.

BOUNDARY CAPTURE STREAM TUBE
INTAKE OPERATING CONDITIONS
LOW SPEED, "SUCKING" CONDITION. ENGINE DEMAND EXCEEDS INTAKE AREA. FLOW ACCELERATES AND CONVERGES INTO INTAKE.
MATCHING POINT (SUBSONIC) CAPTURE AREA MATCHES INTAKE AREA.
HIGH SUBSONIC SPEED AND/OR WITH ENGINE THROTTLED.
INTAKE SPILLAGE CONDITION.
SUITABLE SHAPING OF THE INTAKE COWL CAN INDUCE A FAVOURABLE (FORWARD) SUCTION FORCE AT SUBSONIC SPEED.
SHOCK WAVE
LOW SUPERSONIC SPEED.
PITOT INTAKE WITH DETACHED NORMAL SHOCK.
SUBSONIC FLOW BEHIND SHOCK INTO INTAKE.
OBLIQUE SHOCK
NORMAL SHOCK
MODERATE SUPERSONIC SPEED WITH CENTRE BODY (PRE-COMPRESSION) INTAKE.
FIRST (OBLIQUE) SHOCK DECELERATES FLOW SUPERSONICALLY.
SECOND (NORMAL) SHOCK GIVES SUBSONIC FLOW INTO INTAKE.
SHARP LIPS MAY INDUCE SEPARATION OF THE CONVERGENT FLOW INTO THE INTAKE AT LOW SPEED, LEADING TO PRESSURE LOSS, DISTORTION AND TURBULENCE IN THE DUCT.
AUXILIARY DOORS ADMIT PART OF THE AIRFLOW DEMAND, REDUCING PRIMARY INTAKE FLOW, REDUCING CONVERGENCE, ELIMINATING SEPARATION.

The chin intake location, pioneered by the F-86D as a means of allowing a nose radar to be fitted and featured also on the Fiat G-91, F-8 Crusader, A-7 Corsair and F-16, can give beneficial shielding from incidence effects if the fuselage is locally wider than the intake mouth; the forward fuselage surfaces can perhaps be shaped to generate a favourable pre-entry shock pattern at supersonic speed. Just as a side intake

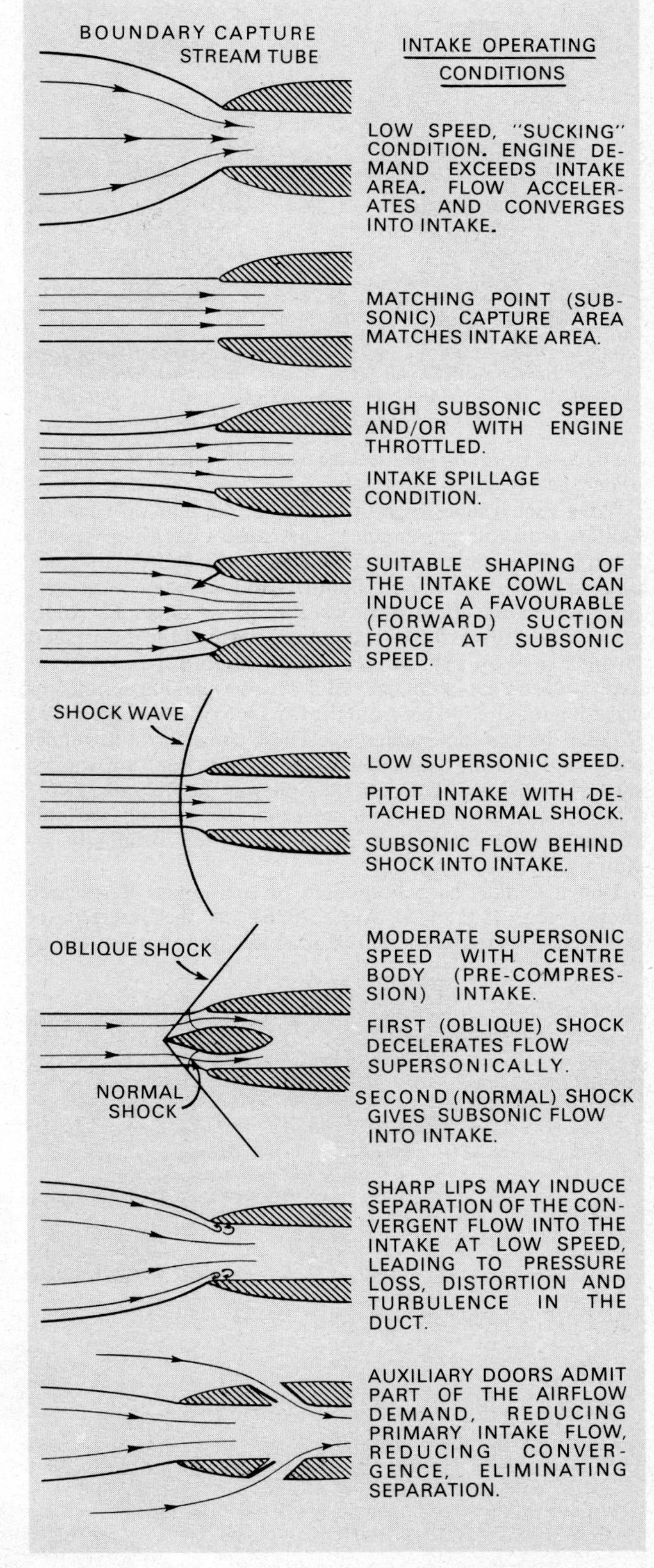

experiences magnified incidence effects, a chin intake is subject to magnified sideslip effects. However sideslip is not generated deliberately in normal flight (an exception is crosswind landing), so the operating range of sideslip is usually substantially less than the range of incidence that has to be catered for. The chin location does however result in a deeper forebody, requiring more fin area to compensate and the enforced rearward location of the nosewheel may restrict

Examples of the centre body supersonic external compression intake are provided by the MiG-21 (above left) and Lightning (above right).

carriage of stores on the fuselage (the F-16 can carry very little under the fuselage).

Wing root leading edge intakes were popular on subsonic fighters with tolerant engines. The earliest example was the Vampire, followed by the Venom and Sea Vixen from the same company; the Grumman Panther and Cougar were very similar, as were the Sea Hawk and the Hunter. The main drawback of this location is the small depth at the intake face, giving a large internal surface area at the forward part of the duct, and the rapid changes of cross-section shape and flow direction required to get from the wing into the fuselage with a circular duct to the engine face. These considerations render wing root leading edge intakes unsuitable for thin-winged supersonic designs. The only example was the Republic F-105 Thunderchief with its unique reversed local sweep, variable internal ramp intakes, a design proposed originally by Antonio Ferri of NASA.

Dorsal intakes have been used on a number of research aircraft (eg, H.P. 115, Avro 707B), in the interests of expediency. Perhaps the only fighter design to have a dorsal intake was the North American F-107, a development of the F-100 (illustrated and described in AIR INTERNATIONAL/July 1978). This intake had a central vertical splitter plate with twin movable ramps as pre-compression surfaces. The main drawback of the dorsal position is, of course, the poor quality of the pre-entry flow in the separated wake from the forward fuselage at high angles of incidence.

The future scene

With the ever-widening operating envelopes of combat aircraft, and the sensitivity of modern reheated by-pass engines to flow distortion, turbulence and swirl, the task of intake design is becoming increasingly difficult. In future we are likely to see alternative forms of variable intake geometry to increase tolerance to extremes of incident flow at subsonic and transonic speeds, with perhaps more emphasis on high performance at the lower supersonic speeds, for good acceleration, than on top Mach number level flight performance. □

(Below) Vertical wedge supersonic external compression side intakes illustrated by the MiG-23BM (left) and JA 37 Viggen (right).

The horizontal wedge internal compression intake, first displayed by the A-5 Vigilante, has since been adopted by such types as the F-14 Tomcat, the F-15 Eagle, the Panavia Tornado and the MiG-25 Foxbat (illustrated left), though these all differ greatly in detail design. The F-18A Hornet (illustrated below) has its intakes shielded by strakes for good characteristics at high incidence. Features of the Hornet's arrangement include a five per cent pre-entry compression wedge, complex diverter paths — up through slots in the strakes, down behind splitter plates and outward between upper lip and wing undersurfaces — and BL bleed holes on the splitter plates ahead of the intake faces, plus cambered lower lips. This provides an example of the complexity of detail design to ensure good characteristics.

The Wellesley

GEODETICS IN ACTION

WELLESLEY, Wellington, Warwick and Windsor: there is an attractive alliteration in the names of the monoplane bombers produced between 1930 and 1945 from the Weybridge home of the aviation interests of Vickers Ltd. By no more than coincidence, the names of this distinguished quartet also alliterate with that of the company's chief designer (structures), B N Wallis*; and through this link, the four bombers had much more in common than just the first letters of their names. Not all were equally successful in their operational deployment, it is true, but all made use of the Wallis structural principles known as geodetic construction. To describe geodetics as a "breakthrough" in construction techniques for metal aircraft might be to over-emphasise its importance; certainly, the system did not become universally accepted, and the Vickers bombers were the only aircraft built and used in large numbers successfully to apply geodetic construction fully. In the early years of the last decade before World War II, however, Wallis can be credited with having evolved and made available to engineers the first wholly novel method of aeroplane construction since the Great War had ended. It fell to the Vickers Wellesley to prove in practice that the system worked.

To understand the place of geodetics in aviation history it is necessary to realise that in 1930 most designers were still groping towards the application of streamlined shapes, and that wood remained as important a constructional material as metal. Stressed-skin metal structures were still a novelty, not a norm; typical structures then in use perforce had much internal bracing, within wings and fuselages, and streamlining of the fuselage was often achieved by adding formers and stringers to the outside of the basic "box", thus reducing still further the usefulness of the interior space.

Turning his mind from airships to aeroplanes, Wallis immediately became concerned with the problems of achieving streamlined shapes with better structural efficiency than before. Undoubtedly, his experience with airship design was relevant, and he concluded that it should be possible to build a streamlined form in which the loads were carried by structural members that followed geodesic lines. A geodesic is the shortest line joining two points on the surface of a spherical body (the same line being known as a great circle course in navigational parlance) and the adjective "geodetic" refers to the application of geodesy, the science of calculating geodesics.

If the shape in question is considered to be a tube, a geodetic line can be drawn as a spiral round the surface of the tube; if a second spiral is then drawn in the other direction, a number of points of intersection are obtained. If a structure is then built along the geodetic lines, with rigid joints at the intersections, shear and torsional loads are balanced out in the opposing geodesics; the result is a structure of excellent strength-to-weight ratio and one that has no internal bracing whatsoever. Such was the basis of Wallis' reasoning, confirmed by such calculations as he was able to make without the benefit of practical tests. Of course, the basic theory had to be modified in practice, since the shapes required were anything but regular tubes or even spheres, and cut-outs had to be provided for cockpits, etc; nevertheless, most surfaces of a streamlined

**The late Sir Barnes Wallis, now best remembered for his development of the dam-busting weapon used by No 617 Squadron in 1943 and for his later work on swing-wings. He had been employed as an engineer by Vickers since 1913, working on airships until the end of 1929. His appointment as chief designer (structures) at Weybridge, where Rex K Pierson was chief designer, aircraft, on 1 January 1930, followed the Vickers decision to close its airship department.*

BEECHCRAFT KING AIR C90

BEECHCRAFT BONANZA F33A

BEECHCRAFT BARON E55

BEECHCRAFT DUCHESS

ıave the same first name?

Beechcraft Baron E55.

(Multi-engine/instrument trainer)

Top Speed	208 kts
Cruise Speed	195 kts
Range	1,912 km
Service Ceiling	5,822 m
Useful Load	924 kg
Seats	4-6

Beechcraft King Air C90 jetprop.

Top Speed	222 kts
Cruise Speed	216 kts
Range	2,372 km
Service Ceiling	8,565 m
Useful Load	1,781 kg
Seats	6-10

There are many other Beechcraft airplanes used daily in training operations around the world. The Beechcraft Skipper, Sundowner, T-34C-1 Turbine Mentor and T44A jetprop King Air all perform remarkably well on training missions.

Whatever your trainer needs may be contact your Beechcraft Distributor soon for more information.

Or, if you prefer, write to: Beech Aircraft Corporation, 9799 East Central, Wichita, Kansas 67201, U.S.A.

All inquiries will be answered promptly.

EAGLE AIRCRAFT SERVICES, LTD.
Leavesden Aerodrome
Watford WD2 7BY, England
Phone: (9273) 79611/7 (Garston, Herts)
Cable: EAGLESERV (Watford) VIA WUI
Telex: (851) 261502 (VIA WUI)

(Above and below left) The Type 246, Vickers' private venture to G.4/31, in its original form as completed in the early summer of 1935. This aircraft subsequently became the Type 281.

aeroplane were curved in two directions, and on any such surface a geodesic could be drawn.

Putting theory into practice required an act of faith on the part both of Rex Pierson, to whom Wallis now reported, and the Vickers directors most immediately concerned with aircraft development. It says much for the clarity with which Wallis himself must have argued the case for geodetics that such support was forthcoming — notably from Sir Robert McLean, chairman of Vickers Aviation. Wallis was himself in no doubt about the advantages of geodetic construction; of the Wellesley, which was the first of his designs fully to exploit the principle, he wrote "this method of aeroplane construction is the most important contribution to aircraft engineering since the completion of the first successful metal aircraft. For example, it permits each wing to be hollow and entirely free from any kind of obstruction — the additional space thus gained can be utilised for extra tankage or other loads, and the complete structure is one of extreme lightness combined with great strength and rigidity, thus making possible a range and load carrying capacity that has hitherto been considered unattainable". In this same note, the system was referred to as the Vickers-Wallis "Geodetic" system, an "entirely new principle" in which "all parts of the structure are formed as geodetics in the streamline shape of the fuselage, and also in the curved profile of the wings".

Biplane versus monoplane

The first aeroplane for which Wallis became responsible at Weybridge was the Vickers Type 207, an unprepossessing biplane to Specification M.1/30 which incorporated some original structural techniques that also owed something to airship practice but were not geodetic. While construction of the Type 207 proceeded, the Weybridge design team turned its attention to another requirement, outlined in Specification G.4/31, for a general-purpose aeroplane for service with RAF units overseas. The specification, intended to produce an aeroplane to replace the Vickers Vincent, stressed the importance of such features as reliability, good forward view for the pilot, short take-off and landing and load-carrying ability. Circulated in June, the specification attracted widespread interest in the industry and was to lead eventually to orders being placed for prototypes of three designs while six others were built as private ventures. Eventually, it was one of the private venture designs that was selected for production, as the Vickers Wellesley, wherein lay a paradox, for the Air Ministry had selected the alternative Vickers *biplane* design to G.4/31 as one of its official prototypes, had listed it as the best of the types evaluated and had actually reached the point of placing a production contract for it.

Aircraft design in the early 'thirties was still at the stage where biplane and monoplane could compete, at least on paper, for the same rôle; there was no concensus of opinion favouring the monoplane and traditional support for the biplane was a long time a'dying. Pierson and his project team therefore played safe by proposing both biplane and monoplane solutions for G.4/31, the biplane and one monoplane project having a Pegasus radial engine and a fixed, trousered main undercarriage while a second monoplane project featured a Kestrel liquid-cooled inline engine. The biplane found official favour and was ordered, as Type 253, in April 1932; its fuselage employed a rudimentary form of geodetic construction but the wing was pure pre-Wallis. Convinced that a very much better aeroplane could be built as a monoplane, Wallis obtained permission from Vickers' Board of Directors to proceed with the design of Type 246 to meet the G.4/31 specification requirements whilst also demonstrating the advantages of geodetic construction.

The fuselage of Type 246 in fact closely resembled that of the Type 253 biplane, in both profile and construction. The geodetic wing was of dramatically high aspect ratio (8·85 to 1) and a retractable undercarriage was now adopted, the main legs folding inwards (under manual power) to put the wheels in the wing roots. With the same Pegasus IIIM3 engine as used in the biplane, the Vickers monoplane came out with a lower tare weight and a better performance in all respects while carrying a larger payload.

Bearing the manufacturer's PV marking O-9, the Type 246 prototype first flew on 19 June 1935 at Brooklands (Weybridge), 10 months after the biplane; flight testing of both aircraft was in the hands of Capt "Mutt" Summers, company chief test pilot. By the time the monoplane first flew the biplane had already been evaluated by the A&AEE at

Martlesham Heath. Both prototypes appeared in the New Types Park at the RAF Display at Hendon in June 1935, but testing of the Type 246 received a set-back on 23 July, when the aircraft made a crash-landing as a result of damage to one of the undercarriage legs during retraction. Meanwhile, the evaluation of other G.4/31 designs had been completed at the A&AEE and — although considerable interest had been aroused by Westland's PV monoplane up to the time it suffered a structural failure and crashed — the Vickers 253 had been officially endorsed as the design best able to meet the requirement and a contract for 150 had been drawn up.

The accident suffered by the Type 246 delayed its submission to the A&AEE for official handling trials, but the results produced in the first few weeks of flight testing could not easily be ignored by the Air Ministry, and aggressive campaigning by Vickers Aviation chairman Sir Robert McLean resulted in cancellation of the order for biplanes and a decision to purchase 96 of the monoplanes instead. News of this contract reached Vickers on 10 September 1935, while the prototype was still being rebuilt; at the same time, a contract was raised for purchase of the prototype itself and a specification was drawn up (22/35) to define the production standard. The Air Ministry had now changed its views considerably since G.4/31 had first been issued, and had dropped the general-purpose and torpedo-carrying provisions from the requirement; the Vickers monoplane was now being bought as a day or night bomber to hasten the re-equipment and expansion of the RAF's bombing force both at home and overseas.

Before it was flown again following its landing accident, the prototype was modified in several respects to bring it closer to the production standard, in accordance with Vickers Type 281 drawings. Noticeably, sliding covers were fitted over the previously open cockpits, a broader-chord rudder was fitted and the fairing round the tailwheel was simplified. An important but less obvious change was the use of hydraulics to retract the undercarriage, and a Pegasus X engine was installed, driving a fixed-pitch Fairey-Reed metal propeller (although, when it crashed, the prototype had been using an experimental variable-pitch propeller). Radio was fitted to Service requirements, with a large aerial mast just behind the front cockpit, and windows were included in the fuselage sides to give light in the cabin separating the two cockpits. There would have been space in the fuselage for an internal bomb-bay, but providing a large cut-out for this purpose was considered to be undesirable in view of the geodetic construction and as an alternative to externally-mounted bombs on the wings Vickers adopted bomb panniers — one under each wing — which were fabricated by Heston Aircraft and each carried up to 1,000 lb (454 kg) of bombs internally. Flying again by early 1936, the prototype Type 281 was now given the RAF serial number K7556, and it was first assessed at the A&AEE in March of that year, by which time it carried an armament of one 0·303-in (7,7-mm) Browning in the starboard wing and a Vickers "K" gun in the rear cockpit.

By mid-'thirties standards, production of the Wellesley, as the new Vickers bomber was named, was a lengthy process, well over a year elapsing from the placing of the contract to the first flight of a production example, which took place on 30 January 1937, at Brooklands. Evolving suitable production techniques for the geodetic structure, and completing exhaustive static tests to assure the RAF that the new form of construction was acceptable, accounted for the delay; but once started, production quickly got into stride and by March 1938, Vickers had delivered all 96 originally ordered plus a second batch of 80 that had been ordered in 1936. Production aircraft were powered, as standard, by the 925 hp Pegasus XX engine driving a de Havilland Hamilton Standard three-bladed two-position propeller; the first eight were built as Vickers Type 287s, after which some strengthening of the wing structure was introduced and production continued as Type 294s. One early production Wellesley was set aside for use as a test-bed for the Bristol Hercules HE.1S sleeve-valve engine, the installation being covered by Vickers Type 289 drawings.

Into service

The Wellesley I entered service as a day and night bombing aeroplane with No 76 (Bomber) Squadron at RAF Finningley, where the unit was formed by splitting off No 7 Squadron's "B" Flight in April 1937. Subsequent deliveries during 1937 allowed Nos 148, 35, 77 and 207 squadrons to equip on the new type, in that order, at home and then Nos 14, 45 and 223 in the Middle East. The use of the Wellesley by the home-based squadrons was never regarded as more than an interim measure; the original G.4/31 specification had been concerned with an aircraft for overseas use and although the Wellesley had moved some way away from the G.4/31 concept, its destiny was still to operate in the Middle East and Africa. By the time war broke out, all the home-based Wellesleys had been withdrawn from front-line service; overseas, No 45 had also re-equipped, passing its Wellesleys on to No 47, as described later. One early production aircraft (the fifth), after serving briefly with Nos 76 and 148 squadrons, was fitted with a Pegasus XVIII to clear tropical use and the strengthened Type 294 wing. It was then fitted with a Pegasus XXII and a fuel jettisoning system as part of the work undertaken by Vickers for the RAF's Long Range Development Unit.

The LRDU had been formed after the success achieved with the Fairey Long-Range Monoplane (AIR INTERNATIONAL/July 1977) and was headed by Wg Cdr O R Gayford, who had been pilot of the Fairey LRM in 1933 when it covered 5,341 mls (8 597 km) in 57 hr 25 min to set a new World Distance Record. As Barnes Wallis had earlier pointed out, it was a characteristic of geodetic construction that much more space was available for fuel than in similar-sized aircraft of more conventional construction; just how right he was can be understood when it is realised that with only slight

(Above) The prototype Wellesley, after modification as the Type 281 and application of the serial K7556. (Immediately below) The fourth production Wellesley (K7716), one of the eight completed to Type 287 standard, and (bottom) the 17th production Wellesley (K7729).

modification the Wellesley bomber could be expected to set a new absolute World Record for distance in a straight line, whereas the Fairey Monoplane four years earlier had to be designed and built specially for the purpose and had no direct operational applications. To take advantage of the Wellesley's inherent performance, the LRDU was set up in January 1938 at Upper Heyford, and five Wellesleys from the second production batch were assigned to it, while the fifth production Mk I, as noted, served as a test-bed for some of the special features, including the Pegasus XXII installation with which it first flew at Filton, Bristol, on 21 January 1938.

Carrying a service load and 1,000 lb (454 kg) of bombs, the Wellesley had a range of about 2,500 mls (4 023 km) under typical conditions. For the record attempt, the RAF was looking for almost three times this distance; to achieve it, not only would more fuel have to be carried and special long-range flying techniques be used; it also would be necessary to achieve the best possible figure for air miles per gallon by reducing drag wherever possible, and one of the most important modifications was the use of an NACA-type long-chord cowling, combined with a new fairing on the front fuselage to mate with the cowling.

The Pegasus XXII was specially adapted to run on 100-octane lead-free fuel, using a higher compression ratio than the Mk XX. A Rotol constant-speed propeller replaced the DH

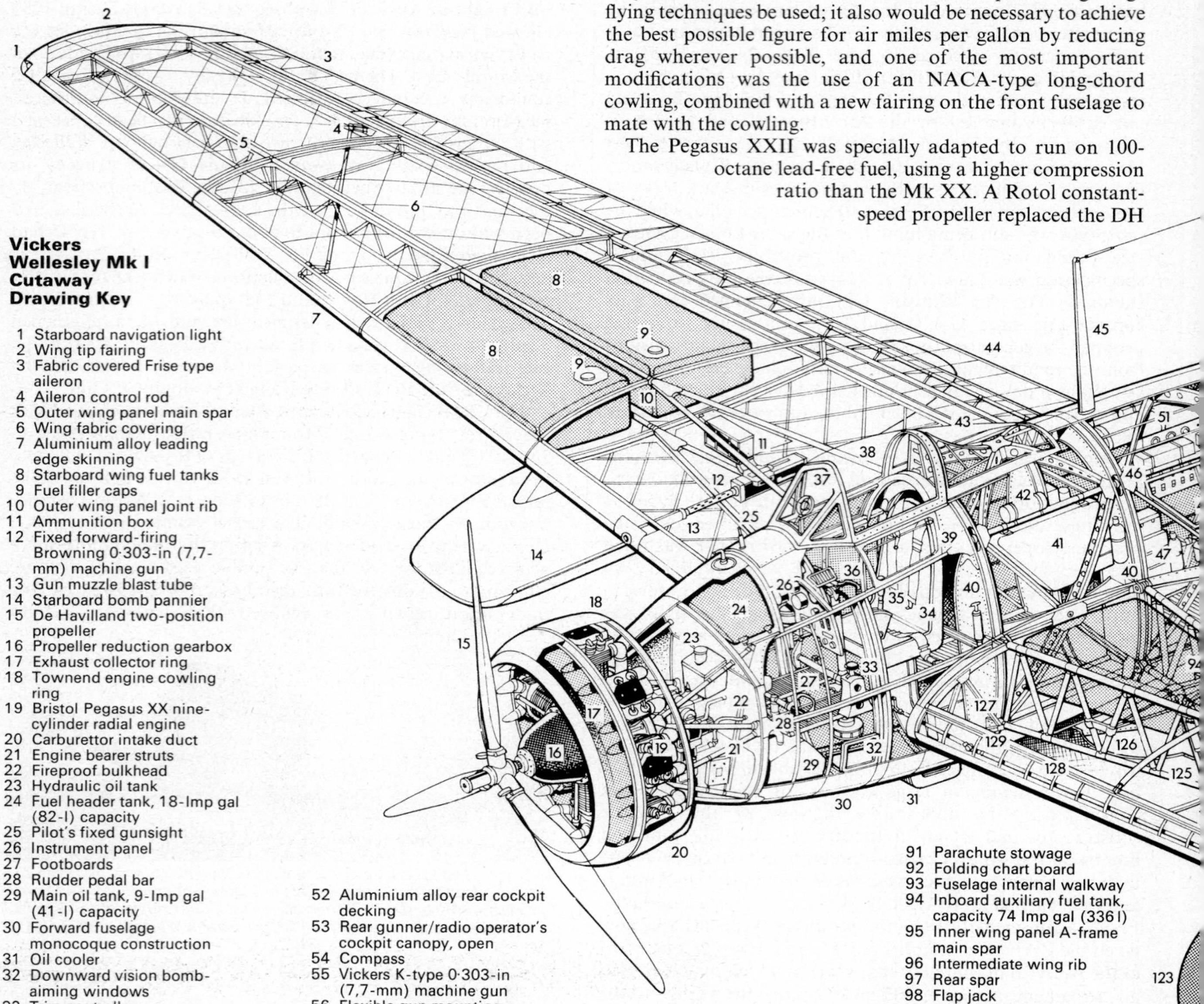

Vickers Wellesley Mk I Cutaway Drawing Key

1 Starboard navigation light
2 Wing tip fairing
3 Fabric covered Frise type aileron
4 Aileron control rod
5 Outer wing panel main spar
6 Wing fabric covering
7 Aluminium alloy leading edge skinning
8 Starboard wing fuel tanks
9 Fuel filler caps
10 Outer wing panel joint rib
11 Ammunition box
12 Fixed forward-firing Browning 0·303-in (7,7-mm) machine gun
13 Gun muzzle blast tube
14 Starboard bomb pannier
15 De Havilland two-position propeller
16 Propeller reduction gearbox
17 Exhaust collector ring
18 Townend engine cowling ring
19 Bristol Pegasus XX nine-cylinder radial engine
20 Carburettor intake duct
21 Engine bearer struts
22 Fireproof bulkhead
23 Hydraulic oil tank
24 Fuel header tank, 18-Imp gal (82-l) capacity
25 Pilot's fixed gunsight
26 Instrument panel
27 Footboards
28 Rudder pedal bar
29 Main oil tank, 9-Imp gal (41-l) capacity
30 Forward fuselage monocoque construction
31 Oil cooler
32 Downward vision bomb-aiming windows
33 Trim controller
34 Pilot's seat
35 Engine throttle control
36 Control column handwheel
37 Windscreen panels
38 Pilot's sliding cockpit canopy cover
39 Cockpit side hatch
40 Wing attachment fuselage bulkheads
41 Water tank
42 Maintenance tool container
43 Canopy aft glazing
44 Starboard split trailing edge flap
45 Aerial mast
46 Upper longeron joint
47 Ration containers and water bottles
48 Cabin side window panel
49 Electrical switch panel
50 W/T spare coils
51 D/F aerial container
52 Aluminium alloy rear cockpit decking
53 Rear gunner/radio operator's cockpit canopy, open
54 Compass
55 Vickers K-type 0·303-in (7,7-mm) machine gun
56 Flexible gun mounting
57 Rear cockpit canopy aft fairing
58 Forced landing flares
59 Aerial lead-in
60 Fuselage fabric covering
61 Telescopic aerial mast stowage
62 Marine distress flares
63 Starboard tailplane
64 Aerial cables
65 Elevator horn balance
66 Starboard elevator
67 Elevator trim tab
68 Fin construction
69 Rudder horn balance
70 Fabric covered rudder construction
71 Rudder trim tab
72 Tail navigation light
73 Formation-keeping light
74 Port elevator construction
75 Elevator tab
76 Tailplane geodetic rib construction
77 Tailplane attachment joints
78 Tailwheel fairing
79 Fixed tailwheel
80 Fuselage geodetic frame construction
81 Upper longeron
82 Bottom longeron
83 Battery
84 Radio racks
85 Air driven emergency generator
86 Trailing aerial winch and fairlead
87 First aid kit
88 Reconnaissance camera
89 Rear gunner's folding seat
90 Spare ammunition drums
91 Parachute stowage
92 Folding chart board
93 Fuselage internal walkway
94 Inboard auxiliary fuel tank, capacity 74 Imp gal (336 l)
95 Inner wing panel A-frame main spar
96 Intermediate wing rib
97 Rear spar
98 Flap jack
99 Flap operating rod
100 Flap shroud construction
101 Port split trailing edge flap
102 Port bomb pannier tail fairing
103 Fabric covered aileron construction
104 Geodetic wing panel framework
105 Aileron hinge control
106 Wing fabric covering
107 Wing tip construction
108 Port navigation light
109 Pitot tubes
110 Aluminium alloy leading edge skinning
111 Tubular main spar booms
112 Retractable landing/taxying lamps
113 Bomb doors
114 Port bomb pannier
115 Bomb stowage, four 250-lb (113-kg) or two 500-lb (227-kg) bombs each side

two-pitch standard unit and an engine-driven vacuum pump was added for instrument actuation. The propeller was hydraulically operated off the aircraft's standard system, and a new system was fitted for actuation of the undercarriage, which was beefed up for the heavier weights of the long-range aircraft. The increased weight resulted primarily from the extra fuel, capacity being increased to 1,290 Imp gal (5 864 l) from the normal maximum of 430 Imp gal (1 955 l). An RAE Mk IV three-axis autopilot was fitted, to relieve the pilot of some of the rigours of flying the aircraft alone for some 48 hrs.

Provision was made for a third occupant to be carried, but the design of the Wellesley was such that dual controls could not easily be fitted, nor was it feasible for pilots to change position during the flight. Sperry blind-flying instruments were fitted, together with gyro-horizon and gyro-compass.

A three-seat layout for the Wellesley had already been studied by Vickers as Type 402*, the RAF being interested in the possibility of operating the type with a separate navigator, rather than having the second crew-man double as gunner,

**Design office numbers were shared between Vickers at Weybridge and Supermarine at Southampton, the latter company using numbers 300-399 inclusive. Thus, Type 402 is closer in time to the earlier Wellesley variants than the number suggests.*

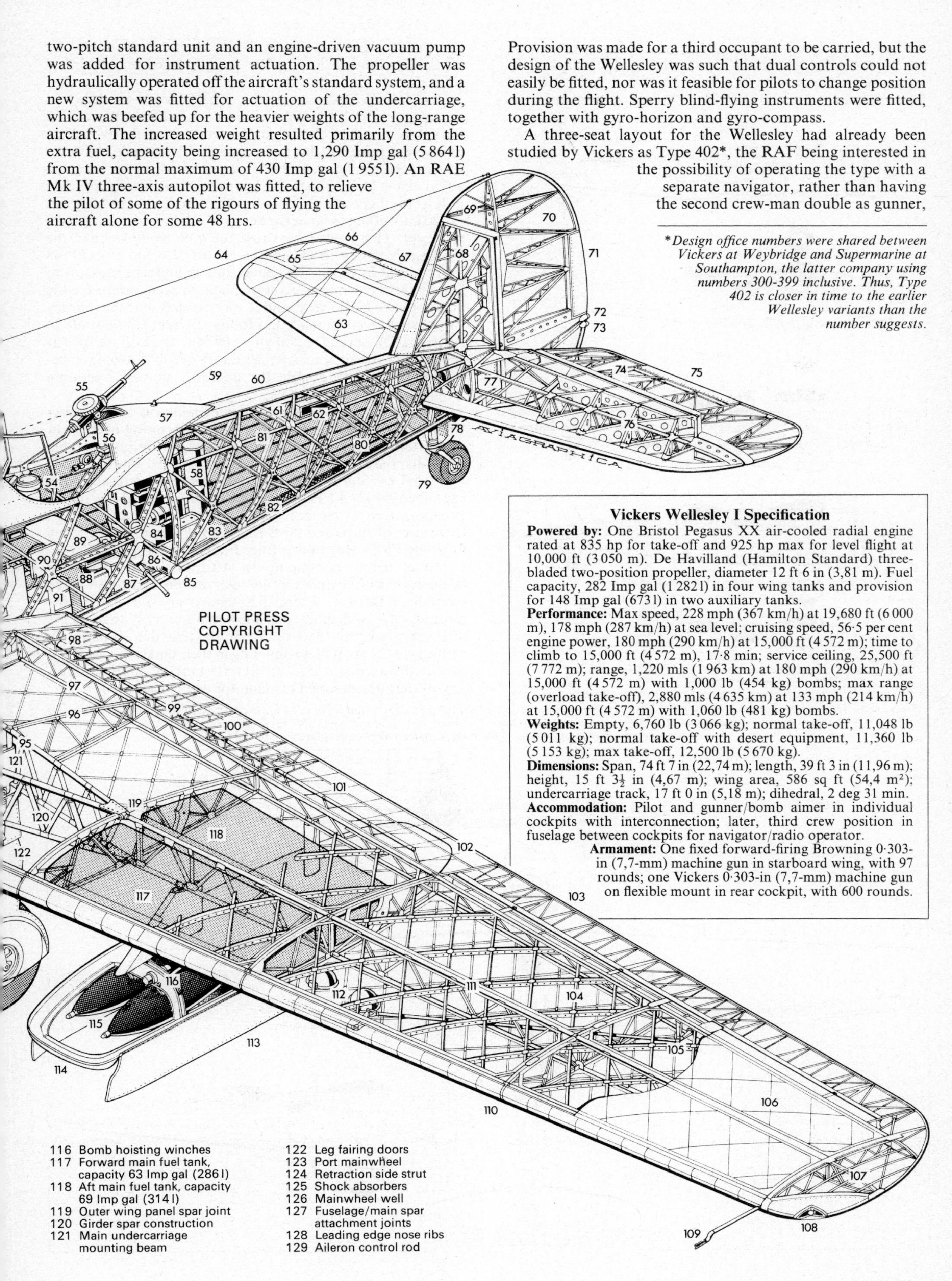

Vickers Wellesley I Specification

Powered by: One Bristol Pegasus XX air-cooled radial engine rated at 835 hp for take-off and 925 hp max for level flight at 10,000 ft (3 050 m). De Havilland (Hamilton Standard) three-bladed two-position propeller, diameter 12 ft 6 in (3,81 m). Fuel capacity, 282 Imp gal (1 282 l) in four wing tanks and provision for 148 Imp gal (673 l) in two auxiliary tanks.

Performance: Max speed, 228 mph (367 km/h) at 19,680 ft (6 000 m), 178 mph (287 km/h) at sea level; cruising speed, 56·5 per cent engine power, 180 mph (290 km/h) at 15,000 ft (4 572 m); time to climb to 15,000 ft (4 572 m), 17·8 min; service ceiling, 25,500 ft (7 772 m); range, 1,220 mls (1 963 km) at 180 mph (290 km/h) at 15,000 ft (4 572 m) with 1,000 lb (454 kg) bombs; max range (overload take-off), 2,880 mls (4 635 km) at 133 mph (214 km/h) at 15,000 ft (4 572 m) with 1,060 lb (481 kg) bombs.

Weights: Empty, 6,760 lb (3 066 kg); normal take-off, 11,048 lb (5 011 kg); normal take-off with desert equipment, 11,360 lb (5 153 kg); max take-off, 12,500 lb (5 670 kg).

Dimensions: Span, 74 ft 7 in (22,74 m); length, 39 ft 3 in (11,96 m); height, 15 ft 3½ in (4,67 m); wing area, 586 sq ft (54,4 m²); undercarriage track, 17 ft 0 in (5,18 m); dihedral, 2 deg 31 min.

Accommodation: Pilot and gunner/bomb aimer in individual cockpits with interconnection; later, third crew position in fuselage between cockpits for navigator/radio operator.

Armament: One fixed forward-firing Browning 0·303-in (7,7-mm) machine gun in starboard wing, with 97 rounds; one Vickers 0·303-in (7,7-mm) machine gun on flexible mount in rear cockpit, with 600 rounds.

navigator and bomb-aimer. A long, glazed canopy was also developed, running from the front cockpit to the rear cockpit, and was flown on one Wellesley that was used for fuel jettisoning experiments; there is no evidence, however, that this was ever known as the Wellesley II, either officially or by Vickers, although it is often so identified in published references.

The five Wellesleys for the LRDU were modified in accordance with Type 292 drawings (while Type 291 covered the development of blind-flying instruments in the Wellesley) and were delivered to the unit in the second quarter of 1938. To gain experience, Sqn Ldr R Kellett, the Unit's senior pilot, led a four-plane formation from Cranwell to Ismailia, Egypt, early in July; the flight was airborne for 32 hrs and covered 4,300 mls (6 920 km), going as far as the Persian Gulf before turning back to Egypt. This flight gave cause for quiet confidence in the Wellesley's ability to exceed the record of 6,306 mls (10 148 km) claimed by the Soviet Union for a flight from Moscow to San Francisco. Final plans were made in preparation for the attempt later in the year, and it was decided that the journey would start from Ismailia and follow a Great Circle route to Australia. A special 1,200-yd (1 097-m) take-off strip was prepared at Ismailia, to cater for the 18,400 lb (8 346 kg) take-off weight, nearly double the aircraft's normal operating weight.

Three Wellesleys took off from Ismailia on 5 November 1938, taking 45 minutes to reach their operating altitude of 10,000 ft (3 050 m) and then setting course across Saudi Arabia for India, the Dutch East Indies and Australia. The flight was again led by Sqn Ldr Kellett, the other two aircraft being captained by Flt Lt H A V Hogan and Flt Lt A N Combe. Winds proved to be more adverse than favourable, but all three aircraft surpassed the Soviet record before the Wellesley flown by Flt Lt Hogan was forced to land at Kupang, Timor, to refuel before continuing to Australia. The other two Wellesleys, with dwindling fuel reserves, pressed on to make landfall at Darwin, where they landed at 04.00 hrs in the morning of 7 November, just a few minutes more than 48 hrs after leaving Egypt. Between them, the two aircraft had only 61 Imp gal (277 l) of fuel remaining in their tanks, but they had flown a distance of 7,157·7 mls (11 519 km) non-stop, setting a record that was destined to stand for eight years.

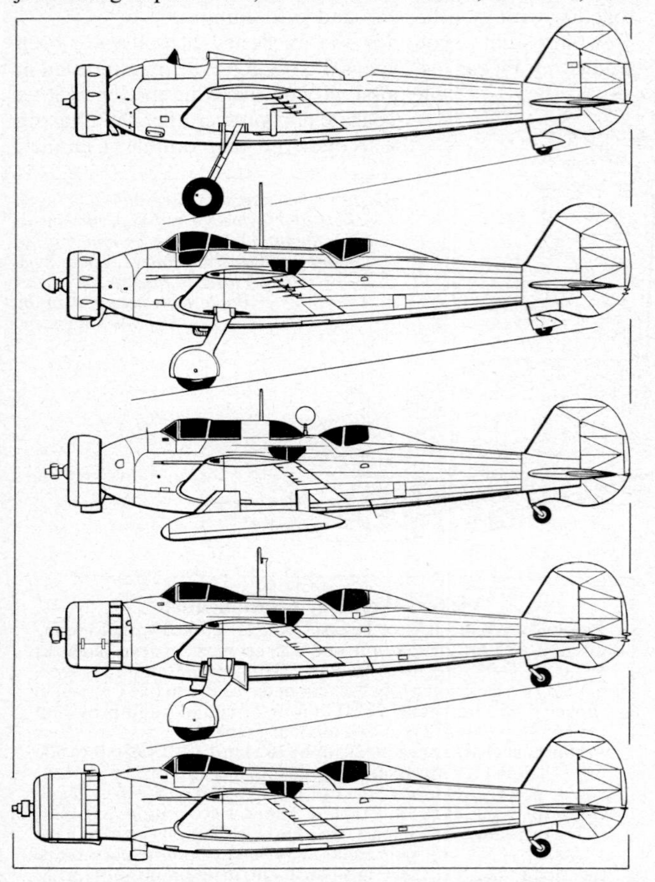

(Above left) The side profile drawings depict (top to bottom) the prototype Wellesley in its original form (1935); the prototype after reconstruction as the Type 281 (1936); the three-seat Type 402 Wellesley; the LRDF Type 292 Wellesley, and the Type 289 Wellesley Hercules test-bed. The general arrangement drawing below depicts the standard Wellesley Mk I.

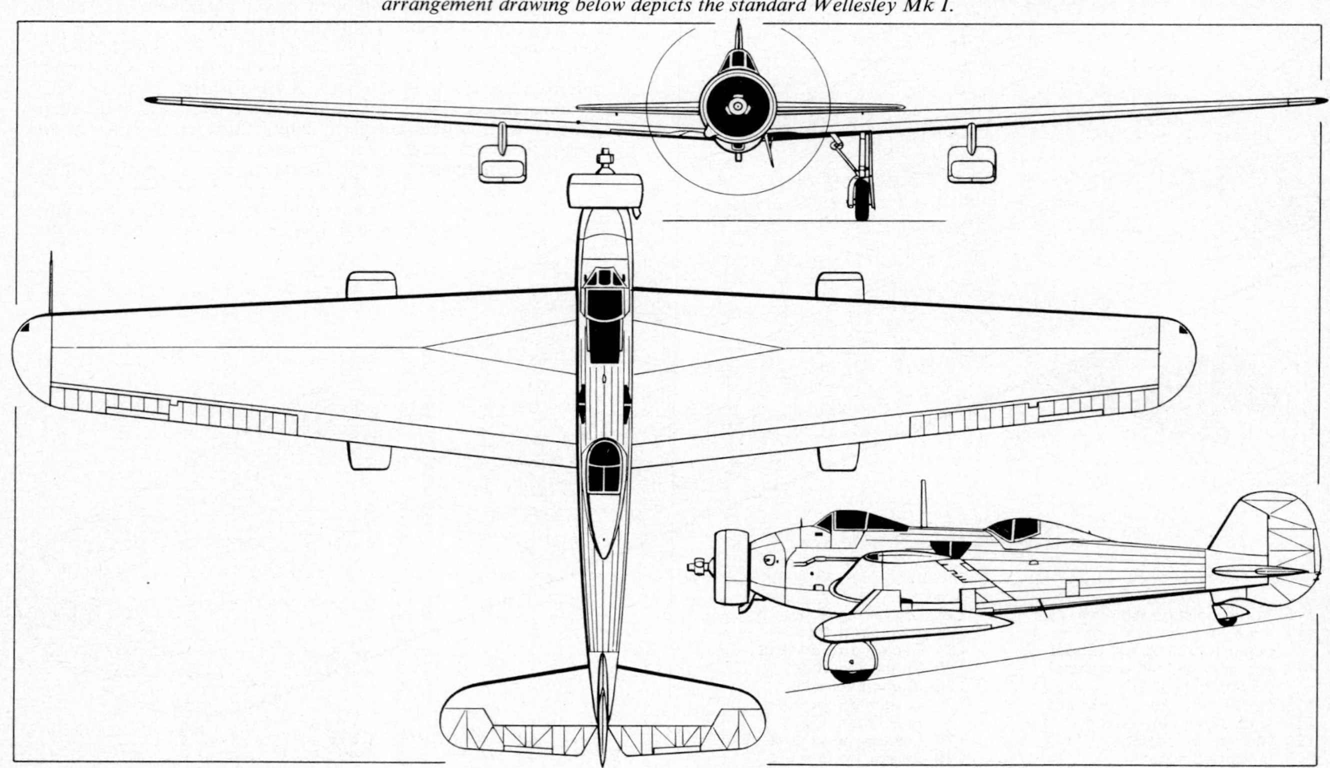

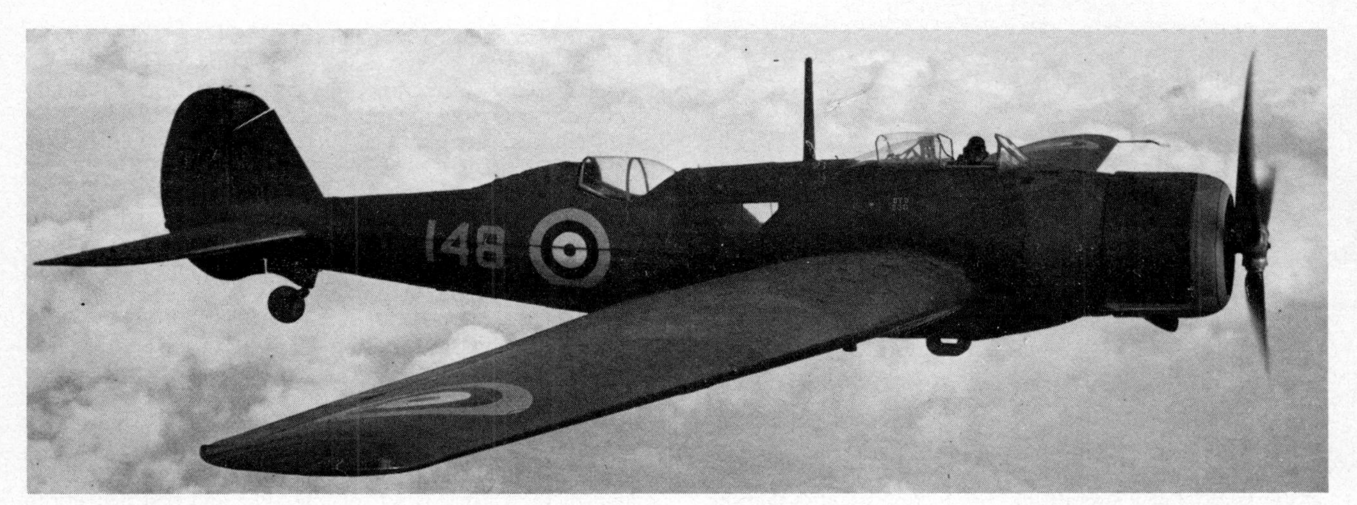

(Above) The fifth production Wellesley (K7717) utilised as a trials aircraft for the Long Range Development Unit after brief service with No 148 Squadron. Note NACA-type cowling and new front fuselage fairing. (Right) One of the Wellesleys (L2637) assigned to the LRDU. This particular machine was the back-up aircraft and did not participate in the Unit's long-distance flights.

By the time the Wellesleys set this record, the war clouds were gathering over Europe and the achievement of the aircraft and its vindication of Wallis' faith in geodetic construction received relatively scant recognition. Nevertheless, the Wellesley had already served its purpose in laying the foundations on which the Wellington was being built and would, in the war that was soon to come, flourish.

Operational use

The outbreak of World War II in September 1939 found the Wellesley still in service as front-line equipment with only three squadrons — all based in the Middle East; No 14 Squadron was at Ismailia, Egypt, while Nos 47 and 223 were in the Sudan, the former at Khartoum, the latter at Summit. Not until June 1940, with Benito Mussolini's declaration of war between Italy and the Franco-British Allies on the evening of the 10th, did any early possibility of active participation in operations face these units. During the previous month, No 14 Squadron had joined the other two in the Sudan, and was now based at Port Sudan airfield, while No 47 had moved to an airfield at Erkowit (renamed Carthago in July 1940). Together, the Wellesley squadrons formed the Advanced Striking Force of Air Commodore L H Slatter's No 203 Group.

While far from being the most modern of operational types, the Wellesleys were considered suitable for active service against the Italians in East Africa; indeed, they were at least as up to date as most of the equipment of the *Regia Aeronautica* in the area — quite apart from which they were all that was available. In line with the Royal Air Force's policy of taking the war to the enemy whenever possible, there was no delay in getting the Wellesleys into action. On the morning of 11 June, eight Wellesleys of No 47 Squadron were off at dawn for a raid on the Eritrean capital, Asmara. This first attack met no fighter opposition, but a lucky shot from the elderly anti-aircraft guns around the city's airfield struck one of the bombers, which was last seen trailing smoke and failed to return; it had crashed in the mountains shortly after leaving the target; No 14 Squadron was also involved in this first day's operations, but because of troubles experienced with the underwing bomb containers, its aircraft were delayed in their take-off until late in the afternoon.

The Italian East African empire was large and spread across wild territory, the towns and military installations being widely separated and thinly garrisoned. Even the considerable range of the Wellesley was not sufficient to reach all targets — certainly in the further reaches of Ethiopia. The No 203 Group bombers were therefore made responsible primarily for taking the war to Eritrea — particularly to the main Red Sea coast bases in the Massawa area — and to Northern Ethiopia. In this task they were joined by Blenheims based in Aden, Italian territory therefore forming the "meat in the sandwich" between the two main British base areas; Southern Ethiopia was left to South African forces, operating from Kenya.

Both the Sudan and Aden possessed a handful of Gloster Gladiator biplane fighters for base defence at this time, but none was available for escort to the bombers. For the early months of the war the Wellesleys had to rely on their altitude performance, and the Blenheims on their speed, for escaping the attentions of Italian interceptors. These attributes were frequently to prove inadequate for coping with determined opposition — and determined it was indeed to prove over Eritrea. The *Regia Aeronautica* personnel in East Africa included some of the most experienced and professional in the whole air force, and one of the units based here, the 412[a] *Squadriglia CT*, enjoyed the benefit of having been fully re-equipped with Fiat CR 42 biplane fighters which were to prove most formidable opponents for the RAF. Indeed, until the arrival of Hurricanes in relatively substantial numbers during the early months of 1941, the *Regia Aeronautica* was to enjoy a greater degree of success for the numbers employed than probably it did on any other front. This was despite a lack of resupply facilities and reserves which was to become an increasingly severe problem as the weeks passed.

continued on page 49

THE DHC-8

ORDERING a new aircraft into production signifies that the design is no longer a "paper aeroplane"; but in this decade of the derivatives it is fair to ask, "How new is new?" For the de Havilland Aircraft of Canada DHC-8 — formerly known as the Dash X and now being marketed as the Dash 8 — the answer is that it is a size-derivative of an established design, the Dash 7. Genesis of the Dash 8 was a direct outgrowth of de Havilland's perception of a market for a 32/36-passenger pressurised twin-turboprop STOL-capable transport to fill the gap between the unpressurised 19-passenger Twin Otter and the pressurised 50-passenger Dash 7. Thus, it is one of numerous designs now being studied and, in some cases, built in the same size category, but differs from most others in having better STOL performance.

The Dash 8 is a $Can150m (£58m) development programme that was announced rather coyly at the Commuter Airlines Association of America convention late last October in Florida, although informal briefings to airlines on the then Dash X project had been made at the Paris Air Show in June 1979. Public announcement of the programme came at the annual meeting of the Air Transport Association of Canada early in November in Toronto, when DHC president John Sandford explained that cash flow from Dash 7 sales would fund the new aircraft; and early in December a conference was held at Downsview, Ontario, by DHC to which other Canadian companies were invited to consider taking part in the programme.

Late in February 1980, another piece in the DHC-8/Dash X/Dash 8 puzzle fell into place when it was announced that the engine chosen for the new STOL transport was the 1,700-shp Pratt & Whitney Aircraft of Canada PT7A-2R (the 1,500-shp PT7A-1 having already been selected by EMBRAER for the EMB-120 Brasilia, another of the new projects in the same size category), in preference to the General Electric CT7. PWAC and DHC signed an agreement for the supply of 200 engines for the Dash 8. Then, on 2 April, came the big surprise when the Province of Ontario placed an order worth $Can9m (£3·5m) for two Dash 8s (with spares) to be used by the norOntair consortium of small airlines (Austin Airways, On Air, and Air Dale) serving 20 communities in the northern parts of the province. The order was small — as is usual for small airlines — but then the first order for the Twin Otter (over 600 sold) was for a single aeroplane for the Ontario Department of Lands and Forests! The significance of the first order for the Dash 8 is that it was placed so soon after programme go-ahead, and that is the first time that de Havilland has received a government order before building and flying a new commercial aeroplane.

Commenting on the order, Provincial Treasurer Frank Miller explained the twofold purpose of the purchase. "While an improved transportation network in northern Ontario is a priority of this government", he said, "we are also aware that the aerospace industry is an important sector of our economy. It is a high-technology sector generating very significant export earnings. It is important that the aerospace industry continues to expand in Ontario. The de Havilland expansion itself could create about 3,000 new jobs and could lead to export sales in excess of $Can3,000m (£1,154m). Through this purchase of Dash 8 aircraft, we are enhancing norOntair's service capability and at the same time providing key incentives to our aircraft-manufacturing industry. We are pleased to be the lead customer of the Dash 8 and are confident that our purchase will inaugurate a successful export campaign".

The norOntair system now uses eight Twin Otters to feed mainline carriers and the Dash 8's 32/36-passenger capacity (four-abreast, 32-in (81,3-cm) pitch) is attractive with increasing traffic since it will relieve congestion on some of the present Twin Otter routes. Also, the new aeroplane is more fuel-efficient and will cruise about 50 per cent faster. First flight of the Dash 8 is set for mid-1983 and first delivery to norOntair for July 1984.

A few days after the norOntair order was announced, de Havilland's 4,600 employees were told that a new plant might be built for Dash 8 production and would employ about 1,500, apart from another 1,000 jobs at the main Downsview plant which is already being expanded for increased production of the Dash 7, Twin Otter and Buffalo. Location of the new plant has yet to be decided.

Dash 8 described

When first mooted as the Dash X, the new de Havilland twin-turboprop transport showed its close relationship with the Dash 7 in that it was essentially a short-fuselage derivative with two fewer engines. However, it differed visibly in having *single* main wheels retracting into fuselage-side fairings instead of into engine nacelles. There were two reasons for this change — the engine was of different layout, and fuselage-mounted main wheels had shorter legs and so were lighter and cheaper. Whereas the PT6 engines of the Dash 7 have air intakes at the rear and exhausts at the front, the PT7 has straight-through flow with a tailpipe, leaving no room for main wheels in the nacelle if the pipe is straight. So it was rational to design a

(Above) The first released illustration of the Pratt & Whitney PT7A turboprop. (Below) Three-view drawing of the Dash 8.

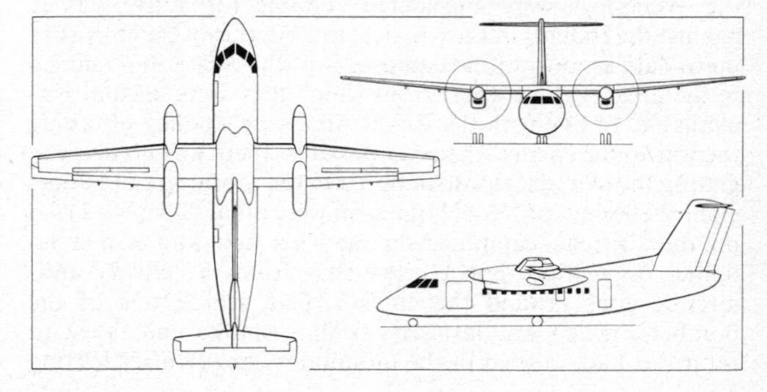

simple engine installation with short nacelles and straight tailpipes, and to retract the wheels into fuselage bulges.

However, service experience with the Dash 7 has confirmed how valuable the wide-track main wheels are for crosswind-landing — particularly when operating onto stub runways at major airports — so it was no surprise to find that the Dash 8 as ordered into production has been designed to have side-venting tailpipes to leave room in the nacelle for *twin*-wheel main undercarriage legs. Additional weight of the longer main-gear legs is compensated for by absence of cross-sectional and wetted-area drags of the fuselage-side fairings and — no less important — commonality is maintained with standard Dash 7 fuselage structure.

Aerodynamically, the Dash 8 clearly owes much to its four-engined progenitor in that it has a high wing and "T"-tail with tandem-element rudder (features originated by de Havilland with the DHC-5 Buffalo). Because of the new engines, the nacelles are longer than the Dash 7's and slimmer, and the twin overwing stovepipe exhausts have given way to nacelle-side vents under the wings. Unlike the fuselage, the wing is completely new and, apart from having smaller area, differs from that of the Dash 7 in having a rectangular centre-section and tapered outer panels instead of straight taper from the roots. Also, dihedral is incorporated on the outer panels only instead of from the roots. The fuselage is basically that of the Dash 7 with about 15 ft (4,57 m) taken out, but the Dash 8 has a different nose that slopes down more sharply. There is a baggage compartment aft of the flight deck. Normal crew complement will be two pilots and one flight attendant.

PT7 development

The PT7 has a specific fuel consumption of 0·503, about 15 per cent better than for the PT6, and drives the propeller at 1,200 rpm. The new engine features axial compressor stages, a two-stage centrifugal compressor, two-stage compressor turbine and two-stage power turbine. Power potential is from the present 1,500-shp (PT7A-1) and 1,700-shp (PT7A-2R) up to at least 2,500 shp. Work on a demonstrator engine started officially in July 1979; a definitive gas-generator core will run in late 1980; and a power-turbine/gearbox assembly will be on test by March 1981. The PT7 has an electronic fuel-control system for ease and precision of power setting that is so important for steep-gradient STOL approaches, and a system to monitor engine condition for maintenance. Weight is about 800 lb (363 kg); the engine has a diameter of 22 in (55,9 cm) compared with 19 in (48,3 cm) for the PT6, but the PT7 is a little shorter.

Acceptance of the Dash 8 and its success in service will be helped by the progressive adoption of three-dimensional area navigation (3D RNAV) and microwave landing systems (MLS) combined with the advantages of steep-gradient (7·5 deg for STOL instead of 3·0 deg for CTOL) take-off and final approach. Thus, like the Dash 7, the new DHC STOL transport will be able to use either stub runways at major airports, via otherwise unused approach airspace, or operate easily from small, local airstrips or specially equipped STOLports. With this versatility and its pedigree of being a fourth-generation turboprop STOL design, the Dash 8 should have a very rosy future. □

DAVID W H GODFREY

De Havilland Dash 8 Specification

Power Plant: Two Pratt & Whitney Aircraft of Canada PT7A-2R turboprops each rated at 1,700 shp for take-off, meeting FAR Part 36 Stage 3 noise requirements.
Performance: Max cruise speed, 300 mph, 260 kt (483 km/h) at 25,000 ft (7 620 m); range with IFR fuel reserves and full payload, 600 naut miles (1 112 km); FAR Part 25 take-off field length, 3,000 ft (914 m); max range with IFR reserves, 1,200 naut miles (2 224 km).
Weights: Gross weight, approx 30,000 lb (13 608 kg).
Dimensions: Span 82 ft 0 in (25,0 m); length 70 ft 11 in (21,6 m); height 24 ft 3½ in (7,4 m); wheel track 25 ft 9½ in (7,9 m).

THE NEW COMMUTERLINERS — II

Saab-Fairchild Airliner

PRELIMINARY details have now been published of the commuter airliner that was the subject of an agreement signed in Stockholm on 25 January 1980 between Saab-Scania AB and Fairchild Industries Inc. The aircraft is the first to be developed on a fully collaborative basis between a European and an American company. First flight is projected for late 1982 or early 1983, with deliveries starting early 1984.

With a circular cross-section fuselage and a cabin pressurised to a differential of 7·0 psi (0,49 kg/cm²), the new commuter airliner is being designed to a combination of fail-safe and safe-life principles and with emphasis upon simplicity of systems, operation and maintenance. The wing carries single-slotted flaps and the tricycle undercarriage, all members of which retract forwards.

A choice of engine has yet to be made, from the available new generation of power plants in the 1,500+ shp bracket, including the jointly-developed Garrett-Volvo TPE331-14, the Pratt & Whitney PT7A and the General Electric CT7.

To market the new aircraft worldwide (except in North America) the two manufacturers are setting up a jointly-owned Swedish company, with a sales office in Paris, and Alan R Buley, formerly president of Fokker-VFW International, has been appointed its chief executive. Fairchild will remain responsible for marketing in the USA. □

Saab-Fairchild Commuter Airliner Specification

Power Plant: Two "new generation" turboprops in the 1,500+ shp class. Fuel capacity, 900 US gal (3 407 l) in two integral wing tanks.
Performance: Max cruise speed, 295 kt (550 km/h); initial rate of climb, 2,000 ft/min (10,2 m/sec); single-engined climb rate, 750 ft/min (3,8 m/sec); balanced field length, under 4,000 ft (1 200 m); design range for commuter operations, four 110-ml (200-km) stages without refuelling.
Weights: Operating weight empty, 14,500 lb (6 600 kg); payload, 7,500 lb (3 400 kg); max zero fuel weight, 22,000 lb (10 000 kg); max take-off weight, 25,000 lb (11 350 kg); max landing weight, 24,500 lb (11 100 kg).
Dimensions: Span, 70 ft 4½ in (21,44 m); length, 63 ft 9 in (19,43 m); height, 21 ft 8 in (6,61 m); undercarriage track, 22 ft 0 in (6,671 m); wheelbase, 23 ft 3 in (7,10 m).
Accommodation: Two pilots and 34 passengers (plus one flight attendant) three-abreast at 30-in (76-cm) pitch, with toilet compartment, wardrobe and provision for galley. Luggage compartment volume, 225 cu ft (6,4 m³).

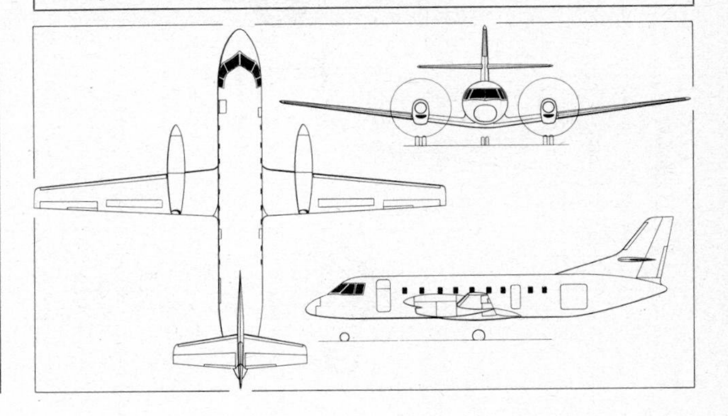

FIGHTER A TO Z

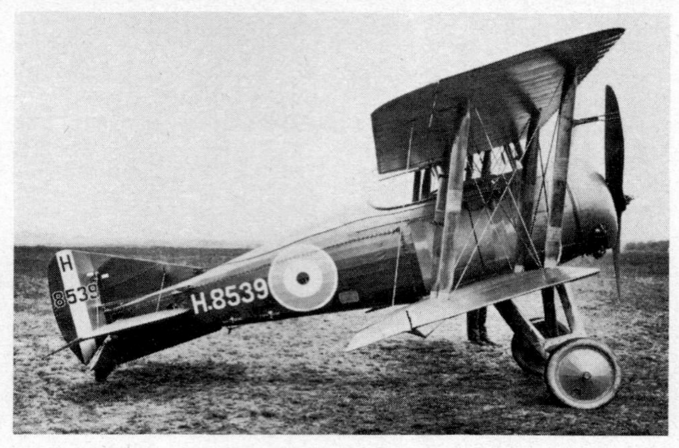

A Mars X Nightjar at RAE Farnborough in 1922. Nightjars of No 203 Sqdn, RAF, operated in the Middle East during the Chanak crisis.

The first production Grebe II, this type entering RAF service in October 1923 and remaining first-line equipment until mid-1928.

GLOSTER MARS X NIGHTJAR — UK

Last of the derivatives of the Nighthawk, the Mars X Nightjar was developed as a single-seat shipboard fighter, and featured a 230 hp Bentley B.R.2 nine-cylinder rotary engine, a special wide-track undercarriage incorporating arrester gear and an armament of two 0·303-in (7,7-mm) synchronised Vickers guns. Although intended for naval use, the 22 Mars X Nightjar fighters resulting from the conversion of Nighthawk airframes by Gloucestershire Aircraft were delivered to the RAF, the first being delivered to the AEE Martlesham on 8 May 1922. The Nightjar entered service in July 1922, but was withdrawn within two years. Max speed, 120 mph (193 km/h) at sea level, 110 mph (177 km/h) at 10,000 ft (3 050 m). Time to 15,000 ft (4 570 m), 23 min. Empty weight, 1,765 lb (801 kg). Loaded weight, 2,165 lb (982 kg). Span, 28 ft 0 in (8,53 m). Length, 18 ft 4 in (5,59 m). Height, 9 ft 0 in (2,74 m). Wing area, 270 sq ft (25,08 m²).

GLOSTER GREBE — UK

Essentially a single-seat fighter version of the lower-powered tandem two-seat Grouse trainer, the Grebe was flown in the summer of 1923 with a 350 hp Armstrong Siddeley Jaguar III, three prototypes being built. The production model, known as the Grebe II, was re-engined with a 400 hp Jaguar IV and, carrying an armament of two synchronised 0·303-in (7,7-mm) Vickers guns, entered RAF service in October 1923. Of wooden construction with fabric skinning, the Grebe II supplanted the Sopwith Snipe, 129 production examples being built during 1923-27, a small number of these being completed as tandem two-seat trainers, and the type remained in first-line RAF service until replaced by the Siskin mid-1928. One two-seat and two single-seat Grebe IIs built against RAF contracts were supplied to the New Zealand government in 1928. Max speed, 162 mph (261 km/h) at sea level. Time to 20,000 ft (6 095 m), 24 min. Endurance, 3 hrs. Empty weight, 1,695 lb (769 kg). Loaded weight, 2,538 lb (1 151 kg). Span, 29 ft 4 in (8,93 m). Length, 20 ft 3 in (6,17 m). Height, 9 ft 3 in (2,82 m). Wing area, 254 sq ft (23,60 m²).

The Grebe II (below) was the first Gloster aeroplane produced in substantial numbers for RAF service.

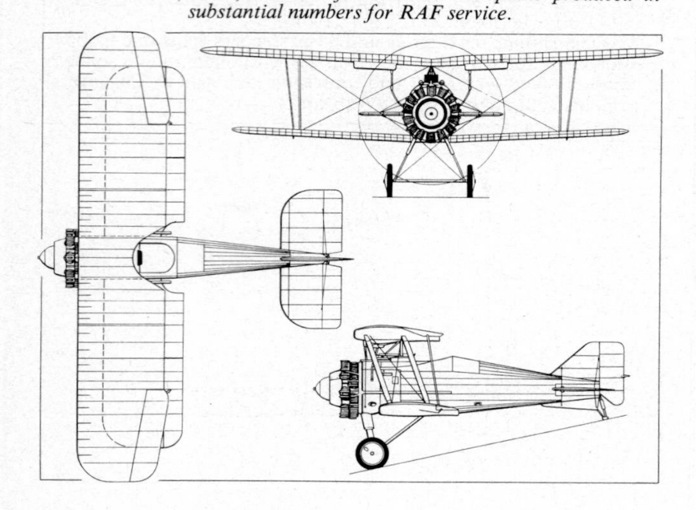

GLOSTER GAMECOCK — UK

In July 1924, Gloucestershire Aircraft began work on an improved Grebe single-seat fighter to specification 37/23 and intended for the 398 hp Bristol Jupiter IV nine-cylinder radial engine. Of wooden construction with fabric skinning and retaining the then-standard armament of two synchronised 0·303-in (7,7-mm) Vickers guns, the prototype was delivered to Martlesham on 20 February 1925, and in the following September an initial order was placed on behalf of the RAF for 30 Gamecock Is powered by the 425 hp Jupiter VI. In the event, a further 60 Gamecock Is were built for the RAF (1925-27), one of these (unofficially known as the Gamecock III) at one time flying with a lengthened fuselage, new and enlarged fin-and-rudder assembly and narrow-chord ailerons. A developed version, the Gamecock II, with a steel-tube upper

The Gamecock I (below) was essentially an improved Grebe and 90 production examples were supplied to the RAF.

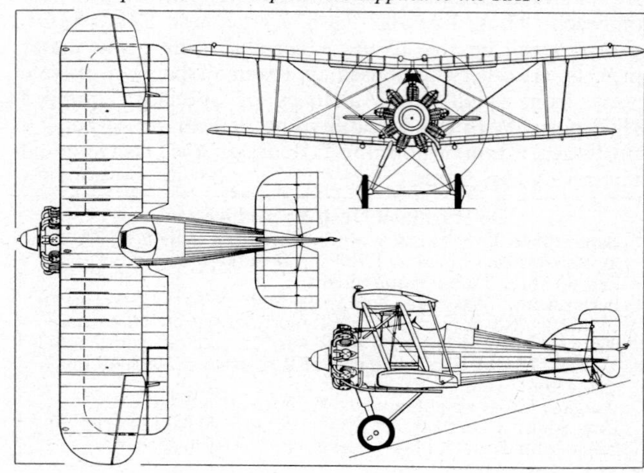

(Above) A Gamecock I serving with No 43 Sqdn, RAF, and (below) a Gamecock II in Finnish service.

wing centre section, narrow-chord ailerons and a larger rudder, appeared in 1928, and was adopted by Finland, two pattern aircraft and a manufacturing licence being acquired. Fifteen Gamecock IIs were built for the Finnish air arm 1929-30 by the State Aircraft Factory (*Valtion Lentokonenetehdas*), these having the lengthened fuselage tested earlier in the UK by the so-called Gamecock III and being powered initially by the 420 hp Gnome-Rhône Jupiter (IV) 9Ab or 9Ak and later by the 480 hp Jupiter (IV) 9Ag. The last Gamecock Is were withdrawn from first-line RAF service mid-1931, Gamecock IIs remaining first-line Finnish equipment until 1935. The following data relate to the Gamecock I. Max speed, 145 mph (233 km/h) at 10,000 ft (3 050 m). Time to 10,000 ft (3 050 m), 7·6 min. Endurance, 2·5 hrs. Empty weight, 1,930 lb (875 kg). Loaded weight, 2,742 lb (1 244 kg). Span, 29 ft 9½ in (9,08 m). Length, 19 ft 8 in (5,99 m). Height, 9 ft 8 in (2,94 m). Wing area, 264 sq ft (24,52 m²).

GLOSTER GORCOCK — UK

Gloucestershire Aircraft's first military aircraft of all-metal construction was the third prototype Gorcock single-seat fighter resulting from a May 1924 contract for three prototypes powered by the Napier Lion 12-cylinder water-cooled engine, the first two combining a steel fuselage with wooden wings and the third having an all-steel structure. The first mixed-construction Gorcock was powered by a 450 hp geared Lion IV and was flown mid-1925, the second Gorcock having a 525 hp direct-drive Lion VIII. Engine difficulties prevented their delivery until 1927, together with the all-metal third Gorcock which had a Lion IV. All three aircraft carried the standard armament of twin synchronised 0·303-in (7,7-mm) Vickers guns and were used for research and development flying, no production being ordered. Although 158 lb (72 kg) heavier than the mixed-construction prototypes, the all-metal prototype, to which the following data refer, was 10 mph (16 km/h) faster. Max speed, 174 mph (280 km/h) at 5,000 ft (1 525 m). Time to 15,000 ft (4 570 m), 10·5 min. Endurance, 1·8 hrs. Empty weight, 2,422 lb (1 099 kg). Loaded weight, 3,337 lb (1 514 kg). Span, 28 ft 6 in (8,69 m). Length, 26 ft 1 in (7,94 m). Height, 10 ft 2 in (3,12 m). Wing area, 250 sq ft (23,22 m²).

(Above) The second Gorcock with a direct-drive Lion VIII engine and Gamecock-style tail unit.

GLOSTER GUAN — UK

The Guan single-seat high-altitude fighter was intended primarily to test the application of turbo-supercharged engines to fighters, and three prototypes were ordered at the beginning of 1925. Of mixed construction, with metal fuselage, wooden wings and fabric skinning, and provision for the standard twin synchronised 0·303-in (7,7-mm) Vickers gun armament, the Guan bore a close family resemblance to the Gorcock, and the first prototype was completed in June 1926 with a geared 450 hp Napier Lion IV with an exhaust-driven turbo-supercharger below the propeller shaft. The second followed early in 1927 with a direct-drive 525 hp Lion VI and turbo-supercharger mounted above the propeller shaft. Difficulties with the turbo-superchargers led to cancellation of the third prototype and abandonment of the development programme. The following data relate to the second Guan. Max speed, 175 mph (282 km/h) at 15,000 ft (4 570 m). Time to 20,000 ft (6 095 m), 12·5 min. Empty weight, 2,972 lb (1 348 kg). Loaded weight, 3,803 lb (1 725 kg). Span, 31 ft 10 in (9,70 m). Length, 22 ft 0 in (6,70 m). Height, 10 ft 2 in (3,12 m). Wing area, 298 sq ft (27,68 m²).

(Above and below) The second prototype Guan with Lion VI engine and turbo-supercharger above the propeller shaft.

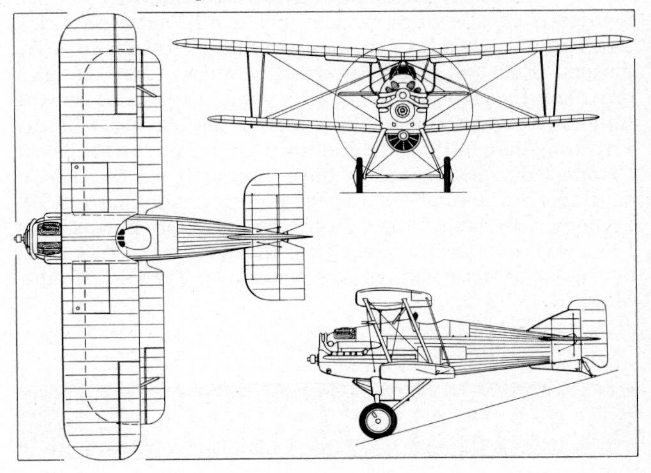

НА ВООРУЖЕНИИ СОВЕТСКОЙ АВИАЦИИ • IN SOVIET SERVICE–9

SINCE FIRST SIGHTED on the fantail operating pad of a *Kresta I* class anti-submarine cruiser engaged in a shakedown voyage in 1967, and shortly afterwards aboard the more radical half-deck *Moskva* during its first passage through the Dardanelles, the Ka-25 has provided both backbone and rib cage of the Soviet shipboard ASW helicopter force. Assigned somewhat whimsically the reporting name *Hormone* in the west and product of the experimental design bureau headed for a quarter-century by the late Nikolai Il'ich Kamov, this compact, relatively unsophisticated machine originated with a specification formulated in the late 'fifties for a dedicated shipboard anti-submarine warfare helicopter seen as a key element in a major shift in Soviet naval strategy.

In the mid-'fifties, the Soviet Union had become aware of the high priority that the United States was assigning the Polaris missile-carrying submarine programme and had digested the unpalatable fact that, within the space of relatively few years, US submarines were likely to be capable of targeting key Soviet industrial and population centres from the Arctic, Norwegian and Mediterranean seas. This threat dictated a hurried shift towards anti-submarine warfare in naval strategy and the utmost urgency being attached to the creation of a new generation of ASW weapons and sensors, and the platforms, both seaborne and airborne, from which to operate them.

Paralleling a massive naval design programme embracing several categories of new and specialised ASW vessels was a programme aimed at enhancing dramatically the ASW capabilities of the Naval Air Force, or *Voenno-morskovo Flota* (AV-MF), in both shore-based and seaborne operations. For *very* long-range maritime surveillance, *Bear* [Tu-95], obsolescent in its intended strategic bombing rôle, provided an ideal airborne platform and was therefore further developed [Tu-142], being restored to production for its new maritime tasks; the open-ocean ASW patrol category was fulfilled by *May* [Il-38], a derivative of the commercial Il-18, and the near-zone ASW task was catered for by *Mail* [Be-12], all of which made their début in AV-MF service from the early, through the mid to the late 'sixties. But as important as any of these — and from some aspects more so — was *Hormone,* the first relatively efficacious ASW helicopter to be fielded by the AV-MF.

Kamov's bureau had been responsible for the first Soviet ship-based helicopter, the Ka-15, dubbed *Hen* under the ASCC reporting name system, which, adopted by the AV-MF in 1954, was a relatively primitive, rudimentarily-equipped two-seater capable of carrying a small depth charge on a rack attached to each side of the fuselage but possessing no ASW sensors. Built in relatively small numbers, *Hen* at least provided the Soviet Navy with some experience in the shipboard operation of helicopters, and it was hardly surprising that, in 1958, the Kamov team, led by chief engineer Vladimir Barshevski, should have been assigned the task of developing a specialised turbine-powered shipboard ASW helicopter, the first of three prototypes of which, flown late in 1960, was to be shown publicly for the first time in July 1961, during the Soviet Aviation Day flypast over Tushino Airport, Moscow.

KAMOV HORMONE

At the time of its début over Tushino, the new Kamov helicopter was assigned the reporting name *Harp*. Sporting mock-ups of air-to-surface missiles on outrigger pylons and aerodynamic fairings under nose and tailboom representing sensor housings, the helicopter conformed to the formula favoured by the Kamov bureau of superimposed co-axial counter-rotating three-bladed rotors and a pod-and-boom fuselage configuration. Two turboshafts — which it was subsequently to transpire were of Glushenkov design — were mounted side by side above the cabin, forward of the rotor driveshaft, these engines making, with the rotors, transmission and auxiliaries, a single self-contained assembly designed for rapid removal and reinstallation. It was evident that the Kamov bureau had aimed at maximum internal capacity with minimum external dimensions and it was to become apparent that it had succeeded in this endeavour admirably.

It would seem that the decision to proceed with series production of the Kamov ASW helicopter was taken in 1961-62 as it is known that deliveries of pre-series machines to the AV-MF commenced late in 1965. Externally, the series model differed little from the prototype demonstrated at Tushino, apart from more angular vertical tail surfaces, the endplate components, unlike those of the prototype, being toed inward, and a revised undercarriage. It is somewhat surprising, therefore, that the new reporting name of *Hormone* was bestowed on the production Ka-25. While *Hormone* and its ASW systems were being evolved, virtually all the larger anti-submarine vessels, or BPKs *(Bolshoy protivo lodochny korabl)*, that had been laid down in Soviet shipyards incorporated helicopter support facilities, with fantail operating pad and a hangar tailored to *Hormone,* the first Soviet Navy ship to feature such being the *Kresta I* class anti-submarine cruiser — essentially an interim design pending construction of the improved *Kresta II.* Pads for temporary *Hormone* operation or re-arming and refuelling of the helicopter were introduced on a number of destroyers. Simultaneously, a pair of *Moskva*-class half-deck anti-submarine cruisers specifically for operation of *Hormone* were being built, these each providing accommodation for 18 helicopters.

In parallel with development of the shipboard ASW helicopter, the Kamov bureau evolved a commercial flying-crane variant, the Ka-25K, which, flown early in 1967, and displayed publicly at the Paris *Salon de l'Aéronautique* of that year, differed essentially in having a detachable gondola in place of the undernose search radar installation and intended for occupancy by one of the two crew members during positioning and unloading of externally-slung cargoes. All ASW equipment was, of course, deleted, and brochure figures indicated a good payload-to-AUW ratio and respectable performance, but the Ka-25K apparently failed to find favour as further development and production were not pursued.

Kamov's *Hormone* possesses no direct western equivalent. Perhaps the closest comparable helicopter in the West is Aérospatiale's SA 330 Puma, which, having some 20 per cent less empty equipped weight and enjoying almost twice the power, understandably offers appreciably higher performance and a better payload-to-AUW ratio. Nevertheless, despite the less than desirable power offered by its paired Glushenkov turboshafts and taking into account the conceptual age of *Hormone* and the stage reached in Soviet rotorcraft development by the time of its début, the performance of this helicopter is competent and it scores in compactness — within

17

an overall length of marginally more than 32 ft (9,75 m) it offers a cabin of sufficient capacity to accommodate up to 12 passengers when not occupied by search equipment, and (in *Hormone-A*) a weapons bay beneath the cabin floor housing ASW torpedoes, nuclear depth charges, or other stores.

Structurally, *Hormone* has a conventional all-metal semi-monocoque fuselage of pod-and-boom type, the Glushenkov turboshafts — which, in late production examples, are reportedly of GTD-3BM type each rated at 990 shp — together with the main reduction gear, oil system, fuel filters, cooling system, hydraulics and powered control system, being mounted as self-contained units above the main cabin and driving two three-bladed co-axial contra-rotating rotors of 51 ft 8 in (15,74 m) diameter, the blades featuring automatic folding. The pilot and co-pilot are seated side-by-side on the flight deck to which access is provided by large aft-sliding doors. Either two or three systems operators are normally housed in the main cabin immediately aft of the flight deck, this measuring 12 ft 11 in (3,95 m) by 4 ft 11 in (1,50 m) by 4 ft 1 in (1,25 m), entry and egress being via an aft-sliding door in the port side to the rear of the main undercarriage bracing. Tip-up seats for 12 passengers may be provided along the cabin sides, and it is believed that a squad of eight fully-armed marines may be accommodated, although there has been no evidence of the use of *Hormone* in the assault troop-carrying rôle during amphibious exercises.

The non-retractable four-wheel undercarriage has two castoring forward wheels and embodies pivoted rear legs enabling their larger wheels to be raised about their wishbone supports in order to adopt a position in which they offer less interference to signals from the nose-mounted radar. An inflatable pontoon, together with its inflation bottles, may be attached to each leg to cater for emergency descent on water. Search radar is housed in an undernose radome possessing a diameter of about 4 ft (1,25 m), and ASW equipment includes towed MAD (Magnetic Anomaly Detection) gear, dunking sonar accommodated in a compartment at the rear of the main cabin — reputedly inoperable at night or in adverse weather — and an electro-optical sensor, but equipment obviously varies from one *Hormone* to another, some displaying an inverted flower pot-shaped fairing, with a transparent top, above the tailboom and others having a blister fairing built into the base of the central tailfin. External racks may be fitted to the fuselage sides for cylindrical fuel tanks, flare and sonobuoy dispensers, and other stores, and there have been reports of small air-to-surface "fire-and-forget" missiles being mounted on outrigger pylons.

The basic ASW version is identified in the west as *Hormone-A,* and this has been exported in small numbers to Syria, Yugoslavia and elsewhere, and has been ordered by India, but there are several other variants in service with the AV-MF, the only one so far identified by application of a suffix to the reporting name being a special electronics version referred to as *Hormone-B*. Used for mid-course guidance of anti-ship missiles, this variant lacks the ventral weapons bay of *Hormone-A,* features a larger, more spherical nose radome, has a cylindrical radome beneath the rear of the main cabin, displays various additional antennae and is fitted with data link equipment.

Possessing an empty weight of the order of 10,500 lb (4 765 kg) and a maximum take-off weight of 16,500 lb (7 484 kg), *Hormone-A* has a maximum speed of approximately 130 mph (209 km/h) and a normal cruise of 120 mph (193 km/h), range on standard internal fuel being some 250 miles (400 km) increasing to about 400 miles (645 km) with external auxiliary tanks. Hovering ceiling at normal loaded weight (ISA) is 1,970 ft (600 m) and service ceiling is 11,000 ft (3 355 m).

By the late 'sixties, *Hormone* was firmly established in AV-MF service aboard the four *Kresta I* class cruisers and the two *Moskva* class half-deck helicopter carriers, the former accommodating one *Hormone* and the latter 18 (usually 16 of the *-A* version and two *-B*s). From the early to mid-'seventies *Hormone* was progressively deployed aboard the 10 *Kresta II* class cruisers as they entered service, followed by a half-dozen larger *Kara* class cruisers, each equipped with one *Hormone,* and, more recently, by the still larger ASW carrier cruisers of the *Kiev* class (each accommodating 27 *Hormone-A*s and three *-B*s), two of which have joined the Soviet Fleet with a third working up. Production of Kamov's ASW helicopter was reportedly phased out in 1975-76, after a run of some 450 machines of which upwards of 275 currently remain in the AV-MF first-line inventory. Undeniably ageing, *Hormone* may be expected to give place to a more sophisticated, higher-performance shipboard ASW helicopter during the mid-'eighties, and, meantime, it may be assumed that its systems and weaponry have been and are being progressively upgraded. □

Configurationally unique among current service helicopters in having superimposed contra-rotating rotors, the Ka-25 is currently the only Soviet shipboard ASW helicopter in AV-MF service. Seen above left and immediately left in its Hormone-A version, this helicopter is exceptionally compact for the capacity that it offers. The flying photograph shows auxiliary fuel tanks attached to the fuselage sides and both photos illustrate the inverted flower pot-type housing above the tailboom.

CANADIAN YELLOW BIRDS

BY ROBERT S GRANT

THE shrill whine of a turbine engine shatters the early morning silence of a remote Canadian northern lake. A uniformed game conservation officer steps down to the right hand float of the shiny yellow de Havilland Turbo-Beaver that has just alighted. Beckoning the occupants of a red canvas-covered canoe to the aeroplane, the officer waits patiently while the canoeists apprehensively dip their way towards the floating aircraft. Fishing licences are produced and checked — all is in order. Moments later, the STOL aircraft is gone; the fishermen are left again to enjoy their private wilderness experience.

Ontario, one of Canada's 10 provinces, has a unique fleet of aeroplanes operated — on duties such as this and many others — under the supervision of the Ontario Ministry of Natural Resources, Aviation and Fire Management Branch. Formed in 1924 as the Ontario Provincial Air Service (OPAS), the first aeroplanes were 13 Curtiss HS-2L flying boats procured from the US Navy. Registered G-CAOA to G-CAON, these boats were the forerunners of numerous aircraft types to serve with the "Yellow Birds" in subsequent years.

For the decade of the 'eighties, a mixture of de Havilland Turbo-Beavers, Otters and Twin Otters, and a pair of Beechcraft King Air 200s are on line. The *raison d'être* of today's provincial fleet is "aggressive fire suppression", but forest fires do not ravage the resplendent coniferous and deciduous forests of Ontario at all times. Consequently, personnel and aircraft meet other flying needs of the Ministry, including the special requirements of the numerous branches, boards and commissions that make up a complex provincial government.

The pilots of the Ontario Provincial Air Service, as it is still called (albeit unofficially), are some of the most highly trained and experienced bush pilots in the world. Before being accepted on staff, the applicant requires bare minimums of 1,500 total flying hours, of which 500 must be on float-equipped aircraft — standards which are higher than those of any major airline in Canada including the federal carrier, Air Canada. Most "rookies" joining the Service will have 3,000-4,000 hours accumulated by working for commercial bush operators, thus acquiring an awareness of natural conditions necessary for survival in a harsh environment. Average age for new pilots is late twenties or early thirties, while average flying time for those already on permanent staff runs to over 7,000 hours.

Once having been accepted, a rookie reports to headquarters at Sault Ste Marie. There, despite his previous experience, he will undergo thorough flying conversion courses, administration, theory and survival training. Pilots are restricted to proficiency on two types only. For each type, 15 hours of flying time is compulsory. One pilot, recently hired, already had 4,000 hours on Turbo-Beavers, but no exceptions were made — he underwent exactly the same programme.

During summer fire seasons, all the float aircraft are equipped for water bombing, water being carried in the floats. Consequently, the change for most new pilots involves learning the techniques applicable to aerial fire fighting. Water loads carried on Turbo-Beavers and single-engined Otters are 140 US gal (530 l) and 220 US gal (838 l) respectively. This small amount of short-term retardant must be placed on target from very low level for effectiveness. Despite hazards associated with single-engined tree top operations, the Ministry, to date, has never had a fatality attributable to water bombing, although on several occasions miscellaneous items (eg, poplar trees, hydro lines, etc) have accompanied aircraft back to base.

Once training courses have been completed, pilots have not seen the last of "school". They will be required to return to Sault Ste Marie at least twice a year for re-training and upgrading. In the field, they will have at least four route and proficiency checks (two per aircraft) per year. Policy also dictates that pilots may use an aircraft for practice at any time, providing it is not on specific duty.

One of the OMNAR Turbo-Beavers (C-FOEV) on skis for winter operations. It cruises at 141 mph (227 km/h) in this configuration and can operate with little trouble into extremely short, slushy lakes.

After arriving on base, the new pilot, complete with smart uniform and gold metal wings still bearing the original OPAS crest of 1924, may move into government-supplied housing or purchase his own. Usually he will be on a six- to nine-month temporary contract. If a permanent year-round vacancy exists, he may be offered first opportunity to fill the position. Once on "classified" staff, the pilot will have a one-year probationary period.

Fire hazards

Today's fire centre system is an interlocking network of regional and district dispatch units that provide information and data for decision making and resource allocation. It is from these centres the MNR pilots receive daily assignments. When the hazard index (ie, fire potential) of the forests is high, all other duties come to a halt, and it is "fire only" for the aircraft, much to the chagrin of other government departments. The Yellow Birds are considered essential in all phases of forest fires, from detection to suppression to mop-up. The water bombing aircraft are utility machines that do far more than deliver water.

Frequently, Turbo-Beavers, being light and swift, supplement the contracted aerial detection aeroplanes to check out "smokes" (fire towers have not been in service for observation in Ontario since 1972). Usually, locating a blaze is not difficult if smoke is thick enough, but the problem lies in pinpointing exact locations so that ground crews can walk to the site. The Ministry of Natural Resources has "fire management" charts to which a plastic gridded overlay is applied. The size of the blaze, intensity, distance from water and best access, are radioed back to the nearest participating fire centre. Otters and Twin Otters are kept on Red Alert, ie, required to be airborne within minutes. The standard fire fighting ground unit is a totally mobile five-man crew and equipment. The de Havilland single Otter can legally carry such a load with the added advantage of converting immediately to a water bomber after the men are on site. Occasionally fires will be a considerable distance from shorelines, calling for a cargo drop through the belly hatch of Otters and Turbo-Beavers; sometimes fire hose is free-dropped, although current Ministry policy does not encourage this procedure.

Northern Ontario often has multiple blazes reported, especially after thunderstorms roll through the hinterlands. Commonly, several water dropping aircraft will work the same fire. The Ministry usually has several heavy water bombers, eg, Cansos, Douglas A-26s or Canadair CL-215s, on contract at designated air bases. With the variances in speeds, restricted visibilities in smoke and hazardous terrain, the danger of mid-air collisions is obvious. Such situations call for the use of "Bird Dogs" — high-flying Turbo-Beavers that serve as flying command posts to expedite an orderly flow of traffic to and

During 1977, seven former CAF Otters were acquired for service with the OMNR Aviation and Fire Management Branch, and were completely overhauled and restored to "better-than-new" standards. The author's photograph below shows two of the Otters heading north for two weeks of winter aerial survey during their first year of service.

(Above) C-FOPI is one of the service's three Twin Otters, photographed at Sioux Lookout during a "fire flap". Wheels are attached to the floats to allow these aircraft to taxi up the ramps under their own power for routine maintenance. (Below) One of the unsuccessful Grumman CS2F-1 Trackers at Thunder Bay. (Photos, Robert S Grant).

from a fire. They also assist in co-ordinating movements between air attack and ground unit crews. To reduce cockpit work load for the bombers, they warn of any potential hazards such as cheekos (standing dead timber — impossible to see in smoke conditions). Precise judgement and absolute control are key words for both "Bird Dog" and bomber aircraft. After "fire flaps" are brought under control and normal operations resume, the Yellow Birds will continue to perform their routine non-fire duties.

Winter operation

The arctic-like winter climate of northern Ontario raises problems in the utilisation of a year-round fleet of aeroplanes. Many of the Yellow Birds return to Sault Ste Marie hangars for scheduled overhauls at this time of year, but permanent air bases will have specific aircraft assigned to them. Kenora, in the northwest, has had one Turbo-Beaver and one Otter every winter for the past three years, but many bases will have their complement reduced by one.

The turbine engine is admirably suited for cold climate. The MNR has few hangar facilities in the north; consequently aeroplanes are operated from the proverbial snow bank. Plug-ins, wing covers, tail covers and engine tents are applied every night before the aircraft is "put to bed". In the morning, the PT6A turboprops of Turbo-Beavers or Twin Otters require little more than 10 minute warm-ups before take-off.

The single-engined Otter, with its huge R-1340 radial engine, is another matter, however. In the pioneering days of the OPAS, it was normal procedure to drain oil onto the snow or ice where it solidified instantly; then it was picked up and plopped into a pail in which it was heated overnight in preparation for being returned warm to the engine in the morning. Today's piston bush aircraft have things somewhat easier. Besides heavy engine and wing covers, the aircraft are "diluted" ie the oil is injected or mixed with gasoline to prevent coagulation in gelid weather. Prior to flight, "burn-off" is necessary — the engine must be run for as long as 90 minutes to boil away the injected gasoline. If the process is rushed and the pilot takes-off, the oil is discharged outside through breather tubes with obvious results. It is hardly a pleasant task for the engineer or pilot who must sit in a cold aircraft, but it is in fact far less tedious than draining oil every night.

Anyone flying over the far northern reaches of Canada's white wilderness, with its confusing mosaic of thousands of lakes stretching unbroken to the horizon, would certainly think that here is a pilot's paradise. Every surface a landing field, few restrictions in length and rarely a crosswind; but in winter there are unseen hazards waiting for the unwary and the inexperienced. Beneath snow surfaces, there may be hidden slush pools. Regardless of low outside temperatures, underneath the crusty layers of snow is an insulated layer of water that may never freeze. When an aeroplane touches down and stops, it will probably become mired instantly in cold wet snow. Much digging will be required before a take-off path on solid ice can be cleared. There are techniques to be used when operating in slush, but every year the snow shovel, standard equipment on any bushplane, is a frequently-used tool. The wind often packs snowdrifts into solid hummocks. When an aircraft ski strikes these obstacles, it can sometimes tear off an entire landing gear leg.

One of the original OPAS Curtiss HS-2Ls at Orient Bay. Timber baulks have been positioned to allow the Liberty engine to be removed for overhaul.

White-out landings during overcast are common. In airline or cloud flying, an aircraft will descend until visual contact is made with the surface, then the pilot will use outside references to land. In the dreaded white-out, however, the basic approach to a lake is visually made, then the pilot goes to the instruments, feeling his way down. In conditions of unbroken snow cover on the surface and overcast sky above; it is impossible to distinguish height above the landing surface. If the snow is soft, it is even difficult quite often to tell when the aircraft has landed.

The largest user of the Yellow Birds throughout the year is the Ontario government's Fish and Wildlife Branch. Summer or winter, they are responsible for a large proportion of flying hours spent in aerial game law enforcement or animal census. Moose survey, considered an essential part of wildlife management programmes, is an annual event in northern Ontario. Both Turbo-Beavers and Otters are used during prime survey months of January or February. Selected plots are flown low level in a search for animal tracks. Once any sign of game is spotted, the aircraft will circle while its crew of observers and the pilot search the forests. Almost without exception, the low-level manoeuvring associated with aerial survey results in plenty of airsickness for those observers so unfortunate as to ride as animal counters.

Aerial census is not confined to moose or caribou, however. During autumn, immediately after the deciduous trees lining the watercourses have dropped their leaves, beaver population surveys are conducted. How does one count a small rodent such as a beaver from the air? Experienced conservation officers search for fresh cuttings and new lodge construction to determine the number of live or dead beaver houses within a designated trapline area. Much care is taken in the management of the beaver in Canada, for the livelihood of many native trappers depends on this small creature that so attracted first European settlers to early Canada and its prosperous fur trade.

Lake surveys are scheduled during winter or summer. In the winter, biologists are transported from lake to lake — usually with Turbo-Beavers fitted with a ski/wheel combination landing gear — where water samples are removed for future analysis. In the summer, these surveys are more complicated and take far longer, the Otter being used to airlift survey teams with camping gear and equipment as well as a boat or canoe carried externally on strong tubular racks.

Timber surveys

The nature of some tasks has changed little since the creation of the OPAS. Formed initially to assess the so called "unlimited" natural wealth of timber in the province, the Service with its Yellow Birds still plays an important rôle today for the Ministry's Timber Branch. Aerial photography is a speciality. Standard equipment on Turbo-Beavers and Otters is a 17-in (43-cm) belly-hatch to which a camera can be mounted. The pilot is required to hold his machine level, both laterally and longitudinally, while Timber personnel manipulate the complicated camera equipment. After film processing, a quick mosaic is constructed and any rough spots are re-flown. Most photo flights call for altitudes at or below 9,500 ft (2 896 m). With photographs, timber stand volume can be estimated — exactly the same work that was carried out from the nose cockpit of the original HS-2Ls. From the photos, the twisting contours and gravel deposits can also be recorded for construction of logging roads. Ground crews will later move into new cutting areas, well informed of the "lie of the land".

The heaviest timber harvesting is planned to take place in winter months when bodies of water are frozen solid enough to support heavy vehicular traffic. Almost weekly, snowshoe equipped Timber Branch men and women are flown to the woodlots, dropped off and picked up later at day's end. This way the commercial logging companies are monitored closely to prevent overharvesting.

Scattered throughout northern Ontario are numerous Indian settlements peopled by Cree and Ojibway natives. There are still many communities in which outdoor toilets and tipis are part of a normal way of life. Usually, these settlements are quiet places, but occasionally violence erupts and crimes are committed. When such is the case, it is hardly practical to fly an entire village of witnesses to southern courts. Judges, complete with attorneys, court reporters and policemen are therefore flown in, usually by a single or Twin Otter. Justice is meted out quickly — and perhaps more fairly in consequence — while the Yellow Bird sits waiting tied to a dock or parked on the ice. The distances are long, and sometimes necessitate extra fuel stops being made in an area where, because of the transportation problem, fuel is tremendously expensive, but this is being alleviated by establishment of fuel caches for exclusive use by MNR aeroplanes.

Keeping in touch with the native people is a time consuming and necessary task for representatives of the provincial government. In the south, highways and secondary roads form a fine network of land transportation, but in the hinterlands, roads are few and poor and do little more than scratch the surface of vast wilderness areas. Ministry of Natural Resources aircraft, by virtue of their STOL ability, are able to provide excellent transportation to almost any location. Airstrips are being constructed in the north, but even so it will be many years before fast floatplanes become obsolete.

When Canada's north country was first being conquered by the aeroplane, mercy flights created great headlines. Any follower of Canadian aviation history will know of dramatic emergency aerial voyages into bush country. The story of Wop May and his dramatic flight 600 mls (966 km) north of Edmonton, Alberta, in mid-winter with a life-saving load of diphtheria serum, is one. A grizzly-mauled mine superintendent flown to Vancouver from northern British Columbia is another. There are many, but the truth is that such "rescues" are now a routine part of northern living, which still reduce suffering and often save lives. The files at Sault Ste Marie bulge with reports of injured tourists being moved from isolated locations to proper medical facilities. Burn victims, gunshot wounds, axe accidents and severed limbs are not uncommon. Drowning victims, fresh or old, have been hauled wrapped in blankets or plastic bags on the floor of many MNR Turbo-Beavers or Otters. During the scourge of poliomyelitis, flights from bush to iron lung were commonplace, winter and summer; thankfully, this is one requirement that has now dwindled to nothing.

The Tracker saga

In 1970, a Grumman CS2F-1 Tracker was purchased from the Royal Canadian Navy at a cost of $Can10,000 (about £4,000). Knox Hawkshaw, a world-renowned authority on aerial fluid delivery systems, supervised extensive modifications and experimentation to the aircraft, converting it to chemical bomber with a capacity of 800 US gal (3 030 l). After field trials, five more of these aircraft were modified at $Can100,000 per copy in 1972. The Trackers, built under licence by de Havilland of Canada in the early 'fifties, were destined for a "one strike concept" in which the long term holding effects of chemical were to smother the fires more effectively than rapid delivery of short term retardants, ie, water. Experts estimated that chemical dropping was at least 10 times more effective than plain water, but since the programme fell short of original expectations, many personnel within the MNR have modified their point of view. The cost of bagged chemical has risen astronomically, making a miss a very expensive affair, while critics point to the billions of gallons of water available at relatively low cost, ie, the cost of a water landing. The land-based Trackers also must return to an airport after each drop, but float aircraft can stay with the fires and work for hours, since water is seldom far distant from any fire in the hinterland. Satellite bases with tanks of pre-mixed chemical were established at strategically located airports and airstrips to help alleviate this problem. Unfortunately, forest fires did not always co-operate and refused to burn within a prescribed radius of the land bases.

An Otter with integral float tanks carrying 220 Imp gal (1 000 l) of water photographed during trials at St Petersburg, Florida.

The Trackers are single purpose aeroplanes — even the contracted Cansos can haul fuel during quiet times. In 1978, severe corrosion was discovered in several of these powerful aircraft resulting in a costly maintenance overhaul. Crew costs were high. Most pilots were hired on a six-month contract and did not always return at the beginning of the next season, thus forcing the training of new personnel, further increasing costs.

In February, 1980, an aircraft journal, *Canadian Aircraft Operator*, carried an announcement that the entire inventory of these R-1820 piston-engined fire bombers was being offered for public sale. At the time of writing, it appeared that Conair of British Columbia would be accepted as bidder, so a return to the original philosophy of the float water bomber is indicated so far as the Ontario operation is concerned.

To that end, the MNR seems favourably inclined towards the well-proven de Havilland of Canada Twin Otter. Three have been in service for several years although only two are converted to carry water bombing floats during fire seasons. (The remaining Twin Otter is kept on IFR status at Toronto International Airport for miscellaneous duties). With a water load of 450 Imp gal (2 046 l), the Twin Otter is a very capable fire suppression machine. It can remain on site for several hours and with the PT6A-27 turboprop engine, reliability is beyond question. It also happens to be the only aircraft currently on the market and in production that fills the bill for a utility aeroplane *cum* water bomber. It is believed that the present Air Service plans the addition of more Twin Otters to the line; unofficial word has been received that three new aircraft have been ordered from de Havilland in Downsview, Ontario.

The 'eighties will probably see the phasing out of piston-engined aircraft within the structure of the Ontario Ministry of Natural Resources, Aviation and Fire Management Branch. Long term studies have been initiated which aim for the utilisation of an all turbine bush fleet. Regardless of what types of aircraft follow, Canadians may rest assured that the highly professional standards of this historic organisation will continue to protect the forests and the people of Ontario. □

An AJ 37 Viggen of F 15 (Hålsinge Flygflottilj) based at Söderhamn in the South Norrland Military Command. F 15 comprises two divisioner (squadrons), one of which serves as the Viggen conversion unit and is equipped with the tandem two-seat SK 37.

(Below) A JA 37 Viggen of F 13 (Bråvalla Flygflottilj) based at Nörrkoping in the East Sweden Military Command. F 13 has three Viggen-equipped divisioner, one fulfilling the reconnaissance rôle with the SH 37 and the others currently working up on the JA 37. F 13 received its first JA 37s during 1979 and is the first flottilj of Flygvapnet to re-equip with this second-generation version of Viggen.

The head-on view (left) and the upper planview (below) both depict the JA 37 Viggen. The complex four-colour camouflage pattern applied to the side and upper surfaces is standard on all versions of Viggen currently serving with Flygvapnet.

(Left) The emblem of F 13 which appears on the vertical fin of the JA 37 Viggen fighter now equipping this unit. F 13 was previously equipped with the J 35F Draken.

Esoteric embellishment

EMBARRASSMENT is a subjective reaction; that which embarrasses one may be totally ignored by another. For example, if we — and we use the pronoun of the first person plural nominative in the belief that aeronautical modelling is still as near exclusive a male preserve as a briar pipe emporium — should attend a function in a brown hacking jacket, beige slacks and (heavens forbid!) a blue striped shirt, we would be totally unconcerned, nay, probably not even notice, if a dozen others be similarly attired. Not so our spouses, however, who would as likely as not climb the nearest wall at encountering *one* dress similar to that they happen to be wearing!

Still pushing the porcine chauvinism bit, we aver that we would care not a jot if the character downing his pint next to us in our local hostelry displays identical exemplary taste in wearing apparel to our own. BUT, if he, or anyone else for that matter, turns up at our local *modelling* club toting a model of, say, an Fw 190A sporting identical finish and markings to the model that *we* are displaying, then, like that of the girl whose knicker elastic snapped while she was being interviewed for a security assistant's job, our visage might well be suffused with the ruddy glow of embarrassment. For we, like all *keen* modellers, believe ardently *vive la différence* when it comes to our favoured pastime!

It is probably true to say that the majority of modellers — by which we mean all those hundreds of thousands that assemble kits as distinct from the out-and-out enthusiasts that form the *crème de la crème* of the modelling community — are content to settle for conformity; adhering to the letter to the assembly and finishing instructions accompanying the kit, and faithfully applying the decals supplied. All well and good, but for those of us who translate from the tyro through the experienced to the skilled in modelling with the passage of years, a desire usually manifests itself to do our own thing; to ensure that our finished models are not indistinguishable from many thousands of others produced from the same kits. In short, we are bitten by the customising bug; whether or not we are in the habit of displaying our creations at club meetings for general edification, we obtain satisfaction from the knowledge that *our* model is unique.

In these days of advanced moulding techniques and, in the cases of most kit manufacturers, more enlightened attitudes towards customer requirements and subject choices, the opportunities to make more than minor improvements to models are becoming progressively fewer. With alternative parts now almost *de rigueur* with the more expensive kits permitting completion of alternative variants, conversions have become almost routine, and particularly when full advantage is taken of available vacuum-formed conversion kits. Thus, the rugged individualist — of which more emerge as our pastime expands in popularity — encounters increasing difficulty in finding suitable outlets for his talents. Of course, the truly *individual* modeller is one who gets his kicks from scratch building, but such is still, proportionately, a rare breed. So what is the answer?

Perhaps the widest choice of possibilities for singular treatment of models nowadays lies in the choice of markings and the finishes that accompany such. For years opportunities for esoteric embellishment of models were inhibited by commercially-produced decal availability, but over the last few years we have seen high-quality decals emerging from Australia, France, Italy, South Africa, Spain and elsewhere, and there are now more than a dozen specialist decal manufacturers — most of them in the USA — with Microscale the most prolific, and there may be as many more of which we are as yet unaware. Hundreds, even thousands, of decal sheets have become available during the latter half of the 'seventies, but owing to the fact that these tend to be expensive to design and manufacture, relatively few of them retail for less than a pound or a couple of dollars a sheet, and this cost factor undoubtedly deters some modellers.

There are, of course, still some limitations as specialist decal manufacturers tend to favour, understandably enough, the more popular aircraft types and especially those which offer the most colourful and decorative schemes. Thus, we have a proliferation of F-14 Tomcats, S-3 Vikings, P-3 Orions and the like, resplendent in their multi-coloured unit markings. Not that we would disparage the choice of such markings as decal subjects, for they are most attractive and representative of a passing era likely soon to be sacrificed on the altar of low-visibility operational necessity. Thus, more esoteric embellishments as yet provide only a minority among commercially available decal sheets, but we have little doubt that the decal sheet manufacturers will progressively emulate those kit manufacturers that provide them with their reason for being in exercising a more imaginative approach to subject matter. In this respect, we would remind readers of the highly original approach to producing decals of the world's smaller and more obscure air arms represented by the *Decal Set* produced by Pat Sedlock of Ohio and reviewed in this column in May last year. Insofar as airliner buffs are concerned, decals provide the main opportunity for customising models, for the number of different aircraft types is closely confined whereas decal sets are legion, offering a fabulous selection of colour schemes. *Vive la différence!*

This month's colour subject

That bulbous Swedish battler, the Saab 37, may not be everybody's idea of aeronautical pulchritude, but there can be little doubt that it is one of the most advanced and efficacious combat aircraft in service use today. Named Viggen, which is loosely translated as the Thunderbolt, but, more strictly, is the three-pronged bolt or dart hurled by Thor, the Nordic god of thunder, the Saab 37 is unique in appearance and comes within that category of *rarae aves*, the canards, although we have seen Viggen described as a tandem monoplane and staggered biplane! However its configuration is described, Viggen is undeniably exotic and it is presumably the exotical shape of this remarkable Swedish fighter that has attracted a half-dozen kit manufacturers.

Three of the kits represent prototypes of Viggen, having been produced at an early stage in the fighter's development, these are by Airfix and Hasegawa (at one time available from the late lamented Frog) in 1/72nd scale, and by Tamiya in 1/100th scale. All three kits make up into very good models but they are all decidedly limited by their early issue in that they do not represent any actual service version. Happily, there are two very good 1/72nd scale kits of Viggen that *do* represent service aircraft, one by Lesney in its "Matchbox" range and the other by Heller, the former being an accurate and well-produced kit enjoying a considerable price advantage, in the UK at least, over its rival, but the latter being, in our opinion and regardless of price, the first choice in its scale. Heller's kit may be completed in AJ 37 attack, SF 37 recce or SK 37 training versions and possesses a total of 78 parts.

The latest kit of Viggen to be released is in 1/48th scale and from Esci, representing the AJ 37 and comprising a total of 89 component parts, all but the four transparencies being formed in light grey plastic with extremely fine raised panel lines. The interior of the cockpit is quite well furnished, with a four-part ejection seat and control column located on a one-piece floor, console and rear bulkhead moulding, plus front housing, instrument panel and weapon sight. All of the many small intakes mounted around the fuselage are separate parts, as are the four air brakes which may be mounted either open or closed. The tandem-wheel main and twin-wheel nose undercarriage units are reproduced in fine detail, and there is engraved detail inside the wheel wells and doors.

A distinctive feature of Viggen is its delta foreplane or canard — who was it said that, to the aeronautically illiterate, Viggen could be described as having a dwarf wing and an elephantine tail? — and the model correctly reproduces its drooped leading edge. Under the wings and fuselage are seven hardpoints and external stores provided with the kit for attachment to these points comprise a single drop tank, two rocket pods and a pair of AAMs. Assembly is not unduly difficult but should be approached with a little circumspection as no locating pegs are provided, and the fuselage shells have rather thin walls so that alignment is by no means automatic. Of course, kits like this are not intended for the complete tyro, and any extra effort and skill demanded is well worthwhile.

The complex multi-coloured camouflage scheme employed by Viggen is likely to be considered as bordering on a modelling nightmare, but it represents something of a challenge and the extensive instruction sheet accompanying Esci's kit shows the scheme in clear four-view drawings. This complex scheme is, incidentally, now shared by *all* service versions of Viggen and as the AJ 37, as modelled by Esci, has been very extensively illustrated, we have elected to illustrate on our colour page the second-generation JA 37 version of Viggen which has just achieved service status and which offers the reasonably skilled modeller not too difficult a conversion task. The decal sheet offers the markings of an AJ 37 of F 7, the *Skaraborgs Flygflottilj* based at Såtenäs, and, incidentally, the first *Flottilj* to convert to this model of Viggen, which it has now been operating since June 1971. The main and console instrument panels are included on the decal sheet. Esci's kit of Viggen has a UK retail price of £4·35.

A quarter-inch Mossie

The supremely elegant de Havilland Mosquito could not have failed to make the "favourite" grade among kit manufacturers, and over the years we have been presented with several kits in 1/72nd scale and even one in 1/32nd scale. Until now, there has been but one in 1/48th scale and this, from Monogram, suffering some built-in although not *too* fundamental errors, such as too tall a fin-and-rudder assembly. It has, errors notwithstanding, proved a deservedly popular kit, which, still widely available, makes up into either the B Mk IV or FB Mk VI. Now, however, pre-eminence of the Monogram kit gives place to Airfix's very fine quarter-scale offering of the Mosquito FB Mk VI, which is easily the most accurate Mossie yet in *any* scale: Airfix has even got the rear contours of the engine nacelles correct and these have hitherto proved the undoing of all Mossie mould makers!

The stylish lines of the immortal "wooden wonder" have been beautifully captured by this 127-part kit moulded, apart from six transparencies, in medium grey plastic, and detail is sufficient to satisfy all but the most fastidious. Surface detail such as is called for on so smoothly finished an aeroplane is finely carried out, and the forming of the more delicate components, such as those of the undercarriage, is exemplary, with every visible detail reproduced to scale — piping, mud-guards, bracings, tyre treads, all truly as complete as one could wish. Completeness extends to the interior of the cockpit, which has virtually every notable feature reproduced and all can be seen through the very clear canopy — there are instruments and other features moulded integrally with the fuselage shells, in addition to all the separate items, producing one of the best cockpit interiors we have seen in 1/48th scale.

Being a fighter-bomber, this variant of the Mosquito has a solid nose, the cone being separate from the fuselage and embodying holes for the battery of 20-mm cannon, which, too, forms a separate part. The propellers have separate blades, spinners and backplates, while the exhaust clusters and flame shields are also separately formed. Apart from the cannon, the FB Mk VI carried a quartet of 0·303-in (7,7-mm) machine guns, and eight rockets could be mounted beneath the wings, these being included in the kit, as are also a pair of 500-lb (227-kg) bombs for underwing mounting as alternative ordnance to the rockets and supplementing the two similar bombs which were carried by the internal bomb-bay. Apart from the cockpit canopy, the transparencies are for the gunsight, the wingtip navigation lights and the landing lights.

The accompanying decal sheet is accurate in register and colour, and offers markings for two different machines, one from No 143 Sqdn, from the Banff Strike Wing, early 'forty-five, and the other from No 418 Sqdn, RCAF, based at Middle Wallop in August 'forty-four, each scheme being detailed by a four-view drawing. Included in Airfix's Series 7, this is a superb kit doing full justice to a superb aircraft.

A little French vampirism

De Havilland's Vampire was the second jet fighter type to enter production for the RAF and during a long and eventful career it was to see service with a wide variety of foreign air forces, yet it has rarely attracted kit manufacturers as a subject, and the Vampire FB Mk 5, numerically the most common of the species, now appears for only the second time in *any* scale in an excellent 1/72nd scale rendering by Heller.

Moulded in silver plastic and including three transparencies, this kit has a total of 43 parts which assemble precisely to make a most attractive model. The interior of the cockpit embodies all of the detail that one can reasonably expect to find in so small a model, the undercarriage is very finely formed and, in fact, there is a highly commendable delicacy about the moulding of the entire model. The tailbooms are each formed in two halves, linked by the tailplane and joining up with the wings at their trailing edges, and the wings themselves mate neatly with the fuselage pod so that alignment is simple to achieve. Attention to fine detail is evidenced by such items as the mass balances on the elevator, separate oleo calipers on the undercarriage legs, and separate air intakes for the turbojet. The instrument panel is engraved and the surface detailing on all parts is very fine, this including interiors of the undercarriage doors.

France's *Armée de l'Air* acquired a total of 67 Vampire FB Mk 5s and naturally one of these is featured by the decal sheet, this being an aircraft of EC 1/4 *Lafayette* in 1951, which is accompanied by markings for an aircraft of No 112 Sqdn, RAF, operating with the 2nd TAF. The accompanying instruction leaflet and drawings are commendably clear. The UK retail price of this kit is 95p, and Heller's Vampire FB Mk 5 is soon to be followed by a French-built derivative, the Mistral.

Cent-cinquante and deux-cents-six

France's Heller company is steadily widening the spectrum of kits in what is termed the "general aviation" category, and is gradually expanding its range of 1/50th scale light aircraft and helicopters, the two latest additions being the Cessna 150 Commuter and the Bell 206 JetRanger. The Cessna 150 series of light monoplanes was in production for almost 20 years and manufactured in prodigious numbers, yet it has never proved a popular subject with kit manufacturers and it is refreshing, therefore, to see it finally receiving the accolade of a very fine kit, while the JetRanger, which is receiving rather more attention from the kit industry, is also welcome, although both kits are somewhat pricey in the UK, with the former at £2·90 and the latter at £3·10.

The Cessna 150 kit comprises 45 parts which include six transparencies, the remainder being moulded in flawless white plastic with a nice satin finish and fine surface detailing. The cabin interior is a delight, both to build and to behold, having a comfortably furnished appearance, and the undercarriage is delicately formed, with the wheels revolving within the spats. The outer wing panels, each in upper and lower panels, are joined at the centre by a panel forming the cabin roof and embodying two oval windows, and the wrap-around front and rear windows are very clear and display the interior to advantage. A separate spinner attaches to the propeller which can then be made up into a sub-assembly with the nose section of the engine cowling. Here, incidentally, a small improvement can be made by fitting short lengths of plastic dowel inside the cowling to represent the cylinders of the engine where visible through the air intakes.

The decal sheet supplied with this kit must be one of the simplest and smallest ever issued, for it consists of just the black registration letters F-WZDR twice. The trim colour has to be applied by the modeller over the basic white, a large drawing illustrating the design. This kit is expensive perhaps, but the quality is undoubtedly there.

The Bell 206 JetRanger is today probably the best-known and most widely used of all small commercial helicopters, most European examples having been built in Italy by Agusta. Heller's kit of this chopper is in every way as good as that of the Cessna 150 and is moulded in the same kind of plastic with its pleasant finish — 44 white and seven transparent component parts in this case. The cabin interior is again very well furnished, and the rotor head assembly and skid-type undercarriage are most realistic. The main rotor consists of eight separate parts. The assembly of this well-planned model presents no problems, and the colour scheme selected — black and white with grey rotor blades — of the Swedish Police is not too difficult to reproduce. The decal sheet is a little more extensive than that accompanying the Cessna kit, offering POLIS in white and an ornate blue-and-yellow badge for application to each side of the fuselage, plus the registration SE-HPB for the sides of the tailboom.

A welcome old-timer

The B.E.2c, one of the most widely used of Allied observation aircraft of WW I, is so obvious a subject for a plastic kit that it seems almost incredible that no major kit manufacturer has yet ventured to produce it, leaving it to one of the more adventurous of the vacuum-formed kit producers, Formaplane, to fill the gap. Because of the delicacy of construction and fragility of appearance of these early warplanes, it has always been our contention that they are more suited to 1/48th scale than to 1/72nd, but the vac-forming process has enabled Formaplane to achieve, in the smaller scale, a satisfying lightness to the components, the wings and tail surfaces being formed as single thicknesses of plastic. This method is effective but renders the fixing of the centre section and interplane struts a delicate and patience-consuming task.

Presumably in deference to the need to maintain a neat underside to the single-surface

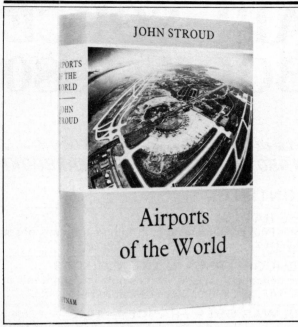

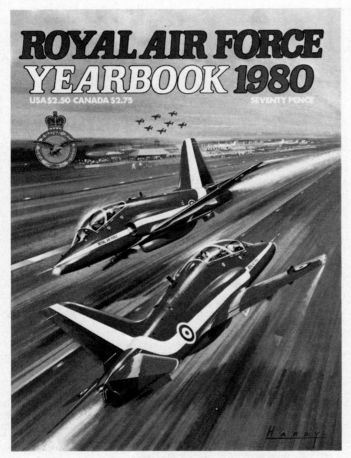

wing panels, the representation of the ribs on the top surface has been made very fine indeed, and anything more than one coat of paint will obscure them! Very narrow strips of 0·005-in thick plastic sheet, brushed into place with liquid cement, will give a more prominent impression of the ribs. The instructions accompanying the kit recommend that the rib lines be lightly scored on the undersides of the wings and tailplane. The engraved details on the fuselage mouldings are well done.

In the usual Formaplane style, the parts are neatly grouped on one sheet of plastic, and every component is there, although some of the smaller items, principally the struts, are perhaps better formed from sheet or from strip. The kit includes lengths of two different diameters of plastic rod, plus a piece of clear sheet for the windscreens. There are no less than 57 parts in all, the moulding standard is high and many small details for the partly-exposed engine and the cockpit interiors are provided, as are also alternative types of fin. Very nice general arrangement, colour scheme and assembly drawings accompany the kit, as do concise instructions, incorporating details of such items as the complex tail skid assembly and the Lewis gun with its spare ammunition drums in a housing on the fuselage side.

This is assuredly a kit to whet the appetite of the WW I period enthusiast who has suffered a dearth of kits for far too long. Our sample kit was provided by BMW Models which can supply the B.E.2c kit by post, the UK retail price being £2·42 plus postage. Incidentally, no decals are provided, but there is more than adequate painting information.

Heller's vliegende hollander

Maintaining its preferred 1/125th scale for airliner kits, Heller has now produced a McDonnell Douglas DC-9-30 in the markings of KLM, Royal Dutch Airlines. This kit consists of 46 parts moulded in a very light shade of grey plastic and five transparencies, and the moulding is to the now customary high standard established by this manufacturer, with finely raised panel lines and engraved details. The cabin window inserts are in four strips and the flight deck transparency is integral with the cabin roof which is clearly marked for painting.

The engine nacelle shapes are well captured, each unit consisting of four parts, and all three undercarriage assemblies are very neat. Separate parts are provided for the flap actuator housings under the wings and, externally, the model has a satisfyingly complete appearance, although there are no internal parts, so a floor and bulkhead could be added to the flight deck with advantage. The attractive KLM scheme is covered by a nicely printed decal sheet which includes the dark blue and white fuselage cheat lines, tail logos, door outlines, registrations and other smaller markings. The basic natural metal, the lighter blue upper fuselage and the white vertical tail must be painted. The UK retail price of Heller's DC-9-30 kit is £3·10. □

F J HENDERSON

WELLESLEY ***from page 33***

Opposing fighters were first encountered by nine Wellesleys from No 223 Squadron during a raid on Gura airfield on 12 June — the second day of the war with Italy. One Wellesley was shot-up so badly that it crashed on landing, while a second was hit by anti-aircraft fire and was badly damaged. Two days later, two of No 14 Squadron's aircraft raided Massawa during the afternoon, but one of these fell victim to a 412[a] *Squadriglia* CR 42. Next evening, the first night raid was undertaken over Eritrea, but not with great initial success. As five bombers prepared to take off from No 223 Squadron's Summit base, the flares aboard one caught fire, and the Wellesley was totally destroyed. Four got into the air, but two were obliged to force-land before they had left Sudanese territory. Of the two which did manage to carrry out their mission, one failed to return — once again a victim of anti-aircraft fire.

No 14 Squadron at this time developed a lower gun position for its Wellesleys, to provide improved protection against fighter attack from below. On 26 June, four of the unit's aircraft featuring this modification joined four unmodified machines from No 47 Squadron to make a dive-bombing attack on Gura airfield. The No 14 Squadron aircraft flew at lower level in the formation, and put their new guns to good use when fighters attacked. Three of the Wellesleys were damaged, but the gunners of each unit were able to claim CR 42s shot down — although Italian records show that only one Italian fighter was actually hit, and managed to force-land with the pilot wounded.

Regular operations by small formations of Wellesleys continued, and on 30 June a detachment of seven from No 47 Squadron arrived at Khartoum to give support to ground forces skirmishing on the frontier. On 8 July, No 14 Squadron enjoyed a most unusual success when four of its Wellesleys were despatched to bomb Zula landing ground jetty, believed to be a seaplane base at the time. Returning from the attack, the Wellesleys encountered a lone Savoia S.81 trimotor bomber flying over the sea, and diving from above, Flg Off C G S R Robinson brought his Wellesley in from behind to shoot this aircraft down into the sea, where it was seen to break up in the water. Throughout July, attacks on Massawa, Asmara, Gura and other targets continued, and fighter interceptions were frequently experienced. Several bombers suffered various degrees of damage during these, and one No 47 Squadron aircraft was lost on the 12th. The biggest operation to date occurred on 30 July when all three squadrons, joined by Blenheims of No 45 Squadron on detachment from Egypt, and a flight of Gladiators, kept up attacks all day on Italian troops at Kassala, on the Gash River.

Raids by bigger formations were becoming more frequent by now, and on 4 August an attack on Massawa harbour was made by Wellesleys from Nos 14 and 47 Squadrons with the Blenheims from No 45 Squadron. Eleven of No 223 Squadron's bombers were detached to Aden on 13 August, from where an attack was launched on the 18th on Addis Ababa, the Ethiopian capital; again it was the airfield that was the main target. The detachment returned to Summit on 22 August and the squadron was out again on 26 August, five Wellesleys attacking Asmara. A long fight with two persistent CR 42s brought a claim for one of the fighters shot down, but at the cost of one Wellesley.

No 14 Squadron lost two more of its Wellesleys to fighters

This early production Wellesley (K7772) was set aside for use as a test-bed for the Bristol Hercules HE.1S sleeve-valve engine. This aircraft subsequently played a major rôle in the flight development of the Hercules which was to take a noteworthy part in World War II, this engine eventually being applied to the Wellington, development of which had run parallel with Wellesley production.

(Left) A Wellesley (K7775 KU-N) of No 47 Squadron, which had received its aircraft from No 45 Squadron in the Middle East and began its war at Khartoum, then moving to Erkowit and flying its first bombing mission on 11 June 1940. (Below) A Wellesley (L2645), originally delivered to No 14 Squadron, photographed in 1942 at St Jean, Palestine.

during the first 10 days of September 1940, but on the 14th the unit received three Blenheim IVs as the first element of a programme of re-equipment with these aircraft. The Wellesleys continued to undertake some operations with the unit for a little longer, but were steadily phased out in favour of the newer aircraft.

On 12 October, No 47 Squadron detached eight Wellesleys to Gedaref landing ground, near the frontier, to assist Ethiopian patriot guerilla forces in the Lake Tana area. Four days later, CR 42s from the 412ª *Squadriglia*, led by a single Savoia S.79, made a dawn attack on the airfield, the fighters destroying all eight Wellesleys, and two Vickers Vincents which were also present, in a devastating strafing attack.

During December, No 47 Squadron moved to Gordon's Tree airfield, Khartoum, but sent a detachment forward to a strip known as "Blackdown", for operations. No 223 Squadron had meanwhile moved to Wadi Gazouza. Only one loss was suffered during the month, when an aircraft from No 47 Squadron fell victim to a CR 42 over Burye on the 6th. Late in 1940, South African forces from Kenya began an advance into Southern Ethiopia, and this was followed on 19 January 1941 by a British drive into Eritrea. While No 223 Squadron remained in the Sudan to undertake reconnaissances and strategic missions, No 47 Squadron moved forward with the ground forces to provide local tactical support. Early in February, a move was made to Agordat, but front-line operations continued to prove costly at times. On 7 February two aircraft on a sortie over the front were shot down by Italian fighters, whilst two days later another early morning strafe caught the Wellesleys on the ground at Agordat. Two were destroyed and four damaged, while two Lysanders and two Hardys were also totally written off. Another Wellesley was lost during a raid on Burye on the 28th, while on 16 March during an attack on the main Italian stronghold at Keren, one more was brought down by five defending CR 42s.

By now, however, Hurricanes of No 1 SAAF Squadron were available to provide a measure of escort, and the Italian air force was in any event rapidly dwindling in numbers. A final airfield strafe at Agordat by a quartette of CR 42s on 18 March managed to destroy only one Wellesley. Seven days later, CR 42s once more intercepted one of the bombers which was badly hit and on fire. Plt Off Kennedy put the aircraft into a steep dive which succeeded in blowing out the flames, and then got his damaged aircraft back to Agordat; he crashed as he attempted to land, but he and the rest of the crew survived, although the gunner was mortally wounded.

In a last desperate foray before Eritrea fell, an Italian destroyer flotilla under the command of Admiral Bonnetti put out from Massawa on 3 April and made for the Port Sudan area. The ships were twice attacked by Swordfish from HMS *Eagle*, intercepted by British destroyers and then bombed by Wellesleys of No 223 Squadron with Blenheims of No 14 Squadron. All the destroyers were sunk, run aground, or were scuttled. One of the Wellesleys was obliged to force-land on the coast near the action, and a second landed alongside to take off the crew, but became stuck itself. The rest then landed, the two aircraft were burned, and the crews were taken aboard the other aircraft of the formation and flown out.

Within days, Massawa, Addis Ababa, Asmara and most of the rest of East Africa fell to British forces, only the fortress at Gondar continuing to hold out, plus a few columns out in the bush. Most RAF and Army units now left for Egypt to join the fight in the Western Desert; included amongst these was No 223 Squadron, which moved to Shandur where it gave up its Wellesleys and became an Operational Training Unit for Martin Maryland crews.

A handful of units — mostly South African Air Force — remained behind to operate over Gondar, and against the diverse enemy units still at large. This force included No 47 Squadron, which on 24 April moved to Asmara, whence it kept up regular small-scale raids on Gondar to maintain the pressure. Despite all attempts by the RAF/SAAF to catch them, the Italians managed to keep a tiny handful of CR 42s operational at Gondar almost to the end. These biplanes could still be deadly, and one managed to shoot down one of the Wellesleys over the fortress on 2 July. By November 1941, all had gone however, as the final offensive on the defences began. Wellesleys joined SAAF Mohawks, Hartebeests and Ju 86s in constant attacks in support of the advancing troops, and on 28 November the garrison finally surrendered. Next month, No 47 Squadron was reclassified as a General Reconnaissance unit, and moved to Massawa to undertake anti-submarine and convoy escort patrols over the Red Sea with its remaining Wellesleys. These duties continued until September 1942, when a move to Shandur in Egypt brought re-equipment and the operational career of the Wellesley was over. □

JAKTVIGGEN ——————————— ***from page 13***
turbine inlet temperature, this having necessitated redesign of the gas generator combustion system and the high-pressure turbine unit. In each of the nine flame tubes fuel is injected through a system of four duplex spray nozzles instead of a single nozzle as employed by the RM 8A. The high-pressure turbine stator of the RM 8B contains impingement-cooled first-stage vanes with slotted trailing edges for cooling air exit, and the high-pressure turbine rotor has a redesigned blade and disc configuration. Total engine weight has risen from the 4,630 lb (2 100 kg) of the RM 8A to 5,181 lb (2 350 kg) and the net results have been increases in the maximum unreheated rating from 14,750 lb (6 690 kg) to 16,200 lb (7 350 kg) and in the maximum reheat rating from 26,000 lb (11 790 kg) to 28,110 lb (12 750 kg) with only nominal increases in fuel consumption. The RM 8B emits appreciably less smoke than the RM 8A owing to its improved combustion system and the target TBO of 600 hours is expected to be achieved in the relatively near future.

The increased thrust offered by the RM 8B more than copes with the higher gross weight of the *JaktViggen* — the take-off weight is roughly one *tonne* more than that of the AJ 37 — resulting from the heavier radar and engine, and some structural reinforcement, particularly in the wing, the structure of which has been stiffened in order to achieve the maximum load factor at high indicated airspeeds and to increase the load spectrum. The decision to incorporate a fixed 30-mm cannon is also partly responsible for the increased weight of the *JaktViggen*. This weapon, another of the significant features of the JA 37, is the Oerlikon KCA cannon, claimed to be the first such weapon to possess an effective range comparable with that of the first-generation AAMs. The weight of its projectile at 12·7 ozs (360 gr) is 50 per cent greater than that of the Aden cannon of similar calibre and imparts an impact energy eight times greater. A gas-operated four-chamber revolver-type weapon, the KCA cannon, which has only a four-degree limiting slip-off angle at 550 yards (500 m), weighs 275·5 lb (125 kg), and is housed in a permanent underbelly pack, which, offset to port, permits retention of a similar arrangement of three underfuselage stores attachment points to that of the AJ 37. The KCA has a muzzle velocity of 3,445 ft/sec (1 050 m/sec) and a rate of fire of 1,350 rpm.

The primary armament of the *JaktViggen* is the "boost-and-coast" BAe Sky Flash (Rb 71), deliveries of which to *Flygvapnet* are now getting under way. A BAe contract with the Swedish Defence Material Administration provided for technical assistance to Saab-Scania and L M Ericsson in interfacing the Sky Flash with the JA 37 airframe and radar, and firing trials with the fourth R&D AJ 37 assigned to the *JaktViggen* development programme commenced in 1978, the three-year integration programme being concluded early this year with a series of trials in which 100 per cent success was claimed. The JA 37 will normally carry a pair of Sky Flash missiles on the inboard wing attachment points and a pair of AIM-9L Sidewinder IR-homers on the outboard attachment points. An additional pair of Sidewinders can be carried by the outboard underfuselage stores attachment points.

The keynote of the *JaktViggen* is operational flexibility. Its short take-off and landing qualities permit dispersal away from the main airfields and operation from secondary fields and roads, endowing it with a high survival probability on the ground. It may be refuelled with its engine running to maintain a high alert status — from which the JA 37 can be airborne in less than one minute — or to reduce turnaround time; it can be refuelled, re-armed and serviced by a team of seven men within 10 minutes and can mount up to 11 sorties in a given 24-hour period. The emphasis placed on cockpit design has resulted in a relatively low workload being imposed on the pilot and the *JaktViggen* is basically easy to fly, offering good low-speed handling characteristics and wide margins to abnormal flight conditions. Small wonder that *Flygvapnet* anticipates affording a major boost in Swedish air defence capability when this advanced warplane achieves full service status.

Sweden's commitment to the *JaktViggen* is immense and this second-generation aeroplane will, according to present planning, take up the larger part of Saab-Scania's airframe production capacity until about the middle of the decade. In so far as *Flygvapnet* is concerned, this very advanced fighter will carry most of the burden of defending Swedish airspace until at least the late 'nineties and possibly into the next century. How "Swedish" its successor will be is, at the present time, very much a moot point and the *Jakt-Viggen* may be the last combat aircraft of exclusively Swedish design or, for that matter, the last to possess such high Swedish content. But if the future of Sweden's unilateral approach to warplane development has now become questionable, there can be little question of the fact that Swedish air defence will shortly begin to rest on the wings of an all-weather all-altitude fighter, which, but for one or two of the very latest US types, is nonpareil and likely to remain so for at least the first half of this decade. □

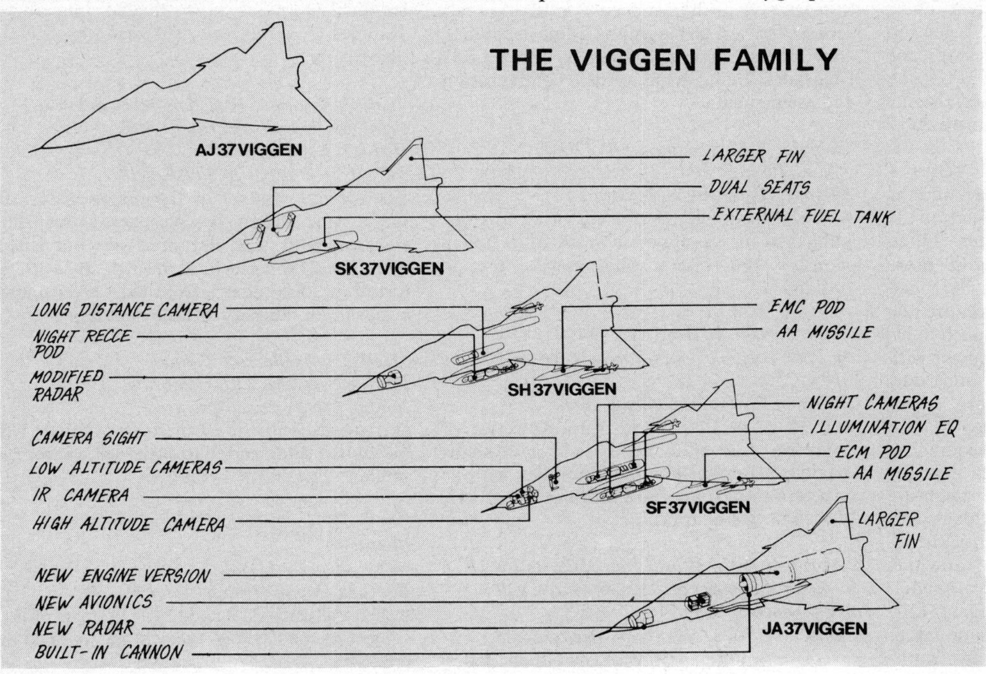

IN PRINT

"The British Bomber since 1914"
by Peter Lewis
Putnam & Co Ltd, London, £8·50
440 pp, 5¼ in by 8½ in, illustrated
THIRD edition of the "bomber half" of Peter Lewis's useful survey of British military aircraft, including prototypes as well as production models. "Bomber" is taken to mean "all types capable of discharging bombs or torpedoes" but fighter-bombers and flying-boats are specifically excluded. The definition leads somewhat surprisingly to the inclusion, in the last few pages of this revised edition, of Navy and Army helicopters armed with air-to-ground missiles.

"Charles A Lindbergh: An American Life"
Edited by Thomas D Crouch
Smithsonian Institution Press, Washington, DC, $8·95 hard binding; $3·95 softcover
119 pp, 6 in by 9 in, illustrated
THIS volume reprints the series of five lectures given at the US National Air & Space Museum on 20 May 1977 to commemorate the 50th anniversary of Lindbergh's 33½-hour nonstop flight, New York to Paris, in 1927. It also reprints NACA Technical Note No 257 (July 1927), by Donald A Hall, which describes the technical preparation of the *Spirit of St Louis*; and it includes an excellent 15-page bibliography, compiled by Dominic Pisano, of material relating to Lindbergh. The text is served by more than 40 photos, most of which tend to be unusual. Collectors of Lindbergh material will find this little book eminently satisfactory. — RKS.

"Ed Heinemann: Combat Aircraft Designer"
by Edward H Heinemann and Rosario Rausa
Naval Institute Press, Annapolis, Md, 21401, $18·95
(available in the UK through Arms & Armour Press, London)
276 pp, 6¾ in by 10 in, illustrated
THIS IS a sketchy but pithy career autobiography by a man who became a legend in his own time as the result of creating such aeroplanes as the Douglas AD, F3D, F4D, A3D and A4D. It is less appreciated that he was also responsible for the Northrop A-17 and BT series attack planes of the 1930s, the Douglas SBD series, the DB-7/A-20 series of World War II and the A-26 thereafter, and the D-558 research aeroplanes, not to mention the seldom remembered DC-5 airliner. Often called "Mr Attack Aviation", with more thought Heinemann might better be called "Mr Weight Control Himself" because the success of his aeroplanes has owed much to his rare ability to combine minimum weight with maximum performance, growth and durability.

In 1926, at age 18, Heinemann started with the Douglas Company as a draughtsman. The vagaries of employment in a young industry subsequently took him through the draughting rooms of the ill-starred International and Moreland aircraft companies, Lockheed, Northrop and back to Douglas. Meanwhile, such men as Gerard Vultee, Dutch Kindelberger, Howard Hughes, Vance Breese, Carl Cover, and Jack Northrop again and again, march through these pages of his autobiography. In 1936, he became chief engineer of Douglas's El Segundo Division (the old Northrop factory), and in 1958 vice president in charge of military aircraft engineering. In 1960, after Donald Douglas, Jr, took over the company, Heinemann was artlessly squeezed out of the organisation, and thereafter Douglas failed to create another combat plane.

No one will be disappointed in this book. It is a "must" for any library relating to US Naval Aviation or the Douglas Aircraft Co and its products. The only complaint that might be made is that there are not 100 more pages than are provided. The lively and always informative text is served by more than 60 photos and 50 three-view drawings. — RKS.

"The Saga of Iron Annie"
by Martin Caiden
Doubleday, New York, $14·95
243 pp, 8¼ in by 11 in, lavishly illustrated
IN A SENSE this book is a hymn to an aeroplane, to the author himself and to his flying buddies, and it would be easy petulantly to dismiss it as "The Rover Boys and Their Aulde Yunkers Arrow-Plane"; but then it must be appreciated that there are thousands of readers who really enjoy this author's form of presentation — though they may not also be readers of this journal. What is more, after all of the hyperbole, bathos and excess verbiage is raked aside, the text reveals a truly fascinating account of a Junkers Ju 52/3m which is claimed to be the only *German*-built "Iron Annie" now in existence (a claim that apparently ignores the Ju 52/3ms still serving in Switzerland).

The aeroplane is apparently Werke Nr 5489, sold to the Norwegian airline Det Norske Luftfartselskap in the 1930s, cannibalised and joined with constituents of the wartime vintage WNr 130714 to create a new machine after 1945. In 1957 it was sold off to a South American operation. In 1968, an American citizen found it among the weeds at Quito, Ecuador, bought it, restored the aeroplane to a marginal flying condition and had it flown to the US. The author bought it in 1975 and had it completely rebuilt in 1976. Today it flies in *Luftwaffe* warpaint with the civil registration N52JU. The book provides many informative accounts of the trials and tribulations encountered in flying and rebuilding this ancient flying machine; its text is served by more than 180 photos.

BOOKS BRIEFLY

"German Fighters over England", edited by Bryan Philpott
96 pp, 6½ in by 9½ in
Patrick Stephens, Cambridge, £2·50 (soft covers), £3·95 (cased)
ANOTHER selection of photographs from the *Bundesarchiv* in Koblenz, including some interesting views of British aircraft shot down over enemy-occupied territory.

"BAC Lightning" by Arthur Reed
Ian Allan Ltd, Shepperton, £5·95
112 pp, 7 in by 9¼ in
NUMBER FIVE in the Modern Combat Aircraft series. Plenty of photographs (some in colour), concise text and a run-down on the 337 Lightnings built, defining their configuration and assignments.

"Dossier B-52", by the staff of JP4
AI Srl, Firenze, Italy, Lire 3,500
80 pp, 7½ in by 10½ in, illustrated
A MONOGRAPH on the Boeing Stratofortress, published in conjunction with the Italian monthly JP4. Useful photographs; text in Italian.

"Commercial Aircraft, 1935-1960", by Enzo Angelucci and Paolo Matricardi
318 pp, 5 in by 7½ in
Sampson Low, Maidenhead, £4·50
VOLUME V in the World Aircraft series of Sampson Low Guides, based on Italian-originated material that includes colour impressions of some 160 aircraft of the period, plus some useful appendices.

"World Aircraft: World War II Parts I & II" by Enzo Angelucci and Paolo Matricardi
320 pp each, 5 in by 7½ in
Sampson Low, Maidenhead, Berks, £4·25 each
TWO more in the Sampson Low Guides series devoted to "World Aircraft". These are translations of Italian volumes, illustrated with three-view line drawings and colour perspective drawings. Part I covers the European nations, Part II the rest of the world.

"Ground Studies for Pilots", by S E T Taylor and H A Parmar
Vol 1: "Radio Aids" (200 pp, £6·95)
Vol 2: "Plotting and Flight" (130 pp, £5·25)
Vol 3: "Navigation General" (230 pp, £6·95)
Granada Publishing, St Albans, 6 in by 9¼ in
THIS third edition of a text book for professional pilots is now divided into three volumes, covering the field comprehensively and clearly.

"British Aviation: Widening Horizons, 1930-1934", by Harald Penrose
HMSO, London, £7·95
340 pp, 5¼ in by 8½ in, illustrated
THE FOURTH volume of the major historical survey undertaken by Westland's one-time chief test pilot. The first three were published by Putnams; this one (and the fifth, 1935-1939, to follow soon) comes from the Government publisher in the RAF Museum series.

"Hellcat", by Barrett Tillman
Patrick Stephens Ltd, Cambridge, £7·95
266 pp, 6 in by 9 in, illustrated
BRITISH edition of the American original (US Naval Institute), and follows the same author's similar work on the Dauntless.

"Le F-16" by Jean-Luc Beghin and Pierre Sparaco
46 pp, 8¼ in by 11½ in
Editions Dupuis, Brussels, Bel Fr 130
HEAVILY illustrated account (in French) of the subject of the "sale of the century", aimed at readers in the 10+ age bracket.

Volume 19 Number 2 August 1980

Editorial Offices:
The AIR INTERNATIONAL, PO Box 16, Bromley, BR2 7RB Kent.

Subscription, Advertising and Circulation Offices:
The AIR INTERNATIONAL, De Worde House, 283 Lonsdale Road, London SW13 9QW. Telephone 01-878 2454. US and Canadian readers may address subscriptions and general enquiries to AIR INTERNATIONAL PO Box 353, Whitestone, NY 11357 for onward transmission to the UK, from where all correspondence is answered and orders despatched.

MEMBER OF THE AUDIT BUREAU OF CIRCULATIONS ABC

Subscription rates, inclusive of postage, direct from the publishers, per year:

United Kingdom	£7·50
Overseas	£8·00
USA/Canada	$20·00

Rates for other countries and for air mail subscriptions available on request from the Subscription Department at the above address.

The AIR INTERNATIONAL is published monthly by Fine Scroll Limited, distributed by Ducimus Books Ltd and printed by William Caple & Company Ltd, Chevron Press, Leicester, England.

Second Class postage approved at New York, NY. USA Mailing Agents: Air-Sea Freight Inc, 527 Madison Avenue, New York, NY 10022.

ISSN 0306-5634

CONTENTS

FRONT COVER An Israel Aircraft Industries Westwind 1124 biz-jet demonstrator.

WRENDEZVOUS WITH WREN

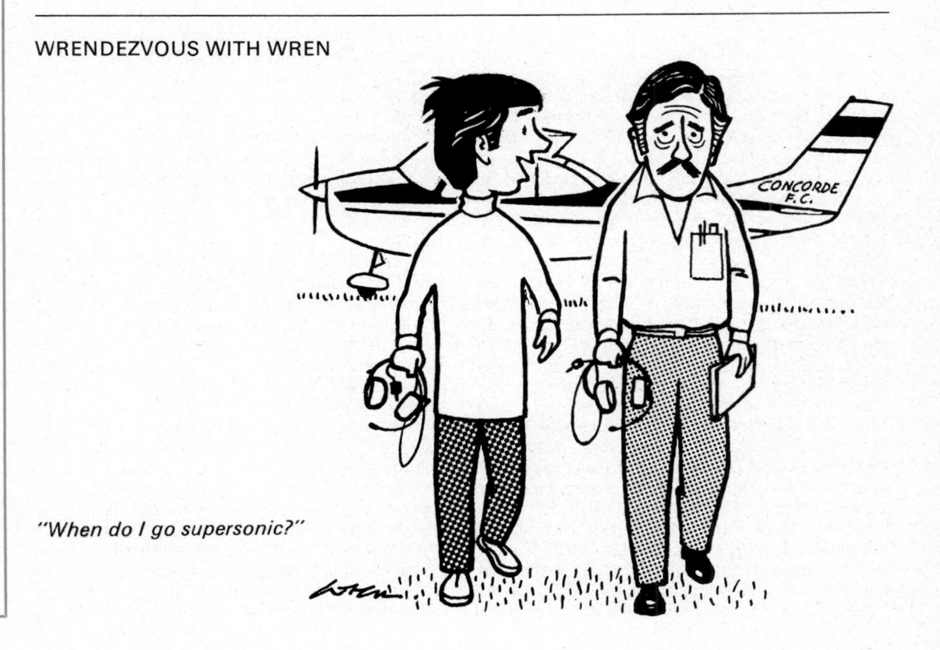

"When do I go supersonic?"

AIRSCENE

MILITARY AFFAIRS

BELGIUM
A *Force Aérienne* source has stated that the service had, at mid-June, only 40 per cent of the fuel that it had at the same time last year owing to escalating fuel costs, and if no additional funding is made available by the government, FAéB pilots will be limited to only three hours flying per month from 1 September until 31 December.

BRAZIL
Some misgivings are being expressed in Brazilian governmental circles concerning the strain that will be imposed on defence expenditure throughout the present decade unless **procurement planning** for the *Fôrça Aèrea Brasileira*, described as **"overly ambitious"**, is trimmed back. Doubts are also being voiced of the ability of Brazilian aviation industry to expand sufficiently to fulfil its share of proposed FAB procurement within the planned timescale without endangering other production programmes and development commitments. An insupportably heavy load will, it is alleged, be imposed upon EMBRAER around mid-decade, when it is anticipated that production of the EMB-312 basic-advanced trainer for the FAB will peak and production of both the AMEX (Aeritalia-Macchi-EMBRAER X) light strike fighter and the EMB-120 Brasilia commuter transport will be starting up. While production of the EMB-326 Xavante is expected to phase out late next year, subject to the receipt of further export orders, EMBRAER currently anticipates that production of the various Bandeirante derivatives will continue through the decade, although production of the EMB-201 Ipanema agricultural aircraft and the various Piper types currently licence built is to be transferred to the Neiva subsidiary. The situation may be further exacerbated by unofficial reports of discussions concerning licence assembly by EMBRAER of at least 50 Dassault-Breguet Mirage 2000 fighters required by the FAB around mid-decade. In addition to the EMBRAER-manufactured or -assembled aircraft, the FAB envisages procurement in the first half of the decade of a number of medium- or heavy-lift helicopters and a further six Lockheed C-130 Hercules transports.

There is some evidence that the differing **operational requirements of** Brazil and Italy will necessitate more extensive differences between Brazilian and Italian versions of the **AMEX** (or AMX) light strike aircraft than originally anticipated. The FAB requirement for a 3,000-lb (1 360-kg) ordnance load to be carried over a distance of 600 miles (965 km) is expected to result in a 13-*tonnes* (28,660-lb) gross weight and consideration is therefore being given to the extension of the wing of the Brazilian AMEX by some 5·9 ft (1,8 m) to restore anticipated take-off, climb and cruise performance at the higher gross weight, or the application of reheat to the Spey 807 turbofan to provide additional take-off thrust, particularly under hot-and-high conditions.

The FAB is currently planning the **replacement of** its Cessna **T-37C** trainers **with** the EMBRAER **EMB-312** (T-27) from late 1982 or early 1983. The FAB has a requirement for approximately 150 EMB-312s with deliveries from mid-1982 and continuing through 1984, but with follow-up contracts (primarily for the COIN rôle) and anticipated export orders on the basis of interest evinced by other Latin-American air forces, EMBRAER is expecting production of this type to continue until 1986-87. The first EMB-312 prototype is expected to make its *official* first flight on the 19th of this month (August), with a second prototype joining the flight test programme on 22 October, and a third early next year. Clearance for FAB service is forecast for mid-1982.

EGYPT
Forty General Dynamics **F-16 fighters** requested by Egypt in February and formally offered by the US Defense Department, together with weapons, spares and support equipment, for $961·1m (£412·5m) under Project *Peace Vector* are **to be delivered** to the Egyptian Air Force **from early 1982.** Thirty of the Egyptian F-16s are to be provided by diverting production from the USAF to which monthly deliveries will be reduced from 15 to slightly more than 13 between December next year and May 1983, the remaining 10 coming from production as yet to be programmed. The 30 F-16s to be taken from USAF deliveries will be replaced between September 1983 and May 1984 at an average rate of three monthly.

The US Defense Department has stated that the **current** Egyptian Air Force **inventory of Soviet aircraft** comprises 100 MiG-21s optimised for the intercept rôle, 100 dual-rôle MiG-21s, 120 Su-7s, 46 Su-20s, 90 MiG-17s, 24 MiG-23s and six MiG-23Us.

According to its C-in-C, the Egyptian Air Force will begin to take delivery of **Chinese-built MiG-21s before** the **end of** the **year.** He added that they will be "modified" aircraft, with "different engines and weapons" to Soviet-built MiG-21s currently in the Egyptian inventory and "easier to maintain". Western intelligence agencies had earlier believed that the Chinese copy of the MiG-21F, designated F-7, had been withdrawn from production at the Xian airframe factory in 1966 after completion of only 60-80 aircraft, but the promised deliveries to Egypt suggest that the difficulties experienced by the Chinese with this fighter have meanwhile been overcome and the type reinstated in production. Chinese personnel are currently assisting in the maintenance of Egyptian MiG-21s.

EIRE
The Irish Air Corps is reportedly planning **procurement of** two **additional** Beech **Super King Air 200s** to bring its fleet of this type to five aircraft. The third Super King Air 200 was delivered on 23 May and is to be used primarily for pilot training, the other two aircraft serving in the fishery protection rôle. The fifth Super King Air is expected to be a Maritime Patrol 200T model with AIL APS-128 radar for the sea surveillance mission.

INDIA
The **first** Indian Air Force **unit** to be equipped **with** the **Jaguar,** No 14 Sqdn, **has** now **attained operational status.** This squadron is currently equipped with Jaguars on loan from the RAF — 15 of the 18 aircraft being assigned to the Indian Air Force on this basis having been delivered to India at the time of closing for press — and the first of the 40 new-production aircraft to be produced by British Aerospace for the IAF prior to the commencement of licence production by HAL is scheduled to be completed next month (September). Final clearance of the overwing-mounted Matra 550 Magic dogfight missiles is now expected to be undertaken in India and a proportion of the IAF aircraft are to be fitted with the Thomson-CSF Agave multi-rôle radar primarily for the maritime strike mission, although no final choice has yet been made between a nose- or podded-installation.

The Indian Navy's **order for** the **Sea Harrier** (see *Military Contracts*/January) has now been **announced** by British Aerospace, although the order, which comprises six single-seat Sea Harrier FRS Mk 51s and two two-seat Harrier T Mk 60s, is referred to as having been placed by an "Asian country". The Indian Navy will take delivery of its Sea Harriers in 1983, by which time the carrier INS *Vikrant* will have undergone extensive modernisation and will have been fitted with a ski-jump ramp. A new small carrier or sea control ship is to be designed to replace the *Vikrant* in the 'nineties.

INDONESIA
The Indonesian Air Force has placed an **order** with Lockheed **for** three C-130H(S) **stretched Hercules** transports for delivery in the last quarter of this year, supplementing two C-130H(S) Hercules purchased last year. The C-130H(S) embodies the same "stretch" as the Hercules C Mk 3 of the RAF, increasing cargo volume by one-third and providing accommodation for 92 (rather than 64) paratroops or 128 (rather than 92) fully-equipped troops. The stretched Hercules join 11 C-130B, two advanced C-130H and one L-100-30 Hercules in the Indonesian Air Force's transport fleet.

The Indonesian Air Force has recently taken **delivery of** the first six of 16 ex-Israeli **Skyhawks** (14 A-4Es and two TA-4Hs) transferred from Israeli surplus stocks with US approval at an estimated cost of $25·8m (£11m).

Deliveries of six GAF **Searchmaster-L** maritime surveillance aircraft to the Indonesian naval air component are to commence **late next year** under the defence co-operation programme between Australia and Indonesia, approximate value of the aircraft being $A10m (£4·95m). These will join 12 Searchmaster-Bs supplied to the Indonesian Navy between 1975 and 1979, the Searchmaster-L differing primarily in equipment fit.

IRAN
According to US sources, the Iranian Islamic Air Force still has **10 per cent of** its Grumman F-14 **Tomcat fighters airworthy,** although these are unable to use their Phoenix AAMs. Approximately 60 per cent of the F-5E Tiger II fleet and about 40 per cent of the F-4 Phantom fleet remain airworthy, but the IIAF is critically short of pilots, some of whom were executed following the revolution and many others relieved of their commissions owing to suspect loyalties.

ISRAEL
The Israeli **Defence Force** is **receiving** a number of ex-US Army **Beech RU-21** battlefield surveillance aircraft as a result of the Camp David agreements. These are being refurbished and fitted with updated surveillance equipment by Beech before delivery to Israel.

JAPAN
The **first** of two prototypes of the Air Self-Defence Force's **F-15J Eagle** fighter was **flown** for the first time at St Louis on 4 June and after completion of a six-week manufacturer's test programme, a six-man Japanese inspection team will take delivery and is scheduled to undertake eight flights with the aircraft from Edwards AFB where the second prototype will make 16 flights in Japanese hands, the two aircraft being ferried to Nagoya in March. The first four of the eight F-15Js supplied to

Mitsubishi in knocked-down component form are now under assembly at the Komaki facility and the first is to fly in July of next year. The ASDF anticipates that the first F-15J Eagle-equipped unit will be the 202nd Sqdn at Nyutabaru Air Base, Miyazaki, Kyushu Island, which will form on its new equipment by 1982.

MALAYSIA
The Royal Malaysian **Air Force** is now scheduled **to receive** the first 22 of 88 refurbished A-4C and A-4L **Skyhawks** (see *Military Affairs*/April) **next summer,** although no announcement has been made concerning the placing of contracts for the refurbishing, the aircraft being sold "as is, where is". The RMAF anticipates having five-six squadrons of Skyhawks operational by the mid-'eighties.

MEXICO
The Mexican naval aviation component, the *Aviacion de la Armada de Mexico,* has recently taken **delivery of** a de Havilland Canada **DHC-5D Buffalo** which augments the service's small transport fleet of C-45s, C-47s, a single Learjet 24D and a miscellany of light aircraft. Earlier, a single DHC-5D Buffalo was delivered to the *Fuerza Aérea Mexicana.*

OMAN
As we close for press, the announcement of a **follow-on order for** an unspecified number of **Jaguar International** tactical strike fighters for the Sultan of Oman's Air Force was understood to be imminent. The SOAF is currently operating 11 Jaguars with its No 5 Sqdn at Thumrait, these including two two-seaters.

PAKISTAN
The Pakistan Government has placed an **order** with Reims-Aviation **for 24 FTB 337** (licence-assembled Cessna Super Skymaster) push-and-pull light twins equipped for the ambulance rôle.

PERU
The **first** announced **export customer for** the Aermacchi **MB 339** basic-advanced trainer is the *Fuerza Aérea Peruana* which requires a replacement for its ageing Cessna T-37Bs which have now seen 20 years of service with the Air Academy at Las Palmas. It may be assumed that the marginally less elderly T-37Cs in the FAP inventory will also call for replacement in the mid-'eighties, but the 24 A-37Bs serving in the light attack rôle were only acquired in the mid-'seventies and are unlikely to need replacing for some considerable time. The quantity of MB 339s ordered has not been revealed, but the contract indicates further diversification of procurement sources on the part of the FAP.

PHILIPPINES
Philippine **Naval Aviation** is **to receive** three Fokker **F27MPA Maritime** patrol and surveillance aircraft and further PADC-built Pilatus Britten-Norman BN-2A-21 Islander/Defenders, plus a further nine PADC-built BO 105 helicopters and 18 US-built helicopters of unspecified type.

SAUDI ARABIA
McDonnell Douglas anticipates commencing the airlift of selected personnel to the Royal Saudi Air Force bases at Dhahran, Taif and Khamis Mushayt from mid-1981 in preparation for the **delivery of** F-15C and F-15D **Eagle fighters** under Programme *Peace Sun* from January 1982. The RSAF is scheduled to receive the first of 45 single-seat F-15Cs and 15 two-seat F-15Ds in that month with the last being delivered in the second quarter of 1984 to equip three squadrons. Both F-15C and F-15D have provision for an additional 2,000 lb (907 kg) of internal fuel by comparison with the F-15A and F-15B that they succeeded in production, but according to US State Department officials, the Saudi government is now seeking the supply of equipment enabling its aircraft to fulfil the long-range strike rôle in addition to the purely defensive rôle for which they were originally ordered. The Saudi government is requesting the supply of conformal tanks (FAST packs) which will give each Eagle a further 10,000 lb (4 540 kg) of fuel capacity and sufficient range to reach Israel, and the necessary racks and release equipment for bombs and air-to-ground missiles. The US State Department has said that the Saudi request is being considered in the context of changes in Middle East and Gulf security (ie, the Soviet invasion of Afghanistan). Israel's ambassador to the USA, Ephraim Evron, reacted to news of the Saudi request with the comment that the ultimate target of any deadly weapons sold to Saudi Arabia would be Israel and that granting the request would unsettle the balance of forces in the region.

SPAIN
The 28 CASA C-101 **Aviojets of** the **second production batch** to be built for the *Ejército del Aire* will be standard C-101EB basic trainers and not the projected armed version of the Aviojet as was widely supposed. The follow-on aircraft will be distributed between the 41 and 42 *Grupos* as replacements for the T-33As and T-6Ds and -6Gs respectively in the refresher training rôle. There would now seem little likelihood that the armed C-101ET Aviojet will be ordered for the *Ejército del Aire,* but CASA believes it to have considerable export potential.

On 24 April, the *Escuela de Helicópteros* at Cuatro Vientos was disbanded, together with its component units, the 751 and 752 *Escuadrones.* At the same time, the Air Academy Selection Centre (*Centro de Selección de la Academia General del Aire*) was transferred from Granada to Los Alcázares, its former CASA-built Jungmann-equipped 781 *Escuadrón,* together with the helicopter-equipped former 751 and 752 *Escuadrones* (of the CSAGA), becoming the *Ala de Enseñanza No* 78 at Granada. Grading will still be performed by 781 *Escuadrón,* and 751 and 752 *Escuadrones* are expected to be redesignated as 782 and 783 *Escuadrones* respectively, while retaining their original equipment.

According to US sources, three **more** ex-US Navy Lockheed **P-3A Orions** are to be delivered to the *Mando Aéreo Táctico* (MATAC) around 1982. These will presumably augment the current fleet of six Orions in *Ala* 22 and provide the basis of a second *Escuadrón.*

SWEDEN
Plans to double the size of the Hercules transport fleet of *Flygvapnet* were implemented in May with a SwKr186m (£19·1m) **order for** three **Lockheed C-130Hs** to supplement the two C-130Es and one C-130H currently included in the inventory of F 7 at Såtenäs.

The joint *Flygvapen/Marinen* **helicopter *Division*** with Boeing Vertol and Kawasaki-Vertol 107-IIs at Berga, south of Stockholm, which has been operating under unified command since 1976, is **to be divided** between the two services once more, the *Flygvapen* element being relocated at F 17 (Kallinge).

The Swedish **Parliament has approved** allocation of SwKr200m (£20·56m) requested for **initial JAS** (*Jakt-Attack-Spaning* — Fighter-Attack-Reconnaissance) aircraft **development** between 1 July and the end of 1981. Funding of JAS has been recommended by the Supreme Commander, Gen Lennart Ljung, as a potential successor to Viggen from 1990 onwards, and Gen Ljung is to submit to the government not later than 1 September 1981 complete data and a firm offer from Swedish industry on the JAS programme, a final decision whether or not to proceed with the programme being taken in the following year as part of a new five-year defence programme. Given a go-ahead, JAS funding will account for some SwKr19,200m (£1,974m) of total appropriations of SwKr20,500m (£2,108m) earmarked for aircraft development and procurement outside the ongoing JA 37 Viggen programme for the period to the year 2000. As currently envisaged, JAS will weigh only half as much as Viggen and its sub-systems could be developed

Photographed recently by a Saab SH 37 Viggen all-weather maritime reconnaissance aircraft over the Baltic, this Tu-22M Backfire-B of the AV-MS appears to have had its in-flight refuelling probe reinstated, this item of equipment having been removed during the SALT negotiations. The radome of the gun-laying radar in the tail is now more pointed, and other minor changes since the preparation of our most recent drawing of this type (see In Soviet Service — 5/June 1979) include outlet fairings above the engine air intakes, additional intakes forward of the tailpipes and more dielectric panels on the dorsal fin. (Photograph courtesy Swedish Air Force.)

Sporting a colourful red-white-and-blue finish, this is the British Aerospace HS.748-2B demonstrator, now with a wide-look interior based on the design of the Concorde passenger cabin, including enclosed overhead baggage lockers. The 20th anniversary of the 748's first flight was celebrated on 24 June (see news item, opposite page).

in collaboration with foreign industry, although the aircraft, as a whole, is expected to maintain a distinct Swedish profile.

UNITED KINGDOM
The Ministry of Defence has announced that facilities for the **basing of** USAF-operated General Dynamics BGM-109 Tomahawk ground-launched **cruise missiles** will be provided **at** RAF **Greenham Common and** the disused airfield of RAF **Molesworth.** The missiles in Britain, totalling 96 at Greenham Common and 64 at Molesworth, are part of the larger total of 464 which it is intended to base in Europe under the terms of a NATO modernisation plan. Britain is the first of the NATO nations to confirm basing arrangements; approximately the same number of Tomahawks are to be based in West Germany and smaller quantities in Italy, Belgium and the Netherlands, according to the plan, but final governmental approvals have still to be given. The missiles, with a range of 1,500 naut mls (2 414 km), will be deployed in hardened shelters, with initial operational capability to be achieved by December 1983 and the entire force of 464 missiles in position by mid-1988.

The **first** two **Tornado** GR Mk 1 interdictor/strike aircraft **to enter RAF** service were delivered on 1 July to the Tri-national Tornado Training Establishment at RAF Cottesmore. The aircraft, one of which is equipped with dual controls, are the first of approximately 50 Tornadoes eventually to be based at Cottesmore and were scheduled to be utilised for the first stage of the instructor flying training programme that was scheduled to commence late last month (July). The TTTE is to be officially opened at Cottesmore in January.

VENEZUELA
On 11 June, British Aerospace completed **contracts to refurbish** 23 **Canberra** B Mk 82, PR Mk 83 and B(I) Mk 88 aircraft of the *Fuerza Aérea Venezolana.* Successive contracts called for the entire FAV fleet of Canberras to be stripped for inspection, renovated in detail and then rebuilt and fitted with updated radio, navigation and weapons equipment, the first reconditioned aircraft being returned to Venezuela in 1977. The FAV first procured Canberras from the UK 28 years ago, in 1952, with an order for six, a further 10 being ordered in 1957 and 14 more in 1965. The FAV anticipates operating its Canberra fleet throughout the remainder of the decade.

AIRCRAFT AND INDUSTRY

CANADA
New **details of** the **Pratt & Whitney PT7,** the engine which, in its PT7A-2R version, will power the de Havilland Dash 8 (see AIR INTERNATIONAL/July 1980), show that it is a completely new design, differing in fundamental respects from the PT6. The three-spool PT7 has two centrifugal stages and no axial stages. The first centrifugal compressor stage is driven by a single-stage axial turbine and the second stage is similarly driven by an axial turbine that has air-cooled blades and air-cooled vanes. A two-stage axial turbine drives the propeller gearbox at the front of the engine by way of a third shaft passing through the other two. The R suffix in the designation of the Dash 8 engine refers to "reserve" rating, the higher power available for the engine-out case. The initial PT7A-1R version of the engine has a take-off performance of 1,590 shp up to 102 deg F and a max continuous rating of 1,500 shp up to 99 deg F with a residual jet thrust of 202 lb (91,6 kg). The max sfc is 0·533 lb (0,242 kg)/eshp/hr at the take-off rating and 0·544 (0,247) at the max continuous rating. Dry weight including standard equipment is 824 lb (374 kg).

FEDERAL GERMANY
The RAAF has donated a Douglas **Dakota to** the **Berlin Airlift Memorial Museum** as a reminder of the work performed by RAAF crews during the Berlin Airlift in 1948-49. Flown from the RAAF base at Butterworth, Malaysia, to Gütersloh by a six-man crew including one who flew 240 missions into Berlin during the Airlift, the Dakota (A65-69) was handed over on 20 June. Originally a USAAF C-47B, A65-69 is one of 12 in service with the RAAF, with which it has operated for 37 years; the remaining aircraft of this type will all have been withdrawn by 30 June 1981.

FRANCE
Avions Pierre **Robin** has rationalised its families of **light aircraft** into two ranges each of three variants and expects to produce a total of 115 of these six types in the course of the present year. The four-seat wooden family now comprises the 110 hp Dauphin 80, the 160 hp Major 80 and the 180 hp Regent 80. Of all-metal construction are the two-seat R 2112 and R 2160, respectively with 112 hp and 160 hp engines, and the four-seat 180 hp R 1180. The R 2160 has also now entered production in Canada where R Robin Inc of Lachute-Montreal has obtained Canadian certification for this variant. In the course of 1980, Robin expects to fly the prototype R 3140 as the first of a new R 3000 family. Five variants have been planned, comprising the R 3100, a 100 hp two-seat club trainer; the R 3120, a light four-seater with 110 hp engine; the four-seat 160 hp R 3140, the four-seat 180 hp R 3170 and the four-seat turbosupercharged 180 hp R 3180 with retractable undercarriage.

Reims Aviation has been granted exclusive worldwide **production rights for** the **Cessna 337** Skymaster series of twin-engined aircraft, nearly 3,000 of which have been sold to date, including almost 500 of the O-2A military versions used by the USAF. Reims has been assembling Skymasters since 1971, and developed the FTB military version and a utility model in 1975; aircraft off the French assembly line are now in service in 16 foreign countries.

INDONESIA
Within the framework of the licensing and technical co-operation agreements concluded in November 1978, Aérospatiale and P T Nurtanio signed new **contracts in** Djakarta on 13 May in **respect of** 15 sets of SA 330 **Puma and** AS 332 **Super Puma** parts. These helicopters will be assembled by Nurtanio for delivery from January 1981 onwards, the recipients being the Indonesian Air Force and Pelita Air Service.

INTERNATIONAL
Fairchild Industries and Saab-Scania jointly announced the selection of General Electric **CT7 turboprops to power** the **commuter airliner** that the two companies are now jointly developing (see AIR INTERNATIONAL/July 1980). The CT7-5 version selected will be rated in excess of 1,500 shp and is derived from General Electric's T700 helicopter turboshaft, commercial versions of which were certificated as the CT7-1 and CT7-2 in 1977/1978. Announcing the decision, Saab-Scania said that the CT7 gives the lightest, most economic aeroplane/engine combination, the lowest fuel consumption per passenger/mile and the most advantageous customer warranty programme of any engine available. In the CT7-5 turboprop version, the new engine is scheduled for FAA certification in 1983, sometime after the prototype of the Saab-Fairchild airliner enters flight test.

Airbus Industrie has confirmed that it will put **two more Super Guppy** outsize **transports** into service, one in spring 1982 and one in spring 1983, to meet the needs of the increasing A300/A310 production rates. Contracts have been placed with UTA for the conversion to be made at Le Bourget, in conjunction with Aero Spacelines of Santa Barbara, Calif. The two Super Guppies used by Airbus at present went into service in November 1971 and September 1973 respectively, and are operated on behalf of the manufacturer by Aéromaritime, a subsidiary of UTA.

Westland Helicopters and Costruzioni Agusta have formed a joint company to undertake the development, manufacture and marketing of a **new medium-weight helicopter** identified as the **EH 101.** Intended to meet the requirements of the Royal Navy and the Italian Navy for a replacement for the Sea King/ASH-3D, the EH 101 is a new designation for the helicopter that has previously been under development, under MoD contract, as the WG.34 Sea King Replacement, now adapted to incorporate specific Italian requirements. With a 25,000-lb (11 340-kg) gross weight, the EH 101 is being developed intially as a military helicopter but it is intended that the basic design should be acceptable in the civil market also. The sales potential is estimated to approach 1,000 units. The joint company, named EH Industries, is to be based in London, and equally owned by Westland and Agusta.

Newest company to woo the Japanese aerospace industry with offers of **joint development of** a new short/medium-range airliner is McDonnell Douglas, which is seeking a partner for its 170-seat **ATMR-2** project. Japan has identified its interest in a 100-150 passenger aeroplane as the Y-X-X and was believed to be close to reaching a preliminary decision by the end of this month (August). Earlier, Fokker had proposed Japanese collaboration around the F29, which already has Dutch government backing and is likely to be powered by the Anglo-Japanese RJ-500 turbofan. Airbus has suggested joint development of the SA-1, the new single-aisle proposal that in its basic form is a 132-seater with RJ-500 or CFM 56-3 engines. Lockheed has invited Japanese participation in the proposed passenger-carrying L-100-30C version of the Hercules and Boeing has made proposals around developments of the 737 and 757. One senior Japanese official is reported to have said that the ATMR-2 is too big and the SA-1 programme too indefinite to match the Y-X-X requirement.

NETHERLANDS

Following termination of the merger between Fokker and VFW, the Dutch company has **adopted** the **title Fokker BV** with effect from 1 June. The Fokker-VFW International company, which had functioned as the marketing organisation of Fokker-VFW, has been wound up and its activities are now fully integrated with Fokker BV. The Fokker annual report for 1979 — drawn up on the basis of an independent company, although the split with VFW did not become effective until early this year — showed an increase in turnover of 17 per cent to Dfl 965m (about £213m) and a net profit of Dfl 4·8m (£1·06m). During the year, 19 F27s were sold to bring the total to 699, and eight F28s were sold for a total of 152; the number of employees increased by more than 500 to 7,935 at 31 December 1979.

SOVIET UNION

Investigation of an accident suffered by an Ilyushin Il-62 operated by Poland's LOT, which crashed at Warsaw in March, showed that a serious fatigue problem had occurred in one engine and led to the **grounding of** all **Il-62s** pending investigation and corrective action. The aircraft were returned to flight status only after modified engines had been fitted, and as priority was given to Aeroflot aircraft, the other operators — LOT, CSA, Tarom and Interflug — are reported to have suffered lengthy and costly delays. The problem is also believed to have had repercussions on delivery of the Il-86, which was expected to enter service with Aeroflot in July.

UNITED KINGDOM

The Manchester Division of British Aerospace is now studying a number of **options to stretch the HS.748** transport in order to capitalise upon the revival of interest in turboprop-engined aircraft in the wake of rising fuel costs. No decisions have been taken as to the timing of such a stretched development but interest is centred upon an aircraft able to carry about 60 passengers compared with the 48-52 at present, with new engines. The new generation of small turboprops such as the General Electric CT-7, Pratt & Whitney PT-7 or Garrett-Volvo TPE331-14 are among possible power plants but may not be quite powerful enough to match the optimum stretch of the aircraft; a more powerful alternative is the General Electric CT64. The 748 recently celebrated (on 24 June) the 20th anniversary of its first flight. Sales now total 349 to 75 operators in 48 countries and with the advent of the new Series 2B — with a large number of detailed improvements, a "wide-body" interior look based on the design of the Concorde (which is only 1 in/2,5 cm wider) and hush-kitted engines — increased sales are expected to lead to production being accelerated from 9 to 12-18 a year.

Formally opened on 3 July by HRH the Duke of Edinburgh, the new **Caledonian Airmotive** turbine engine **facility at Prestwick** Airport is now operational. Established by the Caledonian Airways Group with the assistance of the Scottish Development Agency, Caledonian Airmotive is specialising initially in the overhaul of General Electric CF6-50 engines, with encouragement and technical collaboration from the engine manufacturer. The workshop, on a 20-acre site, is one of the most comprehensively-equipped of its kind in Europe, with the equipment and facilities required for virtually every aspect of engine refurbishing, from initial strip to final re-assembly and testing. A fully sound-insulated test cell has been built and can handle engines of up to the highest thrust at present foreseen. Up to 150 complete engines of CF6-50 size can be handled annually; in many cases, the plant will be handling individual modules rather than complete engines and it is estimated therefore that up to 250 engines a year will be returned to service. Contracts have been signed with British Caledonian to handle the engine overhauls for its five DC-10s and another early customer is Spantax. In due course Caledonian Airmotive expects to handle other variants in the CF6 range and smaller turbofans of other manufacturers.

British Airways has adopted the **Marconi AD 660** Doppler Velocity Sensor (DVS) **for** its **Boeing 737 fleet,** following the selection of this new equipment by Lufthansa. The DVS provides an accurate cockpit indication of speed over the ground, from 10 kt to 800 kt (18,5-1 482 km/h), when the aircraft is at any altitude from the ground up to 45,000 ft (13 716 m). Weighing only 11 lb (5 kg), the AD 660 requires an aperture of only 9 in by 15 in (23 by 38 cm) and is claimed to be the most advanced doppler groundspeed sensor available in the world.

USA

Boeing has obtained the first airline **order** — from Swissair — **for a new version of** the **Boeing 747** with an extended upper deck. The bulged portion of the upper front fuselage is being lengthened by 23 ft (7,01 m) to the rear; with additional windows and a new emergency exit, the extension allows up to 69 passengers to be seated on the upper floor, behind the flight deck, compared with a maximum of 32 at present. In addition, the circular stairway giving access to the upper deck is replaced by a straight stairway at the rear of the extended top deck. The effect of these innovations is to allow up to 44 more passengers to be carried in typical mixed-class layouts. The new configuration, referred to by Boeing as the 747SUD, is available on a range of present models, comprising the -100B, the -100B(SR), the -200B and -200B Combi, but not on the short-body 747SP. The Swissair contract for 747SUDs is for four aircraft to be delivered between March 1983 and December 1984; in addition, the company will delay acceptance of one previously-ordered 747 so that the SUD can be incorporated. Provision is being made to take options on four more 747s for 1986-1988 delivery.

Piper has begun production of a **turbosupercharged version of** the **Seminole,** offering a considerably improved performance compared with the basic version of the four-seat light twin. With 180 hp Lycoming TO-360-E1 engines and a gross weight of 3,925 lb (1 780 kg) — 125 lb (57 kg) more than the original Seminole — the Turbo Seminole has a better cruising speed, service and single-engined ceilings and useful load. Piper claims that the Turbo Seminole, at a suggested list price of $101,500, is able to compete with six-seat twins costing up to $40,000 more.

The **Bell 222** twin turbine helicopter received FAA **approval** on 15 May **for** single-pilot **IFR operations,** in Cat 1 conditions. Also now certificated are new pop-out lightweight floats that eliminate the drag of the 16-in (41-cm) extensions of the stub wings previously required, and save 88 lb (40 kg) in installed weight. IFR operation with the cargo hook and with the new floats is also approved, and at the end of May the FAA certificated a 200-lb (91-kg) increase in gross weight, to 7,850 lb (3 560 kg) without any change in empty weight. Bendix RDR-1400 weather radar has been approved for the Bell 222 and during June the company expected to obtain certification for a 45-US gal (170-l) auxiliary fuel tank mounted in the "hat box" section of the aircraft and approval for a max operating weight, with external load, of about 8,200 lb (3 720 kg).

Sikorsky Aircraft announced **delivery,** on 19 June, **of** the 136th and **last commercial S-61** helicopter, ending a 19-year production span for the civil variants of the helicopter which entered production in military guise in 1959. The final aircraft was delivered to Siller Brothers Inc, of Yuba City, California, for use in support of logging activities; the company already operates another S-61 and two S-64 Skycranes. More than 1,100 examples of the S-61 family have been built, including production by licensees in Italy, the UK and Japan. Commercial production comprised 123 S-61Ns and 13 S-61Ls, the latter being land-based variants without flotation equipment.

CIVIL AFFAIRS

BELGIUM

Scheduled **air services between Belgium and Berlin** have been resumed for the first time since September 1939. The East German carrier Interflug is flying one service a week by Tu-134A between Schoenefeld and the Brussels International airport at Zaventem, but Sabena has shown no signs of interest in a reciprocal service.

HONG KONG

The Hong Kong Government is spending HK$150m (£13m) on consultant design studies for a **new airport to replace** that at **Kai Tek,** now nearing its maximum capacity. The studies are based on a proposal to build the new airport at Chek Lap Kok, a small island off north Lantau (itself the largest of the colony's off-shore islands). If soil and ocean-bed tests at Chek Lap Kok are favourable, the government will make a final decision in 1982 on the construction of the new airport, expected to cost HK$5,500m (£478·3m). The timescale would then provide for a start in 1983 and completion of the first phase by 1990. Linked with the scheme are plans to build a series of bridges to provide a permanent road connecting Lantau Island to West Kowloon by way of the two small islands of Tsing Yi and Ma Wan.

LEBANON

Middle East Airlines achieved a **record profit** of £6·8m in 1979, once again demonstrating its resilience in the face of great operational difficulties springing from the troubles in the Lebanon. Mr Asad Y Nasr has been re-appointed president and chairman of the board of directors, and the company is expected soon to announce its plans for a major re-equipment programme.

UNITED KINGDOM

The Board of Trade has overturned a decision by the CAA, which had favoured licensing British Caledonian as the second operator on the **London-Hong Kong route,** at present served exclusively by British Airways. Previously, the Hong Kong government had issued licences to allow both B.Cal and Cathay Pacific to serve the route, and the CAA decision resulted in intense pressure being put upon the Board of Trade by Hong Kong agencies to obtain British approval for the locally-based Cathay Pacific (in which British Airways has a small stake). In addition, Laker Airways, which had applied for a licence for low-fare services on the route but had won approval from neither authority, appealed to the Board of Trade for the decision to be overruled. Apparently responding to these pressures, Secretary of Trade John Nott announced on 18 June that all four airlines were to receive licences to operate on the route, without restrictions; however, the Hong Kong authorities have yet to authorise Laker on the route, and also has to consider whether to allow more than the 14 flights a week previously approved — seven by British Airways, four by B.Cal and three by Cathay Pacific. The last-mentioned airline planned to inaugurate services on the route on 17 July by Boeing 747 and B.Cal was expected to introduce DC-10s on 1 August. A number of low-fare proposals have been made, including a £100 one-way stand-by fare by B.Cal, approximately half the present lowest fare by British Airways.

Sparrows Aviation, a division of Sparrows International Crane Hire which has been operating a PA-31 Navajo Chieftain since the end of 1978 as a corporate transport for its own requirements, has now obtained an AOC to allow it to **offer** an **executive air service** to other users. The aircraft is based at Bristol Airport.

British Airways has introduced a **change in** its **livery** as applied to its aircraft, ground vehicles and tickets and ticket wallets. The change deletes the word "Airways" and uses the single word "British" in a larger, bolder style. The overall colour scheme and the tail emblem remain unchanged.

Aviation Consultants International, an advisory group established last year in Switzerland, has **set up** its operational HQ in London and has established a UK subsidiary, **Aviation Consultants Ltd.** The company is a group of nine aerospace/aviation consultants and experts, each of whom is already an established authority in his own specialisation; by joining forces in ACI, they are able to offer a very broad band of expertise and can call upon additional resources when necessary. Members of the group are Air Marshal Sir Ivor Broom (chairman of the UK company); Capt Norman Todd (its managing director); Capt Derek Ellis; Arthur Gibson; Dr Ian Perry; Gordon Rose; Dr David Scott (USA); Lt Col R Smith and Richard Weston (Switzerland). The offices are at 2/3 Gough Square, London, EC4.

CIVIL CONTRACTS AND SALES

Airbus A300: Trans-Australia Airlines, which has four A300B4-100s on order and two on option (see this column/February 1980) has taken a third option and has requested earlier delivery than previously announced. The first aircraft will now be delivered in June 1981 with further deliveries in October and November and the fourth in June 1982. ☐ Olympic Airways has converted two of its four options for A300B4-100s to firm orders, making eight in all. The seventh and eighth aircraft will be delivered in the spring of 1982.

Airbus A310: Kuwait Airways has ordered six A310-200s, for delivery starting in 1983.

Boeing 727: Northwest Orient ordered two Advanced 727s, for delivery in January 1981. ☐ Braniff ordered a further seven Advanced 727s. ☐ Republic has contracted for three new 727-200s. ☐ Dan-Air has taken delivery of a 727-200 purchased from Singapore Airlines.

Boeing 737: Air Europe has again increased its purchase of new 737s with an order for a seventh, for delivery in spring 1982; the sixth, recently ordered, is for delivery in March 1981. ☐ Britannia Airways ordered five more 737s, two for delivery in September and December this year, the other three in April/May 1982, bringing the total fleet to 26. ☐ Abelag Airways in Belgium has leased one 737 from Gulf Air. ☐ Air New Zealand has recently ordered another Advanced 737, its ninth.

Boeing 747: British Airways placed orders for three more passenger-carrying 747-200Bs for delivery in January-April 1981, following delivery of a recently-ordered 747F in September 1980. ☐ Swissair ordered four 747-200s and plans to take options on four more for 1986/1988 delivery. The two 747s at present in Swissair service will be sold when the new aircraft, and a fifth previously ordered, are delivered, starting in 1983; they are of a new configuration with extended upper deck (see separate news item). ☐ Iberia ordered three additional 747-200Bs, one of which was delivered in May with two more in March/April 1981.

British Aerospace BAe 146: First orders for the BAe 146 have been placed by Lineas Aereas Privadas Argentinas SA (LAPA) of Buenos Aires. The contract comprises two Srs 100s for delivery in September and October 1982 and one Srs 200 for March 1983, with paid options on three more Srs 200s. The aircraft are for use on domestic routes out of Buenos Aires and LAPA will lease two One Eleven 400s from BAe later this year pending delivery of the 146s.

British Aerospace One-Eleven: LAPA is leasing two Srs 400s until delivery of BAe 146s in 1982. ☐ O & A International purchased one Srs 200 from US Air for corporate use. ☐ AirGo of Dallas is acquiring four Srs 200s from US Air, for conversion to cargo use.

Canadair CL-215: The Yugoslav government is placing orders for four CL-215 water-bombers for 1982 delivery. Canadian export credit facilities have been made available to cover the Can$19·6m (£7·29m) cost.

CASA C-212 Aviocar: Dirgantara Air Service, a domestic operator in Indonesia, ordered three NC-212s from Nurtanio.

Convair 990: Spantax is advertising for sale its entire fleet of 12 CV 990As together with a simulator and full spares package. The decision to sell is believed to be the result of rising fuel costs and the Spanish charter specialist is expected soon to announce selection of a replacement type.

De Havilland Canada Dash 7: Golden Gate Airlines (a merger of Gem State Airlines and Air Pacific) based in Monterey, California, ordered two more, for late 1981 delivery, to make a total of 12 on order or option. The company also has options on 12 Dash 8s.

Fokker F27: Pilgrim Airlines, flying commuter services in the New York area, has acquired one Mk 100 from TAA and one Mk 100 with cargo door from Icelandair. Two more are on order from TAA. ☐ Mississippi Valley Airlines increased its order to four by converting one Mk 500 previously on option.

Fokker F28: East-West Airlines has ordered two Mk 4000s, with first delivery in September 1981, for use jointly by East-West and the newly-formed Northern Airlines. ☐ Bangladesh Biman is to acquire two Mk 4000s, one in 1981 and one in 1982.

Grumman-American Gulfstream 1-C Commuter: Air North has ordered two of the 1-C Commuter conversions of the Gulfstream I. The 37-seat twin-Dart transports will be delivered in September and December.

Lockheed L-1011 TriStar: Gulf Air has taken up an option on one additional L-1011-200, for November delivery.

Lockheed L-100 Hercules: Pacific Western Airlines is offering for sale (through Omni International) three L-100-20 civil Hercules.

McDonnell Douglas DC-9: Pratt & Whitney has identified four customers for the JT8D-217 powered version of the DC-9 Super 80, these being Air California and Republic in addition to the previously-announced Aeromexico (first customer for the uprated version) and Polaris Leasing. In addition, Southern International, not previously listed as a Super 80 customer, has an option on two aircraft with JT8D-217s.

McDonnell Douglas DC-10: Swissair ordered two more Srs 30s to bring its fleet to 13. For delivery in spring 1982, the new aircraft are of extended-range type, with an extra 1,530-US gal (5 800-l) tank in the rear of the cargo compartment to extend range by 800 mls (1 287 km) to a maximum of 6,600 mls (10 620 km). With 54,000 lb st (24 494 kgp) CF6-50-C2B engines, the Srs 30ERs have a new gross weight of 580,000 lb (263 088 kg). Swissair also will convert two Srs 30 delivered earlier this year to ER standard.

MILITARY CONTRACTS

Aermacchi MB 339: A contract has been placed with Aermacchi on behalf of the *Fuerza Aérea Peruana* for an unspecified quantity of MB 339 basic-advanced trainers.

Dassault-Breguet Mirage IIIB: An order has been placed on behalf of the Swiss *Flugwaffe* for two two-seat Mirage IIIBs to make up attrition, contractual value of the order being £7·5m.

Fokker F27MPA: An order is being placed on behalf of the *Marine Luchtvaartdienst* (MLD) for two F27 maritime patrol aircraft under a contract valued at approximately £9m. To replace SP-2 Neptunes in the Netherlands Antilles, the aircraft are for delivery in September 1981 and February 1982.

Lockheed C-130H Hercules: The Indonesian Air Force has placed an order with Lockheed for three stretched C-130H(S) Hercules for delivery in the last quarter of this year. ☐ An order valued at SwKr186m (£19·1m) has been placed on behalf of the Swedish *Flygvapen* for three C-130H Hercules transports. ☐ The Royal Malaysian Air Force has ordered three C-130H-MP Hercules for maritime patrol. Delivery of two of these has been effected with the remaining aircraft to be delivered in the last quarter of this year.

Reims-Aviation FTB 337: The Pakistan Government has placed a contract with Reims-Aviation for 24 FTB 337 light twins for the aeromedical rôle. At the time of closing for press it is not known if these will be operated by the Pakistan Air Force or the Army aviation component.

Under
the curtain
TORNADO
NATO'S No1 in all weathers

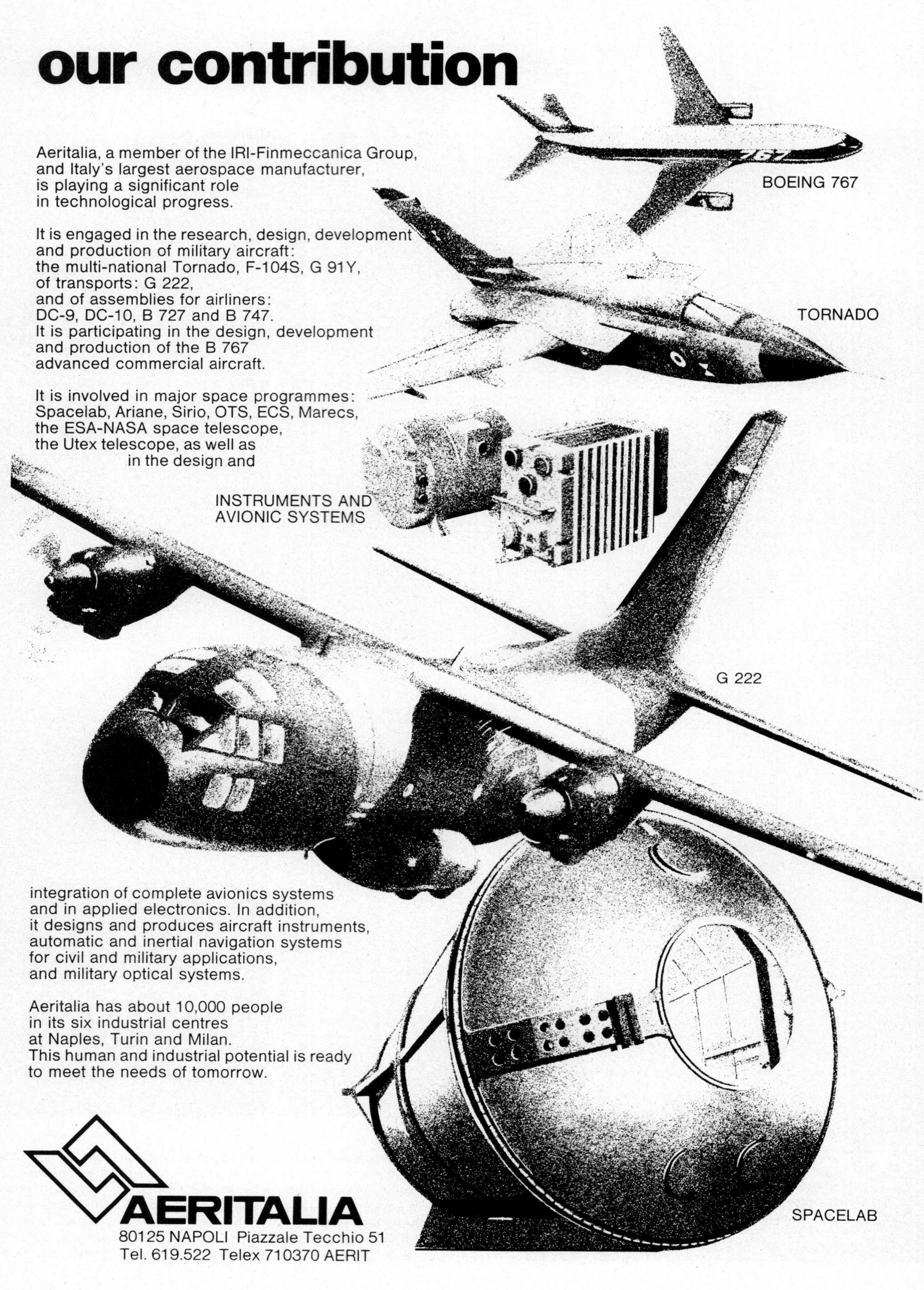
our contribution
Aeritalia, a member of the IRI-Finmeccanica Group,
and Italy's largest aerospace manufacturer,
is playing a significant role
in technological progress.
It is engaged in the research, design, development
and production of military aircraft:
the multi-national Tornado, F-104S, G 91Y,
of transports: G 222,
and of assemblies for airliners:
DC-9, DC-10, B 727 and B 747.
It is participating in the design, development
and production of the B 767
advanced commercial aircraft.
It is involved in major space programmes:
Spacelab, Ariane, Sirio, OTS, ECS, Marecs,
the ESA-NASA space telescope,
the Utex telescope, as well as
in the design and
integration of complete avionics systems
and in applied electronics. In addition,
it designs and produces aircraft instruments,
automatic and inertial navigation systems
for civil and military applications,
and military optical systems.
Aeritalia has about 10,000 people
in its six industrial centres
at Naples, Turin and Milan.
This human and industrial potential is ready
to meet the needs of tomorrow.
BOEING 767
TORNADO
INSTRUMENTS AND
AVIONIC SYSTEMS
G 222
SPACELAB
AERITALIA
80125 NAPOLI Piazzale Tecchio 51
Tel. 619.522 Telex 710370 AERIT

BACK-DOOR SURVEILLANT

MARK THREE NIMROD HERALDS IMMENSE AEW BOOST

With initial flight of the first Nimrod AEW Mk 3 imminent as this issue closes for press, an important stage is reached in one of the most vital of UK air defence programmes: provision of an efficacious high-technology airborne early warning system for the mid-'eighties, when, by consensus, the threat of confrontation between NATO and WarPac is most likely to reach a peak.

WHIMSICAL IN APPEARANCE, with its immense bulbous fore and aft radomes, the bizarre-looking aircraft now commencing first-phase flight testing from British Aerospace's Woodford, Cheshire, facility and scheduled to display its dramatically distinctive lines in public next month at the Farnborough Air Show, offers little in terms of aeronautical pulchritude. But the old adage that "handsome is as handsome does" has never been more apposite than in the case of this aircraft, the Nimrod AEW Mk 3, for it bids fair to upgrade RAF capability more than any single aeroplane type ever procured by the service. The major qualitative advances in WarPac offensive air power of recent years, with concomitant heightening of the dangers of pre-emptive air strike against the west, have increased the urgency attached to injection of effective airborne early warning capability into the overall West European air defence system, and this Mancunian débutante offers heartening indication that such sorely needed capability will not now be long delayed.

Described by Air Chief Marshal Sir Douglas Lowe, Controller Aircraft in the Ministry of Defence (Procurement Executive), at its initial roll-out on 30 April as possibly one of the ugliest and certainly the most expensive aircraft that the RAF has ever ordered, the Nimrod AEW Mk 3 is assuredly of singular appearance and the overall programme cost of the 11 aircraft of this type currently on order is unofficially estimated to total well in excess of a half-billion pounds sterling. If this addition to the RAF's inventory, with which the service anticipates achieving an initial operational capability in 1982, plugs the low-level radar gap, at this point in time offering an open back-door to potential intruders, then so immense a sum of money will have been very well spent indeed.

Originally funded as a fall-back solution to the RAF's airborne early warning needs of the 'eighties to be pursued in the event that Boeing's E-3A Sentry proved unsuitable or a NATO commitment to procurement of the US aircraft — which the UK government supported and in which it had declared its intention of participating — failed to materialise, the Nimrod AEW Mk 3 translated from back-up to chosen back-door surveillant when protracted NATO prevarication over collective AEW aircraft procurement finally began to threaten continued RAF airborne early warning ability*. Although the UK's unilateral approach to meeting the AEW need was inevitably to evoke criticism from some NATO allies, with the finite life of the RAF's small fleet of Shackleton AEW Mk 2s — which is, in any case, of strictly limited operational effectiveness — the UK government concluded that it could afford to gamble no longer on the successful outcome of NATO's AEW deliberations.

Thus, on 31 March 1977, what had been to that time a low-key fall-back development over a number of years — and had, in fact, lain in limbo between 1971 and early 1975 — went into top gear as a high priority programme. Barely more than three years later — and remarkably close to target despite some labour problems in the interim — the milestone of flight test has been reached in the development of this newest of purpose-designed AEW aircraft. When it enters service two years hence, it will, from some important aspects, be a more sophisticated aircraft than the E-3 Sentry, with which NATO will commence direct operations a year or so later, and there is reason to believe that it will be more closely attuned to the European scenario.

Trials quintet

The first of the 11 Nimrod AEW Mk 3s now commencing flight test (XZ286) is to fulfil development work on performance and handling qualities, airframe systems operation and testing of the high-capacity cooling system for the avionics, and, initially at least, it has few of the avionics subsystems. It will eventually be assigned to navigational systems development and will be joined in the test programme later this year by the second aircraft (XZ287), which, scheduled for completion in October, will be to full AEW configuration with the complete radar and avionics suite, and will fulfil the mission avionics system development rôle, testing subsystem operation and system compatibility. The airframes of these aircraft were, in fact, those of the last Nimrod MR Mk

**A Memorandum of Understanding marking the formal launching of the NATO airborne early warning system was finally to be signed on 6 December 1978.*

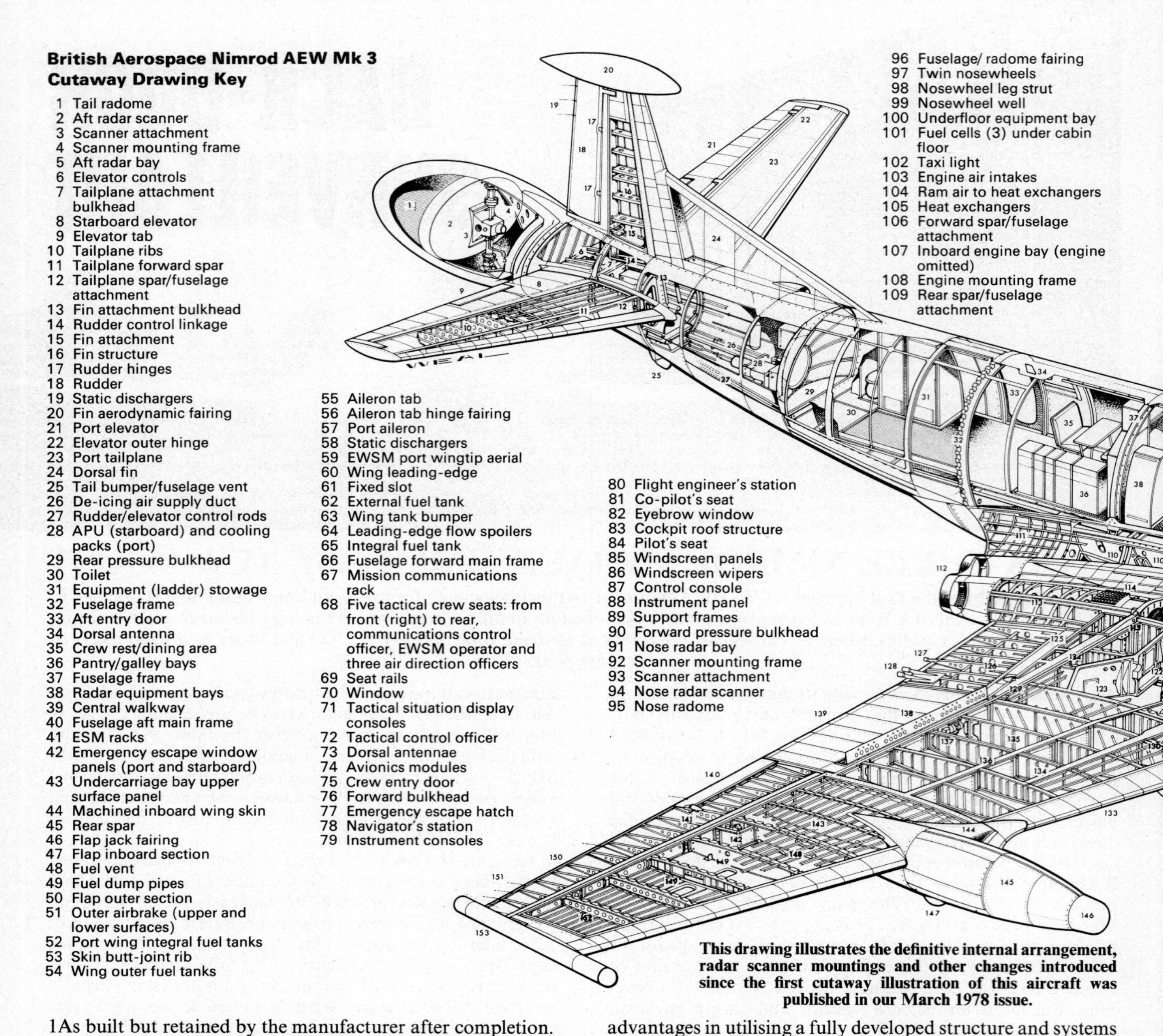

British Aerospace Nimrod AEW Mk 3 Cutaway Drawing Key

1 Tail radome
2 Aft radar scanner
3 Scanner attachment
4 Scanner mounting frame
5 Aft radar bay
6 Elevator controls
7 Tailplane attachment bulkhead
8 Starboard elevator
9 Elevator tab
10 Tailplane ribs
11 Tailplane forward spar
12 Tailplane spar/fuselage attachment
13 Fin attachment bulkhead
14 Rudder control linkage
15 Fin attachment
16 Fin structure
17 Rudder hinges
18 Rudder
19 Static dischargers
20 Fin aerodynamic fairing
21 Port elevator
22 Elevator outer hinge
23 Port tailplane
24 Dorsal fin
25 Tail bumper/fuselage vent
26 De-icing air supply duct
27 Rudder/elevator control rods
28 APU (starboard) and cooling packs (port)
29 Rear pressure bulkhead
30 Toilet
31 Equipment (ladder) stowage
32 Fuselage frame
33 Aft entry door
34 Dorsal antenna
35 Crew rest/dining area
36 Pantry/galley bays
37 Fuselage frame
38 Radar equipment bays
39 Central walkway
40 Fuselage aft main frame
41 ESM racks
42 Emergency escape window panels (port and starboard)
43 Undercarriage bay upper surface panel
44 Machined inboard wing skin
45 Rear spar
46 Flap jack fairing
47 Flap inboard section
48 Fuel vent
49 Fuel dump pipes
50 Flap outer section
51 Outer airbrake (upper and lower surfaces)
52 Port wing integral fuel tanks
53 Skin butt-joint rib
54 Wing outer fuel tanks
55 Aileron tab
56 Aileron tab hinge fairing
57 Port aileron
58 Static dischargers
59 EWSM port wingtip aerial
60 Wing leading-edge
61 Fixed slot
62 External fuel tank
63 Wing tank bumper
64 Leading-edge flow spoilers
65 Integral fuel tank
66 Fuselage forward main frame
67 Mission communications rack
68 Five tactical crew seats: from front (right) to rear, communications control officer, EWSM operator and three air direction officers
69 Seat rails
70 Window
71 Tactical situation display consoles
72 Tactical control officer
73 Dorsal antennae
74 Avionics modules
75 Crew entry door
76 Forward bulkhead
77 Emergency escape hatch
78 Navigator's station
79 Instrument consoles
80 Flight engineer's station
81 Co-pilot's seat
82 Eyebrow window
83 Cockpit roof structure
84 Pilot's seat
85 Windscreen panels
86 Windscreen wipers
87 Control console
88 Instrument panel
89 Support frames
90 Forward pressure bulkhead
91 Nose radar bay
92 Scanner mounting frame
93 Scanner attachment
94 Nose radar scanner
95 Nose radome
96 Fuselage/ radome fairing
97 Twin nosewheels
98 Nosewheel leg strut
99 Nosewheel well
100 Underfloor equipment bay
101 Fuel cells (3) under cabin floor
102 Taxi light
103 Engine air intakes
104 Ram air to heat exchangers
105 Heat exchangers
106 Forward spar/fuselage attachment
107 Inboard engine bay (engine omitted)
108 Engine mounting frame
109 Rear spar/fuselage attachment

This drawing illustrates the definitive internal arrangement, radar scanner mountings and other changes introduced since the first cutaway illustration of this aircraft was published in our March 1978 issue.

1As built but retained by the manufacturer after completion.

The first two Nimrod AEW Mk 3s will be joined in the development programme early next year by the third aircraft (XZ281), which, like the second, will be fully-equipped and will have a similar test commitment of systems proving, all three eventually being brought up to operational standard for 1982 delivery to RAF Waddington, where the Nimrod AEW Mk 3 fleet is to be based. These aircraft have been preceded in the programme by two other trials aircraft, a specially modified Comet Srs 4 (XW626), which, first flown after modification for its test mission on 28 June 1977, has since served as a flight development platform for Marconi Avionics' pulsed Doppler radar system, and a Nimrod MR Mk 1 (XZ283) which has been flying with AEW Mk 3 communications systems since February this year, the pair having so far contributed several hundred hours to early warning Nimrod development.

The Nimrod AEW Mk 3 airframe is, of course, essentially a modification — albeit a relatively extensive one — of that of the Nimrod MR Mk 1, a number of which became available for conversion when the RAF's responsibilities changed from world-wide involvement to a more limited European rôle, rendering a reduction in the service's maritime surveillance fleet desirable. Apart from that of economy, there are obvious advantages in utilising a fully developed structure and systems of proven reliability, and the Nimrod provides an ideal AEW platform in that it couples a desirably high transit speed with the ability to loiter for long periods, adds an economical cruise altitude coinciding with the AEW requirement and combines these characteristics with ease of handling and docility at low speeds.

The admittedly somewhat bizarre appearance of the Nimrod AEW Mk 3 results from the fact that, from the outset, the design team elected to adopt a fore-and-aft arrangement of the radar and thus avoid the radar "shadow" suffered by a dorsal rotodome, such as is employed by the E-2 Hawkeye, E-3 Sentry and Tu-126 *Moss*, simultaneously invoking less aerodynamic drag. The two identical scanners mounted at the extremities of the airframe are synchronised, each sequentially sweeping through 180 deg in azimuth, and provide uninterrupted coverage throughout 360 deg of combined sweep as the arrangement avoids any airframe obscuration effects. Structural flexing is compensated for with automatic roll- and pitch-stabilisation by dual INS, the scanners thus overcoming the cyclic error present in other systems.

The structural redesign dictated by the forward radome was readily accommodated by the comparatively deep fuselage of the basic Nimrod, and the radome itself has been optimised for

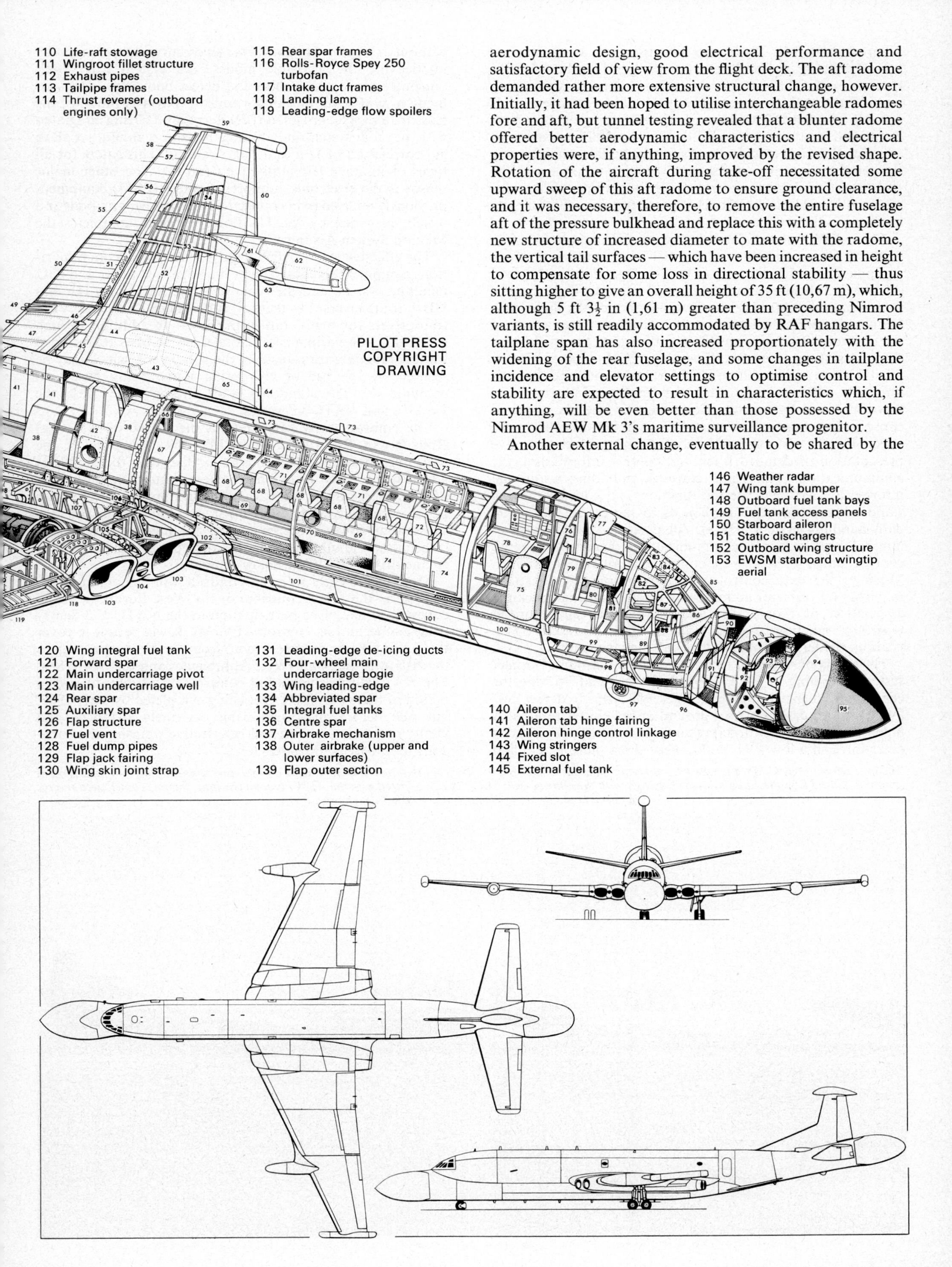

aerodynamic design, good electrical performance and satisfactory field of view from the flight deck. The aft radome demanded rather more extensive structural change, however. Initially, it had been hoped to utilise interchangeable radomes fore and aft, but tunnel testing revealed that a blunter radome offered better aerodynamic characteristics and electrical properties were, if anything, improved by the revised shape. Rotation of the aircraft during take-off necessitated some upward sweep of this aft radome to ensure ground clearance, and it was necessary, therefore, to remove the entire fuselage aft of the pressure bulkhead and replace this with a completely new structure of increased diameter to mate with the radome, the vertical tail surfaces — which have been increased in height to compensate for some loss in directional stability — thus sitting higher to give an overall height of 35 ft (10,67 m), which, although 5 ft 3½ in (1,61 m) greater than preceding Nimrod variants, is still readily accommodated by RAF hangars. The tailplane span has also increased proportionately with the widening of the rear fuselage, and some changes in tailplane incidence and elevator settings to optimise control and stability are expected to result in characteristics which, if anything, will be even better than those possessed by the Nimrod AEW Mk 3's maritime surveillance progenitor.

Another external change, eventually to be shared by the

Nimrod MR Mk 2, is the provision of wingtip pods accommodating the multi-channel port and starboard ESM receivers with their broadband spiral antenna arrays providing omni-directional coverage. The positioning of these pods provide the desired uninterrupted field of view but have demanded particularly careful design to ensure provision of effective electrical transparencies for the aerials while leaving the aerodynamic characteristics of the wing unimpaired. The pods increase wing stresses marginally but fatigue life remains essentially unchanged. Other changes to the aircraft are largely confined to the main cabin area.

The AEW system is installed with the operators in the forward cabin and the radar, IFF and communications equipment towards the rear of the fuselage, and the Nimrod AEW Mk 3 requires a tactical crew of six and a flight crew of four. The navigator is primarily a member of the flight crew but also supports the tactical crew which comprises a tactical air control officer responsible for directing the mission, a communications control officer, an ESM officer for the identification and correlation of ESM intercepts, and three air direction officers responsible for track monitoring and reporting, and fighter direction. Each of the six operator consoles has a tactical situation display, showing the tracks selected by the operator and a tabular display for the selective presentation of detailed track and control information, the communications and ESM consoles providing additional information for their specific functions, all consoles having standard multi-function keyboards for access to the digital data handling system (DHS). All positions have access to internal and external communications networks, overall control being exercised by the communications control officer. Much of the data control is entirely automatic, functions requiring no operator action being track initiation; tracking; association of radar, IFF and ESM, and data storage. Operator functions include system control; track classification; fighter control and data link management.

The Marconi Avionics' radar is a multi-mode pulse Doppler system operating in the E/F band (10 cm) and utilising the changed frequency of moving target reflections to detect low-flying aircraft despite strong ground or sea clutter returns. A high PRF (pulse repetition frequency) is employed for aircraft detection and a low PRF with a very short pulse length and without Doppler is used for ship surveillance, and by interleaving the available modes, the system can simultaneously plot surface ships and detect both high- and low-flying aircraft. Another major sensor system is the IFF, the Cossor Jubilee Guardsman IFF interrogators being integrated with the radar system and utilising the same scanning aerials to aid correlation of IFF and radar returns. This caters for all types of military IFF utilised by NATO. The other major sensor is the electronic support measures (ESM) equipment previously referred to in connection with the wingtip pods and which, provided by the US Loral concern, completes the Mission System Avionics.

The effectiveness of AEW depends heavily on communications equipment to complement the advanced radar and data handling system, and the Nimrod AEW Mk 3 uses HF and UHF transceivers for tactical communications, and VHF transceivers for flight control purposes. In addition to high speed data link equipment, radioteletype facilities are included for low rate data transmission, the equipment, which may be secured by the use of encryption units, being based on common NATO standards and interoperable with the USAF's and NATO's Sentries.

The Nimrod AEW Mk 3 retains the 12,160 lb (5 516 kg) Rolls-Royce RB 168-20 Spey Mk 250 turbofans of the maritime surveillance Nimrods and utilises their fuel supply as a heat sink to cool the avionics systems, thus overcoming the need for large air intakes which would impose severe drag penalties and adversely affect on-station loiter time. The very substantial power requirements of the high-powered radar transmitter and other equipment are to be catered for by four engine-driven 60 kVA primary generators.

Most of the early warning Nimrods will be committed to NATO as the UK's contribution to West European AEW coverage in lieu of its participation in the NATO E-3 Sentry programme, and six Nimrod AEW Mk 3s will be able to cover the entire UK air defence region, from the Norwegian Sea to the Atlantic, the South-West Approaches and the North Sea. The RAF will receive its full complement of aircraft over a period of three years, the fleet being completed by early 1985, but well before mid-decade, this extremely advanced and vitally important aircraft will be effectively closing the back-door to low-flying intruders. □

The first Nimrod AEW Mk 3 is seen here together with the Comet Srs 4 (XW626) that has been serving as a flight development platform for Marconi Avionics' pulsed Doppler radar system. Together with the Nimrod MR Mk 1 (XZ283) fitted with the AEW communications, this has contributed several hundred hours flying to Nimrod AEW Mk 3 development.

(Above and below) The first Nimrod AEW Mk 3 (XZ286), now commencing performance and handling trials, is seen here at British Aerospace's Woodford facility shortly before completion and roll-out. This and the second Nimrod AEW Mk 3 were originally the last two aircraft off the Nimrod MR Mk 1 assembly line.

FROM BETHANY TO TEL AVIV...

...WESTWIND STORY

FROM BETHANY to Tel Aviv, as the eagle flies, is a mere 35 mls (56 km) or so — no distance at all for a modern biz-jet and not a journey of marathon proportions even in Biblical times. For the Westwind, however, the journey from Bethany, its birthplace, to Ben Gurion International Airport and the home of Israel Aircraft Industries where it is now in production, was measured not in tens or even hundreds of miles, but in thousands. For, by a strange quirk of fate, the Bethany where this twin-engined business transport was conceived and built, nearly 20 years ago, was not that village on the slopes of the Mount of Olives where once Jesus talked with Martha and Mary, but a town of much larger proportions in Oklahoma, USA. And the Westwind biz-jet that is now established as the most successful of Israel Aircraft Industries' civil aircraft programmes, with production well into three figures, a solid reputation and a good foothold in the North American market, was the brainchild of a designer with the singularly un-Jewish name of Smith! There is more than a little irony, too, in the fact that an aircraft designed and produced in America, had to be sold by its originators to comply with anti-trust laws, only to reappear as a foreign import that is now capturing a not-unsubstantial share of the US domestic market for aircraft of its class.

Of the origins of the Westwind, and the reasons for the transfer of its production from the USA to Israel, more later in this account. Before going into history, it is worth describing the Westwind as it is today, a well-proven product of an energetic and enterprising company that has had to overcome numerous problems to establish and maintain its position in the marketplace. The basic aircraft now in production is the Westwind I, a designation introduced in 1978 to distinguish an improved model of the Westwind 1124; the 1124 (or sometimes Eleven-24 in earlier references) itself indicated the introduction in 1975 of turbofan engines on the basic aircraft. The most recent development is the Westwind 2, with a series of aerodynamic refinements aimed at increasing the aircraft's range and economy; deliveries of this variant are now beginning.

The Westwind — which in its current version IAI likes to call a "third generation aircraft", with more than 10 years of development and product improvement behind it — is a mid-wing monoplane with engines mounted on the rear fuselage. The entire passenger cabin is ahead of the wing, and is thus uninterrupted by centre-section structure; locating the engines well aft and sweeping-back both the tailplane and the vertical tail surfaces keeps the CG in the right place and the straight tapered wing is thin enough for a maximum operating Mach No of 0·765. Structurally straightforward, the Westwind has a two-spar wing and a semi-monocoque fuselage built in two main sections, the fore section being pressurised to a differential of 8·8 psi (0,62 kg/cm²), with provision for a maximum of 9·0 psi (0,63 kg/cm²).

Main legs of the landing gear are carried on structural beams in the wing close to the fuselage and retract sideways to allow the single wheels to lie flush, but exposed, in wells in the wings. The nosewheel retracts rearwards and is fully enclosed by two doors; actuation of the undercarriage, and of the brakes and nosewheel steering, is hydraulic, a dual 2,000 psi (141 kg/cm²) system being installed in the aircraft for this purpose, and for the wing-mounted speed brake and lift dumper operation. Primary flight controls are mechanically operated and trim tabs are incorporated in the port aileron and rudder; longitudinal trim is by means of the variable incidence tailplane, electrically actuated. Also electrically operated are the high-lift double-slotted flaps on each wing trailing edge. Electrical generation is by means of a starter/generator on each engine, providing 24-volt DC, and two solid-state static inverters to supply 115-volt AC.

Full icing protection is provided, with inflatable de-icing boots on all aerofoil leading edges and hot engine bleed air to heat the engine intakes. Engine bleed air is also used for cabin conditioning, as an alternative — at pilot discretion — to ram air.

The fuel system in the basic Westwind 1124 comprises an integral tank in each wing, two wing-tip tanks and a tank in the centre fuselage (behind the cabin), providing a total capacity of 1,330 US gal (5 035 l). One of the features that distinguishes the Westwind I from the earlier standard is that provision is made for an auxiliary, removable, fuel tank to be fitted in one of the baggage compartments, increasing the capacity by 105 US gal (397l). The wing tip tanks are fixed and are not optional.

One of the most notable features of the Westwind is the spaciousness of the accommodation it offers relative to the size — and price — of the aircraft. More than 15 ft (4,6 m) long, the cabin provides, typically, for seven passengers, and a maximum of 10, in addition to two pilots, and is large enough to include a self-contained toilet at the rear. In the Westwind I, the size of the toilet is increased by lowering the floor to give 7 in (18 cm) more headroom.

Although it is now wholly an Israeli product so far as manufacture and support is concerned, the Westwind relies heavily upon US-made components. There are two reasons: the fact that it began its life as an American product, and because it is geared almost exclusively to the American market — fewer than 10 per cent of all Westwinds sold to date are owned outside the USA. The standard specification has been established through close consultation between IAI and its US distributor, Atlantic Aviation. In contrast to the practice of the majority of biz-jet manufacturers, IAI prefers to furnish and finish the aircraft prior to delivery but Atlantic Aviation continues to play an important rôle not only in marketing and supporting the type in America but in providing vital feedback to the manufacturers — who inevitably had a great deal to learn about selling and supporting a civil aircraft when they embarked on the Westwind. The standard Westwind avionics specification is built around Collins equipment, with the FCS-105 flight control system (a combination of FD-109Z flight director and AP-105 autopilot); NCS-31A RNAV and frequency control, dual VHF-20A communications and VIR-30A navigation, DME-40, ADF-60A and other items. RCA Primus 400 weather radar and dual Sperry C-14 compasses are fitted, and provision is made for Global GNS-500A or CCC Ontrac III VLF/Omega navaids.

Westwind variants

Israel Aircraft Industries was one of the first of the biz-jet manufacturers to switch from turbojet to turbofan power on an existing airframe; its intention to do so was announced in September 1974 and the switch was made with effect from aircraft No 187*. The introduction of the Garrett AiResearch TFE 731-3-1G engines was the most significant new feature, but IAI also made other improvements to make the Westwind more competitive in range and speed with such types as the Learjet 35/36 and the Dassault-Breguet Falcon 10. These improvements included a new drooped wing leading edge, achieved by fitting a glassfibre cuff and first tested in wind tunnels and on a modified Model 1123. This reduced stalling speed by about 5 kt (9 km/h) without any drag penalty at cruising speed, while the engines offered better fuel economy; at the same time, they had enough extra power to allow gross weight to increase from 20,500 lb (9 300 kg) to 22,850 lb (10 365 kg). A stronger undercarriage was introduced to match the higher weights, with new tyres and an improved braking system which, together with the newly-developed Grumman thrust reversers, helped to overcome one of the deficiencies of earlier Westwind models — the landing performance on wet runways. Internal changes included a redesigned flight deck to improve pilot comfort on long flights. Single-point refuelling was a new feature of the 1124, and the APU used in earlier models was deleted. A small dorsal fin was added, providing an easy external distinguishing feature between the 1124 and earlier Westwinds.

Two of the production Model 1123s were converted to serve as Westwind 1124 prototypes, the first of these making its maiden flight at Ben Gurion airport on 21 July 1975. Flight testing for certification showed that the stick shaker could be eliminated from the control circuits and that an earlier 350-kt (648 km/h) speed restriction, that applied when the aircraft was carrying fuel in the tip tanks, could be lifted. The improvements offered by the Westwind 1124 brought an immediate uplift in orders and deliveries from an initial 36-aircraft production batch began early in 1976.

The Westwind I was announced in September 1978 and was phased into production after 53 Westwind 1124s had been built. As already noted, its new features were relatively modest improvements, including a 5 per cent increase in cabin volume,

** Westwind sequence numbers have run consecutively since the start of production of the basic aircraft in the USA. As noted later in this account, the first 150 aircraft were of American manufacture, although some of these were sold by IAI: Nos 151 to 186 were Model 1123s built in Israel.*

Illustrated below and in the heading photograph (opposite page) is the prototype Westwind 2, latest version of the IAI biz-jet and distinguished by the winglets on the tip tanks. Delineation of the fuselage structure is part of the external finish and interior colour scheme designed for the prototype by the Porsche Design Group. Following FAA certification, this aircraft has now been delivered to a customer in Columbia.

achieved primarily by lowering the floor level in the toilet area, and provision for a 700-lb (318-kg) capacity removable fuel tank to be fitted in the starboard side of the forward baggage compartment. RCA Primus 400 colour radar became standard equipment and some further improvements were made in the environmental and fuel systems. The Westwind I demonstrator, displayed by Atlantic Aviation at the 1978 NBAA Convention in St Louis, sported interior and exterior styling by Pierre Cardin, with a black-and-white horizontal striping and red highlights. Within one year of its début, the Westwind I had collected 45 orders and the 100th turbofan-engined Westwind was scheduled to be delivered in mid-1980. By the end of 1980, IAI expects to have delivered 128 Westwinds in the 1124/Westwind I/Westwind 2 family.

Meanwhile, in September 1979, IAI had revealed details of the Westwind 2, production deliveries of which are expected to start in September. News that IAI was working on an advanced version of the 1124 with winglets on the tip tanks had come more than a year earlier, and as the Westwind 2, a prototype (c/n 239) entered flight testing at Tel Aviv on 24 April 1979. At the time of writing, 18 Westwind 2s had been ordered. Certification was obtained from the FAA on 17 April 1980 and the first delivery (of the prototype) was made on 16 May, to Helicol (Avianca) in Columbia.

The winglets that are the most obvious distinguishing feature of the Westwind 2 are part of what the company calls the Sigma wing system, evolved through extensive computer and wind-tunnel testing and with the advantage of flight test results obtained earlier with an Arava fitted with winglets. The winglets, based on NASA research by Richard Whitcomb, are small fixed surfaces, attached to the tip tanks and angled slightly out from the vertical. They serve to reduce the induced drag of the wing, which in turn reduces the induced drag of the winglet itself; a drag reduction of about 4 per cent was

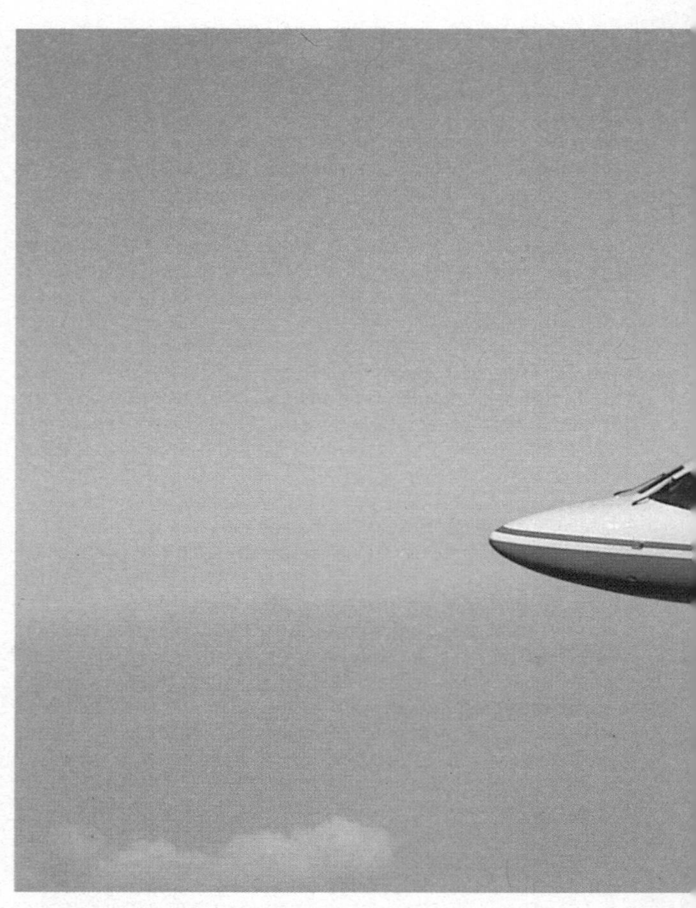

(Below) Another illustration of the prototype Westwind 2 (c/n 239) as demonstrated in public for the first time in the USA during 1979. (Above) A standard production Westwind 1124 (c/n 245) now owned in the USA by Mar Jet Inc of Portland. (Right) An eye-catching finish designed by Pierre Cardin on the Westwind I demonstrator used by Atlantic Aviation in 1978.

N1124P

N240WW

achieved in the cruise, and a larger improvement (up to about 12 per cent) was obtained in the second segment climb, normal climb and loiter.

Combined with the winglets in the Sigma system is a new aerofoil section, which involves an extension of 1 per cent forward of the leading edge, with a modification of the under surface back to 5 per cent of wing chord and of the upper surface back to 40 per cent of chord. The net result of these modifications is to achieve a higher Mach divergence number.

The Westwind 2 prototype, with an eye-catching finish by the Porsche Design Group featuring metallic grey exterior and warm grey-and-blackberry red leather interior furnishing, appeared in public for the first time at the 1979 NBAA Convention at Atlanta. By then, a provisional type certificate had been issued and the aircraft had totalled 220 hrs in 75 flights. Preliminary data indicated that the Westwind 2 would be certificated at higher gross weights and higher speeds than the Westwind I and would offer improved range and better field performance (particularly in hot and high conditions) as indicated in the comparison on the opposite page.

The Westwind 2 retains the same powerplant as the Westwind I, but the wing modifications allow approximately 175 lb (80 kg) more usable fuel to be carried. Collins FCS-80, incorporating the APS-80 autopilot, is being adopted in place of the FCS-105 used previously, with Collins Pro Line solid state avionics.

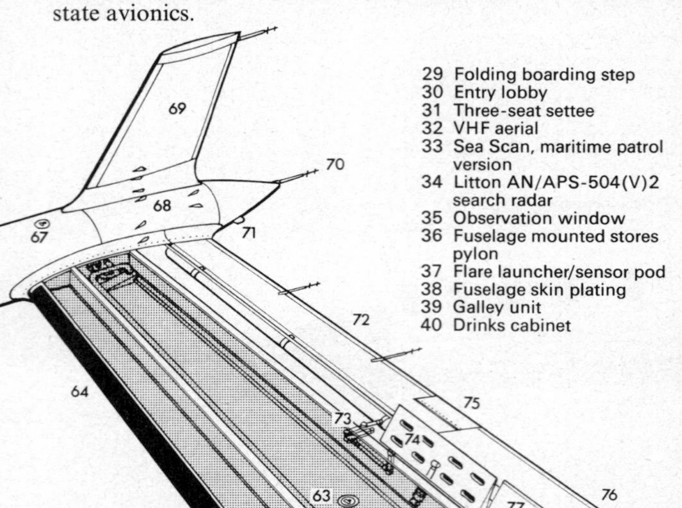

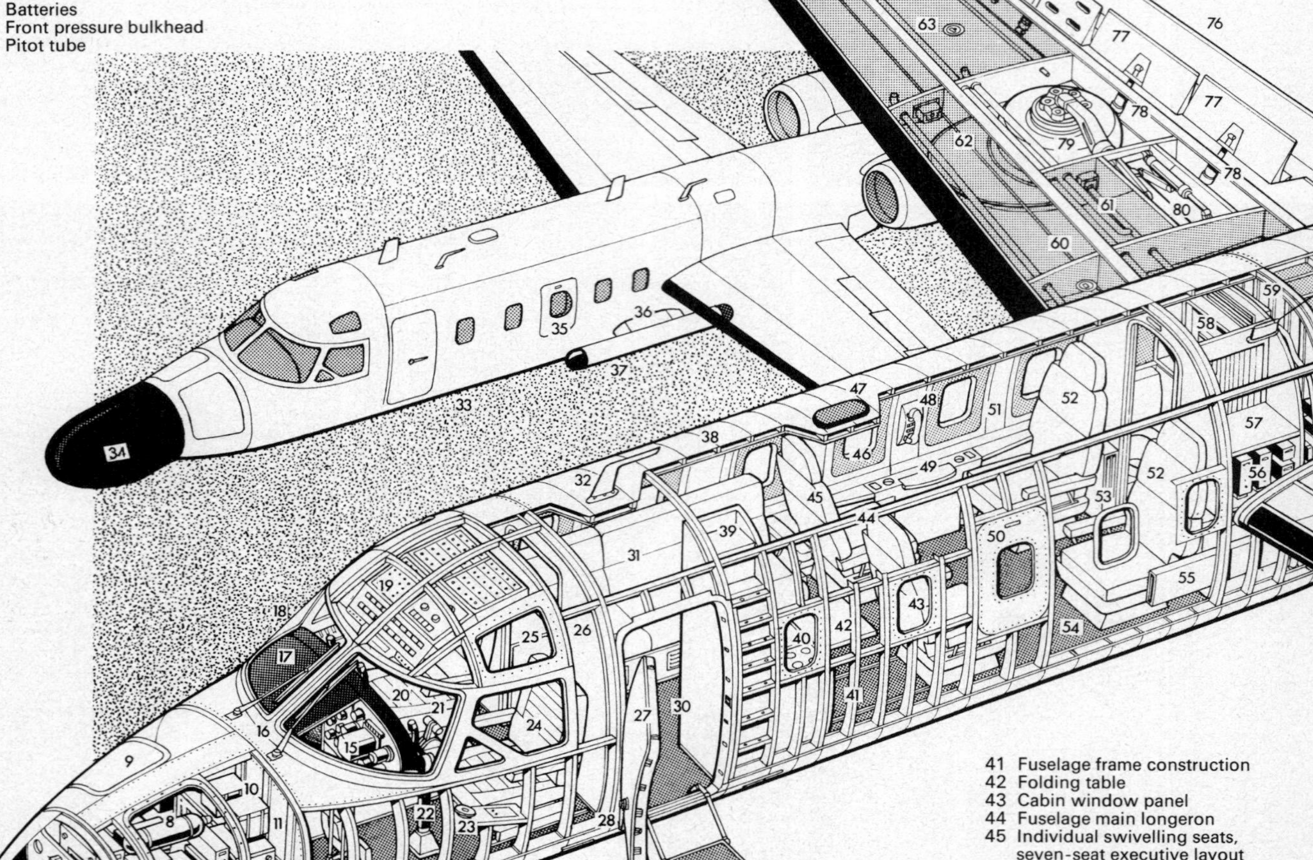

IAI Westwind 2 Cutaway Drawing Key

1 Radome
2 Weather radar scanner
3 Radar tracking mechanism
4 Nosewheel leg door
5 Twin nosewheels
6 Nose undercarriage leg strut
7 Radio and electronics equipment
8 Oxygen bottle
9 Nose compartment access doors
10 Batteries
11 Front pressure bulkhead
12 Pitot tube
13 Cooling air intake
14 Rudder pedals
15 Instrument panel
16 Windscreen wipers
17 Instrument panel shroud
18 Curved windscreen panels
19 Overhead switch panel
20 Co-pilot's seat
21 Engine throttles
22 Control column
23 Nosewheel steering control
24 Pilot's seat
25 Cockpit eyebrow windows
26 Cockpit bulkhead
27 Entry door
28 Door latch
29 Folding boarding step
30 Entry lobby
31 Three-seat settee
32 VHF aerial
33 Sea Scan, maritime patrol version
34 Litton AN/APS-504(V)2 search radar
35 Observation window
36 Fuselage mounted stores pylon
37 Flare launcher/sensor pod
38 Fuselage skin plating
39 Galley unit
40 Drinks cabinet
41 Fuselage frame construction
42 Folding table
43 Cabin window panel
44 Fuselage main longeron
45 Individual swivelling seats, seven-seat executive layout
46 Starboard emergency exit window
47 D/F loop aerial
48 Radio telephone
49 Fold-out table stowage
50 Port emergency exit window
51 Cabin wall trim panels
52 Rearmost forward-facing seats
53 Magazine rack
54 Uninterrupted floor level
55 Air conditioning distribution ducting
56 Rear radio rack

During 1976, IAI began to promote a maritime reconnaissance version of the Westwind as the 1124N, based to some extent upon experience gained in submitting a version of the Model 1123 to the US Coast Guard before the latter's decision to buy the Dassault-Breguet Falcon 20. As originally projected, the 1124N was to be fitted with Litton AN/APS-503 search radar in a retractable ventral radome; a retractable FLIR installation and an LLTV sensor in the cabin; a retractable magnetometer in the rear fuselage; a searchlight in the nose of one of the wing-tip tanks; flare, beacon and chaff dispensers and space for sonobuoy ejectors in the aft fuselage

continued on page 98

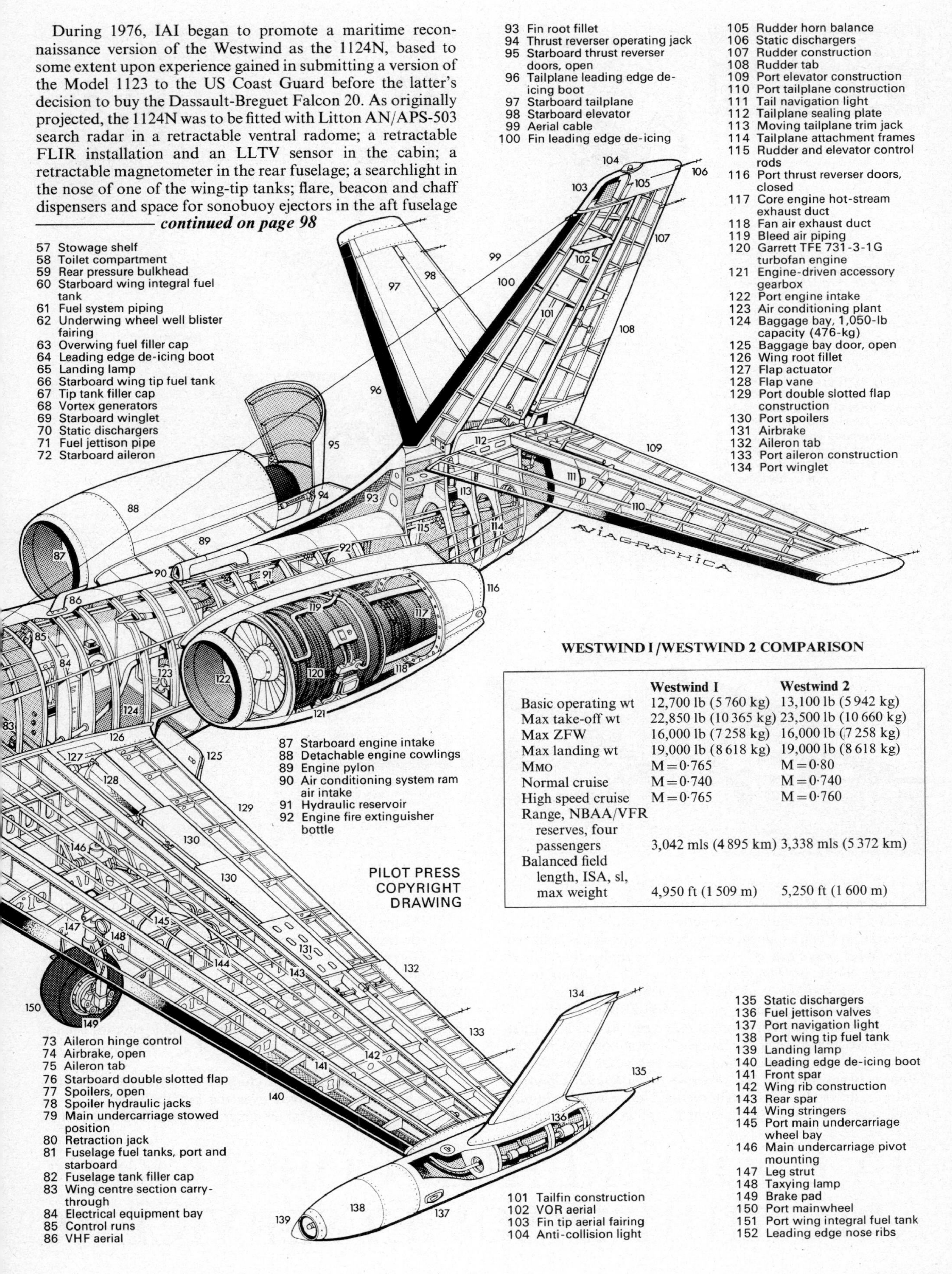

57 Stowage shelf
58 Toilet compartment
59 Rear pressure bulkhead
60 Starboard wing integral fuel tank
61 Fuel system piping
62 Underwing wheel well blister fairing
63 Overwing fuel filler cap
64 Leading edge de-icing boot
65 Landing lamp
66 Starboard wing tip fuel tank
67 Tip tank filler cap
68 Vortex generators
69 Starboard winglet
70 Static dischargers
71 Fuel jettison pipe
72 Starboard aileron
73 Aileron hinge control
74 Airbrake, open
75 Aileron tab
76 Starboard double slotted flap
77 Spoilers, open
78 Spoiler hydraulic jacks
79 Main undercarriage stowed position
80 Retraction jack
81 Fuselage fuel tanks, port and starboard
82 Fuselage tank filler cap
83 Wing centre section carry-through
84 Electrical equipment bay
85 Control runs
86 VHF aerial
87 Starboard engine intake
88 Detachable engine cowlings
89 Engine pylon
90 Air conditioning system ram air intake
91 Hydraulic reservoir
92 Engine fire extinguisher bottle
93 Fin root fillet
94 Thrust reverser operating jack
95 Starboard thrust reverser doors, open
96 Tailplane leading edge de-icing boot
97 Starboard tailplane
98 Starboard elevator
99 Aerial cable
100 Fin leading edge de-icing
101 Tailfin construction
102 VOR aerial
103 Fin tip aerial fairing
104 Anti-collision light
105 Rudder horn balance
106 Static dischargers
107 Rudder construction
108 Rudder tab
109 Port elevator construction
110 Port tailplane construction
111 Tail navigation light
112 Tailplane sealing plate
113 Moving tailplane trim jack
114 Tailplane attachment frames
115 Rudder and elevator control rods
116 Port thrust reverser doors, closed
117 Core engine hot-stream exhaust duct
118 Fan air exhaust duct
119 Bleed air piping
120 Garrett TFE 731-3-1G turbofan engine
121 Engine-driven accessory gearbox
122 Port engine intake
123 Air conditioning plant
124 Baggage bay, 1,050-lb capacity (476-kg)
125 Baggage bay door, open
126 Wing root fillet
127 Flap actuator
128 Flap vane
129 Port double slotted flap construction
130 Port spoilers
131 Airbrake
132 Aileron tab
133 Port aileron construction
134 Port winglet
135 Static dischargers
136 Fuel jettison valves
137 Port navigation light
138 Port wing tip fuel tank
139 Landing lamp
140 Leading edge de-icing boot
141 Front spar
142 Wing rib construction
143 Rear spar
144 Wing stringers
145 Port main undercarriage wheel bay
146 Main undercarriage pivot mounting
147 Leg strut
148 Taxying lamp
149 Brake pad
150 Port mainwheel
151 Port wing integral fuel tank
152 Leading edge nose ribs

WESTWIND I/WESTWIND 2 COMPARISON

	Westwind I	Westwind 2
Basic operating wt	12,700 lb (5 760 kg)	13,100 lb (5 942 kg)
Max take-off wt	22,850 lb (10 365 kg)	23,500 lb (10 660 kg)
Max ZFW	16,000 lb (7 258 kg)	16,000 lb (7 258 kg)
Max landing wt	19,000 lb (8 618 kg)	19,000 lb (8 618 kg)
MMO	M=0·765	M=0·80
Normal cruise	M=0·740	M=0·740
High speed cruise	M=0·765	M=0·760
Range, NBAA/VFR reserves, four passengers	3,042 mls (4 895 km)	3,338 mls (5 372 km)
Balanced field length, ISA, sl, max weight	4,950 ft (1 509 m)	5,250 ft (1 600 m)

MIKOYAN FLOGGER

Two of the most important members of the Flogger family currently in V-VS service are the MiG-23MF Flogger-B (right) and the MiG-27 Flogger-D below, the former optimised for the air-air mission and the latter a dedicated air-ground aircraft. While the majority of Flogger-B fighters retain the light grey air superiority finish, an increasing number are now being camouflaged in a similar fashion to variants with a primary air-ground function, as is seen by this photograph taken at a V-VS base in the Trans-Baikal Military District. The photograph immediately below, taken during Exercise "Sever" last year, depicts MiG-27 Flogger-Ds of a squadron of the FA commanded by a Maj I Ivanov. Comparison of these photographs shows clearly some of the salient differences between these two variants of the basic Flogger design.

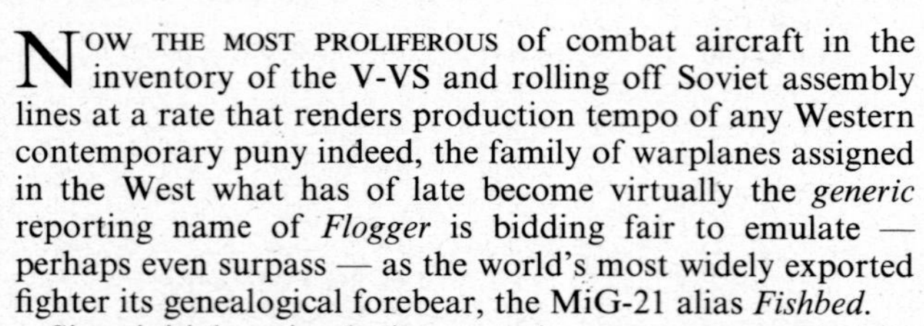

NOW THE MOST PROLIFEROUS of combat aircraft in the inventory of the V-VS and rolling off Soviet assembly lines at a rate that renders production tempo of any Western contemporary puny indeed, the family of warplanes assigned in the West what has of late become virtually the *generic* reporting name of *Flogger* is bidding fair to emulate — perhaps even surpass — as the world's most widely exported fighter its genealogical forebear, the MiG-21 alias *Fishbed*.

Since initial service deployment nine years ago as a straight air combat fighter with the Soviet TacAir component, the *Frontovaya Aviatsiya* (FA), and, some two years later, the air defence organisation, the *Protivo-vozdushnaya Oborona (Strany)*, the basic design has burgeoned into a sizeable family of closely related aircraft, which, possessing extensive commonality of airframe and systems features, now covers almost the entire spectrum of fighter tasks, from interception and air superiority to interdiction and ground attack.

Furthermore, over the past two or three years, members of the *Flogger* family have been exported to countries as disparate as Algeria and Cuba, and to most of the principal WarPac air arms, including those of Czechoslovakia, the DDR and Hungary, while an agreement is now being finalised between the Soviet Union and India for mid-'eighties licence manufacture in the latter country of two members of the family.

By any reckoning, this product of the Mikoyan-Gurevich design bureau has evolved over the past half-decade or so under the aegis of General Designer Rostislav A Belyakov into

НА ВООРУЖЕНИИ СОВЕТСКОЙ АВИАЦИИ • IN SOVIET SERVICE–10

one of the most important families of combat aircraft extant, from viewpoints of both efficacy and quantity, and *Flogger* now provides the backbone of Soviet TacAir — a function which it will presumably also fulfil for all major WarPac air arms in the coming years — with upwards of 1,600 currently serving with elements of *Frontovaya Aviatsiya*, according to the latest assessments of western analysts. A further 500 plus are deployed by the *Istrebitel'naya Aviatsiya P-VO Strany* for home defence tasks, and 100-150 have so far been supplied to other WarPac forces with deliveries accelerating.

Essentially a product of the changes in tactical thinking of the mid-'sixties, with their re-evaluation of the fighter rôle, and the FA's manifest lack of tactical fighters in the category of the F-105 Thunderchief and F-4 Phantom, *Flogger* appears to have been biased in concept towards air-ground operations. The primary aim would seem to have been creation of a flexible combat aircraft combining increased warload/range performance with a field performance no more demanding than that of fighters of the preceding generation. Such favoured variable geometry, although alternative fall-back solutions were investigated in parallel by the Mikoyan-Gurevich bureau, and an aerodynamic trials aircraft, the Ye-231, featuring pilot-selected variable wing sweep with NASA-style outboard hinges, multi-shock lateral inlets *à la* Phantom and a ventral fin folding to afford adequate ground clearance, entered flight test in the winter of 1966-67.

Apart from the significant advance represented by the adoption of VG, the design team had, in conformity with long-standing Soviet practice, apparently endeavoured to evade complexity wherever possible. For example, the use of sophisticated high-lift devices was avoided, the only movable surfaces on the variable-sweep wing panels being plain trailing-edge flaps. The Ye-231 made its public début at Domodedovo in July 1967, whereupon the ASCC, which had previously been scrupulous in avoiding bestowal of *flattering* reporting names on Soviet aircraft débutantes, assigned that of *Flogger** to the newcomer, presumably not intending to reflect its anticipated capabilities. To this the suffix *-A* was later to be added when, at the beginning of the 'seventies, the initial and rather different production derivative of the aerodynamic trials aircraft was first sighted, becoming *Flogger-B*. Shortly thereafter it became known — after some initial confusion with the MiG-25 alias *Foxbat* — that the VG fighter was MiG-23 in Soviet parlance.

Redesign for production

Between aerodynamic trials aircraft and production fighter came a very considerable amount of design development which would seem to have been completed in a commendably short time and paced by the Sergei K Tumansky bureau's development of a turbofan, the R-27, primarily tailored for the new warplane. Airframe development had included some fairly fundamental changes between *Flogger-A* and *Flogger-B*. The movable portions of the wing were shifted forward bodily some 24 in (60 cm), resulting in a shorter fixed wing glove and increasing the gap between the fully swept wing and the horizontal tail, presumably to move the aerodynamic centre forward. Leading-edge flaps were added to the movable wing panels, the flaps being carried by a tapered extension, which, forming a narrow slot with the fixed glove at minimum sweep, produced a substantial dogtooth at mid-sweep. The third major change was in the rear fuselage, which, accompanied by some revision of the fixed vertical surface, was recontoured, marginally deepened and mated with an engine efflux nozzle that was shortened by some 3·5 ft (1,06 m), reducing loads on the fuselage and, presumably, structural weight.

The MiG-23 was evidently configured to offer true multi-rôle adaptability as a *basic* design — adhering to the familiar Soviet principle of minimum cross-section with everything hung outside — but with a range of minimal- to major-change versions optimised for specific tasks, and these have now assuredly taken on the mantle of *Fishbed*. It should be stressed, however, that *Flogger* is not a *true* successor to the earlier warplane in the sense that, unlike its predecessor, it is no simple, lightweight, low-cost dogfighter, but if not designed with *dogfighting* in mind, the air-air rôle was for long given priority in its mission repertoire and for several years enjoyed development and production priority.

The initial series model, which was to become familiar in the West as *Flogger-B*, was configured as a straight air defence aircraft, with few concessions to its strictly limited secondary ground attack task. The capability of this version was to be progressively upgraded with the successive introduction of improved radar, more advanced weaponry and a more powerful Tumansky turbofan during what is now a decade of continuous production. However, displaying no major and readily identifiable external changes, such enhanced versions (eg, MiG-23M and -23MF) are not differentiated between in the ASCC reporting system, all these retaining the *-B* suffix assigned to the first-sighted production *Flogger*.

As first manufactured in series, *Flogger-B* was powered by Tumansky's first production turbofan, the R-27 with a basic maximum thrust of 15,430 lb (7 000 kg) boosted to 22,485 lb (10 200 kg) with maximum reheat, this giving place in 1975-76 to the R-29 with maximum basic and reheat ratings of 17,635 lb (8 000 kg) and 25,350 lb (11 500 kg) respectively to result in what might be referred to as the "second generation" MiG-21MF. Carrying the large and powerful J-band *High Lark* radar, which, in its current service version, has a maximum search range of some 53 miles (85 km) and the ability to track targets at up to 35 miles (55 km), and some — albeit limited — lookdown capability, *Flogger-B* initially toted a quartet of IR-homing AA-2 (K-13A) and radar-homing AA-2-2 *Atoll* missiles as primary air-air armament. These were distributed between stations under each air intake trunk and the fixed wing glove. From the late 'seventies, these have been progressively supplanted by a mix of semi-active radar-homing AA-7 *Apex* medium-range and IR-homing AA-8 *Aphid* dogfight missiles.

All versions of *Flogger-B* mount a 23-mm twin-barrel GSh-

Several WarPac air forces are now operating the MiG-23BM Flogger-F, an example of this multi-role aircraft in service with the Czechoslovak Air Force, photographed during "Družba 79", is seen below.

*One who or that which chastises.

(Above) A MiG-23MF Flogger-B photographed in the landing circuit at a V-VS airfield in the DDR. It will be noted that, although sporting air superiority finish, this aircraft carries rocket pods — primarily air-ground ordnance — on the fuselage pylons. The emblem that may just be discerned on the nose denotes a measure of excellence attained by the unit. (Below left) Flogger-G differs in only minor respects from Flogger-B, the changes most obvious in this photograph being the shorter dorsal fin and the notched trailing edges of the horizontal tail surfaces.

23L cannon on the fuselage centreline, aft of the nosewheel bay, ahead of which is a chisel-nosed housing for a laser rangefinder, and for the secondary ground attack mission, UV-16-57 or similar rocket packs or such drop weapons as 1,102-lb (500-kg) bombs may be carried in lieu of the AAMs, tandem racks at times being applied to the glove hardpoints. A 360 deg coverage is provided by *Sirena* 3 (SO-69) passive warning radar, the aerials for which are mounted in the wing glove and above the rudder, and other equipment includes Doppler navigational radar and ILS. Provision is made on the fuselage centreline for a 176 Imp gal (800 l) fuel tank and wet points are provided in the movable wing panels so that, for ferry purposes, a pair of similar-capacity tanks may be hung from non-swivelling pylons, the fully forward sweep position being mandatory when the wing tanks are carried.

The fuselage of *Flogger* is a conventional semi-monocoque structure of basically circular section flattened on each side of the cockpit forward of the air intake trunks, which, also flat-sided, progressively translate to the circular to mate with the rear fuselage. The inboard face of each air inlet is formed by a large flat boundary layer splitter plate, and two small "blow-in" doors are embodied in each trunk, under the wing glove leading edge. The R-29 turbofan in current production models has five LP and six HP compressor stages, a pressure ratio of 12·4 and a mass flow of 231·5 lb (105 kg) per second. Reheat may be varied from 21,825 lb (9 900 kg) to 23,350 lb (11 500 kg) and slam acceleration from idling to maximum takes between three and five seconds, but dry weight at 3,880 lb (1 760 kg) is some 850 lb (385 kg) more than that of the marginally more powerful Pratt & Whitney F100-PW-100.

The manually-variable main wing panels have a minimum sweep angle of 17 deg — at which a strict *g* limitation appertains and the aircraft is not combat rated — with a mid-sweep angle of 45 deg and a maximum angle of 72 deg, which is also the leading-edge sweep angle of the fixed glove. The wing gaps resulting from sweep variation are sealed by — what Panavia refers to as — spring-loaded "feathers", and the movable panels carry full-span, trailing-edge, three-section flaps, the outboard sections of which are actuated independently at full sweep, and extended-chord leading-edge flaps over the outboard two-thirds. Differentially-operated spoilers in the upper surfaces, forward of the trailing-edge flaps, are used in conjunction with the all-moving horizontal tail surfaces.

The undercarriage comprises an aft-retracting twin-wheel nose member with a wrap-around debris-guard — twin wheels having presumably been adopted in order to accommodate the heavy loads imposed on the nose member with full external stores which are well forward of the CG — and single mainwheels with an ingenious if decidedly complex system of retraction. The extremely heavy retraction mechanism raises the wheels into bays in the rear of the air intake trunks and

Some MiG-23BM Flogger-F fighters in V-VS service are now fitted with unusual tandem ordnance racks on the glove hardpoints, as illustrated above.

despite fuselage mounting afford a comparatively wide track, still leaving adequate room for external ordnance under the glove. The starboard-hinging lower portion of the ventral fin is synchronised with the undercarriage.

Variations on the theme

In conformity with the long-standing Soviet practice of evolving tandem two-seat conversion and operational training variants of each new single-seat combat aircraft, such a version of the MiG-23, the *Flogger-C*, entered service at around the same time or shortly after the initial operational single-seat model. The *Flogger-C* (MiG-23U and -23UM) is a combat-capable aeroplane with provision for the same GSh-23L cannon and quartet of AAMs as *Flogger-B*, but most examples of this two-seater display a smaller nose radome, suggesting provision of a less capable radar, which, in all probability, is the J-band *Jay Bird* similar to that installed in the MiG-21bis *Fishbed-N* and possessing an acquisition range of less than 20 miles (32 km) and having no lookdown capability.

A second cockpit for the instructor is inserted aft of the standard cockpit at some significant expense of internal fuel capacity, the second seat being raised slightly higher than that of the forward seat and a retractable periscope provided for the use of its occupant in weapon training and landings. An active ECM antenna is mounted beneath the wing glove on the starboard side and the ILS antenna is centralised and mounted further forward, but in all other respects, *Flogger-C* is essentially similar to the early production *-B* with which it shares the lower-powered R-27 turbofan.

This two-seat model has been supplied in small numbers to all recipients of single-seat *Flogger* variants, and some of its features (eg, the smaller radar and the repositioned ILS antenna) are common to one of the principal export versions, *Flogger-E*, which, like the *-B*, is essentially an air defence aircraft with some limited ground attack capability. Lacking Doppler navigation equipment and the laser rangefinder, and with the less-capable radar, this downgraded version of the MiG-23 is usually armed with the AA-2 *Atoll* missile, and has been exported to a number of countries, usually in concert with *Flogger-C* and *-F*, including Cuba, Iraq, Egypt, Ethiopia, Libya and Syria.

A shift in emphasis from air defence to ground attack and interdiction led to development to a later timescale of two distinct versions of *Flogger* optimised for the air-ground mission, both of which entered V-VS service in the mid-'seventies and both featuring an identical redesigned forward fuselage embodying a drooped nose to improve ground target acquisition. The first of these, the MiG-23BM, or *Flogger-F*, is as yet the only member of the *Flogger* family serving with the V-VS, apart from the two-seater, to have been exported to non WarPac countries (eg, most of the previously-listed recipients of *Flogger-E*) and was, at one time, believed to be *purely* an export model, although, in fact, it is serving with the FA in very substantial numbers, deliveries to Soviet TacAir elements having commenced 1975-76.

Aft of the cockpit, *Flogger-F* is essentially similar to the *-B,* apart from having an R-29B turbofan which, with the same ratings as the R-29 of the current *Flogger-B*, presumably embodies some minor changes to optimise it for the primary air-ground rôle. From the cockpit forward, *Flogger-F* is entirely new. Instead of the ogival radome that characterises the nose of all members of the family intended primarily for air defence, the nose of this variant is tapered sharply downward in side elevation with a flattened bottom contour, and accommodates a laser rangefinder and marked target seeker at its tip, apparently some form of terrain avoidance radar, Doppler and enlarged nosewheels which have necessitated the introduction of blister fairings in the wheel bay doors. This downward-sloping nose has, incidentally, led to those members of the *Flogger* family to which it is applied being dubbed *Utkonos* (Duck nose) by WarPac forces.

The recontoured nose of *Flogger-F* accompanies a deeper windscreen and sloping quarterlight sills, which, too, afford some improvement in downward view for the pilot, and the flat sides of his cockpit incorporate some armour plate to provide a measure of protection from groundfire. The 23-mm twin-barrel GSh-23L cannon is retained, together with the five external stores stations which can carry up to 9,920 lb (4 500 kg) of ordnance (with reduced internal fuel) for short-range missions, loads including up to six 1,102-lb (500-kg) "iron" bombs — with either two on a double rack on the fuselage centreline and one each on bomb mounts attached to the air intake trunk and wing glove hardpoints, or one under each intake trunk and two on tandem racks under each glove half. Alternative loads include various bomblet packs or rocket pods (eg, UV-16-57), and possibly the AS-7 *Kerry* ASM on the glove hardpoints, this radio command guidance missile having a range of about six miles (10 km) and weighing some 2,650 lb (1 200 kg).

Internal fuel tankage of *Flogger-F* is not overly capacious at

(Above right) This close-up photograph of a MiG-27 Flogger-D shows clearly the complex undercarriage common to all members of the Flogger family and the distinctive position of the ordnance pylons of this variant. (Below) A MiG-23BM Flogger-F of a unit based in the Trans-Baikal Military District.

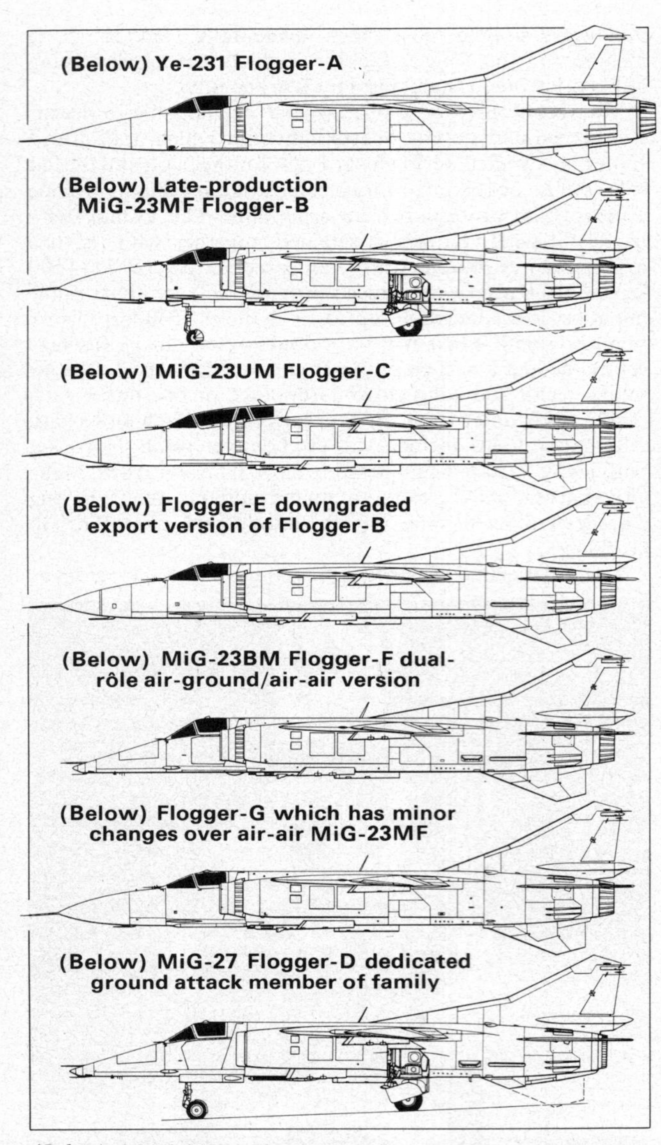

1,265 Imp gal (5 750 l), and this is usually augmented by a 176 Imp gal (800 l) drop tank on the fuselage centreline, while, for ferrying, wet points in the movable wing panels permit two similar tanks to be carried by non-swivelling pylons. Gross weight ranges from 34,170 lb (15 500 kg) clean to a maximum of 44,312 lb (20 100 kg), and performance in clean configuration — which is essentially the same as that of *Flogger-B* — includes maximum speeds ranging from M = 1·1 at sea level to M = 2·3 transiently around the tropopause, a typical combat radius (with centreline fuel tank and minimal allowance for dash or combat) being 590 miles (950 km). At the opposite end of the performance scale, *Flogger-F* lifts off in clean condition at 205 mph (330 km/h) and its approach speed is 174 mph (280 km/h). The data quoted here were provided by the Soviet Union to a potential export purchaser of *Flogger-F* and therefore may be assumed essentially accurate but regrettably included no information relating to field performance, although during a visit to Reims in 1978, *Flogger-G* — with a centreline tank but with much internal equipment deleted and no ammunition for its GSh-23L cannon and therefore presumably approximating to the clean loaded weight of *Flogger-F* — was seen to take-off within 2,625 ft (800 m).

This MiG-23 variant is being supplied to WarPac air forces (eg, Czechoslovakia) and one of the two members of the *Flogger* family that it is proposed that Hindustan Aeronautics will build for the Indian Air Force is the MiG-23BN, which, it can be assumed, will differ from the MiG-23BM alias *Flogger-F* only in terms of equipment specified by the user. Unofficial reports from New Delhi have suggested that this aircraft is being offered to India at a unit cost less than 60 per cent that of Jaguar International; that payment for an initial purchase of complete aircraft, support equipment, pilot and groundcrew training, a number of aircraft in knocked-down component form for assembly by HAL, and subsequent licence manufacture will be spread over 17 years at a nominal interest rate of 2·5 per cent!

Design and designation changes

Whereas *Flogger-F* may be considered as a minimum-change air-ground derivative of the air-air *Flogger-B,* retaining a secondary air defence capability, the second ground attack member of the family, *Flogger-D*, embodied so many changes

(Below) A MiG-21UM Flogger-C tandem two-seat operational trainer in the landing approach. The main undercarriage members are nearly fully extended and the ventral fin is being raised in concert. The small radome of this variant may be clearly seen as can the AAM shoes on fuselage and glove pylons.

A MiG-27 Flogger-D ground attack aircraft of a V-VS unit based in the DDR seen with "everything hanging". The projection above the starboard glove pylon houses a missile guidance antenna.

to optimise it for its rôle that it was deemed to warrant a new designation, entering V-VS service as the MiG-27. Evolved in parallel with *Flogger-F* and incorporating the redesigned nose introduced by that model, albeit with more extensive plate armour in the cockpit sides, *Flogger-D* alias MiG-27 is as yet employed only by the FA and has not been exported, either to WarPac countries or elsewhere.

Commonality with other members of the family is retained by *Flogger-D* insofar as the wings — and their actuating mechanism — and tail surfaces are concerned, and, as previously stated, the nose section (including the larger nosewheels) is shared with *Flogger-F*, but in many other respects it is a very different aeroplane. In developing *Flogger-D* as a dedicated ground attack aircraft, the Mikoyan-Gurevich team consciously — and wisely — sacrificed $M = 2{\cdot}0$ capability to improved low- and medium-altitude mission radius, electing to install a turbofan closely related to the MiG-

continued on page 86

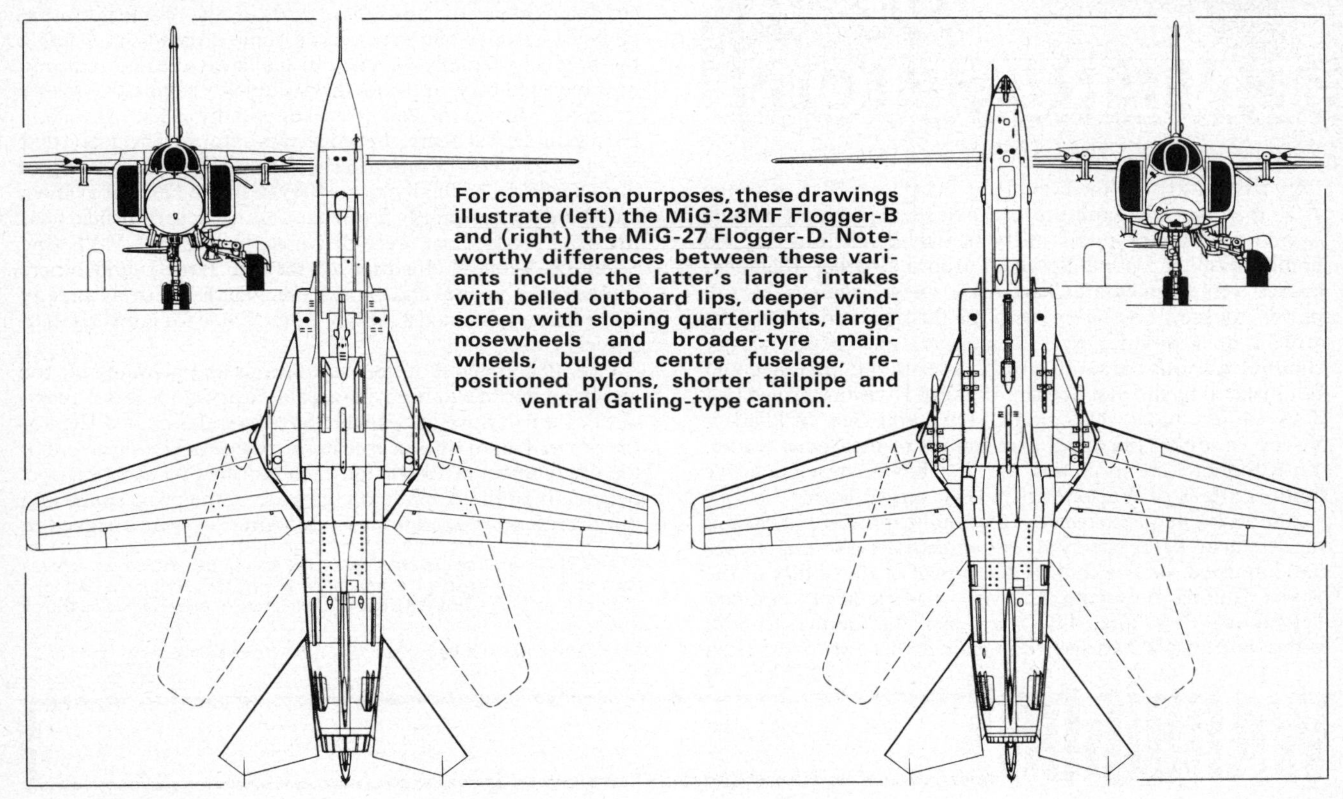

For comparison purposes, these drawings illustrate (left) the MiG-23MF Flogger-B and (right) the MiG-27 Flogger-D. Noteworthy differences between these variants include the latter's larger intakes with belled outboard lips, deeper windscreen with sloping quarterlights, larger nosewheels and broader-tyre mainwheels, bulged centre fuselage, repositioned pylons, shorter tailpipe and ventral Gatling-type cannon.

PE-8: LAST OF A GENERATION

At last light, on the evening of 11 August 1941, with the *Wehrmacht* assault on the Soviet Union barely into its second month, the pilots of 14 heavily-laden four-engined bombers of the 332nd Special Purpose Bomber Regiment coaxed temperamental Charomsky Diesel engines to full power, took-off one by one into the dusk gathering over the airfield at Pushkino, near Leningrad, and began slowly climbing towards the south-west. These aircraft, all that could be mustered by the 81st Special Aviation Division formed two days earlier under the command of Maj-Gen Mikhail V Vodop'yanov on the direct instructions of the Soviet leader, Yosif Stalin, were mounting the first Soviet strategic *heavy* bomber attack of World War II. Their target: Berlin.

The attack had been conceived by Stalin himself as a blow at the very heart of the enemy almost immediately German forces had launched their assault. But sceptical of the ability of the Soviet Union's only comparatively modern heavy bomber, Petlyakov's Pe-8 (alias TB-7), to reach the German capital with a worthwhile load and then regain Soviet territory, he had insisted that the aircraft allocated to this mission first be re-engined with Diesels which offered enhanced range.

The Pe-8, only a couple of dozen examples of which had yet been delivered to the DBA (*Dal'no bombardirovochnaya aviatsiya*, or Long-Range Bomber Force)*, was being built with Mikulin AM-35A 12-cylinder liquid-cooled engines each rated at 1,350 hp for take-off and 1,200 hp at 19,685 ft (6 000 m), and with these possessed a range of barely more than 2,000 miles (3 220 km) when carrying the full 8,818-lb (4 000-kg) warload insisted upon by Stalin — hardly sufficient for a round trip by a necessarily circuitous route between the nearest practical airfield and Berlin which was calculated at upwards of 1,680 miles (2 700 km), and this at max range cruise at best altitude without any allowances for evasive action or over-target dash.

During the previous winter, one example of the bomber had been experimentally fitted with M-40 12-cylinder Vee Diesel engines, which, turbo-supercharged and with nominal ratings of 1,000 hp, had been developed at the TsIAM by A D Charomsky. The re-engined aircraft had demonstrated a range of 4,849 miles (7 820 km) with a 4,410-lb (2 000-kg) bomb load as compared with the 2,920 miles (4 700 km) of which the AM-35A-engined bomber was capable with the same bomb load. Stalin, who was by no means convinced of the efficacy of strategic bombing, had been impressed by this feat and had given Diesel aero engine development his "blessing". Meanwhile, the M-40 engine had been discarded in favour of a more powerful parallel development, the M-30, which had been hurriedly introduced into production despite the protests of Charomsky's team that it was insufficiently developed to be committed to series manufacture at that stage. As the ACh-30B, the production engine was nominally rated at 1,080 hp but offered 1,500 hp for take-off, and heavier and less powerful than the AM-35A, its installation in the Pe-8, while giving the desired range increment, exacted penalties on maximum and cruise speeds, and on operational altitude.

The establishment of the 332nd Regiment† under the command of Major Viktorin I Lebedev specifically for operation of the Pe-8 had virtually coincided with the commencement of hostilities, and in the confusion that reigned, Lebedev had experienced some difficulty in *locating* the bombers actually assigned to his newly-created unit and now required back at the factory as quickly as possible for re-engining. Most of the Pe-8s were supposedly at Kiev/Borispol, but upon arrival there, Lebedev was informed vaguely that they had flown off "in an easterly direction!" After scouring all likely airfields, he finally located seven of the Pe-8s at Poltava and these were promptly flown back to the factory airfield near Moscow. Four more were delivered by the NII V-VS (the Scientific Research Institute of the Air Force), and others trickled back in ones and twos; these, together with six already at the factory, making a total of 22 available for conversion to Diesel power.

Overall command of the preparations and planning for the attack on Berlin had been assigned to Maj-Gen Vodop'yanov, one of the first Soviet aviators to have been designated Hero of the Soviet Union (for his rôle in the rescue of the survivors of the *Chelyushkin* in 1934), and each morning he had to report personally to the Kremlin on the state of the programme and the aircraft serviceability situation. Aircrews were assigned to

**The DBA was to be dissolved later that month but was to provide the nucleus of a new strategic component, the ADD (*Aviatsiya dal'nevo deistviya*, or Long-Range Aviation) that was to be inaugurated in March 1942.*

†332 Bombardirovochnyi aviapolk osobovo naznacheniya.

WARBIRDS

(Above and below right) The first ANT-42 photographed during factory trials in March 1937, at which time all four AM-34 engines had individual radiators. (Heading photo on opposite page) Pe-8 No 66 photographed from the air after its arrival in Washington carrying Foreign Minister Molotov in May 1942.

the unit from Aeroflot, Aviation of the Northern Seas Route (ie, arctic) and test centres, as well as from other V-VS units, and there were soon more crews than aircraft.

Although re-engining of the Pe-8 airframes proceeded at a rapid pace, the inadequate development of the Charomsky Diesels became painfully obvious as the conversions were completed and the aircraft tested. Driving VISh-24 constant-speed propellers and fitted with two-stage centrifugal superchargers, the ACh-30B engines were prone to seizing without any readily obvious reason — revolutions would fluctuate wildly and the engine would then cough and cut! The Diesels were particularly temperamental at altitude and after seizing could rarely be restarted until descent was made to a comparatively low altitude. The fuel flow for each engine was adjusted manually by the pilot, this calling for considerable skill, and the existing problems with the engines were exacerbated by fuel mismanagement, which, too, resulted in stoppages.

Attempts to rectify the shortcomings of the engines, flight testing and crew training all proceeded simultaneously at the factory airfield and Stalin had grown increasingly impatient at the delay in readying the unit for the attack. Finally, all 22 aircraft had received their ACh-30B Diesels and Maj-Gen Vodop'yanov was called to the Kremlin and informed by the Soviet leader that the attack on Berlin would be mounted by every available aircraft on the night of 11-12 August. Vodop'yanov requested that Stettin (now Szczecin) be designated an alternative target in the event that the German capital could not be reached. Stalin reluctantly granted this request, and added, "but you *must* reach Berlin!"

The airfield at Pushkino had been selected as the nearest practical base to the German capital from which to launch the raid, and it was envisaged that the bombers would follow a somewhat circuitous route around the Estonian and Latvian coastlines to evade interception by *Luftwaffe* fighters, then proceed down the Baltic and make landfall north of Stettin. The total distance for the trip out and back was calculated to be 1,680 miles (2 700 km) which was to be flown at long-range cruise of 175 mph (282 km/h), the enemy coastline being crossed at about 23,000 ft (7 000 m). The aircraft were to take-off at last light in order to arrive over Berlin at approximately midnight.

Only 18 of the Pe-8s could be made airworthy for the flight to Pushkino and four of these had to return to the factory airfield with malfunctioning engines, while a fifth nearly came to grief when it was shot at by Soviet anti-aircraft artillery as it made its approach to Pushkino! A day of frenzied preparations followed, and during the afternoon of 11 August, Maj-Gen Vodop'yanov, who was to pilot one of the Pe-8s, gave the crews their final briefing. After some delays, the bombers began taking-off at 2115 hours, but one of the first, piloted by

(Above right) The first ANT-42 in its original form, showing the bulged fairing in the starboard side of the upper decking to accommodate the ATsN engine, which, at the time of the photograph, had still to be installed. (Below) The first ANT-42 after installation of the ATsN, the exhaust staining from which may be seen under the glazing in the upper decking.

Maj Konstantin Yegorov, suffered a double engine failure on one side, plunging into the ground in a steep bank. The remaining 13 began their slow climb-out, turning towards the Baltic, although the aircraft piloted by Capt Aleksandr Tyagunin was first attacked by I-16 fighters and then by Soviet anti-aircraft fire, crashing into the sea.

Vodop'yanov, who was flying with Maj E K Pusep — with whom he had flown in the Arctic — as second pilot, experienced little trouble until, 12 minutes from the German capital at 22,965 ft (7 000 m) altitude, one of the Charomsky Diesels began to falter. He nevertheless pressed on, dropping the 8,818-lb (4 000-kg) bomb load just as he was bracketed by heavy *flak*, a starboard fuel tank being holed and the aircraft suffering other damage. Vodop'yanov calculated that, as a result of the holed tank, he had four hours fuel remaining for a five-hour flight and therefore instructed his navigator, A P Shtepenko, to give him a straight-line course back to base rather than follow the circuitous route by which Berlin had been reached. The aircraft flew into a low pressure area and began to ice up, snow penetrating the flight deck through holes left by *flak* splinters and covering the instruments. The low pressure area was finally cleared, by which time the aircraft was down to some 6,560 ft (2 000 m) over Estonia and somewhere near the frontline. Shtepenko announced, "ETA base 30 minutes" when, at that moment, all four engines seized, the aircraft crashing tail-down into a forest. Miraculously, none of the crew suffered injury and all managed to reach Soviet-held territory.

Vodop'yanov was rushed to Moscow and the next day reported to Stalin in the Kremlin. A number of Party chiefs, Marshals and Generals were present, and the Soviet leader looked grim when he asked for Vodop'yanov's report on the attack. The Major-General answered, "Eleven of our aircraft reached the target, six aircraft regained their base, one was shot down by our own anti-aircraft artillery, one is missing and

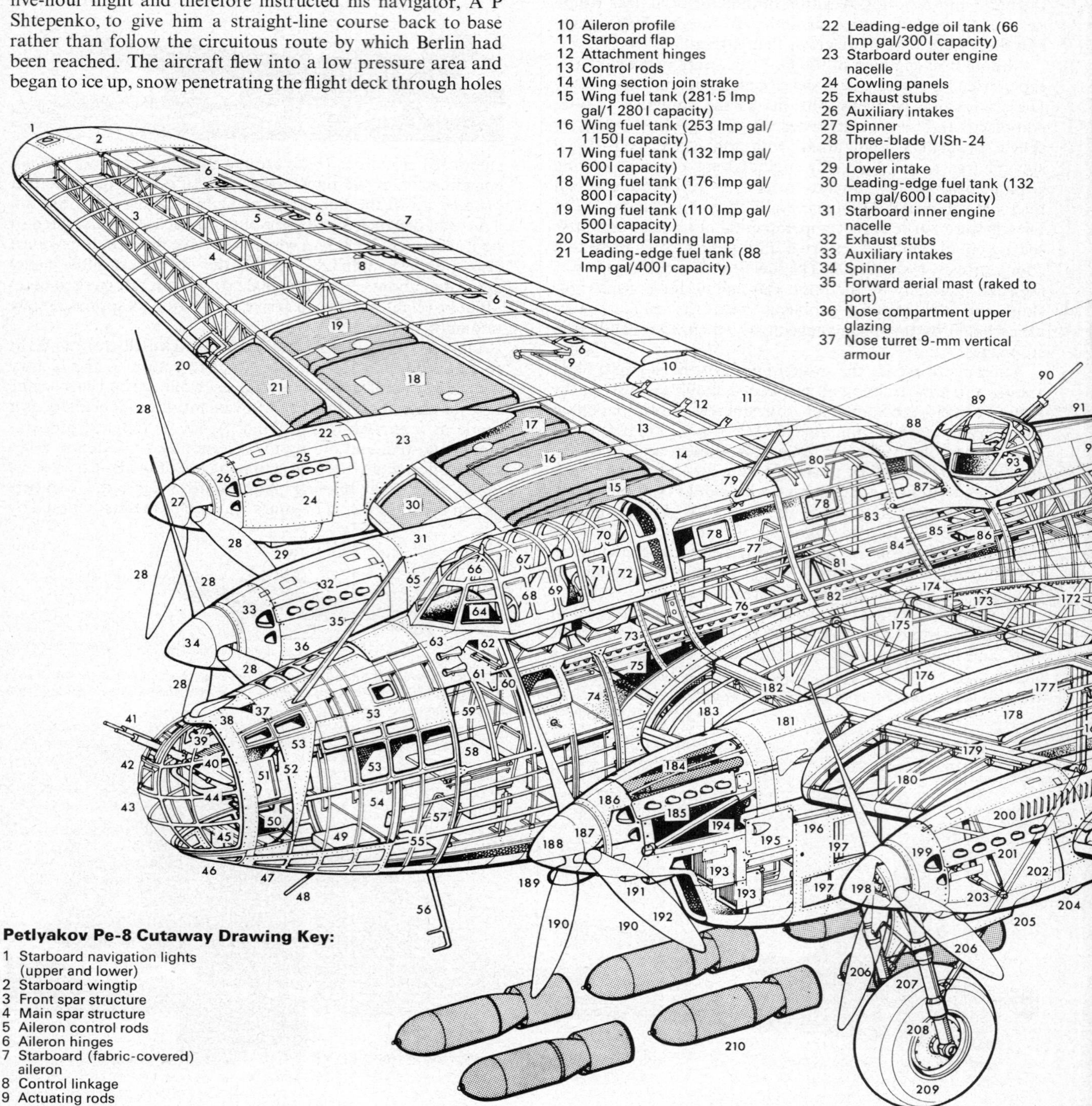

Petlyakov Pe-8 Cutaway Drawing Key:

1 Starboard navigation lights (upper and lower)
2 Starboard wingtip
3 Front spar structure
4 Main spar structure
5 Aileron control rods
6 Aileron hinges
7 Starboard (fabric-covered) aileron
8 Control linkage
9 Actuating rods
10 Aileron profile
11 Starboard flap
12 Attachment hinges
13 Control rods
14 Wing section join strake
15 Wing fuel tank (281·5 Imp gal/1 280 l capacity)
16 Wing fuel tank (253 Imp gal/1 150 l capacity)
17 Wing fuel tank (132 Imp gal/600 l capacity)
18 Wing fuel tank (176 Imp gal/800 l capacity)
19 Wing fuel tank (110 Imp gal/500 l capacity)
20 Starboard landing lamp
21 Leading-edge fuel tank (88 Imp gal/400 l capacity)
22 Leading-edge oil tank (66 Imp gal/300 l capacity)
23 Starboard outer engine nacelle
24 Cowling panels
25 Exhaust stubs
26 Auxiliary intakes
27 Spinner
28 Three-blade VISh-24 propellers
29 Lower intake
30 Leading-edge fuel tank (132 Imp gal/600 l capacity)
31 Starboard inner engine nacelle
32 Exhaust stubs
33 Auxiliary intakes
34 Spinner
35 Forward aerial mast (raked to port)
36 Nose compartment upper glazing
37 Nose turret 9-mm vertical armour

38 Turret mechanism/attachment fairing
39 Turret electric motor drive
40 Ammunition feed
41 Twin 7,62-mm ShKAS machine guns (650 rounds per gun)
42 Nose turret hinged panels
43 Nose turret
44 Machine gun mounting
45 Turret lower support ring
46 Chin fixed glazing
47 Nose (bomb aimer's) optically flat panels
48 Chin machine-gun position (provisional)
49 Bomb aimer's station
50 Bomb-sight
51 Ammunition magazine
52 Nose gunner's sling seat support
53 Nose compartment side glazing
54 Forward fuselage structure
55 Crew forward entry hatch
56 Twin pitot heads
57 Bomb aimer's jump seat
58 Navigator's station
59 Fuselage frames
60 Control cable linkage housing
61 First pilot's rudder pedal assembly
62 Instrument panel
63 Venturi tubes
64 Panel coaming
65 Windscreen panels
66 Tandem-pilot cockpit canopy (offset to port)
67 First pilot's 9-mm contoured armoured seat
68 First pilot's control wheel
69 Canopy sliding section
70 Second pilot's 9-mm contoured armoured seat
71 Second pilot's control wheel
72 Canopy sliding section
73 Cockpit floor support structure
74 Fuselage frame
75 Fuselage/wingroot former frame
76 Aft flight deck area
77 Radio-operator's and aircraft commander's stations
78 Flight deck side windows
79 Intermediate aerial mast (raked to port)
80 Formers
81 Wing spar centre-section tubular structure
82 Centre-section fuel tank (317 Imp gal/1 440 l capacity)
83 Bulkhead
84 Fuselage/wingroot former frame
85 Dorsal turret support structure
86 Dorsal (standing) gunner's fire step
87 External handrail
88 Wind deflector shield
89 Dorsal powered turret
90 Dorsal 20-mm ShVAK cannon (200 rounds)
91 Hinged turtleback (cannon stowage)
92 Fairing
93 Cannon mounting
94 Fuselage structure
95 Ammunition magazine
96 Entry ladder stowage
97 Fuselage structural frame
98 Wingroot fairing
99 Crew aft entry door
100 Door inner frame
101 Fuselage metal panel skinning (1-mm)
102 Aft fuselage side window
103 Rear bulkhead sections
104 Semi-monocoque fuselage structure
105 Fuselage frames
106 Stringers
107 Aft fuselage catwalk
108 Electrical/oxygen leads
109 Fuselage aft frame
110 Tailfin root fairing
111 Starboard tailplane
112 Elevator hinges
113 Starboard elevator
114 Tailfin leading-edge panels
115 Multi-spar tailfin structure
116 Aerial attachment
117 Rudder upper hinge
118 Rudder frame
119 Rudder trim tab
120 Rudder centre hinge
121 Tail navigation light
122 Rudder lower contour cut-out
123 Tail turret deflector plate
124 Powered tail turret
125 Tail gunner's sling seat
126 Cannon mounting
127 Tail 20-mm ShVAK cannon (200 rounds)
128 Elevator tab
129 Port elevator
130 Elevator hinges
131 Tailplane structure
132 Shell ejector chute
133 Ammunition magazine
134 Feed mechanism
135 Multi-spar tailplane attachment points
136 Tailplane root fillet
137 Tailwheel support strut
138 Shock absorber
139 Non-retractable tailwheel
140 Tail surface control rods
141 Fuselage skin panels
142 Lower longeron
143 Port flap structure
144 Wing rib stations
145 Flap profile
146 Port (fabric-covered) aileron
147 Aileron actuating linkage
148 Control rods
149 Hinge point
150 Access panel
151 Aileron outboard profile
152 Port wingtip structure
153 Port navigation lights (upper and lower)
154 Outer rib station
155 Leading-edge panels
156 Front spar structure
157 Wing ribs
158 Main spar structure
159 Port landing lamp
160 Leading-edge fuel tank (88 Imp gal/400 l capacity)
161 Wing fuel tank (110 Imp gal/500 l capacity)
162 Leading-edge oil tank (66 Imp gal/300 l capacity)
163 Wing fuel tank (176 Imp gal/800 l capacity)
164 Inboard nacelle underwing turret
165 Underwing 12,7-mm BT machine gun (220 rounds)
166 Inboard arc-of-fire interruptor frame
167 Machine gun mounting
168 Gunner's folding seat (optional seated/kneeling/prone positions)
169 Inboard nacelle wall entry hatch
170 Wing section join strake
171 Upper wing surface turret access hatch
172 Wing inboard structure
173 Control rod/cable (from cockpit) transition
174 Main spar tubular structure
175 Wing fuel tank (286 Imp gal/1 300 l capacity)
176 Wing fuel tank (99 Imp gal/450 l capacity)
177 Wing fuel tank (281·5 Imp gal/1 280 l capacity)
178 Fuselage bomb-bay
179 Front spar
180 Leading-edge fuel tank (132 Imp gal/600 l capacity)
181 Port inner engine nacelle
182 Front spar tubular structure
183 Leading-edge oil tank (66 Imp gal/300 l capacity)
184 Port inner AM-35A engine
185 Exhaust stubs
186 Auxiliary intakes
187 Fuselage bomb-bay forward wall
188 Spinner
189 Ventral D/F loop bullet fairing
190 Three-blade VISh-24 propeller
191 Lower intakes
192 Radiator intake
193 Twin (inner/outer) radiators
194 Engine bearer
195 Side intake scoop
196 Engine bearer support strut
197 Exhaust/cooling (adjustable) gills
198 Spinner
199 Auxiliary intakes
200 Port inner nacelle external side louvres
201 Exhaust stubs
202 Undercarriage support strut
203 Undercarriage retraction strut
204 Port outer engine nacelle
205 Undercarriage door
206 Three-blade propeller
207 Mainwheel legs
208 Oleo struts
209 Port mainwheel
210 Standard bombload (6 x 220-lb/100-kg bombs)
PILOT PRESS COPYRIGHT DRAWING

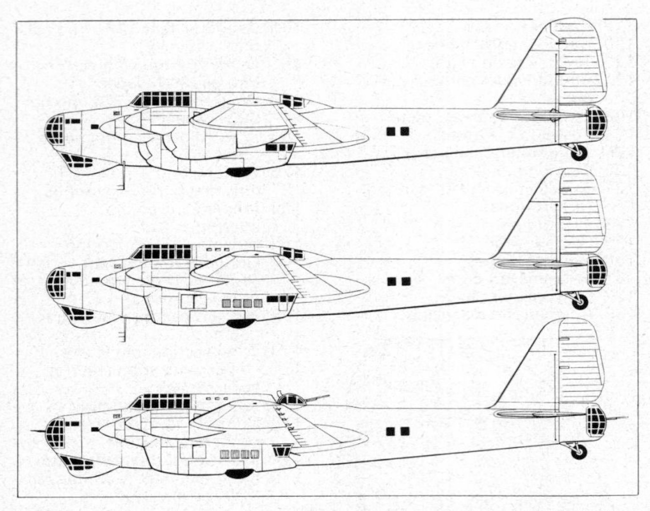

(Top to bottom) The first prototype as flown in 1937 with individual radiators for its AM-34 engines. The first prototype as modified in 1938 with radiators removed from the outer engine nacelles and incorporated in deeper inner nacelles, and venting through multiple grilles. Note revised rudder and balancing. The second prototype with full armament and sliding dorsal panels replaced by rotating turret. Nacelle turrets of definitive design.

the rest made forced landings owing to engine failures. My aircraft crash-landed in a forest!"

Virtually without exception, the Pe-8s engaged on the mission had suffered difficulties with their engines. The inner starboard Diesel of Lt Vasily Bidny's aircraft caught fire after 40 minutes' flying. The fire was extinguished after the engine had been shut down, but at 19,685 ft (6 000 m) near Danzig (now Gdansk), the port outer engine also failed. Unable to maintain altitude on two engines with a full bombload, the aircraft drifted down to 6,560 ft (2000 m) and Bidny released his bombs over Stettin, making a successful forced landing near Leningrad after exhausting the last of his fuel. It transpired that the missing aircraft had been shot down near Helsinki by Finnish anti-aircraft fire after its pilot, Lt Aleksandr Panfilov, became disorientated on the return flight.

Major M Ugrymov had run out of fuel near Veliky Luki, but had made a successful landing near a tractor station and had refuelled the aircraft with buckets and had then regained his base. Maj Aleksandr Kurban had been forced to land at Krasnoye Selo after exhausting his fuel — his engines had failed several times but he had succeeded in restarting them by descending to altitudes of 9,840 ft (3 000 m) and less, consuming a considerable amount of fuel in the process. The other pilots, Maj I Lisachev, Capt Sergei Asyamov, Sr Lt Arsen Churilin and Capt Makarenko, succeeded in reaching Pushkino, but all had tales of engine problems, prompting Vodop'yanov to blurt out at the Kremlin meeting, "I'm ready to tear out those damned Diesels with my teeth! Engines must be reliable for operational flying and flying with these Diesels means the loss of aircraft and men." He added, "And one more thing, we must have homing beacons for without them we wander around like blind kittens." One of those present responded, "What would you like us to do — direct the fascist aircraft straight to your airfield?" At this, Vodop'yanov responded with some heat, "Surely it is obvious that such beacons would be sited well away from the field — we should not have much difficulty in flying the last 50-100 kilometres from the beacon to our base!"

Stalin then terminated the argument, dismissing Vodop'yanov, but, coincidentally, one week later he was ordered to participate in the testing of a Pe-8 with Shvetsov M-82 air-cooled radial engines and, shortly afterwards, the *Pchelka* (Little Bee) homing beacon became available.

End of a line

The Pe-8 was to be the last in a line of bombers, which, born on drawing boards under the aegis of Andrei N Tupolev, the doyen of the Soviet aircraft industry, were in some ways in advance of world standards in concept if not technology. Intended as a successor to the TB-3, the design of a new long-range heavy bomber was initiated early in 1934 by a design brigade at the TsAGI led by Vladimir M Petlyakov assisted by Yosif F Nezval. Petlyakov was later appointed chief designer at the TsAGI Factory of Experimental Design, having gained large aircraft design experience as a deputy to Tupolev in creating the ANT-20 *Maxim Gorki* and in the ANT-26 (alias TB-6) 12-engined bomber abandoned in favour of the new project, which, assigned the official designation TB-7, received the design bureau designation ANT-42.

Design work on the ANT-42 proceeded slowly and produced a relatively conventional cantilever mid-wing monoplane with retractable main undercarriage members and a state-of-the-art all-metal structure, primarily of dural D16. The multi-spar wings were thick enough to provide a crawlway for gunners to reach defensive positions that it was planned to incorporate in the rear of the inboard engine nacelles, the spars themselves being of girder type with steel-tube booms, and the fuselage was an oval-section semi-monocoque with riveted light alloy skinning. The design was not without novelty, however, as Tupolev had proposed the introduction of a separate centralised supercharger unit, or ATsN*, having

**Agregat tsentral'novo nadduva* — central boosting unit.

(Below) The first prototype ANT-42 with definitive radiator arrangement photographed in 1938 while undergoing NII V-VS trials with a ski undercarriage, and (above right) a close-up of the second ANT-42 with the exhaust pipe for the ATsN engine being visible beneath the dorsal gun turret.

(Above) Pe-8 No 66 photographed after its arrival at Leuchars in May 1942, with Hurricanes of No 56 OTU in background. (Below right) One of the Pe-8s fitted with the redesigned nose section with a gimbal-mounted 20-mm cannon replacing the twin-gun turret previously standard.

prevailed upon Vladimir Ya Klimov to develop a reduction gear to enable his M-100 liquid-cooled engine to drive a compressor for four wing-mounted AM-34FRN 12-cylinder water-cooled engines each rated at 930/1,200 hp. The intention was to install the auxiliary engine in the fuselage aft of the flight deck and to starboard above the weapons bay, but if the idea was ingenious, the problems its realisation presented were not simple of solution. The task of designing the reduction gear drive was eventually to be performed successfully at the TsIAM by A A Mikulin assisted by K V Minknev, but special bearings had to be developed to cope with the 25,000-30,000 rpm of the superchargers and special materials were demanded by gas temperatures in excess of 1,000°C and anticipated ambient air temperatures at altitude as low as −60°C.

A commission charged with overseeing the development of the new bomber was headed by Marshal M N Tukhachevsky, Chief of Red Army Ordnance — to be executed on 11 June 1937 on charges of espionage, sabotage and subversive alliances — who took a close personal interest in the programme, as did also Gen Ya A Alksnis, Head of GU-VVS, who, on 23 November 1937, was to be thrown into the Lubyanka prison and die eight months later. This later "removal" of two of the bomber's principal proponents was to prove an unfortunate augury.

Construction work on a single prototype of the ANT-42 commenced on 27 July 1934, more than two years elapsing before, on 9 November 1936, it was to be completed and then without the ATsN-2 to supercharge its propulsive units and so much a fundamental part of its concept. Flight trials were initiated on 27 December 1936, with Gen M M Gromov at the controls, but the first series of factory trials, which were to continue until 20 March 1937, were delayed as a result of damage suffered in a heavy landing made by the test pilot that succeeded Gromov after initial tests. State trials followed between 11 August and 28 October 1937, following which the ANT-42 was returned to the factory for installation of the ATsN-2 supercharger unit, and for the amalgamation of the individual radiators into enlarged nacelles inboard. With the auxiliary engine *in situ*, testing was resumed between 6 March and 30 April 1938, factory and NII V-VS trials being conducted in parallel.

The auxiliary engine concept was considered a secret to be closely-guarded, but visitors to the factory inevitably expressed curiosity when seeing the ANT-42 standing on the factory airfield hardstanding with its propellers still yet the aircraft emitting an awesome noise and vibrating strongly. On such occasions, the chief engineer, Ye K Stoman, would perform a charade of "curing" the problem — simply switching off the hidden auxiliary engine until the visitors had departed — but how many this fooled . . . !

Meanwhile, the flight testing of the first prototype had yielded results that were considered to warrant proceeding with a second and improved prototype, the first studies for which had been initiated in April 1936, and which was foreseen

as a pre-series aircraft. The second prototype was to have improved AM-34FRNV engines, an M-100A as the basis of its ATsN, increased fuel capacity and full armament. The preparation of production drawings for an envisaged pre-series of five aircraft, in fact, began in April 1937, and the second prototype was to make its initial flight on 26 July 1938.

The first prototype ANT-42 weighed 39,680 lb (18 000 kg) empty and had provision for 18,188 lb (8 250 kg) of fuel, which, with maximum overload bombs totalling 8,818 lb (4 000 kg), gave a take-off weight of 70,547 lb (32 000 kg). During trials, the ANT-42 succeeded in demonstrating a level speed of 250 mph (403 km/h) at 26,245 ft (8 000 m) and it was suggested that such placed it beyond the reach of contemporary anti-aircraft artillery and fighters, but this performance was achieved at a loaded weight of 52,600 lb (23 860 kg), without any warload and only part fuel, and Gen Aleksandr Loktionov, who had replaced Gen Alksnis as Head of GU-VVS and was a former rifle brigade commander, expressed little enthusiasm for a programme to which his predecessor and the ill-fated Tukhachevsky had subscribed whole-heartedly. Indeed, it was to be suggested that the ANT-42 could well prove to be yet another record-breaker without practical military application, doubt being expressed that it was capable of carrying the specified bomb load.

The ANT-42 development programme had hardly been aided by the arrest of Vladimir Petlyakov in one of the purges that were so much a part of the Soviet scene at this time, and his incarceration in the special NKVD detention centre established at Factory No 156, most of the progressive development of the bomber falling to the lot of his deputy, Yosif Nezval. Despite this setback and the growth of the tactical air support school of thought at the expense of that propounding strategic bombing tenets, work continued, the first prototype being re-engined with AM-34FRNV engines and its VISh-3B propellers being progressively replaced by VISh-4s and then -24s, testing of this aircraft continuing from 29 September 1938 through 26 March 1939. Factory and NII V-VS testing of the second prototype was undertaken simultaneously from 28 July 1938 until 28 December 1938, but the V-VS remained adamant in its refusal to accept the ATsN — which had been nicknamed the *solovei* (nightingale) by test crews on account of the peculiar whistling sound that it emitted in flight — and Nezval was forced to undertake major redesign, deleting the auxiliary engine and fitting Mikulin AM-35 (later AM-35A) engines each with its own supercharger.

The fate of the entire programme nevertheless hung in the

balance, despite the improvements promised by the switch to AM-35 engines and discarding of the ATsN principle. The future of V-VS strategic bombing in general and that of the ANT-42 alias TB-7 in particular were the subjects of a conference held in the Kremlin early in 1939, and attended by Stalin, Molotov, Voroshilov, various party officials and representatives of the V-VS and the aircraft industry. Aleksandr Filin, the chief of the NII V-VS and one of the few remaining advocates of the strategic bombing concept, staunchly argued in favour of committing the new bomber to series production. Most of Stalin's advisers had concluded from studies of the air war over Spain, then in its closing phases, that the value of air power as a tactical weapon was thoroughly proven whereas its value as a strategic weapon was purely theoretical. In consequence, the Soviet leader was highly sceptical of the wisdom of committing valuable raw materials, skilled labour and factory space to production of an unproven weapon. Few supported Filin openly, as the heavy bomber development programme was inexorably linked with the discredited Tukhachevsky and Alksnis. After further advocacy on the part of Filin, however, Stalin gave way, saying, "Oh well, let it be as you wish, but you haven't convinced me!"

It was in such half-hearted fashion that Petlyakov's heavy bomber was temporarily reprieved, albeit overshadowed by Stalin's lack of enthusiasm, indeed, tacit disapproval, and this was to join with circumstances in bringing about the bomber's early production demise. Preparations for series production of the TB-7, as the bomber was at that time officially designated, were commenced at Factory No 22, on the outskirts of Moscow, and plans were also formulated for a second production source at Factory No 125 then being built at Povolozh'e, Kazan.

The first pre-series TB-7 was rolled out at Factory No 22 in the early summer of 1940, so much time having now elapsed between original conception and initial production that the structure of the bomber was positively primitive by standards that had evolved in the interim. The pre-series aircraft were powered by AM-35s pending availability of the high-altitude AM-35A standardised for production-series aircraft. Developed at the TsIAM by Aleksandr Mikulin, the AM-35A was both a large and extremely heavy engine, with a dry weight of 1,830 lb (830 kg), but with a single-stage supercharger, it offered 1,350 hp for take-off and maximum continuous ratings of 1,200 hp at 19,685 ft (6 000 m) and 1,150 hp at 22,965 ft (7 000 m). Driving VISh-24 constant-speed three-bladed propellers, the AM-35A engines had radiators in the inboard nacelles only, these cooling both inner and outer engines. Provision was made for a maximum of 28,924 lb (13 120 kg) of fuel distributed between 19 thin-gauge unprotected light alloy tanks within the thick TsAGI-40 section wing — five in the centre section, five in each outer wing panel and two in the leading edge on each side.

The crew complement comprised 11 members, with pilot and co-pilot seated in tandem and offset slightly to port. The backs of both pilots' seats were of 9-mm armour and some limited armour protection was provided for the navigator and the engine nacelle gunners. All gun positions were initially fitted with single or twin 7,62-mm ShKAS machine guns, but while the nose turret retained paired ShKAS weapons, larger-calibre guns were fitted in all other positions on the production model, each of the aft-firing engine nacelle positions being provided with a 12,7-mm BT machine gun with 220 rounds and both dorsal and tail turrets being fitted with a 20-mm ShVAK cannon with 200 rounds. The internal weapons bay could accommodate a maximum of 8,818 lb (4 000 kg) of bombs in overload condition, this usually consisting of two 4,409-lb (2 000-kg) bombs, but more normal loads comprised six 220-lb (100-kg), four 551-lb (250-kg) or two 2,204-lb (1 000-kg) bombs.

The empty weight of 36,728 lb (16 660 kg) was some 2,954 lb (1 340 kg) less than the ATsN-equipped second prototype, but with the normal maximum load of 32,540 lb (14 760 kg), the TB-7 was somewhat underpowered at 69,268 lb (31 420 kg) all up and drag was comparatively high — 8·9 per cent of this being contributed by the profusion of round-headed rivets. In consequence, maximum and cruise speeds were unimpressive, although field performance was good, distance to clear a 49-ft (15-m) obstacle ranging from 1,200 yards (1 100 m) to 2,515 yards (2 300 m), depending on the AUW, and the average landing run being 635 yards (580 m).

Production at Factory No 22 was slow in gaining momentum, in part due to shortages of materials and the priority in the supply of AM-35A engines allocated to the MiG-3 fighter, and in part to the somewhat apathetic attitude of the V-VS towards strategic bombing, which, in turn, no doubt influenced factory management attitudes. Furthermore, part of the factory was given over to production of the higher priority tactical Pe-2. Certainly, relatively few of the bombers had been accepted by the V-VS by the time that the *Wehrmacht* initiated Operation *Barbarossa*, and the frenetic re-engining programme was begun in preparation for an attack on Berlin, as already related.

Nezval had, in fact, already been investigating various alternative power plants for the Pe-8 bomber, as the TB-7 was now to be redesignated, and he had also evolved a passenger-

Pe-8 No 66 photographed at Washington in front of Hangar No 20 in early June 1942. Note the open trap above the port inboard nacelle gun position and the fairing aft of the dorsal turret accommodating the stowed 20-mm cannon.

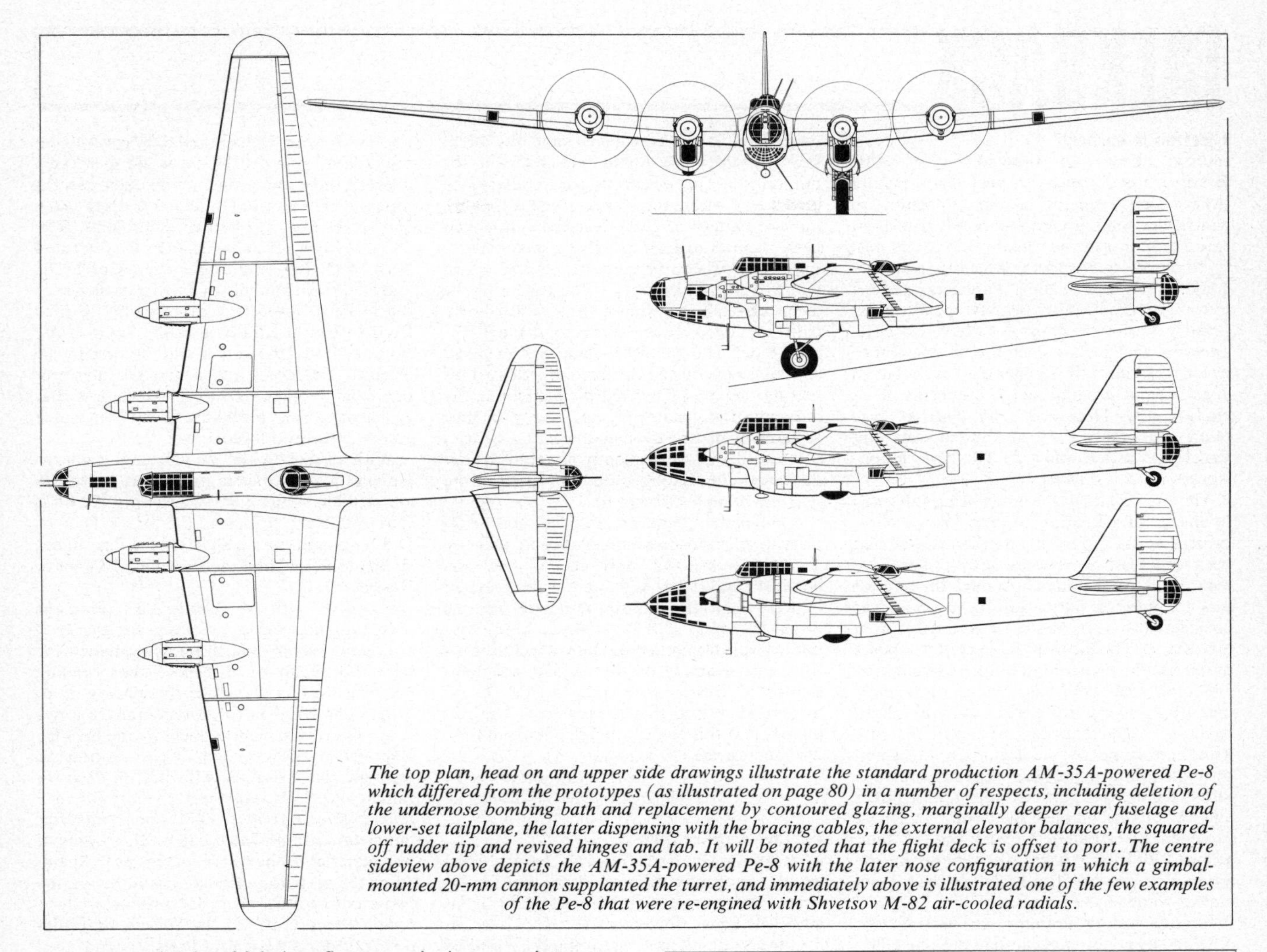

The top plan, head on and upper side drawings illustrate the standard production AM-35A-powered Pe-8 which differed from the prototypes (as illustrated on page 80) in a number of respects, including deletion of the undernose bombing bath and replacement by contoured glazing, marginally deeper rear fuselage and lower-set tailplane, the latter dispensing with the bracing cables, the external elevator balances, the squared-off rudder tip and revised hinges and tab. It will be noted that the flight deck is offset to port. The centre sideview above depicts the AM-35A-powered Pe-8 with the later nose configuration in which a gimbal-mounted 20-mm cannon supplanted the turret, and immediately above is illustrated one of the few examples of the Pe-8 that were re-engined with Shvetsov M-82 air-cooled radials.

carrying version in which Aeroflot was evincing some interest. One example of the bomber had been experimentally fitted with four Mikulin AM-37s offering 1,400 hp for take-off and 1,300 hp at rated altitude, but no noteworthy improvement in performance had been recorded, and another had been fitted with a pair of AM-37s and two Shvetsov M-82 14-cylinder two-row radials, which, with two-speed superchargers, provided 1,700 hp for take-off and a nominal maximum continuous power of 1,540 hp at 6,725 ft (2 050 m). The latter was essentially an installational test-bed and not a proposed production configuration for obvious reasons.

The Charomsky Diesel engine was *officially* favoured as a replacement for the AM-35A, and the loss in speed and altitude performance in which its installation resulted and as revealed by tests conducted in the spring of 1941 were viewed as acceptable penalties exacted in exchange for immensely enhanced range capability. The serious teething troubles being suffered by the Charomsky power plant were hopefully to be resolved — although events were to prove that, if mollified, they had been by no means eradicated by the time Pe-8s powered by this engine attacked the German capital — but the M-82 was seen as a back-up, for the decision to take the AM-35A out of production in order to permit concentration on the low-altitude AM-38 for the Il-2 *shturmovik* rendered the question of a replacement engine of some urgency. In fact, two Pe-8s were being completed with the Shvetsov radials in Factory No 22 when Soviet-German hostilities commenced, and it was in the flight testing of one of these that Maj-Gen Vodop'yanov was to participate shortly after the Berlin attack.

What Pe-8 bombers were available to the V-VS were,

continued on page 101

Petlyakov Pe-8 Specification

Power Plant: Four Mikulin AM-35A 12-cylinder Vee liquid-cooled engines each rated at 1,350 hp at 2,050 rpm for take-off, 1,200 hp at 2,050 rpm at 19,685 ft (6 000 m) and 1,150 hp at 2,050 rpm at 22,965 ft (7 000 m), driving three-bladed constant-speed VISh-24 propellers of 12·8 ft (3,90 m) diam. Maximum fuel capacity (overload condition), 3,431·5 Imp gal (15 600 l) distributed between 19 (one fuselage and 18 wing) tanks.

Performance: (At 55,115 lb/25 000 kg) Max speed, 212 mph (342 km/h) at sea level, 265 mph (427 km/h) at 20,865 ft (6 360 m); max continuous cruise, 230 mph (370 km/h) at 20,340 ft (6 200 m); range cruise, 174 mph (280 km/h); time to 16,405 ft (5 000 m), 14·6 min, to 19,685 ft (6 000 m), 17·4 min; service ceiling, 26,900 ft (8 200 m); absolute ceiling, 33,790 ft (10 300 m); max range, 2,113 mls (3 400 km) at long-range cruise. (At 69,268 lb/31 420 kg) Max speed, 208 mph (335 km/h) at sea level, 255 mph (410 km/h) at 19,685 ft (6 000 m); max continuous cruise, 226 mph (364 km/h) at 19,685 ft (6 000 m); range cruise, 170 mph (273 km/h); time to 19,685 ft (6 000 m), 28 min; service ceiling, 24,605 ft (7 500 m); absolute ceiling, 27,560 ft (8 400 m); max range (overload fuel and 4,410-lb/2 000-kg bomb load), 2,920 mls (4 700 km).

Weights: Empty, 36,728 lb (16 660 kg); empty equipped, 40,520 lb (18 380 kg); max take-off (normal condition), 69,268 lb (31 420 kg); max fuel, 28,924 lb (13 120 kg); max oil, 1,477 lb (670 kg); max bomb load, 8,818 lb (4 000 kg).

Dimensions: Span, 127 ft 11⅘ in (39,01 m); length, 77 ft 4¾ in (23,59 m); height, 20 ft 4 in (6,20 m); wing area, 2,031 sq ft (188,68 m^2); wheel track, 22 ft 11½ in (7,00 m).

Armament: Nose turret with twin 7,62-mm ShKAS machine guns with 650 rpg (later replaced by 20-mm ShVAK cannon with 200 rounds); one 12,7-mm BT machine gun with 220 rounds in each inboard engine nacelle position, and one 20-mm ShVAK cannon with 200 rounds in dorsal and tail turrets. Provision for maximum of 8,818-lb (4 000-kg) bomb load, normal loads consisting of six 220-lb (100-kg), four 551-lb (250-kg) or two 2,204-lb (1 000-kg) bombs.

TALKBACK

Ejection in earnest

HAVING been a subscriber to AIR INTERNATIONAL since its very first days, I believe that I am at last in a position to contribute some hitherto unrevealed historic fact to your magazine which will be of interest to some of your readers. Recently, a former Junkers test pilot, Hans Pancherz, gave a lecture to the Danish Society for Aviation History, during the course of which it became apparent that he had been the first person to evacuate an aircraft — other than as part of an experimental programme — by means of an ejection seat! This event took place at 1150 hours on 15 July 1943, and the aircraft that Pancherz vacated was a Ju 290. The circumstances were as follows:

The Ju 290 was, at this time, being subjected to flutter investigation, testing having commenced at 211 mph (340 km/h) and speed had been progressively increased with successive tests, until, on the day concerned, the aircraft was to undergo flutter testing at what was considered to be its limiting speed of 348 mph (560 km/h). The speed of the aircraft was being monitored by theodolites, but the first flight at 348 mph (560 km/h) was not satisfactorily measured owing to cloud and the flight engineers asked Pancherz to repeat the run. This, too, could not be accurately measured owing to technical problems and Pancherz was instructed to repeat the run yet again. Irritated and anxious to complete the testing, Pancherz exceeded the stipulated speed and, in fact, attained 391 mph (630 km/h), overstressing the elevator as a result. The Ju 290 pitched down violently and entered a steep dive.

For the test programme, an ejection seat operated by compressed air had been installed in the aircraft for the pilot. Activation of the ejection seat theoretically resulted in the jettisoning of the roof hatch and disconnection of the control column (to safeguard against damage to the pilot's knees) automatically before compressed air was metered to the seat. The seat, which had been taken from a Ju 288 and was armoured (the armour plate being retained as it was considered that this might save the pilot's life should he collide with the tail unit during ejection), was intended to attain 12 *g* within a distance of 8·2 ft (2,5 m), but the battery of compressed air tanks had been secured against positive *g* manoeuvres only, and when the aircraft pitched down violently, the tanks broke loose, triggering the compressed air and ejecting the armoured seat, with an unconscious Pancherz, through the roof hatch. Fortunately, Pancherz regained consciousness during the free fall, released his seat harness and deployed his parachute, the only injuries sustained being some damage suffered by his knees when they hit the control column. It was subsequently ascertained that the theodolites had recorded the speed of the seat as 329 mph (530 km/h).

Incidentally, Pancherz insisted that, contrary to all published sources alleging that *two* Ju 390s were flown, only one of these six-engined aircraft was built, and he participated in every flight that this aircraft made, from its initial test of 21 October 1943 at Merseburg until it was dismantled at Dessau in July 1944 (this sole example of the Ju 390 was later burned at Dessau before the arrival of US forces). He added that there was no truth in reports that this aircraft had flown to within a few miles of the US coastline.

Jens Sannom Rasmussen
2450 Copenhagen SV, Denmark

Further Fokker facts

REGARDING Mr F Gerdessen's letter (April issue), concerning delivery of the Fokker D-types, the correct figures established from authentic Schwerin records are: 112 D Is (90 for the German Army, six for the Navy and 16 for the Austrian Army) as you state, but there were 202 D IIs (there being 181 for the German Army, as you claim, plus one for the Navy and 20 for the Austrian Army) and not 177 as Mr Gerdessen suggests, 210 D IIIs (as you state and not 230 as claimed by Mr Gerdessen), 44 D IVs (including the four for Sweden commented on by your correspondent) and 300 D Vs as quoted by you. The Netherlands government did indeed order 10 D IIIs, as Mr Gerdessen alleges, these (and their subsequent Dutch serials) being 350/16 (F 200), 352/16 (F 201), 360/16 (F 202), 1619/16 (F 203), 3022/16 (F 206), 3024/16 (F 207), 3026/16 (F 208) and 3028/16 (F 209), the original series of F 204 and F 205 being unknown. Insofar as the use of the D IV in Sweden is concerned, I learned from Lt Col N Kindberg of the Swedish Air Force staff that the four aircraft ordered by the Swedish Defence Council arrived unarmed, but from Fokker records I ascertained that synchronisation mechanisms and machine guns were sent to Sweden later.

With regard to the D VIIs that came to Holland from Schwerin, there were indeed 98 aircraft, but of these only 22 went to the LVA (Nrs 250-271), 20 went to the MLD (D-20 to D-39), six went to the KNIL in the East Indies (F-301 to F-306) and the remaining 50 went to Russia.

I concur with Mr Gerdessen's comment that Finland placed no order for the G I, although several Finnish pilots evaluated the type thoroughly — I believe that funding problems in fact prevented the placing of an order. The 25 G Is (prototype and 24 series aircraft) ordered clandestinely by the Spanish Republican government were re-ordered through the Estonian Ministry of War in January 1938 (*as stated in Part II of Fokker's Final Fighter/November 1974 issue — Ed*) after imposition of the Dutch ban on the supply of war material to the warring factions in Spain. After the cessation of hostilities in Spain, the Nationalist government tried unsuccessfully to obtain the aircraft via the Société Française des Transports Aériens of Paris.

Ing H A Somberg
Amsterdam-Z, Netherlands

AS THE FOKKER SECTION of "Fighter A to Z" has now ended, I would like to supplement my letter published in the April issue with some additional comments. Firstly, the D XVI. The Dutch Army ordered 14 and not 15 fighters of this type (Nrs 275-288), Nr 277 being the special aerobatic aircraft re-engined with the Mercury. This particular D XVI survived until May 1940. The single example for Italy, it would seem, was never delivered and must have been the same aircraft as that in China. Incidentally, the Dutch D XVIs had split undercarriages and not cross axles (as shown in the general arrangement drawing), although I do not know if the original prototype was later fitted with a split undercarriage. The Conqueror-engined D XVI was *not* rebuilt as the prototype D XVII, this aircraft (c/n 5240) being totally destroyed when it failed to recover from a spin. The D XVII with the Conqueror was thus a completely new aircraft (c/n 5293). It was tested against the Curtiss Hawk and then shipped to the NEI. After a crash (in 1936) it was returned to Holland, repaired by Fokker and supplied to the LVA as Nr 211, the 10 D XVIIs originally supplied to the service being Nrs 201-210.

The prototype of the D XXI was, incidentally, accepted by the NEI Army only with reluctance, being delivered to the NEI early in 1937. It was little used and was lost in a

The Junkers Ju 390 V1 which, according to its test pilot Hans Pancherz, was the only prototype of this final development of the Ju 90/290 family to be built (see letter above from J S Rasmussen).

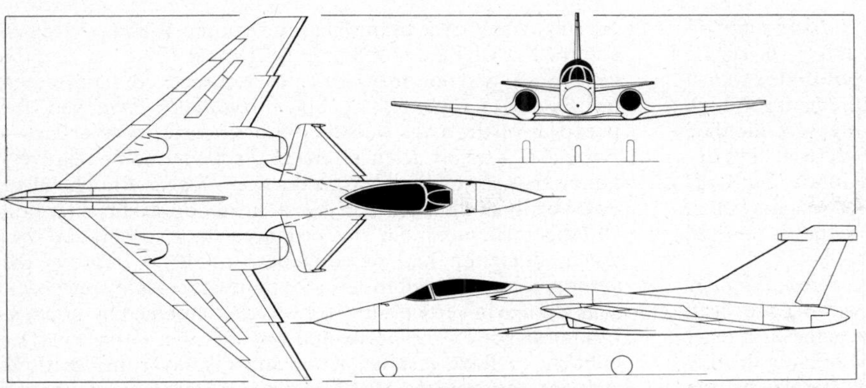

A project drawing of the Aero-Products Chameleon light fighter, as described below by its originator Dan Woodhurst.

Japanese bombing attack on Kalidjati in late February 1942. Although, as you say, the D XXI was offered by the parent company with both fixed and retractable undercarriages, the retractable undercarriage fitted to two VL-built D XXIs was of purely Finnish design. According to my records, the Finnish D XXI made its last flights and was withdrawn in September 1948.

The G I prototype re-engined with Twin Wasp Juniors first flew with these engines on 3 September 1938. The first production G I with Twin Wasp Juniors flew on 19 April 1939, six having been test flown up to 18 September. To 15 May 1940, 10 had been accepted by the LVA and a further six were ready for acceptance. How many of these were, in fact, armed is unclear, as Nr 348 and Nr 355 had been used for gunnery trials and those claimed as having been armed during the "five-day war" (Nrs 343, 345 and 346) were then standing at Schiphol. The unit that was to have been equipped with Twin Wasp Junior-powered G Is, 2-V-2 LvR, was to have been formed on 1 June 1940, but the designated CO, Lt Bierema, was killed on 10 May in a Douglas DB-8A/3N. Some of the American-engined G Is were scrapped in 1940, but at least a dozen served with the *Luftwaffe*, as did at least five Mercury-engined G Is.

F Gerdessen
4204 ES Gorinchem, Netherlands

Light fighter project

WE HAVE read the February 1980 article in AIR INTERNATIONAL on the Piranha and the work being done by the Aerospace Task Force. We believe firmly in the philosophy of the light fighter and have been working extensively on this concept.

Our Chameleon, in the development process at this time, is such a fighter. I enclose some information on this project that I hope will be of interest to your readers.

Mock-up and structural design changes are taking place almost monthly. As can be seen, the canard placement is above and ahead of the wing, the canard's downwash being used effectively by the main wing in reducing the latter's angle of attack.

Testing has shown excellent root lift distribution by placing the wing leading edge chine extension below the fuselage with a laminar flow splitter, thereby achieving measurable even flow at high angles of attack. Air is channelled over the root sections by the engine nacelles, which are separated to minimise contagious engine failure.

Through Coanda effect, a large percentage of the horizontal thrust is recovered with 60 deg of flap. Sustained 9 *g* turn rates can be maintained. The mid-span trailing edge segments make up flaperons which are close to the centre of gravity, thereby reducing trim loads. The inboard segments utilise exhaust flow from the engines to augment the lift coefficient.

Spoilers for roll control incorporate follow-on ailerons and these make up the outboard segments of the wing trailing edge. Studies are in progress to utilise single exhaust deflectors on each nacelle for airbrake and thrust reversers. Engine armour is supplied by lower wing skins and steel bearer spars. One hard point is located on the fuselage centreline and two under each wing.

The engines will have low infra-red qualities because of their location and minimum exhaust signatures through exhaust diffusion. To augment the exhaust diffusion process, retractable flow vanes are employed.

To simplify construction of the fuselage sections, the skins are of flat and flat wrap sections with no compound curves. The cockpit section ahead at the break-away line is of steel tubing, with armour plate in bathtub configuration. The Chameleon has the following characteristics:

Power Plant: Two General Electric J85-GE-21 turbojets each rated at 5,000 lb st (2 268 kgp) or Garrett AiResearch TFE731 series of 6,800 lb st each (3 084 kgp). Fuel capacity, 3,600 lb (1 632 kg) internal, 2,400 lb (1 090 kg) external, giving a total of 6,000 lb (2 722 kg).

Performance (estimated): Max speed, Mach 1·43 at 35,000 ft (10 668 m); economical cruise, Mach 0·85 at 35,000 ft (10 668 m); max rate of climb at sea level, 29,000 ft/min (147 m/sec); combat radius, with fuel for 20 min reserve and 5 min combat, 200 mls (322 km) at sea level; max range, full external fuel, 1,200 mls (1 931 km) at sea level.

Weights (estimated): Empty equipped, 8,000 lb (3 629 kg); military load, 6,000 lb (2 722 kg); max take-off, 20,000 lb (9 072 kg).

Dimensions: Span, 33 ft 4 in (10,15 m); length, 48 ft 4 in (14,72 m); canard span, 13 ft 4 in (4,05 m); height, 13 ft 9 in (4,19 m); wing area, 372 sq ft (34,56 m²); canard area, 75 sq ft (6,97 m²); undercarriage track, 9 ft 4 in (2,84 m); wheelbase, 20 ft 10 in (6,35 m).

Daniel R Woodhurst
Aero-Products Company
Sonoma, California, USA

Don't forget Zrnić

WITH REFERENCE to two entries in the May issue (pages 251 and 256), you mention a pre-war Yugoslav fighter which you call the "IK-Z". Please note that the correct designation of this machine was IK-3 (ie, number *three*), which, logically enough, followed the IK-2 mentioned on pages 250 and 251 of the same issue. For verification, please refer to *Aircraft Profile* No 242.

I can readily understand that in your — very commendable — zeal for authenticity, you have mistaken the numeral "3" for the cyrillic letter "Z" which is almost identical. Also, Rogožarski was in Belgrade proper, the plant across the Sava river, in Zemun, was Ikarus — thus IK! The plane was colloquially known as "Ika-tri", the "a" pronounced as in *lava* and the "tri" pronounced as *tree*, the latter meaning three.

Miroslav Uroshevich
Cincinnati, Ohio 45211, USA

We appreciate your concern for accuracy Mr Uroshevich, but we have not mistaken the arabic numeral "3" for the cyrillic letter "Z". The prefix "IK" did not, as the Aircraft Profile *to which you refer correctly points out, stand for Ikarus but for the designers of the IK-1 and IK-2 (built by Ikarus), Ljubomir* **Ilić** *and* **Kosta** *Sivčev. In the design of the fighter built by Rogožarski, they were joined by Slobodan* **Zrnić** *and the* official *designation assigned to the new aircraft was thus IK-Z, giving credit to the* **three** *members of the design team. The fact that the cyrillic "Z" and the arabic "3" were similar was purely coincidental — as explained in fact, in the* Aircraft Profile *on page 182. This similarity inevitably led to confusion, the IK-Z frequently being referred to in Yugoslavia and elsewhere as the IK-3. Perhaps our use of the correct designation rather than the incorrect but more popularly used designation smacks of purism, but it is not a mistake. — Ed.*

The IK-Z prototype which is the subject of the letter above from Miroslav Uroshevich. The initials IK stood for Ilić and Kosta, and not for Ikarus; consequently the Rogozarski-built IK-Z was not in sequence with the Ikarus-built IK-1 and IK-2 and the '-Z' indicated a third member of the design team, Zrnić.

FLOGGER—————————— ***from page 75***
23's R-29 and sharing a common core but having a larger LP compressor and shorter, simplified two-position exhaust nozzle. Consistent with the primary requirement of high subsonic speeds at low levels and having a simplified afterburner augmenting an estimated 14,330 lb (6 500 kg) dry rating by some 25 per cent, the Tumansky engine of *Flogger-D* breathes via larger-area fixed inlets with belled lips and small fixed splitter plates, and exhausts via a tailpipe that is some 16 in (40 cm) shorter.

To enhance grassfield operational potential, tyres of slightly increased diameter and greatly increased width have been applied to the main undercarriage members and these, in turn, have necessitated enlarging the wheel bays by bulging the bay doors and the adjacent fuselage structure, increasing the fuselage cross-section locally. The twin-barrel GSh-23L cannon common to all other members of the *Flogger* family is replaced by a six-barrel 23-mm Gatling-style rotary cannon — the first time such a weapon has been applied to a Soviet aircraft — of much greater hitting power, and the stores stations under the intake trunks have been moved outboard. The missile pylons common to air defence and trainer *Floggers* are replaced by bomb mounts with distinctive heavy sway bracing and to these may be attached shoes for ASMs (such as AS-7 *Kerry*). In the wing glove leading edges, immediately ahead of the bomb mounts, are housings for an ECM antenna (to port) and a missile guidance antenna. All these changes have resulted in some degradation of speed performance, and *Flogger-D* is believed to have maximum speeds of around M=0·95 at sea level and M=1·6 at altitude, but it is assessed by western analysts as affording markedly improved air-ground capability than other members of its family.

The most recent member of the MiG-23 family to make its public début is *Flogger-G*, six examples of which made courtesy visits to the Finnish base at Kuopio-Rissala in August and the French base at Reims in September 1978. Lacking the laser ranger and one or two other excrescences commonly seen on service aeroplanes — and presumably removed for purposes of the visits outside the boundaries of WarPac — *Flogger-G* is an air defence version displaying some relatively minor changes over recent production *Flogger-Bs*. The most noteworthy of these changes was a shorter dorsal fin extension and this reduction in fin area produced some speculation that the modification had possibly been made to improve the aerobatic capability of the aircraft purely for display purposes. This change in vertical surfaces was accompanied by notched trailing edges on the horizontal tail surfaces. Other changes unlikely to have resulted from any display considerations included the transfer of the Doppler antenna from port to starboard and a redesigned undercarriage nose member, the nosewheels being "spoked" and mounted on a telescopic rather than levered-suspension leg such as is used by all preceding *Floggers*. As the new unit presumably occupied more space, the nosewheel door curvature had been increased to result in a full-length fairing below the fuselage baseline.

While a comparatively simple aeroplane, its control system lacking much of the sophistication built into western variable-geometry aeroplanes, *Flogger* is a vastly more competent aeroplane than any of its predecessors in V-VS service and it has played an important part in the erosion of NATO's technological lead in TacAir over the past half-decade or so. Most important, it is available in very large numbers indeed. Being offered at subsidised prices on credit terms with which the West cannot compete to an increasing number of countries in which the Soviet Union wields or wishes to wield political influence, who can doubt that this family of fighters will be among the world's most widely used before the 'eighties reach the halfway point. □

MiG-23MF Flogger-B fighters of a unit participating in the "Karpaty" Exercise in the Cis-Carpathian Military District in the area of Lutsk, Lvov and Rovno. The emblem indicating that the unit has achieved a prescribed standard of excellence may be clearly seen aft of the radome.

These illustrations depict a MiG-27 Flogger-D of the V-VS Frontovaya Aviatsiya based in the DDR (Group of Soviet Forces in Germany). This displays the standard three-colour upper surface camouflage scheme employed by FA tactical fighters, but the exact pattern varies marginally from aircraft to aircraft.

The side profile above shows clearly the sharply downward inclined nose contour of the MiG-27 (shared with the MiG-23BM) with laser range-finder in the extreme tip, ILS antenna (Swift Rod) below and pitot head (offset to starboard) projecting above. The fairing below and immediately ahead of the aircraft number houses the Continuous-Wave target illumination radar. Note the tandem racks on the wing glove pylon.

The head-on view above shows the repositioned outboard stores stations under the air intake trunks, the active ECM antenna (starboard) and missile guidance antenna (port) above the wing glove pylons, the deepened windscreen with downward sloping sills, the centreline Gatling-type cannon and the fixed inlets with belled outer lips and small fixed splitter plates. The bulges on the vertical tail surface house (lower) the braking parachute and (upper) the Sirena 3 radar warning receiver, below which is the ATC transponder. The other aerials for the Sirena warning radar are mounted in the wing glove.

The planview illustrates the wings at minimum (17 deg) and (ghosted) maximum (72 deg) sweep angles. It should be noted that in this half-and-half drawing, both top surfaces and under surfaces of the portside are illustrated, but the pitot projecting from the nose is shown to starboard. The bulge in the rear nosewheel door necessitated by the larger wheels employed by this (and MiG-23BM) version of Flogger may be clearly seen as may also the marked bulging of the fuselage (under the rear portion of the wing glove) necessitated by the enlarged tyres for improved grassfield operations capability. By comparison with other members of the Flogger family, the MiG-27 has an appreciably shorter tailpipe.

AIR UK

The Long-established Newcomer

RECENT months have seen the emergence of a number of new names on the British air transport scene, some the result of initiatives by newcomers to the business, others reflecting mergers and take-overs in the continuing struggle of the "independent" operators to find a viable *modus operandi*. Of the new names to gain currency in 1979, some were short-lived (British Cargo Airlines, Air Transcontinental) and others are associated, at least for the time being, with the specialised business of carrying IT charter traffic (Air Europe, Orion Airways). One new name — coined towards the end of 1979 and launched operationally on 1 January 1980 — identifies, however, what must be reckoned to be a major force in the UK airline industry. Air UK, which is nominally the result of a merger between four airlines. More realistically, it identifies an integration of two long-established regional operators, and now ranks as Britain's third largest scheduled airline (after British Airways and British Caledonian), with the expectation of carrying 1·7 million passengers on its scheduled and charter services in 1980.

With 1,700 employees (including 300 pilots and 240 cabin staff), a fleet of 40-odd turboprop and turbojet airliners, and a route structure embracing 22 airports in the UK and 11 destinations in Europe, Air UK comes closer to achieving a comprehensive regional network than any of the independent airlines that have emerged in Britain since the end of World War II. Through its constituent companies, it can trace its foundations back through three decades, despite the newness of the Air UK appellation. The process of mergers and take-overs that has finally led to the creation of this "third-force" scheduled carrier in Britain has been characteristic of the whole of British airline operating activities in the post-war era — an era that has seen the launching of a large number of companies to fly passenger or freight, scheduled services or charters. For a variety of reasons that embrace political, financial and technical factors, more of these companies have failed than have succeeded. While the less successful companies have soon fallen by the wayside, the more successful have, by and large, tended to merge with, or sell out to, one another, leading to the creation of the larger and more durable operators of the 'eighties*.

The antecedents

Although the Air UK story begins only a few months ago, it cannot be told without reference to the companies that have been combined in it, under the principal ownership of British and Commonwealth Shipping Co Ltd: Air Anglia, Air Wales, British Island Airways and BIA/Air West. Of these four, Air Anglia and British Island Airways (BIA) are the two principals, and it is the integration of these two relatively long-established and successful airlines that gives Air UK its strength and the real foundation upon which its future success will rest. Each of these companies had itself evolved, by 1979, through a series of mergers and take-overs that had involved several other well-known names among the British "independents" (a term that has long been used to identify those operators outside of the state-owned sector of the UK airlines business, now represented by British Airways).

Air Anglia Ltd had emerged in July 1970 through a merging of three smaller companies: Anglian Air Charter Ltd, Norfolk Airways and Rig-Air Ltd. Of these companies, Anglian Air Charter had been formed in 1950, originally to operate pleasure flights in the Great Yarmouth area of Norfolk; Norfolk Airways started life a year later at Norwich as an air taxi and general charter operator and Rig-Air was formed in 1969 as a jointly-owned subsidiary of these two companies, to provide support for oil-drilling operations in the North Sea. Following the formation of Air Anglia Ltd, scheduled services were started in December 1970 with a modest operation by Islander between Norwich and Aberdeen via Edinburgh. Thereafter, the company achieved rapid growth as a regional

**The process has already led to the creation, as they exist today, of both British Airways and British Caledonian, as related in detail in* AIR INTERNATIONAL*/October 1975 and the issue for October 1972 respectively.*

operator with a fleet of DC-3s gradually giving way to Fokker F27s (10 by 1979) and, eventually, a pair of Fokker F28s — the first and so far only examples on the UK register.

In 1977, Air Anglia was able to announce a profit of more than £1m for the first time, but the step into turbojet operations imposed additional demands on the airline and in April 1979, British and Commonwealth Shipping acquired an 82 per cent interest in the company from Norwich Union. Subsequently, that shareholding was increased to 100 per cent when the shares held by the founders of the company were also acquired.

British Island Airways, as the other major component in Air UK, also can trace its history back to the early post-war years, having been formed — as British United (Channel Islands) Airways — in November 1962 to continue the operations of Silver City Airways and Jersey Airlines, plus some of those of Transair. All these companies had, by 1962, been acquired by British United Airways directly or as a result of the merger between Airwork and Hunting-Clan which had itself created BUA. BUA had also formed British United Airways (Manx) to operate services to the Isle of Man previously flown by Silver City (which had acquired Manx Air Services in 1956), and had acquired Morton Air Services (in which was already incorporated Olley Air Service). In November 1968, British United Island Airways was formed as a combination of BU (CI) A, BUA (Manx) and Morton, and in July 1970 the name was changed to British Island Airways to isolate this company from the British United Airways group, which later that year was sold to Caledonian Airways to form the present B.Cal.

British Island Airways was thus left intact as a subsidiary of British Air Transport Holdings, a company in which British and Commonwealth Shipping held 90 per cent with the balance held by Eagle Star Insurance Group — this now being the ownership of Air UK*. In keeping with its name and its historical association, BIA continued to concentrate upon scheduled services linking the UK with the Channel Islands and the Isle of Man, for which it built up a fleet of Handley Page Heralds — the first of which it had inherited from Jersey Airlines — and became an all-Herald operator when the last DC-3 was retired in 1974. A number of domestic routes were operated, and international operations were expanded from the beginning of 1979, when the company took over all the scheduled services previously flown by British Air Ferries, plus seven more Heralds. Three months previously, BIA had entered the jet era with the acquisition of BAC One-Elevens to operate IT charter flights, principally to the Mediterranean. Unlike Air Anglia, it did not introduce jets on the scheduled services, however.

The other two companies merged with Air Anglia and BIA to form Air UK were also owned by British and Commonwealth by the end of 1979, but had enjoyed only brief independence and little success in their efforts to launch regional commuter services based on Cardiff and Exeter. Air Wales had started operations in December 1977 but had been unable to sustain them, and after it had ceased to operate in 1979, the company was acquired by British and Commonwealth. As a subsidiary of Westward TV, Air Westward began operating in May 1978; it was acquired by B & C in March 1979 and two months later its services were absorbed by BIA, resulting in the creation of BIA/Air West a few months prior to the formation of Air UK.

Towards integration

If experience to date is any guide, it appears that the merging of Air Anglia and BIA operations has been achieved with remarkably few difficulties, and considerably less upheaval than has been experienced by some other airlines in similar situations. Two reasons for this felicitous state of affairs can be given: one certainly is found in the managerial experience and talent that Air UK has assembled from among the teams previously heading the two individual companies, but even more relevant, perhaps, is the fact that BIA and Air Anglia each had similar regional scheduled service operations that were complementary rather than competitive. And although some fleet rationalisation may be called for in future, the fact that the two companies operated different types of aircraft has made initial integration easier than it might otherwise have been.

Historically, BIA had been primarily concerned with the operation of scheduled services between regional airports in the UK and the three islands of Jersey, Guernsey and the Isle of Man, while Air Anglia had concentrated upon serving the business communities in East Anglia and Humberside with links to other UK destinations and across the North Sea to

**Other British and Commonwealth Shipping Group aviation interests include Bristow Helicopters, Airwork Services and Servisair. These are entirely independent of Air UK, although the latter does make use of Servisair for its ground handling at a number of airports in the UK.*

(Below) One of the six Bandeirantes in the Air UK fleet; four are EMB-110P1s with large loading door, as shown here, while two are EMB-110P2s with the standard passenger door. (Heading photo, opposite) One of the four Fokker F27 Mk 200 Friendships added to the Air UK fleet this year, from TAT in France.

continental points. For an initial period, at least, this emphasis is being maintained through the two major operating divisions of Air UK — Island Division and Anglia Division. Also inherited from the former companies are the two prinicipal engineering bases, at Blackpool (Squires Gate) and Norwich Airport (the former RAF airfield of Horsham St Faith), while the company headquarters at Redhill was the former BIA head office. Blackpool remains the centre for Herald engineering and maintenance while Norwich handles the F27, F28 and Bandeirante as well as being the home of the training school for air and ground staff.

The British Airways decision to stop operating a number of its least profitable regional services — some of them being routes that it had itself inherited through the acquisition by British European Airways of the former independent airlines BKS Air Transport, Northeast and Cambrian — allowed Air UK to acquire several new routes on which to operate from the start of the present summer season, and although these did not include any new destinations, they did result in the company becoming the sole operator between Guernsey and London, with services from both Gatwick and Heathrow.

Now flying up to 1,600 services a week on 67 individual routes, Air UK is concentrating on what it believes it does best — providing scheduled services at Britain's regional cities. Its activities embrace several other types of operation, including

(Above and right) Two views of Island Ensign, one of the four Air UK BAC One-Elevens assigned to IT charter flights from Gatwick. These are the only aircraft in the fleet to carry individual names. (Left) A Bandeirante and (below) Fokker F27 at Schiphol Airport, where Air UK provides up to 14 services a day from UK airports.

air
UK
G-CBIA

air
UK
G-CBIA

(Above) One of the Air UK Heralds. Currently the most numerous type in the airline's fleet, the Herald is expected to decline in importance during the next few years. (Below) A One-Eleven at Gatwick and (lower photograph) a Bandeirante at Schiphol.

some night-time flights primarily carrying newspapers (and some of the mail-carrying flights in the Post Office's recently-instituted "Spokes to Speke" operation), the specialised rail-air-rail Silver Arrow/*Flêche d'Argent* operation between London and Paris via Gatwick and Le Touquet and, as already mentioned, a series of inclusive tour charter flights out of Gatwick. However, future plans, at least in the near term, are wholly concerned with developing the regional scheduled services, and Air UK has already identified a number of new routes on which it would like to fly — in addition to several others for which it holds licences but does not yet feel the time is right to launch operations. In particular, the company is interested in developing European services out of London's third airport, Stansted, and has applied for Stansted-Paris rights to join the Stansted-Brussels and Stansted-Amsterdam approval it has already. There is also scope for the development of routes from the established UK provincial points to new "secondary" European destinations, such as the recently-approved Gatwick-Jutland service (to serve Billund and Aarhus).

Operational aspects

Many of the Air UK routes, present and future, offer only modest numbers of passengers and the company sees no early requirement for aircraft any larger than those at present in its fleet — even assuming that the airports in question were able to handle them. Traffic development is more likely to be encouraged, in general, by increased frequency than larger aeroplanes; the objective is to achieve a "bus service with neat and tidy aeroplanes, operating frequently and on time," but the company sees little prospect of joining in the fare-cutting employed by larger airlines as a competitive ploy. A substantial proportion of traffic on Air UK scheduled services is provided by businessmen who will travel anyway, providing the service is reliable; cut fares and promotional gimmicks are unlikely to produce much new traffic on most of the company's routes and with fuel costs continuing to escalate, Air UK is all too well aware that it has a tough fight on its hands to remain profitable in the next few years.

Among the ways in which Air UK might be expected to combat rising costs are higher productivity from its employees and better utilisation from its aircraft. In both respects, improvements are already discernible. There have been virtually no redundancies following the merger, but a modest reduction has been made in numbers of employees, and the output, in terms of capacity tonne km per employee, is improving. After some initial difficulties, an integrated booking system is now working well, using (as originated by Air Anglia) leased capacity in the KLM computer at Schiphol and an increasing number of terminals within the network. Much effort has gone into establishing lines of communication and a feed-back of information for central planning and control purposes, since there was an inevitable tendency at first for the divisions to maintain a degree of independence — by habit if not by intent.

So far as the Air UK fleet is concerned, utilisation will benefit from the addition of the ex-BA routes this year, which are being handled without adding to the fleet. As of January 1980, when the company officially came into existence, the fleet comprised the four 89-seat BAC One-Elevens dedicated to the IT charters; two Fokker F28s, 10 Fokker F27s, 20 Handley Page Heralds and six EMBRAER Bandeirantes. The 85-seat F28s had been acquired by Air Anglia to replace F27s on some of the longer routes, such as Edinburgh-Paris, but Air UK has now leased one of the pair to Air Alsace for an initial six-month period (probably to be extended) while the need for jets rather than turboprops on scheduled routes is re-examined in the light of current fuel costs*; meanwhile, the remaining F28 is operating with 80 rather than 85 seats following some complaints about leg room. Utilisation is expected to be 3,100 hrs this year; the F28s are the only aircraft in the Air UK fleet to date equipped for Cat II operation.

The 10 Air Anglia F27s had been achieving close to 3,000 hrs a year prior to introduction of the F28s but this figure has now slipped to about 2,200 hrs in the current year. All but two of the fleet were Mk 200s; of the two Mk 100s, with lower-rated Dart engines and some operational restrictions, one has been converted to a Mk 200 in the Norwich engineering base and the other is expected to be sold. The fleet is currently being supplemented, however, by four more Mk 200s purchased from TAT in France, and replacing Heralds on a one-for-one basis in the Island Division. These new aircraft excepted, Air UK's F27s are interesting in that they do not have autopilots, a feature that has aided Air Anglia's philosophy to encourage captains and first officers to share the flying of these aircraft on a 50/50 basis; this, the company claims, has in turn produced a high standard of flying skill in its crews and has certainly given first officers the opportunity to acquire experience more rapidly than in many other airlines.

The Heralds — all 50-seat Mk 200s and also averaging 2,200 hrs a year — have served BIA well since it first inherited the original Jersey Airlines' fleet of this type. However, Air UK recognises that the type will become increasingly difficult to maintain — even with the help of BAe Scottish Division, which took over the original Handley Page after-sales commitment — and the fleet is likely to be progressively run down over the next few years. Those in service included seven leased from BAF when the latter's scheduled services from Southend were taken over, but all but two of these are being returned as the TAT F27s are introduced.

The 18-seat Bandeirantes — four are EMB-110P2s and two are EMB-110P1s with the larger cargo-loading door — were ordered in the first instance by British and Commonwealth after that company had acquired both Air Westward and Air Anglia but before the Air UK merger, and they were intended to replace the piston-engined Cessna Titans and Piper Navajo Chieftains that the two companies were using, respectively. All the piston-engined types have now been sold by Air UK, and the Bandeirantes are expected to achieve some 2,000 hrs apiece in their first year, flying the original Air Westward services from Exeter to Southampton/Brussels, Paris, Glasgow and London (Gatwick) as well as a number of the less busy Anglian Division routes, such as Humberside-Glasgow and Norwich-Stavanger. The Bandeirantes are flown as single-pilot aircraft, with a pilot-assistant in the right-hand seat, who acts as cabin attendant; it is also company policy to encourage these pilot-assistants, the majority of them female and all with a PPL and RT training, to achieve a degree of competence in handling a twin-engined aircraft in case of emergency. The company's flying staff also includes one fully-qualified female captain and three first officers (all on Heralds).

Air UK has indicated that it expects its future fleet to be made up of three types: a small turboprop, a medium-size turboprop and a short-haul jet. With the Bandeirante and the F27 clearly filling the first two of these slots for a number of years ahead, only the last-mentioned remains in some doubt — not so much because either the F28 or One-Eleven are unsuitable but because the real need for such a type remains the subject of some uncertainty within the company. If suitable terms could be agreed, there is no doubt Air UK would be interested in operating two or three BAe 146s — the interest dates back to BIA and the HS146 — but "suitable terms" are interpreted by this operator as something akin to the original Eastern Airlines Airbus deal, in which the publicity value of the operation to the manufacturer was considered virtually to offset the cost of leasing the aircraft. British Aerospace has not to date indicated that it would be able to supply 146s for Air UK on such generous terms. It is worth noting that all the Heralds, F27s and One-Elevens have been acquired second-hand and that it may be some years before the company would feel justified in embarking on the purchase of a new multi-million pound jet fleet. Meanwhile, incidentally, one of the One-Elevens is being fitted this year with hush-kits — a legal requirement, as it was acquired after the September 1979 deadline; the three other One-Elevens may be similarly equipped in due course.

Naturally, rationalisation following the merger embraces such things as stewardess uniforms, check-in desks, signs, tickets and stationery, as well as the more immediately obvious logo and fleet livery, but the full change of identity will take up to three years to achieve. Even the aircraft will not be painted in the finally approved Air UK colour scheme until 1982, as and when they become due for overhaul; in the meantime, a rather heterogeneous assortment of schemes will be seen, with the Air UK logo on aircraft in the original BIA and Air Anglia colours, as well as examples of all four types in the smart blue/white/red scheme illustrated in these pages. Even this scheme underwent a change after first being adopted, however, and white vertical tail surfaces have replaced the blue finish seen on the first Herald, F27 and One-Eleven painted up in Air UK colours.

If achieving a uniform livery is the biggest of Air UK's headaches in the next couple of years, the company will have cause to be grateful. Now well into its first summer of operating as a single force, the company is under no delusions as to the challenge that lies ahead. If experience, competence and confidence can be combined to achieve success, however, then this "established newcomer" to the ranks of British airline operators seems well on track for a bright future. □

For example, on the Edinburgh-Paris route, two F27s can be operated for the same fuel as one F28. Although the F28 carries almost as many passengers as two 44-seat F27s, the latter type can offer better frequency which may outbalance any competitive disadvantage due to its slower speed.

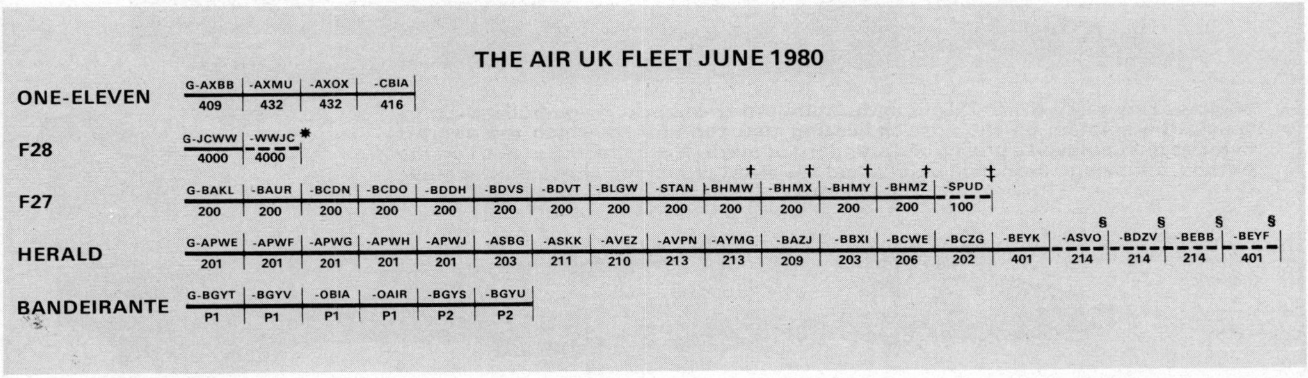

THE AIR UK FLEET JUNE 1980

ONE-ELEVEN	G-AXBB 409	-AXMU 432	-AXOX 432	-CBIA 416															
F28	G-JCWW 4000	-WWJC* 4000																	
F27	G-BAKL 200	-BAUR 200	-BCDN 200	-BCDO 200	-BDDH 200	-BDVS 200	-BDVT 200	-BLGW 200	-STAN 200	-BHMW† 200	-BHMX† 200	-BHMY† 200	-BHMZ† 200	-SPUD‡ 100					
HERALD	G-APWE 201	-APWF 201	-APWG 201	-APWH 201	-APWJ 201	-ASBG 203	-ASKK 211	-AVEZ 210	-AVPN 213	-AYMG 213	-BAZJ 209	-BBXI 203	-BCWE 206	-BCZG 202	-BEYK 401	-ASVO§ 214	-BDZV§ 214	-BEBB§ 214	-BEYF§ 401
BANDEIRANTE	G-BGYT P1	-BGYV P1	-OBIA P1	-OAIR P1	-BGYS P2	-BGYU P2													

**On lease to Air Alsace. †In course of delivery from TAT. ‡To be withdrawn. §To be returned to BAF, off lease, when ex-TAT F27s are delivered.*

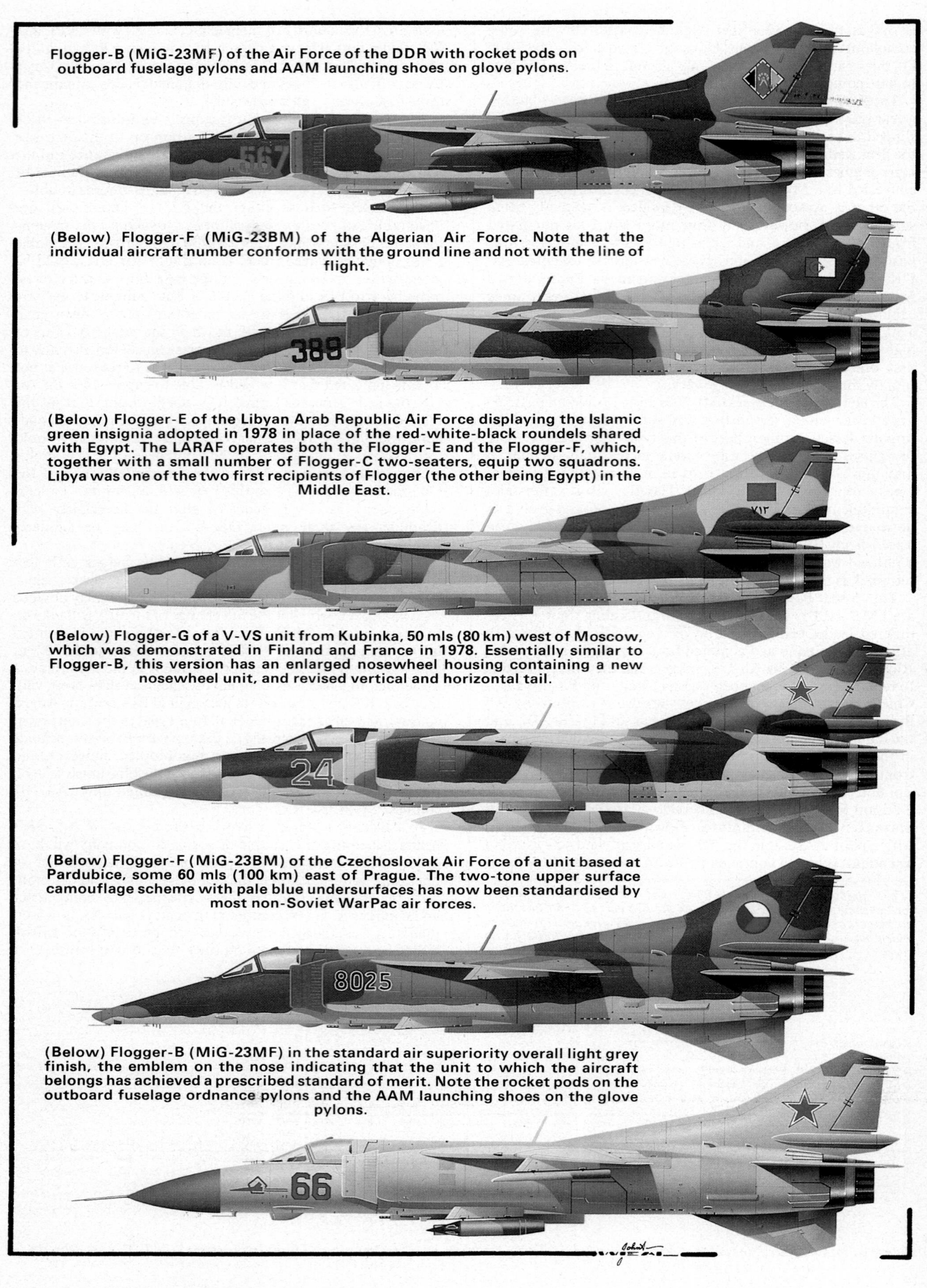

Flogger-B (MiG-23MF) of the Air Force of the DDR with rocket pods on outboard fuselage pylons and AAM launching shoes on glove pylons.

(Below) Flogger-F (MiG-23BM) of the Algerian Air Force. Note that the individual aircraft number conforms with the ground line and not with the line of flight.

(Below) Flogger-E of the Libyan Arab Republic Air Force displaying the Islamic green insignia adopted in 1978 in place of the red-white-black roundels shared with Egypt. The LARAF operates both the Flogger-E and the Flogger-F, which, together with a small number of Flogger-C two-seaters, equip two squadrons. Libya was one of the two first recipients of Flogger (the other being Egypt) in the Middle East.

(Below) Flogger-G of a V-VS unit from Kubinka, 50 mls (80 km) west of Moscow, which was demonstrated in Finland and France in 1978. Essentially similar to Flogger-B, this version has an enlarged nosewheel housing containing a new nosewheel unit, and revised vertical and horizontal tail.

(Below) Flogger-F (MiG-23BM) of the Czechoslovak Air Force of a unit based at Pardubice, some 60 mls (100 km) east of Prague. The two-tone upper surface camouflage scheme with pale blue undersurfaces has now been standardised by most non-Soviet WarPac air forces.

(Below) Flogger-B (MiG-23MF) in the standard air superiority overall light grey finish, the emblem on the nose indicating that the unit to which the aircraft belongs has achieved a prescribed standard of merit. Note the rocket pods on the outboard fuselage ordnance pylons and the AAM launching shoes on the glove pylons.

Who's caning the Canucks?

"MAY I PLEAD a case for some sanity in respect of prices of British kits on the shelves of Canadian stockists," writes Derek Pennington, President of the Toronto branch of the IPMS. "In particular," Mr Pennington continues, "I want to sound a warning to Airfix of the inevitable long-term effect on its sales here of the stratospheric prices now being demanded for both its new and its older kits! It is perhaps difficult to realistically compare the prices of the kits here with those charged in the UK, and such is, in any case, a fruitless exercise as all that counts in the *schoolboy* market on either side of the pond is the price sticker. Nevertheless, a rundown of recent Airfix kit prices quoted by Canadian stockists may be instructive (*Sterling conversions at the rate of exchange appertaining at the time of closing for press have been added in parentheses, and for comparison purposes the current UK retail prices have also been provided* [*in square parentheses*], *but it should be borne in mind that the latter include 15 per cent value added tax which is not, of course, applied to exported kits — Ed*):

1/72nd Sunderland Can$18·50 (£6·90) [£2·60]
1/72nd Superfort Can$18·50 (£6·90) [£3·25]
1/72nd Stirling Can$18·50 (£6·90) [£2·60]
1/72nd Hercules Can$23·50 (£8·77) [£4·50]
1/72nd Hurricane I Can$4·50 (£1·68) [£0·80]
1/72nd F-15B Eagle Can$15·00 (£5·60) [£2·15]
1/48th Hurricane I Can$9·95 (£3·71) [£1·65]
1/48th Mosquito Can$22·50 (£8·39) [£3·25]

"The clincher is the 1/72nd scale Lancaster at Can$25·00 (£9·33) [retailing in the UK at £3·80], and as with Airfix so with Matchbox whose 1/32nd scale kits escalated overnight from Can$14·95 (£5·58) to Can$18·95 (£7·07). It makes no sense to me to pay Can$18·95 for a 1/32nd scale Matchbox Bf 109 when a similar kit is available from Minicraft/Hasegawa for $10·95 (£4·08). We *serious* modellers represent a fairly small slice of the modelling pie in terms of *total* kit sales, and price is the factor determining the size of the remaining slices. In so far as *British* kit manufacturers are concerned, these slices will be meagre indeed if they cannot sell at realistic prices — much as I would *like* an Airfix Mossie, I can buy *three* Monogram items for the same price. The Monogram kits may be old but they are still of good quality. In the April issue. Roy Braybrook concluded his commentary on jet trainer sales potential by saying, *apropos* Hawk trainer price inflation, being the best is simply not good enough. The North American modeller can only echo *Amen*!"

Somebody is certainly caning our Canuck members of the modelling fraternity and it *isn't* Airfix! We have discussed Mr Pennington's complaint with Airfix, a spokesman for the company professing total mystification as to the reason for the inordinately high retail prices applied to Airfix kits in Canada and in which there would seem to be little consistency (the retail prices for the Sunderland and Stirling, which are in Series 6, being the same as that for the Superfortress which is in Series 7)! If value added tax is deducted, the Canadian retail prices are virtually treble those appertaining in the UK and Canadian modellers have every reason to feel outraged. Airfix states that the retail prices of its products in North America are fixed by the distributors, sees no valid reason why these prices should be so high and is "looking into the matter!" We hope that you are giving the matter some urgency, Airfix, because your distributors are bidding fair to price you out of the Canadian market!

This month's colour subject

The importance in the WarPac combat aircraft inventory of the *Flogger* family of variable-geometry tactical fighters has now transcended that of the tailed-delta *Fishbed*. Consequently, omission of this very competent Soviet warplane from any collection of modern fighter models purporting to be representative is no longer excusable. There are now two kits available in 1/72nd scale of *Flogger-B*, alias MiG-23MF, from Airfix and Hasegawa respectively, this being the current member of the family optimised for the air-air rôle, and the latter company is also offering a variation of its kit, which, it alleges, depicts *Flogger-D*, alias MiG-27, which is the version optimised for the tactical strike mission. We say *alleges* advisedly, as, for once, Hasegawa has gone off at half cock, as will be explained.

There is little to choose between the two *Flogger-B* kits and both have been reviewed in this column — Airfix's offering in the June issue — and they make up into creditable representations of the Mikoyan bureau's fighter with every appearance of authenticity; the minor detail errors that we believe to exist would come within the nitpicking category if detailed. In the case of Hasegawa's MiG-27 *Flogger-D* rendering, however, this distinguished Japanese company has not, for once, undertaken adequate research before committing itself to plastic! In fact, the kit represents something of a mélange of the MiG-27 and the MiG-23BM, or *Flogger-F*. The Japanese draughtsman have made the error of assuming the airframe of the MiG-27 to possess a closer affinity with that of the MiG-23 than it actually has!

The distinctive features of the MiG-27 *Flogger-D* are the fixed-ramp air intakes of revised design (Hasegawa has replaced the movable splitter plates of the MiG-23 but has not revised the intake contours), the multi-barrel Gatling type cannon (provided), the shorter engine tailpipe (provided), and increased-width low-pressure tyres (ignored), which, in turn, necessitate not unsubstantial bulging of the fuselage towards the rear of the fixed wing glove (see drawings on page 75). The redesigned, drooped nose to improve ground target acquisition, with attendant deepened windscreen and quarter lights, is common to both the MiG-23BM *Flogger-F* and MiG-27 *Flogger-D*, the former being otherwise similar (apart from cockpit-flanking armour and enlarged nosewheel) to the MiG-23MF *Flogger-B* interceptor.

It is not really practical to rework Hasegawa's purported MiG-27 into a model that genuinely represents the MiG-27, but all is not lost. While it is not possible to add a MiG-27 model to the collection, it is practical to produce a MiG-23BM *Flogger-F* by grafting the nose from Hasegawa's "Mig-27" kit onto the fuselage, wings and tail surfaces of the MiG-23MF *Flogger-B* kit — an expensive undertaking certainly, but perhaps worthwhile for the modeller with a particular penchant for WarPac combat aircraft.

Stepping up the scale to 1/48th, we have recently received a sample of Esci's kit of the MiG-23MF *Flogger-B* and a very nice job the Italian company has made of it, although we have one serious criticism — the cockpit interior. So important in this scale, the cockpit of Esci's *Flogger* is *very* basic, comprising no more than a three-part ejection seat, control column and an instrument panel mounted on a floor section which is also the top of the nosewheel housing. Esci can hardly claim that a sufficiency of detail was unavailable at the time the moulds of this kit were being prepared, for *two years ago* this month the MiG-23 was first seen in the west during a courtesy visit to the Finnish Air Force base at Kuopio-Rissala, and followed this up with a visit to the *Armée de l'Air* at Rheims a few weeks later. Plenty of photos of the cockpit interior of *Flogger* were taken during these occasions, more than sufficient for the production of a competent cockpit by Esci. Admittedly, the version seen at Kuopio-Rissala and Rheims was *Flogger-G*, but there is no reason to suppose that the cockpit of this MiG-23 version differs notably from that of *Flogger-B* depicted by Esci.

The fuselage of Esci's MiG-23 is divided just ahead of the leading edges of the wing gloves, the main section being split horizontally so as to facilitate the incorporation of the swing-wing feature, the forward section, including the cockpit, being split vertically. The nose cone and the jet tailpipe are separate parts. The arrangement of the fuselage assembly suggests that the MiG-27 kit announced by Esci will prove to be a modification of this kit and we hope that the Italians will have avoided the errors perpetrated by the Japanese. The wings have nice sharp leading and trailing edges, obtained by use of inset lower panels, and interlocking teeth endow the "swinging" portions with smooth action. The separate nose cone simplifies the task of adding weight to balance the tail — the accompanying instructions specify 20 grammes, but we used trial and error in order to achieve satisfactory balance.

The main undercarriage members of the MiG-23 family exude complexity, but, as a result of some ingenious planning on the part of Esci, construction is quite simple and the result most satisfying. The only awkward aspects of assembly are provided by the mounting of the free-standing doors over the mainwheels; these are each carried by two slender horizontal supports which have only minimal cementing areas and must, in turn, be *supported* while drying. The twin nosewheels have their mudguards moulded in, but look neat when assembled. The mainwheels are formed in halves and have finely engraved hub details.

Overall, the surface detailing is extremely fine, with raised panel lines and engraved outlines to the control surfaces and air brakes. Many of the parts are very small and finely moulded — there are 92 parts in all, moulded, apart from four transparencies, in light grey plastic — and include various antennae, small strakes, fairings, air intakes and the nose probe. With the windscreen formed separately from the canopy, the latter may be mounted in the open position if so desired, but such renders augmentation of the cockpit interior all the more necessary. The dorsal fin is extended only in flight, folding sideways for take-off and landing to afford the necessary concrete clearance, and this feature is covered by the kit by forming the fin in two parts so that either setting may be selected.

External stores take the form of three auxiliary fuel tanks in two sizes and a quartet of AAMs of two types. Pylon-mounted racks are provided for seven hardpoints, but two of these, applicable to the wet points in the outer wing panels, can only be fitted with the wings in the fully forward position. To complete the armament, the visible portions of the GSh-23L twin-barrel ventral cannon pack are provided as a separate three-part assembly. A very good decal sheet offers markings for V-VS machines in two very different finishes, one having the three-tone camouflage scheme and the other sporting the air superiority light grey finish. The decals include a great many small markings and clearly legible cyrillic stencillings, as well as the national insignia and individual aircraft numbers.

This is a fine kit and quite reasonably priced — if anything is *reasonably* priced — by today's standards at £4·25 in the UK. We have been informed by Humbrol that it has now taken over the UK distribution of Esci kits and will be releasing these as they become available from Italy.

The last Curtiss biplane

"Helldiver" as an aircraft name has, as commented by Capt Eric Brown when writing about the ill-favoured SB2C series in the December issue, always had very strong Hollywood connotations, and although a generic designation for all Curtiss dive bombers, be they biplane or monoplane, is usually associated with the former, which, to many aficionados, best represented the spirit, if not the literal fulfilment, of that evocative appellation. The last of the biplane series was the SBC-4 and it is *this* Helldiver that provides the subject matter for a delightful 37-part 1/72nd scale kit from Heller.

The SBC-4 was ordered — as the Curtiss Model 77 — by a French Purchasing Commission on behalf of the *Aéronavale* in 1939, but the 50 aircraft that actually bore French markings were US Navy SBC-4s relinquished — one wonders if not without some alacrity — at the end of May 1940 as a result of urgent pleas from the French government. In the event, apart from five that were to reach the UK and become Clevelands, these SBC-4s were destined to rot away at Fort de France, Martinique, and it was perhaps just as well for the *Aéronavale* crews who would have been pitted in these aesthetically appealing but operationally ineffectual biplanes against the cannon of the Messerschmitt Bf 109Es and Bf 110Cs. Thus, the operational exploits of the SBC series of Helldiver biplanes were confined to imaginative Hollywood epics. Nevertheless, marking the end of an era in US shipboard combat aircraft development, the SBC-4 is a worthy enough subject for a model and Heller has made a very good job of the kit.

The quality and fit of the parts are excellent, and the surface detailing, which includes the rib effect on the fabric-covered areas of the lower wing, is clearly defined but not exaggerated. Although comprising only five parts, the cockpit interiors look very well through the one-part canopy, while the undercarriage has been given delicate and effective treatment with a minimum of parts. The engine has been fully modelled, and has separate push-rod and exhaust assemblies. Assembly and alignment of the wings is quite simple because the four centre section struts are integrally formed with a section of the fuselage decking, and the interplane struts are rigidly fixed when cemented to the lower wings, thus forming what is, for practical purposes, a jig.

An auxiliary fuel tank is included for mounting beneath the fuselage; camouflage scheme drawings are provided for both British and French examples — full-colour illustrations of the SBC series were included, incidentally, in the number five issue of our companion publication, AIR ENTHUSIAST — and the decal sheet provides both RAF and *Aéronavale* roundels, plus serials to accompany the former, but both British fin flashes and French rudder striping must be applied by hand. The UK retail price of this kit is 95p.

Der Mehrzweckhubschrauber BO 105

Hitherto, Italaerei has confined itself to 1/72nd scale, but this Italian company has now entered the 1/32nd field with a kit of the MBB BO 105 multi-purpose helicopter, which, in recent years, has proved itself one of Europe's most successful choppers, with widespread military and civil applications. The Italaerei kit consists of 100 component parts, all but the eight transparencies being moulded in dark green plastic. Surface detailing is limited to the essentials, but is none the worse for that and is finely wrought.

With the large areas of very clear glazing, the cabin interior *needs* to be competently equipped and happily it is just that, with a floor, rear bulkhead, five seats, control columns, foot pedals, instrument panel, consoles, and two identical — and somewhat passive looking — crew figures which are provided with separately-moulded headsets! The cabin doors, also moulded separately, can be fixed in the open position if so desired. The head assembly of the four-bladed main rotor includes a lot of small parts, some of which demand very careful handling owing to their extremely small size, but the additional care is well worth exerting as the result is very realistic. The two-bladed tail rotor is also well detailed.

The undercarriage consists of two main skids and a tail bumper forming a sturdy support for the model. As an optional installation, the kit includes six rocket launching tubes to be mounted three per side on brackets just above the skid undercarriage attachment points. The kit is primarily for military variants of the BO 105, and markings are provided for armed examples supplied to the *Bundeswehr* and an unarmed example operated by the Dutch *Koninklijke Luchtmacht* on behalf of the Netherlands Army. We understand that this kit is the forerunner of a series of 1/32nd scale helicopters from Italaerei and it certainly provides a promising beginning. Incidentally, the BO 105 has recently appeared in the form of a very nice 1/72nd scale kit from Airfix, and there is another of much earlier vintage in 1/100th scale from Roskopf.

A violent French breeze

Following hard upon its Vampire FB Mk 5, Heller has now released in 1/72nd scale the francisation of this venerable de Havilland jet fighter, the SE 535 Mistral. The *version française*, which first flew on 2 April 1951, differed from the Vampire FB Mk 5 essentially in having an Hispano-Suiza Nene 104 in place of the Goblin and an SNCASO ejection seat, and all but 10 of the 42 component parts of Heller's Mistral kit are common to the preceding Vampire kit. All the new components — the recontoured rear fuselage with its larger jetpipe, the redesigned air intakes, the ejection seat, and the modified undercarriage doors and wheels — are incorporated into one separate frame so that best advantage can be taken of the high proportion of commonality between the component parts of the two kits.

The fit of the parts is exemplary, as it is also with the Vampire kit, and it is moulded in silver plastic with finely wrought surface detailing. The decal sheet is small but well filled with markings for two of the 247 production Mistrals delivered, one operated by EC 1/6 *Oranie* and the other by the *Aéronavale*. The retail price of the Mistral kit in the UK is 95p.

The Red Arrows' latest

With the aerobatic display season in the UK now at its peak, many will already have had an opportunity to see the RAF's famous *Red Arrows* team flying its newly-acquired BAe Hawks, and Airfix has been inspired to reissue its kit of the Hawk T Mk 1 now moulded in red plastic and accompanied by a new decal sheet providing the very distinctive team markings, in blue and white, with serials for all of the team's 10 Hawks — including that unfortunately lost in May after striking the mast of a small yacht during a low-level pass off Brighton — and decals for a camouflaged example from No 79 Sqdn of No 1 Tactical Weapons Unit at RAF Brawdy.

Although the correct *Red Arrows* colour scheme is well catered for by this kit, Airfix has made no provision for the small but important modifications that have been made to the demonstration Hawks, such as the three small pipes above the jetpipe to feed the liquid, which, when mixed with the exhaust gases, produces the coloured smoke which is so much a part of the *Red Arrows*' display routine. The necessary modification is easily made by using fine wire and adds much to the authenticity of the finished model. Being identical, as far as the actual components are concerned, to the original kit, this re-issue includes among its 95 component parts a selection of weaponry to be carried on the external hardpoints, but as these are not applicable to the *Red Arrows* aircraft, the various holes in the lower wing surface which are partly formed but retain a thin covering should be left as they are to maintain a smooth surface. This kit is a good one, both accurate and easily assembled, and as it is of fairly recent vintage, there are no discernible signs of mould wear on the parts. Airfix's *Red Arrows* Hawk is included in Series 3.

Wing struts galore

An item has reached us this month which could well be the answer to a prayer for many a scratch builder or kit converter. Contrail (Sutcliffe Productions of Westcombe, Shepton Mallett, Somerset) has produced a package of aerofoil-section strips. These strips, which are each 1 ft (30,50 cm) in length and moulded in dark grey plastic, comprise nine in total: two 6,50 mm wide, two 4,50 mm wide, two 3,00 mm wide and three 2,00 mm wide. Injection moulded, these strips, being of equal camber each side, are perfect for struts and have the requisite rigidity usually lacking when strips cut from plastic sheet are used. They also remove the lengthy chore of scraping and sanding to streamlined sections.

Although marketed as being for use as wing struts in 1/72nd scale, they possess numerous obvious applications to other scales and for other purposes (eg, undercarriage or float struts, or even rotor blades). Packaged in a plastic bag with a cardboard insert for protection, the strips are finely moulded and the UK retail price is a very reasonable 60p per pack, plus postage, so we fail to see how modellers can possibly afford to miss out on these, as even those not indulging in conversion or scratch building need to replace lost or damaged parts from time to time.

Decal review

Rareliners: (PO Box 6283, Bellevue, Wash 98007) Having recently reviewed favourably Rareliners' decal sheet for an Eastern Provincial Boeing 737, we are very pleased to receive a new release from this concern offering markings for a McDonnell Douglas DC-9-30 of Air Canada in 1/144th scale and tailored to fit the Airfix kit. These decals are of excellent quality and are comprehensive in that they include the broad red cheat line which runs from nose to tail of the fuselage, and also the complete area of red on each side of the fin-and-rudder assembly, upon which is superimposed white maple leaf logos. If the tail is painted white, these logos are not needed, the maple leaf logos then being provided as transparent sections of the red decals. Door outlines are provided as is the legend *Air Canada* in large red letters for application along each side of the fuselage over the cabin windows. The flight deck window decal is an optional item. A choice of registration letters makes it possible to model any one of the four DC-9s in the Air Canada fleet, each with an individual fleet number marked on the vertical tail and the nosewheel doors. The accompanying instruction sheet provides diagrams and clear placing instructions, and the retail price of the sheet is $1·50, plus postage.

Microscale: (Krasel Industries Inc, Santa Ana, CA 92705) The now regular monthly batch of Microscale decal releases this month consists of four sheets in 1/48th scale and relate to the F-4 Phantom, the F-100 Super Sabre and the A-1H Skyraider. Sheet No 48-76 is given over entirely to data for the F-4, consisting mainly of white stencilling but including many red warning signs, ejection seat triangles, yellow arrows, rescue instruction panels and many other items too numerous to list. There are well over 500 separate items on the sheet, each one numbered and keyed to a sheet of diagrams illustrating their placement. Unfortunately, these diagrams are to a small scale, and in three cases heavy shading obliterates certain areas, rendering it impossible to identify the intended location of the decals!

The next two sheets, Nos 48-77 and 48-78, are devoted to the F-100, the first providing for three different aircraft of the USAF, one of which, from the 354th TFW, having a most striking fin design (overall yellow with black horizontal stripes and arrows with the unit emblem superimposed). The other two aircraft, one camouflaged and the other natural metal, are less colourful but offer some interesting features. The camouflaged aircraft, for example, has the inscriptions *Mary Jane* and *Carol Ann* on the port and starboard sides of the nose, and a green-and-white chequered band near the top of the vertical tail surfaces. The sheet carries a mass of other markings, stencillings, warnings, wing walks, rescue signs, etc. The second F-100 sheet relates to only two aircraft, one of which sports a standard scheme but with a large number of small markings over its natural metal finish and the other, while basically natural metal, has large areas of red and white, all of the former and some of the latter being provided as decals, the remainder of the white having to be painted as a background. The recommended kit for these decals is by Monogram, but they are also applicable to Esci's F-100D.

Completing the quartet is sheet No 48-79 for the Monogram A-1H kit, although the more colourful of the two schemes provided is actually for the externally similar A-1J when serving with the 516th FS. This has a basic overall light grey finish but features a diagonal dark blue band, emblazoned with white stars, around the rear fuselage, and an elaborate fin design on a similar theme but embodying the letters "LP" in black. A yellow feline head — presumably a puma — decorates each side of the engine cowling. The A-1H is camouflaged and served with the 56th Special Operations Wing in Vietnam in 1970. The markings are more or less standard apart from the legend *Bubbles or Bust* on each side of the cowling. Some additional small antennae are to be fitted and are noted on the accompanying instruction sheet. There are hundreds of small markings on the sheet in addition to the major ones mentioned above and instrument panels are also included. □ F J HENDERSON

IN PRINT

"Thunderbolt"
by Warren M Bodie
Sentry Books Inc, California, USA, $2·95
74 pp, 8⅛ in by 11 in, illustrated

IN magazine format, this is described as a special edition of the bi-monthly "Wings", and it closely follows the style of production of that magazine, in which much of the material on the Republic P-47 first appeared. The story is told largely through the use of photographs with very lengthy and detailed captions, and embraces operations as well as the design and development history. Numerous rare photographs appear, and Warren Bodie has made an excellent job of the research necessary to put this account together.

"Luftwaffe in Finland 1941-1944, Vol 2"
by Ossi Anttonen
Aviabook, Helsinki, Finland, 50FMK
130 pp, 6¾ in by 10 in, illustrated

COVERS, with the help of 104 photographs, the activities of the *Luftwaffe* in Finland from the beginning of 1943 to September 1944, when Finland signed an armistice with the Soviet Union and co-operation with Germany ceased. The entire text, and the photograph captions, appears in English as well as Finnish. Copies can be ordered from Aviabook, PL40, SF-01531 Helsinki-Vantaa-Lento, Finland, for £6·00 sterling or US$14·00.

"German Bombers over the Med"
by Bryan Philpott
Patrick Stephens Ltd, Cambridge, £2·95 (card), £4·50 (casebound)
96 pp, 6⅝ in by 9⅜ in, illustrated

ANOTHER collection of photographs drawn from the *Bundesarchiv*, Koblenz, many of them previously unpublished, with captions identifying the units and, so far as possible, locations.

"Seven Decades of Progress: A Heritage of Aircraft Turbine Technology"
Edited by William Schoneberger, et al
Aero Publishers, Inc, Fallbrook, California, 92028, USA, $24·95
232 pp, 8¾ in by 11½ in, illustrated

THIS IS not a "coffee table" book; its text is too good for such an appellation. It is an illustrated history of the General Electric Corporation's involvement with gas turbines, ranging from Sanford Moss's work with exhaust driven superchargers in World War I, through the company's activities with Sir Frank Whittle in World War II, to the CF6 series engine currently being used in the A300 and planned for variants of the Boeing 767.

One may wish for more text, but what there is is solid, telegraphic and factual. This is also a beautifully turned out book. Its more than 400 *colour* photos, augmented by simple schematic drawings and some cutaways, are no less than magnificent, artfully edited and brilliantly reproduced on high quality paper. No library relating to jet engine development should be without this volume. — RKS.

"F-5 in Action", by Lou Drendel
"A-26 Invader in Action", by Jim Mesko
Squadron/Signal Publications, Texas, USA
$4·95 each
50 pp each, 8¼ in by 11 in, illustrated

LATEST titles in a useful series for modellers and general enthusiasts alike, with plenty of photographs, finish details, colour profiles and brief text.

WESTWIND **_from page 69_**

and external pods under the wing roots for rescue packs, extra fuel or ordnance. Various of these options remain available to customer specification, but the 1124N has meanwhile evolved into the Sea Scan coast guard and naval tactical support version of the Westwind, in which the radar is mounted in an extended and drooped nose radome. Three specially-equipped Model 1123s were acquired by the Israeli Navy during 1977 and these have subsequently been converted to 1124N Sea Scan standard with turbofan engines and other special equipment. The radar, in this case, is Litton LASR-2, and the Global GNS-500A VLF/Omega navaid is fitted; weapon strongpoints are on the fuselage sides rather than the inner wings and can presumably carry more lethal loads than the officially admitted flare dispensers.

As a maritime surveillance aircraft, Sea Scan has a low-altitude search-endurance of 6·1 hrs and a search range of 1,510 mls (2 428 km) at 3,000 ft (915 m). At higher altitudes, the search range increases to 2,800 mls (4 500 km) and the endurance to more than eight hours.

Another semi-military application for the Westwind I will emerge in 1981 when IAI delivers the four aircraft recently ordered by Rhein Flugzeugbau for use as high speed target tugs. The target towing installation, with a facility for changing targets in flight, is now under development. A version of the Westwind 2 with nose radar installation similar to that of Sea Scan, has been projected to meet the current SAC requirement for a Companion Trainer Aircraft (CTA).

In the beginning

The aircraft now in production as the Westwind had its origins on the drawing board of Ted R Smith, who had founded the Aero Design and Engineering Co in 1950 to manufacture his twin-engined Aero Commander five/seven-seat light transports. Deliveries of the piston-engined Aero Commanders began in February 1952 and the design had progressed through a number of models by 1958, in which year the company was acquired by Rockwell-Standard Corporation. This marked the first entry by Rockwell into the aircraft manufacturing industry; the name of its subsidiary was changed to Aero Commander Inc in October 1960, with Ted Smith remaining VP, Research and Development.

Announced in the spring of 1961 as the Aero Commander Jet 1121, the company's entry into the biz-jet field was an all-new design, the lines of which are perpetuated in the Westwind of 1980. Five years of engineering work and market research had led the company to conclude that "turboprop engines were just a more expensive way of turning a propeller" and that the step from piston engines to turbojets was justified. With its emphasis on a roomy cabin, (originally optimised for only four passengers) and low first cost, (less than $500,000 in 1963) the Jet Commander, as it soon became known, attracted much interest and, by mid-1962, a dozen orders plus letters of

IAI Westwind I Specification

Power Plant: Two Garrett AiResearch TFE731-3-1G turbofans each rated at 3,700 lb st (1 678 kgp) for take-off, with Grumman clam-shell type thrust reversers. Fuel capacity, 1,330 US gal (5 035 l) in integral wing, wing tip and fuselage fuel tanks, plus optional 105 US gal (397 l) auxiliary tank in rear baggage bay.

Performance: Max speed, 471 kt (872 km/h) TAS at 19,400 ft (5 913 m); VMO, 360 kt (667 km/h) IAS up to 19,400 ft (5 913 m); MMO, 0·765 indicated from 19,400 ft (5 913 m) to 45,000 ft (13 716 m); high speed cruise, 438 kt (811 km/h) at 41,000 ft (12 497 m); long-range cruise, 401 kt (1 743 km/h) at 41,000 ft (12 497 m); max operating altitude, 45,000 ft (13 716 m); balanced field length (FAR 25), ISA, sl, max weight, 4,950 ft (1 509 m); landing runway length (FAR 25), ISA, sl, max landing weight, 2,450 ft (747 m); range (standard fuel) 2,806 mls (4 516 km) with seven passengers and 45 min reserve fuel; range (max fuel), 3,042 mls (4 895 km) with four passengers.

Weights: Basic empty weight, 10,186 lb (4 620 kg); basic operating weight (typical), 12,700 lb (5 760 kg); max payload (typical), 3,300 lb (1 497 kg); max zero fuel weight, 16,000 lb (7 258 kg); max take-off weight, 22,850 lb (10 365 kg); max landing weight, 19,000 lb (8 618 kg).

Dimensions: Span, 44 ft 9½ in (13,65 m); length, 52 ft 3 in (15,93 m); height, 15 ft 9½ in (4,81 m); wing area, 308·26 sq ft (28,64 m^2); aspect ratio, 6·5:1; sweepback, 4·62 deg at quarter chord; undercarriage track, 11 ft 0 in (3,35 m); wheelbase, 22 ft 6 in (6,86 m).

Accommodation: Two pilots on flight deck. Standard cabin interior provides seven passenger seats; maximum accommodation, 10 passengers. Cabin length, 20 ft 0 in (6,1 m) overall. 15 ft 6 in (4,72 m) less flight deck; height, 4 ft 11 in (1,49 m), width, 4 ft 9 in (1,45 m). Two baggage compartments in rear fuselage, capacities 40 cu ft (1,13 m^3) and 14 cu ft (0,39 m^3), max combined load 1,050 lb (476 kg).

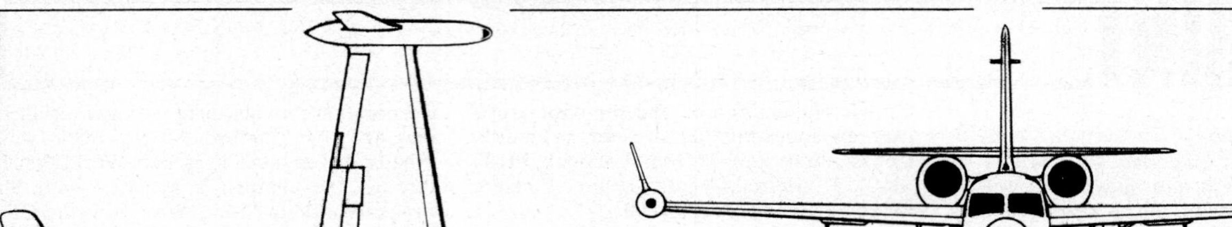
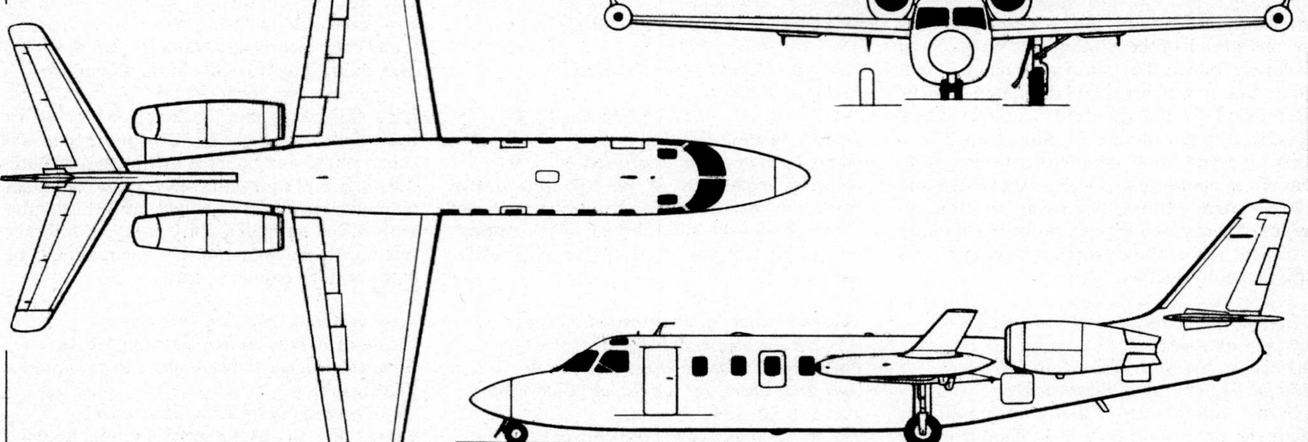

(Below) Three-view general arrangement drawing of the Westwind 2.

intent for four more. The original schedule called for first flight in the last quarter of 1962 and first customer deliveries at the end of 1963 — target dates that proved just a little too optimistic. Two prototypes — as well as a static test specimen — were built and the first of these flew on 27 January 1963.

While certification proceeded, production of an initial batch of 50 aircraft was put in hand and the first of these was flown on 5 October 1964; FAA Type Approval followed on 4 November and the first delivery was made, a year later than originally expected, on 11 January 1965. Prototypes and production Jet Commander 1121s were powered by the 2,850 lb st (1 293 kgp) General Electric CJ 610-1; whereas the prototypes were introduced at a gross weight of 14,000 lb (6 350 kg), however, the production aircraft were certificated at 16,800 lb (7 620 kg), thanks in part to the decision to extend the length of the forward fuselage by 2 ft 6 in (0,76 m) and to increase the basic seating to six in the cabin. The longer fuselage was incorporated in the second prototype prior to its first flight on 14 April 1964. Flight testing revealed that the proposed use of the main landing gear as a speed brake was not acceptable and the wing-mounted speed brakes were then introduced.

The Jet Commander sold steadily if without spectacular results, and additional 50-aircraft batches were authorised to follow the first on the Aero Commander assembly lines at Bethany, Oklahoma. By the beginning of 1957, work on the third of these batches had begun and deliveries were just into three figures as the Rockwell-Standard Corporation began discussions intended to lead to a merger with North American Aviation. By August, the merger discussions were close to reaching a successful conclusion, but the US Justice Department then warned that the nation's anti-trust laws would be violated if the merger proceeded because both companies had in production a comparable product — the Jet Commander and the Sabreliner. For the merger to proceed, urgent action had to be taken by one or other of the prospective partners to divest itself of its biz-jet programme — and since the Sabreliner was already serving in some numbers with the US military, the Jet Commander was the more obvious candidate.

By chance, an IAI purchasing mission was in the USA in the summer of 1967, securing equipment required for various of the company's programmes; also by chance, a confidant of Willard Rockwell was also a friend of the leader of the Israeli mission, Jacob Shapiro. Informed that the Jet Commander

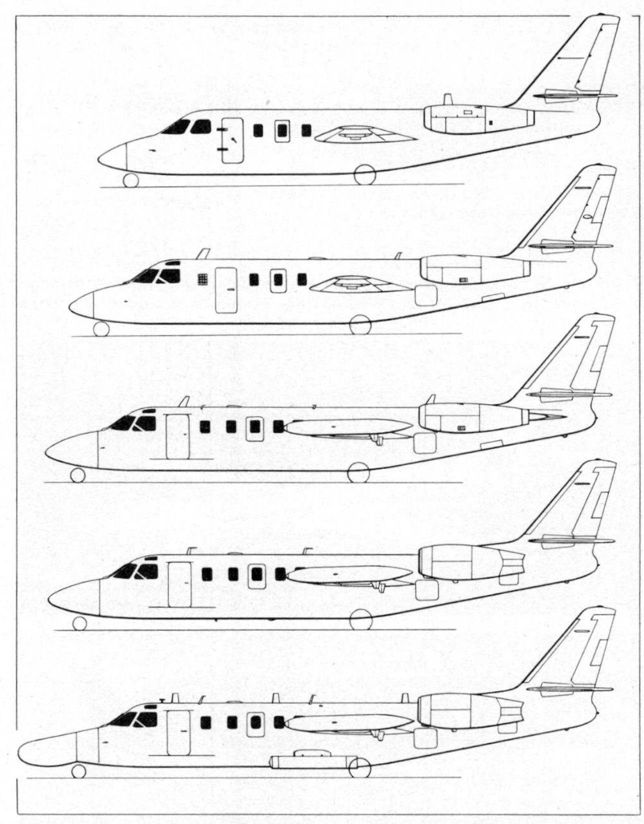

(Above) Side view profiles depicting, top to bottom, the Jet Commander prototype, the Jet Commander 1121 production model, the Commodore Jet -1123, the Westwind -1124 and the Sea Scan.

(Below) The IAI Sea Scan prototype, used to develop the features incorporated on three similar aircraft used by the Israeli Navy. This particular aircraft (c/n 154) was one of the first production Commodore Jet -1123s from Tel Aviv and later became the prototype Westwind -1124 (above right).

(Above) The original short-fuselage prototype of the Jet Commander 1121 on its first take-off and (below) the second flying prototype, with lengthened fuselage.

(Above) The first of the IAI stretched Commodore Jet prototypes, an American-built 1122 converted to 1123, and (below) an IAI-production Commodore Jet 1123.

programme might be up for sale at a bargain price, Shapiro called IAI's founder and leading light, Al Schwimmer; within 72 hrs, Schwimmer was in New York and within two weeks IAI had agreed to purchase the Jet Commander programme, lock, stock and barrel (but not the Commander name), at a reported price of $30m. The Rockwell-North American merger was consummated as planned on 22 September 1967, and by the middle of 1968 the jigs and tools had been relocated at Lod (now Ben Gurion) International Airport, Tel Aviv.

While plans were completed for the transfer of production to Israel, IAI also assumed responsibility for the sale of the final 49 of the 150 Jet Commanders built at Bethany. These included 11 Model 1121As with gross weight increased to 17,500 lb (7 938 kg) and 19 Model 1121Bs powered by the uprated 2,950 lb st (1 340 kgp) CJ610-5 engines; certification of these two variants was granted by the FAA on 19 September 1967 and 23 April 1968 respectively. Sales of these aircraft, from stock, continued through 1969 and 1970, with the name Commodore Jet replacing Jet Commander, as required by the terms of the agreement with Rockwell. Marketing was handled initially by a company set up in New York for the purpose by IAI and called Commodore Jet Inc. Aero Commander also had started development of the Model 1122 with numerous detail refinements plus the new features of the 1121A and 1121B. Three 1121s (c/n 29, 83 and 107) were converted to 1122 standard but plans to put this variant into production were overtaken by events.

With more powerful versions of the CJ610 becoming available, IAI decided to stretch the Model 1121 design before starting production at Tel Aviv. Two of the Model 1122s were set aside for conversion to prototypes of what would become known as the Commodore Jet 1123 in its production form. With 3,100 lb st (1 406 kgp) CJ610-9 engines, the developed aircraft was to have a 22-in (56-cm) fuselage stretch, increasing the basic passenger accommodation from six to eight; double-slotted Fowler flaps in place of the split flap, plus lift dumpers; a reprofiled leading edge; larger tailplane; systems improvements; an APU installation in the rear fuselage and fixed wing-tip fuel tanks on strengthened wings.

The first of the Commodore Jet 1123s made its first flight early in January 1970, but on its third flight on the 21st of that month the starboard flap actuator failed and the asymmetric flap configuration that resulted proved uncontrollable; the four crew members bailed out safely but the prototype was lost and IAI's enthusiasm for the new biz-jet was somewhat dampened, at least temporarily. Testing, with the second prototype, was resumed on 28 September 1970, and certification was obtained on 8 December 1971, at a new gross weight of 20,700 lb (9 390 kg); the first few production 1123s were by then off the line.

Production built up only slowly, with the first few aircraft delivered in 1972, at which time the style "Commodore Jet Eleven-23" was adopted in favour of the earlier "1123". To improve marketing in the USA, Atlantic Aviation was appointed IAI's exclusive distributor for the aircraft and early in 1973, on the latter company's initiative, the name of the Israeli-produced variant was changed to 1123 Westwind in a further effort to give it a distinct identity and to avoid confusion with the Jet Commander/Commodore Jet 1121s. In the course of 1973, Food Fair Inc of Philadelphia became the first operator of the 1123 Westwind in the USA, and Atlantic Aviation delivered its first aircraft, to Litton System Inc. In April of that year, the US Coast Guard leased the 10th production 1123 from IAI for six months to evaluate its potential (alongside a Cessna Citation) as a medium range search and rescue aircraft, and later in the year, Executive Jet Aviation purchased three 1123 Westwinds in QC (quick change) configuration with increased zero fuel and landing weights, modified baggage compartments and increased CG range to allow up to 4,000 lb (1 815 kg) of cargo to be carried in the cabin.

By the middle of 1974, IAI had delivered 25 Westwinds, but production of more than one a month was proving difficult, partly because of labour shortages caused by mobilisation following the Holy Day War in 1973. As already described, work on developing a turbofan-engined variant had started and, as the Westwind 1124, this would appear early in 1976. Production of the Westwind 1123 ended with a total of 36 built.

With the Westwind 1124 and its improved derivatives, IAI appears to have achieved its objective of producing a sound and thoroughly marketable product; certainly its investment in the purchase of the design rights, jigs and tools has been amply repaid and a production rate of four a month has now been established. Work is proceeding on a much more extensively modified new version of the aircraft — possibly to be known as the Westwind 1125 — which IAI plans to have available for deliveries "in the 1982-83 time frame". The company has said that "basic concepts for the design include intercontinental range, long range cruise speed in the Mach 0·8 envelope and highly economical operation". It is likely that this new Westwind will have sweepback on the wings and a newer generation of powerplants; its size probably will not be substantially greater than that of the current model and it is IAI's avowed intention to offer the same excellent value for money that is represented by the Westwind 1123. □

PE-8 from page 83

meanwhile, used in "kopek packages" on small-scale nocturnal raids over shorter ranges than that called for by the Berlin attack and against railheads, airfields and military concentrations behind the frontline. The few longer-range attacks against industrial targets and centres of population mounted primarily for morale-boosting and propaganda purposes were, for the most part, carried out with Ilyushin Il-4s*. Indeed, the ADD, formed as the V-VS's strategic bombing component in March 1942, was to fly 40 per cent of its sorties against battlefield targets and 43 per cent against railway and airfield targets in the immediate rear of the enemy, only 3·29 per cent of all sorties flown being of a strategic nature. Maj-Gen Vodop'yanov requested permission to fly experimental daylight bombing sorties with the Pe-8 and two aircraft were assigned for the trial, one being flown by Vodop'yanov and the other by Maj Nikolaev. Bombing results were reported to be good, but the aircraft were damaged and there is no evidence that the experiment was repeated!

The death knell for Pe-8 production was not long in sounding after the German onslaught began. Demanding on duralumin and other materials now in desperately short supply, and utilising labour and equipment that were required for vitally needed tactical aircraft, coupled with a lack of a clear policy towards the use of strategic air power, the Pe-8 became almost overnight a luxury that could be ill afforded and, in any case, had few supporters. Factory No 125, which had originally been assigned to Pe-8 production, was reallocated to the manufacture of the Pe-2 and, shortly thereafter, the decision was taken to transfer Factory No 22 lock, stock and barrel to Povolozh'e where it was to be amalgamated with Factory No 125 and concentrate on the twin-engined tactical bomber.

Thus, production of the Pe-8 ran down until the transfer of Factory No 22 in October 1941, terminating with the 79th production aircraft. All production examples had been powered by the AM-35A engine — some of those that had been converted for the ACh-30B Diesel for the Berlin attack subsequently had their Mikulin engines reinstated — although a small number of these were to be re-engined with the Shvetsov M-82 radial in 1942-43, and complaints concerning the efficacy of the forward armament had resulted in the last dozen or so aircraft off the line embodying a redesigned nose in which the turret with its twin ShKAS machine guns was replaced by a recontoured proboscis incorporating a gimbal mounting at its tip for a 20-mm ShVAK cannon.

The first knowledge of the Pe-8 gleaned by the Soviet Union's western allies came when, in May 1942, Pe-8 No 66 piloted by Maj E K Pusep, who had flown as co-pilot to Maj-Gen Vodop'yanov on the Berlin attack, landed at RAF Leuchars, near Dundee, after flying from Moscow, via Murmansk *en route* to Washington, via Prestwick and Reykjavik, carrying Foreign Minister Molotov and other senior Soviet officials. The Pe-8, its weapons bay filled with auxiliary fuel tanks, arrived in Washington on 29 May, returning over much the same route in the following month, arriving back in Moscow on 13 June, having crossed German-held territory at first light and maximum altitude in order to evade interception.

A dwindling number of Pe-8s continued in V-VS service throughout the remainder of hostilities, among their more noteworthy operations being bombing attacks on Königsberg (now Kaliningrad) in May 1943, and a series of attacks on German troop concentrations in the Kursk salient in the following July, when, for comparatively short-range missions, they carried up to 11,023 lb (5 000 kg) of bombs. Several Pe-8s survived the war and, with armament removed and gun positions faired over, and sporting civil registrations, these were used as freight transports in the Arctic until the early 'fifties. Earlier this year, an expedition was sent to the Khara-Tumus peninsula, east of the Khatanga River estuary, in Taimyr, to inspect the remains of a Pe-8 that had been force-landed on the south side of the Mys Kosisty after exhausting its fuel. This aircraft is now to be recovered and restored for exhibition in the Monino Air Forces Museum, near Moscow, as the only remaining example of the 79 aircraft of its type to be built.

The Pe-8 was the ultimate development of a generation of bombers born in the early 'twenties — when strategic bomber development was resumed in the Soviet Union after WW II, the basis of this resumption was to be provided, unwittingly, by Boeing with its B-29 Superfortress.* Petlyakov's long-range strategic bomber had not been a singularly outstanding aeroplane and obsolescence had been approaching even before production committal. Too high a proportion of its gross weight was accounted for by its structure and it was underpowered. Perhaps the opponents of its series production had been right, but for the wrong reasons! □

**Ilyushin Il-4s had, in fact, mounted the first Soviet nocturnal bombing attack on Berlin on the night of 8/9 August 1941, aircraft of the 1st Guards Mine/Torpedo Bomber Aviation Regiment (BAP) of the Baltic Fleet under Col E N Preobrazhensky in concert with Il-4s of the 22nd and 30th BAPs flying this mission, operating from Kagal and Aste on Saarema Island, a round distance of some 1,240 miles (2 000 km). Fifteen Il-4s were involved in the first attack, the Soviet Naval Air Force being in overall charge of the Berlin attacks which continued on a small scale until 4 September 1941.*

**The story of the acquisition of the B-29 by the Soviet Union and its subsequent development by the Tupolev bureau was told in "The Billion-Dollar Bomber", July-October 1971 issues.*

The photographs above and below taken at Leuchars in May 1942 show clearly (above) the 20-mm cannon dorsal turret and 12,7-mm gun nacelle position, and (below) the 20-mm cannon tail turret.

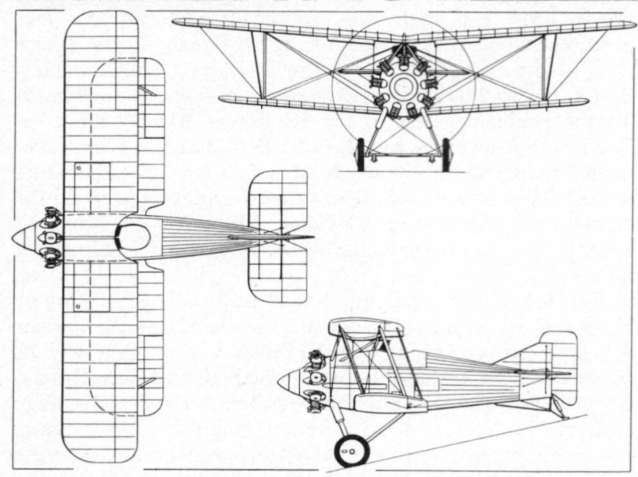

(Above and below) The sole Gambet prototype designed as a shipboard fighter for the Imperial Japanese Navy.

GLOSTER GOLDFINCH — UK

The second all-metal fighter designed by H P Folland, the Goldfinch was ordered in January 1926 as an all-metal version of the Gamecock, but, as initially completed, the prototype embodied a proportion of wood in its fuselage structure. After initial trials, the prototype was reworked, a lengthened, all-metal fuselage and revised tail unit being applied, and in its new form, the prototype Goldfinch was delivered to Martlesham late 1927. Powered by a supercharged 450 hp Bristol Jupiter VIIF nine-cylinder radial, and having two 0·303-in (7,7-mm) Vickers Mk I synchronised machine guns, the Goldfinch offered an extremely good performance, but in competing for a production contract to specification F.9/26 it was bested by the Bristol Bulldog. Max speed, 172 mph (277 km/h) at 10,000 ft (3 050 m). Time to 20,000 ft (6 095 m), 16 min. Empty weight, 2,058 lb (933 kg). Loaded weight, 3,236 lb (1 468 kg). Span, 30 ft 0 in (9,14 m). Length, 22 ft 3 in (6,78 m). Height, 10 ft 6 in (3,20 m). Wing area, 274·3 sq ft (25,48 m²).

GLOSTER GAMBET — UK

During 1926, in which year Gloucestershire Aircraft changed its name to Gloster Aircraft (on 11 November), the company was approached by the Japanese Nakajima concern, which (together with Aichi and Mitsubishi) had been asked to submit a design for a new shipboard fighter for the Imperial Japanese Navy. At this time, H P Folland was designing a shipboard fighter as a company venture. Named Gambet, the prototype was of wooden construction and powered by a 420 hp Bristol Jupiter VI nine-cylinder radial, armament consisting of two 0·303-in (7,7-mm) Vickers guns mounted in troughs in the fuselage sides. This prototype was acquired by Nakajima in July 1927, together with manufacturing rights, and after modification by a team led by Takao Yoshida and installation of a 520 hp Nakajima-built Jupiter VI engine, the Gambet competed against the prototypes of indigenous design and was ordered into production in April 1929 as the Navy Type 3 Carrier Fighter (A1N1). Max speed, 152 mph (245 km/h) at 5,000 ft (1 525 m). Time to 10,000 ft (3 050 m), 7·0 min. Endurance, 3·75 hrs. Empty weight, 2,010 lb (912 kg). Loaded weight, 3,075 lb (1 395 kg). Span, 31 ft 10 in (9,69 m). Length, 21 ft 3½ in (6,47 m). Height, 10 ft 8 in (3,24 m). Wing area, 284 sq ft (26,38 m²).

GLOSTER GNATSNAPPER — UK

The Gnatsnapper was designed to the requirements of specification N.21/26 calling for a single-seat shipboard fighter of all-metal construction and powered by a Bristol Mercury IIA nine-cylinder air-cooled radial. The first of two

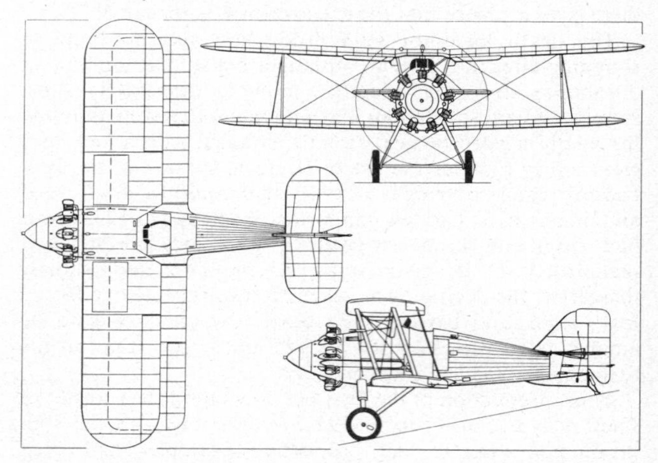

The Goldfinch (above in definitive form and below in original form) was the second all-metal fighter designed by H P Folland.

(Below) The first prototype Gnatsnapper in its original form, with Jupiter VII engine and plain ailerons.

Six guns and a cowled Jupiter VIIF distinguished the SS.19 (above) prototype for the Gauntlet.

(Above and below) The Gauntlet II, the photograph illustrating this type on skis in Finnish service.

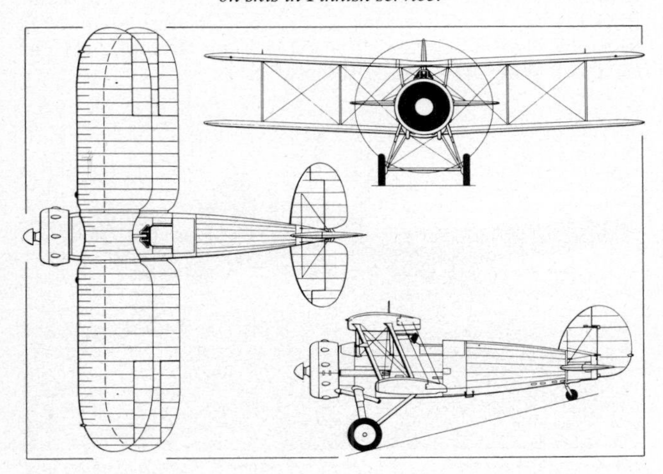

prototypes, temporarily powered by a Jupiter VII engine, flew in February 1928. The Mercury IIA was subsequently installed, but as this did not measure up to anticipated performance or reliability, the Jupiter VII was reinstated for official trials. The second prototype, initially with a Mercury IIA, was not completed until March 1930, but the designated power plant was again discarded shortly thereafter, and the first prototype was re-engined with a 540 hp Armstrong Siddeley Jaguar VIII 14-cylinder radial as the Gnatsnapper II, but suffered damage during official trials. In 1931, it was re-engined once more, with a steam-cooled 525 hp Rolls-Royce Kestrel IIS, as the Gnatsnapper III, subsequently serving as a Rolls-Royce test-bed and hack aircraft. The following data relate to the Jupiter-engined model. Max speed, 165 mph (265 km/h) at 10,000 ft (3 050 m). Time to 15,000 ft (4 570 m), 12·2 min. Endurance, 5 hrs. Empty weight, 2,970 lb (1 347 kg). Loaded weight, 3,625 lb (1 644 kg). Span, 33 ft 6 in (10,21 m). Length, 24 ft 7 in (7,48 m). Height, 10 ft 11 in (3,32 m). Wing area, 360 sq ft (33,44 m²).

GLOSTER GAUNTLET — UK

Competing against the Boulton Paul Partridge, the Armstrong Whitworth A.W.16 Starling II and the Hawker Hawfinch to meet the requirements of F.20/27 for a single-seat fighter built principally of steel or duralumin, the Gauntlet began life as the SS.18 designed to the contemporary F.10/27 specification and flew as such in January 1929, initially with a Mercury IIA engine. This was subsequently replaced by a 480 hp Jupiter VIIF (as the SS.18A) and then by a 560 hp Panther III (SS.18B), the Jupiter later being reinstated (as the SS.19). In its last-mentioned form, it was tested with four wing-mounted 0·303-in (7,7-mm) Lewis guns and two fuselage-mounted Vickers guns of similar calibre, but the wing-mounted guns were later removed (as the SS.19A), and with the 536 hp Mercury VIS engine (as the SS.19B), this was ordered into production in February 1934 with a twin Vickers Mk V-gun armament and a 640 hp Mercury VIS2 as the Gauntlet, the first production aircraft being completed in the following December. Twenty-four Gauntlet Is built by the parent company were to be followed by 204 Gauntlet IIs with revised (Hawker-type) structure. Seventeen were licence-built in Denmark by the Army Aviation Troops' Workshops (after procurement of one pattern aircraft) and ex-RAF Gauntlet IIs disposed of abroad comprised three to Rhodesia, four to South Africa and 25 to Finland. Six were later assigned to the RAAF in the Middle East. The following data relate to the Gauntlet II. Max speed, 230 mph (370 km/h) at 15,800 ft (4 815 m). Time to 20,000 ft (6 100 m), 9 min. Empty weight, 2,770 lb (1 255 kg). Loaded weight, 3,970 lb (1 800 kg). Span, 32 ft 10 in (9,99 m). Length, 26 ft 5 in (8,00 m). Height, 10 ft 3 in (3,10 m). Wing area, 315 sq ft (29,26 m²).

GLOSTER GLADIATOR — UK

A private venture to specification F.7/30, the Gladiator was a derivative of the Gauntlet and flew in prototype form (as the SS.37) on 12 September 1934 with a 530 hp Mercury IV engine. Series production to specification F.14/35 was initiated in the summer of 1935, and the first Gladiator Is were flown in

The last of the RAF's biplane fighters, the Gladiator I and II (the latter being illustrated above and below) were the most widely exported British pre-war fighter types.

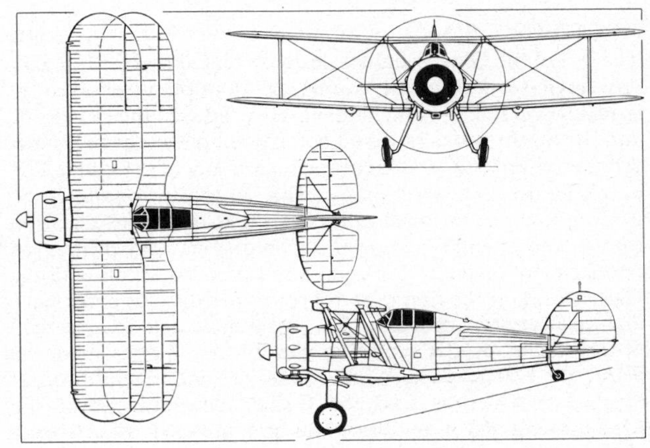

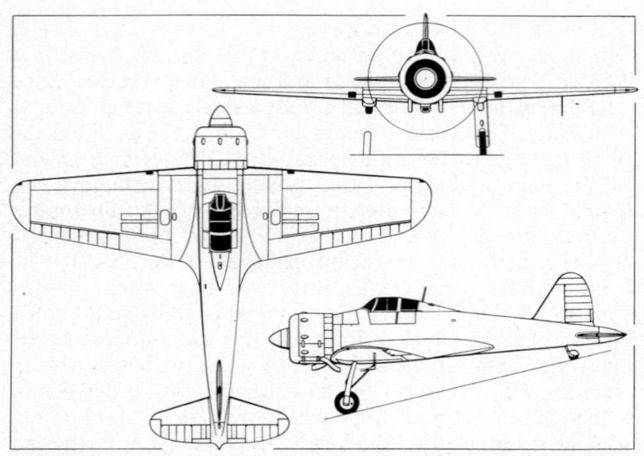

The F.5/34 fighter (above and below) suffered protracted development, the first of two prototypes being seen below.

January 1937. The Gladiator I was powered by an 830 hp Mercury IX engine and (eventually) standardised on an armament of two fuselage-mounted and two wing-mounted 0·303-in (7,7-mm) Browning guns, a total of 378 being built, followed by 270 Gladiator IIs with the similarly-rated Mercury VIIIA or VIIIAS, plus 38 completed as Sea Gladiator (Interim) shipboard fighters and a further 60 built from the outset as Sea Gladiators. Production included 26 Mk Is for Latvia, 14 Mk Is for Lithuania, six Mk Is and six Mk IIs for Norway, 37 Mk Is and 18 Mks IIs for Sweden, 22 Mk Is for Belgium, 36 Mk Is for China, four Mk Is for Eire, two Mk Is for Greece and 15 Mk IIs for Portugal. Ex-RAF aircraft transferred to other air arms comprised 30 Mk IIs for Finland, 17 Mk IIs for Greece, 45 Mk Is (brought up to Mk II standards) and Mk IIs for Egypt, 14 Mk Is and Mk IIs for Iraq, and one Mk I and 11 Mk IIs for South Africa. The following data relate to the Mk II. Max speed, 257 mph (414 km/h) at 14,600 ft (4 450 m). Time to 10,000 ft (3 050 m), 4·5 min. Range, 444 mls (714 km). Empty weight, 3,444 lb (1 562 kg). Loaded weight, 4,864 lb (2 206 kg). Span, 32 ft 3 in (9,83 m). Length, 27 ft 5 in (8,36 m). Height, 10 ft 7 in (3,22 m). Wing area, 323 sq ft (30,00 m^2).

GLOSTER F.5/34 — UK

The last of the Gloster fighter designs created by H P Folland, the single-seat all-metal cantilever monoplane evolved to specification F.5/34 (which ultimately produced the Hurricane and the Spitfire) was powered by an 840 hp Mercury IX nine-cylinder radial engine and carried an armament of eight 0·303-in (7,7-mm) Browning guns. This aircraft, to which no designation was assigned other than that of the specification that it was intended to meet, suffered somewhat protracted development owing to the company's preoccupation with the Gladiator, and the first of two prototypes did not commence flight trials until December 1937, with the second following in March 1938. By the time that the Gloster fighter made its début, the Hurricane had achieved service and the Spitfire had reached production, and the further development of the Mercury-engined monoplane was not pursued. Max speed, 316 mph (508 km/h) at 16,000 ft (4 875 m). Time to 20,000 ft (6 095 m), 11 min. Empty weight, 4,190 lb (1 900 kg). Loaded weight, 5,400 lb (2 449 kg). Span, 38 ft 2 in (11,63 m). Length, 32 ft 0 in (9,76 m). Height, 10 ft 2 in (3,09 m). Wing area, 230 sq ft (21,36 m^2).

GLOSTER F.9/37 — UK

Designed by W G Carter to meet the demands of specification F.9/37 calling for a twin-engined single-seater, the Gloster fighter was of all-metal stressed skin construction and was intended to carry a fuselage-mounted armament of two 20-mm Hispano cannon and four 0·303-in (7,7-mm) Browning machine guns. Two prototypes were ordered, the first of these, powered by two 1,050 hp Bristol Taurus T-S(a) 14-cylinder radials, being flown on 3 April 1939. The aircraft attained a maximum speed of 360 mph (579 km/h) at 15,000 ft (4 570 m), but was badly damaged in a landing accident early in its flight test programme. When testing was resumed in April 1940, it had been re-engined with 900 hp Taurus T-S(a) IIIs with the result that performance suffered, maximum attainable speed in level flight being reduced to 332 mph (534 km/h) at 15,200 ft (4 630 m). The second prototype, meanwhile, had been completed with 885 hp Rolls-Royce Peregrine liquid-cooled engines, flying for the first time on 22 February 1940, and attaining a maximum speed of 330 mph (531 km/h) during subsequent flight testing. Although the handling characteristics of Gloster's F.9/37 contender were considered highly satisfactory and performance with the original engines had proved spectacular, no production was ordered. The following data relate to the Taurus T-S(a)-powered prototype. Max speed, 360 mph (579 km/h) at 15,000 ft (4 570 m). Climb, 2,460 ft/min (12,5 m/sec) at 12,000 ft (3 660 m). Empty weight, 8,828 lb (4 004 kg). Loaded weight, 11,615 lb (5 269 kg). Span, 50 ft 0½ in (15,24 m). Length, 37 ft 0½ in (11,27 m). Height, 11 ft 7 in (3,30 m). Wing area, 386 sq ft (35,85 m^2).

The second Peregrine-powered F.9/37 prototype is illustrated above and the general arrangement drawing depicts the first Taurus-powered prototype.

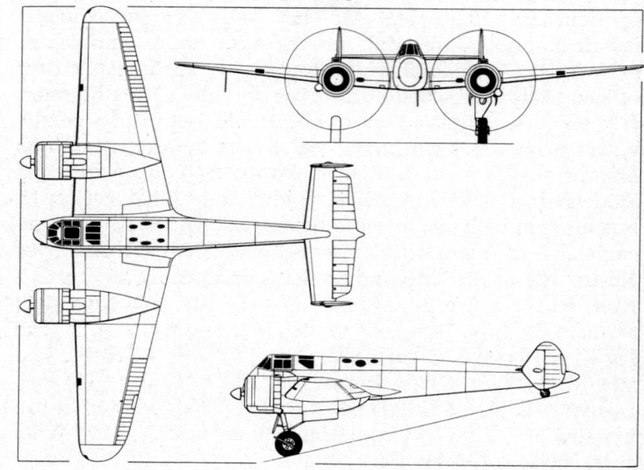

Volume 19 Number 3 September 1980

Managing Editor *William Green*
Editor *Gordon Swanborough*
Modelling Editor *Fred J Henderson*
Contributing Artist *Dennis Punnett*
Contributing Photographer *Stephen Peltz*
Editorial Representative, Washington *Norman Polmar*
Managing Director *Donald Syner*
Publisher *Keith Attenborough*
Financial Director *Claire Sillette*
Advertising Director *Elizabeth Baker*
Advertising Manager *Roger Jewers*
Subscription Manager *Sheilagh Campbell*
Distribution Manager *William Streek*

Editorial Offices:
The AIR INTERNATIONAL, PO Box 16, Bromley, BR2 7RB Kent.

Subscription, Advertising and Circulation Offices:
The AIR INTERNATIONAL, De Worde House, 283 Lonsdale Road, London SW13 9QW. Telephone 01-878 2454. US and Canadian readers may address subscriptions and general enquiries to AIR INTERNATIONAL PO Box 353, Whitestone, NY 11357 for onward transmission to the UK, from where all correspondence is answered and orders despatched.

MEMBER OF THE AUDIT BUREAU OF CIRCULATIONS ABC

Subscription rates, inclusive of postage, direct from the publishers, per year:

United Kingdom	£7·50
Overseas	£8·00
USA/Canada	$20·00

Rates for other countries and for air mail subscriptions available on request from the Subscription Department at the above address.

The AIR INTERNATIONAL is published monthly by Fine Scroll Limited, distributed by Ducimus Books Ltd and printed by William Caple & Company Ltd, Chevron Press, Leicester, England.

Second Class postage approved at New York, NY. USA Mailing Agents: Air-Sea Freight Inc, 527 Madison Avenue, New York, NY 10022.

ISSN 0306-5634

CONTENTS

FRONT COVER British Aerospace Harrier GR Mk 3 tactical fighters of No 1 Squadron from RAF Wittering on exercise.

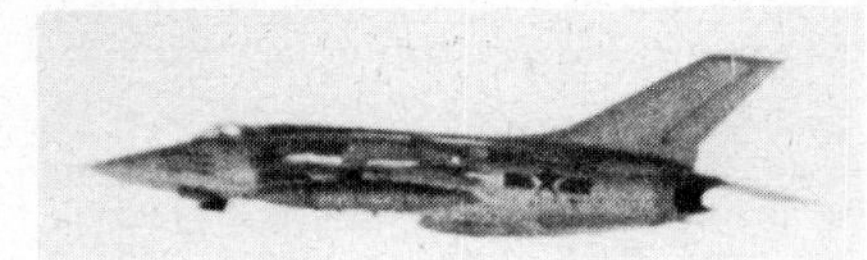

WRENDEZVOUS WITH WREN

"Try to cultivate a spirit of aggression, Dilbury."

AIRSCENE

MILITARY AFFAIRS

BRAZIL

The *Fôrça Aérea Brasileira* is reported to be enthusiastic concerning the **potential of** the EMBRAER **EMB-120 Brasilia** and is planning initial procurement of 25 for transport and communications tasks with deliveries commencing 1984-85 to the *Comando de Transportes Aéreos.* The first prototype Brasilia is scheduled to commence flight testing in May 1982, with the second prototype following in October of that year, and the military version will be capable of carrying up to 30 troops or 6,610 lb (3 000 kg) of freight.

CHILE

The naval air component, the *Servicio de Aviacion de la Armada de Chile,* has recently been revealed as the **latest recipient of** the Pilatus PC-7 **Turbo Trainer**, a batch of four trainers of this type having been delivered in May as replacements for the ageing Beech T-34A Mentors operated by the service. The *Fuerza Aérea de Chile* is also a likely recipient of the PC-7 as it is actively seeking a replacement for its aged T-34As, some of which have now been in service since the early 'fifties. One possibility that has been explored is procurement of additional T-25 Universal trainers from Brazil, but it has been recently stated by EMBRAER, of which Neiva is now a subsidiary, that the Universal is not to be reinstated in production.

GREECE

The **first** two of five new-build two-seat Vought **TA-7H Corsairs** for the Hellenic Air Force were accepted at Grand Prairie, Texas, early in July, these following one A-7H reworked to TA-7H standard and flown in March last year. The TA-7H Corsairs will presumably be shared between the 110ª and 115ª wings currently operating some 55 A-7H Corsairs with one squadron in the former and two in the latter.

INDIA

Many weeks of speculation and rumour concerning the future of the contract with British Aerospace under which the Indian Air Force is receiving the **Jaguar International** were only partly dispelled in July when Mrs Indira Gandhi stated that the government would honour its commitment to the aircraft but would take advantage of optional clauses which might be in India's favour. At present, 40 Jaguars are to be supplied to the IAF direct from BAe, followed by 45 kits of knocked-down parts for Indian assembly. The licence manufacturing contract was not scheduled to be finalised until later this year and it now seems likely that this will not be pursued, and that the 45 aircraft originally to have been supplied as kits will be delivered as complete aircraft.

The Indian Defence Minister, C P N Singh, recently informed Parliament that **no further orders for Sea Harriers** are to be placed after completion of delivery of the six Sea Harrier FRS Mk 51s (plus two Harrier T Mk 60s) currently contracted for. British Aerospace, which had been in process of negotiating the sale of further aircraft to India over and above four which are on option, was apparently given no advance warning of the announcement, and it is difficult to see how India can operate a viable shipboard strike force with such a small number of aircraft.

JAPAN

The Air Self-Defence Force has postponed **selection of** a **successor to** the Kawasaki-built Vertol **V-107-II** (see *Airscene*/June) for at least a further two years owing to heavy and higher-priority budgetary commitments in Fiscal Years 1981 and 1982, six Lockheed C-130H Hercules being scheduled for inclusion in the former and some 30 follow-on F-15J Eagles in the latter. The ASDF is now to request a further three V-107-IIs in the Fiscal 1981 budget in order to provide equipment for a new rescue flight to be based at Akita.

The **first** of two **F-15J Eagle** fighters for the ASDF built by the parent company was officially accepted by Col Yuzo Otsubo of the Defence Agency at St Louis on 15 July and is now undergoing flight testing at Edwards AFB, this aircraft, together with the second F-15J, being scheduled for ferrying to Nagoya in March. McDonnell Douglas is also building six two-seat TF-15Js for the ASDF, and supplying eight F-15Js to Mitsubishi in knocked-down component form, the first of these being scheduled to fly in July next year.

NEW ZEALAND

Boeing Aerospace has been selected to **modernise** the RNZAF's fleet of five 14-year-old Lockheed **P-3B Orions** under a $21m (£8·94m) 44-month contract calling for the upgrading of the data handling and display systems, the radar, the IR detection systems and the inertial navigation equipment. In a second phase of the modernisation programme, the ASW systems of the RNZAF's Orions will be upgraded.

PAKISTAN

An initial batch of 30 PAF **Mirages** are currently **being updated** by the installation of the Litton LW-33 nav/attack system incorporating a Thomson-CSF head-up display. It is anticipated that the entire PAF Mirage fleet will be progressively modified in similar fashion. Unofficial French sources have stated that the Pakistan government is seeking to purchase 35 Mirage 2000 fighters for 1985-86 delivery.

PARAGUAY

By May, the *Fuerza Aérea Paraguaya* had taken **delivery of** five of the nine EMB-326GB **Xavante** trainer/ground attack aircraft ordered from EMBRAER late last year, and 14 FAP pilots were undergoing operational training on the Xavante with the *Fôrça Aérea Brasileira* at the Fortaleza Air Base. The four remaining aircraft are scheduled to be delivered before the end of the year.

PHILIPPINES

The three Fokker **F27MPA** maritime surveillance aircraft now ordered **for** use by the **Philippine Air Force** (see *Airscene*/August) are scheduled to be delivered next year under a deal which includes the training by Fokker of 42 Philippine personnel, these including both air and ground crews, the first courses being scheduled to commence at Schiphol this autumn. It is anticipated that a follow-on order will be placed for a further three F27MPAs, of which two will possess a measure of attack capability, and the rôles of the aircraft will include coastal patrol, fishery protection, and search and rescue.

SAUDI ARABIA

At the time of closing for press, the US State Department had still to announce a **decision concerning** Saudi Arabia's request that conformal fuel pods, multiple ejection racks and the appropriate ordnance be supplied for the **F-15C Eagle** fighters that are scheduled to be delivered to the Royal Saudi Air Force from January 1982 under the *Peace Sun* programme. The Saudi Ambassador to the US, Sheikh Faisal Alhegelan, has said that unless the US government provides the requested equipment, Saudi Arabia will take its arms business elsewhere. Much more than just the equipment requested is "available from other sources and without restriction or condition", the Ambassador commented. The Saudi government is also understood to be requesting the supply of an unspecified number of Boeing KC-135 tankers for use with the F-15Cs, advanced AIM-9L AAMs and, possibly, E-3A AWACS aircraft.

TAIWAN

The US Administration has agreed to General Dynamics and Northrop making **presentations of** their respective **FX** intermediate export fighters to the Nationalist Chinese government, the US State Department having granted the necessary munitions licences allowing the supply of technical and marketing information. Since the US Administration lifted its embargo on sales to Taiwan, the Nationalist Chinese have presented a shopping list of 18 items, headed by FX, but are concerned that any future decision to buy will depend on Sino-Communist pressures on the White House.

UNITED ARAB EMIRATES

The Chief-of-Staff of the UAE Defence Forces, Gen Awad Khalidi, is reportedly actively seeking **replacements for** the ageing Hawker **Hunter** fighters on permanent detachment to Sharjah, these comprising seven single-seat FGA Mk 76s and FR Mk 76s, and two two-seat T Mk 77s. There would seem little doubt that one or other version of the Mirage will be selected as a successor to the Hunter as the Abu Dhabi element of UAE Air Force, which provides the service's backbone, is primarily equipped with Mirage IIIEADs and Mirage 5ADs. A new military air base is currently under construction in Abu Dhabi, south of Tarif, and a new transport airfield is being built at al Hamra.

UNITED KINGDOM

On 28 July, Secretary of State for Defence Francis Pym stated that the RAF's **Buccaneers** were **to resume** normal **flying** immediately following stringent inspection of each aircraft. The inspection, which resulted from the loss of a Buccaneer in Nevada on 7 February attributable to a fatigue failure in the starboard wing, has revealed that over half the Buccaneer force of 65 aircraft showed no signs of fatigue or only minor cracks which have since been repaired, and these have now resumed unrestricted peacetime flying. The remaining aircraft displayed more substantial cracks and the economics of the more extensive repairs that these demand to restore them for frontline flying are under study. Mr Pym added, "Hitherto, we have maintained our full Buccaneer declaration to NATO on the basis of availability in war. It is now clear that, initially and possibly also in the longer term, this declaration must be reduced." It has been suggested unofficially that one and perhaps two Buccaneer squadrons may have to be withdrawn and that force levels are unlikely to be recovered before the squadrons' Tornado re-equipment programme gets into its stride in 1983-84, the Buccaneer OCU and No 208 Sqdn having been scheduled to initiate that programme in 1983. No changes in phase-in of Tornado are likely to result from any decision to scrap or proceed with the repair of those Buccaneers having more substantial cracks.

USA

Having won the fly-off between competing air-launched cruise missiles for the USAF, Boeing began a **second series of** 19 test and evaluation **flights for the AGM-86B** on 12 June with a successful launch from a B-52G over the Utah Test Training Range. The flight originated from Edwards AFB, as will all but two of the series, the exception being two flights to be made next year from the Boeing Military Airplane Co at Wichita, Kansas. In the first phase of the ALCM programme, the USAF will modify 173 B-52Gs to carry 12 AGM-86Bs externally, six on each inboard wing pylon; with the first squadron operational deployment scheduled for December 1982, these B-52Gs will retain their penetration capability and will carry short-range attack missiles and gravity bombs in the fuselage bomb bays. In the second half of the decade, they will then be modified to carry eight AGM-86Bs internally, so that by 1990 they will make up an all stand-off force, each Stratofortress carrying 20 ALCMs. In addition, the USAF is completing the necessary development effort to permit modification of 96 B-52Hs to the same configuration, with the option of starting this conversion programme in 1984. To provide an insurance against unforeseen problems with the B-52 as an ALCM carrier, the USAF is continuing its investigation of a new Cruise Missile Carrier Aircraft (CMCA) and is initially concentrating upon evaluation of a Rockwell B-1 derivative as a Strategic ALCM Launcher (SAL). To this end, the No 3 B-1 will be used for a flight test programme in 1981/82 in which AGM-86Bs will be carried and launched from internal and external points.

Six manufacturers of biz-jets have made tentative proposals to meet the projected **USAF requirement for a companion trainer aircraft** (CTA) for use by Strategic Air Command. Although the CTA programme is not yet firm, funds are available in FY81 to start the evaluation of prospective aircraft and if further funds are then provided the USAF would purchase about 60 aircraft in FY 83/FY 84, with the objective of saving up to 100 million US gallons of fuel (at a current cost of $1·18 per gal) a year. This saving is based on the assumption that the CTA would be used by SAC bomber crews to fly 25 per cent of the mission hours flown at present in B-52s, and with fuel costs constantly rising, the entire first cost of the CTAs might well be covered by the savings over the first 3-4 years. The CTA is expected to be equipped to carry a five-man crew (two pilots, two navigators and an EWO) with appropriate equipment and will be used to fly training missions for the B-52's low-level rôle. The aircraft most likely to be proposed in response to the USAF request for proposals — expected to be circulated shortly after this issue went to press — are the Cessna Citation 2, Dassault-Breguet Falcon 10, Gates Learjet Model 35, IAI Westwind 2, Mitsubishi Diamond and Rockwell Sabreliner. USAF probably will lease two examples of the chosen CTA after source selection next spring, for preliminary evaluation and to develop the crew stations in the cabin.

AIRCRAFT AND INDUSTRY

BRAZIL

EMBRAER has announced that, following its acquisition of the Neiva company (*Airscene*/July 1980), further **work on** the **YT-25B Universal II** (see *Airscene*/January 1979) will be **discontinued** and plans to build a further batch of T-25 Universals have been dropped. Meanwhile, EMBRAER's workforce is again increasing to cope with Bandeirante production and the new development programmes, and passed the 5,000 mark for the first time earlier this year. By the time this issue appears in print, EMBRAER is expected to have flown the Xingu II prototype, featuring a 30-in (76-cm) fuselage stretch and uprated PT6A-41 engines. The first flight target date was 21 July, to be followed on 19 August by the first flight of the EMB-312 (T-27) basic trainer.

CANADA

The promise of a **further loan** of Can$4m from the recently-elected Liberal Government appears to have saved, once again, the programme **to produce the Trident Trigull** light amphibian. After a long fight to obtain backing for the Trigull, which has been fully developed in prototype form, Trident Aircraft set up a new production factory at Victoria, BC, with the backing of the provincial government as well as the previous Liberal government. However, the programme was halted at the beginning of this year, when the first production aircraft was close to completion, after the Federal Progressive Conservative government refused to honour the earlier commitment.

FEDERAL GERMANY

Since making its first flight on 14 June 1979, the Dornier **Skyservant** fitted **with a TNT wing** has made more than 100 flights and has demonstrated a speed range of 34-182 kt (63-337 km/h). The New Technology Wing is now being applied to the Dornier 228 (see *AirData File*/page 151); meanwhile, the TNT test-bed is engaged in an interesting test programme in which seven types of propellers supplied by Dowty-Rotol and Hartzell are being evaluated. These propellers include three- and four-blade types with supercritical blades, extra-wide blades and Kevlar-reinforced blades. In a further phase, the aircraft will test an advanced propeller jointly developed by Dornier, the DFVLR and Propellerwerk Hoffmann. Dornier also plans to test two different spoiler systems for roll control, allowing the entire wing trailing edge to be used for Fowler flaps to improve the low-speed performance.

FRANCE

First flight of the **Mudry CAP-21** was made at Berney on 24 June. Powered by a 200 hp Lycoming AEIO-360-B1B engine with fuel injection, the single-seat CAP-21 is the latest development in the Avions Mudry series of aerobatic monoplanes and is derived from the CAP-20L, from which it differs in respect of the engine and the wing, developed for Mudry by Aérospatiale. Five more CAP-21s are being built and one is expected to be flown by the Swiss aerobatic champion Eric Muller in the forthcoming championships at Oshkosh, USA, in which CAP-20Ls will be flown by the Italian team and part of the French team.

INTERNATIONAL

Aérospatiale and Alitalia have joined forces to continue **studying** a 44/50 seat **regional transport**. The agreement provides for the evolution of a single aircraft for joint development, based on the projects each company has been studying as the Aérospatiale AS.35 (see *AirData File*/August 1979) and the Aeritalia AIT.230 (*AirData File*/March 1980).

An agreement between Aérospatiale and the People's Republic of China signed on 2 July provides for the **assembly in China of** an initial batch of 50 SA 365 **Dauphin II helicopters** and for the subsequent manufacture of the type under licence in China. The deal follows the earlier purchase by China of Alouettes and Super Frelons and adds to the sale to date of 102 SA 365s in the C and N versions and 90 SA 366Gs for the US Coast Guard (now designated HH-65A Dolphin).

JAPAN

In the 12 months of FY 1979 (to end-March 1980), the **Japanese aerospace industry produced** 118 fixed-wing aircraft, 25 helicopters and 108 aero-engines; of the totals, 72 aircraft and 107 engines were delivered to the three services, seven aircraft and one engine to domestic operators and 64 aircraft were exported. Sales of the Mitsubishi MU-2 series reached 638 by the end of May, and 83 MU-300 Diamonds are now on order. Nihon Airplane meanwhile reported that 162 YS-11s remained in service, of 182 built, including 114 in Japan; they are used by a total of 18 operators in seven countries and have totalled 3·2m hours since entry into service in April 1965.

NEW ZEALAND

The **first production Cresco** ag-plane was recently **completed** by Aerospace Industries at Hamilton and has now entered flight test. The prototype Cresco first flew on 28 February 1979 but was subsequently destroyed in a flying accident. Another recent first for the company is the sale of a Fletcher FU-24-954 ag-plane in the USA, through Frontier Aerospace of Long Beach, Calif, where the aircraft are being assembled.

POLAND

Production figures released by the **PZL-Warsaw** indicate that it has produced 530 examples of the PZL-104 Wilga to date, including 110 in 1979; 90 per cent are exported and demand is said to be increasing. The latest Wilga version, the Wilga-80, gained Canadian certification in March 1980 and four examples have been exported to Canada for use as floatplanes. Production of the PZL-106A Kruk ag-plane totals 88, including 24 delivered to East Germany in 1979 with 15 more to go this year. New Kruk versions under development are the PZL-106AR with a PZL-3SR engine driving a slow-running, large-diameter propeller, and the PZL-106AT Turbo-Kruk with a 760 shp Pratt & Whitney PT6A-34AG turboprop. An improved wing of better aerodynamic characteristics is being developed for the Kruk. Production of the PZL-110 Koliber (licence-built SOCATA Rallye) is proceeding and more than 30 have been delivered. A version with a 220 hp PZL-Franklin 6A engine (replacing the 125 hp PZL-Franklin 4A) is being developed. Up to the end of March, PZL-Mielec had completed over 30 M-18 Dromader ag-planes, exports of which include two to Yugoslavia and six of a fire-fighting version to Canada. Development of turboprop versions is underway, to be powered by the PT6A and possibly the PZL-10S, which is the Polish production version of the Soviet TVD-10, for use in the Antonov An-28. Production of the An-28 will begin in Poland in 1984 and it is planned to build 1,200 for export to the Soviet Union by 1990.

UNITED KINGDOM

A successful **maiden flight** was made on 16 July by the first **of the** British Aerospace **Nimrod AEW Mk 3** development aircraft. In a 3½-hr flight under the command of chief test pilot Charles Masefield with Nimrod AEW project pilot John Cruise and a crew of four, the flight envelope was explored up to 25,000 ft (7 620 m) and flutter runs made up to 275 kt (509 km/h). Preliminary slow-speed handling trials were so satisfactory that complete stalls were made through to nose drop, both clean and with gear extended. Two more development aircraft are to fly within the next few months and the AEW Mk 3 should enter service with the RAF early in 1982. Also on 16 July, the Mission Systems Avionics (MSA) for the Nimrod 3 was formally switched on for the first time at the Radlett factory of Marconi Avionics. The MSA comprises nose and tail radar scanners, a very advanced electronic signal processing system, six control and display consoles, a comprehensive communications sub-system for voice and processed data, IFF radar, ESM and other sub-systems. It is described as the most powerful UK airborne electronics system.

Development testing of the Panavia **Tornado F Mk 2** passed another milestone on 18 July with the first **flight of** the **second prototype,** A.02. In the course of a flight lasting 1 hr 10 min, by Paul Millet and Roy Kennard, the aircraft achieved Mach 1·25 at medium altitude and underwent handling trials. One of A.02's main tasks will be weapon system integration and development; it is the first of the F Mk 2s to carry the avionics system developed by EASAMS Ltd (a member of the GEC-Marconi group). The third and last prototype, A.03, is to fly later this year and will be the primary aircraft for evaluation of the Air Intercept radar. By mid-July, prototype A.01 had made 45 flights totalling 61 hrs 44 min.

USA

General Dynamics has proposed, as a private venture, an **extensively modified** development of the **F-16** that it has offered to the USAF as a potential interim advanced tactical fighter with a much enhanced supersonic performance. Identified **as the F-16XL Scamp** (for Supersonic Cruise Aircraft Modification Programme), the new project features the basic F-16 fuselage extended by a 30-in (76-cm) plug just behind the cockpit and a 26-in plug farther aft, with an all-new advanced technology wing of compound delta planform. The wing is called a "cranked arrow" by GD and evolved from wind-tunnel research programmes undertaken by NASA's Langley Research Center, it has a 70-deg leading edge sweep over most of the span, reducing to 50 deg at the tips, which incorporate manoeuvre and spin-resisting leading-edge flaps. Aileron and elevons on the trailing edge are separated by small fairing pods containing the aileron actuators. The wing has a chord of 499 in (12,67 cm) compared with 195 in (4,95 cm) for the F-16A — this chord being the reason for the fuselage plugs — and an area of 646·4 sq ft (60,05 m²). With the same Pratt & Whitney F100 engine as used in the F-16A, the Scamp would have a max speed of M=2·5 and max cruise of M=2·2, compared with M=2·0 and M=0·93 respectively. It would gross 37,500 lb (17 010 kg) compared with 35,400 lb (16 057 kg), would carry more fuel and have better take-off and landing distances. General Dynamics claims that the Scamp, compared with the F-16A, would have twice the supersonic radius, 25 per cent more air-to-air combat mission radius, 20 per cent more air-ground mission radius with double the payload, a 90-kt (167-km/h) increase in sea level penetration speed with 2·5 times the payload and improved manoeuvrability that should double or triple the gun-firing opportunities during combat. Commonality of structure and systems between the F-16A and F-16XL is put at better than 90 per cent and GD has proposed a $40m (£17m) programme to modify two of the FSD F-16As to Scamp configuration for a flight test and demonstration programme that could begin before the end of 1981 if given a go-ahead by this month (September).

On 21 July, the USAF officially named the General Dynamics F-16 the **"Fighting Falcon"** at a special ceremony held at the Hill AFB, Utah. It may be assumed that "Fighting" was incorporated in the name to avoid legal complications that might otherwise be expected to arise with the US distributors of the Dassault-Breguet Falcon series of business executive aircraft.

LearAvia Corp of Reno, Nevada, has raised an initial $10m (£4·25m) of loan capital to finance **development and production of** the **Lear Fan 2100** business aircraft by offering "limited partnerships" in the company. Two hundred such partnerships have been sold, at $150,000 each, to be paid in three increments at six-month intervals. Investors will share in a 7 per cent royalty on each Lear Fan delivery until they have received $300,000 each; thereafter they will share in a 5 per cent royalty for 25 years. In addition to this $30m (£12·75m), the British government is providing $35m (£14·9m) in grants and loans and $15m (£6·38m) in loan guarantees for capital equipment for the production facility that is being set up at Aldergrove, Northern Ireland (see *Airscene*/April 1980). To handle the production programme, Lear Avia has set up a wholly-owned company, Lear Fan Ltd (UK), with Linden S Blue as managing director and chief executive; engineering, research and development will continue at Reno under Lear Fan Corp (US), a subsidiary of the UK company. Orders to date total 127 and about 300 employees are engaged at Reno while the first group of workers recruited in Ulster will soon go to Reno for training. First flight of the Reno-built prototype is expected on 24 October, with certification by May 1982 and deliveries starting in June 1982.

The first of six McDonnell Douglas **KC-10A Extender** flight-refuelling tankers ordered so far by the USAF made its **initial flight** at Long Beach on 12 July. The KC-10A is a military derivative of the DC-10 Srs 30CF convertible-freighter, incorporating a flight refuelling boom, a boom operator's station under the rear fuselage and additional tankage in the cabin.

Late in July, the **Douglas Aircraft** Co received McDonnell Douglas board of directors' approval **to continue** advanced engineering and technical verification **work on the ATMR**, which is now designated the DC-XX. If a launch commitment is made in due course, it will become the DC-11.

Five companies are working on **concept study contracts for a Next Generation Trainer** (NGT) awarded by the USAF, with the objective of selecting a winning design (or two designs) early next year. The contracts were awarded to Cessna, Fairchild, General Dynamics, Rockwell and Vought, but the USAF's Air Training Command will also consider a programme to modernise the Cessna T-37B — which the NGT is intended to replace in the later 'eighties — and off-the-shelf US or foreign-built aircraft. The contract studies are to be submitted to USAF by mid-October. After prototype testing, a production decision could be taken in 1984 with entry into service in 1987 and possible acquisition of about 600.

Swissair has confirmed its choice of Pratt & Whitney **JT9D-7R4G2** turbofans **to power** the five **Boeing 747SUD** (stretched upper deck) transports recently ordered (see *Airscene*/August 1980). The 7R4G2 engine is rated at 54,750 lb st (24 835 kgp) and is the most powerful version of the JT9D so far specified for airline operation as well as being the first application of the -7R4 family in the Boeing 747. Previously, nine airlines have specified engines in this series for Boeing 767 and Airbus A310 transports.

Pratt & Whitney has given **preliminary details of** a new turbojet engine, **the PW 1120,** in the 20,000 lb (9 072 kgp) thrust class, intended for application in new fighter aircraft later in the present decade. The company says that it has identified a market for over 5,000 engines of this size over the next 20 years and has indicated that it could be used to power the planned FX export fighter (for which Northrop proposes the F-5G and General Dynamics is building a J79-powered F-16), the IAI Lavi, the Saab-Scania JAS and the projected European Combat Aircraft. The PW 1120 is based on the hot section of the F100 turbofan, with a new LP compressor, a new LP turbine and a simplified afterburner. It will have an overall length of 170 in (4,32 m) compared with 191 in (4,85 m) for the F100 and a diameter of 33 in (84 cm) compared with 40 in (102 cm). If development of the PW 1120 continues as planned, flight testing will begin in 1983 and qualified engines could be available in 1985.

General Electric is proceeding on schedule with **development testing of the F101DFE** (the "derivative fighter engine" based on the F101 augmented turbofan originally developed to power the Rockwell B-1), that has been funded jointly by USAF/USN to provide a possible alternative to the Pratt & Whitney F100. A total of five engines is involved, the first two of which were tested under the F101X designation. Engines Nos 3, 4 and 5 are to be used next year in flight test programmes, first in an Air Force GD F-16A at Edwards Air Force Base and then in a USN Grumman F-14A at Grumman's Calverton base. One of these three engines recently completed the first of two 1,000 mission-equivalent-hour endurance tests, and a second similar test is likely later this month (September), leading to first flight next January in the F-16, with testing in the F-14 to follow in July. There are no production plans at present for the F101DFE, but General Electric has proposed its use to re-engine the F-14 Tomcats and for installation in later production F-16s.

To investigate the application of propulsive lift technology to aircraft carriers, the NASA Quiet Short-haul Research Aircraft (**QSRA**) —an extensively modified de Havilland C-8A Buffalo — has recently completed more than 500 **landings on** a simulated **aircraft carrier deck** at Crows Landing, a naval landing field near Ames Research Center, Calif. These tests were to be followed in late July by demonstration flights to and from a US aircraft carrier at sea in waters off San Diego. In the flights at Crows Landing, the QSRA touched down at 52 mph (84 km/h) in a 23 mph (37 km/h) headwind, enabling it to stop in the length of the deck without using arrester gear.

Cessna has announced a **delay** of six months **in certification of** the **Citation III,** to April 1982, and an 11-month delay in the start of deliveries, to the last quarter of 1982. The stretch-out is attributed primarily to delays in obtaining tooling and some parts and materials, and to the introduction of some airframe modifications. The latter include a redesign of the ailerons and elevators to reduce a tendancy to float; simplification of the wing trailing edge; a one-piece main cabin entry door to replace the split airstair door; a revision of the hydraulic system and introduction of electrical power for the flap drive system and addition of a back-up electrical system for pitch control in place of a mechanical system. By early July, the two Citation prototypes had totalled 222 hrs in 221 flights and 36 hrs in 31 flights respectively; more than 900 stalls have been made. Cessna says it has a backlog of more than 460 orders for Citations, including the Citation 1 and 2, which are currently being built at the rate of 12 a month; the 700th Citation was delivered during July. More than 130 of the outstanding orders are for Citation IIIs and the earliest delivery date for a newly-ordered aircraft is May 1985.

Grumman Aerospace has completed the **FAA certification of** its **G-111 amphibian,** the civilianised version of the HU-16 Albatross (see *Airscene*/July 1979). The first conversion was undertaken for Resorts International and began flight testing on 13 February 1979; the second G-111 was expected to be in flight test by the time this issue went to press and is to enter service with Resorts subsidiary Antilles Air Boats later this year. Resorts International now has at least 13 HU-16s programmed for conversion to G-111 standard, at the rate of one every two months through 1981; Grumman had previously itself acquired six and has more recently purchased an additional 36 HU-16s in a military surplus sale and intends to convert these to G-111s for commercial sale. To handle the programme, the company is planning to acquire former Fairchild facilities at St Augustine, Florida, in place of the Stuart, Florida, facility used for the first few conversions. Grumman is also discussing with Resorts International a G-111 version with General Electric CT7 turboprops in place of the R-1820-82A piston engines.

Mooney Aircraft plans to introduce a new **six-seat pressurised M-30** in 1985, with prototype testing to start in 1982. The M-30 is of conventional low-wing configuration with a 350 hp Lycoming TIO-540 turbosupercharged piston engine expected to provide a top speed of nearly 300 mph (483 km/h) and a 250 mph (402 km/h) cruise. Range is expected to be 1,150 mls (1 850 km) at 75 per cent cruise power and a 4·7 lb/sq in (0,33 kg/cm^2) pressure differential will give a 10,000 ft (3 050 m) cabin altitude at 25,000 ft (7 620 m). Features of the M-30 include Fowler flaps over 90 per cent of the span, with spoilers instead of ailerons for roll control, advanced flight control and avionics systems, weather radar and airframe de-icing.

Rockwell International's General Aviation Division is now **flight-testing** a prototype of its **Model 1000.** Based on the Turbo Commander 980, it has improved performance, greater range and more cabin space. Full details will be revealed at the NBAA Convention in Kansas City later this year.

First flight of the **Beech** Commuter **C99** was made at Wichita on 20 June, marking the company's re-entry into the commuter airliner market following termination of the original Beech 99 production in 1975. Deliveries of the C99 are to begin in 1981, followed by the Beechcraft Commuter 1900, a 19-passenger derivative of the Super King Air 200, in 1983.

Cessna has **changed** the **name of** its light twin, previously the Model 303 **Clipper, to Crusader.** Two prototypes are now in flight test and deliveries will begin in 1981. At the upper end of the Cessna range, the Model 425 **Corsair** was **certificated** by the FAA on 1 July and customer deliveries are about to start.

Hawk Industries, a general aviation operator and aircraft dealer, has set up a manufacturing division in order to develop a small, specialised **cargo aircraft known as the GafHawk.** Powered by a 1,173 shp Pratt & Whitney PT6A-45B or 1,500 shp PT6A-65 turboprop, the GafHawk is of the simplest possible configuration and construction, with a high wing of parallel chord and a box-like fuselage with rear loading ramp. The aircraft has a gross weight of 14,500 lb (6 576 kg) but will be certificated initially at 12,500 lb (5 670 kg) to comply with FAR Pt 23. Principal dimensions are a span of 71 ft 4 in (21,75 m), length of 46 ft 11 in (14,30 m) and gross wing area of 491·9 sq ft (45,68 m^2). The useful load will be 8,250 lb (3 741 kg) and fuel capacity is 360 US gal (1 360 l). The company has modified a Piper Tri-Pacer to represent a 54 per cent model of the GafHawk and has been flight testing this prototype since 1978.

In Johnson, Kansas, the Mike Smith Aircraft Co is seeking financial backing to build two prototypes of a six-seat turboprop-powered **business aircraft** designed as a follow-on to a prototype that was built two years ago but crashed following engine failure. The **Smith Lightning** features an 850 shp Pratt & Whitney PT6A-42 in the rear fuselage driving a Hartzell three-bladed 90-in (2,29 m) diameter pusher propeller and has an overall configuration reminiscent of the LearAvia Lear Fan 2100. Like the latter aircraft, the Lightning was also designed to use graphite and glassfibre epoxy composites extensively in its construction but after discussing with the FAA the certification programme for such a structure the company has decided to use conventional light alloys for the primary structure. The Lightning has a span of 29 ft 8 in (9,04 m), length of 31 ft 2½ in (9,5 m) and wing area of 110 sq ft (10,22 m^2). With a gross weight of 4,200 lb (1 905 kg) and fuel capacity of 150 US gal (568 l), the Lightning will have a max speed of 460 mph (740 km/h) at 25,000 ft (7 620 m) and will cruise at 437 mph (703 km/h) over a distance of 2,450 mls (3 943 km).

CIVIL AFFAIRS

BELGIUM

Third-level **services from Liege and Charleroi to London** are now being operated on behalf of Sabena **by ASPAIR** (Aviation Spare Parts Europe), a Charleroi-based operator, using a Swearingen Metro. This decision has been taken after political upheaval in the French-speaking Walloon district in Belgium when it was realised that the so-called "Walloon Airlines" were actually being flown by a Flanders-based operator, EAT of Grimbergen. This in turn had resulted from the new convention signed between Sabena and Walloon regional authorities in March (see *Airscene*/May 1980) stipulating the use of a pressurised turboprop instead of the Beechcraft 99 used by former operator Publi-Air. The agreement also specified that Sabena should appoint a third-level operator from the French-speaking region of Belgium.

Air Berlin USA, a subsidiary of Air Florida, started **operations between** West **Berlin** (Tegel) **and Brussels** on 22 July on a once weekly basis. A Boeing 737 is used by the airline, which is expanding into the European market as a result of American open skies policy. The Potsdam 1945 agreement limits flights to and from West Berlin to aircraft belonging to the US, Britain or France. Air Berlin's move was prompted by inauguration of a weekly flight to Brussels from East Berlin Schoenefeld by Interflug in April (this column, last month). In May, Air Berlin began operating a Berlin-Tel Aviv service, using a Boeing 707.

BRAZIL

The **Fundacão Rubem Berta**, a group made up of present and former employees of Varig which owns both the Varig and Cruzeiro do Sul airlines, has **purchased** the entire stock of **Rio Sul**, one of the five third-level airlines in Brazil. Previously the Fundaçao held a 30 per cent share in Rio Sul, which has a fleet of eight EMB-110P Bandeirantes and several Navajo Chieftains.

HONG KONG

Cathay Pacific Airways became, on 17 July, the first airline to take advantage of the recently-approved "open skies" policy on the **London-Hong Kong** route, when its **inaugural** Boeing 747 **service** arrived at Gatwick, departing on the return inaugural later the same morning. Three return flights are operated each week, with one-way fares ranging from £151 to £1,124 respectively for an advance-purchase budget midweek reservation and first-class with sleeper seat. Introduction of the Cathay Pacific services ends a 30-year BOAC/British Airways monopoly on the route and was followed on 1 August by the first B.Cal service. The Laker Airways application to operate on the route had not been approved by the Hong Kong licensing authority at the time of going to press.

UNITED KINGDOM

British Airways has been badly **hit by** the growing **recession** in business world-wide and in the second quarter of 1980 its total traffic fell by 5 per cent compared with the same period of 1979, whereas a 4 per cent growth had been projected. The airline is now suffering the effects of considerable overcapacity, with the continuing delivery of TriStars and Boeing 747s, and the reduction in revenue has created a cash flow problem. To provide additional cash, British Airways is planning to sell some of its early (JT9D-powered) Boeing 747s and most of the remaining 707s. Capacity is also being reduced by the decision taken earlier in the year to retire nine of the 14 Super VC10s that were still operational (these having been flown to Prestwick for open storage during April) and it is now likely that the last of the Super VC10s will be retired completely in 1981, two years earlier than previously planned (with a substantial number of aircrew redundancies in consequence). Costs are also being reduced by cancelling or consolidating services where traffic is low and frequencies in the winter schedules will be reduced. A campaign has been launched to cut 2½ per cent from operating costs across the board and steps are being taken to sell tickets more aggressively.

The earliest date at which the planned **successor company to British Airways** is now likely to be launched is mid-1981, according to Trade Secretary John Nott. Timing of the flotation of the new company, shares in which will be offered for public sale, will depend upon the speed with which British Airways recovers from its current trading downturn, which has resulted in the results for 1979-80 being substantially below earlier forecasts. When the new company is launched, employees with a qualifying length of service will be eligible for a half-price share offer, allowing them to invest up to £2,000 each in the airline and to receive one free share for each one bought at the offer price, provided the shares are held by trustees. A free offer of up to about £50 worth of shares will also be made to all eligible employees, whether they subscribe their own money or not.

Redcoat Cargo Airlines has announced plans to become the **first commercial operator of** freight-carrying **airships** and, if the plan matures, will eventually dispose of its fixed-wing aircraft, the present fleet of which comprises one Canadair CL-44 and one Britannia, plus two Britannias on lease. As a first step towards airship operation, Redcoat will join forces with Airship Industries Ltd to set up a joint company to operate the NR2 airship next year. The NR2 is a modification of Airship Development's AD500 non-rigid airship, first flown last year; since then, Airship Development Ltd has been acquired by Thermo-Skyships Ltd and the joint company has been re-named Airship Industries Ltd, based in the Isle of Man. Thermo-Skyships, which recently raised £1·4m through an offer of shares on the London Stock Exchange, had planned to construct a sophisticated type of passenger-carrying airship with many advanced features, but these plans have been put in abeyance while the company concentrates upon the development of the Skyship R40 against a Redcoat order for four with 10 more on option. The R40 is a helium-filled rigid airship with a length of 600 ft (183 m) and diameter of 120 ft (36,6 m) and will be designed to carry a 40-ton (40 640-kg) payload over a still-air range of 2,500 mls (4 023 km). Powered by four Pratt & Whitney PT6A-50 turboprops, the R40 will cruise at 68 kt (126 km/h) and, Redcoat claims, will be able to operate competitively with the present generation of

Design features of the world's best low-level, all-weather combat aircraft

Tornado is unique. It is the only air defen weapon which gives the Western World t ability to strike by day or by night, in goo weather and bad, against the spearheads ar support centres of land, sea and air attac mounted over a wide front.

Tornado turns to its own advantage the po visibility and bad weather conditions whic more often favour an aggressor. It has t performance, structural characteristics ar advanced systems necessary for high-spee low-level penetration of massed air defenc in which SAMs have a 4 to 1 advantage ov NATO's fighter and reconnaissance aircraft.

Variable-geometry wings, new-technolog engines, and unique terrain-following ar nav/attack systems enable Tornado to meet a foreseeable developments in the threat attack. Over 800 Tornado aircraft will mak the air forces of Great Britain, Germany ar Italy and the German Navy the backbone European air defence through to the 21 century.

ariable-geometry design
ıe combination of variable-geometry wings ith a rugged airframe and new-technology ıgines enables Tornado to reconcile the con-cting demands of an operational envelope hich includes long-range missions at high ıpersonic speeds and at ultra-low-level in ısty conditions; impressive payload/range erformance; ability to operate into and out of ıort or bomb-damaged airfields; and high ıanoeuvrability, even when carrying heavy xternal stores. With wings swept forward ıd high-efficiency slats and flaps deployed, ornado develops very high lift-coefficients hich ensure outstanding shortfield capa-ilities. With wings swept back, Tornado pro-ides the level of ride comfort essential to ıaintain fighting efficiency through long ıissions at terrain-hugging heights and the :ability vital for precise aiming and delivery of veapons. The rugged structure guarantees ›ng fatigue life and, with the VG wing and igh-thrust engines, gives the high-g man-euvrability needed for target acquisition and elf-protection.

\utomatic terrain-following
ornado's claim to be the first genuine *all-veather* supersonic combat aircraft is founded n an automatic terrain-following system vhich enables it to fly at high transonic speeds t altitudes as low as 60m (200ft) in all weather nd light conditions. It also allows landings in :ategory II weather conditions. Ability to enetrate alert enemy defences in any weather further assured by a navigational system of nprecedented accuracy and ground-mapping adar which enables fix-points and targets to e readily identified when flying blind. The ystem gives an order of accuracy many times reater than that possible with conventional ıertial systems and also improves accuracy of veapon aiming and delivery. Acquisition of x-points and targets is also simplified by the bility to superimpose the radar map on the ıoving map in the combined display. A wide ariety of information from major avionic sub-ystems is presented, via a high-speed digital rocessor, on head-up, pilot's map, TV and other electronic displays. Mission data can be fed into the system before take-off simply by inserting a magnetic tape into the cockpit voice recorder.

Fly-by-wire-control
Tornado has a full fly-by-wire control system which ensures optimum handling character-istics throughout the flight envelope, even when carrying heavy external stores. In essence, this irons out the gusts and bumps inseparable from high-speed flight in turbulent conditions and provides the stability needed for accurate delivery of weapons in the lay-down, dive and toss modes.

New-technology engines
The new-technology Turbo Union RB199 3-spool turbofan was designed specifically for Tornado and, in some 4,000 hours of Tornado flying, has proved itself an excellent fighter engine, with crisp handling, freedom from stagnation stalls, exemplary re-light character-istics, and rugged durability. It develops 15,000lb thrust but is only about 12ft long. The twin-engine installation ensures the high thrust/weight ratio essential for high per-formance and unsurpassed manoeuvrability and the fuel economy essential for long endurance and good payload/range capability.

Survival capability
Tornado's survival capability derives chiefly from its ability to escape detection and inter-ception by flying at exceptionally high speeds and low levels and so minimising exposure to enemy counteraction. The aircraft's small size and fact that its engines have a lower infra-red signature than any other current fighter engine also contribute to its ability to avoid detection. In addition, Tornado has an advanced radar warning and ECM suite which provides maximum protection against SAMs and other defence weapons. Crew and essential systems are protected by an armoured windscreen and by heavy structure. Tornado also has potent self-defence capability as a result of its high-g manoeuvrability and two internally-mounted 27mm Mauser cannon.

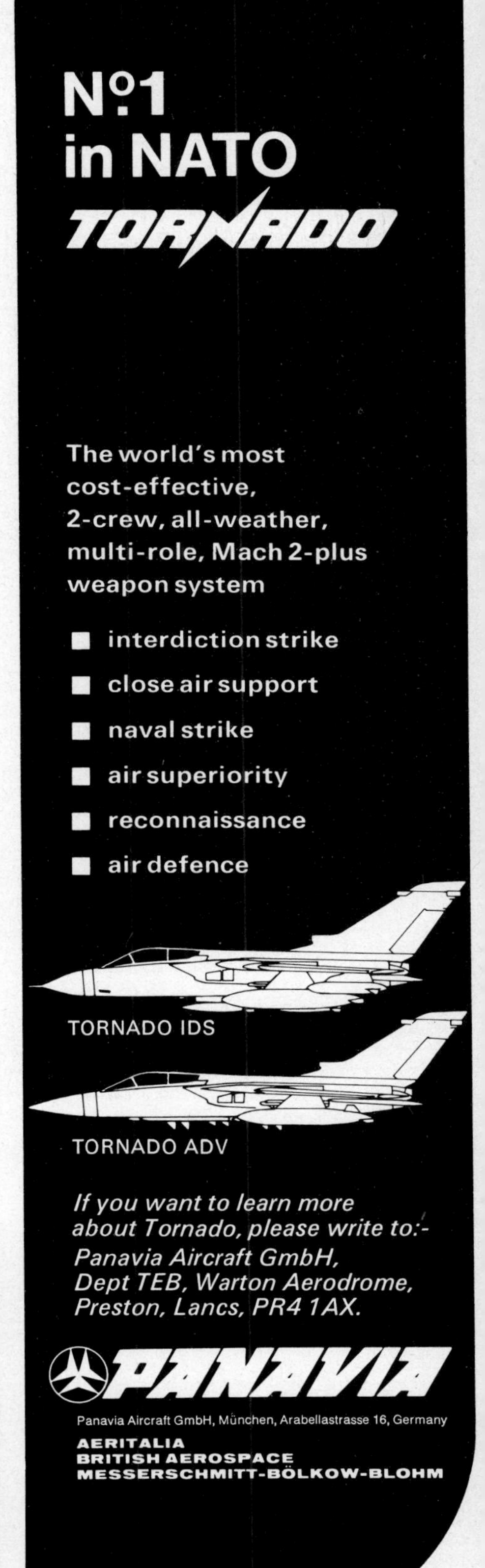

fixed-wing jet freighters because of the lower fuel consumption. The R40s will cost £4m each according to the airline and it is hoped that revenue operations can begin in 1985. Meanwhile, many technical, operational and regulatory problems have to be investigated, and it is for this purpose that the NR2 will be used from next year onwards.

Supplementing the Rothmans' aerobatic team flying four Pitts S2A two-seat aerobatic biplanes, a single-seat **Pitts S2S** is being used to give a separate programme of **solo aerobatic displays** in the UK during the present summer season. The S2S is a more powerful version of the basic S2, with a 260 hp Lycoming engine, and the Rothmans' aircraft, registered G-SOLO, is the first example seen in Europe. Imported and erected by Anvil Aviation, it is being flown by David Perrin, a former member of the Rothmans' team, and gave its first public demonstration at Exeter on 12 July. Rothmans has announced meanwhile that it will not be operating the four-man aerobatic team after the end of this year, although the company "will still maintain its links with aerobatics".

Holidays with a difference are being offered by Pionair Tours Ltd of Horley, Surrey, giving aviation enthusiasts the chance to travel to and from Tangier **in a** vintage **Douglas DC-3**. The aircraft, G-ANAF, features 14 double seats positioned adjacent to the large windows, and is leased from Air Atlantique. Starting in October, Pionair Tours will offer package tours from Gatwick to Jersey, Santander, Seville and Tangier, with pre-flight briefings for the passengers, side-trips for enthusiasts at each point of call and three days in Tangier with a day trip to Gibraltar. The cabin attendant will wear a newly-designed version of a 'forties-style uniform.

USA

A **new airline** is being formed in the New York area with the name **People Express**. The management is drawn from former employees of Texas International, including the president Donald C Burr, and operations are planned to start in the first half of 1981 using short/medium-range jet transports such as the DC-9, Boeing 737 or Boeing 727. Operations will centre upon Newark and will be aimed at the high-density routes on the US East Coast.

CIVIL CONTRACTS AND SALES

Airbus A300: South African Airways has converted to a firm order its previous option on an A300C4 Combi, and has taken options on two more A300s. The Combi will be delivered in the last quarter of 1982 and will join four A300B2-200s and a single A300B4-100.

ATL-98 Carvair: Two Carvairs acquired on lease at the end of 1978 by Nationwide Air to operate vehicle ferry services across the Cook Strait are now available for sale in New Zealand. No licences to permit the proposed Nationwide operation were forthcoming from the NZ government.

Bell Helicopters: The Tunisian government ordered six Model 205A-1s, for delivery this year. ☐ Air Logistics has taken delivery of six Model 206L-1 Long Rangers with six more to follow later this year, making a total of 31 in the fleet, which includes 70 other Bell types. The company also has converted to a firm order previous options on six Model 412s for delivery in 1981.

Boeing 727: Eastern Airlines is leasing five 727-200s from Pacific Southwest, from August, for use on the Eastern Air Shuttle. ☐ Europe Air Service has leased one -200 from Braniff and is expected to acquire three of its own in due course.

Boeing 737: Southwest Airlines of Dallas ordered six more Advanced 737s, according to Boeing; the airline itself had previously announced three of these orders, for delivery late 1980/early 1981; the other three will be delivered in the first quarter of 1982. ☐ Pacific Western Airlines ordered two more 737s, for delivery in November/December 1981 to follow three already on order for earlier 1981 delivery.

British Aerospace HS.125: The Argentine State-owned oil company Yacimientos Petroliferos Fiscales Sociedad del Estado (YPF) has ordered one Srs 700B, bringing the sales total to 496 of which 138 are Srs 700s.

De Havilland Dash 7: Loganair has confirmed an order for one Dash 7, for delivery in August 1981.

De Havilland Dash 8: Commitments for another 18 Dash 8s have been announced by the company since its previous listing (see *Airscene*/July 1980), bringing the total to 73 for 21 companies. Additions to the list of commitments are Rocky Mountain Airways (6); Rio Airlines (3 more to total 6); Henson Airlines (1 more to total 4); Metro Airlines (4); Pilgrim Airlines (1) and BPA Australia (3).

EMBRAER EMB-110 Bandeirante: Among the latest customers is Centreline Air Services, a charter operator based at Biggin Hill, which has taken delivery of an EMB-110P1.

EMBRAER EMB-120 Brasilia: Among the companies holding options are Metro Airlines (5) and Pennsylvania Commuter (2). Letters of intent in respect of 17 aircraft have been written by four other US airlines — Aeromech, Cascade, Boston-Provincetown Airlines and Royale Airlines. According to Pratt & Whitney Aircraft of Canada, supplier of the PT7A turboprops for the Brasilia, total options now stand at 51.

EMBRAER EMB-121 Xingu: The manufacturer has confirmed the sale of five to Belgium (this column/March 1980) for use by Sabena as pilot trainers. Deliveries will begin in December.

Lockheed L-1011 TriStar: Delta ordered one additional TriStar to bring its total order for -100s, -200s and -500s to 51. Delivery will be in April 1982. ☐ Air Portugal's hoped-for order for five TriStar 500s, twice deferred for want of government approval, remains in jeopardy at the time of going to press because of continuing labour problems and strikes that threaten to compound the company's financial problems. A £20m loss for 1979 was recently recorded.

McDonnell Douglas DC-8: Starting on 2 August, Air New Zealand has leased a Srs 63CF from Flying Tiger Line to operate its Los Angeles-Auckland-Los Angeles round trip each week. Next June, it will be replaced by one of ANZ's Srs 50s modified from passenger to all-cargo configuration.

McDonnell Douglas DC-10: Mexicana Airlines signed a contract for two more Srs 15s, for delivery in June 1982. They are the fourth and fifth of the type ordered by Mexicana and will have 315 seats in a one-class layout, with a below-deck galley.

Shorts Skyvan: The Government of Malawi placed a £2m-plus contract for three Skyvans for operation by Air Malawi. The order follows the sale of a Skyvan to the Malawi Police Force last December and brings to 136 the total sold, to 44 operators in 30 countries.

Vickers Vanguard: Field Aviation Ltd has acquired the five Vanguard Merchantman freighters from British Airways and is offering three of these for sale.

MILITARY CONTRACTS

British Aerospace Bulldog: The Scottish Division of BAe has received a £350,000 order for five Bulldog trainers for delivery early next year to an unspecified country in the Middle East.

Fokker F27MPA: The Philippine Air Force has placed an order with Fokker BV for three F27MPA maritime patrol aircraft at an approximate unit cost of \$8·5m (£3·6m).

SEPECAT Jaguar International: The Sultanate of Oman has placed a follow-on order for 12 more Adour 811-powered Jaguar International tactical strike fighters. Previously, 12 had been purchased, including two two-seaters.

Sukhoi Su-22: It has now been confirmed that a \$136m (£57·5m) contract has been placed on behalf of the *Fuerza Aérea Peruana* for a follow-on batch of 16 Su-22 (Fitter-C) tactical strike fighters to equip a third *escuadron*. Previously, the FAP had received 32 single-seat Su-22s and four tandem two-seat Su-22s. The purchase price is to be paid over 12 years at two per cent interest.

MIRAGE 2000 export fighter for the 'eighties

Roy Braybrook describes France's most important new warplane

IF ANY EUROPEAN FIGHTER is to be exported in really large numbers throughout the 1980s and 1990s, then it will undoubtedly be the Dassault-Breguet Mirage 2000. Only that aircraft has the combination of performance and moderate price that is required to provide a true successor to Britain's Hawker Hunter and France's own Mirage III/5 in overseas markets.

Although the Mirage 2000 is a brand-new design, its origins clearly lie in the Mirage III/5 series, of which some 1,400 examples from production lines in four different nations now serve with 20 air forces. To understand the remarkable potential for success of this new aircraft, it is necessary first to refer back to the mid-1950s and analyse the reasons for the success and the shortcomings of its delta-winged predecessor. One must then examine why Dassault-Breguet switched in the mid-1960s to the swept-wing for the Mirage F1, and finally what technological changes occurred in the mid-1970s to make reversion to the delta formula so attractive.

The Mirage III was one of a generation of $M=2{\cdot}0$ fighters that appeared in the years immediately following the Korean War, the other notable examples being the Lockheed F-104 and the MiG-21. All three types represented a dramatic leap forward from the subsonic F-86 and MiG-15 that had fought it out over Korea, since these new aircraft achieved more than 100 per cent increase in speed capability over a generation that had first flown less than ten years earlier. This was arguably the most sensational advance ever in fighter development, being greater in effect than that produced by the switch from piston engines to turbojets in the mid-1940s.

The post-Korea generation got to $M=2{\cdot}0$ by a massive increase in thrust and an equally important reduction in drag. Thrust was boosted by the addition of an afterburner, giving for relatively little weight a sizeable static increase (typically 40 per cent). However, more importantly, in supersonic flight afterburning thrust increased steeply with aircraft speed up to the point that intake pressure recovery fell off markedly. With a multi-shock intake (rather than the simple pitot intake of the transonic F-100, MiG-19 and Super Mystère), there was suddenly scope for a large-scale improvement in speed at high altitude (ie, above heights where structural strength and stiffness were limiting factors), given an airframe of low wave drag.

Assuming the use of a slender fuselage, the key to wave drag reduction is the form of the wing. As a basis for analysing the Mirage III approach, it is instructive to compare the philosophies adopted by Dassault, Lockheed and the Mikoyan design bureau. Lockheed chose a virtually straight wing of low aspect ratio, achieving low wave drag by keeping the exposed area very small and by using the unprecedented thickness/chord ratio of 3·3 per cent. This extreme fineness (the F-104 wing is almost certainly still the thinnest in the world) eliminated any possibility of carrying a significant amount of fuel in the wing, and necessitated a complex fuselage-mounted undercarriage and new methods of construction for the wing and the aileron actuator. The company evidently felt that a sizeable increase in landing speeds was inevitable with the new $M=2{\cdot}0$ generation. In the later F-104G, Lockheed moderated landing performance to some extent by use of a blown flap.

Artem Mikoyan's approach was to achieve low wave drag through the use of a moderately thin 60-degree delta wing, with a much lower wing loading and high lift flaps (trimmed by a highly swept tailplane) to give more conventional landing speeds. The long inboard chord produces a reasonable thickness, allowing some fuel to be carried in the wing and the main undercarriage legs to be buried (although the axles are articulated so that the wheels lie vertically in the fuselage sides). It is arguable that this less extreme Soviet approach was in principle superior to that of Lockheed, since the only fundamental subsequent change to the MiG-21 has been the introduction of blown flaps to improve the view over the nose in approach configuration. In practice, the most significant difference between the two types has been the greater flexibility resulting from the larger size of the F-104, making it a useful ground attack aircraft.

The Dassault approach also adopted the moderately thin delta wing, but it eliminated the horizontal tail in favour of a lower wing loading. The result was a comparatively large wing of straightforward construction, with an extremely useful fuel volume and ample space for a simple, wide-track under-

carriage, yet with good longitudinal distribution of cross-section area for low wave drag.

The tailless delta configuration was first tested by Dassault in the form of the twin-engined MD 550, powered by two Rolls-Royce Viper turbojets of 1,750 lb (800 kg) thrust. This aircraft first flew on 25 June 1955. Boosted by a SEPR rocket of 3,300 lb (1 500 kg) thrust, it reached M = 1·3 in December 1956. The successor to the MD 550 was originally designed around two Gabizo turbojets. However, this engine was cancelled, so the fuselage was redesigned to accommodate an afterburning Atar 101G of 9,900 lb (4 500 kg) thrust. The resulting Mirage III made its maiden flight on 18 November 1956. With a SEPR rocket of similar thrust to that used in the MD 550, it attained M = 1·8 in level flight on 27 January 1957.

A pre-series batch of 10 Mirage IIIAs was then built, with the Atar 9B of 13,200 lb (6 000 kg) and a SEPR 841 rocket of 3,700 lb (1 680 kg). One of these aircraft reached M = 2·0 in level flight on 24 October 1958, and in the following year a speed of M = 2·17 was recorded. With minor changes this aircraft went into production as the Mirage IIIC, the first of which flew on 9 October 1960.

The Mirage IIIC interceptor was joined in 1961 by the dual-rôle Mirage IIIE with increased internal fuel and, in 1967, by the simply-equipped Mirage 5. The latest model of the first Mirage series is the Mirage 50, powered by the uprated Atar 9K50 of 15,870 lb (7 200 kg) in place of the Atar 9C, the thrust of which is unchanged from the engine in the Mirage IIIA. Depending on radar fit, this new aircraft is designated Mirage III/50 (Cyrano IV radar derived from that on the Mirage F1) or Mirage 5/50 (Agave radar as used on the Super Etendard). It is not clear which sub-series is on order for Chile (16 Mirage 50C and 50DC).

Pros and cons

The Mirage III was a remarkable achievement for its day. It was claimed to be the only production aircraft capable of both flying at M = 2·0 with air-air weapons, and taking-off and landing in less than 2,500 ft (760 m) of unpaved runway. Despite its large wing of 376 sq ft (35 m^2) gross area, its thickness/chord ratio of 4 per cent (root) tapering to 3·5 per

Dassault-Breguet Mirage 2000 Specification

Power Plant: One SNECMA M53-5 single-shaft turbofan rated at 12,350 lb (5 600 kg) maximum unreheated thrust and 19,840 lb (9 000 kg) maximum reheated thrust. Internal fuel capacity, 835 Imp gal (3 800 l) with provision for a jettisonable fuel tank of up to 374 Imp gal (1 700 l) under each wing and up to 264 Imp gal (1 200 l) on fuselage centreline.

Performance: Max attainable speed (clean), M = 2·35 or 1,550 mph (2 495 km/h) above 36,090 ft (11 000 m); max sustained speed (clean), M = 2·2 or 1,450 mph (2 335 km/h); max speed at sea level, M = 1·2 or 915 mph (1 472 km/h); time to M = 2·0 at 49,200 ft (15 000 m) from brakes release, 4·0 min; max climb rate, 49,000 ft/min (249 m/sec); service ceiling, 65,000 ft (19 800 m); tactical radius (four AAMs, two 374 Imp gal/1 700 l drop tanks) 435 mls (700 km); landing approach speed, 161 mph (260 km/h).

Weights: Combat, 19,840 lb (9 000 kg); max take-off, 33,070 lb (15 000 kg).

Dimensions: Span 29 ft $6\frac{1}{3}$ in (9,00 m); length, 50 ft $3\frac{1}{2}$ in (15,33 m); wing area, 441·30 sq ft (41,00 m^2); wheel track, 11 ft $1\frac{3}{4}$ in (3,40 m); wheelbase, 16 ft $4\frac{3}{4}$ in (5,00 m).

Armament: Two 30-mm DEFA 554 cannon and (air superiority) two Matra 550 Magic IR-homing short range dogfight missiles and two Matra Super 530D radar homing medium-range missiles. For the strike rôle nine external stations (four beneath the wings and five beneath the fuselage) are available for up to 11,000 lb (5 000 kg) of ordnance, loads including 18 550-lb (250-kg), six 880-lb (400-kg), or three 2,200-lb (1 000-kg) bombs.

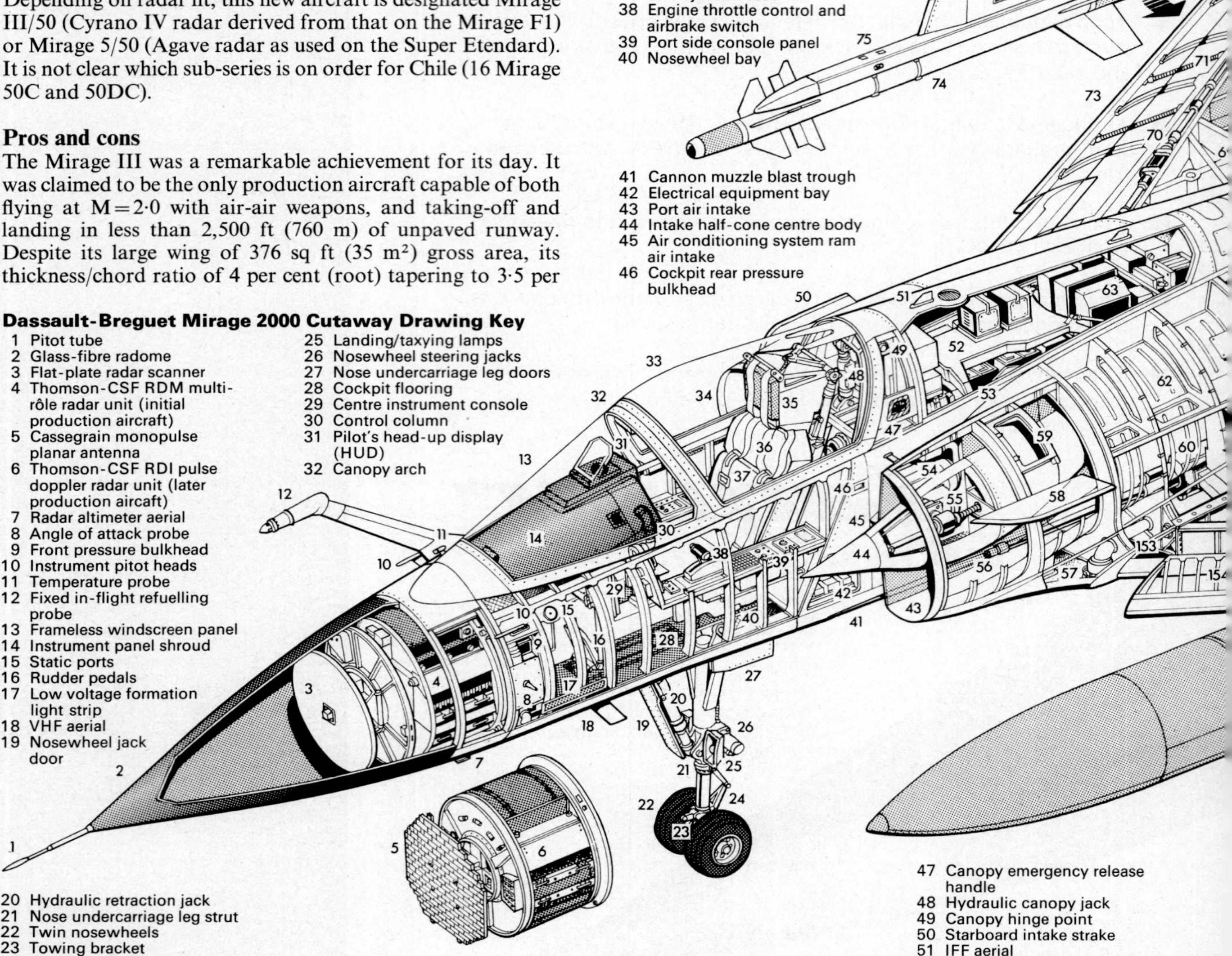

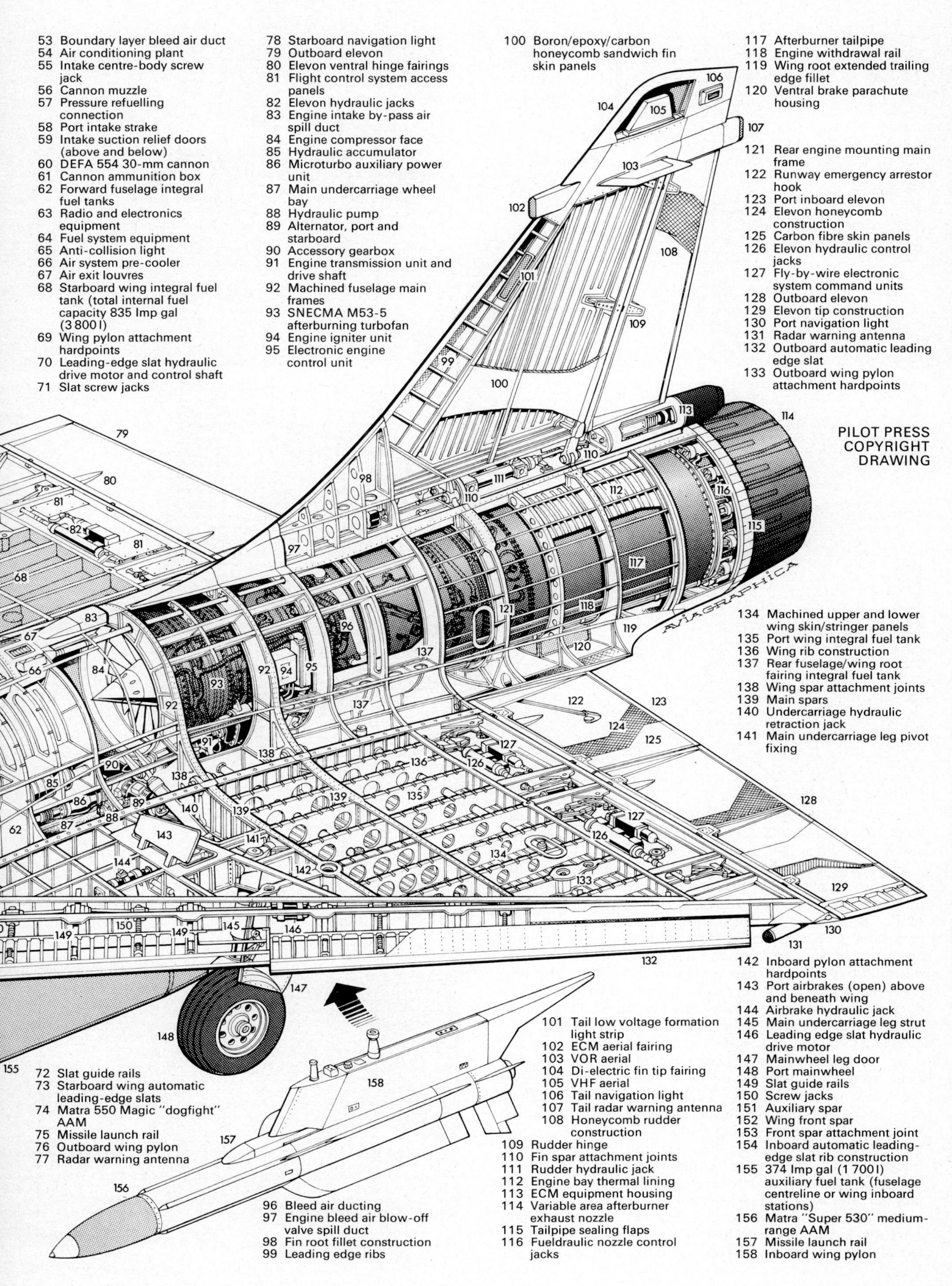
53 Boundary layer bleed air duct
54 Air conditioning plant
55 Intake centre-body screw jack
56 Cannon muzzle
57 Pressure refuelling connection
58 Port intake strake
59 Intake suction relief doors (above and below)
60 DEFA 554 30-mm cannon
61 Cannon ammunition box
62 Forward fuselage integral fuel tanks
63 Radio and electronics equipment
64 Fuel system equipment
65 Anti-collision light
66 Air system pre-cooler
67 Air exit louvres
68 Starboard wing integral fuel tank (total internal fuel capacity 835 Imp gal (3 800 l)
69 Wing pylon attachment hardpoints
70 Leading-edge slat hydraulic drive motor and control shaft
71 Slat screw jacks
72 Slat guide rails
73 Starboard wing automatic leading-edge slats
74 Matra 550 Magic "dogfight" AAM
75 Missile launch rail
76 Outboard wing pylon
77 Radar warning antenna
78 Starboard navigation light
79 Outboard elevon
80 Elevon ventral hinge fairings
81 Flight control system access panels
82 Elevon hydraulic jacks
83 Engine intake by-pass air spill duct
84 Engine compressor face
85 Hydraulic accumulator
86 Microturbo auxiliary power unit
87 Main undercarriage wheel bay
88 Hydraulic pump
89 Alternator, port and starboard
90 Accessory gearbox
91 Engine transmission unit and drive shaft
92 Machined fuselage main frames
93 SNECMA M53-5 afterburning turbofan
94 Engine igniter unit
95 Electronic engine control unit
96 Bleed air ducting
97 Engine bleed air blow-off valve spill duct
98 Fin root fillet construction
99 Leading edge ribs
100 Boron/epoxy/carbon honeycomb sandwich fin skin panels
101 Tail low voltage formation light strip
102 ECM aerial fairing
103 VOR aerial
104 Di-electric fin tip fairing
105 VHF aerial
106 Tail navigation light
107 Tail radar warning antenna
108 Honeycomb rudder construction
109 Rudder hinge
110 Fin spar attachment joints
111 Rudder hydraulic jack
112 Engine bay thermal lining
113 ECM equipment housing
114 Variable area afterburner exhaust nozzle
115 Tailpipe sealing flaps
116 Fueldraulic nozzle control jacks
117 Afterburner tailpipe
118 Engine withdrawal rail
119 Wing root extended trailing edge fillet
120 Ventral brake parachute housing
121 Rear engine mounting main frame
122 Runway emergency arrestor hook
123 Port inboard elevon
124 Elevon honeycomb construction
125 Carbon fibre skin panels
126 Elevon hydraulic control jacks
127 Fly-by-wire electronic system command units
128 Outboard elevon
129 Elevon tip construction
130 Port navigation light
131 Radar warning antenna
132 Outboard automatic leading edge slat
133 Outboard wing pylon attachment hardpoints
134 Machined upper and lower wing skin/stringer panels
135 Port wing integral fuel tank
136 Wing rib construction
137 Rear fuselage/wing root fairing integral fuel tank
138 Wing spar attachment joints
139 Main spars
140 Undercarriage hydraulic retraction jack
141 Main undercarriage leg pivot fixing
142 Inboard pylon attachment hardpoints
143 Port airbrakes (open) above and beneath wing
144 Airbrake hydraulic jack
145 Main undercarriage leg strut
146 Leading edge slat hydraulic drive motor
147 Mainwheel leg door
148 Port mainwheel
149 Slat guide rails
150 Screw jacks
151 Auxiliary spar
152 Wing front spar
153 Front spar attachment joint
154 Inboard automatic leading-edge slat rib construction
155 374 Imp gal (1 700 l) auxiliary fuel tank (fuselage centreline or wing inboard stations)
156 Matra "Super 530" medium-range AAM
157 Missile launch rail
158 Inboard wing pylon
PILOT PRESS COPYRIGHT DRAWING
AVIAGRAPHICA

cent (tip) gave a very low wave drag. The new Mirage 50 can reach M = 1·8 at 45,000 ft (13 700 m) in 4·7 minutes, and can sustain M = 2·0 as high as 60,700 ft (18 500 m).

The simple delta configuration thus combined low wave drag with excellent fuel volume, and permitted the use of traditional methods of construction. However, it also incurred serious penalties in sustained turn rate (the most important performance parameter in air combat) and in landing performance. Sustained turn rate is penalised by the low aspect ratio (1·94) of the delta, causing high induced drag. This is of little significance in intercepting bombers, but means that in a dogfight the Mirage III/5 loses speed rapidly: pulling up the nose has much the same effect as opening the airbrakes.

Manoeuvrability also suffers as a result of excessive trim drag, since high lift coefficients demand disproportionately large trimming downloads on the elevons which are only a short distance aft of the CG. This large trimming download also restricts the net lift coefficient available, hence the aircraft lands fast despite its low wing loading. The delta wing is also subject to large dihedral effect (rolling moment due to sideslip), which limits the crosswind it can tolerate. However, the most significant drawback is that, having no horizontal tail, the delta wing aircraft can have no trailing edge flap.

The Mirage F1, which first flew in December 1966, employed a more advanced form of construction to permit the use of a thin swept wing. This was fitted with leading- and

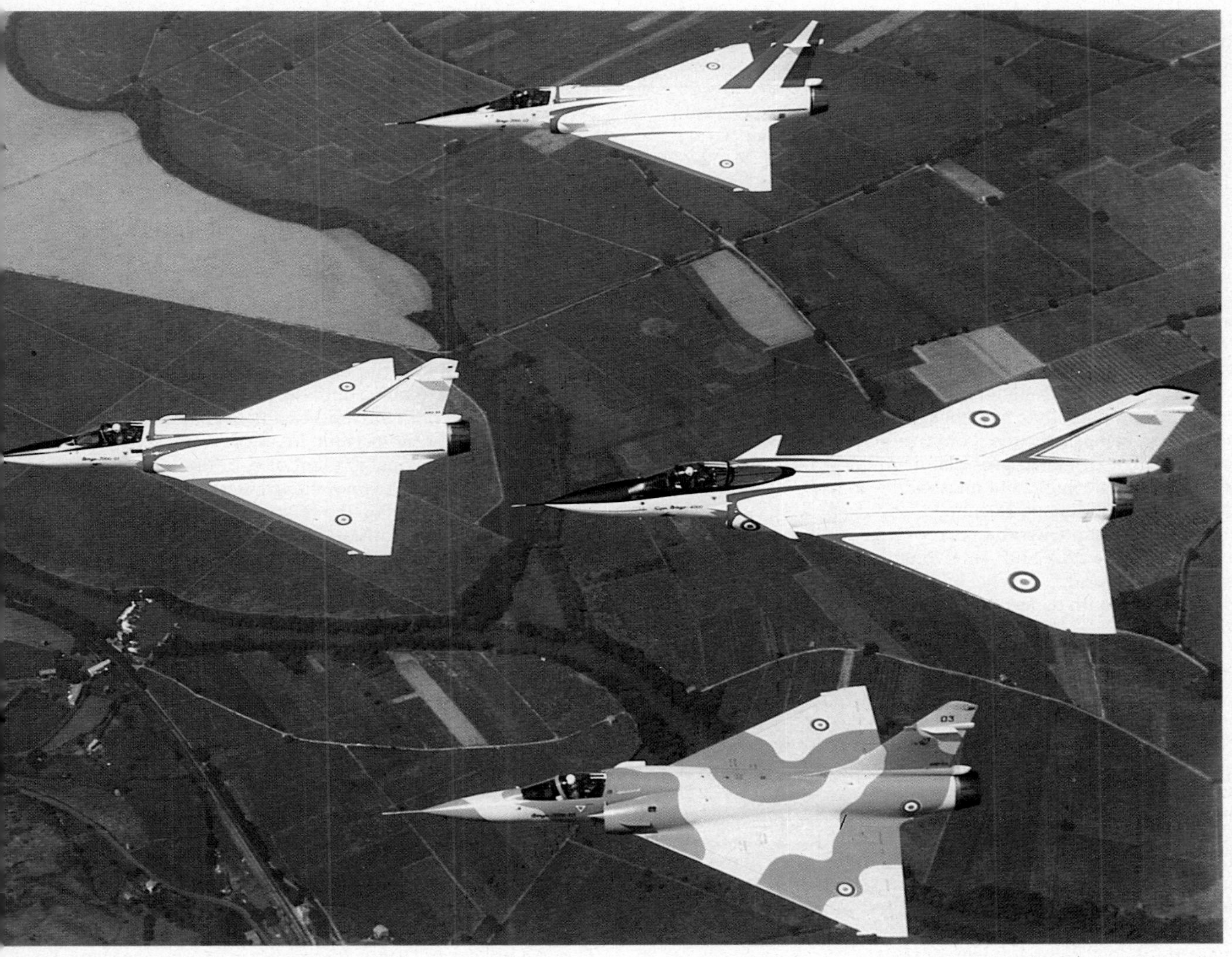

Four prototypes of the Mirage 2000 have flown to date, and all are shown in the photographs on these pages. The fourth aircraft, with the definitive fin-and-rudder, is depicted top left and the third aircraft, in its 1979 air display finish, is centre left. Seen above are the Mirage 2000-01 (leading), -02 (top), -03 (bottom) and the sole Super Mirage 4000 (right) as displayed at the Paris Air Show in June 1979 and the line-up below shows (left to right) the second, first and third prototypes.

trailing-edge flaps, trimmed by a conventional low-set horizontal tail. Although wing loading was substantially increased relative to the Mirage III series, low speed handling is significantly improved, and approach speed reduced by 20 per cent, implying a landing run reduction of 36 per cent. Fitted with the Atar 9K50 as used in the later Mirage 50, the maximum speed of the Mirage F1 is increased to M=2·2, whereas the earlier delta-wing series has a normal limit of M=2·0. However, acceleration times are probably lengthened and supersonic ceiling is reduced to 53,000 ft (16 000 m). Despite the reduction in wing volume, internal fuel capacity is increased by 43 per cent by the use of integral tanks in the fuselage, giving major improvements in range and endurance. Deliveries of the F1 began in 1973, and although a relatively conventional design for its generation, this aircraft has now attracted orders for over 600 units from 10 nations.

When it came to designing a third single-engined Mirage series, the company thus had background experience on both the tailless delta and the conventional swept wing configuration. The delta had proved outstanding in terms of wave drag and usable volume, but unattractive in terms of sustained turn rate and landing performance. The swept wing cured the landing and manoeuvrability problems, but only at the expense of wave drag and wing volume. The aim of the next generation aircraft clearly had to be to combine the advantages of both concepts while somehow eliminating their drawbacks.

The most important single factor motivating Dassault's return to the tailless delta layout was the concept of exploiting negative longitudinal stability. In a conventional arrangement, with the CG ahead of the AC (aerodynamic centre), the lift on the wing-body combination is trimmed by an aerodynamic download on the horizontal tail (or elevons in the case of a tailless delta). If the CG is moved aft, the natural longitudinal stability of the aircraft is decreased, but so is the required trimming download on the tailplane. If the CG is placed on the AC, the aircraft is neutrally stable and requires no tail load to trim. However, if the CG is taken aft of the AC, then the aircraft is longitudinally unstable, and wing lift is trimmed by an *upload* on the tailplane or elevons, which benefits both trimmed lift coefficient and trim drag.

The F-16 is an example of a relatively conventional aircraft designed for negative longitudinal stability (at least in subsonic flight) with a trimming upload on the tailplane. The Mirage 2000 is an example of a tailless delta that uses the same idea. However, this class of aircraft benefits much more from negative stability, since traditionally its maximum lift coefficient is small and its trim drag high. Thus, when the Mirage 2000 is pitched up to high AOA for manoeuvring flight or landing, instead of requiring an aerodynamic download on the elevons to trim (as with the Mirage III/5), it is trimmed by an upload that boosts lift coefficient.

None of the principles involved in the foregoing discussion represents new thinking. It has always been obvious that moving the CG aft would provide more lift, less drag and a faster-reacting aircraft. The problem has been to produce an aircraft that the pilot can fly despite its natural instability. The solution to this problem was provided by the combination of electrically-signalled controls (fly-by-wire or FBW) and an advanced automatic flight control system (AFCS). In such a system the pilot has no direct mechanical connection to the various control surfaces. Instead he uses the control column and rudder pedals to indicate to the AFCS how he wishes the aircraft to respond and the black boxes cause the tailplane, ailerons and rudder to move until the pilot's demands are met. For example, if the pilot moves the control column aft against the resistance of a spring-feel unit, his effort is translated into a demand for a proportional amount of *g*, or (at low speeds) of AOA. The tailplane or elevon is moved by the AFCS until the measured *g* or AOA equals the required value. Lateral stick force is conventionally translated into a roll rate demand, and rudder pedal force into a rudder position demand.

Modern technology has thus made it possible to produce an aircraft that can be flown with far less than normal stability, or even with substantial instability, in much the same way as a missile is guided.

Advanced technology

In designing what is essentially an advanced technology Mirage III, Dassault-Breguet also introduced major improvements in regard to the powerplant, aerodynamics and structural materials. In place of the Atar series of turbojets which power all earlier production models, the Mirage 2000 was given the SNECMA M53 single-shaft turbofan — more strictly a continuous-bleed turbojet — which has a better fuel consumption, produces more thrust and weighs 285 lb (130 kg) less than the most powerful Atar (ie, the 9K50 used in the Mirage 50 and F1).

This new engine had begun flight trials in a Caravelle testbed in July 1973, flew in a Mirage F1E in December 1974, and carried out its 150-hour military qualification test in April 1976. This M53-2 of 18,737 lb (8 500 kg) afterburning thrust was the model to be used in early flight trials of the Mirage 2000. However, this engine was soon superseded by the M53-5 of 19,840 lb (9 000 kg) maximum thrust, which passed its 150-

continued on page 145

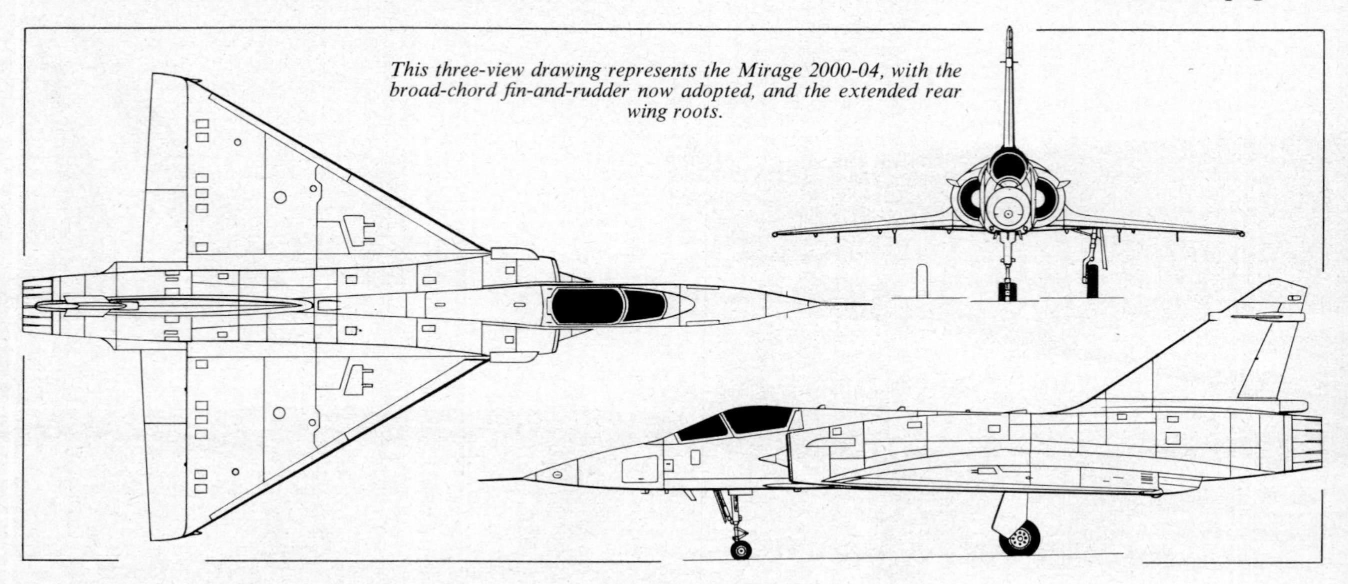

This three-view drawing represents the Mirage 2000-04, with the broad-chord fin-and-rudder now adopted, and the extended rear wing roots.

MULTI
MISSION
Battlefield Lynx
Britains world beating advanced technology helicopter. Fast, agile, all weather, twin engined.
Battlefield Lynx
able to put men and equipment right on the spot, wherever, whatever
Battlefield Lynx
the complete troubleshooter, in full production to meet orders from armed forces throughout the world.

The new Boeing 234: the 44-passenger reason.

As oil exploration and development move further and further offshore, the logistics of support become more and more complex. But the new Boeing 234 Chinook helicopter is going to change much of that by simplifying the movement of personnel and priority cargo.

Nothing else can move men and materials so far, so fast, so effectively. With airliner comfort for 44, a 600-mile range at 140 knots, and a 1,600,000-flight-hour heritage of proven performance, the Chinook will do the job with straight-line efficiency, transporting crew members from shore to platform in a matter of hours instead of days. It's capacity that cuts costs while eliminating layovers, complicated staging, and non-productive travel time.

The further out you go, the more you need the Boeing Chinook. For literature and information, contact Mark John, Boeing Vertol, Philadelphia, Pa. 19142, phone (215) 522-3357.

BOEING VERTOL HELICOPTERS
THE LEADING EDGE
Philadelphia, Pa. 19142

DASHING SUCCESS FROM DOWNSVIEW

A description of the De Havilland Dash 7, by David W H Godfrey, PEng, CEng, MRAeS, AFAIAA

WITH total sales and options approaching 90 and a production rate of three aeroplanes a month by early 1981, the Dash 7 is viewed by The de Havilland Aircraft of Canada as an established success. The steady stream of orders reaching Downsview, Ontario, vindicates the company's faith in this 50-passenger commuter liner that uses short take-off and landing (STOL) performance to great advantage while remaining a simple design bereft of special devices or the need for tricky piloting techniques.

In making a success of the DHC-7, the marketing style of which is DASH 7, de Havilland had a number of barriers to hurdle. It is a relatively small company and had never before developed a four-engined aeroplane; when the DHC-7 project began the company was foreign-owned (by the Hawker Siddeley Group in the UK) and faced some family rivalry (from the HS.748 and, later, the HS.146); the prime potential market in the United States was restricted to third-level airlines (which by regulatory definition were limited to using aircraft of up to 12,500-lb/5 670-kg gross weight and 30 passengers); no government orders were forthcoming initially in Canada; and civil sales potential in Canada was small. So, the DHC-7 had a protracted gestation period despite the evident need, as de Havilland saw it, for a pressurised bigger brother for its highly successful 19-passenger DHC-6 Twin Otter and a replacement for such aircraft as the F.27 Friendship, Viscount, HS.748, Convair 340/440 and DC-3, even the latest of which were based on 1950's technology and engine performance.

Quietly, and much more slowly than it liked, the company pressed on with project work and one-by-one the obstacles were removed or circumvented. Design was no problem since experience with the turboprop-powered DHC-5 Buffalo and Twin Otter was relevant to the DHC-7's flight regime. Also — despite its own experience of advanced-technology STOL with the augmentor-wing Buffalo flying test-bed built for NASA by Boeing; the availability of suitable turbofan engines, and other companies' work with externally blown flaps, upper-surface blowing, jet flaps and the like — de Havilland knew that its airline customers were conservatively minded. So, the DHC-7 design remained very straightforward in having the high wing and "T"-tail configuration of the Buffalo (including its tandem rudder); four of the same basic turboprop engines as used in the Twin Otter; and twice the latter's passenger capacity in a pressurised fuselage. Thus, the 1967 design for a 38-passenger STOL aeroplane was powered by 715-shp Pratt & Whitney Aircraft of Canada PT6A-27s, and featured a fixed undercarriage on the fuselage sides with tandem main gear. Gross weight was set at 26,500 lb (12 018 kg); but changes were in the offing.

Market surveys showed a need for at least 48 seats. Project development resulted in adoption of a wing-mounted retractable undercarriage for higher cruise speeds and better crosswind characteristics (wider track between the inboard engine nacelles than the corners of the fuselage); and slats were deleted because of the difficulty of adequately de-icing such small-chord surfaces, and of the possibility of negative stall at the steep approach attitudes they would make possible. Wing loading, however, remained the same at 45 lb/sq ft (219 kg/m^2). After one year of project definition, design development began early in 1969, but the US recession shortly after damped airline interest in new aircraft and the project was shelved temporarily.

Various partnerships with other companies were considered by DHC, but it seemed that the potential for a STOL-performance airliner was good enough to encourage keeping the DHC-7 an all-Canadian programme. By mid-1971, the logical partner in the programme was the Canadian federal government and it was announced in October 1972 that work was to start at once on two pre-production aircraft that would be powered by 1,120-shp PT6A-50 engines. Meanwhile, US regulations had been changed to permit regional airlines to use aircraft carrying up to 56 passengers.

Initial development costs for Dash 7 airframe and engine totalled $Can82m, shared between DHC, PWAC (then, United Aircraft of Canada), and the federal government (Department of Industry, Trade and Commerce). Concurrently, the Canadian government took an option to buy DHC from Hawker Siddeley, purchasing the company on 26 June 1974.

Flight development and flying controls

Maiden flight of the first pre-production aeroplane (registered C-GNBX-X) was made on 27 March 1975, and the second aircraft (C-GNCA-X) flew on 26 June the same year. A third airframe was used for static-load testing and a fourth for fatigue tests. The first production Dash 7 (C-GQIW) flew on 30 May 1977 and was used, with the pre-production aircraft, for final test flying. Certification by the Canadian Department of Transport to FAR Part 25 was completed on 2 May 1977. Under FAR Part 25 and Part 121 regulations, the Dash 7 is approved for STOL operation with certification for a 7·5-deg glideslope approach angle over a 35-ft (10,7-m) obstacle.

Although it has STOL capabilities, the Dash 7 is flown by normal piloting techniques at all times and does not need special handling methods or variation from standard airline practice. For steep-approach descents (7·5 deg instead of the conventional 3·0 deg), the aeroplane has more than adequate descent-control capability because of the Beta-control propeller system, in which blade-angle is varied directly from the engine-power lever while propeller rpm are kept at a high value. Blade-angle follows throttle movement without perceptible lag, so the pilot has a very rapid and very effective means of altering approach gradient.

During development flying a few minor changes were made. These included drooping the wing leading edge outboard of the flaps, marked by a boundary-layer fence; changing landing flap-angle from 55 to 45 deg; adding vortex generators at the rear of the inboard engine nacelles to correct pressure distribution; insetting the elevator hinges; reshaping the elevator balances and closing the nosewheel doors after landing to avoid build-up of mud, slush or ice.

Conventional flying controls are used, with cable-circuit operation from dual control columns and sets of rudder pedals. The elevator is operated manually via spring tabs. Lateral control is by manually-operated ailerons on each outer wing panel which are operated in conjunction with powered spoilers in the outer wings. The pilot's control ramshorns operate the ailerons while the co-pilot controls the spoilers, each having separate cable circuits. The two sets of ramshorns are interconnected by a member which can be disconnected in case of a lateral control malfunction. Conventional tabs are used for the independent aileron-trim system.

Duplicate hydraulic servo actuators power the lateral-control spoilers, each servo getting its input signal from the lateral-control cable circuit and producing modulated spoiler

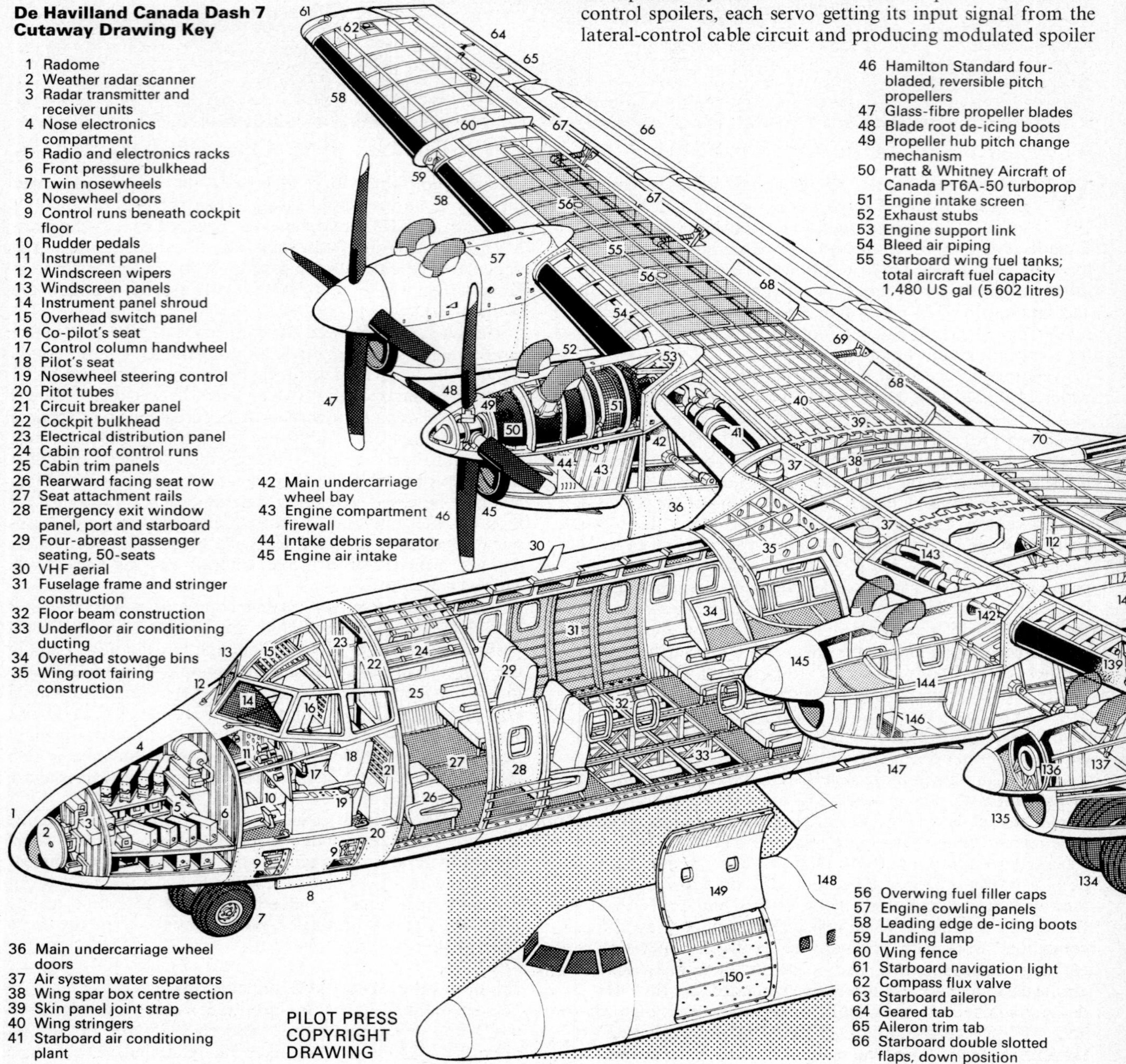

deflections when "up aileron" command movements are made. So, in flight, these spoilers operate differentially to augment the ailerons. On the ground, after nosewheel touchdown has occurred, and the engine-power levers have been pulled back, the spoilers operate symmetrically as lift dumpers. Symmetrically operated ground spoilers are located inboard of the lateral-control spoilers. Similar to those of the Buffalo, the tandem rudder elements are powered by hydraulic actuators attached to the front element at mid-height. The rear element is mounted on the front and is driven as a geared tab by a pushrod linkage at each end.

Double-slotted large-chord flaps cover about 80 per cent of the wing span, extending from the wing roots to the inboard ends of the ailerons. They are operated by linear hydraulic actuators through irreversible mechanical drives and inter-connecting torque shafts. At take-off, the high lift coefficient used is made more profitable by the high propeller thrust available at low flight speeds. The settings of 45 deg for landing and 25 deg for take-off give a C_L max of 3·2 and provide a drag increment that permits adequate glideslope capture from above the 7·5-deg STOL approach angle. Since there is only a small difference between take-off and landing C_L, in the case of an overshoot the flaps may be retracted to the 25-deg setting without the aeroplane sinking.

Stall margins for the horizontal stabiliser are also improved by limiting the power level when the flaps are at the landing

67 Roll control spoilers
68 Ground spoilers
69 Flap screw jacks
70 Wing root trailing edge fillet
71 Fuel transfer pipe fairing
72 Starboard service door
73 Rear seat row
74 Buffet unit
75 Starboard baggage door (open)
76 Fin root fillet
77 Refuelling/defuelling pipe
78 Emergency locator transmitter aerial
79 Fin leading edge
80 Fin construction
81 VOR aerial
82 Elevator control rods
83 Tailplane/fin attachment spar box
84 Upper position light
85 Anti-collision light
86 Tailplane leading edge de-icing boots
87 Starboard tailplane
88 Static discharge wicks
89 Elevator trim tabs
90 Elevator spring tab
91 One-piece elevator
92 Elevator horn balance
93 Tailplane construction
94 Rudder hydraulic jacks
95 Trailing rudder
96 Fore-rudder
97 Tail navigation light
98 Rear fuselage vent
99 Tailcone access door
100 Retractable tail bumper
101 Cockpit voice recorder
102 Sloping fin attachment frames
103 Ventral pressure refuelling connection
104 Rear pressure bulkhead
105 Baggage compartment
106 Baggage restraint net
107 Toilet compartment
108 Wash basin
109 Passenger door upper segment
110 Trailing edge wing root fillet
111 Inboard flap track
112 Wing spar/fuselage main frame attachment joint
113 Flap shroud ribs
114 Port wing integral fuel tank bays
115 Lower passenger door segment/airstairs
116 Handrail
117 Nacelle tail fairing
118 Port double slotted flaps
119 Roll control spoilers
120 Port aileron construction
121 Aileron geared tab
122 Static discharge wicks
123 Aileron horn balance
124 Compass flux valve
125 Port navigation light
126 Wing rib construction
127 Leading edge nose ribs
128 Wing fence
129 Wing tank outboard end rib
130 Landing lamp
131 Leading edge de-icing boots
132 Outboard nacelle hydraulics bay
133 Engine nacelle construction
134 Twin mainwheels
135 Engine air intake
136 Front engine mounting
137 Undercarriage breaker strut
138 Main undercarriage leg strut
139 Hydraulic retraction jack
140 Main undercarriage pivot mounting frame
141 Wing tank inboard end rib
142 Bleed air piping
143 Port air conditioning plant
144 Port inner nacelle construction
145 Propeller spinner
146 Oil cooler
147 HF aerial rail
148 Quick-change passenger/cargo version
149 Cargo door
150 "Ballmat" heavy duty cargo handling floor

AVIAGRAPHICA

De Havilland Dash 7 Specification

Power Plant: Four Pratt & Whitney Aircraft of Canada PT6A-50 turboprops flat-rated at 1,120 shp to 81 deg F (27 deg C) with water injection at sea level. Hamilton Standard 24PF four-blade propellers, feathering and reversing, counterweight type, 11 ft 3 in (3,43-m) diameter. Fuel capacity, approx 1,480 US gal (5 602 l) in integral wing tanks.

Performance: Max cruise speed, ISA, 41,000 lb (18 597 kg), 8,000 ft (2 438 m), 231 kt TAS (428 km/h); cruise speed, 15,000 ft (4,572 m), 227 kt TAS (421 km/h); en route rate of climb, at 44,000 lb (19 958 kg) take-off weight, sea level, 1,200 ft/min (6,1 m/sec); three-engine rate of climb, 700 ft/min (3,5 m/sec); en route ceiling, at 41,000-lb (18 597-kg) weight four engines, 22,800 ft (6 949 m); three-engine ceiling, 14,800 ft (4 511 m); FAR 25 take-off field length, 41,000 lb (18 597 kg), 2,260 ft (689 m) with 25 deg flap; 2,520 ft (768 m) with 15 deg flap; FAR STOL landing field length, 45 deg flap, 42,000 lb (19 051 kg), 1,950 ft (594 m); FAR 25 CTOL landing field length, 45 deg flap, 2,160 ft (658 m); FAR 25 CTOL landing field length, 25 deg flap, 2,990 ft (911 m); range with 50 passengers and baggage, 9,500 lb (4 309 kg) payload, long-range cruise speed at 15,000 ft (4 572 m), IFR fuel reserves, 690 naut mls (1 279 km); max-fuel range, with 6,500 lb (2 948 kg) payload, 1,170 naut mls (2 168 km).

Weights: Operating weight empty (typical), 27,600 lb (12 519 kg); max zero-fuel weight, 39,000 lb (17 690 kg); max usable fuel, 9,925 lb (4 502 kg); extended-range max fuel (DASH 7 No. 28 on and DHC-7R), 14,810 lb (6 717 kg); max payload, 11,400 lb (5 171 kg); max take-off weight, 44,000 lb (19 958 kg); max landing weight, 42,000 lb (19 051 kg).

Dimensions: Span, 93 ft 0 in (28,35 m); length, 80 ft 7·7 in (24,58 m); height, 26 ft 2 in (8,00 m); wing area, 860 sq ft (79,9 m^2); wheeltrack, 23 ft 6 in (7,16 m); wheelbase, 27 ft 6 in (8,38 m); aspect ratio 10:1; baggage, 240 cu ft (6,8 m^3).

Accommodation: Standard layout provides 50 seats four-abreast at 32-in (81-cm) pitch, with toilet and galley at rear of cabin. Baggage compartment in rear fuselage, capacity 240 cu ft (6,80 m^2).

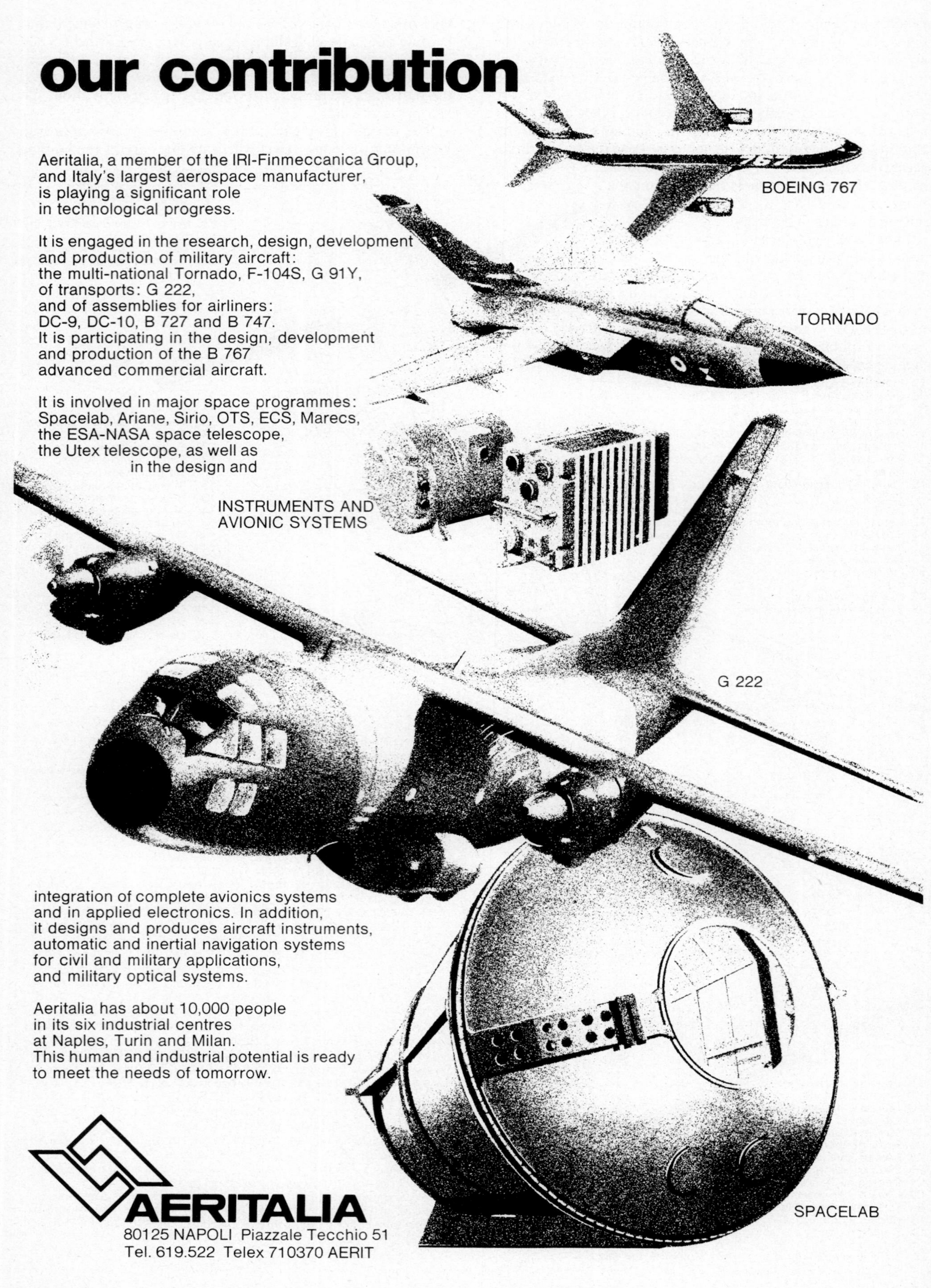
our contribution
Aeritalia, a member of the IRI-Finmeccanica Group,
and Italy's largest aerospace manufacturer,
is playing a significant role
in technological progress.
It is engaged in the research, design, development
and production of military aircraft:
the multi-national Tornado, F-104S, G 91Y,
of transports: G 222,
and of assemblies for airliners:
DC-9, DC-10, B 727 and B 747.
It is participating in the design, development
and production of the B 767
advanced commercial aircraft.
It is involved in major space programmes:
Spacelab, Ariane, Sirio, OTS, ECS, Marecs,
the ESA-NASA space telescope,
the Utex telescope, as well as
in the design and
integration of complete avionics systems
and in applied electronics. In addition,
it designs and produces aircraft instruments,
automatic and inertial navigation systems
for civil and military applications,
and military optical systems.
Aeritalia has about 10,000 people
in its six industrial centres
at Naples, Turin and Milan.
This human and industrial potential is ready
to meet the needs of tomorrow.
BOEING 767
767
TORNADO
INSTRUMENTS AND
AVIONIC SYSTEMS
G 222
SPACELAB
AERITALIA
80125 NAPOLI Piazzale Tecchio 51
Tel. 619.522 Telex 710370 AERIT

setting. Deflection of the flaps to the take-off setting is by mechanical, irreversible screwjacks, the system being designed to "freeze" in the event of failure so that flaps may not be moved asymmetrically. Movement of the flaps from the 25-deg approach angle to 45 deg for landing is via hydraulic jacks that return under air load to the 25-deg take-off setting if there is either hydraulic failure or sudden application of engine power.

Once on the ground, the Dash 7 has three independent means of shedding lift — propellers; inboard spoilers; and outboard spoilers. About 90 per cent of the lift behind the propellers is destroyed by setting the blades to the ground fine-pitch angle. A spin-up signal from the mainwheels at touchdown actuates withdrawal of the power-lever gate so the pilot may move the lever into ground fine-pitch or into reverse. Even in a delicate landing, the additional drag thus caused results in sufficient loss of lift to actuate mainwheel squat switches which activate the inboard spoilers to dump the remainder of wing lift. By this time, the weight is well onto the mainwheels, so spoiler action does not give the impression of a hard landing. When the nosewheels are on the ground, another squat switch actuates the outboard spoilers symmetrically to dump lift and the anti-skid mainwheel brakes take over smoothly. (An early idea to make provision for nosewheel brakes was found to be completely unnecessary.) A useful feature in crosswinds is that full lateral control of the outboard spoilers is available until the nosewheels are on the ground. Since reverse thrust use is not assumed in the aircraft certification, it is worth noting that with a median touchdown point the aeroplane may be brought to a stop within the factored landing distance without either wheelbrakes or spoilers, but by reverse thrust alone.

Structural design and systems

Airframe design of the Dash 7 follows the requirements for FAR Part 25, although more severe criteria were imposed for the case of a high-descent rate landing. The airframe design life is 40,000 flight hours. Fail-safe/alternative load-path practices have been followed and unusually low stress levels were selected to offset the severe fatigue environment of high-frequency short-haul flights at relatively low altitudes (even though the cabin is pressurised). Bonded stringers are used widely, as are window doubler plates to attain minimum weight, provide a smooth exterior surface and prevent crack propagation.

Menasco Manufacturing of Canada supplies the undercarriage, which features high-strength steel for the principal elements. Both main and nosewheel units have a 17-in (43-cm) stroke to provide maximum passenger comfort during STOL landings. The mainwheels have twin-disc hydraulic brakes; the nosewheels have a two-stage shock-absorber with damping to combat braking "nod" and landing "rockover".

There are duplicated 3,000 lb/sq in (211 kg/cm²) hydraulic systems, each with a pair of variable-displacement pumps — one on each engine. Otherwise vacant space in the outboard engine nacelles houses hydraulic reservoirs and ground-servicing connections for each system. A 28-volt DC electrical system provides power for engine starting and for navigation instruments. The DC system comprises four 250-amp starter-generators and two nickel-cadmium rechargeable batteries. There is a 400-Hz three-phase 115/200-volt 20-kVA supply for windshield and propeller-blade anti-icing.

Wing, horizontal stabiliser and engine air intakes have inflatable-overshoe de-icing supplied by engine-bleed air which also powers the cabin air-conditioning and pressurisation systems.

For conditions above 60-deg F (15·6-deg C) at sea level there is an optional water-injection system to supply about 8 lb (3,6 kg) a minute of demineralised water to each engine for at least three take-offs. The Dash 7 is the first application of water-injection to the PT6, but this feature is necessary only at very high-altitude airfields.

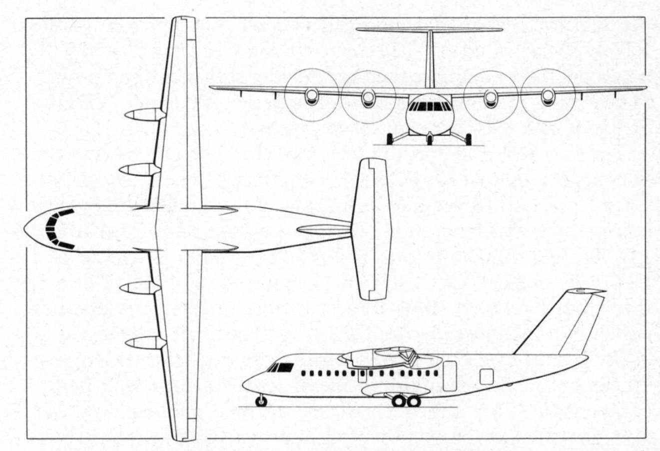

An early three-view of the Dash 7 project showing the fuselage-mounted, tandem leg main undercarriage that was first planned.

Fuel is carried in four integral wing tanks — two of 343 US gal (1 295 l) capacity inboard and two of 444 US gal (1 682 l) outboard — for a total of 1,574 US gal (5 964 l). Fuel can be moved from any tank to any other tank by using the pressure-refuelling manifold as a transfer line. Each tank has two booster pumps — a fuel-driven ejector pump and an electric standby pump. Fuel for starting is provided by the engine-driven pump until self-sustaining speed is reached by the gas generator and the engine then drives its own pump. The engines will run without the booster pumps because the fuel tanks are above the engines. A connection point for pressure fuelling/defuelling at 150 US gal (568 l) a minute is located on the fuselage underside aft of the rear cabin-pressure bulkhead. There are also overwing gravity-fuelling tank fillers.

Turboprops triumphant

In opting to stay with turboprop power, de Havilland of Canada not only retained familiar, proven techniques but accurately predicted that for short-haul operations the far greater low and medium-altitude efficiency of the turboprop would more than compensate for a few minutes added to block time. And the oft-repeated opinion that passengers wanted jets and would not travel in anything with propellers has been completely invalidated. This DHC wisdom has been proven not only by the then-unforeseen fuel shortage, the anticipated alleviation of aircraft-size restrictions for commuter airlines, and deregulation of airlines — but also by the plain fact that when Dash 7 development was complete, the aeroplane's fuel consumption proved to be five per cent better than the most conservative estimates. (It is worth noting in passing that several new, very large aircraft designs are based on using turboprop engines with eight-blade swept-planform propellers being developed by NASA.)

It was not mere patriotism that led to selection of the Pratt & Whitney Aircraft of Canada PT6 engine for the Dash 7 (any more than it was when the 1,700-shp PT7A-2R was chosen more recently for the 32-passenger Dash 8), although the worldwide success of this Canadian power plant in many aircraft *other* than hundreds of Twin Otters was an excellent starting point. Since it first ran in November 1959 and flew in the nose of a Beech 18 in May 1961, the PT6 has moved steadily onward in acceptance and upward in both power and reliability. Civil certification of the 578-shp PT6A-6 was obtained late in 1963 and the family of engines that followed comprises PT6A civil and T74 military turboprops; PT6T civil and T400 military coupled turboshafts for helicopters; ST6 auxiliary power units, and industrial and marine power plants. Initially, as already related, the 38-passenger DHC-7 project was to have 715-shp PT6A-27 engines, but the 50-passenger production design that emerged needed more power — the PT6A-50 flat-rated at 1,120 shp to 81 deg F (27 deg C) and with a new gearbox adequate to take considerably increased power. (The PT6A-55 contemplated for the Series 200 Dash 7 (DHC-7L) is of about 10 per cent more power.)

The first full-scale production model of the engine was the 580-shp PT6A-6 of 1963. The 715-shp PT6A-27, in production since 1967, had 18 per cent more mass flow and featured a new compressor diffuser for increased pressure ratio and lower specific fuel consumption. The PT6T-3, T400 TwinPac and ST6L-73 APU (used in the Lockheed L-1011 TriStar) introduced cooled first-stage turbine-nozzle guide-vanes which are also used in the PT6A-50. These air-cooled vanes allow higher cycle temperatures and greater thermodynamic efficiency, while maintaining metal temperatures well below earlier values, for improved sfc. Additional cooling flow was also provided at the combustion-liner wall and at the turbine disc and blade roots to limit thermal stresses.

A major change for the PT6A-50 was a new reduction gearbox to keep low propeller rpm. Reduction gear ratio is 22·74:1 from a maximum power-turbine speed of 30,017 rpm, giving a propeller rpm of only 1,320. The new gearbox has a 20-kVA alternator drive with an outspeed of 15,866 rpm. As opposed to a gas-generator drive, the power-turbine alternator gives close frequency regulation and engine-acceleration response that are unaffected by alternator load. The larger-diameter gearbox and higher propeller loads require a new exhaust case which has two ports venting over the wing to direct noise away from the ground.

The 11 ft 3-in (3,43-m) diameter propellers created special engine-mounting problems that were solved by designing a lightweight, two-plane bed structure in which low-rate springs at front and rear, combined with a long mounting base, provide good vibration isolation. Combined with low vertical stiffness at front and rear mounting points, high lateral stiffness provides adequate whirl/flutter stability asymmetry. Hard-landing loads are minimised by the long mounting base and by proper positioning of the suspension elastic centre with both bottomed and unbottomed isolation. Steady-thrust loads are carried by the rear, lower mounts which are duplicated and steady torque loads are absorbed by rear, upper and lower mounts.

Propellers are a new design, but are a version of the familiar bracket (counterweight) type that is not only extremely reliable because of its inherent simplicity, but in the event of pitch-change mechanism malfunction sends the blades towards feather rather than brake. Large-chord blades are of glass-fibre reinforced plastics with forged aluminium spars and foam cores. This type of construction reduces the weight

penalty of designing for high thrust while at the same time keeping a low noise level by using low rotational speed. The DHC requirement for a 95 PNdB noise signature at 500 ft (152 m) involved two design parameters — rotational noise factor, which defines noise attributable to other sources such as lift coefficient, and ratio of blade area to disc area.

A study was made to determine the optimum combination of diameter, rpm, number of blades, activity factor and integrated lift coefficient for best take-off and climb performance while maintaining tip speeds at the values set by the noise-signature limits. Propeller diameter is limited by the resultant heavier gearbox to provide a lower propeller speed, and increases in aircraft structural weight to provide necessary airframe clearance to support the higher loads. For a certain

The Dash 7 has been selling steadily since its introduction into service and the sales/options total is confidently expected to pass the 100 mark by the end of this year. The US commuter industry provides an important market for the type, a typical example being Air Wisconsin (above); a number of useful sales have also been achieved in the Middle East, such as to the Emirates Air Service in Abu Dhabi (below left). Military sales to date have been made only to the Canadian Armed Forces, which operates two as CC-132s (below).

diameter, blade activity factor is traded-off against the number of blades to give good take-off thrust and cruise efficiency, and to reduce blade loading.

Four blades were chosen for the Dash 7 propeller because of superior thrust efficiency; also, three blades would have imposed a weight penalty. Many glass-fibre blades of this type have been installed on the P-3 Orion, P-2 Neptune, and on various helicopters over the past 14 years.

Stub runways and STOLports

Several things have coalesced to generate the increasing sales success enjoyed by the Dash 7, but before enumerating these it is important not to forget that in the first place there had to be an aeroplane to sell! And the right type of aircraft was designed not by blind faith or over-optimism, but as a logical extrapolation of de Havilland of Canada's STOL knowhow. However, there is no doubt that the Downsview team *did* have the courage of its own technical convictions despite the far from obvious market and a shameful lack of domestic encouragement.

Allowing commuter airlines to operate larger aircraft in the US — DHC's prime market area — removed a major barrier. But there have been other developments which have accelerated interest in the Dash 7, notably the effect of US airline deregulation, scarcity of fuel, air traffic congestion at major "hub" airports, availability of US area-navigation system installations including miniaturised airborne equipment, and the promised adoption of microwave landing systems. *Each* of these factors has effects on other types of aircraft, but *all* of them combine with steep-gradient approach and departure characteristics of the Dash 7 to make it an extremely attractive proposition not only to the commuter airlines directly, but also to the whole air transport pattern.

The idea of separate STOLports — whether in downtown or rural areas — has been complemented by the concept of STOL aircraft operating between local airstrips and stub runways at major hub airports. Thus, if no airfield exists in an area that needs service — as in some of the new resort towns — then a STOLport is the obvious choice. But *existing* small, local aerodromes are now being used for STOL operations linking them together and to major airports without increasing air traffic congestion at the latter. Indeed, this extremely convenient type of feederline or commuter service may be used to *reduce* traffic congestion while *increasing* access to long-distance flights*.

This has been done in the US, notably by Ransome Airlines, based at Philadelphia, which is an Allegheny Commuter company. Ransome looked into the practicability of using separate STOL arrival routes to hub airports in the US North-east Corridor. This concept originated in the early 1960s, but there were no suitable aircraft (the Breguet 941 Integral, alias McDonnell Douglas 188, was tried out). Now, with the Dash 7 available, the advance of avionics and computers, the fuel shortage, and air traffic saturation at major airports, the "STOL 'n' stub" concept is proving a winner.

Since the Dash 7 has an approach turn radius of less than 2,500 ft (762 m) compared with about 7,500 ft (2 286 m) for aircraft such as the DC-9 or Boeing 737, the de Havilland aeroplane uses far less terminal airspace on the final approach. Also, it is the only aeroplane certificated for a 7·5-deg approach angle and features more precise speed control, better touchdown accuracy, superior deceleration during landing roll, and is much quieter. Required runway length for landing under FAR Part 121 regulations is 1,950 ft (594 m) at maximum landing weight in zero wind. (With maximum wheel braking and full reverse propeller thrust, the Dash 7 can stop within 600 ft/183 m, but the deceleration is greater than would normally be acceptable by passengers except in an emergency.)

Advances in electronic microprocessors have resulted in such systems as the JET Electronics & Technology DAC-7000 3D RNAV which is a considerable improvement over first-generation three-dimensional area-navigation systems. The DAC-7000 used in Ransome Airlines Dash 7s is integrated with the standard Sperry SPZ-700 automatic flight control system to give fully automatic control of aircraft flight path so that the pilots are free to manage aircraft configuration (flaps, trim, undercarriage, ailerons/spoilers, rudder) and speed while monitoring airspace congestion. The RNAV track is displayed on the RCA Primus colour radar so that the pilots may observe their progress along the approach route and determine the presence of severe weather. If air traffic or weather conditions change in any way, any of the approach-path waypoints may be displaced by using a slewing switch on the

continued on page 147

**DHC studies indicate that more than 70 per cent of people boarding a commuter service aeroplane do so in conjunction with a trunk flight.*

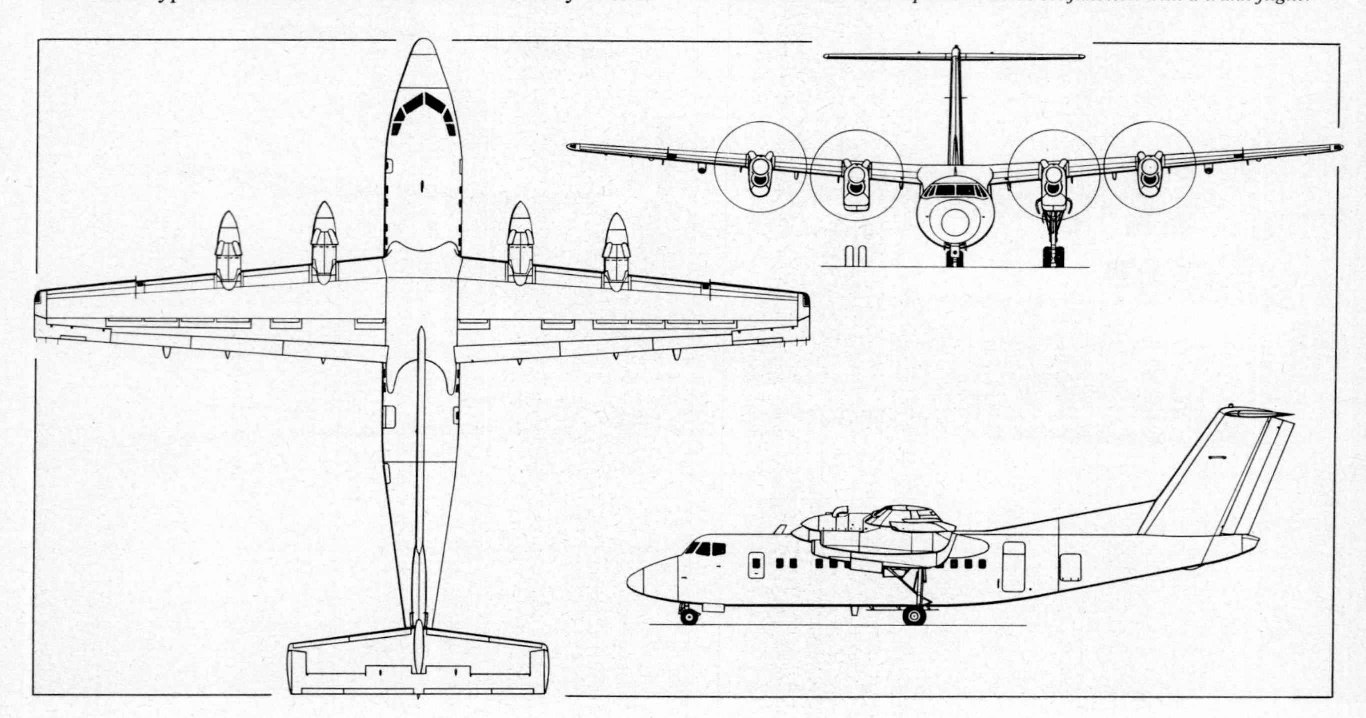

Fully equipped, state-of-the-art flight deck is designed for crew efficiency.

The new

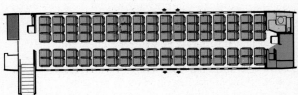

A NEW FIGHTER FOR EUROPE

AT THE BEGINNING OF THE 1970's, two examples of a new generation of fighter thundered into the skies over the International Air Shows. These aircraft were so obviously new in concept that they heralded a new era in fighter design, placing more emphasis on combat agility than maximum speed, and having very much higher thrust-to-weight ratios than had hitherto been thought necessary. In addition, new advances such as fly-by-wire (FBW) coupled with control configured vehicle (CCV) technology allowed unstable configurations with resulting improvements in lift-to-drag ratio. The results of the amalgamation of all these advances were the General Dynamics YF-16 and the Northrop YF-17 prototypes; and, as the F-4 and F-104 had represented the technology of the 1950's, these aircraft reflected twenty years of development and were nothing short of a quantum leap in performance and capability.

The performance improvements that these new aircraft have over their predecessors that would be noticed by a pilot or his adversary are:

- Sustained turn rate up by over 50 per cent.
- Specific Excess Power (SEP) almost doubled.
- Acceleration times halved.
- Incidence limits increased by 50 per cent.
- Structural strength limits increased beyond normal human tolerance.

These aircraft have grown up into the F-16A and the F-18A Hornet, and jointly are set to enjoy even greater success than their predecessors. Both designs have been ordered in large numbers by the USAF, US Navy and Marines, and the F-16 in particular has notched up some very large export orders, notably to the smaller European countries in the "Sale of the Century". The success of this new fighter concept is therefore not in doubt, and the military and commercial success of the resulting designs would seem guaranteed.

Whilst many countries have already decided on their re-equipment plans, the larger countries within Europe have yet to commit themselves to a new fighter. Their requirements call for a later in-service date than the F-18 or F-16, so the opportunity to conceive and produce a new, more advanced fighter has arisen. It has been said that unless a new aircraft offers a 15-20 per cent performance improvement over what is currently available, then it is not worth the expense of pursuing. It is perhaps a difficult task to achieve this advance over the F-18, but a new European fighter would have the advantages of a decade of new technology and of learning from American experience. The military aircraft manufacturers of Britain, Germany and France have a wealth of experience and, if united, could form a team equal to any American company and capable of creating an aircraft better than anything now available.

The requirements

The UK Requirement is outlined in Air Staff Target AST 403 which in its first draught called for a Jaguar/Harrier replacement. This places emphasis on the air-to-ground mission but also requires an ability to provide battlefield air superiority. In the air-to-ground rôle, the requirements are close air support, battlefield interdiction and battlefield surveillance. It was concluded at an early stage, however, that the requirement for a Harrier replacement could not easily be combined with the other aspects of AST 403, and this element would be best met by a development of the existing Harrier. The latter need is therefore now separately defined in AST 409. The aircraft to AST 403 is required in service by 1990/91.

The French Requirement, ACT 92, also calls for a Jaguar replacement and has obvious similarities to AST 403, but with an in-service date of 1992. The German requirement for an aircraft to replace the F-4F was outlined in the German Air Force Command Staff Study 90. This was for an aircraft with a primary air defence mission and a secondary air-to-ground capability. In the air-to-air rôle, the aircraft would have the following missions:

- Air superiority.
- All weather air defence.
- Area defence.
- Long range combat radius.
- Escort for other strike aircraft.
- Interception of cruise missiles and RPV's.

The future for a European fighter lies in successfully combining the requirements in a common design, and at first sight this would seem to be difficult to achieve. Normally, air superiority and ground attack are incompatible. At its most fundamental, air superiority requires high manoeuvrability which normally means a low wing loading and low span loading. A ground attack aircraft needs high wing loading and high span loading to maintain good low-level ride comfort at high attack speeds. It is remarkable therefore that the details of designs so far released indicate so much similarity, and to understand why this is possible it is necessary to look at some of the design proposals.

The designs

Messerschmitt-Bölkow-Blohm's TKF-90 has been the most publicised design, with a full scale mock-up being displayed earlier this year at the Hanover Air Show. It is a single-seat aircraft and has a delta canard layout with a very large wing area which results in low wing loading. The leading edge of the wing is cranked near the tip to provide sufficient wing tip chord for the installation of a tip-mounted missile, and it has a large negative camber at the root which reduces the drag at high incidence with a small drag penalty at low incidence. The canard foreplane is unusually situated ahead of the cockpit and is almost in the plane of the wing; to reduce the intrusion into the pilot's field of view, it has some anhedral, and this would probably allow some degree of direct force mode operation, as would the twin fins. The cockpit is placed high on the fuselage to give the pilot the best all-round view. The two engines are fed by a large two-dimensional chin intake. This is a supersonic wedge intake with a variable lower lip which could be adjusted to different flight conditions. MBB believes that the chin intake is the best arrangement for good intake pressure recovery at high angles of incidence and sideslip.

Although not revealed by the mock-up, there is interest at MBB in post-stall technology. Thrust-to-weight ratios well in excess of unity are commonplace in new fighter designs, so an aircraft could, in effect, sit on its tail with zero airspeed. When decelerating in wing-borne flight an aircraft's incidence increases; any low aspect ratio wing, and a delta in particular, does not produce a conventional abrupt stall, but continues to develop vortex lift up to high incidence. If engine thrust is increased to unload the wing, flight can be envisaged in a transition phase where the aircraft's weight is borne by both engine and wing, with control being provided by articulating nozzles. MBB envisages flight being possible at up to 70 deg incidence with such a system and its TKF-90 layout would lend itself admirably to such use. This aircraft is in the 14-*tonne* class and would probably employ RB.199 engines. The radar would be optimised for the air defence rôle and is probably more akin to the Tornado ADV radar than the lighter varieties.

The Dornier TKF-90 is a far more conventional layout and reflects that company's association with Northrop. It is very similar in layout to the F-18 except that its flying surfaces are more highly swept. It was deliberate policy to stay with a low risk conventional layout within the current state-of-the-art. It was felt that a quantum jump in technology was not required to produce an effective aircraft and that effort would be better spent increasing cost efficiency via weight and size control, resulting in larger fleet sizes. To this end the design is smaller and lighter than MBB's, being more in the 10-*tonne* class (similar to the F-16). One drawback to this type of concept is that all the available engines are too large and the possibility of developing a new engine would have to be considered. MTU has proposed a derivative engine based on RB.199 technology which is the correct size, but which would be an expensive development.

Manoeuvrability is fundamental to the German designs and gives an idea of the Study 90 requirement. Dornier is aiming for a sustained turn rate double that of the F-4F and significantly better than that of the F-16. It would also be better than the lightweight development of the F-18A, the F-18L. A sea level maximum speed of M = 1·2 could be provided, with a top speed of M = 2·0 at altitude, and the take-off and landing ground rolls would be less than 1,500 ft (450 m). A typical air-to-ground weapon load would be 6,600 lb (3 000 kg), consisting of precision-guided munitions, and internal armament would be the 27-mm Mauser gun developed for the Tornado. As regards mission performance, Dornier believes that an intercept with up to an hour of loiter time can be achieved, all on internal fuel.

Avions Marcel Dassault-Breguet Aviation has produced a series of first class fighters since the 1950's and has been the main protagonist of the delta wing planform. It may have come as something of a surprise so soon after the appearance of the Mirage 2000 and the private-venture Super Mirage 4000 to see models of a new fighter design on the French concern's stand at Hanover, but it was *no* surprise to see that a delta had again been adopted, albeit one with a cranked leading edge and a canard foreplane. Two variations of the same basic configuration are proposed, one with a low wing and a single fin, obviously reminiscent of the Mirage 4000, and another with a shoulder wing and twin fins on booms extending from it. Each aircraft has a single seat and twin engines with side intakes mounted beneath the all-moving foreplanes to give some degree of flow straightening at high incidence. The intakes are different from the semi-circular centrebody intakes used on Dassault-Breguet's most recent designs, and show a trend away from intakes optimised for high supersonic speeds.

The modified delta wing will allow carriage of wing tip missiles and also minimises tip stall, allowing operation at high angles of attack with greater manoeuvrability. A leading-edge slot system is proposed and wing loading is expected to be about 70 lb/sq ft (340 kg/m²). Although resembling the Super Mirage 4000, the new projects are closer in size to the Mirage 2000. The two different designs show a fair amount of

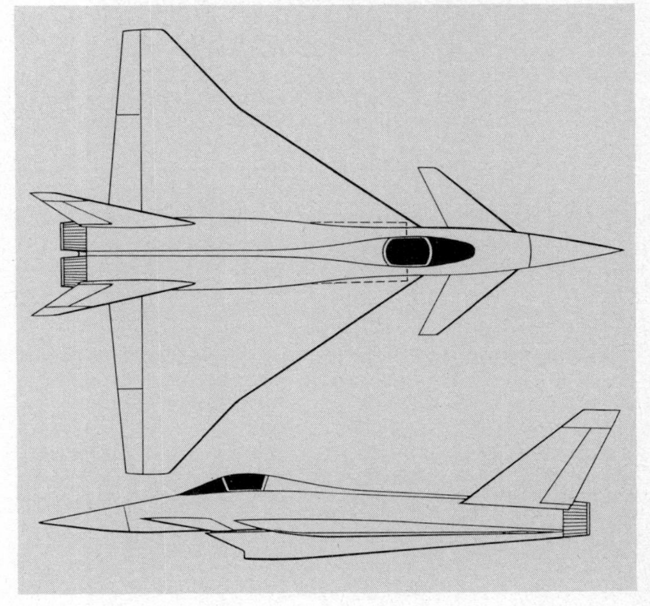

(Above) A full-scale mock-up of the MBB design for the German TKF-90 requirement as displayed earlier in 1980 at Hanover and (below) a provisional drawing showing its configuration.

(Right) Configuration drawings of two design studies by Dassault-Breguet for the French ACT 92 requirement for a highly manoeuvrable fighter to enter service during the 'nineties. The impressions below depict the same two project designs, both of which take advantage of the work Dassault-Breguet has undertaken to bring the Mirage 2000 and Super Mirage 4000 to fruition.

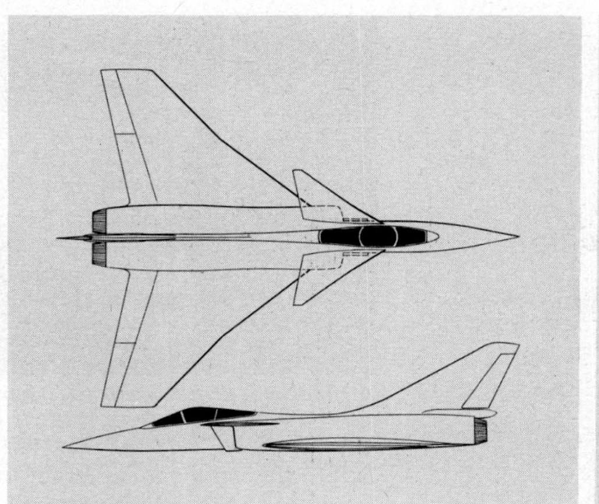

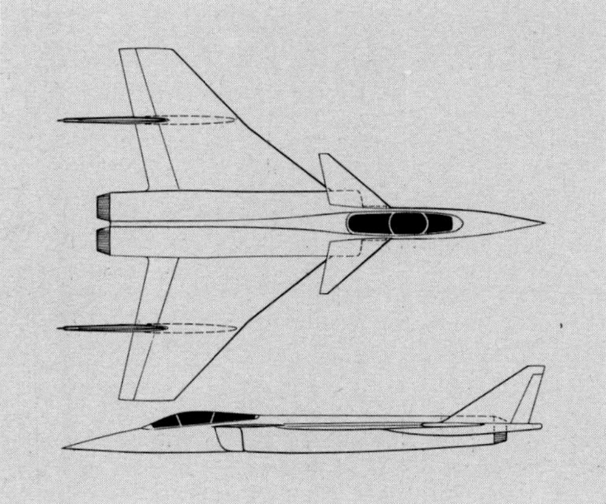

flexibility in layout. The twin boom-mounted fins would give greater directional stability at high incidence and would remove any chance of flow separation and high drag that often accompanies a single fin mounted between two engines. In addition, the booms would provide good locations for ECM equipment. They could, however, also provide serious aeroelastic problems and could therefore be heavy. The choice between high and low wing is usually decided by dictates such as retracted undercarriage location, under-fuselage stores carriage, structural path continuity and underwing stores clearance.

British Aerospace has kept a low profile regarding its submissions to AST 403, but has released a photograph of a model of a typical aircraft to meet this requirement. This design would appear to have a great deal in common with the French designs, with its cranked delta canard planform. The twin engines are more widely spaced to give better survivability in the event of one engine being damaged in combat (debris is less likely to cause damage to the second engine). This also allows a cleaner fin/fuselage junction which in turn is less likely to cause flow separation problems. The intakes are set beneath the wings under the highly swept strake, this allowing flow straightening at high incidence, and the large canard surface is below and behind the cockpit so as not to intrude on the pilot's field of view. It is probably fair to say that this configuration, like those of AMD-BA, represents nothing more definitive than a typical layout, but it does illustrate the tremendous degree of common thinking that exists between the design teams of all three nations.

The powerplants

The obvious choice of powerplant for both Britain and Germany must be the RB.199. It was designed and developed for the tri-national Tornado and is in production. It is small, light and powerful, but has a cycle that was optimised for the Tornado, resulting in a relatively high by-pass ratio and relatively low dry thrust. It is, however, very economical at its dry rating. As such it is probably not ideal for a fighter, but Rolls-Royce claims that because the engine is modular it can be easily adapted to better suit it to other rôles. Two stages of development are envisaged: RB.199 Mk 101 Improved with "fighter reheat" and the RB.199-62R which has a modified compressor as well as reheat improvements, and this engine would appear to be well suited to most European requirements.

France is currently developing the SNECMA M88 augmented turbofan, which is in the 7·5-8·5 *tonne* thrust class (16,500-18,700 lb) and is similar to the developed RB.199 in terms of performance, size and weight, but boasts a simpler two-spool design and a cycle more optimised for a fighter. The claim that the M88 is based on 1980's technology is really making a virtue of adversity in that SNECMA have been very late in entering the military jet engine market; the recent M53 engine can be likened to a Spey, whereas the Atar — which is still being produced — is more like an Avon. Comparing the M88 to the Atar 9K-50 shows the great improvement in technology; it is 57 per cent of the weight and could have 18 per cent greater thrust. In spite of all this, it is a brand new engine and must be at least seven years and millions of francs away from service.

The third engine that could be considered for the European fighter is the General Electric F404 of 7·3 *tonnes* thrust (16,000 lb). This engine, like the RB.199, is in production and powers the F/A-18. It is similar in concept to the M88 in having a two-spool layout and a "fighter" cycle. It has a greater dry thrust than the RB.199, but is not as good in other areas and is less economical at cruise settings due to its lower bypass ratio.

The necessary compromises

Having briefly described the designs and engines, it is interesting to try to identify common ground and to make a guess at a typical compromise aircraft that could meet most of the European requirements — the European Combat Aircraft (ECA).

Almost by popular consent, the layout would be a delta canard with a cranked leading edge, and the reasoning for this is simple and well known to all three countries. The best turning performance is given by the lowest span loading, therefore span should be large. For a given span, the supersonic drag of a wing is largely fixed, a wing of small area with low sweep and relatively high thickness-to-chord ratio will have similar drag to a wing of the same span with greater area but larger sweep and reduced thickness. The arguments for large area are that the resulting low wing loading gives good field performance and also greater manoeuvrability at low airspeeds (an area that is felt to be increasingly important). To achieve good high incidence behaviour a leading edge sweep of at least 55 deg is required.

This all points to the obvious choice of planform — the delta. Deltas cannot normally carry tip missiles, so to achieve

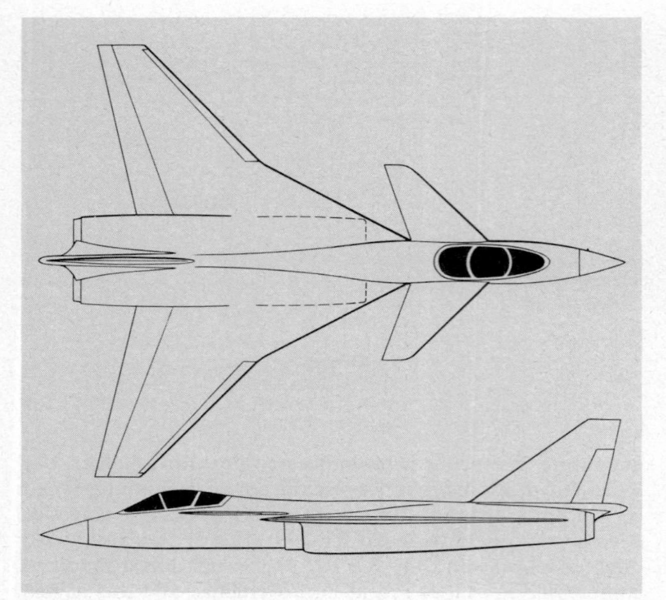

this desirable capability, the tip chord must be extended, and this gives rise to the leading edge crank and also reduces tip stalling. The aircraft would be unstable subsonically with a fly-by-wire system and active controls because of the improvements in lift-to-drag ratio that result. To control the aircraft adequately a tailplane is needed, and a canard would be chosen because with a delta there is little room for anything else. It lifts in the correct direction and it can cause favourable interference with the wing at high incidence, thus improving lift. The foreplane in conjunction with a FBW system also could have the advantage of giving gust alleviation; it can sense a gust

At Warton, British Aerospace has been conducting studies of an advanced fighter to comply with the RAF's AST 403 requirement. One recent version of the design is shown left and above.

before the wing encounters it and can cause the appropriate action to be taken to smooth the ride. This would offset one of the traditional disadvantages of aircraft with low wing loadings and make it possible to offer the same layout for both fighter and attack aircraft.

If post-stall manoeuvring is required, the intake must work well at high incidence and at reasonable yaw angles, and the best arrangement for this is undoubtedly the chin intake. Its main disadvantage is one of credibility, in that it can be visualised as a powerful vacuum cleaner and also raises the cockpit and equipment bays to an alarming height above the ground. In addition it can restrict underfuselage stores carriage and is directionally destabilising. Traditional side intakes do not behave so well at high incidence or high yaw angles, but shielding them in the fashion of the AMD-BA designs can rectify the former. Shielding under the wing in the style of the BAe design would have the same effect, but would probably need large boundary layer diverter slots and these

continued on page 143

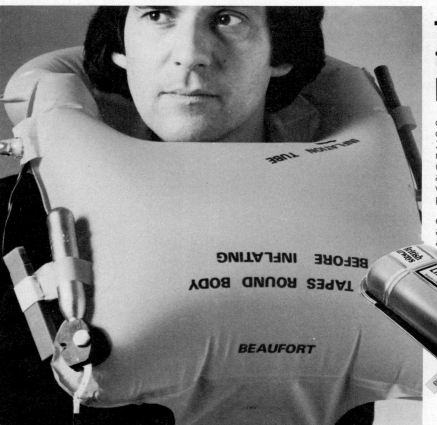

COMING QUIETLY ...
THE BAE 146

SEVEN YEARS — almost to the day when this issue of AIR INTERNATIONAL is published — have elapsed since the decision was made to launch the development and production in Britain of a small new airliner for the feederline market. With first flight still several months away, the time taken to bring this project to fruition might well seem excessive, and the intervening years have indeed seen the fortunes of the aircraft fluctuate. Launched with the blessing — and financial backing — of the British government as the Hawker Siddeley HS.146 on 29 August 1973, the programme was stopped in October 1974, only to be re-launched on 10 July 1978 by British Aerospace as the first new programme undertaken by the nationalised corporation.

The temporary suspension of work on the 146 was occasioned not by any technical difficulties or engineering problems but by doubts about its commercial viability at a time when the airline market was particularly depressed. In the interregnum, work proceeded in a low key to keep the design alive and up-to-date; and market surveys and regular discussions with potential customers left the manufacturers in little doubt that the 146 was as apposite in 1978 as it was in 1973. Since the decision to re-launch, the programme has been accelerating steadily, although not without encountering some difficulties along the way. There has been some slippage in the planned timescale for the flight test programme and the delivery dates for the first dozen or so aircraft off the line, caused by some delays in supplies and aggravated by the national engineering dispute during 1979. Perhaps the biggest hurdle that has confronted the 146 since 1978, however, is one of credibility, more especially since it was not until June of this year that British Aerospace was able to announce the first firm contract for the type.

In fact, the 146 is not setting a precedent in this respect. It is comforting for a manufacturer to be able to launch a new type on the back of nice solid orders from one or two major airline customers — and in the case of the larger types of airliner, there can indeed be no question of launching into production without such orders being placed. By its nature, however, the 146 is more likely to be sold in ones and twos than in twenties and thirties, and to operators that would not wish, or are not able, to make equipment purchase decisions more than a year or two in advance of delivery. Several other types in a similar category to the 146 have been launched with few, if any, orders but are now successfully established in production.

The 5 June announcement that Lineas Aereas Privadas Argentinas SA (LAPA) of Buenos Aires had signed an $85m (£36·2m) contract for three 146 feederliners with three more on option was valuable to British Aerospace, in giving the whole programme greater respectability in the eyes of the public. More encouraging to those working behind the scenes, however, is the knowledge that 20 or so 146s are currently the subject of serious negotiations and letters of intent; that potential airline customers for the type continue to show favourable interest even if they are not yet ready to negotiate; that continuously updated market surveys show little variation in the forecast that some 1,200 new aircraft of 146 type will be needed by the airlines over the next 12-15 years and that British Aerospace should be able to capture one-third of that market with the 146. Encouraging also is the physical presence of the 146 at the Hatfield, Herts, factory of British Aerospace, which is the design, final assembly and flight test centre for the aircraft. Major components for this assembly line are beginning to flow from other British Aerospace factories — notably Manchester, Bristol and Brough — and from the two major overseas suppliers, Avco and Saab-Scania.

Future milestones

By the time the 146 receives CAA certification, in its basic Srs 100 form, at the beginning of August 1982, a dozen aeroplanes will have flown and production will be nudging three a month. In 1979 values, the programme will by then have called for an investment of the order of £250m, including the laying down of production tools and fixtures and the value of work in hand, as well as the design, R&D and flight test costs. Part of the risk is being shared by the two major overseas suppliers — Avco Aerostructures, which is responsible for the entire wing box, and Saab-Scania, responsible for the tailplane, rudder, ailerons and spoilers.

Within British Aerospace itself, the Chadderton factory of the Manchester Division is responsible for the rear fuselage, the Filton factory of the Weybridge/Bristol Division makes the centre fuselage, Brough Division makes the fin and flaps, Scottish Division at Prestwick is responsible for the engine pylons and the Hatfield/Chester Division, as well as having

A FAMILY

F-5G Newest member of F-5 family of tactical fighters and trainers. Designed to meet emerging worldwide needs for defense through the turn of the century.

A single General Electric F-404 engine replaces twin J-85 engines of earlier F-5s. Result: 60 percent increase in available thrust. Mach 2 class.

F-5E Air-to-air combat superiority over anticipated threats. Air-to-ground capability fulfilling user needs. Easy maintenance. Rapid turnaround. All at affordable cost.

Production activity on the BAe 146 at Hatfield is shown in these photographs of (above) the first centre fuselage section to arrive (early June) from Filton, Bristol, and (below left) four Hatfield-produced nose assemblies, including a test specimen (second from left) and the sections for the first three Srs 100 flight test aircraft.

overall responsibility for the project, manufactures the front fuselage (including the flight deck) at Hatfield. Shorts in Belfast supply the engine pods, as a non-risk-sharing subcontractor, and the engines themselves come, of course, from Avco's Lycoming Division. Other major equipment suppliers are Dowty-Rotol for the undercarriage and flap operating system; Dunlop for the wheels and brakes; Smiths, for the SEP 10 flight control system and for fuel gauging; Plessey for the electrical equipment and Flight Refuelling for fuel valves and switches.

Three 146-100s are assigned to the flight test programme, which is now expected to start at Hatfield early in May 1981. The first flight will be made by the Division's chief test pilot Mike Goodfellow accompanied by deputy project pilot Peter Sedgwick; they will be assisted, as the programme builds up, by a team of five or six test pilots, the majority of whom are being newly appointed to the Hatfield staff to cope with the major expansion that the 146 programme represents. With varying degrees of instrumentation, the three pre-production aeroplanes are expected to total about 1,000 hrs on development and certification flying; in addition, some 200 hrs of route proving will be flown prior to first delivery. Of the first three aircraft, one is likely to be retained by the company for continuing development flying and one will become the demonstrator, while the third will eventually be refurbished for sale.

As the test programme nears completion, the need for crew training of customers' pilots will expand; since it is likely that many sales of the 146 will be in small quantities there will be a large number of operators relative to total aircraft production

British Aerospace 146-100 Cutaway Drawing Key

1 Elevator mass balance
2 Twin tabs
3 Elevators, manually operated
4 Fixed tailplane
5 Elevator control linkage
6 Tab linkage
7 Tailplane box
8 Anti-icing ducts to tailplane
9 Detachable fin leading-edge section
10 Two-spar fin structure
11 Fin stringers/rib construction
12 Rudder hydraulic jacks
13 Rudder construction
14 Rear navigation lights
15 Petal-type airbrakes
16 Airbrakes (extended — max 60-deg deflection)
17 Airbrake hydraulic jack
18 Cross-connecting strut (pantograph linkage)
19 Fin/fuselage attachment points
20 APU
21 APU exhaust
22 Air-conditioning packs
23 Rear service door (rearwards hingeing)
24 Twin seats
25 Rear pressure dome
26 Ram air intake
27 Engine air bleed ducts
28 Rear passenger door (rearwards hingeing)
29 Rear toilet
30 Door hinge/mechanism
31 Doorway (airstairs optional)
32 Airstairs stowage (optional)
33 Cabin floor
34 Bulkhead
35 Wingroot fairing
36 Landing gear rear bulkhead frame
37 Fuselage construction
38 Wing skinning, jointed on aircraft centreline
39 Lift spoilers — three identical surfaces each wing
40 Roll spoiler — one each wing
41 Aileron trim and servo tabs
42 Port aileron (honeycomb construction)
43 Port navigation light
44 Vent inlet
45 Fuel lines
46 Port landing light
47 Engine pylons
48 Port engine nacelles
49 Wingroot fairing
50 Wing/fuselage attachment
51 Hat-racks and passenger baggage
52 Hydraulics equipment bay
53 Six-abreast passenger accommodation
54 Cabin floor —sandwich panel with non-metallic core
55 Bulkhead, rear of cargo hold
56 Main forward cargo hold
57 Floor structure
58 Fuselage construction — closed section type stringers bonded to skin
59 Cabin entry door
60 Forward cabin bulkhead
61 Forward passenger door (plug type, outward opening)

and up to 100 hrs may have to be earmarked for pre-delivery crew training for each operator. Additional Training Captains will be added to the Hatfield team for this purpose and the provision of a 146 simulator for use in the Training Centre is planned by British Aerospace.

Before certification of the 146-100 is completed, the first Srs 200 will enter the programme, this being the eighth aeroplane off the line and expected to fly in March 1982. The Srs 200 differs only in fuselage length (stretched to provide three more seat rows) and in operating weights, so flight development and certification will require relatively few hours and should be completed in November 1982. Srs 200s start appearing at regular intervals on the line by the middle of 1982; the first customer aeroplanes of this type will be Nos 13 and 16, and thereafter it is expected that every third aeroplane will be a Srs 200. Naturally, the precise division of production between the two types will eventually be established by the requirements of customers. LAPA, as it happens, is more interested in the larger variant and although its first two aircraft, for delivery in September/October 1982, are Srs 100s, the third, for March 1983 delivery, and the three options, are Srs 200.

One static test airframe (complete except for the front fuselage and the non-load-carrying moving surfaces) is at present under assembly at Hatfield and, with 1,200 strain gauge channels, will enter full-scale testing next August. Two tests will be made to 85 per cent of ultimate load and three tests to 100 per cent of ultimate load. Fatigue testing will be conducted on three separate specimens: a fuselage nose, a centre fuselage and wing and a rear fuselage with tail unit. Representing one complete airframe, these specimens will be tested through 80,000 flight cycles, followed by 60,000 cycles for crack propagation and to investigate residual strength.

Market reflections

The history of the BAe 146 to date, with the stop on development that was imposed scarcely more than a year after it had first been launched, has inevitably thrown a spotlight

British Aerospace 146-100 Specification

Power Plant: Four Avco Lycoming ALF 502R-3 turbofans each rated at 6,700 lb st (3 040 kgp) for take-off. Fuel capacity, 2,540 Imp gal (11 540 l) in centre section and integral wing tanks; optional provision for 300 Imp gal (1 360 l) in wing fillet tanks.
Performance: Design VMO/MMO, 315 kts (583 km/h) CAS, M = 0·70; typical high cruise speed, 425 kts (787 km/h); range with max payload, 650 naut mls (1 204 km); range with 71 passengers and baggage, 980 naut mls (1 816 km) with standard fuel, 1,385 naut mls (2 567 km) at increased gross weight and 1,495 naut mls (2 770 km) with optional increased tankage; balanced take-off field length, 3,500 ft (1 067 m), ISA at sea level.
Weights: Typical operating weight empty, 44,570 lb (20 217 kg); max take-off weight, 73,850 lb (33 500 kg); optional (-100R) increased gross weight version, 80,000 lb (36 288 kg); max landing weight, 71,850 lb (32 590 kg); max zero fuel weight, 61,850 lb (28 055 kg).
Dimensions: Span, 85 ft 5 in (26,42 m); length, 85 ft 10 in (26,16 m); height, 28 ft 3 in (8,61 m); gross wing area, 832 sq ft (77,3 m²); aspect ratio, 8·98:1; sweepback, 15 deg at quarter chord; undercarriage track, 15 ft 6 in (4,72 m); wheelbase, 33 ft 1½ in (10,1 m).
Accommodation: Flight crew of two; max seating, one-class, 88 passengers six abreast at 31-in (79-cm) pitch or 82 at 33-in (84-cm) pitch; alternative five-abreast layouts for 76 passengers at 31-in (79-cm) pitch or 71 at 33-in (84-cm) pitch. Underfloor baggage/cargo compartments with volumes of 258 cu ft (7,30 m³) front and 242 cu ft (6,85 m³) rear.

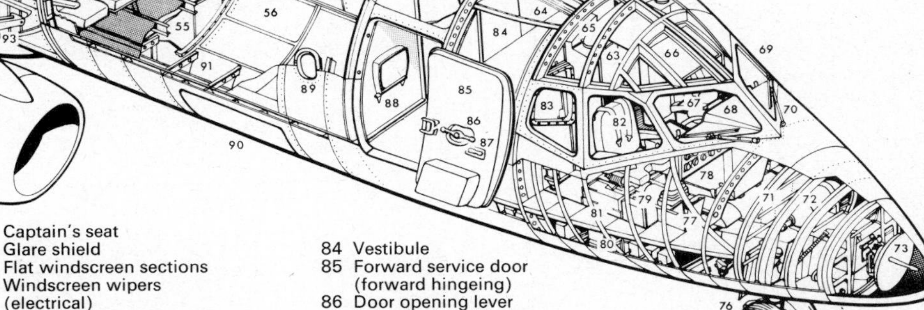

62 Overhead control runs
63 Flight-deck door
64 Forward toilet
65 Air-conditioning outlets
66 Overhead panel
67 Captain's seat
68 Glare shield
69 Flat windscreen sections
70 Windscreen wipers (electrical)
71 Front pressure bulkhead
72 Oxygen bottle (1 812 l)
73 Weather radar
74 Radome
75 Twin nosewheels — hydraulically steered
76 Nosewheel leg flap
77 Rudder pedals
78 Centre instrument console
79 Stringerless front fuselage construction
80 Underfloor electrics bay
81 Side console
82 First Officer's seat
83 Direct-vision panel
84 Vestibule
85 Forward service door (forward hingeing)
86 Door opening lever
87 Locking mechanism lever
88 Attendant's folding seat and cabin galley area
89 Cabin windows
90 Cargo door, plug type
91 Floor support structure
92 Main landing gear retraction jack
93 Side strut
94 Twin mainwheels
95 Main landing gear
96 Shock absorber strut
97 Front landing gear pivot bearing
98 Front wing spar — single-piece machined
99 Flap interconnecting drive shaft
100 Rear cargo door (plug type)
101 Flap tracks
102 Landing gear door
103 Starboard landing light
104 Leading-edge construction
105 Pylon structure box
106 Intake
107 Avco Lycoming ALF 502 R-3 turbofan
108 Gas generator cowling
109 Wing anti-icing duct
110 Tabbed Fowler flaps, one piece each wing
111 Flap track fairings
112 Flap carriage
113 Wing stiffeners
114 Undersurface inspection panels
115 Starboard roll spoiler
116 Fuel lines
117 Wing rib stations
118 Starboard aileron
119 Aileron trim and servo tabs
120 Vent inlet
121 Vent surge box
122 Aileron
123 Starboard navigation light

upon Hatfield's market research. If the aircraft was worth building in 1973, why was it dropped in 1974? If the market requirement changed so suddenly then, could it do so again? Indeed, is it possible to define accurately the requirements of the market sector at which the 146 is aimed? These, undoubtedly, are questions that the board of British Aerospace will have asked both before and since the decision was made to re-launch the 146 in 1978.

In fact, the company's overall forecasts of demand for new aircraft over a 15-year future period have shown very little variation since the HS.146 was first studied: air passenger traffic is growing and is forecast to continue to grow at a rate — slower, it is true, in terms of percentage increase per year, than during the 'sixties — that by 1995 will more than double the revenue passenger-miles flown in 1980. All major traffic forecasts — not just those of British Aerospace — broadly agree on this point. Further analysis of airline routes throughout the world and the kind of equipment required to operate them makes it possible to extrapolate, from this growth figure, the likely need for new aircraft of various sizes. In the short/medium-range sector of the market, a requirement for 1,650 aircraft of 70/140-seat capacity is defined, by 1995. This is the portion of the market for which the 146 is intended, and the British Aerospace objective is to secure one quarter of the total sales — sufficient to make the programme well worthwhile.

Actually to win *any* share of the potential market requires the product not only to be right in size but also in performance, time, cost and some less easily measured parameters. So far as size is concerned, the 146 seats 70 to 88 passengers in its Srs 100 form and up to 110 in the Srs 200*. In performance, it is optimised to operate over stage lengths of about 150 miles (240 km) (with unrefuelled multi-stop capability) and up to a maximum of 1,200 mls (1 930 km). It will fly from field lengths of 3,500-4,000 ft (1 070-1 200 m), ISA at sea level, with comparable standards in hot/high conditions, and because it has four engines it has excellent climb-out and obstacle-clearance capabilities.

So far as first cost is concerned, the target was to put the 146 on the market at a figure \$1·5m below that of the Boeing 737-200 at a comparable delivery date; present indications are that the margin will be closer to \$2m. In operating economics the 146 can offer seat-mile costs 25 per cent below those of the current turboprop twins and air-mile costs 20 per cent below those of current twin-jets. Development of a mixed traffic version with a cargo loading door in the forward fuselage, will also enhance operational flexibility. Structural and system design philosophies — to be reviewed in detail in a later issue of AIR INTERNATIONAL — contribute to the low first cost, simplicity of maintenance and operation and high reliability.

There is no doubt, then, that the 146 looks highly attractive on paper. It is being offered primarily in the category of a replacement for the twin-turboprop types with 50 or more seats and with external noise levels low enough to make it acceptable even in environments where the relatively quiet turboprops can be intrusive. Less tangible influences are at work on the future market, however. Second-hand sales of the early-generation twin-jets could compete with the 146, although these may not now materialise as rapidly as once seemed likely because the introduction of tougher noise restrictions is being stretched out. Rapidly rising fuel costs will make these same twin-jets look less attractive than the 146 to many operators, but this same argument can be used to suggest that the twin-turboprops will find a new lease of life.

The airlines are historically known to be among the first to suffer a downturn in business in times of recession, such as is now setting in throughout the world, and although this may make relatively little difference to long term traffic forecasts it certainly could lead many operators to delay making new equipment purchases. The interaction between these and other factors adds up to a large grey area in the market projections for any new aircraft, the 146 among them. In the circumstances, it may be many years before the commercial success of the programme can be seen to be assured; meanwhile, at a technical level, confidence grows daily as the first aircraft take shape at Hatfield and the sights are set firmly on the first flight milestone next May. □

**Compared with originally-published specifications, the Srs 200 is now 7 in (18 cm) longer, a change that, taken in conjunction with some internal rearrangements, makes it possible to accommodate one more seat row than at first proposed.*

A three-view of the BAe 146 Srs 100 and (bottom right) side view of the Srs 200.

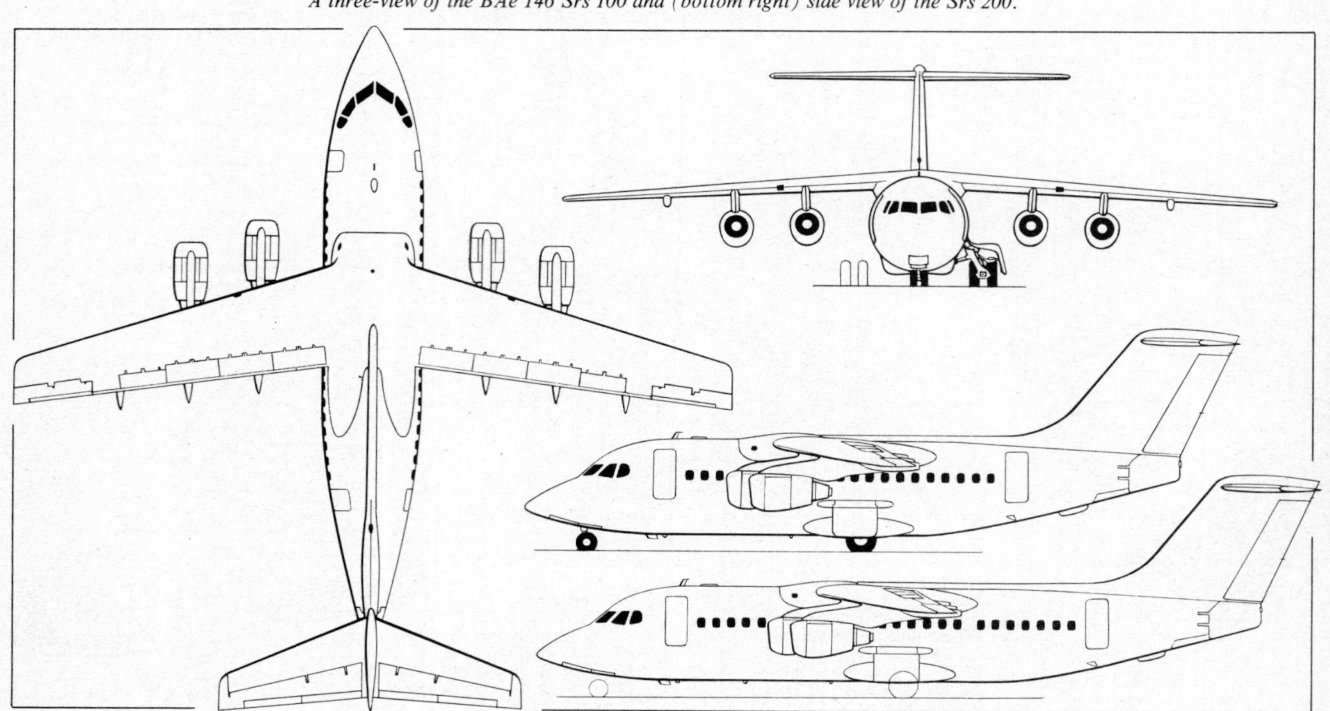

FANTAN: A SINO-SOVIET MÉLANGE

MORE THAN TWENTY-TWO YEARS AGO, in January 1958, when the Soviet Union was still the mentor of China's newly-emerging aircraft industry and ideological differences between the Communist superpowers were only just surfacing, a licence manufacturing agreement was signed for the production of the supersonic MiG-19 in China. Despite the subsequent departure of the Soviet specialists and the inexperience and incomplete training of their Chinese deputies, the MiG-19 programme was persisted with and series production was launched, first at the Shenyang facility and eventually at Tientsin also. Lack of expertise notwithstanding, the Chinese aircraft industry had delivered more than a hundred MiG-19S, or *Chien Chi* 6 (F-6), fighters into the hands of the Air Force of the People's Liberation Army by mid-1964.

Over the years, as experience was gained, both the airframe and its Tumansky RD-9B turbojets were progressively improved, the latter — manufactured by the Shenyang engine plant as the WP-6 — being provided with air-cooled turbine blades of original design and having their TBO doubled to 200 hours. Their installation in the basic day fighter produced the

PROLOGUE

ONCE UPON A TIME, or, more precisely, early in the last decade, reports began to filter out of China, via Hong Kong, of a derivative of the Shenyang- and Tientsin-built copy of the early 'fifties vintage MiG-19S fighter. This, so it was alleged, had fuselage-mounted lateral air intakes and conical nose in place of the circular pitot nose intake characteristic of all known versions of Mikoyan's first production supersonic warplane that rendered it unique among *twin*-engined fighters of its era. With confirmation by western intelligence agencies of the existence of and initiation of production of such an aeroplane, the Air Standards Co-ordinating Committee accordingly assigned to it the reporting name *Fantan*.

Although lacking concrete evidence of *Fantan*, an enterprising Japanese aviation magazine commissioned an artist to produce a conception of the aircraft based solely on the vague description acquired from Hong Kong. There were a number of known precedents of pitot nose intakes being supplanted experimentally by fuselage-mounted lateral intakes, and all of these — the MD 450-30L version of the Dassault MD 450 Ouragan, the MD 453 variant of the MD 452 Mystère II and the YF-93 derivative of the F-86A — had been evolved as a means of providing aerodynamically acceptable accommodation for larger and more efficacious intercept radar.

There were, of course, other precedents of similar experimental nasal surgery for different reasons — such as the MiG-17SN derivative of the MiG-17F which required such for vertically-traversing cannon — but these were unknown in the west at the time, and the Japanese artist, or those briefing him, assumed naturally enough that the reason for this quite fundamental modification to the basic MiG-19S was to permit installation of a worthwhile radar. As, contemporaneously, reference was being made to the designation "F-9" as that of a new Chinese-developed fighter, it took only a small stretch of the imagination to link this with *Fantan*.

Some time elapsed and then a West German aviation monthly reproduced the Japanese drawing, presumably in good faith, as depicting the "Shenyang F-9" — Shenyang being known, by that time, to house a factory that was building the MiG-19S and it apparently being reasoned that this was also likely to be the source of *Fantan*. The highly speculative nature of the drawing went unremarked, and despite the time that had elapsed since it had first seen birth on a Japanese drawing board, it now resurfaced and gained further mileage in the pages of an internationally-known Swiss aviation monthly and its bi-monthly defence companion, but now accompanied by a highly imaginative in-depth technical description of the "Shenyang F-9" under a spurious Russian byline.

Three more years elapsed, and then, early last year, the Chinese finally lifted part of the veil of secrecy that had enveloped *Fantan*, releasing both still photos and a full-colour ciné film sequence of the aircraft, which, at the time, Chinese sources referred to as *Sinshi-6-itsi* (Type 6bis) *Chien* (Fighter), alias F-6bis. It was now patently apparent, at least, from photographic evidence available, that *Fantan* did *not* have a radar nose, as assumed by the Japanese artist so many years earlier, but was an interdiction aircraft; that he had erroneously maintained the relationship between cockpit and wing root of the MiG-19S in his conception and that his air intake ducting bore little relationship to fact. We assume Swiss faces to have blushed with embarrassment at these revelations.

However, the depths of fantasy and confusion to which this Sino-Soviet mélange was to be subjected had still to be plumbed to the full, for a usually authoritative British aviation publication, generally accused of over-conservative reporting and evidently working with an insufficiency of photographic evidence, thereupon published the startling and — as time was to prove — wildly inaccurate assertion that *Fantan* was "no revamped MiG-19, but a new design similar in size and weight to the Jaguar"!

By now, it was obvious to all that the nasal surgery that had resulted in *Fantan* had been prompted by a Chinese requirement for a ground attack aircraft and there was evidence that the Chinese, themselves, were referring to *Fantan* simply as the *Kiang Chi* (Attack Plane). Still more recently, the Beijing aeronautical publication *Hangkong Zhishi* has referred to it as the *Kiang** (Attack) 5, or A-5. Thus, after almost a decade of confusion, we finally know what *Fantan* really looks like and, unless the Chinese change their minds once more, what its designation is. For the rest, in view of Chinese reluctance to provide detail, most must remain surmise for the time being.

**A rather odd transliteration from a Hong Kong-based defence publication emerging as Qiang.*

F-6-*bin*, while limited all-weather capability was introduced with the F-6-*jia* and F-6-*yi*, which approximated to the MiG-19PF and -19PM respectively. Furthermore, the Chinese developed an original tandem two-seat conversion training variant evolved entirely independently of the Soviet MiG-19UTI. Thus, a family of Chinese-developed variants of the basic MiG-19S emerged during the late 'sixties and early 'seventies, and when, it may be assumed, the AFPLA formulated a requirement for a ground attack aircraft with a much better performance than the MiG-17, which — like the contemporary Hunter — offered an extremely poor warload-radius performance by the standards of the day, it was to be expected that the faithful MiG-19 would be viewed favourably as a basis on which to develop the comparatively unsophisticated interdictor now demanded.

The AFPLA requirement obviously called for relatively high speed penetration with a limited load (eg, four 551-lb/250-kg bombs) and also the ability to carry other loads (eg, rocket pods) at lower speeds. In designing the MiG-19, Artem Mikoyan's team had elected to adopt a simple pitot type intake as the best choice for an aeroplane with a design Mach number of the order of M=1·3 — although they were possibly influenced by their lack of experience with any other intake form — despite the fact that the aircraft was *twin*-engined* with its power plants mounted fairly well aft. They thus evolved what was, for its time, the unique configuration of a twin-engined fighter with a nose pitot intake. Such intakes were associated with earlier fighter generations possessing centrally-mounted engines, and adaptation of the basic MiG-19 design for fuselage side air intakes had much to commend it.

There were several precedents for this nasal surgery, but all involved aeroplanes with single, centrally-mounted engines, and were associated with the passing of the "eyeball" fighter and the desire, therefore, to find a convenient location for a large radar dish. The motivation in the case of the Chinese was different. The RD-9B engines and their ducts in the MiG-19 took up very little fuselage depth, and the engines, themselves, were positioned well aft, thus rendering possible the introduction of the internal weapons bay evidently an intrinsic part of the AFPLA requirement. This meant the repositioning of equipment, the sort of equipment to be moved including radios, batteries, oxygen and air conditioning gear, etc, and it must have been immediately obvious that all this could be transferred to the nose if side air intakes be adopted.

The intakes finally chosen were of far higher aspect ratio than normally associated with a twin-engined aeroplane, since the duct cross section was changing not to a half-circle but to a full one. There was, however, proportionately a very long duct over which the change of section could take place. Furthermore, the intake shape selected permitted retention of the inboard wing unchanged — it is not possible to bulge out fuselage contours where there are cannon and wheel doors without fairly dramatic redesign — and maximum commonality of structure with the standard MiG-19 may be presumed to have been a prerequisite. The new forward fuselage grafted on to the rest of the MiG-19 airframe incorporated a sharply-pointed, conical nose, the sides immediately aft of which were flattened to present the belled air intakes with a favourable pre-entry shock pattern at high speeds, and small fixed splitter plates were adopted.

The nosewheel unit was both shifted aft in relation to the cockpit and arranged asymmetrically to make more room in the front fuselage, with widely-spaced nose-gear doors for good access to the nose equipment — although this feature must have resulted in highly adverse effects on directional stability in the gear-down configuration (there have been no signs of the sequencing up of the doors American fashion). The new forward fuselage moved the cockpit forward in relation to the wing leading edge — this was to give an optical impression that the aft fuselage had been stretched, but although such would undoubtedly have been useful in terms of maintaining directional stability, while, from a longitudinal stability viewpoint, it could have been used to eliminate the forward CG shift produced by the new nose, commonality with the standard MiG-19 apparently enjoying a higher priority, the aft fuselage of the progenitor was retained virtually unchanged — and a few knots were gained by redesigning and deepening the dorsal spine, simultaneously virtually eliminating rear view. A more minor change introduced by the new forward fuselage was the replacement of the aft-sliding cockpit canopy by one hinging at the rear to open upwards.

The wing, comprising a single mainspar and three auxiliary spars, was also retained essentially intact, with the wing root-mounted 30-mm cannon remaining *in situ*, only the Fowler-type flap being slightly modified at its trailing-edge root to produce a kink and a minimal area increase. The horizontal slab-type tail remained unchanged, but the vertical surfaces were increased in height to compensate for some inevitable loss in directional stability, and the elongated ventral fin of the MiG-19 gave place to shorter and deeper strakes to port and starboard.

The sum total of these changes was the *Kiang* 5, alias *Fantan*; an aircraft intended as a sort of mini-Buccaneer carrying four 551-lb (250-kg) bombs internally at acceptable low-level penetration speeds. It is not known with certainty when prototype trials were initiated — western visitors, who have seen squadrons of *Kiang* 5s parked on commercial airfields, have been told by Chinese officials that the design is about 10 years old — but it can be assumed that flight testing commenced in the late 'sixties, production subsequently being assigned to the Nancheng factory with initial service entry taking place in 1972-73. It has since undoubtedly been built in very substantial numbers and, although the present production status of the *Kiang* 5 is not known with certainty, there is no reason to believe that it has yet been phased out of the Nancheng facility.

There is no evidence to support the allegations of one western analyst that the wing area of the *Kiang* 5 has been increased by 30 per cent by the addition of a new wing centre section and that the maximum take-off weight has risen by 44 per cent. Indeed, there is ample evidence to refute such assertions. It is improbable that aircraft weight is up by more than 300-400 lb (135-180 kg) relative to the standard diurnal MiG-19, and it would seem almost certain that the insertion of the weapons bay and the equipment repositioning have been at some 15-20 per cent expense of the standard 808 Imp gal (3 675 l) four-cell fuel tank set. Internal capacity, almost invariably augmented by a pair of 167 Imp gal (760 l) drop tanks slung from the outboard (wet) hardpoints, is likely to endow the *Kiang* 5, when carrying full internal bomb load, with a LO-LO-LO tactical radius of the order of 200 nm (370 km), increasing to 350 nm (650 km) HI-LO-HI, with allowance for full-reheat penetration and escape. Ferry range is probably some 1,100 nm (1 850 km).

The WP-6A, or *Wopen* 6A, nine-stage axial-flow turbojets powering the *Kiang* 5 are understood to display improvement over the Tumansky RD-9B from which they derive in TBO rather than performance, and it is fairly safe to assume that the ratings of the original engine are much the same as those offered by the Chinese derivative, namely 5,730 lb (2 600 kg) dry and 7,165 lb (3 250 kg) with maximum reheat, and as the sum total drag with the new inlets and redesigned nose is not inordinately more than that of its progenitor — of course, if one *believes*, as has been stated on one occasion in the west,

**It should be noted that the specification that was eventually to be fulfilled by the MiG-19 had called for a* single *Lyulka AL-5 engine, and a prototype was flown as the I-350, the parallel prototype, the I-360, which, apart from paired small-diameter turbojets, was otherwise similar and was the progenitor of the MiG-19, was something of a "private venture" insofar as anything can be within the Soviet aircraft industry.*

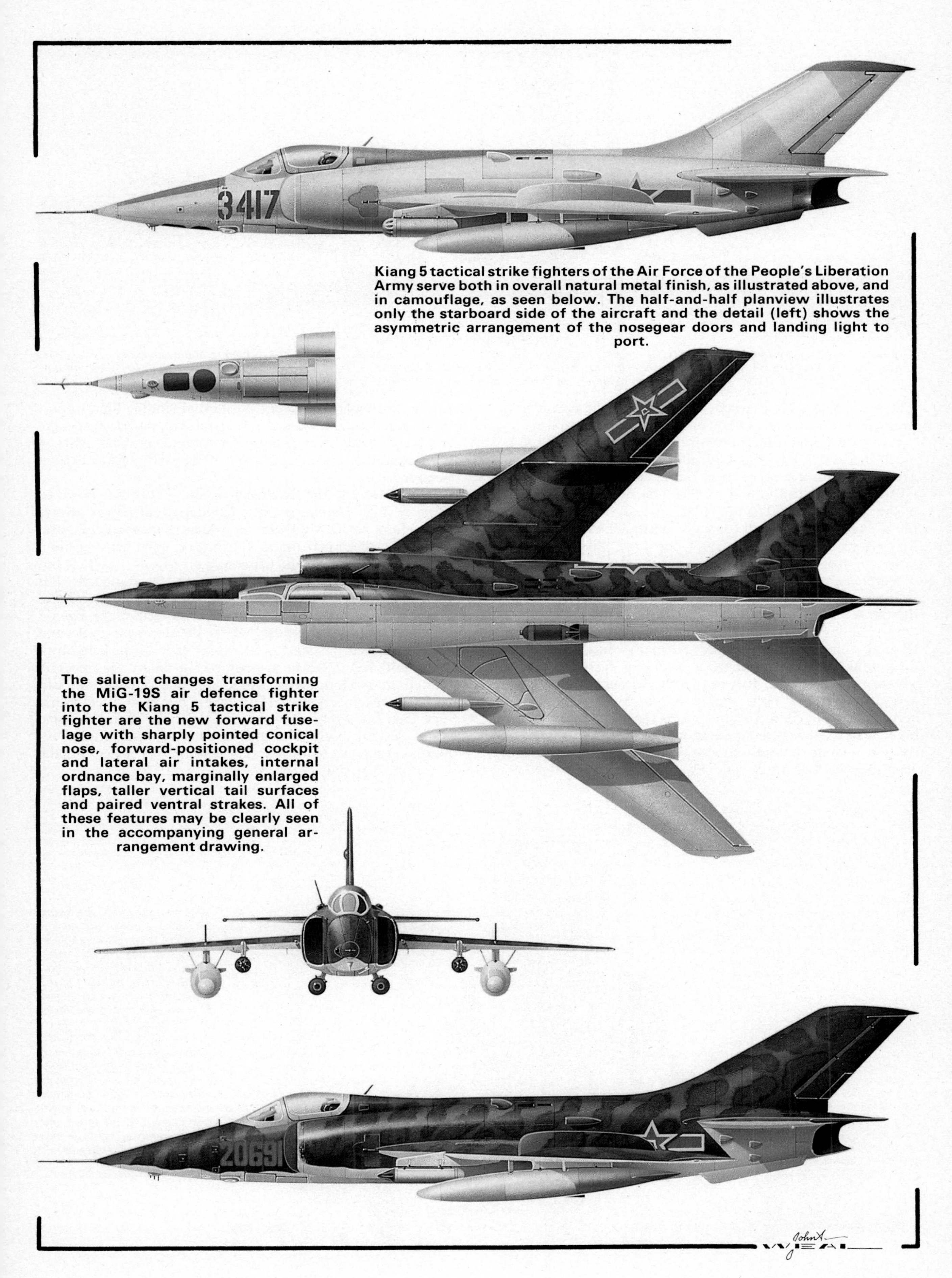

Kiang 5 tactical strike fighters of the Air Force of the People's Liberation Army serve both in overall natural metal finish, as illustrated above, and in camouflage, as seen below. The half-and-half planview illustrates only the starboard side of the aircraft and the detail (left) shows the asymmetric arrangement of the nosegear doors and landing light to port.

The salient changes transforming the MiG-19S air defence fighter into the Kiang 5 tactical strike fighter are the new forward fuselage with sharply pointed conical nose, forward-positioned cockpit and lateral air intakes, internal ordnance bay, marginally enlarged flaps, taller vertical tail surfaces and paired ventral strakes. All of these features may be clearly seen in the accompanying general arrangement drawing.

A fully-armed Kiang 5 ground attack fighter of the Air Force of the People's Liberation Army with 551-lb (250-kg) bombs on the external fuselage stores stations and rocket pods on the projecting inboard wing pylons. The widely-spaced nosegear doors, clearly seen in this photograph, are likely to have highly adverse effects on directional stability in the gear-down configuration.

that the Chinese have accepted the built-in headwind that would derive from a 60 per cent increase in cross section . . . ! — it is to be expected that, in clean condition, there will not be much disparity in speed performance between *Kiang* 5 and MiG-19S, with a maximum of about M = 1·35 at 32,800 ft (10 000 m) down to about M = 0·95 on the deck. Initial climb is of the order of 20,000 ft/min (101,5 m/sec). It is *possible* that the *Kiang* 5 was designed for high subsonic penetration with the pylons jettisoned. A few types have this capability, although dropping the pylons is a very expensive procedure.

Supplementing the internal bay are two external stores stations on the fuselage outboard of the bay doors and beneath the flaps, each apparently capable of lifting a single 551-lb (250-kg) bomb, and four wing hardpoints, those outboard of the main undercarriage members normally being occupied by drop tanks and the inboard hardpoints carrying pylons, which, projecting well forward of the leading edge, usually carry small rocket pods similar to the S-5 type and each accommodating eight 57-mm rockets. Internal equipment is necessarily a subject for speculation, but the various items on the nose include two dielectric panels for a radar altimeter, the usual Soviet-style three-rod IFF antennae, a gun camera housing to starboard, a very substantial landing light to port and a total temperature probe. Other items may be expected to be Chinese derivatives of the ARK-5 radio compass, RSIU-4 VHF communications radio and MRP-48P marker beacon receiver.

In conclusion, the Nancheng-built *Wopen* 6A-powered *Kiang* 5, alias *Fantan*, is no more than what it was always believed to be, a MiG-19S on which a measure of nasal grafting has been performed. It is a very much better ground attack aeroplane than the Chinese-built MiG-17, or F-5, but woefully poor on warload-radius by modern standards. But then, it should be remembered that its *basic* design reaches back some 30 years. One thing would seem certain: the *Kiang* 5 has long since seen the end of its development cycle and speculation that the latest production version is powered by a Xian-built RB.168-25E augmented turbofan, as recently mooted in a Hong Kong-based defence publication, can hardly be taken seriously. If a *Kiang* 5 *has* been fitted with a Spey, then it is purely a design exercise, for a large single engine would destroy both the balance and the feasibility of an internal weapons bay, and this feature was, after all, the primary reason that *Fantan* was developed! □

This photograph of the Kiang 5 shows clearly the asymmetrical arrangement of the nosegear doors, the starboard-mounted gun camera, the di-electric panels for the radar altimeter, the three-rod IFF antennae and the large optical panel offset to port. The barrel of the starboard 30-mm wing root cannon can be seen. The 167 Imp gal (760 l) drop tanks on the pylons outboard of the maingear attachment points are normally carried at all times, but can be replaced by ordnance for short-range missions.

A Question of Cosmetics

THE ADAGIAL ALLEGATION that beauty is in the eye of the beholder assuredly embodies more than a modicum of truth insofar as we modellers are concerned. For some, beauty in a model equates with the simulated oil and exhaust staining, the scuff marks and the repaired ravages of battle favoured by adherents to the school of realism; for others it means a pristine factory roll-out finish, which, if perhaps short on realism, at least shows the aircraft to best advantage. Such beautification rests, of course, entirely with the skills of the individual modeller once he has completed assembly of his kit. But what induced him to part with his money for that particular kit in the first place?

Caprice undoubtedly plays its rôle in kit choice, but rare is the *dedicated* modeller influenced by packaging in his selection of a kit on which to lavish leisure time and expertise. Once *he* has decided on subject matter and what is, in his view, the kit best representing the aircraft of his choice, he will buy it even though it be wrapped in newsprint! So much for the true devotees of the art, but if such rarely yield to the wiles of attractive packaging, does this mean that manufacturers can simply market their kits in labelled plastic bags and save the not inconsiderable cost of full-colour art-bedecked boxes? No way! Those who, more or less, buy on impulse account for a very high proportion of total sales and major contributory factors in *their* purchases are packaging cosmetics — the skills displayed by manufacturers in producing attractive, eye-catching boxes in which to market their kits.

In these days of worldwide and worsening market recession, with shrinking sales, growing stocks and commensurate gloom — particularly within the British kit-producing industry, bedevilled in exporting by the current strength of sterling, and suffering soaring manufacturing costs and crippling interest rates on the financing of swelling inventories — success in attracting the patronage of the impulse purchaser may tip the balance between bankruptcy and solvency. Thus, the highest degree of importance attaches to product presentation. Yet, in recent years, there has been a marked decline in boxtop quality, albeit a downward trend to which UK kit producers, such as Airfix and Lesney, have fortunately — or should it be fortuitously? — not as yet succumbed.

In the USA, box top art is all but dead; its near decease is due not to any lack of awareness of its sales importance, but to regulations insisting that illustrations decorating packaging show precisely what is contained by the box, no more, no less! *Genus homo* has always been divided between the sane, the insane and officials, and the US official mind, in one of its more whimsical flights, has decreed that the boxes containing kits should make no attempt to portray the *real* aircraft in a realistic or artistic setting — Hell, the guy might think that he's buying a *real* B-17 with his few bucks! Thus, eye-titillating and graphic box art has given place to illustrations of built-up models — and not always very *well* built — without scenic background (in case, presumably, some idiot might think that it, too, be contained in the box) and the results are invariably dismal. The reason for the low completion standard of some of the models depicted on the boxes *could* conceivably result from the use of very early test shots of pre-series kits hurriedly assembled to ensure that the boxes that they "decorate" be ready in good time to meet the kit's release date — kits awaiting their packaging equate with burning money. Of course, if one is less charitable, one might be led to suppose that such illustrations are intended to pander to the less skilful modeller who might otherwise complain if his own efforts failed to match up with the results depicted by the box top!

Such are no adequate substitutes for high-quality action paintings, but when it comes to *action*, it would seem that nowadays some European countries are overly sensitive about any illustration with connotations of violence. They no longer permit a combat aircraft to be shown firing guns, dropping bombs or being fired upon by other aircraft or anti-aircraft weaponry; one is led to wonder if those responsible for replacing the traditional drama of box top art with the pacific ever watch TV. The consequence has been that the artwork gracing some recent kit boxes has been markedly muted and docile, with the aircraft represented by the kit presented portrait style. While we will readily admit that the mere sight of the Inspector of Taxes' cypher on an envelope is enough to make us reach a shaking hand for the medicinal elderberry wine, we have difficulty in accepting that a mere picture of a fighter firing guns or launching rockets — surely *raisons d'être* of the species — will prompt young Willie to kick the cat or clobber the boy next door. In similar vein, we have the aversion in some countries to the inclusion of swastikas on illustrations of aircraft that carried such.

Happily, Airfix and Lesney — and particularly the former — seem still to be commissioning some superlative and dramatic paintings with which to beautify their box tops; more's the pity that they so often overprint these with large red stars bearing the legend NEW — not always literally true anyway — which, intended to impart a note of immediacy, only succeed in spoiling artwork for which several hundreds of pounds have presumably been paid. High quality box art has been something of a tradition in the kit manufacturing industry since its early days. A good, interest-evoking package encourages sales, and high sales are in *our* interest as well as those of the kit producer, for, without them, he loses his spirit of adventure; subject choice inevitably diminishes for "play it safe" becomes the keynote of his approach to future products. Let us make a plea to the kit industry, therefore, to halt the decline in packaging standards; if such decline is prompted by reasons of economy, then it could prove a very false economy indeed.

This month's colour subject

This month, the SBAC once more holds its Flying Display and Exhibition at Farnborough. There was a time, not so many years ago, when "Farnborough" was as *British* as was Cheddar cheese, afternoon tea and the Derby; when the world flocked to that Hampshire airfield to see new *British* aircraft, both civil and military, ranging across the entire gamut. In those days, admittedly *before* the birth of AIR INTERNATIONAL, at around this time our editorial staff, then flying the banners of other publications, were metaphorically girding their loins for the rigours of the hospitality chalets, all in the cause of true aeronautical journalism. Today, "Farnborough", as an event, is about as British as *Canadian* Cheddar cheese, but, as usual, our editorial team, older if not wiser, is metaphorically girding its loins . . . oh well, *plus ça change* . . . !

What prompted this soliloquy? This month's choice of colour subject, the Hawk multi-purpose trainer and light tactical aircraft! It occurred to us that the Hawk will be the only *all-British* fixed-wing military aircraft developed from scratch over the past decade to be present at this year's Farnborough — or Farnborough International '80 as it is now called — and even that has an Anglo-French engine. As the only representative of British military airframe design of the 'seventies at this first Farnborough of the 'eighties, it is fortunate that the Hawk is an extremely good and thoroughly efficacious aircraft, and with more than half of the 265 Hawks so far ordered from British Aerospace now delivered, those modellers with a penchant for the current military aviation scene *should* include this aesthetically appealing little aeroplane in their collection. Particularly so as there is now no dearth of alternative finishes and markings, as our colour pages reveal. The first deliveries of the Hawk were made to Kenya earlier this year, deliveries to Indonesia are imminent at the time of closing for press and following close on their tailpipes will be the first aircraft for Finland.

As yet there has been no uncontrollable rush on the part of the kit manufacturers to produce plastic miniature replicas of the Hawk, and so far only two kits have reached the market, one from Airfix and one under Lesney's "Matchbox" trademark, both in 1/72nd scale. Both kits were issued early in the development of the aircraft and, in consequence, omit some minor items, such as the ventral fins and wing fences standardised for production machines. These easily-rectified points apart, both kits are accurate and well produced, our preference being for the Airfix offering which has recently been re-issued, as described in this column last month, to include a new decal sheet with the markings of the RAF's *Red Arrows* display

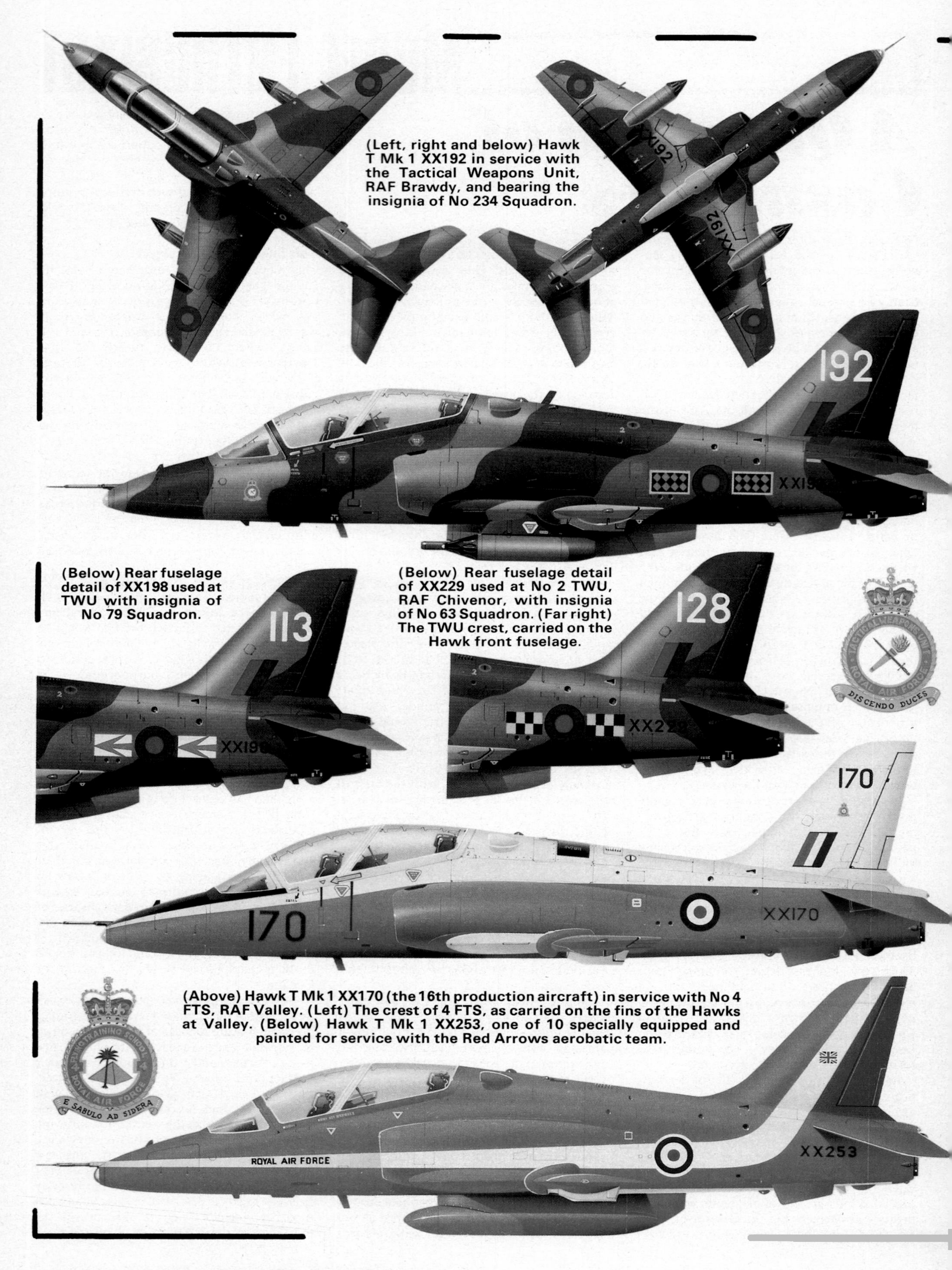

(Left, right and below) Hawk T Mk 1 XX192 in service with the Tactical Weapons Unit, RAF Brawdy, and bearing the insignia of No 234 Squadron.

(Below) Rear fuselage detail of XX198 used at TWU with insignia of No 79 Squadron.

(Below) Rear fuselage detail of XX229 used at No 2 TWU, RAF Chivenor, with insignia of No 63 Squadron. (Far right) The TWU crest, carried on the Hawk front fuselage.

(Above) Hawk T Mk 1 XX170 (the 16th production aircraft) in service with No 4 FTS, RAF Valley. (Left) The crest of 4 FTS, as carried on the fins of the Hawks at Valley. (Below) Hawk T Mk 1 XX253, one of 10 specially equipped and painted for service with the Red Arrows aerobatic team.

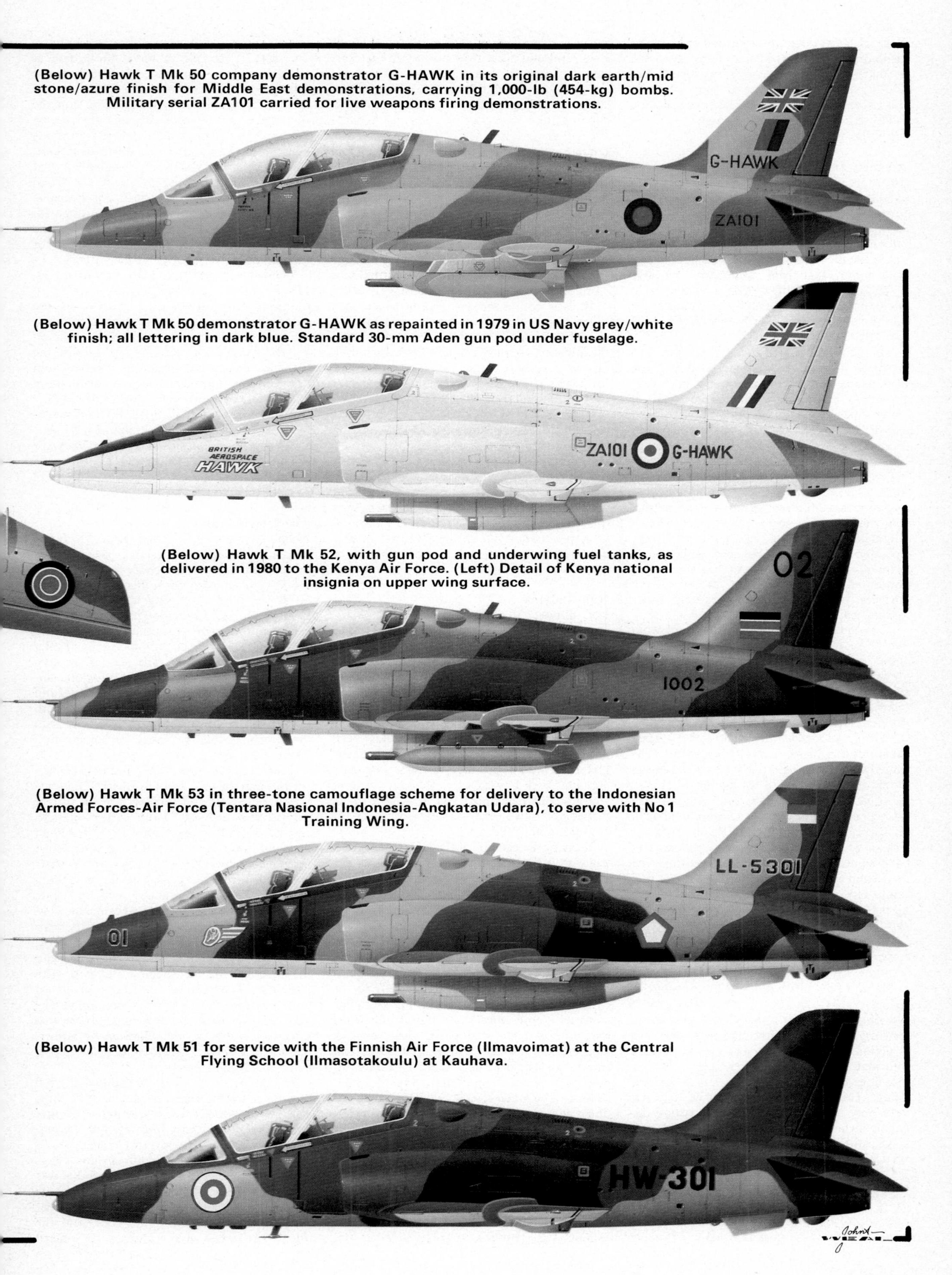

(Below) Hawk T Mk 50 company demonstrator G-HAWK in its original dark earth/mid stone/azure finish for Middle East demonstrations, carrying 1,000-lb (454-kg) bombs. Military serial ZA101 carried for live weapons firing demonstrations.

(Below) Hawk T Mk 50 demonstrator G-HAWK as repainted in 1979 in US Navy grey/white finish; all lettering in dark blue. Standard 30-mm Aden gun pod under fuselage.

(Below) Hawk T Mk 52, with gun pod and underwing fuel tanks, as delivered in 1980 to the Kenya Air Force. (Left) Detail of Kenya national insignia on upper wing surface.

(Below) Hawk T Mk 53 in three-tone camouflage scheme for delivery to the Indonesian Armed Forces-Air Force (Tentara Nasional Indonesia-Angkatan Udara), to serve with No 1 Training Wing.

(Below) Hawk T Mk 51 for service with the Finnish Air Force (Ilmavoimat) at the Central Flying School (Ilmasotakoulu) at Kauhava.

team. If Hawk kits are somewhat thin on the ground at the present time and only available in one scale, there seems little doubt that additional kits will appear as the importance of this aircraft grows and it is to be hoped that the 1/48th scale buffs will be adequately catered for in the not-so-distant future.

An early Halifax

The Handley Page Halifax has hitherto been available only in its Hercules radial-engined form as the Mk III from Airfix, which company has long displayed a penchant for the later marks of the WW II aircraft types that it offers the modeller. Now, in the same 1/72nd scale but this time from "Matchbox", we have a kit of the Halifax Mk I which also encompasses with a number of alternative additional parts the similarly-powered B Mk II and GR Mk II variants.

This kit consists of no fewer than 155 component parts which are moulded in black, dark green, dark earth and clear plastic, thus providing appropriate shades to form a suitable basis for painting. As we have come to expect from "Matchbox", the standard of moulding is very high, with scarcely a vestige of flash to be seen, and the fit of the parts leaves little to be desired, while outline accuracy is hard to fault. Alternative parts provided to cover the three different versions of the Halifax that may be built from this kit include two complete nose sections, one with the power-operated gun turret and the other with a single manually-operated gun in a smoothly-contoured nose, and two sets of vertical tail surfaces, one having tapered and the other vertical leading edges.

The interior fitments are adequate for what can be seen through the transparencies, and there are three crew figures. From the viewpoint of shape, we were well impressed by the engine nacelles, but disliked the flat, blank faces of the intakes, of which there are two different types; these will simply not satisfy the discerning modeller who will wish to open them out and blank them off further aft. The undercarriage is very good and possesses ample strength; an H2S scanner housing may be fitted under the fuselage and the bomb-bay has separate doors which can be mounted open to display the bay's interior. The transparencies, of which there are 30, are very clear, and well-defined frames greatly assist painting. The kit includes many small parts, such as fuel dump pipes, antennae and air intakes, which all help to produce a very satisfying model of this famous bomber.

A good-quality well-printed decal sheet provides markings for a Halifax B Mk I of No 76 Sqdn, RAF Linton-on-Ouse in June 1941, a B Mk II of No 10 Sqdn, RAF Leeming, in February 1942, and a GR Mk II Series Ia of No 58 Sqdn, RAF Coastal Command, St Davids, in 1943. The accompanying instruction sheet provides very clear assembly information and three large-scale four-view drawings offer full painting and marking details. This is a very fine kit which we welcome with only minor reservations concerning the engine air intakes, previously mentioned, and some rather heavy panel lines on the wings and vertical tail.

Flogger frugality

To produce two different kits from essentially one set of moulds is undeniably prudent economy. In fact, it makes damned good business sense, *but* both kits must stand in their own right and accurately portray the aircraft that they purport to represent. Last month, we reviewed in detail the available kits of the Mikoyan *Flogger* family of fighters, highlighting the differences between the MiG-23 *Flogger-B* and the MiG-27 *Flogger-D*, and communicating our hope that Esci, which had announced its forthcoming issue of a kit of the latter, would not emulate Hasegawa in producing a mélange of the MiG-27 and the MiG-23BM. The Esci kit is now to hand and, regrettably, this Italian company has followed in the wake of its Japanese competitor and produced something of a hybrid in exchange for something like two-thirds compatibility of component parts with the earlier *Flogger-B* kit!

We do not propose to waste space with reiteration of the differences between MiG-23 and MiG-27, and we have no doubt that it was the intention of neither Japanese nor Italian kit producer to short-cut the job. It is simply that, for once, their research was inadequate before they committed themselves to plastic. Some 30 of the Esci MiG-27 kit's component parts differ from those of the MiG-23 kit, covering the drooped nose, shorter afterburner, Gatling-type cannon, etc, but no way will it make up into an authentic model of the MiG-27 *Flogger-D*! If cost is not a paramount consideration and you wish to mate the nose of this kit with the rest of the MiG-23 *Flogger-B* kit to produce a MiG-23BM *Flogger-F*, then it can be obtained in the UK at the retail price of £4·25.

Italo Indians

For almost 30 years, Costruzioni Aeronautiche Giovanni Agusta has held licences to build Bell helicopters, the most proliferous of these being the variations on the Iroquois theme. The Iroquois — incidentally the US military appellation for its versions of the Models 204 and 205 — has possibly been built in larger numbers than any other military helicopter, and for long Agusta has been licence-manufacturing an equivalent of the UH-1D Iroquois as the AB 205. Logically enough, Esci has selected this for its first venture into helicopter kits in 1/48th scale, offering it in two separate kits as the UH-1D Iroquois and as the AB 205.

There have been kits of the UH-1B in 1/48th (by Aurora) and 1/50th (by Fujimi) scales, but Esci's kit is the first in 1/48th scale to represent the larger-capacity "Indian" and comprises 103 parts, most of which, apart from 13 transparencies, are moulded in very dark green plastic. The mouldings are of fine quality with just the right amount of surface detailing, some engraved and some raised, resulting in a distinguished model. The cabin interior is extremely well catered for, with all the major controls represented on the framework, authentic-looking seating for the crew, an ammunition box aft of the crew seats and troop seats with delicately-formed framing. All doors are separate and those for the main cabin can be made to slide, while the forward doors can be affixed in the open position if so desired. Particularly noteworthy is the excellent marking of the non-slip cabin floor surface and the diamond-quilted patterning of the ceiling and walls, repeated on the interiors of the doors.

The rotor head has a wealth of detail and includes the transmission housing and jet exhaust — all visible parts are provided as well as some which are enclosed when assembly is completed. Externally mounted, the armament consists of air-to-ground rocket launchers and multiple-barrel machine guns each side, the ammunition belts for the guns leading from the box aft of the crew seats. Also included among the parts is a lifting winch, but no mention is made of this item in the assembly instructions. The decal sheet, while small, is adequate and has instrument panels, a number of small stencillings and South African Air Force as well as US markings, the latter dispensing with all national insignia and identified only by the legend UNITED STATES ARMY on each side of the tailboom.

In most respects identical to that of the UH-1D as far as the mouldings are concerned, omitting only those parts related to the externally-mounted armament, thus comprising 19 less components than the companion kit, the AB 205 kit does, however, utilise the lifting winch which is mounted above the cabin door on the starboard side. A much more extensive decal sheet comes with the AB 205, providing markings for three different machines, respectively from the Italian *Caribinieri*, the *Serviceo de Busqueda y Salvamiento* of Spain's *Ejercito del Aire*, and HTG-64 of the Federal German *Luftwaffe*. The UK retail price of these kits is £4·25 each.

The Czech Arado

An issue from the Czechoslovak Kovozavody Prostejov is always of interest, especially so as, more often than not, this concern selects for its kit a type that is not otherwise available. However, its latest offering, while, as the Avia C 2, presenting a new designation to the kit catalogues, is none other than the Arado Ar 96B which has been produced by Heller comparatively recently. The Ar 96B was, of course, manufactured in Czechoslovakia under German direction during the war years and remained in production (as the Avia C 2) until 1949, while its advanced training service with the Czechoslovak Air Force continued until 1955.

There was no visible difference between the Ar 96B and the C 2, and thus the 1/72nd scale kits from KP and Heller are in direct competition, at least, in the western market, and good as it is, the Czechoslovak product does not quite equal that of the distinguished French company. KP's kit consists of 29 parts moulded in light grey plastic, plus a landing light and a one-piece canopy, which, despite being nicely thin, could have been somewhat clearer in order to show better the very well-detailed cockpit interiors, which have floor, seats, control columns, instrument panels and the turnover frame dividing the two. The distinctive vane applied to the spinners of the Argus engines is formed separately. The undercarriage is delicately formed, as are also the cover doors and the wheel well interiors, the last-mentioned, which are detailed inside, being somewhat shallow.

The quality of the decals accompanying KP kits has much improved of late, and the three schemes provided are interesting. The first covers a trainer employed by the Central Flying School at Prostejov, this having natural metal finish with yellow bands around wings and fuselage; the second is an aircraft that was utilised by the Air Research and Test Institute at Prague-Letňany, with khaki-green upper surfaces and pale blue undersides, and the third represents a civil-registered Air Guard aircraft in natural metal finish with a red engine cowling and red leading edges to the wings and tailplane.

This is a kit that would normally receive an unqualified welcome, but it suffers the misfortune of following so close behind a similar release from so redoubtable a rival as Heller.

Fiat's ninety-one

For long a comparatively important item in the inventory of both the *Luftwaffe* and Italy's *Aeronautica Militare*, but now in process of phasing out the former, the Fiat G.91 has not hitherto been available in 1/48th scale and so Esci's new production of this type in this scale is very welcome. It is both accurate and well-detailed, and may be completed as either a G.91R-1 of the *Aeronautica Militare* or as a G.91R-3 of the *Luftwaffe*, these differing principally in armament and canopy shape, and appropriate alternative parts being provided by the kit.

The mouldings — three in clear and 75 in light grey plastic — are of a high standard, with very fine panel lines and rivet detail. Externally, the model is complete, with very well detailed undercarriage and air brakes, and with engraved detail within their housings, but Esci has fallen down on the cockpit interior, which hardly matches up with the externals, although the ejection seat is good and a full floor is provided, so the application of extra detail is rendered quite practicable. Decals are, incidentally, included for the instrument panels.

Detachable panels in each side of the nose reveal details of the gun armament which differs between the two variants. A further difference concerns the wing hardpoints, the German variant having four whereas the Italian model has only two, this determining the placing of the stores provided by the kit — two drop tanks, two bombs and two rocket launchers. The decal sheet is very good, with comprehensive markings for an AMI machine from the 2° *Stormo* at Treviso St Angelo in 1977, and two *Luftwaffe* examples, one from *Waffenschule* 50 at Furstenfeldbruch in 1970 and the other from LKG 43 at Oldenburg in 1977, colourful unit emblems being included, as well as wingwalk lines, stencillings, etc.

A companion kit issued simultaneously makes up into the G.91PAN version used by the AMI aerobatic team, the *Frecce Tricolore*, this being moulded in dark blue plastic and omitting 24 parts from the G.91R kit, but introducing six new parts for the display smoke containers, etc. The decal sheet provides all the colourful markings of the *Frecce Tricolore*, and the UK retail price of each G.91 kit is £3·35.

Lightweight duo

The growing prolificity of the Italian Esci concern, whose paired G.91s, brace of choppers and MiG-23 *cum* -27 mélange have already been reviewed this month, is underlined by the arrival of yet two more of this company's products via the UK distributor, Humbrol, these comprising a version of Ed Heinemann's bantam bomber, the Skyhawk, and the Franco-German dual-rôle Alpha Jet, both aircraft for which can be claimed light weight combined with no mean ability, and both in 1/48th scale.

The variant of the McDonnell Douglas Skyhawk featured by Esci is the A-4E — don't be misled by the listing of the kit as A-4E/F for the kit lacks the back-pack necessary if it is to represent the later sub-type — and it comprises 85 parts in light grey plastic and a further three as transparencies. Well detailed and neatly moulded, with most of the surface detailing engraved, the kit embodies a number of refinements, such as piping and other features *inside* the wheel wells. The undercarriage is finely formed, a refuelling probe is provided for the starboard side of the nose, the separate leading-edge wing slats can be set in the open position and there is a neat representation of an ejection seat for the well-equipped cockpit.

There is plenty of space in the nose for the recommended 20 grammes of weight to balance the tail, and considerable emphasis is placed on external stores, with a centreline-mounted multiple ejector rack carrying six Mk 82 bombs, and two rocket launchers and two drop tanks provided for mounting in different combinations. A very fine decal sheet includes the instrument panels and a great many small markings and stencillings, and covers two different US Navy aircraft, one from VF-192 when based at Da Nang, Vietnam, in 1966, and the other from VF-43 at NAS Oceania, Virginia, in 1976. A third set of markings is provided for an A-4G of the Royal Australian Navy's No 805 Sqdn. This kit retails in the UK at £3·35.

Insofar as the Alpha Jet is concerned, there have previously been a couple of kits in 1/72nd scale and one, from Heller, in 1/50th scale, but Esci's is the first in 1/48th scale, although, regrettably, it falls rather below the high standard that we have recently come to expect from this Italian company. Moulded in silver plastic and consisting of 77 parts, plus a clear canopy, this is an accurate model with much to commend it, but it suffers rather heavy panel lines on the fuselage and flying surfaces — these are embossed and call for some fairly drastic application of "wet and dry" emery before painting. The plastic exhibits a surfeit of flow marks, although these will be obscured by the paint.

The cockpit interior, with its two ejection seats, is quite well furnished and decals are provided for the instrument panels, and the undercarriage is deserving of commendation for its neat but robust construction and nicely formed wheels. The trailing edges of the wings are reasonably thin, as are also those of the tailplane, but the rudder trailing edge calls for considerable thinning before it may be considered acceptable. The very clear canopy is an excellent moulding with the framing neatly defined. Two bombs and two drop tanks are provided for application to the wing hardpoints and the decal sheet offers a wide selection of markings to cover one machine each from the *Armée de l'Air*, the *Luftwaffe* and the *Force Aérienne Belge*. The kit provides appropriate nose cones for the French and German versions but makes no attempt to differentiate between the Martin-Baker ejection seats of the former and the Stencil seats of the latter. This is, however, an acceptable kit if not representative of the best that Esci can do, and, like the Skyhawk, it retails in the UK at £3·35. □

F J HENDERSON

EUROFIGHTER ***from page 130***

could prove to have high drag, as has been found on the F-18. The AMD-BA solution would not suffer so much of a problem because its intakes are nearer the nose and so have a smaller boundary layer to divert. This is possibly the best solution, therefore, as long as good performance at high yaw angles is not required.

The choice of powerplant will probably depend on the individual country. It is difficult to see Britain and Germany not using the RB.199 now that it has been developed and is progressing well down the learning curve. Similarly, it is highly unlikely that France, after committing itself to an expensive Research and Development programme on the M88, would consider any other engine. The two engines are of similar size so it should not be impossible to accommodate either engine; the RB.199 for Britain and Germany, the M88 for France. Although not clearly shown on models, articulating nozzles could confer significant gains in combat and field performance and, if not used initially, could be fitted as a later development.

European Combat Aircraft — the future

It has been shown that a suitable design for a European Combat Aircraft could meet the requirements of Britain, Germany and France, and this compromise has been the subject of meetings between representatives of BAe, MBB and AMD-BA. The tri-company feasibility study has produced such a measure of agreement that the future looks set for the ECA. However, this agreement is only on a company level, with the companies leading the way for international collaboration, albeit with the tacit agreement of their relevant ministries. This work is largely privately funded; for example, MBB has been told that it must fund ECA work itself. This reflects the German Government's efforts to hold down defence spending and indicates no firm commitment to a German or European design. A purchase of foreign aircraft has not been ruled out. Similarly, in Britain, there is likely to be some continuing enthusiasm amongst the purse-string holders for an off-the-shelf purchase of McDonnell Douglas F-18s, and in France the Dassault-Breguet Super Mirage 4000, already flying as minimum-equipped prototype, remains available in a fall-back position.

Clearly the onus is on the aircraft and aero-engine industries of Britain, Germany and France to ensure that costs are kept as low as possible and that the ECA out-performs any rival. First indications are that it *could* be a world-beater, ensuring that Europe would stay in the forefront of military technology until well into the next century. This is an aircraft that Europe, its air forces and industries cannot afford to lose. □

TALKBACK

Brazil's New Trainer

WE HAVE just received the June Issue of AIR INTERNATIONAL, which includes an article on our new trainer, the EMB-312 (T-27), the prototype of which is scheduled to make its first flight on 19 August. A full scale mock-up of the T-27 is to be exhibited at the Farnborough International air show in September.

We would like to stress that the EMB-312 is now a totally new design and has nothing to do with any previous EMBRAER or other project. It has been developed according to the most up-to-date international concepts to an advanced military specification and has sophisticated radio-navigation, communications and weapons delivery systems.

The design of the EMB-312 is the responsibility of the long-established EMBRAER design team. There has not been any recent change in the EMBRAER organisation and the team is not dependent upon any single individual being transferred from another company in Brazil.

Mario Leme Galvao
Press and PR Manager
EMBRAER, São Paulo, Brazil

Latin "Peashooters"

I WAS PLEASANTLY SURPRISED to see the June choice of colour profiles for the modelling section was the Boeing P-26, one of the most colourful monoplane fighters ever operated anywhere in the world. Regrettably, your artist has omitted the blue centre from the wing star of the Guatemalan aircraft and I feel that attention should be drawn to the fact that the upper wing surfaces of the Guatemalan machines were dark green — this is correctly depicted by your artist but can only just be seen and as attention is not drawn to it in the caption could well be overlooked by modellers.

There were, in fact, seven P-26As forming Guatemala's first fighter squadron, these having been acquired in 1937 from USAAC stocks in the Canal Zone. The only fighter in Guatemalan service prior to the procurement of the P-26As being an old Nieuport 28 of World War I vintage used as an advanced trainer and based at Campo de la Aurora, Ciudad de Guatemala. At the end of World War II, six P-26As were still on charge, and the last serviceable example was not withdrawn until the first F-51D Mustangs arrived in 1950 to re-equip the Escuadrón de Caza. Two of the P-26As were eventually sold in the USA: FAG 0672 (ex 33-123), which was registered N3378G and is currently owned by Edward Maloney, and FAG 0816 (ex 33-135), the subject of your colour profile. It is interesting to note that these aircraft retained their USAAC Technical Data Block on their fuselage port sides, although with appropriate modifications. When 0672 arrived in the USA the following was stencilled just below the windscreen:

FUERZA AEREA
DE GUATEMALA
P26A 0672
SERIAL 33-123

John Andrade
Bewdley, Worcs DY12 2DX

Navy Skytrains

I AM able to update your reference to the US Navy's operation of the C-9B Skytrain II ("Super 80 for the 'Eighties"/June 1980, page 296). At present no regular Navy squadron flies this type, as all the Service's C-9Bs are assigned to units of the Naval Air Reserve Force. They are on the East Coast VR-55 at Norfolk, Va, and VR-58 at Jacksonville, Fla, while West Coast squadrons are VR-56 at Alameda, Ca, and VR-57 at North Island, Ca. Each unit has an establishment of three aircraft.

Anthony Robinson
Ashtead, Surrey

Surviving Sea Fury

PAGE 85 of your February issue shows the Sea Fury T Mk 20 (VX281 alias G-BCOW) together with the statement that it *was* owned by Spencer R Flack and that the aircraft is no longer airworthy. The facts are that the Sea Fury *is* owned by Spencer Flack and it is flying supremely well, and for the record, Spencer and I fitted in a seven-minute aerobatic slot at Cranfield during January of this year.

In addition to running the above T Mk 20, Spencer is restoring one Mk 14 Spitfire, one Hawker Hunter Mk 4 and one Sea Fury Mk 11. The Hunter, as many of your readers may have witnessed, made its début recently at the Biggin Hill Air Fair and, with the exception of a few minor modifications, is now ready for a busy season of displays in the capable hands of Stefan Karwowski.

Charles F Thomas
North Crawley, Bucks

Illustrated below is the colourful Hunter F Mk 51 G-HUNT, which has recently made its début on the UK air show scene, as noted above in the letter from Charles Thomas. Originally serving with the Danish Air Force as E-418, it was marked G9-490 prior to its first flight in civil guise on 20 March 1980. (Above right) The Sea Fury G-BCOW, which continues to be flown at air shows by Spencer Flack.

AIRCRAFT OF THE BATTLE OF BRITAIN

William Green

An essential background book to the Battle of Britain. Contains full technical details of the principal aircraft taking part on both sides – the RAF's Hurricane, Spitfire, Defiant and Blenheim and the Luftwaffe's He 111, Ju 87, Ju 88, Do 17, Bf 109 and Bf 110, with concise descriptions of their development and histories. Illustrated throughout with many unusual photographs, tone profiles and three views, *Aircraft of The Battle of Britain* combines a high standard of pictorial presentation with an authoritative and informative text by one of the world's leading experts.

£1.95 (paperback) 64 pp 7" x 8⅝"
Illustrated throughout

AIRCRAFT VERSUS SUBMARINE

New edition

Alfred Price

The aircraft has always been the natural predator of the submarine. Alfred Price traces 70 years of see-saw technology from the early airships to the Nimrod. Mr. Price, author of the highly acclaimed *Instruments of Darkness* excels at explaining in clear and understandable language the complexities of warfare and expertly describes the actions, aircraft, submarines and personalities involved.

This completely revised and up-dated edition includes the latest available information and photographs on this important aspect of modern warfare.

£8.95 224 pp 9¼" x 6⅛"

JANE'S
Publishing Company Ltd
238 City Road, London EC1

Military Enthusiast

A new magazine from the publishers of Born in Battle.

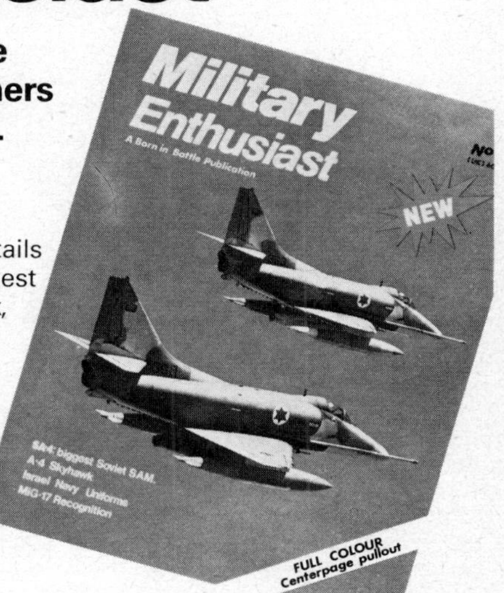

No. 1 on sale at your newsagents from Aug 28th, features details of SA4 – Russia's biggest SAM, the A4 Skyhawk, Israel Navy Uniforms, MIG 17 Recognition and full colour centre page pull out.

36 pages of action, photographs and informed editorial.
To be published six times a year, Military Enthusiast is also available on subscription. For full subscription details of all Eshel – Dramit publications write to Comag Subscription Dept.

COMAG Tavistock Road, West Drayton, Middlesex UB7 7QE England.
Tel: West Drayton 44055. Night Ansaphone West Drayton 48468. Telex: 8813787.

The Official Newspaper of the

ROYAL AIR FORCE

In handy size and popular style. The Newspaper contains 24 PAGES of service news and views, sports fixtures, reports and commentaries.

Feature articles on the Royal Air Force of today — and yesterday, with Pictures, Colour and Cartoons.

Be well informed and send for your copy **NOW!**

The "RAF NEWS" is published fortnightly.
Price: 8p Annual subscription: £4·50 (including postage).

RAF NEWS

Please send, post paid, one copy of the "RAF NEWS" each fortnight for one year. I enclose Cheque/P.O./Money Order, value £4·50. Please send free copy.

To.. (block letters)

Address..

.... Date....................

Orders to be sent to Business Manager, "RAF NEWS", Turnstile House, 94/99 High Holborn, London WC1V 6LL. Cheques, Money Orders, Postal Orders to be made payable to the Accounting Officer, Ministry of Defence and crossed Bank of England A/c Postmaster-General.
AI

THE STRIKING TRAINER

S-005
The cost-effective
Aermacchi MB-339 brings your pupils
— after the initial screening —
to high-performance combat aircraft.
With 4,000 lb of military load
— ranging from two 30 mm cannon
to 1,000 lb bombs — on six underwing
stations, the MB-339 can be
put immediately in front-line service
becoming a powerful CAS or recce/EW tool.
Result: one aircraft performs the whole training,
keeps pilots combat-ready sparing precious
flying hours on more costly aircraft
and improves your Air Force capabilities
with great logistic
and cost
advantages.
Aer Macchi
s. de sigis-80

hour test in May 1979. An even more powerful version is under development: the M53-P2 of 22,046 lb (10 000 kg) thrust, which will, in due course, supersede the M53-5 as the standard engine for the production Mirage 2000. The M53 is a low-bypass (0·32) turbofan of modular construction. It owes its light weight to its basic simplicity: it has only three LP compressor stages, five HP stages, and two turbine stages all on a single spool. It is capable of continuous operation at M = 2·5 at high altitude, and has no restrictions on the use of afterburner in any part of the flight envelope.

Compared to the Mirage III, the Mirage 2000 aerodynamic configuration was refined by computer-aided design to give a highly optimised shape. The wing roots were swelled out with "Karman fairings" to provide additional space for equipment and fuel at minimal drag penalty. The internal fuel capacity of the Mirage 2000 is 835 Imp Gal (3 800 l), representing approximately 30 per cent of clean take-off weight, a figure previously attained only by US naval fighters. In place of the fixed conical camber of the Mirage III wing, automatic leading-edge flaps were provided, giving a maximum of 15 deg droop inboard and 20 deg outboard. These flaps permit the Mirage 2000 to be operated safely up to high AOA. The first public demonstrations took place at the last Farnborough Air Show, with flypasts at 96 kt (178 km/h) at 24 deg AOA, but later flight trials have taken the aircraft to 30 deg AOA. Normal approach speed is 140 kt (260 km/h) compared to 184 kt (340 km/h) for the Mirage III. In order to provide directional stability at high AOA, the fin height was increased relative to that of the Mirage III, and strakes were placed on the outer surface of the intakes to control the shedding of fuselage vortices.

It is noteworthy that in the course of Mirage 2000 development the modifications to the airframe have only been minor. The fin height has been cut down slightly, fin sweep increased, the intake boundary layer diverters redesigned and the Karman fairings extended beyond the trailing edge root. The aircraft originally flew with triplicated FBW with mechanical back-up, but this system has now been replaced by quadruplex FBW on the pitch and roll circuits and simple triplex FBW on the rudder circuit.

In aiming to achieve a combat thrust/weight ratio in the region of unity, weight saving was obviously of crucial importance. One factor that helped in this respect was the thickness of the wing root, providing increased depth in the region of maximum bending moment and thus saving on spar boom weight. Additional weight saving is achieved by the use of advanced materials, notably titanium and carbon-fibre and boron-fibre composites. These advanced composites are used for the vertical tail skins, flight control surfaces, avionics bay door and mainwheel doors. Hydraulic system weight was reduced by adopting a high pressure: 4,000 psi (280 bars). The Messier-Hispano undercarriage represents a mere 2·2 per cent of maximum gross weight — a remarkable achievement.

The resulting aircraft has a weight that is only marginally heavier than that of the Mirage IIIE, and is approximately 1,100 lb (500 kg) lighter than the Mirage F1, while providing far higher performance and a much more effective nav-attack system. Radar range is quoted as four or five times better than for the Mirage III and twice that of the Mirage F1. Its two DEFA 554 cannon have selective firing rates of 1,800 and 1,300 rd/min, according to the type of target. For air-air missions the Mirage 2000 is to be armed with the Matra 550 Magic IR-homing short-range missile and the Matra Super 530D radar-homing medium-range missile, which has snap-up capability against M = 3·0 intruders flying at up to 98,000 ft (30 000 m).

The Mirage 2000 has nine external weapon stations, whereas the Mirage III has only five and the F1 only seven. The new aircraft can carry up to 18 bombs of 550 lb (250 kg), six of

The Mirage 2000-02 demonstrates a low slow fly-by, with wing leading edge slats open.

880 lb (400 kg), or three of 2,200 lb (1 000 kg). External fuel may be carried in two 374 Imp gal (1 700 l) underwing and one 264 Imp gal (1 200 l) centre-line tanks. In a typical ground attack mission with guided weapons, the Mirage 2000 would have an ATLIS laser target marker and TV tracker unit on the centre-line, two AS-30 missiles with Ariel laser seekers and two Magic missiles, and the two internal 30-mm cannon for self-defence.

Due to delays with the definitive intercept radar, the first 80-100 aircraft for the *Armée de l'Air* will be fitted with a multi-rôle doppler radar (RDM — *Radar Doppler Multifonction*), reportedly designated Cyrano 500 and derived from the Cyrano IV in the Mirage F1. By 1985, this will be superseded by the Thomson-CSF/EMD pulse-doppler radar designated RDI (*Radar Doppler à Impulsions*). This is to give an acquisition range of 54 nm (100 km) against a 54 sq ft (5 m²) target. A third type of radar (EMD/Thomson-CSF Antilope 5) is projected for a nuclear strike variant proposed for service in 1986. Dead reckoning navigation, velocity data and attitude reference information is provided by a SAGEM inertial system. The various parts of the weapons system are connected by multiplex digital communication system termed Digibus.

The Mirage 2000 cockpit is of advanced design, with most of the information required to operate the aircraft displayed on the HUD and a head-down three-colour CRT, both developed by Thomson-CSF. The head-down display can show an artificial horizon, radar mapping, TV information from an ATLIS tracker, navigation data and ESM (radar warning) information. Control knobs for communications, weapon selection, etc, are centrally situated on the main instrument panel, rather like the "up-front control" of the F-18. Control knobs used in combat are located on the control column handle and throttle lever (analogous to the MDC "hands-on-throttle-and-stick" concept).

Project status

The programme got the *feu vert* in December 1975, replacing the far more expensive, twin-engined ACF (*Avion du Combat Futur*). The Mirage 2000-01 made its maiden flight on 10 March 1978, followed by 02 on 18 September 1978, 03 on 26 April 1979, and 04 on 12 May 1980. The fifth prototype (Mirage 2000B-01) is a two-seat trainer that will also be used for demonstration purposes. It is expected to fly during the autumn.

The Mirage 2000 is wanted initially by the *Armée de l'Air* for air defence, which will require approximately 130 units. On a later timescale, it is anticipated that a second variant will be developed for low level penetration and tactical reconnaissance and that approximately 200 of this model will be procured. For this second domestic version, of which two prototypes are planned, Aérospatiale is developing the nuclear ASMP *(Air-Sol Moyenne Portée)* stand-off missile with a range of 54 nm (100 km). Four production aircraft were ordered in 1979, to be followed by 22 this year (out of a total of 123 Mirage 2000s planned for procurement over the three-year period 1980-82). Although it was originally envisaged that the aircraft would be in service in 1982, it now appears that deliveries will only start in mid-1983. Export deliveries of a

multi-rôle version with the RDM radar are expected to commence in 1984. Production rate for domestic use will be up to 44 units per year, but capacity is available to double this should export demands require it.

Although the Mirage 2000 was primarily intended for a rather different rôle from that of the General Dynamics F-16 and McDonnell Douglas F-18, ie, bomber interception rather than dogfight duties, it is inevitable that these three types will find themselves in competition in the export market, since they are all supersonic fighters in broadly the same price category.

The F-16 is the smallest, least expensive and most advanced in programme timescale, having entered service in early 1979. It is biased toward the dogfight rôle and in such duties it undoubtedly excels, being a small, highly powered, and extremely manoeuvrable aircraft. However, despite its excellent internal fuel capacity and consequently good warload-radius performance, current indications are that in ground attack configurations it will have an AOA restriction that may prove an embarrassment. In the air defence rôle its radar capability is limited and further development is required if it is to use radar-guided weapons. Carrying two such weapons, its maximum speed is quite possibly well below M=1·5.

The F-18 is the heaviest of the trio — and probably the most expensive — and the best multi-rôle aircraft. Its weight suggests that it will be less penalised in performance by heavy warloads. Its very advanced radar and the fact that it was designed to carry semi-recessed Sparrow or AMRAAM must give it a reasonable capability in medium/low level air-air missions. However, it is definitely inferior to the Mirage 2000 in maximum speed and ceiling and is thus less suited to intercept really high performance intruders.

The Mirage 2000 is approximately the same weight as the F-16, but more expensive and less well powered. It is difficult to believe that this aircraft will be able to equal the two American fighters in the dogfight rôle as long as the thrust of the M53 lags behind that of the F100. Given as much thrust as the F-16, its only fundamental disadvantage would be the lower aspect ratio of the delta wing.

In ground attack the Mirage 2000 is probably similar to the F-16, ie, inferior to the F-18. However, in high altitude air defence the French aircraft must be the winner by a significant margin. It can exceed M=2·3, will have a service ceiling of 66,000 ft (20 000 m), and will be able to reach M=2·0 at 49,000 ft (15 000 m) in four minutes from wheels rolling.

In summary, each of these new Western fighters will provide outstanding effectiveness in its own area of the light/medium fighter spectrum, and all of them will be sold in large numbers. Wherever the operator emphasises the need to intercept even the highest and fastest of intruders, or simply demands an aircraft with the best possible speed and altitude capability, then the Mirage 2000 will be the obvious choice in its class. □

DASH 7 ***from page 124***

control console to automatically enter updated waypoint co-ordinates into the RNAV computer.

Although intended as a non-precision approach aid, the DAC-7000 RNAV provides lateral guidance and a projected guidepath similar to the glideslope/localiser information of a conventional ILS approach. The computer has preprogrammed routes inserted so that it establishes a series of waypoints on an approach route and navigates from each waypoint to the next. Vertical-deviation data are computed along desired descending (or ascending) flight paths to satisfy altitude requirements at each waypoint. Thus, an approach corridor is established whose glidepath angle varies with each course change at a given waypoint. Programming a final waypoint at the runway threshold ends the approach conventionally.

This RNAV system meets FAA requirements and has received approval for IFR operations (1,500-ft/457-m ceiling and 3·0 miles/4,8 km visibility) in vertical navigation (VNAV) as well as all RNAV modes. Pictorial presentation on the RCA Primus digital colour radar permits observation of the intended track through weather and shows any gross errors in the route programme. As experience is gained with RNAV operations, it is expected that weather minima will be reduced.

Ransome Airlines had been limited by air traffic congestion at Washington's National airport so, with FAA co-operation, several possible routes into this airport and into Philadelphia airport were evaluated by assembling airspace not used during conventional IFR conditions so that the Dash 7 could be navigated independently to the final approach. Also, the already saturated primary instrument runway was avoided by landing on an intersecting stub which was quite long enough (2,300 ft/701 m) because of the Dash 7's STOL performance.

The Ransome Dash 7s enter the Runway 33 approach over the DAWSE waypoint at 3,000 ft (914 m) altitude and start to descend along vertical-path segments to meet altitude requirements at each subsequent waypoint. Minimum descent altitude (MDA) corresponds with the IFR minimum. A missed approach point (MAP) is located at the MDA to permit a missed-approach procedure that does not use airspace reserved for conventional jet arrivals. If VFR flight is possible from the MAP, a 3D RNAV guided approach is made to the final waypoint on the threshold of Runway 33. A STOL landing is then made on the runway stub and ends short of Runway 18/36. The RNAV approach corridor to Washington National is separated not only from the conventional jet approach corridor up the Potomac River, but also from service aircraft using Andrews Air Force Base to the east.

Although providing accurate three-axis guidance, RNAV is only as accurate as VOR/DME signals used to derive position data. So, for precision-approach aid on this Ransome route the FAA is installing microwave landing systems (MLS) at both Washington National and Philadelphia airports to evaluate all-weather operations in actual commuter-airline conditions.

In places where STOLports make the most sense, the Dash 7 is again an obvious choice of equipment because of its steep-gradient performance. With a gross take-off weight of 44,000 lb (19 958 kg) and operating under FAR part 25, the Dash 7 needs only 2,260 ft (689 m) for take-off under ISA standard-day sea-level conditions. The STOLport built at Vail, Colorado, by Rocky Mountain Airways has high-intensity runway lights; a visual approach slope indicator (VASI); runway-end identification lights (REIL); a precision microwave guidance system; and a non-directional beacon (NDB).

Prospects and portents

Clearly, the Dash 7 has changed from being a "sleeper" (as was the highly successful F.27 in its early years) into a very active programme. The Series 200 now on offer with 1,230 shp PT6A-55 engines will retain full STOL attributes while offering hot/high performance (probably at a slightly higher gross weight) which will be particularly useful for operators supporting resource exploration in remote areas. In a later timescale, the Series 300 Dash 7 with higher-power engines and higher gross weight will have a 70-in (178-cm) fuselage plug added to increase passenger seating from 50 to 60.

Meanwhile, the twin-engine 32-passenger Dash 8 has been launched, so DHC — with the 19-passenger Twin Otter and the commercial version of the Buffalo, the 44-passenger DHC-5E Transporter — has a wide range of civil transports as same-family options for regional airlines and commuter operators. With this product line-up, de Havilland Aircraft of Canada has consolidated and extended its leadership in development of STOL transport and utility aircraft of rugged simplicity and economical performance, while offering the very latest innovations for both safety and cost-effectiveness. □

The first Meteor I after delivery to the USA in exchange for a Bell XP-59 Airacomet.

GLOSTER METEOR I-III — UK

Developed in accordance with the requirements of specification F.9/40, the first prototype Meteor to fly (actually the fifth prototype airframe) took the air on 5 March 1943 with de Havilland H.1 turbojets rather than the Whittle W.2Bs intended, the first airframe flying with Rover-built W.2B/23 engines on 24 July 1943, these being two of a total of eight prototypes. A pre-series of 20 powered by Rolls-Royce Welland (W.2B/23C) turbojets of 1,700 lb (771 kg) thrust was delivered as Meteor Is, the first of these flying on 12 January 1944, one RAF squadron being fully equipped with this type by the end of the following August. The Meteor II was a proposed version with de Havilland H.1 Goblin engines which was not proceeded with, and the Meteor III was the first major production model, this having a strengthened airframe, increased internal fuel capacity and a sliding cockpit canopy. The Meteor III was intended to have 2,000 lb (907 kg) Rolls-Royce W.2B/37 Derwent I engines, but the first 15 of 210 of this version built retained the Welland, the first of these flying in September 1944. The Meteor III had empty and loaded weights of 10,519 lb (4 771 kg) and 13,920 lb (6 314 kg), but performance and dimensions were similar to those of the Meteor I to which the following data refer. Both marks carried an armament of four 20-mm British Hispano cannon. Max speed, 385 mph (619 km/h) at sea level, 415 mph (675 km/h) at 10,000 ft (3 050 m). Initial climb, 2,155 ft/min (10,9 m/sec).

The Meteor III (above and below) was the first version of the Gloster jet fighter to be built in substantial numbers.

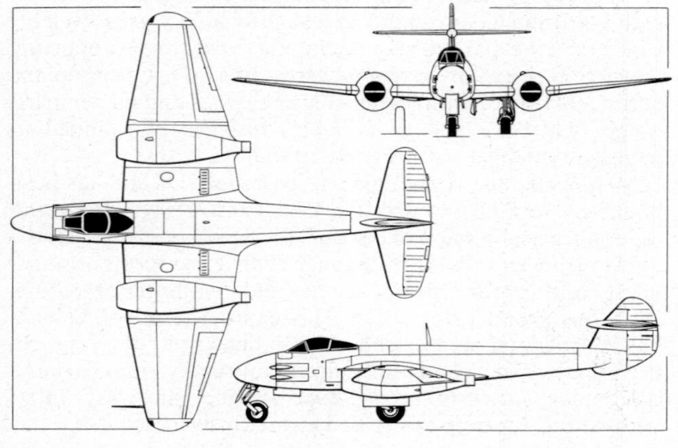

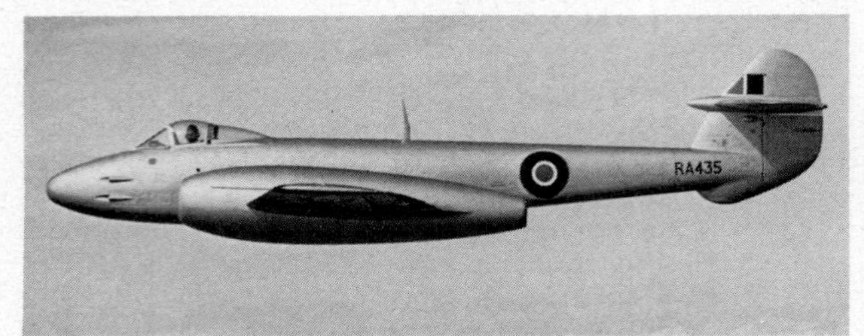

The Meteor F Mk 4 was exported to five air forces and more than 500 were built for the RAF.

Empty weight, 8,140 lb (3 737 kg). Loaded weight, 13,795 lb (6 258 kg). Span, 43 ft 0 in (13,10 m). Length, 41 ft 3 in (12,57 m). Height, 13 ft 0 in (3,96 m). Wing area, 374 sq ft (34,74 m²).

GLOSTER METEOR F MK 4 — UK

On 17 May 1945, a Meteor III flew with enlarged engine nacelles housing 3,000 lb (1 362 kg) Rolls-Royce Derwent 5 turbojets and serving as a prototype for the extensively modified Meteor F Mk 4 which featured further airframe strengthening and a pressurised cockpit, the wing area later being reduced six per cent by clipping the wingtips. Fully rated Derwent 5 engines of 3,500 lb (1 588 kg) were standardised for the series production model which carried the standard armament of four 20-mm British Hispano cannon and a total of 535 was to be built for the RAF (including 46 by Armstrong Whitworth), export deliveries comprising 100 for Argentina, 38 for the Netherlands, 12 for Egypt, 48 for Belgium and 20 for Denmark. The Netherlands subsequently purchased 27 ex-RAF F Mk 4s and two were supplied to France for development work. Deliveries were completed in 1950. One example of a fighter reconnaissance version, the Meteor FR Mk 5, was flown on 15 June 1949, but crashed during this first flight. Max speed, 580 mph (933 km/h) at 10,000 ft (3 050 m). Initial climb, 7,500 ft/min (38,1 m/sec). Range (internal fuel), 610 mls (982 km) at 30,000 ft (9 145 m). Empty weight, 11,217 lb (5 088 kg). Loaded weight, 14,545 lb (6 597 kg). Span, 37 ft 2 in (11,32 m). Length, 41 ft 0 in (12,50 m). Height, 13 ft 0 in (3,96 m). Wing area, 350 sq ft (32,51 m²).

GLOSTER METEOR F MK 8 — UK

Development of an improved Meteor, the F Mk 8, began in 1947, and the first prototype (a modified F Mk 4) flew on 12 October 1948. The F Mk 8 introduced Derwent 8 engines, which had a similar 3,500 lb (1 588 kg) rating to the Derwent 5s that they succeeded, a 30-in (76 cm) increase in fuselage length, entirely new tail surfaces, an ejection seat, new cockpit canopy and some structural strengthening. Deliveries to the RAF commenced at the end of 1949, and a total of 1,183 was to be built for the service and for export. Export deliveries comprised 12 ex-RAF aircraft to Egypt, 23 ex-RAF aircraft to Belgium, 20 aircraft to Denmark, 12 aircraft (plus seven ex-RAF) to Syria, five ex-RAF to the Netherlands, 60 aircraft to Brazil and 11 aircraft to Israel. The RAAF operated the Meteor F Mk 8 in Korea in 1951-3, losing 48 aircraft during hostilities and taking 41 back to Australia at their end, Fokker licence-built 155 for the Dutch and 150 for the Belgian air forces, and Avions Fairey assembled a further 30 from components supplied by Fokker and 37 from sets supplied by the parent company. Fighter-reconnaissance and pure reconnaissance versions were evolved as the FR Mk 9 and PR Mk 10. One hundred and twenty-six of the former were built for the RAF, of which 12 were subsequently supplied to Ecuador, seven to Israel and two to Syria, and the RAF also received 59 of the latter. Max speed, 598 mph (962 km/h) at

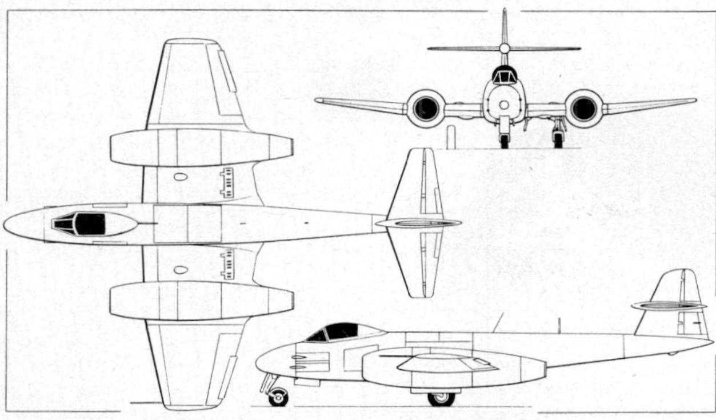

The definitive single-seat production model of the Meteor, the F Mk 8 (above and below) saw some combat flying with the RAAF over Korea in 1951-53.

10,000 ft (3 050 m). Range, 600 mls (965 km). Initial climb, 7,000 ft/min (35,56 m/sec). Empty weight, 10,684 lb (4 846 kg). Loaded weight, 15,700 lb (7 122 kg). Span, 37 ft 2 in (11,32 m). Length, 44 ft 7 in (13,59 m). Height, 13 ft 0 in (3,96 m). Wing area, 350 sq ft (32,51 m²).

GLOSTER E.1/44 — UK

Late in 1944, Gloster began construction of an all-metal single-seat fighter designed around a centrifugal-flow turbojet being developed by Rolls-Royce and to emerge as the Nene. To the requirements of specification E.1/44, the first prototype was completed in July 1947, but suffered irreparable damage when the vehicle transporting it to the A&AEE was involved in an accident. A second prototype was completed and flown on 9 March 1948, this being powered by a 5,000 lb (2 268 kg) Nene 2 turbojet and having provision for four 20-mm Hispano cannon. After initial flight testing the tail assembly was redesigned to improve handling. A third prototype was flown in 1949, and a fourth was nearing completion when it was

(Above) The third E.1/44 prototype which flew from the outset with the definitive tail, and (below) the second prototype with the original tail.

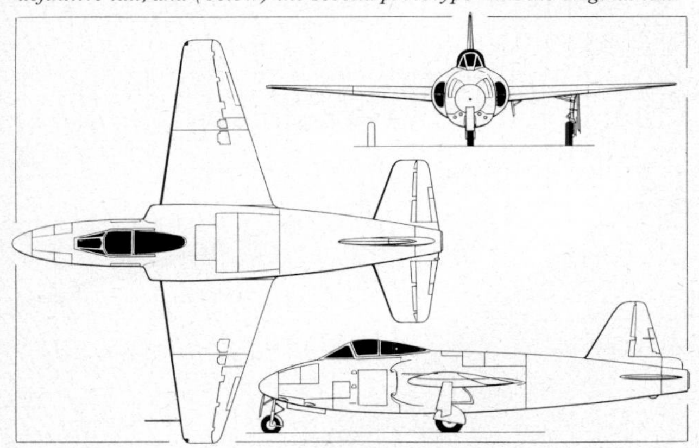

(Above) A Javelin F(AW) Mk 4, and (below) the Javelin F(AW) Mk 9 which featured limited reheat.

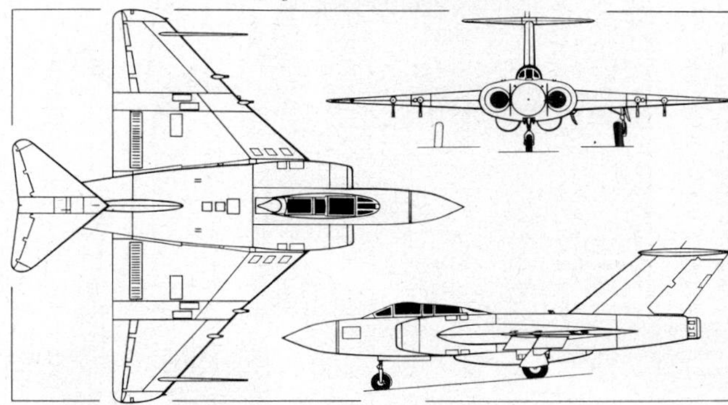

decided that the single-engined fighter lacked the development potential of the twin-engined Meteor, further work being discontinued. Max speed, 620 mph (998 km/h) at sea level. Endurance, 1 hr. Time to 40,000 ft (12 190 m), 12·5 min. Empty weight, 8,260 lb (3 747 kg). Loaded weight, 11,470 lb (5 203 kg). Span, 36 ft 0 in (10,97 m). Length, 38 ft 0 in (11,58 m). Height, 11 ft 8 in (3,55 m). Wing area, 254 sq ft (23,60 m²).

GLOSTER JAVELIN — UK

Designed to meet the requirements of specification F.4/48 for a two-seat twin-engined all-weather interceptor fighter, the Javelin was of tailed-delta configuration and the first of seven prototypes was flown on 26 November 1951. The initial production model, the Javelin F(AW) Mk 1, was flown on 22 July 1954, was powered by two 8,000 lb (3 628 kg) Armstrong Siddeley Sapphire ASSa 6 turbojets and carried an armament of four 30-mm Aden cannon. Forty F(AW) Mk 1s were followed by 30 F(AW) Mk 2s which differed essentially in having US (APQ 43) in place of British (AI 17) radar, the first example of this version flying on 31 October 1955. The next fighter version (paralleling production of 22 T Mk 3 trainers) was the F(AW) Mk 4, which, flown on 19 September 1955, differed in having a fully-powered all-moving tailplane, 50 being built. The F(AW) Mk 5 was similar apart from carrying additional fuel in the wings and having provision for four de Havilland Firestreak AAMs, 64 being built, together with 33 F(AW) Mk 6s which bore the same relationship to the Mk 5 as did the Mk 2 to the Mk 1 in that they were equipped with US radar. The F(AW) Mk 7 introduced 11,000 lb (4 990 kg) Sapphire ASSa 7 engines, a modified flying control system, an extended rear fuselage with raised topline, and other changes. Armament comprised two 30-mm Aden cannon and four Firestreak AAMs, and 142 were built. The final production version of the Javelin was the F(AW) Mk 8 with Sapphire ASSa 7R engines with limited reheat boosting output to 12,300 lb (5 579 kg) above 20,000 ft (6 095 m) and US radar. Forty-seven were built during 1957-59, and 76 of the earlier F(AW) Mk 7s were brought up to similar standard as F(AW) Mk 9s during 1960-61. The Javelin was finally withdrawn from RAF service in 1967. The following data relate to the definitive F(AW) Mk 8. Max speed, 701 mph (1 128 km/h) at sea level, 614 mph (988 km/h) at 35,000 ft (10 670 m). Time to 50,000 ft (15 240 m), 9·25 min. Loaded weight, 37,410 lb (16 969 kg). Span, 52 ft 0 in (15,85 m). Length, 56 ft 3 in (17,14 m). Height, 16 ft 0 in (4,88 m). Wing area, 927 sq ft (86,12 m²).

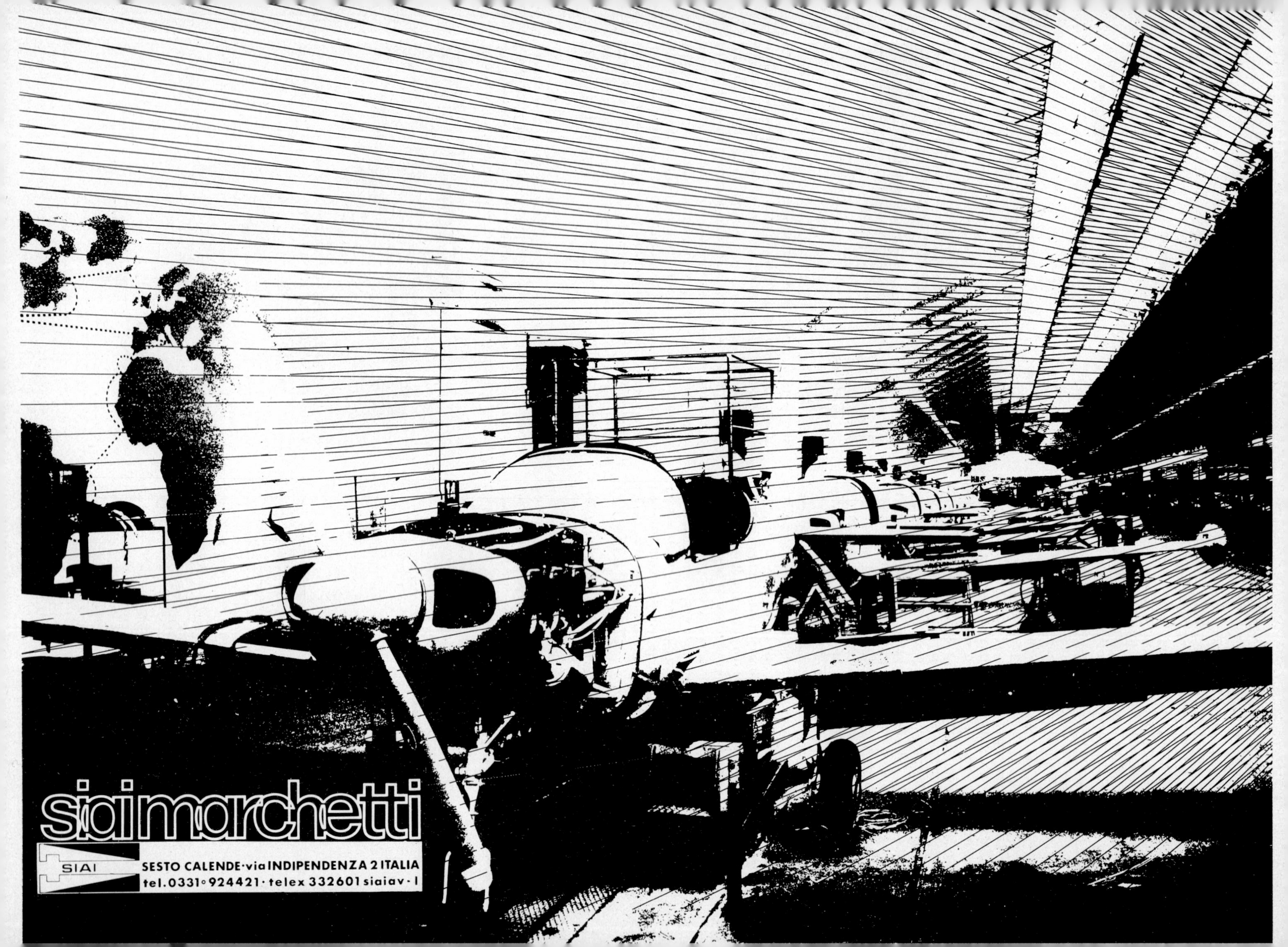
siaimarchetti
SIAI
SESTO CALENDE · via INDIPENDENZA 2 ITALIA
tel. 0331 ∘ 924421 · telex 332601 siaiav - I

ARGENTINA

FMA IA 63

LATEST ADDITION to the growing range of turbofan-powered two-seat basic-advanced trainers with a secondary light strike capability, the Fábrica Militar de Aviones (FMA) at Córdoba anticipates commencing cutting metal shortly on the tandem two-seat IA 63 conceived to meet the requirements of a *Fuerza Aérea Argentina* specification calling for a successor for the Morane-Saulnier Paris for service from 1985-86. Being developed in collaboration with Dornier — although according to recent statements from Brazil, that country, too, is likely to collaborate in the programme — the IA 63 is most closely comparable with the CASA C-101 Aviojet and is likely to be similarly powered by a Garrett AiResearch TFE 731 turbofan, although a definitive choice of engine had not been announced at the time of closing for press, and the Pratt & Whitney JT15D-4 and -5 were among other turbofans under consideration.

Embodying some equipment commonality with the IA 58 Pucará, the IA 63 bears the closest configurational resemblance to the forthcoming and notably smaller Siai-Marchetti S.211, and the FAéA requirement calls for a maximum take-off weight for the pilot training mission of 8,820 lb (4 000 kg) with a load factor of +7 *g* to −3 *g*, this reducing in external stores configuration to +4·5 *g* to −2 *g*, provision being made for a hardpoint in each wing to suit the aircraft for light weapons training and light strike rôles. Meeting MIL F-18 372 requirements and scheduled to commence its flight test programme late 1982 or early 1983, the IA 63 is believed to possess considerable export potential in Latin America and is considered to be an ideal complement to the AMEX (being developed jointly by Italy and Brazil in the same timescale). The FAéA requirement for this type for the pilot training rôle is estimated at 50-60 aircraft.

Power Plant: One turbofan in the 3,000-3,500 lb (1 360-1 590 kg) category.

Performance: (Estimated) Max speed, 460 mph (740 km/h); cruise, 404 mph (650 km/h) at 13,125 ft (4 000 m); limiting Mach number, M=0·8; max range (with external fuel), 920 mls (1 480 km) at 13,125 ft (4 000 m); take-off distance to clear 49 ft/15 m obstacle, 4,265 ft (1 300 m); landing distance from 49 ft (15 m), 4,265 ft (1 300 m).

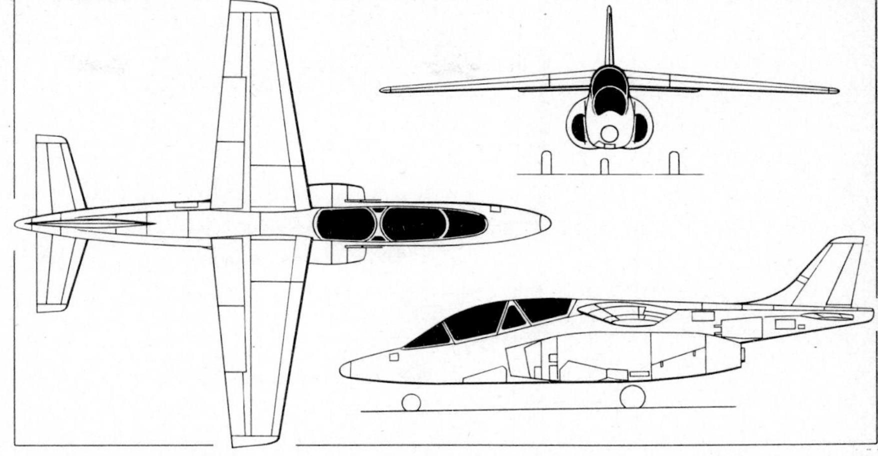

Three-view drawing of the IA 63 basic jet trainer projected by the Fabrica Militar de Aviones in Cordoba, Argentina.

Weights: Normal loaded (clean) for pilot training mission, 8,820 lb (4 000 kg).

Dimensions: Span, 31 ft 9 in (9,68 m). Length, 36 ft 10¾ in (11,25 m); height, 12 ft 0¼ in (3,67 m). Wing area, 206·46 sq ft (19,18 m²).

FEDERAL GERMANY

DORNIER 228

THE latest developments of the Dornier Do 28 Skyservant design (and originally designated Do 28E as members of that family), Dornier 228 prototypes are expected to fly early in 1981 and to make their public début at the Paris Air Show in June next year. Two prototypes are being built, one in Dornier 228-100 configuration and one as the Dornier 228-200 with a lengthened fuselage.

The Dornier 228 represents a considerable stretch of the original Do 28D-2 on which it is based, retaining little but the basic fuselage cross section and the general structural philosophy. Its most important new feature is the wing, which is Dornier's TNT (*Tragflügels Neuer Technologie* or new technology wing), a prototype of which was first flown on a converted Skyservant on 14 June 1979. Associated with this wing is the introduction of turboprop engines, mounted in wing nacelles in place of the piston engines previously carried on sponsons.

Models of the Dornier 228, latest derivative of the Skyservant family, show (left to right) the 228-100, the larger 228-200 and a 228-100 in military finish.

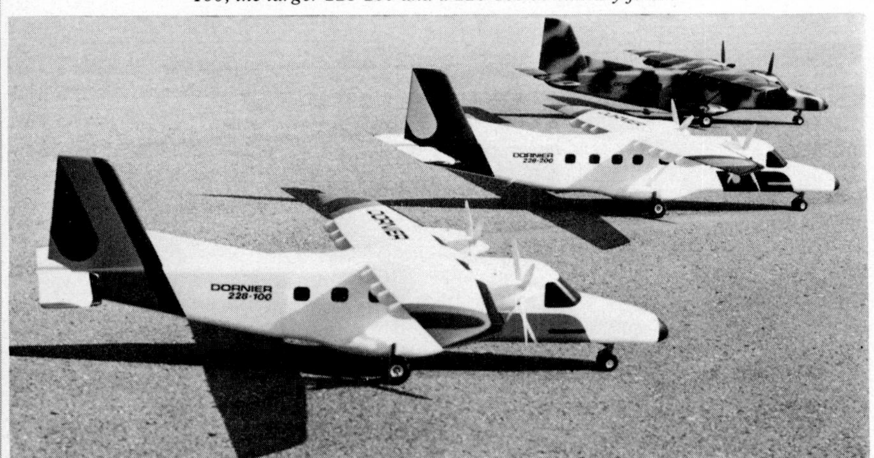

Compared with the Skyservant, both versions of the Dornier 228 have longer fuselages, the 228-200 itself being 5 ft (1,52 m) longer than the 228-100. As well as a lengthened cabin, which allows the 228-100 to carry seven more passengers than the Do 28D-2, the new fuselage features a longer and reprofiled nose. The tail unit remains largely identical with that of the Skyservant, apart from the use of a larger dorsal fin, but the undercarriage is completely new and is now retractable into fuselage-side fairings.

The Dornier A-5 aerofoil section used in the TNT wing is similar to the NASA-developed Whitcomb GA(W)-1 supercritical section, although not quite so thick or so "droopy" over the front 40 per cent of chord. The company claims that the section gives better lift/drag characteristics, especially in the take-off and initial climb, than the GA(W)-1 section and that as applied to a twin-engined aircraft such as the Dornier 228, offers performance improvements of up to 25 per cent compared with older, conventional aerofoils.

The Dornier 228 is designed to provide the basis for a family of related aircraft covering a wide variety of civil and military rôles. The basic 228-100 carries 15 passengers and the 228-200 provides 19 seats plus a larger rear baggage compartment; both versions incorporate the passenger/cargo double door that is a standard feature of the Skyservant and have a nose baggage compartment. All-cargo and mixed passenger/cargo versions will be available and executive interiors have been designed. Military and quasi-military rôles include maritime surveillance, observation/calibration, training, air ambulance, search-and-rescue and troop and supply dropping.

The following data are based on the use of Garrett TPE331 turboprops, which will power the prototypes, but the engine mounts are being designed to cater for installation of a range of alternative power plants. The aircraft is designed to the American FAR 23 and SFAR 41 requirements and will initially be certificated by the German (LBA) authorities, with US, UK, Australian and French certification following. Structural design is based on a service life of 30,000 flights without replacement of major structural parts.

Power Plant: Two Garrett AiResearch TPE 331-5 turboprops each rated at 715 shp for take-off, up to ISA+18 deg C, driving Hartzell four-bladed all-metal constant-speed fully-feathering and reversing propellers of 8 ft 11 in (2,73-m) diameter. Fuel capacity approxi-

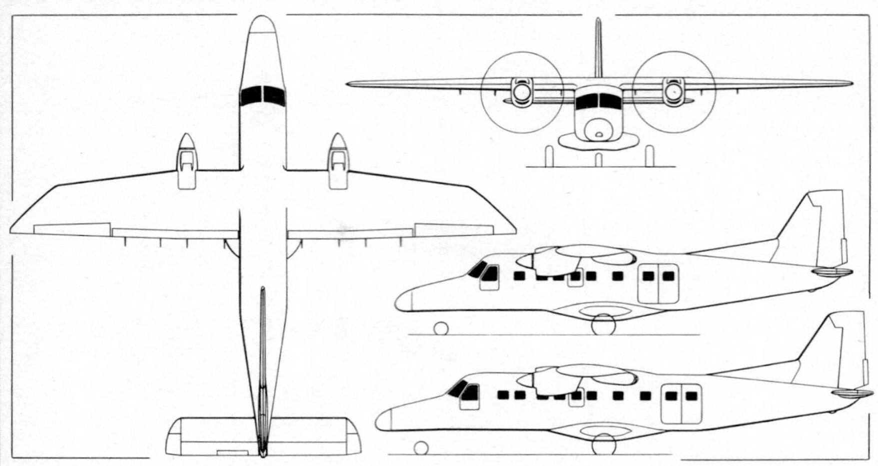

Three-view drawing of the Dornier 228-100 and additional side-view (bottom) of the 228-200.

mately 600 US gal (2 250 l) in two integral wing tanks.

Performance: Max cruising speed, 200 kt (370 km/h) at sea level, 233 kts (432 km/h) at 10,000 ft (3 050 m); max range cruise, 179 kts (332 km/h) at 10,000 ft (3 050 m); initial rate of climb, 2,050 ft/min (10,4 m/sec); single-engine climb rate, 530 ft/min (2,7 m/sec); service ceiling, 29,600 ft (9 020 m); single-engined ceiling, 14,000 ft (4 265 m); take-off distance to 50 ft (15,2 m), 1,720 ft (525 m); range with max passenger payload (228-100), 1,065 naut mls (1 970 km); range with max passenger payload (228-200), 620 naut mls (1 150 km); range at max cruise speed (228-100), 935 naut mls (1 730 km); range at max cruise speed (228-200), 555 naut mls (1 030 km).

Weights: Operating weight empty (IFR equipped, two pilots, passenger transport version), (228-100), 7,040 lb (3 193 kg), (228-200), 7,370 lb (3 343 kg); max payload (228-100), 4,870 lb (2 207 kg), (228-200), 4,540 lb (2 057 kg); max zero fuel weight (both versions), 11,900 lb (5 400 kg); max take-off weight (both versions), 12,570 lb (5 700 kg); max landing weight, 12,570 lb (5 700 kg).

Dimensions: Span, 55 ft 7 in (16,97 m); overall length (228-100), 49 ft 3 in (15,03 m), (228-200), 54 ft 3 in (16,55 m); overall height, 15 ft 9 in (4,86 m); wing area, 344 sq ft (32,0 m²); undercarriage track, 10 ft 8 in (3,30 m); wheelbase (228-100), 18 ft 1 in (5,53 m); (228-200), 20 ft 6 in (6,29 m).

Accommodation: Flight crew of two. Standard passenger version seats (228-100) 15 or (228-200) 19 in single seats each side of central aisle at 30-in (76-cm) pitch; cabin width, 4 ft 4 in (1,35 m) and height, 5 ft 1 in (1,55 m). Front baggage hold volume, 31 cu ft (0,88 m³); rear baggage hold volume (228-100), 32 cu ft (0,9 m³), (228-200), 80 cu ft (2,28 m³), each with separate external access door.

UNITED KINGDOM

SHORTS 360

A GROWTH VERSION of the Shorts 330 commuterliner offering a 20 per cent increase in passenger capacity and enhanced cruise performance, the Shorts 360 will differ from its progenitor primarily in having some 10 per cent more power, a 3-ft (91-cm) plug in the fuselage ahead of the wing, and an entirely redesigned and aesthetically more attractive rear fuselage and tail surfaces. Considered by the manufacturers to be complementary to the 330 rather than a successor, the 360 will be the end product of a programme estimated to involve a total of £15m in non-recurring costs and will enter flight test in the last quarter of next year, with certification scheduled for a year later. The manufacturers are confident that, at a unit price of $3m-$3·25m (as compared with about $2·7m for the smaller-capacity 330) in 1980 terms, the 360 will possess a significant first-cost advantage over the potential competition and will also benefit from at least a year's lead in the market, and is seeking sales of 275-350 aircraft over the remainder of the decade.

The most noteworthy design change featured by the Shorts 360 is the new rear end previously mentioned, which, now gracefully tapered with a swept single tail, in marked contrast to the characteristic "sawn off" appearance of the 330's rear fuselage with its angular twin fins and rudders, produces an important reduction in drag. Two additional seat rows raise capacity to 36 passengers and considerable importance has been attached to the provision of adequate baggage space, 6 cu ft (0,17 m³) being available per passenger, or 7·2 cu ft (0,204 m³) if the overhead lockers are included.

Power Plant: Two Pratt & Whitney (Canada) PT6A-65R turboprops each having a maximum rating of 1,294 shp and driving 9 ft 3 in (2,82 m) diam Hartzell five-blade low-speed propellers. Fuel in main tanks in wing centre section/fuselage fairing with total capacity of 480 Imp gal (2 182 l).

Performance: High speed cruise, 243 mph (391 km/h) at 10,000 ft (3 050 m); range (max passenger payload), 265 mls (426 km) at high speed cruise at 10,000 ft (3 050 m) with allowances for 100-mile (160-km) diversion and 45 min hold, (max fuel), 655 mls (1 054 km) same conditions; take-off distance (ISA sea level at MTOW), 4,330 ft (1 320 m), (ISA + 20°C sea level), 4,720 ft (1 439 m); landing distance (ISA sea level at MLW), 3,930 ft (1 198 m).

Weights: Operational empty, 16,490 lb (7 480 kg); max useful load, 9,210 lb (4 178 kg); passenger payload, 7,020 lb (3 184 kg); max take-off, 25,700 lb (11 657 kg); max landing, 25,400 lb (11 521 kg).

Dimensions: Span, 74 ft 8 in (22,75 m); length, 70 ft 6 in (21,49 m); height, 22 ft 7 in (6,88 m); wing area, 453 sq ft (42,08 m²); cabin length, 36 ft 2 in (11,02 m); cabin height, 6 ft 4 in (1,93 m); cabin width, 6 ft 4 in (1,93 m).

Accommodation: Crew of two on flight deck, plus cabin attendant. Standard seating for 36 passengers in 11 rows of two-plus-one, with wide aisle, and one row of three at rear of cabin. Baggage compartments in nose (45 cu ft/1,27 m³) and aft of cabin (170 cu ft/4,81 m³), plus overhead baggage lockers (45 cu ft/1,27 m³).

(Above) An artist's impression and (below) three-view drawing of the Shorts 360, latest derivative of the Shorts 330 commuterliner.

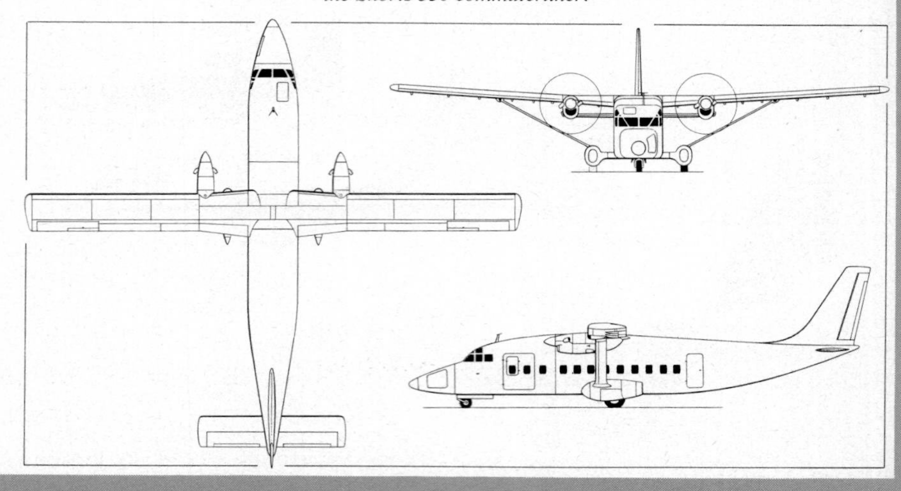

Volume 19 Number 4 October 1980

Editorial Offices:
The AIR INTERNATIONAL, PO Box 16, Bromley, BR2 7RB Kent.

Subscription, Advertising and Circulation Offices:
The AIR INTERNATIONAL, De Worde House, 283 Lonsdale Road, London SW13 9QW. Telephone 01-878 2454. US and Canadian readers may address subscriptions and general enquiries to AIR INTERNATIONAL PO Box 353, Whitestone, NY 11357 for onward transmission to the UK, from where all correspondence is answered and orders despatched.

MEMBER OF THE AUDIT BUREAU OF CIRCULATIONS ABC

Subscription rates, inclusive of postage, direct from the publishers, per year:

United Kingdom	£7·50
Overseas	£8·00
USA/Canada	$20·00

Rates for other countries and for air mail subscriptions available on request from the Subscription Department at the above address.

The AIR INTERNATIONAL is published monthly by Fine Scroll Limited, distributed by Ducimus Books Ltd and printed by William Caple & Company Ltd, Chevron Press, Leicester, England.

Second Class postage approved at New York, NY. USA Mailing Agents: Air-Sea Freight Inc, 527 Madison Avenue, New York, NY 10022.

ISSN 0306-5634

CONTENTS

FRONT COVER: Westland WG30 prototype helicopter demonstrating in the air mobility rôle, embarking troops.

WRENDEZVOUS WITH WREN

"I can't wait to see this chap's display."

AIRSCENE

MILITARY AFFAIRS

AUSTRALIA

The RAAF is seeking governmental approval and A$48m (£23·4m) funding for procurement and **conversion** to the tanker/transport rôle **of** three **ex-Qantas Boeing 707-338C** aircraft. It is estimated that the unit cost of the secondhand aircraft will be of the order of A$5m (£2·44m) but that the actual conversion, which is expected to be undertaken in Australia, will cost some A$12m (£5·85m) per aircraft.

At the time of closing for press, it was being unofficially suggested in Canberra that the definitive **choice in the TFF** (Tactical Fighter Force) **contest** between the F-16 Fighting Falcon and F-18 Hornet, scheduled to be announced this month (October) **may be deferred** until the end of the year in order to give the latter aircraft extra time in which to meet its specification. The F-18 has been widely reported as frontrunner in RAAF preference, but the F-16 has of late been gaining ground, in part as a result of its competitor's technical and budgetary problems, and in part owing to the 44 per cent industrial offsets being offered by General Dynamics which exceed by 14 per cent the Australian offset goal. The programme cost of the F-16 (covering 75 aircraft of which all but two would be assembled in Australia) is being unofficially quoted as A$858m (£419m) in 1980 terms as compared with A$1,372m (£699·5m) for the F-18.

The Australian **Defence Department** is currently **seeking** four General Dynamics **F-111s** from the USA **as attrition replacements** for the four RAAF F-111Cs lost as a result of accidents. The possibility of acquiring ex-USAF aircraft is currently in preliminary consideration stage and availability and cost have still to be ascertained. If aircraft are procured it is likely that they will be F-111As which differ in a number of major respects from the F-111Cs of the RAAF which were built specifically to Australian requirements. Of the 20 remaining F-111Cs, four are being adapted for the reconnaissance mission; the first was completed by GD last year.

The **RAAF** has announced that it **will finally retire** the Douglas **C-47** from its inventory on 30 June next year after just short of two score years of service. The RAAF has received a total of 138 C-47s in that time.

AUSTRIA

The *III.Hubschraubergeschwader* of the **Army Aviation Force** *(Heeresfliegerkräfte)* at Linz-Hörsching **has** now **relinquished** the last of its aged **AB 204B** helicopters and completed re-equipment with the AB 212, deliveries of 12 of which commenced in May. The second batch of 12 AB 212s ordered for the Army Aviation Force will re-equip the AB 204B *Hubschrauberstaffel* of the *I.Hubschraubergeschwader* at Tulln-Langenlebarn next year.

The **Army Aviation Force,** which was expected to announce the selection of a fighter in June with which to re-equip its Surveillance Wing, or *Überwachungsgeschwader,* **has** once **again deferred** a **decision** for a further six months at the behest of the Austrian government. According to the Finance Minister, Dr Hannes Androscit, budgetary considerations are unlikely to permit the actual placing of an order before 1982, by which time the contention and vacillation over Austrian fighter procurement will have lasted some 14 years.

CANADA

As a result of the **partial waiver** by the US government **of** the $878,000 (£370,465) **R&D levy on** each **CF-18 Hornet** for the Canadian Armed Forces, the latter are now expected to receive a total of 137 aircraft whereas the number would have been reduced to 129 had the full levy been imposed. The partial waiver is conditional upon Canada making an equal gesture on US imports. The reduced R&D levy will yield some $140m (£59m), which, combined with the long-term fixed-price contract negotiated with McDonnell Douglas, will probably result in the CAF paying a unit price well below that paid by the US Navy for its Hornets, but the preferential treatment accorded Canada has resulted in some objections in the US Congress in which some factions have pointed out that, on the basis of more recent estimates, a more realistic R&D levy would be $1·3m (£549,000) per aircraft.

FEDERAL GERMANY

The *Luftwaffe* is reportedly becoming increasingly **disenchanted with** the results of the tri-national industry **study** recommending joint development **of the TKF-90.** According to *Luftwaffe* chief-of-staff Gen Friedrich Obleser, his service takes the view that its requirements for a tactical fighter and those of the RAF and *Armée de l'Air* for a close air support aircraft "are too far apart to economically justify a joint project." The type of aircraft recommended by the tri-national industry study is too expensive for the *Luftwaffe,* according to Gen Obleser.

In an overall **progress report on Tornado,** Gen Obleser stated recently that 95 per cent of the development programme has now been completed and that pilot familiarisation time for conversion to the Tornado is estimated to average eight hours compared with 14 hours for the F-4F Phantom or F-104G Starfighter. The average transition time for *Luftwaffe* squadrons from the Phantom to the Tornado will be about nine months and during the transition the squadrons will be withdrawn from active operations. He added that the current production rate of 8-9 aircraft monthly is being raised to 12 aircraft, that the Tornado programme is on schedule and that the first of 112 Tornados for the *Marineflieger* will be introduced into service in 1982. According to the Federal German Ministry of Defence, the flyaway price of the Tornado has remained constant since 1976 — excluding inflation and exchange rate fluctuations — and at the end of last year, the flyaway cost based on 805 aircraft was DM35·26m (£8·64m). The first *Luftwaffe* instructor crew has completed training at MBB's Manching facility, and the first *Luftwaffe* Tornados were expected to begin arriving at the Tri-national Tornado Training Establishment at RAF Cottesmore last month (September). The ratio of maintenance man-hours to flying hours is already approaching the originally specified 33:1.

FINLAND

On 17 July, the **first batch of** six **MiG-21bis** *(Fishbed-N)* **fighters** to re-equip Hävllv 31, the combat component of the Karelia Wing, or *Karjalan Lennosto,* flew into Kuopio-Rissala to initiate replacement of the unit's aged clear-weather MiG-21F *(Fishbed-C)* fighters. Although the quantity of MiG-21bis fighters being procured for *Ilmavoimat* has not been revealed, late in 1977, when the decision to procure this third-generation MiG-21 was first revealed, the Defence Headquarters announced that up to 30 would be acquired. No programme cost has been announced.

The **first** of four British Aerospace **Hawk T Mk 51s** to be supplied from the UK for *Ilmavoimet* service was to be **delivered** last month (September) and the other three were to follow by the end of the year. Meanwhile, the first airframe for assembly by Valmet OY was despatched overland last July and should fly at Halli early in 1981; a total of 46 Hawk 51s is to be built by Valmet, primarily from UK components with a small content of locally-manufactured parts.

A **follow-on order for** five **Mil Mi-8** helicopters (see *Military Affairs*/July) has now been placed on behalf of *Ilmavoimat,* the total programme cost being reportedly some FMk 121m (£14m). Although *Ilmavoimat* is understood to have expressed a preference for one of the western contenders for the order (ie, Lynx, S-76 Spirit and SA 365N Dauphin 2), the service's choice was overruled by the government in favour of the Soviet helicopter.

INDIA

A **follow-on batch of** three **Sea King** Mk 42A ASW **helicopters** was recently delivered to the Indian Navy's Cochin NAS by Belfasts of TAC Heavy Lift. The three Sea Kings join in Indian Navy service the 11 survivors of 12 Sea King Mk 42s delivered in two batches of six in 1971 and 1973 to equip Nos 330 and 336 squadrons which deploy their helicopters to the carrier INS *Vikrant* and are home-based at Cochin. The Sea King Mk 42A differs from the earlier Mk 42 in having uprated engines and transmission, six-bladed tail rotors and Canadian Fairey Beartrap haul-down deck attachments to suit them for operation from *Leander* class frigates. The Indian Navy is reportedly considering the purchase of a further nine Sea Kings over the next three-four years.

Although the Indian government has dropped its option on a second batch of **Sea Harrier** FRS Mk 51s (see *Military Affairs*/September), Mrs Indira Gandhi has ordered a further **re-evaluation** of the aircraft to determine once and for all if it is the most suitable successor to the aged Sea Hawk aboard the INS *Vikrant,* or if, in view of the carrier's relatively limited remaining service life, any Sea Hawk replacement is required. It has been popularly supposed that the Sea Harrier is another of the victims of the game of denigrating decisions of the former Desai government, but a decision to procure Sea Harrier was, in fact, taken by the former government of Mrs Gandhi, initial procurement only being finalised and ratified by the succeeding government. One of the arguments used by the anti-Harrier lobby has been that, as ordered by the Indian government, the Sea Harrier is essentially a first-generation V/STOL aircraft whereas it is in the Indian Navy's interest to await availability of a second generation aircraft such as the AV-8B. However, an independent reappraisal of the Indian Navy's policy and prospects has indicated that, apart from funding problems, the *Vikrant* from which the Sea Harrier is intended to operate has only another five years or so of useful life remaining and a replacement is highly unlikely, rendering procurement of the shipboard V/STOL aircraft illogical.

INDONESIA

Following completion of deliveries to No 14 Sqdn of the TNI-AU (*Tentara Nasional Indonesia — Angkatan Udara,* or Indonesian Armed Forces — Air Force) in July of 12 F-5E Tiger IIs and four two-seat F-5Fs, it is being reported that a similar quantity of the **Northrop fighter** is now **likely to** be procured to **re-establish** a **naval** (TNI-AL) **combat aviation**

element, the service having been restricted to surveillance and SAR rôles since the withdrawal of its two MiG-19 and two MiG-21 squadrons as a result of the Soviet spares embargo. The prospective naval squadron for the F-5 is No 300 Sqdn previously equipped with the MiG-21.

Hawk trainers, scheduled to participate in the National Day flypast over Jakarta on the 5th of this month (October), will shortly **replace** the **T-33A** in service with the TNI-AU's No 11 Sqdn. The initial TNI-AU Hawk — the 126th from overall production but, in fact, the 140th to fly — made its first flight at Dunsfold on 6 June and was formally accepted at a ceremony at Dunsfold in July by the Indonesian ambassador, Mr Saleh Basarah. The first four of the eight Hawk T Mk 53s on order were flying out to Jakarta last month (September), staging by way of Malta, Cairo, Bahrein, Karachi, Bombay, Calcutta and Bangkok.

The first of eight British Aerospace Hawk T Mk 53s for Indonesia, seen on a pre-delivery test flight. As noted on this page, the first four Hawk T Mk 53s were being delivered during September.

INTERNATIONAL
The **training of** a total of 370 **crewmen to man** the **NATO** fleet of 18 Boeing **E-3A Sentry** AWACS aircraft **has** now **been initiated** at Tinker AFB, Oklahoma, and is scheduled to be completed in the autumn of 1982. The training courses at Tinker AFB vary from three to 55 weeks, according to the future assignment of the trainees. NATO is expected to take delivery of its first E-3As in the first or second quarter of 1982 at Geilenkirchen Air Base, Germany, where the entire fleet is to be based.

JAPAN
The Air Self-Defence Force anticipates requesting **funding of** some £5·9m in the Fiscal 1981 budget to initiate the development of the **MT-X,** a subsonic basic trainer to replace the T-33A and T-1. The ASDF hopes to complete development by Fiscal 1987 with a total development cost of about £67·5m. Mitsubishi, Kawasaki and Fuji are currently competing for the development contract.

PAPUA NEW GUINEA
The Australian Ministry of Defence has approved the sale of two **additional GAF Nomads** to the Papua New Guinea Air Force. To be delivered next year, the aircraft will join three Nomads provided by the Australian government in 1977-78. The estimated cost of the aircraft, support equipment, initial spares supplies and technical support for three years is £2m.

SAUDI ARABIA
Although no definitive response has yet been made by the Carter administration to the Saudi request for the supply of conformal fuel tanks and the necessary racks and release equipment for bombs and air-to-ground missiles with the F-15 Eagles to be supplied to the RSAF, it has been announced that two **additional F-15s** are to be sold to Saudi Arabia for $53m (£22·37m). These will be retained in the USA and delivered to replace any RSAF F-15 that may be lost or damaged beyond economical repair in order to maintain the fleet at its initial 60 aircraft strength level.

SOVIET UNION
It has now been confirmed that the Ilyushin **Il-76** *(Candid)* freighter airframe is **serving as** the basic **platform for** the new Soviet **Airborne Warning and Control System** (AWACS) which is expected to achieve initial operational capability 1984-85. The Il-76 AWACS aircraft, which will operate in conjunction with interceptors possessing look-down shoot-down capability, is expected to appear in substantial numbers during the second half of the present decade.

In recent months, the V-VS is reported to have deployed at least one and possibly two **regiments of Tu-22M** *Backfire-B* long-range strike **aircraft** to new airfields that have been built **close to** the **Chinese border.**

UNITED KINGDOM
RAF Chivenor was **re-activated** as a full-flying station at the beginning of August, with the arrival of six Hawk T Mk 1s to form the nucleus of No 2 Tactical Weapons Unit. The Hawks were drawn from No 63 Squadron, one of the three units previously making up the TWU at RAF Brawdy. Additional aircraft from this squadron will be joined early in 1981 by the Hawks of No 234 Squadron to make a total of about 50 at Chivenor, sufficient for three overlapping courses that will train some 60 students a year. A unique aspect of the courses at No 2 TWU will be that navigators as well as pilots will fly on training sorties to familiarise themselves with fast jet operations. Chivenor has been used only by a search-and-rescue flight of Whirlwinds since 1974, when the Hunters of No 229 OCU moved out.

USA
The US Navy has awarded six-month **study contracts** to six contenders **for the VTXTS** basic/advanced jet training system. The awards, made in late August, follow evaluation of nine proposals submitted in response to a US Navy request last March, and are made in respect of new twin-jet designs proposed by Northrop (teamed with Vought), Grumman (teamed with Beech) and McDonnell Douglas (teamed with British Aerospace), the Rockwell T-2X modernised version of the T-2C Buckeye, and the British Aerospace Hawk and Dassault-Breguet Alpha Jet. The two European manufacturers have made their submission jointly with McDonnell Douglas (Douglas Aircraft Co division, Long Beach) and Lockheed. Unsuccessful in this first phase of the VTXTS programme were new projects by General Dynamics (teamed with American Airlines) and Rockwell, and the Aermacchi MB 339.

AIRCRAFT AND INDUSTRY

AUSTRALIA
Ansett Airlines of Australia announced the selection of the General Electric **CF6-80A to power** its five **Boeing 767s,** delivery of which begins in October 1982, with two more in January 1983 and the last in July 1984.

BRAZIL
Following the recent presentation of a full-scale mock-up of the **EMB-120 Brasilia** at EMBRAER's International Operator's Meeting in Rio de Janeiro, the company has announced a number of **design changes** to meet the suggestions of potential customers. Among these changes will be an increase in the size of the baggage compartments from 180 to 240 cu ft (5,1-6,8 m³) with max load up from 882 lb to 1,323 lb (400-600 kg); pressurised rear baggage compartment also will be sealed off from the cabin and given its own external access door. The main landing gear will be extended aft, by lengthening the strut, to avoid CG penalties due to the increased baggage weight, and all passenger seats will be moved forward slightly to reduce the forward CG limit from 6 per cent to 4 per cent. EMBRAER also will eliminate the recessed centre aisle to obtain a flat floor surface, for easier conversion to cargo configuration; to accommodate this change without reducing cabin height, the cabin cross section will be increased by 3 in (7,6 cm) to 7 ft 6 in (2,29 m).

As scheduled at the time the contract for prototypes was signed on 6 December 1978, the EMBRAER **EMB-312** basic trainer made its **first flight** at São Paulo on 19 August. The fully-aerobatic EMB-312 basic trainer (see AIR INTERNATIONAL/June 1980) is destined for service with the *Fôrça Aérea Brasileira* as the T-27 and deliveries to the *Academia da Fôrça Aérea* (Air Force Academy) at Pirassununga, São Paulo, will begin in the second half of 1982. Powered by a flat-rated 750 shp Pratt & Whitney PT6A-25C turboprop, the T-27 has four wing hardpoints to carry up to 1,235 lb (560 kg) of external stores.

CANADA
Certification of the Canadair **Challenger** was granted by the Canadian Transport Department on 11 August, 22 months after first flight (on 8 November 1978). More than 1,500 hrs were completed in over 800 flights up to certification, and five aircraft were ready for immediate delivery; the production rate is now building from two-three a month to a maximum of seven a month by late 1981 against a backlog of 128 firm orders for the standard aircraft and 40 orders and deposits for the Challenger E and standard Challenger with GE engines. Deliveries of the last-mentioned will begin in first half of 1983 and of the Challenger E a year later, at current prices of US$7·8m and $8·9m, compared with $7m for the Avco-Lycoming ALF 502L version ordered today for delivery in mid-1982.

CHINA
Four 475 shp Pratt & Whitney **PT6A-10 turboprops** are being delivered by the Canadian company to the China National Aero-Technology Import and Export Corporation and will be used **to power** two prototypes of the **Y-11T** light transport. The Y-11T is a development of the piston-engined Y-11, some 15 examples of which have now been built at the Harbin aircraft factory. In addition to having improved performance, the Y-11T will feature an enlarged cabin to carry 16 passengers or a payload of 3,300 lb (1 500 kg). First flight is expected before the end of 1981.

FRANCE
As briefly noted last month, the Aerospatiale **SA 366N Dauphin** helicopters ordered by the US Coast Guard has been **designated HH-65A** and named **Dolphin.** The first of 90 Dolphins ordered in June 1979 made its first flight at Marignane on 23 July and is to be delivered to the US later this year for final fitting of equipment, including avionics. Most of 1981 will be required for flight testing and FAA

With financial backing from the National Research Development Corporation, NDN Aircraft Ltd has embarked upon its second new aircraft project, the NDN 6 Fieldmaster. Powered by a 750 shp Pratt & Whitney PT6A-34AG turboprop, the Fieldmaster is an agricultural aeroplane at the top end of the size range, with a number of novel features. The prototype is expected to fly in mid-1981; full details will appear in our next issue.

certification in the USA, with the first delivery to the USCG next October.

INDONESIA

With effect from aircraft No 29, **Nurtanio** has switched from **production of** the **Aviocar** NC-210 Srs 100 to the **Srs 200.** With uprated TPE 331-10-5-1C turboprops, the Aviocar 200 has a number of new features and refinements based on experience gained with the early production Srs 100s. In addition, the Srs 200 has been certificated to carry up to 28 passengers, compared with a maximum of 19 in the Srs 100. This is achieved by using a four-abreast layout at a pitch of 30 in (76 cm), and introducing an additional emergency exit at the rear of the cabin, starboard side. Two seats, at the rear of the cabin to port, ahead of the rear entrance door, are rearwards-facing and two at the front of the cabin, also to port, can be replaced by a small toilet compartment. Nurtanio has also announced that the US operator Federal Express has indicated that it will option 50 of the CN-235 short-haul transports under joint development by CASA and Nurtanio.

ITALY

Four AerMacchi **MB 339A** basic/advanced jet trainers have recently **completed** an **intensive flying trial** at the Official Test Centre *(Reparto Sperimentale di Volo)* of the AMI at Pratica di Mare. In eight months, a total of 1,470 hrs was flown, simulating about 3,000 hrs in typical training squadron use with 4,200 landings. The lead aircraft completed 535 hrs of testing and 60 hrs on demonstration and ferry flights in the period.

General Electric Co has signed an agreement with **Alfa Romeo** in Italy covering a licence **manufacturing** and technical assistance programme for **the T700** turboshaft (subject to US and Italian government approval). The T700, which powers the Sikorsky UH-60 and SH-60, the Hughes AH-64 and the Bell 214ST, is a candidate for application in the Westland/Agusta EH-101 anti-submarine helicopter and has already been selected to power the Westland WG34A prototypes.

JAPAN

Mitsubishi is intensifying its marketing efforts in Europe with the appointment of a **distributor** for the MU-2 Marquise and Solitaire and MU-300 Diamond **in the UK.** Business Aviation Consultants Ltd of Guernsey has become distributor for the UK, Eire, the Channel Islands and Gibraltar, and will use its sales organisation Colt Aviation, based at Staverton Airport, Cheltenham. The company made a first appearance at the Farnborough Air Show last month.

TAIWAN

The first prototype of the **XAT-3** basic trainer powered by two Garrett AiResearch TFE731 turbofans was scheduled **to commence** its **flight test** programme in August. Designed and built by the Aero Industry Development Centre at Taichung, the XAT-3 has been developed with consultancy assistance from the Northrop Corporation. The XAT-3 is similar in configuration and general appearance to the design proposed to the US Navy by Northrop to meet the service's VTXTS requirement.

UNITED KINGDOM

Rapid **progress with** flight testing of the Panavia **Tornado F Mk 2** has been aided by the aircraft's excellent handling characteristics throughout the flight envelope and the ADV prototype 01 has now covered virtually the whole of the flight envelope previously cleared for the IDS version, the Tornado GR Mk 1. This includes clearance to 800 kts (1 482 km/h) indicated airspeed, as achieved by the earlier Tornado version in 1979. The Flight Test department at Warton has reported that testing of the ADV Tornado to date has shown better-than-predicted results in supersonic acceleration (especially in the transonic phase), in stick force per *g*, in directional stability and in rudder and taileron effectiveness. These bonus points all contribute to the manoeuvrability, ease of handling and fighting capability of the Tornado F Mk 2.

Pilatus Britten-Norman has added a **turboprop version of** the **Islander** to its range, with the first flight of the BN-2T at Bembridge on 2 August. The new variant is powered by 320 shp Allison 250-B17C turboprops, and replaces the earlier Turbine Islander proposal by Fairey Britten-Norman, which used 400 shp Lycoming LTP101s and first flew on 6 April 1977. The BN-2T was among the Pilatus Britten-Norman exhibits at Farnborough last month (September), in Maritime Defender configuration, but it has been developed for commercial use as "a quick response to the world-wide deteriorating Avgas fuel supply situation". Deliveries will start early in 1981.

British Caledonian has selected the General Electric **CF6-80A1** engines **to power** its fleet of Airbus **A310s** and has ordered 16 engines to power three A310s on firm order and three on option, with four spares. Delivery of the A310s is scheduled for 1984, for use on the B.Cal routes to West and North Africa and within Europe.

Aircraft Designs (Bembridge) Ltd announced during August that construction of the prototype **Sheriff** light twin has now started, with the **first metal cut.** First flight is expected during 1981 and the company still hopes to market the "minimum twin" at a cost of about £35,000, of which the total material cost is no more than £8,000. The prototype will be built on the Isle of Wight but production will probably take place outside the UK to minimise labour costs.

A further stage in construction of the first **BAe 146** feederjet (see AIR INTERNATIONAL/September 1980) was reached in mid-August when the first set of **production wings** from Avco Aerostructures in Nashville was **delivered** to Hatfield. The wings (in two pieces, to be joined at the centre section which is built integrally with the centre fuselage) are trucked from Nashville to New York and then flown across the Atlantic by Boeing 747F freighters (Seaboard World in the first case). Also received at Hatfield in August was the first rear fuselage from BAe's Manchester Division.

Vickers-Slingsby is now in **production** with a batch **of** 25 **Venture T Mk 3** motorised gliders for Air Cadets' use, ordered to supplement the 15 Mk 2s previously delivered. The Venture is a British production version of the Scheibe Motor-Falke and the T Mk 3 version differs in having an electric self-starting system. A converted T Mk 2 made the first flight with this system on 3 February 1979 and the first production T Mk 3 (Slingsby T-61F) flew on 4 October 1979, with deliveries to the Gliding Schools starting earlier this year. **Vickers-Slingsby** also has recently signed (on 26 June) an agreement with Fournier Aviation permitting it **to build** in the UK a new version of the **RF-6B** with a 120 hp engine and wheel spats.

USA

Modifications to the McDonnell Douglas F-18 Hornet wing to raise roll rate to specification are now expected **to add four-five months to** the **test programme** and delay achievement of initial operational capability until at least December 1982. Roll rate with the existing wing at M = 0·9 at 10,000 ft (3 050 m) is 80 deg/sec below that specified. Wing modifications include increases in the torsional stiffness of the inner and outer wings, the strengthening of the trailing-edge box and the extension of the ailerons to the wingtips; they are expected to add 142 lb (64,5 kg) to the structural weight. The redesigned wing will be incorporated on the Hornet production line with effect from the No 17 F-18; aircraft Nos 15 and 16 will have the modification applied out of sequence and Nos 10-14 are being retrofitted.

Boeing Vertol announced the **first flight of** the Model 234 **Commercial Chinook** on 20 August at Eddystone, Philadelphia. The flight lasted 30 minutes and the aircraft is one of six ordered by British Airways Helicopters for delivery in mid-1981 onwards. Two more will enter the flight test and certification programme this year.

Lockheed-Georgia has received a USAF contract worth $68m to start the production of **new wing torsion boxes for** retrofit to 77 **C-5A** Galaxy transports in MAC service. Award of the contract coincided with the start on 14 August of a 55-flight test programme using one of the two sets of wings built for test and evaluation; the other set has completed the first of two simulated 30,000-hr fatigue tests. The first of the production conversions will be delivered from Marietta in mid-1982 and by mid-1983 the programme will handle three C-5As every two months until completion in July 1987.

The **fifth** and last Sikorsky **YSH-60B Seahawk** prototype made its **first flight** at Stratford, Conn, on 14 July, by which time the other four aircraft had completed nearly 300 hrs of flight testing. The No 1 YSH-60B was then in the hands of the Naval Air Test Center (NATC) at Patuxent River, Md; No 2 was in flight qualification testing at Sikorsky's West Palm Beach facility; No 3 was being used for avionics qualification tests by IBM Federal Systems Division at Owego, NY, and No 4 was about to be delivered to NATC.

Bell Helicopter has delivered the **second XV-15** tilt-rotor research aircraft **to** NASA's **Dryden**

Flight Research Center at Edwards AFB, following completion of the contractor portion of flight trials. The first XV-15 is already at Ames Research Center, Mountain View, Calif. In the course of the next year or so, the aircraft at Dryden will be used to expand the performance envelope and the aircraft at Ames will then undertake specific research tasks within the limits established. The two XV-15s have so far totalled 278 hrs of testing, of which 60 hrs were in flight (almost all on the second aircraft). More than 100 conversions have been made in flight from helicopter to aircraft mode and *vice versa*. A maximum speed of 346 mph (557 km/h) has been achieved at 16,000 ft (4 877 m).

Pratt & Whitney has reached a further stage in the application of its JT9D turbofan with the **introduction** into service **of** the **JT9D-7Q3** rated at 53,000 lb st (24 040 kgp). Now in use in the most recent Boeing 747-200 to join the Iberia fleet, the -7Q3 is the highest-rated commercial jet in operation. It incorporates the gas-path components of the -59A/70A version of the JT9D together with the external configuration of the -7, permitting installation in the current 747-200 nacelle. The result is a combination of increased performance, reduced aircraft drag and lowered propulsion system weight which significantly improves the performance of the Boeing 747. Pratt & Whitney has also announced **certification of** the 56,000 lb st (25 400 kgp) **JT9D-59D and JT9D-7Q2,** the most powerful turbofans currently available for commercial use.

General Electric has received a USAF contract to start **full-scale development of** its **GEPOD 30** lightweight gun pod containing the 30-mm GE-430 four-barrel cannon and 350 rounds. The gun is derived from the GAU-8/A weapon used in the Fairchild A-10, and can use the whole range of ammunition fired by that gun. The GEPOD 30 has a rate of fire of 2,400 rpm and weighs 1,800 lb (816 kg) fully loaded. Two prototype GEPOD 30s have been built by GE's Aircraft Equipment Division under a company-funded programme and have been flight tested against ground targets on the Northrop F-5E, Vought A-7D and YA-7E, and McDonnell Douglas F-4E. The USAF contract provides for the two prototype pods to be refurbished and four more to be built, and includes provision for long lead funding for 60 production units. The USAF has a long-term requirement for 520 GEPOD 30s.

Deliveries of the General Dynamics **F-16** passed the 200 mark in mid-July when the 128th Fighting Falcon (an F-16B) was accepted by the USAF for service at MacDill AFB. The balance of 72 F-16A/Bs are in service with the Belgian, Danish, Dutch, Norwegian and Israeli air forces.

Production of the Rockwell **Sabreliner 65** appears likely to suffer an **interruption** in 1982, with the possibility that production will not be continued in its present form beyond that date. By the end of 1981, Rockwell will have built 75 Sabreliner 65s, but will then have to vacate the El Segundo plant (adjacent to Los Angeles International Airport and owned by Northrop) where wings and fuselages are built at present, for final assembly at Perryville, Mo. The need to relocate production plus an unexpected increase in the lead-time on some bought-out parts will impose a gap of at least nine months on the production sequence, and Rockwell is investigating several alternatives including introduction of an improved Sabreliner 65A, termination of the programme and continuation of the Sabreliner 65 in its present form. All but four of the 75 aircraft to be built at El Segundo have been sold.

Piper **delivered** the **500th Cheyenne** turboprop twin on 13 August, six years after the type was first introduced. The milestone aircraft was a Cheyenne I but the total includes the more powerful, higher performance Cheyenne II (which is the current designation of the original model in the series) and the larger Cheyenne III, deliveries of which began on 30 June this year. Piper says that its current order-book for the Cheyenne III is worth $75m and covers production a year ahead.

First flight of the first production Learjet **Longhorn 50** series was made on 11 August at Tucson, Arizona. Two prototypes had then completed 435 hrs of flight testing and certification is expected around the end of the year. The first 20 production Longhorn 50s are in various stages of assembly.

Certification of the Swearingen **Metro IIA** under the FAA's new Special Federal Aviation Regulation (SFAR) 41 for commuter aircraft to operate at weights above 12,500 lb (5 670 kg) is an industry first. The Metro IIA is the new variant of the 19-passenger Metro II, certificated at 13,100 lb (5 942 kg) with a further increase to 13,230 lb (6 000 kg) expected before year-end. More than 200 Metro IIs are now in service or on order for 24 US airlines and 18 operators elsewhere in the world.

Bellanca Aircraft appeared to have lost its long struggle to remain solvent with the announcement on 24 July that the Alexandria Bank and Trust Company was taking immediate action to foreclose on the company's mortgage as it was **in default** on its obligations in respect of loans exceeding $3·2m. The company has filed for protection under US Federal laws that allow a margin of time for reorganisation before bankruptcy becomes final. Production of the Eagle agricultural biplane, which is handled by Bellanca under a separately-funded arrangement, is continuing, but all production work on Bellanca's own products has ended; during July, deliveries were continuing of aircraft already completed, including the second production T-250 Aries.

Shown publicly for the first time at Farnborough last month, the single-seat derivative of the tandem-seat MB-339 trainer (right) is known as the MB-339K Veltro (Greyhound) 2, perpetuating the name of the wartime MC-205V single-seat fighter, perhaps the most efficacious of Italian warplanes of WW II. The Veltro 2 light close-support aircraft has two 30-mm DEFA cannon and can carry up to 4,000 lb (1 815 kg) of ordnance on six wing pylons.

A successful flight over a distance of 2 mls (3,2 km) was made on 7 August at Edwards AFB by the **solar-powered Gossamer Penguin,** a development of Dr Paul MacCready's man-powered Gossamer Albatross. Although not the first solar-powered flight, this appears to be the most successful to date and the Gossamer Penguin is the first to use a system of direct power from the solar cells mounted above the centre section, without intermediate batteries. The pilot on this occasion was Janice Brown, a qualified glider pilot. A further development by Dr MacCready is the Solar Challenger, which will be of more conventional tractor aeroplane configuration than the Gossamer Penguin, having a span and length of 42 ft (12,8 m) and 32 ft (9,75 m) respectively, a weight of 60 lb (27,2 kg) empty and 215 lb (97,5 kg) loaded, including 50 lb (22,7 kg) for the 30,000 miniature photo-electric cells on the wing and tail surfaces. The Solar Challenger is expected to be able to fly at up to 40 mph (64 km/h) for distances of up to 100 mls (161 km) on solar power alone and to have reasonable performance as a glider.

CIVIL AFFAIRS

FEDERAL GERMANY

Through its extensive use of **helicopters,** the ADAC service in Federal Germany now provides emergency facilities **for road accident casualties** within reach of 70 per cent of the population. The helicopter fleet has recently been increased to 18 for the *Katastrophenschutz* (emergency rescue service operated by ADAC) with the leasing of a BO 105 named *Christoph* 18; in addition, five helicopters of the German Army and three private aircraft are available when needed. During September, ADAC organised an Aeromedical Evacuation Congress, attended by more than 500 medical experts, engineers, doctors and government agency representatives from 42 countries; this congress would, it was hoped, help to encourage the wider use of helicopters to assist in road accidents in other countries.

FRANCE

The GIFAS has announced that the **dates of** the next **Paris Air Show** (the 34th) will be Thursday 4 June to Sunday 14 June 1981. The first day will be reserved for the press and there will be no public admittance on 5, 9, 11 and 12 June.

INTERNATIONAL

The long-standing objective of creating a **joint Arab airline** to operate transatlantic services appears to be nearing fulfilment and flights to and from New York could begin next spring. Initial members of the consortium are likely to be Jordan (Alia), Kuwait (Kuwait Airways), Saudi Arabia (Saudia), Lebanon (MEA), and the United Arab Emirates (Gulf Air), with the possibility that Iraq will also join in. Participating airlines will contribute equipment purchased to a common specification; the consortium will not buy aircraft or ground equipment in its own right, but the services will be operated under a common name – possibly Arabair.

ITALY

For use at its flight training centre, **Alitalia** has **ordered** four Siai Marchetti **SF-260s and** two Piaggio **P166-DL3** turboprop twins.

UNITED KINGDOM

British Airways recorded a **pre-tax profit** of £20m in the year ended 31 March 1980, compared with £90m in the previous year. Profit after tax and dividend payments was £4m, down from £62m in 1978/79. The target set by the government of a six per cent return in real terms was not met, but a net dividend of £7m was paid on the Public Dividend capital of

£160m. Although the airline achieved its original revenue expectations, costs increased at a higher rate than anticipated and the cost of fuel proved to be the highest single adverse factor with the airline's total fuel bill going up by 72 per cent from £240m to £413m.

Coinciding with celebrations to mark the 50th anniversary of Gatwick airport, the **first British Caledonian service to Hong Kong** departed on 1 August. The airline is the third to operate the London-Hong Kong route, joining British Airways and Cathay Pacific; the application by Laker Airways awaited approval by the Hong Kong Licensing Authority at the time of going to press. B.Cal inaugurated its service with its newly-delivered sixth DC-10 Srs 30, named *Robert the Bruce, The Scottish Warrior,* in a three-class layout with 23 first-class Skylounger seats, 54 executive class and 172 economy class. Fares ranging from £99 (one-way, stand-by) to £1,100 (one-way, first class, Skylounger) are offered by B.Cal, which is operating four services a week, by way of Dubai in each direction.

B.Cal has brought forward the **launching** date for its **London-Dallas service** from next Spring to 26 October. Effective from that date, four flights a week are being flown as an extension of the service to and from St Louis. The change of plan is a consequence of the restrictions imposed upon the frequency of B.Cal's Hong Kong service, which it had planned as a daily operation. The reduction of this service to four times a week as a result of the "open skies" policy that allows Cathay Pacific to serve the route also, has left B.Cal's seventh and last DC-10 Srs 30 (delivered early October) uncommitted. This aircraft will now replace the Boeing 707 on the London-St Louis route, with the Dallas extension.

USA

Western Airlines has been **designated** as the US operator **for Denver-London and Anchorage-London** routes. On the latter, it will compete with British Airways but on the Denver route it will be the sole operator for three years, under the terms of the revised Bermuda Two air services agreement. After three years, B.Cal will be allowed to serve the Denver route also. Western is the 13th airline licensed to operate scheduled services between the UK and the USA, joining three British, six US and three foreign operators. It has not yet announced starting dates for the new services and in view of the current business recession and other difficulties it may be reluctant to start at present. Under US regulations, Continental Air Lines and Northwest Orient have been named as the back-up companies for the Denver and Anchorage routes respectively, and will assume the licences if Western does not start the services in due time.

Pan American is adopting a new system for **naming its aircraft,** all of which bear Clipper names in keeping with the airline's tradition dating from 1931. With immediate effect, the Clipper names are to have a common theme for each aircraft type in the fleet; the only exception will be the Boeing 707s and DC-10 Srs 30s at present in the fleet, as these are being phased out or sold. The themes for the other types are as follows: Boeing 747-100, seas or oceans; 747SP, patriotic names; 747F, commercial names; TriStar 500, birds; DC-10 Srs 10, celestial names; Boeing 727-200, action names and 727-100, people categories. All Pan American Clippers bear genuine Clipper Ship names, with the sole exception of Clipper Lindbergh, named to honour the aviation pioneer.

Pan American will resume **services to Paris** from New York on 1 April next when it introduces a daily service between Kennedy and Orly Airports, using Lockheed L-1011-500 TriStars. The airline suspended its Paris service five years ago as part of a rationalisation of transatlantic services offered by Pan Am and TWA.

A year after the CAB rejected plans for a **merger between Continental** Air Lines **and Western** Airlines, the two companies have again drawn up proposals with a view to merging. The effects of deregulation and the current business recession on the US airline industry are thought to have made it likely that the CAB would now take a different view of merger proposals.

CIVIL CONTRACTS AND SALES

Aérospatiale Caravelle: Air Inter has purchased from Sterling Airways the latter company's last five Caravelle XIIs, to join seven already in Air Inter service. One will be delivered at the end of 1980, one late in 1981, one early in 1982, one early in 1983 and the last late in 1983.

Boeing 727: Air France ordered one additional 727-200. ☐ VASP of Brazil has leased two 727-200s from Interlease for two years; the aircraft are ex-Singapore Airlines. ☐ Braniff sold 15 of its older 727-200s to American Airlines, for delivery by next January. ☐ Air Canada ordered three -200s for February/June 1982 delivery.

Boeing 737: Tunis Air has ordered two more 737-200s, for delivery in April and June 1981. ☐ Fiji-based Air Pacific is leasing one 737 from Air New Zealand until 31 October 1981. ☐ Interlease acquired two 737s from Western and sold one to the Government of Mexico as a presidential transport and the other to a Far East airline. ☐ C P Air ordered six more 737s, for delivery between June 1981 and June 1982; all are to be the latest high gross weight version.

Boeing 747: Recent orders confirmed by Boeing are from Air France for one and from UTA for two. ☐ Japan Air Lines announced it will order two 747s subject to government approval, in continuation of its fleet modernisation. ☐ Aerolineas Argentinas has acquired the 747SP that was delivered new to Braniff in October 1979.

Boeing 757: Eastern Air Lines has again re-ordered the 757 by increasing its firm order by four to 27, in addition to 24 on option. They take the place of four 727s previously ordered by Eastern, and will be delivered in late 1984. ☐ Boeing has now confirmed the order from Transbrasil (this column/June 1980) for five 757s, with GE CF6-32 engines. Deliveries start in 1983.

British Aerospace 748: Air Illinois has ordered a second 748, a Srs 2B, for December delivery and has taken options on three more for delivery 1982-1984. Under recently-completed arrangements, Aero Spacelines of Goleta, Calif, will complete 748s for delivery in the USA; the first will be the new aircraft for Air Illinois.

Canadair CL-44: Redcoat Air Cargo has acquired one CL-44, previously operated by British Cargo Airlines, to add to its fleet of two Britannias.

Convair 440: Nor-Fly Charter sold one CV-440 to Gulf Air Transport of Louisiana.

Dassault-Breguet Falcon 20: Recent orders include a contract from the Government of Indonesia for one aircraft for electronic calibration. Operated by the Civil Aviation Department, it will be fitted with an IR tracking system.

Dassault-Breguet Falcon 50: HM the King of Morocco has ordered one Falcon 50 for his personal use. The Fiat Company in Italy is also among customers for the business trijet.

EMBRAER EMB-110 Bandeirante: Tennessee Airways has acquired two EMB-110P1s for commuter service in the Tennessee, Kentucky and North Carolina area. ☐ Eagle Airways took delivery of the first Bandeirante, an EMB-110P1; it is the first in New Zealand.

EMBRAER EMB-120 Brasilia: Included in the total of over 50 options and letters of intent, are six for AeroMech, five for Imperial Airlines and three for Air Midwest.

McDonnell Douglas DC-10: JAL announced on 15 August that it would order two more Srs 40s, for late 1981/early 1982 delivery. With JT9D-59A turbofans rated at 53,000 lb st (24 040 kgp), they will bring the JAL DC-10 fleet to 19.

Pilatus Britten-Norman Islander: The Mexican government ordered 15 Islanders to serve as freight carriers in underdeveloped areas.

Shorts 330: LAPA, operating domestic services from Buenos Aires, has two 330s on order, in addition to three YS-11s in service and two BAC One-Elevens to be delivered soon for use pending the arrival in 1982 of the first BAe 146s.

Sikorsky S-76 Spirit: Sales rose to a total of 371 for 85 operators in 23 countries. On 31 July, Sikorsky delivered the 76th S-76 to Petroleum Helicopters of New Orleans — the second of 11 ordered by PHI for offshore oil duties.

MILITARY CONTRACTS

Agusta Bell AB 205 Iroquois: The Zambian Air Force is currently taking delivery of an unspecified number of AB 205 helicopters to supplement six of this type procured in the early and mid-'seventies.

Bell AH-1S Cobra: The US Army has placed an order for 12 AH-1S Cobra helicopters with Bell Helicopter Textron on behalf of the National Guard with deliveries scheduled to commence in April. Initial funding for the contract, which includes related support equipment, totals $8,429,419 (£3·558m).

Bell UH-1N Iroquois: Bell Helicopter Textron has received a $7,387,500 (£3·118m) contract for the supply to the Tunisian government of six "Bell 205A-1 commercial utility helicopters". The contract, which is being administered by the US Army Troop Support and Readiness Command, in fact covers UH-1N Iroquois military helicopters for the Tunisian armed forces which are being supplied as part of an arms aid package.

GAF Nomad: The Papua New Guinea Defence Force is to receive two additional Nomad utility aircraft under a £2m contract which includes support equipment, spares supplies and technical support for three years, deliveries being scheduled for next year.

Lockheed C-130H Hercules: A single C-130H Hercules has been purchased for the Tunisian Republican Air Force, the contract value, including support equipment and spares, being approximately $24m (£10·17m).

Mil Mi-8: Five Mi-8 medium-lift helicopters have been ordered for the Finnish Air Force under a £14m contract.

VC 10 Transport to Tanker

ARMIES, it has been said, march on their stomachs. By a similar analogy, fighting air forces of the 'eighties might be said to depend for their military effectiveness upon their air refuelling tankers. Not every air force, it is true, has operational requirements that call for the use of tanker aircraft, but among the world's major exponents of air power, the USA, the Soviet Union, the UK, France and Canada would all be hard pressed to fulfil their military commitments without these "filling stations in the sky".

So far as the RAF is concerned, tankers are an integral part of the front-line force, operating in support of Strike Command's combat element and, particularly, its air defence force. The addition to the front-line, in the course of the next few years, of 165 Panavia Tornado F Mk 2 air defence fighters will make even greater demands upon the tanker force if the full capabilities of the new aircraft are to be enjoyed, demands that the present total of 23 Victor K Mk 2s (16 in front-line service, plus the remainder with the OCU or in reserve) will find it impossible to meet. The planned acquisition of an additional squadron of tankers, in the form of converted VC10 and Super VC10 commercial transports, therefore has an importance out of all proportion to the size of the contract.

The RAF's intention to form a squadron of VC10 tankers (with nine aircraft) was first announced in parliament during 1978, when the Under-Secretary of State for Defence said that effectively the new squadron would be "equivalent to increasing our fighter and strike-attack forces but at markedly less cost". After completion of feasibility studies during 1978, the contract to convert nine aircraft was awarded to British Aerospace in May 1979 and was then said to be valued at about £40m.

(Heading illustration) An impression of a VC10 K Mk 3 tanker trailing its two wing-mounted drogues for the benefit of a pair of Tornado F Mk 2s. (Below) The 14th and last of the RAF's VC10 C Mk 1s receiving attention at Cyprus.

Deliveries of the new tankers to the RAF will not begin until 1982, and are expected to be completed during 1983. By that time, the two squadrons flying the Victor K Mk 2s, Nos 55 and 57, will have moved from their present base at RAF Marham to RAF Scampton, making room at the former base for two of the first squadrons of Tornado GR Mk 1s. The VC10 tanker squadron (perhaps to be No 214, the number of a third Victor tanker squadron that was disbanded in 1977) is likely to be based in the southern half of England, possibly at RAF Brize Norton where it would join the VC10 C Mk 1 strategic transports of No 10 Squadron.

The tanker programme

The nine aircraft now undergoing modification to tanker configuration at the Filton plant of British Aerospace's Aircraft Group are of two different types, comprising five Standard VC10s built as Type 1101s for BOAC and subsequently operated by Gulf Air after sale by British Airways; and four Super VC10s built as Type 1154s for East African Airways and operated by that company until 1977, when they were put into storage. Apart from the difference in fuselage length (the Super VC10 is 13 ft/3,96 m longer than the Standard) and in power plant (the Super having the more powerful Conway R.Co.43D Mk 550 engines compared with the Standard's R.Co.42 Mk 540s), the East African Airways aircraft also incorporated a freight door in the forward fuselage side and, being the last aircraft to leave the Weybridge production line, had a number of progressive modifications.

For obvious operational and engineering reasons, the RAF wanted as high a degree of commonality as possible across the VC10 fleet — including not only the tankers but also the 13 transports already in service, which themselves have several features making them different from any specific commercial model. There was, of course, no question of modifying the Super VC10s to have the Standard fuselage — or *vice versa* — but a common engine is being used for the tankers, in the shape

Since entering service in 1967, the RAF's VC10 C Mk 1s have undergone two changes of titling. Originally they bore the legend Transport Command as shown on the first aircraft (above); this later changed to Air Support Command (below left); now, only Royal Air Force is displayed, as shown on the previous page.

(Below) A fine study of the VC10 C Mk 1 James McCudden VC, *showing the Super VC10 type installation of the Conway 301 engines, with extended pylons and upset nacelles.*

of the Super's Conway Mk 550B, which is interchangeable with the Conway 301, the military equivalent which powers the RAF's C Mk 1s. The freight doors on the Type 1154s are being rendered inoperative. Whereas the commercial Super VC10s have thrust reversers on all four engines, all the tankers will have outboard reversers only, as on the Standard VC10s and the RAF's C Mk 1s. For the tankers, a common installation of additional fuel cells in the fuselage has been adopted (although the Super in theory could have carried more) and such features as the flight refuelling probe in the nose and the APU in the extreme rear of the fuselage are to the same standard as the RAF's transport VC10s. The two types of tanker are distinguished by their designations: VC10 K Mk 2 for the five Standards (which when modified take the new Type number of 1112 in the Weybridge drawing office sequence) and VC10 K Mk 3 for the four Supers (Type 1164).

Investigation into the feasibility of converting these particular aircraft to tanker configuration began late in 1977, when both Gulf Air and EAA had already put the aircraft up for sale. By April 1978, the MoD had drawn up Air Staff Requirement (ASR) 406 to define the RAF's needs and placed a contract to formalise the study. Following acceptance of the British Aerospace submission, work has proceeded under Specification K294DP. As the original home of the VC10, the Weybridge design office has overall responsibility for design of the conversion and management of the programme; physically, the work is being done at Filton (part of the same Weybridge-Bristol Division of the BAe Aircraft Group) where the aircraft had meanwhile been collected and temporarily stored.

The conversion work is being done in the big Brabazon hangar at Filton, where Concordes were previously assembled. One Standard and one Super have been selected to serve as prototype/development aircraft and these will make their first flights, respectively, towards the end of 1981 and early in 1982. Meanwhile, the other seven airframes, stripped of their flaps and slats, will have been wrapped in Driclad bags for protection while they are stored in the open air awaiting conversion. These protective PVC covers, with internal dehumidification, allow the aircraft to be moved on their own wheels; as the programme proceeds, up to five aircraft will be in the hangar at any one time for conversion.

The AAR system

Like the Victor K Mk 2s that they will complement (see AIR INTERNATIONAL/December 1976), the VC10 tankers have three refuelling points — one under each outer wing and one in the underside of the rear fuselage. When fighters are being refuelled, the normal procedure is for two aircraft to make contact with the wing drogues, one after the other (so that successive link-ups can be monitored from the tanker's flight deck); then, when refuelling is complete, simultaneous separation is effected.

To convert the VC10 commercial passenger transports to military AAR (air-to-air refuelling) aircraft there were, therefore, two principal requirements — the provision of the three refuelling units and the installation of additional fuel tanks to boost the aircraft's already considerable fuel capacity. This, in the commercial Standard VC10, is 17,940 Imp gal (81 555 l) in four integral wing tanks and a centre section transfer tank; the Super VC10 carries a total of 19,315 Imp gal

(87 805 l), thanks to the addition of an integral tank in the fin — a feature also of the RAF's VC10 C Mk 1 transports. These original capacities have been supplemented, in the tankers, by installing a series of five cylindrical tanks in the fuselage of each version.

These fuselage tanks, of metal construction with internal bags, are mounted on two heavy gauge beams that replace two of the standard seat rails and allow the tanks to be moved down the fuselage into their final position. Installing the tanks in the four K Mk 3s is simplified by the existence of the forward freight doors, through which the tanks will be loaded before the doors are finally closed and made inoperative. In the case of the five K Mk 2s, however, a section of the forward fuselage roof will have to be removed to allow the tanks to be inserted. Once the tanks are in position, a heavy A-frame is installed in front of each tank to meet the 9*g* crash case.

The new fuselage tanks are refuelled through a riser pipe in the wheel bay, and are interconnected to vent through the centre tank to the wing vent pipe. Fuel in these tanks feeds by gravity from front to rear — valves at the base of each tank preventing reverse flow — and from the rear tank to the aircraft centre section tank which retains its function of the primary transfer tank. Two extra pumps are now fitted in this central tank, and there are four new pumps in the wing tanks to meet the requirement to feed fuel outwards to the underwing refuelling pods — using the previously installed fuel jettison line in modified form — and to the fuselage hose drum unit (HDU).

The VC10 tankers have their own in-flight refuelling provision, using the system previously developed for the C Mk 1 aircraft but not normally used by that type operationally. The system uses a nose-mounted probe with a fuel line running through the lower port side of the fuselage into the fuel gallery. Valving and pumps in the tankers thus allow for the entire aircraft fuel capacity to be transferred to receiver aircraft and the whole capacity to be re-charged in flight — although for obvious reasons these theoretical maximum transfers are never achieved!

Of the three refuelling points fitted, the rear fuselage HDU installation requires the largest modification of the airframe, since it involves cutting a hole in the pressurised structure. In the case of the Standard aircraft, there is in fact little room to spare for this installation, which has to be aft of the large wheel-well in the fuselage and ahead of the carry-through structure for the rear engine mountings. The same constraints do not apply to the longer fuselage of the Super VC10, but the HDU is located in the same position relative to the rear of both types of aircraft. The entire fuselage installation, featuring a Flight Refuelling Mk 17B HDU, in fact occupies much of the space taken up by the rear underfloor freight hold, which is removed. New pressure bulkheads are provided fore and aft of the cut out for the HDU, with a pressure floor over the top and new sidewalls. The hose drum unit is, of course, remotely controlled and includes 81 ft (24,7 m) of hose.

To carry the wing refuelling pods, new structure is provided between the spars, and pylons are permanently attached under the wing. The aircraft can be flown with pods removed but the pylons remain in place. The position of the pylons on the wing is somewhat farther outboard than the minimum required for multiple refuellings and the minimum desirable for structural reasons, in order to be clear of the trailing edge flaps. The installation is designed to accept either the Flight Refuelling Mk 20B refuelling pod or the newer and lighter Mk 32; in the latter, the ram air turbine drives the fuel pump which also powers the HDU, whereas in the Mk 20 a separate hydraulic pump is used to drive the HDU. As already noted, the wing

BAC VC10 Mk 1 Specification

Power Plant: Four Rolls-Royce Conway 301 (R.Co.43D) turbofans, each rated at 21,800 lb st (9 888 kgp) for take-off. Thrust reversers on outboard engines only. Fuel capacity 17,925 Imp gal (81 480 l) in integral wing tanks and 1,440 Imp gal (6 546 l) in fin tank.
Performance: MMO, 0·86; max cruising speed, 568 mph (914 km/h); long-range cruising speed, 425 mph (684 km/h) at 30,000 ft (9 150 m); initial rate of climb, 3,050 ft/min (15,5 m/sec); range with max payload, 3,900 mls (6 275 km).
Weights: Max payload, 57,400 lb (26 030 kg); max take-off weight, 323,000 lb (146 510 kg); max landing weight, 235,000 lb (106 600 kg).
Dimensions: Span, 146 ft 2 in (44,55 m); length, 158 ft 8 in (48,36 m); height, 39 ft 6 in (12,04 m); gross wing area, 2,932 sq ft (272,4 m²); wheelbase, 65 ft 10½ in (20,08 m); undercarriage track, 21 ft 5 in (6,53 m).
Accommodation: Flight crew of four (two pilots, navigator, engineer). Standard seating for 150 passengers in rearwards-facing six-abreast seats.

The three-view drawing below depicts the VC10 K Mk 3, with additional side view of the shorter K Mk 2.

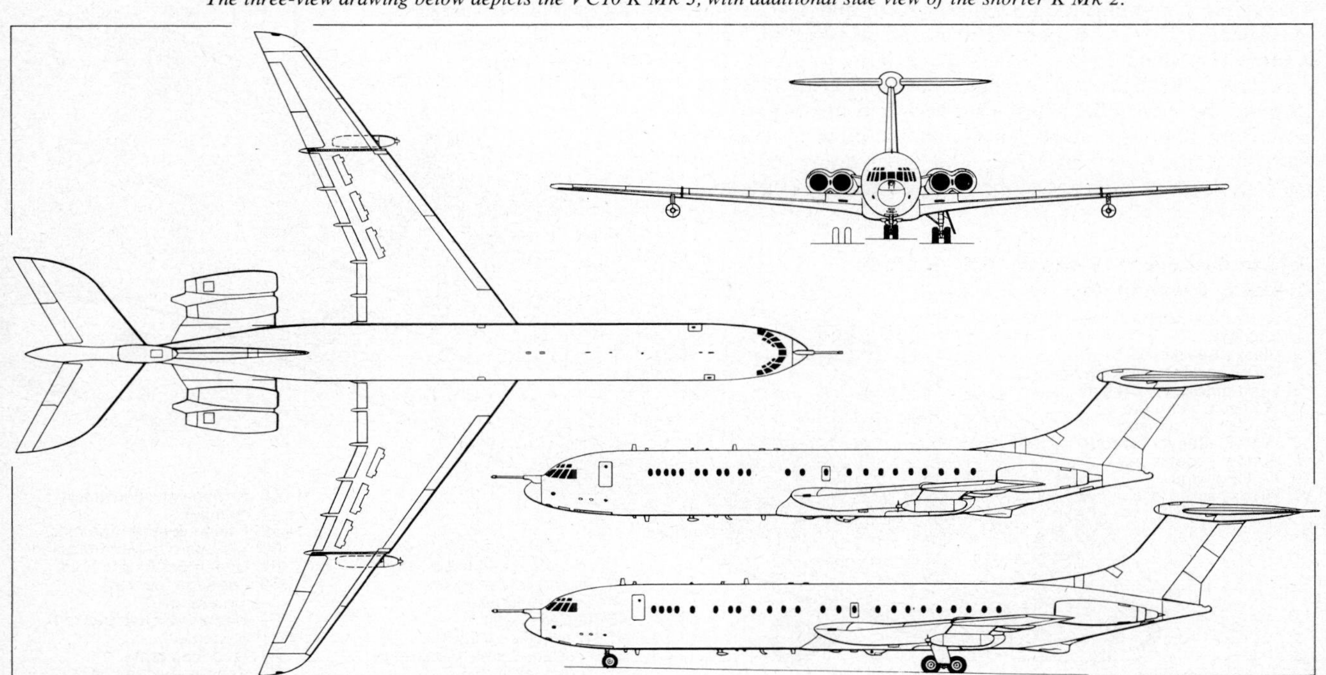

pods are fed by fuel diverted from the existing fuel jettison pipes in each wing; air for the Mk 20B is tapped from the anti-icing duct (carrying engine bleed air) in the wing leading edge. Each of the wing pods trails 50 ft (15,25 m) of hose.

Another modification for the tankers is the installation of a Turboméca Artouste 520 auxiliary power unit in the tail cone, to standardise with the C Mk 1 and make the aircraft independent of most ground support equipment including starting trucks. The APU provides compressed air for engine starting and can drive a 40 k VA generator to operate essential electrical services on the ground. There is also an ELRAT (emergency electrical ram air turbine) in a retractable, drop-out installation under the centre fuselage. Just behind the ELRAT the tankers have another new feature comprising a closed-circuit TV camera in a small fairing; remotely controlled, this camera can be trained on the fuselage HDU or either wing pod. For night operations, a series of flood-lights is also being fitted, trained to illuminate the aircraft for the benefit of the receiving aircraft; these light installations are on each side of the wing pod fairings and in the fuselage underbelly to illuminate the underside of the wing, in the wing flap actuator fairings at the wing trailing edge "kink" to illuminate the rear fuselage and in the rear end of the fuselage HDU fairing to light the engine nacelles.

Like the VC10 C Mk 1s, the tankers will have a primary flight crew of four, comprising two pilots, flight engineer and navigator. The flight engineer's station is on the starboard side of the flight deck and is modified to include the AAR operating requirements including the CRT display for the CCTV. The navigator's station is aft-facing on the port side of the flight deck. Both engineer and navigator have swivelling seats so that they can face forwards and between the two is a sliding, forward-facing supernumerary seat. A toilet, galley and miscellaneous stowage unit are located immediately aft of the flight deck. At the front end of the cabin, ahead of the fuel tanks, seats are being retained for the use of ground personnel who may need to be carried for overseas deployments. Standard rear-facing triples are used, but as the Standard and Super VC10s have different cabin door positions, these seating compartments will differ between the K Mk 2 and K Mk 3, with, respectively, six triples and five triples plus a double seat.

Avionics fit in the tankers is based upon that of the C Mk 1s, and will include OMEGA for long-range navigation, dual VHF/UHF communication, dual HF, ADF and TACAN as the primary aid to air-to-air refuelling contacts. Weather radar is carried in the nose.

Access to the flight deck and passenger compartment will be through the service door in the starboard front fuselage; the port front door is modified to permit the crew to leave by parachute in case of emergency. All other doors, port and starboard, are being made inoperative, as are two of the four emergency exits in the centre cabin, and many of the cabin windows (approximately every second unit) are being blanked out. All windows are retained at the front end, for the small passenger compartment, and overhead luggage racks are also retained in this area, being removed from the remainder of the cabin. The forward underfloor freight hold is unchanged from the commercial standard and this will allow the underwing pods to be carried internally if required during ferry flying; alternatively the hold may be used to transport spares. Spare drogues are carried at the forward end of the tank compartment and a 26-man dinghy is located in the passenger compartment ceiling.

The military origins

In its C Mk 1 version, the VC10 has been in service with the RAF since 7 July 1966, the date on which the first of 14 aircraft of this type was delivered. Entering service with No 10 Squadron at RAF Brize Norton, the VC10 flew its first scheduled service for what was then Transport Command (later Air Support Command, now an integral part of Strike

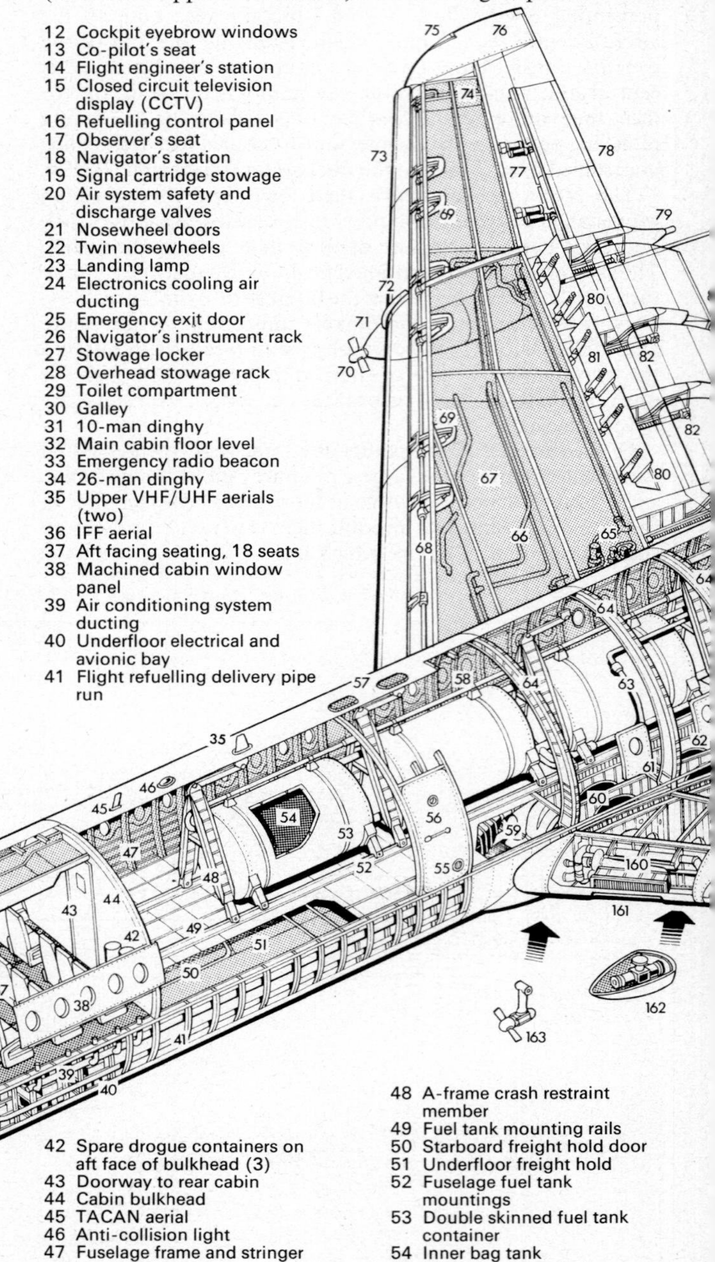

British Aerospace (Vickers) VC10 K Mk 2 Cutaway Drawing Key

1 In-flight refuelling probe
2 Radome
3 Glide slope aerial
4 Radar tracking mechanism
5 Front pressure bulkhead
6 Windscreen wipers
7 Windscreen panels
8 Instrument panel shroud
9 Rudder pedals
10 Taxying lamp
11 Pilot's seat
12 Cockpit eyebrow windows
13 Co-pilot's seat
14 Flight engineer's station
15 Closed circuit television display (CCTV)
16 Refuelling control panel
17 Observer's seat
18 Navigator's station
19 Signal cartridge stowage
20 Air system safety and discharge valves
21 Nosewheel doors
22 Twin nosewheels
23 Landing lamp
24 Electronics cooling air ducting
25 Emergency exit door
26 Navigator's instrument rack
27 Stowage locker
28 Overhead stowage rack
29 Toilet compartment
30 Galley
31 10-man dinghy
32 Main cabin floor level
33 Emergency radio beacon
34 26-man dinghy
35 Upper VHF/UHF aerials (two)
36 IFF aerial
37 Aft facing seating, 18 seats
38 Machined cabin window panel
39 Air conditioning system ducting
40 Underfloor electrical and avionic bay
41 Flight refuelling delivery pipe run
42 Spare drogue containers on aft face of bulkhead (3)
43 Doorway to rear cabin
44 Cabin bulkhead
45 TACAN aerial
46 Anti-collision light
47 Fuselage frame and stringer construction
48 A-frame crash restraint member
49 Fuel tank mounting rails
50 Starboard freight hold door
51 Underfloor freight hold
52 Fuselage fuel tank mountings
53 Double skinned fuel tank container
54 Inner bag tank
55 Wing inspection light

Command as 38 Group) on 4 April 1967. Initially, these aircraft operated regular services between the UK and Hong Kong, Singapore and Bahrein; from 1969, a regular transatlantic service to New York and/or Washington was also flown. Changing UK defence commitments have subsequently eliminated the commitment to operate the Far Eastern routes but the VC10s continue to fly the transatlantic

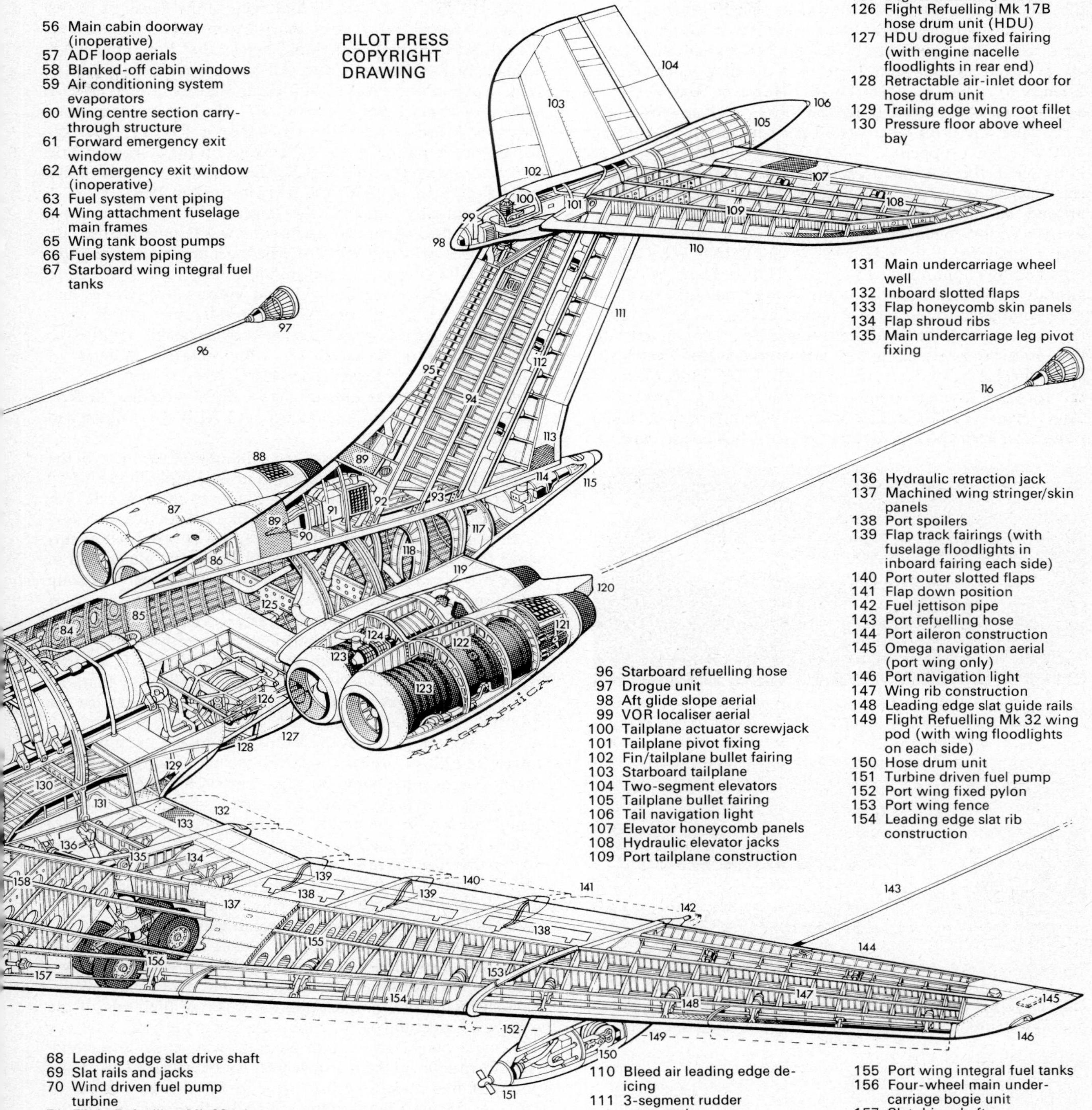

56 Main cabin doorway (inoperative)
57 ADF loop aerials
58 Blanked-off cabin windows
59 Air conditioning system evaporators
60 Wing centre section carry-through structure
61 Forward emergency exit window
62 Aft emergency exit window (inoperative)
63 Fuel system vent piping
64 Wing attachment fuselage main frames
65 Wing tank boost pumps
66 Fuel system piping
67 Starboard wing integral fuel tanks
68 Leading edge slat drive shaft
69 Slat rails and jacks
70 Wind driven fuel pump turbine
71 Flight Refuelling Mk 32 wing pod
72 Wing fence
73 Starboard leading edge slat segments, open
74 Vent surge tank
75 Starboard navigation light
76 Wing tip fairing
77 Aileron hydraulic jacks
78 Two-segment ailerons
79 Fuel jettison pipe
80 Starboard spoilers, open
81 Spoiler twin hydraulic jacks
82 Flap screw jacks
83 Starboard slotted flaps, down position
84 Unfurnished fuselage interior
85 Rear service door (inoperative)
86 Fin root fillet
87 Starboard engine cowlings
88 Starboard thrust reverser (outboard engine only)
89 HF notch aerials
90 Ram air intake
91 Air system intercooler
92 Intercooler exhaust grille
93 Fin spar attachment joints
94 Tailfin construction
95 Bleed air leading edge de-icing
96 Starboard refuelling hose
97 Drogue unit
98 Aft glide slope aerial
99 VOR localiser aerial
100 Tailplane actuator screwjack
101 Tailplane pivot fixing
102 Fin/tailplane bullet fairing
103 Starboard tailplane
104 Two-segment elevators
105 Tailplane bullet fairing
106 Tail navigation light
107 Elevator honeycomb panels
108 Hydraulic elevator jacks
109 Port tailplane construction
110 Bleed air leading edge de-icing
111 3-segment rudder construction
112 Rudder hydraulic jacks
113 Honeycomb trailing edge panels
114 Rolls-Royce/Turboméca Artouste Mk 520 APU
115 Extended tailcone
116 Centre refuelling hose and drogue unit
117 Aft pressure bulkhead
118 Sloping fin frames
119 Engine pylon fairing
120 Exhaust nozzle tail fairing
121 Thrust reverser, outboard engine only
122 Machined engine mounting beams
123 Rolls-Royce Conway Mk 550B turbofans
124 Bleed air system compressor, inboard engines only
125 Engine mounting beams
126 Flight Refuelling Mk 17B hose drum unit (HDU)
127 HDU drogue fixed fairing (with engine nacelle floodlights in rear end)
128 Retractable air-inlet door for hose drum unit
129 Trailing edge wing root fillet
130 Pressure floor above wheel bay
131 Main undercarriage wheel well
132 Inboard slotted flaps
133 Flap honeycomb skin panels
134 Flap shroud ribs
135 Main undercarriage leg pivot fixing
136 Hydraulic retraction jack
137 Machined wing stringer/skin panels
138 Port spoilers
139 Flap track fairings (with fuselage floodlights in inboard fairing each side)
140 Port outer slotted flaps
141 Flap down position
142 Fuel jettison pipe
143 Port refuelling hose
144 Port aileron construction
145 Omega navigation aerial (port wing only)
146 Port navigation light
147 Wing rib construction
148 Leading edge slat guide rails
149 Flight Refuelling Mk 32 wing pod (with wing floodlights on each side)
150 Hose drum unit
151 Turbine driven fuel pump
152 Port wing fixed pylon
153 Port wing fence
154 Leading edge slat rib construction
155 Port wing integral fuel tanks
156 Four-wheel main undercarriage bogie unit
157 Slat drive shaft
158 Inner wing spars
159 Leading edge slat telescopic de-icing air duct
160 Freon air system cooling unit, starboard unit deleted
161 Ram air intake
162 Ventral CCTV camera fairing (and wing floodlights in fuselage under-belly fairing)
163 Emergency ram air turbine generator (Elrat)

route and are used for a wide variety of mobility exercises, aeromedical and VIP flights.

The RAF had first ordered VC10s in September 1961 when a contract for five was placed with Vickers-Armstrongs (Aircraft) Ltd, but it is relevant to recall that that order had been preceded almost a decade earlier by one for six Vickers 1000 military transports. Designed to Specification C132D, the Vickers 1000 (or Type 716) was to be a 120-seat strategic transport with four Conway engines, and its development also gave rise to the commercial VC7 project, which could have given Britain an important lead over the first generation of Boeing 707s and Douglas DC-8s. However, the RAF re-assessed its needs and cancelled the Vickers 1000 in November 1955 when the prototype was 80 per cent complete and the VC7 was then dropped.

By 1960, the RAF had again raised a requirement for a strategic jet transport and Specification C239 was written around the commercial VC10. Following the initial order for five placed in September 1961, six more were ordered in 1962 and a final three in July 1964 when BOAC reduced its outstanding commitment for Super VC10s. These last three aircraft were then already in preliminary manufacture but were completed to the same standard as the earlier C Mk 1s, that is to say with the Standard fuselage length combined with the uprated engines and fin fuel tanks of the Super. First flown at Weybridge on 26 November 1965, the C Mk 1 incorporated the forward fuselage freight door (thus being Type 1106, rather than Type 1105 as first ordered, without the door) and a number of special features to permit the loading and carriage of standard freight pallets or individual cargo items as an alternative to the 150 troops in six-abreast rearwards-facing seats. For the casevac rôle, the C Mk 1 could carry 76 stretchers while 48 triple-seat units were stored in the underfloor freight holds and a typical mixed load would be 36 stretchers with six attendants and 69 passengers.

(Above) One of the RAF's VC10s was made available to Rolls-Royce in 1969 for use as an FTB for the RB.211 turbofan, installed on the port side of the fuselage in place of the two Conways.

(Above) The Standard VC10 'RVF after its sale by British Airways for personal use by the President of the United Arab Emirates. (Below) The Standard VC10 'SIX sold by B.Cal for personal use of the Sultan of Oman.

The VC10s gave the RAF a much-needed increase in airlift capability during the 'sixties and became the flagships of the transport force. It was a nice touch by the RAF, therefore, to give these 14 aircraft individual names that honoured RAF winners of the Victoria Cross. All but one of the 14 C Mk 1s remain available for service at present; the exception is XR809 *Wing Commander Hugh Malcolm VC* which was converted to serve as a test-bed for the Rolls-Royce RB.211. The test installation replaced the two Conways on the starboard side and, re-registered as G-AXLR, this aircraft resumed flight testing on 6 March 1970, and was scrapped in 1976.

As eventually ordered, the military VC10 was a close relative of the commercial aircraft and was required to operate in the three principal rôles of passenger transport, freighter and casualty evacuation. Before the contract for this version was placed, however, the RAF and Vickers-Armstrongs had studied a number of options and considerable project work was completed on what became known as the Multi-Rôle VC10, designed to cover — with suitable changes of equipment — no fewer than seven rôles, comprising, in addition to the three already listed, flight refuelling tanker, bomber, maritime reconnaissance and ALBM (air-launched ballistic missile) carrier.

This Multi-Rôle VC10 featured a Standard fuselage with the freight door, uprated Conways and fin fuel tank, Super VC10 wing with a total of eight strong points (four each side) for external stores, and interchangeable front fuselage/nose section. For the flight refuelling rôle, it was proposed at this stage that the fuselage HDU should simply be plugged-in in place of the rear freight hold door in the port side. The wing refuelling pods would have been carried on the outermost of the underwing strong points and the extra fuel in the fuselage was to be carried in eight cylindrical tanks in two side-by-side rows. This would have given an increase of some 10,500 Imp gal (47 735 l) in total fuel uplifted, considerably more than the extra capacity offered by the installation now adopted for the VC10 K Mk 2 and K Mk 3.

To make a bomber of the VC10, the project team had the interesting idea of resurrecting the technique adopted in the same design office some 30 years earlier for the Wellesley, proposing to fit eight panniers or cocoons on the wing strong points, each with the ability to carry eight 1,000-lb (454-kg) bombs for a total load over short ranges of 64,000 lb (29 030 kg). In this rôle, the nose installation would have included H_2S radar bomb-sight together, possibly, with a visual bomb-aiming panel. For the ALBM rôle, eight Douglas Skybolts could be carried rather than the bomb panniers.

As a maritime reconnaissance patrol aircraft, the Multi-Rôle VC10 would have carried its offensive weapons in two panniers, on the inboard wing pylons, and the fuselage would have needed more modification for this rôle than any of the others, with a visual bomb-aiming station in the nose, a battery of 12 sono-buoy launchers ahead of the wing and a retractable ASV 21 radome in the rear fuselage. An ECM aerial was to be pod-mounted above the fuselage and MAD was located on one wing tip. Six 1,300-Imp gal (5 910 l) cylindrical tanks in the rear fuselage would have given the MR variant a range of well over 6,000 mls (9 660 km).

The commercial origins

Delivery of the nine VC10 tankers by the end of 1983 will mean that the RAF will have received 23 of the 54 VC10s built (including 22 Supers); with the premature retirement this year of most of the Super VC10s remaining in service with British

The Standard VC10 'TDJ after sale by B.Cal to the Ministry of Defence for use by Aero Flight at the RAE, Bedford. Special instrumentation accounts for the nose probe.

Airways, additional aircraft are also available for conversion and it is not inconceivable that these could provide a second squadron of VC10 tankers at a later date, following a period in storage. In service both with the RAF and commercial operators, the VC10s have proved exceptionally reliable and well-liked by crews and passengers alike. Clearly enough, however, the type was anything but a commercial success — a fact that has to be attributed in no small measure to the vacillation and obstructive tactics of BOAC in the early 'sixties, at the time the VC10 was about to enter service.

The VC10 had evolved, it will be recalled, in the period from 1956 to 1958, following the cancellation of the Vickers 1000 and the commercial VC7. A year after dropping its interest in the VC7, BOAC had ordered (prior to first flight) 15 Boeing 707s and had then begun discussing with British manufacturers the development of a jet transport for service on the eastern routes. After first considering the D.H.118 (sometimes referred to as the Comet 5), BOAC eventually selected the Vickers project in May 1957 and announced its intention to order 35. By January 1958, when the order was confirmed, the design had been developed and enlarged to have transatlantic capability as well as the "hot and high" performance necessary on the routes to the Middle and Far East and Africa. The contract for 35 was supplemented by options on 20 more; subsequently, BOAC was to claim that this figure was based on Vickers "minimum requirement" to launch a new type rather than the airline's commercial needs.

The VC10 was notable, at the time of its inception, for its rear-engined layout, being the first large four-engined transport to have this configuration. Its advantages included a "clean" wing which could be designed for maximum lift without having regard to engine installation, and low noise levels in the cabin which made the VC10 one of the most popular transports of the 'sixties and 'seventies with regular travellers. The care taken by the design team to obtain a high standard of structural integrity, ease of maintenance and — through extended flight testing — excellent handling characteristics all added to the high reputation of the VC10 in service. It suffered, however, from a relatively high empty weight resulting from the extra structure in the rear fuselage to carry the rear engine loads, and, as time went on, from the relatively high fuel consumption and excessive external noise levels of the Conway engines, which could not easily be replaced. More than anything else, however, the commercial programme suffered from BOAC's equivocal attitude towards the introduction of its new aircraft and the constant changes and reductions in contracts.

Soon after ordering the 35 VC10s in the Standard (Type 1101) version, BOAC concluded that a larger derivative could be used to advantage on the "Blue Riband" North Atlantic route. Vickers projected a Super VC10 with a fuselage stretch of 28 ft (8,5 m) and extra fuel carried in wing-tip fuel tanks. Ten of these Supers were ordered in June 1960 but within a year the airline had decided that this variant would be too specialised; instead, a more modest stretch of 13 ft (3,9 m) was adopted and the additional fuel capacity was provided in the fin rather than at the wing tips. In 1961, the contracts were changed from 35 Standards and 10 Supers to 12 Standards and 30 of these smaller Supers. Included in the latter quantity would be seven Type 1152 convertible passenger/freighters incorporating the side freight-loading door, and 23 Type 1151 passenger transports, but during 1964 — just as the first of the Standard aircraft was entering service — BOAC's management indicated that it wished to reduce or cancel its order for Super VC10s and to buy additional Boeing 707s instead. Intensive negotiations eventually led to the State airline retaining on order 17 Super VC10s; three others, as previously noted, would be completed as Type 1106 for the RAF and 10 were cancelled at an early stage of production.

Other contracts for Standard VC10s came from Ghana Airways for four (of which one was not in the end built and one

continued on page 189

WG30 : TOWARDS PRODUCTION

SINCE making its début at the Paris Air Show last year, the Westland WG 30 has been making steady but largely unpublicised progress. Although the company is not yet ready to announce firm orders for this private venture development of the Lynx, it is sufficiently confident that these will come to lay down an initial production batch of 20 aircraft. Production jigs and tooling are now beginning to appear at Yeovil and long-lead time items have been ordered.

The first WG 30 appeared at Paris having made its first flight on 10 April 1980; it was then finished externally to represent a civil version and the second prototype, shown in the indoor exhibition, also had its cabin furnished to represent the civilian rôle. Since then, the first machine has done a good deal of flying, the current total being over 210 hrs, and has undergone a number of small modifications, particularly around the rear end. As planned right from the start, the direction of rotation of the tail rotor has been reversed, with benefit to the external noise levels. A more obvious change is the addition of a low-set tailplane with end-plate fins, replacing the earlier half-tailplane on the starboard side that was a carry-over from the Lynx.

(Opposite page) Photographs of the WG 30 prototype in military guise, in which it can carry 14 fully-equipped troops or 22 troops with standard equipment. (Top of page) Milan anti-tank missile teams boarding the WG 30. (Below) An illustration that clearly shows the new tail unit on the WG 30 prototype.

Indicative of the primary interest in the WG 30 in a military rôle is the olive drab finish now sported by this prototype. Both within NATO and elsewhere, the WG 30 is gaining attention for its potential in the air mobility rôle, especially when teamed with the armed versions of the Army Lynx or other types of attack helicopters.

The second prototype of the WG 30, since its appearance at Paris, has been stripped of its interior furnishing and used for a comprehensive series of structural integrity tests, which continued through most of 1979 and into the early months of 1980. It has now been put into rebuild and will emerge to full production standard for flight testing to begin in the spring of 1981. This should then lead to certification by the end of that year, clearing the way for deliveries to begin, in either civil or military guise, in 1982.

The potential civil rôle of the WG 30 was confirmed at last month's Farnborough International by the appearance of a full scale mock-up in British Airways colours. With its ability to carry 17-21 passengers, the WG 30 is expected to have immediate application in the high-density short-haul end of the helicopter market. There is the obvious possibility that, at a later stage, advantage could be taken of the projected development by Rolls-Royce Small Engines Division of versions of the Gem offering max contingency ratings of 1,220 shp and even 1,600 shp compared with the 1,120 shp contingency and 1,060 shp take-off ratings of the Gem 41 used at present in the WG 30. □

KC-10A
BOOSTING US AIR MOBILITY

TWO DOZEN YEARS AGO, on 31 August 1956, the first jet-powered flight refuelling tanker/transport, Boeing's KC-135A Stratotanker, entered flight test to launch a dramatic upgrading of the USAF's ability to deploy combat aircraft, men and supplies on a global scale. In the near quarter-century that has since elapsed, the world scene has been transformed: extremely capable aircraft though the KC-135A has remained, events such as the 1973 Middle East conflict, when many countries denied landing rights to USAF Military Airlift Command aircraft, highlighted the need for a tanker/transport of greatly enhanced capability; one able under most circumstances to dispense with the need for forward basing when supporting the deployment of forces to distant trouble-spots.

Acceptance of this need led to establishment of a requirement for a so-called Advanced Tanker/Cargo Aircraft (ATCA); an aircraft capable of virtually doubling the non-stop range of, for example, a fully-loaded C-5A Galaxy, combining the tasks of both tanker and cargo aircraft by refuelling fighters and simultaneously carrying their support equipment and support personnel in overseas deployment, and possessing such range as to render demands on vital fuel supplies in the theatre of operations superfluous. Such an aircraft is the McDonnell Douglas KC-10A Extender which effected its inaugural flight on 12 July last, just 50 days short of the 24th anniversary of the KC-135A's début. Considerably larger and almost double the all-up weight of the Stratotanker that it will supplement in service, the Extender reflects in capability the immense advances in technology that have taken place over the conceptual quarter-century between the two aircraft, and when it commences operation with USAF Strategic Air Command next year, it will endow the service with a highly significant mobility enhancement.

Flown three months after its official roll-out from the Long Beach facility of the Douglas Aircraft Company Division of McDonnell Douglas, and now well into a five-month Qualification Operational Test and Evaluation at Yuma, Arizona, which is preceding a six-month Phase I of the Follow-on Test and Evaluation at Barksdale AFB, Louisiana, the designated home base of the future KC-10A Extender fleet, the McDonnell Douglas tanker/transport is essentially a derivative of the DC-10 Series 30CF convertible freighter. Selected as the USAF's ATCA after competitive evaluation with a version of the Boeing 747, the KC-10A is currently the subject of contracts covering six aircraft, but additional quantities to be procured over the first half of this decade will be determined by available funding, current planning calling for procurement of up to 20 by mid-decade.

Adaptation of the basic commercial DC-10-30CF to KC-10A configuration has included the installation of seven unpressurised bladder-type fuel cells located in the under-deck vented cavities, three forward and four aft of the wing. Protected by keel beams and strategically-placed energy absorption material, these cells accommodate a maximum of 117,500 lb (53 298 kg) of fuel and are interconnected with the standard wing tankage which houses a further 238,565 lb (108 213 kg). The refuelling boom, which is "flown" by means of a digital fly-by-wire control system, is appreciably more advanced than that utilised by the KC-135, offering significant advantages in operational safety, efficiency and fuel flow rates. It features larger disconnect and control envelopes, automatic load alleviation, position rate sensing to ensure disconnect within control limits, and other advanced features. An additional feature of the KC-10A's refuelling system is the provision of a hose reel unit to cater for the probe-and-drogue refuelling system utilised by USN, USMC and NATO aircraft (as well as certain of the older fighter types operated by ANG and Reserve units).

The aerial refuelling operator's station is located aft of the rear lower fuselage fuel tanks and is accessible from the upper deck. Embodying a periscopic observation system to afford a wide field of view for traffic management, the station provides the operator with an aft-facing crew seat instead of a prone position as offered by the KC-135, and two additional seats are provided for an instructor and an observer when carried. By comparison with the basic DC-10-30CF, the cargo handling system has been improved to accommodate a broader spectrum of loads. Adapted in part from the commercial model, it is augmented by powered rollers, powered winch provisions for assistance in fore and aft movement of cargo, an

extended ball mat area to permit loading of larger items and pallet couplers which allow palletising of cargo items too large for a single pallet. These features, coupled with the 102 by 140 in (259 by 355 cm) forward portside upward-hinging cargo door endow the KC-10A with the ability to transport a very significant proportion of all the tactical support equipment required by a fighter squadron.

Several configurations exist for personnel accommodation, one such catering for a crew of five, plus six seats for additional crew and four bunks. The same area offers space for installation of 14 more seats for support personnel. Another arrangement makes room for a further 55 support personnel, together with the necessary utility, toilet and stowage modules, raising personnel capacity to 80.

The pre-delivery flight test programme consists of some 300 flying hours performed by a combined test team of McDonnell Douglas, FAA and USAF personnel, and during the test programme, the KC-10A will refuel a variety of USAF aircraft, including the C-5A Galaxy, the F-4 Phantom, the F-15 Eagle and the A-10 Thunderbolt using the boom, while the hose-and-drogue system will be used in refuelling tests with various US Navy aircraft, including the S-3 Viking and the A-4 Skyhawk.

The combined aerial refuelling and cargo-carrying capabilities of the KC-10A Extender will enable it to handle an appreciably wider variety of missions than can be assigned to the KC-135 Stratotanker, but the McDonnell Douglas tanker/transport is not viewed as a successor to the older Boeing aircraft — at least, not in this decade — but rather as complementary to it, and when the first four Extenders enter service at Barksdale AFB next year, they will have significantly reduced the USAF's reliance on foreign bases. □

McDonnell Douglas KC-10A Extender specification

Power Plant: Three 52,500 lb (23 814 kg) General Electric CF6-50C2 turbofans.
Performance: Max cruise, 595 mph (957 km/h) at 31,000 ft (9 450 m); long-range cruise, 540 mph (870 km/h); range (max cargo), 4,373 mls (7 037 km); unrefuelled ferry range, 11,500 mls (18 503 km); critical field length, 11,000 ft (3 353 m).
Weights: Operational empty (cargo configuration), 244,471 lb (110 892 kg), (tanker configuration), 240,245 lb (108 975 kg); design max take-off, 590,000 lb (267 624 kg).
Dimensions: Span, 165 ft 4 in (50,42 m); length, 181 ft 7 in (55,35 m); height, 58 ft 1 in (17,70 m); wing area, 3,647 sq ft (338,80 m²).

The first KC-10A Extender is seen in the photographs on these pages during its Qualification Operational Test and Evaluation at Yuma. It will shortly be entering a further phase in its evaluation programme, flying from Barksdale AFB, the designated base for the future USAF KC-10A fleet.

The Black Knights and the Green Mountain Boys

ELECTRONIC WARFARE IN NORAD

During the mid-'fifties, the USA and Canada co-operated in establishing a continental air defence system. Primarily designed to detect and foil a Soviet air attack, this system was designated the North American Air Defence Command (NORAD), the agreement being signed on 12 May 1958. As established, NORAD included continent-spanning radar and communications lines such as the DEW Line; airborne radar pickets and all-weather fighter interception squadrons. Over 20 years later NORAD persists; its aircraft and ground equipment have since been upgraded, although not as completely as some would prefer. An important component within NORAD is the training which keeps air and ground units at a peak of readiness, and one of the most vital aspects of this training focuses on electronic countermeasures (ECM). In order to exercise its operational units, NORAD maintains two specialised electronic warfare (EW) squadrons. These are No 414 Sqdn of the Canadian Armed Forces, and the 134th Defence Systems Evaluation Squadron of the USAF Vermont Air National Guard, and by a coincidence these two units are both now flying types of aircraft — the Avro CF-100 and the Martin B-57 — that are in the final phase of deployment. Larry Milberry has visited the two squadrons to prepare this account for AIR INTERNATIONAL.

THE NAME of the game is jamming, evasion and deception. By these methods, which really have not changed radically since the inception of NORAD in the 'fifties, the aircraft of No 414 Squadron and the 134th DSES seek to conceal their approach, the size of their force, and course changes; to overload "enemy" defence systems; to generally confuse those defences, and, in the process, to protect themselves. Each squadron flies two or three major exercises per month. No 414 operates mainly in the 22nd through 25th NORAD regions, of which the 22nd — which stretches from Alaska to the East Coast — is the largest region and home for the squadron. Because of its location (at North Bay in Ontario) and the availability of the 134th, the Canadian unit only rarely operates in the 20th and 26th NORAD regions in the southern USA, or in Alaska.

Electronic warfare missions vary considerably and include frequent trips to fighter bases to exercise interceptor crews. Almost daily, EW aircraft head out to military flying zones, where they fly parallel tow-lines, giving fighter after fighter a chance to locate and "splash" the EW target plane. In addition, whenever EW aircraft are on cross-country flights deploying to distant bases, ground radar facilities *en route* are routinely exercised. At least once a month there are large scale regional EW exercises and one big "coast" exercise, devised to include the entire continent either east or west of the

(Above) One of the B-57Cs of the 134th DSES, in USAF three-tone camouflage, over the Vermont countryside earlier in 1980. (Below) Three EB-57Bs (in grey finish with red high-visibility markings) and two B-57Cs on the flight line at Burlington. (Heading, opposite page) Examples of the three aircraft types used for EW training by No 414 Squadron, CAF, in line-astern formation over Ontario.

(Above) A pair of CF-100 Mk 5Ds in flight near North Bay, earlier this year, and (below left) the crew boarding a CF-100, showing the Black Knights insignia on the forward fuselage.

Mississippi valley. Frequently such massive exercises are flown at night when the required airspace is available and civil aviation won't be too badly disrupted.

So far as the Canadian Armed Forces are concerned, EW had its beginnings in the post-war RCAF in 1955. At that time Dakotas of 104 Composite Unit, Winnipeg, were assigned to the EW rôle, an EW Fairchild C-119 Flying Box Car being acquired the following year. By nature it made an impressive chaff dispenser! In 1959, the RCAF's Electronic Warfare Unit was formed at St Hubert and by 1965 the unit was flying some 28 CF-100s and three C-119s. During this period, most of the EWU CF-100s were Mark 5Cs with two main capabilities: jamming airborne radar and chaff dropping. There were also a few Mark 3 trainers. On 15 September 1967 the EWU became No 414(EW) Squadron and once again the famous Black Knight squadron took to the skies. No 414 Squadron had initially been formed in the UK in 1941. Equipped with Tomahawks and Lysanders, it provided army co-operation duties, soon being re-equipped with Mustang Is and gradually gaining combat experience. In an early operation the squadron was active over Dieppe during the disastrous Commando landing there, and for most of the war it specialised in ground attack, photo reconnaissance and forward air control. By war's end, the squadron was flying Spitfires and at disbandment in August 1945 had logged 6,087 sorties.

The squadron was re-formed on 1 April 1947 and assumed the task of photo reconnaissance in the Arctic. Flying Dakotas from various northern detachments, it had covered over 300,000 square miles (777 000 km²) by 31 October 1950 when it was again disbanded. The unit was to re-form three more times: in 1952 as a Sabre squadron at Bagotville and Baden; in 1957 as a CF-100 and later CF-101 squadron at North Bay; and finally in 1967 as an EW squadron at St Hubert. In 1968 it relocated to Uplands near Ottawa; then, in the summer of 1972, squadron commander Lt Col Fern Villeneuve led a mass formation of 16 CF-100s and nine T-33s to the current home at CFB North Bay, near Lake Nipissing in mid-northern Ontario.

EW in Canada

Today, the squadron is special in more than just its rôle; it is the only Canadian squadron still operating more than two aircraft types; the only squadron to be the sole flying unit at any Canadian air base and the only one still flying the venerable CF-100.

Besides its NORAD duties, No 414 occasionally works with other units. It has flown in the big *Maple Flag* TAC exercises held twice a year at Cold Lake, Alberta. In 1979 it operated from Bermuda on Maritime Command fleet exercises, at which time its CF-100s flew missions simulating aggressors attacking naval vessels and launching anti-shipping missiles, with the CF-104s of No 417 Sqdn simulating the missiles themselves. With the CF-100s jamming fleet radars, life was generally made difficult for the defenders. At TAC exercises at Cold Lake and places like Eglin AFB in Florida the crews from No 414 and the 134th have usually been such spoilers as to ruin their chances of getting invited back for the next shoot!

As presently established, No 414 operates some 28 aircraft, comprising seven CF-100 Mark 5Ds, 18 T-33s and three Dassault-Breguet CC-117 Falcons; three of the T-birds are with the detachment at Uplands. There are 21 pilots and 13 navigator/EWOs (Electronic Warfare Officers). Pilot turnover is about one-third annually, and somewhat less for EWOs.

Aircraft utilisation varies from type to type. The T-33s are usually operated as "silent" targets, but they also fly with underwing chaff or jamming pods. The Falcons are airborne jammers although one (No 507) was modified in 1979 to drop chaff from a dispenser in the rear fuselage. At present only the CF-100s have full EW capability: jamming both air and ground radars, communications jamming, and dropping chaff. By the time the Avro Canada aircraft are phased out next year, the Falcons will all have been upgraded to have full EW capabilities.

The Lockheed T-birds also serve in the training rôle, since

No 414 is the Canadian Forces T-33 conversion unit; other T-33s serve as target tugs at Comox where they tow drogues for naval gunnery practice, and four others are based at Baden in Germany as utility aircraft for 1 CAG. It seems certain that this rugged aircraft has several years of useful service ahead of it in Canada and will out-live the CF-100s.

The Falcons were acquired in 1968 in a deal that saw an initial batch of Canadair CL-215 water bombers sold to France as an off-set. The Falcons first joined No 412 Sqdn at Uplands where they served as utility transports, frequently in the VIP rôle, but in a budgetary cut they were taken away from the air force and turned over to their present owner, the Treasury Board. By the mid-'seventies it was clear that an EW aircraft was needed to replace the CF-100s, and three Falcons were then assigned to No 414, the first arriving at North Bay in October 1977. The remaining four still flown by No 412 Sqdn are expected to turn up at North Bay by mid-1981. There is no doubt that the crews favour the Falcon over both the CF-100 and the T-33. Besides being a good EW aircraft, it represents a great step forward in avionics, comfort and other aspects over the 'fifties technology of the other two types. Even so, the Canadian Forces' Falcons are hardly the latest in biz-jets; still flying with their General Electric CF700-2C turbojets, they will soon be re-engined with the -2D2 version.

From a historic viewpoint, No 414 Squadron's most exciting aircraft are its CF-100s. Most aircraft of this vintage have long since gone to the scrapyard, so by international standards the CF-100 is a regular flying museum piece — as, indeed, is the B-57 serving with the 134th Squadron in the USAF. Although it acquired the name Canuck 30 years ago, at least unofficially, the CF-100 has over the years endeared itself to its admirers and crews as the "Clunk", a term that apparently derives from the noise made when its landing gear retracts.

The striking all-black CF-100 prototype first flew on 19 January 1950. Within three years, the first production examples were entering squadron service at North Bay. They went on to provide NORAD's first line of defence over Canada for eight years, and also served in Europe with NATO. Of the 692 built, 53 were acquired by Belgium, the only nation other than Canada to operate the type. Production ceased in 1958 with the final aircraft being rolled out under the nose of a CF-105 Arrow.* Although still a fine aircraft, the CF-100 had by 1958 been surpassed technologically by fighters like the F-101 and F-106 already in squadron service with the USAF's Air Defence Command squadrons assigned to NORAD. The RCAF had expected to replace its CF-100s with Arrows but political events killed that prospect in 1959. Instead, 60 surplus USAF F-101s and two squadrons of Bomarc SAMs were procured as CF-100 replacements. Nonetheless, the dependable characteristics of the CF-100 coupled with the need in the RCAF for an EW aircraft saved it from impending extinction and since its retirement as a fighter the CF-100 has served nearly 20 years in the EW rôle. The seven CF-100 Mk 5Ds at North Bay* are, with one exception, the last flying. The exception is 100760, which has been used for several years at St Hubert as a flying test bed by Canadian Pratt & Whitney.

For a detailed account of the CF-100, see AIR ENTHUSIAST/FOUR; for an article on the CF-105 Arrow, see AIR ENTHUSIAST/EIGHT.

Today's CF-100 embodies several features unfamiliar to the production Mk 5. A package of EW gear, weighing over 1,000 lb (454 kg), occupies the former gun pack housing in the belly, and 6,000 lb (2 720 kg) of extra fuel is carried in a fuselage tank and the big tip tanks. Hence, gross weight is up from 37,000 lb (16 783 kg) for the standard Mk 5 to 40,000 lb (18 145 kg) for the Mk 5D. The original fighter's wing tip extensions are no longer used, somewhat affecting original service ceiling, and a pair of big chaff dispensers is now carried underwing attached to the hard points provided on all production CF-100s.

Old age has led to some flying restrictions *g*-wise but otherwise the CF-100 cruises at a respectable 440 knots (815 km/h) at up to 45,000 ft (15 716 m). The Clunk's powerful Orenda 11 turbojets still provide remarkable take-off and climb performance, the climb to 40,000 ft (9 145 m) taking five minutes.

At present No 414's CF-100s are limited to 75 hours of flight per month. That restricts aircrew time to about 10 hours each, and the crews make up their monthly flying time on T-birds and Falcons. No new CF-100 pilots are being trained as this takes about 60 hours and with time running out on the CF-100s would be a wasteful process. Unnecessary wear and tear is also prevented by use of an ancient CAE CF-100 simulator, on which pilots and EWOs spend 2-3 hours each per month.

As the CF-100 reaches the end of its life, monthly utilisation will be upped to 90 hours in order to use up all remaining engine life. In this way no one will ever be able to say that the tax payer didn't get his money's worth out of the CF-100!

The serial numbers and airframe hours as at the end of 1979, of the aircraft serving with No 414 Squadron are as follows: 100472 (5,359 hrs); 100476 (4,749 hrs); 100500 (5,253 hrs); 100504 (5,298 hrs); 100784 (4,922 hrs); 100785 (4,830 hrs); 100790 (4,872 hrs).

(Below) One of the 134th Squadron's Martin B-57Cs at Burlington, unusual in having the all-black finish of a night intruder aircraft. (Above right) The rotary bomb doors of an EB-57B, packed with "black boxes", awaits installation.

When the CF-100 100757 was delivered from North Bay to the National Aeronautical Collection in Ottawa during 1979 it made the trip on a pair of engines each down to its final hour!

The USAF counterpart

The 134th Defence Systems Evaluation Squadron is based at Burlington, on the east shore of Lake Champlain amidst the scenic Vermont mountains. It's an Air National Guard unit and part of the 158th Defence Systems Evaluation Group. Formed in 1946, the 134th was a fighter squadron initially equipped with P-47s and P-51s. From those early days onward members of the 134th have been known as the Green Mountain Boys.

The squadron entered the jet age when it converted to Lockheed F-94s in 1954. These were superseded in 1958 by Northrop F-89s which were themselves replaced in 1965 by Convair F-102s. During these years pilots of the 134th saw combat duty in Korea and South-East Asia. In 1974 the unit changed rôles when it re-equipped with Martin B-57 Canberras. The new rôle was electronic warfare, and initially nine EB-57Bs and two B-57Cs were acquired; for the most part these were aircraft that had seen EW service with other units such as the 4313th DSES from Stewart AFB, New York, while some had seen combat with the 8th and 13th Bomb Squadrons in South-East Asia.

Further B-57s were acquired in 1976 from the Kansas Air Guard and present strength stands at 15 EB-57Bs, three B-57C trainers* and five T-33s. When the 17th DSES from Malstrom AFB, Montana, disposed of its B-57s in July 1979 the 134th became the last USAF squadron still flying that historic aircraft; the 20 or so aircraft of the 17th were then flown into storage in Arizona where they serve as the chief source of replacement aircraft and spares for the 134th.

(Above left) A Canadair T-33A-N Silver Star — one of 18 on the strength of No 414 Squadron — carrying an EW pod under the port wing. (Below) One of No 414 Squadron's CC-117 Falcons shares the flight line at North Bay with a CF-100 Mk 5D.

The squadron's rôle is essentially similar to that of No 414 Squadron. It exercises fixed and mobile ground radar units, and NORAD squadrons flying F-101s, F-106s, F-4s and F-15s. Exercises are flown throughout the seven NORAD regions. Its aircraft frequently work with Canadian CF-101 squadrons at Comox, Bagotville and Chatham. There are also periodic overseas commitments, which in 1979 included exercises in Iceland and Korea. On the Korean exercise, four B-57s from Burlington made the trans-Pacific hop in 11 stops totalling 40 hours in the air. A C-141 served as shepherd aircraft for the flight.

Our recent visit to the 134th on behalf of Air International took place on a Monday, the day when B-57s are usually sent "on the road" (that is, on Temporary Detachment). Activities for the day saw one B-57 tasked to McChord, Washington; one to Great Falls, Montana; and one to Jacksonville, Florida. These aircraft were to work with Air National Guard F-106 squadrons. Two other aircraft flew to Pease AFB, New Hampshire, to work with ground radar units. A B-57C trainer was allocated for a recurrency ride for the squadron commander, Lt Col Ed Govette, while Lt Col David Ladd was lined up to take the author on a familiarisation ride in a second B-57C. With the steady demand for EW training by NORAD elements it is indeed rare to find all the aircraft of the 134th at Burlington on the same day.

As an Air Guard unit, the 134th is under command of the state governor and is partially state funded. In times of emergency such units can be federalised on a moment's notice. Traditionally, Guard budgets are not excessive and as a result units become highly efficient operations, working on a "do-more-with-less" basis that affects everything, right down to the judicious use of chaff.

Personnel with the 134th fall into different categories. Some, like the CO, are full-time Government Service people, while others are weekenders in the tradition of the citizens' army or the British territorials. Among the squadron's weekend pilots are men who work during the week as teachers, bankers and salesmen in nearby communities. A third category includes regular air force personnel attached to the squadron in advisory rôles. Aircrew strength at present numbers 30 pilots and 18 EWOs, with a dozen crews always available to fly.

New pilots are still trained on the B-57 and become qualified after 150 hours, the three B-57Cs being the training workhorses. There is no simulator available. T-33s, while having an EW rôle, also serve the squadron in the training and proficiency rôles.

Pilots with the 134th have to be strictly the best available to cope with the rigours of EW flying; a crew may find itself in Florida on one mission, the rugged mountain region of the West Coast on the next, then on to the wind-swept central plains, followed by an exercise in the Arctic. All forms of weather and terrain can be experienced within a short time span. The Squadron's EWOs are equally experienced and competent.

In NORAD, the EW emphasis is on radar jamming; there is the capability of communications jamming but this is not widely used. Among the EWOs of No 414 Squadron and the 134th as much effort is put into techniques used as into the electronic wizardry. An astute EWO can sometimes foil an intercept more by using his wits than his chaff or jammers. An EWO's success depends on his ability to judge a situation as one requiring old-fashioned cat-and-mouse flying, or the use of electronics. It is also a fact that of all the EW equipment carried on the CF-100s and B-57s, the most effective is also the most prosaic — chaff!

Respected veterans

The aircraft of NORAD's two electronic warfare squadrons make for an interesting comparative study of vintage military jets. The CF-100 and B-57 share many similarities. To begin, they each originated from the immediate post-war era. The CF-100 was Canada's first indigenous jet fighter, while the Canberra from which the B-57 derived was Britain's first jet bomber. That both types are still operational today is a fine testimony to the aircraft industries over 30 years ago. Each type is a neatly proportioned though boxy-looking twin, with a generally similar engine arrangement although the CF-100's Orendas hug the fuselage while the B-57's Wright J-65s (licence-built Armstrong Siddeley Sapphires) are mounted farther out on the wing. The latter feature gives rise to the B-57s only undesirable flying characteristic: as the engines are so far out, a control problem may result from failure of one of them.

Two other similarities of the CF-100 and B-57 are the tandem cockpit arrangement, and the big wing-tip fuel tanks usually carried. On the ground, however, they are readily distinguishable by their stances; the CF-100 sits high while the B-57 seemingly hugs the ground as closely as possible. The B-57 has somewhat larger dimensions than the CF-100 and tips the scale fully loaded by 10,000 lb (4 540 kg) over the CF-100. Engine output for the two aircraft is about equal, as is the cruising speed of 440 knots (815 km/h), and range of 1,200 mls (1 931 km). The B-57's payload far exceeds that of the CF-100, however; its EW load, including two 675-lb (300-kg) chaff dispensers, being some 3,700 lb (1 680 kg).

There is one other aspect shared by these two old soldiers which can only be described as lamentable. Both types are about to be forced into retirement. Whatever the strength of the airframes and utility of the equipment they carry, their Orenda and J-65 engines are fast running out of time. Replacement engines and spares have become very scarce. Within months of the CF-100's planned September 1981 phase-out, the B-57s are expected to join the ghost squadrons adorning the Arizona desert. Aircraft number 52-1551 has already been earmarked for preservation in the Smithsonian, and there is some talk of McDonnell Douglas F-4 Phantoms being issued as the follow-on type for service with the 134th. Ironically, both the CF-100 and B-57 are long-life airframe types. Aircraft of the 134th are at about the 8,000 hr point and accumulating time at the rate of 400 hrs per year towards an airframe limit of 10,000 hrs at present. Years ago, Canada's National Research Council pegged the CF-100's ultimate airframe life at 20,000 hrs!

Like No 414 Sqdn, the 134th is a high-spirited outfit. Both squadrons are naturally proud of their heritage, their special rôles and their antique aircraft, but for the 134th there is a special reason for pride. It achieves something unique by virtue of being an Air National Guard unit. It has been based at Burlington for over 34 years. Its men and women are nearly all from Burlington and environs; everyone knows everyone and long-term service is a tradition. There are many pilots, many men in the engineering shops, and many on the flight line with over a decade of service with the squadron — even a handful who were there in the days on the P-47.

In 1983 NORAD will celebrate its 25th anniversary. It seems unfortunate that two such stalwarts as the CF-100 and B-57 will not be at the party. Meanwhile, a special send-off is in preparation at CFB North Bay. In September 1981 thousands will visit the base for a CF-100 reunion and airshow, the highlight of the event being the last fly-past of the CF-100. It is certain that at least one of the aircraft on static display that weekend will be a B-57 of the 134th. □

**Serial numbers and flight hours (to April 1980) of the EB-57B Canberras of the 134th DSES are as follows: 52-1499 (6,889 hrs); 52-1500 (7,920 hrs); 52-1504 (8,179 hrs); 52-1505 (5,551 hrs); 52-1506 (8,159 hrs); 52-1509 (7,262 hrs); 52-1511 (8,283 hrs); 52-1516 (8,659 hrs); 52-1519 (7,355 hrs); 52-1521 (6,505 hrs); 52-1526 (9,147 hrs); 52-1545 (8,646 hrs); 52-1548 (8,990 hrs); 52-1551 (7,519 hrs) and 52-1564 (6,153 hrs). The three B-57Cs are 53-3831 (8,302 hrs); 53-3840 (8,432 hrs) and 53-3856 (8,292 hrs).*

TALKBACK

Vietnam air war

IN A RECENT issue of the Soviet publication *Aviatsiya i Kosmonavtika* appeared an article by Gen-Maj Dao Din Luen, C-in-C of the Vietnam People's Army Air Force, presenting some details of the history of his air arm which may interest your readers. The Vietnam People's Army Air Force (VPAAF) was, according to its C-in-C, formed a quarter-century ago, in May 1955, when, after the conclusion of hostilities with the French, an aerodrome section was formed, but it was not until May 1959 that the first air transport unit was formed, and nearly five years more elapsed before, in February 1964, the first fighter regiment was organised. This flew its first operational sorties on 3 April 1965, and on that and the following day claimed the destruction of four F-105 Thunderchiefs and AD-6 Skyraiders.

The article relates a number of incidents as highlights of the subsequent fighting with the US and South Vietnamese forces, but does not attribute dates to many of these events (eg, the attack by pilots Bien and Man on 12 F-105s over Vinfu in which two of the F-105s were destroyed and the aircraft of "USAF MiG specialist Jim Karl" was damaged; the attack by MiG-17s flown by pilots Ai and Bai on the US 7th Fleet in the Gulf of Tonking in which the destroyer *Heybeck* was damaged, and the battle with 36 US aircraft off Kha Van Tyukl in which Col John Folin, deputy CO of the Korat-based wing, was shot down). There are *some* incidents, however, to which specific dates are applied, such as the destruction of four F-105s by pilots Do, Koka, Khuen and Dinya on 30 April 1967, three of the USAF pilots being taken prisoner; the destruction of three F-4 Phantoms over Khatai by pilots Tin, Khai and Mai on 12 May 1967, one of the US pilots being Col Norman Hardison, and the destruction by night over Tkhanshan by Hero of the People's Army Fam Tuan of a B-52 Stratofortress.

To 31 December 1972, when "the destructive US air attacks ceased", the VPAAF had engaged in more than 400 air combats in which it had destroyed 320 US aircraft of 17 types, 88 US aircrew having been captured. In the spring of 1975, with the capture of Da Nang, a number of enemy aircraft were captured and VPAAF crews were converted to the Cessna A-37. Within six days, on 28 April, five of the A-37s acquired by the VPAAF flew their first operational sorties with an attack on the airfield at Tanshonnat. On 16 May 1977, the VPAAF became an independent component of the forces of the Vietnam People's Republic, and for its operational achievements was to be awarded the title of "Hero Air Force", two regiments being named "Hero Regiments" and eight companies becoming "Hero Companies". Twenty-two airmen of the VPAAF have received the Hero of the Vietnam People's Army award, 248 commissioned and non-commissioned personnel have been awarded Ho Chi Minh badges, and the VPAAF as a service has been awarded the Order of Ho Chi Minh, First Class.

F J French
Felixstowe, Suffolk IP1 17EF

Covert Hercules

I AM writing to correct an erroneous caption used for one of the C-130 photos on page 193 of "AIR INTERNATIONAL"/April 1980 issue. The photo depicts an MC-130E at Rhein-Main airbase, Germany, but states that this aircraft is a "drone launcher/retriever". As an MC-130E pilot belonging to the unit to which that bird is assigned I can assure you that it is not used to "shoot" or "snatch" drones — this being the speciality of the DC-130 version.

The MC-130E, code named *Combat Talon* (but known as "Blackbird" to the aircrews), is a specially modified model of the C-130E Hercules and is used for Special Operations. Our speciality is covert infiltration and exfiltration at ultra low altitudes at night, using special avionics for terrain masking, navigation and airdrops. MC-130s are the descendants of the black "Carpetbagger" B-24s of World War II.

Lt Bernard V Moon II
New York, USA

Canberra confusion

THE INTERESTING letter from Simon Murdoch, published in AIR INTERNATIONAL/May 1980, raises some questions about the identities of the *Luftwaffe* Canberras and includes one specific error I would like to correct. The reference to the serial D9568 is certainly wrong: this should be D9569.

The problem arises in trying to relate the successive re-allocation of serial numbers to these three Canberras, the original c/ns of which are not in doubt. It is also certain that the original markings (YA+151, 152 and 153, then 00+01, 02 and 03) were assigned in sequence with the c/ns, as listed by Mr Murdoch.

It does seem that the next allocation of fuselage serials was out of sequence, but several alternative versions of the allocation have now been published and Mr Murdoch offers yet another. From information I received some years ago from a *Luftwaffe* serving officer I believe the correct sequence to be:

00+01 to D9569 to 99+34
00+02 to D9566 to 99+35
00+03 to D9567 to 99+36

I would be interested to learn if any reader can confirm beyond doubt that these are correct.

P H T Green
Irby, South Humberside

Scrapped Shorts

I HAVE read with interest the article "The Belfast Goes Civil" (AIR INTERNATIONAL/June 1980) and, in particular, the reference to the seven aircraft sold to Rolls-Royce Limited.

The article states that four aircraft were broken up by Rolls-Royce Ltd after removal of the Tyne engines. In fact, the aircraft, less the engines and other instrumentation, were sold to the Bird Group of Companies who subsequently broke them up in order that the constituent metals and other materials could be sold for re-use.

Richard P Thwaites
Group Company Secretary
The Bird Group of Companies
Stratford-upon-Avon, Warks

G-91s in Angola

WITH REFERENCE to Mr F Willemsen's letter in AIR INTERNATIONAL/April 1980 issue, on the German *Luftwaffe* ("Talkback", page 205), this needs a minor clarification. The 40 G-91R.4s handed over to the *Força Aérea Portuguesa* (FAP) in 1966 mentioned have been engaged in the colonial war in Guinea-Bissau, Angola and Mozambique and at least 10 have been shot down by SAM 7 or AAG (anti-aircraft guns). At least three of the others remain in the FAPA/DAA (Angolan Popular Air Force and Anti-Aircraft Defence) inventory.

Nijunza Kambrukwnha
Luanda

A Jug in need

IN FEBRUARY this year, my "Pride and Joy" had an engine failure during the take-off roll at the Tulsa International Airport. The plane crashed into a wooded area at the end of the runway and sustained severe damage to the fuselage and right wing. It was a P-47D aeroplane which had been restored to its World War II flying configuration and colours. It was one of only three P-47s remaining on active flight status in the world today.

After the accident I trucked the wreckage to

continued on page 188

(Left) MiG-21s receiving the attention of ground crews at an unknown base in North Vietnam during the period of hostilities against South Vietnam. Some details of the Vietnam People's Army Air Force are contained in the letter above from F J French, based on information published in the Soviet Union. The reference to a B-52 being shot down by a VPAAF fighter is controversial, as USAF records indicate that all 17 Stratofortresses lost to enemy action were destroyed by surface-to-air missiles.

THE SMELL OF THE AIRPLANES

BY ROY BRAYBROOK

ILLUSTRATIONS BY CHRIS WREN

I FEEL OBLIGED to return to the subject of air shows, if only to have an excuse to tell a story which appeals to my sense of humour. By way of introduction, I should add that those readers who have lived with this series from as far back as July 1979, may recall that we then kicked around various ideas to make air displays safer and more dramatic. Whereas most of my thoughts fall on the human analogue of radar-absorbent material (I am painfully aware that the modelling column draws far more fan-mail than *Personal View*), this particular article did actually stimulate some response.

Total strangers came up to me and pointed out that at the Queen's Silver Jubilee show at Finningley in 1977, the Royals could not have been barbecued by the RAAF F-111 "torching" jettisoned fuel, since that part of the act was omitted when Themselves were present. Sailplane enthusiasts wanted to know why there had been no mention of T-shirts declaring "Glider Pilots Do It Silently".

Two readers told me that my reference to the Atlantic crash at Farnborough in 1968 was at fault, ie, that there had been more to it than the drag of the port propeller unfeathering pulling the aircraft down out of a steep left-hand approach. One said that severe turbulence had been an important factor. The other told me that a spectator's ciné film had indicated a runaway of the rudder at the critical moment. All very interesting information, although the fact remains that following that crash all asymmetric power demonstrations have been banned at the world's three major shows, ie, Paris, Farnborough and Greenham Common.

Out of all the conversations that arose from that article, the point that came across most strongly was that the only way to really liven up an air show is to include a firepower demonstration. Hence the following story.

Once upon a time there was a Latin American country, which I recall mainly for its excellent beer, attractive *muchachas*, an unbelievable alpaca rug that I bought in the Indian market and some very useful initialled glasses that I liberated from the Bolivar. It had been governed for some years by a tri-service socialist *junta*, but one day word got around that the navy had decided to play monopoly, steam its old cruisers into the harbour of the capital, and train their guns on anyone who was too stupid to understand the more subtle aspects of internal politics.

This rumour went down like a lead balloon with the air force, which felt it was just as good at subtle messages as the navy. A firepower demonstration was therefore arranged in the bay, where the crowds on the cliffs could watch a simulated battle in which wooden targets in the shape of ships would be duly sunk by the glorious aviators.

Comes the great day, the population of the capital watches as every Mirage that can be coaxed off the concrete beats hell out of the targets with cannon, rockets and bombs. This goes

"... sense of smell..."

down very well with the crowds, but the political message is blurred by the fact that (a) the targets — being wood — fail to sink, and (b) two Mirages are lost. To the best of my recollection, one flew into the sea and another was hit by a ricochet.

To come to the punch-line, the joke that went around the bars that night was that *if the "battle" had gone on for another half-hour, the "ships" would have won*!

Having attended a couple of British Army firepower demonstrations at Lulworth Cove, with some very spectacular use of tank guns and artillery (and this year the Euromissile Milan anti-tank missile), I am keen to see what an air force can provide in comparison.

It is not really true that — as MoD (Def Sales) argues — Britain has three defence equipment exhibitions, since the SBAC Show is far removed from an aviation equivalent of the British Army (or Royal Navy) Equipment Exhibition. To make Farnborough equate with BAEE, Def Sales would have to organise a simultaneous firepower demonstration by the RAF at Larkhill on Salisbury Plain for invited military guests and the press. I trust DPF (Defence Promotions & Facilities) will remember who started the idea!

There are various precedents for the use of Larkhill for air-to-ground firings in front of official delegations, and earlier this year a Royal Artillery show for the public included rocket firings by a US Army AH-1S HueyCobra. Switzerland has regular air-to-ground firing competitions (*Flugmeisterschaft*) at a site up in the mountains, but these events are open to only

THE SNORES OF THE CROWD!

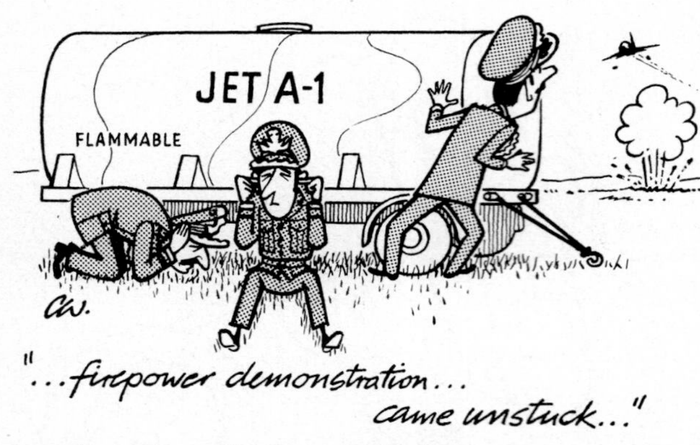

"...firepower demonstration... came unstuck..."

a small number of invitees. Aerial firepower demonstrations (including the use of napalm) have taken place in Israel, but the best known are probably those held annually by the US Navy at Pt Mugu (on the coast near Los Angeles), where firings can be made with little risk to the crowd.

Unfortunately, firepower demonstrations have been known to come badly unstuck. Press reports earlier this year spoke of an accident in Portugal, in which the reviewing stand was actually strafed by the aircraft! I am told that in the early postwar years firepower was occasionally demonstrated to important visitors to Boscombe Down and West Raynham (then RAF Central Fighter Establishment). There is said to have been a well-known incident in which the famous Zurakowski (flying a Hornet) almost hit a Soviet delegation with his RPs!

Associated with any use of firepower, there must be some element of risk, although at a venue such as Pt Mugu this is minimised by the targets being quite evidently in the blue area and the spectators on the concrete-coloured stuff.

Of course, there will always be some slight risk at any form of air display. To digress for a moment, what I object to extremely strongly is the idea of any spectator having a heart attack induced by some cretin in a noisy, high-speed multi-million aircraft (or leading formation of same), who decides to liven things up by making his entrance at low level and full throttle from *behind* the crowd. Any demonstration pilot who finds it necessary to induce a state of shock in the spectators or terrify young children has no right in the business. It is moronic to imagine that everyone in a crowd of thousands is completely fit and I would ban such pilots for life. In any event, when I have my coronary, I want it to be induced by something much more satisfying!

Smoke and Flame

Going to the opposite extreme, one of the more accomplished display pilots to take part in the 1980 UK air show season makes considerable use of very low noise levels. Stefan Karwowski (a New Zealander who has flown with the Carling Pitts team in Canada and was formerly the solo demonstration pilot on Hunter and Jaguar for SOAF*), flying the Hunter Mk 51 from the Spencer Flack collection, has developed a display which includes a high-speed inverted pass with engine at flight idle. The aural impact is enhanced by the fact that the aircraft has been extensively cleaned up, with gun blast deflectors and link collectors removed, and all unnecessary apertures faired over, producing an extremely low airframe sound level. His demonstration also includes a tight, low turn in front of the crowd, again with the engine throttled back so that the audience gets the full effect of two very powerful wing vortices.

In essence, the problem for any demonstration pilot is to find some means to produce an impact on the senses without actually endangering life. The senses in question are traditionally restricted to sight and sound, although BAe's Bill Bedford has said that the sense of smell should not be ignored: "A really exotic high-performance aircraft should somehow leave behind the fragrance of Chanel No 5"! And Philip Meeson's Pitts Special a hint of Smitty or a whiff of Marlboro?

Having applauded the RAAF's trick of "torching" jettisoned fuel, I note with concern the report in the April issue of this journal that the technique is now banned by that service on the grounds that it may have caused the loss of an F-111 in October 1978.

If flames are out of the question, then smoke is the obvious eye-catcher. I learn from the sales literature of that well-known US smoke-maker Frank Sanders that the technique was first used in 1929 at the Cleveland Air Races, when a gentleman named Lund injected oil into the engine exhaust of the Taper-Wing Waco.

Smoke can enliven any display, and was used to good effect in the case of the Royal Netherlands Air Force F.27M Troopship which won the International Display Sword at Greenham Common in 1979. Although these F.27M demonstrations have been received very enthusiastically in the UK, the fact is that on his home ground the pilot (Maj Doors) normally does most of his show with one engine out! On the subject of outstanding demonstrations by transport aircraft, one example that is universally acclaimed is de Havilland Canada's flying of the Buffalo.

With modern high performance aircraft it is possible to make a visual impact by sudden changes of aircraft attitude and flight path. In March, I attended a demonstration of the F-16 by Neil Anderson for the Hellenic Air Force evaluation team and the flying included the closest thing to square turns that I have ever seen. This was a very good example of a demonstration aimed not at pleasing a crowd, but at convincing hard-nosed professionals of the aircraft's acceleration, climb and turn rate, and the pilot's ability to manoeuvre with reckless abandon.

On occasion a pilot enlivens his show with a manoeuvre that others will not (and possibly cannot) use. It is probably fair to say that John Farley's dramatic "rocket climb" in the V/STOL Harrier has no real operational significance, but no other aircraft (not even the Yak-36) can duplicate it.

Dassault-Breguet's Saget is widely regarded as Europe's leading high-speed aerobatic pilot and there is no sign of others rushing to imitate his horizontal rolling circles in the Alpha Jet. I have never met Saget, but Macchi's Franco Bonazzi (another of Europe's top demonstration pilots) tells me that what makes the Frenchman unique is his application of light aircraft aerobatics to high-speed military types.

"...wingtip vortices..."

Sultan of Oman's Air Force.

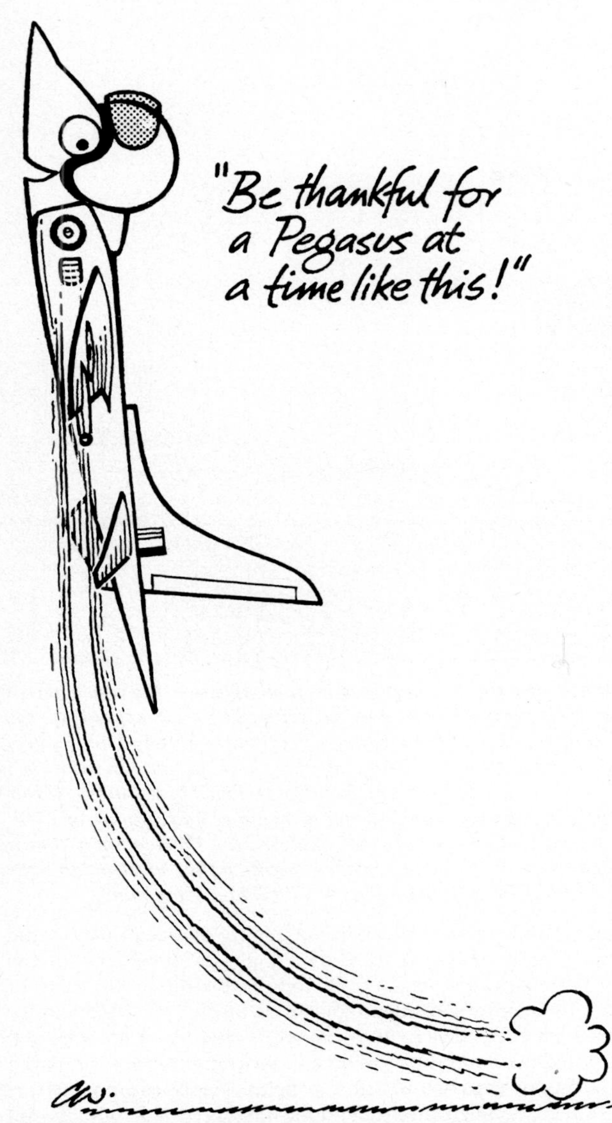

"Be thankful for
a Pegasus at
a time like this!"

Apparently Saget teaches aerobatics weekends at Villacoublay. Whether his rolling circles in the Alpha Jet prove anything beyond his own superlative skill is not clear: perhaps the message is that you need a really good rudder to do it, and that of the Alpha Jet is powered, whereas the rival Hawk's rudder is "manual".

Following the loss of a Tornado during a rehearsal for this year's Hanover Show in what some reports described as a repeat of the A-10 looping accident at Paris in 1977, I wonder if loops are really worth including in the programme for anything but the most highly powered aircraft. A really well executed loop may give the pilot considerable satisfaction, but from the spectator's viewpoint it is a slow-moving, drawn-out, neck-straining affair. Recovery height varies not only with speed and height of entry to the loop, but also with the timing and amount of flap, buffet and afterburner. I am told that the RAF has banned looping manoeuvres with the Lightning due to variations in afterburner response.

In commenting on my earlier effort on the subject of air displays, one reader said that — like car racing — such events are now less exciting because of the current obsession with eliminating all risk to human life. I checked this analogy with my tame expert on motor racing and found it to be total nonsense. Due to the development of energy-absorbing chicken-wire barriers, you can now have vehicles hurtling at the crowd at far higher speeds and with no risk to the spectators.

Regrettably, air shows have no equivalent of the chicken-wire barrier, and accidents will consequently continue to put at risk not only the life of the driver, but also those of people on the ground. Having talked to some of the experts, what particularly worries me is the number of air show accidents that were predicted days in advance by other pilots taking part, and the number of complaints that the pilots have against the air traffic controllers and their own employers.

Le Bourget is a particularly difficult case for ATC, since it mixes all-day flying displays with normal airport movements. However, it is clearly unacceptable to have the controller spoil the pilot's concentration by telling him in the middle of a difficult manoeuvre that he is to land on a different runway!

Complaints against the aircraft manufacturers centre on the limited time available for practice prior to the show. It has been suggested to me that the responsibility for a pilot going ahead with his display should be taken out of his hands and given to an inspector appointed by the show organisers, who would have to certify to the pilot having had adequate practice, including routine variations of his act to deal with (for example) changes in weather.

Beyond this, the pilot's company should ensure that his condition is not endangered by marketing commitments in the evenings, and that prior to flying he is not harrassed by sales or press contacts. Despite all these precautions, there will still be the pilot who kills himself by making an off-the-cuff change to his routine under pressure of competition. Human beings have a habit of getting carried away, first figuratively and then literally.

Nonetheless, since so many air show accidents could have been avoided through proper precautions, I wonder how many company heads have read of such tragedies and written to their chief test pilots to ask what can be done to eliminate them. Precious few, I suspect.

At the end of the day, when we have done our best to liven things up and simultaneously cut down the loss of lives, what does an air show achieve? Beyond entertaining the masses, it is hoped that it plays some part in selling aeroplanes, although the link between shows and sales is difficult to prove. The Red Arrows gave some brilliant displays on their two-seat Gnats, yet not one of the type was ever exported.

Perhaps the best thing ever said on this subject was in reference to Rockwell's Bob Hoover, one of the great showmen of the aviation game, a pilot who does things with a Shrike Commander (for example) that normal demonstration pilots only do in a Pitts Special. According to the legend, someone once said: "Of course, I would never buy a Shrike Commander. It may be a superlative machine, but in the back of my mind there would always be that terrible nagging suspicion that *HE* might have flown it!" □

New on the airshow circuit in 1980 was the Pitts S 2S G-SOLO, flown in Rothmans colours by David Perrin.

EMIL ÜBER ENGLAND

Two score years ago this month, the epic aerial conflict of all time, the Battle of Britain, completed its final phase — the emasculated Jagdflieger were withdrawn from the assault on Southern Britain — the Schlacht um England — suffering, like their opponents, the squadrons of RAF Fighter Command, from physical and nervous strain: neither side had been defeated; both were battered and weary. Forty years on, W J A "Tony" Wood takes a fresh look at the rôle played in the "Battle" by one of the classic fighters in aviation's annals, the Messerschmitt Bf 109E, alias Emil, then at the zenith of its career and, to that time, apparently enveloped by a nimbus. It was Emil's lot to be a principal in the drama that unfolded over England's southern counties in that dramatic summer and autumn of 1940, and on these pages, W J A "Tony" Wood sets the scene for its participation in the "Battle", and analyses the shortcomings that it suffered and the advantages that it enjoyed compared with its principal opponents in the historic conflict that ensued, and the unfavourable conditions, both geographical and tactical, under which it was pitted against RAF Fighter Command.

UP TO AND INCLUDING the operations of July and early-August 1940, the German Fighter Arm, or *Jagdwaffe*, had accomplished all the tasks set before it since the beginning of the war. Prior to the commencement of hostilities, on 1 September 1939, the tactical, operational and logistical development of the *Jagdwaffe* had proceeded apace. Within the *Reich* itself, manoeuvres, which encompassed the swift movement of fighter forces, had been practised before and during the Austrian *anschlüss*, the annexation of Czech-Sudetenland and prior to the Munich Crisis, while active combat experience in Spain through the medium of the *Legion Condor* brought back a tactical dividend of incomparable value. It was a combat-ready and tactically experienced *Jagdwaffe* that supported the invasion of Poland and swept aside the meagre opposition afforded by a few squadrons of obsolescent PZL P.7 and P.11c fighters.

Even in the limited defensive actions involving diurnal defence of the *Reich*, the Bf 109Es and Bf 110Cs of *Jafü Deutsche Bücht* (German Bight) had inflicted casualties of such gravity upon RAF Bomber Command as to force it to resort to nocturnal bombing for which it was ill-prepared. A small force, consisting of I/ZG 1, I/ZG 76, and II/JG 77, had furnished adequate support of Operation *Weserübung* on 9 April 1940, when the *Wehrmacht* invaded Denmark and Norway. The first real test of the capabilities of the *Jagdwaffe* came on 10 May 1940, when Germany turned upon France, Holland and Belgium. Due to the pace of operations lasting until 25 June 1940, attrition was comparatively heavy, but not even the most modern fighters of the Anglo-French alliance, which included the Hawker Hurricane Mk I, the Bloch 152 and the Morane-Saulnier MS 406, could match those of the *Jagdwaffe*, the Bf 109Es, or *Emils*, in terms of numbers or efficacy, nor their pilots in terms of experience and combat skill.

The success of the *Jagdwaffe* in the West during May and June 1940 lay not so much in the quality of its equipment and crews, both of which were of a high standard, but in the dynamic nature in which units followed within a few miles of the advancing front-line. Conceived as part of a tactical air force *par excellence*, the *Luftwaffe* fighter units enjoyed unparalleled mobility: advanced working parties prepared airstrips or repaired existing airfields, signal equipment was installed and teleprinter-telephone lines were laid, light 20-mm and 37-mm *Flak* units giving protection, while relays of Ju 52/3m's flew in everything from B4 aviation fuel, oil and ammunition to deck-chairs and tents. Within at most a day and often even hours of occupying a strip, the fighters could be turned-around and launched on operations in support of the advance.

During the *Kanalkampf* of July and the first 10 days of August 1940, the Bf 109Es of *Jagdgeschwader* 51 operated from grass strips in the Pas-de-Calais, before being joined by those of III/JG 3 on 12 July, and elements of JG 26 and JG 52 towards the latter end of the month. During this time Obstlt Max Ibel's JG 27 supported *VIII Fliegerkorps*. Periods of bad weather led to difficult conditions on the soggy, grass airfields, but in the air the *Jagdgeschwader* encountered no immediate problems. The area of the Channel and the Straits of Dover, wherein the bulk of the initial shipping strikes took place, lay well within the combat radius of *Emil*. *Major* Theo Osterkamp headed JG 51 until succeeded in his post of *Geschwaderkommodore* by the supremely successful Maj Werner Mölders on 27 July, thereafter becoming *Jafü* 2 in succession to Obstlt Karl von Döring. Both Johannes Fink and Osterkamp conducted the *Kanalkampf* with skill and vigour, continually probing the defences of No 11 (Fighter) Group under Air Vice-Marshal Keith R Park. The *Emils* gave escort cover and top-cover to the Do 17Z bombers and Ju 87s during the strikes, and were often released for freelance fighter sweeps, termed *Frei Jagd* (Free Chase), in which formations of Bf 109Es in up to

Gruppe strength roved over the Channel and the South Coast at heights varying from deck-level to 25,000 ft (7 620 m).

Although reluctant to do so, Air Chief Marshal Dowding (C-in-C Fighter Command) was committed to countering the attacks against merchant shipping in the Channel in addition to the defence of Dover. These tasks he could conduct with economy of effort due to the extraordinary advantage proffered on his Command by dint of radar. Facing seawards the radar early-warning system consisted of a belt of Chain-Home (CH: AMES Mk I) stations that had a pick-up range of 150 miles (241 km) on a target flying at 15,000 ft (4 570 m). As *Kampfgeschwader* 2's Dorniers struggled for height, therefore, Dowding's Groups could be passed information of their position and strength before they passed abeam Amiens from their bases near Cambrai. The CH system was backed by Chain-Home Low radars that could locate a target in the Channel flying at any altitude above 150 ft (46 m). The system had cost millions and had been the subject of unremitting research and labour.

The early-warning radars were but a part of a comprehensive system of Fighter Control which, aided by the Observer Corps, was able to plot enemy raids while, at the same time, control its own fighters by VHF R/T and IFF (Identification: Friend-or-Foe). The Germans also had radar. The FuMG 80 *Freya*, developed by the GEMA concern, was in service as an early-warning radar with properties similar to, if not better, than its British counterpart, but on the Channel coast there was only one located at Wissant which was employed for coast-watching. Whereas the RAF could "see" by day or by night, the *Luftwaffe* was thus to remain blind.

Despite the advantage of radar, the RAF Fighter Control System could not differentiate between fighters and bombers in a formation, and there were to be several occasions during *Kanalkampf* when Hurricanes and Spitfires were bounced by *Emils* engaged on a *Frei Jagd* mission. The RAF fighters were invariably at a disadvantage in terms of height and the position of the sun as they climbed southwards over the Channel. On 19 July 1940, the long suspected deficiencies of the Defiant were thrown into stark relief when No 141 Squadron was all but annihilated in a dogfight with Bf 109Es south of Folkestone. Weighed down by its heavy turret, the ponderous Defiant was to suffer very heavy loss until a belated Air Ministry order of 31 August 1940 relegated the type to the nocturnal rôle, or to use by day only in the most favourable circumstances. Thankfully for Fighter Command, the Defiant provided only a very small proportion of its overall inventory.

The *Kanalkampf* also highlighted the weakness of Fighter Command's combat tactics. The basic RAF formation was the section of three, flying in Vic (V-formation) with sections in echelon or in line-astern. Operations in France and over Dunkirk had largely put paid to the ludicrous Fighting Area Attacks which had been the standard procedure during the 1930s. Following a near disaster on 23 May, No 54 Sqdn had pursued the policy of employing the pair of fighters, while No 19 Sqdn preferred a section of six in loose pairs. During July 1940, Sqdn Ldr P K Devitt's No 152 Sqdn regularly employed the section of two and four when in fighter-versus-fighter combat.

Other squadrons followed slowly in the development of formation tactics which were best suited to the cut and thrust of a dogfight. The *Jagdwaffe*, on the other hand, had used the basic *Rotte* (pair) and *Schwarm* (finger-four) to maintain fluidity with cohesion in formations up to *Gruppe* strength. Developed by the incomparable Mölders, the *Rotten* and *Schwärme* formations were to be copied and were to form the basis of fighter formation tactics to this day. Both were ideal for *offensive* fighter operations but, unfortunately for the *Luftwaffe*, were to be of minimal value when used in a tight *defensive* capacity for the escort of bomber formations.

The relative merits

The fighter battles that took place during *Kanalkampf* offered a unique opportunity to compare the relative merits of pilots and machines of the opposing air forces. Notwithstanding the dangers posed by the *Frei Jagd* tactics upon RAF squadrons on occasion, both sides often fought purely fighter-versus-fighter combats over the Channel within equal distance of their recovery airfields. In terms of combat experience, a far greater

(Head of opposite page) On page 199, Julius Neumann recalls his experiences with Emil. Here Bf 109Es of Oblt Neumann's Schwarm are seen shortly before his last mission. (Above right) Emils of III/JG 26 dispersed on Caffiers airfield, near Calais, during the "Battle of Britain", and (below) Emils of II/JG 27 at St Trond airfield, Belgium, where the unit was based 19-22 May 1940.

An engine change being carried out under decidedly primitive conditions on a Bf 109E-3 of III/JG 26 at Caffiers airfield, near Calais, during the "Battle of Britain".

percentage of German fighter pilots had seen action than had their counterparts in the RAF. This was to count in the ensuing battles of attrition. Those who had not served in the *Legion Condor*, or been rotated from Poland and Norway, had seen continuous action since 10 May 1940. Moreover, freshmen fighter pilots were leaving a well-organised and efficient training system at the rate of 800 per month.

Prospective fighter pilots, after basic training at a *Fl. Ausbildungs Regt* and *A/B Schule* where they received 120-150 hours flying, passed on to *Jagdflieger-Vörschule* for 8-10 hours on Bf 108B and Ar 96B types before a period of up to 50 hours on the Bf 109E. The *Luftwaffe* enjoyed a surplus of fighter pilots in 1940, and successful candidates were assigned to an operational *Ergänzungs-Staffel* or the *IV Gruppe* of the parent *Jagdgeschwader*. Fighter pilot training in the RAF, by comparison, was still in a state of upheaval following the pre-war expansion and mobilisation phase. The output of pilots from RAF Training Command was relatively low, and as yet was not complemented by the production of pilots and crews from the newly-constituted Empire Air Training Scheme. The Operational Training Units were not formed until December 1940, while the output of "fighter" pilots from the Group Pools of Nos 11 and 12 (Fighter) Groups produced a combined average of a mere 44 per month during the first quarter of 1940. Experienced officer and NCO pilots, those who had seen active service in France and sparring over Dunkirk, were to be killed or wounded at a rate that was to inflict the gravest crisis upon RAF Fighter Command during the summer and autumn of 1940. These men could not be replaced in the time available, and the Command was forced to rely on a steadily diminishing number of exhausted men of experience who could do little with the freshmen pilots arriving on squadron with less than 10 hours *total* on either the Hurricane or Spitfire.

In terms of the relative qualities, there was little to choose between *Emil* and the Spitfire, whilst the Hurricane fought at some disadvantage. Given equal opportunity for engaging in combat, the quality and experience of the pilot was the over-riding factor in all three machines. In later air conflicts, the qualitative merits of the machine were to have a greater influence on the outcome of a battle and the eventual attainment of air superiority in an operational theatre. Examples of this were to be provided by the superiority of the Bf 109F-4/Trop over the Hurricanes and Curtiss P-40s of the Desert Air Force in 1942, the Fw 190A-3 over the Spitfire VB in Channel sparring during the same year, and the P-51B Mustang and the P-47D Thunderbolt with water-injection over the opposing *Luftwaffe* fighters in April 1944. But in the summer of 1940, the qualitative performance and handling parameters of the Hurricane, Spitfire and *Emil* were comparatively even. The advantage, as in every combat since 1914, went to the man who used height, sun and surprise, and who was able to fly his aircraft to and beyond its limits without fear.

The manufacturer's performance figures for its particular product were invariably the optimum that could be achieved under ideal conditions. The conclusions and performance parameters of Rechlin, in the case of the *Luftwaffe*, and A&AEE (Boscombe Down) for the Royal Air Force, were often obscured by an over-optimistic approach in an attempt to denigrate an enemy type without attempting to establish its true potency. Standard performance figures for the Spitfire Mk IA indicated a maximum True Air Speed of 362 mph (582 km/h) at 18,500 ft (5 640 m), but Fighter Command's *standard* figure for the Mk IA was 344 mph (554 km/h) on the pilot being ordered to "Gate", or fly at maximum speed. Gate for the Hurricane Mk I was 313 mph (503 km/h) by comparison with the oft-quoted maximum TAS of 324 mph (520 km/h) at 16,250 ft (4 970 m). The operational ceilings of the Hurricane and Spitfire were 30,250 ft (9 250 m) and 34,000 ft (10 350 m) respectively; time to 15,000 ft (4 570 m) for the Spitfire Mk I was 6·2 min, and for the Mk I Hurricane 7·25 min which, even for the standards of 1940, was slow.

In their handling qualities, both aircraft were excellent: the Hurricane was sedate compared with the sensitive Spitfire, which was viceless save for a vicious flick if pulled around the corner too hard. Both were armoured; both were armed with eight Browning 0·303-inch (7,7-mm) Mk II* machine guns, harmonised to 200 yards (183 m) and aimed by a GM2 Mk II reflector sight. A reliable weapon, the Browning had a muzzle velocity of 2,440 ft/sec (743 m/sec) with Mk VII ball ammunition and a rate of fire of 1,150 rounds per minute. A three seconds burst fired approximately 10 lb (4,5 kg) of ball, incendiary-tracer and de Wilde ammunition.

The Hurricane Mk I, fitted with the 1,030 hp Merlin III and the Rotol or de Havilland CS propeller, bore the brunt of RAF Fighter Command's defensive commitment during the summer of 1940; it was to be the last period in which it could be considered adequate for the interceptor duties placed upon it. Compared with the Spitfire and Bf 109E, the Hurricane was aerodynamically and structurally obsolescent even prior to the outbreak of war, but it was to give invaluable service, representing as it did a compromise between speed and armament on the one hand and an uncomplicated production process resulting in high rate of supply and ease of maintenance on the other.

The overall impression presented by *Emil* was of a fighter design that had been compromised by the need for heavier armament and increased engine power to keep in step with fighter development in France and Britain. The design, as envisaged in the spring of 1934, was essentially a lightweight, high-performance point-defence fighter fitted with the traditional fuselage-mounted armament of two rifle-calibre machine guns and the possibility of a third firing through the propeller spinner. The French development of the 20-mm Hispano-Suiza cannon and the British adoption of an anti-bomber armament of eight 0·303-inch machine guns rendered the Messerschmitt's armament patently inadequate. Attempts to fit a 20-mm cannon in the fuselage position were not to meet with success until the advent of the *Friedrich*-series of 1941. The retro-fit of a 7,92-mm MG 17 in each of the wings compromised the strength of the single mainspar, and the structural integrity of the light wing was compromised still further by the insertion of coolant radiators with adoption of the DB 601 engine for the Bf 109E, coupled with, from the E-3 sub-type, enlarged cavities for MG FF 20-mm cannon with their bulky T.60-FF canular magazines.

The inboard wing was reinforced and strengthened by 12-gauge skin, but the structural weakness was never totally made good. Limitations of IAS in the dive were promulgated in Pilot's Notes with special emphasis on care in the application of rolling *g* forces, to the fascination of the British whose Royal Aircraft Establishment was still conducting structural tests on *Emil*'s wing as late as October 1944! While this German fighter was to remain structurally sound for all normal manoeuvres provided that the pilot flew within its limits, there was no doubt that the aircraft had to be handled with a degree of circumspection not encountered in the Spitfire and Hurricane. In addition to the wings, the undercarriage, although of wider track than that of the Spitfire, suffered from greater torsional loads in crosswind and sideslip.

The Messerschmitt Bf 109E-1, E-3 and E-4 were the primary versions to serve with the *Jagdflieger* during the *Schlacht um England*: the Bf 109E-7 fighter-bomber entered the fray during August 1940, fitted with either a ETC 500/IXb or ETC 50/VIIId bomb-rack with the associated battery, fuse-box and release switch. The standard powerplant of all variants was the twelve-cylinder inverted-Vee Daimler-Benz DB 601A-1 or Aa (modified supercharger) rated at 1,085 hp (1,100 *pferdestärke*: PS) at 14,760 ft (4 500 m). The Robert Bosch PZ12 fuel-

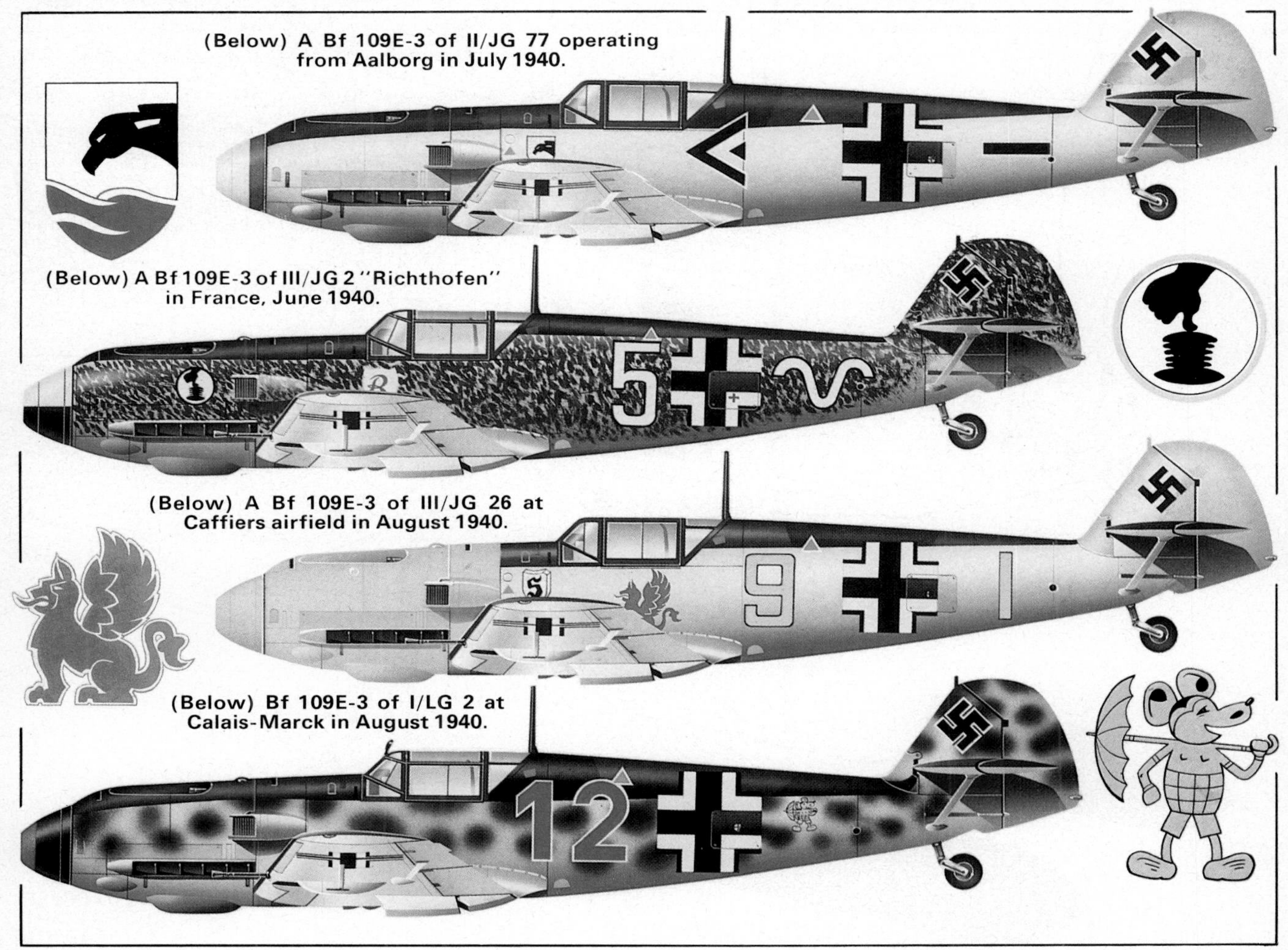

(Below) A Bf 109E-3 of II/JG 77 operating from Aalborg in July 1940.

(Below) A Bf 109E-3 of III/JG 2 "Richthofen" in France, June 1940.

(Below) A Bf 109E-3 of III/JG 26 at Caffiers airfield in August 1940.

(Below) Bf 109E-3 of I/LG 2 at Calais-Marck in August 1940.

injection pump fed one L'Orange (Sch.9-2137G) fuel jet per cylinder to confer several of the advantages of direct-fuel injection on a combat engine: engine acceleration and response to the throttle was immediate and, unlike the Hobson and Rolls-Royce/SU carburettors of the Merlin, the engine ran normally under negative-*g* conditions. The fuel injection system, however, demanded a high standard of maintenance.

The maximum TAS of the Bf 109E-1/E-3, as indicated in the official D.Luft.T handbook, was 285 mph (458 km/h) at sea-level, rising to 345 mph (555 km/h) at 16,400 ft (5 000 m). The operational ceiling was 33,760 ft (10 290 m). The wing-loading, and therefore the handling characteristics and some of the performance attributes, was high for a fighter of 1940: at half-fuel weight, the loading of the Bf 109E-3 was 31·4 lb/sq ft (6,43 kg/m^2) as compared with the 23·7 lb/sq ft (4,85 kg/m^2) of the Spitfire. The British conducted copious studies and trials of the Bf 109E following the acquisition of an example from the French in May 1940 and, as late as September 1940, Messrs M B Morgan and D E Morris of RAE concluded the following:

1. The take-off is fairly straightforward. Landing is difficult until the pilot gets used to the aircraft. Longitudinally the aircraft is too stable for a fighter. There is a large change of directional trim with speed. No rudder trim is fitted: the lack of this is severely felt at high IAS, and limits the pilot's ability to turn to the left when diving.

The fin area and dihedral are adequate. The stall is not violent and there is no subsequent tendency to spin. The CLmax (max coefficient of lift) is 1·4 (flaps up) and 1·9 (flaps down). No vibration or "snaking" develops in a high-speed dive. Aileron snatching occurs as the slats open. All the controls are far too heavy at high IAS. Aerobatics are difficult.

2. The Messerschmitt 109E-3 is inferior to the Hurricane and Spitfire as a fighter. Its manoeuvrability at high speeds is severely curtailed by the heaviness of the controls, while its high wing loading causes it to stall readily under high normal accelerations and results in a poor turning circle.

At 400 mph IAS (644 km/h) a pilot, exerting all his strength, can apply only one-fifth aileron, thereby banking through 45° in about four seconds. The minimum radius of turn without height-loss at 12,000 ft (3 650 m) at full throttle is calculated at 885 ft (270 m) for the Messerschmitt 109E and 696 ft (212 m) for the Spitfire. The cockpit is too cramped for comfort.

No mean adversary

The RAF squadrons engaged in combat with *Emil* found little evidence to support the assertion that the German type was "inferior to the Hurricane and Spitfire as a fighter." The RAF fighters were light on the controls in the low and medium speed régimes but, in common with the Messerschmitt, they, too, were extremely hard to manoeuvre during high IAS dives. The rate of roll of the Spitfire, for example, was very low and was to be improved only in 1941, after pressure from operational squadrons brought in metal-skinned ailerons. Allied pilots found that the Bf 109E's poor pitch control at high IAS was particularly alarming: in a dive at 400+ mph IAS (644+ km/h) maximum backwards force of the control column brought the nose up very slowly, with the pilot being unable to apply *g* sufficient even to "grey-out". But few *Luftwaffe* pilots

continued on page 196

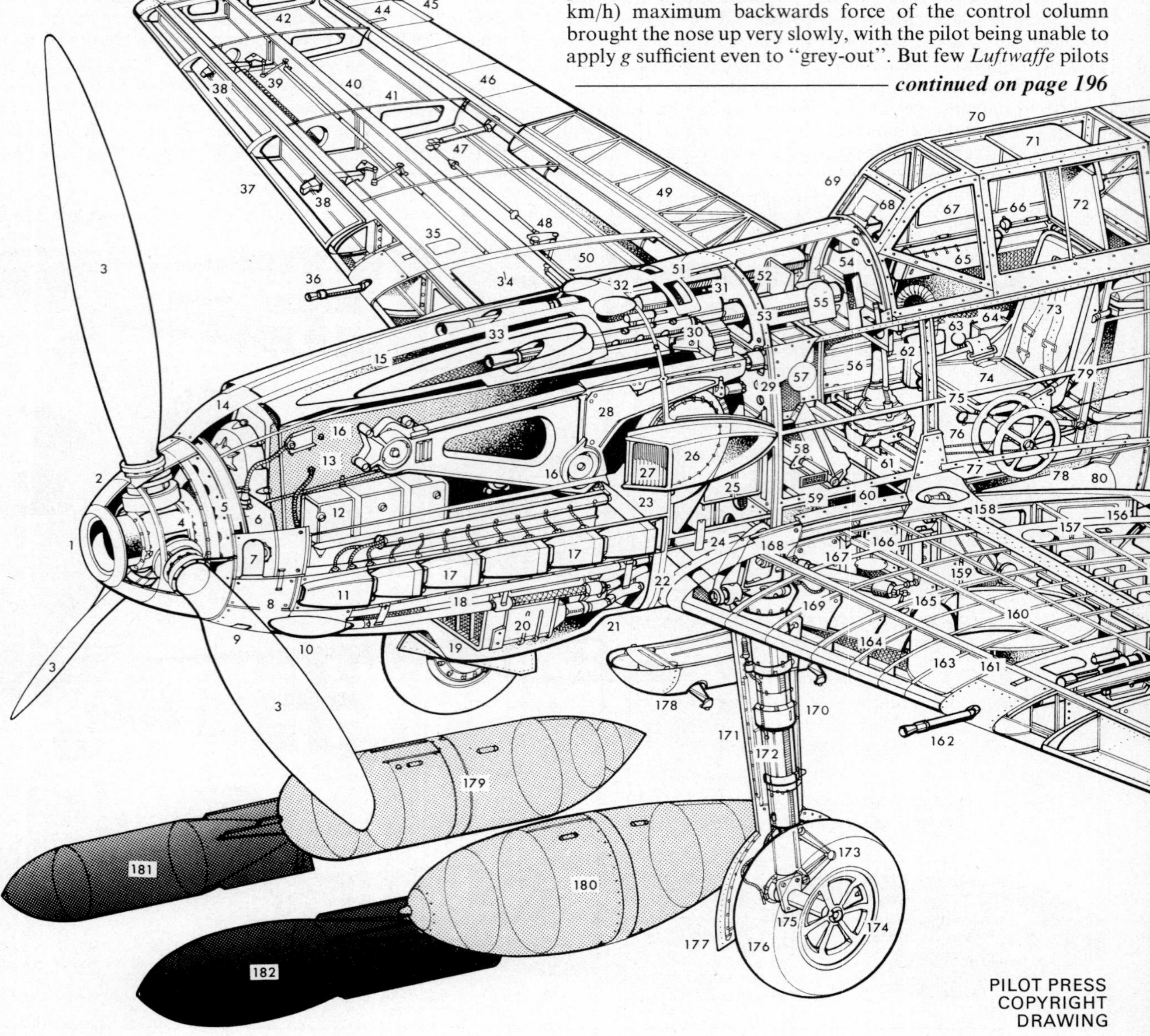

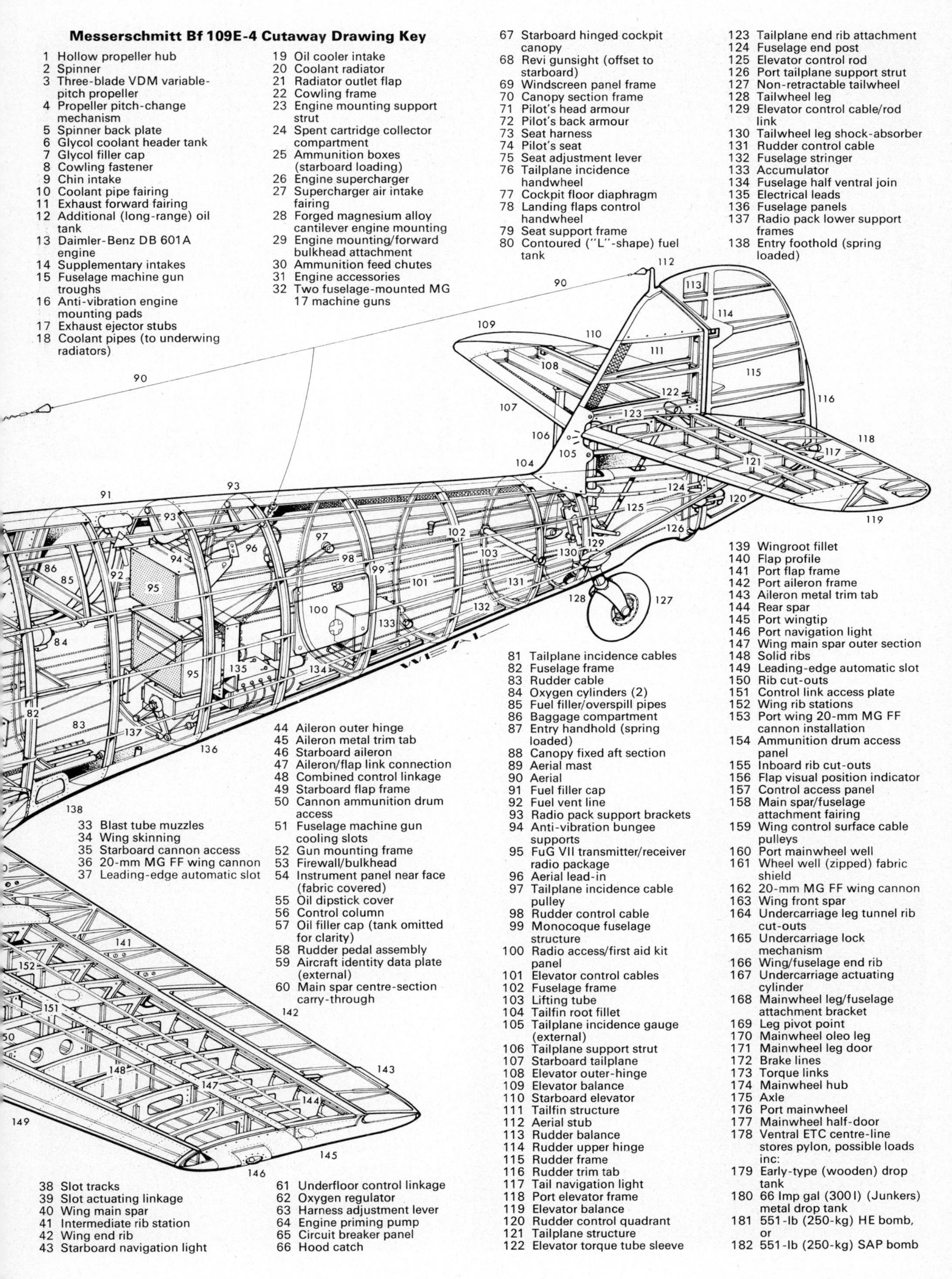

Messerschmitt Bf 109E-4 Cutaway Drawing Key

1 Hollow propeller hub
2 Spinner
3 Three-blade VDM variable-pitch propeller
4 Propeller pitch-change mechanism
5 Spinner back plate
6 Glycol coolant header tank
7 Glycol filler cap
8 Cowling fastener
9 Chin intake
10 Coolant pipe fairing
11 Exhaust forward fairing
12 Additional (long-range) oil tank
13 Daimler-Benz DB 601A engine
14 Supplementary intakes
15 Fuselage machine gun troughs
16 Anti-vibration engine mounting pads
17 Exhaust ejector stubs
18 Coolant pipes (to underwing radiators)
19 Oil cooler intake
20 Coolant radiator
21 Radiator outlet flap
22 Cowling frame
23 Engine mounting support strut
24 Spent cartridge collector compartment
25 Ammunition boxes (starboard loading)
26 Engine supercharger
27 Supercharger air intake fairing
28 Forged magnesium alloy cantilever engine mounting
29 Engine mounting/forward bulkhead attachment
30 Ammunition feed chutes
31 Engine accessories
32 Two fuselage-mounted MG 17 machine guns
33 Blast tube muzzles
34 Wing skinning
35 Starboard cannon access
36 20-mm MG FF wing cannon
37 Leading-edge automatic slot
38 Slot tracks
39 Slot actuating linkage
40 Wing main spar
41 Intermediate rib station
42 Wing end rib
43 Starboard navigation light
44 Aileron outer hinge
45 Aileron metal trim tab
46 Starboard aileron
47 Aileron/flap link connection
48 Combined control linkage
49 Starboard flap frame
50 Cannon ammunition drum access
51 Fuselage machine gun cooling slots
52 Gun mounting frame
53 Firewall/bulkhead
54 Instrument panel near face (fabric covered)
55 Oil dipstick cover
56 Control column
57 Oil filler cap (tank omitted for clarity)
58 Rudder pedal assembly
59 Aircraft identity data plate (external)
60 Main spar centre-section carry-through
61 Underfloor control linkage
62 Oxygen regulator
63 Harness adjustment lever
64 Engine priming pump
65 Circuit breaker panel
66 Hood catch
67 Starboard hinged cockpit canopy
68 Revi gunsight (offset to starboard)
69 Windscreen panel frame
70 Canopy section frame
71 Pilot's head armour
72 Pilot's back armour
73 Seat harness
74 Pilot's seat
75 Seat adjustment lever
76 Tailplane incidence handwheel
77 Cockpit floor diaphragm
78 Landing flaps control handwheel
79 Seat support frame
80 Contoured ("L"-shape) fuel tank
81 Tailplane incidence cables
82 Fuselage frame
83 Rudder cable
84 Oxygen cylinders (2)
85 Fuel filler/overspill pipes
86 Baggage compartment
87 Entry handhold (spring loaded)
88 Canopy fixed aft section
89 Aerial mast
90 Aerial
91 Fuel filler cap
92 Fuel vent line
93 Radio pack support brackets
94 Anti-vibration bungee supports
95 FuG VII transmitter/receiver radio package
96 Aerial lead-in
97 Tailplane incidence cable pulley
98 Rudder control cable
99 Monocoque fuselage structure
100 Radio access/first aid kit panel
101 Elevator control cables
102 Fuselage frame
103 Lifting tube
104 Tailfin root fillet
105 Tailplane incidence gauge (external)
106 Tailplane support strut
107 Starboard tailplane
108 Elevator outer-hinge
109 Elevator balance
110 Starboard elevator
111 Tailfin structure
112 Aerial stub
113 Rudder balance
114 Rudder upper hinge
115 Rudder frame
116 Rudder trim tab
117 Tail navigation light
118 Port elevator frame
119 Elevator balance
120 Rudder control quadrant
121 Tailplane structure
122 Elevator torque tube sleeve
123 Tailplane end rib attachment
124 Fuselage end post
125 Elevator control rod
126 Port tailplane support strut
127 Non-retractable tailwheel
128 Tailwheel leg
129 Elevator control cable/rod link
130 Tailwheel leg shock-absorber
131 Rudder control cable
132 Fuselage stringer
133 Accumulator
134 Fuselage half ventral join
135 Electrical leads
136 Fuselage panels
137 Radio pack lower support frames
138 Entry foothold (spring loaded)
139 Wingroot fillet
140 Flap profile
141 Port flap frame
142 Port aileron frame
143 Aileron metal trim tab
144 Rear spar
145 Port wingtip
146 Port navigation light
147 Wing main spar outer section
148 Solid ribs
149 Leading-edge automatic slot
150 Rib cut-outs
151 Control link access plate
152 Wing rib stations
153 Port wing 20-mm MG FF cannon installation
154 Ammunition drum access panel
155 Inboard rib cut-outs
156 Flap visual position indicator
157 Control access panel
158 Main spar/fuselage attachment fairing
159 Wing control surface cable pulleys
160 Port mainwheel well
161 Wheel well (zipped) fabric shield
162 20-mm MG FF wing cannon
163 Wing front spar
164 Undercarriage leg tunnel rib cut-outs
165 Undercarriage lock mechanism
166 Wing/fuselage end rib
167 Undercarriage actuating cylinder
168 Mainwheel leg/fuselage attachment bracket
169 Leg pivot point
170 Mainwheel oleo leg
171 Mainwheel leg door
172 Brake lines
173 Torque links
174 Mainwheel hub
175 Axle
176 Port mainwheel
177 Mainwheel half-door
178 Ventral ETC centre-line stores pylon, possible loads inc:
179 Early-type (wooden) drop tank
180 66 Imp gal (300 l) (Junkers) metal drop tank
181 551-lb (250-kg) HE bomb, or
182 551-lb (250-kg) SAP bomb

BACKFIRE PROLIFERATES

BEING ENCOUNTERED with increasing frequency over international waters around the Soviet periphery, from the Baltic Sea to the Sea of Japan, the long-range strike and maritime recce-strike aircraft known in the West as *Backfire* is assuming steadily greater importance in the inventories of the long-range strategic component of the V-VS and the shore-based element of the naval air arm whose capabilities it is now dramatically enhancing. With output — supposedly to have been limited to 30 annually under the commitments made at the Vienna Summit in June of last year — now reportedly rising from 2·5 to 3·5 monthly at the recently-expanded production facility devoted to *Backfire* manufacture south of Kazan, on the Kuybyshev-Volga lake, this potent warplane is posing a significant and growing threat, both as a primary strategic and tactical weapon directed against NATO in Europe and as a means of inflicting great damage on maritime reinforcement from the USA.

This variable-geometry warplane has provided a subject for

The photographs of Backfire-B (reproduced by courtesy of the Swedish Air Force via FLYGvapenNYTT) carrying the AS-4 Kitchen air-to-surface missile were taken during intrusions of Swedish airspace over the Baltic. The photographs above and on opposite page showing Backfire without refuelling probe were taken last year by J 35F Drakens, while that of Backfire with refuelling probe (below) was taken by an aircraft of the same type in the previous year. The general arrangement drawing on the opposite page supersedes that published in AIR INTERNATIONAL in June last year.

44
John Weal

controversy among western analysts since satellite reconnaissance first revealed a prototype of the initial model, *Backfire-A*, on the ground at the factory airfield near Kazan in July 1970. The primary area of disagreement over this aircraft has been its range capability. While there can now be little doubt that its primary functions *are* peripheral attack and naval missions, these providing the principal threat *currently* posed by *Backfire*, there is equally little doubt that it *does* pose at least some measure of intercontinental threat.

The supplement to the overview of the United States Military Posture for Fiscal 1981 by the Chairman of the US Joint Chiefs of Staff, Gen David C Jones, USAF, comments: "... detailed technical analysis now indicates that the aircraft [*Backfire*] *has* intercontinental strike capabilities", adding that these are enhanced by in-flight refuelling, "an option for which all *Backfires* are believed capable". In his Annual Report to Congress for the same Fiscal Year, US Secretary of Defense Harold Brown, was somewhat more guarded in attributing intercontinental capability to *Backfire*, stating: "It [*Backfire*] undoubtedly has *some* intercontinental capability in the sense that it can, for example, surely reach the United States from Soviet home bases on a one-way high-altitude subsonic unrefuelled flight with recovery in the Caribbean area. With Arctic staging, refuelling and certain high-altitude cruise profiles, it can probably execute a two-way mission to much of the United States."

However, if not academic, the question of *Backfire*'s intercontinental capability is perhaps of less immediate concern to NATO than its more manifest threat to Europe and the re-supply sealanes, with the menace that it presents the latter of overriding concern. Indeed, the naval *Backfire* fleet could well overtake the Soviet submarine force as the most serious threat to NATO maritime power by the mid-'eighties. With upwards of 150 of the production *Backfire-B* — referred to by Soviet delegates to the SALT II deliberations as the Tu-22M* — aircraft now deployed by the NavAir element, the *Aviatsiya Voenno-morskovo Flota* (AV-MF), and Long-Range Aviation, or *Aviatsiya Dal'nevo Deistviya* (ADD), it would seem that deliveries are continuing to be divided more or less equally between these components of the V-VS.

The differences between the *Backfires* for the AV-MF and the ADD appear to be confined to avionics and weaponry, the version most frequently encountered by western fighters in Soviet incursions on the fringes of national airspace being the maritime strike variant. The AV-MF *Backfire-B* has been appearing with increasing frequency of late over the Baltic, along the periphery of Swedish airspace, and has been intercepted by Viggens and Drakens of *Flygvapnet*. Although US intelligence reports have referred to the primary armament of *Backfire-B* in naval service as comprising *two* AS-4 *Kitchen* stand-off weapons — presumably mounted side-by-side on launching pylons beneath the air intake trunks — with the replacement of these missiles by the later AS-6 *Kingfish* in progress, most examples of this aircraft encountered over the Baltic carry *one Kitchen* semi-recessed in the fuselage, as illustrated by the accompanying photographs and drawings.

AS-4 *Kitchen* was first developed as a stand-off weapon for *Bear* and *Blinder*, and was, in fact, first seen on a *Blinder-B* as early as 1961, the mounting employed for this weapon by the earlier aircraft being essentially similar to that utilised by the AV-MF *Backfire-B*. This stand-off weapon, which features short-span delta wings and cruciform tail surfaces, the ventral component of which folds to starboard until launching, has undoubtedly undergone considerable development over the score of years in which it has been in production. Apparently propelled by a liquid rocket motor and featuring inertial guidance with infra-red terminal homing, *Kitchen*, in the form mated with *Backfire-B*, has an overall length of some 36 ft (11,0 m) and a span of approximately 11·5 ft (3,5 m). Weighing about 14,330 lb (6 500 kg), it attains speeds in excess of M = 2·0 and has a low-altitude range of the order of 160 naut miles. The AS-6 *Kingfish*, which is much the same size as *Kitchen*, has been seen on *Badgers* of the AV-MF, both over the Baltic and the Sea of Japan, but has yet to be seen on *Backfire*, which is expected to be its primary carrier.

AV-MF *Backfire-B*s have jettisonable stores racks well aft, beneath the air intake trunking, which are likely to carry ECM and ECCM pods, and, perhaps, decoy missiles. No gravity bombs can be accommodated by the internal weapons bay when the semi-recessed stand-off weapon is mounted, the unoccupied portion of the bay presumably being given over to fuel. The primary weapon of the ADD *Backfire-B* is as yet uncertain, but a new 745-mile (1 200-km) range cruise missile expected to be deployed from 1982-83 is known to have been mated with *Backfire* which may be expected to serve as its primary launch platform.

It is undeniable that *Backfire* is immeasurably enhancing the capabilities of both the AV-MF and the ADD, and the shore-based element of the former, in particular, is having its ability to strike enemy shipping at great distances from base radically transformed by the introduction of this highly capable warplane. □

**The service designation "Tu-22" had previously been applied in the west to the bomber and reconnaissance aircraft assigned the ASCC reporting name* Blinder *and known to possess the design bureau designation Tu-105. There have been examples of an identical design bureau designation being applied to two totally different aircraft, but a service designation has not, hitherto, been repeated, and as the suffix "M" invariably implies a limited design modification — and* Backfire *is, by no stretch of the imagination, a limited design modification of* Blinder *— it must be assumed that the designation "Tu-26" earlier credited to* Backfire *by western intelligence agencies is therefore incorrect.*

TALKBACK ***from page 176***

my home in Del Rio, Texas. I am presently involved in an active rebuild and restoration of the plane. Due to the damage suffered when the aircraft hit several large trees I am desperately trying to locate any of the major airframe components for the P-47.

If there are any of your readers who could help me locate and obtain any parts for the P-47, their assistance would be more than appreciated. I would welcome any information passed to me and invite any interested in the restoration to stop by our hangar for a visit.

Keep the green side up and the grey side down!

Major Robin P Collord
9056 Frazier
Del Rio, Texas, USA

Boeing restored

ENCLOSED is a photo of the newly-refurbished Boeing 80-A. Boeing Air Transport was the first to hire registered nurses 50 years ago and they first flew on this type of aircraft. Boeing Air Transport became United Air Lines later on. This aircraft will be the centrepiece of the soon-to-be-constructed Pacific Northwest Aviation Historical Foundation (which may be shortened to Pacific Museum of Flight) or "Red Barn Air Park", which includes the original Boeing "Red Barn" building.

Paul A Ludwig
Seattle, USA

VC10 ——— *from page 165*

other was transferred before delivery to BUA) and from BUA for two. East African Airways bought five Super VC10s, these being the last of the type built. Further details of deliveries and operators are tabulated separately.

The first VC10 to fly was a company-financed prototype, entering its test programme on 29 June 1962 with a take-off from the small airfield at Weybridge on the site of the original Brooklands race track. All the VC10s and Super VC10s were flown out of Weybridge in this way but were based, for flight testing, at nearby Wisley. There, it was soon discovered that the VC10 had a serious drag problem that would require a number of modifications and aerodynamic "fixes" to restore the specific range to the guaranteed figures. While work was proceeding on these modifications, attention was also focused upon the low speed handling, especially after the fatal accident suffered by the prototype BAC One-Eleven in October 1963 had cast suspicion on the T-tailed layout.

Several hundred hours of development flying were devoted to these aspects of VC10 performance and handling in 1963/64, and by comparison with the prototype as first flown the production aircraft incorporated a number of changes that included Küchemann wing tips adding 6 ft (1,8 m) to total span; so-called "beaver tail" fairings between the jet pipes on each pair of engines; re-alignment of leading-edge slats to obtain the optimum wing profile in cruising flight; extensions aft of the engine pylons at their roots; engines moved outboard from the fuselage by 11 in (0,29 m) and set at 3 deg greater incidence to the fuselage datum; wing leading edge chord increased by 4 per cent from root to outer wing fence; and addition of a stick-pusher in the control circuit to inhibit the angle of incidence during the approach to the stall.

With all these modifications fully investigated, the VC10 was granted an unrestricted C of A on 23 April 1964 and BOAC flew the first revenue service six days later, from London to Lagos. Differences in the flying characteristics of the Standard and Super, as well as manufacturing considerations, dictated that the modified engine installation should apply only to the Super VC10s and the extended wing leading edge should apply to the Supers and the BUA and Ghana Standards, but not to the BOAC Standards. These differences therefore apply to the tankers, the K Mk 2s differing from both the C Mk 1s and the K Mk 3s in having the early wing and unmodified engine installation.

Flight testing of the Super VC10 began on 7 May 1964 and this version entered service with BOAC on 1 April 1965. The last of the 17 was not delivered to BOAC until the end of May 1969. Plans to keep the bulk of the Super VC10 fleet in service until 1983 have recently been amended by British Airways in the light of its current over-capacity caused by the introduction of additional Lockheed TriStars and Boeing 747s at a time of slackening traffic growth. Consequently, nine of the 14 Super VC10s in service at the beginning of the year were withdrawn from service in March and the five that remain now share with a single Standard VC10 of Ghana Airways the only commercial flying undertaken by the type. The story of the VC10 is far from over, but for the future it is the operation in military rôles by the RAF that provide the focus of interest. □

VC10 PRODUCTION AND DISPOSITION

Construction number	Type number	Initial identity	First flight	Delivery	Remarks
803	1100	G-ARTA	29 Jun 62	30 Jan 68	Prototype. Converted to Type 1109 for Laker Airways, used by MEA (as OD-AFA) then B.Cal. and scrapped 1974.
804	1101	G-ARVA	8 Nov 62	8 Dec 64	BOAC/BA. Sold to Nigeria Airways (as 5N-ABD) and WO 20 Nov 69.
805	1101	G-ARVB	21 Dec 62	6 Feb 65	BOAC/BA. Scrapped Oct 76.
806	1101	G-ARVC	21 Feb 63	1 Dec 64	BOAC/BA. To Gulf Air (as A40-VC). Conversion to K Mk 2 (as ZA144).
807	1101	G-ARVE	15 Apr 63	1 Oct 64	BOAC/BA. Scrapped Oct 76.
808	1101	G-ARVF	6 Jul 63	4 Sep 64	BOAC/BA. To Sheikh Zayad Bin Sultan Al-Nahyan (Abu Dhabi Royal Flight).
809	1101	G-ARVG	17 Oct 63	12 Jun 64	BOAC/BA. To Gulf Air (as A40-VG). Conversion to K Mk 2 (as ZA141).
810	1101	G-ARVH	22 Nov 63	8 Jul 64	BOAC/BA. Scrapped Sep 76.
811	1101	G-ARVI	20 Dec 63	22 Apr 64	BOAC/BA. To Gulf Air (as A40-VI). Conversion to K Mk 2 (as ZA142).
812	1101	G-ARVJ	25 Feb 64	23 Apr 64	BOAC/BA. To Gulf Air for personal use of the Ruler of Qatar. Out of service.
813	1101	G-ARVK	28 Mar 64	2 May 64	BOAC/BA. To Gulf Air (as A40-VK). Conversion to K Mk 2 (as ZA143).
814	1101	G-ARVL	2 Jun 64	16 Jun 64	BOAC/BA. To Gulf Air (as A40-VL). Leased to Air Ceylon. Conversion to K Mk 2 (as ZA140).
815	1101	G-ARVM	9 Jul 64	22 Jul 64	BOAC/BA. Out of service.
816-818	1101	—	—	—	To have been G-ARVN, 'VO and 'VP for BOAC. Not built.
819	1103	G-ASIW	30 Jul 64	30 Sep 64	BUA/B.Cal. To Air Malawi (as 7Q-YKH). Out of service.
820	1103	G-ASIX	16 Oct 64	31 Oct 64	BUA/B.Cal. To Sultan of Oman Royal Flight (as A40-AB).
821-822	—	—	—	—	Not built.
823	1102	9G-ABO	14 Nov 64	27 Jan 65	Ghana Airways
824	1102	9G-ABP	21 May 65	18 Jun 65	Ghana Airways. Leased to MEA and WO Dec 68.
825	1103	G-ATDJ	18 Jun 65	1 Jul 65	Intended as Type 1102 9G-ABQ for Ghana Airways. Delivered to BUA/B.Cal. Sold to MoD/RAE Bedford (as XX914). Out of service.
826	1106	XR806	26 Nov 65	19 Apr 67	RAF C Mk 1. *George Thompson, VC.*
827	1106	XR807	25 Mar 66	17 Nov 66	RAF C Mk 1. *Donald Garland, VC/Thomas Gray, VC.*
828	1106	XR808	9 Jun 66	7 Jul 66	RAF C Mk 1. *Kenneth Campbell, VC.*
829	1106	XR809	28 Jul 66	31 Aug 66	RAF C Mk 1. *Hugh Malcolm, VC.* To Rolls-Royce and first flown as RB.211 test-bed (as G-AXLR) on 6 Mar 70. Out of service.
830	1106	XR810	29 Nov 66	21 Dec 66	RAF C Mk 1. *David Lord, VC.*
831	1106	XV101	11 Jan 67	31 Jan 67	RAF C Mk 1. *Lanoe Hawker, VC.*
832	1106	XV102	5 May 67	25 May 67	RAF C Mk 1. *Guy Gibson, VC.*
833	1106	XV103	14 Jun 67	5 Jul 67	RAF C Mk 1. *Edward Mannock, VC.*
834	1106	XV104	14 Jul 67	3 Aug 67	RAF C Mk 1. *James McCudden, VC.*
835	1106	XV105	3 Oct 67	20 Oct 67	RAF C Mk 1. *Albert Ball, VC.*
836	1106	XV106	17 Nov 67	1 Dec 67	RAF C Mk 1. *Thomas Mottershead, VC.*
837	1106	XV107	22 Mar 68	17 Apr 68	RAF C Mk 1. *James Nicolson, VC.*
838	1106	XV108	7 Jun 68	18 Jun 68	RAF C Mk 1. *William Rhodes-Moorhouse, VC.*
839	1106	XV109	18 Jul 68	1 Aug 68	RAF C Mk 1. *Arthur Scarf, VC.*
840	1102	—	—	—	Intended as 9G-ABU for Ghana Airways. Not built.
851	1151	G-ASGA	7 May 64	13 Feb 65	BOAC/BA.
852	1151	G-ASGB	29 Sep 64	30 Apr 65	BOAC/BA.
853	1151	G-ASGC	1 Jan 65	1 Feb 65	BOAC/BA. To IWM Duxford Apr 80.
854	1151	G-ASGD	11 Feb 65	3 Mar 65	BOAC/BA. Out of service Apr 80.
855	1151	G-ASGE	6 Mar 65	27 Mar 65	BOAC/BA.
856	1151	G-ASGF	24 Mar 65	2 Apr 65	BOAC/BA.
857	1151	G-ASGG	17 Sep 65	21 Jun 65	BOAC/BA.
858	1151	G-ASGH	2 Oct 65	4 Nov 65	BOAC/BA. Out of service Apr 80.
859	1151	G-ASGI	28 Jan 66	12 Feb 66	BOAC/BA. Out of service Apr 80.
860	1151	G-ASGJ	22 Feb 67	3 Mar 67	BOAC/BA. Out of service Apr 80.
861	1151	G-ASGK	1 Sep 67	27 Oct 67	BOAC/BA.
862	1151	G-ASGL	27 Dec 67	25 Jan 68	BOAC/BA. Out of service May 80.
863	1151	G-ASGM	25 Feb 68	6 Mar 68	BOAC/BA. Out of service May 80.
864	1151	G-ASGN	1 May 68	7 May 68	BOAC. WO Sep 70.
865	1151	G-ASGO	11 Sep 68	27 Sep 68	BOAC/BA. WO Mar 74.
866	1151	G-ASGP	20 Nov 68	6 Dec 68	BOAC/BA.
867	1151	G-ASGR	12 Feb 69	31 May 69	BOAC/BA.
868-875	1151	—	—	—	To have been G-ASGS to 'GZ for BOAC. Not built.
876-880	1151	—	—	—	To have been for BOAC. Not built.
881	1153	5X-UVA	3 Sep 66	30 Sep 66	EAAC. WO Apr 72.
882	1153	5H-MMT	12 Oct 66	31 Oct 66	EAAC. Conversion to K Mk 3 (as ZA147).
883	1153	5Y-ADA	21 Mar 67	31 Mar 67	EAAC. Conversion to K Mk 3 (as ZA148).
884	1153	5X-UVJ	19 Apr 69	30 Apr 69	EAAC. Conversion to K Mk 3 (as ZA149).
885	1153	5H-MOG	16 Feb 70	28 Feb 70	EAAC. Conversion to K Mk 3 (as ZA150)

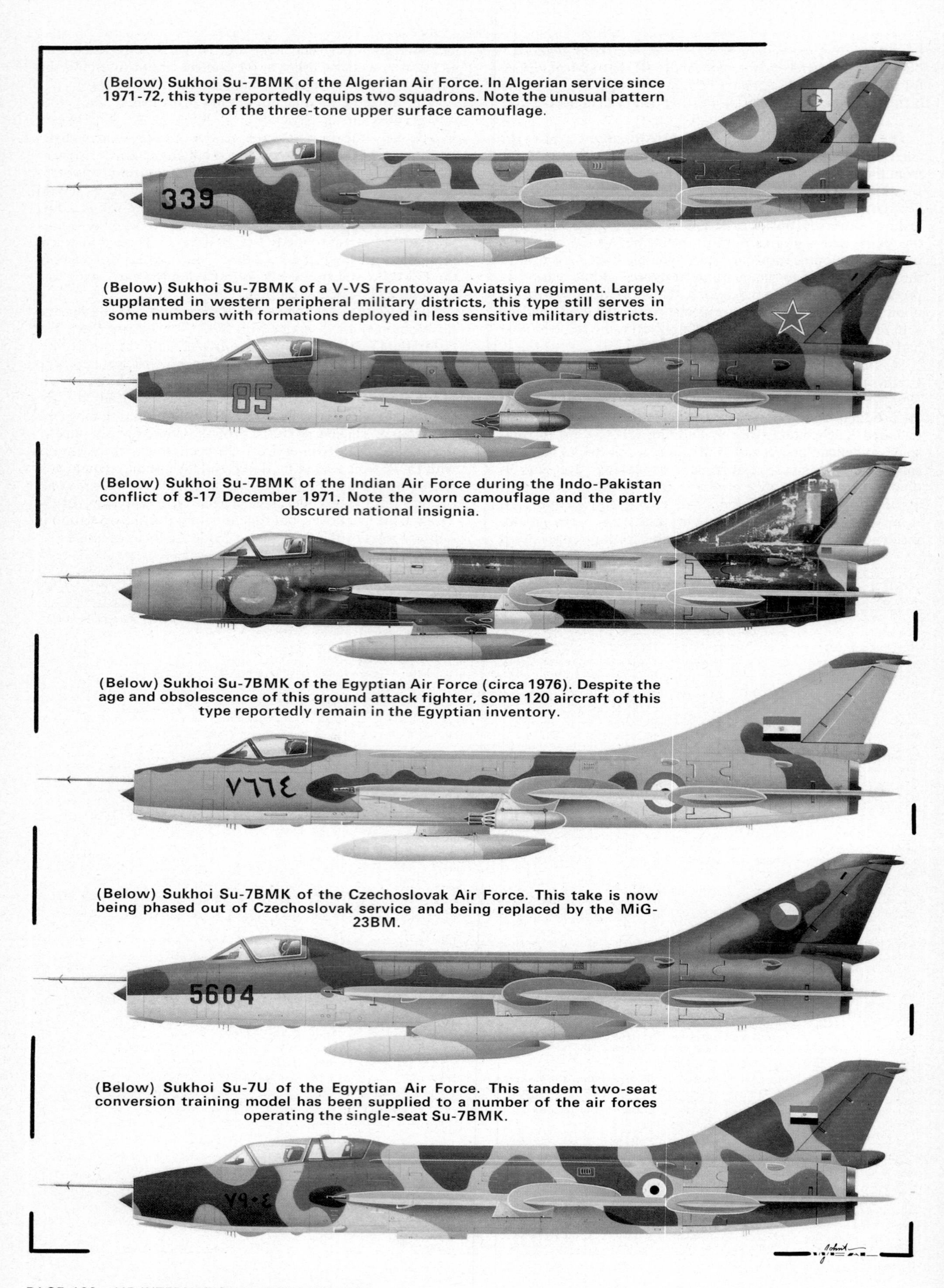

(Below) Sukhoi Su-7BMK of the Algerian Air Force. In Algerian service since 1971-72, this type reportedly equips two squadrons. Note the unusual pattern of the three-tone upper surface camouflage.

(Below) Sukhoi Su-7BMK of a V-VS Frontovaya Aviatsiya regiment. Largely supplanted in western peripheral military districts, this type still serves in some numbers with formations deployed in less sensitive military districts.

(Below) Sukhoi Su-7BMK of the Indian Air Force during the Indo-Pakistan conflict of 8-17 December 1971. Note the worn camouflage and the partly obscured national insignia.

(Below) Sukhoi Su-7BMK of the Egyptian Air Force (circa 1976). Despite the age and obsolescence of this ground attack fighter, some 120 aircraft of this type reportedly remain in the Egyptian inventory.

(Below) Sukhoi Su-7BMK of the Czechoslovak Air Force. This take is now being phased out of Czechoslovak service and being replaced by the MiG-23BM.

(Below) Sukhoi Su-7U of the Egyptian Air Force. This tandem two-seat conversion training model has been supplied to a number of the air forces operating the single-seat Su-7BMK.

Nurturing nostalgia

THERE ARE THOSE TO WHOM nostalgia is noisome, but with change being so rarely for the better nowadays, there is a growing school of thought that anything evoking nostalgia should be nurtured. Just as nostalgia for *real* ale in British hostelries led to a campaign by those bemoaning the loss of the beer engine, so it would seem that there is at least the beginning of a movement by modellers towards more *real* aeroplanes — "real" in this instance equating with a propeller up front and two sets of wings for preference!

In truth, such nostalgic subject matter is a little more demanding on modelling skill than is the modern aeroplane, the tyro being likely to look askance at the intricacies of interplane struts and bracing wires that are so much a part of the biplane. Thus, the kit manufacturer with finger metaphorically applied to the modelling pulse and endeavouring to cater for its nuances must be engaged in some pretty heavy soul-searching before following the trend towards nostalgia, for a substantial portion of the kit market is made up of tyros.

Venturesome or no, one or two of the major kit manufacturers are, if not exactly throwing caution to the winds, chancing the arm attached to their pulse-gauging finger and once more delving into the 'twenties and 'thirties for biplane subject matter, as indicated by the first new kit review this month, which, covering a 1/48th scale Hawker Fury biplane, heralds the return of Airfix to that genre after a very long absence.

There has always been a certain number of biplane kits available, but such have achieved a reputation in the industry for being no better than moderate sellers. Perhaps the first sign of changing tastes came when Lesney released in its "Matchbox" series its 1/72nd scale Hawker Fury I biplane to be agreeably surprised by the comparatively ready response with which it was greeted; certainly sufficient for this company to venture a Boeing P-12E and, later, an Armstrong Whitworth Siskin IIIA. Subsequently, "Matchbox" was to plunge much deeper with a Supermarine Stranraer and, very recently, a Handley Page Heyford, followed by a Curtiss SBC-3 Helldiver. Long may sales warrant the company pursuing this trend.

Monogram was tempted to issue the occasional biplane kit once upon a time — the WW I kits released by this company last year were Aurora retreads — and we still cherish its 1/32nd scale Grumman F3F and 1/72nd scale Boeing F4B-4, Curtiss F11C-2 and Curtiss P-6E, all of which are still thoroughly worthwhile acquiring despite age. Heller, which has displayed as much originality as any and more than most in its choice of kit subjects, has yet to find much attraction in 'tween wars biplanes, its only excursion into this category being the Curtiss SBC-4, although the Nieuport-Delage NiD 622 *sesquiplane* must not be forgotten. Esci, largely preoccupied with modern, or at least, relatively recent turbojet-powered aircraft and WW II monoplanes, has at least ventured one biplane, the 'thirties Henschel Hs 123, presumably on the basis that it strayed into WW II, but it at least indicates that there could be prospects of further biplanes from this Italian company.

Now Airfix, as already mentioned, has demonstrated its belief that the market for 'tween wars biplanes is sufficiently buoyant to warrant a 1/48th scale Fury I; let us hope that the buoyancy proves sufficient to encourage investment in more subjects of the period. What a field day the conversion addicts would have if a kit of the Fury's larger stablemate, the Hart, was to be added to Airfix's range. There were all of a dozen varieties of this aeroplane.

It could well be that the future will hold some pleasant surprises for biplane *aficionados* who are more numerous today than hitherto, a fact to which kit manufacturers are gradually awakening.

This month's colour subject

A quarter-century ago, in 1955, the prototype of a large single-seat tactical fighter, the S-1 powered by a massive Lyulka turbojet and the first progeny of the resuscitated design bureau of the late Pavel O Sukhoi, was undergoing flight test in the Soviet Union. The first Soviet design to feature a movable intake shock cone and a slab-type all-flying horizontal tail, the S-1 attained 1,348 mph (2 170 km/h), or M=2·05 under test, this being 230 mph (370 km/h), or M=0·34, above the maximum attainable speed called for by the specification to which design work had commenced in 1953. Seen briefly in public over Tushino in June 1956, the S-1 served both to rehabilitate Sukhoi as a major Soviet combat aircraft designer and to provide the basis for the ground attack fighter that was to be manufactured in vast numbers as the Su-7 from the late 'fifties, throughout the 'sixties and into the 'seventies. It was to see service with a half-score of air forces — indeed, it remains in service with the majority of them today — in progressively improved versions. In fact, the Su-7 was to be built in far larger numbers than *any* dedicated ground attack fighter to-date. Yet, despite its numerical importance and a career that has embraced operational use in wars on the Indian subcontinent and in the Middle East, the Su-7 is as yet represented by only *one* kit!

Kits of Soviet combat aircraft of whatever vintage remain thin on the ground — although, as recorded in this column over the last year or so, the kit industry has shown a willingness to expend plastic on the MiG-23, the MiG-25 and, after a style, the MiG-27 — and in view of the fact that a wealth of authentic reference material on the Su-7 has been available for some considerable time, it might have been expected that one or other of the more enterprising western kit manufacturers would have been attracted to *Fitter-A*, as this fighter is known in the West. But, no, it had been studiously ignored by all until, late last year, VEB Plasticart in the DDR released an Su-7 kit in 1/72nd scale.

Reviewed in this column in January, the VEB Plasticart kit has every appearance of accuracy, both in dimensions and outline, comprises a total of 46 component parts and offers straightforward assembly. The levered-suspension undercarriage units are neatly formed and the high-pressure tyred wheels are all moulded separately. The cockpit interior is sparsely equipped, although relatively little can be seen through the very clear but small two-part canopy. The panel lines are much too heavily embossed and call for rubbing down, as do also the trailing edges of the flying and control surfaces. Four rocket pods and two drop tanks are included in the kit, and the decal sheet, which comprises Soviet, Czechoslovak and Polish markings, is good, but, as noted when this kit was first reviewed, calls for varnishing prior to application in order to frustrate a tendency on the part of the subjects to break up while fixing. The UK importers of this kit are Cotswold Aeromodels (7 Eldorado Road, Cheltenham, Glos), and as one of the still deplorably few current Soviet military aircraft subjects available it is well worth getting.

Quintessence of elegance

To most of those with a penchant for the biplane fighters of the 'twenties and 'thirties, the late Sir Sydney Camm's Fury biplane represents the very essence of aeronautical pulchritude. Although hardly a favourite subject for kit manufacturers, it is probably the very elegance of this graceful fighter that has rescued it from being totally ignored, as have been the vast majority of its contemporaries, and many years ago a very fine kit in 1/48th scale was produced by a regrettably short-lived company entitled Inpact, and this kit is, we believe, still obtainable under the Life-Like label. Rareplanes produced a 1/72nd vac-form of the Fury, and Lesney was also attracted to the type, offering a similar scale injection-moulded kit. Now Airfix, in its recently-introduced 1/48th scale series, has presented us with a Fury kit that bids fair to establish itself as definitive.

Consisting of 47 component parts moulded in silver plastic, plus a clear windscreen, the kit captures the delectable lines of the Fury with complete precision, the surface detailing being carried out with just the right degree of emphasis, differentiating nicely between the fabric- and metal-covered areas. In finishing this model, it is *vital* to achieve a highly-polished aluminium effect on the cowlings and other metal parts, and a dull finish — rather like that of plastic — on the fabric to achieve the contrast so characteristic of the period, when so much time was devoted to keeping the machines immaculate.

Building a biplane is never quite as simple as a monoplane, but even the tyro will find little to tax his abilities with this one as the wings are each in one piece, fixing the dihedral angle. The centre section struts are an integrated assembly and these, together with the N-type interplane struts, render alignment virtually automatic. A particularly nice feature of this kit is the seven-part reproduction of the Rolls-Royce Kestrel IIS engine which may be displayed by removing the upper part of the cowling. There is some scope for extra detailing on the engine and small details can be added to the open cockpit, but this in no way may be construed as a criticism.

The rigging of the Fury is quite simple and, of course, essential, as are the squadron markings emblazoned on the upper wing and the fuselage sides, and without which the feel of the period in which the Fury saw its heyday is lost. There is an excellent decal sheet offering the parallel bars of No 1(F) Sqdn, or the black-and-white checks of No 43(F) Sqdn. Furies — as distinct from the *Yugoslav* Furies — did, of course, see some limited wartime operational use with the South African Air Force, and so those with a penchant for camouflage can finish the aircraft as serving with No 1 Squadron, SAAF, or, alternatively, in the scheme adopted by the RAF after the Munich crisis of 1938. Incidentally, the story of the Fury biplane was related in detail in the number three issue of our companion publication, AIR ENTHUSIAST, which included details of markings and finishes. Certain items are deserving of special mention, such as the offset fin intended to counteract torque and a number of very small parts, including separately moulded control horns for the rudder and ailerons. This kit is in Airfix's Series 4, retailing in the UK for £1·65 and we like it! If you are not yet on the nostalgia kick, then this offering is more than likely to start you off.

The Hornets are swarming

We had fair warning from the trade fairs earlier in the year to expect a deluge of kits for the McDonnell Douglas F-18 Hornet and this is now descending on us with a vengeance. The first to reach us were to 1/48th scale from Esci and to 1/32nd scale from Minicraft/Hasegawa, and now both of these concerns are competing in the 1/72nd scale arena with almost simultaneous releases. Under the circumstances, comparisons are unavoidable, but we could not come up with a clear recommendation because, although there are minor differences of interpretation visible in the completed models, the major variation is in constructional approach, the two kits differing appreciably in this aspect yet yielding similar results.

Esci has chosen to mould the wings integrally with the upper fuselage, leaving the tailplane separate, while Hasegawa has elected to do exactly the opposite. We have a preference for the finer surface detailing of the Hasegawa product, but in no way could that of the Esci product be considered poor — it is just a little on the heavy side on the wings. Both kits are moulded in white plastic, the Esci kit having 62 parts and the Hasegawa kit having 55, detailing being of a similar standard and the difference in the number of parts being explained mainly by the respective methods of construction employed. The wheel wells on the Esci model are deeper set and look rather better, but Hasegawa offers more internal detail in that area. Both kits include two Sidewinder and two Sparrow AAMs, and good decals with all appropriate lettering, insignia and small markings. Hasegawa has opted for the second and third FSD aircraft, while Esci has selected the fifth and sixth. Which kit to choose? Really, we cannot be specific, but whichever you choose you will not be disappointed.

Hawthorne's felis tigris

When, on 30 May 1959, the No 1 prototype Northrop N-156F fighter was rolled out of the Advanced Production Hangar at Hawthorne as a company-sponsored project and the tangible result of a highly expensive gamble, few, let alone Welko Gasich, then Northrop's Chief of Advanced Design, with whom primary responsibility for the success or failure of the programme rested, could have realised what a well-timed gamble it was to prove. Intended to halt the upward spiral of fighter size, weight and complexity, the Northrop warplane was, with the passage of the years, to prove itself a lightweight only physically and anything but a lightweight in capability. For a time, the gamble appeared to have failed and, after a period on backburner, the entire programme was virtually "mothballed", but then, in May 1962, it paid off when the US Department of Defense announced selection of the N-156F as a defensive weapon for supply to favoured nations under the MAP. From that time, the programme has never looked back, and today, with deliveries of its extensively developed Tiger II version approaching the 1,100 mark and the basic design bidding fair to take on yet a further lease of life with the F-5G, what began as a long shot has evolved into one of the best investments that any military aircraft manufacturer has made over the past two or three decades.

Kits of the original production single-seat F-5A and two-seat F-5B have been produced in the past in or about 1/48th scale, but the honour of marketing the first 1/48th scale kit of the more efficacious F-5E Tiger II went recently to Monogram and this product now faces direct competition from another fine Tiger II kit in the same scale from Esci. The Italian company's kit is arranged in generally similar fashion to other F-5 kits, with the upper wing panels and horizontal tail surfaces moulded integrally with the upper fuselage, the lower wing panels being formed with the lower fuselage. The design of the aircraft lends itself well to this treatment and the result is effective. Thus, the major proportion of the airframe comprises only two pieces, yet there are 71 component parts in this kit, all but the three transparencies being in light grey plastic, so the extent of the detail provided by Esci may be appreciated.

The representation of the panelling and rivet detail is very fine, and we particularly like the undercarriage which is intricately detailed, this detail also extending to the finely-contoured doors. Among the smaller parts are eight separately-formed intakes and fairings. The encapsulated cockpit presents a satisfyingly complete appearance, the ejection seat being an outstanding feature. The decals cover three different machines: an "aggressor" from the USAF's 527th TFTAS, 10th TFW, at Alconbury *circa* 1977, and Thai and Taiwanese examples. Distributed by Humbrol, this fine kit retails at £3·35 in the UK.

. . . and Bethpage's

The appellation of "Tiger" has, of course, been used for fighters before its bestowal on the Northrop F-5E, Grumman's F11F-1, alias F-11A, single-seat shipboard fighter of the 'fifties being so named. The Bethpage-built Tiger was hardly the most successful of Grumman's fighters, enjoying a relatively brief service life, the first deliveries being made (to VA-156) in March 1957, the phase-out from first-line use commencing barely more than two years later and the last unit (VF-111) relinquishing its Tigers in April 1961. It never achieved the performance with which it was widely credited, but it could lay claim to being the US Navy's first genuine supersonic shipboard aeroplane, being capable in clean condition of 728 mph (1 171 km/h) at 35,000 ft (10 670 m), or about M=1·085. Thus, the Grumman Tiger has at least some noteworthiness; it certainly possesses aesthetic appeal.

We have a 1/48th scale kit from Lindberg dating back more than two decades, but we cannot recall a single 1/72nd scale kit of this Grumman "cat". Happily, Hasegawa has now filled the gap with a very nice kit, our sample of which was actually manufactured in the USA by Minicraft Models of Torrance, California, which company furnished our review copy. The kit consists of 47 parts very neatly formed in light grey plastic, plus three transparencies. The surface detailing is very fine and there is some excellent engraving on such parts as the wheels, undercarriage struts and doors, and jet outlets.

The kit includes four Sidewinder AAMs with two drop tanks as alternative stores for the inboard hard points. The decals, which are particularly good, are for a gull grey-and-white example from VF-21, featuring a shark's mouth in black, white and yellow, as well as black-and-yellow horizontal fin stripes. There are also markings for the *Blue Angels* aerobatic team, which employed this aircraft for a number of years, these being in yellow.

Twin-boom Swede

Heller has now firmly established a reputation as easily the most adventurous of the major kit producers, and those with a yen for the more exotic or esoteric aircraft types have every reason to be grateful to this French company. Who else, other than a vac-form producer, would have risked an arm and a leg with a kit of the twin-boom Saab 21A single-seat fighter of the late 'forties? Not absolutely unique in configuration — the pre-war De Schelde S.21 (the numerical designation being pure coincidence) that never flew, the wartime Vultee XP-54, the Mansyu Ki-98 still under construction when Japan surrendered and the SO 8000 Narval, which, like the Saab 21A, was a product of the 'forties, were the other examples of this layout — this Swedish fighter was designed by a team led by Frid Wanström in 1941, and was perhaps the first product of the Swedish penchant for the unusual in aeronautical design that was to result in such as the Draken and Viggen. The Saab 21A first flew on 30 July 1943, and production as the J 21A for *Flygvapnet* subsequently totalled 298 aircraft.

Heller has made an excellent job of its 1/72nd scale kit of this marginally offbeat warplane, this consisting of 40 parts moulded in olive green plastic and a further four in clear plastic. The mouldings are first class, with very neat external detailing, the panel lines generally being raised and the fabric-covered control surfaces are finely textured. The lower wing panel, being in one piece, sets the dihedral, and the assembled wing has slots in its trailing edge to accommodate the tail booms, giving positive alignment. The booms are split vertically and incorporate the vertical tail surfaces, a one-piece tailplane linking the rear ends. The cockpit is well furnished and includes a convincing representation of the ejection seat — the J 21A having been one of the first service aircraft to provide this means of escape for the pilot — as well as the controls and instrument panel. The canopy is in three sections and thus enables alternative settings to be selected. There is adequate room in the nose of the fuselage nacelle to place weights for balancing the model on its tricycle under-carriage, and decals are provided for two machines, one each from F 6 and F 9, and include unit crests. The UK retail price of this kit is 95p.

Yet another violent windstorm
Competing with the Hornet in popularity among kit manufacturers is the Panavia Tornado, which, during its years of development flying has featured as a kit four times, the latest, from Esci, being the third in 1/72nd scale and the best so far, superseding both Airfix and Italaerei/Revell kits in this scale. The fundamental design of the Tornado has remained unchanged since its début, but successive aircraft have displayed noticeable detail differences and the Esci kit gets closer to the definitive production aeroplane than either predecessor.

Making up into a very attractive model with particularly good — mostly engraved — surface detailing and moulding of a very high standard in a light grey shade of plastic, Esci's Tornado features a fuselage formed in upper and lower sections to incorporate the operative swing wings, and the fit of these components is very good. Highlights of the kit are the undercarriage legs and wheels, the ejection seats and the exhaust nozzles, all of which are extremely well presented. The cockpit interior is adequate but could be augmented with advantage. Optional open or closed positions are possible with the canopy and the dorsal air brakes. Two carriers under the fuselage are each provided with four Mk 82 bombs on twin shoes, while the outer hardpoints carry two Kormoran ASMs and two ALQ-119 ECM pods. The decal sheet, to the usual high Esci standard, has markings for the first Italian prototype (P-05) and a pre-series German example, but does not include any British markings.

A modern rarity
At this, the beginning of the 'eighties, there are only *two* amphibian flying boats in production, the Canadair CL-215 and the Shin Meiwa US-1, and the question of whether or not such aircraft are anachronistic is still unsettled. But anachronism or no, the CL-215 has been more or less in continuous production since the late 'sixties, with a fourth series under way, the most recent order being from the Yugoslav government for four as water-bombers for 1982 delivery. This sturdy Canadian amphibian has finally received the accolade of a plastic kit and from who else but Heller.

In 1/72nd scale, Heller's kit is quite superb. One might go so far as to say that this French company has excelled itself, with every external and a great deal of internal detail reproduced. The mouldings, 95 in yellow and nine in clear plastic, are exemplary, and the surface detailing is just right. The forward section of the hull planing bottom is a separate moulding mating neatly with the main fuselage shells, and the interior is fitted out from bow to stern, with a fully-equipped flight deck, a spacious cabin and reproductions of the water collecting and dumping gear employed for water-bombing. The interior of the cabin features framing on the walls and rivet detailing on the floor, and the wheel well interiors are equally well formed and detailed. The Pratt & Whitney R-2800 two-row radials are modelled in full relief, and the characteristic nacelles enclosing them have been captured to perfection. The boarding ladder provided for the rear entrance door can be used to support the tail when the model is posed on the ground, but weights may be placed in the nose for balancing purposes if preferred.

CL-215s have been employed by the French *Securité Civile* since the late 'sixties, and the decals accompanying the kit cover the essential markings for one of these machines. The plastic closely simulates the basic colour, but there are large areas of red to be painted, these being clearly indicated by the four-view general arrangement drawing. This is quite a large model, with a wing span of 15·6 inches (39,7 cm), and even if this boat does not appeal to you as a subject, do have a look at this kit. You may well be tempted.

More Fokker fodder
A new injection-moulded 1/72nd scale kit of a WW I aeroplane is something of an event nowadays and we were pleased to receive just such a kit recently from Veeday Models (POB 1, Wiveliscombe, Taunton, Somerset), but, the choice of subject, the B.E.2c — the Fokker fodder of 1915-16, when it was the prey of Albatros, Halberstadt, Roland and Pfalz — is to be regretted as this type was so recently the subject of a vacuum-formed kit issued by Formaplane, and it is sad that such duplication should occur in a field which, so sparsely sown, offers so many possibilities for choice. This said, the kit may be judged on its merits and for a limited-production injection-moulded kit it is surprisingly good, with nicely formed parts and a good standard of surface detailing.

The upper wing is in one piece, thus fixing the dihedral angle, and has correctly formed under-camber and good rib effect, these features also applying to the two lower wing panels. White plastic is used for the 34 parts, and only the smaller pieces display any marked degree of flash, which is, in any case, easily removed. The wing alignment calls for some care, but assembly in general is straightforward enough, only some cleaning out of the mating surfaces being necessary to get a good fit. The engine has separate cylinder banks and exhaust pipes, and there is a neatly moulded four-blade propeller. Seats are provided for the cockpits.

The kit includes decals for four large and two small RFC roundels and two Union Jacks, the blue of the roundels being of the correct light shade in use at the time. Assembly instructions are supplied together with a good three-view drawing. This kit is available from Veeday Models at £1·95 plus 25p postage.

Super detail
A new departure, at least, in our experience, is the series of kits of super-detailing items produced by Waldron Model Products (1385 Stephen Way, San Jose, CA95129). This company's list of products is a long one and is devoted to cockpit details of British, US and German WW II fighters, principally in 1/32nd and 1/48th scales. We have received a sample kit comprising side consoles for the F4U-1D Corsair in 1/32nd scale (applicable to the Revell kit).

The instrument faces and panels — 20 pieces in all — are printed in black, in fine detail on thin aluminium sheet and have to be carefully cut out and stuck in position with cyano-acrylate glue. The kit also includes five small plastic blocks to supplement the consoles provided with the F4U-1D kit. A very clear instruction sheet positions every part and describes all necessary component modifications. Our sample was supplied by Croydon Impex and we are impressed with the precision of the product. Among the numerous listed items are such as seat belt and shoulder harness buckles, even a miniature continuous hinge.

Decal Review
Microscale: Following on August's selection of decals in 1/48th scale, we now have a quartet in 1/72nd scale which exhibits a commendable variety in selection. Sheet 72-252 is covered entirely with black lettering in four sizes for aircraft of the USMC, mainly depicting the title of the Corps, either in full or abbreviated as U.S.MARINES. The height of the letters ranges from 1,0 mm to 4,0 mm, and there are also the names of four USMC bases, Anacostia, Quantico, Cherry Point and El Toro, in two sizes. Sheet 72-253 for the Cessna T-37A/B (Hasegawa) has a selection of markings for six different USAF aircraft, one in basic natural metal finish, three in white, one overall red and the remaining example in a bicentennial red-white-blue scheme which provides the most colourful section of a very full sheet.

Sheet 72-254 is for the F-100 Super Sabre (Minicraft/Hasegawa) and comprises two schemes based upon natural metal finishes but embodying large areas of colour. One machine, from the 354th TFW, has the fin and rudder painted bright yellow, with black bands and arrows, and the unit badge superimposed — this was featured on Sheet 48-77 in 1/48th scale reviewed in this column in August. Its companion, which has large areas of red-and-white striping, was also featured in 1/48th scale on Sheet 48-78. Finally, Sheet 72-255 is for the recently issued Minicraft/Hasegawa kit of the F11F-1 Tiger (reviewed elsewhere in this column), four aircraft being included, all of which utilised the light gull grey-and-white scheme. The interest here is centred on the fin markings which, without exception, are attractive and colourful, the units represented being VA-156, VF-33, VF-51 and VF-121.

Cleveland IPMS (Croydon Impex, 10 Stoneyfield Rd, Old Coulsdon, Surrey): From the UK distributors we have received samples of sheets of decals produced by the Cleveland Branch of the IPMS (USA). These decals come as 8 in (20,2 cm) by 7 in (17,8 cm) sheets with lettering and numbers in the "cut off corner" style in four sizes, 12,5, 8,5, 1,5 and 1,0 mm high. We have received sample sheets in black and white, but understand that red and yellow will also be available. These are very useful decals and Croydon Impex expects the price to be 50p per sheet or £1·75 for the set of four, these prices seeming reasonable. Croydon Impex also tells us that there are plans to stock the Italian CMPR decals recently reviewed in this column. Readers should contact Croydon Impex direct for more information. □

F J HENDERSON

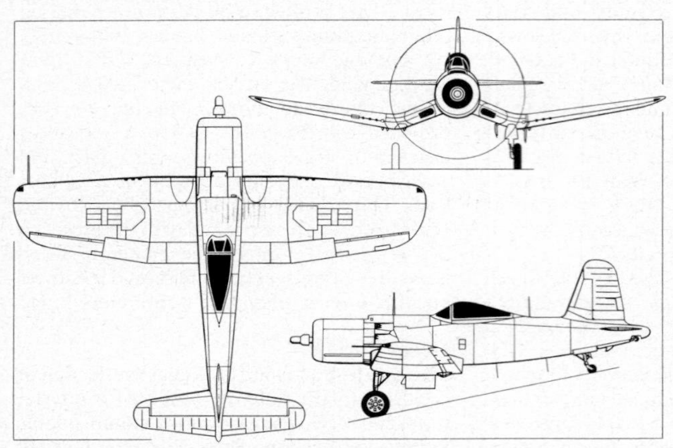

The general arrangement drawing above depicts the shipboard F2G-2 version of the Goodyear-developed low-altitude interceptor derivative of the Corsair.

(Above) One of the eight XF2G-1s and (below) one of the five shipboard F2G-2s completed.

GOODYEAR F2G **USA**

Essentially a higher-powered low-altitude interceptor derivative of the Vought Corsair which was being built by the Goodyear Aircraft Corporation as the FG-1, the F2G embodied extensive redesign to take maximum advantage of the 50 per cent increase in take-off power offered by a 28-cylinder Pratt & Whitney R-4360-4 Wasp Major single-stage engine rated at 3,000 hp. Two FG-1 airframes were rebuilt as XF2G-1s, the first of these flying in May 1944, prior to which, in March 1944, Goodyear had been awarded contracts for 418 shore-based F2G-1s and 10 shipboard F2G-2s. An all-round vision "bubble"-type cockpit canopy was adopted, the tail surfaces were enlarged, internal fuel capacity was increased and provision was made for either four or six wing-mounted 0·5-in (12,7-mm) guns. A total of eight prototypes was completed, but as a result of the contractual cut-backs accompanying the end of hostilities in the Pacific, only five F2G-1s and five F2G-2s were delivered. The following data relate to the F2G-2. Max speed, 399 mph (642 km/h) at sea level, 431 mph (694 km/h) at 16,400 ft (5 000 m). Initial climb, 4,400 ft/min (22,35 m/sec). Range (internal fuel), 1,190 mls (1 915 km). Empty eight, 10,249 lb (4 649 kg). Loaded weight (normal), 13,346 lb (6 054 kg). Span, 41 ft 0 in (12,50 m). Length, 33 ft 9 in (10,29 m). Height, 16 ft 1 in (4,90 m). Wing area, 314 sq ft (29,17 m²).

GORBUNOV 105 **USSR**

Early operational use of the LaGG-3 single-seat fighter revealed it to be overweight and a difficult aircraft to fly for any but experienced pilots. One of the three principal members of the design team responsible for creating this fighter, Vladimir P Gorbunov, was assigned the task of redesigning the aircraft to overcome its major shortcomings, this being referred to both as the *samolet* (aircraft) 105 and as the LaGG-3 *oblegchennyi* (lightened). The Klimov M-105PF-1 12-cylinder liquid-cooled engine rated at 1,260 hp at 2,625 ft (800 m) was retained, but the rear fuselage was cut down aft of the cabin, the leading-edge wing slats and aileron mass balances were removed and armament was revised, comprising a lightweight hub-mounted B-20 (MP-20) 20-mm cannon and a single 12,7-mm UB machine gun. By comparison with the LaGG-3, empty equipped weight was reduced by 660 lb (300 kg). Flight trials with the *samolet* 105 were undertaken in 1942, but development had by now been overtaken by that of the La-5 and only prototypes were completed. Max speed, 354 mph

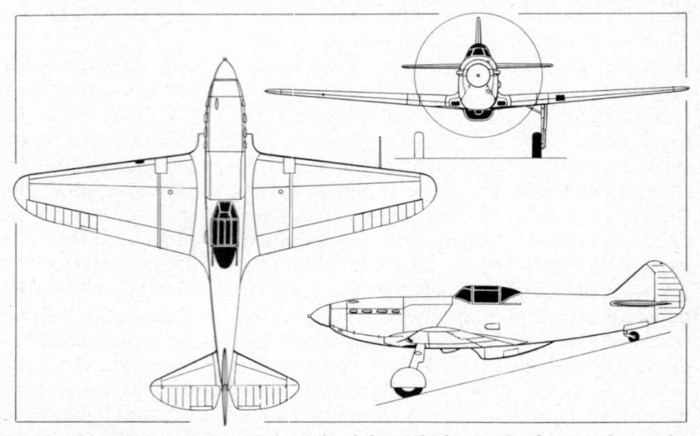

(Above) The samolet 105 evolved by Vladimir Gorbunov from the LaGG-3 in an attempt to overcome some of the latter's shortcomings.

(Above and below) The Go 229 V2 alias Ho IX V2, one of the most radical of WW II's experimental fighters to be flight tested.

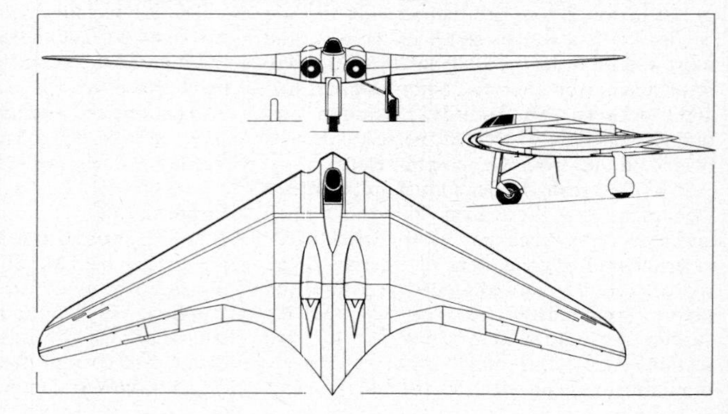

Progenitor of a long line of fighters, the GL-1 or Type A (above and below) was the first aircraft designed by Charles Gourdou and Jean Leseurre.

(570 km/h) at sea level, 387 mph (623 km/h) at 13,120 ft (4 000 m). Time to 16,405 ft (5 000 m), 6·0 min. Loaded weight, 6,316 lb (2 865 kg). Span, 32 ft 1⅞ in (9,80 m). Length, 28 ft 11 in (8,81 m). Height, 14 ft 5¼ in (4,40 m). Wing area, 188·37 sq ft (17,50 m^2).

GOTHA GO 229A (HO IX V2) GERMANY

Among the most unorthodox and advanced fighters evolved during WW II was a turbojet-driven pure flying wing evolved by Reimar and Walter Horten flown in February 1945, by which time it had been assigned the RLM designation Go 229, the development and production programmes having been allocated to the Gothaer Waggonfabrik. Conceived by the Horten brothers in 1943, the first prototype, the Ho IX V1, was completed as a glider for aerodynamic trials, the second prototype of the revolutionary single-seat fighter being powered by two 1,962 lb (890 kg) Junkers Jumo 004B turbojets. This, initially designated Ho IX V2, was of mixed construction, the centre section being of welded steel tube and the remainder being of wood, with plywood skinning overall. In the early summer of 1944, prior to the commencement of testing of the turbojet-powered prototype, the designation Go 229 was applied and a further seven prototypes and a pre-series of 20 were ordered. Gotha introduced relatively minor changes and provision was made for an armament of four 30-mm MK 103 or MK 108 cannon. During high-speed trials with the V2 in March 1945, a level speed of 497 mph (800 km/h) was recorded, but the aircraft was destroyed after only two hours' flying when the starboard engine failed during a landing approach. The Go 229 V3 was being prepared for flight testing when the factory was occupied by US forces. The following data are manufacturer's estimates for the Go 229A-0. Max speed, 590 mph (950 km/h) at sea level, 607 mph (977 km/h) at 39,370 ft (12 000 m). Range (internal fuel), 1,180 mls (1 900 km). Initial climb, 4,330 ft/min (22 m/sec). Empty weight, 10,140 lb (4 600 kg). Loaded weight, 16,550 lb (7 507 kg). Span, 54 ft 11¾ in (16,75 m). Length, 24 ft 6 in (7,47 m). Height, 9 ft 2¼ in (2,80 m). Wing area, 565·15 sq ft (52,50 m^2).

GOURDOU-LESEURRE GL-1 (TYPE A) FRANCE

The first aircraft to be designed by Charles E P Gourdou and Jean A Leseurre, the GL-1, also known as the Type A, was a single-seat parasol monoplane fighter powered by a 180 hp Hispano-Suiza 8Ab eight-cylinder water-cooled engine. Of mixed construction, with an all-metal fuselage primarily of steel tube with plywood covering and a fabric-covered wing with steel spars and wooden ribs, the GL-1 was officially evaluated at Villacoublay on 10 May 1918. Structurally overweight, the prototype was tested with one of its two 7,7-mm Vickers guns removed and with reduced fuel, demonstrating in this configuration level speeds higher than contemporaries powered by a 300 hp Hispano-Suiza engine. Although the design team believed that the structural weight problem could be resolved, official testing indicated that the wing offered an insufficient load factor, and redesign was therefore undertaken to result in the GL-2 alias Type B. Max speed, 150 mph (242 km/h) at 3,280 ft (1 000 m). Time to 3,280 ft (1 000 m), 2·41 min. Endurance, 1·5 hrs. Empty weight, 1,323 lb (600 kg). Loaded weight, 1,733 lb (786 kg). Span, 29 ft 6⅓ in (9,00 m). Length, 21 ft 7⅘ in (6,60 m). Height, 7 ft 6½ in (2,30 m). Wing area, 179·22 sq ft (16,65 m^2).

GOURDOU-LESEURRE GL-2 (TYPE B) FRANCE

By comparison with its progenitor, the GL-1, the GL-2 (Type B) had an entirely new and heavily reinforced wing, new horizontal tail surfaces mounted higher on the rear fuselage, and revised rudder and undercarriage. The 180 hp Hispano-Suiza 8Ab engine was retained and armament comprised two synchronised 7,7-mm Vickers guns. The number of pairs of inclined wing bracing struts was increased from two to four, each pair attaching to the wing at half-span and three-quarter-span, the cantilevered portion thus being only one-quarter of the half-span, resulting in an extremely rigid structure, the wing load factor being 10·4 as compared with 3·5 for the GL-1. Twenty GL-2s were ordered and, built by Mayen et Zodiac, the first being delivered to Villacoublay late November 1918. Subsequent aircraft were fitted with a taller rudder and enlarged fin to rectify a directional control deficiency, but with the termination of hostilities, *Aéronautique Militaire* interest in the GL-2 waned and development was cancelled. Max speed, 152 mph (245 km/h) at sea level. Time to 16,405 ft (5 000 m), 17·5 min. Empty weight, 1,257 lb (570 kg). Loaded weight, 1,874 lb (850 kg). Span, 30 ft 10 in (9,40 m). Length, 21 ft 1⅛ in (6,43 m). Wing area, 202·37 sq ft (18,80 m^2).

The GL-2, or Type B, illustrated above and below, was the first Gourdou-Leseurre fighter to enter production, the start of deliveries coinciding with the end of WW I.

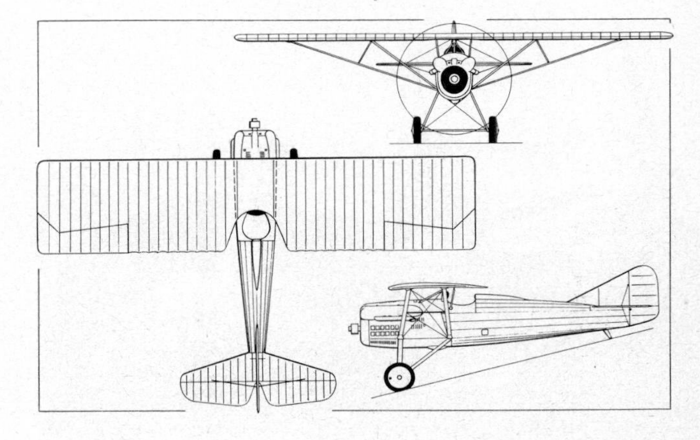

complained of the controls of the Messerschmitt. Experience gave confidence, and high-*g* pull-outs were feasible with liberal use of the powerful stabiliser trimmer. The evidence of *Emil*'s poor turning ability at high IAS to the left was nonsense: captured on 9 June 1941, the *Staffelkapitän* of 7./JG 2, *Oberleutnant* Werner Machold confirmed that:

> Contrary to the statements by previous Messerschmitt 109 pilots, this man maintains that it is not difficult to execute a left-hand turn at high speed. On the contrary, he would always try to force his opponent into a left-hand turn. It should be mentioned, however, that this man is very powerfully built.

To have the ability to out-turn one's opponent was very important, but not supremely so. Messerschmitt pilots found that their acceleration, top speed and initial rate of climb matched those of a well-flown Spitfire Mk I: as an evasive manoeuvre the negative-*g* push-over (ie, the start of an outside loop) gave the German pilot an initial advantage in acceleration. The pursuing RAF pilot had to half-roll and pull after the fleeing target, unless he had anticipated this frequent *Luftwaffe* tactic by swinging well out to one side and maintaining positive-*g* as he pulled around after it.

On the other hand the Messerschmitt pilots were aware of the Spitfire's good acceleration and high speed, while the turning ability of both the Hurricane and the Spitfire in the band 12,000-18,000 ft (3 658-5 486 m) was exceptionally good. Thus, they adapted their tactics accordingly. If engaged in a turning-circle with RAF fighters, they assessed the experience of their opponents by how well or badly they flew, and either stayed in the turn to fight it out or evaded: some German pilots favoured a steep spiral climb that the Hurricane found difficult to follow, while the less confident went into the *Abschwung* to use the Bf 109E's high acceleration in the dive. The paramount rule of every fighter leader was to position his formation up-sun and at superior altitude in relation to his opponents. If the leader could achieve surprise, then there was little excuse for letting the advantage slip: over the Channel during the *Kanalkampf* neither side held a clear advantage; over Southern England the tactical advantage was, in general, ceded to the RAF.

The weapons system of the Bf 109E-1, consisting of four Rheinmetall MG 17s, was inadequate. A considerable improvement in firepower came with the installation of the MG FF 20-mm cannon in the E-3 and the improved MG FF/Ms in the E-4 sub-variant. In performance this weapon was inferior to the Hispano-Suiza 404 20-mm cannon of French design, but the MG FF was in front-line service whereas the British were still conducting trials with the HS 404. The muzzle velocity was 1,920 ft/sec (585 m/sec) which reduced effective range, while the rate of fire was 520 rounds per minute. Sixty rounds contained in the canular magazine consisted of *Panzergranate* (SAP), *Brandsprenggranate* (thick-cased incendiary) and *Minenmunition* (thin-cased HE/I); the order of belting was usually alternate SAP and *Minen*, with every fifth an incendiary round. With two MG 17s and two MG FF/Ms, the weight of fire of a three-second burst was about 18 lb (8 kg). This was deceptively low in terms of the damage that could be inflicted by the 20-mm HE rounds on an airframe. The weapons were aimed by a Zeiss *Revi* C 12/c or C 12/d reflector sight, with the weapons cocked and fired by a trigger and button on the KG 13 control column. Visibility from *Emil*'s cockpit was excellent, until the 8-mm head-and-shoulder armour was fitted which severely reduced the search view to the rear. The pilot sat in a semi-reclining position (considered uncomfortable by the British) that enabled him to withstand the effects of *g* in the turn.

Emils of III/JG 27 being refuelled and re-armed between missions from Carquebut airfield during the summer of 1940.

The emphasis on the survivability of German pilots was increased as the offensive progressed. The British considered that the hood-jettison mechanism of the 109 was an outstanding feature. Towards the end of July 1940, the old kapok life-jacket was replaced by the Swp 734 model which, like the yellow one-man dinghy, was inflated by a small CO_2 bottle: one pilot of 1./JG 77 remarked bitterly that his capture had been due to his dinghy automatically inflating itself during combat and, forced hard against the instrument panel and roof, he had had no option but to land. In addition the pilot wore a seat-type parachute, had a Type N.4002 Very-pistol with flares and pyrotechnics, and carried an automatic weapon, Pervitin pills and sachets of yellow-green sea-dye marker. The cockpit was indeed cramped. If he came down in the Channel, an embryonic air-sea rescue service (denied immunity after 29 July 1940) came to his aid, in addition to the E- and R-boats, or he might reach one of the innumerable "lobster-pots" (Lw rescue floats) that dotted the Channel. In spite of the efforts to recover downed German crews, the Channel often won, and *die Kanal* itself was to become bitterly despised and feared by the Bf 109E pilot of 1940.

Advent of Adlerangriff

The *Kanalkampf* reached a crescendo of activity on 8 August 1940, when, as an unpremeditated part of the general escalation in operations, VIII Fl Kps *Stukas* and Bf 109Es made a determined attack on Convoy CW.9 *Peewit*. Two days later *Zerstörergeschwader* 2's Bf 110C-2 fighters were mauled by Hurricanes and Spitfires over Portland, to confirm the *Fuhrüngsstab*'s fear that no great reliance could be placed on future long-range escort missions by this comparatively unwieldy twin. Recent experience had shown that the Bf 110C and D-1 were totally outclassed by RAF single-engined fighters: there had been notable recent occasions when *Staffeln* of 110s had been forced into defensive circles while urgent R/T requests were made for support by Bf 109Es. The unsuitability of the Bf 110C *Zerstörer*, to fulfil its intended rôle on deep and medium penetration operations dramatically reduced the chances of the *Luftwaffe*'s impending offensive resulting in acceptable losses. In the recent battles, the *Kampfgeschwader* crews had come up against stiff fighter opposition for the *first* time, and had noted, to their alarm, that RAF fighter pilots appeared to be totally undeterred by the manually-operated single 7,9-mm MG 15 and MG 17 machine guns that constituted the standard defence of the German bombers. If offensive operations were to succeed on penetration raids over England, the bomber leaders maintained, then close fighter escort was essential.

On *Adlertag* — "Day of Eagles", as the opening day of the aerial assault on Britain had been dramatically dubbed — 13 August 1940, the *Emil*-equipped units of *Luftflotte* 2 (apart from the Bf 109E-1/B and E-4/B fighter-bombers of 3./Ekdo 210), were provided by the *Stab* and three *Gruppen* each of *Jagdgeschwader* 3, 26, 51 and 52, and the *Geschwaderstab* and I/JG 54 under *Jafü* 2 (Obstlt Osterkamp), while *Luftflotte* 3 included the *Stab* and three *Gruppen* each of JG 2, JG 27 and

JG 53 *Pik-As* under Obstlt Werner Junck as *Jagdfliegerführer* 3.

Lack of co-ordination at command level and variable weather on *Adlertag* marred the conduct of the *Luftwaffe*'s operations on this, the start of the maximum effort designed to establish air superiority and ultimately bring Great Britain to the point of surrender. In the course of a record 1,485 sorties the *Luftwaffe* struck at Eastchurch airfield in the morning, with attacks on Portland, Southampton and airfields in Hampshire and Kent in the afternoon: 45 German aircraft, including a large number of the vulnerable Ju 87B-2s, were brought down in return for the loss of 13 RAF fighters. This operational effort was exceeded on 15 August 1940, when all three *Luftflotten* directed attacks on RAF airfields: the majority of attacks succeeded in arriving over their objectives, which included Hawkinge, Lympne, Driffield, Manston, Martlesham, Rochester (Short Bros: Stirling production), Middle Wallop and Worthy Down. RAF Fighter Command put up 974 sorties to lose 34 Cat.3 with 17 pilots killed and 16 wounded. Far short of the RAF's exaggerated claim of 182 destroyed, the *Luftwaffe*'s loss, at 75, was nevertheless little short of disastrous.

The fighting of *Schwarz Donnerstag* (Black Thursday) ultimately caused a major recasting of *Luftwaffe* strategy: firstly, the casualties suffered by *Luftflotte* 5 off Northumberland and North-East England effectively put Gen Hans-Jurgen Stümpff's command out of the offensive; secondly, the success of Nos 12 and 13 Groups in the North swung the battle back to South-East England where the *Luftwaffe* could operate over shorter distances; and thirdly, the Ju 87B and the Bf 110C *Zerstörer* were confirmed as being unfit for operations over England except under the most favourable circumstances. Concerned over the failure of the *Stuka* and the conduct of the offensive since the start of *Adlerangriff* — "Attack of the Eagles", as the overall assault was known — Göring held a conference that evening at Karinhall. On the subject of fighter-escorts he had this to say:

> "The fighter escort defences of our *Stuka* formations must be readjusted as the enemy is concentrating his fighters against our *Stuka* operations. It appears necessary to allocate three *Jagdgruppen* to each *Stuka gruppe*: one of these *Jagdgruppen* remains with the *Stukas* and dives with them to the attack; the second flies ahead of the attack at medium altitude and engages the fighter defences and the third protects the whole attack from above. It will also be necessary to escort the *Stukas* returning from the attack over the Channel."

In an indirect manner, the *Oberbefehlshaber der Luftwaffe* had opened what was to be a lasting, and increasingly bitter, chastisement of the *Luftwaffe* Fighter Arm that was to endure until the end of the Second World War. Within three days of *Schwarz Donnerstag*, on what was to be the hardest-fought day of the entire offensive, 71 German aircraft failed to return or were destroyed in crashes: StG 77 alone lost 16 Ju 87s. Twenty-seven RAF fighters were destroyed or assessed at Cat.3, and 10 pilots were killed in action. From 15 to 18 August inclusive, the *Luftwaffe* had lost 194 aircraft in actions that demonstrated to Göring the fact that Dowding's forces were far from being beaten down and, as a corollary to this, that the *Jagdwaffe* was either incompetent or being mis-used.

At the conference at Karinhall on the morning of 19 August 1940, the *Oberbefehlshaber* announced: "Until further notice the main task of *Luftflotten* 2 and 3 will be to inflict the utmost damage possible on the enemy fighter forces. With this are to be combined attacks on the ground organisation of the enemy bomber forces conducted, however, in such a manner as to avoid all unnecessary losses." The staunch counter-offensive being conducted by RAF Bomber Command during this time, by day and by night, was causing other services concern. A considerable proportion of the effort of the *Jagdwaffe* was directed, to the exclusion of the overriding considerations of the offensive, towards a defensive commitment against raids on the Channel ports and its own airfields. Göring then gave the *Luftflotten* and *Fliegerkorps* commanders a free hand in the

During the final phase of the "Battle of Britain", Emils were increasingly employed in the fighter-bomber rôle over Southern England. Here a Bf 109E-4/B of III/JG 26 is seen with a 551-lb (250-kg) bomb in readiness for one of these missions.

selection of specific targets, while reserving the decision to attack Liverpool and London for himself. In addition he decided to phase out Richthofen's *VIII Fliegerkorps* from active operations over England and pronounced that while the Bf 110 *Zerstörer* remained on operations it was to be given a top-cover of Bf 109Es.

He then turned his attention to fighter commanders. He attributed the heavy losses recently suffered by the *Stuka* and *Kampfgruppen* to the lack of aggression on the part of the *Jagdflieger*. He suggested that the fighter force had failed to fulfil its allotted task, asserting that its pilots had been more concerned with adding to their scores in combat with RAF fighters than with the vital task of covering the bombers. They undoubtedly preferred the *Frei Jagd*, the pure fighter sweep, to the difficult close-escort and escort-cover missions around and in the vicinity of the bomber formations. But, he insisted, the *Jagdflieger* should exercise greater responsibility toward their charges: in the air they should fly close alongside and on the ground they should visit and liaise with the bomber crews and ascertain their problems. Henceforth, he pronounced, if the fighter pilots abandoned an escort mission using the excuse of bad weather, then they would face summary court-martial!

Several *Kommodöre* and *Gruppenkommandeure* had revealed the fact that they were past their prime as combat pilots, and Göring went on to state that in the future the most successful pilots would become the *Verbandsführer* (formation leaders). After decorating Werner Mölders and *Major* Adolf Galland (Kdr III/JG 26) with the *Deutsches Kreuz* in Gold, he informed the latter that he was to be appointed the *Geschwaderkommodore* of JG 26, and thereafter a wave of promotions took place. *Major* Gunther Lützow took over JG 3, *Major* Hannes Trautloft the *Grünherz* JG 54, and Wolfgang Schellmann the élite *Jagdgeschwader 2 Richthofen;* other up-and-coming youngsters, such as Otto Bertram, Edu Neumann, Rolf-Peter Pingel, Gerd Schöpfel and Walter Oesau took up the posts of *Gruppenkommandeure*. But the promotions of these successful pilots had come too late, for their hands were already tied to the tactical demands of the bombers!

Error compounds error

On the following day the Ops 1a section of the *Luftwaffenführrungsstab* (Operations Staff) at OKL issued a directive in compliance with Göring's orders to authorise an all-out offensive against RAF Fighter Command. The directive charged the *Luftwaffe*:

> To continue the fight against the enemy air force until further notice, with the aim of weakening the British fighter forces. The enemy is to be forced to use his fighters by means of ceaseless attacks. In addition, the aircraft industry and the ground organisation are to be attacked by individual aircraft by day and by night, if weather conditions do not permit the use of complete formations.

The *Oberkommando der Luftwaffe* (High Command) had known for some time that the bulk of Fighter Command's

The cockpit of Emil was comparatively small and narrow. The instruments on the upper panel surmounted by a clock (top centre) are (left to right) the altimeter, compass and boost pressure gauge in the upper row, and ASI, turn-and-bank indicator, rpm indicator and propeller pitch indicator in the lower row. The lower panel carried the oil pressure and fuel contents gauges, and the oil and water temperature gauges. The undercarriage selector handle is seen on the upper right of the lower panel.

forces were concentrated around London, at the airfields of Hornchurch, Debden, North Weald, Kenley, Northolt and Biggin Hill, within Park's No 11 (Fighter) Group. These Sector Airfields were a vital link in Fighter Command's defensive system, and the assault on the network of airfields in Nos 10 and 11 Groups during the critical period of 24 August to 6 September 1940 was to bring the *Luftwaffe* to within grasp of achieving air superiority over the "enemy fighter force" based in Southern England. With effect from 20 August, *Jafü* 3's fighter units were transferred from Cherbourg and Normandy, to airfields in the Pas-de-Calais, to be joined by the *Zerstörer* element from *X Fliegerkorps* in Norway. This massive concentration of fighters was to furnish escort and support on medium-penetration attacks on No 11 (Fighter) Group's defensive network in South-East England. But there was an irremedial flaw in the offensive plan.

Whilst operating by day within British airspace, the *Luftwaffe*'s bombers needed fighter-escort: the Bf 110 *Zerstörer* had the range with which to accompany the bombers, but not the ability to survive the fighter opposition. The *Emil* had demonstrated that it could achieve, if employed correctly, an element of air superiority over the Channel and the South Coast. But the *Jagdgruppen* were now faced with the task of protecting the bombers at all times to the limit of their radius of action. It was now that the entire *Luftwaffe* offensive by day was to be confined, in its plans and objectives, by the limitations in range and endurance of *Emil*.

The Bf 109E carried 88 Imp gal (400 l) of fuel. When allowance was made for start-up and take-off, the range was 286 miles (460 km) and the endurance 55 minutes at 16,400 ft (5 000 m) with maximum continuous rpm: at the most economical cruise setting, at the same altitude, the range was 413 miles (825 km) and the endurance 1 hr 50 min. These were figures that bore no relation to operations. On a *Frei Jagd* mission, with an allowance for 10 minutes of combat, the maximum radius was about 125 miles (200 km). Therefore, from Audembert, near Cap Gris Nez, a fighter sweep could extend to a line drawn through Portsmouth-Reading-Luton-Ely-Norwich, while a unit based at Cherbourg could operate over Dorset and Hampshire as far north as Andover. But the *Frei Jagd* tactics were now shelved, to be replaced by the close-escort and escort-cover rôles.

It took at least 30 minutes for the Bf 109Es to assemble over a specified point with the bombers before setting course: when escorting the slower He 111s the Messerschmitt pilots had to weave above and behind the bombers, but were able to throttle back sufficiently to formate on the faster Ju 88A-1 and Do 17Z-2. With the fighter pilot's endurance reduced to 50 minutes after forming up and cruising at approximately 180 mph (290 km/h), he could afford to accompany the bombers over a radius of only 75 miles (120 km), sufficient to the southern outskirts of London only and not beyond. This limitation was to prove to be a critical factor, and effectively drew the teeth of the *Jagdwaffe*.

Long-range fuel tanks had been used in Spain: the Heinkel He 51B-2 fighter carried a 37·5 Imp gal (170 l) drop tank on operations with the *Legion Condor* during 1937-38, and the Junkers Ju 87R-1 was currently equipped with an excellent 66 Imp gal (300 l) tank made by Norddeutsche Kühlerfabrik in co-operation with the Junkers concern. Erhard Milch later stated that the use of drop tanks on *Emil* had been raised many months prior to the crisis now facing the *Jagdwaffe*. At the conference of 15 August 1940, he maintained, the subject was again raised as the "fighter pilots were refusing to use drop tanks unless their aircraft were armour plated". In fact there was a moulded plywood tank available, but this leaked after warping and the pilots were justifiably concerned as to its incendiary proclivities.

The Bf 109E-7 was entering service equipped with the racks, fuel pipes and booster pump required for the use of the Junkers/NKF 66 Imp gal (300 l) tank; there were as many as two to three *Gruppen* equipped with the Bf 109E-1/B and E-4/B that had the necessary racks and lacked only the fuel system. With the drop tank, the Bf 109E's radius of action was 200 miles (320 km), sufficient, from the Pas-de-Calais, to cover the aero engine and airframe factories in the British Midlands, and force RAF Fighter Command to bases beyond the Humber.

Notwithstanding the blame and bungling that could be apportioned to the *Luftwaffe* High Command for this crucial oversight, could not the *Kommodöre* and *Kommandeure* at the frontline, those with first-hand knowledge of the limitations of their equipment, have been more vociferous in their demands for a jettisonable tank? As it was their silence was deafening. The Junkers/NKF tank arrived at the front in early-November 1940, and by that time the issue was resolved: the combat radius of 200 miles (320 km) during the Battle of Britain "would have been just the decisive extension of our penetration", claimed the *Geschwaderkommodore* of JG 26 after the war. And he was almost certainly right!

After the critical phase against the airfields in the South-East, the *Luftwaffe* turned at last to the bombing of London. It was to be the final error in the conduct of the *Schlacht um England*. On 1 September 1940, the *Luftwaffenführrungsstab* issued orders for the attack on some 30 airframe, engine and component factories giving succour to the RAF, but political as well as tactical considerations now came into play and, on 3 September, the decision to bomb London was taken in order to draw RAF Fighter Command into a final battle of attrition. Kesselring's original objective, now sanctioned by Hitler as a *Vergeltungsangriff* (reprisal attack) in return for RAF Bomber Command's raid on Berlin, now reduced some of the intolerable pressure that had been placed on Fighter Command. On the afternoon of 7 September 1940, 372 bomber sorties were directed against the East India Docks and the eastern suburbs of London, followed that night by a further 255 sorties. Concentrated daylight attacks ensued during the weeks to come. Again German losses began to be serious, and differences of opinion arose between the *Jagdwaffe* and the sorely-tried bomber leaders, with accusations and counter-accusations that resulted in the direct intervention of Göring in the dispute.

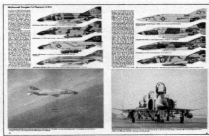

The *Jagdwaffe*, already committed to escort work, wished to embody a more fluid system of bomber protection: this consisted of *Schwärme* providing escort, escort-cover and top-

cover at heights up to 30,000 ft (9 150 m), whilst a number acted as forward-support in the traditional *Frei Jagd* rôle. The bomber leaders, alarmed at the high casualty rate being sustained and the apparent inefficiency of the Bf 109 pilots, pressed for a rigid escort in *Rotten* (pairs) and *Ketten* (threes), with a form of wider escort in close formation, in addition to a top cover. It was a case of the bomber men telling the fighter pilots how to do their job and the latter were justifiably incensed. The matter was settled by the *Oberbefehlshaber* who accorded to the views of the bomber leaders. The *Jagd-* and *Zerstörergruppen* were ordered to fly in and around the bomber groups, and to remain in position until attacked. Thus, the fundamental advantages of surprise, initiative, altitude, speed, and, above all, fighting spirit, were ceded to the pilots of Fighter Command.

With the failure of the *Jagdwaffe* to gain air supremacy over Southern England in the time allotted, the plans for *Unternehmen Seelöwe* (Operation Sealion — the invasion of the British Isles) were postponed "indefinitely" by the *Führer* on 17 September 1940. By night, the *Luftwaffe* turned its attention to the systematic bombing of industrial and area targets in a campaign that was to last until May 1941. On the day of Hitler's decision to postpone *Seelöwe*, the *Luftwaffe* reverted to smaller formations of bombers with escorts of 100-200 fighters, but with support in the form of the deadly *Frei Jagd* missions. The limitations in the range of *Emil* continued to restrict the area of the assault, however.

The top priority in target selection remained Greater London, but aircraft factories and RAF fighter airfields were again included in the order of attack. On 27 September 1940, another change in tactics occurred: small formations of 20-30 Ju 88A-1 bombers were used with an escort of 200-300 Bf 109s and Bf 110s, and the Bf 110C-4 fighter-bombers were once again employed on fast, low-level missions on precision targets. At the beginning of October 1940, the *Oberbefehlshaber* directed that one *Staffel* of each *Gruppe* in each *Jagdgeschwader* be diverted to the Jabo rôle (*Jagd-Bomber*: fighter-bomber). Accordingly the Bf 109E was fitted with the ETC 500/IXb rack which usually carried an SC 250 bomb of 551 lb (250 kg), or the ETC 50/VIIId that could hold a cluster of four 110-lb (50-kg) SC 50s. Jabo tactics had been evolved by I *(Jagd)*/LG 2 over the previous months and much of its knowledge was passed to the *Gruppen*. The tactics hereafter summarised were drawn from the reports of *Luftwaffe* personnel captured by the British in October and November 1940:

1. One P/W stated that the whole of I and II (*Jagd*)/LG 2 were equipped with the Me 109 fighter-bomber, and that three *Staffeln* of JG 27 are to convert to the Jabo rôle, with the remainder acting as top-cover during operations. The 2./JG 52 also operates as a Jabo unit at St Inglevert.
2. Apparently no definitive procedure has yet been evolved for Jabo work on the Me 109E, but a dive is usually made at an angle of 15-20 deg using the *Revi* and the pull-out made at around 3,000 ft (910 m). Pilots say that they aim the nose of the aircraft ahead of the target. In a 15-20 deg dive, a point is picked some 200 yards (183 m) ahead. The IAS builds up to around 340 mph (546 km/h) and at 80 deg to 430-480 mph (690-770 km/h). The Me 109 can be dived at 80 deg but the pilot must pull back before bomb-release to prevent the bomb from striking the propeller. The maximum attainable IAS is reduced by 10-15 mph (16-24 km/h) by the ETC rack alone, and by double that amount when the bomb is carried. The highest Jabo 109s have been seen at 23,000 ft (7 000 m). The Jabos tend to jettison their bombs when E/A are around so as to obtain greater manoeuvrability.
3. The whole of III/JG 26 took part in an operation on 5 November 1940, in addition to several other *Gruppen*. All of 9./JG 26 carried bombs. *Oberstleutnant* Adolf Galland claims more than 50 victories and seems to be beating *Major* Werner Mölders. The *Staffelkapitän* of 9./JG 26 (Oblt Heinz Ebeling) had three years' service with 95 war-flights and claims 18 "kills" on operations against England. He stated that 9./JG 26 never flew more than three sorties per day: rest days are more or less regular.
4. The affairs of III/JG 26. The *Gruppe* is based on a field 4-5 miles (6-8 km) SSE of Guines, on the edge of a rectangular wood: there are no hangars and the 109s are dispersed on the edges among the trees. Personnel are billeted in Guines and drive by car to the airfield every morning at dawn. The third *Staffel* of each *Gruppe* of JG 26 is equipped with Me 109 Jabos. Only one spare aircraft is available to 9.*Staffel*. In July 1940, 9./JG 26 underwent fighter-

EMIL RECALLED

(As related to Alfred Price by Oberleutnant *Julius Neumann who flew with* II Gruppe *of* Jagdgeschwader *27 during the campaign in France and the Battle of Britain)*

THE BF 109E, OR EMIL, called for some skilful handling during take-off and landing, and at the fighter school near Berlin, we tyros were introduced to this potent warplane via the rather more docile and comfortable Bf 108, which shared with the single-seater Willi Messerschmitt's unmistakable "signature". This gave us some experience in piloting a reasonably fast monoplane with a retractable undercarriage and a variable-pitch propeller, reducing the hazards that we would undoubtedly have faced had we gone to *Emil* "cold".

The first idiosyncrasy encountered when learning to fly the Bf 109E was provided by the fighter's take-off — it demanded quite a lot of right rudder to hold it straight, the propeller torque resulting in a predilection for breaking left. Fortunately, one soon became accustomed to this tendency. The landing, too, presented something of a problem for novices. As one reduced speed for the approach, control sloppiness increased. At about 90 mph (145 km/h), the wing slots opened automatically and one immediately felt the extra lift that they imparted. The stalling speed with undercarriage and flaps down was about 60 mph (90 km/h), and below that speed *Emil* would drop a wing violently and without warning. Under such circumstances, the fighter fell like a stone and unless a reasonable amount of height was available there was no time to recover! It was vital to get both mainwheels on the ground simultaneously, or else the aircraft would swing in the direction of whichever wheel touched first, and as often as not the result was a broken undercarriage leg.

Quite a few Bf 109Es were written off during pilot conversion, but once pilots had accustomed themselves to these less endearing characteristics accidents were rare, even at primitive forward landing grounds such as those we utilised in France, and at speed *Emil* had few vices and handled beautifully. For its day it was very fast and offered an excellent rate of climb. Up to its maximum horizontal speed it was very light on the controls and easy to handle, although the controls did stiffen up considerably in the dive.

Until the end of the campaign in France, few of us had experienced much aerial combat in *Emil*. A handful of pilots had flown earlier versions of the Bf 109 in combat in Spain, but many of these had soon been promoted to staff positions. The Polish Air Force had been rapidly overwhelmed and thus little dogfighting experience had been gained during that short campaign, while in France it proved difficult to compare *Emil* with the Morane-Saulnier 406 or Curtiss Hawk as we saw so very little of them, and on the rare occasions that they were encountered, they were not, in my opinion, handled aggressively. Some pilots, such as Mölders and Galland, had some combat with Moranes and Curtisses, but these were the exception rather than the rule. Personally, I saw only one Morane during the entire French campaign and this was disappearing into the distance, and my sole "kill" was a Dutch Fokker T V bomber which I shot down over Belgium.

During the campaign in the West, my *Jagdgeschwader*, JG 27, operated as part of *Generalmajor* Baron Wolfram von Richthofen's *VIII Fliegerkorps* and our primary tasks were the close support of our ground forces and providing escort for the *Stukas*, and it was not until the Dunkirk withdrawal that we really had an opportunity to test the mettle of *Emil* in dogfighting. We now met RAF fighters in numbers for the first time; they represented a foe as aggressive and as well-equipped as we were. For the initial phase of the Battle of Britain, my *Gruppe* moved to Crépon, near Caen, and from the beginning of August we were frequently in combat and I succeeded in shooting down a Hurricane. In escorting *Stukas*, the English south coast was beyond our radius of action from Crépon and immediately before these operations we would move to one of the forward landing grounds near Cherbourg, top up our tanks and fly from there.

I cannot compare *Emil* with the Spitfire or Hurricane, never having flown either, but we were told that there was no better fighter in the world than the Bf 109E and we had every reason to accept this assertion. We knew the Spitfire and Hurricane to be

bomber training at a depot near Rheims for a week, but has since evolved its own methods. This usually takes the form of a mass attack in which each *Schwarm* dives in line-abreast. Height is normally maintained at 26,000 ft (7 900 m) before diving at the pre-briefed angle — normally between 40 and 60 deg. Prior to pulling out at about 16,000 ft (4 900 m) the pilots start to count: they start at 23 and release between the count of 27-28 by which time the 109 is just getting its nose to the horizon. Only the *Staffelkapitän* gives the word for release on the R/T, with the rest keeping in time by counting. If the weather is clear or if RAF opposition is intense, bombs are released on Dover harbour.
5. It is said that Obstlt Adolf Galland, the *Kommodöre* of JG 26, is now specialising in picking off lone or straggling aircraft. In contrast, Hptm Schöpfel, the *Kommandeur* of *III Gruppe*, goes "bald-headed" into the thick of everything he can see. He is credited with bouncing 15 Hurricanes from out of the sun, shooting down four and returning with his windscreen totally obscured by the oil of the fourth.

The massed daylight attacks of the *Luftwaffe* finally ceased towards the end of October 1940, and on 1 November the *Luftwaffe* returned to the *Kanalkampf* with the Ju 87s making their reappearance: these were given thorough fighter escort by the *Jagdgruppen* which continued to operate Jabo and *Frei Jagd* missions over parts of Southern England. The final large scale mission for JG 26 occurred on 5 December 1940, when support was given to II (*Jagd*)/LG 2 on a Jabo mission to London. During the epic phases of the *Schlacht um England*, from 1 July to 31 October 1940, the *Luftwaffe* had lost 1,789 aircraft of all categories in service with operational units engaged in operations against Britain: the total number destroyed in combat (*Feindflug*) and on operations (*bei Einsatz*) had included 600 Bf 109Es and 235 Bf 110s. Over the same period the Metropolitan Air Force (home-based elements of the RAF) lost 1,603 Cat.3 destroyed, of which 1,140 were single and twin-engined fighters and 367 bombers. The results were about even. The epic aerial conflict of all time was over.

Both *Luftflotten* 2 and 3 followed a course of conservation during the winter of 1940-41; units were either posted back to Germany for re-fit, or remained in the West, while some moved to Austria in preparation for the Balkan foray in the spring of 1941. In retaliation for the offensive RAF Circus operations, Rhubarbs and sweeps launched under the aegis of the new AOC-in-C Fighter Command, Air Marshal W Sholto Douglas, *Jafü* 2 and 3 commenced another round of Jabo and *Frei Jagd* operations in early-April 1941: sweeps were flown over Kent and Sussex, with the Jabos attacking Manston, Hawkinge and Lympne. The *Emil* was now losing the race in the quest for improved performance, however, being hard put to keep pace with the latest Spitfire Mk V series. Some *Emils* were fitted with the Daimler-Benz DB 601N-1 engine (1,175 hp at rated altitude) to become the Bf 109E-4/N and the E-7/N. The use of nitrous-oxide gas to act as an anti-detonant and increase power output above the rated altitude was tested. The system, known as GM-1 or *Ha-Ha*, evinced considerable interest from the British when a Bf 109E-7/Z equipped with GM-1 (WNr 5983 of 7./JG 2) forced landed at Worth Matravers, Dorset, on 9 June 1941. This particular aircraft had been on a Jabo mission in search of shipping.

As the *Luftwaffe* transferred its units to the East in preparation for the invasion of the Soviet Union during May and June 1941, the remaining *Emils* of JG 2, JG 26 and I/JG 52 were based in France and Belgium to play their part in the defence of the Western Front, along with the new Bf 109F and the Fw 190A-1. Save for the few *Emils* of the reconnaissance units the characteristic square wing tips and strutted tailplane of *Emil* were by now a rare sight in the skies over England, however. The last to fall on English soil was, in fact, to be that of Uffz Kurt Thüne of 1.(F)/123 who put his Bf 109E-7/Z (WNr 4970) down in a field near Buckfastleigh, Devon, after an engine failure on 7 January 1942. Thereafter, *Emil*, acting in the time-honoured mien of any old soldier, merely faded away. □

good, and we believed that we were opposed by a pilot-aircraft combination closely comparable with our own, but we considered that our tactics were the better. Insofar as I was concerned, my greatest worry in attacks on the UK was the long overwater flight — about 80 miles (130 km) in each direction by the shortest possible route; there could be no deviations for tactical planning and there was no margin for navigational error. Some of the other fighter *Geschwader* had been issued with rubber dinghies, but we in JG 27 had only our life jackets and the knowledge that some four hours in the sea was about as much as we could take without dying of exposure.

On Sunday, 18 August 1940, I flew my final and most memorable sortie in *Emil*. On that day we were to fly escort for more than a hundred Ju 87s of *Stukageschwader* 3 and 77 which were to attack targets in the Portsmouth area — the largest such *Stuka* attack attempted to that time. My *Geschwader* put up 70 *Emils* from all three *Gruppen* for the close escort of the dive bombers supplemented by 32 more *Emils* from JG 53, while JG 2 sent off a further 55 in a huge free hunting patrol intended to scour the area of British fighters. Because of the low cruise of the *Stukas* and our own short radius of action, the timing of the take-off was critical — five minutes too early meant we would have to break off our escort mission that much earlier — so we sat on the ground until the dive bombers had taken-off, assembled and overflown our field. We rapidly overhauled them, but to maintain station we had to weave our *Emils* from side to side.

Soon after crossing the British coastline I caught sight of a few small specks on the horizon: RAF fighters! In no time at all, a tremendous dogfight was in full swing as we endeavoured to keep the Spitfires and Hurricanes off the *Stukas*. I succeeded in getting on the tail of one of the enemy fighters and chased him in a high speed dive while he jinked from side to side to avoid my fire. We were soon down to about 165 ft (50 m) above the sea and heading towards the Isle of Wight. I knew that I had scored some hits and my quarry began to leave a thin trail of black smoke. Now, I thought, I have him cold! I glanced aft to make sure that my tail was clear before going in for the kill and was startled to see two smoke trails behind us — a black one and a white one. The white trail was coming from my *Emil*!

Although I had had no idea that my aircraft had been hit, the glycol system had evidently been punctured. I glanced at the engine temperature gauge and saw that the needle was hard against the upper stop, realising at the same time that the cockpit was getting uncomfortably hot. My engine began to splutter, so I broke off the chase and tried to gain height in order to bale out. At that moment, the engine cut dead and flame began to appear from the joint in the cowling. I was only some 100 ft (30 m) above the ground, jettisoned the canopy and prepared to crash land, side-slipping into a small field. The port wing struck the ground first and took the force of the landing, and my *Emil* spun round and slithered to a halt in a cloud of dust, my head receiving a hefty blow from the windscreen when it was jerked violently to one side.

That was the last I was to see of *Emil* for nearly 40 years, and then, last year, I visited the Battle of Britain exhibit at the RAF Museum, Hendon. Here the curator kindly allowed me to sit in the *Emil* included in the exhibit. I immediately felt at home. Everything came easily to hand despite the lapse of time. It was like meeting an old friend again after many years. Had the tank been full and there been a runway in front of me . . . ! □

IAT

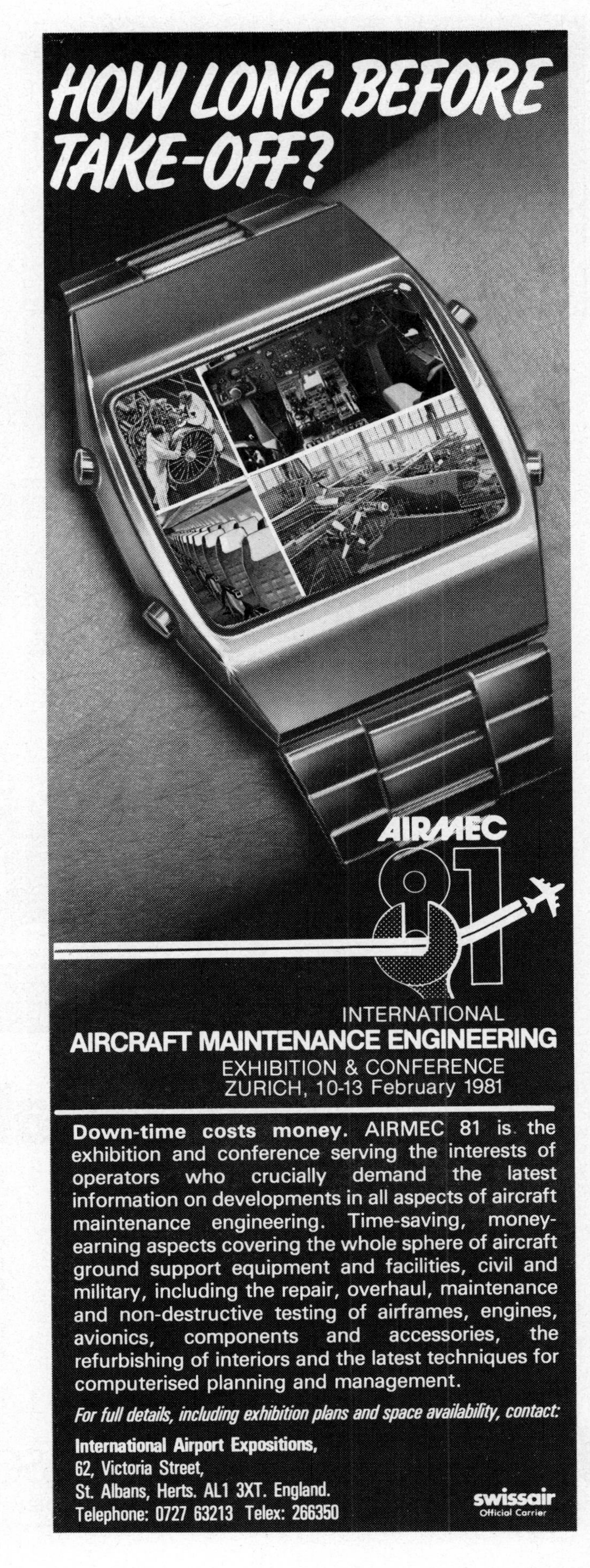
HOW LONG BEFORE TAKE-OFF?
AIRMEC
81
INTERNATIONAL
AIRCRAFT MAINTENANCE ENGINEERING
EXHIBITION & CONFERENCE
ZURICH, 10-13 February 1981
Down-time costs money. AIRMEC 81 is the exhibition and conference serving the interests of operators who crucially demand the latest information on developments in all aspects of aircraft maintenance engineering. Time-saving, money-earning aspects covering the whole sphere of aircraft ground support equipment and facilities, civil and military, including the repair, overhaul, maintenance and non-destructive testing of airframes, engines, avionics, components and accessories, the refurbishing of interiors and the latest techniques for computerised planning and management.
For full details, including exhibition plans and space availability, contact:
International Airport Expositions,
62, Victoria Street,
St. Albans, Herts. AL1 3XT. England.
Telephone: 0727 63213 Telex: 266350
swissair
Official Carrier

The signal-sorters

Integrating given combinations of VHF, UHF, HF, VOR, ADF and other receiver signals into a single interface obviously requires flexibility on the part of an aircraft's Communication Control System equipment.

Flexibility in CCS

And flexibility is exactly what the Racal Six-Ninety Series CCS offers.

These small, highly sophisticated units provide for the selection, control and interface of audio signals from onboard equipment and intercom.

Modular principle

Already in use in military and civil aircraft all over the world, the Series is based on a modular principle which allows equipment to be custom engineered to fit any aircraft from Chinook to Hawk.

Complete range

The station boxes shown above are just two from the complete range, which includes equipment suitable for almost any application.

For full details of the Six-Ninety Series, contact the address below.

RACAL ACOUSTICS for sound communications

Racal Acoustics Limited, Beresford Avenue, Wembley, Middlesex HA0 1RU, England.
Telephone: 01-903 1444. Telex: 926288. Telegrams & Cables: Acoustics Wembley.

RACAL

BRAZIL

EMBRAER EMB-110P3 BANDEIRANTE

BRAZILIAN state-owned manufacturer EMBRAER has launched development of a pressurised version of the highly successful Bandeirante twin-turboprop transport, with the designation EMB-110P3. Basis for this development is the EMB-110P2, the principal version currently in production for the commuter airline.

The cabin of the P3 is to be pressurised to a differential of 2·5 psi (0,18 kg/cm²), giving a cabin equivalent altitude of 10,000 ft (3 050 m) at an actual height of 17,000 ft (5 182 m). The accommodation remains unchanged, at 19 passenger seats, but the fuselage is shortened by 29½ in (75 cm) as a result of introducing a T-tail. Uprated PT6A-65 engines are introduced and the undercarriage is modified to have twin wheels on each leg, main and nose. Slightly extended wingtips, of the type used on the EMB-121 Xingu and EMB-120 Brasilia, are also featured.

Power Plant: Two Pratt & Whitney PT6A-65 turboprops each rated at 1,173 shp for take-off, driving three-bladed propellers.

Performance: Max cruising speed, 308 mph (495 km/h) at 10,000 ft (3 050 m); range with 19 passengers, 700 naut mls (1 297 km) at max cruise speed and 790 naut mls (1 463 km) at economic cruising speed at 1,500 ft (457 m).

Weights: Operating weight empty, 8,657 lb (3 927 kg); max zero fuel weight, 12,500 lb (5 670 kg); max payload, 3,840 lb (1 743 kg); max take-off weight, 15,430 lb (7 000 kg); max landing weight, 14,770 lb (6 700 kg).

Dimensions: Span, 51 ft 3½ in (15,63 m); overall length, 51 ft 0½ in (15,56 m); overall height, 16 ft 7 in (5,06 m); wing area, 313·2 sq ft (29,1 m²); aspect ratio, 8·09:1; undercarriage track, 15 ft 9 in (4,80 m); wheelbase, 15 ft 6 in (4,73 m).

Accommodation: Flight crew of two and 19 passengers in cabin pressurised to a differential of 2·5 lb/sq in (0,18 kg/cm²), three abreast at a pitch of 31 in (79 cm). Cabin length, 46 ft 6½ in (14,19 m); max cabin width and height, 5 ft 3 in (1,60 m); cabin volume (including flight deck), 660 cu ft (18,7 m³).

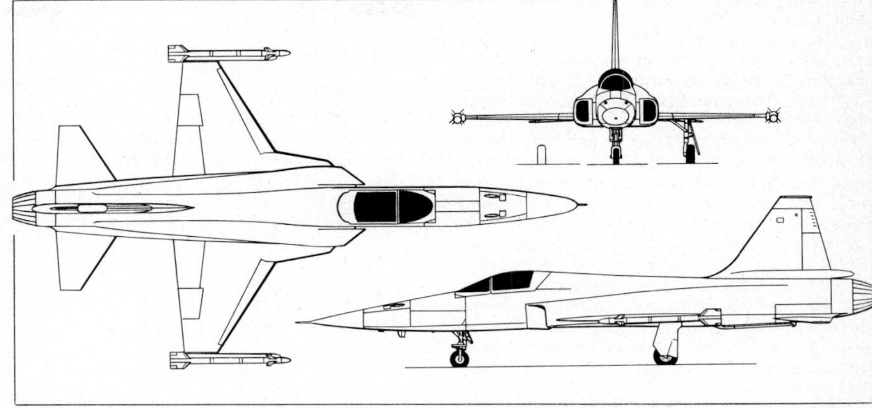

Three-view drawing and (below) an artist's impression of the Northrop F-5G, the single-engined derivative of the Tiger II.

(Above) An impression and (below) three-view drawing of the EMBRAER EMB-110P3, a pressurized version of the Bandeirante now under development.

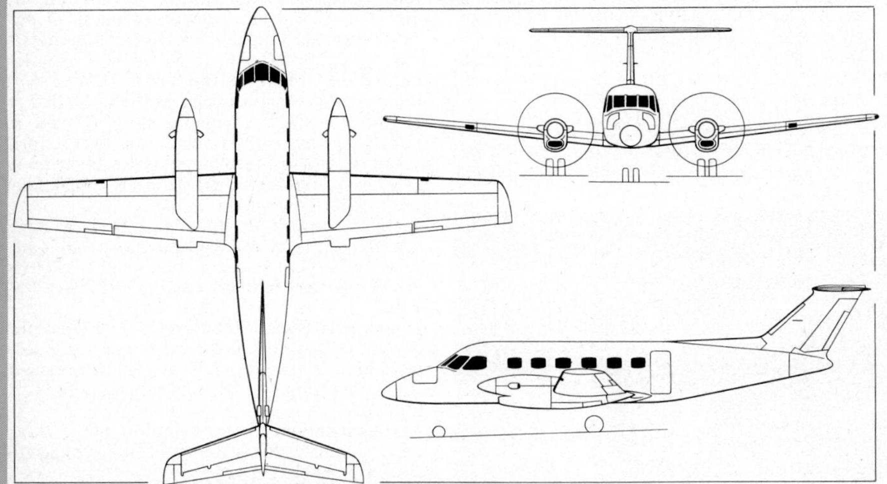

USA

NORTHROP F-5G

AS one of the principal contenders for future export business as a lightweight international fighter, under the aegis of the US government's FX programme, the Northrop F-5G is proceeding on schedule towards a prototype first flight in the late summer of 1982. The FX fighter is intended to be wholly company-funded and for export only, as a successor for the Northrop F-5 series. In addition to the F-5G itself, downgraded versions of the GD F-16 and possibly the MDC/Northrop F-18 are expected to be offered; General Dynamics is already working on a version of the F-16 with General Electric J79 engine for this purpose.

The F-5G has grown out of studies made by Northrop over the past six years, and its improvements when compared with the F-5E are derived primarily from the use of a more powerful engine, combined with relatively modest airframe and system changes. A number of engine options were studied before Northrop decided in March 1979 to use the General Electric F404 (the engine that powers the F-18 Hornet, in the 16,000 lb st/7 258 kgp F404-GE-400 version). By comparison, the F-5E Tiger II is powered by a pair of 5,000 lb st (2 268 kgp) J85-GE-21 engines. The F-5G therefore has an increase of some 60 per cent in maximum thrust, for a 17 per cent increase in empty weight, and will be able to achieve a max rate of climb of more than 50,000 ft/min (254 m/sec) at sea level and a max speed of the order of M = 2·1.

Installation of the single F404 engine, with a single variable-geometry nozzle, in place of the side-by-side pair of J85s, results in modification of the rear fuselage profile, which is considerably slimmer in plan view. The F404 has internal cooling and less air space is therefore needed between the outside of the engine and the inner skin of the fuselage structure. Because this new rear fuselage profile changes the aerodynamic characteristics, Northrop designers have added long, narrow "step" fairings to the lower fuselage on each side, extending from the wing to aft of the tailplane; these fairings help to maintain the longitudinal stability unchanged. To improve longitudinal stability at high angles of attack, the front fuselage is flattened slightly to have a shark nose profile.

The air intakes on each side of the fuselage are slightly enlarged in cross-section area, are extended forwards a few inches and are moved outward from the fuselage to accommodate the thicker boundary layer flow that results from the higher speeds to be achieved. In the central fuselage area, equipment is rearranged and fuel cells reshaped; together with a 5-in (12,7-cm) plug inserted just aft of the cockpit, this allows an equipment compartment to be installed in the upper fuselage, giving easier access to avionics equipment for servicing.

The small inboard leading-edge extensions on the F-5E's wing are being lengthened forwards and modified in shape, as necessary for the redesigned air intakes and also to increase the maximum lift co-efficient of the F-5G's wing.

Internal and structural changes include a banjo frame round the engine to carry the fin loads into the fuselage; a modified drag chute fairing at the base of the fin; graphite composite skins on the rear fuselage and tailplane; increased skin thickness on the inner wing sections to cater for the higher weight of the single-engined version and to allow the limiting load factor to increase from 7·33 *g* to 9 *g*; heavy-duty wheels and brakes and a dual fly-by-wire system with mechanical back-up for longitudinal control. (The F-5E has a dual hydro-mechanical control system.)

Northrop calculations indicate that at 30,000 ft (9 145 m) the F-5G will be able to accelerate from M=0·9 to M=1·2 in 30 sec and to M=1·6 in 80 sec. The sustained rate of turn at that altitude is estimated to be 6 deg/sec at M=0·8; at lower altitudes, 11 deg/sec will be sustained and the peak rate will be 19·3 deg/sec.

With the same internal fuel capacity as the F-5E, the F-5G will have about 10 per cent more combat radius and 20 per cent better range/endurance as a result of the new engine's lower sfc. Wing and fuselage strong points will carry the same loads as on the F-5E, but the F-5G is being designed primarily for the air-to-air rôle, with two AIM-9 Sidewinders at the wing tips to supplement the two built-in 20-mm cannon in the front fuselage. In a typical combat air patrol mission, the F-5G will carry three 275 US gal (1 041-l) external tanks to achieve a combat radius of 300 naut mls (555 km), including allowance for acceleration, supersonic manoeuvering and a 20-min reserve. For a HI-LO-HI interdiction mission with two drop tanks, Sidewinders and seven Mk 82 bombs, the F-5G achieves a 360 naut ml (666-km) combat radius.

Numerous different equipment configurations have already been produced for the 27 nations that have purchased F-5 variants and most of these will remain available for the F-5G; they include such items as fire control radar, dual radar/EO display, inertial navigation platforms, laser target designators, laser-guided ordnance, nose-mounted cameras, in-flight refuelling, anti-skid brakes and ECM equipment. The new General Electric GEPOD 30 gun-pod carrying a 30-mm gun, has been flown on an F-5 and is available for use on the F-5G. A two-seat version of the F-5G will be available if required.

Power Plant: One General Electric F404 turbofan rated at approximately 16,000 lb st (7 258 kgp) for take-off with afterburning. Fuel capacity, 4,440 lb (2 014 kg).

Performance: Max speed, M=2·1 at 37,000 ft (11 278 m) equivalent to a true airspeed of 1,200 kts (2 230 km/h); max speed at sea level, M=1·05, equivalent to 694 kts (1 285 km/h); initial rate of climb, 50,300 ft/min (256 m/sec); time to 40,000 ft (12 192 m) from brake release, 2·3 min; take-off distance, 1,450 ft (442 m).

Weights: Empty, 11,220 lb (5 089 kg); take-off weight, clean, 17,110 lb (7 761 kg); max take-off weight, 26,140 lb (11 857 kg).

Dimensions: Span, 26 ft 8 in (8,13 m); length, 48 ft 6 in (14,78 m); height, 14 ft 10 in (4,52 m); wing area, 186 sq ft (17,28 m^2).

Armament: Two 20-mm M39A2 cannon in front fuselage. Four wing pylons and fuselage centreline strong point carry up to 7,000 lb (3 175 kg) of ordnance. Two AIM-9 Sidewinder AAMs at wing-tips.

One of the armament options for the Northrop F-5G is the General Electric GEPOD 30, shown here carried on the centreline fuselage station of the second production F-5E in use for development flying. The GEPOD 30, recently ordered into production by the USAF, contains a 30-mm gun with a 2,400 rounds per minute rate of fire.

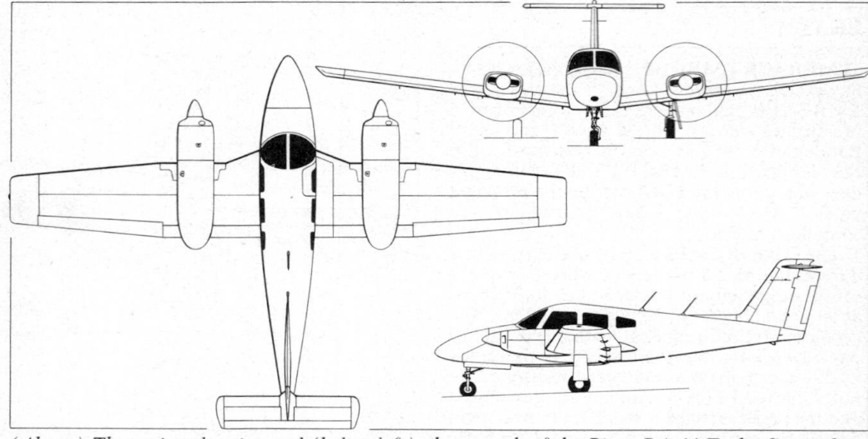

(Above) Three-view drawing and (below left) photograph of the Piper PA-44 Turbo Seminole, a new variant in the 1981 range.

PIPER PA-44-180T TURBO SEMINOLE

THE addition of a turbosupercharged version of the Seminole to the Piper range of light twins makes available a four-seat aircraft of unusually good performance. It is expected to offer competition for the six-seat twins with more powerful engines, since it can achieve competitive speeds with a saving of up to $10 an hour in fuel costs. Piper believes that many of the larger aircraft are used by operators who do not really need more than four seats but have regarded the smaller aircraft as lacking in overall performance.

The Turbo Seminole is certificated to operate at altitudes up to 20,000 ft (6 100 m) and has a built-in oxygen system with the oxygen bottle located behind the baggage compartment. At a base-price of $17,310 (£7,400) the Turbo Seminole is at least $5,500 (£2,350) cheaper than its nearest four-seat competitor, the normally-aspirated Beech Duchess.

Power Plant: Two Lycoming TO-360-E1 flat-four piston engines, oppositely rotating, each rated at 180 hp and driving Hartzell two-bladed constant speed fully-feathering propellers. Fuel capacity, 110 Imp gal (500 l).

Performance: Max speed, 195 kts (362 km/h); max cruising speed, 167 kts (309 km/h) at 10,000 ft (3 050 m); cruising speed at 75 per cent power, 183 mph (339 km/h); initial rate of climb, 1,290 ft/min (6,56 m/sec); single-engined rate of climb, 180 ft/min (0,91 m/sec); max certificated operating altitude, 20,000 ft (6 100 m); single-engined ceiling, 12,500 ft (3 810 m); take-off distance to 50 ft (15,2 m), 1,500 ft (457 m); landing distance from 50 ft (15,2 m), 1,190 ft (363 m); range, 875-920 naut mls (1 621-1 704 km).

Weights: Empty weight, 2,435 lb (1 105 kg); useful load, 1,508 lb (684 kg); max cabin load, 1,365 lb (619 kg); max zero fuel weight, 3,800 lb (1 724 kg); max take-off weight, 3,925 lb (1 780 kg).

Dimensions: Span, 38 ft 6½ in (11,75 m); length, 27 ft 7 in (8,41 m); height, 8 ft 6 in (2,59 m); wing area, 180 sq ft (16,72 m^2); undercarriage track, 10 ft 6 in (3,19 m); wheelbase, 8 ft 5½ in (2,58 m).

Accommodation: Four including pilot. Baggage volume, 26 cu ft (0,74 m^3); baggage capacity, 200 lb (91 kg).

Volume 19 Number 5 November 1980

Editorial Offices:
The AIR INTERNATIONAL, PO Box 16, Bromley, BR2 7RB Kent.

Subscription, Advertising and Circulation Offices:
The AIR INTERNATIONAL, De Worde House, 283 Lonsdale Road, London SW13 9QW. Telephone 01-878 2454. US and Canadian readers may address subscriptions and general enquiries to AIR INTERNATIONAL PO Box 353, Whitestone, NY 11357 for onward transmission to the UK, from where all correspondence is answered and orders despatched.

MEMBER OF THE AUDIT BUREAU OF CIRCULATIONS ABC

Subscription rates, inclusive of postage, direct from the publishers, per year:

United Kingdom	£7·50
Overseas	£8·00
USA/Canada	$20·00

Rates for other countries and for air mail subscriptions available on request from the Subscription Department at the above address.

The AIR INTERNATIONAL is published monthly by Fine Scroll Limited, distributed by Ducimus Books Ltd and printed by William Caple & Company Ltd, Chevron Press, Leicester, England.

Second Class postage approved at New York, NY. USA Mailing Agents: Air-Sea Freight Inc, 527 Madison Avenue, New York, NY 10022.

ISSN 0306-5634

CONTENTS

FRONT COVER: A Lightning F Mk 6 of No 11 Squadron on the approach to Akrotiri during deployment from RAF Binbrook for weapons training.

WRENDEZVOUS WITH WREN

"Certainly — what kind of favour?"

AIRSCENE

MILITARY AFFAIRS

ANGOLA

The single example of the Fokker **F27 Maritime** displayed at Farnborough International 80 in the insignia of the FAPA/DAA (*Fôrça Aérea Populare de Angola/Defesa Anti-Aviões,* or Angolan Popular Air Force and Anti-Aircraft Defence), and **delivered to Angola** last month (October), is to be flown and maintained on behalf of the FAPA/DAA by TAAG-Angola Airlines. To be based at Luanda, the F27 Maritime is to be employed on sea surveillance, offshore installation control, fishery protection and SAR tasks along Angola's 995-mile (1 600-km) coastline. TAAG-Angola Airlines is also apparently responsible for the operation and maintenance of the bulk of the FAPA/DAA transport fleet, which now comprises one F27-600, one C-130E Hercules, seven An-26s, 10 An-2s, three C-47s, six BN-2A Islanders and four Aérospatiale N.262s. The operational strength of the FAPA/DAA is currently based on one interceptor squadron with 11 MiG-21MF and MiG-21bis fighters, and one close air support squadron with seven MiG-17Fs and the two surviving Fiat G.91R-4s. There is a helicopter force of 10 Mil Mi-8s and 13 SA 316B Alouettes, advanced training is performed on three MiG-15UTIs, and four PC-6 Turbo-Porters serve in the liaison and utility rôles.

AUSTRALIA

Defence Minister Dennis Killen has announced that the carrier HMAS *Melbourne* is to be replaced by a **helicopter carrier** capable of operating V/STOL fixed-wing aircraft, and it is understood that the Australian government has reached agreement in principle to procure a *Guiseppe Garibaldi* class 13,000-*tonne* vessel which should enter service with the RAN in 1985. The *Garibaldi* class vessel has apparently been selected in preference to Spanish and US contenders for the contract and, according to Mr Killen, a V/STOL fixed-wing aircraft for operation from the vessel will be selected in 1983, the only obvious candidates being the Sea Harrier and the AV-8B.

Several companies, including Israel Aircraft Industries, have responded to an RAAF **RFP** (Request for Proposals) **for updating** its 87 **Mirage IIIs,** and the service will issue a specification to which tenders will be invited once the proposals have been studied. The refurbishment programme is vital if the Mirage IIIO is to be retained in first-line service until the selected TFF aircraft is completely absorbed into the inventory in 1986-87.

Major **procurement programmes** currently in the pipeline embrace tri-service requirements **for** up to 120 **light and medium helicopters** to be procured during the first half of this decade. The primary requirement is for the replacement of the RAAF's fleet of 40 plus UH-1B, -1D and -1H Iroquois helicopters currently fulfilling a variety of tasks, and a similar requirement specified by the Army suggests that the Army Aviation Corps is proposing to assume some of the ground and troop support tasks hitherto performed by the RAAF. RAN interest in new helicopters centres on the requirement to equip the four FFG-7 missile frigates currently on order for ASW tasks, the first two of which being scheduled for delivery during the course of the New Year, with the recently-ordered fourth vessel to be delivered during 1984. Ten ASW helicopters are required for the first three FFG-7s, and the Australian Defence Department is seeking maximum commonality between the helicopters required by the three services, Aérospatiale and Sikorsky having proposed a single-type/multi-variant solution and Westland having proposed a package comprising both the Lynx and the WG30. The RAAF and RAN also have requirements for a new light helicopter for which the SA 350 Ecureuil is reportedly favoured, some 30 helicopters apparently being involved in the bi-service requirement.

AUSTRIA

A four-man team from the **Army Aviation Force** (*Heeresfliegerkräfte*) headed by Col Josef Bernecker, the service's chief test pilot, spent a week at Fort Worth in September **evaluating the F-16** Fighting Falcon, both Col Bernecker and the chief engineer of the Army Aviation Force, Col Manfred Münzer, flying a two-seat F-16B several times. Evaluation of the F-16 initiated the latest in numerous fighter evaluations made on behalf of the *Heeresfliegerkräfte* over the past 14 years, although the Austrian Finance Minister has recently stated that budgetary considerations are unlikely to enable a fighter order to be placed before 1982. The *Heeresfliegerkräfte* has a requirement for up to 24 aircraft to re-equip its Surveillance Wing (*Überwachungsgeschwader*), short-listed types being both the F100- and J79X-powered versions of the F-16, and the Mirage 50, although, as delivery is not anticipated before 1984-85, it is likely that the Northrop F-5G will be added to this list, its predecessor, the F-5E Tiger II, having been frontrunner in the last Austrian round of evaluations.

BELGIUM

The Belgian Army's air component, the *Aviation Légère de la Force Terrestre/Licht Vliegwezen van het Landmacht*, is currently **studying** the Aérospatiale SA 365 Dauphin 2, the MBB-Kawasaki BK 117 and the Westland Lynx to meet both its anti-armour and liaison/observation **helicopter requirements** in the second half of the decade, having eliminated smaller types, such as the Gazelle and Hughes 500MD. It is believed that procurement of a smaller quantity of larger, more capable helicopters will prove more cost effective, and current plans envisage acquisition of a total of 48 of the selected type to replace the 68 surviving Alouette IIs of the 100 purchased in 1958. Twenty-eight of the new helicopters will each be equipped with eight missile launching tubes and will equip two anti-armour squadrons, one squadron being attached to each of the two divisions of the 1(BE) Corps in Germany from 1984 onwards, and the remaining 20 helicopters will be assigned to the liaison/observation rôle. A definitive choice of helicopter is scheduled to be made in 1982.

The *Force Aérienne Belge/Belgische Luchtmacht* is requesting **offers for** 53 Lockheed F-104G and TF-104G **Starfighters** which will become surplus to the service's requirements between the end of this year and the beginning of 1984. The aircraft each average some 3,000 hours and approaches have been made by a Texas broker who has indicated interest in the Starfighters for refurbishment and resale, by the Lockheed Aircraft Service Company, and by a dealer acting on behalf of Taiwan (with which country Belgium has no diplomatic relations), the last-mentioned being considered the most likely purchaser. In addition, Belgium is expected to make a deal with Turkey to supply 16-18 F-104Gs from the Belgian inventory at a greatly reduced price by means of the NATO programme assistance fund.

DENMARK

The Royal Danish Air Force is undertaking a refit and **update programme for** the weapon delivery and navigation system (WDNS) in its **Saab 35XD Drakens**. As part of this programme, which will return the modified aircraft to service by 1984, orders have been placed in the UK for Marconi Avionics 900-Series head-up displays, incorporating the "Snapshoot" facility, and for Ferranti Type 105D lightweight laser rangers, which are lightweight derivatives of the Type 105 used in the Fairchild A-10. The new WDNS for the Draken is being integrated by Lear Siegler Inc's Instrument Division as system manager, and includes a Lear Siegler computer and Kearfott inertial platform.

EGYPT

The **training** of Egyptian Air Force pilots **on the F-16** Fighting Falcon is scheduled **to commence** at MacDill AFB, Florida, in the **autumn of next year,** following English language training (to commence in January) and a short course on Northrop F-5s at Williams AFB, Arizona. The EAF is scheduled to receive an initial batch of 40 F-16s through the *Peace Vector* programme, with deliveries commencing in 1982.

Deliveries to the EAF of a **third batch of Mirage** 5SDE **fighter-bombers** are now being completed, increasing total Egyptian procurement of the Dassault-Breguet aircraft to 62, plus six two-seat Mirage 5SDD trainers. The initial batch of 40 aircraft (including six two-seaters) was funded by Saudi Arabia from 1975 onwards, this being supplemented by a further 14 aircraft in 1977, the third batch also consisting of 14 aircraft.

FEDERAL GERMANY

The **first fully-operational Alpha Jet-equipped** *Jagdbombergeschwader,* **JaboG** 43, as LeKG 43 is to be redesignated in January, is now in process of **accepting its** new **equipment** at Oldenburg. The *Geschwader* is to receive a total of 51 Alpha Jets, of which 10 will be dual-control models, to equip two *staffeln* each of which will have 18 aircraft constantly on line, the remaining 15 aircraft being held in reserve or in maintenance. LeKG 41, to be redesignated JaboG 41 on the commencement of re-equipment at Husum mid-year, will have a similar statutory strength. The Alpha Jet OCU, JaboG 49 at Fürstenfeldbrück commissioned on 20 March with 32 dual-control Alpha Jets, will also eventually have an inventory of 51 aircraft of which 18 will form the weapons training detachment at Beja, Portugal.

The *Heeresflieger*, the Army's **air component,** is now in the initial stages of **phasing into service** 302 MBB **BO 105** light helicopters (212 PAH anti-armour models and 90 VBH liaison and observation models), the initial operating unit of the BO 105 PAH-1 being the weapons school *(Heeresfliegerwaffenschule)* at Buckeburg. The *Waffenschule* will eventually have an inventory of some 30 PAH-1s, and operational deployment will be within three *Panzerabwehrregimenten,* or anti-tank regiments, based at Celle, Roth and Fritzlar, and attached to the I, II and III Army Corps respectively.

FINLAND

The Finnish **Air Force,** *Ilmavoimat,* **has leased** two Fokker F27-100 **Friendships** from Kar-Air to replace its grounded C-47s. The period of the lease is six years and a clause in the lease gives *Ilmavoimat* the option of buying the aircraft after four years. *Ilmavoimat* has also purchased four Piper Arrow IVs for interim use as primary trainers pending availability of sufficient Valmet Vinkas, deliveries of which have only now commenced following a delay of more than a year.

The Air Force, *Ilmavoimat*, took **delivery of** its first two **L-70 Vinka** (Miltrainer) primary trainers from Valmet last month (October) at Halli, and the manufacturer anticipates delivering a further three aircraft to the service before the end of this year. By the time that the first Vinkas were handed over, Valmet had flown some 500 hours with the prototype, 150 hours with the first production aircraft and 20 hours with the company demonstrator, the last test flight for Type Certification (FAR 23) having been made on 22 September.

FRANCE

It has been officially announced that **France** is **to build two** 32,000 *tonne* **nuclear-powered** aircraft **carriers** to replace the *Clémenceau* and *Foch*, and the first of the new carriers is scheduled to join the French Navy in 1991. The *Clémenceau*, which underwent major refit last year, is currently expected to remain in service until the early 'nineties, and the *Foch*, which is now undergoing refit, is likely to be retained until the end of the century.

GREECE

The US Defense Department has informed Congress of a proposed **letter of offer** to Greece covering the sale **of** eight Bell **AH-1S Cobra** anti-armour helicopters equipped with TOW missiles at a cost of $35m (£14·58m). It is assumed that the Cobras are intended for the Hellenic Army's air component, the *Aeroporia Stratou*, the helicopter element of which is currently equipped with Bell UH-1Ds and Agusta-Bell AB 205s.

INDIA

The agreement reached last year between India and the Soviet Union for **procurement of** the **MiG-23** (see *Airscene*/January) has now been **scaled down** and acquisition of the air-air MiG-23MF (*Flogger-B*) has been temporarily shelved pending the outcome of a comparative evaluation between the Soviet fighter and the Dassault-Breguet Mirage 2000. It was earlier planned to purchase 80 MiG-23MF fighters for IAF service from the mid-'eighties, the bulk of these being assembled by HAL at Nasik from knocked-down components. Procurement of the two-seat MiG-23UM (*Flogger-C*) and MiG-23BN (*Flogger-F*) optimised for the air-ground rôle is proceeding and a total of 85 aircraft is involved, comprising 15 two-seaters and 70 single-seaters, the contract finalised last year calling for the first batch to be supplied in flyaway conditions, with initial deliveries in 1982, and the balance being supplied in knocked-down component form for assembly at Nasik.

The controversy surrounding the IAF's METAC (Medium Tactical Transport Aircraft) requirement has re-opened following **cancellation of** the agreement reached last year (see *Airscene*/December 1979) between the Indian and Soviet governments for the **licence manufacture** by HAL **of** the Antonov **An-32** (*Cline*). Choice of the An-32 as the METAC was strongly influenced by price, which was less than half that of the closest contender (DHC-5D Buffalo) and barely one-third that of the other frontrunner in the contest, the Tyne-engined Aeritalia G 222T. The Antonov bureau, which had developed the An-32 from the An-26 specifically to meet the hot-and-high requirements of the METAC specification, had introduced a number of modifications (eg, leading-edge wing slats, undercarriage revisions and a slight increase in maximum troop capacity) at the request of the IAF in order to meet the most critical aspects of the requirement. But despite the statement (on 24 October 1979) by the then Indian Defence Minister that agreement for supply of the An-32 to the IAF had been reached, no contracts were signed and the Soviet Union refused to persist with development of the aircraft and to initiate production without such contracts. A further evaluation of potential medium tactical transports is now being undertaken by the IAF, with the DHC-5D Buffalo apparently being viewed with most favour, but an early decision appears unlikely and the programme is expected to be scaled down from the IAF's "95 aircraft requirement".

It has now been confirmed that rumoured IAF interest in the photographic reconnaissance version of the **MiG-25** (see *Airscene*/October 1979) has been translated into a **firm order** for eight aircraft to replace the Canberra PR Mk 7s of No 106 Sqdn. The aircraft, which will reportedly be essentially similar to the *Foxbat-B*, are to be delivered to India late 1982 or early 1983.

The IAF is expected to **phase out** the last **of** its **Gnat** lightweight fighters by March-April of next year. Nos 9 and 18 squadrons, formerly equipped with the Gnat, have now re-equipped with the Ajeet, and of the remaining Gnat squadrons (Nos 2, 22 and 24) two will convert to the Ajeet and one to the MiG-21bis over the next few months.

The Indian Navy anticipates receiving its **first Kamov Ka-25** *Hormone* **helicopter** this month (November) with the belated arrival of the first of three *Krivak* class destroyers from which the Ka-25s are intended to operate. INAS 333, formed specifically for the operation of the Ka-25, has now completed crew training in the Soviet Union and will deploy one helicopter aboard each destroyer, a total of five Ka-25s being on order. The Indian Navy was reluctant to procure the Kamov helicopter as it considered it irrational to add in small numbers yet another operational aircraft type to its inventory and particularly so as the six *Godevari* class frigates now being built in India, with the first scheduled for commissioning in 1982, will each accommodate two Sea Kings. However, the Soviet Union refused Indian requests that the *Krivak* class vessels be adapted to accommodate the Sea King, insisting that the destroyers be accepted with the standard Soviet weapons systems. Delivery of the vessels to India is now some two years late and it may be assumed that the Ka-25s (like the Il-38s serving with Indian Naval Aviation) are refurbished ex-AV-MF aircraft.

INTERNATIONAL

The first two **German** production **Tornadoes** were **delivered to** the Trinational Tornado Training Establishment (TTTE) at RAF **Cottesmore** on 2 and 3 September, the aircraft being GT 005 and GT 004 respectively. The arrival of the German aircraft brought the number of Tornadoes at Cottesmore to five, the others being BS 002, BT 002 and 004, the last-mentioned having arrived on 2 September. Three service instructor aircrews have now taken up their duties at the TTTE. During the peak period of training there will be almost 50 Tornadoes at the TTTE, 40 per cent of which will be provided by the RAF, 45 per cent by the *Luftwaffe* and *Marineflieger*, and the remainder by the *Aeronautica Militare*.

JAPAN

Defence Agency **requests for** the Fiscal **1981 budget show** an **increase of 9·7 per cent** over the previous year and include 58 new aircraft for the three services at a total cost of £288·3m as follows: (ASDF) three Mitsubishi F-1s, four Grumman E-2Cs, six Lockheed C-130Hs, nine Mitsubishi T-2s, two Kawasaki KV-107-2s and one Mitsubishi MU-2; (MSDF) 11 Mitsubishi SH-3Bs, four Beech King Air C90s, one Fuji KM-2 and one Mitsubishi S-61A; (GSDF) two Mitsubishi LR-1s (MU-2s); six Fuji UH-1Hs and eight Kawasaki OH-6Ds. During Fiscal 1981, the ASDF will form an F-15J Eagle test squadron and the sixth and last F-4EJ Phantom squadron (the 306th at Komatsu AB), in addition to the service's first "aggressor" training unit with five T-2s and two T-33As (at Tsuiki AB). The MSDF proposes to reconstitute the current P-2J-equipped Okinawa Air Unit as the 5th Air Group and to form a new ASR squadron (initially with two S-61As) at Iwojima.

MALAYSIA

Vought, Lockheed Air Services, Grumman and McDonnell Douglas are all bidding for the sizeable refurbishing contract resulting from procurement by the **Malaysian** government of 88 ex-US Navy **A-4 Skyhawks** to be withdrawn from storage at the Davis-Monthan AFB, Arizona. The Royal Malaysian Air Force is understood to require a number of two-seat Skyhawks for conversion and continuation training, but it is not yet known if these will be conversions of single-seaters. The RMAF anticipates operating the A-4 for "at least eight years" and the fatigue life remaining to the aircraft being purchased is reported as "more than adequate" to meet this requirement. Although no refurbishing contract had been announced by the time of closing for press, the RMAF anticipates receiving 25 per cent of the aircraft "next summer".

The US Defense Department has informed Congress of a proposed **letter of offer** to the Malaysian government **covering** the sale of two Northrop **RF-5Es** for the RMAF at a cost of $38·2m (£15·9m).

NETHERLANDS

The Dutch decision to procure **additional F-16 Fighting Falcons** was confirmed mid-September when details of the 1981 budget were released. It was stated that the KLu plans to order 24 more F-16s and has earmarked £2m for preliminary funding in the budget. A Dutch official spokesman has told the five-nation steering committee of the F-16 multinational co-production programme that the 24 aircraft will be the first batch of a total of 111 aircraft, 30 of which will be utilised to make up attrition suffered by the 102 aircraft currently on order for the KLu, the remaining 81 replacing the service's fleet of NF-5s. Although it is anticipated that the additional KLu F-16s will be assembled by Fokker after completion of current F-16 contracts mid-1984, the Dutch have not excluded the possibility of a direct off-the-shelf purchase from General Dynamics as studies have indicated that such could save some £83m. The Dutch decision for a unilateral procurement programme for additional F-16s came after they had failed to convince the Belgians of the desirability of advancing their replacement date for the Mirage 5. Suffering serious economic problems and still undecided as to the most suitable successor for the Mirage, the Belgian government still believes that a decision is unnecessary before 1982-83. The Dutch order (which will almost inevitably be placed with Fokker), unaccompanied by follow-on orders from Belgium, Norway and Denmark, could lead to a change in the current five-nation memorandum of understanding which could possibly be replaced by a bilateral agreement between Holland and the USA.

SPAIN

The **Army** aviation component, FAMET (*Fuerzas Aeromoviles de Ejercito de Tierra*), is scheduled **to receive** the first 10 of 60 MBB BO 105C **helicopters** to be assembled in Spain by CASA before the end of **this year**. Of the 60 helicopters (of which a further 30 will be delivered by CASA during 1981), 28 will each be armed with six HOT anti-armour missiles and a single fixed 20-mm cannon, 18 will be cannon-equipped reconnaissance models and the remainder will be unarmed liaison helicopters. Crew training at the *Centro de Instruccion y Applicacion* of FAMET at Los Remedios, Madrid, has been underway for several months on 11 pre-series BO 105s originally obtained by the Federal German *Heeresflieger* for use by its *Versuchsstaffel*, the operational trials unit, at Celle and rendered surplus to requirements earlier this year with the initial deliveries of the first BO 105 PAH-1 helicopters. The ex-*Heeresflieger* helicopters have been purchased outright for FAMET and will continue in the training rôle after delivery of the CASA-assembled BO 105s.

TURKEY

Some **criticism** has been voiced in Ankara **of** the **replacement of** the more aged of the Turkish Air Force's fleet of **F-104G** Starfighters **with** well-worn ex-KLu **F-104G** Starfighters, deliveries of 25 of which commenced in August, and plans to acquire yet more second-hand F-104Gs from Belgium (see separate item). By means of the NATO programme assistance fund, these F-104Gs are being purchased at a token unit price of $75,000 (£31,250) as compared with a normal price of a well-maintained F-104G of between $2m and $4m (£833,000 and £1,667,000), according to avionics and other equipment. The F-104G primarily equips the 141 *Filo* at Mürted and the 191 *Filo* at Balikesir, within the Turkish 1st Tactical Air Force, these two squadrons operating the survivors of the 38 MAP F-104Gs delivered from 1963 and supplemented in the early 'seventies by 11 F-104Gs transferred from Spain. The ex-KLu F-104Gs are apparently intended primarily to make up attrition suffered by these squadrons, but if the ex-Belgian aircraft are also acquired, it is anticipated that sufficient aircraft will be available to form a third F-104G squadron. In reply to press criticism that the Air Force is replacing "old F-104s with more old F-104s", the Central Command commented that the second-hand F-104Gs will adequately meet Turkey's most pressing needs until the mid-'eighties, by which time Turkey will be producing its own fighters! This comment presumably refers to the long-delayed plans for the licence manufacture by the TUSUS organisation of the Northrop F-5E Tiger II and, later, the F-5G, but a contract has still to be signed and a factory has still to be built, suggesting that statements that the F-5E will be in production in Turkey by December of next year are somewhat optimistic. Prior to the arrival of the ex-KLu aircraft, the Turkish Air Force had received totals of 55 F-104Gs and eight TF-104Gs, proposals in the late 'seventies to transfer 20 F-104Gs from *Aeronautica Militare Italiana* surplus stocks having failed to see fruition.

UNITED KINGDOM

British Aerospace hopes to be awarded shortly a two-year feasibility study on the RAF's "large aircraft replacement programme" under which it is hoped to select a **single basic replacement for** virtually **all** of the service's current range of **large aircraft** in the 'nineties. Preliminary consideration is now being given to programmes to replace the Nimrod MR Mk 2, the Victor and, eventually, VC10 tankers, and the Hercules and VC10 transports with one basic airframe. The Ministry of Defence believes that the use of a single basic airframe would be a sensible and cost-effective way of replacing the RAF's fleet of large aircraft and a major step towards the aim of dramatically reducing the number of individual aircraft types the service operates. British Aerospace will, under the anticipated contract, study how new versions of the A300 Airbus might meet up to four very different specialist rôles in RAF service.

AIRCRAFT AND INDUSTRY

ARGENTINA

The *Fábrica Militar de Aviones* (FMA) has now decided to install the Garrett-AiResearch **TFE 731-3 turbofan in** the first three prototypes of the **IA 63 basic jet trainer** and the fourth prototype will be powered by the Pratt & Whitney JT15D-5 for comparison purposes. The design of the IA 63 has now been defined and the first metal will be cut early next year to meet a late 1982 or early 1983 first flight date. Design development of the IA 63 is being undertaken in close co-operation with Dornier, a number of whose engineers are now working at Córdoba while a number of FMA engineers are now working with Dornier in Germany, the German company having been responsible for the design of the supercritical wing. Several variants of the IA 63 are currently foreseen, including a single-seat light CAS version and a light strike model optimised for naval use, the *Comando de Aviacion Naval*'s basic/advanced trainer needs being fulfilled by the recently-placed order for the MB-339 (see *Military Contracts*), the IA 63 time scale having been unsuited to the Navy's training requirements. Since publication of preliminary details of the IA 63 (*AirData File*/September), the FMA has issued a number of revised figures, the clean take-off weight with fuel for a 621-mile/1 000-km range having been reduced to 7,562 lb (3 430 kg), the maximum level speed (at 13,125 ft/4 000 m) and stalling speed (in landing configuration at 7,652 lb/3 430 kg) now being quoted as M=0·73 and 83 knots (154 km/h) respectively, and range (in ferry configuration) being quoted as 932 mls (1 500 km). These figures are understood to be based on the use of the 3,480 lb (1 580 kg) TFE 731-2-2N rather than the approx 3,700 lb (1 680 kg) 731-3 for which the FMA has now opted.

AUSTRALIA

Through a contract signed on 27 August between Hawker de Havilland Australia and British Aerospace, **Australia** has become a participant **in the Airbus** production **programme**, with an initial contract to produce 150 aircraft sets of wing in-spar ribs.

CANADA

Steps taken by **Canadair to restore** the guaranteed **performance of** the **Challenger** — particularly in respect of range — will lead to the introduction of a fuselage fuel tank of 241 US gal (912 l) capacity and an increase in max take-off weight to 40,125 lb (18 200 kg). Compared with the original guarantee of a 4,000 naut ml (7 403-km) range to dry tanks, the Challenger as certificated in August at a gross weight of 34,500 lb (15 650 kg) can achieve only 2,870 naut mls (5 316 km), with NBAA IFR reserves. However, the first 15 customer aeroplanes are being delivered for operation at a gross weight of 36,000 lb (16 330 kg), which will allow an extra 1,500 lb (680 kg) of fuel to be carried with the normal payload, and modification to the wing ribs, wheels and brakes will then allow the weight to go to 38,500 lb (17 464 kg) and the full integral wing tankage of 14,960 lb (6 786 kg) to be carried. Effective with aircraft No 60, in August 1981, Canadair will introduce the extra 1,640 lb (744 kg) of fuel capacity in the form of two free-standing tanks under the cabin floor; these will bring the basic operational weight up to 22,675 lb (10 285 kg) from 20,300 lb (9 208 kg) but with the increase in take-off weight will provide an increase of 250-300 naut mls (463-555 km) in range. Kits to retrofit the earlier aircraft will be provided by Canadair at no cost to the operator. A series of aerodynamic improvements is being studied to reduce drag in order to obtain improved range and to restore some of the losses in field performance consequent upon the higher weights. These include a drooped leading edge, possible leading edge devices, winglets and changes in the nacelle pylon and tailplane junction fairings. Further reference is made to these improvements in *AirData File*/page 248, together with the latest data for Challenger E.

CHINA

According to reports from Peking, **flight testing of the Y-10** four-engined airliner (see *Airscene*/July 1980) has recently begun. The aircraft is said to seat 120-140 passengers, to have the same general configuration as the Boeing 707 and to be powered by four Pratt & Whitney JT3D turbofans. The same sources are also quoted as saying that China is building its own versions of the Antonov An-12 and An-24 turboprop transports.

FEDERAL GERMANY

Dornier has received a contract from the *Bundesministeriums für Forschung und Technologie* (BMFT — Ministry of Research and Technology) to cover a three-year **development** and flight-test **programme on** the **Do 24TT** (*Technologieträger* — technology vehicle) amphibian. The Do 24TT will comprise an existing Do 24 boat hull on which will be mounted a new wing incorporating features of the TNT already flown on the Do 28 Skyservant test-bed, with three Pratt & Whitney PT6A-45 turboprops, and a land undercarriage. First flight is expected to be made in mid-1982 and the Do 24TT is intended to provide the basis for development of a 30-seat ocean-going flying boat or amphibian for military or commercial use. The Dornier company has been studying projected developments of the original Do 24 flying boat for many years and started definition of the Do 24TT in March 1979.

FRANCE

Flight **testing of** the **stretched** version of the Aérospatiale **Super Puma,** the **AS 332L**, began at Marignane in late-September. The AS 332L (see *Airscene*/March 1980) has a 2 ft 6 in (76,5 cm) section inserted in the front fuselage, increasing the cabin volume by 67,1 cu ft (1,9 m^3) and allowing three-four more passengers to be accommodated, according to version. Fuel capacity is increased by 110 Imp gal (500 l) to 453 Imp gal (2 060 l), giving this variant a range of 553 mls (890 km), but an extra 227 Imp gal (1 030 l) can be carried in auxiliary internal and external tanks to stretch the range to 720 mls (1 160 km). The prototype AS 332L is the fourth production Super Puma; the first two are in use for certification trials and the third is the first customer aircraft, for Petroleum Helicopters.

First flight of the two-seat Fournier **RF-6B with** a **120 hp** Lycoming O-235-L2A **engine** in place of the original 100 hp R-R Continental O-200A was made at Nitray on 14 August. Production of the earlier variant totalled 43 aircraft. Following certification, the new version will be put into production in the UK by Vickers-Slingsby (see *Airscene*/October 1980) and Fournier will market the British-built aircraft in France and French territories overseas. The French company will in future concentrate its production effort upon the RF-9 powered sailplane.

INTERNATIONAL

The most recent information concerning the **EH 101** ASW and medium-lift **helicopter project** (see *Airscene*/August) from EH Industries Limited, the Anglo-Italian management company jointly owned by Westland Helicopters and Agusta, indicates that anticipated maximum all-up weight has now risen to some 28,660 lb (13 000 kg) and that disposable load at 13,227 lb (6 000 kg) will be some 50 per cent greater than that of the Sea King. The first third of this decade will be spent in defining the EH 101 and prototype trials are unlikely to commence before 1985, with deliveries commencing "in the late 'eighties". It is anticipated that prototype trials will be conducted with General Electric T700 turboshafts, but a definitive decision regarding engines for the series production EH 101 is unlikely to be taken much before mid-decade and the forthcoming Rolls-Royce/Turboméca RTM321 is being "viewed with some interest". While the EH 101 has been conceived primarily to meet the needs of the Royal Navy and Italian *Marinavia* for a Sea King replacement from the late 'eighties/early 'nineties, and the aim is to evolve a helicopter in which the versions for the two services will employ common airframe, power plant, dynamic components, basic systems and basic avionics, the only major differences being in specialised rôle equipment, the strictly limited potential market for helicopters in this category has resulted in increased emphasis now being placed on the development of a baseline aircraft with considerable potential commercial appeal. EH Industries will sub-contract development and production of the EH 101 in approximately equal shares to Westland Helicopters and Agusta, and there will be no duplication of component production, but both companies will establish assembly lines and EH Industries is seeking the sale of at least 750 EH 101 helicopters, both military and commercial, in the first decade-and-a-half of production, approximately one-third being military, including procurement of about 60 of the ASW model by the Royal Navy.

MBB and Kawasaki have formally launched **production of the BK 117** multi-purpose helicopter with approval for an initial batch of 100 to be laid down. Meanwhile, the backlog of orders and options has now passed the 100 mark. The development programme to date embraces the P1 ground test vehicle at Gifu, engaged on endurance trials; the P2 (Ottobrunn) and P3 (Gifu) flying prototypes, which have completed 245 hrs; the P4 (Ottobrunn) for static trials and fatigue tests and the S01 pre-production machine which is to be used with P3 for certification flying. Flights have been made at weights up to 6,283 lb (2 850 kg), compared with the initial certification figure of 6,173 lb (2 800 kg), or 6,614 lb (3 000 kg) with external loads. The envelope explored includes a speed of 150 kt (277 km/h), altitude of 15,000 ft (4 575m) and 2*g* turns at 100 kt (185 km/h) at max weight.

ITALY

Siai-Marchetti began flight testing during July at Vergiate a version of the **SF 260 powered by** a 260 hp **Allison** 250B-17C **turboprop.** The engine, similar to that used in the Siai-Marchetti SM 1019, offers several advantages for users of the SF 260 in the training rôle, including better "hot and high" performance, lower operating costs and easier fuel availability. The installation increases the length of the SF 260TP to 24 ft 2½ in (7,38 m) from 23 ft 3½ in (7,10 m).

SWITZERLAND

Piltatus can now claim total firm **sales of** 160 PC-7 **Turbo Trainer** basic trainers to eight air forces on four continents, all customers to-date also having options on additional aircraft, these currently totalling a further 120 trainers. The firm orders comprise 16 for Burma (deliveries completed), 12 for Bolivia (deliveries completed), 10 for the Chilean Navy (two remaining to be delivered), 12 for Guatemala (deliveries completed), 52 for Iraq (45 remaining to be delivered), 38 for Mexico (30 remaining to be delivered) and 20 for two as yet unidentified air forces. Negotiations with a ninth air force (reportedly in South-East Asia) for a substantial number of Turbo Trainers were in their final stages at the time of closing for press and production tempo at Stans, at present averaging 4·5 aircraft monthly and rising to 5·0 per month, will rise still further to 6·0 monthly early next year in order to meet delivery schedules up to the beginning of 1982. Approximately 80 Turbo Trainers are expected to have been delivered by the end of this year. The extended operational evaluation of two production Turbo Trainers by the Swiss *Flugwaffe* is virtually complete, the two aircraft having been utilised for a full year in regular training courses at the *Flugwaffe*'s basic and advanced flying schools. Preliminary results indicate that their use has enabled pupils to graduate to much higher training standards in considerably less flying time than fellow students on piston-engined equipment and, in consequence, it is anticipated that an initial Turbo Trainer production order for the *Flugwaffe* will not now be long delayed. Among several foreign services that have recently evaluated the Turbo Trainer, the Canadian Armed Forces are understood to be looking favourably on the Swiss aircraft as a potential successor to part of their CT-114 Tutor fleet.

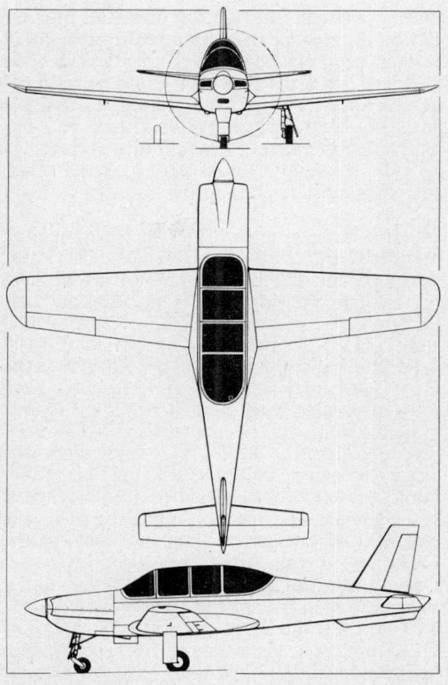

***Modifications** are being made **to** the Aérospatiale **TB-30 Epsilon** to overcome a pitch-yaw coupling problem revealed during flight testing of the two prototypes (which made their first flights on 22 December 1979 and 12 July 1980 respectively). The first prototype was expected to resume testing last month (October) in the form depicted in this drawing, with revised wing-tips and a completely new rear fuselage and tail unit. Overall dimensions of the Epsilon are increased by these modifications to a span of 25 ft 11½ in (7,92 m) and length of 24 ft 10½ in (7,59 m).*

TAIWAN

At the time of going to press, **first flight** was **imminent** in Taiwan **of** the **XAT-3** basic jet trainer, developed at the Aircraft Industry Development Centre (AIDC) with technical assistance from Northrop Corp. Similar assistance had been extended by Northrop to CASA at the initial design stage of the CASA-101 Aviojet, which the XAT-3 resembles in overall configuration; also of the same general appearance is the Northrop-Vought submission in the US Navy VTXTS competition. The XAT-3 is powered by a pair of Garrett AiResearch TFE 731 turbofans and with a gross weight of about 11,000 lb (5 000 kg) is reported to have a max level speed of M = 0·85. There is a local requirement for about 60 aircraft of XAT-3 type.

UNITED KINGDOM

British Airways Helicopters has publicly indicated its **interest in** the **Westland WG 30,** a cabin mock-up of which was shown at Farnborough in BA livery. Captain Jock Cameron, BAH managing director, said that a "firm agreement" between the two companies was likely to be signed before year-end, making British Airways the first customer for the WG 30, and that by the mid-'eighties BAH could need about 25 of these helicopters. A pacing factor, however (see "WG 30: Towards Production"/October 1980) is likely to be the availability of the uprated Gem 60-series, needed to give the WG 30 the ability to carry a full 17-passenger payload on typical North Sea oil support operations, for which rôle it is needed by BAH as a Sikorsky S-61 replacement. Westland's management has recently authorised production of an initial batch of 20 WG 30s.

Exhibited in the static park at Farnborough prior to having made its first flight, the **Nash Petrel** is a two-seat **light tourer** and glider tug developed from the single-seat Procter Kittiwake, two examples of which were built to the designs of Roy Procter some years ago. A 160 hp Lycoming O-320-D2A engine powers the prototype, which has a gross weight of 1,680 lb (762 kg), span of 29 ft 4 in (8,94 m) and length of 20 ft 5 in (6,22 m); engines of 118 to 180 hp can be fitted according to the intended rôle. With a fixed tricycle undercarriage, low wing and side-by-side seating, the Petrel is semi-aerobatic and has been designed to retain the excellent handling characteristics of the Kittiwake. Construction of an initial batch of five is planned by Nash Aircraft Ltd of Farnham Trading Estate, Surrey.

USA

In what is known as the **Multinational Staged Improvement Program** (MSIP), General Dynamics is proceeding with two separate modification programmes **for the F-16** Fighting Falcon. One of these programmes, Engineering Change Proposal (ECP) 425, provides for the introduction of an enlarged tailplane, with 30 per cent greater area and of revised construction in which titanium is wholly eliminated, and mechanical fastening takes the place of bonding used at present to attach the graphite epoxy skins to the aluminium honeycomb. This new tailplane will overcome manufacturing difficulties that have been encountered, will be considerably cheaper and will not be dependent upon scarce titanium supplies. It also will serve to improve F-16 handling, which has suffered with weight growth, particularly when the CG is at the aft limit and behind the centre of lift; the Fighting Falcon is now cleared for operation at weights up to 35,400 lb (16 057 kg) subject to limitations on the angle of attack in certain external load configurations, and a further increase to 37,000 lb (16 783 kg) is expected. Some of this weight growth is associated with the future addition of new avionics and weapons, to provide for which the second modification programme, ECP 350, is being undertaken. This comprises a number of internal structural and wiring changes that can best be made at the production stage, although the equipment installation will come in the 1983-86 period. ECP 350 serves to strengthen the equipment racks in the fuselage bay; increases the capacity of wing pylons No 3 and 7 from 1,000 lb (454 kg) to 3,500 lb (1 588 kg) each; provides for fitting a landing parachute in the base of the fin (to meet a Norwegian requirement) and strengthens the air intakes to allow carriage of pods containing terrain-following radar one side and low-altitude navigation targeting infrared (Lantirn) the other side. The strengthened wing pylons will permit carriage of the advanced medium-range AAM and new internal equipment will include an advanced jamming system and a new fire control radar.

Boeing and USAF have begun a year-long test programme for the modernisation of the B-52G/H Stratofortress fleet in SAC service, with a **first flight** on 3 September at McConnell AFB, Kansas, **of a B-52G** carrying the new **offensive avionics system** (OAS). This system is common to both the B-52G and B-52H, but only the former models are to be converted in due course to carry Boeing AGM-85B air-launched cruise missiles (ALCM), whereas both are to be adapted to carry the Boeing AGM-69A short-range attack missile (SRAM). The single OAS prototype will therefore progressively test the SRAM wing pylon, the SRAM internal launcher, the ALCM wing pylon and the ALCM rotary launcher (which can accommodate SRAM also), and will make 52 flights totalling 400 hrs, including one missile launch of each type from wing pylons and one each from the rotary launcher. SAC plans to have the ALCM-equipped B-52G operational in the first squadron by the end of 1982 (see *Airscene*/September 1980).

The **YAV-8C prototype**, in use to develop a series of new features that the US Marine Corps plans to introduce progressively on its fleet of AV-8A Harriers, was **lost** on 5 September when it crashed into the sea after taking off from the USS *Tarama* amphibious assault ship. The pilot ejected safely, using the Stencel SIIIS seat; the speed was 90·5 kt (167 km/h) at 26 ft (8 m) above the sea with the aircraft pitched 10 deg nose up, and the ejection was the 13th using this type of seat, all with complete success. A second YAV-8C is available to continue the programme, which embraces the introduction of a new VHF radio, a chaff and flare dispensing system, lift improvement devices, a radar warning system and secure voice equipment. The AV-8C modification may also introduce the General Electric GE525 (GAU-12) 25-mm five-barrel Gatling-type gun, in one of the ventral pods, replacing the 30-mm Aden gun usually carried, while ammunition is carried in the other pod, with a suitable cross feed system between the two. A trial installation of this new weapon system was to be flown in October with firing trials starting in November, but loss of the YAV-8C may delay this programme.

Loss of the McDonnell Douglas/Northrop **TF-18** two-seat Hornet on 8 September shortly after its departure from Farnborough, where it was displayed daily throughout the period of the show, led to a temporary grounding of the eight other Hornets engaged in the flight development programme. Both pilots ejected safely after power was lost on the starboard engine and control problems occurred; preliminary evidence indicated a failure in the LP turbine of the General Electric F404 engine, causing disintegration and consequential damage to the airframe. The aircraft was the first of two two-seaters in the batch of nine FSD aircraft; its place will be taken by the other two-seater (the ninth aircraft), which will continue the accelerated service test portion of the programme. Total Hornet hours up to the time of the crash were 2,246.

Lockheed has announced that work on the **L-400 Twin Hercules** has been **suspended**, nine months after the decision was taken to proceed with full scale development. The go-ahead was given in response to the firm interest shown by several potential customers, including Spain and Venezuela, but funding priorities in these nations have since changed and the prospect of orders being placed for the Twin Hercules has receded. Work on the L-400 could be resumed at any time in the future should the market situation change; meanwhile, Lockheed has expressed interest in the possibility of finding a partner for joint development of the Twin Hercules, perhaps in another country.

Hughes Helicopters exhibits at Farnborough included the 500MD **Defender II**, latest development of the multi-mission Model 500 in the **light gunship** rôle. The principal new feature is the Martin Marietta mast-mounted sight (MMS), which was shown in its first experimental application on the 500MD at the Paris Air Show last year and has now been fully integrated into the helicopter's weapons system. Removal of the earlier M65 nose-mounted sight for the TOW missiles allows the weight to be redistributed and the twin-TOW launchers can now be attached to the standard fuselage-side hardpoints. Operating at the original gross weight of 3,000 lb (1 360 kg), the Defender II can carry the 30-mm Hughes Chain Gun (developed for the AH-64) under the fuselage in place of the TOW installation, and with the gun fitted can still carry a pair of GD Stinger AAMs; other optional equipment includes a pilot's night vision sensor, a radar warning system and an advanced avionics/mission equipment package. A four-bladed tail rotor, developed for the commercial Model 500D, cuts perceptible external noise by about 50 per cent.

The McDonnell Douglas **DC-9 Super 80** was **certificated** by the FAA on 26 August, at the conclusion of a 10-month programme during which 795 flights were made, totalling 1,085 hrs. The FAA certification permits operation of the Super 80 by a two-pilot crew, although the size of the crew complement remains a controversial issue with some pilot unions, including ALPA in the USA. The manufacturer claims that the Super 80 is the "world's quietest commercial jetliner" on the basis of FAA testing, which shows that it surpasses the most stringent requirements of FAR Part 36 Stage 3 (although it was required only to comply with Stage 2 of this Regulation). A total of 87 firm orders has been placed for Super 80s, with 28 more on conditional order, for 10 airlines and two leasing companies. First to operate the Super 80 was to be Swissair, which took delivery of the first of 15 on order on 12 September and was inaugurating service on 5 October on the Zurich-London and other European routes.

The Swearingen **Metro III, introduced** at the NBAA Convention in late September, is a refined version of the Metro II commuter, the principal new features of which are a 10-ft (3-m) extension of wing span and the use of 950 shp Garrett AiResearch TPE 331-11 turboprops in place of the 840 shp engines used previously. Slow-running propellers reduce noise levels, and the uprated engines improve performance and allow the gross weight to be increased from 12,500 lb (5 670 kg) to 14,000 lb (6 350 kg). First orders for the Metro III have been placed by Crossair in Switzerland and Austrian Air Service.

Current Boeing thoughts on the **projected Boeing 737-300,** as expressed at Farnborough, are to insert two fuselage plugs to increase the length by 7 ft (2,14 m) to add two seat rows, and to fit new high by-pass ratio engines such as the CFM56-3 or RJ500 of 20,000 lb st (9 072 kgp) each. The basic wing would be retained, with some structural strengthening for the higher weights, revised leading and trailing edge flaps and wing-tip flutter booms fitted. A small dorsal extension of the fin would be required and the nosewheel leg would be lengthened by 7·2 in (18 cm) to give the new engines the necessary ground clearance.

CIVIL AFFAIRS

CHINA

An **air services agreement** between the **USA and China** will allow one designated airline of each nation to operate a service linking New York, San Francisco and Honolulu on the one hand with Beijing (Peking) and Shanghai on the other hand, with an intermediate technical stop (no traffic rights) in Tokyo. The service will be operated once a week by each airline in the first instance and it is expected that Pan American will be designated as the US carrier.

UNITED KINGDOM

A series of **route cuts** and frequency reductions is announced by **British Airways** following a serious short-fall in expected revenues in the current financial year (since April). A pre-tax loss of £17m was recorded in the first quarter and earnings were 11 per cent below target. About 50 routes are being cut, representing 8 per cent of the normal winter capacity and the status of these routes will be reviewed next spring. Among the cuts, effective from 1 November, is the Concorde service to Bahrain and Singapore. Reductions in North Atlantic frequencies have released one Boeing 747 for immediate sale and the Super VC10 fleet has been reduced to two, for final retirement next spring (see *Airscene*/September 1980). No cuts are planned in announced orders for new aircraft but delivery of the Boeing 757s may be stretched out.

Britannia Airways has won a two-year extension of its contract with Gibraltar Airways to operate a scheduled **service**, on the latter's behalf, **between London** (Gatwick) **and Gibraltar.** The company flies a Boeing 737 three times a week on this service, which it introduced for an initial two-year period in April 1979 in succession to the earlier service from Heathrow flown by British Airways Tridents. The Gibraltar service is Britannia's only scheduled service. The company is one of Britain's largest inclusive tour and charter operators, flying one third of all "package" holidaymakers from the UK, and has recently announced its 1979 financial results, in which a pre-tax profit of £11·8m was recorded on total turnover of £107m; the profit after tax was £3m, or less than £1 for every passenger carried. The recent introduction of a new fleet livery has been accompanied with the introduction of names for the all-Boeing 737, 25-aircraft fleet, using names of famous travellers, explorers and aviation pioneers. The US Export-Import Bank has recently announced that it plans to approve a private loan guarantee of $223·5m (£93m) for Britannia to buy up to five Boeing 767s; the company has to date announced an order for only two, for spring 1984 delivery, but during September **Britannia** announced that it had **selected** the General Electric **CF6-80A to power the 767s** and had placed a $28m (£11·7m) order for 14 of these engines.

Less than a year after its formation, by a merger between BIA and Air Anglia, **Air UK** has been forced to announce a series of **cutbacks** designed to combat the effects of a decline in business and sharply increased operating costs. Service on 12 routes is being suspended "until there are signs of an up-turn in the economy and people begin to fly in the numbers needed to sustain them" and frequency is being reduced on five other routes. The operating fleet for the winter period is being reduced by 10 aircraft, to comprise 14 Fokker F27s, eight Heralds and three Bandeirantes, plus the four One-Elevens committed to IT operations. The second Fokker

F28 in the fleet has already joined the first on lease to Air Alsace, for a minimum three-year period; one Bandeirante is on charter to Bristow and two others are available for lease and some or all of seven Heralds withdrawn from service may now be cannibalised. The fleet reductions will result in the Squires Gate, Blackpool, engineering base being closed, and this and other changes will lead to 400 redundancies. Meanwhile, Air UK has won a licence to operate scheduled services between Stansted and Paris, with effect from April 1981. A twice-daily service is planned but no starting date has been announced.

USA

Following its nomination to operate Anchorage-London and **Honolulu-London** services, **Western Airlines** announced that it will inaugurate **service** on the new route on 31 October, with two flights a week by DC-10. By operating by way of Anchorage, the service cuts some 500 mls (800 km) off the previous most direct London-Honolulu route via San Francisco; Western's fares offer reductions of some £84 on the excursion fares now available by way of SF and up to £634 off the one-way first-class fare, as well as reduced flying time. Substantial savings also are offered on the London-Anchorage leg.

CIVIL CONTRACTS AND SALES

Aérospatiale AS 332 Super Puma: Petroleum Helicopters has ordered six, including three of the first AS 332C production models and three AS 332L stretched versions.

Airbus A310: Kuwait Airways ordered five more A310s, adding to six previously ordered. Total A310 orders now 76 firm and 68 on option.

Bell 214B: Mitsui and Co, Bell's Japanese dealer and licensee, ordered six 214Bs for resale to commercial operators in Japan engaged in electrical power construction projects and for general use. Delivery will be completed early in 1981, when Bell will end 214B production unless substantial new orders are received.

Boeing 727: Alitalia ordered one — its 18th — for delivery in December 1982.

Boeing 737: Federal Express Corp sold two of its four Boeing 737-200QCs to Aramco Services for operation in Saudi Arabia in support of oil construction and extraction activities. □ Indian Airlines has taken delivery of one additional 737, not previously announced. □ LAN-Chile ordered two, for delivery November 1980 and November 1981. □ Ecuadorian domestic carrier TAME ordered one 737, delivered at the end of September. □ Air Pacific ordered one 737, for October 1981 delivery. □ Southwest Air Lines of Okinawa will take delivery of its fifth 737 in October 1982. □ New German charter operator Supair International ordered two for 1982 delivery. □ Air Malta leased one from Transavia for November operation, with two more to follow in April, all on two-year lease.

Boeing 757: American Airlines has confirmed that it holds unpaid options on a number of Boeing 757 delivery positions, but is not close to confirming an order. The options were made available by Boeing to American and several other customers for the 727-200 who might wish to convert existing orders for the latter type to orders for the 757.

British Aerospace HS 125: Manufacturers Hanover Corp of New York City bought two Srs 700s, bringing the sales total to 500, including 142 Srs 700s.

British Aerospace BAe 146: Second announced sale of BAe 146s is for two aircraft to be delivered in November 1982 and March 1983 to an unnamed US scheduled airline.

De Havilland DHC-7 Dash 7: The manufacturer states that negotiations with Prinair for the sale of two Dash 7s (announced earlier this year, with an option on two more) have been terminated because financial terms could not be agreed.

EMBRAER EMB-110 Bandeirante: Alexandria Aviation ordered two P1s, for operation by Euroair of Biggin Hill on charter duties. □ Loganair ordered one more P1. □ Air Littoral ordered one P2. □ Comair Inc of Cincinnati became 12th US commuter airline to buy the Bandeirante with order for one P1 and options on two more.

EMBRAER EMB-120 Brasilia: The option total rose to 86 with a letter of intent given by CSE Aviation for 10 and an option on three taken by Britt-Air.

Fokker F27: Angolan state oil company Sonangol has ordered one F27 Mk 500 for March 1981 delivery, for oil-support duties. It will be in combi configuration with forward cargo door. □ Air New Zealand ordered two more Mk 500s, for delivery in July and October 1981.

Fokker F28: Air Alsace has taken a three-year lease on the second Air UK F28, following earlier lease of the same company's first F28.

Handley Page Dart Herald: Air Algerie has leased four from British Air Ferries, for domestic operation. □ Air UK retired seven from service, will offer for sale or lease, or cannibalise.

Hawker Siddeley Argosy: IPEC in Australia sold one of its three Argosy 100s to World Vision, to be operated by Kris-Air out of Hong Kong on refugee relief flights into Kampuchea and other SE Asian countries.

Ilyushin Il-76M: Syrianair has taken delivery of one Il-76M freighter, becoming the third operator of the type after Aeroflot and Iraqi Airways.

Lockheed L-100-30 Hercules: PEMEX (Petroleos Mexicanos), the Mexican government-owned oil consortium, has acquired one -30, delivered in September. Mexico is the 48th country to acquire Hercules, total orders for which have now reached 1,609.

Lockheed L-1011 TriStar: Delta Air Lines has converted one option to a firm order for a L-1011-1, to bring its total fleet to 40 by June 1982. □ BWIA ordered two more L-1011-500s, for delivery in mid-1982.

McDonnell Douglas DC-8: ORBIS, an affiliate of Baylor College of Medicine in Houston, has acquired one DC-8 to be used, after modification by Tiger Air, as a flying hospital, to make training facilities and equipment available to eye doctors around the world.

McDonnell Douglas DC-10: Egyptair has finally dropped its options on four DC-10s, citing recent losses as the reason. The first two aircraft are close to completion and will be available for lease or sale by the manufacturer at the end of the year.

Saab-Fairchild 340: First customers, as announced at Farnborough but subject to final contracts being concluded, are Crossair for five with five on option, Swedair for five-seven, and Stillwell Aviation as Australian distributor, for 12.

Shorts 330: Orders have been announced for four more 330s by members of the Allegheny Commuter Group — two for Suburban Airlines and one each for Crown Airways and Pennsylvania Commuter Airlines. Orders now total 70.

Shorts 360: First customer for Shorts' new derivative of the Model 330 is Suburban Airlines of Reading, which ordered four, including the first production aircraft in late 1982 and three more in 1983. Suburban is a member of the Allegheny Commuter Group, operating in the states of New York, New Jersey and Pennsylvania.

Swearingen Metro III: First orders have been placed for the new Metro III by Crossair of Switzerland, for three, and Austrian Air Service, for two. Deliveries will begin in spring 1981.

MILITARY CONTRACTS

Aermacchi MB-339: An order has been placed on behalf of Argentina's *Comando de Aviacion Naval* for 10 MB-339 two-seat basic/advanced trainers for 1981 delivery. This is the second export order for the MB-339, the previous order (see *Military Contracts*/August) placed on behalf of the *Fuerza Aérea Peruana* now being known to call for 14 aircraft.

Agusta/Boeing Vertol CH-47C Chinook: The Egyptian government has placed a contract valued at £58·5m with Agusta for 15 CH-47C Chinook helicopters, the contract including spares support and technical back-up with the first delivery scheduled for late this year.

British Aerospace Bulldog: The £350,000 order for five Bulldog trainers for an unspecified customer announced earlier this year (see *Military Contracts*/September) is now known to have been a follow-on order from Jordan with deliveries scheduled for early in the New Year.

CASA C-212-200 Aviocar: Spain's *Ejército del Aire* has placed an order with CASA for four Series 200 C-212 Aviocars equipped for search-and-rescue duties.

Fokker F27 Maritime: One F27 Maritime sea surveillance aircraft has been ordered on behalf of the Angolan Popular Air Force and Anti-Aircraft Defence, FAPA/DAA, and was scheduled to be delivered to Luanda last month (October). See *Military Affairs*.

North American QF-86F Sabre: Sperry Flight Systems has been awarded a contract by the US Naval Weapons Center for the conversion of 10 F-86F fighters as QF-86F target drones. The 10 conversions will be completed by November 1981 and the value of the contract is approximately $350,000 (£145,830), with potential follow-on orders for the conversion of a further 90 F-86Fs.

Pilatus PC-7 Turbo Trainer: Latest announced order for the Turbo Trainer is for 10 aircraft for the *Servicio de Aviacion de la Armada de Chile*, eight of which had been delivered at the time of closing for press.

Westland Lynx: Orders have been placed for 14 Lynx AH Mk 1s for the British Army and 10 Lynx HAS Mk 2s for the Royal Navy, bringing total numbers of Lynx helicopters ordered for the UK armed forces to 114 for the Army and 80 for the Navy.

Westland/Aérospatiale Gazelle: Orders have been placed by the Ministry of Defence for a further 38 Gazelle helicopters for delivery to all three British military services from April 1982.

THE YEAR OF THE HAWK

THE BRITISH AEROSPACE (*née* Hawker Siddeley) Hawk has now been in service with the Royal Air Force for four years, and with some 140 aircraft delivered, over 60,000 hrs have been flown at the two principal training establishments — No 4 FTS, RAF Valley, and the Tactical Weapons Unit at RAF Brawdy. Since the arrival of the first two Hawk T Mk 1s at Valley on 4 November 1976, the story has been one of undramatic but solid achievement, with the Hawks smoothly taking over the advanced jet flying training and weapons training tasks from, respectively, the Gnat and the Hunter.

As the Hawk is more than 20 years later in concept than the aircraft it has replaced, substantial improvements were to be expected in the various parameters by which a modern training aeroplane is judged: parameters that are less concerned with the higher end of the performance spectrum than with the niceties of handling — which must balance vicelessness with enough "bite" to be representative of the most advanced combat aircraft — and with reliability and maintainability factors that have a critical bearing on training costs. In these respects, the message that has come back from the RAF is one of complete satisfaction. In the words of the CFI at Valley, Wg Cdr Doug McGregor, the Hawk "is allowing us to produce fast jet pilots better trained than ever before". Compared with previous types of training aircraft, the Hawk has been found to require, in round figures, only half the maintenance manhours per flying hour and the specified rates for maintenance and reliability performance have in fact been bettered.

With the solid foundations of RAF operating experience now laid, the Hawk has passed, during 1980, a number of new milestones that will help to expand both its utility and its marketability in future. These milestones include the first export deliveries; flight testing of a number of small but important aerodynamic refinements and of uprated engines; initial Sidewinder firing trials and the winning of a study contract to continue the effort to sell Hawk to the US Navy to meet its VTXTS requirement. Also noteworthy was the placing of the first repeat order for Hawks by the RAF, and the introduction of Hawks for the 1980 season by the Red Arrows. The year also saw the first live ejection from the Hawk, and although this was possibly a milestone the manufacturers and the RAF would have preferred not to have reached, the effectiveness of the Martin Baker zero-zero seats was demonstrated in extremely critical circumstances and without loss of life or serious injury.

Exports begin

At the time of writing, British Aerospace has delivered the first Hawks to two of the three export customers who, to date, have ordered a total of 70 Hawks. First to go, in mid-year, were a trio of Hawk Mk 52s to what British Aerospace continues to identify (in accordance with the terms of its customer's contract) as "an African air force". It is widely, if unofficially, known, that the country in question is Kenya. Prior to delivery, six Kenya Air Force pilots attended a conversion course at the Flight Test Centre at Dunsfold, including a week at ground school and four-and-a-half weeks flying, during which time each pilot went solo on the Hawk. For the first delivery, two of the Hawks were flown by BAe test pilots, and the third by a KAF pilot; the formation staged through Sigonella (Sicily), Cairo and Khartoum to Nairobi, where the Hawks were welcomed by Kenya's Permanent Secretary for Defence and Chief of Staff.

Kenya has ordered 12 Hawk Mk 52s. In common with the other aircraft for export, they have five weapon stations (one on the fuselage and two on each wing) whereas the RAF aircraft have only three stations. They also have a customer-specified avionics fit and — an exclusive feature so far — a braking parachute.

The first Hawk Mk 53 for the Indonesian Armed Forces — Air Force was handed over on 10 July at Dunsfold to the Indonesian Ambassador, HE Saleh Basarah, this being the first of eight on order, for service with the No 1 Training Wing of the TNI-AU at Jakarta. Four of the eight were leaving the UK in September and after flying out by way of Malta, Cairo, Bahrain, Karachi, Bombay, Calcutta and Bangkok, were expected to fly-past at the Indonesian Armed Forces Day celebrations on 5 October.

Delivery of the Finnish Hawk Mk 51s has also begun. *Ilmavoimat* was the first export customer to order the Hawk, in December 1977: 50 are to be acquired, of which four are being delivered this year (the first in September) as complete aircraft from the UK and the remainder will be assembled in the period 1981-85, by Valmet OY at Halli; of these, the first was despatched by land and sea in July and should fly early next year. Most of the airframe components will be supplied by British Aerospace but Valmet is building the tailplanes, fins and rudders and is also assembling the Rolls-Royce Adour 851 turbofan engines. The Hawks differ from the RAF standard in having Saab gunsights and in their avionics fit; they are to be used primarily to replace Fouga Magisters at the Central Flying School *(Ilmasotakoulu)* at Kauhava.

Engine and airframe development

As mentioned above, the standard engine for the export Hawks (to date) is the Adour 851, itself the export version of the Adour 151 that powers the RAF Hawk T Mk 1. This non-afterburning turbofan has a basic thrust of 5,200 lb st (2 360 kgp) at sea level. As part of its planned development of uprated Adours for the Hawk, Jaguar and other applications, Rolls-Royce Turboméca Ltd — the joint Anglo-French company responsible for design, development and production of the engine — has offered the Adour 861 with a basic thrust of 5,700 lb st (2 585 kgp) at sea level. This engine, if produced, will be a version of the RT.172-56 featuring a revised LP compressor and HP and LP turbines that offer improved surge margins as well as higher thrust. Installationally interchangeable with the Adour 851, the Mk 861 not only provides some 8-10 per cent more thrust for take-off, depending on ambient temperature, but 15-20 per cent more at speeds up to M = 0·8 at sea level, which is particularly valuable in respect of performance with heavy and high-drag external loads. Conversion of earlier engines to the new standard will be possible.

Since May 1979, the company demonstrator Hawk Mk 50 (registered G-HAWK and bearing the military serial number ZA101 to allow it to make live weapons trials) has been flying with a specially-modified Adour that achieves the Mk 861 thrusts although it does not have the new internal features of the later engine.

G-HAWK has been used during 1980, in conjunction with a programme of wind-tunnel testing, to obtain higher lift coefficients from the basic wing, without changing the aerofoil section. This work, which is supported by an MoD development contract, was undertaken initially to reduce the minimum approach speed (VPA MIN) in order to demonstrate compliance with the US Navy VTX specification (115 kts/213 km/h). Although the Hawk was originally designed to have a double-slotted flap across the entire trailing edge between the ailerons, early flight testing led to the outboard flap vane being cut back in order to obtain required characteristics for the RAF. For the G-HAWK trials, the original flap configuration was restored, and the size and location of the "breaker strips" (small metal wedges) on the leading edge, that serve to control the way in which airflow breaks away at the approach to the stall, was changed.

These modifications served to increase the maximum lift coefficient on the approach by about one-third and to reduce the stalling speed by about 12 kts (22 km/h). The size and location of the wing fences has subsequently been varied on G-HAWK in order to obtain improved characteristics in the full range of external store configuration handling. As a result, the clean Hawk with half fuel now has a stalling speed of less than 90 kts (167 km/h).

The combination of uprated engine and improved lift coefficients goes hand-in-hand with the application of heavy external loads to the Hawk, which has now flown with 6,500 lb (2 950 kg) underwing. Each of the five stores stations (including the fuselage centreline) is stressed to carry 1,120 lb (508 kg) up to a factor of 8 *g*; when heavier loads are carried, there is a lower *g* limit imposed. Twin store carriers on the wing pylons make it possible to carry up to eight bombs — eg, four 1,000 lb (454 kg) and four 500 lb (227 kg); in another configuration, four 1,000-lb (454-kg) bombs were carried outboard and two 100 Imp gal (455 l) drop tanks inboard. To improve the landing performance in extreme conditions, an enlarged diameter braking parachute is also available, measuring 8 ft 6 in (2,59 m) compared with 7 ft (2,13 m) and this has been flown on G-HAWK.

Sidewinders for the RAF

The five-station Hawk has been demonstrated carrying a pair of AIM-9 Sidewinder air-to-air missiles on the outer wing positions, as one of more than 50 possible weapon configurations. However, the missiles have not been fired from this position, as none of the customers to date has called for this particular armament. The decision to adapt a proportion of the RAF's Hawks to carry Sidewinders as a means of supplementing the UK air defence force therefore called for a full clearance programme to be conducted. Also, as the RAF aircraft are operated in three-station configuration (with the necessary structure for the outer wing stations included, but without electrical cables or "plumbing") it became necessary to clear the Sidewinder (AIM-9G as well as AIM-9L) installation on the inboard wing pylons. The first phase of this work has now been completed and a number of firings has been made, without any problems being encountered.

(Heading photo, opposite) The first Hawk 53 of eight ordered by the Indonesian Armed Forces — Air Force. Deliveries began in September. (Below) Air Vice-Marshal Peter Latham, AOC 11 Group, RAF, arrives at RAF Chivenor in a Hawk bearing the insignia of No 63 Squadron to establish at this base the newly-formed No 2 Tactical Weapons Unit.

ZA101
ZA101
G-HAW

Including the 18 additional aircraft ordered earlier this year, the RAF has a total of 193 Hawk T Mk 1s on order and it is expected that kits will be procured to convert about half of this total to carry Sidewinders. Details of deployment have not been revealed by the MoD but it seems safe to assume that the Hawks used by the Tactical Weapons Units will be those modified and that in the event of hostilities they would be flown by TWU instructors and other qualified pilots for the defence of key installations. The Sidewinders will not, of course, be carried while the aircraft are engaged in their normal training duties, which as far as the TWU is concerned embrace low-level tactical flying (pilot and navigator), air combat, air weaponry and forward air control.

The expansion of the RAF air defence force, with the creation of a third Lightning squadron and the forthcoming introduction of the Tornado F Mk 2s, has increased the training requirement on the Tactical Weapons Unit. As a result, the Unit was divided into two with effect from 1 August this year, with No 1 TWU remaining at Brawdy and No 2 TWU taking up residence at RAF Chivenor. Two of the three squadrons at Brawdy (Nos 63 and 234) will be fully established at Chivenor by early 1981 with some 40 Hawks.

(Opposite page) The company demonstrator Hawk 50 has been much used for the development of weapons load carrying and for the aerodynamic refinements described in this account; it is shown here carrying four 1,000-lb (454-kg) and four 500-lb (227-kg) bombs on twin carriers on the four wing hardpoints, plus the centre-line gun pod. (Top) One of the Hawk T Mk 1s of the RAF's TWU at RAF Brawdy on a rocket firing sortie; it carries the markings of No 234 Squadron. (Below) An Indonesian Hawk 53; the first of these export Hawks flew on 6 June, being the 140th of the type to fly.

Few readers will be unaware that Hawks, as well as being in service with the TWUs and 4FTS, are now flown by the Red Arrows, who are completing their first full season on the type after 16 years on the Gnat. In the hands of what is undoubtedly the world's premier formation jet aerobatic team, the Hawk has already given excellent service and has been described by Team Leader Sqn Ldr Brian Hoskins as "the best aircraft I have flown in the aerobatic rôle. It is extremely manoeuvrable, stable in formation and rolls beautifully along its own axis". The Red Arrows aircraft are standard T Mk 1s with some small modifications, the most significant of which concerns the centreline pod, used to carry the dyes to be injected into the jet exhaust, by way of pipes over the jet pipe, for the production of red, white or blue "smoke". The other most obvious difference is the colourful finish for the 10 aircraft (including one reserve).

It was during one of the early displays of the 1980 season, on 17 May, that the Red Arrows team suffered one of its rare accidents and the first Hawk was lost. While performing over the sea for the benefit of spectators on the front at Brighton, one of the Hawks struck the top of the mast of a yacht that is reported to have moved into the display area after the display had started (the report of the official inquiry into the accident has not yet been published). The impact severed the wing tip and left one aileron uncontrollable; although the pilot was able to pull the nose up, he had no lateral control and the aircraft rolled inverted. Ejection was initiated in this position at little more than 100 ft (31 m) of altitude and the parachute deployed as the pilot was about to enter the water; he suffered only minor injury. A replacement aircraft has now been modified to Red Arrows standard.

The US Navy requirement

A major opportunity now exists for the British Aerospace Hawk to meet the US Navy requirement for a new basic/advanced jet trainer to enter service in 1986/87. Needless to say, competition was intense and in the first phase of the VTXTS programme seven prime contractors made nine separate aircraft proposals to the Navy; six of these proposals — including the Hawk — have been selected for the second phase, a six-month study period leading to selection of one or more finalists. The request for proposals had been issued in December 1979, with a return date of March 1980, and as the VTXTS cipher indicates, the requirement is not just for a naval training aeroplane (VTX) but for a complete training system (TS).

At the present time, US Naval student pilots begin their training with 70 hrs on the Beech T-34C. They are then divided into three streams, one to specialise on helicopters, one to proceed to multi-engine training (on the Beech T-44A) and one — the largest group — to become strike or fast jet pilots. For this last-mentioned group, training is given at present on the Rockwell T-2C Buckeye followed by the McDonnell Douglas TA-4J Skyhawk. The US Navy inventory comprises some 314 TA-4Js, of which about half are assigned to the pilot training programme, and some 205 T-2Cs, all but about 20 as pilot trainers. Allowing for increased training efficiency and high utilisation from a new type, it is assumed that the Navy will buy some 300 of the winning VTXTS; this number could well increase if the same type is selected to fill certain other specialised tasks, and there is the attractive possibility that it will provide the basis for meeting the USAF's requirement, in a later timescale, for a T-38A Talon replacement.

British Aerospace is one of six companies awarded contracts during August to continue studies of the Hawk as a trainer meeting the requirements of the US Navy's VTXTS.

In seeking a trainer to meet VTXTS, the Navy indicated that it wished to consider all options from updated versions of existing types through off-the-shelf buys to development of new aircraft. In keeping with this objective, the submission made in March covered three available European trainers, five original designs by American manufacturers and a derivative of the T-2C. The European designs were the Hawk (submitted by British Aerospace in partnership with the Douglas Aircraft Co division of McDonnell Douglas), the Alpha Jet (submitted by Dassault-Breguet in partnership with Lockheed) and the Aermacchi MB-339. Original designs were submitted by General Dynamics teamed with American Airlines (in respect of the training system aspect), Grumman teamed with Beech, Northrop teamed with Vought, Rockwell's Columbus Division and McDonnell Douglas (with British Aerospace in partnership on the indigenous Douglas design from Long Beach as well as the Hawk). Rockwell also submitted the T-2X improved Buckeye. The MB-339 and the original designs by Rockwell and GD were eliminated in August, leaving six to proceed into the next study phase.

Of the nine original proposals, the Hawk is unique in being single-engined. All the new designs, as well as the Alpha Jet and T-2X, favoured the use of twin engines, with the Pratt & Whitney JT15D the choice in most cases. The single-versus-twin engine argument need not be reiterated here; suffice to say that the Navy did not indicate a preference in its VTXTS specification (the TA-4J is single-engined) and that the 60,000 hrs flown by the RAF on the Hawk without a single engine failure that endangered the aircraft powerfully reinforce the British Aerospace philosophy.

To meet VTXTS, the Hawk needs only minimum modification. As already described, compliance with the VTX carrier approach speed requirement of 115 kt (213 km/h) has already been demonstrated, with a margin of some 7 kts (13 km/h), and in other performance parameters the Hawk meets or exceeds the requirements. An arrester hook would be added, the nosewheel and leg would require modification for catapult launching, and all undercarriage units would be modified for carrier landings, to absorb vertical velocities of about 23 ft/sec (7,0 m/sec) compared with 15 ft/sec (4,6 m/sec) at present. Naval instrumentation and avionics would be installed, including head-up and CRT displays.

The submission of the Hawk for VTXTS has been a valuable exercise for British Aerospace and has increased the company's confidence that the aircraft is as good as any basic/advanced trainer either available or planned. Export sales, it has to be said, have not matched some of the early projections, but this is not because the Hawk is losing out to the competition but because economic and other factors have imposed restraints on air forces that need to buy new trainers but cannot afford to do so while also re-equipping front-line units. In this context it is worth recalling that single-seat strike variants of the Hawk have been projected and could be developed relatively easily if a positive market requirement was identified. Typically, a single-seat Hawk could have a built-in armament of two 30-mm cannon (thus freeing the fuselage centreline for carriage of bombs or fuel tanks; additional internal fuel and a new front fuselage with a single cockpit.

Such developments are still some way in the future, however. For the present, the emphasis remains firmly upon the two-seat Hawk which, as this year's milestones show, is beginning to reap the benefits inherent in its design. □

ACE QUALIFYING AT AKROTIRI

IT IS 0700 HOURS and the temperature, already well into the eighties, will climb into the high nineties before much more of the morning has passed. Despite the early hour, the flight line presents a scene of considerable activity as a half-dozen fighters, their drab grey-and-green North European camouflage unseemly in the bright eastern Mediterranean sunlight, are readied for the day's tasks. This comparative tranquillity of scene is suddenly disrupted by the pulsating roar of paired Avons as a banner-towing Canberra gathers speed down the runway, takes-off and climbs away in a southerly direction towards the firing range to initiate the morning's activities, soon to be followed by the first of the fighters, which, between them, will fly more than a score of sorties by 1300 hours.

The venue is RAF Akrotiri, on the Akamas peninsula, in Britain's Western Sovereign Base Area of the 3,000 square mile (7 770 km^2) island of Cyprus. The fighters are Lightnings or Phantoms of one or another of the nine air defence squadrons on detachment from the UK or RAF Germany for its annual Armament Practice Camp (APC). The temperature may vary 10 or 15 degrees and the squadron emblems sported by the fighters may change, but in all other essential respects this scene will be repeated every working day for 10 months of the year as each squadron, in turn, spends a month honing its air-air gunnery proficiency to achieve NATO ACE (Allied Command Europe) qualification.

Air-air gunnery is essentially a visual skill, which, despite the advent of the AAM as the primary fighter weapon, is as vital a faculty as ever was in short-range close-in manoeuvring combat, and proficiency can only be achieved and maintained by practice using live ammunition. The RAF is therefore singularly fortunate in having facilities available at Akrotiri, where, not only does good weather permit an intensive target firing programme for most of the year, but an adjacent clear sea area allows live firing without hazarding shipping.

RAF Akrotiri, which for the past two years has provided the locale for the APCs, is a comparatively young station, which, named after an adjacent village, in fact celebrated its quarter-century last month (October). Originally established as a Near East Air Force strike and reconnaissance base, and ideally situated in that all approaches and departures can be made over the sea, RAF Akrotiri became the service's largest multi-rôle station, with three operational wings, a fully-developed air defence system, supporting engineering and administrative units and some 4,000 service personnel, with a total RAF community of the order of 11,000. The station was heavily involved in the 1974 emergency, when nearly 25,000 British civilians and tourists of all nationalities were flown out of the island, but as a result of the Defence Review of the following year, all the fixed-wing squadrons and their supporting elements were redeployed, leaving Akrotiri with one squadron of Whirlwind helicopters.

The period of relative inactivity that was to follow was to prove short-lived, however, for the decision to centre the APCs on Akrotiri has contributed in major extent to restoring this as one of the RAF's busiest bases. In its heyday as an NEAF base, RAF Akrotiri operated 24 hours a day, seven days a week, 365 days of the year. Today, the base is restricted to an eight-hour operating window during the week's five working days, although, in practice, it does open up outside that window for special high priority flights. But despite the fact that it is normally open only 160 hours monthly, during those hours it handles an average of 80 aircraft with more than 4,500 passengers and some 330 *tonnes* of freight, apart from its intensive APC activities and those of the Whirlwind Mk 10 helicopters of No 84 Squadron's "A" Flight which is home-based at Akrotiri. Providing the air head for the United Nations Forces in Cyprus, Akrotiri handles numerous foreign military and civil charter flights on their behalf; advantage is taken of the generally excellent winter flying conditions by training detachments from UK operational conversion units, and earlier this year, the *Red Arrows* and *Falcons* teams spent some time at Akrotiri working-up prior to their display season. In fact, in any one month, as many as 20 different types of aircraft can stage through the base, demanding considerable versatility on the part of Akrotiri's ground personnel.

Commanded by Gp Capt A Parkes BSc, RAF Akrotiri is spread over much of the 50 square miles (130 km^2) or so of the Western Sovereign Base Area established, together with the similarly-sized Dhekelia SBA to the east, when Cyprus became a fully independent and self-governing Republic. Apart from the two SBAs, there are a number of retained sites and training areas, which, Cypriot territory, are used on a privilege basis. Most of Akrotiri's aircraft are transient, the only permanent flying unit being the previously-mentioned No 84 Sqdn, the four Whirlwinds of this squadron's "A" Flight maintaining a 15-minute SAR standby with two helicopters whenever an APC is operating and one on 90-minute standby around the clock. The other permanent operational unit is No 34 Sqdn RAF Regiment which operates as a field squadron for the defence of the airfield. RAF Akrotiri parents No 280 signals

(Above and top right) A Lightning F Mk 6 of No 5 Sqdn photographed (by Peter Scott/Rolls-Royce) over the Cypriot countryside after completing a firing sortie during the Squadron's recent Armament Practice Camp at Akrotiri. (Right) A Lightning T Mk 5 of No 5 Sqdn that accompanied the Binbrook Wing's F Mk 6s for the APCs of the component squadrons, and (below) Binbrook Wing Lightning F Mk 6s — a No 11 Sqdn aircraft in the foreground and two more of the squadron's aircraft plus one of No 5 Sqdn, but all flown by pilots of the latter squadron during AIR INTERNATIONAL's visit — awaiting their turn to fly academic sorties.

unit which mans the radar on Mount Olympus, this being the 6,400-ft (1 950-m) tip of Troodos, the highest point on the island, and also provides a parenting service for the Air Headquarters at Episkopi, other RAF units in Cyprus and also for Army units on the peninsula.

Commenting that Akrotiri is probably the most popular of RAF bases, Gp Capt Parkes told AIR INTERNATIONAL that, at times, it is one of the busiest. "On the broader scene," he continued, "we have recently been involved in two major events, RAF Akrotiri having been the mounting and reception base for the Iran evacuation and also the staging post for Operation *Agila* which involved the positioning and subsequent withdrawal of troops, police and civilian administrators in Zimbabwe to supervise the ceasefire and elections. Such events highlight the importance of RAF Akrotiri. Night flying in the UK in summertime when darkness lasts for only a few hours inevitably attracts many complaints from the local populace, so this summer we alleviated the problem, at least, insofar as the Lyneham area was concerned, by exporting the noise generated by the Hercules OCU to Akrotiri. Indeed, apart from the Armament Practice Camps, RAF Akrotiri is nowadays a very busy, active station.

"A unique point about Akrotiri is the fact that we have troops from five different Corps working here. Consequently, if we add the total service personnel, their dependants and

A Binbrook Wing Lightning F Mk 6 taxying in at Akrotiri after completing a shoot (left), and No 5 Squadron's T Mk 5, the task of which at Akrotiri was primarily dual checks but also flew range safety missions, coming in to land.

locally-employed civilians, the station population in a working day swells to something of the order of 4,000 people. Of course, the population tends to be more transient than permanently based, a fact presenting some problems, but as one of the few remaining permanent RAF overseas bases, Akrotiri offers good value for the taxpayers' money."

Armament Practice Camp

At the time of AIR INTERNATIONAL's recent visit to RAF Akrotiri, No 5 Squadron, one of the component units of the Binbrook Wing, had just succeeded its sister squadron, No 11, which had flown the nine Lightning F Mk 6s and one T Mk 5 — in fact a mix of the two squadrons' aircraft — out from Binbrook several weeks earlier over the somewhat more than 2,000 miles (3 220 km), allowing for the doglegs necessary in transit, with the aid of six refuellings by Victor tankers for the single-seaters and 10 refuellings for the two-seater.

No 5 Sqdn, commanded by Wg Cdr Terry Adcock, was, in fact, the first operational unit to equip with the Mk 6 version of the Lightning, having been re-formed at Binbrook on 8 October 1965, taking delivery of this more efficacious and, insofar as the RAF was concerned, definitive version of the fighter from December and operating it continuously since that time. Fifteen years is a *long* time in the life of a first-line fighter and the Lightning was evolving more than a decade before it reached No 5 Sqdn, but the pilots' enthusiasm and affection for this now quite venerable warplane was impressive. If perhaps lacking in sophistication by today's standards, the Lightning F Mk 6, we were assured by every pilot, remains an excellent air-air fighter and its passing from the RAF's first line in the mid 'eighties and with it the era of the single-seat interceptor in the RAF — at least, until the ECA or something of its ilk hopefully appears in the 'nineties — will be deeply regretted.

Flt Lt Tim Neville, whose task was that of IWI (Interceptor Weapons Instructor), while admitting that the Lightning presents its pilot with a fairly high workload, stressed that it is "a pilot's aeroplane and, being highly responsive, thoroughly satisfying to fly. It is an excellent turning aircraft and, consequently, effective in traditional air combat manoeuvres, but it is in the vertical plane that it excels — if we use the vertical and our opponent elects to turn and engage he is dead!" Wg Cdr Terry Adcock added that the Lightning may appear inelegant to some but its lines exude sturdiness and, in fact, in his view it is probably one of the most robust fighters ever built. "Nowadays," he commented, "it is necessary to conserve the *g* life of the airframe and we therefore rarely pull more than 3·5 *g*, but nevertheless, all our pilots enjoy the Lightning and gain much satisfaction from it. It has, of course, something of a reputation as a "gas-guzzler", burning about 20 Imp gal (90 l) a minute of its 1,200 Imp gal (5 455 l) at tactical speeds and this consumption increasing tenfold in a climb with full reheat selected, and I, for one, would like to see the overwing ferry tanks reintroduced. But then, the Lightning was conceived as a UK-based pure interceptor to meet a high-altitude high-performance threat. One thing is for sure; in a "hot" situation we would all be happy to be flying the Lightning and none of us is looking forward to the day when we join the ranks of the WEWOLS*."

Each Armament Practice Camp (APC) lasts a total of five weeks of which four are devoted to intensive air-air gunnery practice, the remainder comprising the first few days of general shake-down and the last few days occupied in recovery. The participating unit flies between 0700 and 1300 hours each working day. "A" Flight occupying the shooting position for the first two weeks, with "B" Flight running the operational side, and the position being reversed for the second two weeks. Each of the squadron's 16 pilots flies a total of nine live firing sorties, after a ciné camera work-up, against banner targets towed over a 2,000 square mile (5 180 km²) range to the south of the Island by Canberra B Mk 2s of No 100 Sqdn.

Two Canberras normally fly either two or three two-hour sorties each day, 30 minutes of each sortie being occupied by transiting and finding a clear area. The pilot of the Canberra target tug also serves as range safety officer, and he normally flies at about 180 knots (333 km/h), a speed limitation imposed by the breaking strain on the 300-yard (274-m) cable towing the 24 ft by 6 ft (7,3 m by 1,8 m) banner. After about one-and-a-half hours the banner begins to tear and every effort is therefore made to minimise banner time to reduce wear. Sqn Ldr Alex Ford, CO of the No 100 Sqdn detachment, admitted

**WEWOL: We were on Lightnings!*

that the limitations of the banners currently used are inhibiting, but said that higher-speed banners are expected to be available for next year's APCs. "The APCs," he said, "keep us pretty busy throughout most of the year. We fly the Canberras out from RAF Marham in two legs with a night stop at Naples primarily to suit the Akrotiri air window, each leg taking about 2 hr 45 min. Our pilots each do more than one deployment to Akrotiri annually, some doing as many as four, although the intensive flying here imposes something of a strain as does the heat in the cockpit during the summer months, our B Mk 2s having strictly limited-duration cold air units!"

Sqn Ldr Ford explained that, with one fighter on the banner, the Canberra follows a simple race-track pattern, but with two aircraft on the banner a figure-of-eight is adopted. As a safety factor, the Canberra assumes 30 deg of bank once the fighter has positioned itself, and the latter must not come within 300 yards (274 m) and a 12 deg angle-off or else its pilot is scratched. There is thus comparatively little risk of a bullet strike on the towplane, although there is, of course, always the possibility of a runaway gun.

Each fighter pilot flies a number of ciné camera sorties until he has demonstrated that he can consistently achieve the required safety parameters of range and angle-off. The IWI then clears the pilot "live" (ie, cleared to fire live 30-mm shells against the banner). He then flies six academic shoots in order to gain ACE qualified. The ACE qualification is a percentage score based on hits made against rounds fired and the standard is laid down by SHAPE (Supreme Headquarters Allied Powers Europe), this standard being common to all air forces in NATO. There are many factors affecting the number of hits on the banner, some of these being outside the pilot's control, such as gun movement, velocity jump and bullet spread. These factors mean that less than 50 per cent of the rounds fired have a chance of hitting the banner and clearly rendering the pilot's task a difficult one.

After completing his six academic firing sorties — always assuming that the pilot has not ACE qualified in fewer shoots — he then flies what is known as a limited academic sortie in which he is permitted a maximum of five passes, commencing with the usual ciné dry run, after which he is cleared to fly the operational shoot. For this only 20 rounds are provided each gun and the sortie consists of one ciné and two live passes. In this instance, the fighter meets the towplane head-on, the Canberra then going into orbit and both firing passes having to be completed within 540 deg of turn. The banners are dropped over the airfield by the Canberras after each sortie and the scores achieved are carefully recorded, the hits obtained by each individual pilot being identified by staining produced by the coloured dyes applied to the bullets. The score is always based on a full shoot even if the pilot has failed to expend all his ammunition. As the Seed Trophy is awarded each year to the squadron displaying the most prowess in air-air gunnery during its APC, there is considerable competitive spirit.

In addition to their air-air gunnery sorties, the squadrons mount theatre familiarity flights and practice intercept (PI) missions, and one of the many valuable benefits of the annual APCs is the experience that they provide the squadrons in long-distance tanker refuelling sorties during the one-hop transits to and from Akrotiri. Normally each squadron flies its own aircraft to Akrotiri for its APC, but this year, for reasons of airspace management convenience, the two Binbrook-based Lightning F Mk 6 squadrons operated as a wing, No 11 Sqdn flying the aircraft to Cyprus and No 5 Sqdn flying them back. Both transits were accomplished with the aid of six Victor tankers operating in relays of three, four single-seat Lightnings accompanying each of two tankers and the remaining single-seater and the two-seater accompanying the third. The return "hop" from Akrotiri to Binbrook was made via Sicily, during which leg each F Mk 6 received three refuellings — with the T Mk 5 receiving five — at which point the relay of tankers changed, and then via Palermo, Nice and Boulogne, with a similar number of refuellings, the average transit speed being M = 0·75.

There can be little doubt as to the considerable value of the annual Armament Practice Camps in maintaining the RAF's air-air gunnery capability at peak efficiency, nor of the cost effectiveness of the use of RAF Akrotiri as their venue, but perhaps most impressive insofar as this writer was concerned was the fact that the APC being conducted during AIR INTERNATIONAL's visit and involving the Binbrook Wing provided ample evidence that, despite its age, the Lightning remains, as it ever was, a superb fighting vehicle that, somewhat short-legged and demanding in pilot workload though it may be, will give a very good account of itself against any potential adversary if called upon to do so for some years to come. □

(Below left) Wg Cdr Terry Adcock and the IWI examine the banner after a firing sortie for the individual scores, and (below right) Lightnings being re-armed at Akrotiri between firing sorties.

VERSATILITY UNLIMITED -the Boeing KC-135 Story

by Al Lloyd

FEW military aircraft production programmes undertaken since the end of World War II can compare with the Boeing KC-135 in size, speed of execution, cost-effectiveness and operational success. In a period of $8\frac{1}{2}$ years, Boeing built no fewer than 820 of these four-jet tankers (including 88 closely-related different-rôle variants); built at an average rate of seven a month throughout that period, these aircraft were delivered to the USAF at the lowest cost per pound of airframe weight of any military aircraft then in production in the USA. Between June 1958 and July 1959, the production rate peaked at 15 aircraft a month and when Boeing completed delivery of the last of the KC-135s at the beginning of 1965, it was able to announce that the production value of the 820 aircraft built was about $1·66 billion, or some $2m per copy.

The USAF certainly has had value for its money. Since the end of 1965, when the last of the piston-plus-jet KC-97 Stratofreighters was withdrawn from service with Strategic Air Command, the KC-135As have been the sole air refuelling tankers in general service with USAF*. The force is managed by SAC but has responsibilities far beyond the operational support of SAC's own strategic bombers (B-52s and FB-111s); KC-135As also serve the 4,400 fighters of Tactical Air Command, the transports (C-5s and C-141Bs) of Military Airlift Command, and aircraft of the US Navy and Marine Corps, and NATO air forces in Europe. Included in the force are a number of units manned by the Air National Guard, these units sharing with the regular squadrons in maintaining the Tanker Task Forces (TTF) that are deployed at various bases around the world to support specific operational missions on a regular or transient basis.

Of the total production quantity of 820 of the Boeing jet tanker family, no fewer than 732 were built to a common standard (subject to the usual progressive introduction of production-line modifications) as KC-135As. Such consistency was itself unusual for so long a production run of a multi-engined aircraft, but it has been more than offset by the extent to which subsequent modification programmes have produced distinctive variants. Apart from the KC-135A, six other designated variants came off the production line, but the -135 family has subsequently grown to a current total of 37 variants that are identifiable by prefix and suffix letter designations, with a number of sub-variations within certain series. Furthermore, because the KC-135A retains such an important rôle in the USAF inventory, it is the subject of ongoing modifications and development programmes which will produce further variants in years to come; the most important of these is the programme to fit CFM-56 turbofans in about half of the 640 KC-135As (and KC-135Qs) that remain in the active inventory in 1980, as described later in this account.

Boeing's tanker boom

The Boeing company's first association with air-to-air refuelling dates back to 1929, when a Boeing Model 40-B was used as a tanker and a Model 95 mailplane served as the receiver for trials in which a trailing hose extended from the

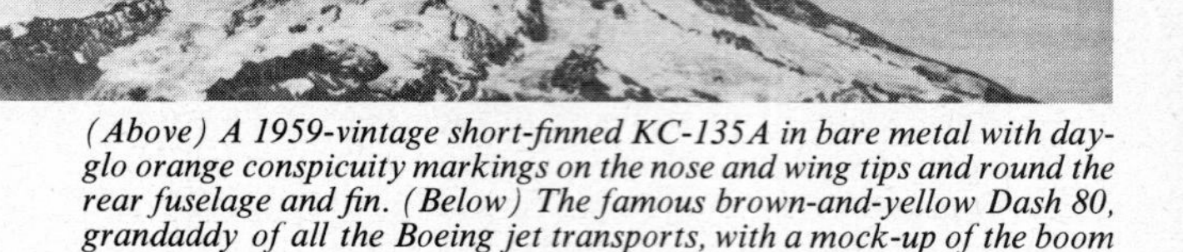

(Above) A 1959-vintage short-finned KC-135A in bare metal with day-glo orange conspicuity markings on the nose and wing tips and round the rear fuselage and fin. (Below) The famous brown-and-yellow Dash 80, grandaddy of all the Boeing jet transports, with a mock-up of the boom operator's position under the rear fuselage.

former was grasped by a crew member in the latter so that the nozzle could be inserted into the fuel tank filler pipe. These experiments had no practical outcome, however, and the more relevant origins of the KC-135A are to be found in the request from USAF's Air Materiel Command in November 1947 that Boeing should investigate air-to-air refuelling methods and installation.

The studies then begun led eventually to the development of Boeing's "flying-boom" system, first used on B-29 Superfortresses converted for use as tankers. In the interim period, the USAF had put into service a number of B-29s modified to use the British-developed hose-type refuelling system, in which a hose trailed by one aircraft was "hooked" in flight by a weighted line trailed by the receiver. To improve on this system, Flight Refuelling Ltd developed the "probe-and-drogue" system which has become the standard for aircraft of the RAF and has been widely used by the US Navy up to the present time, and was also used for some time by the aircraft of USAF's Tactical Air Command. Comparative evaluation of the FR and Boeing systems led the USAF to opt for the latter however, and to follow the 116 boom-equipped KB-29Ps, the

**The HC-130Ps of the Aerospace Rescue & Recovery Service are equipped only to refuel helicopters, using the probe-and-drogue method.*

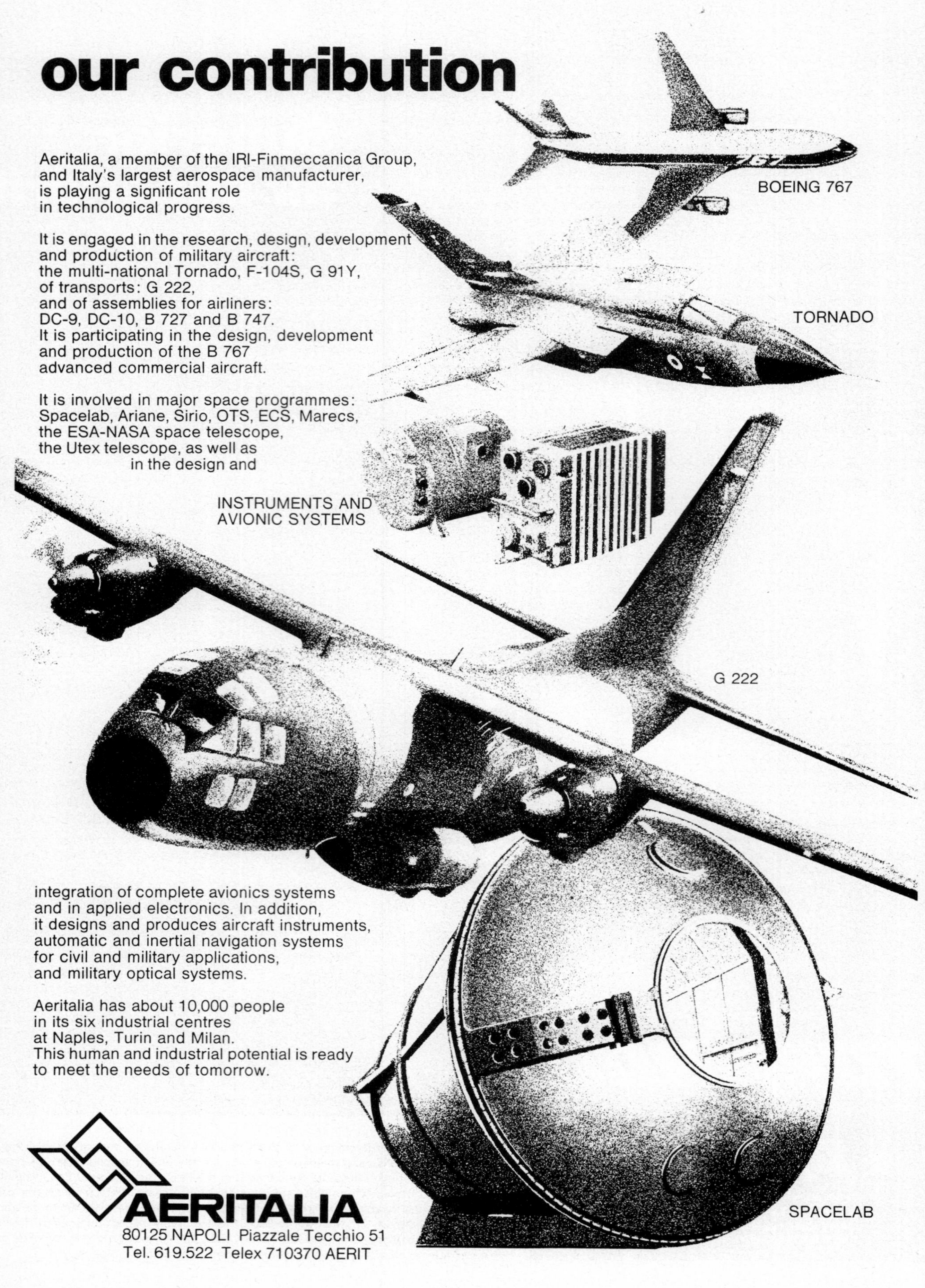
our contribution
Aeritalia, a member of the IRI-Finmeccanica Group,
and Italy's largest aerospace manufacturer,
is playing a significant role
in technological progress.
It is engaged in the research, design, development
and production of military aircraft:
the multi-national Tornado, F-104S, G 91Y,
of transports: G 222,
and of assemblies for airliners:
DC-9, DC-10, B 727 and B 747.
It is participating in the design, development
and production of the B 767
advanced commercial aircraft.
It is involved in major space programmes:
Spacelab, Ariane, Sirio, OTS, ECS, Marecs,
the ESA-NASA space telescope,
the Utex telescope, as well as
in the design and
integration of complete avionics systems
and in applied electronics. In addition,
it designs and produces aircraft instruments,
automatic and inertial navigation systems
for civil and military applications,
and military optical systems.
Aeritalia has about 10,000 people
in its six industrial centres
at Naples, Turin and Milan.
This human and industrial potential is ready
to meet the needs of tomorrow.
BOEING 767
TORNADO
INSTRUMENTS AND
AVIONIC SYSTEMS
G 222
SPACELAB
AERITALIA
80125 NAPOLI Piazzale Tecchio 51
Tel. 619.522 Telex 710370 AERIT

USAF acquired a total of 814 KC-97 Stratofreighters. The first of the KC-97 tankers entered service in 1951, and as the importance of these aircraft become more completely appreciated in support of SAC operations world-wide, it soon became obvious that a new tanker was going to be needed to match the performance of the front-line jet bombers and fighters. Adding jet pods to some of the KC-97s and to 136 Superfortresses that were also modified to KB-50 tankers was no more than an interim solution.

Formal expression of the future requirement came towards the end of 1953, when the USAF indicated a need for 800 jet tankers to support the SAC fleet of B-52s and B-58s. Boeing, Convair, Douglas, Fairchild, Lockheed and Martin were invited to respond to the RFP in May 1954, but Boeing had already pre-empted the field by completing the design and launching construction of a prototype jet tanker-transport well ahead of the USAF's formal action. Clearly, the Seattle company's close contact with the USAF in developing and producing the KB-29, KB-50 and KC-97 tankers had given it a close insight into SAC's needs. A series of design studies, conducted under the same Model 367 designation that applied to the KC-97, had led eventually to the 367-80 configuration and the famous "Dash 80" prototype. Built as a private venture at a cost of $16m, the Boeing 367-80 was intended not only to meet USAF's tanker needs but also to serve as a prototype for a commercial jet transport, the potential for which had already been so clearly demonstrated by the de Havilland Comet. Rolled out on 14 May 1954, the Dash 80 took to the air on 15 July and only three weeks later — before the refuelling capabilities had even been demonstrated, let alone proved — the USAF announced that it would purchase 29 of the Boeing aircraft; the official contracts were completed on 5 October 1954, at which time the KC-135A designation was adopted. Less than two years would elapse before the first production KC-135A Stratotanker (serial 55-3118) would roll-out at the company's Renton factory on the shores of Lake Washington, to fly on 31 August 1956.

Although both the KC-135 family (Boeing Model 717) and the commmercial 707/720 family have a common origin in the Dash 80 prototype, it is wrong to regard the tanker as a military variant of the commercial transport; the 707 was developed from the prototype in a parallel programme — making its first flight some 18 months after the first KC-135A, on 20 December 1957 — and the two types share little but their overall configuration and the basic wing box. The 707 differs, notably, in having a slightly larger fuselage diameter with a double lobe cross section, which meant that Boeing could not build the two types in common fuselage jigs. This difference was emphasised when the USAF later bought some commercial 707s off-the-shelf for VIP (and Presidential) use and designated them as C-137s rather than C-135s.

To achieve a better strength-to-weight ratio, the -135 structures were designed to a "safe-life" philosophy, whereas the 707/720 structures are "fail-safe", as required to meet FAA regulations. In material terms, the tanker utilises a 7178 aluminium alloy while the commercial model is largely fabricated in the 2024 alloy.

Among the differences between the KC-135A and the early production commercial 707s (the 707-100 series with JT3C-6 turbojet engines*) was the lack of air intakes at the root of the engine pylon where it joined the engine cowling. On the 707s, these intakes served the turbo-compressors (driven by engine bleed air) that pressurised the cabin; on the KC-135A, engine bleed air was utilised directly for pressurisation and the intakes were therefore not needed. The absence of windows in the fuselage was another obvious difference, as well as the flying boom and boom operator's station in the underside of the rear fuselage.

Less obvious but equally significant were the differences in dimensions. The span of the -135 and the 707-100 is 130 ft 4 in (39,72 m) while the 707-300/400 spans 145 ft 4 in (44,30 m). Fuselage lengths (excluding the tailplane, which projects

**Boeing Sales Department identifies the original short-bodied commercial jet transport as the -120 with turbojets and -120B with JT3D turbofans; the long-bodied versions with Pratt & Whitney engines were -320 and -320B, while the -420 had RR Conway turbofans. Engineering Department designations for these same aircraft were -100, -100B, -300, -300B and -400 respectively.*

(Above) A KC-135A taking off from Hickham AFB, Hawaii, showing the adaptation to fit a refuelling drogue to the refuelling boom.

(Above right) In overall grey finish, this KC-135A is in the markings of the 160th ARG, Ohio Air National Guard, Rickenbacker AFB, Ohio. (Below) A tall-finned KC-135A, 1963-vintage, in Corogard finish with the SAC "Milky Way" band and crest round the centre fuselage.

(Above) An early short-finned KC-135A showing the yellow stripe, to assist receiver pilot alignment, stretching along the underside of the fuselage from the director lights to the boom operator's pod. (Below) A close-up of the director lights and the alignment stripe under the front fuselage.

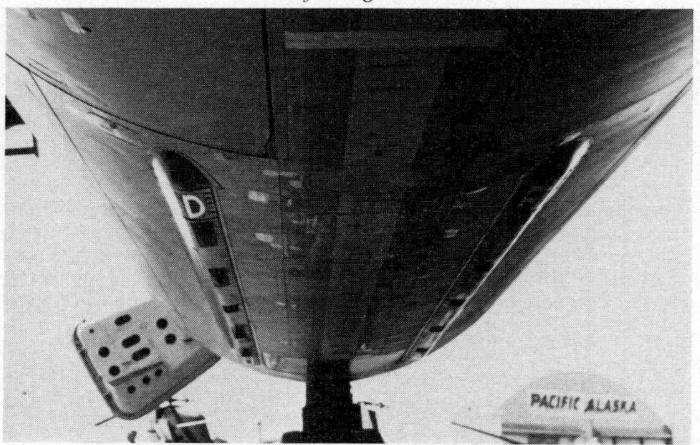

beyond the end of the fuselage) are 128 ft 10 in (39,27 m) for the -135, 138 ft 10 in (42,32 m) for the 707-100 and 145 ft 6 in (44,35 m) for the 707-300/400. The difference in fuselage diameter is a mere 4 in (10 cm), the smaller -135 being an exact 12 ft (3,66 m) at its maximum — 5 in (12,7 cm) larger than the Dash-80. The wing planforms of the -135 and 707-100 are similar with 338-in (8,59-m) root chords and 112-in (2,84-m) tip chords, single-sweep leading edges, and single-sweep trailing edges with the exception of the wing trailing edge root fillets. The 707-300 has a 347·1-in (8,82-m) root chord and a tip chord of 112 in (2,84 m), single sweep leading edge and double-swept trailing edge — the break in the trailing edge being inboard of the inboard nacelle.

Delivery of the KC-135As to the USAF began on 30 April 1957 and SAC put its new Stratotankers into service on 18 June that year, with the 93rd Air Refuelling Squadron at Castle AFB, Calif. By that date, a total of 215 KC-135As was on order; 130 more were ordered in April 1958 and further increments were placed annually to bring the total order book to the following:

732 KC-135A Stratotankers (SAC)
17 KC-135B Stratotankers (SAC)
10 RC-135B (SAC)
15 C-135A Stratolifters (MATS)
30 C-135B Stratolifters (MATS)
4 RC-135A (MATS)
12 C-135F Stratotankers (French Air Force)

The last of the KC-135As was delivered to USAF at Seattle on 12 January 1965 and was assigned to the 380th Aerial Refuelling Squadron at Plattsburgh AFB, NY. The following month, the production line closed with delivery of the last RC-135B, although the final aircraft to be handed over were the four RC-135As, retained until January 1966 for installation of special equipment.

The KC-135A in detail

The KC-135A was designed, in the first instance, to meet the air refuelling/transport needs of Strategic Air Command, with tanks in the lower fuselage and in the wings to carry both air refuelling and aircraft fuel. The main cabin area is available for cargo/troop transport purposes — 80 to 160 troops or up to 83,000 lb (37 650 kg) in payload — and a main cargo door measuring 72 in by 114 in (1,83 × 2,90 m) is located in the port side forward of the wing. A normal crew of four comprises a pilot, co-pilot, navigator and boom operator. Four J57-P-59W or J57-P-43WB turbojet engines equipped with water injection power the aircraft (although the first production batch lacked water injection and operated at a lower gross weight). Thrust reversers are not fitted. A single HF probe antenna is mounted at the top of the vertical fin, extending forwards.

Primary flight control is provided through manual, non-hydraulically boosted systems for the ailerons, spoilers, elevators and rudder. Aerodynamic balance panels and balance tabs assist the flight crew in operating the primary flight controls. Secondary flight controls consist of Fowler flaps on the wing trailing edge, with split fillet flaps, speed brakes and an adjustable horizontal stabiliser.

The inboard ailerons are used throughout all flight speed régimes, whereas the outboard ailerons are used for low speed flight only. When the flaps are retracted, a lockout mechanism in the aileron control system disengages the outboard ailerons, which are moved by direct cable control — not a control tab. A force-relief tab reduces control wheel forces. Normal flap operation is through the hydraulic system. A manual or electric back-up flap operating system is provided, the former on all KC-135A and KC-135A-derived models, the RC-135B and its derivatives, and the electric back-up system on other models of the -135.

Early KC-135As were delivered with a manually-operated rudder. These aeroplanes had a height of 38 ft 5 in (11,71 m) and were identifiable by the fin cap being mounted directly above the rudder; they were retrofitted, and later production -135s were delivered, with a powered rudder. This change, which resulted in a 40-in (1,02-m) fin extension, significantly improved aircraft stability and control at lower speeds, and is identifiable by the fin extension above the rudder with the fin cap installed on top. The overall height of the aircraft was increased to 41 ft 8 in (12,7 m).

The KC-135A's fuel system is made up of 22 tanks, 12 in the wing and nine in the fuselage, with a total capacity of 31,200 US gal (118 105 l). Each wet wing has two main tanks and an outboard reserve tank, while the centre wing tank is made up of six bladder cells. Four bladder cells comprise the forward body tank, which is located in the lower fuselage just ahead of the front wing spar; the aft body tank is behind the main landing gear wheel wells and consists of five bladder cells. There is one tank above the cabin floor, in the aft end of the fuselage. In normal operation, direct tank-to-engine fuel feed uses the main wing tanks; however, any engine can be fed through a cross-feed system from any tank. The body fuel tanks normally provide fuel for refuelling; all onboard fuel may be used by the engines; and all but 1,000 US gal (3 785 l) may be used for refuelling. Usable fuel quantities are approximately 5,800 US gal/37,700 lb (21 955 l/17 100 kg) from the forward tank and 6,378 US gal/41,457 lb (24 143 l/18 805 kg) from the aft tank. The fuel nozzle pressure is regulated to approximately 45-50 psi (3,2-3,5 kg/cm²) and the fuel flow rate is approximately 5,850 lb/min (2 654 kg/min) in the basic aircraft, although there are plans to increase this through a future modification programme as noted later.

The flying boom refuelling system in the KC-135A is similar in concept to that pioneered by Boeing on the KB-29, KB-50 and KC-97; it comprises a rigid boom that can be lowered and telescopically-extended from the underside of the tanker and then "flown" by a boom operator until the tip makes contact with a refuelling receptacle in the receiver aircraft that is formating behind and below the tanker. Fuel is pumped from the fuselage tanks through check valves, directly into the air refuelling manifold, to the air refuelling line valve, through the air refuelling pressure regulator and fuel flow transmitter, and then out through the boom. Some aircraft are equipped with a reverse-flow refuelling system so that a receiver aircraft can assist the tanker should the latter itself be short of fuel.

All -135 aircraft have a boom operator's station pod bulging beneath the rear fuselage; in some of the special-duty variants, the station is not used. On tanker aircraft, this station has positions for a boom operator, an instructor and a student operator. Three pallets ("ironing boards") with safety harnesses, communications equipment and oxygen equipment are available for each crew member. One set of boom operating controls is installed in the compartment, consisting of an instrument panel, boom hoist lever and boom telescope lever for use by the operator's left hand and a ruddevator control stick for use by the operator's right hand. A periscope may be used to increase the operator's field of vision.

Two types of air refuelling booms may be used on the KC-135A — high speed and standard speed — using interchangeable booms. Use of the high speed boom with matched ruddevators places no restrictions over and above the normal clean aeroplane placard speeds, whereas aircraft equipped with standard speed booms are restricted to 330 knots (611 km/h) calibrated air speed or Mach 0·85, whichever is less. High speed booms have extended latch fairings to reduce drag and are placarded HIGH SPEED BOOM on the latch fairing. The ruddevators that control the "flight" of the boom must be matched to the boom, and high-speed ruddevators are placarded HIGH SPEED BOOM on both the upper and lower surfaces; they are also identifiable by the full-span one-piece trim tab, as compared to the half-span three-piece tab on the standard-speed ruddevators. The refuelling boom consists of two concentric tubular sections capable of extending over a range of 28 to 47 ft (8,5-14,3 m). Nominal travel of the boom is in a cone within 30 deg left and right azimuth and an elevation of +12·5 deg and −50 deg.

Two rows of lights are mounted on the bottom of the fuselage between the nose and main wheel wells, and serve to provide instructions to the receiver aircraft pilot for corrections in forward, aft, up and down movement. A fluorescent yellow stripe 8 in (20 cm) wide and 65 ft (19,8 m) long, between the director lights and the boom pod, serves as an additional visual aid to the receiver aircraft pilot for maintaining longitudinal alignment behind the tanker aircraft.

Many of the KC-135 variants are also equipped with an air refuelling receiver (ARR) system. An ARR slipway and receptacle, covered by slipway doors when not in use, are installed on the top centreline of the fuselage slightly aft of the pilots' station, the receptacle being manifolded into the aeroplane's air refuelling system.

From its inception, the KC-135A was designed to operate in the boom/receptacle mode. By 1960, it had become apparent that the Stratotanker could also be used to support TAC fighters then fitted for probe-and-drogue refuelling, and a hose and drogue were designed to be attached to the KC-135A boom. For this purpose, a collapsible drogue and coupling were fitted to 42 in (1,07 m) of hose and 48 in (1,22 m) of rigid tubing, which in turn was attached to an adapter, thus forming the entire hose and drogue assembly, almost 13 ft (3,96 m) long and approximately 121 lb (54,9 kg) in weight. Aeroplane performance with the drogue installed is degraded by an increase in fuel consumption of approximately 1 lb (0,45 kg) of fuel per hour.

Tanker variants

Fifty-six KC-135As have been modified into KC-135Qs for use by SAC. These aircraft have specialised avionics for rendezvous with the SR-71As and a fuel system capable of

(Above) One of the four RC-135As operated by the 1370th Photo Mapping Wing, showing the camera ports in the fairing that extends from the nose wheel bay to the wing leading edge. These aircraft did not have refuelling equipment installed but have now been converted to KC-135Ds for use as tankers.

(Above right) One of the three short-finned "boomless tanker" KC-135As supplied to MATS prior to delivery of their own C-135As. This aircraft eventually became an RC-135D. (Below) A turbofan-engined, tall-finned C-135B in MATS markings with day-glo orange conspicuity markings.

Boeing KC-135 Cutaway Drawing Key

1 Detachable radome
2 Weather radar scanner
3 Radar array
4 Forward pressure bulkhead
5 Forward fuselage structure
6 Pilot's side console
7 Rudder pedal assembly
8 Central console
9 Instrument panel
10 Windscreen defrost/rain removal
11 Windscreen panels
12 Co-pilot's seat
13 Eyebrow windows
14 Ditching external handholds
15 Overhead console
16 Crew instructor's seat
17 Pilot's seat
18 Crew instructor's console
19 Escape spoiler
20 Entry and escape hatch
21 Nosewheel hydraulic actuator
22 Entry/escape tunnel
23 Crew entry door
24 Ladder
25 Twin nosewheels
26 Fuselage frame
27 AC power shield
28 Electrical equipment racks
29 Supernumerary crew station
30 Navigator's stool (celestial observation)
31 Navigator's seat
32 Navigator's instrument panel
33 Overhead storage rack
34 Celestial observation windows
35 Window defrost
36 Electronics rack
37 Flight deck door
38 Circuit breaker panel
39 Toilet
40 Battery
41 Cargo door frame
42 Forward fuselage underfloor fuel tanks (four tanks): capacity 5,800 US gal (21 955 l)
43 Floor support beam
44 Cargo deck: 5,000 lb and 10,000 lb (2 268-4 540 kg) tie-down fittings
45 Cargo door hinges
46 Main cabin air supply risers (starboard)
47 Door upper frame
48 Cabin air duct
49 Fuselage frame
50 Engine inlet nose cowl
51 No 3 engine nacelle
52 Oil filler access
53 Surge bleed outlet
54 Nacelle pylon
55 Pylon strut access
56 Wing leading-edge
57 No 3 main fuel tank: capacity 2,275 US gal (8 612 l)
58 Fuel filler access
59 Starboard inner pylon light (fuselage illumination)
60 Pylon strut attachment
61 Wing front spar
62 No 4 main tank: capacity 2,062 US gal (7 805 l)
63 Leading-edge wing flap
64 No 4 engine nacelle
65 No 4 engine fuel air starter tank
66 Oil cooler chin intake scoop
67 Engine inlet nose cowl
68 Nacelle pylon
69 Dry bays
70 No 4 reserve tank capacity 434 US gal (1 643 l)
71 Wing outer leading-edge
72 Starboard navigation light
73 Starboard wingtip
74 Starboard outer aileron
75 Aileron lockout mechanism
76 Flap torque tube linkage
77 Aileron balance tab
78 Actuating links
79 Bus quadrant
80 Starboard outer spoilers
81 Starboard outer flap
82 Flap track
83 Snubber
84 Trim actuator
85 Aileron control tab
86 Starboard inner aileron
87 Hinge fairing
88 Actuator linkage
89 Starboard inner double-slotted flap
90 Flap track
91 Starboard inner spoilers
92 Wing rear spar
93 Dorsal identification light
94 Cabin air duct
95 Starboard midships escape hatch
96 Centre-facing troop seating (80)
97 Troop seat support rails
98 Centre-section wing tank: capacity 7,306 US gal (3 314 l)
99 Port midships escape hatch
100 Wing centre-section top skin
101 Keel beam antenna bay
102 Bulkhead section
103 Fuselage light (wing illumination)
104 Wingroot/fuselage fillet plate
105 Front spar pick-up point
106 Port landing lights
107 Air-conditioning pack (port) intake scoop
108 Leading-edge structure
109 Wing front spar
110 Inboard wing stringers
111 No 2 main tank inner wall: capacity 2,275 US gal (8 612 l)
112 Stiffeners
113 Engine bleed air manifold
114 Water injection manifold
115 Four-wheel main landing-gear
116 Torsion links
117 Landing-gear trunnion
118 Wing rear spar
119 Angled ribs
120 Pylon/wing fairing
121 Pylon strut access
122 No 2 engine pylon
123 Nacelle
124 Engine inlet nose cowl
125 Oil cooler chin intake scoop
126 Pratt & Whitney J57-P-59W turbojet
127 Engine drive alternators
128 Oil tank
129 Tail pipe
130 Exhaust outlet cone
131 Nacelle support aft fairing
132 Leading-edge wing flap
133 Wing ribs
134 Lower surface inner stringers
135 No 1 main tank: capacity 2,062 US gal (7 805 l)
136 Front spar
137 Fuel filler access
138 Strengtheners
139 Dry bays
140 Pylon fairing
141 Strut access
142 Hinged cowling panels
143 Engine inlet nose cowl
144 Nacelle frame
145 Pylon structure
146 Pylon support strut
147 Fixed aft panels
148 Nacelle support aft fairing
149 Wing outer leading-edge
150 No 1 reserve tank: capacity 434 US gal (1 643 l)
151 Rear spar

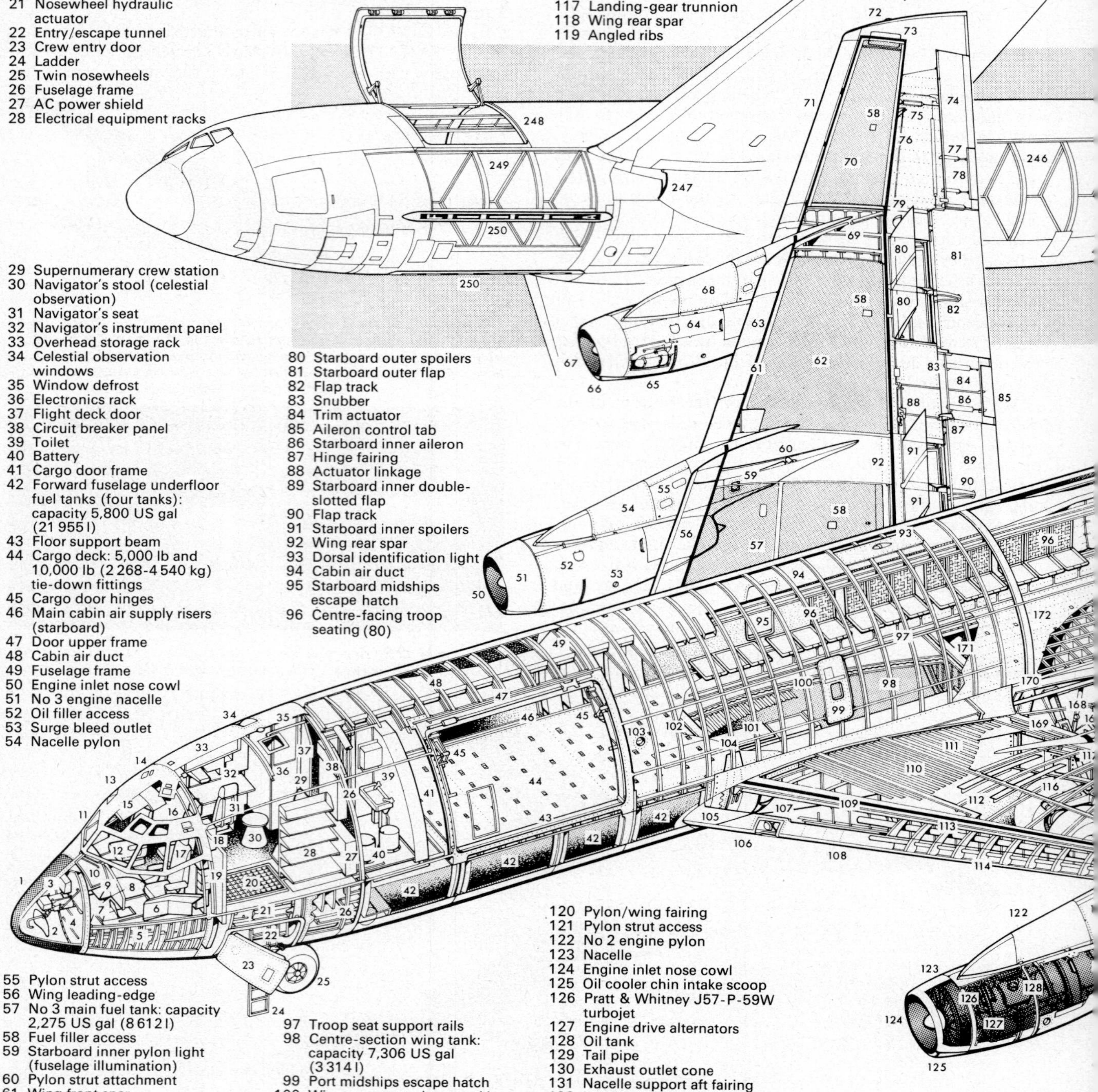

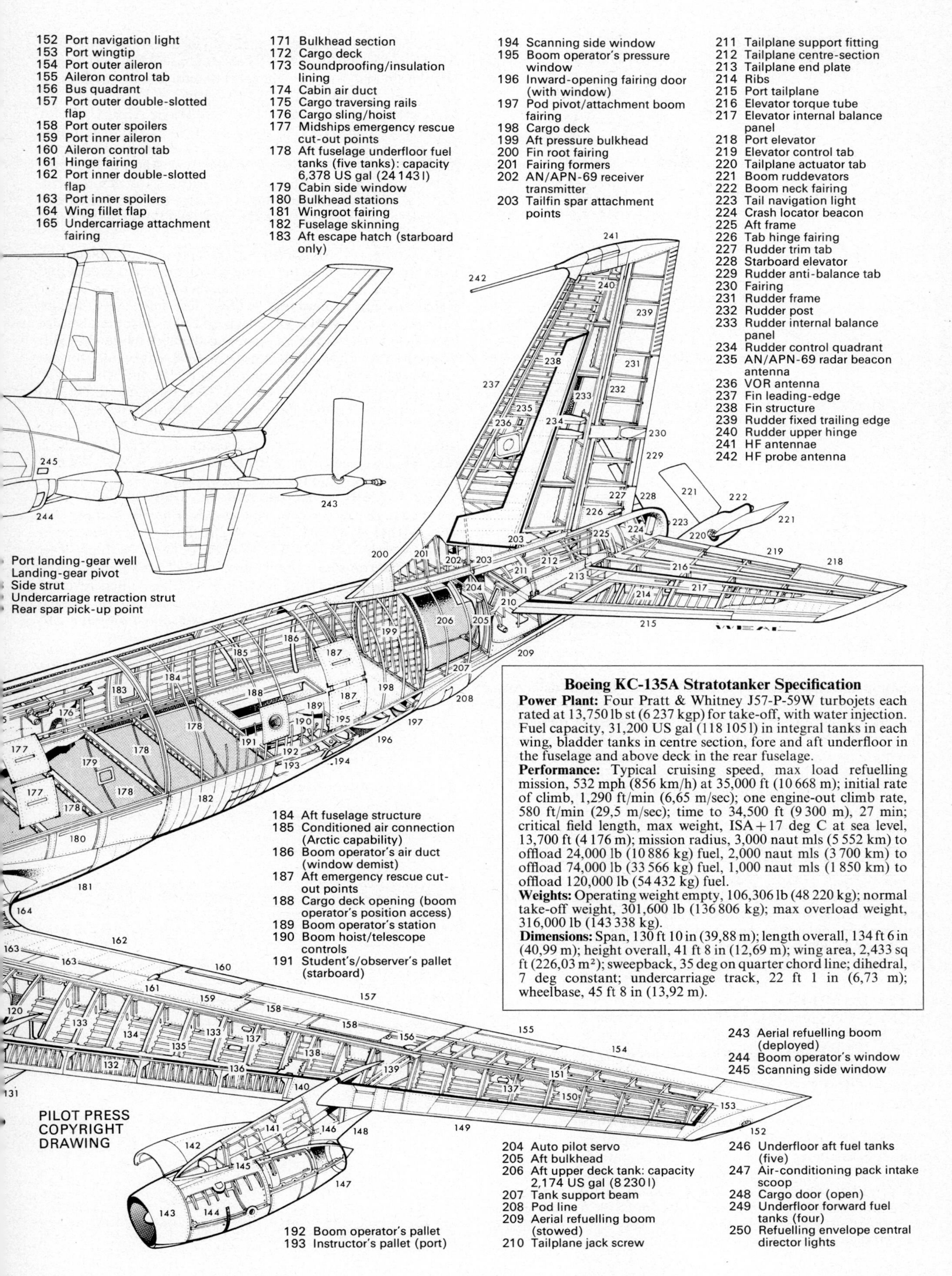

Boeing KC-135A Stratotanker Specification

Power Plant: Four Pratt & Whitney J57-P-59W turbojets each rated at 13,750 lb st (6 237 kgp) for take-off, with water injection. Fuel capacity, 31,200 US gal (118 105 l) in integral tanks in each wing, bladder tanks in centre section, fore and aft underfloor in the fuselage and above deck in the rear fuselage.

Performance: Typical cruising speed, max load refuelling mission, 532 mph (856 km/h) at 35,000 ft (10 668 m); initial rate of climb, 1,290 ft/min (6,65 m/sec); one engine-out climb rate, 580 ft/min (29,5 m/sec); time to 34,500 ft (9 300 m), 27 min; critical field length, max weight, ISA+17 deg C at sea level, 13,700 ft (4 176 m); mission radius, 3,000 naut mls (5 552 km) to offload 24,000 lb (10 886 kg) fuel, 2,000 naut mls (3 700 km) to offload 74,000 lb (33 566 kg) fuel, 1,000 naut mls (1 850 km) to offload 120,000 lb (54 432 kg) fuel.

Weights: Operating weight empty, 106,306 lb (48 220 kg); normal take-off weight, 301,600 lb (136 806 kg); max overload weight, 316,000 lb (143 338 kg).

Dimensions: Span, 130 ft 10 in (39,88 m); length overall, 134 ft 6 in (40,99 m); height overall, 41 ft 8 in (12,69 m); wing area, 2,433 sq ft (226,03 m²); sweepback, 35 deg on quarter chord line; dihedral, 7 deg constant; undercarriage track, 22 ft 1 in (6,73 m); wheelbase, 45 ft 8 in (13,92 m).

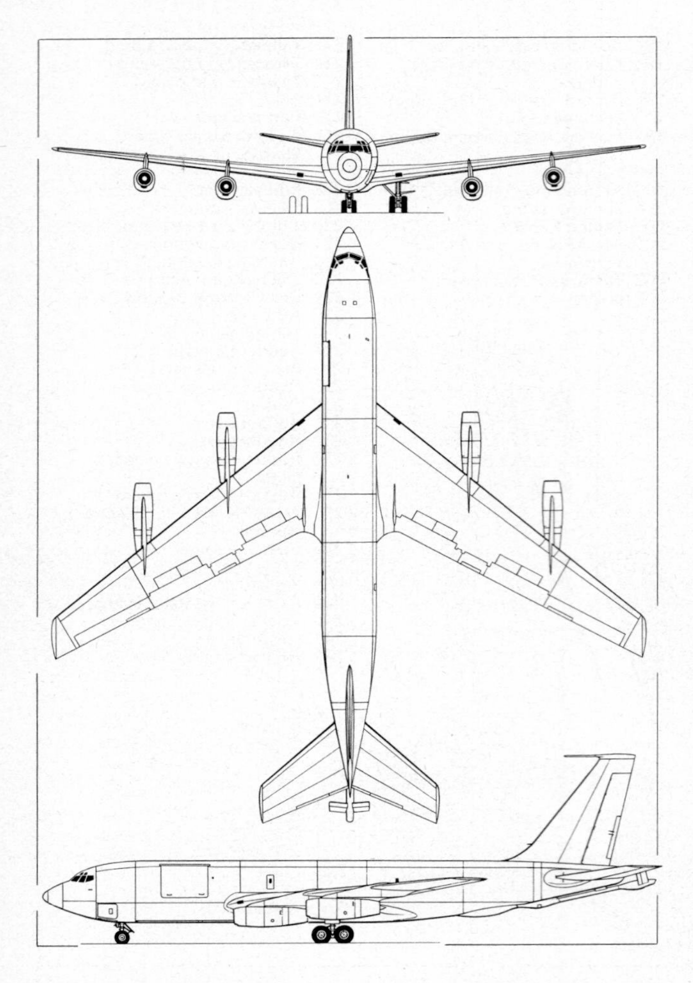

handling the specialised JP-7 fuel for the "Blackbirds". An extra TACAN antenna has been installed externally. Some aircraft are "partials" operated by various SAC refuelling units in conjunction with their regular KC-135As; the only refuelling unit equipped exclusively with the KC-135Q is the 100th Air Refueling Wing located at Beale AFB, California.

Twelve C-135Fs were procured by the French Air Force (*Armée de l'Air*) in 1964, to provide a global capability for the Strategic Air Force Mirage IV bombers. Using the probe and drogue refuelling system, these aircraft were originally assigned to three units — 91st, 93rd and 94th *Escadres de Bombardement*. On 1 July 1976, the 93rd *Escadre* was disbanded and all of the C-135Fs were reassigned to the 91st and 94th *Escadres*. Procured from Boeing through US government channels, the C-135Fs carry USAF serial numbers 63-8470 thru' 63-8474 and 63-12735 thru' 63-12740; one of the 12 is no longer in service.

C-135s for MATS

Fifteen C-135A and 30 C-135B Stratolifters were procured by the USAF for use by MATS as long range logistics transports starting in 1961, as a stop-gap measure pending delivery of the Lockheed C-141 StarLifters. The C-135As had the same engines as the KC-135A whereas the C-135Bs introduced Pratt & Whitney TF33-P-5 turbofans, with thrust reversers. Able to carry up to 126 troops or 89,000 lb (40 370 kg) of cargo, the C-135s had the refuelling boom and associated gear deleted, although retaining the boom operator's station; they were built with the taller fin and powered rudder of later KC-135As, but pending delivery of the first C-135As, Boeing modified three short-tailed KC-135As to an interim C-135A configuration and the first of these flew on 19 May 1961. The first C-135B flew on 15 February 1962.

The fleet of C-135Bs was equally divided between the 1611th Air Transport Wing of MATS at McGuire AFB, NJ, for use by the 18th and 41st Air Transport Squadrons, on the Eastern Transport Air Force (EASTAF) routes to Europe and the Middle East; and the 1501st ATW at Travis AFB, Calif, for the 44th ATS on WESTAF routes to the Far East. In addition, McGuire received 13 C-135As and Travis received one; one other C-135A was assigned to the Los Alamos Scientific Laboratories at Los Alamos, New Mexico (as described in Part Two of this account) but in practice the Travis and Los Alamos aircraft (serials 60-376 and 60-377) were operated alternately.

Beginning in 1965, the Boeing transports were replaced by Lockheed C-141As as the mainstay of the airlift Command (MAC), and the C135A/B fleet was then dispersed in the Air Force Systems Command (AFSC) test fleet, SAC reconnaissance fleet, MAC VIP fleet and Air Weather Service fleet. Two C-135As were assigned to the 89th Military Airlift Wing (MAW) of MAC at Andrews AFB, Maryland, for use as administrative support aircraft in 1975, one with a VIP interior installed. In 1977, two C-135As (60-376 and 60-378) were assigned to the 55th Strategic Reconnaissance Wing (SRW) of SAC at Offutt AFB, Nebraska, for administrative support duties. The other remaining C-135A (60-377) is currently assigned to the 4950th Test Wing, AFSC, Wright-Patterson AFB, Ohio for R&D missions.

Five C-135Bs, converted into VC-135Bs in 1975, were assigned to the 89th MAW, Andrews AFB (serial numbers 62-4125, -4126, -4127, -4129 and -4130). They were operated in consort with the VC-137s (see Part Two) as high level government transports but by August 1977, only two (62-4126 and -4127) remained with the 89th MAW. The others reverted to C-135Bs; one (64-4125) was assigned to the 435th Tactical

continued on page 236

(Left) Three-view drawing of the Boeing KC-135A in its standard form, with definitive tall fin. (Below, top to bottom) Side views of the early short-finned KC-135A; the short-finned C-135A; the RC-135A; the tall-finned C-135B with turbofan engines and the KC-135RE with CFM-56 turbofans.

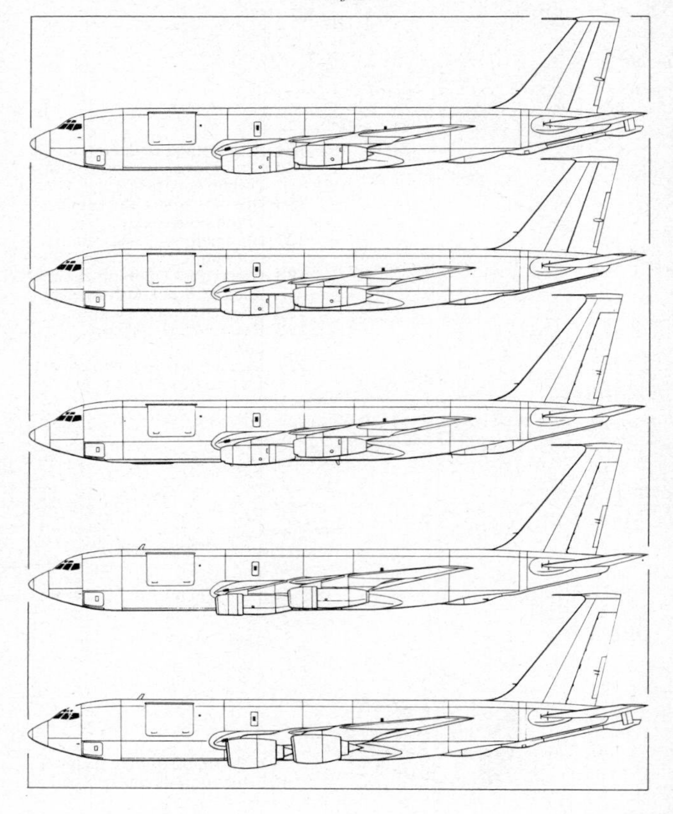

Mitsubishi Ki.46 . . .

. . . the Aesthetic Asiatic

UNQUESTIONABLY among the most graceful warplanes of any nation deployed during World War II and included with the most efficacious, Mitsubishi's ballerina-like Type 100 Command Reconnaissance Aircraft, or Ki.46, was unique in being the only land-based warplane designed from the outset specifically for the strategic reconnaissance rôle to see operational usage by any combatant. From its first clandestine overflights of Malaya before Japanese forces launched hostilities until its surveillance of the Superfortress bases in the Marianas as these hostilities drew to their close, this supremely elegant creation of the immense Mitsubishi conglomerate served Imperial Japan as a far-seeing eye. Ranging across the vast expanses of the Pacific, the Ki.46 was a painful thorn in the side of the Allies over Malaya, the Dutch East Indies, New Guinea, Burma, China and the Philippines; indeed, wherever Japanese forces were engaged this warplane was to be encountered and, to the perturbation of the Allies, such was its performance that until virtually the final phases of the war it fulfilled its task with impunity.

The fact that Japan alone among the future combatants of World War II had considered the strategic reconnaissance mission of sufficient importance to warrant development of an aircraft solely for its fulfilment was not, in itself, surprising in view of the geographical scale of operations envisaged by Japanese militarists in the late 'thirties, when concluding that a Pacific conflict was no longer merely desirable but inevitable. What *was* surprising was the extent of the advance in the state of the art demanded when, in 1937, the Imperial Army's Air Headquarters, or *Koku Hombu*, formulated its specification for a dedicated strategic reconnaissance aircraft. Issued to Mitsubishi on 12 December 1937, this called for an aircraft possessing a six-hour endurance and a speed performance enabling it to evade interception by any fighter existing or known to be under development! The design team was given an entirely free hand in the means that it employed in meeting these primary requirements.

The task was assigned to Tomio Kubo and Joji Hattori, who, from the outset, placed all emphasis on aerodynamic cleanliness, adopting the minimum practical fuselage cross section and the thinnest available wing section, while the Aeronautical Research Institute of the University of Tokyo devoted its attention to the development of close-fitting, low-drag cowlings for the Mitsubishi Ha-26 14-cylinder two-row radials that had been selected to power the new aircraft, which, meanwhile, had been assigned the *Kitai* (Experimental Airframe) designation Ki.46. The basic design that evolved was an all-metal stressed-skin low-wing monoplane with a fully retractable undercarriage, the cockpits of the pilot and radio-operator/gunner being separated by the main fuel tank bay close to the aircraft CG. The wing comprised a single main spar and two auxiliary spars, provision being made for fuel tanks fore and aft of the main spar, both inboard and outboard of the engine nacelles, these combining with the main tank to provide a total capacity of 328 Imp gal (1 490 l). All fixed surfaces had flush-riveted light alloy skinning, the flaps were metal skinned, and the ailerons and movable tail surfaces were fabric covered. The fuselage was an oval-section flush-riveted semi-monocoque, and some measure of defence was provided by a single 7,7-mm Type 89 machine gun on a flexible mounting in the rear cockpit. The Ha-26-*Ko* engines each possessed a military rating of 875 hp at 11,810 ft (3 600 m), offering 780 hp at 2,540 rpm for take-off and driving 9 ft (2,75 m) diameter three-bladed Sumitomo (Hamilton Standard) constant-speed propellers.

The Ki.46 was subjected to the most intensive wind tunnel programme conducted in Japan to that time and emerged as a highly refined design, the first prototype being completed during the course of October 1939 at the Kagamigahara plant, north of Nagoya, where it was to enter flight test early in the

(Head of page and below) The most widely utilised version of the Type 100 Command Reconnaissance Aircraft was the Ki.46-Otsu, the first Ha-102-engined model which saw service throughout the Pacific conflict.

following month. Responsible for initial trials was Major Yuzo Fujita, the Imperial Army's foremost test pilot and a member of the staff of the Technical Branch of the *Koku Hombu* that had formulated the specification to which the Ki.46 had been evolved. From the outset, it was obvious that the Ki.46 possessed insufficient power to achieve the 373 mph (600 km/h) maximum speed at 13,125 ft (4 000 m) called for by the specification, clocking only 336 mph (540 km/h) at this altitude during speed trials, but in every other respect the new reconnaissance aircraft met or exceeded requirements, and there was reason to suppose that development of the Ha-26 with a two-speed supercharger as the Ha-102 then in progress would enable the shortfall in speed performance to be made good.

Production had already been authorised of a pre-series of aircraft as the Type 100 Command Reconnaissance Aircraft Model *Ko** with similar Ha-26-*Ko* engines to the prototypes, and the Kagamigahara plant was instructed to proceed with these while development was pursued of an Ha-102-engined model, the Ki.46-*Otsu**, as the initial operational version. The pre-series Ki.46-*Ko* aircraft began to appear in the late spring of 1940, these being assigned as available to a specially-created unit for intensive service evaluation and the Shimoshizu Army

**The* Kanji *characters* Ko, Otsu, Hei, *etc, possessed a sequential significance in word meaning if not always in actual practice,* Ko *signifying "premier" or "primary",* Otsu *indicating "secondary",* Hei *standing for "tertiary", and so on.*

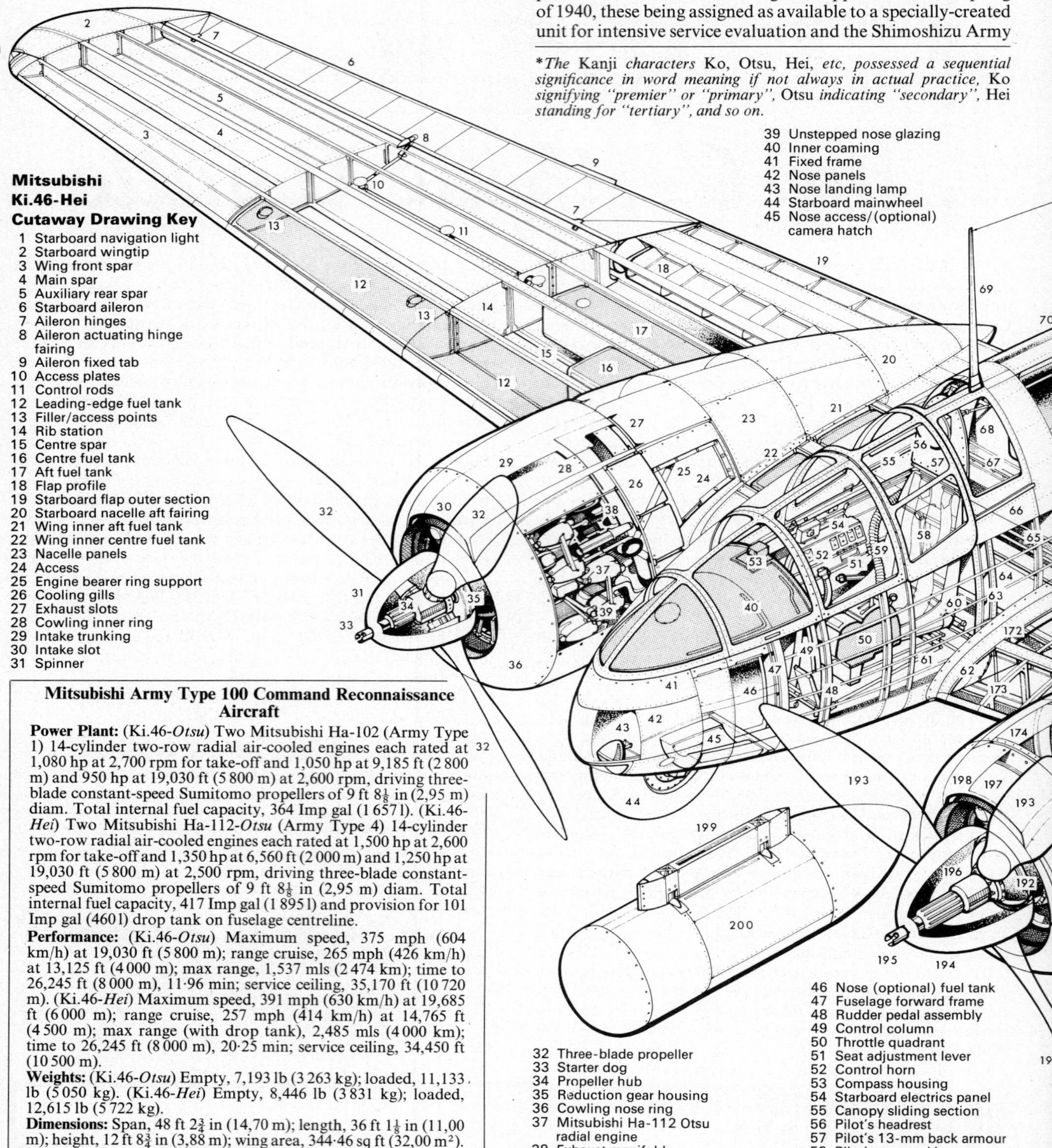

Mitsubishi Ki.46-Hei Cutaway Drawing Key

1 Starboard navigation light
2 Starboard wingtip
3 Wing front spar
4 Main spar
5 Auxiliary rear spar
6 Starboard aileron
7 Aileron hinges
8 Aileron actuating hinge fairing
9 Aileron fixed tab
10 Access plates
11 Control rods
12 Leading-edge fuel tank
13 Filler/access points
14 Rib station
15 Centre spar
16 Centre fuel tank
17 Aft fuel tank
18 Flap profile
19 Starboard flap outer section
20 Starboard nacelle aft fairing
21 Wing inner aft fuel tank
22 Wing inner centre fuel tank
23 Nacelle panels
24 Access
25 Engine bearer ring support
26 Cooling gills
27 Exhaust slots
28 Cowling inner ring
29 Intake trunking
30 Intake slot
31 Spinner
32 Three-blade propeller
33 Starter dog
34 Propeller hub
35 Reduction gear housing
36 Cowling nose ring
37 Mitsubishi Ha-112 Otsu radial engine
38 Exhaust manifold
39 Unstepped nose glazing
40 Inner coaming
41 Fixed frame
42 Nose panels
43 Nose landing lamp
44 Starboard mainwheel
45 Nose access/(optional) camera hatch
46 Nose (optional) fuel tank
47 Fuselage forward frame
48 Rudder pedal assembly
49 Control column
50 Throttle quadrant
51 Seat adjustment lever
52 Control horn
53 Compass housing
54 Starboard electrics panel
55 Canopy sliding section
56 Pilot's headrest
57 Pilot's 13-mm back armour
58 Pilot's seat and harness

Mitsubishi Army Type 100 Command Reconnaissance Aircraft

Power Plant: (Ki.46-*Otsu*) Two Mitsubishi Ha-102 (Army Type 1) 14-cylinder two-row radial air-cooled engines each rated at 1,080 hp at 2,700 rpm for take-off and 1,050 hp at 9,185 ft (2 800 m) and 950 hp at 19,030 ft (5 800 m) at 2,600 rpm, driving three-blade constant-speed Sumitomo propellers of 9 ft 8⅛ in (2,95 m) diam. Total internal fuel capacity, 364 Imp gal (1 657 l). (Ki.46-*Hei*) Two Mitsubishi Ha-112-*Otsu* (Army Type 4) 14-cylinder two-row radial air-cooled engines each rated at 1,500 hp at 2,600 rpm for take-off and 1,350 hp at 6,560 ft (2 000 m) and 1,250 hp at 19,030 ft (5 800 m) at 2,500 rpm, driving three-blade constant-speed Sumitomo propellers of 9 ft 8⅛ in (2,95 m) diam. Total internal fuel capacity, 417 Imp gal (1 895 l) and provision for 101 Imp gal (460 l) drop tank on fuselage centreline.

Performance: (Ki.46-*Otsu*) Maximum speed, 375 mph (604 km/h) at 19,030 ft (5 800 m); range cruise, 265 mph (426 km/h) at 13,125 ft (4 000 m); max range, 1,537 mls (2 474 km); time to 26,245 ft (8 000 m), 11·96 min; service ceiling, 35,170 ft (10 720 m). (Ki.46-*Hei*) Maximum speed, 391 mph (630 km/h) at 19,685 ft (6 000 m); range cruise, 257 mph (414 km/h) at 14,765 ft (4 500 m); max range (with drop tank), 2,485 mls (4 000 km); time to 26,245 ft (8 000 m), 20·25 min; service ceiling, 34,450 ft (10 500 m).

Weights: (Ki.46-*Otsu*) Empty, 7,193 lb (3 263 kg); loaded, 11,133 lb (5 050 kg). (Ki.46-*Hei*) Empty, 8,446 lb (3 831 kg); loaded, 12,615 lb (5 722 kg).

Dimensions: Span, 48 ft 2¾ in (14,70 m); length, 36 ft 1⅛ in (11,00 m); height, 12 ft 8¾ in (3,88 m); wing area, 344·46 sq ft (32,00 m²).

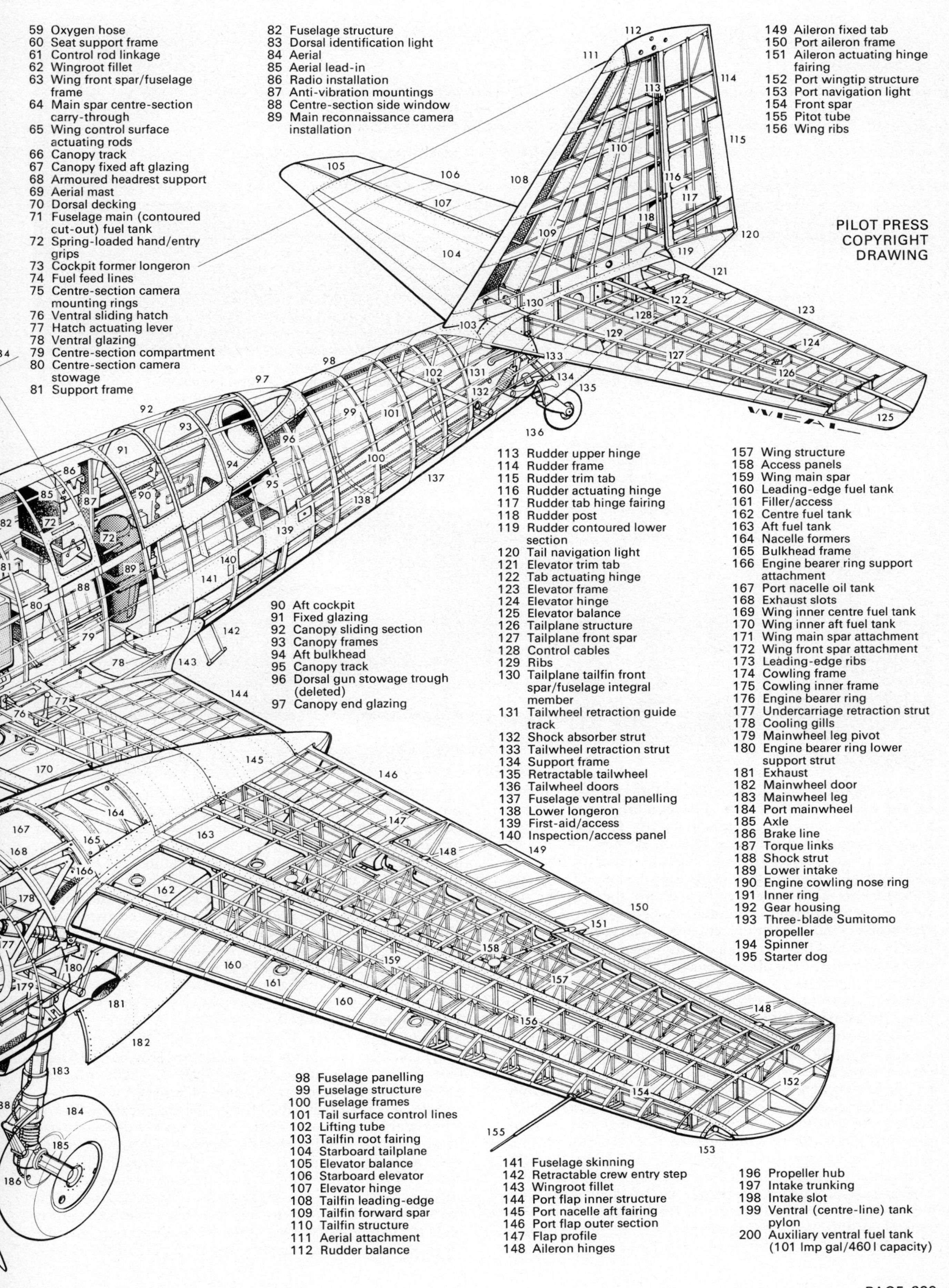

59 Oxygen hose
60 Seat support frame
61 Control rod linkage
62 Wingroot fillet
63 Wing front spar/fuselage frame
64 Main spar centre-section carry-through
65 Wing control surface actuating rods
66 Canopy track
67 Canopy fixed aft glazing
68 Armoured headrest support
69 Aerial mast
70 Dorsal decking
71 Fuselage main (contoured cut-out) fuel tank
72 Spring-loaded hand/entry grips
73 Cockpit former longeron
74 Fuel feed lines
75 Centre-section camera mounting rings
76 Ventral sliding hatch
77 Hatch actuating lever
78 Ventral glazing
79 Centre-section compartment
80 Centre-section camera stowage
81 Support frame
82 Fuselage structure
83 Dorsal identification light
84 Aerial
85 Aerial lead-in
86 Radio installation
87 Anti-vibration mountings
88 Centre-section side window
89 Main reconnaissance camera installation
90 Aft cockpit
91 Fixed glazing
92 Canopy sliding section
93 Canopy frames
94 Aft bulkhead
95 Canopy track
96 Dorsal gun stowage trough (deleted)
97 Canopy end glazing
98 Fuselage panelling
99 Fuselage structure
100 Fuselage frames
101 Tail surface control lines
102 Lifting tube
103 Tailfin root fairing
104 Starboard tailplane
105 Elevator balance
106 Starboard elevator
107 Elevator hinge
108 Tailfin leading-edge
109 Tailfin forward spar
110 Tailfin structure
111 Aerial attachment
112 Rudder balance
113 Rudder upper hinge
114 Rudder frame
115 Rudder trim tab
116 Rudder actuating hinge
117 Rudder tab hinge fairing
118 Rudder post
119 Rudder contoured lower section
120 Tail navigation light
121 Elevator trim tab
122 Tab actuating hinge
123 Elevator frame
124 Elevator hinge
125 Elevator balance
126 Tailplane structure
127 Tailplane front spar
128 Control cables
129 Ribs
130 Tailplane tailfin front spar/fuselage integral member
131 Tailwheel retraction guide track
132 Shock absorber strut
133 Tailwheel retraction strut
134 Support frame
135 Retractable tailwheel
136 Tailwheel doors
137 Fuselage ventral panelling
138 Lower longeron
139 First-aid/access
140 Inspection/access panel
141 Fuselage skinning
142 Retractable crew entry step
143 Wingroot fillet
144 Port flap inner structure
145 Port nacelle aft fairing
146 Port flap outer section
147 Flap profile
148 Aileron hinges
149 Aileron fixed tab
150 Port aileron frame
151 Aileron actuating hinge fairing
152 Port wingtip structure
153 Port navigation light
154 Front spar
155 Pitot tube
156 Wing ribs
157 Wing structure
158 Access panels
159 Wing main spar
160 Leading-edge fuel tank
161 Filler/access
162 Centre fuel tank
163 Aft fuel tank
164 Nacelle formers
165 Bulkhead frame
166 Engine bearer ring support attachment
167 Port nacelle oil tank
168 Exhaust slots
169 Wing inner centre fuel tank
170 Wing inner aft fuel tank
171 Wing main spar attachment
172 Wing front spar attachment
173 Leading-edge ribs
174 Cowling frame
175 Cowling inner frame
176 Engine bearer ring
177 Undercarriage retraction strut
178 Cooling gills
179 Mainwheel leg pivot
180 Engine bearer ring lower support strut
181 Exhaust
182 Mainwheel door
183 Mainwheel leg
184 Port mainwheel
185 Axle
186 Brake line
187 Torque links
188 Shock strut
189 Lower intake
190 Engine cowling nose ring
191 Inner ring
192 Gear housing
193 Three-blade Sumitomo propeller
194 Spinner
195 Starter dog
196 Propeller hub
197 Intake trunking
198 Intake slot
199 Ventral (centre-line) tank pylon
200 Auxiliary ventral fuel tank (101 Imp gal/460 l capacity)
PILOT PRESS COPYRIGHT DRAWING

(Above) A Ki.46-Otsu of the 81st Sentai's 2nd Chutai. The 81st was one of the first Sentais formed on the Ki.46 and saw service over China, Indochina, Malaya, Sumatra, Java and Burma. (Below) A Ki.46-Otsu of the 82nd Sentai, which, formed in the autumn of 1944, operated over China, Korea and Manchuria.

Flying School for pilot training. The teething troubles suffered by the Ki.46-*Ko* during these first months of service were mostly of a comparatively minor nature, the most serious being associated with the fuel and oil systems, the former tending to create vapour locks and the latter overheating under certain conditions, and these problems were to take some time to resolve and then by the rerouting of some fuel runs and comparatively substantial changes to the oil system. One problem that did not immediately reveal itself and was to remain with the Ki.46 throughout its subsequent service life was a weakness in the oleo-pneumatic shock absorber leg of the main undercarriage which was to display a tendency to fail at the attachment point. Oxygen supply reliability was also to prove itself a problem never to be satisfactorily overcome.

From the viewpoint of the pilot, the Ki.46 possessed no serious vices. Although the nose-up attitude of the aircraft tended to produce restricted forward view until the tail came up, the handling characteristics during take-off were generally good. The rudder was not as effective as might have been desired and aileron response tended to be lethargic, but the rôle that the Ki.46 was intended to fulfil did not call for extreme agility and it was generally considered that the controls were adequately effective throughout the speed range.

Full-scale production of the Ki.46-*Otsu* had meanwhile been launched at Mitsubishi's No 11 Plant at Nagoya, the first example of this model being completed and flown in March 1941. Structurally, this differed in only minor details from the pre-series Ki.46-*Ko*. Its Ha-102 (Army Type 101) engines utilised the same bearers and engine cowlings to those of the Ha-26-*Ko* that they replaced but drove marginally larger propellers of 9 ft 8⅛ in (2,95 m) diameter and offered 1,080 hp at 2,700 rpm for take-off, with nominal ratings of 1,050 hp at 9,185 ft (2 800 m) and 950 hp at 19,030 ft (5 800 m) at 2,600 rpm. Fuel capacity was augmented by the introduction of tanks in the wing leading edges, total capacity being raised to 364 Imp gal (1 657 l), and various economies reduced empty weight by 256 lb (116 kg) to 7,194 lb (3 263 kg), maximum loaded weight rising from 10,630 lb (4 822 kg) to 11,133 lb (5 050 kg).

Enter Dinah

The additional power provided by the Ha-102 engines fully made good the shortfall in level speed performance, 375 mph (604 km/h) being attainable at 19,030 ft (5 800 m), and endurance at 5·8 hours at 265 mph (426 km/h) was only 12 minutes less than that called for by the specification. Tomio Kubo and his team were elated by the success of Ki.46-*Otsu* trials, elation shared by the *Koku Hombu* which was convinced with some justification that Japan had created the most advanced vehicle for strategic reconnaissance extant and one virtually immune from interception. The first Ki.46-*Otsu* reconnaissance aircraft were completed in parallel with the last of 34 (including prototypes) of the Ki.46-*Ko* version, and the more powerful model, together with a number of the Ha-26-

powered pre-series aircraft, was hurriedly assigned to a half-dozen independent companies *(Dokuritsu Dai Shijugo Chutais)* activated between July and September 1941 at the Kagamigahara air base specifically for the strategic reconnaissance rôle. These *chutais* — the 50th, 51st, 70th, 74th, 76th and 81st — were despatched as formed to Manchuria from where they were immediately redeployed to strategically situated bases enabling them to reconnoitre — on occasions under local Imperial Navy command — virtually the entire South-East Asian scene of future operations, the 51st *Chutai*, for example, moving, in September, to Kompong Trach, Cambodia, from where it flew clandestine overflights of Malaya with Ki.46-*Ko* aircraft.

The Ki.46 was soon ubiquitous in South-East Asia and much of China; wherever Japanese forces were to strike the target was first reconnoitred by this outstanding aircraft which had little difficulty in evading fighter interception, and even when the USAAF was to deploy P-38F Lightnings to the Pacific and the RAAF was to receive some Spitfire Vs for the defence of Northern Australia, which was being reconnoitred by Ki.46s based on Timor, the successful interception of the Mitsubishi reconnaissance aircraft remained very much the exception. Nevertheless, the advent of more efficacious Allied fighters was obviously but a matter of time, and in the summer of 1942, work was proceeding on a version of the aircraft offering an even more advanced performance, the Ki.46-*Hei*.

It was at this time that the Directorate of Intelligence of the Allied Air Forces (Southwest Pacific Area) assigned the reporting name *Dinah* to the Ki.46, which, by now was viewed as one of the most troublesome (to the Allies) of any aircraft fielded by Japan and certainly one of the most respected. Apart from poor reliability of the oxygen supply system and proneness of the main undercarriage legs to fatigue failure, both air and ground crews thought highly of the characteristics of the Ki.46, which, despite a comparatively light structure, was surprisingly robust. It was trusted by its pilots who were confident of their ability to evade enemy fighters — which was just as well as they were seated ahead of a large, unprotected fuel tank, were provided with no form of armour protection and the single 7,7-mm machine gun could hardly be considered to represent a serious means of defence — and the fact that the radio equipment was unreliable was of little consequence as, on most missions, the strictest radio silence was maintained throughout. Various cameras could be installed in the rear cockpit, varying from 24 cm to 1,0 m in focal length, and the Ki.46 was extensively employed for the so-called *Ichi-Kohka Sosaku* (one-pass scouting) type of mission, taking-off from one base, overflying the target and continuing on to land at another base.

The Ki.46-*Hei* took advantage of the availability of the Mitsubishi Ha-112-*Otsu* (Army Type 4) engine, which, with direct fuel injection, offered 1,500 hp at 2,600 rpm for take-off, 1,350 hp at 2,500 rpm at 6,560 ft (2 000 m) and 1,250 hp at 2,500 rpm at 19,030 ft (5 800 m). To cater for the increased fuel consumption of the more powerful engines, the fuel system was redesigned and an additional unprotected tank introduced ahead of the pilot in the extreme nose, raising total internal fuel capacity to 417 Imp gal (1 895 l), while provision was made for a 101 Imp gal (460 l) ventral drop tank by means of which maximum endurance was raised slightly to six hours. The aft-

(Above) The refined Ki.46-Hei which first entered service in the summer of 1943, the example illustrated having originally been flown by the 17th Chutai (the stylised characters for "17" being faintly seen on the fin) and subsequently abandoned after suffering damage in a strafing attack. (Below) One of the prototypes of the turbo-supercharger-equipped Ki.46-Tei.

(Above and below left) A Ki.46-Hei KAI interceptor of the 16th Independent Fighter Company which operated from the home islands and from Okinawa during the final phase of the Pacific conflict.

firing 7,7-mm machine gun was discarded together with the characteristic stepped pilot's windscreen, the latter giving place to a new windscreen producing an unbroken curve from the extreme nose to the rear of the radio operator's glazed canopy. While improving the aerodynamics of the airframe and adding a few knots to the speed, this new windscreen was to prove unpopular as it resulted in some distortion of vision.

Two prototypes of the Ki.46-*Hei* were completed at Nagoya in December 1942, and the new model demonstrated a maximum speed of 391 mph (630 km/h) at 19,685 ft (6 000 m) and a range of 2,485 miles (4 000 km) at 257 mph (414 km/h), but higher weights impaired climb rate and ceiling was marginally reduced. Production of the Ki.46-*Hei* was initiated to supplement rather than succeed the Ki.46-*Otsu*, both models being produced in parallel at the Nagoya facility, the earlier version not being phased out until late 1944, by which time a total of 1,093 examples of the -*Otsu* variant were to have been built. The two models frequently operated side-by-side in mixed units, but, initially at least, the Ki.46-*Hei* presented maintenance personnel with a number of problems, these being mostly associated with the fuel injection system of the Ha-112-*Otsu* engine, and these were only finally resolved after the creation of special field teams which visited operational bases to iron out the maintenance problems.

The Ki.46-*Hei* offered a notably improved altitude performance (ie, between 26,245 ft/8 000 m and 32,810 ft/10 000 m) and in an attempt to improve still further on this aspect of the flight envelope, work began in 1943 on a version powered by exhaust-driven turbo-supercharger-equipped Ha-112-*Otsu Ru* engines as the Ki.46-*Tei*. Mounted in the tails of the engine nacelles, the Ru-102 turbo-superchargers enabled the engines to retain their rated power of 1,250 hp up to 26,900 ft (8 200 m). Space availability prevented the installation of intercoolers, the intake air therefore being cooled by methanol. Numerous problems were encountered with this turbo-supercharging system, and flight testing with the first of four Ki.46-*Tei* prototypes did not commence until February 1944 and was to continue into the following year — in February 1945, one of these prototypes, undoubtedly aided by strong tailwinds, succeeded in covering a distance of 1,430 miles (2 301 km) at an average speed of no less than 435 mph (700 km/h) — although production plans had meanwhile been shelved.

A more militant Dinah

On 14 June 1944, B-29 Superfortresses of the USAAF's 20th Bomber Command flew from bases in Chengtu to attack a target in the Japanese home islands for the first time. On this occasion, the intruding force, making a nocturnal attack, did not take full advantage of the high-flying attributes of the Boeing bomber, but in so far as the *Koku Hombu* was concerned, the writing was clearly on the wall; attacks from altitudes that could barely be reached let alone fought at by most existing home defence fighters now seemed imminent. Fighters optimised for the high-altitude rôle were under development but a more immediate solution to the problem was called for; extemporisation was necessary and the most suitable aircraft for adaptation as an extemporary high-altitude interceptor was the Ki.46-*Hei*.

Lacking the climb rate and agility desirable in a fighter — factors which had led to the discarding of a projected fighter adaptation of the Ki.46 in the summer of 1943 — the reconnaissance aircraft had only its high-altitude speed and considerable endurance to commend it as a B-29 interceptor, but these characteristics were now considered sufficient to warrant reactivation of the Ki.46 fighter project, and in May 1944, a month before the B-29 made its début over Japan, work had, in fact, been resumed on such an extemporary interceptor, this task receiving the highest priority in June.

Modification design work was hastily completed, and preparations were made by the 1st Army Air Arsenal at Tachikawa to set up a conversion line to which, from August, Mitsubishi's Nagoya plant delivered Ki.46-*Hei* aircraft straight from assembly. The conversion consisted of the removal of the forward fuel tank and the photographic equipment, and the introduction of a stepped windscreen for the pilot, an entirely new nose mounting two 20-mm Ho-5 cannon with 200 rpg, and, aft of the main fuel tank, an obliquely-mounted 37-mm Ho-203 cannon firing forward and upward, this being provided with eight 25-round magazines loaded by the observer.

Designated as the Army Type 100 Air Defence Fighter, or Ki.46-*Hei* KAI, the first example of the interceptor to leave the

Tachikawa conversion line was flown in October 1944, aircraft being delivered during the following month to the 106th *Sentai* which had been formed at Kagamigahara on 24 October and was to operate this improvised fighter until its disbandment on 30 May 1945. Others were to be assigned to the 16th and 17th Independent Fighter Companies *(Dokuritsu Hiko-Chutais)*, the latter being based at Chofu, Tokyo, and simultaneously, the Ki.46-*Hei* KAI was issued to another Independent Fighter Company, the 81st, formed for the defence of Mukden, Manchuria. Subsequently, the 82nd and 83rd *Chutais* were established with this type for home defence duties, and the 28th *Sentai* at Togane, in the Eastern Defence Sector, was to operate the Ki.46-*Hei* KAI in concert with the Kawasaki Ki.102-*Otsu*. Other aircraft of this type were to operate in the armed reconnaissance rôle with the 16th *Dokuritsu Hikotai* which also operated prototypes of the Ki.46-*Tei*.

Some 200 aircraft were converted for the B-29 interception task with which they enjoyed only qualified success, being inhibited by poor climb rate and inadequate firepower. The obliquely-mounted 37-mm weapon proved ineffectual and the airframe, sturdy enough for the rôle for which it was designed, lacked the ability to absorb much battle damage. In fact, it had little more than a good high altitude performance to commend it, this including speeds of 379 mph (610 km/h) at 19,685 ft (6 000 m) and 356 mph (573 km/h) at 29,530 ft (9 000 m). Development of a similar conversion of the Ki.46-*Tei* was proposed but abandoned when little progress was made with overcoming the problems encountered with the Ru-102 turbo-superchargers.

Conversions of the Ki.46-*Hei* for the fighter rôle continued at Tachikawa until late March 1945, and another conversion of the basic aircraft but one produced in smaller numbers was the Ki.46-*Otsu* KAI for the pilot training task at the Shimoshizu Army Flying School, a second cockpit for the instructor being inserted in the main fuel bay of the standard aircraft, the main tank being reduced in size and the instructor occupying an elevated seat beneath a separate canopy with a stepped windscreen.

Production of the Ki.46-*Otsu* and -*Hei* continued unabated throughout most of 1944, but late in the year the Nagoya facility suffered extensive damage as a result of an earthquake which seriously disrupted production, further extensive damage being inflicted by B-29 attacks. Some production of the Ki.46-*Hei* was transferred to a new factory at Toyama in consequence, but this was to contribute fewer than 100 aircraft to the total of 611 reconnaissance aircraft of this version built, these bringing the grand total of Ki.46s manufactured to 1,742, which, incidentally, was the largest number of reconnaissance aircraft of any single type built by *any* of the combatants.

The final phase of the Pacific conflict saw Ki.46-*Hei* aircraft mounting a constant surveillance of the Marianas B-29 Superfortress bases from Shimoshizu, near Tokyo, with a refuelling stop on Iwo Jima. Even at that late stage in the war, the Allies had still to resolve the problem of successfully intercepting this aircraft, although *when* intercepted, the Ki.46-*Hei*, lacking defensive armament and the 13-mm back and head armour provided the pilot being no more than a gesture towards protection, presented an easy "kill". The Allies were not alone in respecting the capabilities of this Mitsubishi reconnaissance aircraft, the *Technische Amt* of Germany's *Reichsluftfahrtministerium* having been sufficiently impressed to recommend negotiation of a manufacturing licence under the Japanese-German Technical Exchange Programme at one stage.

The task of the reconnaissance aircraft lacks something of the drama of that of fighter or bomber, but it can be equally vital and particularly so in a far-ranging conflict such as took place in the Pacific, a fact of which the Imperial Army's Air Headquarters was fully aware, and in catering for this task Japan created in the Ki.46 one of the truly outstanding aircraft of World War II. □

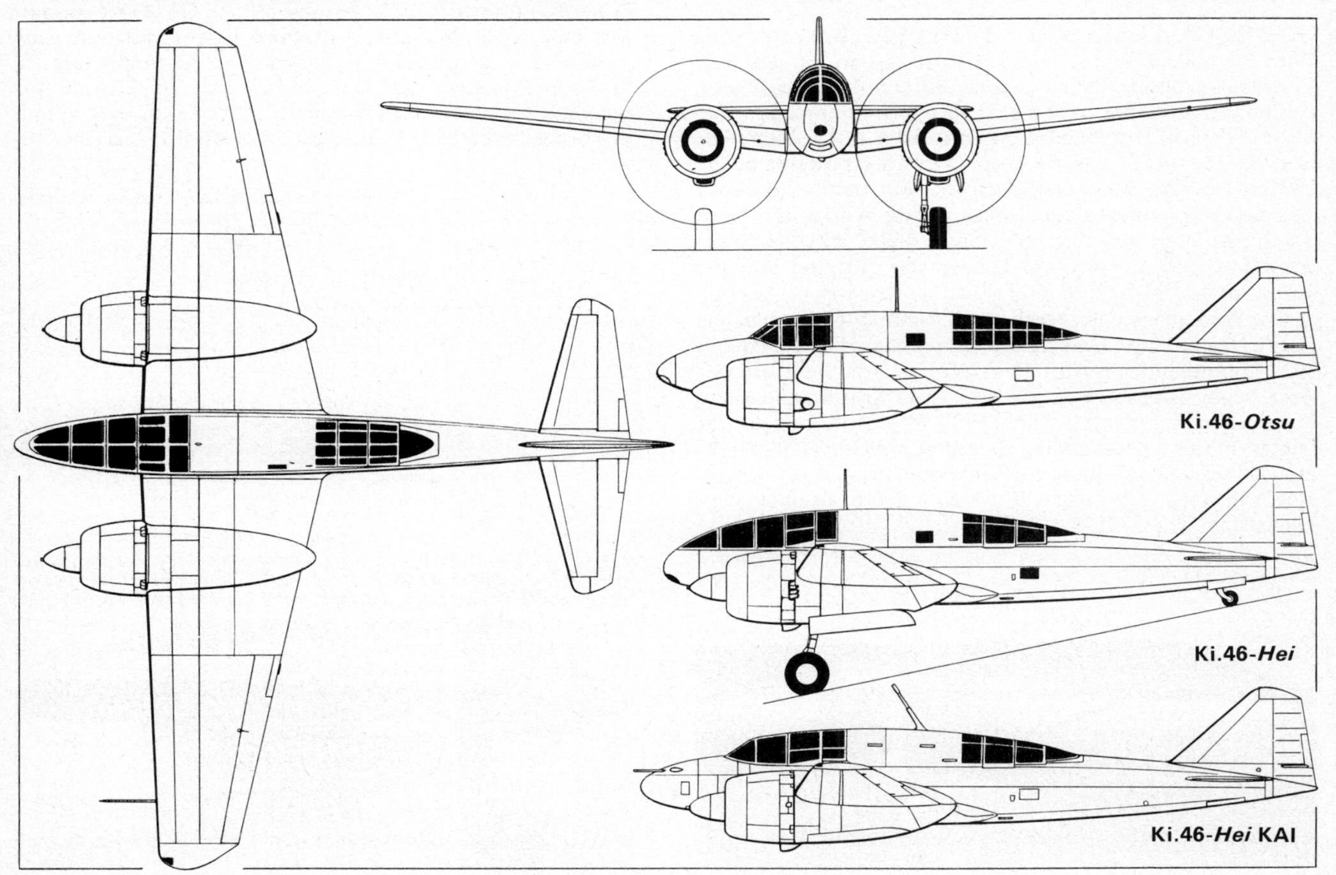

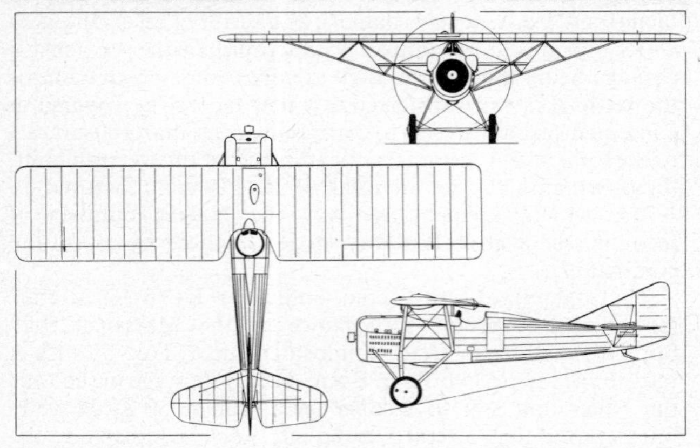

The primary operator of the GL-21 (above and below) was Finland, an example in Finnish service being illustrated by the photograph.

GOURDOU-LESEURRE GL-21(TYPE B2) FRANCE

With the end of World War I, Charles Gourdou and Jean Leseurre established their own company at St Maur les Fossés, continuing development of the GL-2 fighter monoplane as the GL-21 (Type B2) exhibited at the Paris *Salon de l'Aéronautique* of 1920. The GL-21 was, like its predecessors, powered by the 180 hp HS 8Ab water-cooled engine, but the broad chord ailerons with horn-balance areas laying within the wing planform were replaced by longer-span and narrower constant-chord ailerons, the rudder was enlarged and the series model introduced additional undercarriage bracing struts. Armament comprised two 7,7-mm Vickers machine guns in the fuselage. One GL-21 was purchased by Finland in 1923, followed by a further 18 in 1924, an additional aircraft later being assembled in Finland from spares, and these remained in Finnish service until 1931. A total of 30 single-seat fighters of this type was built. Max speed, 149 mph (240 km/h) at 3,280 ft (1 000 m). Range, 280 mls (450 km). Empty weight, 1,455 lb (660 kg). Loaded weight, 2,116 lb (960 kg). Dimensions as for GL-2.

A GL-22 alias Type B3 in service with the Estonian Air Force. A parallel development to the GL-21, the GL-22 differed primarily in employing a new wing profile.

GOURDOU-LESEURRE GL-22 (TYPE B3) FRANCE

Evolved from the GL-2 in parallel with the GL-21, the GL-22 (Type B3) also made its début in 1920. It differed from the GL-21 primarily in having a new wing profile, steel-tube in place of light alloy wing bracing struts, a modified frontal radiator and a revised cockpit interior. The HS 8Ab engine and twin Vickers gun armament were retained, but some structural revision reduced empty weight by 154 lb (70 kg). The prototype, like that of the GL-21, was initially flown with twin undercarriage struts on each side, but a triple-strut arrangement was adopted for the series model. With gun armament the aircraft was designated GL-22 C1 (C = *Chasse*), but without armament it was designated GL-22 ET1 (ET = *Entrainement de Transition*) and was intended for the advanced training rôle. The first order for the GL-22 was placed with Gourdou-Leseurre on 13 December 1920, 20 examples of the single-seat fighter subsequently being built for export to Estonia, Latvia and Czechoslovakia, 30 of the training version being supplied to France's *Aviation Marine*. In addition, a manufacturing licence was acquired by the newly-established Zmaj concern in Yugoslavia. Max speed, 153 mph (247 km/h) at sea level, 137 mph (220 km/h) at 16,405 ft (5 000 m). Endurance, 2·5 hrs. Time to 16,405 ft (5 000 m), 17·5 min. Empty weight, 1,301 lb (590 kg). Loaded weight, 1,940 lb (880 kg). Dimensions as for GL-2.

GOURDOU-LESEURRE GL-23 (TYPE B4) FRANCE

The GL-23 single-seat fighter of 1925 was a further development of the basic GL-2 design in which the HS 8Ab engine and standard GL-22 C1 fuselage and armament were mated with the longer span wing and enlarged rudder first applied to the experimental tandem two-seat GL-22 ET2 (Type B5) trainer of 1922. A total of nine GL-23 C1 aircraft was built at St Maur, two of these having different wing profiles for comparison purposes. One example had its fuselage elongated by 25·6 in (65 cm) to provide for accommodation of a single casualty stretcher aft of the pilot, this being presented at Le Bourget on 24 April 1925 as the GL-

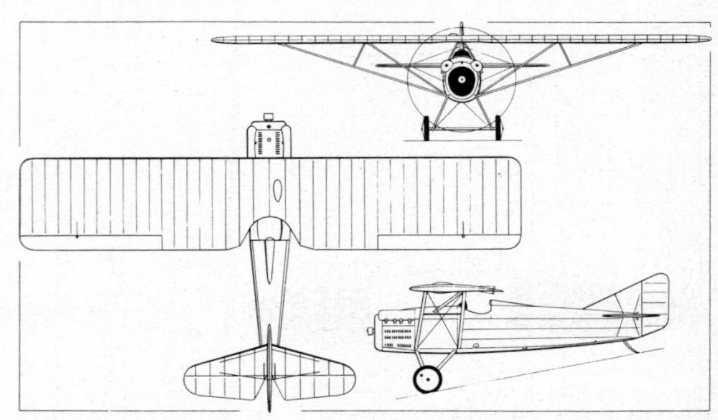

The GL-23, illustrated by the general arrangement drawing above, was essentially a longer-span derivative of the GL-22, but the GL-31 (below) was an entirely new design, development of which was early abandoned.

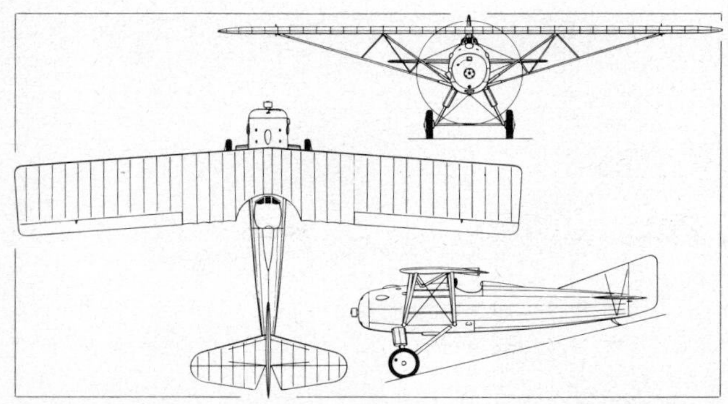

(Above and below) The GL-40 was designed to fulfil a requirement for a high-altitude fighter, but development did not progress beyond one prototype.

23 TS, one other example being completed (as the LGL 23 TS) in the following year. Max speed, 130 mph (210 km/h) at 3,280 ft (1 000 m). Range, 373 mls (600 km). Empty weight, 1,455 lb (660 kg). Loaded weight, 2,116 lb (960 kg). Span, 36 ft 1 in (11,00 m). Length, 21 ft $3\frac{9}{10}$ in (6,50 m). Height, 7 ft $9\frac{1}{3}$ in (2,37 m). Wing area, 251·88 sq ft (23,40 m²).

GOURDOU-LESEURRE GL-31 (TYPE I3) FRANCE

Although retaining the basic parasol monoplane configuration of preceding Gourdou-Leseurre fighters and similar construction (ie, all-metal structure apart from wooden wing ribs and fabric skinning), the GL-31 single-seat fighter was an entirely new design whereas its predecessors had all been extrapolations of the original GL-2. Designed to the requirements of the 1921 C1 programme, the GL-31 C1 was powered by a 420 hp Gnôme-Rhône 9A Jupiter air-cooled radial and had provision for two fuselage-mounted 7,7-mm Vickers guns and two unsynchronised Darne guns of similar calibre in the wings. The rectangular wing planform characteristic of all earlier Gourdou-Leseurre fighters gave place to a trapezoid with marked leading-edge taper and the profusion of wing bracing struts was supplanted by one pair of struts on each side. In the event, the 1921 C1 programme was overtaken by that of 1923 and the GL-31 by the Gourdou-Leseurre contender for the later programme, the GL-32, and the sole prototype did not fly until 1926, development being discontinued thereafter. Max speed, 161 mph (260 km/h). Range, 373 mls (600 km). Empty weight, 1,929 lb (875 kg). Loaded weight, 2,976 lb (1 350 kg). Span, 34 ft $5\frac{1}{3}$ in (10,50 m). Length, 23 ft $7\frac{1}{2}$ in (7,20 m). Height, 8 ft $10\frac{1}{3}$ in (2,70 m). Wing area, 226·05 sq ft (21,00 m²).

GOURDOU-LESEURRE GL-40 (TYPE G) FRANCE

The GL-40 single-seat high-altitude fighter actually preceded the GL-31, flying for the first time in 1922. Also a contender in the 1921 C1 programme, the GL-40 was powered by a 300 hp Hispano-Suiza 8Fb water-cooled engine fitted with a Rateau turbo-supercharger. The constant-chord wing, which featured slight sweepback, was braced by a similar four-pair strut arrangement as that of the GL-2 and its derivatives, and Lamblin radiators were attached to the undercarriage legs. The GL-40 was capable of altitudes in excess of 26,245 ft (8 000 m) and, in fact, was claimed to have attained 39,587 ft (12 066 m) on 10 October 1924 with Jean Callizo at the controls. However, this claim was subsequently alleged to have been fraudulent. Only one prototype of the GL-40 was built. Max speed, 161 mph (260 km/h) at 22,965 ft (7 000 m). Range, 497 mls (800 km). Empty weight, 2,392 lb (1 085 kg). Loaded weight, 3,329 lb (1 510 kg). Span, 47 ft $6\frac{9}{10}$ in (14,50 m). Length, 31 ft $2\frac{2}{5}$ in (9,51 m). Height, 9 ft 7 in (2,92 m). Wing area, 376·75 sq ft (35,00 m²).

GOURDOU-LESEURRE GL-50 (TYPE F) FRANCE

In April 1919, *Général* Duval, France's *Directeur de l'Aéronautique*, formulated a programme for the replacement of the principal categories of combat aircraft serving with the *Aéronautique Militaire*, two of these being CAP (*Chasse, Reconnaissance d'Armée et Protection*) and CAN (*Chasse et Reconnaissance d'Armée de Nuit*) two-seaters. Although this programme was overtaken in the following year (the CAP category being discarded), Gourdou-Leseurre designed and built prototypes to meet both requirements, the GL-50 CAP2 (Type F) and the GL-51 CAN2 (Type H), which embodied considerable commonality. The GL-50 was powered by a 300 hp Hispano-Suiza 8Fb water-cooled engine and was intended to have a Rateau turbo-supercharger, although, in the event, this was not to be fitted, and armament comprised two fixed forward-firing 7,7-mm Darne machine guns and two guns of similar calibre on a swivelling mount in the rear cockpit. A long-span, untapered wing was fitted and the arrangement of the bracing struts was similar to that of contemporary Gourdou-Leseurre single-seaters. The GL-51 CAN2 was essentially similar apart from having a 380 hp Gnôme-Rhône 9Ab Jupiter radial engine, a reduced loaded weight (3,968 lb/ 1 800 kg) and a marginally higher maximum speed (140 mph/ 225 km/h). Both prototypes were flown in 1922, but no production followed. The following data relate to the GL-50. Max speed, 131 mph (210 km/h). Loaded weight, 4,431 lb (2 010 kg). Span, 47 ft $10\frac{4}{5}$ in (14,60 m). Length, 30 ft $8\frac{1}{8}$ in (9,35 m). Height, 9 ft $4\frac{1}{5}$ in (2,85 m). Wing area, 430·57 sq ft (40,00 m²).

(Above and below) The GL-50 was intended as a two-seat multi-rôle fighter, the GL-51 developed in parallel being essentially similar apart from having a radial engine.

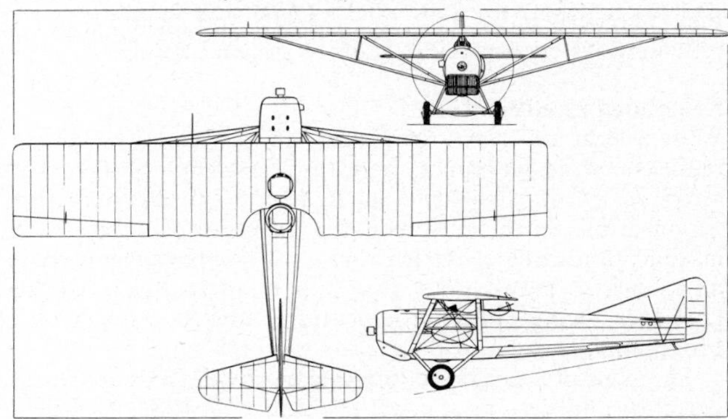

One of the 12 C-135Fs delivered to the Armée de l'Air *in 1964, refuelling a Mirage IV by means of the probe-and-drogue system. The 11 surviving C-135Fs were returned to Wichita in 1978/79 to have their lower wing skins replaced.*

BOEING KC-135 ——— ***from page 226***

Airlift Wing of MAC at Ramstein Air Base, Germany, for use as a VIP transport for high level government officials within USAFE direction and the other two were transferred to the 55th Strategic Reconnaissance Wing (SRW), SAC, Offutt AFB, to serve in a staff support rôle. These changes resulted in three KC-135As then serving as staff support aircraft being reallocated back to the tanker fleet. In December 1977, the two remaining VC-135Bs were also redesignated C-135Bs as part of the Carter Administration "low profile" programme; in addition, the 89th MAW at Andrews was downgraded to the 89th MAG as a cost savings measure and whereas the VC-135Bs had carried the 89th MAW colours of white, light blue and gold, the C-135Bs were now painted an overall white to preserve the austerity image.

Four RC-135As (serials 63-8058 to 63-8061) were delivered to MATS in 1965-1966, these actually being the last production-line aircraft in the KC/C-135 family delivered to the Air Force. The prime mission of these aircraft was photomapping and geodetic surveying, for which purpose they were operated by the 1370th Photo Mapping Wing, Air Photographic and Charting Service (APCS), MATS, Turner AFB, Georgia. A camera compartment replaced a portion of the normally-installed forward fuselage fuel tank, with two 30-in (76-cm) diameter, 2·5 in (6,3 cm) thick optically-ground camera windows in the bottom of the compartment; an external track-mounted door slid aft to expose the camera windows.

By July 1972, all four RC-135As had been reassigned to SAC for command support missions out of Offutt AFB. The photomapping equipment was removed and passenger seats were installed, although the camera compartment remained. By the end of 1980 these aircraft will have been further modified into KC-135Ds to serve in the tanker rôle. The reason for this new designation is that many of the aeroplane systems are not the same as those on the KC-135A because they were originally built to a MATS specification and a refuelling system was not part of the original RC-135A.

Scheduled modifications

With a fleet of over 760 aircraft in service, slow tanker replacement programmes, and the versatility of the -135 airframe, efforts to extend its structural life are on-going. Engineering work packages for inspection, repair and modification are currently in progress. These packages include an acoustic crack detection system, structural fatigue packages, wing splice modification, and a wing reskin programme.

The acoustic crack detection system provides for early crack detection and warning to concealed skin in the lower surface of the wing centre section. Early crack detection will increase structural integrity by ensuring that small cracks will be repaired prior to becoming large enough to reduce the wing residual strength to potential catastrophic failure levels. The system includes transducers in the wing which are wired to a single black box in the main cabin of the aircraft. Monitoring of the black box will reveal potential problems in the wing structure should the cracks occur. Fleet-wide system installation on affected high-time aircraft is scheduled for 1981 (average KC-135A hours is at present about 8,000, far below the typical figure of 65,000 hrs for commercial Boeing 707s).

Four structural fatigue packages are being installed on various -135 airframes. Each package is destined to remove certain structural fasteners from the aircraft and inspect the fastener holes where a history of fatigue testing has demonstrated fatigue crack development. The fastener holes are inspected for minute cracks, reamed to oversize in order to clean up any actual/potential defects in the holes, and fitted with new oversized fasteners. Different areas are dealt with by each package, the packages being worked at progressively increased airframe hours.

The Wing Station (WS) 360 splice is a manufacturing joint which is perpendicular to the wing rear spar; its centreline bisects the inboard spoilers at the rear and intersects the inboard engine at its forward end. Analysis showed that this area has a potential for a high number of fatigue cracks in the fastener holes in the internal doubler. Modification consists of the installation of an external, aerodynamically faired, doubler plate across the lower wing production break. This doubler provides an external load path of sufficient strength to carry 100 per cent of the design limit load in the event of a complete failure of the internal splice plate. The modification is being incorporated into high-time tankers, with fleet completion scheduled for 1981.

Engineering Change Proposal (ECP) 405 provides for replacement of the lower wing skin between Wing Stations 737, left and right, in the area between the outboard engines. The original 7178-T6 aluminium alloy skin is replaced with skin fabricated from the same 2024-T351 material used on commercial Boeing jetliners, thereby doubling the service life (in flight hours) on the -135 fleet, from 13,000 to 26,000 hrs. In addition, the stiffeners, spars and rib chords are replaced. This modification affects approximately 1,500 sq ft (139,35 m²) of structure on the 2,433 sq ft (226,03 m²) of wing. The Boeing Military Airplane Company at Wichita began incorporation of the first ECP 405 retrofit kit in November 1975 under a 14-aircraft competitive bid programme; it was completed on 12 February 1976 and 140 aircraft had received the ECP 405 modification by March 1980. Between March 1978 and October 1979 the entire fleet of 11 *Armée de l'Air* C-135Fs also underwent ECP 405 modification. The programme is scheduled for completion on all -135s by 1988.

Avionics changes are also being accomplished on the -135 fleet. New solid state electronic equipment is providing a quantum jump in reliability and weight reduction in aircraft systems. Forties-vintage vacuum tube type Doppler navigation systems are being replaced by new lightweight, solid-state systems exhibiting a higher mean-time-between-failure (MTBF) rate. To comply with ICAO requirements for flying the North Atlantic Track System, inertial navigation systems are also being installed on the -135s; flight testing of a combined INS/Doppler navigation system began in 1978 and was completed by January 1979. Single INS units were installed beginning in January 1979, and the combined INS/DNS units have been available for installation since April 1980. Total retrofit of the INS/DNS units is programmed for the 1982-1983 time frame.

Future updates

Boeing and the Air Force have for some years been studying several ways in which the performance of the -135 family can be improved, primarily as a means of reducing fuel consumption in order to save operating cost. Three areas are of particular interest, covering skin drag, the addition of winglets and, most important, the retrofitting of CFM-56 engines. Another package of improvements is at present under study as the Improved Aerial Refuelling System (IARS).

A study is underway to determine the fuel penalty caused by the surface roughness of the external paint. Originally, all -135 aircraft were delivered in a natural metal finish, and later with the airframe painted with a metallic-coloured paint for corrosion control purposes. This silver anti-corrosive finish was Corogard — an aluminium-filled, vinyl-modified polysulphide that is flexible and resists attack by the MIL-H-5606 hydraulic fluid used in military aircraft. Its major drawback is that it has a higher drag coefficient than the polyurethane paints used on commercial aircraft. However, polyurethane paint requires greater maintenance. Currently, most -135 aircraft are being painted with aliphatic polyurethane, which is a gloss grey with a lower drag coefficient than the Corogard.

Winglets were installed on one NKC-135A (55-3129) for tests by NASA at the Dryden Flight Test Center, Edwards AFB, California, under a contract signed on 10 June 1977. Small, vertically canted winglets, approximately 9 ft (2,74 m) long, were mounted on the wingtips of this aircraft, which was first flown on 24 July 1979. Preliminary studies indicate a 7-8 per cent lift-to-drag ratio improvement with a corresponding reduction in fuel consumption. If tests prove the installation beneficial, the Air Force could realise an annual fuel saving of about 45 million US gal (170 m litres); fleet installation of the winglets could begin as early as 1983.

The IARS update programme has recently received USAF funding for the research and development phase and is likely to be applied in due course to some or all of the KC-135s. It

KC-135A DEPLOYMENT

Strategic Air Command has prime responsibility for the -135 fleet; maintenance is programmed through the Oklahoma City Air Materiel Area (OCAMA), Air Force Logistics Command. Regular Air Force units within SAC which operate the KC-135A tankers are as follows (correct at April 1980):

3rd Air Division
  43rd Strategic Wing, Andersen AFB, Guam
  376th Strategic Wing, Kadena AB, Japan
7th Air Division
  306th Strategic Wing, Mildenhall RAF, England
  11th Strategic Group, Fairford RAF, England

8TH AIR FORCE
19th Air Division
  2nd Bombardment Wing (H), Barksdale AFB, LA
  7th Bombardment Wing (H), Carswell AFB, TX
  340th Air Refueling Group (H), Altus AFB, OK
  384th Air Refueling Wing (H), McConnell AFB, KS
40th Air Division
  305th Air Refueling Wing (H), Grissom AFB, IN
  379th Bombardment Wing (H), Wurtsmith AFB, MI
  410th Bombardment Wing (H), K.I. Sawyer AFB, MI
42nd Air Division
  19th Bombardment Wing (H), Robins AFB, GA
  68th Bombardment Wing (H), Seymour Johnson AFB, NC
  97th Bombardment Wing (H), Blytheville AFB, AR
45th Air Division
  42nd Bombardment Wing (H), Loring AFB, ME
  380th Bombardment Wing (M), Plattsburgh AFB, NY
  416th Bombardment Wing (H), Griffiss AFB, NY
  509th Bombardment Wing (M), Pease AFB, NH

15TH AIR FORCE
4th Air Division
  28th Bombardment Wing (H), Ellsworth AFB, SD
12th Air Division
  22nd Bombardment Wing (H), March AFB, CA
  96th Bombardment Wing (H), Dyess AFB, TX
14th Air Division
  320th Bombardment Wing (H), Mather AFB, CA
  100th Air Refueling Wing (H), Beale AFB, CA
  307th Air Refueling Group (H), Travis AFB, CA
  93rd Bombardment Wing (H), Castle AFB, CA
47th Air Division
  92nd Bombardment Wing (H), Fairchild AFB, WA
57th Air Division
  5th Bombardment Wing (H), Minot AFB, ND
  319th Bombardment Wing (H), Grand Forks AFB, ND

Commencing in the summer of 1975, SAC began delegating part of its air refuelling operation to the Air National Guard and Air Force Reserve — the first time a strategic mission was allocated to non-regular forces. Reserve/Guard units operating the KC-135A are as follows (current at April 1980):

AIR FORCE RESERVE

10TH AIR FORCE
  452nd Air Refueling Wing (H)
    336th Air Refueling Squadron (H), March AFB, CA
  931st Air Refueling Group (H)
    72nd Air Refueling Squadron (H), Grissom AFB, CA
  940th Air Refueling Group (H)
    314th Air Refueling Squadron (H), Mather AFB, CA

AIR NATIONAL GUARD
101st Air Refueling Wing, Bangor, ME
126th Air Refueling Wing, Chicago, IL
141st Air Refueling Wing, Fairchild AFB, WA
171st Air Refueling Wing, Pittsburgh, PA
128th Air Refueling Group, Gen Billy Mitchell Field, WI
134th Air Refueling Group, Knoxville, TN
151st Air Refueling Group, Salt Lake City, UT
157th Air Refueling Group, Pease AFB, NH
160th Air Refueling Group, Rickenbacker AFB, OH
161st Air Refueling Group, Phoenix, AZ
170th Air Refueling Group, McGuire AFB, NJ
189th Air Refueling Group, Little Rock AFB, AR
190th Air Refueling Group, Forbes ANG Base, KS

C-135A Operating units
55th Strategic Reconnaissance Wing, Offutt AFB, NE
4950th Test Wing, Wright-Patterson AFB, OH

C-135B Operating Units
4950th Test Wing, Wright-Patterson AFB, OH
55th Strategic Reconnaissance Wing, Offutt AFB, NE
89th Military Airlift Group, Andrews AFB, DC
435th Tactical Airlift Wing, Ramstein AF, Germany

C-135C Operating units
Det. 1, 890th Military Airlift Group, Hickam AFB, HA
Det. 1, 4950th Test Wing, Andrews AFB, DC

C-135F Operating Units
91st *Escadre de Bombardement, Armée de l'Air*
94th *Escadre de Bombardement, Armée de l'Air*

This NKC-135A is being used by NASA at the Dryden Flight Test Center, Edwards AFB, to evaluate the benefits that might be derived from the use of the 9-ft (2,74-m) long winglets. Fuel savings resulting from the reduced lift-to-drag ratio could offset the cost of introducing the modification on a fleet-wide basis.

embraces four major items, some of which are an outgrowth of Boeing's own development work for the 13 Boeing 707-3J9C tanker-transports delivered to the Imperial Iranian Air Force*; they comprise the installation of high rate of flow pumps, a tail-mounted floodlight, an improved probe-and-drogue system and a head-up display for the boom operator.

The new pumps will increase the maximum rate of flow through the boom from 900 to 1,200 US gal/min (3 407-4 542 l/min), thus matching the capabilities of the newer receiving aircraft now entering service. A new tail-mounted floodlamp will better illuminate the whole of the receiver, and not just the refuelling receptacle; tests have already been made with such a lamp installed in a fairing at the top rear of the KC-135A's fin. The possibility of installing an HDU (hose drum unit) in the belly of the KC-135A, forward of the boom operator's position, is receiving attention, as an alternative to the hose-and-drogue adaptor kit previously developed by Boeing, which has operational limitations. Installation of this kit renders the boom inoperative, whereas the option now being studied would allow the KC-135A to use either system on the same flight. Use of a head-up display at the boom operator's position would enhance the efficiency with which boom hook-ups are achieved and, with the other improvements, allow a larger number of refuellings to be completed in a given time.

The CFM-56 programme

On 13 January 1978, the USAF awarded Boeing a contract to study the possibilities of re-engining the KC-135, and to estimate the improvements that could then be achieved over a "baseline" mission involving a 2,000 naut-ml (3 700-km) transit, off-loading 91,000 lb (41 278 kg) of fuel and flying a further 1,000 naut mls (1 850 km) to recovery base. Among the proposals studied by Boeing were the following:

KC-135H with TF33-P-7 engines (as on the C-135B) and a Boeing 707-320B wing). Fuel offload would increase by 55,000 lb (24 950 kg) or range by 2,000 naut mls (3 700 km).

KC-135P7 with TF33-P-7 engines on the KC-135A wing. Fuel off-load increased by 23,000 lb (10 433 kg) or range by 900 naut mls (1 667 km).

KC-135ME with CFM-56 or JT10D turbofans on inboard pylons only. Fuel offload up by 26,000 lb (11 794 kg) or range up by 1,100 naut mls (2 038 km).

KC-135X: As KC-135H but with CFM-56 or JT10D engines. Fuel off-load up by 61,000 lb (27 670 kg) or range up by 2,600 naut mls (4 816 km).

KC-135Y: As KC-135X with new technology wing. Offload up by 69,000 lb (31 300 kg) or range up by 3,200 naut mls (5 927 km).

These studies were interesting in showing the extent to which performance could be improved, but had to be related to cost. Boeing estimates of unit costs, assuming a substantial proportion of the KC-135 fleet was to be converted, ranged from a low of $3·7m for the KC-135ME to $10·6m for the KC-135Y. In the event, none of these options was chosen; on 23 January 1980 the USAF signed an initial contract with the Boeing Military Airplane Co to proceed with the design of a CFM-56 retrofit for the KC-135A, without changing the wing. This variant is currently referred to as the KC-135RE.

Meanwhile, in a joint private venture with General Electric and SNECMA (manufacturers of the CFM-56 through CFM International), Boeing had installed four of these new turbofans on a 707-300, which made its first flight on 27 November 1979. In 86 flights, this aircraft accrued 164 hours and 20 minutes, and aircraft performance, engine performance and noise reduction were found to be as predicted. Minor problems encountered in testing necessitated tests with chined nacelles to improve the flaps-down stall speed by 3·5-7 knots (6,5-13 km/h), and installation of surge bleed valves to improve engine low-RPM stability. Test results surpassed the FAA requirements for bird ingestion, fan blade-out and water ingestion conditions. Earlier in 1980, the re-engined test-bed 707 made an 18-state, 20-stop tour of SAC, Air National Guard and Air Force Reserve bases operating the KC-135As, demonstrating the benefits of the re-engining to military officials and community leaders.

Funds are included in the 1981 Defence budget to provide for the conversion of one KC-135A to the new configuration, with first flight scheduled to be made on 1 October 1982; a 200-hr flight test programme would be conducted at Edwards AFB, being completed by May 1983. The USAF hopes to convert up to 300 KC-135As, but the initial objective is a 100-aircraft programme, with funds for the first 10 of these to be included in the FY82 budget. If this programme goes to plan, deliveries of KC-135REs to the USAF would begin in 1984. In addition, the *Armée de l'Air* has already announced its intention to fit CFM-56s to its 11 C-135Fs. The modified aircraft are expected to have an increased gross weight of 325,000 lb (147 420 kg), up from 316,000 lb (143 338 kg), with a strengthened undercarriage. For a given mission, the KC-135RE will be able to offload up to twice as much fuel; there will also be important advantages in the take-off performance in hot-and-high conditions, in reduced external noise levels and reduced fuel consumption by the tanker fleet. One estimate puts the final saving from the re-engined KC-135 tanker fleet at some 2·3 million barrels a year, or about 3 per cent of the USAF's *total* annual fuel consumption.

The forthcoming introduction into the USAF inventory of more than 30 McDonnell Douglas KC-10A Extender tankers will give a major boost to the Air Forces' aerial refuelling capabilities, but will do little to reduce the significance of the KC-135 fleet; large numbers of tankers continue to be needed to meet daily operational tasks and the larger fuel load carried by each KC-10 is valuable only in respect of certain specific missions (see AIR INTERNATIONAL/October 1980). The airframe life of the KC-135s poses little limitation, as already noted; fitting new engines, plus the various other updates described in the foregoing accounts will produce a tanker well able to meet USAF needs up to the year 2010 or beyond. □

The concluding instalment of this account, to be published next month, will give details of the EC-135, RC-135 and other special-purpose variants of the basic aircraft.

**The Boeing 707-3J9Cs delivered to the IIAF between 1974 and 1976 were unique in having the flying-boom system married to commercial-type 707 airframes. Six of these aircraft also had Beech Model 1080 hose-and-drogue pods under each wing tip (see AIR INTERNATIONAL/December 1976) to serve the IIAF Grumman F-14 Tomcats. Boeing had earlier made a trial installation of these pods on a company-owned 707 and two of the five Canadian Armed Forces Boeing 707s were so fitted in 1971. The RAAF is currently considering converting three ex-Qantas 707-320Cs to tanker configuration.*

IN PRINT

"Legion Condor 1936-1939; Eine illustrierte Dokumentation"
by Karl Ries and Hans Ring
Verlag Dieter Hoffmann, Mainz-Ebersheim, DM68
288 pp, 8¼ in by 11¾ in, illustrated

TWO acknowledged exponents of World War II *Luftwaffe* literature, Herren Ries and Ring, have here combined forces and talent to produce what is arguably the definitive pictorial work of reference on the part Germany played in the air war over Spain between 1936-1939.

In 288 pages, and almost 500 pictures, they have achieved that acme of pictorial compilation: the breath of life. Every page exudes the flavour of the times.* This is not just another lumping together of contemporary photographs on a common theme, but rather a carefully chosen, knowledgeable and objective selection of illustrations which accompany the reader through 16 chronological chapters charting the causes, the course and the outcome of the Spanish Civil War as seen through the eyes of the Legion. One minor criticism for the English-speaking market is that the text, unlike many of the authors' previous books, is not bi-lingual but in German alone. Much interesting detail is inevitably lost.

However, drawing heavily on their own specialised fields of *Luftwaffe* markings and personnel respectively, the authors present a fascinating collection of photos depicting the Legion's aircraft in a wide variety of hitherto unknown and unsuspected finishes and markings, together with portraits and informal group shots of many a youthful face and familiar name destined soon to gain fame on a wider stage. And there is much more besides; illustrations of Italian and Spanish aircraft, the latter both Nationalist and Republican, and ranging from such antiquities as the de Havilland D.H.9 up to "modern" American tourers. There is also a leavening of the tanks and armoured vehicles as used by both sides (the most intriguing perhaps being several very DIY Republican armoured lorries), plus some evocative shots of the towns and landscape which the combatants fought for and over.

All this, together with maps, tables and close on 40 pages of comprehensive appendices (unit emblems, codes, serials, successes and losses, etc), makes for an absorbing volume by any yardstick, and one which more than justifies its rather steep cover price at today's rate of exchange. — JW

"Legion Condor 1936-1939" reviewed on this page is heavily illustrated throughout, the vast majority of these illustrations having remained unpublished hitherto. Two of these photographs reproduced here depict (above) a Bf 109D of 2./J88 and (below) a trio of He 51s of 1./J88, that in the foreground being flown by Staffelkapitän Harro Harder.

"The Encyclopaedia of World Air Power"
Consultant Editor Bill Gunston
Hamlyn Publishing Group Ltd, Feltham, Mddx, £15·00
384 pp, 9 in by 11¾ in, illustrated

IF EVER there has been a *tour de force* among books devoted to the current military aviation scene then that book must be *"The Encyclopaedia of World Air Power"*, with its sixteen hundred or so illustrations! The first section of this book, comprising some 50 pages, is devoted to succinct descriptions of the world's air forces, each illustrated with national insignia in full colour — these being, incidentally, noticeably more up-to-date than those included in other recent books surveying world air power — and, for the most part, photos of representative aircraft equipment. The major proportion of the book, consisting of 300-plus pages, is concerned with the aircraft themselves and is a picture buff's delight, with hundreds of illustrations — black-and-white and full colour photos, general arrangement and comparison drawings, colour profiles and some superb, albeit oddly arranged, double-page three-view colour drawings by Keith Fretwell — that will satiate the gourmand and provide plenty for the gourmet.

The final section of the book surveys air-launched missiles, although, regrettably, only a proportion of these missiles are actually illustrated — with the amount of money that has obviously been expended on illustrating this lavish publication, this reviewer would have imagined that the added cost of a few line drawings of missiles could have been no more than a drop in the bucket. The aircraft coverage of this book is genuinely encyclopaedic and its content offers many hours of fascinating browsing. The retail price may sound rather high, even in these days of grossly inflated book prices, but will not seem inordinate once you have hefted this weighty tome from its shelf and perused its packed pages.

"Air Power: The World's Air Forces"
Edited by Anthony Robinson
Orbis Publishing Ltd, London, £9·95
304 pp, 8¾ in by 11¾ in, illustrated

BOOKS purporting to provide a detailed survey of the world's air arms are now legion and *"Air Power"* can be numbered among the better of them. Essentially a spin-off from the weekly part-work *Wings* in being assembled from a series of articles that appeared in that publication, *"Air Power"* is none the worse for that — unless, of course, you subscribed to *Wings* — and is a handsome volume superbly illustrated throughout in colour and of a standard of printing that is a credit to the Hong Kong printing house responsible. Overall it is a competent reference albeit suffering in some measure from the fact that the diverse authors contributing the component parts of this volume have adopted differing standards of detail, while the chapter ostensibly devoted to the Warsaw Pact air forces (but, in fact, making no reference to any air arm other than that of the Soviet Union and then only in rather sweeping generalities) would seem to have been intended for a somewhat more juvenile readership. An odd feature of the book concerns national insignia, which, scattered through the relevant chapters, are as often as not unaccompanied by identification. Theoretically, the insignia illustrations mate

**Even down to what the well-dressed airman wore when perforce patronising 3./J.88's exposed and draughty thunderbox in the depths of a Spanish winter!*

BEECHCRAFT KING AIR B100

BEECHCRAFT KING AIR E90

BEECHCRAFT KING AIR F90

BEECHCRAFT SUPER KING AIR 200

BEECHCRAFT KING AIR C90

KING AIR B100.

Top Speed	265 kts
Cruise Speed	262 kts
Range	2,454 km
Service Ceiling	8,576 m
Useful Load	2,160 kg
Seats	8-15

KING AIR F90.

Top Speed	267 kts
Cruise Speed	251 kts
Range	2,919 km
Service Ceiling	9,084 m
Useful Load	1,991 kg
Seats	8-10

KING AIR E90.

Top Speed	249 kts
Cruise Speed	245 kts
Range	3,009 km
Service Ceiling	8,419 m
Useful Load	1,863 kg
Seats	6-10

KING AIR C90.

Top Speed	222 kts
Cruise Speed	216 kts
Range	2,372 km
Service Ceiling	8,565 m
Useful Load	1,781 kg
Seats	6-10

For more information, contact your nearest Beechcraft Distributor. Or, if you prefer, write to: Beech Aircraft Corporation, 9799 E. Central, Wichita, Kansas 67201, U.S.A.

EAGLE AIRCRAFT SERVICES, LTD.
Leavesden Aerodrome
Watford WD2 7BY, England
Phone: (9273) 79611/7 (Garston, Herts)
Cable: EAGLESERV (Watford) VIA WUI
Telex: (851) 261502 (VIA WUI)

with adjacent photographs of the aircraft of the air force concerned, but there are a number of instances where the insignia cannot be *seen* on the aircraft and others where obsolete insignia is illustrated with the current insignia seen in the photographs, or *vice versa*. The colours of some of the markings — particularly the blues — are decidedly odd in places, but, overall, this book is good value for money by today's standards and to be recommended.

"The Stirling Bomber"
by M J F Bowyer
Faber & Faber, London, £10
226 pp, 6 in by $9\frac{1}{8}$ in, illustrated

OF THE four-engined bombers that served the RAF during World War II, the Short Stirling was the least successful — the inevitable consequence, perhaps, of being first. The Specification which produced the Stirling defined a quantum jump in heavy bomber design, requiring an aeroplane that would have greater range with heavier bomb load than any previous RAF bomber, without sacrificing performance. Both for the Directorate of Operational Requirements at the Air Ministry and for Shorts' design team at Rochester, the Stirling was a step into the unknown, and it was to suffer the price of being a pioneer.

Operationally, the Stirling was soon overtaken and surpassed by the Halifax and the Lancaster; left to serve out the war in rôles other than bombing, it has until now attracted only scant attention from the writers of World War II history. With this book, Mike Bowyer goes a long way to redressing the balance. An avowed Stirling enthusiast since the early war days when "as an impressionable teenager, I had thrilled to the sight of those mighty machines", he traces in this volume the difficult gestation of the giant bomber, its important contribution to the Bomber Command offensive until 1943 and its later use on other duties.

The latter included troop transport and glider towing in support of the invasion of Europe in 1944, passenger and freight transport, service with the Special Duty squadrons in support of SOE operations and electronic warfare in No 100 Group. All these activities are faithfully recorded. Appendices give details of Stirling production, Stirling squadrons and other operating units, and list by serial number the aircraft used by each squadron and their fates.

There are many interesting photographs, a number of them not previously published, and a series of drawings depicting the camouflage schemes and markings.

"Halifax"
by K A Merrick
Ian Allan Ltd, Shepperton, Surrey, £9·95
224 pp, $6\frac{7}{8}$ in by $9\frac{1}{2}$ in, illustrated

AFTER all the publicity enjoyed by the Avro Lancaster — deservedly regarded as the most outstanding heavy bomber of World War II — it is good to see both the Halifax and the Stirling enjoying a somewhat belated recognition of their respective contributions to the war effort. This "illustrated history of a classic World War II bomber" is the second Halifax book to appear recently (see "Raider", reviewed in the February 1979 issue) and it makes a good companion volume to Mike Bowyer's "Stirling" reviewed on this page.

The genesis of the Halifax, by way of the twin-engined H.P.55 and H.P.56, is traced somewhat sketchily, but can be found in more detail in Chris Barnes' excellent history of "Handley Page Aircraft Since 1907" (Putnam, 1976) and in other works dealing with the pre-war evolution of bombers for the RAF. The account of operational initiation, the early trials and tribulations and the consequent development of the Mk II and later marks sets the scene for the chapters that follow. These describe, in adequate and interesting detail, the use of the Halifax to support the Bomber Command offensive and the major development effort that went on at the same time to improve its efficiency.

Unlike the Lancaster, the Halifax bomber saw quite extensive service in the Middle East, North Africa and Italy, as described in one of the chapters here. At home, it took on several other important rôles, serving with Coastal Command for maritime reconnaissance, as a troop transport and glider tug, as an agent-dropper for the SOE and with No 100 Group on electronic countermeasures. As a cargo carrier, the Halifax sported a pannier suspended in the bomb-bay and this in turn gave rise to the post-war civil versions including the Halton, which entered service with BOAC soon after the war ended. All these many aspects of the Halifax story are fully covered in a well-illustrated volume, which has the inevitable and necessary appendices listing RAF user-units, production details, a list of civil-registered Halifaxes and a summary of design data for all the many variants.

On the nostalgia trail

Farnborough Commentary
by Raymond Baxter
Patrick Stephens Ltd, Cambridge, £6·95
112 pp, 8 in by $9\frac{1}{4}$ in, illustrated

ANYONE who, like the author of this volume (and the writer of this review), has attended all the Farnborough air shows will almost certainly enjoy a nostalgic journey through these pages. Raymond Baxter, as a BBC commentator throughout that time, has enjoyed a privileged view of successive Farnboroughs, often from a seat in one or other of the aircraft on display, so he has some interesting and amusing anecdotes to tell. He has, moreover, a professional way with words which makes for pleasant reading.

At more than 6p a page, however, it has to be said that the book is not outstanding in value-for-money terms. There are, it is true, more than 200 photographs — the majority depicting aircraft displaying at Farnborough although there are 17 of the author — but none are in colour. There is not a lot of space left for words, but Raymond Baxter does succeed in capturing much of the atmosphere, drama and sheer pleasure that characterised the Farnborough shows of the 'fifties and 'sixties. Readers who did not have the opportunity to attend those shows may not find it so easy to understand the enthusiasm he describes or to appreciate just how much it has changed (not necessarily for the better) by being enlarged to include "foreigners" (ie, non-British exhibits).

Civil registers

THE civil aircraft enthusiast, spotter and registration collector are well served by a number of recent publications from the specialist publishers. The titles listed below have reached us for review.

The two Air-Britain registers follow the customary format but "Airline Fleets '80" introduces some changes, including the addition of major US third-level airlines, to bring the total number of operators listed to 875 in 159 countries. Both spiral-bound and perfect-bound editions are available, the quoted prices being inclusive of postage from the Air-Britain Sales Department, 9 Rook Close, Elm Park, Hornchurch, Essex, RM12 5QH.

The two MCP registers, like the previously-published "British Civil Aircraft Registers", are historically complete from the start of the respective listings (in Norway, N-1 issued in 1919 and in Belgium, O-BABA in 1920). Every registration is listed, with details of aircraft, c/n, owner, and eventual disposition.

"Southern Europe and the Middle East Civil Aircraft Registers 1980"
Edited by Ian P Burnett
An Air-Britain Publication, £4·50
132 pp, 7 in by $9\frac{1}{4}$ in, illustrated

"1980 Registers of Germany, D- DM-"
Compiled by P M Gerhardt
An Air-Britain Publication, £6·00
154 pp, 7 in by $9\frac{1}{4}$ in, illustrated

"Airline Fleets '80"
An Air-Britain Publication, £6·00
269 pp, $4\frac{5}{8}$ in by $6\frac{5}{8}$ in

"Belgian Civil Aircraft since 1920"
by John Appleton and Armand Thys
Midland Counties Publications (£3·95 soft-back or £5·95 hardback), from 24 The Hollow, Earl Shilton, Leicester, LE9 7NA
128 pp, $5\frac{7}{8}$ in by $8\frac{1}{4}$ in, illustrated

"Norwegian Civil Aircraft since 1919"
Compiled by Kay Hagby
Midland Counties Publications (address as above), £3·95 softback or £5·95 hardback
120 pp, $5\frac{7}{8}$ in by $8\frac{1}{4}$ in, illustrated

New editions

"Aircraft Annual 1981"
Edited by Martin Horseman
Ian Allan Ltd, Shepperton, Surrey, £3·95
130 pp, 7 in by $9\frac{1}{4}$ in, illustrated

A DOZEN articles and photo-features provide something for most tastes, ranging in their content-matter from World War I to the present day and embracing military and civil, with many photographs.

"The Soviet War Machine"
Edited by Ray Bonds
Salamander Books Ltd, London, £7·95
250 pp, $8\frac{1}{4}$ in by $11\frac{3}{4}$ in, illustrated

ONE of the well-known Salamander "War Machines", making a second appearance in a slightly revised and updated version. Useful compilation covering the strategy, tactics and weapons of the Soviet Air Force, Navy and Army.

"Jane's Weapon Systems 1980-81"
Edited by Ron Pretty
Jane's Publishing Co Ltd, London, £40
934 pp, $8\frac{1}{4}$ in by $12\frac{1}{2}$ in, illustrated

THE ANNUAL revision of an important Yearbook, now in its 11th edition. By its nature, this one lacks the wider appeal of the "Aircraft" and "Ships" Yearbooks but it is not one iota less valuable in its more specialised field, which it covers authoritatively and comprehensively.

Plaudits for the Peripherals

EVERY LEISURE INDUSTRY attracts to its periphery like bees to a honeypot a range of small organisations operating within the shadow of the mainstream companies; peripheral concerns metaphorically scooping up the fall-out left by the activities of the leaders forming the vertebrae of that industry's backbone and fulfilling functions non-viable in the context of *big* business. The model aircraft kit industry is no exception and many are the small companies around its fringe supplementing the output of the hardcore of established kit producers.

Some of these peripherals are transient, soon wilting and dying, while others flourish and their appellations become, if not exactly household names, then comparatively well-known to the modelling fraternity — what reader of this column can lay hand on heart and declaim that he has never heard of, say, Rareplane or Modeldecal? Producing vac-forms, limited-run injection-moulded components, conversion kits, decals and other adjuncts to our pastime, they invariably have two things in common: they are run by enthusiasts and they are small — frequently little more than one-man businesses. Their enthusiasm and size are vital to their survival, for they cater primarily for the cadre of truly dedicated modellers who have built up a high degree of expertise over the years but represent a strictly limited proportion — perhaps 10 per cent or less — of the overall market for aircraft kits.

The peripherals make an extremely valuable contribution to the modelling scene which grows in importance with the passage of the years. For example, the increasing discernment of the modelling fraternity is being paralleled by a demand for decals other than those accompanying the kits and concerns such as Microscale and Modeldecal, to mention but two from a blossoming fringe industry, have responded in sterling fashion to establish what is now accepted as a highly desirable back-up for the major kit producers around which the whole of this leisure industry might be said to rotate.

Vac-forms, too, are now well established, catering primarily to the tastes for the more exotic or esoteric subject matter of the more skilled modeller, but more recent of conception are the limited-production injection-moulded components now often incorporated in what are primarily vacuum-formed kits. These are made by an injection process utilising small machines and dispensing with the immensely expensive hardened-steel moulds necessary for conventional injection moulding, and the cost is low enough to render runs even as short as a thousand kits a viable proposition. The results now being obtained by such small organisations as Guano in the USA and Veeday in the UK are highly encouraging; they have succeeded in manufacturing by this method and successfully marketing complete injection-moulded kits at prices well within the reach of most modellers and, what is more, within the average modeller's ability to translate into models standing comparison with most of those that they make from conventional kits. For proof, one has only to look at the recently-released IK-2 from Guano and B.E.2c from Veeday.

Yet another facet of this expanding fringe business takes the form of accessories, which, although as yet barely more than lining up for take-off, has considerable promise. We have had items such as drop tanks and bombs, and aerofoil-section strips for struts, and last month we reviewed in this column the first kits of cockpit details for the larger-scale models which may be utilised to achieve true exhibition standards. For long may these peripherals prosper for they provide a service which we need and, owing to sheer economics, can never be provided by the major kit producers.

Failures recalled

"You win a few and you lose a few" — a saying that might be viewed as apposite to the British aircraft industry (or, indeed, any aircraft industry) during WW II, for it had its share of spectacular successes and a leavening of abysmal failures. Two of its failures, if not exactly abysmal, were the Armstrong Whitworth Albemarle and the Blackburn Botha, both of which were built in large numbers despite being found unsuited for their intended rôles because once production momentum had been built up widespread disruption would have followed in the wake of sudden and total cancellation. Thus, the Albemarle, designed as a reconnaissance bomber, saw service as a special transport and glider tug, and the Botha, intended as a general reconnaissance and torpedo-bomber, served out its days as an operational trainer. These undistinguished aircraft are never likely to find favour with the major kit manufacturers and Contrail has elected to replace the existing vacuum-formed kits that have been listed in its catalogue for some time past with two completely new 1/72nd scale kits of the Albemarle and Botha representing a major improvement on what has gone before.

Contrail has made a fine job of both kits, including, in each case, injection-moulded engines, propellers, wheels, undercarriage struts and exhaust pipes, and very good decals. All of the vac-formed parts — 32 for the Albemarle and 22 for the Botha — are cleanly moulded and of more than adequate thickness, with a considerable amount of fine surface detailing, while the assembly instructions, three-view drawings and detail photographs are of a very high standard, including all necessary painting information. Flight deck interiors are well catered for, and these kits exhibit a high standard of production throughout. We have no information as to price at the time of closing for press, but readers can contact Sutcliffe Productions (The Orchard, Westcombe, Shepton Mallet, Somerset) for more information, although most specialist model shops can supply these kits.

This month's colour subject

Avions Marcel Dassault-Breguet Aviation has, over the years, come in for a lot of criticism over its high-pressure and often less-than-candid marketing practices — behind-the-scenes activities in India to persuade the powers-that-be to jettison the Anglo-French Jaguar in favour of the purely French Mirage 2000 have seen much press mileage of late, particularly in the UK — but, in our view, if the heat gets too great one should get out of the kitchen; no amount of pressure, covert or overt, will today persuade a major air force to accept an incompetent aeroplane and Dassault-Breguet's aeroplanes are anything *but* that! Indeed, this highly virile French company's Mirage series of fighters have successively demonstrated an expertise that other, less successful European aircraft manufacturers can but envy!

The swept-wing Mirage F1 is now busily emulating the success of the delta-winged Mirage fighters that preceded it and with production rate currently running at about a half-dozen per month — small beer by US or Soviet standards perhaps — this versatile fighter has been rolling off the assembly line for almost a decade yet more customers always seem to appear on the horizon. The Mirage F1 has fared quite well at the hands of the plastic kit manufacturers and is today represented by three kits, two to 1/72nd scale and one to 1/48th scale. In the former, there is a choice between Airfix and Heller, both making up into good, well detailed models, but the French company's kit has an edge, particularly in the finish of the component parts and general finesse. On the other hand, the Airfix product scores when it comes to price, so far as the UK is concerned at least, so choice may well depend upon whether or not the extra touch of class justifies to the individual modeller the additional cost. In the larger 1/48th scale category, Esci has comparatively recently produced a Mirage F1 kit, which, distributed in the UK by Humbrol, is an accurate and well-detailed product to be unhesitatingly recommended.

Phantom precursor

Our first impression on opening up Airfix's new kit of the McDonnell F2H Banshee was one of surprise not evoked by the kit itself but by the box which seemed to be about twice as large as was necessary to comfortably house its contents! Is this really an appropriate kit for inclusion in Series 4, Airfix? In our view, it should have been placed fairly and squarely in Series 3, but here it is, reminiscent of the "before and after" slimming advertisements, with a skeletal figure wearing the suit of a very obese individual!

Insofar as the kit itself is concerned, this is certainly a nice enough product, and as the first

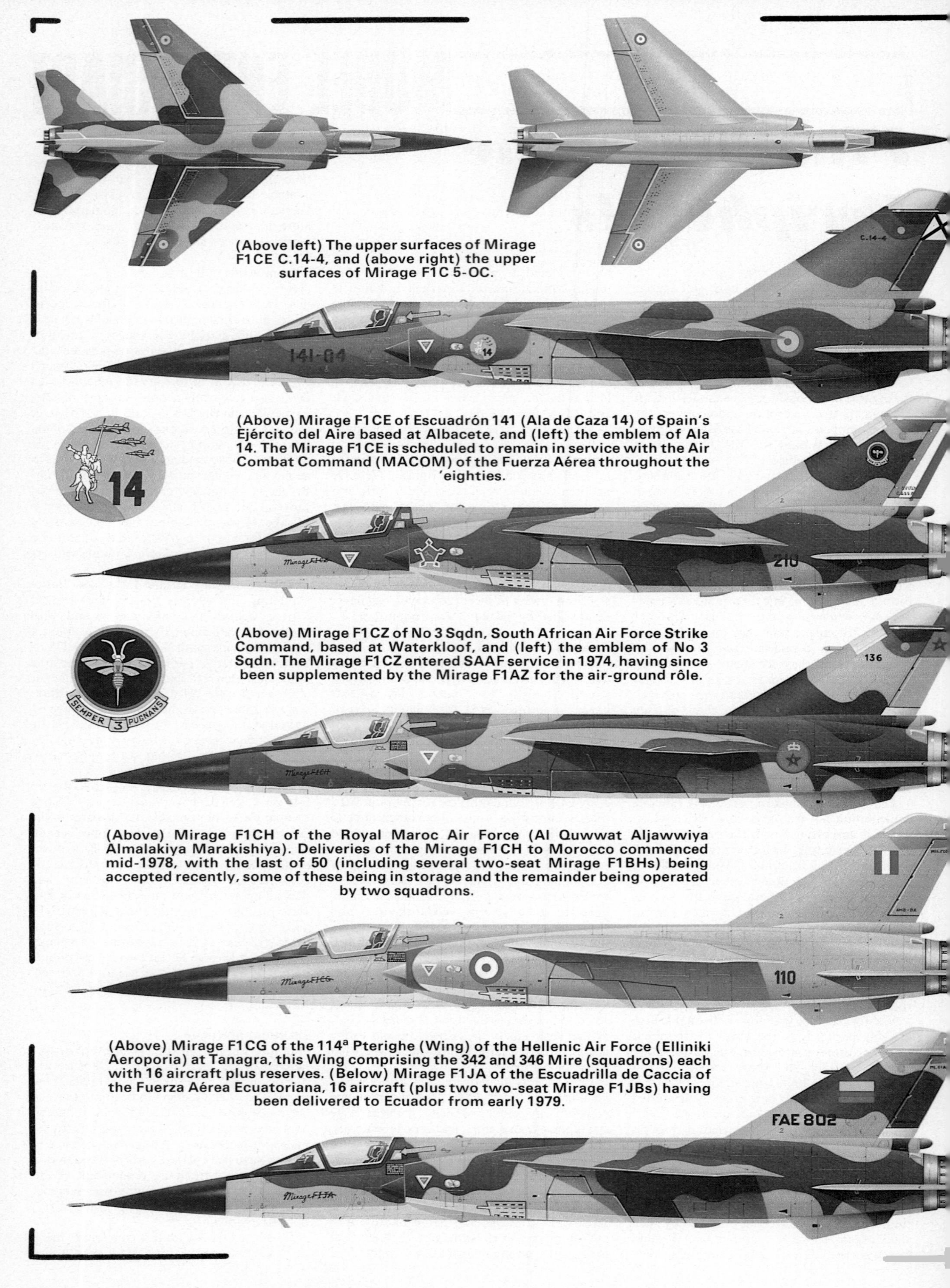

(Above left) The upper surfaces of Mirage F1CE C.14-4, and (above right) the upper surfaces of Mirage F1C 5-OC.

(Above) Mirage F1CE of Escuadrón 141 (Ala de Caza 14) of Spain's Ejército del Aire based at Albacete, and (left) the emblem of Ala 14. The Mirage F1CE is scheduled to remain in service with the Air Combat Command (MACOM) of the Fuerza Aérea throughout the 'eighties.

(Above) Mirage F1CZ of No 3 Sqdn, South African Air Force Strike Command, based at Waterkloof, and (left) the emblem of No 3 Sqdn. The Mirage F1CZ entered SAAF service in 1974, having since been supplemented by the Mirage F1AZ for the air-ground rôle.

(Above) Mirage F1CH of the Royal Maroc Air Force (Al Quwwat Aljawwiya Almalakiya Marakishiya). Deliveries of the Mirage F1CH to Morocco commenced mid-1978, with the last of 50 (including several two-seat Mirage F1BHs) being accepted recently, some of these being in storage and the remainder being operated by two squadrons.

(Above) Mirage F1CG of the 114ª Pterighe (Wing) of the Hellenic Air Force (Elliniki Aeroporia) at Tanagra, this Wing comprising the 342 and 346 Mire (squadrons) each with 16 aircraft plus reserves. (Below) Mirage F1JA of the Escuadrilla de Caccia of the Fuerza Aérea Ecuatoriana, 16 aircraft (plus two two-seat Mirage F1JBs) having been delivered to Ecuador from early 1979.

and so far the only injection-moulded kit in 1/72nd scale of the aircraft that really placed the now-distinguished McDonnell concern on the map is particularly welcome. Conceived during the closing months of WW II, the Banshee was to be built in six major models delivered between August 1948 and October 1953, a total of 892 production aircraft being built, its career including service in the Korean conflict. The basic version selected by Airfix for its kit is the F2H-2, characterised by a slightly longer fuselage and wingtip tanks, and there are 57 component parts moulded in midnite blue plastic, plus a very clear one-piece transparent canopy.

We cannot fault this kit on outline accuracy and the surface detailing is neatly realised, part being engraved and part being raised but all fine. The fit of the component parts is good throughout, and the ailerons and rudder have been formed as inset sections in order to ensure adequately thin trailing edges. All three undercarriage units are nicely simulated, but in each case the wheel well is too shallow, a fault which we would hardly expect to encounter in a modern kit. The cockpit interior, which includes a pilot figure, is no more than adequate, but the kit includes a good selection of external stores, these including the wingtip fuel tanks, and four bombs and four rockets, each with its individual pylon.

An alternative nose section is provided to produce the F2H-2P photographic model, the basic nose having to be cut away along lines scored inside the fuselage to effect the transformation, but Airfix has not included the appropriate transparent panels for the cameras — three each side — which are simply marked in outline on the plastic. These panels were rectangular and flat, and so may quite easily be added by the modeller, but we would have liked to have seen them included in the kit — the boxtop illustration shows them clearly enough! The decal sheet is good and offers markings for a US Navy F2H-2 from VF-172 and a USMC F2H-2P from VMJ-1, both of which were Korean conflict participants. This kit is retailed in the UK at £1·65.

Alpha Jets ad infinitum

With the advent of a 1/72nd scale kit from Airfix, we calculate that there are now no fewer than five currently-available kits of the Dassault-Breguet/Dornier Alpha Jet, two to the same scale by "Matchbox" and Heller, and two larger versions by Heller (1/50th) and Esci (1/48th). Confining ourselves to consideration of the smaller-scale versions only, we can eliminate the "Matchbox" offering as this kit, admittedly a very early effort, is simply not in the same class as the competition, while the new Airfix kit has formidable competition from the preceding Heller offering both as regards quality and price.

Treating the Airfix kit on its own merits, however, it is very well proportioned and accurate, with 64 well-fitting components in a medium shade of grey plastic with a one-piece clear canopy. The surface detailing is generally very fine, with just a hint of heaviness here and there, while the encapsulated cockpit interior is good, although we admit to a twinge of sympathy for the two pilot figures whose legs have been amputated at the knees — we appreciate that plastic is expensive nowadays, but there are limits beyond which economies are self-defeating! Both German and Belgian versions of the Alpha Jet are catered for by means of alternative nose tips, and there is a selection of ordnance applicable mainly to the former which also has an arrester hook not

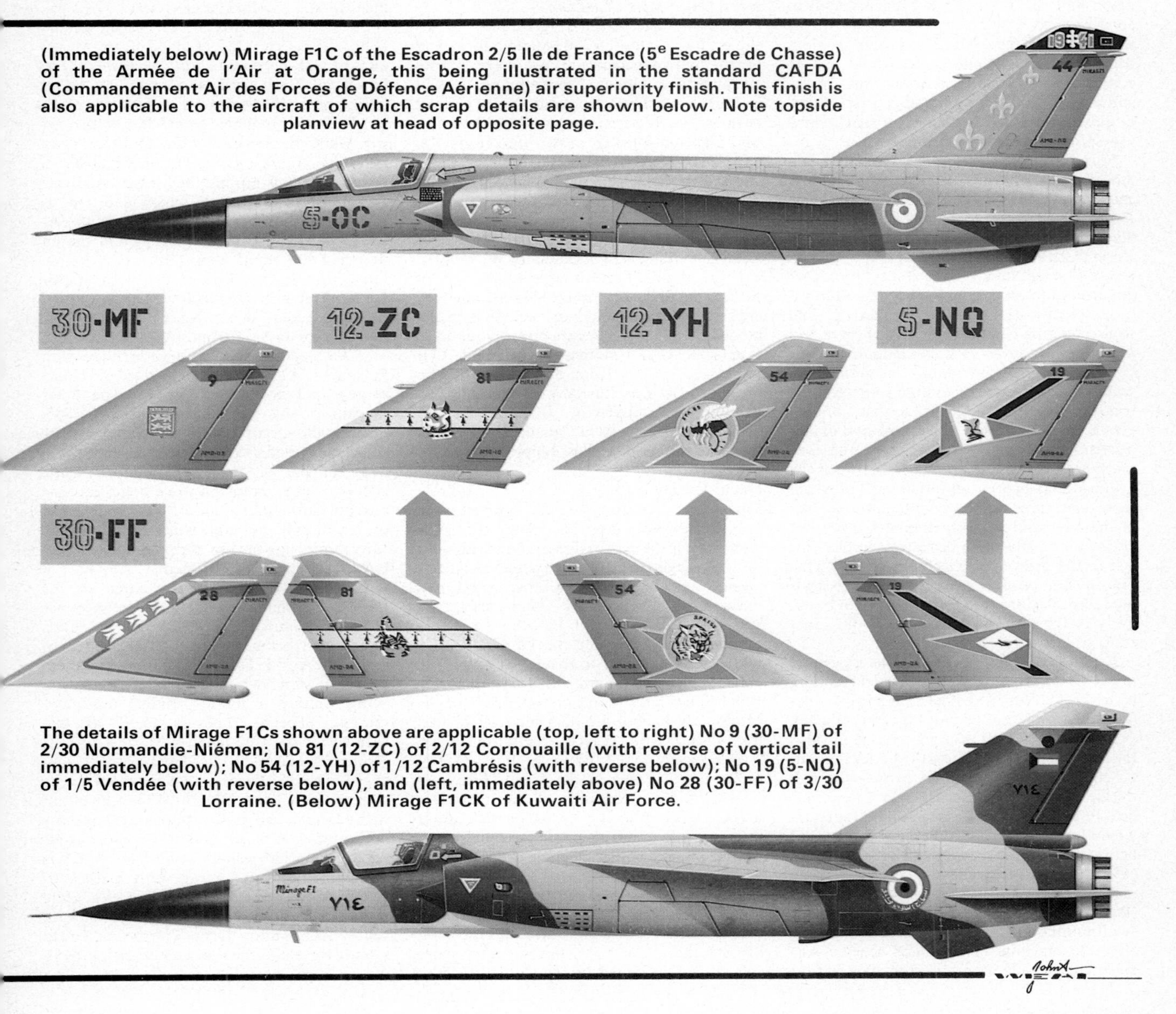

(Immediately below) Mirage F1C of the Escadron 2/5 Ile de France (5e Escadre de Chasse) of the Armée de l'Air at Orange, this being illustrated in the standard CAFDA (Commandement Air des Forces de Défence Aérienne) air superiority finish. This finish is also applicable to the aircraft of which scrap details are shown below. Note topside planview at head of opposite page.

The details of Mirage F1Cs shown above are applicable (top, left to right) No 9 (30-MF) of 2/30 Normandie-Niémen; No 81 (12-ZC) of 2/12 Cornouaille (with reverse of vertical tail immediately below); No 54 (12-YH) of 1/12 Cambrésis (with reverse below); No 19 (5-NQ) of 1/5 Vendée (with reverse below), and (left, immediately above) No 28 (30-FF) of 3/30 Lorraine. (Below) Mirage F1CK of Kuwaiti Air Force.

featured by Belgian machines. The *Luftwaffe* Alpha Jet has a 27-mm Mauser cannon mounted asymmetrically beneath the fuselage and the kit includes this item in satisfying detail. The decals cover an aircraft ascribed to *Jagdbombergeschwader* 49 at Fürstenfeldbruck and one of an unspecified unit of the *Force Aérienne Belge*. Being included in Series 3, this kit retails at £1.20 in the UK and represents reasonable value by present standards.

Like the Hawk, featured as our colour subject in the September issue, the Alpha Jet is now entering service with several air arms and, in consequence, a number of different national markings and several colour schemes are now applicable — a Togolese example was demonstrated at Farnborough International 80.

French 'thirties elegance . . .

The mid-'thirties witnessed the "golden age" of air racing in the USA dominated by overpowered diminutive projectiles which gave the impression of being large radial engines with the minimum of supporting airframe appended. Then, in 1936, a slim, elegant and relatively low-powered monoplane built by the veteran French Caudron concern and piloted by Michel Detroyat wrested the Greve and Thompson trophies from the US contenders and would almost certainly have swept the board but for its withdrawal following complaints — apparently quite unfounded — that the French entry was sponsored by its government.

Prior to this, the Caudron C.450/460 racing monoplanes, of which four were built, had emerged as victors in the '34, '35 and '36 *Coupe Deutsch* events, and had also held the world's landplane speed record for a year, from December 1934 until December 1935 — a class record that still stands. Even Heller has not yet got around to producing a kit of the Caudron racer, but we do now have a superb 1/32nd scale rendering from Williams Brothers of San Marcos, California, as a companion to their Gee Bee and Wedell-Williams kits to the same scale. Moulded, apart from the single canopy transparency, in an appropriate shade of blue plastic, the kit consists of 60 parts and makes provision for building any one of the four machines. The major differences between the Caudrons lay in their undercarriages of which there were three different configurations, two of these being fixed with streamlined fairings and spats, and the other being retractable. This last-mentioned was applicable to No 6909, the Greve/Thompson winner, and if this version is modelled, the lower wing panels have to be cut away — they are clearly marked on the inner surface — to form the wheel wells.

Externally, simplicity of line was a keynote of the Caudron racer and the model resulting from this kit reproduces the clean, simple lines faithfully, while, at the same time, reproducing every visible feature inside the cockpit and also the forward portion of the six-cylinder Renault air-cooled engine which may be seen through the air intake in the nose. The very fine surface detailing includes the flush-mounted radiators which formed panels on the port side of and below the engine cowling. The decals are extensive and of excellent quality, including markings applicable to all four aircraft at all stages of their racing careers. In fact, only a small number of these decals can be used for any one machine. The colour scheme was essentially simple, being overall blue with a thin tricolour band diagonally around the fuselage, to which was added racing numbers on the wings and fuselage, and the manufacturer's descriptive legend on the fin and rudder. The kit is accompanied by a full 1/32nd scale drawing with every variation of detail and marking clearly shown. This is an outstanding kit with tremendous appeal for those with a feeling for the era of which it was a representative.

. . . and American brute force

Representative of the powerful radial-engined racers specially designed for the US National Air Races of the mid 'thirties and typical of the competition that the previously-described Caudron had to face was the LTR.14 *Pesco Special*, originally built in 1936 as the Turner-Laird Meteor by Lawrence Brown Aircraft to the ideas of that flamboyant air racing personality, Col Roscoe Turner. When the Meteor's wing loading proved to be too high, the aircraft was modified by Matty Laird and, as the *Pesco Special* with a 1,000 hp Twin Wasp engine, it was flown by Turner to victory in the 1938 Thompson Trophy Race, repeating its success in the following year after being rechristened *Miss Champion*.

Airframe has selected this racer as the subject for its latest 1/72nd scale vac-form, and for the more experienced it will make up into an attractive model, especially as the kit includes a very fine set of decals for the aircraft both as *Pesco Special* and as *Miss Champion*. The vacuum-formed parts total only 16, covering the basic structures of fuselage, wings and tail surfaces, plus the undercarriage legs, spats and canopy. Among those parts *not* included are the engine, wheels, propeller and cockpit interior, and so a high degree of scratch-building skill is called for in completing this model, There is little in the way of surface detailing on the mouldings, but they are well formed and we feel that many modellers will find the extra effort required to supplement the kit contents is worthwhile. Our sample kit came from John Tarvin who produced it for Burnaby Hobbies (5209 Rumble Street, Burnaby, BC, Canada V5J 2B7). Specialist shops in Canada, the UK and the USA should be able to supply the kit.

Decal Review

Microscale: To describe the producers of Microscale decals as prolific would seem to be understating the case as Krasel Industries seem to be averaging a new sheet weekly, and this month we have no fewer than eight new releases, all of them for 1/48th scale. The subject aircraft are all jets, but we have representative types for the USAF, the US Navy and the USMC to ensure variety.

Sheets Nos 48-80 and -81 are both for F-100D Super Sabres and are intended for the Monogram kit but are also suitable for that from Esci. The first sheet covers two machines, both basically in natural metal finish. One of these, *Pretty Penny* of the 481st TFS *Green Crusaders*, has a drawing of the lady after which it was presumably named on each side of the nose, with unit badges and green flashes on the fin, while the other machine, from the 20th TFW, sports multi-coloured fin flashes plus red flashes on each side of the fuselage, plus four badges, three on the fuselage and one on the fin. There are two more aircraft on No 48-81 and these are, if anything, rather more colourful. One Super Sabre from the 450th TFS (FW-263) has a stylised white bird motif on a purple band outlined in white and black on the fin, and a similarly outlined purple-and-white checked nose, a large cobra in green and yellow decorating the fuselage. The other machine featured is from the 49th TFW and has its entire vertical tail and the nose painted in a red, yellow and blue design. Buzz numbers and a host of small markings are included for all four schemes.

Sheets 48-82 and -83 cover respectively USMC and US Navy F-8 Crusaders, two machines from each service and all in the basic gull grey and white scheme. From VMF(AW)-235 comes an F-8E with red areas superimposed with white stars on nose, fin and ventral strakes, while an F-8C from VMF(AW)-334 sports a stylised red bird motif on each side of its fin and red lightning flashes on each ventral strake. The US Navy aircraft are an F-8E of VF-24 aboard the USS *Hancock* and an F-8H of VF-111 aboard the USS *Shangri-La*, each with very elaborate fin decorations in red and white, and, in the case of the second aircraft, a shark's mouth for the air intake. As with the Super Sabre sets, there is a plethora of smaller markings. The recommended kit is by Esci (ScaleCraft).

Sheet No 84 offers two exceptionally colourful A-7Es. One of these, from VA-83 aboard USS *Forrestal*, sports what we take to be a Ram's Head, with its nose pointing, rather oddly, vertically downward on each side of the fin. This motif is in black and white, with a red eye, while the rudder is white and the fin tip light blue. There is also a diagonal blue band, edged in yellow, around the forward fuselage. A similar band, but in black and red, is featured by the other A-7E, this time from VA-195 aboard the USS *Kittyhawk*, and the fin design of this aircraft almost defies description, incorporating a bird's head with multi-coloured feathers, these colours being repeated on the rudder. Sheet No 85 provides the markings of an A-7E from VA-94 *Shrikes*, also USS *Kittyhawk*, displaying a white rudder with red and black stars, and black-edged red bands at top and bottom of the fin. The other machine on this sheet, an A-7B from VA-205, has a highly-decorative Bi-centennial scheme comprising eight vari-coloured flashes and a "76" emblem for superimposition on a white rudder, a large green-and-white bomb-carrying bird appearing on the fin. All four A-7s are in the usual gull grey and white basic scheme. Microscale suggests use of the Monogram kit, but Esci's kit can also be used.

The last two sheets of this batch are for USMC F-4 Phantoms, the three on Sheet 48-86 being comparatively prosaic, the units represented being VMFA-232 (two aircraft) and VMFA-235. The basic colouring of these aircraft is standard, the individual decoration being confined to the fins, rudders and nose radomes. Sheet 48-87 covers three F-4Bs, one lettered for the Commander Marine Aircraft Group 32 (MAG-32), this having large black-edged orange fin flashes and black checks on its white rudder. From VMFA-312 is a Phantom with a large area of its fin-and-rudder assembly decorated with black and white checks outlined in red and yellow, while VMFA-323 is represented by an aircraft with black-and-yellow coiled snakes on each side of a white rudder, and black bands superimposed with yellow diamonds on the fin. The recommended kits are Revell for the F-4J and Entex fôr the F-4B. □

F J HENDERSON

ARGENTINA

FMA IA 58B & IA 66 PUCARÁ

WITH 44 delivered to the *Fuerza Aérea Argentina* by the beginning of September, when production was running at two per month with planned increase to three (and possibly four) monthly by the end of next year, the Pucará twin-turboprop close air support aircraft is now thoroughly established in service and the Fábrica Militar de Aviones at Córdoba is placing increased emphasis on variant development, both for indigenous use and for export. In FAA service, the initial series version of the Pucará, the IA 58A with Turboméca Astazou XVIG engines, has built up a reputation for sturdiness and flexibility, resulting in a hardening of foreign interest and three export contracts for two Latin American countries (unofficially reported to be Dominican Republic and Venezuela) and one Middle Eastern country are now in the final stages of negotiation, with announcement of the signing of the first of these believed to be imminent at the time of closing for press.

The latest variant of the Pucará, which was scheduled to commence its flight test programme at Córdoba early last month (October), is the Garrett-AiResearch TPE331-powered IA 66. The design of the TPE331 engine mount and nacelle has been undertaken by Volpar Incorporated of Van Nuys, Calif, on behalf of the FMA, the US company also being responsible for the first installation, the Pucará wing, complete with TPE331-11 engine being returned to Córdoba for application to the IA 66 prototype airframe on 29 August. The recently-certificated TPE331-11, which drives a Dowty Rotol R316 four-bladed metal propeller in its IA 66 installation, is rated at 1,000 shp, and the FMA believes that its availability as an option to the Astazou will markedly improve the prospects of the Pucará on the export market. Work will shortly commence on two pre-series examples of the TPE331-powered IA 66, which, intended for evaluation by the FAA, are scheduled to be completed in March.

The FMA envisages offering the IA 66 with both Garrett-AiResearch and Turboméca engines, and one version of this aircraft for which a final decision as to engine type has still to be made is a special airline pilot trainer variant to be delivered to the INAC (National Institute of Civil Aviation) at Moron next year, although the first of three-four Pucarás to be utilised by the INAC will have TPE331s. The IA 66 trainer will have full dual control and the special school by which it will be operated will effectively provide the FAA with a pool of commercial pilots possessing Pucará training available to the service in an emergency. A further version of the Pucará now under development for the FAA is a maritime surveillance and attack model, with search radar and a reconnaissance camera fit. Changes are to be embodied in the cockpits aimed at increasing crew comfort for long-endurance missions — the official requirement calls for a 10-hour endurance but this can be achieved by the standard IA 58A when carrying maximum external ferry fuel and few changes in the fuel system are therefore called for.

Flight development of the IA 58B Pucará-B, the prototype of which (AX-05) — actually a modification of the 25th series aircraft — commenced its test programme in the late spring of last year, is continuing and the prototype has now completed more than 150 hours flying; the two TPE331-engined pre-series IA 66s to be delivered for FAA evaluation next spring will be of Pucará-B configuration, although earlier proposals to introduce the -B model on the assembly line with the 61st series Pucará are not now being pursued. The latest programme calls for the 101st and subsequent Pucarás to be of the -B model and this version, with either Turboméca or Garrett-AiResearch engines, will be available for export late 1982.

The Astazou-powered IA 58B Pucará-B prototype differs from the current series production IA 58A primarily in having the two 20-mm Hispano HS 804 cannon in the underside of the forward fuselage replaced by a pair of 30-mm DEFA 553 cannon, the quartet of 7,62-mm FN-Browning machine guns being retained. The larger-calibre cannon have been accommodated by deepening the forward fuselage by 6·3 in (16 cm) with a nominal increase in empty equipped weight, the maximum external stores load remaining 3,307 lb (1 500 kg) and maximum take-off weight being unchanged. Apart from slight increases in take-off and landing run, the performance of the IA 58B remains essentially similar to that of the IA 58A. In addition to introducing heavier cannon armament and the modifications to the fuselage structure that their installation entailed, the Pucará-B also has a new avionics fit. The UHF, VOR/ILS and ADF sets, which are now duplicated, may be operated from either forward or aft cockpit, and provision is made for the Omega navigation system and weather radar. The following data relate to the Pucará-B prototype.

Power Plant: Two 1,022 ehp Turboméca Astazou XVIG turboprops each driving Hamilton Standard 23LF/1015-0 three-bladed metal propellers of 8·53-ft (2,60-m) diam. Total internal fuel capacity, 281·5 Imp gal (1 280 l) divided between two wing and two fuselage tanks, and provision for three 70·4 Imp gal (320 l) external tanks.

Performance: (at max take-off weight) Max speed, 311 mph (500 km/h); max diving speed, 466 mph (750 km/h); max cruise, 298 mph (480 km/h) at 19,685 ft (6 000 m); econ cruise, 267 mph (430 km/h); initial climb, 3,543 ft/min (18 m/sec); service ceiling, 32,810 ft (10 000 m); range (internal fuel), 838 mls (1 350 km); endurance (at 12,606 lb/5 718 kg), 5 hr 37 min, (at 13,095 lb/5 940 kg), 5 hr 23 min; min take-off run, 1,158 ft (353 m); min landing run, 1,827 ft (557 m).

Weights: Max take-off, 14,991 lb (6 800 kg).

Dimensions: Span, 47 ft 6¾ in (14,50 m); length, 46 ft 9 in (14,25 m); height, 17 ft 7 in (5,36 m); wing area, 326·1 sq ft (30,30 m²).

CANADA

CANADAIR CHALLENGER AND CHALLENGER E

CANADAIR LTD brought the No 7 Challenger to Farnborough for its first appearance in the UK, just 22 months after first flight and three weeks after obtaining Type Approval from the Department of Transport Canada. The aircraft was bearing the colours of TAG, Canadair's distributor in the Middle East and a major customer for the basic Model 600 version of the Challenger, powered by 7,500 lb st (3 402 kgp) Avco Lycoming ALF 502L engines. Canadair currently has a backlog of 128 orders for this version, and expects to have delivered 17 by the end of this year; production will then build during 1981 to a peak of seven a month.

(Above and below) The prototype Pucará-B which has now completed more than 150 hours testing and will be joined next year by two similarly-configured TPE331-engined IA 66 Pucarás.

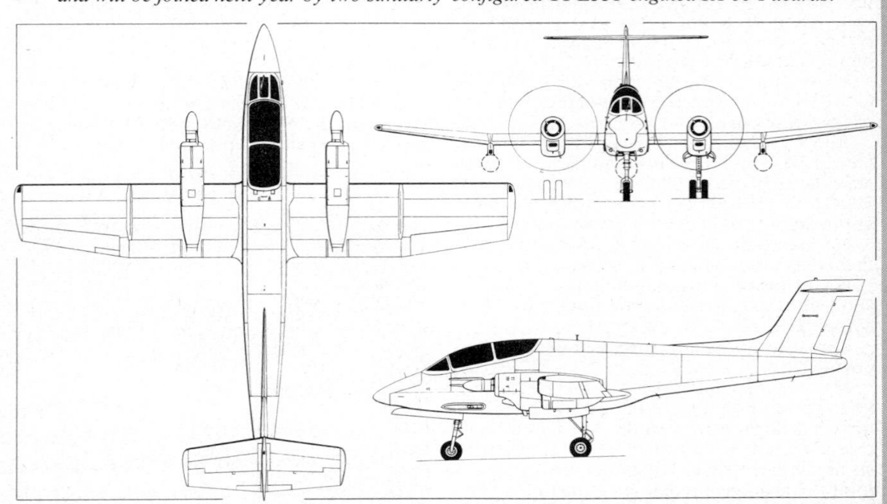

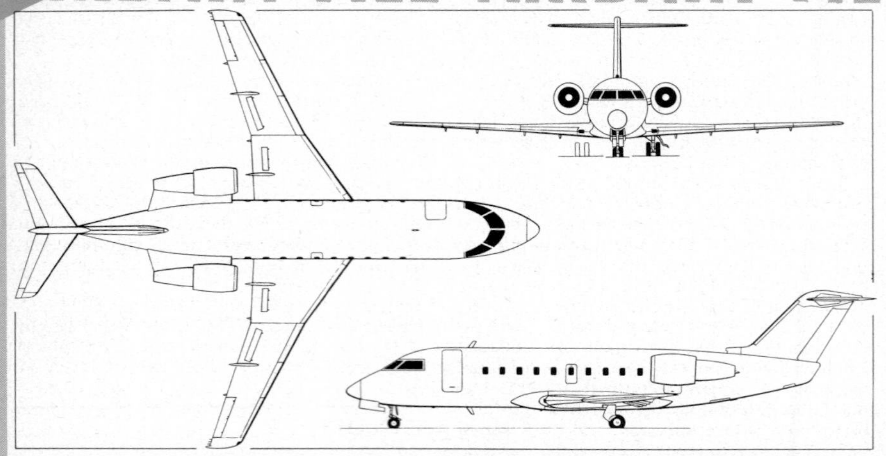

(Above) A revised three-view of the Canadair CL-610 Challenger E showing the extended span, leading-edge devices, changed spoiler configuration and revised engine pylons. (Below) CL-600 Challenger No 7 in TAG markings at Farnborough.

Certification proved to be a longer and more difficult task than expected, principally because it was the first modern jet aeroplane certificated by Transport Canada to the latest and most stringent regulations, the precise interpretation of which had not previously been established. By 11 April, when the Type Approval was awarded, the four trials aircraft had made nearly 850 flights totalling some 1,500 hrs, including exhaustive stalling tests that called for more than 2,000 stalls to be made in every possible combination of configuration and condition of entry. In addition, the fatigue test specimen had made nearly 11,000 simulated flights, representing more than 9,000 hrs.

The Type Approval included a number of restrictions, the lifting of which depends on completion of certain other tests or meeting certain conditions. Canadair spelled out these initial restrictions as follows:

Maximum operating altitude 40,000 ft (12 192 m) pending completion of tests on crew oxygen equipment.

Airspeed limit of 317 kt/M=0·79 (587 km/h) IAS and take-off and landing max weights limited to 33,000 lb (14 970 kg) and 30,500 lb (13 835 kg) respectively, pending approval of the tail loads survey report.

No flight into known icing conditions until flights in natural icing have been completed.

No operations from standing water, slush or snow until tests in these conditions have been completed.

Thrust reversers not to be used until testing completed.

Most of the outstanding work needed to clear these limitations was being undertaken on Challenger No 2, while No 4 (which is owned by Avco Lycoming) has been earmarked as the fleet leader for engine proving in a joint Canadair/Lycoming 1,000-hr programme. Aircraft No 2 is assigned to a performance improvement programme, in which No 9 will also participate, with special reference to aerodynamic improvement, and No 5 is the Canadair demonstrator.

Now that the initial task of certification has been completed, Canadair is turning its attention to a number of possible improvements and refinements, some of which are directed towards the forthcoming Model 610 Challenger E while others will have application on all models in the family. These improvements include an eventual increase in gross weight to 40,125 lb (18 200 kg) from 36,000 lb (16 329 kg) for the basic Model 600; a drooped wing leading edge (which will be flying on test by the end of the year); a split nozzle in place of the present confluent nozzle design and possibly the addition of winglets which wind tunnel testing suggests could add 150 mls (241 km) to the range.

The company holds 48 orders or paid options for the stretched Model 610 Challenger E and the Model 601, the latter being the standard size aircraft powered by the Challenger E's General Electric CF 34 engines. Since formal go-ahead for the stretched version was announced on 14 March 1980, the specification has been revised somewhat and the data available at Farnborough are quoted below. These show increases in weights (see *AirData File*/September 1979) and a 45-in (1,14-m) increase in wing span, achieved by inserting a 22·5-in (57-cm) section each side at the wing root. Leading edge flaps and slats are likely to be introduced on the Challenger E and flap and spoiler configurations are also being changed.

First flight of the Challenger E is now expected to be made in the second quarter of 1982, with deliveries starting in mid-1983. It will be preceded by the first Model 601, which will fly late in 1981 with deliveries starting a year later.

The following specification refers to the Model 610 Challenger E.

Power Plant: Two General Electric CF34-1A turbofans each rated at 9,140 lb st (4 146 kgp) with APR (five-minute limit) and 8,650 lb (3 924 kgp) without APR; max continuous power, 8,980 lb st (4 073 kgp). Fuel capacity, 2,633 US gal (9 967 l) in wing and centre section tanks plus 813 US gal (3 078 l) in fuselage tank; systems total 3,446 US gal (13 044 l).

Performance: High speed cruise, M=0·83, 476 kt (882 km/h); long-range cruise, M=0·75, 431 kt (800 km/h); max certificated altitude, 45,000 ft (13 716 m); range (NBAA IFR reserves, 200 naut ml/370 km alternate), 3,240 mls (6 000 km) with wing fuel only, 4,150 naut mls (7 687 km) with wing and fuselage fuel.

Weights: Basic operating weight, 27,950 lb (12 678 kg); max fuel (wing only) 17,800 lb (8 074 kg); max fuel (wing and fuselage), 23,300 lb (10 569 kg); payload with full fuel, 2,000 lb (907 kg); max take-off (wing fuel only), 47,500 lb (21 546 kg); max take-off (full fuel), 53,000 lb (24 041 kg); max landing weight, 45,000 lb (20 412 kg); max zero fuel weight, 32,350 lb (14 674 kg).

Dimensions: Span, 65 ft 7 in (19,99 m); length, 77 ft 2 in (23,52 m); height, 20 ft 8 in (6,30 m); wing area, 490 sq ft (45,52 m²); aspect ratio, 8·77:1; sweepback, 25 deg at quarter chord; wheelbase, 32 ft 5⅛ in (9,89 m); undercarriage track, 10 ft 5 in (3,18 m).

Accommodation: Flight crew of two; typical layouts provide 14, 15 or 17 passenger seats in cabin length of 37 ft 0 in (11,28 m). Cabin interior max width, 8 ft 2 in (2,49 m); width at floor line, 7 ft 2 in (2,18 m); headroom, 6 ft 1 in (0,94 m); volume, 1,505 cu ft (42,62 m³).

DE HAVILLAND CANADA DHC-8

BY THE END of Farnborough week, de Havilland's backlog of option commitments for the Dash 8 had risen to 90, placing the company in the lead among the group of manufacturers now offering commuter aircraft in the 30/40-seat category. The largest single new commitment came from Innotech Avia-

An impression of the de Havilland Dash 8, commitments for which had risen to 90 by the time the company displayed the latest Dash 8 model at Farnborough.

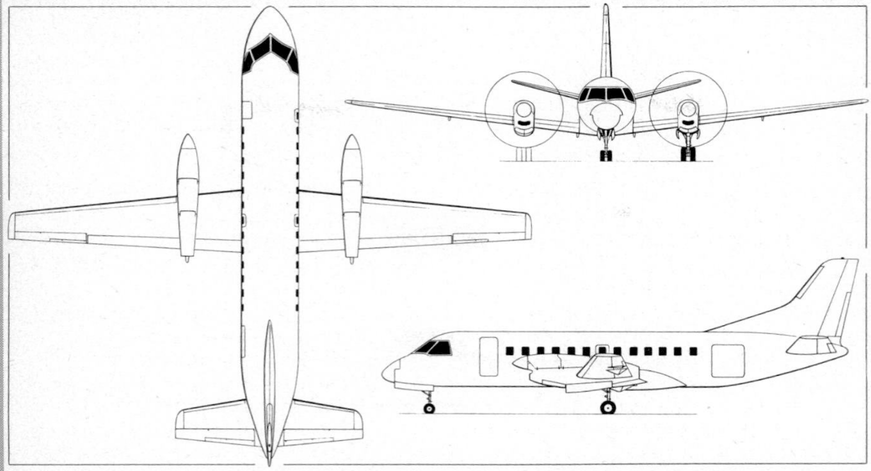

(Above) A preliminary three-view of the Saab-Fairchild 340 as now revised, with low-mounted tailplane and (below left) a model showing the original configuration.

tion as a result of an agreement giving that company exclusive rights to distribute the Dash 8 as a corporate transport in North America. Innotech has taken options on seven "green" Dash 8s from the first year of production (starting in mid-1984), and the company will supply customer interiors, spares and field support.

De Havilland also announced at Farnborough that the Canadian federal government has now agreed to provide financial support for the Dash 8, which to date had been funded from the company's own resources. Research and development on the 32/36-passenger Dash 8 are expected to cost more than $Can150m (£53·3m) and production will call for employment of 2,500-3,000 more workers by the mid-1980s. A new site is to be selected for final assembly and testing of the Dash 8, to supplement expansion at the Downsview plant near Toronto.

First flight of the Dash 8 is set for mid-1983 with deliveries to the launch customer, NorOntair, in 1984. The most recent additions to the option list, in addition to Innotech, are Suburban Airlines (3), Perimeter Airlines (2), Torontair (1), Widerøe's Flyveselskap (6), Home Oil of Canada (1) and World Projects and Trading Corp (1).

Although a full specification for the Dash 8 has yet to be released by de Havilland, data issued at Farnborough showed some revisions by comparison with the initial release (see AIR INTERNATIONAL/July 1980), as follows:

Power Plant: Two Pratt & Whitney PT7A-2R turboprops each rated at 1,800 shp for take-off. Four-bladed, large diameter propellers.

Performance: Max cruising speed, 260 kt (482 km/h) at 25,000 ft (7 620 m); max operating altitude, 25,000 ft (7 620 m); range with IFR fuel reserves and max payload, 400 naut mls (741 km); range with IFR reserves and 32-passenger payload, 600 naut mls (1 112 km); max range with IFR fuel reserves, 1,100 naut mls (2 038 km); FAR 25 take-off and landing field lengths, 3,000 ft (914 m) at sea level, ISA + 15 deg C.

Weights: Max payload, 7,500 lb (3 402 kg); max take-off, approx 30,000 lb (13 608 kg).

Dimensions: Span, 84 ft 0 in (25,60 m); length, 75 ft 6 in (23,01 m); height, 25 ft (7,62 m); undercarriage track, 26 ft 0 in (7,92 m).

Accommodation: Flight crew of two; up to 36 passengers four-abreast at 31-in (78-cm) seat pitch.

INTERNATIONAL

SAAB-FAIRCHILD 340

ONE OF the several new projects for commuter airliners in the 30/40-seat category publicised at Farnborough this year, the Saab-Fairchild 340 has been firmed up since the first details were published earlier in the year (see AIR INTERNATIONAL/July 1980) and with effect from 1 September the company has been willing to guarantee the key performance parameters. These, as quoted at Farnborough, are: a max field length of 4,000 ft (1 219 m); minimum cruising speed of 298 mph (480 km/h); minimum range of 932 mls (1 500 km) with 34 passengers and max empty weight of 14,400 lb (6 532 kg).

The first phase of project definition and specification work — which began in January and involved a 100-strong team drawn from Saab and Fairchild and working at Farmingdale, Long Island — has been completed and the second phase has now begun, centred upon Linköping, Sweden. This phase embraces detail design, development, test and evaluation up to certification in December 1983. The two flight test aircraft are scheduled to fly in October 1982 and January 1983 respectively, with the first production aircraft available by the end of 1983.

Production of the SF 340 is to be shared on an equal basis, with Fairchild building wings, tail unit and engine nacelles at its Republic Company Division in Farmingdale and Maryland, while Saab builds the fuselage and is responsible for final assembly and flight testing at Linköping. Certification will be to American FAR-25 and joint European JAR-25 standards, and the commuter will be the first airliner to be certificated simultaneously to these latest standards. Marketing is being handled in the USA, Canada and Mexico by the Swearingen Aviation Corp (a Fairchild subsidiary) and in the rest of the world by Saab-Fairchild HB, a jointly-owned company set up for the purpose.

To help establish the design parameters of the SF 340, Saab and Fairchild invited the views of eight commuter operators — Crossair in Switzerland, Cimberair in Denmark and Air Wisconsin, Air Midwest, Metroflight, Pocono Airlines, Cochise Airlines and Golden Gate Airlines in the USA — and representatives of these companies formed an Operator Advisory Board. At Farnborough, Saab-Fairchild HB was able to announce that one of these companies, Crossair, was in the final stages of negotiating a contract for five SF 340s with five more on option, to become the first confirmed customer; in addition, Swedair was negotiating for five-seven aircraft and Stillwell Aviation was discussing an agreement for the Australian distributorship which would lead to the placing of a firm order for 12. Contracts in the Swearingen marketing area were expected to be announced during October.

An important milestone in phase I development was the selection of General Electric as the engine vendor, the SF 340 being the first announced application for the CT7 turboprop derived from the T700 helicopter turboshaft. Saab-Fairchild claims that the CT7 offers 5-15 per cent lower fuel consumption than its competitors; specifically, the fuel cost for the 34-seat SF 340 operating 10 flights a day on a 100-naut ml (185-km) sector works out at $430,000 a year (fuel at $1·50/US gal), compared with $510,000 and $610,000 for 30-seat and 32-seat aircraft with Pratt & Whitney PT7 engines.

Wind-tunnel testing (using a 1/5th half-scale model for high lift system selection, a 1/14th scale model to validate the configuration at low and high speeds and a 1/5th scale model to verify and refine the configuration) has led to a recent decision to relocate the tailplane from the fin to the fuselage, giving it 15 deg of dihedral, to avoid pitch up beyond the stall. Other minor changes shown in the accompanying three-view drawing include increased cockpit glazing, plug-in doors with separate self-contained airstairs and repositioned emergency exit over the wing.

The Saab-Fairchild 340 has a circular-section fuselage pressurised to 7 psi (0,49 kg/cm²). The basic airframe structure is designed for long life in short-haul operation, with extensive use of large panels with metal-to-metal bonded stiffeners. Fatigue testing will be conducted for 45,000 hrs and 90,000 landings. The two-spar wing has a single-slotted, externally-hinged four-position flap extending over the whole span inboard of the ailerons. Basic flying controls are fully manual, with electrically-operated trim tabs. A 3,000 psi (211 kg/cm²) hydraulic system operates the landing gear, brakes, nosewheel steering, anti-skid system and flaps. All three undercarriage legs have twin wheels and retract forwards to allow for gravity extension in case of hydraulic failure.

Power Plant: Two General Electric CT7-5 turboprops each flat-rated to 30 deg C at sea level for 1,654 shp at take-off, Dowty Rotol R320 four-bladed propellers of composite construction and 10 ft 6 in (3,20 m) diameter. Fuel capacity, 880 US gal (3 331 l) in two integral wing tanks.

Performance: Max cruising speed, 260 kts (482 km/h) at 20,000 ft (6 100 m); long range cruise, 211 kts (391 km/h) at 20,000 ft (6 100 m); FAR 25 take-off field length required, 3,200 ft (975 m) ISA at sea level, 4,400 ft (1 341 m) ISA + 15 deg C at 5,000 ft (1 525 m); range with max payload, 550 naut mls (1 019 km); range with 34 passengers (IFR reserves), 780 naut mls (1 445 km); max range, 1,570 naut mls (2 908 km) with 23 passengers.

Weights: Typical OWE, 14,700 lb (6 668 kg); fuel capacity, 5,900 lb (2 676 kg); weight-limited payload, 7,300 lb (3 311 kg); max take-off and landing weight, 25,000 lb (11 340 kg); max zero fuel weight, 22,000 lb (9 980 kg).
Dimensions: Span 70 ft 3½ in (21,4 m); length, 63 ft 11 in (19,5 m); height, 22 ft 6 in (6,8 m); aspect ratio, 11:1; wheelbase, 23 ft 6 in (7,2 m); undercarriage track, 22 ft 0 in (6,7 m).
Accommodation: Flight crew of two with provision for single-pilot operation; 34 passengers three-abreast at 30-in (76-cm) seat pitch. Baggage compartment on main deck, volume 225 cu ft (6,4 m³).

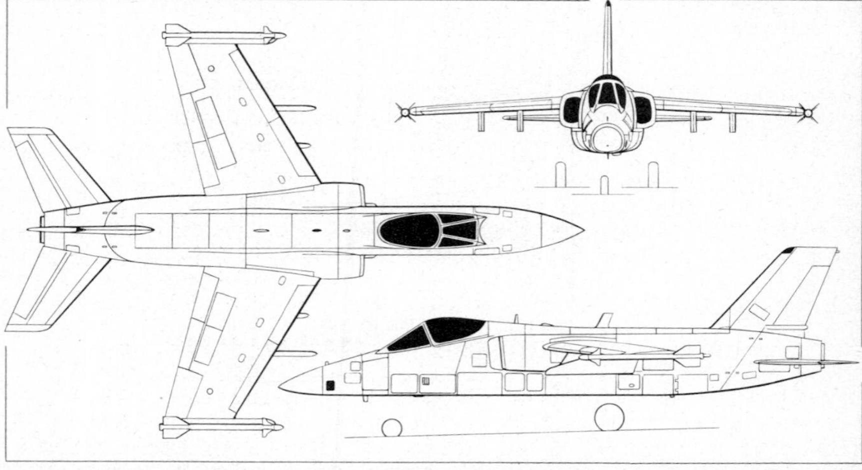

Seen in model form at Farnborough in its definitive configuration and illustrated (above) by a new general arrangement drawing and (below, right) by an artist's impression, the Aeritalia/Aermacchi AM-X tactical fighter has a span (excluding missiles) of 29 ft 1¾ in (8,88 m), a length of 44 ft 1 in (13,44 m) and a height of 13 ft 8⅙ in (4,17 m).

ITALY

AERITALIA AIT-230-208

SINCE starting the project development of a commuter transport during 1979, Aeritalia has revised the basic design to offer larger capacity and to take advantage of the new generation of engines now on offer. Whereas the AIT-230-204 (as described in *AirData File*/March 1980) would have been powered by PT6A-65 turboprops and accommodate 30 passengers, the current AIT-230-208 has been enlarged to use the more powerful PT7A or General Electric CT7 and to seat 38-42 passengers. This project is the basis on which Aeritalia and Aérospatiale concluded an agreement in July to study the possibility of jointly developing a 40/50-seat commuter liner, to operate over ranges of 808-932 mls (1 300-1 500 km) at a speed of 497 mph (800 km/h). As now studied, the AIT-230 closely resembles the Aérospatiale AS.35, and the two companies should find little difficulty in merging the two projects into a single design, should they so decide. Subject to satisfactory market reaction and joint government backing, initial deliveries could begin in 1985.

The AIT-230 is meanwhile being continued so that Aeritalia could, if necessary, proceed with the project alone. The intention is to achieve a design that, after full design definition, could go straight into production without an intermediate prototype phase. The AIT-230 is described as a multi-purpose light turboprop transport, the basic version of which would be a passenger transport for the upper end of the commuter market; other variants would be for commercial cargo use, capable of accepting standard containers, and for military use with good field performance in hot and high conditions. The Italian company regards the AIT-230 as part of an evolving family of designs, including the G 222, and one which could make use of the company's growing experience in the mass production of structural components in advanced composites.

The basic AIT-230 is sized to make use of the new engines of 1,800-2,000 shp; this provides a fuselage seating 38 in a four-abreast single-aisle layout (or 42 at reduced pitch). Provision would be made for subsequent development of a 50-passenger version, requiring a longer fuselage and increased wing area. The cabin would be pressurised to a differential of 6 psi (0,42 kg/cm²).

Key features of the design noted by Aeritalia are the double-radius fuselage cross-section, providing spacious overhead baggage stowage and a good degree of passenger seating comfort; high-mounted cantilever wing having a rectangular centre-section and trapezoid-shaped outer sections with integral fuel in the torsion box; large-scale use of metal bonding in primary structures and of advanced composites in non-structural parts. The AIT-230 will have mechanical flight controls with electric trim; protection against icing on the aerodynamic surfaces, engine inlets, propellers and windshields; full air conditioning by engine bleed; hydraulic operation of the flaps, landing gear, nosewheel steering and brakes; auto-pilot in basic aircraft, with full IFR capability, digital cockpit displays and weather radar fitted.

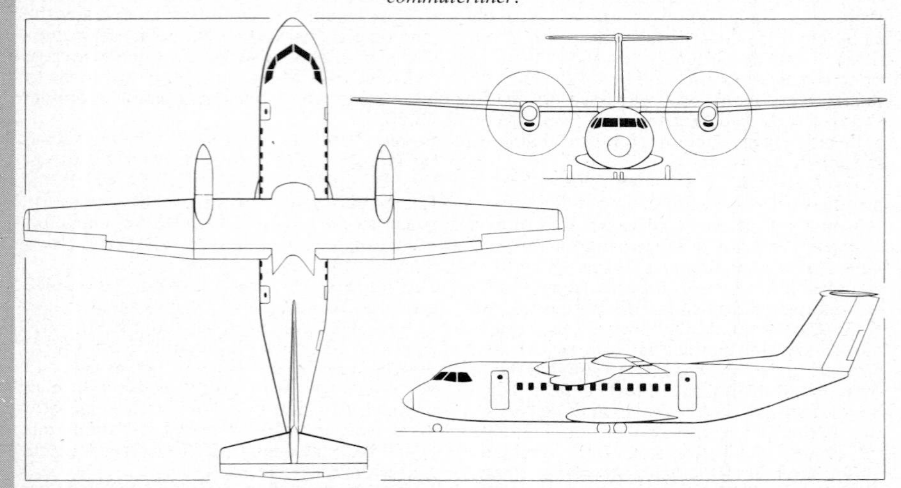

Three-view of the AIT-230-208, the latest version of the Aeritalia project for a 40/50-seat commuterliner.

Power Plant: Two new generation turboprops of about 1,800 shp each; eg, Pratt & Whitney PT7A-2R/1, flat-rated at 1,800 shp at sea level up to 72 deg F with 1,950 shp emergency rating at sea level up to 82 deg F, or General Electric CT7-7, flat-rated at 1,728 shp, sea level up to 86 deg F. Hamilton Standard four-bladed propellers of 12-ft (3,66-m) diameter. Fuel capacity, 4,050 lb (1 837 kg).
Performance (PT7A-2R engines): Max cruising speed, 283 kt (524 km/h) at 20,000 ft (6 100 m); initial rate of climb, 1,925 ft/min (9,78 m/sec); cruising ceiling, 25,000 ft (7 620 m); single-engine ceiling, 15,000 ft (4 572 m); FAR 25 take-off field length required, 3,870 ft (1 180 m); FAR 135 landing field length required, 3,280 ft (1 000 m); range with max cargo payload, 95 naut mls (176 km); range with 38 passengers and baggage, 710 naut mls (1 315 km); range with max fuel and 25 passengers, 1,480 naut mls (2 741 km).
Weights: Typical OWE (passengers), 19,522 lb (8 855 kg); typical OWE (cargo), 18,721 lb (8 492 kg); max take-off weight, 30,910 lb (14 020 kgp); max zero fuel weight, 29,210 lb (13 250 kg); max landing weight, 30,688 lb (13 920 kg).
Dimensions: Span, 75 ft 5 in (22,98 m); length, 66 ft 8 in (20,30 m); height, 20 ft 9 in (6,32 m); wing area, 516·7 sq ft (48,0 m²); wheelbase, 23 ft 10 in (7,28 m); undercarriage track, 13 ft 10½ in (4,23 m).

Accommodation: Flight crew of two and 38 passengers four-abreast at 32-in (81-cm) seat pitch, or 42 at 29-in (74-cm) seat pitch, with toilet, galley, and rear baggage compartment of 230 cu ft (6,5 m³) capacity.

AERMACCHI MB-339K VELTRO 2

WITH the tandem two-seat MB-339 basic/advanced trainer now established in production and in the early phases of service with Italy's *Aeronautica Militare*, and with the first export orders (14 for the *Fuerza Aérea Peruana* and 10 for Argentina's *Comando de Aviacion Naval*) in house, Aeronautica Macchi has now begun to exploit the development potential of the basic design and, on 30 May 1980, flew the first example of a private-venture single-seat light close air support version, the MB-339K. Named Veltro (Greyhound) 2, perpetuating that of the wartime MC-205V single-seat fighter, and appropriately registered I-BITE, the MB-339K made its public début at Farnborough International '80, by which time it had flown some 25-30 hours, and is now the subject of a marketing drive with deliveries being offered within 20-24 months at a unit price of the order of $3m. The MB-339K displayed at FI '80 is not considered by Aeronautica Macchi as a prototype but as the first *production* example, having been built on production jigs and tools, and sets of components are now in hand for three additional single-seaters, which, like all future single-seaters, will be built on the same assembly line as the two-seat MB-339.

The MB-339K, the programme cost of which is estimated by Aeronautica Macchi to be of the order of $6m, is intended solely for export, there being no indigenous market for an aircraft in this category, and is aimed primarily at the air forces of third level countries with a need for a dedicated light CAS aircraft offering maximum availability and minimum ground support requirements at a comparatively low cost. Possessing a high level of commonality with its two-seat predecessor, the MB-339K is largely new forward of the aft-sloping bulkhead aligning with the wing root air intakes and utilises experience gained with the MB-326K (which serves with the air forces of Ghana, Tunisia, Dubai, South Africa and Zaïre) in having an essentially similar twin-DEFA 553 30-mm cannon installation.

By comparison with the two-seat MB-339, the MB-339K has substantially increased internal fuel capacity, offering an improved payload-radius envelope, and a higher maximum take-off weight catering for the higher load capacities of its six wing hardpoints, the inner and mid-points being stressed for 1,000 lb (453,6 kg) and the outer points being stressed for 750 lb (340 kg). With a typical military load of about 2,400 lb (1 089 kg), such as four 500-lb (226,8-kg) Mk 82 bombs and 125 rounds for each DEFA cannon, the radius of action with 5 min combat varies from 200 nm (370 km) LO-LO-LO, with 30 nm (55 km) penetration at 425 knots (787 km/h) and 30 nm escape at 450 knots (518 km/h), to 350 nm (648 km) HI-LO-HI with 10 per cent fuel reserve. Flexibility is such as to allow a wide range of different missions. For example, a typical armed reconnaissance mission (one photographic pod, full cannon ammunition, two Matra 550 Magic IR missiles and two 93·5 Imp gal/425 l pylon tanks) can be performed at a distance of 455 nm (843 km) from base, while a 150 nm (278 km) LO-LO-LO close air support mission can be flown with six LAU-3/A expendable launchers each with 19 2·75-in (6,98-cm) rockets representing, with full cannon ammunition, a military load of 2,765 lb (1 254 kg).

MB-339 production is now running at 2·0-2·5 monthly, but is building up to 3·0 per month to be attained early in the New Year and is currently expected to peak at 4·0 monthly late 1981, this including both single- and two-seat models with Aeronautica Macchi looking for the export sale of 300-400 by the late 'eighties. In view of the sale to date of 761* (including licence-built examples) of its progenitor, the MB-326, such a target would not seem unduly optimistic.

Power Plant: One 4,320 lb (1 960 kg) Fiat-built Rolls-Royce Viper 632-43 turbojet. Total internal fuel, 446·75 Imp gal (2 031 l) distributed between fuselage and wingtip tanks, plus provision for two 93·5 Imp gal (425 l) jettisonable pylon tanks.

Performance: (combat configuration) Max speed, 553 mph (889 km/h) at sea level; limiting speed, 575 mph (926 km/h)/Mach = 0·85; max climb, 7,500 ft/min (38 m/sec) at sea level; service ceiling, 44,500 ft (13 565 m); time to 30,000 ft (9 145 m) from brakes release, 9·15 min; take-off ground roll (clean), 1,870 ft (570 m), (at max take-off weight), 2,985 ft (910 m); landing speed, 102 mph (165 km/h); landing run, 1,345 ft (410 m).

Weights: Operational empty, 6,997 lb (3 174 kg); loaded (clean), 10,974 lb (4 978 kg); max take-off, 13,558 lb (6 150 kg).

Dimensions: Span, 36 ft 2 9/10 in (11,05 m); length, 36 ft 0 in (10,97 m); height, 12 ft 9½ in (3,90 m); wing area (including ailerons and flaps), 178·83 sq ft (16,61 m²).

(Above and below) The MB-339K Veltro 2 close air support derivative of the MB-339 basic/advanced trainer, which was publicly demonstrated at Farnborough for the first time.

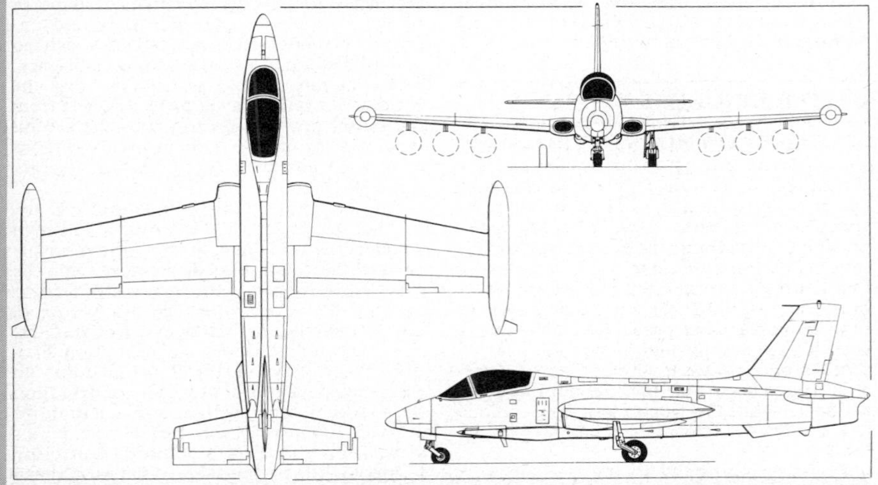

NETHERLANDS

FOKKER F29

FOKKER BV made its first Farnborough appearance following the dissolution of the VFW-Fokker partnership, and the Dutch company showed that it was vigorously pursuing its independence with the well-established F27 Friendship and F28 Fellowship, and also with the projected F29 twin-turbofan airliner. The company has been working on the evolution of this aircraft for several years, at first as a relatively simple "stretch" of the F28 and more recently as a more extensive redesign of the Fellowship that has been tailored closely to the anticipated needs of the short-haul carriers for an aircraft of relatively large capacity.

The F29 effort has now reached the point where, in Fokker's own words, it represents "... a major challenge to supply the short-haul needs of the world's flag carriers." An estimated 100m Dutch guilders (£21·6m) has been spent to date (of which the Netherlands

**There has been some confusion concerning sales of the MB-326, some figures for totals having included options. The correct figures are as follows: Italy (AF) 2 prototypes, 124 MB-326s, 2 MB-326Gs and 2 MB-326Ks, (Alitalia) 4 MB-326Ds; Australia 97 MB-326Hs; Argentina (Navy) 8 MB-326GBs; Brazil 182 EMB-326GB Xavantes (9 of which to Paraguay and 6 to Togo); Dubai 6 MB-326Ks and 2 MB-326Ls; Ghana 9 MB-326Fs and 6 MB-326Ks; South Africa 151 MB-326Ms and 100 MB-326Ks; Tunisia 8 MB-326Bs, 8 MB-326Ks and 4 MB-326Ls; Zambia 23 MB-326GBs and Zaïre 17 MB-326GBs and 6 MB-326Ks. In addition to these orders which (apart from small proportions of the Brazilian and South African licence-built totals) have been fulfilled, Aeronautica Macchi is building an additional small quantity against options held by Dubai and Tunisia, and Brazil and South Africa have options on 50 additional EMB-326GB Xavantes and 50 additional MB-326Ks respectively.*

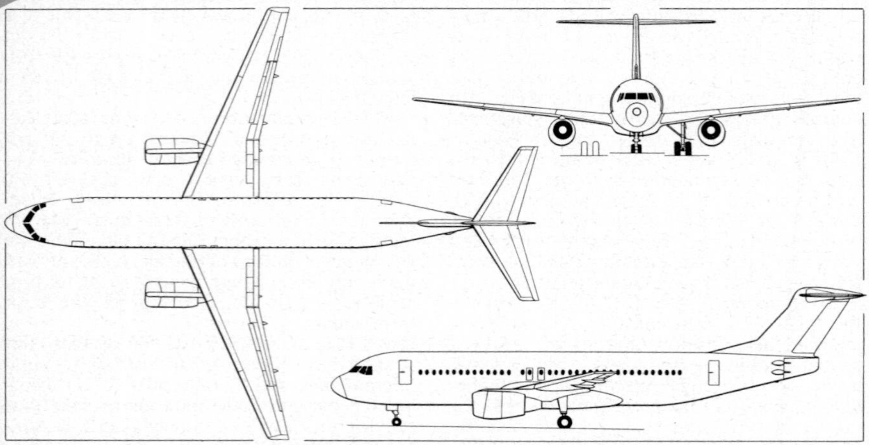

Three-view of the Fokker F29 as presented at Farnborough. With definition nearing completion, the company hopes to reach a launch decision within the next few months.

government has contributed 60 per cent) and negotiations with prospective partners and launch customers were at an advanced stage in September.

The current Fokker objective is to reach a launch decision in mid-1981, based on concluding joint risk-sharing agreements with two partners; it is widely assumed that one of these partners will be the Japanese industry consortium that is looking for such a new project in the YXX category, and which was thought likely to reach a decision favourable to Fokker before the end of this year. A second partner, preferably in North America, is regarded as essential by Fokker. The market for aircraft of the F29 category is estimated by Fokker to total 1,500 by the end of the century.

As now planned, the F29 is a 138/156-seat airliner capable of being stretched to 162/179 seats, with a fuselage diameter sized to permit six-abreast seating with a single aisle. About 6,000 hrs of wind tunnel testing have been completed, and combined with computer research have led to some recent improvements in wing technology resulting in a reduction of about 6 per cent in wing area without any decrease in lift; as a result, the original design objectives have been maintained so far as cruising performance is concerned, but the weight reduction provides an extra row of seats, reduced drag and improved fuel consumption. On a 500-naut ml (926-km) sector, the fuel saving per seat is now some 5 per cent better than earlier estimates for the F29; the high aspect ratio, supercritical wing is estimated to give a fuel saving of 7-10 per cent over the current-technology twin jets; an additional 4-6 per cent improvement is claimed from other design aspects and the engines are expected to give a 17-19 per cent reduction, so that the total saving in fuel per seat with the F29 can be as high as 35 per cent over optimum ranges.

Although Fokker's original F29 projects were based on the Rolls-Royce RB.432, this engine (which has meanwhile become the R-R/ Japanese Aero Engines RJ500-01) is now joined as a candidate to power the new transport by the General Electric/SNECMA CFM56-3 of similar thrust. Latest market inputs have led Fokker to increase the design range from 1,500 to 1,700 naut mls (2 778-3 149 km), and increased weight variants could eventually carry 138 passengers for 2,500 naut mls (4 630 km).

Based on a mid-1981 launch, the F29 in its initial version could be flying in 1983 with customer deliveries starting in 1985. The stretched aircraft could be available two-three years later.

Power Plant: Two wing-mounted high bypass turbofans of 20,000 lb st (9 072 kgp) each; eg, Rolls-Royce/Japanese Aero Engines RJ500-01/D4 or CFM International CFM56-3. Fuel capacity, 41,000 lb (18 600 kg) in wing integral fuel tanks.

Performance: MMO = 0·79, VMO = 330 kts (611 km/h) EAS; economic cruising speed, M = 0·75, 430 kts (796 km/h) at 37,000 ft (11 278 m); max cruising altitude, 37,000 ft (11 278 m); FAR take-off field length required, 7,000 ft (2 134 m) at max weight, sea level, ISA + 15 deg C; FAR landing field length required, 4,000 ft (1 219 m), wet surface, mission weight; range, 820 naut mls (1 519 km) with max payload, 1,700 naut mls (3 149 km) with 138 passengers and baggage; max range, 2,850 naut mls (5 280 km) with 15,000-lb (6 804-kg) payload.

Weights: Typical OWE (RJ500), 74,340 lb (33 720 kg); typical OWE (CFM56), 74,950 lb (34 000 kg); max take-off weight, 131,770 lb (59 770 kg); max landing weight, 121,910 lb (55 300 kg); max zero fuel weight, 111,990 lb (50 800 kg).

Dimensions: Span, 107 ft 10½ in (32,88 m); length, 128 ft 11 in (39,30 m); height, 36 ft 6½ in (11,14 m); wing area, 1,163 sq ft (108,0 m²); sweepback, 21 deg at quarter chord; aspect ratio, 10:1; wheelbase, 40 ft 4½ in (12,31 m); undercarriage track, 22 ft 5½ in (6,85 m).

Accommodation: Flight crew of two and 138 passengers six-abreast at 34-in (86-cm) seat pitch or 156 passengers six-abreast at 30-in (76-cm) seat pitch. Cargo volume (underfloor) 1,296 cu ft (36,7 m³) in two holds.

UNITED KINGDOM

NDN AIRCRAFT NDN 6 FIELDMASTER

AS ITS second project, to follow the NDN 1 Firecracker basic trainer, NDN Aircraft Ltd has embarked upon the development of an agricultural aeroplane. After first studying the possibility of adapting the Firecracker for this rôle, NDN Aircraft came to the conclusion that a much larger aircraft had better market prospects. Although there are many agricultural monoplanes in production, the market itself is expected to double over the next 20 years, from a present level of about 1,400 aircraft a year; of this total, about one-third are sold within the Communist bloc nations and of the remainder, over half within the USA.

There is a clear trend among ag-plane users in favour of larger-capacity aircraft, and the Fieldmaster is an attempt to respond to this demand; the only aircraft with comparable load-carrying ability are the jet-powered M-15 Belphagor (which, because of its high fuel consumption and, therefore, operating costs, is unlikely to achieve sales outside of the Communist bloc) and the M-18 Dromader, which is already attracting considerable attention in Western markets.

Although the Fieldmaster appears at first glance to be of conventional ag-plane configuration, it has several advanced features that promise to give it an outstanding performance and some operating characteristics that will be specially attractive to agricultural users. These features spring from the innovative approach to aircraft design of Desmond Norman, founder of NDN Aircraft and the co-designer of the best-selling Islander/Trislander utility transport; before becoming involved in the Britten-Norman venture, Norman had also acquired first-hand experience of the agricultural aeroplane business through Crop Culture (Aerial), which had an 80-strong fleet of ag-planes, and as a director of Snow Aeronautical, where the Snow S-2 design originated. Also closely involved in Fieldmaster development is Andy Coombs, as technical director of NDN Aircraft; he also was formerly closely connected with design of the Islander.

The most important new design feature of the Fieldmaster is its integral hopper, which is part of the primary fuselage structure. Located close to the aircraft's CG, the hopper carries the engine bearers at its front end, the cockpit and rear fuselage structure at the rear and the wing attachment at the lower edge each side; an internal baffle accommodates the carry-through structure for the wing loads. After investigating stainless steel as the structural material for the hopper, the designers have opted for titanium (supplied by IMI, fabricated by Middleton Sheet Metal). Although titanium is some 10 times as expensive as steel, it is lighter and offers exceptionally good fatigue and corrosion resistance. NDN Aircraft estimates that the use of titanium may increase the Fieldmaster's first cost by about £3,000, but that the extra revenue that can be earned because of its lower weight will offset this penalty in the first year of operation.

The integral hopper, which has a capacity of 698 US gal (2 642 l), has an additional advantage in that a smaller fuselage cross section can be used for a given capacity. Combined with the use of a turboprop engine (the widely accepted Pratt & Whitney PT6A), this leads to a better streamlined shape of fuselage, smaller frontal area drag and improved propeller efficiency, all of which go toward better performance and fuel efficiency. The company claims, incidentally, that the Fieldmaster is the first ag-plane designed from the outset for turboprop power; the several types now flying with turboprops are without exception adaptations of earlier piston-engined types.

Another important innovation on the Fieldmaster concerns the use of a full-span auxiliary aerofoil flap, into which is incorporated the liquid spray dispersal system. The spray bar is clipped to the rear spar of the flap and liquid is ejected through a series of 40 nozzles directly into the downwash of the flaps, thus achieving excellent crop penetration. Flap deflections of 6·8 deg will be used for all spraying applications, in which configuration the aircraft automatically adopts a nose-down attitude, improving still further the pilot's view. Conventional ailerons for roll control are located on the trailing edge of the wing ahead of the auxiliary flaps, and because their effectiveness is enhanced by the airflow over the flaps, they are smaller than would otherwise be the case.

The Fieldmaster is being designed as a two-seater so that a loader or other assistant can be carried in a "buddy seat" behind the pilot, and removable dual controls will be available for flight training and check-out procedures. Sufficient fuel tankage will be built-in to achieve a ferry range of 1,000 mls (1 610 km); the tanks are in the outer wings for maximum safety in case of an accident.

A tricycle undercarriage has been adopted for the NDN 6, as the designers believe that the majority of ag-plane pilots will be familiar with tricycle techniques through their basic flying training. Many of the present generation of ag-planes are tail-draggers for the sake of rough-field operations, but at the heavier end of the range, where the Fieldmaster fits, this aspect is less relevant. In any case, the undercarriage is of very wide track, with levered suspension main wheels and a twin nose wheel.

NDN Aircraft has obtained the financial backing of the National Research Development Corporation for the launching of the Fieldmaster; the cost up to certification, using a single prototype plus structural test specimens, is put at approximately £500,000 (excluding the value of NDN's input of technology transferred from the Firecracker programme). The NRDC contribution, understood to be about £400,000, will be repaid in the form of a levy on sales of production Fieldmasters.

First flight of the prototype is expected to be made soon after the middle of next year and certification should be completed by September 1982. It is the company's intention to certificate the Fieldmaster to the full relevant BCARs, without special limitations for agricultural use, and to obtain full clearance for spinning at all CG and load combinations.

Production is expected to be handled by NDN Aircraft at the company's new factory now being built at Sandown Airport on the Isle of Wight, and deliveries could begin as soon as certification is obtained. Quantities varying between two and seven a month are regarded as viable by the company and, in view of the promising performance forecast for the Fieldmaster, do not seem to be over-ambitious. Estimating that the direct labour content will be about 2,700/2,800 hrs, NDN Aircraft anticipates that the Fieldmaster will enter the market at a first cost of about £150,000.

Power Plant: One Pratt & Whitney PT6A-34AG turboprop rated at 750 shp, driving a Hartzell three-bladed reversing and feathering propeller of 8 ft 10 in (2,69 m) diameter. Fuel capacity, 208 Imp gal (946 l) in four integral wing tanks.

Performance: Max speed, clean, 163 kt (302 km/h); cruising speed, 149 kt (276 km/h); stalling speed (flaps down), 59 kt (109 km/h); initial rate of climb, 1,200 ft/min (6,1 m/sec); take-off ground run, 580 ft (177 m); landing distance (with reverse thrust), 280 ft (85 m); max range, 1,020 naut mls (1 889 km).

Weights: Empty equipped, 3,500 lb (1 588 kg); useful load, 5,000 lb (2 268 kg); certificated gross weight, 8,500 lb (3 856 kg).

Dimensions: Span, 50 ft 3 in (15,32 m); length, 36 ft 2 in (10,97 m); height, 11 ft 5 in (3,48 m); wing area, 338 sq ft (31,42 m²); undercarriage track, 16 ft 8 in (5,08 m); wheelbase, 11 ft 0 in (3,35 m).

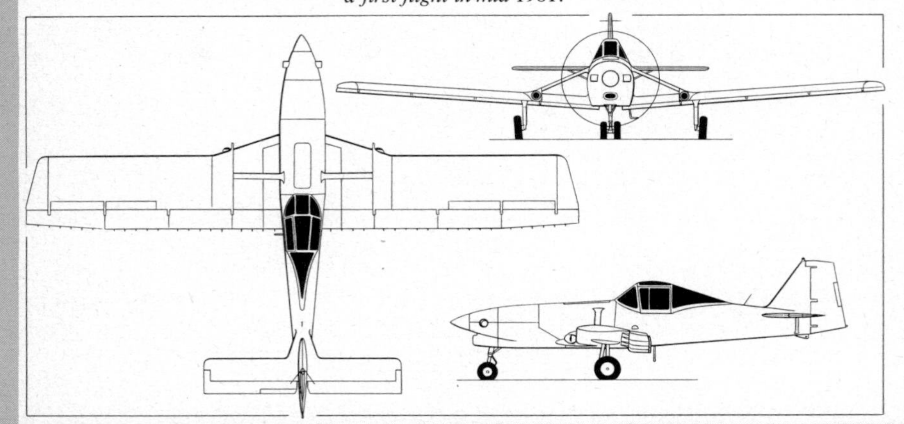

Three-view of the NDN-6 Fieldmaster, the new agricultural aeroplane now under construction for a first flight in mid-1981.

Making its first public appearance at Farnborough, the Pilatus Britten-Norman BN-2T Turbine Islander demonstrator was in Defender configuration with nose radar.

PILATUS BRITTEN-NORMAN BN-2T TURBINE ISLANDER

INITIAL ORDERS were announced in the course of the Farnborough air show for the new turboprop version of the Islander, two each having been purchased by Hawker Pacific and Heli Orient, the company's distributors, respectively, in Australasia and the Far East. Deliveries will begin early next year.

The BN-2T Turbine Islander was first flown at Bembridge, IoW, on 2 August 1980, and is now being given a high priority by the company in view of the increasing difficulties in ensuring supplies of Avgas (the fuel for piston-engined aircraft) in various parts of the world. Specific instances have already occurred of Islander sales being lost because the potential operator could not be certain of future Avgas supplies.

The BN-2T is the second turbine-engined Islander variant; an earlier prototype, developed by Fairey Britten-Norman and first flown on 6 April 1977, had Lycoming LTP 101 turboprops but did not prove wholly successful. The BN-2T is powered by Allison 250-B17C engines, derated in this application to give 320 shp for take-off and 300 shp for maximum climb. Little change to the structure of the Islander is necessary for the turboprop installation, but because the engines are lighter than the piston Lycomings, the extended wing-tip fuel tank option is not available on the BN-2T and alternative means of carrying additional fuel are under study, including the use of underwing long-range tanks of the type already available for the Defender military version of the Islander.

Preliminary performance data for the BN-2T follow:

Power Plant: Two 400 shp Allison 250-B17C turboprops each derated to 320 shp for take-off and 300 shp for max climb. Max usable internal fuel load, 871 lb (395 kg).

Performance: Max cruising speed, 180 mph (290 km/h) at sea level and 197 mph (317 km/h) at 10,000 ft (3 050 m); best range speed, 162 mph (261 km/h); initial rate of climb, 1,100 ft/min (5,59 m/sec); single-engined climb rate, 225 ft/min (1,14 m/sec); service ceiling, over 20,000 ft (6 100 m); single-engine ceiling, over 10,000 ft (3 050 m); take-off distance to 50 ft (15,2 m), 1,070 ft (326 m); landing distance from 50 ft (15,2 m), 1,080 ft (329 m); range with max fuel, no reserves, 515 mls (829 km); range with max fuel, IFR reserves, 385 mls (620 km).

Weights: Aircraft prepared for service (APS) weight, 4,120 lb (1 869 kg); disposable load, 2,480 lb (1 125 kg); max take-off and landing weight, 6,000 lb (2 722 kg).

Dimensions: Span, 49 ft 0 in (14,92 m); length, 35 ft 7¾ in (10,9 m); height, 12 ft 4¾ in (3,77 m); wheelbase, 13 ft 1¼ in (4,0 m); undercarriage track, 11 ft 10 in (3,6 m).

Accommodation: Pilot and nine passengers in normal commuter configuration.

USA

McDONNELL DOUGLAS F-15 STRIKE EAGLE

A JOINT VENTURE between McDonnell Douglas and Hughes Aircraft to gain USAF acceptance of an all-weather interdiction version of the F-15 air superiority fighter, the Strike Eagle represents an investment of some $50m (£20·8m) on the part of the two companies. An adaptation of the second two-seat F-15B, the Strike Eagle, demonstrated at Farnborough after a 5 hr 20 min unrefuelled crossing from Loring AFB, Maine, to RAF Mildenhall (about 2,700 naut miles/5 000 km), was scheduled to commence full-scale test late last month (October) after installation of the

The private-venture Strike Eagle all-weather interdiction development of the McDonnell Douglas F-15 seen, above, with conformal fuel tanks and 22 500-lb (226,8-kg) Mk 82 bombs.

synthetic aperture radar (SAR) Hughes AN/APG-63 set forming the heart of the nav/attack system. The SAR represents an advance in digital electronics providing a high-resolution ground mapping capability to a resolution of about 10 ft (3,00 m) without affecting the radar's air-air capability. Night and adverse weather capability is provided by a Pave Tack forward-looking IR and laser designator pod carried under-wing, and a moving target indicator aids the weapon system operator (the second crewman) in locating and tracking moving ground targets.

When displayed statically at Farnborough, the Strike Eagle was fitted with five of the new supersonic MER 200 multiple weapon racks (qualified for speeds up to M=1·4) — one under each wing, one under each conformal FAST (Fuel and Sensor Tactical) Pack and one under the fuselage — carrying a total of 22 Mk 20 Rockeye dispenser bombs. In addition, the two wing racks each carried a pair of AIM-9L Sidewinder AAMs, and other weaponry incorporated in the ground display of the Strike Eagle's potential armament included 2,000-lb (907-kg) Mk 84 bombs, HARM anti-radiation missiles, AGM-65 Maverick television-guided missiles, AGM-84A Harpoon anti-ship missiles and Matra Durandal dibber bombs, demonstrating the versatility of the interdiction model.

The initial flight test phase now commencing concentrates on confirming the operation and resolution of the radar, weapons separation from the reinforced FAST tanks and in-flight firing trials with a 30-mm General Electric GAU-8 gun pod. The radar trials are expected to be completed early in the New Year, after which blind bombing testing will commence using the fully integrated system. This system will provide a manoeuvring attack capability to avoid overflying the target.

McDONNELL DOUGLAS DC-XX

FOLLOWING the July decision by the McDonnell Douglas board to continue advanced engineering development of the Douglas Aircraft Company's DC-XX project for a short/medium-range medium-capacity airliner, the company came to Farnborough with the latest specification, showing several recent changes in this project. Previously identified as the ATMR II (see *AirData File*/February 1980), the DC-XX is destined to enter production as the DC-11 if the launch decision is taken in due course; the programme now in hand will continue in any case until the end of this year.

The Douglas philosophy is to offer "wide-body" standards of accommodation in an aircraft designed to compete with the Boeing 757 (and, if launched, the Airbus SA1/SA2). This is achieved by adopting a unique (to date) twin-aisle layout with six-abreast seating. Such an arrangement necessarily requires the use of a somewhat greater fuselage diameter than a six-abreast single-aisle layout for the same number of passengers, but the company believes that the added passenger appeal will offset any penalty that might be suffered in operating cost, especially in the more sophisticated North American markets; a cost, in fact, that is met by filling two extra seats on each flight. Nevertheless, economic considerations have led to the recent decision to increase the diameter of the fuselage by 4 in (10 cm), to 173 in (4,39 m), so that seven-abreast (twin-aisle) layouts will be possible if required by the operators.

The increased diameter also has the effect of raising the floor, thus increasing the underfloor capacity, and of shortening the undercarriage. A small change in wing planform has reduced aspect ratio from 9·8 to 9·2, helping to offset the extra weight of the larger fuselage. Weights have gone up, however, and the company has been glad, therefore, to take advantage of the higher powers now being offered by Pratt & Whitney for the JT10D. Originally, the ATMR II was based on the 32,000 lb st (14 515 kgp) JT10D-232, but the engine manufacturer has now offered a somewhat larger version that can be used in either the Boeing 757 (the JT10D-236 at 36,000 lb st/16 327 kgp) or the DC-XX (the JT10D-234, derated to about 34,000 lb st/15 422 kgp).

Douglas has been looking at active controls for the DC-XX, and has concluded that the longitudinal system should be active, permitting a smaller tailplane area. The wings will not use active controls but feature an advanced aerofoil section, and an improved high-lift system with three-position slats on the leading edge and double-slotted flaps. Considerable use of advanced composite materials is planned.

Subject to a firm launch decision being made, the DC-XX is expected to enter service no earlier than the end of 1985; present airline difficulties are likely to delay introduction beyond the date that is technically feasible. Meanwhile, McDonnell Douglas is continuing to seek risk-sharing partners, possibly to be found within North America since little interest in the project has been shown in Japan and Europe is rather heavily committed to the Airbus programmes.

Power Plant: Two advanced-technology high-bypass turbofans underwing; eg, 34,900 lb st (15 830 kgp) Pratt & Whitney JT10D-234, 36,500 lb st (16 556 kgp) General Electric CF6-32C1 (Improved) or 37,400 lb st (16 965 kgp) Rolls-Royce RB.211-535C2A. Fuel capacity, 85,580 lb (38 819 kg).

Performance (JT10D): Range with max payload, 1,450 naut mls (2 686 km); range with 180 passengers and baggage, 2,600 naut mls (4 816 km).

Performance (CF6 or RB.211): Range with max payload, 1,300 naut mls (2 408 km); range with 180 passengers and baggage, 2,300 naut mls (4 260 km).

Weights: Typical OWE, 127,700 lb (57 925 kg); weight-limited payload, 52,300 lb (23 723 kg); max take-off weight, 213,500 lb (96 844 kg); max landing weight, 194,000 lb (87 998 kg).

Dimensions: Span, 131 ft 5 in (40,05 m); length, 148 ft 5 in (45,23 m); height, 44 ft 4 in (13,50 m).

Accommodation: Flight crew of two/three and 180 passengers, mixed class, 14 five-abreast at 38-in (96,5 cm) seat pitch and 166 six-abreast at 30-in (76-cm) seat pitch or 244/255 one-class seven-abreast. Underfloor cargo capacity, 1,843 cu ft (52,19 m³), or 13 containers plus 376 cu ft (10,65 m³) bulk.

Three-view of the McDonnell Douglas DC-XX as presented at Farnborough, with enlarged fuselage diameter and JT10D-234 turbofans mounted closer inboard than on earlier ATMR II projects.

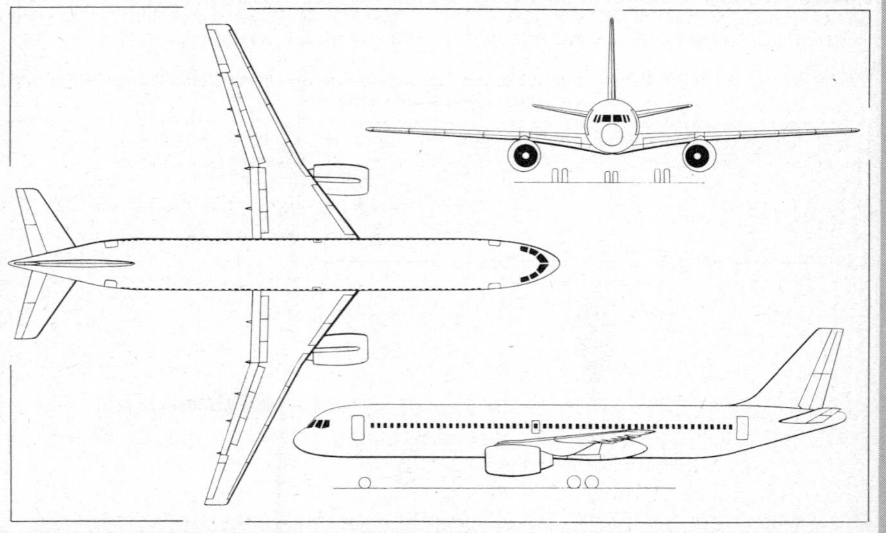

Volume 19 Number 6 December 1980

Editorial Offices:
The AIR INTERNATIONAL, PO Box 16, Bromley, BR2 7RB Kent.

Subscription, Advertising and Circulation Offices:
The AIR INTERNATIONAL, De Worde House, 283 Lonsdale Road, London SW13 9QW. Telephone 01-878 2454. US and Canadian readers may address subscriptions and general enquiries to AIR INTERNATIONAL PO Box 353, Whitestone, NY 11357 for onward transmission to the UK, from where all correspondence is answered and orders despatched.

MEMBER OF THE AUDIT BUREAU OF CIRCULATIONS ABC

Subscription rates, inclusive of postage, direct from the publishers, per year:

United Kingdom	£8·75
Overseas	£9·25
USA	$23·00
Canada	$26·00

Rates for other countries and for air mail subscriptions available on request from the Subscription Department at the above address.

The AIR INTERNATIONAL is published monthly by Fine Scroll Limited, distributed by Ducimus Books Ltd and printed by William Caple & Company Ltd, Chevron Press, Leicester, England.

Second Class postage approved at New York, NY. USA Mailing Agents: Air-Sea Freight Inc, 527 Madison Avenue, New York, NY 10022.

ISSN 0306-5634

CONTENTS

FRONT COVER A Fokker F27-200MPA on a pre-delivery flight over the North Sea, prior to delivery to Spain's Ejército del Aire for service with Escuadron 802 in the search and rescue rôle in the Canary Islands.

Merry Christmas - Happy New Year

Buenas Navidades - Feliz Año Nuevo

Frohe Weihnachten - Ein Glückliches Neues Jahr

Joyeux Noël - Heureuse Année

Buon Natale - Buon Anno

AIRSCENE

MILITARY AFFAIRS

BRAZIL

The *Fôrça Aérea Brasileira* (FAB) is currently planning **introduction of** the EMBRAER **EMB-312** (T-27) basic trainer into the FAB Academy at Pirassununga during the **second half of 1982** as a successor to the Cessna T-37 and, subsequently, the Neiva T-25 Universal, thus maintaining the rapid tempo that has characterised development of the new trainer. The initial FAB contract for the EMB-312 is understood to involve 168 aircraft with deliveries to the service attaining five per month by the end of 1982. Production tempo is subsequently to rise to 10-12 aircraft monthly to cater for export orders which EMBRAER confidently predict and of which at least three are reportedly under initial negotiation, apart from an order for three aircraft to be supplied early 1983 to the Oxford Air Training School for use in the training of up to 120 pilots on behalf of an unspecified African government. The projected fly-away unit cost of the EMB-312 is slightly in excess of £370,000, and the second prototype is scheduled to join the flight test programme this month (December). The *official* first flight of the EMB-312 took place at São José dos Campos on 19 August, but the aircraft was, in fact, first airborne on 16 August.

Assembly has now begun of what is expected to be the **final batch of** EMB-326GB **Xavantes** for the *Fôrça Aérea Brasileira*, this comprising 15 aircraft to replace those withdrawn from FAB production for export (six to Togo and nine to Paraguay) and complete the service's current orders for 167 aircraft. An option exists on 50 additional Xavantes but it is not now anticipated that this will be taken up.

FEDERAL GERMANY

Delivery last month of a **modified F-4F** Phantom to *Jagdgeschwader* 74 at Neuberg marked commencement of the service **phase-in** stage of the *Peace Rhine* programme involving the capability upgrading of the remaining 168 aircraft of this type in the inventory of the *Luftwaffe*. The primary purpose of the *Peace Rhine* programme is integration of new conventional weapons systems with the F-4F which will thus be capable of carrying the full range of weaponry fitted to the F-4E of the USAF. The *Peace Rhine* programme has so far received DM300m (£69·2m) funding and the modified F-4F can carry the AIM-9L Sidewinder as well as the ASMs and electro-optically guided bombs of the F-4E, and makes provision for later application of AMRAAM. After initial deliveries to JG 74, the modified F-4F is to be assigned to JaboG 36 at Rheine-Hopsten, which will commence conversion early next year, followed by JG 71 at Wittmundhaven from late 1981, and JaboG 35 at Pferdsfeld from early 1982. The primary rôles of the units will remain unchanged but their potential operational versatility will be greatly increased.

FRANCE

M Yvon Bourges has recently **confirmed** planned **procurement of** the EMBRAER EMB-121 **Xingu** for the *Armée de l'Air* (25) and *Marine* (16) for training and communications rôles with deliveries to France commencing in July. The first French Xingu is scheduled to leave the EMBRAER assembly line in May and eight will be delivered by the end of 1981, 19 during 1982 and the remaining 14 in 1983. Twenty-eight per cent of the total cost will be made up of French-supplied equipment.

The **1981 defence budget** includes provision for procurement of a further 21 Mirage F1s and 22 Mirage 2000s to bring total *Armée de l'Air* purchases of these fighters to 246 and 48 respectively. Provision is also made for five Transall C.160 transports, three Dassault-Breguet Guardian maritime surveillance aircraft for the *Marine* and 22 HOT missile-equipped SA 342 Gazelle helicopters for the *Aviation Légère de l'Armée de Terre*. Funding is also being provided to maintain a force of 15 Mirage IV bombers in service until 1983, and for the re-engining of two DC-8s serving in the VIP transport rôle with CFM56 turbofans.

IRAQ

The Iraqi government is **negotiating** the **purchase of** the Dassault-Breguet/Dornier **Alpha Jet** as the third and final stage in the modernisation of the Iraqi Air Force training fleet which commenced in 1979 with procurement of 40 FFA/Repair AG AS-202/18A Bravo primary trainers and is continuing with current deliveries of 52 PC-7 Turbo Trainer basic trainers. The Iraqi Air Force is currently operating 24 L 39Z Albatross trainer-cum-light strike aircraft and it is understood that the number of Alpha Jets under discussion is also 24.

At the time of closing for press, the **commencement of deliveries of** the **Mirage F1** to the Iraqi Air Force was reportedly imminent. The initial Iraqi order called for 32 single-seat Mirage F1EQs and four two-seat F1BQs, a follow-on order for a further 24 aircraft having been announced at the beginning of this year. When hostilities began between Iraq and Iran, the Iraqi government requested that Mirage deliveries be accelerated, and it is understood that Dassault-Breguet have accordingly brought forward the commencement of deliveries to early this month from next February.

JAPAN

Adm Tsugio Yada, chief of the MSDF, has announced that **no more** Shinmeiwa **PS-1** ASW **flying boats** are to be procured as the rôle performed by the flying boat will be fulfilled by the P-3C Orion. Additional procurement will take place, however, of the US-1 amphibious ASR version. Total procurement of the PS-1 has been 23 of which four have been lost in accidents.

The **ASDF has decided against** the **purchase of additional** Kawasaki **C-1 transports,** stating that the shortfall in needed capacity owing to inadequate numbers of C-1s will be made up by the planned procurement of 14 C-130H Hercules, six of which are expected to be purchased in Fiscal 1981. The ASDF's request to buy the C-130H is expected to be attacked by the opposition parties who are demanding an explanation as to why the ASDF now wishes to acquire the C-130H when, in 1966, it was rejected after an evaluation with the C-1, which, it was stated, possessed range and payload capabilities adequate for the service's needs.

The ASDF is to commence feasibility **studies of** the **service life extension of** the **F-4EJ** Phantom with £1·42m funding in Fiscal 1981. The programme is expected to extend the service life of the F-4EJ from 3,000 to 5,000 hours, and for study purposes, one-sixth of the F-4EJ fleet will be fitted with load sensors. Simultaneously, the ASDF hopes to upgrade the combat qualities of the F-4EJ by means of a new fire control system with look-down capability and by the introduction of wing leading-edge slats. The first and last F-4EJs to have entered the ASDF inventory are currently scheduled to reach their life limitations in 1986 and 1995, but the service hopes to retain the F-4EJ in service beyond the year 2000, thus saving more than £1,665m by postponing procurement of replacement aircraft.

KENYA

The US Defense Department has issued a letter of offer to the Kenyan government for the sale of two **additional** two-seat **Northrop F-5Fs** at a cost of $14m (£5·8m), informing US Congress that the Kenya Air Force is suffering from a lack of F-5Fs for conversion training. The Kenya Air Force has been operating 10 F-5E Tiger IIs and two F-5Fs at Nanyuki since early last year.

OMAN

A major increase in the transport support capability of the Sultan of Oman's Air Force will result from **procurement of** one Lockheed **C-130H** Hercules at a cost, including crew training, ground support equipment and spares for two years, of $24·8m (£10·3m).

NEW ZEALAND

The **Royal New Zealand Air Force anticipates replacing** its last three active de Havilland **Devons** operated in the communications rôle by No 42 Sqdn at Ohakea **with** three Cessna 421 **Golden Eagles** by mid-1981.

Defence Minister Gill has announced that the government has agreed that the RNZAF should enter into **negotiations** with Air New Zealand **for procurement of** one or more **Boeing 737s** when these become surplus to the airline's requirements.

THAILAND

It is reported from Indonesia that the Royal Thai Air Force has taken an **option on** 20 Nurtanio-CASA NC-212-200 **Aviocar** utility transports following a visit to Nurtanio's Bandung facility by an RTAF team headed by AM Surapong Susapong. The Thai government has already purchased six NC-212 Aviocars equipped with cloud seeding gear, two of these having been delivered, with the delivery of a further two imminent and the remaining two to be delivered next year. The RTAF is currently seeking replacements for its aged Fairchild C-123 Providers and Douglas C-47s and it seems likely that the Aviocar has been selected to replace at least a proportion of these.

SWEDEN

The first production BAe **Sky Flash** AAM for *Flygvapnet* was **handed over** to the Swedish Defence Material Administration on 20 October, this being the first supplied under a £60m production contract signed in December 1978. Sky Flash will form the primary armament of the Saab JA 37 Viggen interceptor currently being delivered to *Flygvapnet*.

UNITED KINGDOM

On 2 October, the **first** two examples of a new version of the Westland Sea King, the **HAS Mk 5,** were **handed over** to the Royal Navy. Sea King HAS Mk 5 offers enhanced submarine search capability as a result of the combination of a new Decca 71 radar and tactical air navigation system, sonobuoy dropping equipment and its associated Marconi LAPADS data processing equipment. Provision is made for the later installation of MEL Sea Searcher radar. The Sea King HAS Mk 5 has a crew of four, with the dunking sonar operator also monitoring the LAPADS equipment at an additional crew station, and the cabin has been enlarged for the extra equipment by the repositioning of the rear bulkhead farther aft. Seventeen Sea King HAS Mk 5 helicopters are currently on order for the Royal Navy, and the existing HAS Mk 2 fleet will be progressively brought up to the new standard.

AIRCRAFT AND INDUSTRY

CANADA

Canadair has **resumed production of** the **CL-215** multi-purpose amphibian in a new 300,000 sq ft (27 870 m²) building at Dorval International Airport. Deliveries will begin in late 1981, with four aircraft destined for Yugoslavia, Previously, in two production runs, Canadair has built 65 CL-215s and these are in service with the provincial fire-fighting authorities in Quebec and Manitoba, and in France, Greece, Spain, Thailand and Venezuela.

De Havilland Canada has announced a $Can60m (£21·4m) **expansion programme to handle Dash 8** development, following the decision of the federal government to provide financial support for the new commuterliner (see *AirData File*/November 1980). The expansion plans include the construction of a new warehouse at Downsview, to be used for prototype tooling, construction and assembly of parts for the Dash 8 prototype (and subsequently as a warehouse); two new hangars for Dash 8 component and sub-assembly manufacture at Downsview, and construction of a new final assembly and test facility at a site still to be selected, from more than 60 proposals made by Canadian committees.

FEDERAL GERMANY

MBB is seeking certification of the **BO 105** at an **increased gross weight** of 5,290 lb (2 400 kg), up from 5,070 lb (2 300 kg), following successful testing of the BO 105M (PAH-1) military version at this weight.

FRANCE

Aérospatiale subsidiary SOCATA has adopted the **name Trinidad for the TB.20**, the 235 hp version of the TB.10 Tobago with a retractable undercarriage. First flight was reported to be imminent as this issue went to press. By the end of September, the company had delivered 122 Tobagos and had sold a total of 168 (including the lower-powered TB.11 Tampicos).

First flight of the **AS 332L**, the stretched version of the Super Puma, was made on 10 October. As noted in this column last month, this is the fourth production Super Puma, and it features a fuselage stretch of 2 ft 6 in (0,765 m); the gross weight is unchanged at 17,195 lb (7 800 kg), as are all other major characteristics, including fuel capacity. The maximum number of seats increases from 18 to 22. The introduction of swept-back tips to the rotor blades is expected to permit an increase in gross weight to 17,637 lb (8 000 kg) by the time the AS 332L is certificated and to 18,078 lb (8 200 kg) later; with underslung load, a max weight of 20,723 lb (9 400 kg) is expected to be approved.

The fifth example of the Dassault-Breguet **Mirage 2000**, and the first **two-seater** (2000B-01), made its **first flight** at Istres on 11 October. With the fuselage lengthened by only 8 in (0,20 m), the Mirage 2000 retains most of the characteristics of the single-seater, although fuel capacity is reduced from 880 Imp gal (4 000 l) to 858 Imp gal (3 900 l). The single-seat Mirage 2000 is to be developed for a gross weight of 36,817 lb (16 700 kg), including 13,228 lb (6 000 kg) of external stores.

Dassault-Breguet has announced its decision to put the **Mystère-Falcon 20H into production**, with certification expected in May 1981. The 20H was announced during the Paris Air Show in 1979 as a civil derivative of the Falcon 20G Guardian, powered by 5,440 lb (2 450 kgp) Garrett AiResearch ATF 3-6 turbofans, and a prototype in civil guise first flew on 30 April 1980. The Falcon 20H also features a 180-Imp gal (820-l) fuel tank in the rear fuselage, similar to that in the Falcon 50, bringing total capacity to 1,320 Imp gal (6 000 l). The range with eight passengers and a 45-min fuel reserve is 2,440 naut mls (4 550 km), compared with 1,780 naut mls (3 300 km) for the Falcon 20F. Customer deliveries of the Falcon 20H are not expected to begin until the last quarter of 1982, with priority in engine deliveries being given to the HU-25As for the US Coast Guard. Delays in certification of the ATF3-6, which had difficulty in meeting the FAA bird-impact requirements, have already caused Dassault-Breguet to postpone launching the Falcon 20H.

INTERNATIONAL

Rolls-Royce/Turboméca announced completion of type approval and full military **clearance for the Adour 811**, an uprated version of the engine that will power the Jaguars now on order for export to India and Oman. The Adour 811 is rated at 8,400 lb st (3 810 kgp) for take-off with reheat, some five per cent more than the Adour 804; the dry thrust is increased by more than 10 per cent at high subsonic speed at low level. An equivalend version without reheat, the Adour 851, will be available for future examples of the British Aerospace Hawk (see "The Year of the Hawk"/November 1980).

Bell and Mitsui & Co Ltd have signed an agreement providing for the **production in Japan of** the **Bell 214ST** SuperTransport. The 18-seat 214ST is the largest of Bell's family of single-rotor helicopters and is to enter commercial service early in 1982. Mitsui is purchasing a batch of these helicopters from Bell for sale in Japan and as the first phase of the programme production of the empennage will be undertaken by Fuji for supply to the Bell line at Fort Worth. Progressive phases are expected to lead eventually to production of the complete 214ST in Japan, where nearly 800 Bell helicopters of other types have already entered service and more than 600 have been built under licence.

AIR INTERNATIONAL IN 1981

THE EFFECTS of inflation will already be well-known to the majority of our readers, not only in the United Kingdom but also in other European countries and in North America, where steadily rising costs have unfortunately become a fact of life. While the publishers of AIR INTERNATIONAL continue to make every possible effort to minimise the effects of inflation and to absorb, so far as possible, the recent sharp rises in printing and paper costs and distribution charges, some of these rises must perforce be passed on to readers. Increases in the cover prices of the majority of UK aviation magazines have already been announced in the course of 1980; now, with effect from the January 1981 issue, the price of the UK edition of AIR INTERNATIONAL must be increased to 70p. The subscription rates, effective from January 1981 (or, in the case of existing subscribers, at the next renewal after that date) will be: in the UK, £8·75; overseas, £9·25; USA, $23·00 and Canada $26·00.

Closely following its selection as one of the six finalists in the US Navy VTXTS competition to find a new flight jet training system, the Dassault-Breguet/Dornier **Alpha Jet** made a three-week **tour** of military bases **in the USA** during September. The tour was sponsored by Lockheed, which is teamed with the manufacturers for the VTXTS submission, and the aircraft flew from Istres to Teterboro, NJ, by way of Iceland, Greenland and Canada on 31 August. The Alpha Jet used for the demonstration tour was No 58 off the German production line, painted in US Navy colours. The study contracts awarded by the US Navy (see *Airscene*/October 1980) are for completion by mid-February and will lead later in 1981 to the elimination of three or possibly four of the six contenders, with two or three going through to a demonstration and validation phase prior to selection of the winner in the autumn of 1983. The six study contracts are each valued at between $400,000 and $500,000 (£164,000–£205,000).

ISRAEL

Israel Aircraft Industries has adopted the name **Astra** for the latest **development in** its **Westwind line** of biz-jets (see "From Bethany to Tel Aviv"/August 1980). Scheduled to be available in 1984, the Astra combines the fuselage of the Westwind 2 with an advanced new Sigma 2 wing mounted below the cabin floor. Powered by Garrett AiResearch TFE 731 turbofans, the Astra is designed to cruise at Mach=0·80 and to have a 3,000-naut ml (5 550-km) range. It will accommodate up to 10 passengers.

JAPAN

Mitsubishi Aircraft International announced a 60-day slip in **certification** (to FAR Part 25) **of** the **Diamond I** biz-jet, to February 1981, and a 90-day slip in the start of deliveries, to March 1981; the original schedule will, however, be recovered after the first 10/12 aircraft. The delay in certification is largely attributable to changes in FAA procedures following the DC-10 accident in May 1979. The Diamond I order backlog is now 102; with effect from aircraft No 111, the price has been set at $2,215,000 (£427,000) plus escalation from March 1981, with a $35,000 (£14,650) increase to be made at aircraft No 141 or after certification, whichever is first. An increase in gross weight of 210 lb (95 kg), to 14,100 lb (6 400 kg), has also been announced. The first production Diamond has now flown and arrived at San Angelo, Texas, in August in time to be seen by some 60 customers attending the first owner/operator symposium for the type. Two more Diamonds will join this and the two prototypes to complete certification.

NETHERLANDS

Fokker BV has formed a new wholly-owned **subsidiary in the USA** to handle marketing, sales and support of all Fokker commercial aircraft products, including the F27 and F28, in North America. Based in Washington, Fokker Aircraft USA Inc is expected to participate in expanding the market for the F27 and F28 among US commuter airlines, following the introduction of these aircraft by Swift Aire Lines, Mississippi Valley Airlines, Altair Airlines and Empire Airlines. The company's senior executives are Stuart Mathews, president, and Leroy Simpson, vice-president.

NORWAY

Braathens SAFE has become the last of the existing customers for the Boeing 767 to announce its choice of engine, with **selection of** the Pratt & Whitney **JT9D-7R4D**. The Norwegian company is the seventh 767 customer to select the P & W engine, the others being Air Canada, China Airlines, Pacific Western Airlines, TWA, United and Western.

NEW ZEALAND

Flight **testing of** the second prototype Aerospace Industries **Cresco** is placing special attention upon the flutter characteristics, reported to be the cause of the loss of the first prototype early in 1980. Following certification with the Avco Lycoming LTP 101 turboprop, the company is expected to develop a version of the Cresco with the Pratt & Whitney PT6A engine as an alternative.

SPAIN

CASA has obtained FAA certification, through the latter's Brussels office, for an **increase** of 330 lb (150 kg) **in** the gross **weight of** the **C.212-200 Aviocar**, to 16,424 lb (7 450 kg). The landing weight is increased by 772 lb (350 kg) to 16,204 lb (7 350 kg) and the zero fuel weight by 1,100 lb (500 kg) to 15,540 lb (7 050 kg). The changes allow the payload to be increased by 20 per cent and allow the Aviocar to transport 26 passengers and their baggage over short ranges.

SWEDEN

To pursue **development of** the **JAS project** for a multi-rôle combat aircraft to replace the Viggen, four major Swedish companies have formed an industrial consortium, and discussions have begun with companies in Europe and the USA to seek risk-sharing partners for various of the aircraft sub-systems. The consortium comprises Saab-Scania (system management, system integration and basic airframe design), Volvo Flygmotor (power plant), LM Ericcson (radar) and SRA Communications (display and recording subsystems). Saab is already testing possible configurations for the aircraft with a view to meeting the 1 June 1981 target for submission to the Swedish government of a formal offer on the JAS, and selection of suppliers for all major sub-systems was expected to be made by the end of this year. Research and development up to the spring of 1982 is being jointly funded, with the government contributing SKr200m (£20m). The production programme, if then launched, is expected to cost at least £2,000m for about 300 aircraft to enter service from 1990 onwards.

UNITED KINGDOM

The RAE Bedford and the RSRE Malvern have jointly developed a **Laser True Airspeed System** (LATAS) that has now **entered** the **flight test** stage fitted in an HS 125 operated by the RAE. Using invisible CO_2 laser light that is inherently safe to the human eye, LATAS has the ability to measure airspeed several hundred metres ahead of the aircraft in which it is fitted. Thus sudden changes in the speed and direction of the wind (which may include downdraughts) can be detected in time for the pilot to take action to avoid a large sink rate developing.

McAlpine Helicopters Ltd has extended its agreement with Aérospatiale's Helicopter Division to cover **distribution** in the UK **of the SA 365N** Dauphin, in addition to the AS 355E Twin Squirrel and AS 350B Squirrel. Since taking on the distribution of the smaller helicopter two years ago, McAlpine has sold 15 AS 350Bs in the UK and has ordered 10 AS 355Es plus a single SA 365N. McAlpine also has recently acquired an ATC 112H helicopter IFR procedure trainer, for installation in its enlarged facilities at Hayes, Middlesex.

Practavia Ltd of Wycombe Air Park is now **marketing** in the UK plans and kits for **the Scamp**, a single-seat all-metal biplane for amateur construction. Including the VW car engine conversion in kit form, the Scamp can be built for less than £2,500; six different kit stages are available, so that construction can be started for an outlay of only £195 on the first kit. The VW engine is available in 1600cc or 1835cc versions and can be purchased "ready-to-fly" from Practavia. With the larger engine, the Scamp is aerobatic and uses less than 3 gal (13,5 l) of fuel an hour; more than 500 examples are reported to be under construction in the USA.

In view of the upsurge of interest in the turboprop engine and the continuing sales of the BAe HS748 and Fokker F27, Rolls-Royce has embarked upon an **engine demonstrator programme** aimed at reducing the fuel burn of the **Dart** by about 5 per cent over typical 100-250 naut mls (185-463 km) stage lengths. Further savings of about 3 per cent can be made by changes in aircraft operating techniques. The improvements are obtained with minor improvements to the compressor and turbine blades, and, if test running, to start this year, confirms predictions, they will be offered on future RDa 7 engines. A simple, lightweight hushkit that has demonstrated a 10 EPNdb reduction in low-power noise levels is already available. Nearly 7,000 Darts have now been sold.

USA

The first **DC-8** Srs 61 for **conversion to Srs 71** with CFM 56 turbofans has now arrived at Tulsa, where the work will be done by McDonnell Douglas under contract to Cammacorp, which is managing the programme. The aircraft is one of 29 DC-8s that United Airlines plans to have converted to Super 70 series configuration, and is expected to fly in mid-May 1981, leading to FAA certification by year-end. Major sub-contractors in the programme, in addition to Douglas and CFM International, are Grumman Aerospace with responsibility for the nacelles and pylons, and Garrett AiResearch for air conditioning and APUs. A total of 70 DC-8s will be converted under contracts held by Cammacorp from United, Flying Tiger, Spantax, Capitol, Delta, Transamerica and Jet Aviation (Switzerland), with 40 others under option; Japan Air Lines and SAS are reported among the option holders. The Flying Tiger contract covers 13 DC-8 Srs 63s, for which a separate certification programme will be needed in 1981/82. In addition, the French *Armée de l'Air* has announced that it will convert one DC-8 Srs 62, used by GLAM for regular transport flights between Europe and French Polynesia, and funding for two more conversions is included in the French Defence Budget for 1981. Unless GLAM acquires additional Super Sixty aircraft, these additional DC-8s will be Srs 50s, of which the unit has three in service plus a single Srs 30.

Gulfstream American has again emerged as the **purchaser of Rockwell's General Aviation Division**. A letter of intent was signed early in October and the deal was expected to become firm during November, after this issue went to press. The Rockwell GA product line now comprises three versions of the Turbo Commander, the single-engined Commander range having been discontinued and the Commander 700 light twin transferred wholly to Fuji. Gulfstream has also dropped production of its single-engined aircraft and its Cougar light twin and is seeking to sell its Ag-Cat line. The principal Gulfstream product is now the **Gulfstream III**, which obtained FAA **certification** on 22 September and for which the company holds more than 70 orders. Work is also continuing on the G-159C stretched Gulfstream I commuter and a modification of Gulfstream IIs to G III standard, but the Hustler programme is at low ebb and deposits on production positions have been refunded. The prototype Hustler 500, with combination turboprop/turbojet power, is still likely to be completed before the end of this year, but interest now centres upon a corporate transport derivative of the Peregrine 600, which is itself a Hustler variant proposed to meet the USAF requirement for a new primary trainer (see *AirData File*/October 1979). The Peregrine has not been selected by USAF for further evaluation but Gulfstream is continuing work on a prototype and is planning to develop a corporate version powered by a pair of 1,500 lb st (680 kgp) turbofans side-by-side in the rear fuselage; suitable engines are being projected by Garrett, Teledyne, General Electric and Williams Research in connection with the USAF NGT programme.

Lockheed-Georgia has adopted a **new** system of **designations for** the various configurations of the **Hercules** now in production or on offer. Primarily for marketing and engineering use, the new system does not affect US military designations in the C-130 series and has the biggest impact upon projected rather than current models. The basic designations C-130H and L-100 are retained for the military and commercial models; in future, a change of length from these basic models will be indicated by digits recording the amount of stretch in inches, while configuration changes for specific missions will be shown by suffix letters. An exception is being made in the case of the L-100-30, where the -30 is already so widely used that it will be retained, rather than changing to L-100-180 as would be required under the new system. In detailing the new system, Lockheed listed no fewer than 13 projected Hercules variants that were current at mid-year (not counting the L-400 Twin Hercules, now suspended). These new projects, with their former designations (if different) in parenthesis, were the ECX-130 advanced Tacamo version, KCX-130 advanced tanker, C-130H-MSL missile launcher, C-130H-MSC (C-130MX ALCC) missile control aircraft and C-130H-SC (SC-130) sea control variant, all proposed for the USAF; the C-130H-30 (C-130H(S) and L-382T) foreign military versions with 180-in (4,57-m) body stretch, now in production for Indonesia, and C-130H-MP (PC-130H) maritime patrol/search and rescue version, as recently delivered to Malaysia; and the commercial L-100-30PX (L-100-31) passenger transport (also known as the L-382N), the L-100-30QC cargo/passenger convertible, the L-100-30C cargo/passenger combi, the L-100-30MP maritime patrol/search and rescue version, the L-100-220 (L-100-30M) with 220-in (5,59-m) body stretch and the L-100-260 (L-100-40) with 260-in (6,60-m) body stretch.

Northrop is likely to adopt the **modified wing root extensions** designed for the F-5G (see *AirData File*/October), **on** future production **F-5Es**. The larger extensions have already been flight-tested on an F-5E and have demonstrated a substantial improvement in lift coefficient that can be used with advantage by the F-5E as well as the F-5G. Northrop is building a pre-production batch of four F-5Gs, with first flight in late summer of 1982 followed by initial deliveries in 1983 and large scale production in 1984. The US government has given licences for Northrop to discuss the F-5G with 21 prospective customers and application has been made for 13 more. The fly-away unit cost is being quoted as below $6m (£2·5m).

With a continuing brisk demand, **Learjet production** is being **increased** in the course of 1981 and by the early months of 1982 should be running at 17 aircraft a month, including five Longhorn 50s and 12 Century III models made up of a mixture of CJ610-engined Learjet 20s and TFE731-engined Learjet 30s. The addition of the **Model 25G** to the Century III range has been **announced**, following an agreement between Gates Learjet and The Dee Howard Company providing for the application of the latter's aerodynamic improvement package to the Learjet. The Model 25G will

Superior air superiority

TORNADO *NATO'S No1 in all weathers*

The measure of the effectiveness of the Tornado Air Defence Variant is that it has the ability to establish and maintain the air superiority which ensures that dog-fight situations do not even develop. By combining the latest missile, radar and systems technology, it provides innovative solutions to the problems of electronic stand-off combat, typified by ability to detect and identify hostile aircraft at 100 nm range and to destroy them at 25 nm range with missiles with exceptional snap-down manoeuvre capability. And Tornado ADV can do all this independently of AEW or ground radar to provide a completely autonomous area defence capability.

PVA 47

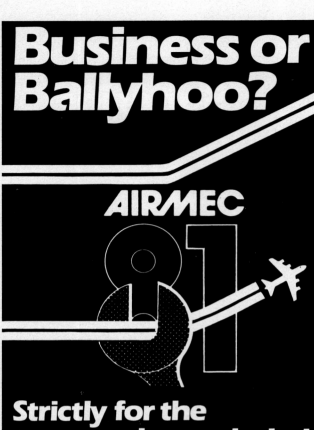

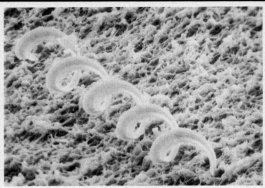

feature an inboard section glove on each wing to carry extra fuel; a new nacelle pylon configuration to improve cruise performance; a new tip-tank fin cuff; pressure-tuned leading edges and a new span-flow limiter. Similar features have already been certificated by Dee Howard as a retro-fit package for the 24 as the XR Learjet, and the range of the Learjet 25G will be more than 20 per cent greater than that of the current Model 25s. A series of improvements has been announced for the Learjet 30, with a 300-lb (136-kg) increase in take-off weight and 1,000-lb (454-kg) increase in landing weight, a flap pre-select system as standard and optional IPECO crew seats in the cockpit.

Gates Learjet announced a four/five month **slippage in** the **Longhorn 50** series **certification**, now expected in March/April 1981. The production build-up will also be slower than first planned. First to be certificated will be the Longhorn 55, followed later by the long-range Model 56; the landing weight of both these models is to be increased by 1,000 lb (454 kg) to 17,000 lb (7 711 kg). The company has now dropped the shorter-range Longhorn 54 from its plans although this could be certificated later if customer interest requires. The three Longhorn 50s in flight test, including the first production aircraft that made its maiden flight on 11 August, had completed more than 460 hrs by end-September, and all three aircraft had been flown to the planned max certificated altitude of 51,000 ft (15 550 m).

Cessna announced **delivery of** the **750th Citation** on 18 September, when a Citation II was handed over to Minster Machine Co of Ohio. Deliveries of Citations are now out-stripping all other biz-jets on an annual basis. Proceeding towards an April 1982 certification target, Cessna has completed 400 hrs of Citation II testing in 372 flights (279 hrs on No 1 and 93 hrs on No 2) up to late September. Flights have now been made to the planned maximum certificated altitude of 51,000 ft (15 550 m) and the max diving speed of Mach = 0·88 (400 kt/740 km/h CAS) has been attained.

Swearingen has adopted the designations **Merlin IIIC** and **Merlin IVC** for the newest **versions** of its business twins, featuring a number of detailed refinements and, in the case of the Merlin IVC, the same 10-ft (3,05-m) wing span extension that is applicable to the Metro III (this column last month). Certificated at a gross weight of 14,000 lb (6 350 kg), the Merlin IVC will carry 13 passengers for 970 naut mls (1 797 km) and eight passengers for 1,500 naut mls (2 778 km). Gross weight of the Merlin IIIC will be 13,215 lb (5 995 kg), and the range with six passengers will be 2,230 mls (3 590 km).

With its first Comanchero **conversions of** the Piper pressurised **Navajo** already in flight test and plans to deliver up to 12 in 1981, Schafer Aircraft Modification of Clifton, Texas, is now offering a similar turboprop conversion of the Navajo Chieftain. The Comanchero has 750 shp Pratt & Whitney PT6A-135 turboprops (flat-rated to 620 shp) replacing the Avco Lycoming TGIO-541-E1A piston engines; the planned Chieftain conversion, to fly in mid-1981, will have PT6A-27s flat-rated to 500 shp replacing the 350 hp TGIO-540-F2BD engines. Turboprop versions of the Cessna 310, 340 and 402 are also planned by Schafer.

Piper has introduced a new variant of its turboprop twins as the **Cheyenne IIXL**. Powered by 750 shp PT6A-135 turboprops (flat rated to 620 shp) it also differs from the Cheyenne II (the basic model in the Cheyenne range) in having the fuselage lengthened by 24 in (61 cm). The cabin seats six-to-eight and the XL has generally comparable performance to the Cheyenne II.

Advanced Systems Technology Inc (Astec) of Everett, Washington, has now completed 24 of its **Eagle conversions of** the Cessna **Citation** (see *AirData File*/January 1978) and is planning to continue at the rate of 10 a year. Citations from c/n 350 onwards, of Citation I type, can be converted to Eagle I standard with the same inner wing glove plus a 14-in (36-cm) wing-tip extension that allows an increase in gross weight, additional fuel capacity and increased cruising speed and range. Astec also is proposing the **TF-25 conversion of** the **Learjet** 24 or 25, in which 3,000 lb st (1 360 kgp) Pratt & Whitney JT15D-5 turbofans would replace the CJ610-8A turbojets. The principal advantage would be in range and noise level, since there would be only a 100 lb (45 kg) increase in installed thrust. Flight testing of the TF-25, using JT15D-4s initially, is expected to begin late next year, with certification of the definitive version in late 1983.

Having previously announced its interest in developing a 13-passenger commuter version of the Super King Air 200 as the Beech 1300 and a stretched-fuselage 19-passenger derivative as the Beech 1900, Beech is now looking at market reactions to a **projected** 12-seat executive version of the latter which it designates as **Beech 1200.** Deliveries could begin in 1983 if the programme goes ahead, and the Beech 1300 will be dropped in any case.

First **orders** are reported to have been placed **for** the **OMAC-1** turboprop-engined 6/8-seat business transport of canard configuration (see *AirData File*/February 1980). First flight, originally set for November, has slipped to next March or April, and some design changes have been made including increased sweep-back on the inboard leading-edge and additional Krueger flaps on the trailing edge. The OMAC-1 is powered by a 700 shp Avco Lycoming LTP-101-700A-1 and at 5,700 lb (2 586 kg) gross weight it is expected to cruise at 285 mph (459 km/h) and to have a range of 3,390 mls (5 456 km/h) at 250 mph (402 km/h). The Reno-based OMAC Inc takes its initials from Old Man's Aircraft Co.

While production of the Mooney M20 series (M20J or Model 201 and M20K or Model 231) continues at the rate of two per working day, **Mooney Aircraft** Corp has announced that first flight of its new **M30 prototype** is expected next February. The six-seat M30 will feature a cabin pressurised to a differential of 4·7 lb/sq in (0,33 kg/cm²) and will have a swept-back tail unit, contrasting with the swept-forward fin and rudder that is a hall-mark of the present Mooney designs. With a 350 hp Avco Lycoming TIO-540 turbosupercharged engine, and a gross weight of 3,790 lb (1 720 kg), the M30 will have a cruising speed of 298 mph (480 km/h) and a range of 1,130 naut mls (2 093 km) at 65 per cent power. Since the Republic Steel company acquired Mooney seven years ago, more than 2,000 aircraft have been produced, including more than 1,050 Model 201s, over 450 Model 231s and about 400 of the 180-hp Rangers, now out of production.

Boeing has delivered the first example of the **747** at the **new gross weight** of 833,000 lb (377 850 kg), the highest certificated weight of any civil aircraft to date. Powered by 53,000 lb st (24 040 kgp) Pratt & Whitney JT9D-7Q engines, the aircraft is a Boeing 747F delivered on 10 October to Cargolux; previous highest certificated weight was 820,000 lb (371 950 kg).

Flight **testing of** the Pratt & Whitney **JT9D-7R4D** turbofan for the Boeing 767 began on 3 October, with one of these engines fitted in the inboard port position on the Boeing 747 prototype, which has remained in Boeing ownership.

US Navy has acquired the **Convair 880** previously operated by the FAA and will use it **as a flight refuelling tanker** for the flight development programme of the F-18 Hornet. A hose drum unit (for probe and drogue refuelling) from a Douglas KA-3D tanker is being fitted in the Convair 880 by Flight Systems Inc and the aircraft is expected to be in service by the end of this year.

Production of the **Great Lakes 2T-1** sporting biplane — claimed to be the oldest certificated aeroplane still in production — has been **transferred** from Oklahoma to Eastman, Georgia, following acquisition of the Great Lakes Aircraft Co by R Dean Franklin. The company was formed in February 1972 by Doug Champlin, who acquired the manufacturing rights in the biplane that had first been certificated in 1929 and of which 264 examples had been built up to the time the original company collapsed in 1932; of those, 56 were still known to be flying in 1972. At Wichita, Kansas, and Enid, Oklahoma, the new company had built 137 more of the biplanes up to the time of its sale in 1979; these aircraft incorporate a few small changes including ailerons on the lower, as well as upper, wings, an inverted-flight fuel and oil system and a 180 hp Lycoming engine. Dean Franklin has announced that a production rate of one Model 2T-1A-2 every seven working days is projected at the new plant in Georgia.

CIVIL AFFAIRS

BELGIUM

Following its inauguration of a Brussels-West Berlin service earlier this year (see *Airscene*/ September 1980), **Air Berlin** USA inaugurated on 22 October a once-weekly **service** linking **Brussels** with **Orlando**, Florida. The service is flown by Boeing 707s.

EGYPT

Using two Boeing 737-200s wet leased from Maersk Air, **Arabia-Arab International** Airlines was to **begin** regular **operation** of domestic services in Egypt on 1 December. Based in Cairo, the company also plans to fly scheduled services to Malta and Luxembourg, and has obtained traffic rights to operate to Rio de Janeiro, Sydney and Seoul. Owned jointly by Egyptian and Saudi Arabian investors, Arabia-Arab International has arranged to purchase one of the Maersk 737s at the end of this year, another at the end of 1981 and a third in 1982, after a year-long lease starting in March 1981. Three new-build 737s will then be acquired in the second half of 1982 and options are being taken on three more.

FEDERAL GERMANY

The new West German charter company **Supair** was expected **to start operations** on 10 November, flying from Munich and Stuttgart to destinations in the Mediterranean area and West Africa. The company expects to benefit from basing its aircraft in the southern German cities, which do not have other resident operators. The initial fleet comprises two 737-200s purchased from Maersk Air; they will be replaced by two new-build high-gross-weight 737-200s ordered from Boeing for delivery in spring and autumn of 1981 and two more similar 737s are on option for November/December 1981 delivery. In the longer term, Supair plans to add CFM 56-engined DC-8s to its fleet.

INDIA

Under its recently-appointed new chairman and chief executive, Raghu Raj (formerly chairman of the Industrial Development Bank of India), **Air India** is reported to be planning a major change of **fleet equipment policy** as one of several measures to combat growing losses. Previous plans to standardise on the Boeing 747 fleet and to replace early 747s among the present fleet (nine 747s and 10 Boeing 707s) with later models are to be abandoned and a smaller three-engined wide-body will be selected as the mainstay of the future fleet.

PORTUGAL

The Portuguese government has approved a four-year plan intended to secure the **financial recovery of Air Portugal** (TAP), which is reported to have been near to bankruptcy in recent months. Government subsidies will be provided to cover debts that accrued from TAP operations in Angola and Mozambique in 1976; the airline's capital will be more than doubled over the next two years and a government subsidy will be provided for the loss-making "social" services to the Azores and Madeira. Approval of the plan allowed Air Portugal to resume negotiations for the purchase of up to five Lockheed TriStar 500s, an earlier order for which has twice been postponed (see *Civil Contracts and Sales*).

UNITED KINGDOM

Sir John King has been named to succeed Ross Stainton as **chairman of British Airways**, with effect from 1 February next, and on a part-time basis. As chairman of Babcock International, Sir John is known to support the government's plans to offer for public sale about half of the shares in British Airways, but this plan has meanwhile been postponed until 1982 at the earliest, because of the poor financial results at present being achieved by the airline. Also with effect from 1 February, Alexander Dibbs, chairman of the National Westminster Bank, will become part-time non-executive deputy chairman of British Airways, succeeding Kenneth Wilkinson, who retires as deputy chairman in December and becomes a part-time member of the board. Chief executive Roy Watts will then become, in addition, executive deputy chairman.

The British transatlantic tour operator **Jetsave** has **signed with British Airways** to carry some 250,000 IT passengers on the latter's scheduled services in 1981. The deal will allow Jetsave to utilise space on BA flights from London to New York, Washington, Los Angeles, Miami and San Francisco (and return), instead of using charter flights. The company will continue to use Transamerica charter flights for its operations from North of England to the USA and CP Air for its flights to and from Canada.

British Airways is to adopt the **names of** major **British cities for** its fleet of RB.211-engined **Boeing 747s**, of which it has 10 so far. The first to be named in this series was christened "City of Birmingham" during October. In the same month, BA took delivery of its first all-cargo 747F, which is also the first of the freighter variants to be powered by Rolls-Royce engines.

British Caledonian has **named** its seventh **DC-10 Srs 30 "James S McDonnell** — The Scottish American Aviation Pioneer" in honour of the founder and chairman of the McDonnell Douglas Corporation, who died in August. The aircraft was used on 26 October to inaugurate the airline's combined London-St Louis-Dallas/Ft Worth service, now operated at a four-times-a-week frequency. The St Louis service had been inaugurated in April with Boeing 707-320C equipment, in which the average monthly load factor had increased from 26 per cent in April to 79 per cent in August. B.Cal's other DC-10s are named after famous Scots: Robert Burns, Sir Alexander Fleming, David Livingstone, Sir Walter Scott, James Watt and Robert the Bruce; an eighth Srs 30 will be delivered next Spring.

USA

Pan American is bringing to an **end** the period during which it has used a **dual** Pan Am/National **identity** following the merger between the two airlines last January. Former National aircraft are progressively being repainted in standard Pan Am livery and the "single image" approach is being pressed in all respects. A world-wide campaign began in October to promote the benefits resulting from the merger and full integration of the two airlines.

CIVIL CONTRACTS AND SALES

Aérospatiale Caravelle: Transeuropa of Spain sold one Super Caravelle to CTA in Switzerland (its fourth); CTA in turn leased one to Finnair.

Airbus A300: Cruzeiro do Sul has converted an option to a firm order for one B4-200 to be delivered in June 1982 (making four in all). ☐ Egyptair has converted options on two B4-200s to firm orders, to make five in all; delivery will be made in the third quarter of 1982. Delivery was recently made of the first two B4-200s to Egyptair, joining three that the company operates on lease from Hapag Lloyd; the third will be delivered in September 1981.

Airbus A310: Kuwait Airways has increased its order for A310s from six to 11. Delivery is to begin in 1983. Total A310 orders are now 76 plus 68 on option.

Boeing 727: The 100th customer for the Boeing 727 is Wistair International, which ordered one for delivery in executive configuration during 1981. Boeing has now sold 1,812 Model 727s, including 11 for executive use; others have been purchased second-hand for the latter rôle.

Boeing 737: Supair of Munich ordered two Advanced 200s for 1982 delivery, plus two more on option (see separate news item). ☐ Maersk Air has sold two 737-200s to Supair, leased one to Guyana Airways (delivered new, direct to Guyana) and leased two more to Arabia-Arab International Airlines. Pelican Cargo at Gatwick is leasing one 737 in cargo configuration from Britannia Airways for livestock charter flights.

Boeing 767: United Airlines converted to firm orders previously-held options on nine 767s, adding to 30 already announced. Options are now held on a further 30 aircraft. Orders now total 161 for 13 airlines, with 129 on option.

British Aerospace HS 748: Air Virginia has ordered one Srs 2B with an option on a second. Delivery will be made in April after fitting out by Aero Spacelines.

CASA C-212 Aviocar: Nurtanio has delivered, from the Indonesian production-line, the first of three ordered by Sabang Merauke Raya Air Charter (SMAC). Largest aircraft in the SMAC fleet, they will operate scheduled and charter services in north and central Sumatra. ☐ Recent CASA 212-200 purchasers in the USA include commuter operators Air Miami, Chaparral Airlines and Key West.

De Havilland Canada Dash-7: Air Niugini has ordered three Dash-7s for delivery in September/December 1981 and April 1982, and has taken options on two more for later in 1982. The sale brings Dash-7 orders to 65 (of which 28 have been delivered) plus 54 on option. ☐ Brymon Airways will order two more (to make four in service by mid-1982) after winning a three-year contract from Chevron UK to use two Dash-7s for an Aberdeen-Unst (Shetlands) service.

Lockheed L-1011 TriStar: TAP Air Portugal has now signed a firm contract for three Dash 500s, with an option on two more. Deliveries begin in 1983.

McDonnell Douglas DC-9: Midway Airlines, operating primarily from Chicago, purchased two Srs 10s to inaugurate Chicago-La Guardia service on 30 October and has an option on a third Srs 10, and on two Super 80s for 1984/85 delivery.

Sikorsky S-76: Recent orders, bringing the total to 412, include 10 more for Bristow Helicopters (making 38); Toronto Helicopters, two (making seven); Shirley Air Services of Edmonton, Alberta, for five and EXXON USA for four.

MILITARY CONTRACTS

Aérospatiale SA 365N Dauphin 2N: Saudi Arabia has ordered 24 SA 365N Dauphin 2N anti-submarine helicopters with deliveries commencing in 1984. Twenty of the helicopters will each be equipped to carry four Aérospatiale AS 15TT anti-ship missiles.

Aérospatiale SA 330 Puma: The Qatar Emiri Air Force has placed an order for an unspecified number of SA 330 Puma medium utility helicopters.

Bell 206B JetRanger III: The Canadian Armed Forces has placed an order for 14 JetRanger III helicopters which are to be based at Portage La Prairie, Manitoba, and will supplement the CAF fleet of CH-136 Kiowas.

Boeing E-3A Sentry: Boeing has received from NATO notification of the placing of an order with a total value of $1,470m (£612m) for 18 E-3A Sentries to be delivered during the period 1982-85.

De Havilland DHC-5D Buffalo: The Ecuadorian Army aviation component, the *Servicio Aereo del Ejercito*, has placed an order for one DHC-5D Buffalo, the purchase being financed by means of a loan of Can$9m from the Bank of Nova Scotia.

Gates Learjet 35A: Finland has signed a letter of intent for the purchase of three Learjet 35As at approximately $22m (£9m) to replace *Ilmavoimat* Il-28s as target tugs in SAM and AAM training.

Hughes 500D: A contract has been placed on behalf of the Royal Jordanian Air Force for eight Hughes 500D helicopters for pilot training.

Lockheed C-130H Hercules: The Sultan of Oman's Air Force is to purchase one C-130H Hercules, contractual value, including crew training, support equipment and spares, being $24·8m (£10·3m).

Northrop F-5F: The Kenya Air Force is to receive two additional two-seat F-5Fs at a cost of $14m (£5·8m).

Rockwell OV-10 Bronco: The Philippine Air Force is to receive 18 OV-10 Bronco observation aircraft at a cost of $113m (£47m). ☐ The Royal Thai Air Force is to receive a supplementary batch of eight OV-10 Broncos at a cost of $58m (£24m).

Sikorsky S-76: An order has been placed on behalf of the Royal Brunei Malay Regiment for seven S-76 helicopters.

Maritime Friendship

FROM 15,000 ft (4 572 m), the sea below looks tranquil and inviting; sunlight sparkles from the crests of waves that distance has diminished to mere creases on the surface below. On the far horizon, a coastline is edged by a silver strand, indented here and there by the outflowings of streams that rise in the high hills beyond. We could be flying off the coast of South America, of Africa, of Australia . . . or cruising above the Mediterranean, maybe, or returning to base in the Caribbean. Water covers three-quarters of the earth's surface and the regular flier has ample opportunity to witness such scenes of natural splendour.

But the sea is not always tranquil; coastlines can be the sites of multifarious activities, not all of them legal, and friendly sunlight is all too often usurped by storm clouds or the shades of night. Nature has many faces, and those whose duties take them into the air must come to terms with them all. And if those duties happen to be concerned with overwater patrol and surveillance, then the help of an aeroplane like the Fokker F27 Maritime will not come amiss, whatever the weather.

At the time of writing, 11 examples of the Maritime have been sold by Fokker (and six delivered) — figures, it is true, that scarcely seem to indicate the pinnacle of success. Nevertheless, the F27 appears already to have captured a greater share of the market than any other among the great variety of maritime surveillance types on offer, and is certainly the market leader in its size/performance class. The market itself for this category of aircraft has developed almost from nothing in the space of a decade, principally because of the international trend towards the establishment of EEZs (exclusive economic zones) at a distance of 200 naut mls (370 km) from national coastlines, and because of the dramatic growth in off-shore industrial activity related to oil and gas extraction from under the sea bed.

The precise size of the market that has thus been created is hard to define; so, too, are the precise characteristics of the aircraft that is needed. Whilst virtually every nation with a seaboard can be classified as a potential customer for a maritime patrol aircraft of some kind, the range/speed/equipment/size/cost equation has so many variables that it can be used to show that almost any aeroplane is "ideal" for the task. Those that have been offered in the past few years range from single piston-engined lightplanes to advanced high-performance twin jets; no doubt the largest part of the market is being, and will be, satisfied by twin-turboprop aircraft but even in this class there is a wide diversity of size, from the newly-announced Pilatus Britten-Norman BN-2T, through such types as the Beech Super King Air 200 and the GAF N22 Searchmaster to the British Aerospace Multi-rôle HS748 and the Fokker F27 Maritime itself.

Fokker* took the decision to go ahead with what is now called the F27 Maritime in July 1975 after a two-year period of market studies, discussions with governments and evaluation of available equipment for the projected missions. At first, the new type was called the F27 MPA (maritime patrol aircraft), and to establish the final configuration and provide a demonstrator, modification of an existing F27 Mk 100 airframe was put in hand (c/n 10183, which had been used by THY as a normal passenger airliner from 1961 to early 1974, and had then been traded-in and stored at Ypenburg). The F27 was, of course, already a best-seller by the time Fokker decided to offer a Maritime version, with a total of 628 sold by the end of 1974 (including the 206 examples built by Fairchild in the USA). As it happened, the decision also coincided with an upsurge in orders for the F27 which no doubt helped to create within the company a climate favourable towards the new variant; sales in 1975 totalled 27, the best annual figure since 1970.

So much has been written in recent years about the maritime patrol and surveillance rôle that it is scarcely necessary to repeat here the mission objectives for which Fokker designed the F27 Maritime. The primary mission was considered to be coastguard duty — the observation of ships along coastal

**At the time of the launch decision, the Dutch company was Fokker-VFW BV, one of the jointly-owned subsidiaries of Zentralgesellschaft VFW-Fokker mbH. This arrangement had resulted from the merger in 1969 between the original Dutch company and the German VFW company. The merger was dissolved earlier in 1980 and Fokker BV is now again an independent company solely under Dutch ownership. For convenience, the name Fokker is used rather than the strictly more accurate Fokker-VFW throughout this article.*

routes, surveillance duties for offshore industries and patrolling territorial fishing waters; included in these duties would be oil pollution control, not only to monitor the threat from wrecked tankers but also to detect illegal flushing of tanks by ships at sea. The secondary mission would be search and rescue, while the basic ability of the F27 to serve as a troop, personnel or freight carrier gave a built-in tertiary rôle.

Early experience of the F27 operating in a maritime environment had been obtained through the use of one aircraft since 1972 by the Icelandic Coast Guard *(Landhelgisgaezlan)*. This particular aircraft (c/n 10260) had been acquired by Iceland in 1972 after service with All Nippon Airways in Japan and, as TF-SYR, it had proved to be a useful tool in the Cod War that followed Iceland's unilateral declaration of a 200 naut ml (370 km) EEZ. Soon after development of the F27 Maritime began, Fokker announced the sale to the Icelandic Coast Guard of a second Mk 200, this being a new-build aircraft (c/n 10545) that was duly delivered in January 1977 as TF-SYN. Although having some special features for its maritime rôle, this aircraft was not a true Maritime, however, and is not now listed by Fokker as such.

The F27 Maritime prototype meanwhile had entered flight testing at Schiphol on 28 February 1976. It had been converted from its original Mk 100 basis to the standard of a Mk 400 airframe, by means of substituting 2,140 shp Rolls-Royce Dart 536-7R (RDa7) engines for the original 1,670 shp Dart 514-7 (RDa6) versions, fitting the large cargo door in the front port fuselage side and bringing the structure and systems up to current standard. Specific to the maritime rôle was the installation of search radar, long-range and other navigation equipment, VHF/UHF direction finding and various other communication systems. Observation windows were fitted, together with a general-purpose launch chute for the dropping of all types of marine markers and flares, and a camera bay was developed to provide for installation of a high-precision mapping camera.

To achieve the long endurance needed for search and patrol

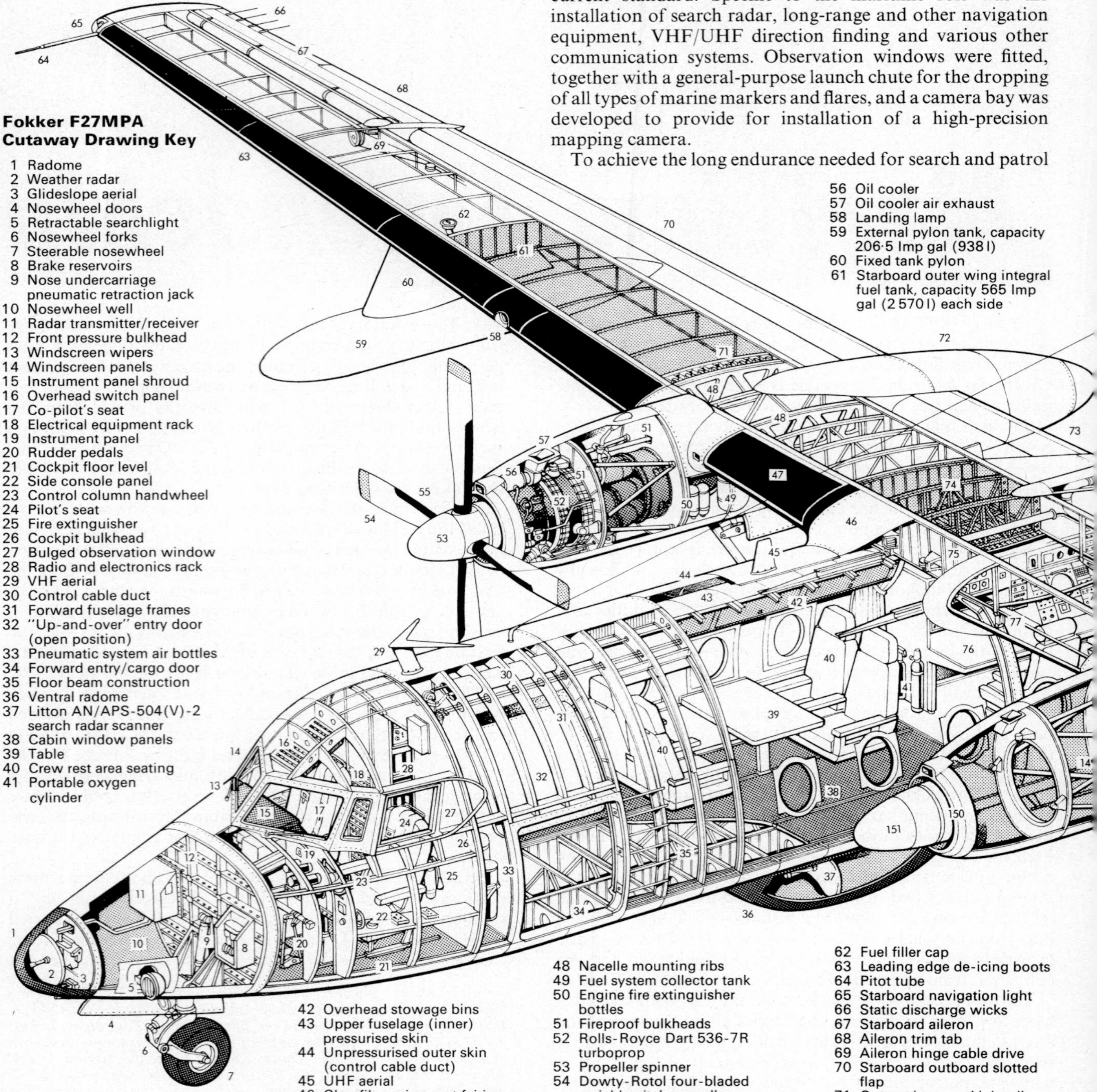

Fokker F27MPA Cutaway Drawing Key

1 Radome
2 Weather radar
3 Glideslope aerial
4 Nosewheel doors
5 Retractable searchlight
6 Nosewheel forks
7 Steerable nosewheel
8 Brake reservoirs
9 Nose undercarriage pneumatic retraction jack
10 Nosewheel well
11 Radar transmitter/receiver
12 Front pressure bulkhead
13 Windscreen wipers
14 Windscreen panels
15 Instrument panel shroud
16 Overhead switch panel
17 Co-pilot's seat
18 Electrical equipment rack
19 Instrument panel
20 Rudder pedals
21 Cockpit floor level
22 Side console panel
23 Control column handwheel
24 Pilot's seat
25 Fire extinguisher
26 Cockpit bulkhead
27 Bulged observation window
28 Radio and electronics rack
29 VHF aerial
30 Control cable duct
31 Forward fuselage frames
32 "Up-and-over" entry door (open position)
33 Pneumatic system air bottles
34 Forward entry/cargo door
35 Floor beam construction
36 Ventral radome
37 Litton AN/APS-504(V)-2 search radar scanner
38 Cabin window panels
39 Table
40 Crew rest area seating
41 Portable oxygen cylinder
42 Overhead stowage bins
43 Upper fuselage (inner) pressurised skin
44 Unpressurised outer skin (control cable duct)
45 UHF aerial
46 Glassfibre wing root fairing
47 Inboard leading edge de-icing boot
48 Nacelle mounting ribs
49 Fuel system collector tank
50 Engine fire extinguisher bottles
51 Fireproof bulkheads
52 Rolls-Royce Dart 536-7R turboprop
53 Propeller spinner
54 Dowty-Rotol four-bladed variable pitch propeller
55 Propeller blade root de-icing boots
56 Oil cooler
57 Oil cooler air exhaust
58 Landing lamp
59 External pylon tank, capacity 206·5 Imp gal (938 l)
60 Fixed tank pylon
61 Starboard outer wing integral fuel tank, capacity 565 Imp gal (2 570 l) each side
62 Fuel filler cap
63 Leading edge de-icing boots
64 Pitot tube
65 Starboard navigation light
66 Static discharge wicks
67 Starboard aileron
68 Aileron trim tab
69 Aileron hinge cable drive
70 Starboard outboard slotted flap
71 Outer wing panel joint rib
72 Nacelle tail fairing
73 Inboard slotted flap

missions, Fokker adopted as standard the wing centre section bag tanks that were an existing option for commercial F27s, and also added two underwing tanks that had previously been developed to allow the F27 to be ferried over long distances and for military users of the basic aircraft. These changes brought the total fuel capacity to 2,463 US gal (9 323 l), or 1,961 US gal (7 423 l) if the pylon tanks were not fitted.

The Maritime prototype (registered PH-FCX and in an attractive "naval" finish featuring dark blue with red trim and a white fuselage top) completed a first phase of testing in five months, amassing some 45 hours. Much of the work was devoted to checking out the performance of the AIL/Litton AN/APS-503F search radar fitted in the belly radome, and to achieving the optimum radome shape for minimum drag. The principal long-range navigation aid selected for the Maritime was the Litton LNT-72 INS, the accuracy of which was also confirmed in the early flight tests.

Production programme

The F27 Maritime demonstrator appeared in public for the first time at Farnborough International 76, by which time Fokker had completed the first sale, of two aircraft for the Peruvian Navy to operate in the coastguard rôle. The Icelandic Coast Guard had by this time decided that the F27 Mk 200 then on order (as already noted) would not be equipped to the full Maritime standard — in particular, it lacked the search radar — and the Peruvian aircraft were thus destined to be the first production examples of the Maritime. These two aircraft

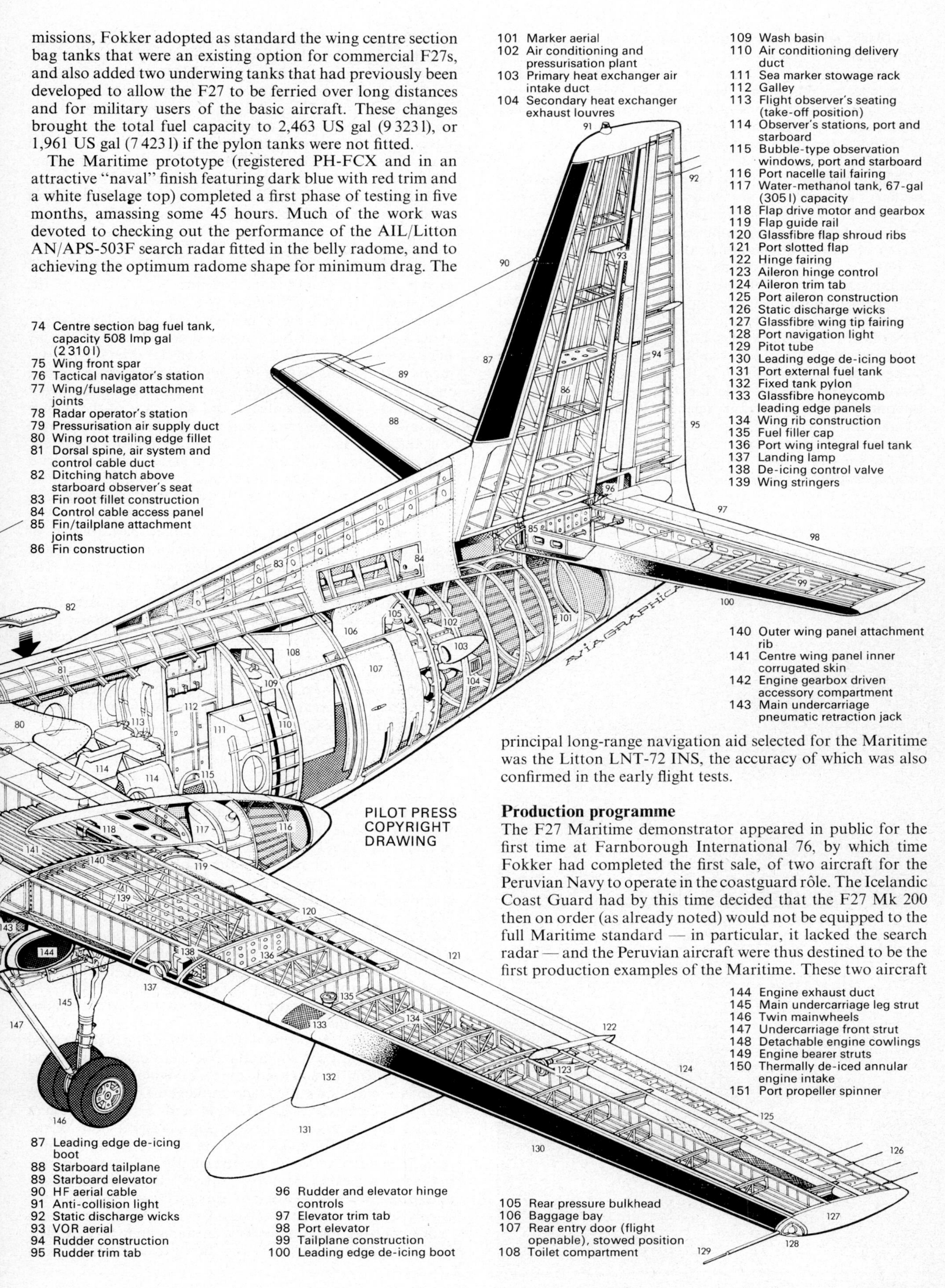

(c/n 10548 and 10549) made their first flights on 14 June and 28 September 1977 and the first of the duo was delivered on 17 September. Delivery of the second was delayed slightly when Fokker leased this aircraft back from the Peruvian government in order to demonstrate the Maritime to the French authorities — who had, and at the time of writing still have, a requirement for this class of aircraft; it was finally delivered to Peru on 25 February 1978.

While the Peruvian aircraft were required to operate in the primary design rôle, the next Maritimes ordered from Fokker were for use in the secondary rôle of search and rescue. This order was for three and was placed on behalf of the Spanish *Ejercito del Aire* for operation by the *Servicio de Salvamiente y de Busqeda* (search and rescue service) in the Canary Islands. Equipped to a similar standard to that of the Peruvian aircraft, the Spanish Maritimes are, however, basically Mk 200 airframes, lacking the forward freight door and reinforced floor of the Peruvian Mk 400s. First of the trio made its initial flight at Schiphol on 23 November 1978 and deliveries were made in March, April and July 1979. These aircraft are now based at Gando air force base (the military side of Las Palmas International Airport) and are operated by *Escuadron* 802 as a component of the *Mando Aereo de Canarias*. This unit's responsibilities extend over some 1·5 million square miles (3,89m km²) of ocean, through which pass major shipping routes between Europe and the American continent and South Africa.

Additional contracts for Maritimes have been announced this year and include one for the Angolan government; this

(Above and below) Two views, from opposite ends of the cabin, of the radar operator's station on the starboard side of the cabin of the F27 Maritime. The large CRT display for the Litton search radar is prominent.

aircraft (c/n 10595) made an appearance at Farnborough International 80 and provided, incidentally, the first confirmation of the appearance of the newly-adopted insignia of the People's Republic of Angola. Delivery was being made to Angola in October. Three Maritimes have been ordered by the Philippine Air Force, for delivery in January, November and December 1981, and the Netherlands government has ordered two for use in the Dutch Antilles region of the Caribbean, where they will be operated by the *Marine Luchtvaartdienst* (MLD) in place of SP-2 Neptunes when delivered in September 1981 and February 1982.

Surveillance features

Production F27 Maritimes have the Litton AN/APS-504(V)-2 search radar, a slightly later and improved version of the equipment first used in the prototype demonstrator. The later radar was installed in the latter aircraft for Phase 2 of its trials, which brought total flying on this aircraft to some 125 hrs by the summer of 1977. In this second phase, several improvements and additional items of equipment were tested; among the former were changes made to the flare launcher, the layout of the VHF/UHF/DF antenna and the shape of the bubble windows at the observer stations. Bubble windows were introduced on the sides of the cockpit to improve the pilots' view. Additional equipment tested included a low light-level TV system and a plotting table connected to the INS, which gave a visual indication of the aircraft's exact position at all times.

The radar has 360-deg scan and three basic modes of operation — search and mapping, beacon interrogation and ground-stabilised display with true ground range. The operator's display is a 7-in (17,8-cm) CRT, on which high revolution mapping of ground features, including coastlines, is presented. Clutter elimination by means of a digital CFAR processor is an optional feature. Complementing the excellent search characteristics of this radar is the Litton LTN-72 long-range inertial navigation system (INS) which provides a self-contained means of navigating the aircraft to predetermined search areas with great accuracy and can then be used to direct the aircraft through programmed search patterns.

A Honeywell AN/APN-198 radar altimeter is fitted to provide the necessary degree of accuracy and safety in low-altitude operations. Bendix RDR-1300 weather radar provides the pilots with information on the weather ahead of the aircraft. As well as providing a back-up navigation aid, Collins DF-301E direction finding equipment is carried as a primary aid for rescue missions, with the ability to determine the bearings of all radio transmissions in the VHF/AM, VHF/FM and UHF frequency range of the aircraft communications systems.

The communication equipment comprises Collins 618T-3 HF for long-range air/air or air/ground use; Collins 618M-3 VHF/AM for short-range voice communication with civil aircraft and ground stations, Sylvania AN/ARC 160 for VHF maritime short-range air/ship links and Collins AN/ARC 159 UHF/AM for short-range communications with military aircraft and ground stations.

Despite the sophistication of the equipment carried, visual search still plays an important rôle, particularly in rescue missions when there are individual survivors in the sea. The observation windows fitted each side near the back of the cabin offer an excellent field of view and extensive human engineering studies have been made in respect both of the windows and of the special observer seats located alongside them. The standard Maritime interior also includes a rest area in the forward cabin, with four seats of VIP standard, a table and space for a bunk; the opportunity for crew members to rest during lengthy missions is considered to be an important factor contributing to efficiency during search periods. The tactical mission consoles, for the radar operator and

Illustrated above and below is the F27 Maritime recently sold to Angola. After being displayed at Farnborough International 80 this aircraft — the most recent Maritime completed – was delivered in October.

navigator/TACCO, are located side-by-side in the central cabin area.

On surveillance missions, it is frequently necessary to take photographs of ships, and to include evidence of time and location on the film. Data from the INS can be fed into hand-held cameras of suitable type, by way of outlets at the observation station and flight deck. Alternatively, an additional wing strong point can be used to carry a camera pod with vertical, oblique and forward-looking camera positions and its own built-in power supply by way of a ram-air turbine.

If photo-mapping is a required rôle, a special camera bay can be provided in the Maritime, permitting installation of an accurate mapping camera such as the Wild RC-10 or the Bendix multi-spectral scanner to detect and record oil spills. A universal launcher tube and marker storage box are located in the rear cabin.

Another new option for the Maritime, to be used for the first time on the aircraft ordered by the *Marine Luchtvaartdienst*, is a searchlight fitted in the nose of the starboard wing pylon tank. To accommodate the Spectrolab Nightsun SX-16 high-power airborne searchlight, the pod will be lengthened by 3 ft 1½ in (0,95 m), but the aerodynamic characteristics will be little changed and the fuel capacity will be the same. The SX-16 has a 14-in (36-cm) parabolic reflector and a peak beam value of 60 million candlepower, using a xenon arc lamp. A focus motor moves the reflector so that beam widths of 1 deg or 10 deg can be selected, and the searchlight can be steered, by a joystick or pistol grip at the co-pilot's station, from horizontal to 45 deg down in elevation and from 10 deg left to 60 deg right in azimuth. Development of the new pod was to begin on the prototype Maritime before the end of this year and preliminary indications are that the beam should be able to illuminate a target from 10,000 ft (3 050 m) and give a clear picture from 7,500 ft (2 286 m).

In a striking blue/white/red finish, this is the F27 Maritime prototype, converted from a commercial F27 Mk 100 and first flown in February 1976. The underwing long-range fuel tanks, which are a standard feature of the Maritime, are not being carried in this photograph.

Aircraft such as the Maritime typically spend much of their flying life in the highly corrosive salt-laden air close to the surface of the sea. Fokker already has acquired much useful operational experience in this respect through the use of F27s by several operators in conditions that expose them to similar atmospheres, such as Iberia on its short routes in the Canary Islands, the Icelandic Coastguard and Air New Zealand. Based on this experience and further research at Amsterdam, Fokker has adopted the interfaying sealing method, which employs a corrosion-inhibiting solution, for application at a number of points on the Maritime airframe. Specifically, the interfay sealing is applied to the under-fuselage, the chine connection, box structure under all doors, the fuselage mainframes to which wing and tailplane are attached, the fore and aft bulkheads, wing trailing edge/rear spar connections and parts of the outer wing. Certain other areas are given an extra coat of white paint. A windscreen de-salting system is also fitted.

As part of Maritime development, extensive model ditching tests have been made. These led to the conclusion that the aircraft ditches well, even in the critical conditions of beam and head seas with waves of the same length as the aircraft's main dimensions. Although ditching inevitably detaches the ventral radome, this in no way reduces the aircraft's ability to float. Confidence is high that should a ditching be necessary, the aircraft would survive intact and would remain afloat. To enhance the crew's ability to evacuate the aircraft in such a case, an additional overhead escape hatch has been introduced in the production Maritime, in the rear fuselage starboard side; of the same dimensions as the standard F27 emergency exit windows, it can be reached by climbing on the observer seat, and a step/handrail is fitted on the outside of the fuselage below the hatch.

As already noted, the Maritime can be based on a Mk 200 or a Mk 400 airframe, the latter incorporating the larger freight loading door in the forward fuselage. In either case, the aircraft retains the ability to operate as a personnel transport, with up to 38 passengers in the cabin. The rear door can be opened in flight to allow dinghies or life support equipment to be dropped during rescue missions. Another optional rôle — already developed for certain military users of the F27 — is target towing; for naval users of the Maritime, this may be a useful additional facility, allowing ship-to-air firing practice when sleeve targets are towed by means of a tow-reeling system such as the Marquardt RMK-19.

Maritime antecedents

The Maritime is the seventh major variant of F27 to enter production in the Netherlands and, as the foregoing account makes clear, it has already made a useful contribution to continuity of production of what has become the best-selling turboprop transport produced outside of the Soviet Union. Fokker sales now total over 500, and after reaching an all-time low in 1977, when orders for only six new F27s were secured, sales have again revived to the point that the production rate can be increased, to a current level of 1½ aircraft a month. To the Fokker sales must be added the 206 aircraft built under licence by Fairchild in the USA, bringing the grand total to 715 at the time of writing.

Project work leading eventually to construction of the F27 began at Fokker's Amsterdam works soon after the end of

continued on page 296

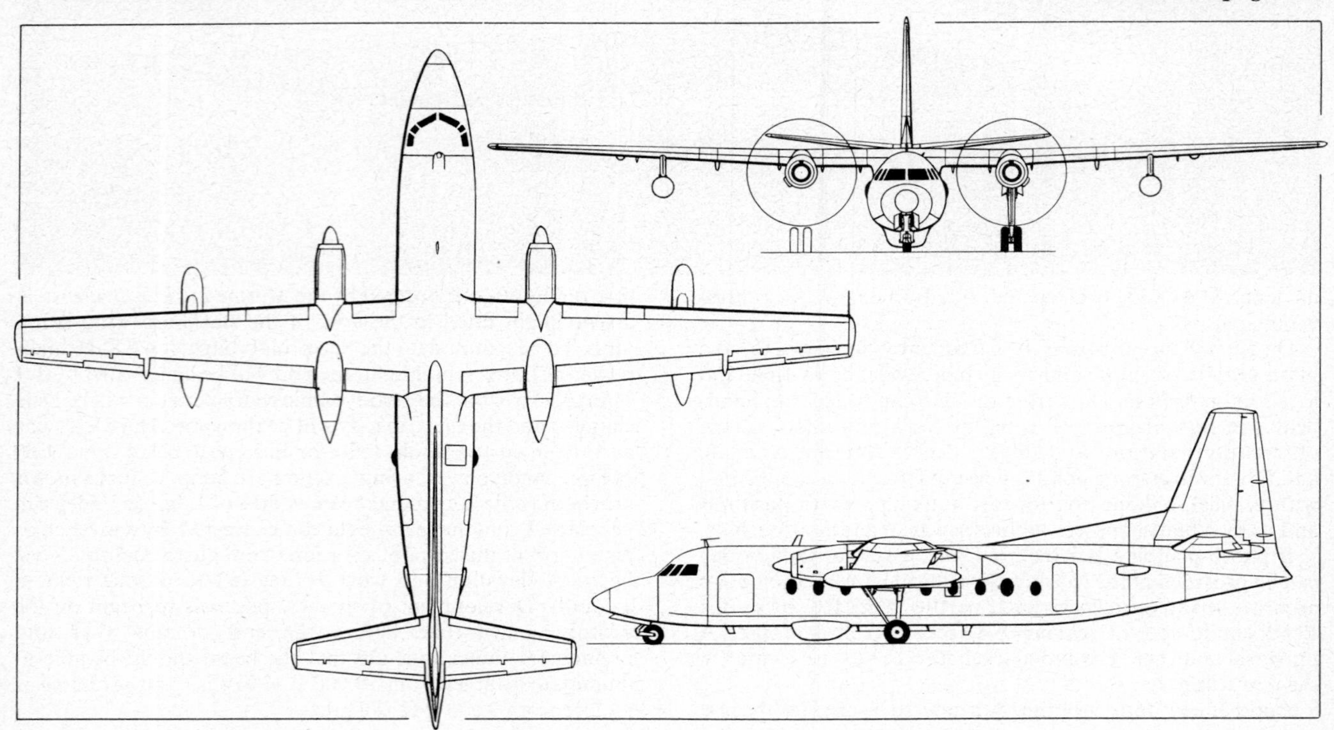

THE LAST OF THE WHIRLWINDS

A familiar sight in RAF livery for more than a quarter-century, the veteran Whirlwind has now reached the twilight of its service career. AIR INTERNATIONAL recently visited what has, for some time past, been the last-remaining RAF unit fully equipped with this long-serving helicopter. No 84 Squadron fulfils an exacting dual rôle in Cyprus with its now-venerable Whirlwinds and anticipates that conversion to the Wessex from late next year will coincide with the final demise of the earlier helicopter, which, for almost a score of years, was numerically the service's most important.

INELEGANT even by helicopter standards, its almost porcine fuselage reflecting basic 'forties Sikorsky technology, the olive-and-grey camouflaged Whirlwind of No 84 Squadron's "B" Flight threaded its way through a narrow, rugged defile in hot, turbulent air. The surrounding terrain, burned a uniform *café au lait* and offering temperatures that at times climb as high as 45°C, was perhaps the least hospitable offered by the extraordinarily varied topography of the 3,572-square mile (9 251-km²) island of Cyprus. Slowing to a hover, XK986 descended precisely on to a rudimentary, gravel-covered pad, which, barely larger than the diameter of the rotor blades, had been carved from a scrub-spattered hillside beneath a four-man DANCON (Danish Contingency Area) observation post.

Operating into and out of OP Delta 12 at Selemani, the problems of harsh terrain and altitude compounded by turbulence and high temperatures, calls for consummate helicoptering skill, but barely more so than does OP Delta 13 at Varisha, or, indeed, any other of the 17 DANCON observation posts otherwise accessible by nothing more sophisticated than goat tracks that come within the "parish" of No 84 Squadron's "B" Flight, or Nicosia Detachment. That "parish" — the tortuous "buffer zone", or Green Line, meandering 130 miles (210 km), varying in width from a few yards to a few miles, and separating the Blue (Greek) and Red (Turkish) lines that, since 1974, have divided the two Cypriot ethnic communities — offers an exacting operational tasking rôle.

The demands that it imposes on the helicopters that, along with numerous other tasks, fly resupply and personnel transportation missions to all of the remote DANCON observation posts every two days, would be found arduous by far more youthful helicopters than the vintage Whirlwinds, with high levels of sturdiness and reliability as prerequisites. But age notwithstanding, the Whirlwinds continue to demonstrate these qualities. Sqn Ldr Roger Wedge, OC RAF Detachment at Nicosia, admitted to AIR INTERNATIONAL that, while No 84 Squadron is looking forward to the twin-engined "luxury" offered by the Wessex, with its higher performance and greater suitability for Cypriot summer temperatures, the Whirlwind will not be relinquished without some regrets, the Squadron having developed an abiding affection for the ageing Westland-built helicopter over a nine-year association.

This Cyprus-based Squadron, currently commanded by Sqn Ldr Nick Hibberd, which re-formed on Whirlwinds at RAF Akrotiri in January 1972, is not, of course, the only remaining RAF operator of this helicopter type. A few remain on the strength of No 32 Squadron at Northolt and a few more are still flying from Shawbury with No 3 Squadron for "peripheral duties", these including senior officer familiarisation, some

(Head of page) A Whirlwind HAR Mk 10 of No 84 Squadron's "B" Flight taking-off from the otherwise unused Nicosia Airport for a re-supply flight to DANCON observation posts in the buffer zone, and (below) during a rapid turnaround at the DANCON Charlie Company camp at Limnitis, a Turkish enclave.

conversion training and a course for Harrier pilots*. Yet others remain with No 22 Squadron's "A" Flight at Chivenor and "D" Flight at Leconfield. But No 84 is the only squadron that remains *fully* Whirlwind-equipped, and the quartet of helicopters that its "B" Flight employs in the UNFICYP (United Nations Force in Cyprus) support rôle average some 50 per cent more flying hours monthly than UK-based Whirlwinds.

The Whirlwind HAR Mk 10s equipping No 84 Squadron, most of which have now accumulated between six and seven thousand hours, are admittedly elderly. Work on the Gnôme-engined Whirlwind began at Yeovil in the mid-'fifties, and this more efficacious development of the original Sikorsky design, which had first flown as the S-55 in 1949 — quieter, 10 knots (18 km/h) faster, with greater range and endurance, and more lifting power —began to supplant the piston-engined "iron chicken" in the early 'sixties, the first HAR Mk 10 having joined No 225 Squadron in November 1961. The Gnôme-engined Whirlwind is thus closing on its score of years in RAF service, though, in truth, XK986, included in "B" Flight's inventory and in which AIR INTERNATIONAL visited the DANCON observation posts, had originally been a Wasp-engined HAR Mk 2 and, having come off the Yeovil line in the 'fifties, its airframe had seen something more than 20 years of use.

The old adage that many a good tune is played on an old fiddle would seem singularly apposite in the case of the Whirlwind, which, if now long of tooth (or should it be rotor blade?), continues to offer high and reliable utilisation under the wide-ranging conditions encountered on a daily basis by No 84 Squadron's component elements which fulfil two very different primary tasks. These elements comprise "A" Flight commanded by Flt Lt Geoff Trott and possessing the primary rôle of search and rescue from Akrotiri, in the British Western Sovereign Base Area, and "B" Flight providing UNFICYP support from the otherwise-disused Nicosia Airport, a few miles to the west of Nicosia City. This division of

**Harrier pilots undergo a week's course on Whirlwinds at Shawbury to provide experience in confined-area flying.*

(Opposite page) Two of No 84 Squadron "A" Flight's quartet of Whirlwind HAR Mk 10s that primarily fulfil the SAR rôle from RAF Akrotiri. It will be noted that each of the helicopters is marked (on the tail rotor arm) with the symbol of one of the four suits of playing cards. The Whirlwinds of "B" Flight (above and below) carry no RAF insignia but sport the Scorpion emblem of No 84 Squadron on a pale blue field on each side of the fuselage nose.

responsibilities, which admittedly occasionally overlaps, has existed since the Squadron was re-formed nine years ago, both flights having four Whirlwinds on strength and, because of the degree of specialisation involved in the differing primary tasks, there is no interchangeability between "A" and "B" crews.

In addition to their SAR rôle, the yellow-painted Whirlwinds of "A" Flight possess secondary communications and VIP flying tasks, and also provide support for British troops within the Sovereign Base Areas. One Whirlwind is maintained at 90-minute SAR standby around the clock for 365 days of the year, and during the Armament Practice Camps (APCs) held at Akrotiri for each of the RAF's nine air defence squadrons (see *ACE Qualifying at Akrotiri*/November), two of the Whirlwinds maintain a 15-minute and a one-hour SAR standby whenever fighters are airborne.

In the two years since Akrotiri became the venue for the APCs, "A" Flight has been called upon only once to rescue a participating pilot, this event having taken place in September 1979, when the pilot of a No 5 Squadron Lightning found himself back on dry land within 20 minutes of "banging out" over the sea. The Whirlwinds of "A" Flight have, of course, participated in other rescues, such as that involving the crew of a Turkish-based USAF F-4 Phantom which ejected 40 miles (64 km) north-east of Cyprus in November 1978, and as Cyprus possesses no life-boat service, many rescue operations are mounted at the request of the Cypriot authorities, as, indeed, are many of the medevac and casevac missions. These are often flown to assist remote communities, sometimes entailing landing and taking-off within the confines of small villages by night or in inclement weather, feats demanding the highest level of skill from the helicopter crews.

The topography of Cyprus is such that the Whirlwinds may be operating at altitudes of the order of 6,000 ft (1 830 m) down to sea level during a single mission, and a recent task involving exceptional navigational skill entailed lifting to hospital as rapidly as possible a diver suffering from the bends. The Whirlwind pilot was told that the patient must not under any circumstances be flown above 500 ft (152 m) and could lose his life if he did not reach hospital within the hour. The direct route to the hospital involved flying over mountain ranges at altitudes far greater than the limitation imposed, whereas a circuitous route around the coast to stay within the altitude limitation would have taken far too long. The pilot was therefore faced with no option but to navigate through the ravines and valleys between the mountains in order to remain sufficiently low, and the diver was duly delivered to hospital well within the time limit.

The Akrotiri-based Whirlwinds fly an average of some 80 hours monthly and all major servicing of both "A" and "B" Flight helicopters is undertaken by the workshops on base. It would be idle to suggest that either airframe or Gnôme turboshaft of the Whirlwind remains youthful, and the effects of age inevitably increase the maintenance workload, although, according to Flt Lt Peter Barnard, the Squadron Engineering Officer, not as yet inordinately. The Gnôme removal rate is now comparatively high, removals attributed to FOD (Foreign Object Damage) at 3·3 per 1,000 flying hours being particularly high and almost triple the figure for Whirlwinds based in the UK. In view of the type of terrain in which No 84's Whirlwinds — and especially those of "B" Flight — are operating, this is scarcely cause for surprise. The overall Gnôme removal rate is virtually double that of UK-based helicopters, but, apart from FOD, there would seem to be no significant dominating cause for this. Of course, most of the Cyprus-based Whirlwinds are operated more intensively than their counterparts at home.

A Whirlwind approaches the small gravel-covered helipad of one of the DANCON observation posts. Situated on hilltops that are virtually inaccessible to anything but a helicopter (or a goat), the observation posts supplied by "B" Flight demand a high level of helicoptering skill from its crews.

Flying more than 1,500 hours annually — of which about 25 per cent are on training and the remainder on tasking — the Nicosia-based quartet of Whirlwinds of "B" Flight has had primary responsibility for the re-supply of isolated observation posts, mostly in DanCon, since the creation of the Green Line in 1974, each of the OPs in the Squadron's "parish" being visited on a thrice-weekly basis, with mail, food, water and various other essential supplies. Apart from the re-supply missions, "B" Flight is responsible for the transportation of personnel between the OPs, the four-man team at each OP being changed every two weeks — replacing the teams of all the OPs can be undertaken in a single morning.

In addition to the direct support of the OPs, "B" Flight is responsible for general communications tasks within the Green Line, for medevac and for co-operation in troop training with the contingents from Austria, Canada, Denmark, Sweden and the UK. Normally operating six days a week, "B" Flight maintains a 30-minute standby during the day and a one-hour standby throughout the night, and also possesses a SAR commitment. One of the Whirlwinds had, in fact, just returned from a SAR mission at the time of Air International's visit. An Austrian soldier had hired a ski-boat during the previous afternoon and had last been seen at about 19.45 hours. As he failed to return to his hotel, "B" Flight had been alerted and, at first light, a Whirlwind had taken-off to search the area. As soon as the morning mists cleared, the small boat had been spotted and its occupant rescued. The medevac tasks performed by "B" Flight average about one per week and frequently take place at night.

Of the four Whirlwinds on strength, one is normally on base servicing at Akrotiri, and the Nicosia Detachment is responsible for its own primary star servicing and rectification, which includes interchange. The Detachment has a total of 63 personnel, including 34 RAF groundcrew and 18 locally-employed civilians, the latter primarily manning the airfield crash service which operates on a round-the-clock basis. A 24-hour service is also provided by the Detachment's Air Traffic Control, which, manned by three ATC assistants, affords a safety watch keeping service for aircraft operating within the Green Line.

The Whirlwinds of No 84 Squadron, both the yellow-painted machines sporting RAF insignia and the camouflaged machines bedecked with the distinctive pale blue bands denoting that they are in United Nations service, have for long been such a part of the Cypriot scene that their passage over the citrus and olive groves or the scrub-strewn hills no longer arouses curiosity from the local population. But many Cypriots have good reason to be grateful for the sturdiness and reliability of the veteran Whirlwinds and the skill of their crews, air and ground alike, and when, in a year or so's time, these long-serving helicopters finally depart from the island's skies to make way for the more efficacious Wessex, there will be many to recall the Whirlwind's sojourn on the island of Cyprus with affection. □

VERSATILITY UNLIMITED

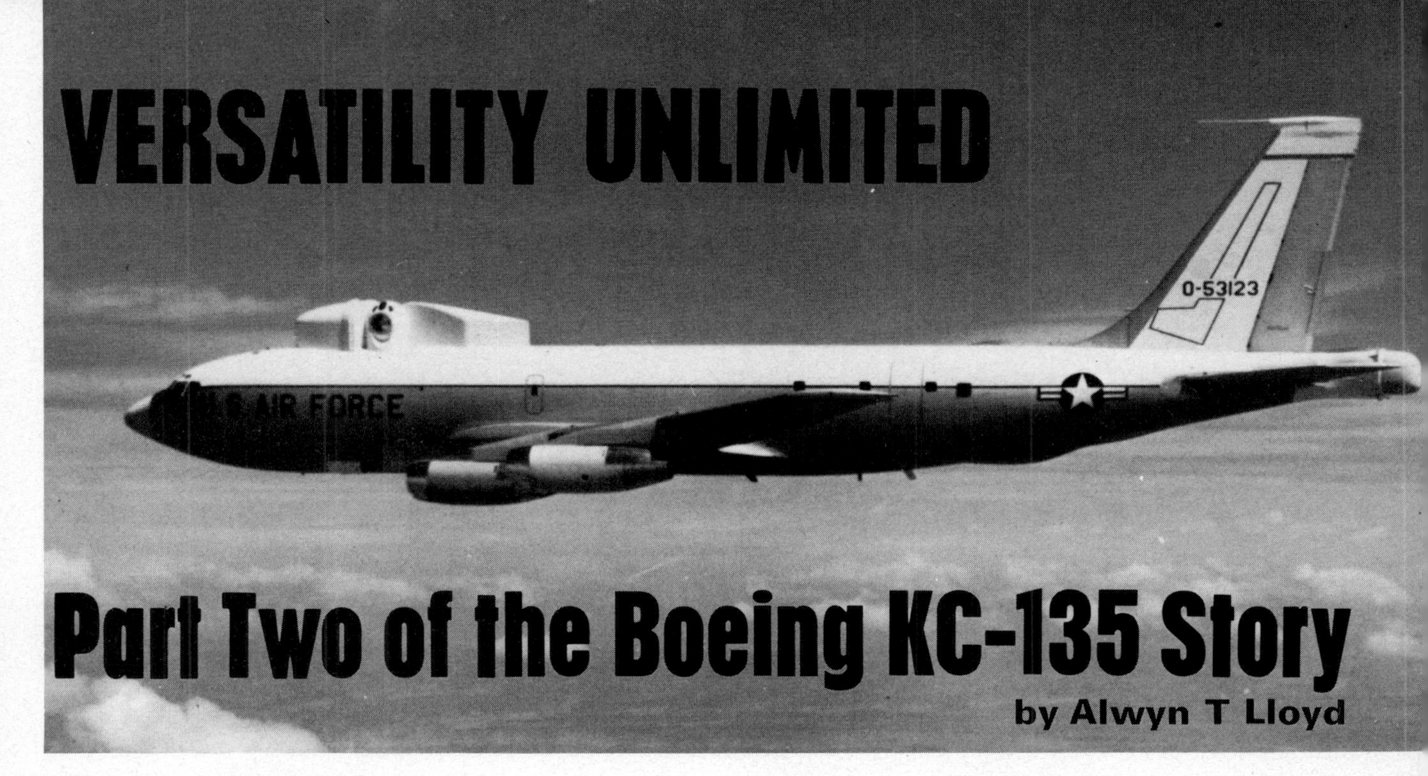

Part Two of the Boeing KC-135 Story

by Alwyn T Lloyd

On 3 February next year, Strategic Air Command will celebrate the 20th anniversary of its Project *Looking Glass* — the programme under which an airborne command post (ABNCP) has been continuously airborne 24 hours a day. Carrying a battle staff headed by a general officer, the *Looking Glass* ABNCP plays a vital rôle in maintaining the command communications structure in the event of a war situation developing, having the ability to maintain contact with the SAC underground headquarters, the USAF Command Post and the National Military Command Center. This SAC ABNCP is also the keystone of the Post Attack Command and Control System (PACCS), which provides for continued command and control of SAC forces in the event of the destruction of SAC headquarters.

The SAC ABNCP is just one of a number of such aircraft now in service with the USAF airborne command and control squadrons, aircraft that are among the many special-purpose derivatives of the KC-135A Stratotanker described in Part One of this account. Typically, these aircraft carry a normal flight crew and a group of highly-qualified officers whose functions embrace command, operations, intelligence, logistics and communications. In common with certain other SAC aircraft, the *Looking Glass* ABNCP is capable of controlling the launch of Minuteman missiles. Other ABNCP EC-135s are operated by the Joint Chiefs of Staff, US Commander-in-Chief Europe, Commander-in-Chief Atlantic and Commander-in-Chief Pacific. Each of these, like the SAC aircraft, would provide command and control of assigned forces of the relevant command in the event of the destruction of the ground-based headquarters.

Most of the command post variants of the Stratotanker carry EC-135 designations, as enumerated in subsequent paragraphs. Mention must also be made, under this heading, of seven KC-135As modified, without change of designation, for radio relay use by SAC. These aircraft have the outward appearance of a KC-135A tanker with the exception of large numbers of blade antennae along the top and underside of the fuselage. A data relay link system and a UHF radio relay system were added to the basic aircraft avionics.

Two of these KC-135As reverted in 1978 to standard tanker configuration. Since then, the other five have had much of the special avionics removed, leaving only the mounts, wiring and antennae installed. They are now operated by various units within SAC. One other KC-135A (serial 61-316) was converted into an airborne command post in 1967. This aircraft had increased communications and navigation capability and was operated by USAF Strike Command, MacDill AFB, Florida, until 1975, when it reverted to KC-135A status. The aircraft had HF probe antennae mounted over the wingtips; additional static dischargers were located on the wingtips, fin tip, elevator tips and refuelling boom ruddevators, and various antennae were installed along the fuselage. The STRICOM insignia was carried on the vertical fin.

The EC-135 variants

Seventeen KC-135Bs were delivered to the US Air Force as new production aircraft for command post duties and were immediately redesignated as EC-135C and EC-135J aircraft. Apart from having the special equipment installed for the command post rôle, they differed from KC-135As in being powered by TF33-P-9 turbofans. Other models in the EC-135 series, with the A, G, H, K, L and P suffix, were modified KC-135s as described below and consequently were powered by the original J57 turbojets.

EC-135A: Six KC-135As were converted into EC-135As in 1965, but one has since reverted back to KC-135A tanker status. EC-135As serve as radio relay link aircraft in support of the SAC Post Attack Command Control System, and are operated from Ellsworth AFB, South Dakota, by the 4th

(Top of page) This modified and highly instrumented NKC-135A (55-3123) is currently serving as the Airborne Laser Laboratory at the AF Weapons Laboratory, Kirtland AFB. This photograph shows one of the earlier laser installations in a dorsal turret; earlier still, the same NKC-135A was a test-bed for the Northrop A-LOTS pod carried by the EC-135Ns. (Below) One of three NC-135As equipped to monitor above-ground nuclear weapon tests and used for solar and cosmic research studies.

(Above) The first production KC-135B in its original configuration. The designation was changed to EC-135C immediately after delivery to the USAF.
(Below) An early production C-135B as delivered in MATS livery.

(Below) Bearing the white top and blue trim of a VIP aircraft operated by the 89th MAW, this VC-135B lacks the cabin windows of the same unit's VC-137 variants of the commercial Boeing 707 (see Part One of this account).

Airborne Command and Control Squadron. All of these aircraft are equipped with the air refuelling receiver (ARR) system, and the refuelling boom is retained. Additional HF probe antennae are mounted over each wingtip.

EC-135C: Fourteen of the 17 KC-135Bs were redesignated as EC-135C airborne command posts for use by SAC; one has since been modified to EC-135J. These fan-powered aeroplanes, equipped with both a refuelling boom and an ARR system, have additional HF probe antennae installed at each wingtip. Two wire antennae extend from the vertical fin to the mid and forward fuselage areas. A trailing wire antenna is housed in a fairing on the lower fuselage, right of the centreline and forward of the main landing gear wheel well. Blade antennae are installed along the belly and the upper fuselage centreline. The EC-135Cs are operated by the 2nd ACCS, SAC, Offutt AFB, Nebraska and the 4th ACCS, SAC, Ellsworth AFB, South Dakota.

EC-135G: Four EC-135Gs were derived from KC-135As in 1965. These aircraft, with refuelling booms and AAR systems, serve SAC as Airborne Launch Control Centre and Radio Relay link aircraft. Blade antennae are located on the top of the fuselage and along the belly; HF probe antennae are located over each wingtip and two wire antennae run from the vertical fin to the forward fuselage. The EC-135Gs are operated by the 4th ACCS, SAC, Ellsworth AFB, South Dakota, and the 305th ARW, SAC, Grissom AFB, Indiana.

EC-135H: Five KC-135As were converted into EC-135Hs in 1968, with an ARR system installed and the refuelling boom retained. Blade antannae are spaced along the aircraft belly and the top of the fuselage, HF probe antennae are installed over each wingtip and a saddle-shaped antenna is located over the fuselage centreline aft of the overwing exit hatches. Two wire antennae are installed at the vertical fin and run forward to masts on the fuselage top, and a trailing wire antenna pod is located forward of the right-hand main landing gear wheel well. Four EC-135Hs are operated by the 10th ACCS, USAFE, Mildenhall AFB, England, and serve as ABNCPs for the US Commander-in-Chief-Europe (USCINCEUR). The fifth aircraft is operated by the 6th ACCS, TAC, Langley AFB, Virginia, as an ABNCP for the Commander-in-Chief-Atlantic (CINCLANT).

EC-135J: PACAF operates the three EC-135Js which were originally converted from KC-135Bs and a fourth converted from an EC-135C. On these aircraft, two wire antennae run from the vertical fin to masts on the forward fuselage, HF probe antennae are installed over each wingtip and a saddle antenna appears over the mid-fuselage area. They serve as ABNCPs and support the Commander-in-Chief-Pacific (CINCPAC), being operated by the 9th ACCS, PACAF, Hickham AFB, Hawaii.

EC-135K: Three KC-135As were converted into EC-135Ks to serve as airborne command posts for the Tactical Air Command. On these aircraft, the refuelling boom has been replaced by a fuel dump tube. HF probe antennae are mounted over each wingtip; two wire antennae were installed over the fuselage, and a third such antenna was added in 1966. One of the EC-135Ks (55-3118) has the distinction of being the first KC-135A off the assembly line on 18 July 1956, when it was christened "City of Renton". After an extensive flight test programme, it was delivered to the Air Force in January 1961. Shortly thereafter, it was modified into the first EC-135K under the *Oxeye Daisy* programme. Aircraft 62-3536, the second to become an EC-135K, had served as a zero "G" trainer for the astronauts. Both aircraft were operated by the 18th ACCS, TAC, Seymour-Johnson AFB, North Carolina but in November 1977, the latter crashed on a night take-off from Kirtland AFB, New Mexico. Consequently, in 1979, KC-135A 59-1518 was pulled from storage (after earlier use by the FAA) for conversion into the third EC-135K as a replacement. Currently, the original EC-135K is assigned to the 8th TDCS, HQ TAC, Tinker AFB, Oklahoma.

A Boeing KC-135A (left) refuels a KC-135B, showing the ARR system that is one of the distinguishing features of the latter (fan-engined) version, later redesignated EC-135C.

EC-135L: Five EC-135Ls are operated by SAC as airborne radio relay link aeroplanes and are part of the PACCS network. Eight were originally converted from KC-135As in 1965, with the refuelling boom retained and an ARR system installed. These aircraft also have a reverse refuelling capability which would allow them to refuel from a bomber. Blade antennae are installed along the top of the fuselage and along the belly. A red-and-white radio frequency radiation hazard warning band is located near the refuelling boom pod and provides a visual identity clue to the EC-135Ls, which are operated by the 70th ARS, 305th ARW, SAC, Grissom AFB, Indiana.

EC-135P: Five KC-135As were originally modified into EC-135Ps for use in various ABNCP programmes, but two have since reverted to KC-135A tankers; the refuelling boom, with reverse refuelling capability, was retained and an ARR system was installed. Two HF probe antennae are installed over the wingtips on the EC-135Ps, a pair of wire antennae extend from the vertical fin to masts on the forward fuselage and blade antennae are installed over the length of the fuselage, top and

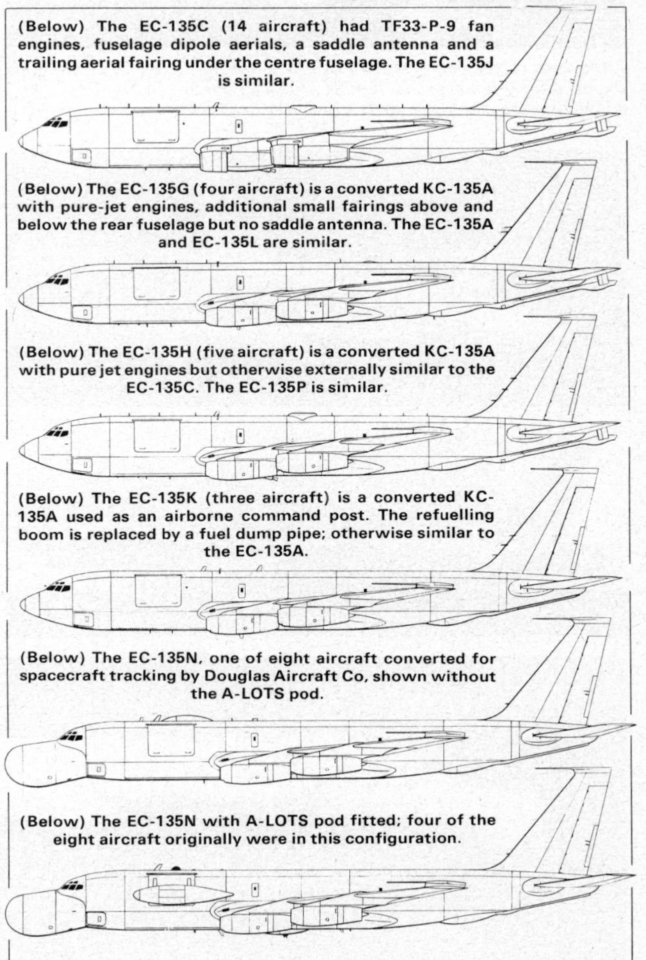
(Below) The EC-135C (14 aircraft) had TF33-P-9 fan engines, fuselage dipole aerials, a saddle antenna and a trailing aerial fairing under the centre fuselage. The EC-135J is similar.

(Below) The EC-135G (four aircraft) is a converted KC-135A with pure-jet engines, additional small fairings above and below the rear fuselage but no saddle antenna. The EC-135A and EC-135L are similar.

(Below) The EC-135H (five aircraft) is a converted KC-135A with pure jet engines but otherwise externally similar to the EC-135C. The EC-135P is similar.

(Below) The EC-135K (three aircraft) is a converted KC-135A used as an airborne command post. The refuelling boom is replaced by a fuel dump pipe; otherwise similar to the EC-135A.

(Below) The EC-135N, one of eight aircraft converted for spacecraft tracking by Douglas Aircraft Co, shown without the A-LOTS pod.

(Below) The EC-135N with A-LOTS pod fitted; four of the eight aircraft originally were in this configuration.

(Above) One of the four EC-135Gs, photographed in August 1980. (Below) One of the five EC-135Hs, in a display fly-past with the refuelling boom fully extended.

(Above) A rarely-photographed EC-135J; turbofan engines identify this as one of the original production KC-135Bs. (Below) One of TAC's EC-135K airborne command posts; this is the original first-production KC-135A.

bottom. A trailing wire antenna fairing is located forward of the right hand main wheel well and a saddle antenna is located on the fuselage top in line with the wing root trailing edge. A red-and-white radio frequency radiation hazard warning band is located on the belly near the refuelling pod. The 6th ACCS, TAC, Langley AFB, Virginia, currently operates two of the EC-135Ps for CINCLANT; all five were originally operated by the 9th ACCS, PACAF, Hickham AFB, Hawaii, for CINCPAC, prior to three being reassigned to the 6th ACCS; one EC-135P was destroyed in January 1980.

Reconnaissance aircraft

The SAC reconnaissance aircraft fleet is used to gather information on potential adversaries on a world-wide basis. All such operations are classified, but it is known that several aircraft types, including a number of RC-135 models, are used on these missions. The airborne reconnaissance crew stations are similar between the various RC-135 models; however, the specialised intelligence gathering equipment varies. All SAC RC-135s have an airborne refuelling receiver (ARR) system installed, thereby affording the aircraft vastly increased range.

To date there have been no fewer than ten RC-135 variants in the SAC inventory. The missions are similar; however, the internal equipment and external appearance varies considerably, and exterior configurations make identification of the different models possible. Significant variations also occur within a given type of RC-135, a condition which must play havoc with maintenance — constant awareness of the nuances on the part of the maintenance planners and maintenance technicians is a must. A plethora of antennae and bulges adorn the RC-135s, with HF, VHF and UHF wire, probe, blade and di-electric panel antennae found on various parts of the aircraft, plus side-looking radar (SLAR) cheeks installed on some aircraft. Extended noses house specialised radar antennae. All of SAC's RC-135 aircraft are assigned to the 55th Strategic Reconnaissance Wing. Offutt AFB, Nebraska.

RC-135B/RC-135C: Ten RC-135Bs, with TF33-P-9 turbofans fitted, were delivered to the Air Force in 1964-65, and immediately went to Martin Aircraft Company, Baltimore, Maryland, for reconnaissance equipment to be installed. In production, a fuel dump tube was installed in lieu of a refuelling boom. In 1967, these 10 aircraft were redesignated as RC-135Cs following modification during which the boom operator's compartment was converted into a camera bay. Large side-looking radar (SLAR) cheeks were installed along the forward fuselage area, and two additional HF probe antennae were added over each wingtip, identical to one HF probe which is mounted atop of the vertical fin. All of these aircraft have since been converted to RC-135Us and RC-135Vs.

(Left) One of SAC's EC-135Ls serving as part of the Post Attack Command and Control System network and operated by the 70th ARS in the 305th ARW. (Below) A good air-to-air study of one of the EC-135N spacecraft trackers with A-LOTS pod fitted.

RC-135D: In 1962-63, four KC-135As were modified into RC-135Ds, with an ARR system installed and the refuelling boom replaced by a fuel dump tube. An integral static boom/pitot system was installed at each wingtip. These aircraft, one of which crashed in January 1969, were readily identifiable for a long period of time because of their thimble-shaped nose radar antenna and long, tubular external side antenna fairings extending forward from the wing roots. Later pictures showed that the tubular fairings had been removed, however. During 1975-79, the RC-135Ds were de-modified and reconverted into KC-135A tankers.

RC-135E: A C-135B, (the MATS turbofan-powered transport) was converted into the sole RC-135E. This aeroplane had a thimble-shaped nose radar antenna like that on the RC-135Ds, but the most distinctive features were the two pods mounted inboard of the number two and number three engines and the wide glassfibre band wrapped around the forward portion of the fuselage. A fuel dump tube was located under the aft fuselage and an integral static boom/pitot system was installed at each wingtip. This aeroplane is no longer in service.

RC-135M: Six C-135Bs, with TF33-P-5 turbofans, were modified into RC-135Ms in 1967-68. An integral static boom/pitot system was installed at each wingtip and a thimble-shaped nose radar antenna was fitted. The factory original fuel dump tube remained on the aircraft and the production refuelling pod was replaced by a double-lobed antenna fairing. A flat-sided, teardrop-shaped antenna was mounted on each side of the fuselage forward of the horizontal stabiliser. Three RC-135Ms remain in service, the other three having been converted to RC-135Ws.

RC-135S: Two RC-135Ss were developed from C-135Bs and were similar to the RC-135Ms in respect of radar antenna fairings and integral wingtip static boom/pitot system. In addition to the aft fuselage antennae carried by the RC-135M, two similar flat-sided antennae are mounted between the base of the fin and the other antennae. One probe antenna is mounted on the lower part of the main cargo door and three similar antennae are on the right side of the fuselage forward of the wing. Prior to 1972, both aircraft had a small round window located between the upper and middle probe antenna on the right side of the fuselage, the middle antenna being installed with the aft end higher.

In 1972, one of the RC-135Ss was modified to have the middle probe antenna installed parallel to the other two antennae, and the single window was replaced by three large round windows. Subsequently, the second aircraft was modified in a similar manner, but with a large rectangular sliding door also installed over the forward-most round window. When this door was installed, the upper probe antenna was deleted. In 1972, modifications resulted in the upper surface of the right wing and the inboard surfaces of the number three and four engine struts and pods being painted black for anti-glare purposes.

RC-135T: In 1971, a single KC-135A was converted into a KC-135R and then further modified to RC-135T. This also had the wingtip static boom/pitot system and a thimble-shaped nose radar. A fence-like antenna was installed on the top of the fuselage along the centreline, and a single wire antenna was strung between the fin and a mast located on the forward portion of the fuselage located to the right of the aircraft centreline. This aircraft is currently operated by SAC for command support and training.

RC-135U: Three RC-135Cs were converted into RC-135Us in 1971. Photographs of these elusive aircraft show them to be highly modified with avionics gear. A single over-wing probe antenna is carried on the right wing, two wire antennae extend from the fin to masts on the forward fuselage area and the wingtips have been extended and reshaped to house antennae. Numerous static dischargers are located at the wingtips, vertical fin tip and horizontal stabiliser tips. The standard KC-135A nose radome is installed, but a large antenna fairing is located on the lower nose aft of the standard antenna. A large, flat-bottomed, oval-shaped fairing is installed midway between the nosewheel well and the wing leading edge and a pair of large SLAR cheeks is fitted, with strut-mounted probe antennae located above each of the SLAR fairings. A modified fairing is installed aft of the refuelling pod, a large fairing is installed on the aft fuselage tail cone and a long fairing is located between the rudder and the vertical fin cap. A fuel dump tube is carried in lieu of a refuelling boom. One of these aircraft has been converted into an RC-135V.

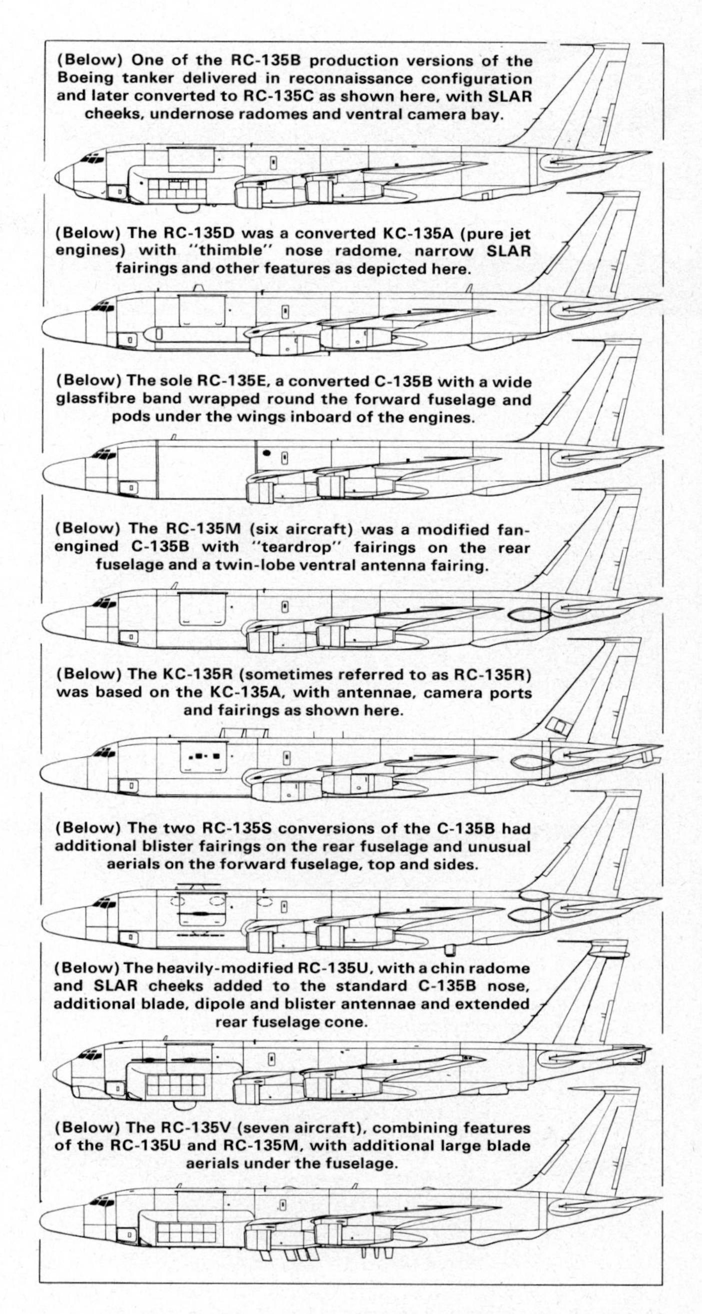
(Below) One of the RC-135B production versions of the Boeing tanker delivered in reconnaissance configuration and later converted to RC-135C as shown here, with SLAR cheeks, undernose radomes and ventral camera bay.

(Below) The RC-135D was a converted KC-135A (pure jet engines) with "thimble" nose radome, narrow SLAR fairings and other features as depicted here.

(Below) The sole RC-135E, a converted C-135B with a wide glassfibre band wrapped round the forward fuselage and pods under the wings inboard of the engines.

(Below) The RC-135M (six aircraft) was a modified fan-engined C-135B with "teardrop" fairings on the rear fuselage and a twin-lobe ventral antenna fairing.

(Below) The KC-135R (sometimes referred to as RC-135R) was based on the KC-135A, with antennae, camera ports and fairings as shown here.

(Below) The two RC-135S conversions of the C-135B had additional blister fairings on the rear fuselage and unusual aerials on the forward fuselage, top and sides.

(Below) The heavily-modified RC-135U, with a chin radome and SLAR cheeks added to the standard C-135B nose, additional blade, dipole and blister antennae and extended rear fuselage cone.

(Below) The RC-135V (seven aircraft), combining features of the RC-135U and RC-135M, with additional large blade aerials under the fuselage.

RC-135V: Seven RC-135Cs and one of the RC-135Us described above were modified into RC-135Vs in 1973-77. The standard KC-135A nose radome has been replaced by a thimble-shaped nose radome, and standard KC-135A wingtips were installed on the RC-135U during modification; the SLAR cheeks remain. An integral static boom/pitot system and an overwing-mounted probe antenna are installed at the right wingtip, two long wire antennae are installed between the fin and masts on the forward fuselage and four large blade antennae are located beneath the fuselage.

RC-135W: Several RC-135M aircraft are being converted into RC-135Ws. These aircraft do not have a refuelling boom. The thimble-shaped nose radome remains and SLAR cheeks are added. Integral static boom/pitot probes are installed at each wingtip, a single HF probe antenna is mounted over the right wingtip and a single wire antenna is strung between the fin and a mast on the fuselage located in a line just aft of the wing leading edge to the left of the aircraft centreline.

Miscellaneous reconnaissance versions

KC-135R: Four KC-135As were modified into KC-135Rs at various points in time: one (59-1514) in 1963, one (58-126) in 1970, (58-124) and finally (55-3121) which became the RC-135T in 1971. One photograph of 58-126 reveals that the KC-135R retained the refuelling boom, had an RC-135D-type thimble-shaped nose radome installed, and wingtip integral static boom/pitot systems. Fence-like antennae were carried along the fuselage top centreline, two small camera ports were cut into the main cargo door and a large flat-sided, teardrop-shaped antenna was located forward of the horizontal stabiliser. Two of the KC-135Rs reverted to KC-135A status in 1976.

WC-135B: Ten C-135Bs were modified into WC-135Bs, although only seven have remained in this configuration, to be operated by Military Airlift Command for weather reconnaissance. Originally delivered as transports in 1962, they were converted for weather duties in 1965 and were at first operated alternately by the 55th Weather Reconnaissance Squadron, McClellan AFB, California, and the 56th Weather Reconnaissance Squadron, Yokota AFB, Japan. Subsequently, all WC-135Bs were operated by the 55th WRS, assigned to the 9th Weather Reconnaissance Wing, Air Weather Service, MATS. In 1975, Air Weather Service ceased to be a flying organisation and the 9th WRW was disbanded; the 55th WRS then became part of the 41st Rescue and Weather Reconnaissance Wing, MAC. In March 1977, one WC-135B was assigned to the 552nd AWACS Wing, TAC, Tinker AFB, Oklahoma, where it has been used for training missions in support of the E-3A programme; the six remaining WC-135Bs are still operated by the 55th WRS.

continued on page 291

(Above) One of the four original RC-135As, now converted to KC-135D tankers as described in Part One of this account. (Below) One of the 10 RC-135Bs in original production configuration.

(Above) An RC-135C (converted RC-135B) showing the side-looking radar (SLAR) cheeks below the "US AIR FORCE" legend on the fuselage. (Below) The sole RC-135E, featuring a large nose radome and a wrap-around glassfibre antenna on the front fuselage.

(Right) One of SAC's RC-135Ms, showing the distinctive teardrop-shaped antenna fairings on the rear fuselage. (Below) The RC-135D was the first variant to feature the "thimble" nose radome and the long tubular fairings on the fuselage sides.

Henschel Hs 129...

...der geflügelte Büchsenöffner

A WINGED CAN-OPENER — *ein geflügelter Büchsenöffner*! In such irreverent fashion, the personnel of the Technical Office, or *Technische Amt*, of the State Ministry of Aviation *(Reichsluftfahrtministerium)* in Berlin were, in the spring of 1937, referring to the latest proposal of the *Luftwaffenführrungsstab*: a dedicated close air support aircraft, or *Schlachtflugzeug*.

For long, Hermann Göring, the *Oberbefehlshaber der Luftwaffe*, had dogmatised that intervention of aircraft in a land battle was militarily ineffectual, having little value other than in its effect on morale. Analysis of the first months of the Spanish Civil War, that crucible of so much military development, had already brought about radical rethinking in Berlin, however, and one change was to be seen in the attitude of the *Oberbefehlshaber* and his staff towards the armoured close air support or assault aircraft.

The concept was not revolutionary, having evolved during World War One, and its resurrection by the Ob.d.L. had engendered little enthusiasm on the part of the *Technische Amt*. There was a consensus that the weight of armour necessary to render vital elements comparatively impervious to concentrated small arms fire would inevitably result in a cumbersome, short-range aeroplane restricted in use to conditions of *Luftwaffe* air superiority.

Time was to prove such doubts more than justified, for the requirement was to result in what was almost certainly the most pilot-taxing and perhaps the least adroit of any combat aircraft ever to be built in numbers for the *Luftwaffe*. But in that spring of 1937, the Ob.d.L. was waxing enthusiastic over the potential of an aircraft dedicated to knocking out enemy strongpoints and armour. Misgivings notwithstanding, therefore, the *Technische Amt* had framed an outline specification for a *Schlachtflugzeug*, inviting four companies to tender their proposals by 1 October 1937.

Apart from defining the desired performance parameters in the broadest terms, the specification confined itself to indicating that these were to be attained on a total of 900-1,100 hp and stipulating armour protection for cockpit, engines and other elements, and provision of a fixed forward-firing armament of at least paired 20-mm cannon.

The specification was accompanied by what was essentially a précis of all *desirable* characteristics, despite *Technische Amt* awareness of their contradictions; that some could be achieved only at the expense of others equally desirable. A preference was expressed for the power to be divided between two engines in order to enhance survivability; it was suggested — but not stipulated — that accommodation be restricted to one crew member for reasons of weight, no call for rear defence being foreseen. Minimum dimensions were desirable to present the smallest possible target to defensive groundfire, and it was recommended that reasonable low-altitude agility be sought to facilitate evasive action after a bombing or firing run.

Of the four companies invited to tender, the Gothaer Waggonfabrik failed to respond and the Hamburger Flugzeugbau proposed the P.40; a *two*-seater powered by a *single* DB 600 engine and sharing the assymetric configuration of the Ha 141 then under construction and viewed by the *Technische Amt* as something of an aeronautical aberration. The Focke-Wulf Flugzeugbau tendered a *two*-seat adaptation of the Argus-powered twin-boom Fw 189 tactical reconnaissance aircraft, prototype construction of which was just commencing, and alone among the contenders, the Henschel Flugzeugwerke attempted to adhere to the recommendations of the *Technische Amt* in proposing the smallest practical single-seat twin-engined aircraft.

The concept of Dipl-Ing Friedrich Nicholaus, Henschel's proposed *Schlachtflugzeug* was intended to utilise a pair of inverted-vee Argus air-cooled engines and enclose the pilot in an armoured shell. It was of conventional design and construction in all respects but one: the cross section of the fuselage was *triangular*. This eccentricity was not the result of any caprice on the part of the designer; it was dictated by the need to mate with the armoured cockpit shell embodying acutely angled flat sides, which, trials had revealed, deflected a high proportion of bullet strikes. The primary disadvantage of so unorthodox a cross section was that, in order to avoid an unacceptably broad base, an extremely narrow cockpit had to be accepted. The pilot's head was in the apex of the triangle and the factor determining the actual cross-sectional size was the width of the average pilot's shoulders!

One of the pre-series Hs 129A-0 CAS aircraft presumably photographed during the evaluation trials. The somewhat ferocious nose decoration seen on this particular aircraft (GM+OG) is not believed to have been associated with a particular unit.

From the outset, the *Technische Amt* considered the Henschel proposal to possess most technical merit, presumably on the basis that it conformed most closely with its recommendations. The Focke-Wulf contender, on the other hand, proffered the advantages of extensive commonality with the forthcoming tactical reconnaissance Fw 189. Both companies were therefore instructed to proceed with design definition and mock-up construction, the Hamburger Flugzeugbau proposal being rejected out of hand.

The first mock-up inspections were carried out in the spring of 1938, and Dipl-Ing Kurt Tank's suggestion that the Fw 189 V1 be rebuilt for close air support trials after completion of initial handling in basic reconnaissance form was accepted. The strong predilection for the Henschel project nevertheless remained, the Focke-Wulf contender being seen essentially as a back-up programme for production development only in the event that the preferred submission proved unacceptable.

A claustrophobic calamity?

Several unsatisfactory features were found during the initial inspection of the Henschel mock-up, those arousing most censure from the traditionalists in the *Technische Amt* inspectorate being the extremely cramped accommodation foreseen for the pilot and the lack of lateral view that was to be conferred by the armoured cockpit canopy, a combination which, it was suggested, might well induce claustrophobia. However, the aircraft had virtually been designed *around* the armoured cockpit shell, which was an integral part of the concept, and no radical changes could be introduced without fundamental redesign of the entire airframe. Not without some reluctance, the *Technische Amt* accepted the cockpit as a *fait accompli*, perhaps consoled by the thought that the *Schlachtflugzeug* was intended for short-endurance missions only.

In September 1938, after two further mock-up inspections and some augmentation of wing area as the result of one of these, the projected aircraft was assigned the RLM designation Hs 129 and a contract issued for the construction of three prototypes and preparation of jigs and tooling for a pre-series of aircraft. This contract was fulfilled by Henschel with considerable expedition, the first prototype, the Hs 129 V1, commencing its test programme within eight months, in April 1939, being followed within seven weeks by the second and third prototypes, the Hs 129 V2 and V3, work having meanwhile commenced on a batch* of pre-series Hs 129A-0 aircraft.

From the outset of the test programme, the flying characteristics of the Hs 129 prototypes were viewed as little short of calamitous, the worst fears of the *Technische Amt* being realised. Throughout its development the aircraft had suffered serious weight escalation — the empty equipped weight was some 12 per cent in excess of that calculated at the time of the final mock-up inspection — and the Argus As 410A-0 engines available were developing only 430 hp each for take-off rather than the 465 hp anticipated. Without ammunition and with fuel in the fuselage tank only, the Hs 129 was unable to reach the level speeds and climb rates that had been anticipated for the fully loaded aircraft.

The take-off run was found to be excessive, acceleration was poor and the climb abysmal. Rolling and pulling out of comparatively shallow dives demanded strenuous effort. In fact, control forces were inordinately heavy under all circumstances; as speed was increased control heaviness grew commensurately, until, in a 45 deg dive, the controls became almost immovable. Early in the flight test programme, the Hs 129 V1 failed to recover from a shallow dive and was totally destroyed, Henschel being instructed to replace this prototype in the development programme with the first pre-series aircraft which thus became the Hs 129 V4.

Various palliatives were applied in attempts to achieve at least minimally acceptable handling characteristics. Electrically-operated tabs were added to the rudder and elevators, and series As 410A-1 engines were fitted, these affording the full 465 hp at 3,100 rpm for take-off. Flight development was shared between company pilots and pilots seconded from the *Erprobungsstelle* at Rechlin, where it was planned that service evaluation trials would be held by *Lehrgeschwader* 2 with the Hs 129A-0 pre-series aircraft already under assembly at Schönefeld.

The test pilots were unanimous in asserting that the Hs 129 had little to commend it, declaring it underpowered, unwieldy, excessively fatiguing to fly, positively dangerous in turbulence at low altitude and almost impossible to fly on one engine. The claustrophobic effects of the cockpit were confirmed and pilots particularly disliked the close proximity of the windscreen to their faces and the inadequate lateral vision. Dipl-Ing Nicolaus and his team had placed emphasis on forward vision and, in consequence, the windscreen was deep proportionately to the size of the cockpit. In order to minimise the size of the armoured shell, however, the seat was so positioned that the lower portion of the pilot's legs projected beneath the windscreen into the nose and his face was thus within barely more than a foot of the armourglass screen. Theoretically, the close proximity of the pilot's eyes to the windscreen, the depth of the screen and the brevity of the downward-sloping nose resulted in a good forward view. In fact, a measure of opacity of the 75-mm armourglass and a tendency towards fogging between this flat screen and the curved outer plexiglas screen at times seriously impaired vision.

No importance had been attached to lateral vision and to provide the pilot with maximum protection, the aft-sliding 6-mm armour canopy embodied only small armourglass inserts providing just sufficient lateral view for the pilot to monitor engine instruments on the inner faces of the engine nacelles. Insufficient space had been available to place these on the instrument panel, which was unusually small as a result of the limited cockpit width and substantial windscreen depth, the latter dictating low positioning of the panel. This, in turn, had necessitated adoption of an unusually small control column as a column of more orthodox size would have tended to have obscured the flight instruments. This minuscule stick was also disliked by the test pilots.

The universal condemnation of the Hs 129 by test pilots and their recommendation that development of the aircraft be discontinued failing total redesign might well have resulted in the abandonment of the project but for the fact that the *Luftwaffenführrungsstab* was attaching increasing urgency to the service introduction of a dedicated close air support aircraft. Both the Hs 129 V2 and V3 participated in

**No reliable details have survived concerning the exact number of pre-series Hs 129A-0 aircraft, such having seldom been included in RLM acceptance lists, but there is some evidence to indicate that it was an unusually large batch — possible as many as 20 aircraft — as it was intended to use pre-series aircraft for comprehensive service evaluation as well as for test and development tasks.*

comparative trials with the Fw 189 V1b, as the first prototype Fw 189 had been designated after modification for the close air support rôle. Fitted with an armoured cockpit shell of similar concept to that of the Hs 129, but accommodating two crew members, and having similar Argus engines, the Focke-Wulf aircraft was both heavier and larger, and while its handling characteristics were *marginally* better, its performance proved even poorer than that of its Henschel competitor. The Fw 189 V1b evoked no more enthusiasm than did the Hs 129, and, in the event, was written off as a result of an accident during a demonstration flight, although Focke-Wulf continued work on a genuine close air support prototype, the Fw 189 V6, and this was later to be evaluated by the 5.*(Schlacht)/Staffel* formed by *Lehrgeschwader* 2 during the summer of 1940 for the service trials of the Hs 129A-0.

Built like a loco

Differing from the prototypes in only minor respects, the Hs 129A-0 was most noteworthy for the sturdiness of its structure — the name Henschel had been associated with locomotive construction since the mid years of the previous century and Rechlin pilots maintained that the company's traditional constructional methods had been utilised in building its close support aircraft.

The abbreviated nose portion of the armoured shell was formed from four trapezoidal spot-welded 12-mm armour plates, the remainder of the shell consisting of a 12-mm armour floor, inclined side panels of 6-mm armour, a 75-mm armourglass windscreen set within a 6-mm armour frame, an aft-sliding 6-mm armour canopy and an armoured seat. The light-metal stressed-skin fuselage centre section was built integrally with the wing centre section and bolted to the armour shell. The wing itself was built around two heavy mainspars and an auxiliary spar reinforced by transverse solid girders, conventional ribs giving place to reinforced pressed-metal frames stiffening the stressed skinning. The entire wing trailing edge was hinged, the outer sections acting as slotted ailerons and the inner sections as slotted flaps. The rear fuselage and tail were stressed-skin all-metal units, the latter having aerodynamically- and mass-balanced elevators and rudder with electrically-operated trim tabs. The incidence of the tailplane was adjustable on the ground and the elevators were interchangeable.

The As 410A-1 12-cylinder inverted-vee air-cooled engines were each rated at 465 hp at 3,100 rpm for take-off and 315 hp at 2,820 rpm, the undersides of their nacelles incorporating 5-mm armour plate and their fuel being distributed between three self-sealing tanks, one of 44 Imp gal (200 l) capacity immediately aft of the cockpit and two each of 45 Imp gal (205 l) between the mainspars inboard of the engines. The undercarriage had cantilever mainwheel legs which retracted aft hydraulically into bays in the tails of the engine nacelles, a proportion of each mainwheel remaining exposed after retraction and projecting below the nacelle to provide a measure of protection in the event of a wheels-up landing. The tailwheel was non-retractable. Gun armament comprised two 7,9-mm MG 17 machine guns with 1,000 rpg in the lower forward fuselage and paired 20-mm MG FF cannon with 250 rpg in the flanks of the fuselage, their breeches enclosed by external metal fairings and the blast tubes passing either side of the pilot. As insufficient room existed within the cockpit for a weapons sight, a Revi C 12/C was fitted externally, just forward and to starboard of the windscreen centre, the intention being that the pilot would align the angled fins of the sight with the horizon to assist aim in a diving attack.

The service evaluation conducted by 5.*(Schlacht)*/LG 2 and commencing in the summer of 1940 merely served to affirm in the eyes of the *Luftwaffe* the unacceptability of the Henschel *Schlachtflugzeug*. It had been anticipated that the Hs 129 would carry two 110-lb (50-kg) SC 50 bombs on underwing racks in addition to the standard cannon armament and that these would be launched in a diving attack, but the stick force per *g* during pull-out rendered an angle of about 15 deg the maximum feasible. The roll rate was barely adequate for changing line during such shallow attacks and any small change of speed demanded constant trimming. Although the Hs 129 was very stable about all axes, it was difficult to fly in turbulence and its sluggish responses rendered any evasive action comparatively ineffectual. The so-called *Panzerkabine* came in for still more criticism after several collisions on the ground were attributed to the inadequate view that it offered.

While operational evaluation was in progress, Henschel had initiated series production of the Hs 129A-1 which differed from the pre-series aircraft in having a redesigned cockpit canopy intended to improve lateral vision, and some rearrangement of the control surfaces and electrically-actuated trim tabs to reduce stick forces. Seven Hs 129A-1s were completed during the closing months of 1940, but the *Luftwaffe* refused to accept these and the assembly line was halted pending reconsideration of the entire programme.

Franco-teutonic mélange

Many of the shortcomings of the Hs 129 stemmed from the fact that it was seriously underpowered, but no engine of suitable size and power was available from the German aero industry. With the fall of France, the small-diameter 14-cylinder Gnôme-Rhône 14M air-cooled radial became available in quantity. While this power plant did not commend itself on the score of its bulk and the fact that its dry weight was twice that of the Argus, it offered the near 50 per cent increase in take-off power that was being sought by Dipl-Ing Nicolaus and his team who launched two parallel developments based on use of the more powerful French engine: one being a straightforward adaptation of the basic Hs 129 airframe and

An Hs 129B-1 of 4./Sch.G.2 in process of being towed along a road in the vicinity of Tripoli in December 1942. Tow wires are attached to each mainwheel axle and alignment of the tailwheel is ensured by means of a manually-directed bar and yoke.

Henschel Hs 129B-2 Cutaway Drawing Key

1 Starboard navigation light
2 Pitot head
3 Leading-edge panels
4 Front spar
5 Wing rib stations
6 Rear spar
7 Aileron hinge fairings
8 Starboard aileron
9 Aileron tab
10 Aileron actuating hinge
11 Control rod
12 Aileron profile
13 Starboard flap
14 Flap actuating linkage
15 Control runs
16 Starboard nacelle aft fairing
17 Exhaust pipes
18 Starboard oil tank location
19 Starboard engine control gauges (external)
20 Exhaust collector ring
21 Cooling louvres
22 Gnôme-Rhône 14M 4/5 radial engine
23 Cowling frame ring
24 Propeller hub
25 Spinner
26 Three-blade Ratier (handed) propeller
27 Cowling panel fasteners
28 Chin intake fairing
29 Armoured nose cap
30 Camera/intake apertures
31 Starboard mainwheel
32 Nose cap release
33 Armoured nose side panels
34 Rudder bar assembly
35 Nose forward armour weld line
36 Infantry assault badge nose stencil
37 External Revi C 12/C gunsight
38 Armoured glass windshield (75-mm)
39 Windshield frame leather crash pad
40 Rear-view mirror
41 Cockpit canopy upper glazing
42 Armoured sliding canopy
43 Armoured bulkhead
44 Contoured seat/headrest (armoured)
45 Angle-of-dive lines painted on side window
46 Sliding window section
47 Abbreviated instrument panel (see 19 and 153)
48 Cannon trough
49 Control column linkage
50 Machine gun trough
51 Seat support frame
52 MG 131 barrel support collar
53 Blast tube/wingroot fairing
54 Cannon blast tube support/side-armour forging
55 Cannon blast tube
56 Butterfly panel (MG 131 wingroot access)
57 MG 151/20 barrel blast tube
58 MG 131 ammunition feed
59 Port wingroot MG 131 machine gun
60 MG 131 service access
61 Cannon barrel sleeve
62 Fuselage fuel tank (44 Imp gal/200 l capacity)
63 Side armour panel (6-mm)
64 Fuselage frame
65 Aerial mast
66 Butterfly panel (starboard cannon service access)
67 Butterfly panel (port cannon service access)
68 MG 151/20 cannon breech
69 Ammunition feed
70 Magazine (250 rounds of 20-mm ammunition)
71 Cannon aft support fuselage cross member
72 Cannon breech fairing
73 Starboard fairing
74 Fuselage frame
75 Aerial lead-in
76 Entry handhold
77 Radio installation
78 Radio tray support
79 Access panel
80 First-aid kit
81 Fuselage aft frames
82 Stringers
83 Control runs
84 Dorsal decking
85 Aerials
86 Elevator balance
87 Elevator outer hinge
88 Starboard tailplane
89 Tailfin leading-edge
90 Tailfin structure
91 Aerial attachment
92 Tail navigation light
93 Rudder balance
94 Rudder structure
95 Rudder post
96 Rudder tab
97 Tab actuating hinge
98 Tail cone
99 Access panel
100 Port elevator frame
101 Elevator tab

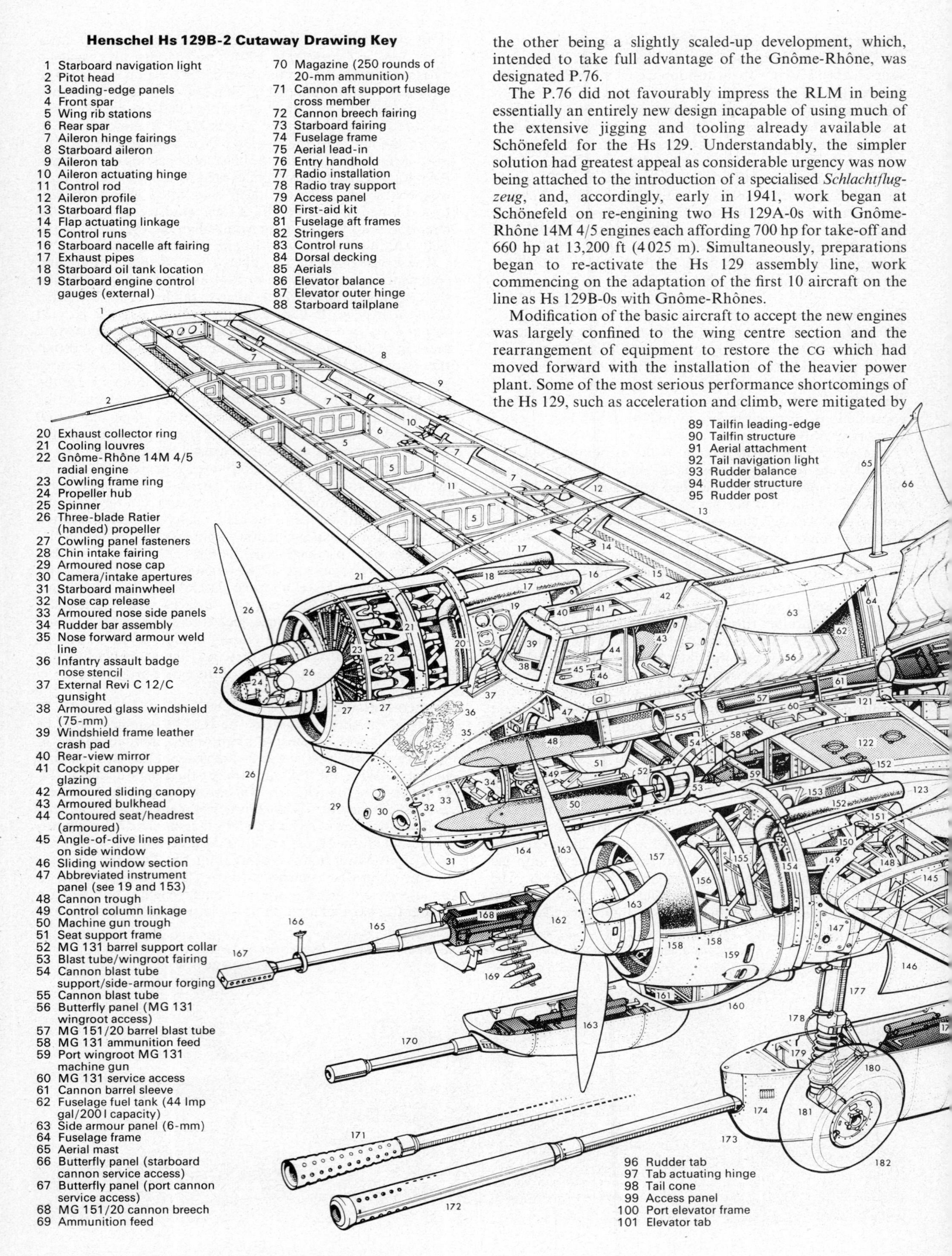

the other being a slightly scaled-up development, which, intended to take full advantage of the Gnôme-Rhône, was designated P.76.

The P.76 did not favourably impress the RLM in being essentially an entirely new design incapable of using much of the extensive jigging and tooling already available at Schönefeld for the Hs 129. Understandably, the simpler solution had greatest appeal as considerable urgency was now being attached to the introduction of a specialised *Schlachtflugzeug*, and, accordingly, early in 1941, work began at Schönefeld on re-engining two Hs 129A-0s with Gnôme-Rhône 14M 4/5 engines each affording 700 hp for take-off and 660 hp at 13,200 ft (4 025 m). Simultaneously, preparations began to re-activate the Hs 129 assembly line, work commencing on the adaptation of the first 10 aircraft on the line as Hs 129B-0s with Gnôme-Rhônes.

Modification of the basic aircraft to accept the new engines was largely confined to the wing centre section and the rearrangement of equipment to restore the CG which had moved forward with the installation of the heavier power plant. Some of the most serious performance shortcomings of the Hs 129, such as acceleration and climb, were mitigated by the installation of the more powerful engines while remaining essentially poor and the general handling characteristics were basically unchanged. Testing of the Hs 129B-0 at Rechlin generated little more enthusiasm than had its Argus-engined forerunner, but series production was already committed and enjoyed the highest priority, deliveries of the series Hs 129B-1 commencing in January 1942, in which month three aircraft were accepted. A *Schlachtflieger* training unit, 4./SG 101, had meanwhile been established at Paris-Orly, this becoming the recipient of most of the surviving Hs 129A-0s, together with several Hs 129B-0s.

The Hs 129B-1 retained the paired MG 17 machine guns but, like the Hs 129A-1, replaced the MG FF cannon with MG 151s of similar calibre, and provision was made for the application of a series of special *Rüstsätzen* (equipment or

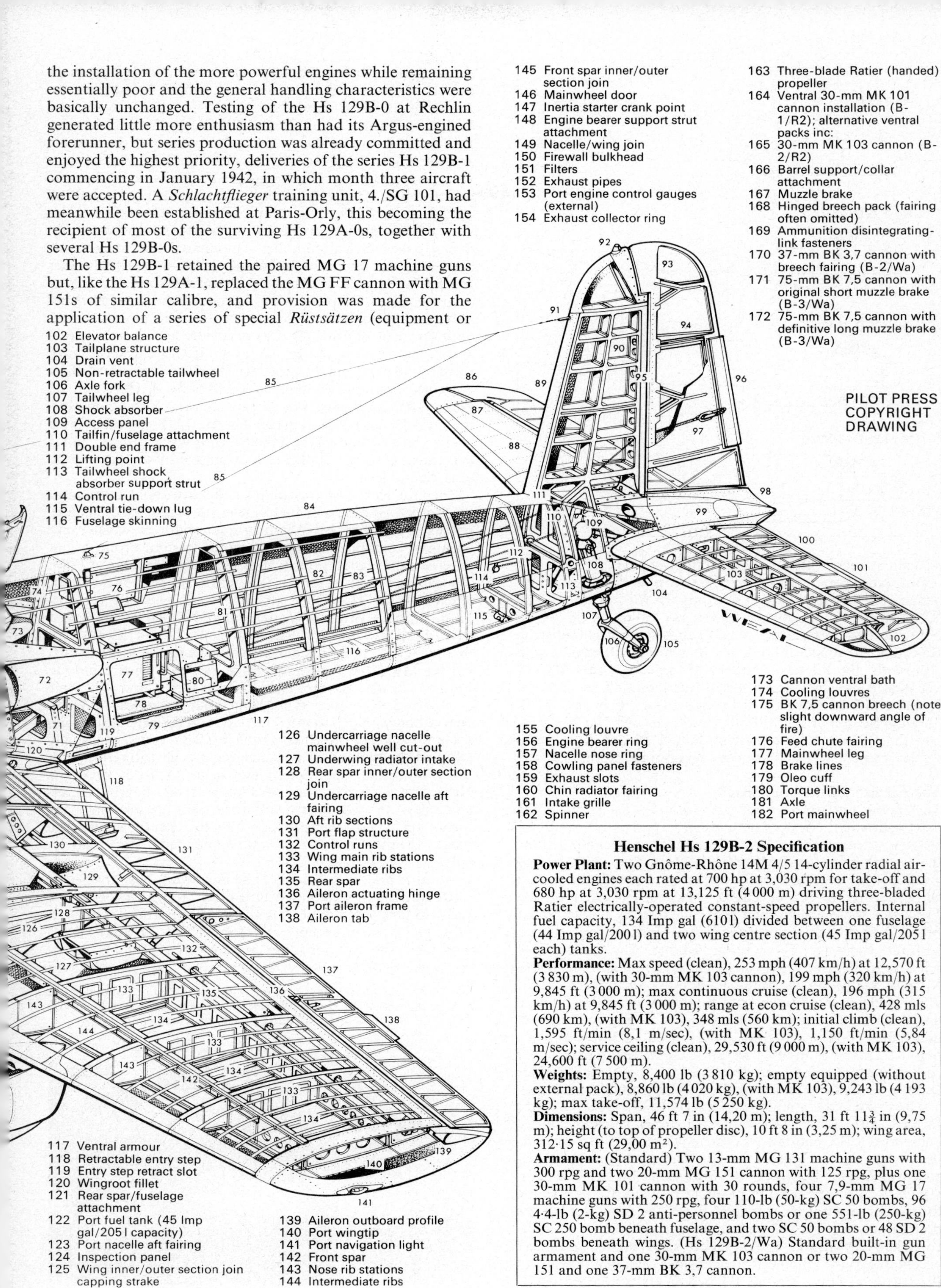

102 Elevator balance
103 Tailplane structure
104 Drain vent
105 Non-retractable tailwheel
106 Axle fork
107 Tailwheel leg
108 Shock absorber
109 Access panel
110 Tailfin/fuselage attachment
111 Double end frame
112 Lifting point
113 Tailwheel shock absorber support strut
114 Control run
115 Ventral tie-down lug
116 Fuselage skinning
117 Ventral armour
118 Retractable entry step
119 Entry step retract slot
120 Wingroot fillet
121 Rear spar/fuselage attachment
122 Port fuel tank (45 Imp gal/205 l capacity)
123 Port nacelle aft fairing
124 Inspection panel
125 Wing inner/outer section join capping strake
126 Undercarriage nacelle mainwheel well cut-out
127 Underwing radiator intake
128 Rear spar inner/outer section join
129 Undercarriage nacelle aft fairing
130 Aft rib sections
131 Port flap structure
132 Control runs
133 Wing main rib stations
134 Intermediate ribs
135 Rear spar
136 Aileron actuating hinge
137 Port aileron frame
138 Aileron tab
139 Aileron outboard profile
140 Port wingtip
141 Port navigation light
142 Front spar
143 Nose rib stations
144 Intermediate ribs
145 Front spar inner/outer section join
146 Mainwheel door
147 Inertia starter crank point
148 Engine bearer support strut attachment
149 Nacelle/wing join
150 Firewall bulkhead
151 Filters
152 Exhaust pipes
153 Port engine control gauges (external)
154 Exhaust collector ring
155 Cooling louvre
156 Engine bearer ring
157 Nacelle nose ring
158 Cowling panel fasteners
159 Exhaust slots
160 Chin radiator fairing
161 Intake grille
162 Spinner
163 Three-blade Ratier (handed) propeller
164 Ventral 30-mm MK 101 cannon installation (B-1/R2); alternative ventral packs inc:
165 30-mm MK 103 cannon (B-2/R2)
166 Barrel support/collar attachment
167 Muzzle brake
168 Hinged breech pack (fairing often omitted)
169 Ammunition disintegrating-link fasteners
170 37-mm BK 3,7 cannon with breech fairing (B-2/Wa)
171 75-mm BK 7,5 cannon with original short muzzle brake (B-3/Wa)
172 75-mm BK 7,5 cannon with definitive long muzzle brake (B-3/Wa)
173 Cannon ventral bath
174 Cooling louvres
175 BK 7,5 cannon breech (note slight downward angle of fire)
176 Feed chute fairing
177 Mainwheel leg
178 Brake lines
179 Oleo cuff
180 Torque links
181 Axle
182 Port mainwheel

Henschel Hs 129B-2 Specification

Power Plant: Two Gnôme-Rhône 14M 4/5 14-cylinder radial air-cooled engines each rated at 700 hp at 3,030 rpm for take-off and 680 hp at 3,030 rpm at 13,125 ft (4 000 m) driving three-bladed Ratier electrically-operated constant-speed propellers. Internal fuel capacity, 134 Imp gal (610 l) divided between one fuselage (44 Imp gal/200 l) and two wing centre section (45 Imp gal/205 l each) tanks.

Performance: Max speed (clean), 253 mph (407 km/h) at 12,570 ft (3 830 m), (with 30-mm MK 103 cannon), 199 mph (320 km/h) at 9,845 ft (3 000 m); max continuous cruise (clean), 196 mph (315 km/h) at 9,845 ft (3 000 m); range at econ cruise (clean), 428 mls (690 km), (with MK 103), 348 mls (560 km); initial climb (clean), 1,595 ft/min (8,1 m/sec), (with MK 103), 1,150 ft/min (5,84 m/sec); service ceiling (clean), 29,530 ft (9 000 m), (with MK 103), 24,600 ft (7 500 m).

Weights: Empty, 8,400 lb (3 810 kg); empty equipped (without external pack), 8,860 lb (4 020 kg), (with MK 103), 9,243 lb (4 193 kg); max take-off, 11,574 lb (5 250 kg).

Dimensions: Span, 46 ft 7 in (14,20 m); length, 31 ft 11¾ in (9,75 m); height (to top of propeller disc), 10 ft 8 in (3,25 m); wing area, 312·15 sq ft (29,00 m²).

Armament: (Standard) Two 13-mm MG 131 machine guns with 300 rpg and two 20-mm MG 151 cannon with 125 rpg, plus one 30-mm MK 101 cannon with 30 rounds, four 7,9-mm MG 17 machine guns with 250 rpg, four 110-lb (50-kg) SC 50 bombs, 96 4·4-lb (2-kg) SD 2 anti-personnel bombs or one 551-lb (250-kg) SC 250 bomb beneath fuselage, and two SC 50 bombs or 48 SD 2 bombs beneath wings. (Hs 129B-2/Wa) Standard built-in gun armament and one 30-mm MK 103 cannon or two 20-mm MG 151 and one 37-mm BK 3,7 cannon.

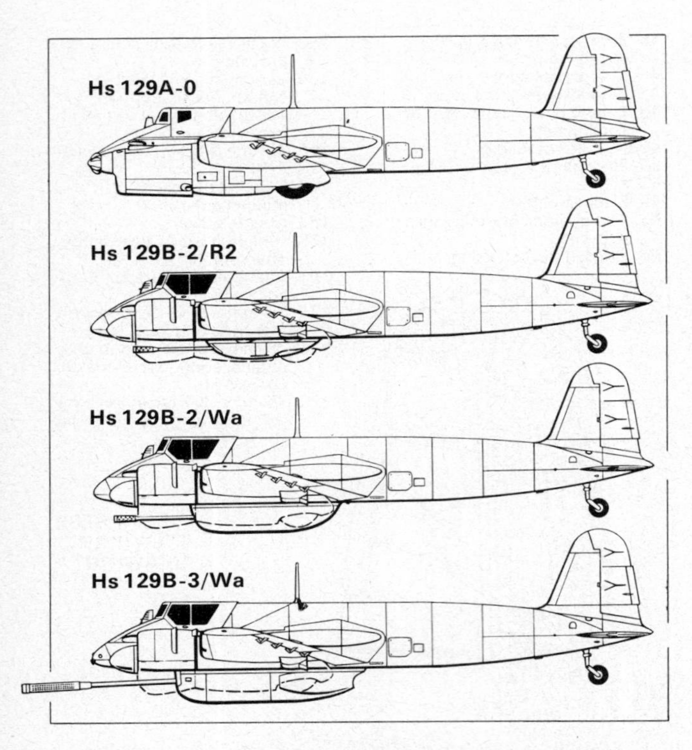

armament sets) which could be fitted and replaced by unit maintenance personnel as and when the operational situation demanded, the type of target dictating the *Rüstsatz* fitted. The R1 (*Rüstsatz* 1) consisting of either two 110-lb (50-kg) SC 50 bombs or two packs each of 48 SD 2 anti-personnel bombs; the R2 comprised a pannier housing a 30-mm MK 101 cannon with 30 rounds; the R3 was a battery of four additional MG 17 machine guns which, unenclosed, was mounted beneath the fuselage with 250 rpg; the R4 consisted of either one 551-lb (250-kg) SC 250 or four SC 50s, or a total of 96 SD 2 bombs, and the R5 was an internally-mounted Rb 20/30 or 50/30 vertical camera, its installation reducing ammunition capacity.

The Büchsenöffner committed

The first Hs 129B-1s were hurriedly assigned to 4.*Staffel* of the newly-activated *Schlachtgeschwader* 1 at Lippstadt in northwest Germany, and, with 12 aircraft on strength, left for the Eastern Front on 10 May 1942, its Henschels still suffering a number of teething troubles which were mostly associated with the Gnôme-Rhône engines. Heartily disliked by the *Luftwaffe*, these engines had proven extremely unreliable, at best refusing to give full rated power and at worst seizing without warning. The Gnôme-Rhône was particularly sensitive to dust and sand which plagued airfields on the South Russian steppes in the summer months, and the record of 4./Sch.G.1 was most noteworthy for low serviceability returns. So troublesome were the Gnôme-Rhône-engined aircraft under the conditions existing on advanced *Luftwaffe* airfields that a further five months were to elapse before reasonably competent filters had been developed for the French engines and the formation of units on the Hs 129B could be resumed.

The second unit to equip with the Hs 129B, 4./Sch.G.2, was formed with 12 aircraft at Deblin-Irena, Poland, on 30 September 1942, and this was to enjoy even less success in its initial months of operation than had the first Henschel-equipped *Staffel*. Deployed to North Africa on 10 November, 4./Sch.G.2 lost one-third of its aircraft in transit, three of the four losses resulting from engine failure, and upon reaching its destination, only four of the remaining eight aircraft could be considered operational. The desert sand proved even less acceptable to the Gnôme-Rhône engines than had the dust of the Russian steppes, despite the new filters, and after two or three missions, during the course of which engine failures were responsible for the loss of two aircraft behind Allied lines, the surviving Hs 129Bs were withdrawn to Tripoli for overhauls. In the event, these were still in process when the arrival of the British 8th Army necessitated the destruction of the aircraft and the evacuation of the personnel of the *Staffel* to Bari.

In the meantime, production of the Hs 129B-1 at Schönefeld had averaged 23 aircraft monthly during the second half of 1942, a total of 219 being completed during the course of the year, but acceptances by the *Luftwaffe* were somewhat erratic owing to the increasing number of modifications that had to be applied to the aircraft once they had left the assembly line. Insofar as service pilots were concerned, once they had accustomed themselves to the rigours of the *Panzerkabine*, they were dismayed to discover that their new mount carried no more than the Ju 87D, was decidedly less manoeuvrable and barely 20 mph (32 km/h) faster. It was extraordinarily sturdy and competently protected its pilot from groundfire, but these desirable features were offset by the fact that its Gnôme-Rhône engines were incapable of absorbing any but the most trivial battle damage. The Hs 129B *could* be flown back to base on one engine if the *Rüstsatz* was jettisoned, but it demanded constant application of muscle by the pilot to fly straight and level.

The importance of providing an effective aerial antidote to the Soviet T-34 tank with its 45-mm armour and the even more potent KV-1 with its 75-mm armour, both of which were beginning to appear in numbers on the Eastern Front, began to receive the highest priority during the early months of 1943. The *Rüstsatz* 2 comprising a 30-mm MK 101 cannon had been applied to the Hs 129Bs issued to a so-called *Panzerjäger Staffel* formed within *Jagdgeschwader* 51 which was deployed operationally in January 1943. With its Hs 129B-1/R2 aircraft, Pz.Jäg./JG 51 enjoyed some successes against Soviet armour, but the MK 101's shells proved incapable of penetrating the frontal armour of the later Soviet tanks and the unit relinquished the cannon in favour of 8·8-lb (4-kg) SD-4 hollow-charge bombs which were found to be more effective, although accurate delivery presented problems. The *Staffel* eventually adopted the method of approaching a tank formation with three aircraft in line abreast and in a 10-15 deg dive, the Henschels endeavouring to release their bombs simultaneously. It was tacitly admitted that attacks in tight formation would have been more effective, but the inadequate lateral vision from the *Panzerkabine* rendered such inadvisable.

Another *Staffel*, 8./Sch.G.1, had meanwhile been formed at Lippstadt and sent to the Eastern Front, to which 4./Sch.G.2 had also been committed after its evacuation from Tripoli and subsequent re-equipment, and former JG 27 and JG 53 personnel had provided the nucleus of a fifth Hs 129B-equipped *Staffel*, 8./Sch.G.2, which had been deployed to

The 75-mm BK 7,5 anti-armour cannon-equipped Hs 129B-3/Wa. It will be seen that the MG 131 machine gun troughs have been faired over but those of the MG 151 cannon are retained.

Tunis-El Aouina. The comparatively high attrition suffered by the Hs 129B-equipped *Schlachtflieger* combined with Henschel's apparent inability to boost production tempo frustrated plans to equip more units, and when, on 10 October 1943, the *Schlachtflieger* were reorganised, there were still only five Hs 129B-equipped *Staffeln*, these now being gathered in a new *Gruppe*, the IV *(Panzer)/Schlachtgeschwader* 9, under the command of *Hauptmann* Bruno Meyer. By this time, 8./Sch.G.2, which had enjoyed somewhat more success than the preceding Hs 129B-equipped unit in North Africa, having operated under the control of the *Fliegerführer Tunis* with an operational strength fluctuating between seven and 16 aircraft, had also arrived on the Eastern Front, all five Hs 129B *Staffeln* coming under the control of the *Führer der Panzerjäger*.

Four of the five Hs 129B units participated in the *Wehrmacht* offensive launched on 5 July as Operation *Zitadelle* in an attempt to regain the initiative on the Eastern Front. The Hs 129Bs operated from Mikoyanovka under the overall command of Hptm Meyer, and three days after the launching of *Zitadelle*, a Soviet armoured brigade intent on making a flank attack on the II *SS Panzerkorps* was sighted west of Byelgorod. The four Hs 129B *Staffeln*, each with 16 aircraft, attacked the Soviet tanks from astern and abeam in relays — as one *Staffel* attacked, a second was *en route* to the target, a third was refuelling and re-arming and the fourth was returning to base to refuel for a further sortie. The Hs 129Bs enjoyed complete success, the Soviet armoured brigade taking heavy losses and the surviving tanks being scattered in complete confusion.

With the reorganisation of the *Schlachtflieger* which followed on the appointment of *Oberst* Ernst Kupfer as the first *Waffengeneral der Schlachtflieger*, the five individual Hs 129B *Staffeln* were redesignated as follows: 4./Sch.G.1 became 10.(Pz)./SG 9, 8./Sch.G.1 became 11.(Pz)./SG 9, 4./Sch.G.2 became 12.(Pz)./SG 9, 8./Sch.G.2 became 13.(Pz)./SG 9 and Pz.Jäg./JG 51 became 14.(Pz)./SG 9. Although these were the only *Luftwaffe* units to be operating the Henschel close air support aircraft at this time, they were joined on the Eastern Front by a similarly-equipped close air support unit of the FARR (*Fortelor Aeriene Regal ale România*, or Royal Air Forces of Romania). This, the *Grupul* 8 *Asalt* (8 Assault Group) had been formed with three squadrons (*Escadrile* 41, 42 and 43) and operated under *Luftflotte* 4, although it roamed freely over the areas covered by both *Luftflotten* 4 and 6, breaking up Soviet concentrations of armour and attacking targets of opportunity. The FARR had been the recipient of the seven Hs 129A-1 aircraft that had been built in 1940 and refused by the *Luftwaffe*, utilising these for the assault training rôle, and was to receive a total of 62 Hs 129Bs.

Advent of the Waffenträger

Production of the Hs 129B-1 had, during the course of 1943, given place to the Hs 129B-2, which embodied as standard the numerous minor changes and modifications introduced on the initial series model as a result of operational experience, and replacement of the MG 15s with MG 131s of 13-mm calibre. It was initially intended that the B-2 would accept the same *Rüstsätze* as the B-1, but the increasing emphasis on the use of the aircraft as a *panzerjäger* had resulted in the decision to equip the aircraft with specialised anti-armour weaponry at the factory rather than deliver it with provision for alternative *Rüstsätze* to be applied in the field. The Hs 129B was thus designated a *Waffenträger*, or "weapon-carrier", the designation becoming Hs 129B-2/Wa.

In its basic form, the Hs 129B-2/Wa was equipped with a similar built-in armament to that of the Hs 129B-1, and the initial version carried a single 30-mm MK 103 cannon in a ventral fairing, this offering a flatter trajectory and a higher muzzle velocity than the MK 101. As an alternative weapon to the MK 103, the 37-mm BK 3,7 anti-tank gun could also be fitted, but in order to provide adequate space for the 37-mm shell magazine, the two MG 131 machine guns had to be removed from the lower portion of the fuselage centre section. Both weapons proved comparatively efficacious when employed against the "softer" sides and rear of the Soviet tanks, although neither could penetrate their frontal armour.

Late in 1943, 11.(Pz)./SG 9 was pulled back from the Eastern Front to serve primarily as an anti-armour weaponry development unit, which, based at Udetfeld, was redesignated *Erprobungskommando* 26 on 20 January 1944. This unit was to be responsible for the testing of a variety of potential Hs 129B-mounted anti-armour weapons against captured Soviet tanks. Weapons tested included the 210-mm Wfr.Gr *(Werfer-Granate)* 21 and 280-mm Wfr. Gr.28 tube-launched rocket projectiles, the 70-mm *Panzerblitz* 1 and 55-mm *Panzerblitz* 2 missiles, and even a pack housing a *Gero* flame-thrower with 66 Imp gal (300 l) of fuel. By far the most sophisticated anti-

continued on page 303

(Above left and below) An Hs 129B-1/R2 (Werk-Nr 141859) of 4./Sch.G.1 photographed, probably at Mikoyanovka, during the summer of 1943. This unit, commanded by Oblt Dornemann, played an important rôle in Operation Zitadelle, being redesignated 10.(Pz)./SG 9 shortly thereafter.

PERSONAL VIEW BY ROY BRAYBROOK

ILLUSTRATIONS BY CHRIS WREN

ENGINES
AIRFRAMES

CHARTING A COURSE FOR V/STOL

THE FUTURE development of V/STOL might be described as a free-fire zone for wise sayings. The late Sir Sydney Camm used to say that V/STOL would never amount to much until it could be combined with the in-flight performance of an F-4. McDonnell Douglas clearly support the notion that V/STOL aircraft cannot achieve competitive warload-radius performance without the development of lightweight advanced composite materials for the airframe. My own contribution on this subject is that nobody will ever produce an advanced V/STOL aircraft until the airframe designer has learned to be really rude to the engine designer!

However, in fairness to my friends in the rotating machinery business, I must admit that my scepticism regarding their willingness to push engine development out to new frontiers is based on bitter experience in the far-off 1960s, when V/STOL appeared to be forging ahead at a staggering rate (if only to catch up with the in-flight performance of the F-4).

What I objected to then was the way in which the BS.100 engine proposal was formulated for the Hawker P.1154 supersonic strike fighter. That powerplant was basically an unscaled Olympus high-pressure compressor with the addition of a fan sized to give the required take-off thrust. Instead of being optimised for the job, it was merely an engine of convenience, designed around an existing surge-free compressor. Considering that this was Britain's best chance of a supersonic V/STOL engine, I felt that this was an unsatisfactory approach. For a project engineer who knew something of engine design and was not afraid to be scathing in his criticism of the equipment supplier, it was, in fact, possible to extract a far more advanced powerplant proposal.

It is now almost 20 years since I was single-handedly dragging the engine manufacturer into step on advanced V/STOL technology, and in that period of time significant changes have occurred. One such change is that Rolls-Royce has now taken the lead in pressing the case for further V/STOL development, leaving British Aerospace a poor second in the UK and well down on the international scale.

A discussion of how V/STOL should progress is therefore a useful means to examine some of the various interests of R-R and BAe, which — although generally compatible — are seldom identical. Moreover, this is a particularly appropriate time to return to the subject of V/STOL, since the next several months should see the publication of some key documents and the taking of crucial decisions on short-term developments. The coming months should also see worthwhile progress toward planning a new generation of V/STOL combat aircraft, the first such aircraft capable of worthwhile supersonic speed in level flight.

Tin vs plywood

For the UK, the most important V/STOL decision to be taken this year is whether the Royal Air Force is to have BAe's so-called "GR5" or the McDonnell Douglas AV-8B to satisfy ASR.409 in replacing existing Harrier GR Mk 3s and some Jaguars. In the beginning, there were many differences between the GR5 (or "big-wing Harrier") and AV-8B, but the contest has now become a classic case of what R-R refers to as "Fitzgerald's Law Of Marketing", namely, the longer the competition, the closer the proposals. Thus, the GR5 has taken on board the LIDs (Lift Improvement Devices) of the AV-8B under the name CADs (Cushion Augmentation Devices), and has also adopted improved air intakes and zero-scarf nozzles. Conversely, the AV-8B now has a raised cockpit and will have to adopt leading edge extensions if it is to approach RAF manoeuvrability requirements, both of these features originally only occurring on the GR5. The AV-8B will almost certainly be offered for export with a radar nose, to counter BAe proposals to combine the big wing of the GR5 with the Ferranti Blue Fox radar of the Sea Harrier.

Both aircraft would have an uprated Pegasus and would offer major improvements over the present-day Harrier GR3 and AV-8A in terms of warload-radius performance, manoeuvrability, number of weapon stations and outrigger track (which has always restricted road operations). However, some fundamental differences remain.

The AV-8B is already flying in technology demonstrator (YAV-8B) form, a converted AV-8A with most of the features of the production aircraft, although not the raised cockpit or the definitive wing and centre fuselage profiles. Assuming that Congress forces series production on a reluctant Department of Defense, the AV-8B will be the first combat aircraft to enter service with an advanced composite wing. This graphite composite material (sometimes referred to as "advanced technology plywood") saves approximately 330 lb (150 kg) relative to the custom-built "tin wing" of the GR5, but it clearly introduces an element of risk due to the very limited amount of prior service experience.

The AV-8B wing uses a NASA supercritical profile with a

"NO, MINISTER, THE 'S' IN STOL STANDS FOR 'SHORT' NOT 'SUPERSONIC...'"

pronounced concave region on the undersurface toward the trailing edge in order to promote lift on the rear part of the chord. All the indications are that this has been a disappointing exercise from an aerodynamic viewpoint, and that it will be difficult to make major improvements to the wing profile due to the form of construction.

The AV-8B also differs from the GR5 in having a more advanced trailing edge flap system to achieve favourable interaction with the jets in STO, a more advanced cockpit in terms of instruments and controls, and ARBS (Angle-Rate Bombing System) for accurate weapon delivery in steep dive attacks. In the event of the AV-8B being accepted by the RAF, the ARBS would have to be replaced by a Ferranti inertial nav-attack system, and the aircraft would have to be strengthened in various areas to meet UK bird-strike criteria.

The GR5 exists only in wind tunnel model form, and is based on a rather different approach to wing design. This derives from Harrier and Airbus experience and is aimed at optimising manoeuvre performance at low levels, rather than achieving the highest possible drag rise Mach No. In view of the manufacturer's background experience with subsonic swept wings, it is hardly surprising that the resulting aircraft is said (on the basis of tunnel tests) to be somewhat more manoeuvrable than the AV-8B.

More surprising is the claim that the GR5 has a 50 kt (93 km/h) advantage in maximum speed at sea level, and that its lower drag more than offsets the far greater internal fuel capacity of the AV-8B. The air intakes of the GR5 are claimed to give a better pressure recovery than those of the AV-8B, cancelling out the benefits of the lighter weight of the US aircraft in terms of disposable load in vertical landing. The basic cost of the GR5 is claimed to be in the region of 20 per cent less expensive than that of the AV-8B.

Notwithstanding the evidently superior aerodynamics of the GR5, it is clear from the desperate political campaign now being mounted by BAe that the RAF is currently inclined to accept the AV-8B with detail improvements (some of which are being tested on the YAV-8B). It might also be deduced from BAe's vigorous defence of its ability to have the aircraft in service by the required 1985/86 timescale that the RAF takes the view that the GR5 is too new a design to complete development in time.

The AV-8B production programme is far larger than that envisaged for the GR5: the USMC plans on some 336 production aircraft (following four Full-Scale Development AV-8Bs), whereas the RAF requirement is for only 60 aircraft, with a possible follow-on order for 40 at some later stage.

Nonetheless, in 1979 McDonnell Douglas sought RAF support for the AV-8B on the grounds that this would ensure production go-ahead. An attractive package of work for the UK was put forward, apparently guaranteeing more manhours for BAe and R-R if the GR5 was dropped in favour of the AV-8B. More recently, it has been generally accepted that RAF adoption of the AV-8B is of no great significance from a US Government viewpoint, but MDC persists with its UK marketing effort (AV-8B participation at Farnborough was cancelled only because the aircraft could not be prepared in time). It might be inferred from the very attractive offsets proposed that the US manufacturer is more concerned with eliminating BAe as a future V/STOL competitor than simply with securing the RAF order.

The interests of BAe and R-R in this matter are quite different. For the engine manufacturer a Pegasus is a Pegasus, whether the aircraft it powers was designed in the US or UK, and the more Pegasus on order the better. For the airframe manufacturer an increase in shopfloor workload over the next few years would be particularly welcome, but abandoning the GR5 would almost certainly lead to redundancies in the Kingston design office. It would also kill any chance of further Harrier exports, notably to China. Whereas today's Harrier

could be retrofitted with the GR5 wing in the mid-1980s, the rear aerodynamic loading of the AV-8B wing makes it unsuitable for mounting on existing fuselages. Hence China (which at present is still potentially a large-scale customer for a modified GR Mk 3) would be buying a dead-end development from the UK if the RAF were to adopt the AV-8B.

It may, of course, be argued that the Chinese sale has now dragged on for so long that it is unlikely to materialise, whether or not the aircraft on offer has any further development potential. However, abandoning the GR5 would almost certainly produce a hiatus in V/STOL development in the BAe Kingston-Brough Division. If this lasted for several years, it is difficult to see how the division could exploit its V/STOL experience in a later generation of vectored-thrust aircraft. This is a particularly serious threat, since it is only in the Harrier that Britain can still claim a world aerospace lead.

Further complications arise from the fact that the vectored-thrust aircraft (as developed at Kingston) is not the only V/STOL option for BAe, since the Warton Division has its own ideas on the subject. Britain's MoD might therefore defend its action in choosing the AV-8B by arguing that the vectored-thrust concept has little supersonic potential, and that BAe should keep its V/STOL know-how alive by concentrating the experts at Warton. Moreover, the twin spectres of design redundancies at Kingston and of losing the UK's only aerospace technology lead could be eliminated by MoD promising to sponsor (or share in) a supersonic V/STOL technology demonstrator, such as R-R at Bristol has been advocating for some time.

Technology demonstrator

If the vectored-thrust engine is to be used in a supersonic fighter, then it will need plenum chamber burning (PCB) to avoid the unreheated turbofan's loss of thrust with forward speed. Used in take-off, PCB makes possible a proportionally smaller, lighter engine. Such an engine is better matched to cruise thrust demands and hence operates at a lower specific fuel consumption (sfc) and with less spill drag on the intake.

The disadvantages of PCB are that it adds complication, virtually eliminates any possibility of operating from unprepared surfaces, and threatens to recirculate hot gases to

(Above) An artist's impression, prepared by Rolls-Royce Ltd, of a possible future supersonic V/STOL aircraft powered by a single augmented vectored-thrust engine. This engine would be derived from the Pegasus and would have a plenum chamber burning (PCB) thrust-augmentation system in the front nozzles and a single thrust vectoring rear tailpipe and nozzles. (Below) Another possible supersonic V/STOL layout, with a single intake, PCB and two thrust-vectoring nozzles.

the air intakes. Without special preventative measures, the temperature rise in the air reaching the engine could eliminate the thrust increase produced by PCB.

It is also worth noting that PCB is a relatively new technology, quite unlike the main combustion system, since it involves combustion with relatively low pressure air in a short, curved duct. The PCB system used by R-R is, in fact, a combination of ramjet technology and the form of burning used in the very short reheat of the RB.199.

Trials with PCB on the Pegasus began late in 1962, and these were followed by BS.100 tests. A total of 650 hours of full-scale PCB development running had been accumulated by 1965, when official interest in PCB terminated with the cancellation of the P.1154 programme. However, in 1979 PCB research on a Pegasus 2 engine began again under MoD funding to provide information on the effects of inlet flow distortion and water ingestion, to check cross-lighting between the two nozzles (eliminating the danger of asymmetric light-up), and to establish altitude performance in a special test cell.

The next steps are to develop PCB for the production Pegasus Eleven and to explore the use of such a powerplant installed in an airframe, looking at PCB firstly in V/STOL and secondly in high speed (hopefully supersonic) flight. It is proposed to investigate take-off and landing considerations in a very low-cost programme, with a PCB Pegasus fitted in an airframe recovered from a crashed Harrier, the aircraft suspended from a large gantry to allow static tests to be carried out at a variety of heights from the ground.

However, there are difficulties in planning even this simple test. Rolls-Royce feels that the only way to reduce hot gas recirculation to an acceptable figure is to droop the front nozzles and toe them in, so that as the aircraft unsticks the jets meet just above the ground, thus eliminating the central fountain of rising hot air. While BAe agrees that drooped nozzles make for a better engine installation from considerations of forward flight, the feeling at Kingston is that the sharp toe-in advocated by R-R would produce an unacceptable loss of vertical thrust component, and loss of the very useful ground cushion effect produced by the "four-poster" jet arrangement of the standard Pegasus.

It has always been the philosophy at Kingston to have the jets almost vertical, and to optimise the ground cushion effect and minimise recirculation by strakes and (if necessary) cross-dams on the fuselage undersurface. For these gantry tests, it seems likely that the BAe approach will be tried first, and that the R-R drooped, toed-in PCB nozzles (involving more extensive changes to both engine and airframe) will only be pursued if the BAe concept fails to control hot gas recirculation.

In order to produce a supersonic V/STOL demonstrator quickly, R-R is proposing a Pegasus Eleven with droop-and-trail PCB, the nozzles circular in cross-section and variable in area (derived from those of the RB.199 in Tornado). Static thrust would be approximately 27,000 lb (12 250 kg). The company argues that by 1986 such an engine should take a demonstrator to the region of M = 1·6. However, it is difficult to imagine any simple adaptation of the Harrier reaching anything like this speed, since the airframe was designed for minimum weight rather than low wave drag. The wing and intakes (at least) would have to be completely rehashed, which — in combination with the revised front nozzle position — suggests that it might be better to start with a completely new airframe design.

The case for a brand-new aircraft as a supersonic V/STOL demonstrator is strengthened by the fact that the thrust centre of the PCB engine is 7 in (17,8 cm) farther forward than for the standard engine. Assuming that PCB is to be used for V/STOL (which appears essential to check the results of the gantry tests), then the CG of the aircraft must be moved forward by a similar distance. Rolls-Royce suggest inserting a structural plug to shift the front fuselage forward. Alternatively, it might be possible to use the front fuselage of the two-seat Harrier T Mk 4 (without the tail ballast that normally goes with this). In either case, the larger vertical tail of the T Mk 4 would probably be necessary to offset the adverse effect of the longer nose on directional stability.

Having moved the CG forward, it would then be necessary to move the aerodynamic centre (AC) forward by a similar amount to maintain the same longitudinal stability. This might be achieved by a 9·3-in (23,6-cm) forward extension of wing chord, with the adverse effect on flutter speed cancelled out by adding mass balance to the leading edge. This chord extension would also produce a reduction in thickness/chord ratio of approximately 10 per cent. The end product thus emerges as an extensively rehashed Harrier with only a marginal supersonic potential.

Conversely, the idea of producing a brand-new airframe for a technology demonstrator has gone out of fashion in the UK, and it can be argued that even France (ie, Dassault-Breguet) is going away from this approach. Nonetheless, such an aircraft could be produced at moderate cost by making use of some components (eg, cockpit, landing gear) from existing aircraft, and by minimising the need for structural testing by designing an over-strong airframe and severely restricting its life. A case can therefore be made for developing from scratch a supersonic V/STOL technology demonstrator around a PCB Pegasus Eleven, although the programme cost would still be over £50m in present day terms.

The considerable expenditure necessary for such a programme (which would eliminate several smaller R&D projects from the MoD budget) means that its advocates would have to argue the potential benefits very convincingly. This country is unlikely to spend such an amount purely to hold a design team together. The fact that a PCB powerplant has supersonic potential can hardly be in doubt. The case for the demonstrator therefore appears to come down to providing a general data base for a new supersonic vectored-thrust engine.

While agreeing that such a data base is highly desirable, I find it difficult to believe that the UK will fund a new single-purpose research aircraft to carry out work that ideally would be done on a multi-application supersonic engine testbed. What appears to be needed is a large supersonic aircraft that is sufficiently high off the ground to take a Pegasus pod under the belly, in much the same way that the RB.199 was tested subsonically under a Vulcan. Such a testbed, used in combination with a modified Harrier to investigate the V/STOL aspects of PCB, might be a more reasonable approach than developing a new aircraft specifically to look at PCB in both V/STOL and supersonic flight.

It is possible that one Concorde might eventually find application as a supersonic powerplant testbed. An alternative might be to use a prototype of the Rockwell B-1, which suggests a joint research programme with the US. This approach would spread the R&D cost, and it would make practical sense, as America is just as interested as the UK in the supersonic development of vectored-thrust engines.

Next generation

Where is this line of development leading? In the case of the Royal Navy, there is said to be a draft AST for a Sea Harrier replacement to enter service in the mid-1990s. This may be the timescale on which the RN genuinely feels the Sea Harrier will be obsolete, or it may be a cynical 10 years in advance of when the RN actually hopes to receive a Sea Harrier replacement.

For the US Navy, the next fighter will be the F-18 replacement, presumably entering service around the year 2005. However, some sources predict a much earlier timescale for a new fighter, in line with the first of the big carrier replacements around 1990. This aircraft for the US Navy is the key to supersonic V/STOL fighter development, and the best timescale indication we shall get in the near future will come from the recommendations of the SEBAMS (Sea-Based Air Master Study) report, probably to be published around the end of the year.

However, even if a production supersonic fighter is required in only 10 years, the question remains, whether it should have an engine based on the vectored-thrust concept or some alternative form of jet lift. This argument is really a throw-back to the 1960s, and my own view remains that (in the case of a high performance fighter) jet lift is best obtained by the vectored-thrust concept, since it is simplest and can provide enhanced in-flight manoeuvrability.

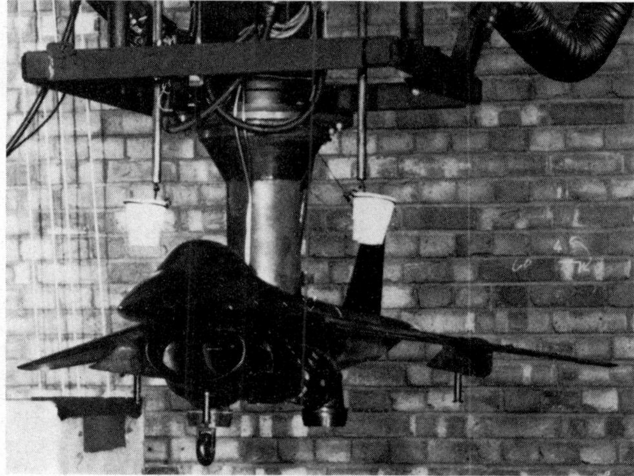

British Aerospace has been investigating a number of possible supersonic V/STOL configurations in the content of a Harrier successor for the RAF. This Kingston project is of similar layout to the aircraft shown in the artist's impression on the opposite page (lower illustration).

Looking to this next fighter generation, R-R is advocating development of a new vectored-thrust engine of around 18 tonnes PCB thrust. In my view one of the most important points in the "definition" of such an engine is that (unlike the Pegasus) it should be applicable to more than one aircraft category. It may be recalled that the Pegasus had too high an sfc for either the AW.681 or production Dornier Do 31. Rolls-Royce appear less optimistic that this aim can be achieved, planning instead on a core engine in the widely-envied General Electric GE-1 tradition, serving as basis for a whole family of powerplants.

There remains the question whether the supersonic V/STOL fighter should have one engine or two. During the P.1154 studies, the idea of replacing its single BS.100 engine with two vectored-thrust Speys was rejected on the (biased) assessment that two engines would increase empty weight, and because the twin-Spey aircraft could not be deck-landed on a single engine. I believe that, since the naval market is now the driving force behind the supersonic V/STOL fighter, a twin-engine configuration warrants further study, and R-R might therefore be better advised to look at a core suitable for a nine-tonne engine. Aside from which, they might quicken the pace of V/STOL progress by being really rude to the airframe designers! □

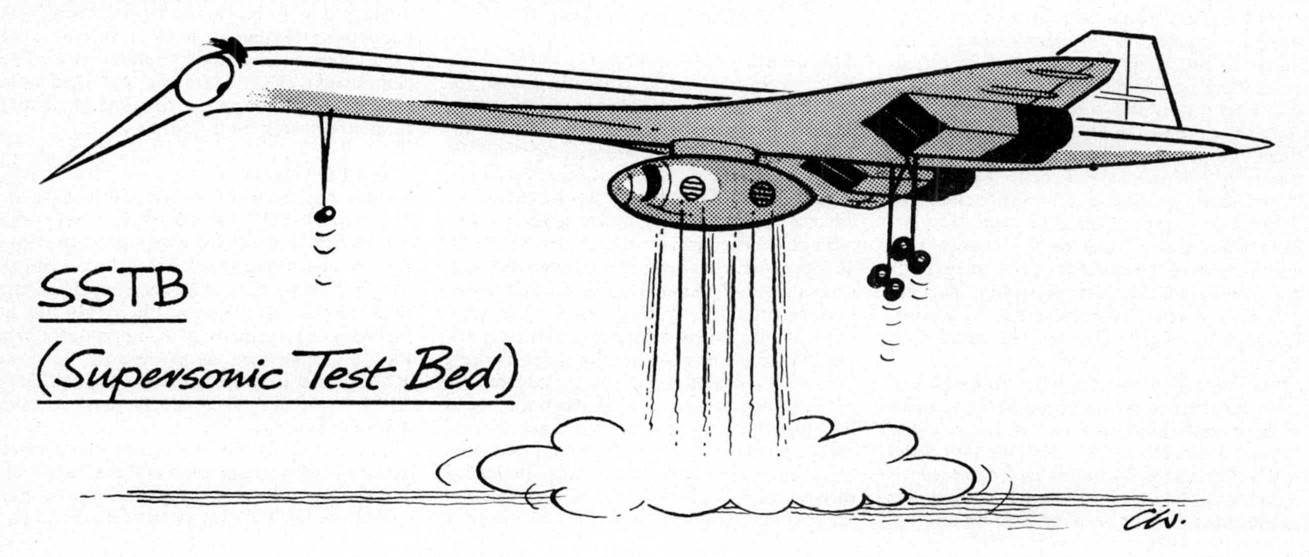

Of Pipers and Tunes

HE WHO PAYS the piper calls the tune. At least, so it was once said, but, in truth, nowadays that would appear as hoary and obsolescent an adage as that also mooting the proposition that the customer is always right! Regrettably, with the passage of the years, all too many companies have come to view their customers as necessary nuisances to be tolerated but dissuaded from demanding anything but minimal consideration, especially when it comes to after-sales service. Many are the tales of woe to be heard of difficulties experienced in endeavouring to persuade a supplier to fulfil his legal obligations and the trend is pervasive; the model kit business is certainly not escaping its miasma.

In so far as the principal kit manufacturers are concerned, there is, of course, not much direct communication with the eventual purchasers of their products — a modeller is hardly likely to bypass his local retail outlet and call in at, say, the factory in Haldane Place, Wandsworth, to buy an Airfix kit! Under normal circumstances, the only contact twixt manufacturer and modeller comes about when component parts are missing from a kit. Nevertheless, most manufacturers *avow* awareness of the value of amicable relations with the modellers, who, after all, keep them in business, and, for that matter, with the stockists and modelling press forming vital links in the chain leading to ultimate sales of kits.

Such avowals notwithstanding, of late things seem to go awry ever more frequently, at least, if our postbag may be taken as any sort of guide. The most recent of many examples of paying the piper and then getting a tune other than that called for comes from reader Maurice Gordon who resides in San Pedro do Estoril, Portugal. His experiences might be hilarious if they did not reveal such ineptitude and casual treatment of a money-paying customer on the part of one of the major British kit producers. Mr Gordon, an ex-de Havilland employee with a penchant for the Tiger Moth and whose local flying club pranged its last example of this fabulous old-timer comparatively recently, was inspired by our review of the 1/32nd scale "Matchbox" Tiger Moth kit included in this column in February to send to the kit's manufacturer, Lesney Products, a cheque for £10·00. This amply covered the purchase price of two kits plus ancillary costs, such as postage, packing etc. The cheque was duly cashed by Lesney Products in April, but no kits arrived in Portugal.

Our reader, understandably concerned at his failure to receive even an acknowledgement of the receipt of his order and cheque, wrote to Lesney Products again. The weeks passed without response, but mid-August, by which time Mr Gordon was beginning to suspect that Lesney was now to be numbered among the victims-of-the-recession statistics, a parcel finally arrived. Hallelujah! The long-awaited Tiger Moth kits! Not so, the parcel contained two kits of the Messerschmitt Bf 109E. An error on the part of Lesney's despatch department? No way! The kits were accompanied by a note informing Mr Gordon that the Tiger Moth was out of stock and that the German fighter had therefore been substituted! Unbelievable! This might be considered to equate with boarding a plane for Paris and being delivered to Brussels as, insofar as the crew is concerned, one destination is as good as another, or ordering steak and chips in a restaurant and getting prunes and custard as, to the chef, it's all food!

Quite apart from the fact that at the time Mr Gordon's cheque was cashed, Lesney almost certainly *had* a stock of Tiger Moth kits, it is barely credible that a company of such size and stature should be so inept in its dealings with its customers; scarcely conceivable that any employee of a specialised model kit manufacturer could be so stupid as to substitute a Bf 109E for a Tiger Moth in fulfilling a specific order. There was a time when we regarded Lesney Products as a company that prided itself on its approach to public relations, providing regular publicity information, efficiently providing review samples of new products and even arranging visits to its factory to show the modern and efficient methods of production and distribution in which it justifiably took pride. More recently, information releases on new products have become, at best, sporadic and review kits no more than occasional. If Lesney Products has an explanation to offer for its ineptness insofar as Mr Gordon is concerned we shall be pleased to publish it, for the ever increasing number of instances of ineptitude on the part of British kit manufacturers in dealing with their customers is doing the industry no good abroad.

This month's colour subject

Forty years ago, on 25 November 1940, the first example of what was to become one of the most controversial warplanes of WW II was eased off the Baltimore runway by "Bill" K Ebel, the Glenn L Martin Company's chief engineer, to initiate a career that was to attract adverse criticism and renown in fairly equal quantities. The aircraft was, of course, the B-26 Marauder, which established new standards in both aerodynamic cleanliness and speed performance for aircraft in its category. Created and flown within 20 months of the request for proposals, the Marauder marked, in some respects, a quantum advance in medium bomber design, but the advances at the high speed end of the performance spectrum that its début betokened had been achieved at some cost to the opposite end of the spectrum; the Marauder was way ahead of the comparatively unsophisticated training procedures that had been evolved for less demanding warplanes.

The Marauder's service début was marred by an alarming series of crashes; the rather colourful epithet of "Flying Torpedo" bestowed on the Marauder by the popular press soon gave place to such appellations as "Widow Maker" and "Flying Prostitute" — several less printable names were coined by aircrews crediting the new bomber with decidedly lethal propensities. Investigation boards deliberating on whether or not production of the Marauder should be persisted with were to be convened on no less than four occasions. But in truth, the Marauder possessed no really vicious characteristics. Its landing speed at 130 mph (209 km/h) was admittedly high and it did demand a high standard of training from its pilots, not suffering fools gladly, but in return it offered a level of operational immunity unapproached by any contemporary; the Marauders of the US 9th Air Force were to suffer the lowest operational attrition of any US combat aircraft in the ETO, this reaching a point below one-half of one per cent on tactical operations against heavily defended targets. In retrospect, the B-26 Marauder may be truly adjudged a classic.

By comparison with most WW II twin-engined bombers, the Marauder has been well served by the kit manufacturers, with, by our reckoning, six different versions. Of the two kits in 1/48th scale that have been offered, the very early product of Aurora, may be disregarded, even if it is still to be found, for it is almost an antique and decidedly crude. The Monogram kit to the same scale is, on the other hand, excellent, being accurate and well detailed, and easily the best version in any scale. This is truly Monogram at its finest. No less than four different kits exist in 1/72nd scale, varying considerably in their vintage and quality, the "Matchbox" kit being the latest and, in our opinion, the best, while the Airfix kit is also good, although of earlier date.

Revell's B-26B — all available kits are of this Marauder sub-type — is older and suffers a number of inaccuracies, particularly around the nose, while the even earlier Frog kit, unlikely now to be obtainable anywhere, was good for its time but not to be considered in the same category as its more youthful rivals. The definitive kit of the Marauder in 1/72nd scale has yet to appear, and at the time of writing cannot been seen on the horizon.

A NATO veteran

For Heller's second offering in 1/48th scale, the Republic F-84F Thunderstreak has been chosen and a worthy companion it provides for this distinguished French company's earlier Mirage IIIC. For long much of the backbone of NATO tacair, the F-84F has so far been represented by comparatively few kits, although two good versions exist in 1/72nd scale. In this larger scale, Heller's kit is the first and, for all practical purposes, the definitive version.

The quality of the mouldings, the surface detail and the general finish of this kit are a joy to behold — there are some flow marks but such seem virtually inseparable from mould-

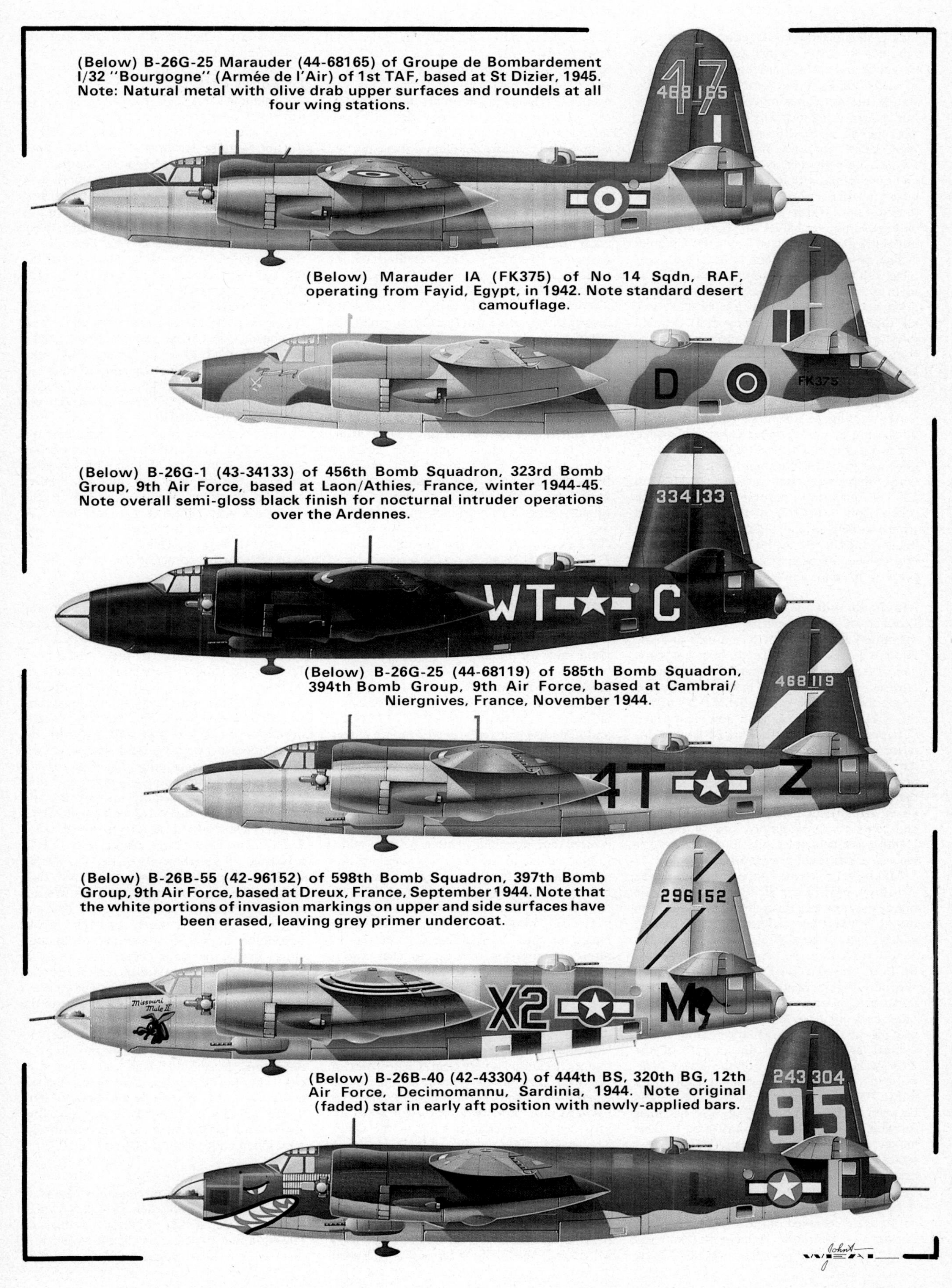

(Below) B-26G-25 Marauder (44-68165) of Groupe de Bombardement I/32 "Bourgogne" (Armée de l'Air) of 1st TAF, based at St Dizier, 1945. Note: Natural metal with olive drab upper surfaces and roundels at all four wing stations.

(Below) Marauder IA (FK375) of No 14 Sqdn, RAF, operating from Fayid, Egypt, in 1942. Note standard desert camouflage.

(Below) B-26G-1 (43-34133) of 456th Bomb Squadron, 323rd Bomb Group, 9th Air Force, based at Laon/Athies, France, winter 1944-45. Note overall semi-gloss black finish for nocturnal intruder operations over the Ardennes.

(Below) B-26G-25 (44-68119) of 585th Bomb Squadron, 394th Bomb Group, 9th Air Force, based at Cambrai/Niergnives, France, November 1944.

(Below) B-26B-55 (42-96152) of 598th Bomb Squadron, 397th Bomb Group, 9th Air Force, based at Dreux, France, September 1944. Note that the white portions of invasion markings on upper and side surfaces have been erased, leaving grey primer undercoat.

(Below) B-26B-40 (42-43304) of 444th BS, 320th BG, 12th Air Force, Decimomannu, Sardinia, 1944. Note original (faded) star in early aft position with newly-applied bars.

ings in silver plastic. The kit comprises 54 parts moulded in silver, apart from four transparencies and a white pilot figure, and for a kit of such quality the assembly is delightfully simple, the completed model of the old "coke bottle" capturing its portly lines to perfection. The cockpit area, with ejection seat, instrument panel consoles and control column, forms a sub-assembly, as does also the tailpipe and nose intake with its splitter plate, with the nose undercarriage member and housing well incorporated. These assemblies are enclosed within the fuselage halves, and both intake and outlet are blanked off well inside the fuselage.

The nosewheel member is moulded complete with wheel, but is finely formed, while the main undercarriage members are exceptionally good, with the wheels made in separate halves, all three wheel wells having fully-detailed interiors. Apart from the one-piece canopy, the transparencies include an armourglass panel and lenses for the upward-facing identity light and the nose gear-mounted landing light. The air brakes may be affixed in either open or closed configuration and there are four underwing pylons, drop tanks being provided for two of these. The decal sheet is extremely good and provides markings for three aircraft. One of these is an *Armée de l'Air* aircraft from EC 1/9 *Limousin* in natural metal finish, the others from JaboG 33 of the *Luftwaffe* and from the Belgian 2nd Fighter-Bomber Wing, being camouflaged. A fine four-view drawing is provided for each scheme. The UK retail price of this kit is £3·95.

Maximum mileage

Esci has, of late, demonstrated anxiety to get maximum mileage from its moulds and the latest releases from this Italian company *almost* repeat previous — and very recent — releases. The Bell 205 has made two previous appearances, as the Agusta-Bell AB 205 and as the UH-1D Iroquois, and now reappears, moulded in white, with khaki-coloured interior parts, representing a Royal Norwegian Air Force machine serving with UNO on rescue tasks in the Sinai in 1978. Apart from the decals and the omission of armament, this kit is virtually identical to preceding releases and remains, quite simply, one of the best 1/48th scale helicopter kits that we have yet seen. The UK retail price is £4·25.

Making its second appearance is Esci's Northrop F-5E Tiger II also in 1/48th scale first released earlier this year. In its latest form the kit reveals few differences from that in which it was originally released, but emphasis is now placed on the "Aggressor" version of the F-5E as used by the US Navy's "Top Gun" Weapons Fighter School at NAS Miramar, the finish being a camouflage of light blue, dark blue and white overall. The decal sheet provides all the necessary markings for such an aircraft as well as for an aircraft of the *Überwachungsgeschwader* of the Swiss *Flugwaffe* in a two-tone grey overall air superiority finish. There are minor external differences between the US Navy and *Flugwaffe* machines for which the kit offers alternative parts. This makes up into a very fine miniature representation of the full-scale original and its retail price in the UK is £3·35.

A tangible spectre

All things considered, the US Navy's variants of the F-4 Phantom II have not suffered overexposure in kit form, with Revell's 1/32nd scale F-4J kit and 1/72nd scale kits of the F-4B from Airfix and Revell, so a new kit in 1/48th scale from Esci which may be completed as either F-4B or F-4J is very welcome. This is an accurately designed and immaculately turned out kit comprising no less than 87 parts moulded primarily in light grey plastic and with the best surface detailing of the engraved variety that we have yet seen sported by an Esci kit. This fine engraving extends, incidentally, even to the wheel well interiors.

The lower wing panel is formed in one piece from tip to tip, fixing the dihedral angle on the outer sections, and assembly presents no particular problems. The detailing of the undercarriage is very fine and the gear doors are nicely contoured, while the cockpit interior, with its two four-part ejection seats, instrument panels (with decals), consoles and controls looks well equipped. The clear canopy, being made in four sections, can be assembled in various configurations. The differences between the F-4B and F-4J models are catered for by the provision of alternative parts, such as two pairs of afterburner outlets and different undernose fairings, while armament provided includes four AIM-7 Sparrow and four AIM-9 Sidewinder AAMs, the latter being carried on paired mountings on the underwing pylons. The decal sheet is exceptionally good, with markings for two aircraft, one being an F-4B of VF-111 *Sundowners* (USS *Coral Sea*, 1972) and the other being an F-4J of VF-74 *Bedevilers* when serving aboard USS *Nimitz*. Both aircraft are basically light gull grey and white, but the individual markings are attractive and a mass of small stencillings appears on the decal sheet. The kit is priced at £4·25 in the UK and we consider it good value for money.

L'élégance française

There can as yet have been no more elegant a jet trainer than the Fouga CM 170 Magister and none has enjoyed a longer service career, one bidding fair to continue throughout this new decade. It is appropriate that Heller should finally have decided to devote plastic to this graceful little aeroplane, even though there is already a very good representation in the same 1/72nd scale by Airfix. The new Heller kit is more than marginally better, being moulded in blue plastic to the very high standard now established by this premier French manufacturer, both as regards the finesse of the detailing and the fit of the component parts.

Heller's Magister consists of 62 parts, including four transparencies, and the kit affords a number of neat touches and a number of minute and very delicately formed components, such as the undercarriage units and the tiny elevator hinges which demand some deft use of tweezers. The amount of detail incorporated into the cockpit area is at least adequate for the size of the model and the one-piece canopy is very clear. Clear lenses are provided for the navigation lights on the wingtip tanks and for the landing light on the fuselage nose, and two additional tanks are provided for attachment beneath the wings. The basic blue colour of the plastic is compatible with that of the *Patrouille de France* scheme and the white striping is included on the decal sheet, although the red striping is omitted. The decals include the serials of 11 different *Patrouille* aircraft and there is an alternative set of markings for a Magister of WS 50 of the *Luftwaffe*. At a retail price of 99p in the UK, this is a kit well worth acquiring for it builds up into a little gem.

Long-lived Lark

Aérospatiale's SA 316 Alouette (Lark) III helicopter possesses a long, long production and development history, ranking as one of Europe's most successful — from both commercial and operational standpoints — rotorcraft, yet we have had to wait until now for a 1/72nd scale kit of this distinguished machine. Needless to say, manufacturer of this kit is Heller and its 61-part product has been well worth waiting for. In view of the large transparent areas, the cabin interior is of the utmost importance in any model of the Alouette III, and Heller has ensured that it is well furnished, with seats having separate supporting frames, floor, controls and a rear bulkhead. The engine and rotorhead, being fully exposed, are also vital features and Heller has provided us with two entirely different engines so that the model may be completed as either the SA 316 or more powerful but generally similar SA 319.

Assembly of this model is precise and the finish of the blue plastic parts is every bit as good as it is for the Magister kit reviewed earlier in this column. The small decal sheet provides markings for an SA 316 of the *Aéronavale* and an SA 319 of the *Armée de l'Air*, the former being painted overall blue and the latter dark green. This is an excellent kit of an interesting helicopter, at 99p in the UK.

More Guano droppings

Our friends at the Guano Aeroplane and Zeppelin Works have been at their backroom moulds again and have come up with a neat little conversion kit for the "Matchbox" 1/72nd scale Hawker Fury biplane to translate it into a Yugoslav Fury with cantilever mainwheel legs and Dowty internally-sprung wheels *à la* Gladiator. The parts are neatly injection-moulded in grey and comprise the main undercarriage legs and wheels, a new radiator housing and grille, a carburettor air intake and two underwing gun fairings — nine parts in all. Full assembly instructions and clear diagrams are provided with the kit which retails at the modest price of 50p in the UK or $1·00 in the USA (from, respectively, J R B Edwards, 19 Larchwood Glade, Camberley GU15 3UW and W F Moore, 5802 North East 59th St, Seattle, Washington 98105). We are asked to point out a possibility of delay in delivery up to as much as eight weeks depending upon the stock and production situation at the time orders are received. Incidentally, this conversion kit cannot be used to produce a Spanish Fury unless a new nose is fashioned to represent the contours of the Spanish fighter's Hispano-Suiza engine.

Also from Guano comes a revised issue of its set of Royal Yugoslav Air Force and Croatian Air Force decals in 1/72nd scale which now cover the Hawker Fury and Hurricane, the IK-2 and IK-Z, the Fiat G 50 and the Bf 109E. These are very good decals, comprising four sheets, and are available from the previously-mentioned addresses at £1·25 and $2·50.

Novel internals

A novel idea has been developed by Modelaid (128 Cardinal Ave, Morden SM4 4SX) which has produced cockpit interiors printed on photographic paper, these being folded into

Continued on page 303

(Above left) One of the two RC-135S reconnaissance aircraft, with unusual fairings and antennae on the forward fuselage. (Above right) A KC-135R, showing the original jet engines and refuelling boom retained. (Below) The RC-135V is a further re-designation of the RC-135C, with large blade aerials under the fuselage. (Right) A "family tree" showing the derivation of variants from the production versions listed in the left-hand column.

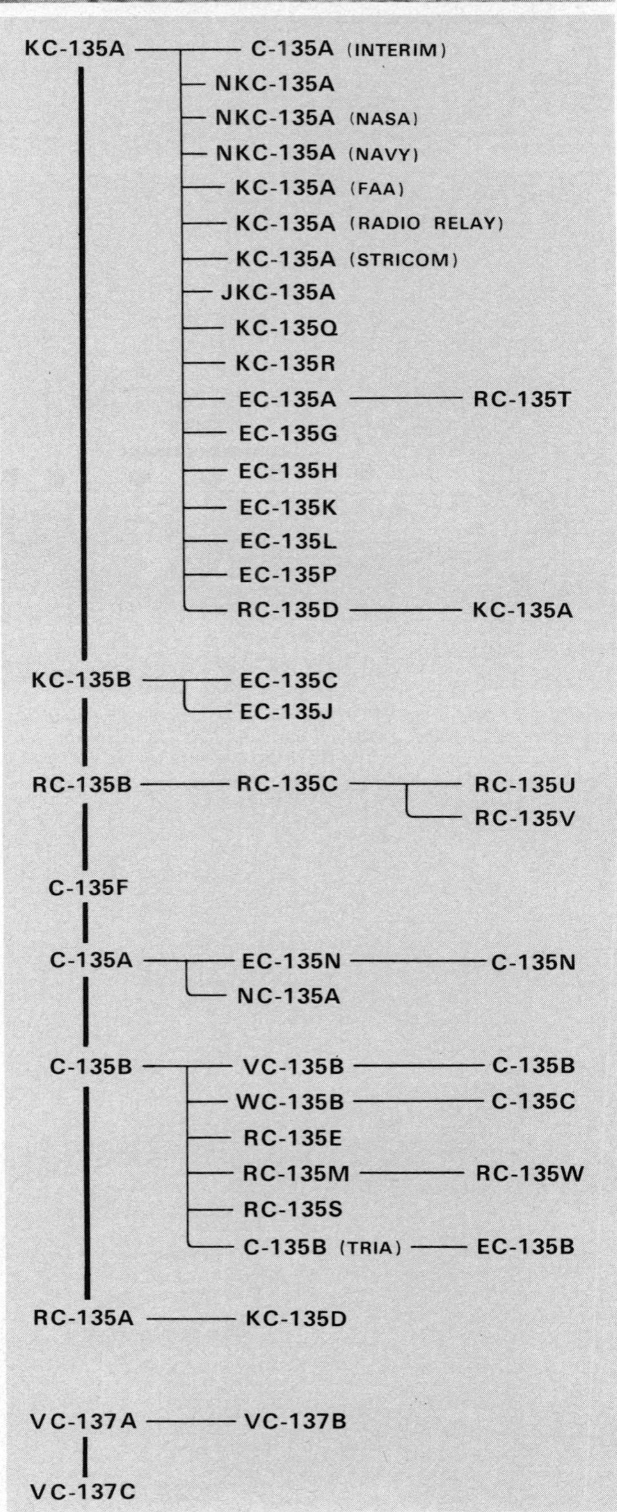

KC-135 ***from page 276***

The WC-135Bs are powered by four TF33-P-5 turbofan engines and have an ARR system installed. Being C-135Bs originally, no refuelling booms were ever installed; however, a fuel dump tube is located under the aft fuselage of each aircraft. These aircraft are equipped with U-1 foils on each side of the fuselage to trap air particles for air sampling studies, with external stiffeners installed on the fuselage sides in the area of the foils.

Research and non-military -135s

The -135 aircraft have served in the past, and continue to serve, in several capacities other than tanker, airborne command post and reconnaissance. USAF -135s are assigned for test purposes to the 4950th Test Wing, Air Force Systems Command while the non-military -135s have been assigned to both the Federal Aviation Administration (FAA) and the National Aeronautics and Space Administration. In the latter category, the FAA operated two KC-135As to certify high altitude jet routes, flight check these routes and perform regular flight check operations. The aircraft allocated for this purpose were 59-1481 and 59-1518, carrying civilian registration N96 and N98 respectively: neither aircraft had the refuelling boom installed. Aircraft N96 was assigned to Hickam AFB, Hawaii, in 1966 to check the Pacific navigational aids. Both aircraft were used for flight check operations within the United States. Aircraft N98 operated with the FAA out of Oklahoma City, Oklahoma, until 1975 when it was returned to the US Air Force and put into storage; subsequently this aircraft was modified to EC-135K status for TAC. Aircraft N96 was transferred to the National Aeronautics and Space Administration (NASA) in 1976, and is now based at Ellington AFB, Texas with the NASA fleet number 960.

Test versions of the -135 used by the USAF have carried numerous designations including EC-135N, C-135N, C-135B T/RIA, JKC-135A, NKC-135A, and NC-135A. Test versions of the C-135B and C-135C are also in the inventory.

EC-135N/C-135N: In 1967, eight Military Airlift Command turbojet-powered C-135As were converted by the Douglas Aircraft Company's Modification Division in Tulsa, Oklahoma, into EC-135Ns. The most notable feature of these aircraft is the 10-ft (3,28-m) long nose radome which houses a 7-ft (2,13-m) diameter parabolic dish antenna — the largest of its kind ever flown. (The AWACS antenna carried on the E-3A is not of the same design.) The primary mission of these

(Above, top) One of the NKC-135As (with refuelling boom retained) used for ionospheric measurement tests; the large number of windows led to the nickname "piccolo tube". (Above, centre) An NKC-135A used by Aeronautical Systems Division (ASD) for radiation airborne measurements. (Below) An RC-135U, showing the SLAR cheeks, wing and fin antennae and extended rear fuselage.

(Above, top) An early photograph of one of the three commercial Boeing 707-153s procured by the USAF as high-level government transports, designated VC-137As and operated in MATS markings. (Above, centre) A later photograph of the same aircraft, after conversion to VC-137B with fan engines and in the blue/white finish adopted by MAC for its VIP fleet. (Below) Air Force One, the second of the two VC-137Cs; note that the ventral fin of the commercial 707-320C is not fitted.

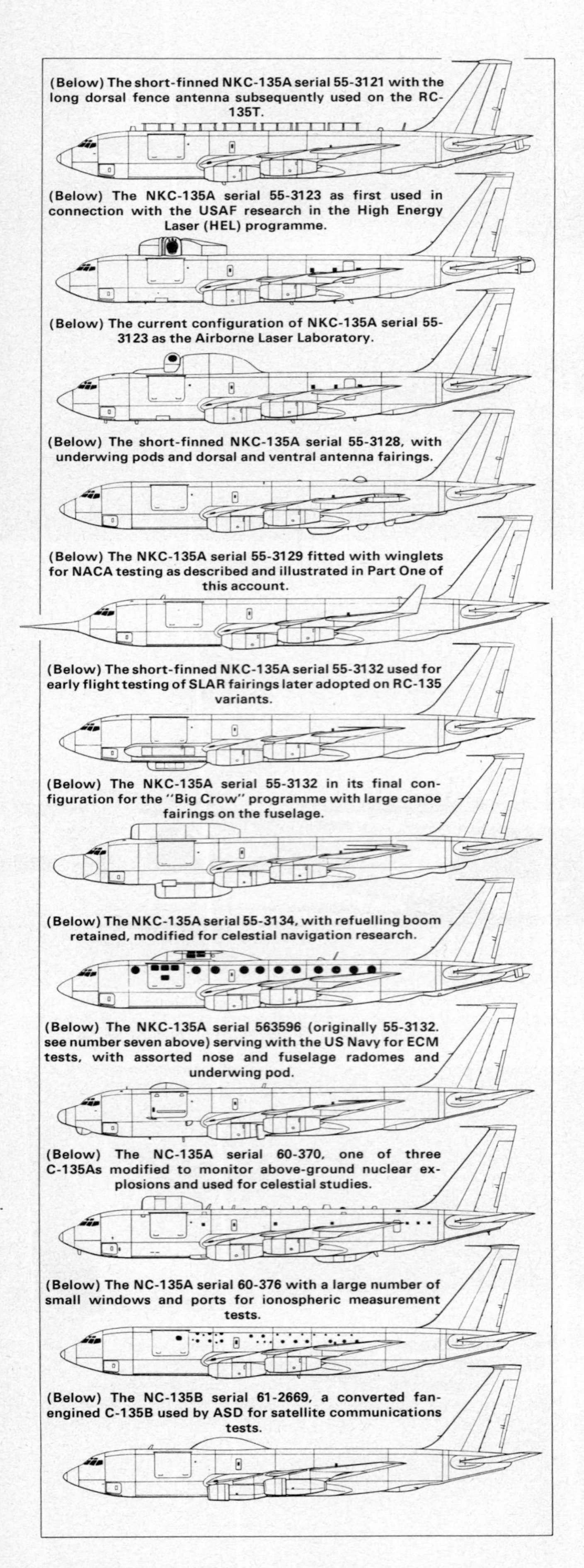

(Below) The short-finned NKC-135A serial 55-3121 with the long dorsal fence antenna subsequently used on the RC-135T.

(Below) The NKC-135A serial 55-3123 as first used in connection with the USAF research in the High Energy Laser (HEL) programme.

(Below) The current configuration of NKC-135A serial 55-3123 as the Airborne Laser Laboratory.

(Below) The short-finned NKC-135A serial 55-3128, with underwing pods and dorsal and ventral antenna fairings.

(Below) The NKC-135A serial 55-3129 fitted with winglets for NACA testing as described and illustrated in Part One of this account.

(Below) The short-finned NKC-135A serial 55-3132 used for early flight testing of SLAR fairings later adopted on RC-135 variants.

(Below) The NKC-135A serial 55-3132 in its final configuration for the "Big Crow" programme with large canoe fairings on the fuselage.

(Below) The NKC-135A serial 55-3134, with refuelling boom retained, modified for celestial navigation research.

(Below) The NKC-135A serial 563596 (originally 55-3132. see number seven above) serving with the US Navy for ECM tests, with assorted nose and fuselage radomes and underwing pod.

(Below) The NC-135A serial 60-370, one of three C-135As modified to monitor above-ground nuclear explosions and used for celestial studies.

(Below) The NC-135A serial 60-376 with a large number of small windows and ports for ionospheric measurement tests.

(Below) The NC-135B serial 61-2669, a converted fan-engined C-135B used by ASD for satellite communications tests.

One of the WC-135Bs used by MAC (and, originally, MATS) for meteorological duties. They were converted from C-135Bs.

aircraft was the tracking of the Apollo/Saturn spacecraft, and they were operated by the Air Force Eastern Test Range (6549th Test Squadron), AFSC, Patrick AFB, Florida.

Four of the Apollo/Range Instrumented Aircraft (A/RIA) also have provisions for the Airborne Lightweight Optical Tracking System (A-LOTS), which is pod-mounted on struts on the main cargo door. The A-LOTS is the largest airborne telescope in the world, being a 22-in (51-cm) telescope with a focal length in excess of 200 in (5,1 m). A high speed 70-millimetre motion picture camera and two television cameras are attached to the telescope. An A-LOTS sighting station is located at the top centreline of the fuselage adjacent to the main cargo door, the sighting blister being a hemisphere of 30-in (76-cm) diameter. A fairing may be installed over the sighting dome when the A-LOTS is not required for a mission.

The remaining four EC-135Ns do not have the A-LOTS provision, but carry a large black-and-white theodolite target on the right side of the nose. Two HF probe antennae are installed over the wingtips and some aircraft carry the wingtip mounted integral static boom/pitot system. A trailing wire antenna is housed in a pod under the wing centre section, forward of the mainwheel wells, and located along the aircraft centreline.

These aircraft operated over the Atlantic and Pacific Oceans, and the Gulf of Mexico, covering the manned space launches. Operating in pairs, they covered 5,000 square miles (12 950 km^2) of ocean, permitting continuous voice communications between the Apollo spacecraft and the shipboard and ground stations. After completion of the Apollo Programme, the Apollo/Range Instrumented Aircraft (A/RIA) designation was changed to Advanced Range Instrumented Aircraft (ARIA). By 1980, all eight aircraft had been demodified and redesignated as C-135Ns. They are now assigned to the 4950th Test Wing, ASD, AFSC, Wright-Patterson AFB, Ohio, where they are used to support the AFSC test mission.

C-135B T/RIA/EC-135B: Four Military Airlift Command fan-engined C-135Bs were modified into Telemetry/Range Instrumented Aircraft (T/RIA) by the Douglas Company's Tulsa Division in 1967. These have the same duckbill platypus noses as the EC-135N aircraft, but do not have A-LOTS provisions. Air Force Systems Command operated these special C-135Bs out of Patrick AFB, Florida, to provide communications support for the space programme; one aircraft was lost from the inventory and a second aircraft became an RC-135S. In late 1978 and early 1979, the two remaining aircraft were modified into the ARIA configuration utilising equipment removed from the non-fan-powered EC-135N aircraft. After modification they were redesignated as EC-135Bs.

NC-135A: NASA had three former MAC C-135As (serials 60-369, 60-370 and 60-371) modified into NC-135As. In 1964, these aircraft were primarily allocated for weapons test diagnostics should above-ground nuclear tests be resumed. When not used for atomic tests, they were used to view solar eclipses, for comet photography, or cosmic ray studies. Subsequently they were assigned to the Atomic Energy

Commission and used by Lawrence Livermore Laboratory, Los Alamos Scientific Laboratory, and the Sandia Laboratories. By 1969, these NASA aircraft had been reassigned to AFSC, and in 1977, aircraft 60-369 and 60-370 were placed in storage. In 1979, aircraft 60-369 was assigned to Air Training Command, Chanute AFB, Illinois, where it is being used as a ground trainer; 60-370 is being scrapped and the Special Weapons Center, AFSC, Kirtland AFB, New Mexico, retains 60-371.

Test C-135A/C-135B/C-135C: In 1969, three MAC C-135As (serials 60-376, 60-377 and 60-378) became part of the AFSC test force. Between 1975 and 1976, Air Force Logistics Command had control of 60-376, but in 1976, this and 60-378 were transferred back to MAC and aircraft 60-377 was retained in the AFSC inventory to perform photographic missions.

Air Force Systems Command (AFSC) also obtained four C-135Bs from MAC in 1969, for use in the TRIA programme, and a fifth C-135B to support the Air Force Avionics Laboratory satellite communications test programmes. The latter aircraft (serial 61-2662) remains in the AFSC inventory in support of Department of Defense missile and space programmes.

One WC-135B (serial 61-2669) became an AFSC avionics testbed under the "Speckled Trout" programme in 1975 and was redesignated C-135C. This aircraft is assigned to Detachment 1, 4950th Test Wing, AFSC, Andrews AFB, Maryland.

JKC-135A/NKC-135A: In 1968, five temporary test versions of the KC-135A had evolved and were identified as JKC-135As. By 1969, these aircraft were redesignated as NKC-135As when they assumed permanent test status with the AFSC. The permanent test fleet of NKC-135As then totalled 14 aircraft.

EC-135 Unit Assignments

SAC
2nd ACCS, Offutt AFB, Ne
4th ACCS, Ellsworth AFB, S D
305th ARW, Grissom AFB, In

USAFE
10th ACCS, Mildenhall AFB, England

TAC
6th ACCS, Langley AFB, Va
8th TDCS, Tinker AFB, Ok

PACAF
9th ACCS, Hickham AFB, Hi

Reconnaissance -135 Unit Assignments

SAC RC-135s
55th SRW, Offutt AFB, Ne

MAC WC-135Bs
55th WRS, McClellan AFB, Ca

TAC WC-135B
552nd AWACS Wg, Tinker AFB, Ok

Test -135 Unit Assignments

AFSC
Special Weapons Test Center, Kirtland AFB, N M
4950th Test Wing, Wright-Patterson AFB, Oh
Det. 1, 4950th TW, Andrews AFB, Md

NASA
Ellington AFB, Tx

US NAVY
Fleet Electronic Warfare Group,
Naval Electronic Systems Command,
Tulsa, Ok

(Above) The NKC-135A used for the "Big Crow" missile vulnerability testing, showing the large radomes above and below the fuselage and the non-standard nose radome. (Below) One of the two NKC-135As (BuNo 563596) on loan to the USN's Naval Electronic Systems Command, for electronic warfare research. Note the underwing radome between the engine pods.

These aircraft perform such rôles as countermeasures testing, airborne laser laboratory testing, water spray testing to simulate rain and icing conditions, satellite communications testing, ionosphere sampling, missile vulnerability testing, instrumented refuelling boom testing, reconnaissance strike equipment testing, and weightlessness testing. Some of these aircraft were nicknamed "piccolo tubes" because of the large number of windows that were added.

In 1975, two NKC-135As (serials 55-3134 and 56-3596) were loaned to the US Navy's Naval Electronic Systems Command. These aircraft, the only examples of the -135 family to serve in US Navy markings, are maintained and operated by McDonnell-Douglas, Tulsa, Oklahoma, under a Navy contract. The aircraft have been modified to perform electronic warfare research with the Fleet Electronic Warfare Group.

The Special Air Missions VC-137s

As explained in Part One, VC-137s are not part of the Model 717 (-135) family of aeroplanes, but are commercial 707s purchased by the USAF. Operated by the 89th Military Airlift Group, MAC, Andrews AFB, Maryland, they provide airlift support to the President of the United States and top governmental officials. Basically 707s, the VC-137s have specialised electronics and interior furnishings. The passenger cabins are divided into three sections, with a communications centre located in the forward cabin area, an airborne headquarters contained in the mid-cabin area and the aft cabin configured like a standard 707. The flight crew of these aircraft consists of a pilot, co-pilot, navigator, flight engineer and radio operator. The cabin crew includes a steward and security personnel.

VC-137A/VC-137B: Three VC-137As (serials 58-6970, -6971 and -6972) were Boeing 707-153s delivered to the US Air Force in May and June 1959. Four commercial Pratt & Whitney JT3C-6 turbojets were first fitted, but with retrofit of JT3D-3 turbofan engines, the designation of these aircraft was changed to VC-137B.

VC-137C: In October 1962, the US Air Force took delivery of its first VC-137C (serial 62-6000). A second VC-137C (serial 72-7000), was delivered in August 1972 and is now the prime Presidential transport, operated with the code name "Air Force One"; the earlier VC-137C is retained as the back-up. These are government VIP versions of the commercial Intercontinental 707-300B jetliner, and carry the Boeing designation 707-353B; thus, they have greater wing-span and overall length than the VC-137A/Bs, and were fitted with JT3D-3 turbofans from the start. □

The first customer to receive examples of the fully-equipped F27 Maritime was the Peruvian Navy, which took delivery of the two aircraft illustrated here late in 1977. During 1979 the Spanish Air Force received three Maritimes for search and rescue duties; one of these is illustrated on the cover of this issue.

MARITIME **—*from page 266***

World War II, when decisions were being taken intended to re-establish the company as a major aircraft manufacturer. An aircraft in the category of a DC-3 replacement appeared to be attractive and after conducting extensive market surveys among airlines and holding discussions with other manufacturers engaged in similar studies (notably Boeing and Canadair), Fokker evolved the P.275 project in 1950, for a shoulder-wing twin-Dart 32-seater. By 1952, this had evolved into the F27, with a pressurised fuselage seating up to 40 passengers and, with the financial support of the Dutch government, prototype construction was launched in September 1953.

The first of two flying F27 prototypes flew on 24 November 1955 at Schiphol; powered by Dart 507 engines, it had a fuselage length of 73 ft (22,25 m), but before even the first flight a decision had been made to stretch this length by 3 ft (0,91 m) to give one more seat row and from the second prototype onwards this was the definitive size. On 26 April 1956, Fairchild Engine and Airplane Corp signed an agreement with Fokker covering production of the F27 in the USA, and tooling-up began at Hagerstown, Md, while Fokker continued with the flight test programme and the marketing effort proceeded into high gear. The sales breakthrough came early in 1956, when Fokker obtained contracts from TAA in Australia, and Braathens SAFE and Aer Lingus in Europe, while West Coast Airlines, Bonanza and Piedmont ordered F27s from Fairchild*. By the end of 1956, Fokker had sold 14 and Fairchild had sold 22 F27s; in 1957, the two companies sold 15 and 23 respectively, but there was then something of a hiatus, sales dropping to 8 and 16 in 1958 and causing Fokker some financial embarrassment; a recovery occurred in 1959 and production finally became established on a firm basis in

**Although the aircraft produced by Fokker and Fairchild were, initially, virtually identical, there was a small difference in the marketing style adopted for the designation. Fokker used "F.27" while Fairchild used "F-27"; however, Fokker has more recently dropped the full point and for consistency the now-current "F27" is used throughout this account.*

both countries.

Certification of the F27, to the then very new requirements of the American CAR 4B and SR 422 regulations, was obtained on 29 October 1957, by which time the first production aircraft were well into final assembly. The first series production F27 off the Fokker line flew on 23 March 1958 and Fairchild followed with their initial aircraft on 14 April 1958. Commercial services began on 28 September 1958, when West Coast Airlines put its first Fairchild F27 into operation; Aer Lingus was first to operate the Fokker-built aircraft, in December of that year.

The initial production standard aeroplane was identified by Fokker as the F27 Mk 100, powered by Dart 511 (RDa6) engines with 12-ft (3,66-m) diameter propellers. The Fairchild equivalent was the F27 (no letter suffix) with Dart 511-7E or Dart 574-7 engines. During 1958, Fokker re-engined the original prototype with the more powerful Dart 528 (RDa7) engines and this version went into production as the F27 Mk 200 and Fairchild F27A, operating at higher weights and with improved payload/range and field performance. The Fairchild F27F was similar, with an executive interior for corporate use and optional increased tankage. Later production Mk 200s had Dart 532-7 engines and currently use the Dart 536-7R.

To increase the operational utility of the F27, Fokker designed a large cargo-loading door for the front port side of the fuselage; together with a strengthened fuselage floor for freight-carrying, this was introduced in 1960 as the Mk 300 Combiplane, based on the Mk 100 airframe with Dart 514-7E (RDa6) engines. This had its equivalent in the Fairchild F27B, only three of which were built. In response to growing military interest, Fokker offered the Mk 300M Troopship, which featured a military interior and large despatch doors, for paratroops and supply dropping, each side at the rear of the cabin.

With the uprated Dart 532-7 (RDa7) engines, the Combiplane became the F27 Mk 400, or Mk 400M in its military version, these soon succeeding the Mk 300/300M. Fairchild offered the equivalent F27G, with Dart 529-7E, but without any sales success. The F27J was a later Fairchild variant for airline use, incorporating a number of small improvements for the North American environment, with Dart 532-7 engines, and the F27M was a special variant for Lloyd Aereo Boliviano with Dart 532-7Ns and large diameter propellers for better hot-and-high performance.

Fairchild production of the Fokker transport ended in July 1973 with 128 examples built. The company had also, by that time, delivered a total of 76 of the larger FH-227s (the FH designation reflecting the change in company name from Fairchild to Fairchild-Hiller in 1964). The FH-227 incorporated a 6-ft (1,83-m) plug in the forward fuselage ahead of the wing to increase the standard passenger capacity to 52, with Dart 532-7 engines. Variants up to FH-227E were designated, with relatively minor changes, and post-production modification by California Airmotive produced the "Cargonaut" version with the forward cargo door installation.

Fokker was a little slower than Fairchild in offering a stretched F27, and when the Mk 500 did appear, the stretch was slightly less, totalling 4 ft 11 in (1,5 m) disposed ahead of and behind the wing. First flight was made on 15 November 1967, and versions with and without the forward cargo door have since been produced, without change of designation; power is provided by the Dart 532-7. With the Mk 200 and Mk 400, the Mk 500 remains in production as one of the principal variants. Also still available is the Mk 600, which is in effect the Mk 400 without the heavy duty floor, but still with the forward cargo door and facilities for quick-change of the interior.

The F27 Mk 700 designation applies to a single Mk 100 retrofitted with the forward cargo door, and the Mk 800 designation was briefly applied to a Mk 600 version with a special rough-field landing gear (and optional APU in the rear starboard engine nacelle), but this is now identified as the Mk 600RF. Similar rough-field modifications are available for the Mk 500. In addition to the main variants identified by these designations, there have naturally been numerous production line modifications in the course of 20-odd years, important among which has been the quite recent introduction of a new look interior with overhead luggage bins and an improved flight deck layout with additional instrumentation.

There also have been many project studies of F27 variants, of which the more interesting have included the F27MS, a short-field military variant with a redesigned rear fuselage including a loading/supply dropping ramp; the P.301 STOL transport powered by four PT6A-50 turboprops, and the P.305 with pod-mounted turbofans replacing the Darts. A flying-boat variant, with a hull built on to the under-fuselage and retractable wing-tip floats, was also studied.

Interesting as these proposals may have been, the *forte* of the F27 is its ability to provide reliable and economic transport over short ranges, and its success has been achieved primarily through commercial operation — in the hands of well over 100 airlines around the world. Military and quasi-military operations are relatively less important but, as the development of the Maritime has shown, are an aspect that the manufacturer cannot afford to neglect. The F27 is now well placed to take advantage of the growing interest in turboprops among the airlines that are finding small turbojet/turbofan transports too fuel-expensive for short-haul, low-traffic routes. Present plans already call for Fokker to increase the F27 production rate to two a month by 1982, and preliminary studies are now in hand for a further increase, to 2½-3 a month, thereafter — not an unsatisfactory situation, surely, for an aeroplane that has just celebrated the 25th anniversary of its first flight. □

Fokker F27 Maritime Specification

Power Plant: Two Rolls-Royce Dart RDa7 Mk 536-7R turboprops each rated at 2,370 eshp with water methanol injection and 2,020 eshp dry for take-off. Dowty Rotol four-bladed constant-speed fully-feathering propellers of 11 ft 6 in (3,5 m) diameter. Fuel capacity, 1,130 Imp gal (5 140 l) in integral wing tanks plus 508 Imp gal (2 310 l) in centre section bag tank plus 206·5 Imp gal (938 l) in each of two underwing pylon tanks; total capacity, 2,051 Imp gal (9 326 l).
Performance: Max speed, 256 kt (474 km/h) at 20,000 ft (6 100 m); cruising speed at 38,000-lb (17 235-kg) weight, 250 kt (463 km/h) at 20,000 ft (6 100 m); typical search speed, 145-175 kt (269-324 km/h) at 2,000 ft (610 m); initial operating ceiling, max gross weight, 23,000 ft (7 010 m); service ceiling, 25,000 ft (7 620 m); time to climb to 20,000 ft (6 100 m) at normal weight, 27 min; take-off field length, normal take-off weight, wet power, 3,340 ft (1 018 m) ISA at sea level and 3,680 ft (1 122 m) ISA plus 20 deg C at sea level; single-engined take-off distance, normal take-off weight, wet power, 5,480 ft (1 670 m) ISA at sea level and 6,000 ft (1 830 m) ISA plus 20 deg C at sea level; unfactored landing distance, 30,000-lb (13 620-kg) weight, 1,750 ft (530 m) ISA at sea level; landing distance required (civil certification), 2,910 ft (887 m); max range, with 30-min loiter and 5 per cent flight fuel reserve, 2,700 naut mls (5 000 km) at 23,000-25,000 ft (7 010-7 620 m), range with 10,000-lb (4 540-kg) payload, transport mission, 810 naut mls (1 500 km); time on station (high-altitude transit to and from base, loiter at 2,000 ft/610 m at 160 kt/296 km/h, 8 hrs at 200 naut mls (370 km), 6 hrs at 400 naut mls (740 km), 4 hrs at 650 naut mls (1 204 km).
Weights: Manufacturer's weight empty, 27,600 lb (12 519 kg); operational equipped weight, 29,352 lb (13 314 kg); max fuel load, 16,300 lb (7 394 kg); water methanol and oil, 655 lb (297 kg); normal take-off weight, 45,000 lb (20 412 kg); max overload weight, 47,500 lb (21 546 kg); max landing weight, 41,000 lb (18 598 kg); max zero fuel weight, 39,500 lb (17 917 kg).
Dimensions: Span, 95 ft 2 in (29,00 m); length, 77 ft 3½ in (23,56 m); height, 28 ft 6½ in (8,70 m); wing area, 754 sq ft (70,00 m²); wheelbase, 28 ft 8 in (8,74 m); undercarriage track, 23 ft 7½ in (7,20 m).
Accommodation: Flight crew of two with third seat on flight deck for observer or engineer. Typical cabin crew for maritime surveillance comprises two observers, radar operator and tactical commander/navigator.

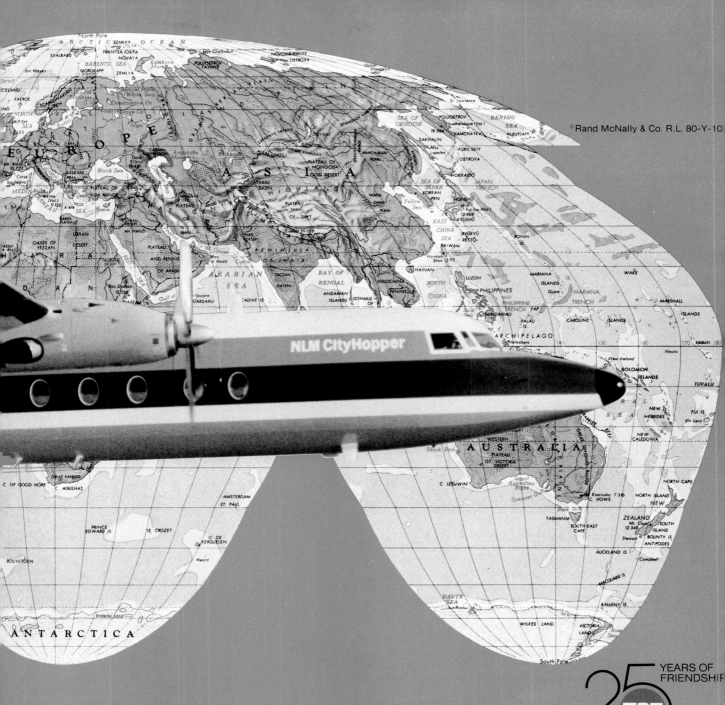

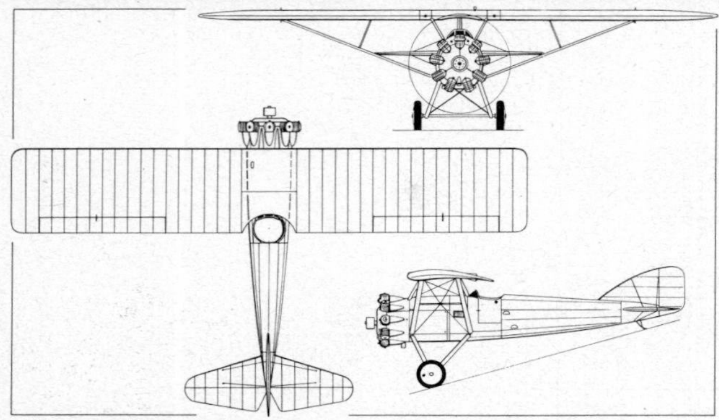

(Above and below) The LGL-32 was the only Gourdou-Leseurre fighter to be built in really substantial quantities.

(Below) The LGL-321 was a more powerful version of the LGL-32, the sole example being a re-engined pre-series aircraft.

(LOIRE-) GOURDOU-LESEURRE LGL-32 FRANCE

From late 1925 (until 1928) Gourdou-Leseurre operated as a subsidiary of the shipbuilding concern Ateliers et Chantiers de la Loire, and during the three years of this association, aircraft designed and built by Gourdou-Leseurre received the prefix LGL. The first so designated was the LGL-32 single-seat fighter which was to be the first and only aircraft of Gourdou-Leseurre design to be built in really substantial quantities. Designed to participate in the 1923 C1 programme, the LGL-32 was powered by a 420 hp Gnôme-Rhône 9Ac Jupiter (the similarly-rated 9Ady being standardised after the five pre-series aircraft) and carried two synchronised 7,7-mm guns. Flown in 1925 and adjudged runner-up to the Nieuport-Delage NiD 42, the LGL-32 received an initial production contract (for 16 aircraft) on 16 September of that year and entered service late 1927, a total of 380 eventually being delivered to the *Aéronautique Militaire* and a further 15 to the *Aviation Maritime*, remaining first-line equipment until 1934. In addition, 63 examples were exported of which 50 were delivered to Rumania (in 1928) and 12 to Turkey, a total of 475 being built (415 at St Nazaire and 60 at St Maur) during 1927-30. Surprisingly, during March-June 1937, Gourdou-Leseurre produced a further batch of 12, ostensibly for French private pilots, but in fact for the Basque government fighting the Spanish Nationalists, one of these having previously been converted as a dive bomber (under the designation GL-633). At the end of 1927, the first pre-series LGL-32 was re-engined with a 600 hp Jupiter as the LGL-321. Max speed, 155 mph (250 km/h) at sea level. Range, 310 mls (500 km). Time to 16,405 ft (5 000 m), 12 min. Empty weight, 2,123 lb (963 kg). Loaded weight, 3,032 lb (1 376 kg). Span, 40 ft $0\frac{1}{4}$ in (12,20 m). Length, 24 ft $9\frac{1}{8}$ in (7,55 m). Height, 9 ft $8\frac{1}{4}$ in (2,95 m). Wing area, 268·03 sq ft (24,90 m^2).

(LOIRE-) GOURDOU-LESEURRE LGL-32HY FRANCE

In 1927, after completing 150 hours flying, the prototype LGL-32 was fitted with twin wooden floats and, retaining its 420 hp Gnôme-Rhône 9Ac and with much of its fuselage re-covered with light alloy, was flown as the LGL-32Hy single-seat fighter seaplane. On 28 March 1927, the LGL-32Hy attained an altitude of 30,479 ft (9 290 m) after taking-off from the Seine, but no production order was placed by the *Aviation Maritime* and development was discontinued. Max speed, 140 mph (225 km/h). Range, 311 mls (500 km). Empty weight, 1,845 lb (837 kg). Loaded weight, 2,756 lb (1 250 kg). Span, 40 ft $0\frac{1}{4}$ in (12,20 m). Length, 27 ft $6\frac{3}{5}$ in (8,40 m). Height, 10 ft $9\frac{7}{8}$ in (3,30 m). Wing area, 268·03 sq ft (24,90 m^2).

(LOIRE-) GOURDOU-LESEURRE LGL-33 FRANCE

Employing essentially the same airframe as the LGL-32, the LGL-33 flown in April 1925 differed primarily in having a 450 hp Lorraine-Dietrich 12Eb 12-cylinder W-type water-cooled engine. The greater engine weight — by comparison with the Jupiter of the LGL-32 — dictated modification of the bracing struts in order to shift the wing further aft to cater for the changed CG and the rudder was enlarged. The LGL-33 offered better low-altitude speed than the Jupiter-engined fighter, but a lower climb rate, and the sole prototype crashed as a result of a structural failure while being flown by André Christiany in 1927, no further development being undertaken. Max speed, 161 mph (260 km/h) at sea level. Time to 6,560 ft (2 000 m), 3·5 min. Empty weight, 2,511 lb (1 139 kg). Loaded weight, 3,492 lb (1 584 kg). Span, 40 ft $0\frac{1}{4}$ in (12,20 m). Length, 26 ft $4\frac{1}{8}$ in (8,03 m). Height, 9 ft $8\frac{1}{4}$ in (2,95 m). Wing area, 268·03 sq ft (24,90 m^2).

The LGL-32Hy (above) was a conversion of the original LGL-32 prototype as a fighter seaplane, and the LGL-33 (below) was a Lorraine-Dietrich-powered derivative of the basic design.

The first (above) and second (below) LGL-341 prototypes which differed essentially in engine cooling arrangements. An insufficient performance advance over the LGL-32 militated against series production.

(LOIRE-) GOURDOU-LESEURRE LGL-34
FRANCE

Seeking enhanced performance with minimal changes to the basic LGL-32 airframe in 1927, Loire-Gourdou-Leseurre produced prototypes of the LGL-34 and LGL-341 single-seat fighters, these differing primarily in the type of power plant installed, the LGL-34 having a 450 hp Hispano-Suiza 12Ga 12-cylinder W-type water-cooled engine and the LGL-341 having a 500 hp Hispano-Suiza 12Hb 12-cylinder vee-type water-cooled engine. Although the wing employed by these fighters was of similar span to that of the LGL-32, the gross wing area was increased by 30 sq ft (2,60 m²), the ailerons were inset and the rear cabane struts were moved forward. The LGL-34 was marginally lighter than the more powerful LGL-341 and the performances of the two aircraft were closely comparable. In May 1928, a second LGL-341 prototype was flown, this discarding the frontal radiator (featured by both the LGL-34 and first -341) in favour of Lamblin-type radiators attached to the forward undercarriage legs. Although the HS-engined fighters offered improved level speed and climb rates by comparison with the LGL-32, these were considered insufficient to warrant production orders. The following data relate to the second LGL-341. Max speed, 168 mph (270 km/h) at sea level, 158 mph (255 km/h) at 16,405 ft (5 000 m). Range, 373 mls (600 km). Empty weight, 2,628 lb (1 192 kg). Loaded weight, 3,666 lb (1 663 kg). Span, 40 ft 0¼ in (12,20 m). Length, 24 ft 11⅕ in (7,60 m). Height, 9 ft 8¼ in (2,95 m). Wing area, 296·02 sq ft (27,50 m²).

(LOIRE-) GOURDOU-LESEURRE LGL-351
FRANCE

In 1926, the STAé (*Service Technique de l'Aéronautique*) conceived a lightweight fighter programme aimed at arresting the upward spiral of fighter costs. Known unofficially as the "Jockey" programme, this envisaged an armament restricted to two 7,7-mm Vickers guns with 300 rpg, a range of 248 mls (400 km) and a maximum speed of at least 168 mph (270 km/h) at 16,405 ft (5 000 m). Among the many contenders for this requirement was the LGL-351 C1. Exhibited at the 1926 *Salon de l'Aéronautique* in Paris as the "LGL-33 Renault", the LGL-351 was powered by a 450 hp Renault 12Ja 12-cylinder liquid-cooled vee engine and employed the same wing as the LGL-33. The LGL-351 was flown in 1927 and was joined in the same year by a second example, the LGL-354, which, envisaged as an export version, possessed greater fuel capacity and provision for an armament of four 7,7-mm guns. The "Jockey" programme proved unsuccessful, development of the LGL-351 being discontinued, and despite outstanding success at an exhibition held in Copenhagen in August 1927, the LGL-354 found no purchaser, being redesignated LGL-35 in 1929. The following data relate to the LGL-351. Max speed, 155 mph (250 km/h) at 3,280 ft (1 000 m). Range, 280 mls (450 km). Empty weight, 2,330 lb (1 057 kg). Loaded weight, 3,155 lb (1 431 kg). Span, 40 ft 0¼ in (12,20 m). Length, 26 ft 4⅛ in (8,03 m). Height, 9 ft 10 in (3,00 m). Wing area, 268·03 sq ft (24,90 m²).

GOURDOU-LESEURRE GL-410 & GL-450
FRANCE

With the establishment by the Ateliers et Chantiers de la Loire of its own design department at St Nazaire. Établissement Gourdou-Leseurre became a separate entity once more, producing the GL-410 and GL-450 to meet the requirements of the 1928 C1 programme, both being based on the LGL-32. Whereas the GL-410 was powered by a supercharged Gnôme-Rhône Jupiter 9Asb engine and had a revised wing of trapezoidal form, the GL-450 had an unsupercharged Jupiter 9Ae and retained the LGL-32 wing. Both engines were rated at 480 hp and both fighters employed independently articulated wheels in place of the old-style cross-axle that had characterised all preceding Gourdou-Leseurre fighters. Two examples of the GL-410 and one example of the GL-450 were built, both being evaluated at Villacoublay during 1932, but in the meantime, the 1928 C1 programme had been overtaken by the 1930 programme and neither Gourdou-Leseurre fighter could meet its more exacting requirements. The following data relate to the GL-450 (figures for the GL-410 being essentially similar). Max speed, 199 mph (320 km/h) at 16,405 ft (5 000 m). Range, 373 mls (600 km). Empty weight, 2,138 lb (970 kg). Loaded weight, 3,042 lb (1 380 kg). Span, 40 ft 0¼ in (12,20 m). Length, 24 ft 9⅛ in (7,55 m). Height, 9 ft 8¼ in (2,95 m). Wing area, 268·03 sq ft (24,90 m²).

The GL-410 (below) and the GL-450 (above) were based on the LGL-32 and differed from each other in having supercharged and unsupercharged engines respectively. The former had a wing of trapezoidal shape.

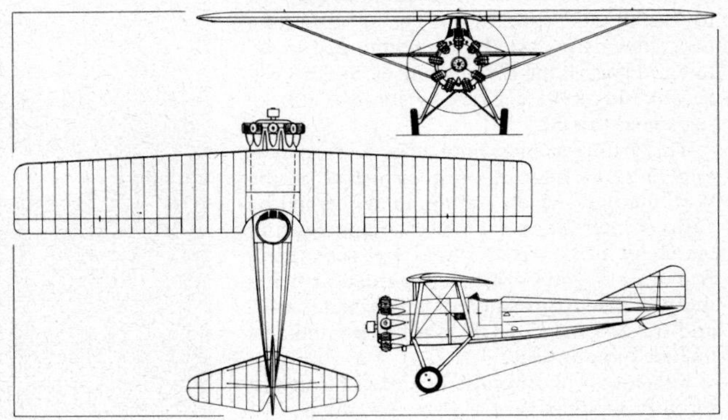

TALKBACK

Zimbabwe's Spitfire

(Above and below) Photographs from Anthony Brooks of the Spitfire 22 recently restored to flying condition in Zimbabwe. It now carries the serial number PK350, having previously served in the Southern Rhodesian Air Force as SR64; the code letters derive from the name of the present owner, Jack Mullock, in whose hands it made the first flight since restoration on 28 March this year.

I ENCLOSE two photographs of the Zimbabwe Air Force Spitfire Mk 22, taken at Thornhill air base when the Spitfire was brought around for demonstration purposes recently.

The aircraft was originally grounded in 1953 and was rebuilt by technicians of Air Trans Africa. They were able to obtain most spares from Air Force stores, with the exception of the propeller—which had to be imported from Germany. It is now flown by the owner of Air Trans Africa, Jack Mullock.

In the background is the last surviving Provost in the Air Force. These aircraft have been replaced by Siai Marchetti Warriors, known locally as Genets. The latter are used for training and during the war were used as ground support aircraft against the terrorists and to protect convoys (one aircraft per convoy). It appears now that Zimbabwean pilots will be trained overseas, for some obscure reason best known to the powers that be.

Anthony Brooks
Gwelo, Zimbabwe

Britannia's Boeing fleet

IN THE August 1980 issue of AIR INTERNATIONAL (page 58) Britannia is credited with having ordered five more Boeing 737s, giving us a fleet total of 26 in 1982. In fact we have six more due, which will bring our fleet to 29 in 1982.

The discrepancy arises, I suggest, from confusion over secondhand purchases, leasing arrangements and so forth. The 23 aircraft we operate at present are:

G-AVRL G-AXNB G-BAZH G-BGNW
G-AVRM G-AXNC G-BAZI G-BGYJ
G-AVRN G-AZNZ G-BECG G-BGYK
G-AVRO G-BADP G-BECH G-BGYL
G-AWSY G-BADR G-BFVA G-BOSL
G-AXNA G-BAZG G-BFVB

All but two of these aircraft were delivered to us new over the period from July 1968 to April 1980, the exceptions being G-AZNZ and G-BGNW, which were purchased secondhand from United Airlines and New Zealand National Airways Corporation respectively. The six 737s on order are due in September 1980 (G-BHWE), December 1980 (G-BHWF), May 1981, April 1982 (two) and May 1982 respectively.

Part of the confusion probably arises from the fact that G-BOSL is registered to OSL, the villa and apartment holiday operator which contracts Britannia for much of its flying.

However, G-BOSL was built and equipped to Britannia's specification, is in Britannia livery and is operated and maintained as an integral part of the Britannia fleet. So also will be our May 1981 delivery, which will also be registered to OSL.

This arrangement is little different from that applying to a number of other aircraft in the fleet, many of which are nominally owned by various international finance companies and merchant banks from whom we lease them. Britannia is quite properly regarded as being the permanent operator of all these aircraft, and those owned by OSL should be similarly included in our fleet.

I enclose a photograph of G-BGYL in our recently modified livery. Towards the end of June 1980 we reached the notable milestone of becoming only the fifth airline in the world to achieve half-a-million flying hours with 737s. Britannia also has, of course, two Boeing 767s on order, for delivery in Spring 1984.

D A Cox,
Customer Services Manager (UK)
Britannia Airways Ltd, Luton, Beds

Flack's Furies

I SEE that in the September issue of AIR INTERNATIONAL, a reader has provided some additional information regarding Spencer Flack's Sea Fury G-BCOW, alias "253". While this data is no doubt correct, its publication at this stage could lead to some mis-identification, as it is Spencer's "new" Sea Fury, the appropriately-registered G-FURY, which will have been seen by many at air displays this summer.

This aircraft made its first flight at Langley on 8 January 1952 in the hands of George Bullen, and on 31 January was delivered to RNAS Anthorn, serialled WJ244. After a long period of storage, it was issued to the Airwork FRU at Hurn on 7 October 1957, receiving the side number "026". Retired to Lossiemouth Aircraft Holding Unit on 19 May 1960, WJ244 was struck off charge on 5 November 1962 and sold to Hawker Siddeley at Dunsfold, where it was placed in storage on 16 April 1964.

Acquired by the Historic Aircraft Museum, it remained at Southend as a "spare" (WJ288 was the main Sea Fury exhibit there) until it was bought by Spencer Flack. After being returned to an airworthy condition in June 1980, it adopted the reserved registration G-FURY and was painted in a scarlet colour scheme similar to the owner's Hunter G-HUNT later that month.

From an examination of G-FURY, I have been able to ascertain its correct constructor's number as 41H 642111, and a check on G-HUNT showed its c/n to be 41H 680277.

Paul A Jackson
Enfield, Middx

One of the most recent additions to the Britannia Airways fleet, the Boeing 737 G-BGYL, in the newest livery. As noted at left, Britannia now has 23 Boeing 737s in service with six more to be delivered by 1982.

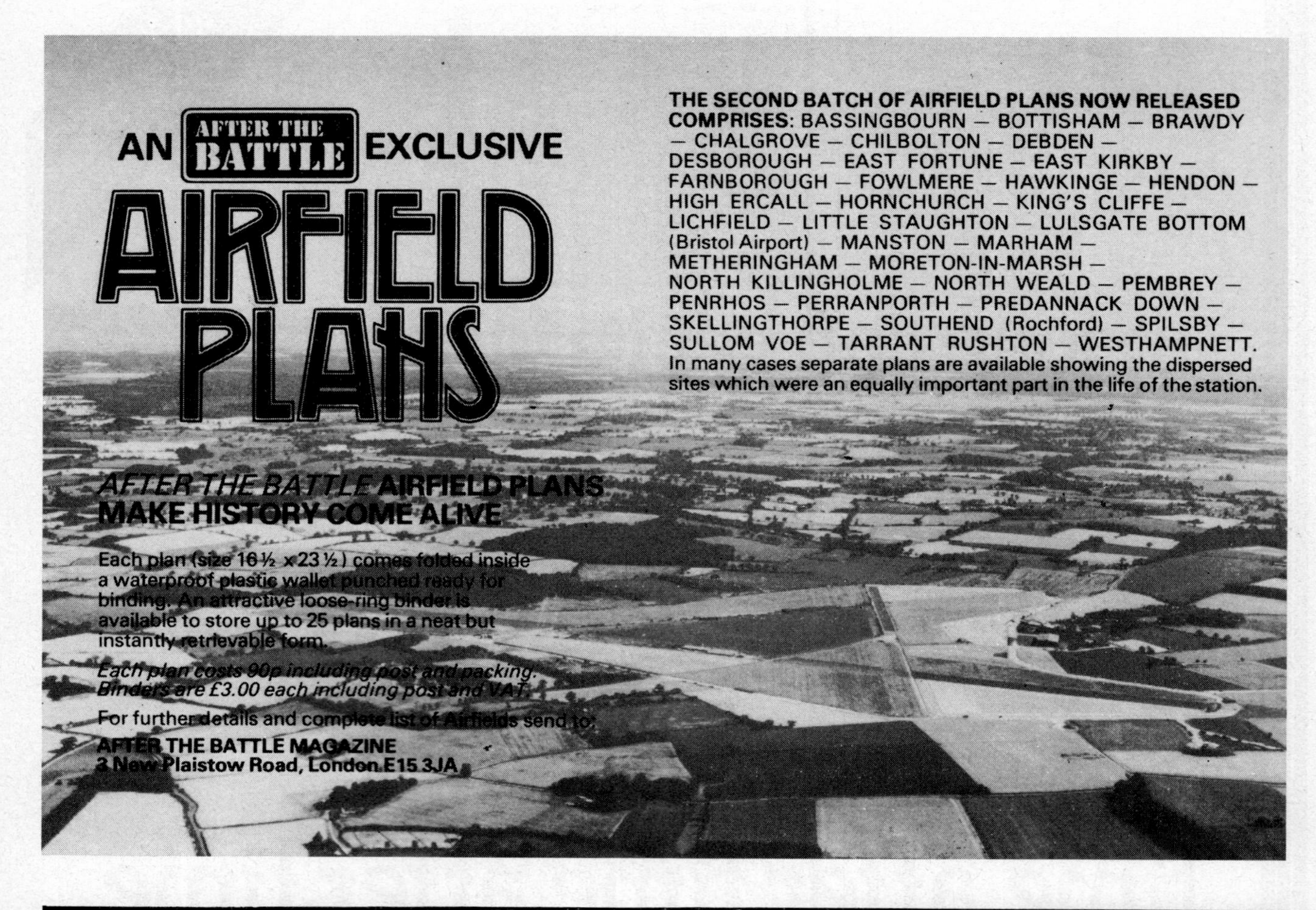
AN AFTER THE BATTLE EXCLUSIVE
AIRFIELD PLANS
THE SECOND BATCH OF AIRFIELD PLANS NOW RELEASED COMPRISES: BASSINGBOURN — BOTTISHAM — BRAWDY — CHALGROVE — CHILBOLTON — DEBDEN — DESBOROUGH — EAST FORTUNE — EAST KIRKBY — FARNBOROUGH — FOWLMERE — HAWKINGE — HENDON — HIGH ERCALL — HORNCHURCH — KING'S CLIFFE — LICHFIELD — LITTLE STAUGHTON — LULSGATE BOTTOM (Bristol Airport) — MANSTON — MARHAM — METHERINGHAM — MORETON-IN-MARSH — NORTH KILLINGHOLME — NORTH WEALD — PEMBREY — PENRHOS — PERRANPORTH — PREDANNACK DOWN — SKELLINGTHORPE — SOUTHEND (Rochford) — SPILSBY — SULLOM VOE — TARRANT RUSHTON — WESTHAMPNETT.
In many cases separate plans are available showing the dispersed sites which were an equally important part in the life of the station.
AFTER THE BATTLE AIRFIELD PLANS MAKE HISTORY COME ALIVE
Each plan (size 16½ x 23½) comes folded inside a waterproof plastic wallet punched ready for binding. An attractive loose-ring binder is available to store up to 25 plans in a neat but instantly retrievable form.
Each plan costs 90p including post and packing. Binders are £3.00 each including post and VAT.
For further details and complete list of Airfields send to:
AFTER THE BATTLE MAGAZINE
3 New Plaistow Road, London E15 3JA

IN PRINT

"Red Stars in the Sky"
by Carl-Fredrik Geust, Kalevi Keskinen, Klaus Niska and Kari Stenman
Tietoteos Publishing Co, Espoo 21, Finland, 30 Markka
48 pp, $8\frac{1}{4}$ in by $11\frac{5}{8}$ in, illustrated

THE Tietoteos Publishing Company and the last three named of the quartet of compilers of this publication are already well-known to the aviation historically-minded throughout the world for their series of monographs of the principal combat aircraft operated by the Finnish air arm during WW II and noteworthy for the rarity and interest of their pictorial content. They are now joined by Carl-Fredrik Geust in producing *Red Stars in the Sky*; a slim, card-covered production with colour limited to the covers which, at first sight, appears somewhat expensive, being £3·45 at the current rate of exchange. If you have an interest in WW II Soviet aviation, however, you will find the content matter to be pure gold and cheap at the price.

Apart from three pages in both English and Finnish describing the organisation of the V-VS in WW II and briefly summarising the HSU award and the assignment of the "Guards" prefix and other honours to operational units, the text is restricted to two-language captions to 96 photos which are supplemented by 18 full-colour profiles (reproduced on the covers), 24 tone profiles (accompanied by colour notes) and a page of line drawings of I-16s. The photographs, in particular, are extremely interesting, very few of them having been published hitherto, and ranging from close-ups of individual markings to aircraft in their operational venue, the units being almost invariably identified and, in many cases, the pilots that flew them. Many are the real gems among the photos, such as those depicting two-seat training versions of the P-40K and the Spitfire IX, and Fw 190D-9s actually *in service* with a fighter unit of the Baltic Fleet.

This publication is devoted exclusively to fighters and is stated by the publishers to be the first in a series, which, it may be assumed, will cover other categories of Soviet WW II aircraft. If the photographic content of succeeding issues are as unique as that of the issue reviewed here, then the *Red Stars in the Sky* series will find a place in the reference libraries of enthusiasts the world over.

Among the illustrations included in "Red Stars in the Sky", reviewed on this page, is the photograph (above) of an early La-5 of the 159 IAP inscribed Eskadrilya Valeri Chkalov *and operating on the Karelian Isthmus in the summer of 1944. (Below) Another of the many previously unpublished photos illustrating this book is this depicting a two-seat training conversion of a P-40K Warhawk in 1945, the conversion having been undertaken by the No 1 Aircraft Depot in Leningrad.*

"Staggerwing! The Story of the Classic Beechcraft Biplane"
by Robert T Smith and Thomas A Lempicke
Staggerwing Unlimited, PO Box 964, New Milford, Conn, 10776, $27·95 (plus $1·40 postage USA and Canada; $5 postage overseas)
254 pp, $8\frac{1}{2}$ in by 11 in, illustrated

WHAT was the first aeroplane to fly across the North Atlantic without even starting its engine? It was the Beechcraft B17R Staggerwing c/n 71, NC15816, owned by air racer Jimmy Haizlip who carried it "in his baggage", so to speak, when he flew to Europe aboard the *Hindenburg* in May 1936. The B17R was on board as cargo for sales demonstrations in Europe. Of such type of information this book is filled — as long as it relates to Beechcraft 17s.

A lovely aeroplane deserves a lovely book; the Staggerwing was such an aeroplane and this is such a book. First published 14 years ago and long since out of print, this collector's item is now available again in a wholly new, revised and enlarged edition. The text is served by more than 600 photos and drawings, including cutaways and exploded views of the whole aeroplane and its individual systems. The book is printed on high quality coated stock and includes nine pages in colour. Included are lists of all Model 17s and their national registrations. Anyone with an affection for this aeroplane of singular eye appeal will find great enjoyment in the pages of this beautifully turned out product. — RKS.

"German Fighters Over Russia"
by Bryan Philpott
Patrick Stephens Ltd, Cambridge, £4·95 casebound, £3·50 softbound
96 pp, $9\frac{3}{8}$ in by $6\frac{5}{8}$ in, illustrated

THIS is No 16 in the growing series of "World War 2 Photo Albums" from PSL, comprising once again, a carefully captioned selection of photographs drawn from the *Bundesarchiv*, a treasure trove of German war-time photographs stored at Koblenz.

For Serial Addicts

THIS REVIEWER, having enjoyed some 40 years of "aviation enthusiasm", can still clearly remember the many hours of painstaking effort he devoted, long ago, to compiling lists of serial numbers of British military aeroplanes. To the uninitiated, "collecting serial numbers" could be dismissed as a meaningless pastime, but we had realised, even then, that they provided a most useful aid to the study of aircraft development, a guide to production sequences and quantities, and a check on identities. The fact that the country was at war meant that, for these self-same reasons, serial numbers were not easily collected — and that itself added zest to the effort.

In post-war years, as the hobby of spotting and aviation studies matured, serial number collecting soon became respectable, and today it is commonplace for a full serial number breakdown to accompany any article describing a military aircraft type, British or otherwise. Several books have already been devoted to the subject of British military serial numbers — notably Bruce Robertson's "British Military Aircraft Serials" (Patrick Stephens, 1979), a series of Air Britain Monographs covering the pre-war K, L, N and P serial batches, and the "British Military Aircraft Serials and Histories" booklets (Alan W Hall Publications).

Perhaps the ready availability of these comprehensive serial number lists takes some of the fun out of collecting (yes, we enjoyed those hours of laborious searching and recording) but they certainly make a valuable contribution to the study of aircraft procurement and utilisation by the British Armed Forces. Now come more serial number books — one small, two modest, one massive — that take the process a stage further (see details below).

The "small one" is a partner for the well-known Ian Allan "Civil Aircraft Markings", which has appeared annually for more than a quarter-century to provide a pocket-guide to all the civil-registered aircraft likely to be "spotted" in Britain. In "Military Aircraft

Markings", Peter March provides a similar listing of all the RAF/RN/MoD serial numbers of aircraft currently (or soon to be) flying over Britain, plus those of the USAF aircraft based in the UK, and those of the Irish Air Corps.

The listing of serials of contemporary aircraft such as the Harrier, Sea Harrier and Tornado that are still in production might seem to conflict with customarily-observed security regulations (although the quantities of aircraft ordered are, of course, common knowledge). Even more eye-brow raising, in this respect, is "the big one" — the British Aviation Research Group's splendid "British Military Aircraft Serials and Markings".

This surely must be the ultimate in spotters' aids, for it comprises — basically — a number-by-number, line-by-line list of serial numbers with blank columns in which the book's owner can record details of the user squadron or unit, the code marking carried, when and where seen and other remarks. (The remarks column in some cases includes printed details of subsequent identities or disposal for aircraft no longer current.) From XA100 onwards (issued in 1953) the listing is complete (to ZB609, carried on the first Hawk Mk 52 prior to delivery to Kenya). In addition, pre-XA100 serials still in use are listed and there are separate sections devoted to the serials of historical aircraft preserved in the UK and preserved abroad, and RAF and RN instructional airframes.

Making this book more than a list of serials, though, is the information given about each allocation of number or numbers, to indicate the construction numbers, when and where built and subsequent conversions or modifications. The compilers have had great success in tracking down details of cancelled contracts, such as the Vickers V1000, Avro 720, TSR 2 and assorted marks of Swift, and are also able to record, for the first time, details of the Vickers Wild Goose and Swallow production batches as well as the large numbers of target aircraft that have been purchased over the years (including the Shelduck D.1, the Chukar D.1 and D.2, and the MATS-B). Hovercraft and aircraft simulators also now carry serial numbers in the same overall sequence, and are duly listed.

To facilitate writing-up, the bulk of the book is printed on good-quality but matt-surfaced paper. Interspersed, on better stock, are pages of more than 300 photographs which provide an excellent garnish for this attractive dish. Line drawings, with colour coding, illustrate current British unit and squadron markings.

Although not presented as such, this volume effectively depicts the pattern of aircraft procurement by the British services over the past 25 years. The cost may look high for a "list of serial numbers" but it is difficult to believe that any student of British aircraft development will be able to resist buying a copy.

Serial numbers occupy only about one-third of the very useful "Directory of British Military Aviation & US Military Aviation in Europe" — useful not only to the enthusiast but also, one must assume, to those who have more sinister reasons for wanting to know the strength and capabilities of NATO forces in Europe. As the author says in his introduction, "much of the information ... will have been published before"; nevertheless, by collating it, adding to it, and presumably also confirming its accuracy, he provides an exceptionally complete overview of RAF, RN and Army flying units, their location and equipment (overseas as well as in the UK). Similar information is included for the USAFE in Europe. The serial listing usefully brings together all the information for each aircraft type, including mark number differences and subsequent conversions.

Moving farther afield, the fourth title in this serial quartet is concerned with "New Zealand Military Aircraft and Serial Numbers". This provides a comprehensive study — for the first time in a single book — of all the aircraft that have been used by the RNZAF and its predecessors. With a number of rare photographs, this extensively-researched volume will prove invaluable to all students of the RNZAF, and will also appeal to those enthusiasts with a special interest in British aircraft. The listings include c/ns and subsequent identities, where known.

"Military Aircraft Markings"
by Peter R March
Ian Allan Ltd, Shepperton, £1·25
80 pp, 4¾ in by 7¼ in, illustrated

"British Military Aircraft Serials and Markings"
Compiled by BARG
Available from Mr D J Allen, BARG Sales Officer, 32 Nash Close, Farnborough, Hants GU14 0HL, £9·95 plus £1·50 p&p
420 pp, 8½ in by 12 in, illustrated

"A Directory of British Military Aviation and US Military Aviation in Europe"
by Paul S Mercer
Available from Jackson Publications, 36 Moat Road, Loughborough LE11 3PN, £4·00 including post and packing
110 pp, 8¼ in by 11¾ in, illustrated

"New Zealand Military Aircraft and Serial Numbers"
by C F L Jenks
Available from Aviation Historical Society of New Zealand, PO Box 12-009, Wellington North, New Zealand, NZ$4·75 plus postage (15c in NZ, 75c overseas, surface mail; $2·40 air mail to Europe/UK, $1·70 air mail to North America, Australia and Asia).
32 pp, 8¼ in by 11¾ in, illustrated

Books in Brief

"Flying Start"
by Mary Francis
Pelham Books Ltd, London, £7·50
168 pp, 6¼ in by 8¼ in, illustrated
A REVISED and updated edition of the book first published in 1969 as "A Beginner's Guide to Flying", providing a very good, easily understood primer for the student pilot.

"Fortresses sur l'Europe"
by Roger Anthoine
Editions Rossel, Brussels, Belgium, 490 FB
336 pp, 6 in by 8¾ in, illustrated
A FRENCH-language account of the air war over the European mainland from August 1943 to the end of the war. Special attention is given to 17 August 1943, when the USAAF mounted its first major long-range bombing raid (against Schweinfurt).

"Superfortress: the Boeing B-29"
by Steve Birdall
Squadron/Signal Publications, Texas, USA, $7·95
80 pp, 11 in by 8¼ in, illustrated
ONE of the larger Squadron/Signal volumes, in "upright" format. The emphasis is on photographs with extended captions, plus short texts on B-29 characteristics, operations, etc, and eight pages of colour photographs and profiles.

"McDonnell Douglas F-15"
by the editors of Aviation Journal
Koku Journal Co Ltd, Tokyo, Japan
120 pp, 8¼ in by 11¾ in
SECOND in this Japanese publisher's Great Aircraft Series, containing a large selection of photographs (many in colour) and drawings, useful for model makers. Text is in Japanese.

"Panavia Tornado" by Bill Gunston
Ian Allan Ltd, Shepperton, Surrey, £5·95
112 pp, 7 in by 9½ in, illustrated
THE SIXTH of the "Modern Combat Aircraft" series. Although it has yet to enter service — deliveries to the TTTE at Cottesmore are now underway — the Tornado is already established as West Europe's most important warplane of the 'eighties. Many more books and articles remain to be written. Meanwhile, this volume tells the story of the Tornado so far — its origins, its characteristics and its capabilities.

Beechcraft B17R NC 15816, the example owned by racing pilot Jimmy Haizlip and "flown" across the Atlantic in May 1936, aboard the airship "Hindenburg". A useful book on the Beech Staggerwings has recently been republished in an enlarged and updated edition, as noted opposite.

MODEL ENTHUSIAST–*from page 290*

MODEL ENTHUSIAST -from page 290

shape to fit into a model. The results are surprisingly good, aiding in affording the cockpit a really complete appearance once the seat, control column and other three-dimensional items are added. The idea is simple enough and certainly effective, and two 1/72nd scale packs are now available, No 1 being for two Messerschmitt Bf 109Gs and No 2 for three Harriers (two for the Hasegawa and one for the Airfix kit). The Harrier installation demands some small kit modifications, but these are fully covered, together with all other relevant information, by the clear instruction sheet provided. Each pack costs 53p.

Lib derivatives . . .

Based on the Monogram 1/48th scale kit of the Consolidated B-24J Liberator is a Combat Models vacuum-formed conversion kit which can be utilised to produce any one of several variants of the basic aircraft, including the Liberator Mk I of the RAF, the Liberator GR Mk V of the same service, the USAAF's B-24D and C-87 transport, the US Navy's PB4Y-1 and, most radical and possibly the most attractive, the extensively modified PB4Y-2 Privateer, with its completely different rear end. This kit has 81 parts, of which 10 are transparencies, covering variations in the tail area, differing lengths and contours of fuselage noses, engine cowlings, turrets and many smaller items too numerous to mention.

An added bonus is a set of parts to make a Bat glide bomb as carried by some PB4Y-2s in the Pacific late in WW II. There are four large sheets of drawings (to 1/48th scale), many detail sketches and comprehensive building instructions. There are also colour chips for non-specular sea blue and intermediate blue. This conversion kit is priced at $12·95, plus postage, which, added to the cost of the Monogram kit, will result in a rather expensive end product, but it certainly offers the modeller a challenge and great possibilities.

. . . and a pair of Messerschmitts

Combat Models has gone for another WW II aircraft that never quite measured up to expectations as subject matter for a companion 1/32nd scale vac-form, the Messerschmitt Me 410A-1 and paired this with a *double* kit of the Messerschmitt Bf 109 to the same large scale. The Me 410A-1 kit consists of 39 component parts and, with minor reservations as in the case of the Whirlwind, these are again well formed. Similar reservations apply to the surface detailing. There are differences in the construction methods adopted, particularly where the wing is moulded in halves and joined through the fuselage by spars. In the case of this aircraft, the accompanying 1/32nd scale plans do not attain the high standards of those accompanying the Whirlwind kit, and there are no sections shown, although a great deal of interior detail is provided. The decal sheet is of very good quality and the kit price is $18·95, plus postage.

The Bf 109 kit makes *two* complete models — not conversions — and there is a choice of F, G, H and K series sub-types. With so many disciples of the Bf 109 cult ready to pounce on the smallest error, we hesitate to be too dogmatic on the question of accuracy, but we feel that this kit can form the basis of some very fine and convincing models. It would certainly seem that a great deal of care has been expended in its preparation. The kit affords possibilities for building some of the more off-beat variants of the Messerschmitt fighter from the 90 parts supplied, five of these parts being transparencies to cater for various canopy configurations.

The accompanying drawings and instructions are profuse and include detailed plans — reprinted from *Koku Fan* magazine — for the Bf 109G-6, a reprint of a 12-page *Luftwaffe* handbook in the original German covering the Bf 109G-8, and still another reprint — this time from the IPMS (US) Quarterly — giving extensive coverage of the construction camouflage, markings and other aspects of many variants. There are even colour chips of six different camouflage shades. Among the more unusual types which can be built from this kit are the extended-span Bf 109H-0 and the two-seat Bf 109G-12. Two sheets of decals come with the kit and the price is $17·95 plus postage. □ F J HENDERSON

HENSCHEL——*from page 283*

armour weapon tested, however, was the SG 113A *Förstersonde* (Ranger Probe) automatic mortar which was built into three aircraft and tested by EKdo 26 at Tarnewitz. The *Förstersonde* comprised a romboid-shaped container in which six individual mortars were installed vertically, each tube housing a single shell with a 77-mm soft jacket and a 45-mm armour-piercing core. The sophistication of the weapon was provided by a photo-electric cell attached to the nose of the aircraft and which, actuated by the electro-magnetic field created by a tank, triggered the mortars which fired their shells vertically downwards. In the event, the reliability of this weapon proved insufficient for operational use.

The *Schlachtflieger* had begun to demand larger-calibre weapons than the 30-mm and 37-mm cannon mounted by the Hs 129B-2/Wa, and during the early months of 1944, studies were conducted of the feasibility of fitting a 75-mm PaK 40 *(Panzerabwehrkanone)* which had been designed for ground-based anti-tank use. In May 1944, aerodynamic trials were conducted at Travemünde with a wooden mock-up of an immense ventral housing and projecting cannon barrel. These trials proved the feasibility of the installation and, somewhat surprisingly, the large housing had little effect on the handling characteristics of the aircraft. Three Hs 129B-2/Wa aircraft were then adapted to carry the PaK 40L cannon and thoroughly evaluated by EKdo 26 against Soviet tanks of various types. The weapon had been modified for aircraft installation in several respects, a large muzzle recoil brake being fitted and mechanical operation being replaced by electro-pneumatic operation. Designated BK 7,5 in this form, the cannon was provided with a dozen 26-lb (12-kg) rounds, the rate of fire being 40 rounds per minute, and thus, after closing to a distance of 550 yds (500 m) of the target tank, the pilot could fire four shells in one pass. Firing trials were completed by EKdo 26 during August-September 1944, and some two dozen aircraft were fitted with the 75-mm cannon on the Schönefeld assembly line under the designation Hs 129B-3/Wa, these being among the last examples of the Henschel *Schlachtflugzeug* built.

The Gnôme-Rhône engines of the Hs 129B remained troublesome, but all efforts to find substitutes had been frustrated. During the course of 1942, proposals had been made to adopt the Isotta-Fraschini Delta RC 16/48 12-cylinder inverted-vee air-cooled engine which was rated at 840 hp at 17,390 ft (5 300 m), and a variant so powered was projected as the Hs 129C. This was, in one of its forms, to have had paired 30-mm MK 103 cannon mounted ventrally and possessing limited traverse, but the Delta engine suffered

(Above and below) Hs 129B-2/R2 aircraft of IV(Pz)./SG 9 at Czernovitz in March 1944. The upper photo shows clearly the proximity of the pilot's head to the windscreen. The photo below shows the aircraft being refuelled and re-armed.

The infantry assault emblem was stencilled on the nose of many Hs 129B CAS aircraft, as seen above. The Revi C 12/C was mounted asymmetrically to starboard ahead of the windscreen.

protracted development delays and no example of the Hs 129C was completed.

By mid-1944, fuel shortages had begun to curtail the operations of the Hs 129B *Staffeln* on the Eastern Front and Soviet tanks had become so numerous that the *Schlachtflieger*, constantly harassed by V-VS fighters, played a progressively less effective rôle in the course of operations. Attrition suffered by the IV/*(Panzer) Gruppe des Schlachtgeschwaders* was heavy; all component *Staffeln* were below strength and the number of Hs 129Bs available to attack the advancing Soviet armour was further reduced with the capitulation of Rumania on 23 August 1944. Furthermore, the *Wehrmacht* armour was to find itself the target for Hs 129Bs when, on 21 September, the FARR initiated operations against its erstwhile allies, 24 of the Henschel aircraft equipping *Escadrilă* 41 of the *Grupul Asalt-Picaj* (Assault and Dive Bombing Group) in the somewhat half-hearted attacks made by Rumanian forces in support of their newfound Soviet allies.

Henschel's Schönefeld assembly line had finally attained its target output of 40 Hs 129Bs monthly in June 1943, and maintained this with difficulty until the following November, total output for the year being 414 aircraft. Thereafter, output steadily declined and only a further 225 were completed during the course of 1944, bringing total production to 859 aircraft, all production of the Hs 129 being cancelled at the end of September 1944 in favour of the "emergency fighter programme".

During the final months of 1944, 10. and 14.(Pz)./SG 9 introduced the BK 7,5-equipped Hs 129B-3/Wa on the Eastern Front, but although this immense weapon was capable of knocking out even the formidable *Josef Stalin* tank with one shot, the comparatively few of this version of the aircraft available dictated their use piecemeal, sorties being largely confined to attempts to knock out Soviet tanks that had already penetrated the German lines. These two *Staffeln* were, by the beginning of 1945, the only surviving components of the IV/*(Panzer) Gruppe*, and as their strength dwindled so the Hs 129 faded from service.

It is unlikely that many *Luftwaffe* pilots regretted the passing of the Henschel *Büchsenöffner*, with its claustrophobic *Panzerkabine*, its mulish handling characteristics, muscle-tiring controls, those "damned French engines" and generally sluggish performance. One ex-Hs 129 pilot recalls: "The flying characteristics of the Henschel were so bad under some conditions that, for years, they provided me with a subject for nightmares! The rudder was particularly heavy and unsuited for the type of mission that we flew as it made last-minute corrections in aiming very difficult. Anything but the shallowest dive became a real pull-out job and both hands were needed on that damned silly little stick to which we gave the same nickname as a certain appendage of the male anatomy. Perhaps the most straightforward characteristic of the Henschel was the landing, but even during that it could become quite a handful if there was any turbulence, despite its stability and heavy controls. Insofar as we pilots were concerned, the only aspect of the aircraft that did not come in for any criticism was the emergency kit (machine pistol, steel helmet and gas mask) in the portside wing centre section!" □

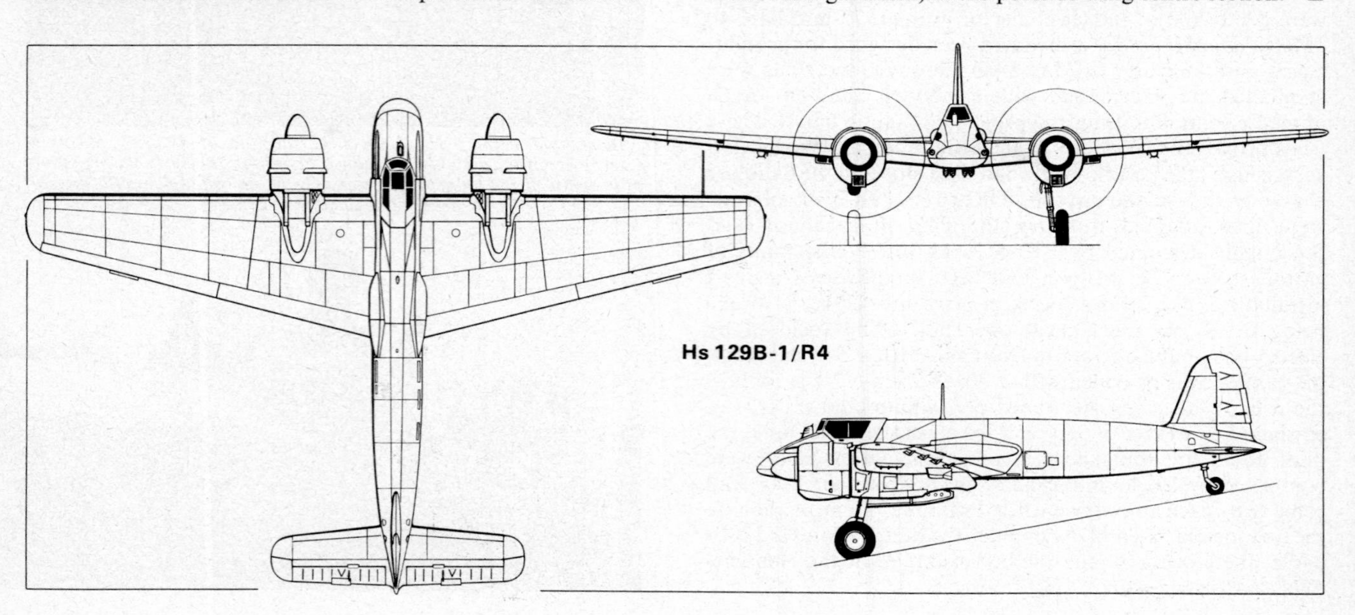